South India

Sarina Singh
Stuart Butler, Virginia Jealous, Amy Karafin,
Simon Richmond, Rafael Wlodarski

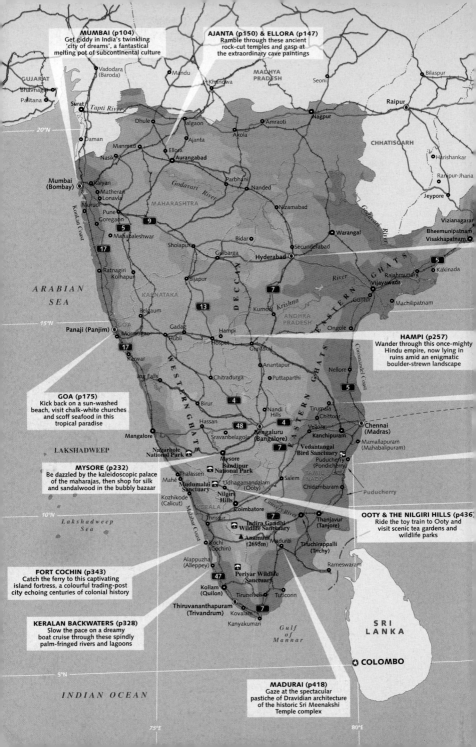

MUMBAI (p104)
Get giddy in India's twinkling 'city of dreams', a fantastical melting pot of subcontinental culture

AJANTA (p150) & ELLORA (p147)
Ramble through these ancient rock-cut temples and gasp at the extraordinary cave paintings

HAMPI (p257)
Wander through this once-mighty Hindu empire, now lying in ruins amid an enigmatic boulder-strewn landscape

GOA (p175)
Kick back on a sun-washed beach, visit chalk-white churches and scoff seafood in this tropical paradise

MYSORE (p232)
Be dazzled by the kaleidoscopic palace of the maharajas, then shop for silk and sandalwood in the bubbly bazaar

OOTY & THE NILGIRI HILLS (p436)
Ride the toy train to Ooty and visit scenic tea gardens and wildlife parks

FORT COCHIN (p343)
Catch the ferry to this captivating island fortress, a colourful trading-post city echoing centuries of colonial history

KERALAN BACKWATERS (p328)
Slow the pace on a dreamy boat cruise through these spindly palm-fringed rivers and lagoons

MADURAI (p418)
Gaze at the spectacular pastiche of Dravidian architecture of the historic Sri Meenakshi Temple complex

GUJARAT
Vadodara (Baroda)
Bhavnagar
Palitana
Surat
Tapti River
Daman
20°N
Dhule
Jalgaon
Manmad
Nasik
Ajanta
Ellora
Aurangabad
Mumbai (Bombay)
Kalyan
Matheran
Lonavla
Murud
Pune
Goregaon
5
Mahabaleshwar
17
MAHARASHTRA
Godavari River
Ratnagiri
Kolhapur
Konkan Coast
ARABIAN SEA
Belgaum
KARNATAKA
Panaji (Panjim)
GOA
Mormugao
Karwar
17
Jog Falls
Gadag
Hubli
13
Bijapur
DECCAN
15°N
Hospet
Hampi
Guntakal
Anantapur
Chitradurga
Birur
4
Nandi Hills
Bengaluru (Bangalore)
48
Hassan
Sravanbelagola
7
Mangalore
Nagarhole National Park
Thalassery
Mahé
Mudumalai Sanctuary
Mysore
Bandipur National Park
Udhagamandalam (Ooty)
Nilgiri Hills
Kozhikode (Calicut)
KERALA
Coimbatore
Indira Gandhi Wildlife Sanctuary
10°N
Lakshadweep Sea
Thrissur
Anamudi (2695m)
Madurai
Kochi (Cochin)
Alappuzha (Alleppey)
47
Periyar Wildlife Sanctuary
Kollam (Quilon)
Tirunelveli
Tuticorin
Thiruvananthapuram (Trivandrum)
Kovalam
7
Kanyakumari
Gulf of Mannar
SRI LANKA
COLOMBO
5°N
INDIAN OCEAN
75°E
80°E

MADHYA PRADESH
Mandu
Khandwa
Seoni
Bilaspur
Raipur
Harishankar
Amraoti
Nagpur
Akola
CHHATISGARH
Rampur-Jharia
Parbhani
Nanded
Jeypore
Vizianagaram
Bheemunipatnam
Visakhapatnam
Nizamabad
Bidar
Warangal
Secunderabad
Gulbarga
Hyderabad
EASTERN GHATS
Rajahmundry
5
Kakinada
River
Krishna
7
Kurnool
ANDHRA PRADESH
Guntur
Machilipatnam
Ongole
Coromandel Coast
Nellore
5
Tirumala
Chittoor
Tiruvalla
Vellore
Kanchipuram
Chennai (Madras)
Mamallapuram (Mahabalipuram)
Vedantangal Bird Sanctuary
Puducherry (Pondicherry)
Salem
Chidambaram
Puducherry
TAMIL NADU
WESTERN GHATS
7
Cauvery River
Thanjavur (Tanjore)
Tiruchirappalli (Trichy)
Rameswaram
9
Nagpur
Puttaparthi

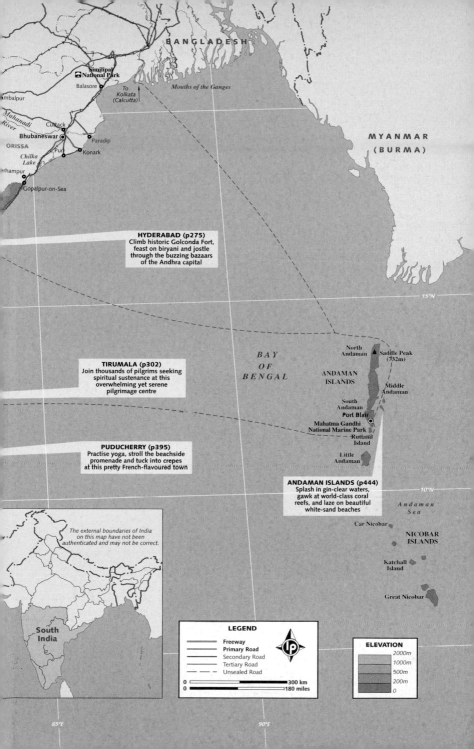

BANGLADESH

Similipal
National Park
Balasore

To
Kolkata
(Calcutta)

Mouths of the Ganges

MYANMAR
(BURMA)

*Mahanadi
River*
Cuttack
Bhubaneswar
Paradip
ORISSA
Puri
Konark
*Chilka
Lake*
erhampur
Gopalpur-on-Sea

ambalpur

HYDERABAD (p275)
Climb historic Golconda Fort,
feast on biryani and jostle
through the buzzing bazaars
of the Andhra capital

15°N

TIRUMALA (p302)
Join thousands of pilgrims seeking
spiritual sustenance at this
overwhelming yet serene
pilgrimage centre

BAY
OF
BENGAL

North
Andaman
Saddle Peak
(732m)

ANDAMAN
ISLANDS

Middle
Andaman

South
Andaman
Port Blair
Mahatma Gandhi
National Marine Park
Rutland
Island

PUDUCHERRY (p395)
Practise yoga, stroll the beachside
promenade and tuck into crepes
at this pretty French-flavoured town

Little
Andaman

ANDAMAN ISLANDS (p444)
Splash in gin-clear waters,
gawk at world-class coral
reefs, and laze on beautiful
white-sand beaches

*Andaman
Sea*

10°N

Car Nicobar

NICOBAR
ISLANDS

*The external boundaries of India
on this map have not been
authenticated and may not be correct.*

Katchall
Island

Great Nicobar

South
India

LEGEND

Freeway
Primary Road
Secondary Road
Tertiary Road
Unsealed Road

0 ——————— 300 km
0 ——————— 180 miles

ELEVATION

2000m
1000m
500m
200m
0

85°E

90°E

South India Highlights

Travellers, Lonely Planet staff and authors share their top experiences of South India. Do you agree with their choices, or have we missed out your favourite? Go to lonelyplanet .com/bluelist and tell us *your* highlights.

1 KERALA BACKWATERS

Watching the Kerala backwaters (p328) slip by from a houseboat. Nets like cobwebs catch the dawn light as fishermen start their day. The houseboat slides past tiny villages, children duck each other under the water and wave, or race you along the bank, or ignore you, absorbed in a game of cricket. The sun at noon pounds out of a bright blue sky, and you retreat under the awning. There's nothing to do but read and watch the water. Water lilies open as the day goes on, then slowly close. Afternoons segue into lazy evenings, the orange sun creeping across the ripples and setting them ablaze before the moon casts her own wavering reflection. Sleep is under a mosquito net and a fan in the warm, tropical night.

Janet Brunckhorst, Lonely Planet, Melbourne

CHOWPATTY BEACH, MUMBAI

I loved strolling along elegant Marine Drive to Chowpatty Beach (p115), as the sun sets, joining hundreds of families promenading and snacking on plates of *bhelpuri*.
Sam Trafford, Lonely Planet, Melbourne

GREG ELMS

PAUL BIGLAND

HAMPI

We cycled around the sights of Hampi, from the towering Virupaksha Temple (p258) past the boulder-strewn landscape to the grand, domed Elephant Stables (p260).
Sarah Tattum, Traveller

MARK DAFFEY

MYSORE

The Maharaja's Palace (p233) at Mysore is bright with ornate decoration and carving, worth exploring before stocking up at the technicolour Devaraja Market (p235).

Peter Bradbury, Traveller

CELEBRATION SEASON

Marching bands in procession to decoratively lit marquees, accompanied by bright fireworks, signal the wedding season is in full swing.

sunphlower, Bluelist contributor

5

6 GET INVOLVED

We helped make our own roti. It didn't look great but, heck, we made it! Many street vendors seemed happy to let us have a go (or at least pretend to) for that great photo to send to friends back home.

leerick, Bluelist contributor

7 PERIYAR WILDLIFE SANCTUARY

Tigers, leopards, elephants and deer roam the misty mountains of the Periyar Wildlife Sanctuary (p334) in the Western Ghats. The park is home to a variety of birds and reptiles. For animal spotting hop on an early morning or late afternoon cruise.

global8, Bluelist contributor

DENNIS JOHNSON

8 GOA

India is an assault on the senses. Feel the sand between your toes, sun on your back and a breeze in your face walking along the beaches in Goa (p192).

sunphlower, Bluelist contributor

FORT COCHIN

A wander through this charismatic town (p343) is a world tour through medieval Europe, coastal China, ancient Jerusalem and old India. It's a quiet and intriguing spot to explore just overflowing with history, spices and interesting shops.

global8, Bluelist contributor

TONY WHEELER

9

MUMBAI

Millions crowd near roped-off paths into the ocean at Chowpatty Beach for Ganesh Chaturthi (p108), to immerse statues into the water as the horde's excitement turns fever-pitch. Claustrophobic. Intimidating. Wonderful.

jamesgraham, Bluelist contributor

KAREN TRIST

10

RICHARD I'ANSON

11 ELLORA CAVES

My favourite experience? Feeling overwhelmed by the ornate Buddhist, Jain and Hindu cave temples (p147) carved from the rock.

Paul Brown, Traveller

PAUL BEINSSEN

12 TEMPLE SOUNDS

Visit any Hindu temple in India and take in the sounds that surround you. Garland-offerers, security guards shouting orders, devotional bands playing traditional music and people praying – it's a quintessential Indian experience.

cyshki, Bluelist contributor

Mother

13 **TAMIL NADU TEMPLES**

We spent time exploring temples (p367) in Tamil Nadu, and we were bowled over by the amazing colourful *gopurams* (gateway towers).

Stuart Macdonald, Traveller

ENJOYING THE JOURNEY
Riding on bumpy local buses, watching the world pass by.

LeahN, Thorntree user

14

MARGIE POLITZER

HYDERABAD
Head to Laad Bazaar (p278) in Hyderabad to stock up on bangles, and watch your arm glitter and glow. If you can't find a colour and size to fit, you must be too fussy!

fdangerfield, Bluelist contributor

15

GREG ELMS

NIC BOTHM

16 TRAIN JOURNEYS

We made the journey from Mumbai to Goa on the Konkan Railway (p503); some of the most beautiful scenery in India.

Gayatri Ganesh, Traveller

PAUL BEINSS

17 CHAI, CHAI

Cup after cup of hot, spiced chai fuelled us through our trip – refreshing, reassuring and never very far away.

Clare Lewis, Traveller

Contents

South India Highlights 4	
The Authors	**16**
Destination South India	**19**
Getting Started	**20**
Itineraries	**25**
Snapshot	**33**
History	**35**
The Culture	**49**
Food & Drink	**75**
Environment	**86**
Activities	**97**

Mumbai (Bombay) 104

History	105
Orientation	108
Information	108
Sights	111
Activities	117
Walking Tour	118
Courses	118
Mumbai for Children	119
Tours	119
Sleeping	120
Eating	124
Drinking	127
Entertainment	129
Shopping	130
Getting There & Away	131
Getting Around	134
GREATER MUMBAI	**135**
Elephanta Island	135
Sanjay Gandhi National Park	136

Maharashtra 137

NORTHERN MAHARASHTRA	**139**
Nasik	139
Around Nasik	142
Aurangabad	143
Around Aurangabad	146
Ellora	147
Ajanta	150
Jalgaon	153
Lonar Meteorite Crater	153
Nagpur	154
Around Nagpur	155
Sevagram	155
Around Sevagram	156
SOUTHERN MAHARASHTRA	**156**
Konkan Coast	156
Matheran	158
Lonavla	160
Karla & Bhaja Caves	162
Pune	163
Around Pune	170
Mahabaleshwar	170
Around Mahabaleshwar	172
Kolhapur	173

Goa 175

NORTH GOA	**181**
Panaji (Panjim)	181
Old Goa	187
Torda	190
Mapusa	190
Fort Aguada & Candolim	190
Calangute & Baga	194
Anjuna	199
Vagator & Chapora	201
Chapora to Arambol	204
Arambol (Harmal)	204
Terekhol (Tiracol) Fort	206
SOUTH GOA	**206**
Margao (Madgaon)	206

Chandor 208
Loutolim 209
Bogmalo & Arossim 209
Colva & Benaulim 210
Benaulim to Palolem 213
Palolem & Around 213
CENTRAL GOA 215
Ponda & Around 215
Bondla Wildlife Sanctuary 215
Molem & Bhagwan Mahavir Wildlife Sanctuary 216
Dudhsagar Falls 216

Karnataka 217
SOUTHERN KARNATAKA 219
Bengaluru (Bangalore) 219
Around Bengaluru 232
Mysore 232
Around Mysore 240
Bandipur National Park 241
Nagarhole National Park 242
Kodagu (Coorg) Region 243
Hassan 246
Belur & Halebid 247
Sravanabelagola 249
KARNATAKA COAST 250
Mangalore 250
Dharmastala 253
Udupi (Udipi) 253
Malpe 253
Amgol 254
Murudeshwar 254
Jog Falls 254
Gokarna 254
CENTRAL KARNATAKA 257
Hampi 257
Hospet 263
Hubli 264
NORTHERN KARNATAKA 264
Badami 264
Around Badami 267
Bijapur 268
Bidar 271

Andhra Pradesh 273
Hyderabad & Secunderabad 275
Nagarjunakonda 295
Warangal 297
Around Warangal 298

Visakhapatnam 298
Around Visakhapatnam 300
Vijayawada 300
Around Vijayawada 301
Tirumala & Tirupathi 302
Around Tirimula & Tirupathi 304
Puttaparthi 304
Lepakshi 305

Kerala 306
SOUTHERN KERALA 308
Thiruvananthapuram (Trivandrum) 308
Around Trivandrum 314
Kovalam 315
Around Kovalam 319
Padmanabhapuram Palace 319
Varkala 319
Kollam (Quilon) 323
Around Kollam 326
Alappuzha (Alleppey) 326
Around Alleppey 331
Kottayam 331
Around Kottayam 333
THE WESTERN GHATS 334
Periyar Wildlife Sanctuary 334
Munnar 337
Around Munnar 339
Parambikulam Wildlife Sanctuary 340
CENTRAL KERALA 340
Kochi (Cochin) 340
Around Kochi 352
Thrissur (Trichur) 352
Around Thrissur 355
NORTHERN KERALA 355
Kozhikode (Calicut) 355
Wayanad Wildlife Sanctuary 357
Kannur (Cannanore) 358
Bekal & Around 360
LAKSHADWEEP 360
Bangaram Island 361
Agatti Island 362
Kadmat Island 362
Minicoy Island 362

Tamil Nadu 363
CHENNAI (MADRAS) 364
History 366

Orientation 367
Information 367
Dangers & Annoyances 371
Sights 371
Activities 374
Courses 374
Tours 374
Sleeping 374
Eating 376
Drinking 377
Entertainment 378
Shopping 378
Getting There & Away 379
Getting Around 381
NORTHERN TAMIL NADU 382
Chennai to Mamallapuram 382
Mamallapuram (Mahabalipuram) 382
Around Mamallapuram 388
Vedantangal Bird Sanctuary 388
Kanchipuram 389
Vellore 392
Tiruvannamalai 393
Gingee (Senji) 395
Puducherry (Pondicherry) 395
Auroville 402
CENTRAL TAMIL NADU 403
Chidambaram 403
Around Chidambaram 405
Kumbakonam 405
Around Kumbakonam 406
Cauvery Delta 407
Thanjavur (Tanjore) 408
Around Thanjavur 411
Tiruchirappalli (Trichy) 411
SOUTHERN TAMIL NADU 415
Trichy to Rameswaram 415
Rameswaram 416
Madurai 418
Kanyakumari (Cape Comorin) 423
THE WESTERN GHATS 426
Kodaikanal (Kodai) 427
Around Kodaikanal 431
Indira Gandhi (Annamalai) Wildlife Sanctuary 431
Coimbatore 431
Around Coimbatore 434
Coonoor 434

Kotagiri	435	Middle & North Andaman	459	**Glossary**	**521**
Udhagamandalam (Ooty)	436	Little Andaman	461		
Mudumalai National Park	442			**Behind the Scenes**	**526**
		Directory	**462**		
Andaman &				**Index**	**532**
Nicobar Islands	**444**	**Transport**	**491**		
Port Blair	450			**World Time Zones**	**546**
Around Port Blair		**Health**	**506**		
& South Andaman	455			**Map Legend**	**548**
Havelock Island	456	**Language**	**515**		
Neil Island	458				

Regional Map Contents

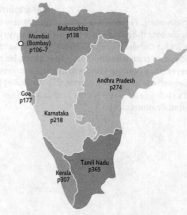

Mumbai (Bombay) p106–7

Maharashtra p138

Goa p177

Andhra Pradesh p274

Karnataka p218

Kerala p307

Tamil Nadu p365

Andaman & Nicobar Islands p446

The Authors

SARINA SINGH
Coordinating Author

After finishing a business degree in Melbourne, Sarina bought a one-way ticket to India where she completed a corporate traineeship with the Sheraton. She later ditched hotels for newspapers, working as a freelance journalist and foreign correspondent. After four years in India, Sarina returned to Australia, pursued post-graduate journalism qualifications and wrote/directed *Beyond the Royal Veil*, a television documentary that premiered at the Melbourne International Film Festival. She has worked on numerous Lonely Planet books, including *Rajasthan*, *India*, *North India* and *Pakistan & the Karakoram Highway*. She has also written for various international publications, including *National Geographic Traveler*, and is the author of *Polo in India*; further details at www.sarinasingh.com.

Life on the Road

In India, you can unexpectedly find yourself up close and personal with moments that have the power to alter the way you view the world and your place in it... It was a sultry subcontinental afternoon in 1990. To escape a sudden monsoonal downpour, I dashed into a museum and found myself tagging behind a bunch of tourists. Suddenly the group's guide, a crinkle-faced old man with thick silvery hair and a wispy beard, pointed directly at me: 'You, with the strong Jupiter vibrations, you're on the wrong path!' I froze in puzzled embarrassment as the other tourists spun around and speared me with inquisitive stares. The somewhat agitated guide scuttled over, beseeching me to start writing – only then would I be going the 'right' way... That evening, while jostling my way through a people-packed bazaar in the old city, a willowy lady selling spice-cakes beckoned me over and insisted – with the same peculiar urgency as the museum guide – that I write about 'all this'. It was too much serendipity to ignore.

STUART BUTLER
Maharashtra, Goa

Stuart Butler is an English-born, French-based photojournalist who has travelled extensively in India over the past decade in search of empty surf, unlikely stories and fodder for his camera lenses. When not struggling to grasp the mathematics behind Indian train timetables he writes about his travels, which have taken him beyond the borders of India to places as diverse as the coastal deserts of Pakistan and the jungles of Colombia. These stories feature frequently in the world's surfing and travel media and can be seen on his website www.oceansurfpublications.co.uk.

VIRGINIA JEALOUS
Tamil Nadu (sans Chennai section), Andaman & Nicobar Islands

Virginia made her first trip to India (carrying Lonely Planet's very first *India* guidebook) in 1984. Infected by her father's obsession with the subcontinent, and the Books About India that he dealt in, she's visited several times, equally enchanted by the country's wildlife, enthralled by its cultural complexities and flummoxed by its idiosyncrasies. Updating the Tamil Nadu and Andaman & Nicobar Islands chapters gave her the chance to revisit some birding hot spots, where the racket-tailed drongo was a big favourite, but the famed Nicobar pigeon continued to elude her. She dreams of inventing one perfect adjective to describe India, but isn't even close yet.

AMY KARAFIN
Tamil Nadu (Chennai section), Andhra Pradesh

Amy Karafin grew up on the US Jersey shore, where she developed a keen curiosity about the horizon that developed into a phobia of residence. Indian in several former lives, she headed straight to India after university for an extended trip that would turn out to be karmically ordained. She spent the next few years alternating between New York and faraway lands until, fed up with the irony of being a travel editor in a Manhattan cubicle, she relinquished her MetroCard and her black skirts to make a living closer to the equator. She currently divides her time between Mumbai (Bombay), New York and Dakar.

SIMON RICHMOND
Karnataka

In 1999 Simon first encountered southern India on a journey that included snorkelling in the Andaman Islands, trekking in the Nilgiri Hills and drifting through the Kerala backwaters on a *kettuvallam* (rice barge) houseboat. A year later he travelled through northern India at the tail end of an overland haul from İstanbul to Kathmandu for Lonely Planet. In 2004 he covered the maximum city of Mumbai, the beaches of Goa and the architectural and cultural wonders of Maharashtra. Simon is the author of several other Lonely Planet guides, including *Cape Town*, *Malaysia, Singapore & Brunei*, *Russia* and *Trans-Siberian Railway*.

LONELY PLANET AUTHORS

Why is our travel information the best in the world? It's simple: our authors are independent, dedicated travellers. They don't research using just the internet or phone, and they don't take freebies in exchange for positive coverage. They travel widely, to all the popular spots and off the beaten track. They personally visit thousands of hotels, restaurants, cafés, bars, galleries, palaces, museums and more – and they take pride in getting all the details right, and telling it how it is. Think you can do it? Find out how at lonelyplanet.com.

RAFAEL WLODARSKI Mumbai (Bombay), Kerala

After completing degrees in marketing and psychology in Melbourne, Rafael vowed never to use either of them and set off on a six-month around-the-world trip. Seven years and four passports later and he is yet to come home. Rafael spent most of his twenties travelling overland through the Middle East, the Indian subcontinent and North and South America. He managed to get lost in India for six months along the way, and relished coming back to Kerala to update this edition of *South India*. He currently calls 'sunny' London home and spends a lot of time in Brick Lane re-living his memories with the aid of fish curry.

Destination South India

Like a giant wedge plunging into the Indian Ocean, peninsular South India is the steamy Hindu heartland of the subcontinent, and an infinitely different place from the landlocked mountains and sun-baked deserts of the north.

Thousands of kilometres of sea-kissed coastline frame fertile plains and undulating hills, all kept deliciously lush by the double-barrelled monsoon. This is the India for those seeking the happy-go-lucky beach life of Goa; the ancient Hindu temples of Tamil Nadu and Karnataka; the upbeat urban jungles of Mumbai (Bombay) and Bengaluru (Bangalore); the breezy palm-fringed backwaters of tropical Kerala; the phenomenal trekking and wildlife-watching opportunities of the hills and plains; and the unfettered rural and tribal culture of Andhra Pradesh.

When it comes to ethnic groups, festivals, landscapes and traditions, South India is spectacularly diverse, presenting the traveller with a scintillating smorgasbord of things to see and do. And then of course there's the food! From traditional favourites such as podgy *idlis* (rice dumplings), addictive dosas (savoury crepes) and fiery Goan curries, to a gamut of global fare – from wood-fired pizzas and spinach lasagne to squishy sushi and crunchy nachos – found in the south's bigger cities and tourist centres.

South India offers a delightfully mellow pace of travel, with most of its sites easily accessible and the beach never too far away. No matter where your wanderings take you, you'll quickly discover that India is an invigorating assault on *all* the senses, an experience that's impossible to define because it's so incredibly different for everyone. Ultimately, it's all about surrendering yourself to the unknown: this is the India that nothing can quite prepare you for because its very essence – its elusive soul – lies in its mystery.

PAUL BIGLAND

Getting Started

Vibrant, inspiring, mystifying, confronting, thought-provoking and frustrating in equal measure, there's no doubt that India presents the traveller with a positively mind-bending array of experiences. But toss aside any stereotypes you may harbour, because the south is India's 'gentler' side, with far fewer touts and scam-artists than the north, and oodles of blissful beaches to flee to whenever you need some seaside therapy. If you haven't visited this part of the world before, set aside the first few days to simply acclimatise to the subcontinent's bamboozling symphony of sights, sounds, tastes and smells.

As South India spans a large area and has a wealth of natural and historic attractions, deciding where to go will be one of your greatest challenges (for ideas, see Itineraries, p25). The key is to try not to squeeze in too much, as travelling often involves considerable distances and stamina. Remember to allow a few weeks of pretrip preparation to sort out your visa and immunisations. Before arriving, nut out a rough itinerary – you don't want to miss that spectacular festival by three days or plan to be relaxing on a Goan beach during the summer or monsoon – but also factor in a certain amount of flexibility, as things don't always run to clockwork in India. Indeed, more than a few travellers have had their holidays marred by not being able to get their preferred train seats, or being delayed by rescheduled buses and the like. Another reason to introduce flexibility into your itinerary is because India has an uncanny way of throwing up wonderful surprises and guiding you off the beaten track.

Finally, read up on India as much as you can prior to your trip, especially its cultural framework (also see The Culture, p49). Doing so will enhance your appreciation of the subcontinent's sights and traditions and will better equip you to hold more informed conversations with locals.

DON'T LEAVE HOME WITHOUT...

- A visa (p486) and travel insurance (p474)
- Advice about vaccinations (p506); some must be administered over a period of weeks
- Nonrevealing clothes (women *and* men) – covering up will win you more respect and is essential when visiting sacred sites
- Sunscreen and sunglasses – the sun packs a mighty punch
- A well-concealed money-belt
- A torch (flashlight) – for power blackouts and unlit lanes at night
- Earplugs to block out night din and for long bus/train journeys
- A small alarm clock – budget and midrange hotels often lack clocks and can be notorious for missing wake-up calls
- Flip-flops (thongs) – for communal or grotty bathrooms
- A shower cap and universal sink plug (uncommon except at top-end hotels)
- Tampons – sanitary pads are widely available but tampons are usually restricted to big (or touristy) cities
- Mosquito repellent (a mozzie net is also useful)
- A sense of adventure – remember, India rewards those who go with the flow

MONSOON MAGIC

Kerala is the first place the southwest monsoon strikes, in early June, drenching the state as it sweeps in eastward from the Arabian Sea. As it rises over the Western Ghats, it cools and soaks the windward slopes before dropping over the leeward side, parts of which receive only about a quarter of the rainfall dumped on the windward side. Within about 10 days the monsoon has usually travelled as far as northern Maharashtra, and by early July it has covered most of the country. Karnataka's Western Ghats are among the wettest parts of South India.

A second soaking occurs in Tamil Nadu and Kerala in November and early December when the retreating monsoon (commonly referred to as the northeast or winter monsoon) blusters in from the Bay of Bengal. The coasts of Andhra Pradesh and Tamil Nadu are occasionally hit by cyclones during these months.

WHEN TO GO

Except in the elevated hills of the Western Ghats, South India is hot year-round and can be roughly divided into two main seasons – dry and wet (monsoon). There are two monsoon periods – the northeast and southwest monsoons – with dates varying slightly across the region. As the climate is tropical, you won't find the large variations in temperature found in northern India.

In general, October to March is the best time to visit South India. It's relatively dry and cool, although in November and the beginning of December parts of Tamil Nadu and Kerala get a drenching as the northeast monsoon retreats across them. In the beach resorts of Goa some facilities (such as beach shacks) don't open until late October and, in the weeks immediately after the monsoon (ie in October), there may be strong rips, which can make swimming hazardous. Accommodation prices in popular tourist places, such as Goa, Kerala and the offshore islands, peak around Christmas and New Year.

See Climate Charts (p466) for more climate information.

Temperatures start to rise rapidly in most places in late March, and by May South India sizzles. The peak travel season in the mountains is April to June, where the altitude provides cool relief from the scorching plains. Conversely, the Western Ghats can get misty and quite cold in winter (late December and January), and the nights are often cold regardless of the time of year.

The climate in the Andaman and Nicobar Islands is tropical, with temperatures averaging 29°C, but this is moderated by sea breezes. The islands receive most rain during the southwest monsoon (May to September), and during the cyclonic storms in October and November. Lakshadweep has similar tropical weather.

Apart from the weather, the timing of certain festivals may also influence when you wish to visit (see the Festivals In... boxed texts at the start of each regional chapter and p471).

COSTS & MONEY

In terms of finances, South India has something to please all pockets. Accommodation ranges from basic beachside shacks to swanky five-star hotels, with some charming midrange possibilities that won't break the bank. A multipriced array of eateries means you can chomp to your heart's content without spending a fortune, and it's also possible to zip around economically thanks to a comprehensive public transport network.

As costs vary throughout South India, the best way of ascertaining how much money you'll need for your trip is to peruse the relevant regional chapters of this book. Be prepared to pay more in the larger cities such as Mumbai (Bombay) and Bengaluru (Bangalore), as well as at popular tourist destinations.

SCINTILLATING SOUTH INDIA

There's much more to South India than simply sightseeing:

- Activities (see p97)
- Courses (see p467)
- Festivals (see p471)
- Shopping (see p478)
- Volunteering (see p487)

In regard to sightseeing, foreigners are often charged more than Indian citizens for entry into tourist sites (admission prices for foreigners are sometimes given in US dollars, payable in the rupee equivalent), and there may also be additional charges for still/video cameras.

Accommodation is likely to be your biggest expense (see p462). Costs can vary depending on the season – high-season prices for hotels can be 50% more, but usually only at popular tourist spots – and depend on whether you're travelling solo or with a group. High season is from around November to February in most regions, with a specific peak season of mid-December to early January in coastal resorts. High season in the mountains (such as at hill stations) is from around April to June. Accommodation rates can shoot up during festivals or other special events, with some hotels charging at least double the normal rate during these times (see p465 for details).

Dining out is terrific value, with meals for as little as Rs 40 at budget eateries, and usually little more than double that for a satiating midrange restaurant meal. As with accommodation, prices vary regionally (for details see the Eating sections of individual chapters).

Regarding long-distance travel, there's a range of classes on trains and several bus types, resulting in considerable flexibility vis-à-vis comfort and price – regional chapters supply specific costs; also see p495. Domestic flights have become a lot more price competitive thanks to the recent deregulation of the Indian airline industry (see p495). Within towns there's economical public transport (see p498), or you may like to consider hiring a car with driver, which is surprisingly good value if there are several of you to split the cost (see p497).

So how exactly does this all translate to a daily budget? Roughly speaking, if you stick to a tight budget you can manage on around Rs 450 to 600 per day (but budget for at least double that in some big cities and tourist hubs). This means staying in basic lodgings, travelling on the cheaper buses and train classes, eating simple meals and doing limited sightseeing. If you wish to stay in midrange hotels, dine at nicer restaurants, do a reasonable amount of sightseeing and largely travel by autorickshaw and taxi, you're generally looking at anywhere between Rs 900 and Rs 1700 per day. Of course, you'll be able to subsist on less in South India's smaller, less touristy towns.

HOW MUCH?

Sarong Rs 60

Mars Bar Rs 25

Bellybutton bindi Rs 15

Haircut/shave Rs 55/20

Toothpaste (100g) Rs 27

TRAVEL LITERATURE

Maximum City: Bombay Lost & Found, by Suketu Mehta, is an incisively researched and elegantly written epic, equal parts memoir, travelogue and journalism, which focuses on the exhilarating city of Mumbai – gang warfare, riots, Bollywood, bar girls and more.

William Sutcliffe's *Are You Experienced?* is the hilarious tale of first-time backpacker Dave, who accompanies his best friend's girlfriend to India in

TOP PICKS SOUTH INDIA

Bay of Bengal   Thailand

RIVETING READS

There is nothing better than getting lost in a book, and there's certainly no dearth of novels offering brilliant insights into India – the below titles are some splendid places to kick off your reading spree. For additional recommended reading, see opposite, p66 and the boxed text (p109).

- *The Inheritance of Loss* by Kiran Desai (see p67)
- *Shantaram* by Gregory David Roberts
- *The God of Small Things* by Arundhati Roy
- *A Fine Balance* by Rohinton Mistry (see p66)
- *A Suitable Boy* by Vikram Seth

FANTASTICAL FESTIVALS

South India has an awesome assortment of major and minor festivals – for complete details, see p471 as well as the Festivals In...boxed texts at the start of each regional chapter.

- Nehru Trophy Snake Boat Race – August; Kerala (p309)
- Ganesh Chaturthi – August/September; especially in Mumbai (Bombay; p108) and Pune (p141)
- Ellora Dance & Music Festival – December/January; Aurangabad (p141)
- Feast of St Francis Xavier – December; Old Goa (p178)
- Festival of Carnatic Music & Dance – December/January; Chennai (Madras; p366)

TREMENDOUS TRIPS

With South India's dazzling mix of dramatic landscapes and waterways, the memories you'll collect while travelling are bound to blaze bright in your memory long after your Indian sojourn has ended. Here is a smattering of the most unforgettable trips.

- Toy train to Udhagamandalam (Ooty; p441) – the miniature steam train to Ooty chugs past some truly jaw-dropping mountain scenery
- Backwater cruise from Alappuzha (Alleppey) to Kollam (Quilon; see The Backwaters (p328) – cruising the lush Keralan backwaters is undeniably one of the glowing highlights of a trip to South India

- Mumbai to Goa by train (p133) – travel down the scenic Konkan Coast on one of India's newest stretches of rail line
- Island-hopping in the Andamans (p449) – kick back on the ferry deck and hop from one glorious island to another in the tropical Andamans
- Cycling in Goa – take an unhurried bike ride from charming Panaji (Panjim; p181) to atmospheric Old Goa (p187)

an attempt to seduce her. Sutcliffe cleverly portrays the backpacker scene in India.

Chasing the Monsoon, by Alexander Frater, is an Englishman's story of his monsoon-chasing journey from Kovalam (in Kerala) to Meghalaya (in the northeast states). It perceptively captures the significance of the monsoon both on the land and for the people.

Inhaling The Mahatma, by Christopher Kremmer, is the author's riveting and multifarious encounter with India, from his stint as a foreign correspondent in the early 1990s, to his marriage to an Indian woman and life beyond.

Geoffrey Moorhouse's *Om: An Indian Pilgrimage* provides an erudite window into the lives of a diverse bunch of people in South India, from coir makers to holy men. This book offers an insight into some of South India's ashrams.

Indian Summer, by Will Randall, is the story of the author's personal experience of unexpectedly finding himself in Pune teaching at a school for street kids, then suddenly fighting to save the school from being shut down.

Anita Desai's *Journey to Ithaca* is the beguiling tale of two young Europeans, Matteo and Sophie, who go to India seeking spiritual enlightenment. While Matteo's ashram experience is spiritually affirming, Sophie's isn't quite so rosy.

In *Divining the Deccan,* Bill Aitken rides through the little-visited centre of South India on a motorbike, painting a lively portrait of the region and including some enlightening historical and cultural details.

INTERNET RESOURCES

Best Indian Sites (www.bestindiansites.com) Proffers links to popular websites including handy search engines.

Incredible India (www.incredibleindia.org) The official Indian government tourism site, with national travel-related information.

Lonely Planet (www.lonelyplanet.com) Apart from plenty of useful links, there's the popular Thorn Tree, where you can swap information with fellow travellers to South India and beyond.

Maps of India (www.mapsofindia.com) A nifty variety of maps, including thematic offerings, such as those pinpointing South India's hill stations, wildlife sanctuaries and states.

South India (www.southindia.com) True to its name, this vast portal focuses on South India, with links to everything from flight and train timetables to hospitals and state-specific travel information.

South India Tourism (www.south-india-tourism.com) Provides information on various facets of the South Indian tourism scene, from festivals and Ayurveda to temples and beaches.

World Newspapers (www.world-newspapers.com/india.html) Has links to India's major English-language national and regional publications, enabling you to stay tuned to what's happening where.

Itineraries

CLASSIC ROUTES

SOUTH INDIA EXPRESS   Three to eight weeks

Start in **Mumbai** (Bombay; p104), then head northeast to **Aurangabad** (p143) to visit the amazing rock-cut caves at **Ellora** (p147) and **Ajanta** (p150). Next, scuttle south to **Pune** (p163) to meditate and play 'zennis' (Zen tennis). It's a long but easy trip to **Bijapur** (p268), with the Golgumbaz (p268), then south to the former Vijayanagar capital of **Hampi** (p257). Continue on to **Bengaluru** (Bangalore; p219), India's IT powerhouse, detouring to the pilgrimage centre of **Sravanabelagola** (p249), and the temples of **Halebid** (p248) and **Belur** (p248). Next stop is the erstwhile maharaja's capital of **Mysore** (p232) and, for a change of pace, slide down the Western Ghats to **Udhagamandalam** (Ooty; p436), with a stop at **Mudumalai National Park** (p442). Take the toy train to Mettupalayam and west to **Kochi** (Cochin; p340). From here you can travel to the **Periyar Wildlife Sanctuary** (p334) to gawk at wild animals. It's a comfortable trip from here to **Madurai** (p418) and its remarkable Sri Meenakshi Temple. After soaking up Madurai's tremendous temples, hop on a train to **Chennai** (Madras; p364).

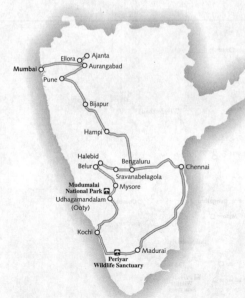

From Mumbai to Chennai, this route includes some of the best of South India's city life and temple towns, as well as trekking and wildlife. Three weeks will cover the main stops, but add a few more weeks to cover the 3500km.

SAVOURING THE SOUTH
Two months

Mumbai (p104), the rambunctious capital of Maharasthra, is a splendid jumping-off point for exploration of India's steamy south. Make sure you time your trip to avoid the sticky monsoon – the sunniest skies are from around October to February. Don't forget to pack plenty of sunscreen!

Kick off in cosmopolitan Mumbai, the beating heart of star-studded Bollywood (p116), making the most of the fabulous shopping (p130), eating (p124) and drinking (p127) before heading inland to **Ajanta** (p150) and **Ellora** (p147) to marvel at Maharashtra's finest cave art. Sashay southwest to **Goa** (p175) to simply flop on the soft sand and splash in the cool ocean at one of the state's palm-fringed beaches before dosing up on history inland at enigmatic **Hampi** (p257), with its temple ruins and giant boulders.

Next, hang out with yuppies at the hip party bars of **Bengaluru** (p228), then get giddy on the waft of incense in spicy **Mysore** (p232) with its opulent Maharaja's Palace (p233). Tuck into a wholesome banana-leaf thali (p238), before cruising south to tropical Kerala, stopping at historical **Kochi** (Cochin; p340) to enjoy a traditional performance of Kathakali (p349). Cruise Kerala's languorous backwaters from **Alappuzha** (Alleppey; p326), before dipping your toes in the warm waters around **Varkala** (p319).

For a change of tempo, head northeast from Varkala to **Periyar Wildlife Sanctuary** (p334) to spot wild elephants before boggling at the intricacy of the awe-inspiring temples of **Madurai** (p418). Pop into **Tiruchirappalli** (Trichy; p411) and **Thanjavur** (Tanjore; p408) before slowing the pace in French-flavoured **Puducherry** (Pondicherry; p395), a cheerful coastal town where you can toss up between curries or crepes. Feast on more fine food in Tamil Nadu's chaotic capital, **Chennai** (p376), before fleeing north to admire the intriguing Mughal-era relics of **Hyderabad** (p275).

A slice of the steamy south, this itinerary visits divine beaches, intriguing cave temples, lush jungle reserves, a maharaja's palace and some of South India's most scintillating cities. Add on a couple of weeks to the journey if you prefer to savour it more slowly.

SAND, SEA & SACRED SITES   Two to three months

This itinerary, beginning in **Mumbai** (p104) and ending in **Chennai** (p364), blends some of the south's most sublime temples with its most breathtaking beaches. If you're keen to beach it up to the max, consider tagging the sun-washed **Andaman Islands** (p444) onto the end of this itinerary.

Start at Mumbai's Chowpatty Beach (p115), overlooking the vast Arabian Sea, with a plate of delicious *bhelpuri* (p78). Take a cruise to the magnificent rock-cut temples on **Elephanta Island** (p135), then travel south by train to beach-blessed **Goa** (p175). Whether you're seeking something mellow or something party-charged, this beach-bursting state has something to suit everyone (see The Beach Files, p192); old favourites include Arambol (Harmal; p204), Vagator (p201) and around Palolem (p213). Continue to the sacred seaside town of **Gokarna** (p254), with its more hushed appeal than touristy Goa. Next, veer inland to the ruined Vijayanagar temples at **Hampi** (p257), with its peculiar boulder-strewn landscape, and the Hoysala temples of **Belur and Halebid** (p247).

Connect through the coastal towns of **Mangalore** (p250) and **Kochi** (Cochin; p340) to Kerala's palm-packed seaside strip and indulge in some serious beach therapy in **Varkala** (p319) and **Kovalam** (p315), before taking the train northeast to the awesome Sri Meenakshi Temple in **Madurai** (p420). Continue north through the historic temple towns of **Tiruchirappalli** (Trichy; p411), **Thanjavur** (p408) and **Chidambaram** (p403), breaking the journey at pretty **Puducherry** (p395) where you can pick up lovely handmade paper (p401) for friends back home.

Continuing north, detour inland to the captivating **Arunachaleswar Temple** (p394) in Tiruvannamalai, and follow the coast to carving-covered **Mamallapuram** (Mahabalipuram; p382), home to the ancient rock-carved Shore Temple (p383). Finally, conclude your southern sojourn with an unhurried stroll along Chennai's **Marina Beach** (p371).

Kicking off in Mumbai and winding up in Chennai, this route brings together the best of South India's beaches and temples – you'll feel chilled out and spiritually charged at the same time! Treat yourself to an additional month to really squeeze the most out of it.

ROADS LESS TRAVELLED

HILL HAPPY   Three to six weeks

A great way to avoid the tourist treadmill is to ditch the coastal towns and go trekking in the beautiful national parks and hills of the Western Ghats.

From Mumbai take the toy train up to **Matheran** (p158), a traffic-free hilltop retreat with tranquil walks and panoramic lookouts. Head back down via Lonavla and Pune before winding your way back up into the hills to **Mahabaleshwar** (p170), a hill station popular with families and famous for its berry farms. From here it's a bit of a trek south to **Madikeri** (Mecara; p243) in the Kodagu (Coorg) hills, but worth it for the rewarding trekking and fragrant coffee plantations. Journey east to Mysore, and head back up into the hills again. Four adjoining national parks – **Bandipur National Park** (p241) and **Nagarhole National Park** (p242) in Karnataka, **Mudumalai National Park** (p442) in Tamil Nadu and **Wayanad National Park** (p357) in Kerala – form the Nilgiri Biosphere Reserve, and together they offer some of the most phenomenal wildlife viewing, trekking and jungle camps in South India. From Mudumalai it's an enjoyable trip to **Udhagamandalam** (Ooty; p436), a sprawling Raj-era hill station set amid forested hills. If you still haven't had your fill of hiking and hill stations, head south from Coimbatore through the Palani Hills to **Kodaikanal** (Kodai; p427), a much quainter and quieter town than Ooty. From Kodaikanal you can take a Kochi-bound bus to **Munnar** (p337), which boasts the world's highest tea plantations as well as dramatic mountain scenery. Another 70km south of here is the **Periyar Wildlife Sanctuary** (p334), a marvellous place for wildlife watching, jungle treks and lake cruises.

Verdant national parks, pretty forests and cool hill stations make a welcome change from the coast and plains. This 1500km route whisks you through impressive hill stations and wildlife-watching areas. You could wrap the trip up in just three weeks, but an extra week will give you some breathing space.

THE WORLD HERITAGE WHIRL   Four to six weeks

Of the 26 World Heritage sites scattered throughout India, 10 are in the south and most of these are ancient monuments or temples.

In Mumbai, one of the newest additions to the list is the **Chhatrapati Shivaji Terminus** (p114) – better known as Victoria Terminus – the main train station, and its riotous blend of Gothic architecture makes this one of the most original train stations on the planet. **Elephanta Island** (p135), just out of Mumbai, sports rock-cut cave temples dedicated to Lord Shiva. The finest historical attractions in Maharashtra are undeniably the rock-cut cave temples at **Ellora** (p147), which were created over a period of five centuries by Buddhist, Hindu and Jain monks, and the caves and Buddhist frescoes at **Ajanta** (p150), which predate those of Ellora.

Meanwhile, the churches and convents of Goa's former capital, **Old Goa** (p187) are among India's most striking and should not be missed. They include the Basilica of Bom Jesus (p188), Se Cathedral (Sé de Santa Catarina; p187) and the Convent & Church of St Francis of Assisi (p187). **Hampi** (p257) is a favourite as much for its atmosphere as for its eye-catching temples harking back to the Vijayanagar empire. Just north, the temples of **Pattadakal** (p267) may be less well known, but the Virupaksha Temple, with it's beautifully carved columns depicting scenes from the great Hindu epics, is still worth a peek. At **Mamallapuram** (Mahabalipuram; p382), the Shore Temple (p383) and Five Rathas (p385) are among a large group of monuments from the Pallava dynasty, while at **Thanjavur** (p408), the Brihadishwara Temple (p409) is the crowning glory.

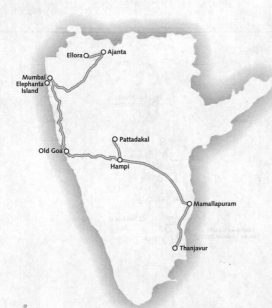

India's southern World Heritage sites include exquisite rock-cut caves, lofty churches, ancient temples and even a city railway station. You could manage the trip in a month, but a couple of extra weeks will make the experience that bit more rewarding.

ISLAND MAGIC
Two to four weeks

If you're hankering for deserted beaches, snorkelling and diving, the Andamans are hard to beat. The island chain, 1000km east of the mainland in the Bay of Bengal, can be reached by boat or air from Chennai or Kolkata (Calcutta). From Chennai, you'll arrive by air or sea into the capital, **Port Blair** (p450), a busy town with little tropical allure but some commendable museums and legacies of the island's colonial past. After a visit to Port Blair's Cellular Jail National Memorial (p451) and **Ross Island** (p455), book a ferry to **Havelock Island** (p456), where you can indulge in scuba diving, snorkelling and fishing. For something quieter, stay on nearby **Neil Island** (p458). From Havelock there are ferries to **Rangat** (p459), with a possible stop at **Long Island** (p447). From Rangat a bus runs up through Middle Andaman to **Mayabunder** (p459), where you can take a boat to tiny **Avis Island** (p459). From Mayabunder, travel overland to **Diglipur** (p460) on North Andaman (or take an overnight ferry from Port Blair to Diglipur), a remote area where you can climb Saddle Peak or laze on deserted beaches.

Back in Port Blair, hire a moped or catch a bus and head down to **Wandoor** (p455), the jumping-off point for the **Mahatma Gandhi Marine National Park** (p455) and Jolly Buoy and Red Skin Islands.

Travel in the dreamy Andaman Islands is a trip unto itself, with inimitable beaches, turquoise waters and superb snorkelling and diving. This route covers about 800km to 1000km of land and ferry travel. You'll need a minimum of two weeks; permit restrictions limit you to 30 days.

TAILORED TRIPS

TEMPLES & PILGRIMAGES

If there's one thing that will have a lingering impact on you during and after your South Indian wanderings, it's spirituality. To bask in South India's spiritual splendour, consider this itinerary, which follows in the footsteps of countless pilgrims and spiritual seekers. There's a particularly well-worn pilgrimage route through Tamil Nadu, which includes the temple towns of **Kanchipuram** (Kanchi; p389); **Tiruvannamalai** (p393); **Chidambaram** (p403); **Kumbakonam** (p405); **Thanjavur** (p408); **Tiruchirappalli** (Trichy; p411), with the Rock Fort Temple and Sri Ranganathaswamy Temple; **Madurai** (p418) for the renowned Sri Meenakshi Temple; **Rameswaram** (p416), one of the holiest Hindu pilgrimage places in India; and **Kanyakumari** (Cape Comorin; p423), where pilgrims flock not only for the Kumari Amman Temple, but also to see the sun rise and set at the southernmost tip of India.

Over in Andhra Pradesh, the Venkateshwara Temple at **Tirumala** (p302) receives as many as 100,000 pilgrims *per day*! In Karnataka, **Sravanabelagola** (p249) is a very auspicious pilgrimage centre for Jains who come to honour the statue of Gomateshvara (Bahubali), perched upon a hill. **Gokarna** (p254), apart from being a chilled-out beach paradise, is one of South India's most sacred sites for Shaivites who gather here to worship at the Mahabaleshwara Temple. Meanwhile, **Nasik** (p139) is Maharashtra's holiest pilgrimage town and host (every 12 years) to the illustrious Kumbh Mela (p472).

ASHRAM HOPPING

If you're seeking spiritual sustenance, South India has more than enough to keep you in deep contemplation for at least one lifetime. To get an insight into ashrams (spiritual communities), see p102.

In Pune, the **Osho Meditation Resort** (p165) is the ashram of the late Bhagwan Rajneesh, which has long attracted travellers from around the globe. Serious devotees of Buddhist meditation should head for the **Vipassana International Academy** (p142) in Igatpuri. At Sevagram is the peaceful **Sevagram Ashram** (p155), established by Mahatma Gandhi in 1933.

At Puttaparthi, **Prasanthi Nilayam** (p304) is the ashram of Sri Sathya Sai Baba, while in Tiruvannamalai, the **Sri Ramanasramam Ashram** (p394) draws devotees of Sri Ramana Maharashi. Puducherry is well known for the **Sri Aurobindo Ashram** (p398), established by a French woman known as The Mother. Just outside Puducherry is **Auroville** (p402), the impressive ashram offshoot that has developed into a large and harmonious international community. The **Isha Yoga Centre** (p434) in Poondi, is a little-known ashram, yoga retreat and place of pilgrimage. On the tropical Keralan backwaters near Kollam (Quilon) is the **Matha Amrithanandamayi Mission** (p328), the ashram of Matha Amrithanandamayi, known as the 'Hugging Mother' because of the *darshan* (blessing) she practices, often happily hugging thousands in a session.

CHASING THE FESTIVALS

The fantastical explosion of colour and sheer exuberance of Indian festivals make for a truly unforgettable experience – the trick is to be in the right place at the right time (see also p471).

Ganesh Chaturthi (August/September; p108) is celebrated all over South India, but is best experienced in Mumbai and Pune when these cities really burst to life. The **Ellora Dance & Music Festival** (December/January; p141) is a cultural event set against the stunning backdrop of the Kailasa Temple. Goa turns it on with India's most memorable Christian festivals, the biggest being the **Feast of St Francis Xavier** (3 December; p178) in Old Goa.

Some of Karnataka's biggest bashes are in Bengaluru, such as **Karaga** (April; p220), with a colourful procession at Dharmaraya Swamy Temple. One of the greatest **Dussehra** (September/October; p220) festivals would have to be in Mysore. **Vasantahabba** (February; p220) showcases traditional and contemporary Indian dance and music. **Thrissur Pooram** (April/May; p309) offers spectacular elephant processions, while Alappuzha (Alleppey) hosts the inimitable **Nehru Trophy Snake Boat Race** (August; p309). The **Mamallapuram Dance Festival** (December/January; p366) is a splendid cultural event, as is the **International Yoga Festival** (January; p366) in Puducherry. The holy nine-day **Brahmotsavam** (September/October; p275) is held at Tirumala, while in Hyderabad, the **Deccan Festival** (February; p275) pays tribute to Deccan culture and includes traditional music and dance.

BLISSFUL BEACHES & BACKWATERS

Sun-worshippers will love South India's gorgeous west-coast beaches, which have been luring travellers for decades. Throw in the postcard-perfect Keralan backwaters and you have the ultimate tropical-holiday package.

Begin with a bang in manic **Mumbai** (p104), soaking up the carnival atmosphere of Chowpatty Beach, before making your escape to India's favourite beach state, Goa. After visiting its capital **Panaji** (Panjim; p181) and the ruined former Portuguese capital of **Old Goa** (p187), select a beach that tickles your fancy (see The Beach Files, p192) for immediate sun and sand therapy. Hit the rails southwards and get off at Karwar for **Gokarna** (p254), a dusty pilgrimage town leading to a string of secluded beaches popular with the chillum-puffing crowd. If visiting during the monsoon, a worthwhile

detour from here is to **Jog Falls** (p254), India's highest waterfalls. Leaving Karnataka you enter the slender coastal state of Kerala. Pass through **Kozhikode** (Calicut; p355) and your next stop is the delightful island stronghold of Kochi's **Fort Cochin** (p343), reached from mainland Ernakulam. From there, head to **Alappuzha** (Alleppey; p326) for a serene houseboat journey through the dazzling backwaters of Kerala (p328). A short trip south, **Varkala** (p319) offers dramatic cliffs and beaches. Your final stop is near the southernmost tip of India: **Kovalam** (p315) is blessed with a small sweep of crescent beaches offering the perfect place to let your hair down.

Snapshot

No matter where your South Indian wanderings take you, if there's one thing you can count on it's that you'll never be short of conversation: whether it's chatting with a Keralan couple about local cuisine on a bone-shaking bus trip, or swapping cyber stories with IT yuppies in a swanky Bengaluru (Bangalore) bar, breaking the ice with strangers is delightfully easy.

Much of the current affairs talk on the streets of South India mirrors that up north, with political directives made in Delhi largely influencing what happens down south. Without a doubt, cricket is the most perennially talked about topic, and showing an interest in the game is usually a sure-fire way of making instant friends. If you're not a cricket aficionado, simply getting up to speed with some star players, such as Mumbai-born Sachin Tendulkar, is going to work wonders. Apart from cricket, the razzle-dazzle world of Bollywood is another hot chitchat topic. Indeed the most avidly discussed subject in early 2007 was the widely publicised racist slurs that Bollywood star Shilpa Shetty copped from some of her fellow (British) housemates while on the UK's reality TV show, *Celebrity Big Brother*. The ensuing racism debate made front-page headlines throughout India and lime-lighted the prolific sense of national pride and identity that has been forged on the subcontinent six decades after the British were booted out.

Also making recent headlines was the legal challenge to India's antigay law, which has existed since the mid-19th century. Prominent personalities, including Keralan-born Booker Prize–winner Arundhati Roy, have added their voices to the growing chorus of public opposition to this controversial law which, its critics purport, patently contradicts the government's assertion that India is a tolerant and liberal-minded nation; also read p53. Another headline-grabbing story was the 2006 renaming of two major South Indian cities, Bangalore and Pondicherry, to their precolonial names of Bengaluru and Puducherry. The decision, aimed at proliferating national pride, comes some years after other cities, such as Mumbai (Bombay) and Chennai (Madras), reverted back to their original names in a bid to celebrate Indian heritage.

Meanwhile, in the national political arena the renascent Congress Party seized power from the Bharatiya Janata Party (BJP) in the 2004 elections largely thanks to notable South Indian support (see also p46). The new government, headed by Prime Minister Manmohan Singh, has been at the vanguard of the country's phenomenal economic growth, which has averaged 8.1% over recent years. However, despite India's galloping economy, vast sections of the population have seen minimal benefit from the boom. Indeed the most pressing challenge for Singh's government is to spread both the burden and bounty of India's economic prosperity. Quite a formidable task given that in the world's biggest democracy, the gap between the haves and the have-nots is far from shrinking, and poverty is set to spiral upwards if India's population growth rate continues to race beyond that of its economic growth. Despite central government initiatives to rein in the ballooning birth rate, overpopulation lies at the crux of many of South India's most pressing problems. The government has also attracted criticism for failing to adequately address its AIDS crisis, with India now recording the planet's highest number of HIV-positive cases.

When it comes to the environment, climate change, deforestation, pollution, tourism-related development (especially in Goa; see the boxed text, p216) and ever-expanding industrialisation are just some of the issues that

FAST FACTS

Population: 1.027 billion (2001 census)

GDP growth rate: 8.5% (2006)

Inflation: 5.2%

Unemployment rate: 8.6%

Population growth rate: 1.4%

Families living in one-room homes: 41%

Literacy rate: 53.7% (women) and 75.3% (men)

Revenue earned by IT industry in 2006: US$10 billion

Proportion of females to males: 933:1000 (2001 census)

Life expectancy: 65.6 years (women) and 63.9 years (men)

both the central and South Indian state governments are grappling with – for more details, see p93. Water is becoming an increasingly hot political potato, with various state governments ardently battling to secure exclusive rights to rivers and dams. One particularly prominent case, the region's longest-running water dispute (between Karnataka and Tamil Nadu) over the waters of the Cauvery River, was finally settled – but not without controversy – by the Supreme Court in 2007 (see p95).

Many national political issues make frequent front-page headlines in South India, especially the thorny situation between India and Pakistan over the disputed northern region of Kashmir. Unresolved since the subcontinent's partition in 1947, the festering Kashmir impasse has been the catalyst for intensely rocky relations between the two countries ever since. From the time he came to power, Singh has reiterated his government's unwavering commitment to solving the Kashmir quandary. However, bridge-building endeavours between India and Pakistan came to an abrupt halt following the July 2006 train bombings in Mumbai that killed over 200 people and left more than 700 wounded. Bilateral talks concerning Kashmir later resumed, but they faced renewed pressure following the February 2007 bomb blasts on a train travelling from Delhi to Lahore (Pakistan), which left 68 commuters dead and threatened to subvert the Indo-Pakistan peace process. The Indian and Pakistani governments refused to let the attack succeed in its objective of sabotaging relations, vowing to press on with constructive dialogue. At the time of writing, those responsible for both blasts had not been identified.

On a more optimistic note, South India has been going from strength to strength in terms of its IT industry, with southern cities such as Bengaluru, Mumbai, Pune, Hyderabad and Chennai attracting massive global interest. The south's burgeoning IT industry has played a key role in revolutionising India's once-ramshackle economy, with analysts forecasting an even rosier future (see the boxed text, A Software Superpower, p55).

A newly emerging market is that of medical tourism (foreigners travelling to India for competitively priced medical treatment coupled with a holiday), which has projected earnings of US$2 billion by 2012 (it currently averages US$330 million per annum). Wellness spas – which include post-operative Ayurvedic treatments and other internationally fashionable home-grown therapies – are set to mushroom in southern centres, especially Kerala and Goa, as the medical tourism sector swells. On the general tourism front, the good news for South India is that recent reports indicate an upswing in the number of foreign tourists heading to the sultry south, which not only translates to a boost in revenue for southern state coffers, but also in increased employment and benefits to associated enterprises (particularly cottage industries), as well as preservation of cultural traditions such as dance and music.

History

South India has always laid claim to its own unique history, largely resulting from its insulation by distance from the political developments up north. Southern India, the cradle of Dravidian culture, has a long and colourful historical tapestry of wrangling dynasties and empires, interwoven with the influx of traders and conquerors arriving by sea. Evidence of human habitation in southern India dates back to the Stone Age; discoveries include hand-axes in Tamil Nadu and a worn limestone statue of a goddess, believed to be between 15,000 and 25,000 years old, from an excavation in the Vindhya Range.

India's first major civilisation flourished around 2500 BC in the Indus river valley, much of which lies within present-day Pakistan. This civilisation, which continued for a thousand years and is known as the Harappan culture, appears to have been the culmination of thousands of years of settlement. The Harappan civilisation fell into decline from the beginning of the 2nd millennium BC. Some historians attribute the end of the empire to floods or decreased rainfall, which threatened the Harappans' agricultural base. The more enduring, if contentious, theory is that an Aryan invasion put paid to the Harappans, despite little archaeological proof or written reports in the ancient Indian texts to that effect. As a result, some nationalist historians argue that the Aryans (from a Sanskrit word meaning 'noble') were in fact the original inhabitants of India and that the invasion theory was actually invented by self-serving foreign conquerors. Others say that the arrival of the Aryans was more of a gentle migration that gradually subsumed Harappan culture, rather than an invasion. Those who defend the invasion theory believe that from around 1500 BC Aryan tribes from Afghanistan and Central Asia began to filter into northwest India. Despite their military superiority, their progress was gradual, with successive tribes battling over territory and new arrivals pushing further east into the Ganges plain. Eventually these tribes controlled northern India as far as the Vindhya Range. As a consequence, many of the original inhabitants, the Dravidians, were forced south.

India: A History, by John Keay, is an insightful and readable account of subcontinental history spanning from the Harappan civilisation to Indian independence.

INFLUENCES FROM THE NORTH

While the Indus Valley civilisation may not have affected South India, the same cannot be said for the Aryan invasion. The Aryanisation of the south was a slow process, but it had a profound effect on the social order of the region and the ethos of its inhabitants. The northerners brought their literature

INDIA, THE GREAT SURVIVOR

India's story is one of the grand epics of world history. Throughout thousands of years of great civilisations, invasions, the birth of religions and countless cataclysms, Indian history has always been a work in progress, a constant process of reinvention and accumulation that can prove elusive for those seeking to grasp its essential essence. And yet, from its myriad upheavals, a vibrant, diverse and thoroughly modern nation has emerged, as enduring as it is dynamic and increasingly well-equipped to meet the challenges of the future.

TIMELINE	3500–2000 BC	2000–1500 BC
	Indus Valley civilisation known as the Harappan culture	Aryans invade North India and push towards the south; Dravidian culture takes root

(the four Vedas – a collection of sacred Hindu hymns), their gods (Agni, Varuna, Shiva and Vishnu), their language (Sanskrit) and a social structure that organised people into castes, with Brahmins at the top (see p50).

Over the centuries other influences flowed from the north, including Buddhism and Jainism (see p58). Sravanabelagola (p249) in Karnataka, an auspicious place of pilgrimage to this day, is where over 2000 years ago the northern ruler Chandragupta Maurya, who had embraced Jainism and renounced his kingdom, arrived with his guru. Jainism was then adopted by the trading community (its tenet of ahimsa, or nonviolence, precluded occupations tainted by the taking of life), who spread it through South India.

Emperor Ashoka, a successor of Chandragupta who ruled for 40 years from about 272 BC, was a major force behind Buddhism's inroads into the south. Once a campaigning king, his epiphany came in 260 BC when, shocked by the horrific carnage and suffering caused by his campaign against the Kalingas (a powerful kingdom), he renounced violence and embraced Buddhism. He sent Buddhist missionaries far and wide, and his edicts (carved into rock and incised into specially erected pillars) have been found in Andhra Pradesh and Karnataka. Stupas were also built in southern India under Ashoka's patronage, mostly along the coast of Andhra Pradesh (also see State of Good Karma, p296), although at least one was constructed as far south as Kanchipuram in Tamil Nadu.

The appeal of Jainism and Buddhism, which arose about the same time, was that they rejected the Vedas and condemned the caste system. Buddhism, however, gradually lost favour with its devotees, and was replaced with a new brand of Hinduism, which emphasised devotion to a personal god. This bhakti (surrendering to the gods) order developed in southern India about AD 500. Bhakti adherents opposed Jainism and Buddhism, and the movement certainly hastened the decline of both in South India.

MAURYAN EMPIRE & SOUTHERN KINGDOMS

Chandragupta Maurya was the first of a line of Mauryan kings to rule what was effectively the first Indian empire. The empire's capital was in present-day Patna in Bihar. Chandragupta's son, Bindusara, who came to the throne around 300 BC, extended the empire as far as Karnataka. However, he seems to have stopped there, possibly because the Mauryan empire was on cordial terms with the southern chieftains of the day.

The identity and customs of these chiefdoms have been gleaned from various sources, including archaeological remains and ancient Tamil literature. These literary records describe a land known as the 'abode of the Tamils', within which resided three major ruling families: the Pandyas (Madurai), the Cheras (Malabar Coast) and the Cholas (Thanjavur and the Cauvery Valley). The region described in classical Sangam literature (written between 300 BC and AD 200) was still relatively insulated from Sanskrit culture, but from 200 BC this was starting to change.

A degree of rivalry characterised relations between the main chiefdoms and the numerous minor chiefdoms, and there were occasional clashes with Sri Lankan rulers. Sangam literature indicates that Sanskrit traditions from the old Aryan kingdoms of the north were taking root in South India around 200 BC. Ultimately, the southern powers all suffered at the hands of the Kalabhras, about whom little is known except that they appeared to have originated from somewhere north of the Tamil region.

The Wonder That Was India, by AL Basham, offers detailed descriptions of the Indian civilisations, major religions, origins of the caste system and social customs – a terrific thematic approach to bring the disparate strands together.

Emperor Ashoka's ability to rule over his empire was assisted by a standing army consisting of 9000 elephants, 30,000 cavalry and 600,000 infantry.

Harappa (www.harappa .com) provides an illustrated yet scholarly coverage of everything you need to know about the ancient Indus Valley civilisations, including a link to recent archaeological discoveries.

321–184 BC	272–232 BC
The Mauryan empire, effectively India's first empire	Reign of Emperor Ashoka; Buddhism spreads in South India

By around 180 BC the Mauryan empire, which had started to disintegrate soon after the death of Emperor Ashoka in 232 BC, had been overtaken by a series of rival kingdoms that were subjected to repeated invasions from northerners such as the Bactrian Greeks. Despite this apparent instability, the post-Ashokan era produced at least one line of royalty whose patronage of the arts and ability to maintain a relatively high degree of social cohesion have left an enduring legacy. This was the Satavahanas, who eventually controlled all of Maharashtra, Madhya Pradesh, Chhatisgarh, Karnataka and Andhra Pradesh. Under their rule, between 200 BC and AD 200, the arts blossomed, especially literature, sculpture and philosophy. Buddhism reached a peak in Maharashtra under the Satavahanas, although the greatest of the Buddhist cave temples at Ajanta (p150) and Ellora (p147) were built later by the Chalukya and Rashtrakuta dynasties.

South Indian Customs, by PV Jagadisa Ayyar, strives to explain a range of practices, from the smearing of cow dung outside homes to the formation of snake images beneath banyan trees.

Most of all, the subcontinent enjoyed a period of considerable prosperity. South India may have lacked vast and fertile agricultural plains on the scale of North India, but it compensated by building strategic trade links via the Indian Ocean.

THE FALL & RISE OF THE CHOLA EMPIRE

After the Kalabhras suppressed the Tamil chiefdoms, South India split into numerous warring kingdoms. The Cholas virtually disappeared and the Cheras on the west coast appear to have prospered through trading, although little is known about them. It was not until the late 6th century AD, when

THE GLOBAL LINK

India's trading links with the outside world stretch back a long way. There is evidence that trade between western Asian cultures, such as the Persians and Egyptians, and the west coast of India was taking place at least a thousand years before Christ. Indian teak and cedar were used by Babylonian builders as far back as the 7th century BC. But a major breakthrough came with the discovery of the monsoon winds, which enabled ships (such as Arab dhows) to travel between western Asia and India with relative ease. The extraordinary reach of the Roman empire during the period of the Pax Romana at the beginning of the Christian era assured the flow of goods between India, western Asia and Europe along two major routes: overland across Persia to North India, and by water (primarily from the Red Sea and the Persian Gulf) to South India.

An anonymous Greek document, the *Periplys Maris Erythraei*, written some time in the 1st century BC, describes various ports along the coast of India. Proof that Roman traders were active in South India has been unveiled over the years in the form of caches of gold coins, Roman pottery and glass. British archaeologist Sir Mortimer Wheeler, digging at Arikkamedu near Puducherry (Pondicherry), uncovered a Roman trading settlement as well as pieces of pottery that had been manufactured near Rome itself. At Rameswaram further south, pottery made in Tunisia when it was under Roman control has been uncovered. And at Iyyal, in central Kerala, more than 200 gold coins minted in Rome in the 2nd century AD were discovered in 1983 by workers excavating clay for bricks.

Goods exported from South India included ivory, precious stones, pearls, tortoiseshell, pepper and aromatic plants. Indian merchants used trade routes established by the Mauryan empire and natural corridors such as the Narmada River and Ganges River valleys to move around India. Longer routes traversed vast tracts of Central Asia to link China with the Mediterranean. There is evidence Indian traders were also established in Red Sea ports, and after the decline of the Roman trade, they ventured in the other direction to Southeast Asia in search of spices and semiprecious stones.

850	1336
The Chola empire comes to power in South India	Powerful Vijayanagar empire founded at Hampi

the Kalabhras were overthrown, that the political uncertainty in the region ceased. For the next 300 years the history of South India was dominated by the fortunes of the Chalukyas of Badami, the Pallavas of Kanchi (Kanchipuram; p389) and the Pandyas of Madurai (p418).

The Chalukyas were a far-flung family. In addition to their base in Badami, they established themselves in Bijapur, Andhra Pradesh and near the Godavari Delta. The Godavari branch of the family is commonly referred to as the Eastern Chalukyas of Vengi. It's unclear from where the Pallavas originated, but it's thought they may have emigrated to Kanchi from Andhra Pradesh. After their successful rout of the Kalabhras, the Pallavas extended their territory as far south as the Cauvery River, and by the 7th century were at the height of their power, building monuments such as the Shore Temple (p383) and Arjuna's Penance (p385) at Mamallapuram (Mahabalipuram). They engaged in long-running clashes with the Pandyas, who, in the 8th century, allied themselves with the Gangas of Mysore. This, combined with pressure from the Rashtrakutas (who were challenging the Eastern Chalukyas), had by the 9th century snuffed out any significant Pallava power in the south.

At the same time as the Pallava dynasty came to an end, a new Chola dynasty was establishing itself and laying the foundations for what was to become one of the most important empires on the subcontinent. From their base at Thanjavur (Tanjore), the Cholas spread north absorbing what was left of the Pallavas' territory, and made inroads into the south. But it wasn't until Raja Raja Chola I (r 985–1014) ascended the throne that the Chola kingdom really started to emerge as a great empire. Raja Raja Chola I successfully waged war against the Pandyas in the south, the Gangas of Mysore and the Eastern Chalukyas. He also launched a series of naval campaigns that resulted in the capture of the Maldives, the Malabar Coast and northern Sri Lanka, which became a province of the Chola empire. These conquests gave the Cholas control over critical ports and trading links between India, Southeast Asia, Arabia and East Africa. They were therefore in a position to grab a share of the huge profits involved in selling spices to Europe.

History & Society in South India, by Noboru Karashima, is an academic compilation focusing on the development of South Indian society during the Chola dynasty and the rule of the Vijayanagars.

Raja Raja Chola's son, Rajendra (r 1014–44), continued to expand the Chola's territory, conquering the remainder of Sri Lanka, and campaigning up the east coast as far as Bengal and the Ganges River. Rajendra also launched a campaign in Southeast Asia against the Srivijaya kingdom (Sumatra), reinstating trade links that had been interrupted and sending trade missions as far as China. In addition to both its political and economic superiority, the Chola empire produced a brilliant legacy in the arts. Sculpture, most notably bronze sculpture (see p70), reached astonishing new heights of aesthetic and technical refinement.

Music, dance and literature flourished and developed a distinctly Tamil flavour, enduring in South India long after the Cholas had faded from the picture. Trade wasn't the only thing the Cholas brought to the shores of Southeast Asia; they also introduced their culture. That legacy lives on in Myanmar (Burma), Thailand, Bali (Indonesia) and Cambodia in dance, religion and mythology.

But the Cholas, eventually weakened by constant campaigning, succumbed to expansionist pressure from the Hoysalas of Halebid (p247) and the Pandyas of Madurai, and by the 13th century were finally supplanted

1424	1498
Bahmani dynasty founded as rivals to the Vijayanagars	Vasco da Gama sails to Calicut (now Kozhikode) in Kerala

by the Pandyas. The Hoysalas were themselves eclipsed by the Vijayanagar empire, which arose in the 14th century. The Pandyas prospered and their achievements were much admired by Marco Polo when he visited in 1288 and 1293. But their glory was short-lived, as they were unable to fend off the Muslim invasion from the north.

MUSLIM INVASION & THE VIJAYANAGAR EMPIRE

The Muslim rulers in Delhi campaigned in southern India from 1296, rebuking a series of local rulers, including the Hoysalas and Pandyas, and by 1323 had reached Madurai.

Mohammed Tughlaq, the sultan of Delhi, dreamed of conquering the whole of India, something not even Emperor Ashoka had managed. Earlier Muslim rulers had seemingly been more preoccupied with looting temples than establishing empires. He rebuilt the fort of Daulatabad (p146) in Maharashtra to keep control of southern India, but eventually his ambition led him to overreach his forces. In 1334 he had to recall his army in order to quash rebellions elsewhere and, as a result, local Muslim rulers in Madurai and Daulatabad declared their independence.

At the same time, the foundations of what was to become one of South India's greatest empires, Vijayanagar, were being laid by Hindu chiefs at Hampi.

The Vijayanagar empire is generally said to have been founded by two chieftain brothers who, having been captured and taken to Delhi, converted to Islam and were sent back south to serve as governors for the sultanate. The brothers, however, had other ideas; they reconverted to Hinduism and around 1336 set about establishing a kingdom that was eventually to encompass southern Karnataka, Tamil Nadu and part of Kerala. Seven centuries later, the centre of this kingdom – the enigmatic ruins and temples of Hampi (p257) – is now one of South India's biggest tourist drawcards.

The Bahmanis, who were initially from Daulatabad, established their capital at Gulbarga in Karnataka, relocating to Bidar in the 15th century. Their kingdom eventually included Maharashtra and parts of northern Karnataka and Andhra Pradesh – and they took pains to protect it.

Not unnaturally, ongoing rivalry characterised the relationship between the Vijayanagar and Bahmani empires until the 16th century when both went into decline. The Bahmani empire was torn apart by factional fighting and Vijayanagar's vibrant capital of Hampi was laid to waste in a six-month sacking by the combined forces of the Islamic sultanates of Bidar, Bijapur, Berar, Ahmednagar and Golconda. Much of the conflict centred on control of fertile agricultural land and trading ports; at one stage the Bahmanis wrested control of the important port of Goa from their rivals (although in 1378 the Vijayanagars seized it back).

The Vijayanagar empire is notable for its prosperity, which was the result of a deliberate policy giving every encouragement to traders from afar, combined with the development of an efficient administrative system and access to important trading links, including west-coast ports. Hampi became quite cosmopolitan, with people from various parts of India as well as from abroad mingling in the bazaars.

Portuguese chronicler Domingo Paez arrived in Vijayanagar during the reign of one of its greatest kings, Krishnadevaraya (r 1509–29). It was during

A History of India, by Romila Thapar (Vol 1) and Percival Spears (Vol 2), is one of the more thorough introductions to Indian history, from 1000 BC to Independent India.

A History of South India from Prehistoric Times to the Fall of Vijayanagar, by Nilakanta Sastri, is arguably the most thorough history of this region; especially recommended if you're heading for Hampi.

ENTER THE PORTUGUESE

By the time Krishnadevaraya ascended to the throne, the Portuguese were well on the way to establishing a firm foothold in Goa. It was only a few years since they had become the first Europeans to sail across the Indian Ocean from the east coast of Africa to India's shores.

On 20 May 1498 Vasco da Gama dropped anchor off the South Indian coast near the town of Calicut (now Kozhikode; p355). It had taken him 23 days to sail from the east coast of Africa, guided by a pilot named Ibn Masjid, sent by the ruler of Malindi in Gujarat.

The Portuguese sought a sea route between Europe and the East so they could trade directly in spices. They also hoped they might find Christians cut off from Europe by the Muslim dominance of the Middle East. The Portuguese were also searching for the legendary kingdom of Prester John, a powerful Christian ruler with whom they could unite against the Muslim rulers of the Middle East. However, in India they found spices and the Syrian Orthodox community, but not Prester John.

Vasco da Gama sought an audience with the ruler of Calicut, to explain himself, and seems to have been well received. The Portuguese engaged in a limited amount of trading, but became increasingly suspicious that Muslim traders were turning the ruler of Calicut against them. They resolved to leave Calicut, which they did in August 1498.

---

his rule that Vijayanagar enjoyed a period of unparalleled prosperity and power.

Paez recorded the achievements of the Vijayanagars and described how they had constructed large water tanks and irrigated their fields. He also described how human and animal sacrifices were carried out to propitiate the gods after one of the water tanks had burst repeatedly. He included detail about the fine houses that belonged to wealthy merchants, and the bazaars full of precious stones (rubies, diamonds, emeralds, pearls), textiles, including silk, 'and every other sort of thing there is on earth and that you may wish to buy'.

Tamil Nation (www .tamilnation.org) proffers everything you need to know about Tamil culture, politics and heritage.

Like the Bahmanis, the Vijayanagar kings invested heavily in protecting their territory and trading links. Krishnadevaraya employed Portuguese and Muslim mercenaries to guard the forts and protect his domains. He also fostered good relations with the Portuguese, upon whom he depended for access to trade goods, especially the Arab horses he needed for his cavalry.

ARRIVAL OF THE EUROPEANS & CHRISTIANITY

The Career and Legend of Vasco da Gama, by Sanjay Subrahmanyam, is one of the best recent investigations of the person credited with 'discovering' the sea route to India.

And so began a new era of European contact with the East. After Vasco da Gama's arrival (1498) came Francisco de Ameida and Alfonso de Albuquerque, who established an eastern Portuguese empire that included Goa (first taken in 1510). Albuquerque waged a constant battle against the local Muslims in Goa, finally defeating them in 1512. But perhaps his greatest achievement was in playing off two deadly threats against each other – the Vijayanagars (for whom access to Goa's ports was extremely important) and the Bijapuris (who had split from the Bahmanis in the early 16th century and who controlled part of Goa).

The Bijapuris and Vijayanagars were sworn enemies, and Albuquerque skilfully exploited this antipathy by supplying Arab horses, which had to be constantly imported because they died in alarming numbers once on Indian

| French establish colony at Pondicherry (now Puducherry) | Hyder Ali assumes power over Mysore kingdom |

soil. Both kingdoms bought horses from the Portuguese to top up their warring cavalries, thus keeping Portugal's Goan ports busy and profitable.

The Portuguese also introduced Catholicism, and the arrival of the Inquisition in 1560 marked the beginning of 200 years of religious suppression in the Portuguese-controlled areas on the west coast of India. Not long after the beginning of the Inquisition, events that occurred in Europe had major repercussions for European relations with India. In 1580 Spain annexed Portugal and, until it regained its independence in 1640, Portugal's interests were subservient to Spain's. After the defeat of the Spanish Armada in 1588, the sea route to the East lay open to the English and the Dutch.

Today the Portuguese influence is most obvious in Goa, with its chalk-white Catholic churches dotting the countryside, Christian festivals and unique cuisine, although the Portuguese also had some influence in Kerala in towns such as Kochi (Cochin). By the mid-16th century, Old Goa had grown into a thriving city said to rival Lisbon in magnificence, and although only a ruined shadow of that time, its churches and buildings are still a stunning reminder of Portuguese rule. It wasn't until 1961 – 14 years after national Independence – that the Portuguese were finally forced out by the Indian military.

The Dutch got to India first but, unlike the Portuguese, were more interested in trade than in religion and empire. Indonesia was used as the main source of spices, and trade with South India was primarily for pepper and cardamom. So the Dutch East India Company set up a string of trading posts (called factories), which allowed them to maintain a complicated trading structure all the way from the Persian Gulf to Japan. They set up trading posts at Surat (Gujarat) and on the Coromandel Coast in South India, and entered into a treaty with the ruler of Calicut. In 1660 they captured the Portuguese forts at Kochi and Kodungallor.

The English also set up a trading venture, the British East India Company, which in 1600 was granted a monopoly. Like the Dutch, the English were at this stage interested in trade, mainly in spices, and Indonesia was their main goal. But the Dutch proved too strong there and the English turned instead to India, setting up a trading post at Madras (now Chennai). The Danes traded off and on at Tranquebar (on the Coromandel Coast) from 1616, and the French acquired Pondicherry (now Puducherry) in 1673.

MUGHALS VERSUS MARATHAS

Around the late 17th century the Delhi-based Mughals were making inroads into southern India, gaining the sultanates of Ahmednagar, Bijapur and Golconda (including Hyderabad) before moving into Tamil Nadu. But it was here that Emperor Aurangzeb (r 1658–1707) came up against the Marathas who, in a series of guerrilla-like raids, captured Thanjavur and set up a capital at Gingee near Madras.

Although the Mughal empire gradually disintegrated following Aurangzeb's death, the Marathas went from strength to strength, and they set their sights on territory to the north. But their aspirations brought them into conflict with the rulers of Hyderabad, the Asaf Jahis, who had entrenched themselves here when Hyderabad broke away from the declining Mughal rulers of Delhi in 1724. The Marathas discovered that the French were

Thousands were burned at the stake during the Goa Inquisition, which lasted more than 200 years. The judgment ceremony took place outside the Se Cathedral in Old Goa.

In 1839 the British government offered to buy Goa from the Portuguese for half a million pounds.

White Mughals, by William Dalrymple, tells the true, tragic love story of a British East India Company soldier who married an Indian Muslim princess and is interwoven with harem politics, intrigue and espionage.

1858	1869
British government assumes formal control over India	Birth of Mohandas (Mahatma) Gandhi at Porbandar, Gujarat

THE LEGENDARY SHIVAJI

The name Chhatrapati Shivaji is revered in Maharashtra, with statues of the great warrior astride his horse gracing many towns, and street names and monuments being named (or renamed in the case of Mumbai's (Bombay's) Victoria Terminus, among others; see p114) after him. So who was this man and why was he so adored?

Shivaji was responsible for leading the powerful Maratha dynasty, a sovereign Hindu state that controlled the Deccan region for almost two centuries, at a time when much of India was under Islamic control. A courageous warrior and charismatic leader, Shivaji was born in 1627 to a prominent Maratha family at Shivneri. As a child he was sent to Pune with his mother, where he was given land and forts and groomed as a future leader. With a very small army, Shivaji seized his first fort at the age of 20 and over the next three decades he continued to expand Maratha power around his base in Pune, holding out against the Muslim invaders from the north (the Mughal empire) and the south (the forces of Bijapur) and eventually controlling the Deccan. He was shrewd enough to play his enemies (among them Mughal emperor Aurangzeb) off against each other and, in a famous incident, he killed Bijapuri general Afzal Khan in a face-to-face encounter at Pratapgad Fort (p172).

In 1674 Shivaji was crowned *chhatrapati* (king) of the Marathas at Raigad Fort (p173). He died six years later and was succeeded by his son Sambhaji, but almost immediately the power Shivaji had built up began to wane.

providing military support to the Hyderabadi rulers in return for trading concessions on the Coromandel Coast. However, by the 1750s Hyderabad had lost a lot of its power and became landlocked when much of its coast was lost to the British.

Down in the south, Travancore (Kerala) and Mysore were making a bid to consolidate their power by gaining control of strategic maritime regions, and access to trade links. Martanda Varma (r 1729–58) of Travancore created his own army and tried to keep the local Syrian Orthodox trading community onside by limiting the activities of European traders. Trade in many goods, with the exception of pepper, became a royal monopoly, especially under Martanda's son Rama Varma (r 1758–98).

Mysore started off as a landlocked kingdom, but in 1761 a cavalry officer, Hyder Ali, assumed power and set about acquiring coastal territory. Hyder Ali and his son Tipu Sultan eventually ruled over a kingdom that included southern Karnataka and northern Kerala. Tipu conducted trade directly with the Middle East through the west-coast ports he controlled. But Tipu was prevented from gaining access to ports on the eastern seaboard and the fertile hinterland by the British East India Company.

THE BRITISH TAKE HOLD

The British East India Company at this stage was supposedly interested only in trade, not conquest. But Mysore's rulers proved something of a vexation. In 1780 the Nizam of Hyderabad, Hyder Ali, and the Marathas joined forces to defeat the company's armies and take control of Karnataka. The Treaty of Mangalore, signed by Tipu Sultan in 1784, restored the parties to an uneasy truce. But meanwhile, within the company there was a growing body of opinion that only total control of India would really satisfy British trading interests. This was reinforced by fears of a renewed French bid for

1885	1942
Founding of the Indian National Congress (Congress Party)	Mahatma Gandhi launches the Quit India campaign, demanding Indian independence

land in India following Napoleon's Egyptian expedition of 1798–99. It was the governor general of Bengal, Lord Richard Wellesley, who launched a strike against Mysore, with the Nizam of Hyderabad as an ally (who was required to disband his French-trained troops and in return gained British protection). Tipu, who may have counted on support from the French, was killed when the British stormed the river-island fortress of Seringapatam (present-day Srirangapatnam, near Mysore; p240) in 1799.

Wellesley restored the old ruling family, the Wodeyars, to half of Tipu's kingdom – the rest went to the Nizam of Hyderabad and the British East India Company – and laid the foundations for the formation of the Madras Presidency. Thanjavur and Karnataka were also absorbed by the British, who, when the rulers of the day died, pensioned off their successors. By 1818 the Marathas, racked by internal strife, had collapsed.

By now most of India was under British influence. In the south the British controlled the Madras Presidency, which stretched from present-day Andhra Pradesh to the southern tip of the subcontinent, and from the east coast across to the western Malabar Coast. Meanwhile, a fair chunk of the interior was ruled by a bundle of small princely states. Much of Maharashtra was part of the Bombay Presidency, but there were a dozen or so small princely states scattered around, including Kolhapur, Sawantwadi, Aundh and Janjira. The major princely states were Travancore, Hyderabad and Mysore, though all were closely watched by the Resident (the British de facto governor, who officially looked after areas under British control).

THE ROAD TO INDEPENDENCE

The desire among many Indians to be free from foreign rule remained. Opposition to the British began to increase at the turn of the 20th century, spearheaded by the Indian National Congress (Congress Party), the nation's oldest political party. The fight for independence gained momentum when, in April 1919, following riots in Amritsar (Punjab), a British army contingent was sent to quell the unrest. Under direct orders of the officer in charge the army ruthlessly fired into a crowd of unarmed protesters attending a meeting, killing well over 1000 people. News of the massacre spread rapidly throughout India, turning huge numbers of otherwise apolitical Indians into Congress supporters. At this time, the Congress movement found a new leader in Mohandas Gandhi (see the boxed text, p45).

After some three decades of intense campaigning for an independent India, Mahatma Gandhi's dream finally materialised. However, despite his plea for a united India – the Muslim League's leader, Mohammed Ali Jinnah, was demanding a separate Islamic state for India's sizeable Muslim population – the decision was made to split the country.

The partition of India in 1947 contained all the ingredients for an epic disaster, but the resulting bloodshed was far worse than anticipated. Massive population exchanges took place. Trains full of Muslims, fleeing westward, were held up and slaughtered by Hindu and Sikh mobs. Hindus and Sikhs fleeing to the east suffered the same fate. By the time the chaos had run its course, more than 10 million people had changed sides and at least 500,000 had been killed.

Nehru became the first prime minister of India and, tragically, Gandhi was assassinated in 1948 by a Hindu fanatic from Pune, who believed Gandhi was responsible for dividing the sacred motherland. The repercussions of Partition

You've probably seen *Gandhi*, starring Ben Kingsley and 300,000 extras, but watch it again because few movies capture the grand canvas that is India in tracing the country's path to independence.

15 August 1947

India becomes independent and is divided into two countries: India and Pakistan

30 January 1948

Mahatma Gandhi assassinated in Delhi by Hindu zealot

remain apparent today: the still-disputed territory of Kashmir has witnessed bloody conflict between India and Pakistan since Independence.

CARVING UP THE SOUTH

While the chaos of Partition was mostly felt in the north – mainly in Punjab and Bengal – the south faced problems of its own. Following Independence in 1947 the princely states and British provinces were dismantled and South India was reorganised into states along linguistic lines. Though most of the princely states acceded to India peacefully, an exception was that of the Nizam of Hyderabad. He wanted Hyderabad to join Islamic Pakistan, although only he and 10% of his subjects were Muslims. Following a time of violence between Hindu and Islamic hardliners, the Indian army moved in and forcibly took control of Hyderabad state in 1949.

The Wodeyars in Mysore, who also ruled right up to Independence, were pensioned off. But they were so popular with their subjects that the maharaja became the first governor of the post-Independence state of Mysore. The boundaries of Mysore state were redrawn on linguistic grounds in 1956, and the extended Kannada-speaking state of Greater Mysore was established, becoming Karnataka in 1972.

The Proudest Day – India's Long Road to Independence, by Anthony Read and David Fisher, is an engaging account of India's pre-Independence period.

Kerala, as it is today, was created in 1956 from Travancore, Cochin (now Kochi) and Malabar (formerly part of the Madras Presidency). The maharajas in both Travancore and Cochin were especially attentive to the provision of basic services and education, and their legacy today is India's most literate state. Kerala also blazed a trail in post-Independence India by becoming the first state in the world to freely elect a communist government in 1957.

Andhra Pradesh was declared a state in 1956, having been created by combining Andhra state (formerly part of the Madras Presidency) with parts of the Telugu-speaking areas of the old Nizam of Hyderabad's territory.

Tamil Nadu emerged from the old Madras Presidency, although until 1969 Tamil Nadu was known as Madras State. In 1956, in a nationwide reorganisation of states, it lost Malabar district and South Canara to the fledgling state of Kerala on the west coast. However, it also gained new areas in Trivandrum district, including Kanyakumari. In 1960, 1049 sq km of land in Andhra Pradesh was exchanged for a similar amount of land in Salem and Chengalpattu districts.

The creation of Maharashtra was one of the most contested issues of the language-based demarcation of states in the 1950s. After Independence, western Maharashtra and Gujarat were joined to form Bombay state, but in 1960, after agitation by pro-Marathi supporters, the modern state of Maharashtra was created, separating from Gujarat while gaining parts of Hyderabad and Madhya Pradesh.

The French relinquished Puducherry in 1954 – 140 years after claiming it from the British. It's a Union Territory (controlled by the government in Delhi), though a largely self-governing one. Lakshadweep was granted Union Territory status in 1956, as were the Andaman and Nicobar Islands.

Throughout most of this carve-up, the tiny enclave of Goa was still under the rule of the Portuguese. Although a rumbling Independence movement had existed in Goa since the early 20th century, the Indian government was reluctant to intervene and take Goa by force, hoping the Portuguese would

1948	1961
First war between India and Pakistan over Kashmir	India kicks Portuguese out of Goa

MAHATMA GANDHI

One of the great figures of the 20th century, Mohandas Karamchand Gandhi was born on 2 October 1869 in Porbandar, Gujarat, where his father was chief minister. After studying in London (1888–91) he worked as a barrister in South Africa, where the young Gandhi became politicised, rallying against the discrimination he encountered. He soon became the spokesman for the Indian community and championed equality for all.

Gandhi returned to India in 1915 with the doctrine of ahimsa (nonviolence) central to his political plans, and committed to a simple and disciplined lifestyle. He set up the Sabarmati Ashram in Ahmedabad, which was innovative for its admission of Dalits (the Scheduled Caste, formerly known as Untouchables; see p52 for more details).

Within a year, Gandhi had won his first victory, defending farmers in Bihar from exploitation. This was when he first received the title 'Mahatma' (Great Soul) from an admirer. The passage of the discriminatory Rowlatt Acts (which allowed certain political cases to be tried without juries) through parliament in 1919 spurred him to further action and he organised a national protest. In the days that followed this hartal (strike), feelings ran high throughout the country. After the massacre of unarmed protesters in Amritsar in 1919, a deeply shocked Gandhi immediately called off the protest.

By 1920 Gandhi was a key figure in the Indian National Congress, and he coordinated a national campaign of noncooperation or *satyagraha* (passive resistance) to British rule, with the effect of raising nationalist feelings while earning the lasting enmity of the British. In early 1930 Gandhi captured the imagination of the country, and the world, when he led a march of several thousand followers from Ahmedabad to Dandi on the coast of Gujarat. On arrival, Gandhi ceremoniously made salt by evaporating sea water, thus publicly defying the much-hated salt tax; not for the first time, he was imprisoned. Released in 1931 to represent the Indian National Congress at the second Round Table Conference in London, he won over the hearts of the British people, but failed to gain any real concessions from the government.

Jailed again on his return to India, Gandhi immediately began a hunger strike, aimed at forcing his fellow Indians to accept the rights of the Untouchables. Gandhi's resoluteness and the widespread apprehension throughout the country forced an agreement, but not until Gandhi was on the verge of death.

Disillusioned with politics and convinced that the Congress leaders were ignoring his guidance, he resigned from his parliamentary seat in 1934 and devoted himself to rural education. He returned spectacularly to the fray in 1942 with the Quit India campaign, in which he urged the British to leave India immediately. His actions were deemed subversive and he and most of the Congress leadership were imprisoned.

In the frantic bargaining that followed the end of WWII, Gandhi was largely excluded, and watched helplessly as plans were made to partition the country – a tragedy in his eyes. He toured the trouble spots, using his own influence to calm intercommunity tensions and promote peace.

Gandhi stood almost alone in urging tolerance and the preservation of a single India, and his work on behalf of members of all communities inevitably drew resentment from some Hindu hardliners. On his way to a prayer meeting in Delhi on 30 January 1948, Mahatma Gandhi was assassinated by a Hindu zealot.

Historical reminders of Gandhi's life and work can be found throughout South India: his ashram is at Sevagram (p155) in Maharashtra; the house where he stayed during many visits to Bombay (now Mumbai) and where he launched the Quit India campaign in 1942 is now a museum (Mani Bhavan; p116); and the former palace where he was imprisoned by the British for nearly two years is in Pune (p163), Maharashtra. There is also a fine museum devoted to Gandhi's life in Madurai (p421) and a memorial in Kanyakumari (p425).

1964	1965
Prime Minister Jawaharlal Nehru dies	Second India–Pakistan war over Kashmir

leave of their own volition. The Portuguese refused, so in December 1961 Indian troops crossed the border and liberated the state with surprisingly little resistance. It became a Union Territory of India, but after splitting from Daman and Diu (Gujarat) in 1987, it was officially recognised as the 25th state of the Indian Union.

MODERN INDIA

Jawaharlal Nehru, India's first prime minister, tried to steer India towards a policy of nonalignment, balancing cordial relations with Britain and Commonwealth membership with moves towards the former USSR. The latter was due partly to conflicts with China and US support for its archenemy Pakistan. Adding uncertainty, wars with Pakistan in 1965 (over Kashmir) and 1971 (over Bangladesh) contributed to a sense among many Indians of having enemies on all sides.

The Nehrus and the Gandhis is Tariq Ali's astute portrait-history of these families and the India over which they cast their long shadow.

The hugely popular Nehru died in 1964 and his daughter, Indira Gandhi (no relation to Mahatma Gandhi), was elected as prime minister in 1966. Indira Gandhi, like Nehru before her, loomed large over the country she governed. Unlike Nehru, however, she was always a profoundly controversial figure whose historical legacy remains hotly disputed.

In 1975, facing serious opposition and unrest, she declared a state of emergency (which later became known as the Emergency). Freed of parliamentary constraints, Gandhi was able to boost the economy, control inflation remarkably well and decisively increase efficiency. On the negative side, political opponents often found themselves in prison, India's judicial system was turned into a puppet theatre and the press was fettered.

Blind to the impact of her reforms, Gandhi was convinced that India was on her side. Her government was bundled out of office in the 1977 elections in favour of the Janata People's Party (JPP). The JPP founder, Jaya Prakash Narayan (JP), was an ageing Gandhian socialist, who died soon after, but is widely credited with having safeguarded Indian democracy through his moral stature and courage to stand up to Congress' authoritarian and increasingly corrupt rule. Once it was victorious, it quickly became obvious that Janata had no other cohesive policies, nor any leader of Narayan's stature. Its leader, Morarji Desai, proved unable to come to grips with the country's problems. With inflation soaring, unrest rising, and the economy faltering, Janata fell apart in late 1979. The 1980 election brought Indira Gandhi back to power with a larger majority than ever before.

DEATH OF A BANDIT

On 18 October 2004, the elusive bandit Veerappan was shot dead by police in an ambush near a remote forest village in Tamil Nadu. It was big news given that the moustachioed outlaw had managed to evade police for more than 30 years. Dubbed the 'forest brigand', Veerappan was a notorious elephant poacher, sandalwood smuggler and cold-blooded murderer. Feared by his adversaries, he headed a loyal gang in his jungle stronghold and plied his illegal trade, dodging police task forces from three states. Veerappan was bold, very bold: in 2000 he kidnapped movie idol Rajkumar and held him hostage for three months; in 2002 he kidnapped Karnatakan politician H Nagappa, who was later found dead. In a finale that reads like something from a movie script, Veerappan went down in true gangster style – with all guns blazing.

1966	1984
Indira Gandhi becomes prime minister of India	Indira Gandhi assassinated; her son Rajiv Gandhi becomes prime minister

Dependent upon a democracy that she ultimately resented, Indira Gandhi grappled unsuccessfully with communal unrest in several areas, violent attacks on Dalits (the Scheduled Caste or Untouchables), numerous cases of police brutality and corruption, and the upheavals in the northeast and Punjab. In 1984, following an ill-considered decision to send in the Indian army to flush out armed Sikh separatists (who were demanding a separate Sikh state to be called Khalistan) from Amritsar's Golden Temple, Indira Gandhi was assassinated by her Sikh bodyguards. Her heavy-handed storming of the Sikhs' holiest temple was catastrophic and sparked brutal Hindu-Sikh riots that left more than 3000 people dead (mostly Sikhs who had been lynched). The quest for Khalistan has since been quashed.

Indira Gandhi's son, Rajiv, became the next prime minister, with Congress winning in a landslide in 1984. However, after a brief golden reign, he was dragged down by corruption scandals and the inability to quell communal unrest, particularly in Punjab. In 1991 he was assassinated in Tamil Nadu by a supporter of the Liberation Tigers of Tamil Eelam (LTTE; a Sri Lankan armed separatist group). Over the years thousands of Tamil refugees had fled to India from war-torn Sri Lanka, most settling in Tamil Nadu.

Bombay & Mumbai: The City in Transition, by Patel Sujata, is a series of essays giving a perceptive window into South India's powerhouse metropolis, its past, and political and economic future.

Narasimha Rao assumed the by-now-poisoned chalice that was leadership of the Congress Party and led it to victory at the polls in 1991.

The December 1992 destruction of the Babri Masjid (p105) by Hindu zealots in Ayodhya (revered by Hindus as the birthplace of Rama), in Uttar Pradesh, sparked widespread communal violence. In Mumbai alone, hundreds of people were killed and an estimated 1100 were wounded after a series of bomb blasts in March 1993.

Meanwhile, Tamil Nadu also faced tumultuous times. The fiercely independent and conservative Tamils have been led alternately by the DMK (Dravida Munnetra Kazhagam) and its offshoot the AIADMK (All-India Anna Dravida Munnetra Kazhagam) since 1957, both parties pushing strong Dravidian 'Tamil Nadu for Tamils' and anti-Hindi language policies, and for more independent powers.

Of all the South Indian states, Goa has probably changed most since Independence, in the rampant development of both tourism and industry (mainly petrochemicals and mining). It has also had more shifts in power since 1987 than there are sun-beds on Calangute Beach, with ministers from the Congress Party and the Hindu nationalist Bharatiya Janata Party (BJP) frequently crossing the floor (switching parties) or resigning.

On a national level, after losing the 1996 election to the BJP, the Congress Party eventually swept back to power in 2004, winning the central government elections largely on the back of major support from South Indian voters, particularly in Andhra Pradesh and Tamil Nadu. The BJP's planned national agitation campaign against the foreign origins of the Italian-born Congress leader, another Gandhi – Sonia, the Italian-born widow of the late Rajiv Gandhi – was subverted by her unexpected but widely lauded decision to step aside. The Congress Party's highly respected former finance minister, Manmohan Singh, was sworn in as prime minister (see p33).

From 1989 to 2007, it's estimated that at least 70,000 people were killed during the conflict in Kashmir.

Singh was passionate about resuming peace talks with Pakistan over the disputed territory of Kashmir, however, these talks came to an abrupt halt when communal tensions soared following the July 2006 train bombings in Mumbai that left over 200 people dead. The Indian government pointed

1991	**26 December 2004**
Rajiv Gandhi assassinated by a supporter of the Sri Lankan-based Liberation Tigers of Tamil Eelam (LTTE) while campaigning in Tamil Nadu	Indian Ocean tsunami claims over 15,000 lives in South India and the Andaman and Nicobar Islands

TSUNAMI!

South India was hit hard by the 26 December 2004 tsunami that slammed into the coast of Tamil Nadu and the Andaman and Nicobar Islands. More than 15,000 people died and many more were injured or left homeless. Worst-affected areas were the Nicobar Islands, 1000km east of the Indian mainland in the Bay of Bengal – although the more northerly Andaman Islands were largely spared – and the central coast of Tamil Nadu. The tsunami had a severe affect on the fishing industry, as not only were fishermen grounded for several months, but the demand for seafood declined – many believed the fish were contaminated from feeding on the flesh of victims. The salt farmers of Tamil Nadu also suffered when thousands of tonnes of stock salt was washed away from the salt pans.

Infrastructure and property reconstruction in India's tsunami-affected regions has, overall, made significant progress but still continues in some areas.

the finger at Pakistan, claiming that its intelligence had played a hand in the blasts – an accusation that Islamabad vehemently denied. Singh later recommenced peace talks with Pakistan, but with suspicions running high on both sides of the border, the road to reconciliation was a shaky one. Then, adding further pressure to the peace process was the February 2007 terrorist bomb attack on a train travelling from Delhi to Lahore (Pakistan) that killed 68 commuters. The Indian and Pakistani governments vowed not to let the attack – designed to disrupt India–Pakistan relations – freeze bilateral peace talks. At the time of writing, investigations were being conducted by Indian authorities to identify – and bring to justice – the culprits (also see p34).

Political Resources – India (www.politicalresources.net/India.htm) contains extensive links to the major players and political parties in India.

On a more optimistic note, 21st-century South India has been riding the IT wave, with southern cities such as Bengaluru (Bangalore), Mumbai, Pune, Hyderabad and Chennai leading India's hi-tech push into the cyber age – for more details, see A Software Superpower, p55.

Seven bombs are detonated on suburban trains in Mumbai leaving over 200 people dead

Bomb blasts on a train travelling from India to Pakistan kill 68 people

The Culture

THE NATIONAL PSYCHE

In a country with such an extraordinary melange of traditions and customs, it might seem impossible to pin down one element that neatly defines the national psyche. However, despite the incredibly intricate tapestry that is India, there is one common thread that weaves through the entire nation: religion. Whether it's a mother in Mumbai (Bombay) performing *puja* (prayers) at a little shrine tucked away in a corner of the home, or Goan children belting out hymns at church each Sunday, spirituality plays a paramount role in defining and guiding people from all walks of life.

Along with religion, family lies at the heart of Indian society. For the vast majority of people, the concept of being unmarried and without children by one's mid-30s (at the very latest) is unimaginable. Despite the steadily rising number of nuclear families (primarily in larger cities such as Bengaluru, formerly Bangalore, and Mumbai), the extended family remains a cornerstone in both urban and rural India, with males – usually the breadwinners – generally considered the head of the household, and two or three generations of a family often living under one roof.

With religion and family considered so sacrosanct, don't be surprised or miffed if you're constantly grilled about these subjects, especially beyond the larger cities, and, receive curious (possibly disapproving) looks if you don't 'fit the mould'. Apart from religion and marital status, frequently asked questions include age, profession and possibly even income. Such questions aren't intended to offend, and it's also acceptable for you to ask the same questions in return.

National pride has always existed on the subcontinent but has swelled in recent years as India attracts increasing international kudos in the fields of IT, science, literature, film and sport (chiefly cricket). The country's robust economy – which is one of the world's fastest growing – is another source of prolific pride.

In 21st-century India the juxtaposition of time-honoured traditions and New Age flies in the face of some common stereotypes about the country. Sure you'll still stumble across the widely-flogged clichés, from snake charmers to ox-pulled carts, but there's certainly a whole lot more to modern-day India than the glossy tourist brochures would have you believe.

LIFESTYLE

Although the lifestyle of a rice farmer in rural Karnataka bears little resemblance to that of a middle-class IT professional in downtown Bengaluru, certain cultural and caste traditions are shared by most layers of society. Indeed the country's first prime minister, Jawaharlal Nehru, adeptly encapsulated India's essence by describing it as being 'a bundle of contradictions held together by strong but invisible threads.'

Traditional Culture

MARRIAGE, BIRTH & DEATH

Marriage is a supremely auspicious event for Indians and although 'love marriages' have spiralled upwards in recent times (mainly in urban hubs such as Mumbai), most Hindu marriages are arranged. Discreet inquiries are made among friends and within the community. Desirable attributes in a potential partner include a good job, a respectable family background, upstanding character and reasonable looks. If a suitable match is not found,

Matchmaking has embraced the cyber age with websites such as www.shaadi.com and www.bharatmatrimony .com catering to tens of millions of Indians and NRIs (Non-Resident Indians).

the help of professional matchmakers may be sought, or advertisements may be placed in newspapers and/or on the internet. The horoscopes are checked and, if propitious, there's a meeting between the two families. The legal marriage age in India is 18.

Dowry, although illegal, is still a key issue in many arranged marriages (primarily in traditional-minded communities), with some families even plunging into debt to raise the required cash and merchandise. In 2005 there were 6787 registered cases of dowry-related deaths (many cases go unreported) in India.

The wedding ceremony is officiated by a priest and the marriage is formalised when the couple walk around a sacred fire seven times. Despite the existence of nuclear families, it's still the norm for a wife to live with her husband's family once married and assume the household duties outlined by her mother-in-law. Not surprisingly, the mother-daughter-in-law relationship can be a thorny one, as reflected in the many Indian TV soap operas, which largely revolve around this theme.

In big cities, such as Mumbai and Bengaluru, the average cost of a wedding is pegged at around US$12,000.

Divorce and remarriage is slowly becoming more common (predominantly in India's bigger cities) but is still generally frowned upon by society. Divorce is certainly not as widespread and acceptable as it is in the West. Among the higher castes, widows are expected not to remarry and are admonished to wear white and live pious, celibate lives (also see p64).

The birth of a child is a momentous occasion, with its own set of special ceremonies that take place at various auspicious times during the early years of childhood. These include four important Hindu ceremonies, performed by the child's parents: *jatakarma* (casting of the horoscope), *nama karma* (name giving), *annaprasana* (feeding the first solid food, usually rice) and *chaula* (the first hair cutting).

Hindus cremate their dead (apart from infants who are buried), and funeral ceremonies are designed to purify and console both the living and the deceased. An important aspect of the proceedings is the *sharadda*, paying respect to one's ancestors by offering water and rice cakes. It's an observance that's repeated at each anniversary of the death. After the cremation the ashes are collected and, 13 days after the death (when blood relatives are deemed ritually pure), a member of the family usually scatters the ashes in a holy river such as the Ganges, or in the ocean.

The Caste System

Although today the caste system is weakened, it still wields considerable power especially in rural areas, where the caste you are born into largely determines your social standing in the community. It can also influence one's vocational and marriage prospects. Castes are further divided into thousands of *jati*, groups of 'families' or social communities, which are sometimes but not always linked to occupation. Conservative Hindus will only marry someone of the same *jati*.

Caste is the basic social structure of Hindu society. Living a righteous life and fulfilling your dharma (moral code of behaviour) raises your chances of being born into a higher caste and thus into better circumstances. Hindus are born into one of four *varnas* (castes): Brahmin (priests and teachers), Kshatriya (warriors), Vaishya (merchants) and Shudra (labourers). The Brahmins were said to have emerged from the mouth of Lord Brahma at the moment of creation, Kshatriyas were said to have come from his arms, Vaishyas from his thighs and Shudras from his feet.

Traditional South Indian Brahmins live with particularly strict 'rules' of lifestyle and behaviour. These include dietary protocols (which dictate a strictly vegetarian regimen and no 'hot' foods, such as garlic or chilli), a simple dress

DOS & DON'TS

South India has oodles of time-honoured traditions, and while you won't be expected to get everything 'right', common sense and courtesy will take you a long way. If in doubt about how you should behave (eg at a temple), watch what the locals do, or simply ask. Refrain from kissing and cuddling in public as this isn't condoned by society.

Dress Etiquette

Dressing conservatively (women *and* men) wins a far warmer response from locals. Nudity in public is not on no matter where you are, and while bikinis may be acceptable on Goa's beaches, you should cover up (eg swim in shorts and a T-shirt) in less touristy places – use your judgement. For more advice about appropriate dress for women, see p489 and also see Dangers & Annoyances, p178.

Eating & Visiting Etiquette

If you're lucky enough to be invited to someone's home, it's considered good manners to remove your shoes before entering the house and to wash your hands before the main meal. Wait to be served food or until you are invited to help yourself – if you're unsure about protocol, simply wait for your host to direct you.

It's customary to use your right hand for eating and other social acts such as shaking hands; the left hand is used for unsavoury actions such as toilet duties. If drinking from a shared water container, hold it slightly above your mouth (thus avoiding contact between your lips and the mouth of the container).

Photographic Etiquette

You should be sensitive about taking photos of people, especially women – always ask first. Taking photos of funerals, religious ceremonies or of people bathing will almost certainly cause offence. Flash photography may be prohibited in certain areas of a shrine, or may not be permitted at all – inquire if you're unsure.

Religious Etiquette

Whenever visiting a sacred site or festival, always dress and behave respectfully – don't wear shorts or sleeveless tops (this applies to men and women) and refrain from smoking. Loud and intrusive behaviour isn't appreciated, and neither are public displays of affection or kidding around. You must remove your shoes (tip the shoe-minder a few rupees when retrieving them) before entering a non-Christian place of worship. You're permitted to wear socks in most places of worship – often necessary during warmer months, when floors can be uncomfortably hot.

Head cover (for women and sometimes men) is required at some places of worship, so consider carrying a scarf just to be on the safe side. There are some sites that don't admit women and some that deny entry to non-adherents of their faith – inquire in advance. Women may be required to sit apart from men. Jain temples request the removal of leather items you may be wearing or carrying and may also request menstruating women not to enter.

Religious etiquette advises against touching locals on the head, or directing the soles of your feet at a person, religious shrine or image of a deity. Protocol also advises against touching someone with your feet or touching a carving of a deity.

Non-Hindus aren't permitted to enter most Keralan temples or the inner sanctums of temples in other states.

Other Traveller Tips

To augment your chances of receiving the most accurate response when seeking directions from people on the street, refrain from posing questions in a leading manner. For instance, it's often best to ask, 'Which way to the zoo?' rather than pointing and asking, 'Is this the way to the zoo?' This is because you may receive a fabricated answer (usually 'yes') if the person can't quite decipher your accent or simply didn't hear you properly. There's no malicious intent in this misinformation – it's just that 'no' can sound so unhelpful!

It's also worth noting that the commonly used sideways wobble of the head doesn't necessarily mean 'no'. It can translate to: yes, maybe, or I have no idea.

TRADITIONAL CLOTHING

Commonly worn by Indian women, the elegant sari comes in a single piece (between 5m and 9m long and 1m wide) and is ingeniously tucked and pleated into place without the need for pins or buttons. Worn with the sari is the choli (tight-fitting blouse) and a drawstring petticoat. The *palloo* is that part of the sari draped over the shoulder. Also widely worn by South Indian women is the *salwar kameez*, a traditional dresslike tunic and trouser combination accompanied by a dupatta (long scarf).

Traditional attire for men in South India includes the lungi and the *mundu*. The lungi is roughly like a sarong, with its end usually sewn up like a tube, while the *mundu* is like a lungi but is always white.

There are regional and religious variations in costume – for example, you may see Muslim women wearing the all-enveloping burka.

---

code, and a certain social etiquette for every occasion. Historically, Brahmin groups fled to South India to escape oppression by Muslim rulers, who often targeted Brahmins to win the support of lower Hindu castes.

Beneath the four main castes are the Dalits (formerly known as Untouchables), who hold menial jobs such as sweepers and latrine cleaners. Some Dalit leaders, such as the late Dr Ambedkar, sought to change their status by adopting another faith; in his case it was Buddhism. To improve the Dalits' position, the government reserves considerable numbers of public-sector jobs, parliamentary seats and university places for them. Today these quotas account for almost 50% of sought-after government jobs. The situation varies regionally, as different political leaders chase caste vote-banks by promising to include them in reservations. The reservation system, while generally regarded in a favourable light, has also been criticised for unfairly blocking tertiary and employment opportunities for those who would have otherwise got positions on merit.

At the very bottom of the social heap are the Denotified Tribes. They had been known as the Criminal Tribes until 1952, when a reforming law officially recognised 198 tribes and castes. Many are nomadic or semi-nomadic, forced by the wider community to eke out a living at the fringes.

Two insightful books about India's caste system are *Interrogating Caste*, by Dipankar Gupta, and *Translating Caste*, edited by Tapan Basu.

Contemporary Issues
AIDS IN INDIA

According to the latest reports, India has surpassed South Africa as having the world's highest number of HIV-positive cases. There are currently 5.7 million reported cases in India, however, analysts believe this is a conservative estimate as many go unreported. Apart from sex workers, truck drivers and intravenous drug users also fall into the high-risk category. There are at least 12,000 sex workers in Mumbai alone, with an estimated 55% of those believed to be HIV-positive.

Areas with the highest incidence of HIV/AIDS include the southern states of Maharashtra, Andhra Pradesh, Karnataka and Tamil Nadu. On a positive note, recent medical reports indicate that the epidemic in South India is slowing down as a result of greater public awareness.

In a country of over one billion people, health officials warn that unless the government radically increases educational programmes (especially promotion of condom use – something that prostitutes claim they can't enforce, as many clients refuse to wear condoms) the number of HIV-positive cases could climb to at least 12 million by 2010. Campaigners say that India's antigay laws (see opposite) make it ambiguous to accurately assess the extent of the epidemic, and also hamper treatment and education efforts.

For health advice, see also p510.

CHILD LABOUR

Despite national legislation prohibiting child labour, human-rights groups believe India has an estimated 60 million (not the officially quoted 12 million) child labourers – the highest rate in the world. Poorly enforced laws, poverty and lack of a social-security system are cited as major causes of the problem. The harsh reality for many low-income families is that they simply cannot afford to support their children, so send them out to work in order to survive.

Recognising the need for tougher anti–child labour laws, in 2006 the government ordered a ban against the employment of children (aged below 14) as labourers in households and the hospitality trade. Combined, these areas are said to employ around 260,000 children, however, activist groups put the figure closer to 20 million. Employers who contravene the ban face possible imprisonment of up to two years, a fine of Rs 20,000, or both. The government has promised to appropriately rehabilitate the displaced child labourers, but critics are sceptical as to how effectively it will be able to do so. If rehabilitation is inadequate, they believe that many jobless children will turn to begging and/or crime. The government's latest ban is an addendum to existing legislation that already forbids the employment of children under the age of 14 in what it classifies as 'hazardous jobs' (eg glass factories and abattoirs).

The South Indian state of Kerala has India's lowest rate of child labour (one in 100); the national average is eight in 100.

The majority (approximately 53%) of India's child labourers work in the agricultural industry, while others work on construction sites, or as rag pickers, household servants, carpet weavers, brick makers and prostitutes. There are also a considerable number of children making *bidis* (small handmade cigarettes), inhaling large quantities of harmful tobacco dust and chemicals. Meanwhile in Kanchipuram (Tamil Nadu), an estimated 4000 school-aged children work full time in the silk industry – see the boxed text, p390.

GAY & LESBIAN ISSUES

Although difficult to accurately pinpoint, India is believed to have between 70 and 100 million gay, lesbian and transgender people. Section 377 of the national legislation forbids 'carnal intercourse against the order of nature' (that is, anal intercourse) and the penalties for transgression can be up to 10 years imprisonment plus a fine. Although this colonial-era law, which dates back to 1861, is rarely used to prosecute, it's allegedly used by authorities to harass, arrest and blackmail gay people.

In 2006 more than 100 high-profile personalities, including Nobel prize-winning economist Amartya Sen, and literary stalwarts Vikram Seth and Arundhati Roy, signed an open letter supporting a legal challenge that has been lodged with the Delhi High Court. The challenge seeks to overturn the country's antiquated antigay law; at the time of writing, a court decision had not been reached.

HIJRAS

India's most visible nonheterosexual group is the *hijras*, a caste of transvestites and eunuchs who dress in women's clothing. Some are gay, some are hermaphrodites and some were unfortunate enough to be kidnapped and castrated. Since it's traditionally unacceptable to live openly as a gay man, *hijras* get around this by becoming, in effect, a sort of third sex. They work mainly as uninvited entertainers at weddings and celebrations of the birth of male children, and as prostitutes.

Learn more about *hijras* in *The Invisibles*, by Zia Jaffrey, and *Ardhanarishvara the Androgyne*, by Dr Alka Pande.

While the more liberal sections of certain cities – such as Mumbai and Bengaluru – appear to be becoming more tolerant of homosexuality, gay life is still largely suppressed. As marriage is so highly regarded on the subcontinent, it's believed that most gay people stay in the closet rather than risk being disowned by their families and society. Nevertheless, freedom of expression is growing. For instance, in 2003 Mumbai hosted the Larzish festival – India's first queer film festival – now held annually in November. This was quite a coup for the gay community, considering the hullabaloo raised by religious zealots over Deepa Mehta's film *Fire* (with lesbian themes), which was famously banned by the ultraconservative Shiv Sena party in 1998.

For details about gay support groups, publications and websites, check out p473.

POVERTY

Chandni Bar, directed by Madhur Bhandarkar, offers a realistic and disturbing window into the lives of women who, driven by poverty and often family pressure, work as dancers/prostitutes in Mumbai's seedy bars.

Raising the living standards of India's poor has been high on the agenda for governments since Independence. However, India presently has one of the world's highest concentrations of poverty, with an estimated 350 million (and growing) Indians living below the poverty line, 75% of them in rural areas. Many others live in horrendously overcrowded urban slums.

The major causes of poverty include illiteracy and a population growth rate that is substantially exceeding India's economic growth rate. Although India's middle class is ballooning (especially in urban centres such as Bengaluru and Mumbai), there's still a marked disparity when it comes to the country's distribution of wealth.

In 2006 the average annual wage in India was US$710. An estimated 35% to 40% of the population survive on less than US$1 per day. Hardest hit are rural dwellers, who earn, on average, four times less than urban Indians. India's minimum daily wage, which varies from state to state, averages Rs 55 (US$1.30), although this certainly isn't always the case in reality. Wages between industries vary, with state governments setting different minimums for different occupations, and there are sectors that have no minimum wages at all, working to the advantage of employers. Women are often paid less, especially in the areas of construction and farming.

Poverty accounts for India's ever-growing number of beggars, predominantly in the larger cities. For foreign visitors this is often the most confronting aspect of travelling in the subcontinent. Whether you give something is a matter of personal choice; however, your money can often be put to better long-term use if donated to a reputable charity. Or, you could lend a hand by working as a volunteer at a charitable organisation – for volunteering possibilities see p487.

POPULATION

India has one of the world's largest Diasporas – over 25 million people in 130 countries – who pumped US$23 billion into India's economy in 2005 alone.

India has the world's second-largest population and is tipped to exceed China as the planet's most populous nation by 2035. According to the latest census (2001), Mumbai is India's most populated city, with an urban agglomeration population of 16,368,084; Kolkata (Calcutta) ranks second with 13,216,546, with Delhi and Chennai (Madras) third and fourth respectively. Despite India's many urban centres, the nation is still overwhelmingly rural, with an estimated 75% of the population living in the countryside.

Despite two South Indian cities having the country's biggest populations, the majority of India's population is concentrated in the north, with around 360 million people living in South India. Maharashtra is the most populous South Indian state, with around 97 million people. Nationally, men outnumber women (933 females to 1000 males), so Kerala is unique in having more

A SOFTWARE SUPERPOWER

The burgeoning IT industry, born in the boom years of the 1990s and founded on India's highly skilled middle class and abundance of relatively inexpensive labour, has made India a major player in the world of technology.

The industry currently employs over one million Indians, with that figure expected to rise to more than two million by 2008, and a further two million or so benefit through indirect employment. When this is added to the trend towards large-scale outsourcing, whereby call centres attached to Western companies move offshore to India, the scale of the revolution in India's once-ramshackle economy starts to become apparent. In 2006 outsourcing was a very healthy US$10 billion industry, a figure that is forecasted to more than double by 2010.

The IT boom has transformed cities such as Hyderabad (p275), nicknamed 'Cyberabad' by many locals, and Bengaluru (Bangalore; p219), known as 'India's Silicon Valley', into IT world leaders. Tamil Nadu, Karnataka and Andhra Pradesh now produce more than 50% of India's software exports.

From the societal perspective, the IT boom has spawned a new breed of Indian yuppie. Many of these young professionals (mostly in their twenties or early thirties and unmarried) are ditching traditional spending patterns (eg for household appliances and retirement) and spending a hefty chunk of their incomes on more hedonistic pursuits such as dining out, shopping and globetrotting.

The average wage rise per annum in the Indian IT industry is 15%, with middle managers enjoying considerably higher increments. An Indian call-centre operator receives an average income of between Rs 10,000 and Rs 12,000 per month. This is at least several thousand rupees higher than that paid by the average Indian company, but a fraction of the cost of what the overseas-based company would pay back home. Meanwhile, talented young Indian managers who have worked with an international company for just a few years may be rewarded (and, from the company's perspective, hopefully deterred from being poached by other companies) with incomes of between Rs 150,000 and Rs 200,000 (even higher in some cases) per month – up to 80% more than the national average income for a middle manager.

Apart from the financial carrot, another incentive used by international companies to lure well-qualified job seekers is the high standard of work-place comfort (eg state-of-the-art equipment, modern cafeterias, possibly even gyms), which counter the drawbacks associated with the job (eg boredom, erratic working hours, verbal phone abuse). Many call centres put their staff through rigorous training courses to get them up to speed with the countries they'll be calling (usually the UK, USA and Australia). These often include lessons on how to mimic foreign accents and staff may also be given pseudo Western names as another means of bridging the cultural divide.

Despite the IT boom playing a critical role in boosting the economy, the industry does have its detractors, particularly those who claim that the country's IT growth is an entirely urban phenomenon with little discernible impact upon the lives of the vast majority of Indians. Whatever the pros and cons, IT will certainly go down in history as one of India's great success stories.

women than men (1058 females to every 1000 males). For further census statistics, click on www.censusindia.net, and for regional populations see the Fast Facts boxed texts at the start of regional chapters.

In South India a large proportion of the population is Dravidian. Over the millennia, however, invasion, trade and settlement have made the population as diverse as anywhere in the country. Invaders and traders from the north, such as Aryans, introduced their traditions to various parts of South India over the years. Christians from the Middle East also arrived on Kerala's coast around AD 100. Arabian and Chinese people came to the Malabar and Coromandel Coasts as traders, and were followed by the Portuguese, the Danes, the French, the Dutch and the British.

ADIVASIS

India's Adivasis (tribal communities; Adivasi translates to 'original inhabitants' in Sanskrit) have origins that precede the Vedic Aryans and the Dravidians of the south. Today there are around 84.3 million Adivasis in India, with some 450 different tribal groups. The literacy rate for Adivasis, as per the last census (2001), is just 29.6%; the national average is 65.38%.

At least 20 million people in South India belong to tribal communities. For thousands of years they have lived more or less undisturbed in the hills and densely wooded regions that agriculturalists regarded as unappealing. Many still speak tribal languages not understood by the politically dominant Hindus, and they follow customs foreign to both Hindus and Muslims. Major Adivasi communities in South India include the Lambanis and Halakkis of northern Karnataka, and the Todas of the Nilgiri Hills of Tamil Nadu (see the boxed text, p439). For information about the Andaman and Nicobar Islands tribal communities, see Island Indigenes, p449.

Although there has obviously been some contact between the Adivasis and Hindu villagers on the plains, this has rarely led to friction since traditionally there has been little or no competition for resources and land. But this is changing. In the past few decades the majority of Adivasis have been dispossessed of their ancestral land and turned into impoverished labourers. Although they still have political representation thanks to a parliamentary quota system, the shocking dispossession and exploitation of Adivasis has often been with the connivance of officialdom – a record the government would prefer to forget and one it vehemently denies. Instead, it points to the millions of rupees said to have been sanctioned into Adivasi schemes. Although some of this has indeed been used positively, corruption has snatched a large portion and unless more is done, the Adivasis' future is uncertain with one of the biggest threats being the erosion of their ancient traditions and culture.

Tourism has had a mixed impact on South India's tribal communities – if you plan on taking a tribal tour, seek out culturally responsible operators. Also see Close Encounters of the Worst Kind, p460.

Find out more about Adivasis in the following texts:

- The Todas of South India – A New Look by Anthony Walker
- Tribes of India – The Struggle for Survival by Christoph von Fürer-Haimendorf
- Archaeology and History: Early Settlements in the Andaman Islands by Zarine Cooper
- The Tribals of India by Sunil Janah

SPORT

The world's second most populous nation has copped derisive criticism for its dismal performances in recent Olympic Games, with critics pointing the finger at paltry sponsorship commitment and lack of public interest. The weightlifter Karnam Malleswari was the only Indian to win a medal (bronze) at the 2000 Sydney Olympic Games, making her the first Indian woman to ever win an Olympic medal. Meanwhile, at the 2004 Athens Olympics, India only managed one medal (silver), won by Rajyavardhan Singh Rathore for the men's double-trap shooting.

Through scintillating text and pictures, *The Illustrated History of Indian Cricket*, by Boria Majumdar, adeptly explores this popular sport, from its origins right up to modern times.

Cricket

Cricket is, without a doubt, India's most beloved sport. Indeed cricket is more than merely a sport – it's a matter of enormous national pride, especially evident whenever India plays against Pakistan. Matches between these two countries – which have had rocky relations since Independence – attract frenzied support, and the players of both sides are under colossal pressure to do their country proud.

Today cricket is big business in India, attracting juicy sponsorship deals and celebrity status for its players, especially for high-profile cricketers such as star batsman Sachin Tendulkar and Sikh ace-bowler Harbhajan Singh (fondly dubbed the 'turbanator'). The sport has not been without its dark side though, with Indian cricketers among those embroiled in match-fixing scandals some years back.

India's first recorded cricket match was in 1721. It won its first test series in 1952 at Chennai against England. International cricket matches are played at several centres in South India, mainly during the cooler months. These include the M Chinnaswamy Stadium in Bengaluru in (p229), the MA Chidambaram (Chepauk) Stadium in Chennai (p364), the VCA Stadium in Nagpur (p154) and the Wankhede Stadium in Mumbai (p129).

Match tickets are usually advertised in the local press (and often on the internet) a few weeks in advance.

Get up-to-date cricket information at Cricinfo (www.cricinfo.com).

Keeping your finger on the pulse of Indian sporting news is just a click away on Sify Sports (www.sify.com/sports).

Football (Soccer)

In South India football has a passionate following, especially in Goa and Kerala. The local newspapers carry details of major matches, and tourist offices can assist with more information if you're keen to attend as a spectator.

In 2007 India slipped to the 165th spot in the FIFA world rankings.

Horse Racing

One of the many legacies of the British Raj is a fondness for horse racing, particularly in parts of South India. Mumbai's racing season runs from November to the end of April, with races taking place on Sunday and Thursday afternoons at the Mahalaxmi Racecourse (p130). Horse racing is also popular in Bengaluru (p229), Mysore (p232) and Hyderabad (p275), where the seasons usually run from around May to July and from November to February.

South India's highest race course is at Udhagamandalam (Ooty), where races take place from mid-April to June (see p438).

Tennis

When it comes to tennis, the biggest success story is the doubles team of Goa-born Leander Paes and Chennai-born Mahesh Bhupathi, who won Wimbledon's prestigious title in 1999 – the first Indians ever to do so. Among more recent wins, Paes (partnered by the Czech Republic's Martin Damm) nabbed the 2006 US Open men's doubles, while Bhupathi (partnered by Switzerland's Martina Hingis) seized the 2006 Australian Open's mixed doubles.

Meanwhile, at the 2005 Dubai Open, Indian wild card Mumbai-born Sania Mirza made waves when she thrashed US Open champion Svetlana Kuznetsova. Mirza, then ranked 97th, 90 spots behind Kuznetsova, became the first Indian woman to win a Women's Tennis Association Tour title. In the 2006 Doha Asian Games, Mirza won silver in the women's singles category and gold in the mixed doubles (her partner was Leander Paes). In early 2007 Sania Mirza's world ranking was 53rd in singles, and 25th in doubles.

Traditional Sports

Kambla (buffalo racing) is a local pastime in rural southern Karnataka between November and March. A pair of good buffaloes and their handlers can cover about 120m in around 14 seconds! For more details, see Buffalo Surfing (p255).

Kerala is renowned for its ancient martial arts form, Kalarippayat (see the boxed text, p349); you can see it practised at the *kalari* (training school) in Thiruvananthapuram (Trivandrum) – see p312 – and at some hotels around the state.

MEDIA

Despite often having allegiances to particular political parties, India's extensive print media enjoys widespread freedom of expression. There are more than 4500 daily newspapers and many thousand more weekly/monthly magazines and journals nationwide, in a range of vernaculars. For listings of major English-language dailies and news magazines, see p463. Most major publications have websites.

For online links to major Indian English-language newspapers, head straight to Samachar (www.samachar.com).

Indian TV was at one time dominated by the dreary national (government-controlled) broadcaster Doordarshan (www.ddindia.gov.in); the introduction of satellite TV in the early 1990s revolutionised viewing habits by introducing several dozen channels. Satellite TV offers a great variety of programming, from Indian and American soap operas to current affairs shows. There are also a number of South Indian regional channels broadcasting in local dialects.

Programmes on the government-controlled All India Radio (AIR; www.allindiaradio.org), one of the world's biggest radio service providers, include news, interviews, music and sport. There are also a number of private channels that offer more variety than the government broadcaster, including talkback on an array of subjects, from relationship problems to peer-group pressure.

Consult local newspapers for TV and radio programme details.

RELIGION

The majority of South Indians are Hindu, although, given the region's history, there's more mixing and melding than the census figures on religious affiliation may suggest. Goa has a considerable Christian population, Hyderabad is home to a sizeable Muslim community, while Mumbai is home to a dwindling community of Parsis (Zoroastrians), among its jumble of other religions.

For a comprehensive overview of the world's religions, including Hinduism, Buddhism, Sikhism, Islam and Jainism, check out www.religionfacts.com.

Religion-based communal conflict has long been a bloody part of India's history, but tensions between religious groups, including Hindus and Muslims, are much less noticeable in the south than up north. In Goa and Kerala the Christian population lives in remarkable harmony with the Hindu majority, although in other states there have been isolated incidences of retribution against Christian missionaries seeking to convert Hindus.

A fantastical melange of religious festivals and events are celebrated across South India, including Diwali (p472), a major Hindu festival, and Christmas as a major Christian one. For comprehensive details, see p471 and the Festivals In...boxed texts at the start of each regional chapter.

Hinduism

India's major religion, Hinduism, is practised by approximately 82% of the population and along with Buddhism, Jainism and Zoroastrianism, it's one of the world's oldest extant religions, with roots extending beyond 1000 BC. Hinduism has no founder, central authority or hierarchy and isn't a proselytising religion.

Shakunthala Jagannathan's *Hinduism – An Introduction* unravels the basic tenets of Hinduism; if you have no prior knowledge, this book is a terrific starting point.

Essentially, Hindus believe in Brahman, who is eternal, uncreated and infinite; everything that exists emanates from Brahman and will ultimately return to it. The multitude of gods and goddesses are merely manifestations – knowable aspects of this formless phenomenon. Brahman is *nirguna* (without attributes), as opposed to all the other gods, which are manifestations of Brahman and therefore *saguna* (with attributes).

GODS & GODDESSES

All Hindu deities are regarded as a manifestation of Brahman, who is often described as having three main representations, the Trimurti: Brahma, Vishnu and Shiva. Following are some prominent deities in South India.

> **THE KARMA CODE**
>
> Hindus believe that earthly life is cyclical; you are born again and again (a process known as samsara), the quality of these rebirths being dependent upon your karma (conduct or action) in previous lives. Living a righteous life and fulfilling your dharma (moral code of behaviour) will enhance your chances of being born into a higher caste and better circumstances. Alternatively, if enough bad karma has accumulated, rebirth may take animal form. But it's only as a human that you can gain sufficient self-knowledge to escape the cycle of reincarnation and achieve moksha (liberation).

Brahma

Only during the creation of the universe does Brahma play an active role. At other times he is in meditation. His consort is Saraswati, the goddess of learning, and his vehicle is a swan. He's sometimes shown sitting on a lotus that rises from Vishnu's navel, symbolising the interdependence of the gods. Brahma is generally depicted with four (crowned and bearded) heads, each turned towards a point of the compass.

Vishnu

The preserver or sustainer, Vishnu is associated with 'right action'. He protects and sustains all that is good. He is usually depicted with four arms, holding a lotus, a conch shell (as it can be blown like a trumpet it symbolises the cosmic vibration from which all existence emanates), a discus and a mace. His consort is Lakshmi (below), the goddess of wealth, and his vehicle is Garuda, a half-bird, half-beast creature. Vishnu has 22 incarnations, including Rama, Krishna and Buddha.

There are around 330 million deities in the Hindu pantheon; those worshipped is a matter of personal choice or tradition.

Vishnu's most renowned temple is the Venkateshwara Temple (p302) at Tirumala in southern Andhra Pradesh.

Shiva

Shiva is the destroyer, but without whom creation couldn't occur. At Chidambaram (Tamil Nadu), he is worshipped as Nataraja, lord of the *tandava* (cosmic dance; see p403), who paces out the cosmos' creation and destruction. Shiva's creative role is phallically symbolised by his representation as the frequently worshipped lingam. With 1008 names, Shiva takes many forms, including Pashupati, champion of the animals, and Nataraja.

Sometimes Shiva has snakes draped around his neck and is shown holding a trident (representative of the Trimurti) as a weapon while riding Nandi, his bull. Nandi symbolises power and potency, justice and moral order. Shiva's consort, Parvati, is capable of taking many forms.

Lakshmi

Lakshmi is Vishnu's consort and the goddess of wealth. In Tamil Nadu the *kolams* (see the boxed text, p74) that grace the thresholds of homes and temples are created with the hope of tempting Lakshmi, and hence prosperity, inside.

Murugan

One of Shiva's sons, Murugan, is a popular deity in South India, especially in Tamil Nadu. He is sometimes identified with another of Shiva's sons Skanda, who enjoys a strong following in North India. Murugan's main role is that of protector, and he is depicted as young and victorious.

Ganesh

The jolly elephant-headed Ganesh is the god of good fortune, remover of obstacles, and patron of scribes (the broken tusk he holds was used to write sections of the Mahabharata; see below). How exactly Ganesh came to have an elephant's head is a story with several variations. One legend says that Ganesh was born to Parvati in his father Shiva's absence – Ganesh grew up not knowing his father. One day, as Ganesh stood guard while his mother bathed, Shiva returned and asked to be let into Parvati's presence. Ganesh, who did not recognise Shiva, refused. Enraged, Shiva promptly lopped off Ganesh's head, only to later discover, much to his horror, that he had slaughtered his own son! He vowed to replace Ganesh's head with that of the first creature he came across. This happened to be an elephant.

Ayyappan

Ayyappan is another of Shiva's sons who is identified with the role of protector. It's said that he was born from the union of Shiva and Vishnu, both male. Vishnu is said to have assumed female form (as Mohini) to give birth. Ayyappan is often depicted riding on a tiger and accompanied by leopards, symbols of his victory over dark forces. Today the Ayyappan following has become something of a men's movement, with devotees required to avoid alcohol, drugs, cigarettes and general misbehaviour before making the pilgrimage.

SACRED HINDU TEXTS

The Mahabharata

A sadhu is someone who has surrendered all material possessions in pursuit of spirituality through meditation, the study of sacred texts, self-mortification and pilgrimage.

Thought to have been composed some time around the 1st millennium BC, the Mahabharata focuses on the exploits of Krishna. By about 500 BC the Mahabharata had evolved into a far more complex creation with substantial additions, including the Bhagavad Gita (where Krishna proffers advice to Arjuna before a battle).

The story centres on conflict between the heroic gods (Pandavas) and the demons (Kauravas). Overseeing events is Krishna (an incarnation of Vishnu), who has taken on human form. Krishna acts as charioteer for the Pandava hero Arjuna, who eventually triumphs in a great battle with the Kauravas.

The Ramayana

Composed around the 3rd or 2nd century BC, the Ramayana is believed to be largely the work of one person, the poet Valmiki. Like the Mahabharata, it centres on conflict between the gods and demons.

Two impressive publications containing English translations of holy Hindu texts are The Bhagavad Gita, by S Radhakrishnan, and The Valmiki Ramayana, by Romesh Dutt.

The story goes that the childless king of Ayodhya, Dasharatha, called upon the gods to provide him with a son. His wife duly gave birth to a boy. But this child, named Rama, was in fact an incarnation of Vishnu, who had assumed human form to overthrow the demon king of Lanka, Ravana. The adult Rama, who won the hand of the princess Sita in a competition, was chosen by his father to inherit his kingdom. But at the last minute Rama's stepmother intervened and demanded her son take Rama's place. Rama, Sita and Rama's brother, Lakshmana, were duly exiled and went off to the forests, where Rama and Lakshmana battled demons and dark forces. Ravana's sister attempted to seduce Rama. She was rejected and, in revenge, Ravana captured Sita and spirited her away to his palace in Lanka. Rama, assisted by an army of monkeys led by the loyal monkey god Hanuman, eventually found the palace, killed Ravana and rescued Sita. All returned victorious to Ayodhya, where Rama was crowned king.

WORSHIP

Worship and ritual play a paramount role in Hinduism. In Hindu homes you'll often find a dedicated worship area, where members of the family pray to the deities of their choice. Beyond the home, Hindus worship at temples. *Puja* is a focal point of worship and ranges from silent prayer to elaborate

---

SACRED CREATURES & PLANTS

Animals, particularly snakes and cows, have long been worshipped throughout India. The cow represents fertility and nurturing, while snakes (especially cobras) are associated with fertility and welfare. Naga stones (snake stones) serve the dual purpose of protecting humans from snakes and propitiating snake gods.

Plants can also have sacred links, such as the banyan tree, which symbolises the Trimurti (p58), while mango trees are symbolic of love – Shiva is believed to have married Parvati under one. Meanwhile, the lotus flower is believed to have emerged from the primeval waters and is connected to the mythical centre of the earth through its stem. Often found in the most polluted of waters, the lotus has the remarkable ability to blossom above their murky depths. The centre of the lotus corresponds to the centre of the universe, the navel of the earth; all is held together by the stem and the eternal waters. This is how Hindus are reminded their own lives should be – like the fragile yet resolute lotus, an embodiment of beauty and strength. So revered is the lotus, that today it's India's national flower.

---

ceremonies. Devotees leave the temple with a handful of *prasad* (temple-blessed food) that is humbly shared among friends and family. Other forms of worship include *aarti* (the auspicious lighting of lamps or candles) and the playing of soul-soothing bhajans (devotional songs).

Islam

Islam was introduced to South India from around the 13th century by Arab traders who settled in coastal Kerala and Karnataka. About 10% of South India's population is Muslim, although this figure is higher in parts of Andhra Pradesh, Karnataka and Kerala. Most are Sunni, although Iranian traders and adventurers also introduced the Shiite following to the region. Although the Mughals, an Islamic dynasty whose empire encompassed a large part of India from the 16th to 18th centuries, controlled northern India for around two centuries, they never really gained a stronghold in the far south, which is one reason there are so many intact ancient Hindu temples in Tamil Nadu.

Islam, which is monotheistic, was founded in Arabia by the Prophet Mohammed in the 7th century AD. The Arabic term *islam* means to surrender, and believers (Muslims) undertake to surrender to the will of Allah (God). The will of Allah is revealed in the scriptures, the Quran. God revealed his will to Mohammed, who acted as his messenger.

Following Mohammed's death, a succession dispute split the movement, and the legacy today is the Sunnis and the Shiites. The Sunnis emphasise the 'well-trodden' path or the orthodox way. Shiites believe that only imams (exemplary leaders) can reveal the true meaning of the Quran.

All Muslims, however, share a belief in the Five Pillars of Islam: the shahadah (declaration of faith: 'There is no God but Allah and Mohammed is his prophet'); sala (prayer; ideally five times a day); the zakat (tax), in the form of a charitable donation or some form of commercial goodwill; sawm (fasting; during Ramadan) – for all except the sick, the very young, the elderly and those undertaking arduous journeys; and the haj (pilgrimage) to Mecca, which every Muslim aspires to do at least once.

A Handbook of Living Religions, edited by John R Hinnewls, provides a succinct and readable summary of all the religions in India, including Christianity and Judaism.

Christianity

Christians comprise around 2.3% of the population, with around 75% living in South India. Christianity is said to have arrived in South India (specifically the Malabar Coast) with St Thomas the apostle in AD 52. However, scholars say that it's more likely Christianity arrived around the 4th century with a

Syrian merchant (Thomas Cana), who set out for Kerala with 400 families to establish what later became a branch of the Nestorian church. Today the Christian community is fractured into a multitude of established churches and new evangelical sects.

The Marriage of East and West, by Bede Griffiths, is the famous book by the equally famous monk who lived for many decades in Tamil Nadu. The author examines the essence of Eastern and Western thought in an attempt to forge a fresh approach to spirituality.

The Nestorian church sect survives today; services are in Armenian, and the Patriarch of Baghdad is the sect's head. Thrissur (Trichur; p352) is the church's centre. Other Eastern Orthodox sects include the Jacobites and the Syrian Orthodox churches.

Catholicism established a strong presence in South India in the wake of Vasco da Gama's visit in 1498. Catholic orders that have been active in the region include the Dominicans, Franciscans and Jesuits. The faith is most noticeable in Goa, not only in the basilicas and convents of Old Goa (p187), but in the dozens of active whitewashed churches scattered through towns and villages. Protestantism arrived with the Danish, the Dutch and the English, and their legacy lives on today in the Church of South India.

Evangelical Christian groups have made inroads both into the other Christian communities, and lower caste and tribal groups across South India. In the past, some congregations have been regarded as being aggressive in seeking converts, and in 'retaliation' a number of Christian communities have been targeted by Hindu nationalist groups.

Jainism

St Thomas the Apostle landed in Kerala in around AD 52, then lived for some time in a cave in present-day Chennai. A church now occupies the site.

Jainism is followed by about 0.4% of the population, with the majority of Jains living in Gujarat and Mumbai. Jainism arose in the 6th century BC as a reaction against the caste restraints and rituals of Hinduism. It was founded by Mahavira, a contemporary of the Buddha and evolved as a reformist movement against Brahminism. Jainism revolves around the concept of ahimsa, or nonviolence.

Apart from Mumbai, South India's small community of Jain people is centred on coastal Karnataka; the 17m-high sculpture of Gomateshvara (one of the world's tallest monoliths; see p249) at Sravanabelagola is at one of Jainism's most-visited centres of pilgrimage.

Buddhism

Buddhism developed in India when it was embraced by Emperor Ashoka during his reign (272–232 BC) and today it comprises around 0.76% of the country's population.

Set in Kerala against the backdrop of caste conflict and India's struggle for independence, *The House of Blue Mangoes*, by David Davidar, spans three generations of a Christian family.

It appears that Buddhist communities were quite influential in Andhra Pradesh between the 2nd and 5th centuries; missionaries from Andhra helped establish monasteries and temples in countries such as Thailand. However, Buddhism's influence waned as Hinduism waxed in South India, about 1000 years after it was first introduced. It underwent a sudden revival in the 1950s when the Dalit leader, Dr Ambedkar, converted to Buddhism and brought many Dalit followers with him. Today these Neo-Buddhists, as they are often called, number about six million and are concentrated in Dr Ambedkar's home state of Maharashtra.

There are several communities of Tibetan refugees in South India, who have established numerous new monasteries and convents since the 1960s. The Bylakuppe area of Karnataka is one of the more easily accessible Tibetan settlements – see p245 for more information.

Judaism

There are believed to be less than 8000 Jews left in India, most of who live in Mumbai and parts of South India. South India's Jews first settled in the region from the Middle East as far back as the 1st century. Jews became es-

---

TEACHINGS OF THE BUDDHA

Buddha taught that existence is based on Four Noble Truths: that life is rooted in suffering; that suffering is caused by craving worldly things; that one can find release from suffering by eliminating craving; and that the way to eliminate craving is by following the Noble Eightfold Path. This path consists of right understanding, right intention, right speech, right action, right livelihood, right effort, right awareness and right concentration. By successfully complying with these, one can attain nirvana.

---

tablished at Kochi (Cochin), and their legacy continues in the still-standing synagogues and trading houses – see p344.

Zoroastrianism

Parsis, adherents of Zoroastrianism, number roughly between 75,000 and 80,000 – a mere drop in India's billion-plus population. Historically, Parsis settled in Gujarat and became farmers; however, during British rule they moved into commerce, forming a prosperous community in Mumbai; see The Parsi Connection, p119, for more details.

Zoroastrianism, founded by Zoroaster (Zarathustra), had its inception in Persia in the 6th century BC and is based on the concept of dualism, whereby good and evil are locked in continuous battle. While Zoroastrianism leans towards monotheism, it isn't quite: good and evil entities co-exist, although believers are enjoined to honour only the good. Humanity therefore has a choice. Unlike Christianity, there is no conflict between body and soul: both are united in the good versus evil struggle. Humanity, although mortal, has components, such as the soul, which are timeless; a pleasant afterlife depends on one's deeds, words and thoughts during earthly existence. But not every lapse is entered on the balance sheet and the errant soul is not called to account on the day of judgment for each and every misdemeanour.

Zoroastrianism was eclipsed in Persia by the rise of Islam in the 7th century and its followers, many of whom openly resisted this, suffered persecution. In the 10th century some emigrated to India, where they became known as Parsis.

Mumbai's Parsi (Zoroastrian) community still use the Towers of Silence to dispose of their dead, but a scarcity of vultures has meant they have had to resort to chemical methods in recent years.

Sikhism

South India is home to a small population of Sikhs – the majority of the country's 1.9% of Sikhs lives in North India, especially Punjab.

Sikhism, founded in Punjab by Guru Nanak in the 15th century, began as a reaction against the caste system and Brahmin domination of ritual. Sikhs believe in one god and, although they reject the worship of idols, some keep pictures of the 10 gurus as a point of focus. The Sikhs' holy text, the Guru Granth Sahib, contains the teachings of the 10 Sikh gurus, among others. Like Hindus and Buddhists, Sikhs believe in rebirth and karma. In Sikhism, there's no ascetic or monastic tradition ending the eternal cycles of rebirth.

Fundamental to Sikhs is the concept of Khalsa, or belief in a chosen race of soldier-saints who abide by strict codes of moral conduct (abstaining from alcohol, tobacco and drugs) and engage in a crusade for *dharmayudha* (righteousness). There are five *kakkars* (emblems) denoting the Khalsa brotherhood: *kesh* (the unshaven beard and uncut hair symbolising saintliness); *kangha* (comb to maintain the ritually uncut hair); *kaccha* (loose underwear symbolising modesty); *kirpan* (sabre or sword symbolising power and dignity); and *karra* (steel bangle symbolising fearlessness). Singh, literally 'Lion', is the name adopted by many Sikhs.

Travels Through Sacred India, by Roger Housden, is a very readable account of popular and classical traditions, and contains a gazetteer of sacred places and a summary of ashrams and retreats.

A belief in the equality of all beings lies at the heart of Sikhism. It's expressed in various practices, including *langar*, whereby people from all walks of life – regardless of caste and creed – sit side by side to share a complimentary meal prepared by hard-working volunteers in the *gurdwara's* (Sikh temple) communal kitchen.

To understand the intricacies of Sikhism, read *A History of the Sikhs*, by Khushwant Singh, which comes in Vol 1 (1469–1839) and Vol 2 (1839–2004).

Tribal Religions

Tribal religions have so merged with Hinduism and other mainstream religions that very few are now clearly identifiable. It's believed that some basic tenets of Hinduism may have originated in ancient tribal culture.

Village and tribal people in South India have their own belief systems, which are much less accessible or obvious than the temples, rituals and other outward manifestations of the mainstream religions. The village deity may be represented by a stone pillar in a field, a platform under a tree or an iron spear stuck in the ground under a tree. Village deities are generally seen as less remote and more concerned with the immediate happiness and prosperity of the community; in most cases they are female. There are also many beliefs about ancestral spirits, especially of those who died violently.

To learn more about some of South India's tribal groups, see the Nehru Centenary Tribal Museum (p281), Island Indigenes (p449) and Hill Tribes of the Nilgiri (p439).

WOMEN IN SOUTH INDIA

South Indian women have traditionally had a greater degree of freedom than their northern sisters. This is especially so in Kerala. Unique in many ways, Kerala is the most literate state in India and is also famous for its tradition of matrilineal kinship. Exactly why the matrilineal family became established in this region is subject to conjecture, although one explanation is that it was in response to ongoing warfare in the 10th and 11th centuries. With the military men absent, women invariably took charge of the household. It has also been argued that the men would very likely form alliances wherever they found themselves, and that the children of these unions would become the responsibility of the mother's family. Whatever the reason, by the 14th century a matrilineal society was firmly established in many communities across Kerala, and it lasted pretty much unchallenged until the 20th century. Kerala was also India's first state to break societal norms by recruiting female police officers in 1938. On top of that, it was the first state to establish an all-female police station (1973).

In other parts of South India, such as Tamil Nadu, women also had more freedom than was the norm elsewhere in India. Matriarchy was a long-standing tradition within Tamil communities, and the practice of marriage among cousins meant that young women did not have to move away and live among strangers. Dowry deaths and female infanticide were virtually unknown in South India until relatively recent times, but the imposition of consumerism on old customs and conventions, making dowries more expensive, has resulted in increased instances.

For further reading about women in India, there are some good websites including the All India Democratic Women's Association (AIDWA) at www.aidwa.org.

Women throughout India are entitled to vote and own property. Although the percentage of women in politics has risen over the past decade, they're still notably underrepresented in the national parliament, accounting for only 10% of parliamentary members. In an ongoing bid to improve women's parliamentary representation, campaigners continue to fight for the Women's Reservation Bill (which proposes a 33% reservation of seats for women) to be passed.

Although the professions are still very much male dominated, women are steadily making inroads, most noticeably in the bigger cities. For village women it is much more difficult to get ahead, and an early marriage to a suitable provider (often arranged years beforehand) is usually regarded as essential.

According to reports, every six hours a married woman in India is beaten or burnt to death, or emotionally harassed to the point of suicide. In October 2006, following persistent women's civil rights campaigns, the Indian parliament passed a landmark bill (on top of existing legislation) that gives women who are suffering domestic violence increased protection and rights. Prior to this legislation, although Indian women could lodge police complaints against abusive spouses, they were not automatically entitled to a share of the marital property or to ongoing financial support. The new law purports that any form of physical, sexual (including marital rape), emotional and economic abuse entails not only domestic violence, but also human rights violations. Perpetrators face imprisonment and fines.

Under the new law, abused women are now legally permitted to remain in the marital house; in the past many were thrown out and made destitute. In addition, the law prohibits emotional and physical bullying in relation to dowry demands. Although the government has been widely lauded for taking this long-overdue step, critics point out that a sizeable proportion of women (especially in rural areas) will remain oblivious of their new rights unless there are sufficient government-sponsored awareness programmes. They also suggest that many women, especially out of India's larger cities, will be too frightened to seek legal protection because of the social stigma and alienation that is often a consequence of speaking out.

Although the constitution allows for divorcées (and widows) to remarry, few do so, simply because divorcées are generally considered outcasts from society. Even a woman's own family will often turn its back on a wife who seeks divorce. Divorce rates in India are among the world's lowest, despite having risen from seven in 1000 in 1991 to 11 in 1000 in 2004. Although no reliable post-2004 statistics are yet available, divorce rates are reportedly growing by 15% per annum, with most cases registered in urban India.

Although sexual harassment has increased in recent years, India has less reported sex crimes than most Western nations. Authorities claim that a rape occurs every 30 minutes in India (in the USA it averages one every two minutes), with around 50% of the victims aged under eighteen. Statistical data can be deceiving, as the majority of rapes in India go unreported. Indeed, it's estimated that only one in every 70 rape cases is registered with authorities, with only 20% of the accused being convicted.

Women travellers should also see p489.

Unveiling India, by Anees Jung, draws on the author's experiences growing up in Hyderabad as a child in purdah (custom of keeping women in seclusion) and those experiences of other women from both rural and urban backgrounds.

THE CURSE OF BEING A WOMAN

In low-income families, girls can be regarded as a liability because at marriage a dowry must often be supplied, posing an immense financial burden. For the urban, middle-class woman, life is materially much more comfortable, but pressures still exist. Broadly speaking, she is far more likely to be given an education, but once married is still usually expected to 'fit in' with her in-laws and be a homemaker above all else. Like her village counterpart, if she fails to live up to expectations – even if it's just not being able to produce a grandson – the consequences can sometimes be dire, as demonstrated by the gruesome practice of 'bride burning', where the husband or a member of his family inflicts pain, disfigurement or death on his wife. It may take the form of dousing with fuel and setting alight or scalding with boiling water, and is usually intentionally designed to look like an accident or suicide.

It is claimed that for every reported case of 'bride burning', around 250 go unreported and that less than 10% of the reported cases are pursued through the legal system.

ARTS
Literature

South India's main languages – Tamil, Kannada, Telugu, Malayalam and Marathi – each have a long literary history. Tamil is considered a case apart (some early works date from the 2nd century) because it evolved independently from the others, which all have their roots in Sanskrit.

In the 19th century, South Indian literature began to reflect the influence of European genres. Where literature had once been expressed primarily in verse, now it was widely seen in prose. By the end of the 19th century, South Indian writers were pioneering new forms; among them Subramania Bharati and VVS Aiyar, who are credited with transforming Tamil into a modern language.

India boasts an ever-growing number of internationally acclaimed authors who are especially revered for evoking a sense of place and emotion through deliciously sensuous and insightful language. Modern South Indian literature in English has been a wildly successful cultural export thanks to superstars such as Mumbai-born Salman Rushdie, who bagged the Booker Prize in 1981 for *Midnight's Children* (opposite), and Keralan writer Arundhati Roy, who won the 1997 Booker Prize for her novel *The God of Small Things*.

One of India's most legendary writers is RK Narayan, who hails from Mysore. Many of his stories centre on the fictitious South Indian town of Malgudi; his most well-known works include *Swami and His Friends*, *The Financial Expert*, *The Guide*, *Waiting for the Mahatma* and *Malgudi Days*.

Family Matters and *A Fine Balance*, by Rohinton Mistry, are expertly crafted accounts of contemporary Indian society, both set in Mumbai. The plots have a touch of melodrama, but they're still an excellent read.

A Matter of Time, by Shashi Deshpande, centres on the problems a middle-class family faces when the husband walks out. Deshpande, who is from Bengaluru, takes the reader back through several generations to demonstrate how family tradition impacts on contemporary behaviour.

Sharanpanjara (Cage of Arrows), by Karnatakan author Triveni, is hailed as one of the great novels in the Kannada language (now available in English). The story centres on an upper-class Mysore woman facing the stigma of mental illness.

For details about English-language Indian literature, from historical to contemporary times, check out Indian English Literature (www.indianenglish literature.com).

THE LEGENDARY RABINDRANATH TAGORE

Bengalis are credited with producing some of India's most celebrated literature, a movement often referred to as the Indian or Bengal Renaissance, which flourished from the 19th century with works by Bankimchandra Chatterjee. But the man who to this day is credited with propelling India's cultural richness onto the world stage is Rabindranath Tagore.

The brilliant and prolific poet, writer, artist and patriot Rabindranath Tagore (or 'Rabi Babu' as he's known to Bengalis) launched India's historical and cultural greatness far beyond the shores of his homeland. He won the Nobel Prize for Literature in 1913 with his mystical collection of poems *Gitanjali* (Song Offering), and in later years his lecture tours saw him carrying his message of human unity around Asia, America and Europe.

Born to a wealthy, prominent family in Calcutta (now Kolkata) in 1861, Tagore began writing as a young boy and never stopped, dictating his last poem only hours before his death in 1941. But for all his internationalism, Tagore's heart was firmly rooted in his homeland; a truth reflected in his many popular songs, sung by the masses, and in the lyrics of the national anthems of both India and Bangladesh. In 1915 Rabindranath Tagore was awarded a knighthood by the British, but he surrendered it in 1919 as a protest against the horrific British-lead Amritsar (Punjab) massacre that left more than 1000 Indians dead.

For a taste of Rabindranath Tagore's work, read his *Selected Short Stories*.

The Revised Kama Sutra, by Richard Crasta, takes an irreverent look at growing up in Mangalore in the 1960s and 1970s. It's a book that leaves you with a lasting insight into the local life of Mangalore and other South Indian cities.

Nectar in a Sieve, by Kamala Markandaya, is a harrowing, though at times uplifting, account of a woman's life in rural South India, and the effect of industrialisation on traditional values and lifestyles.

The first part of Salman Rushdie's *The Moor's Last Sigh* is set in Kochi, (Cochin; Kerala), while his *Midnight's Children* is a stunning story of India from Independence until the disastrous Emergency of the mid-1970s.

Karma Cola, by Gita Mehta, amusingly and cynically describes the collision between India looking to the West for technology and modern methods, and the West descending upon India in search of wisdom and enlightenment.

Meanwhile, Trinidad-born Indian writer VS Naipaul has written widely about India, and his book *A Million Mutinies Now* has to be one of the most penetrating insights into Indian life. Naipaul has won many awards including the Booker Prize (1971) and the Nobel Prize for Literature (2001).

India's latest shining literary star is India-born Kiran Desai who won the 2006 Man Booker Prize for her superb novel, *The Inheritance of Loss,* which, through a handful of engaging characters, intimately explores a gamut of issues including migration, globalisation, economic disparity and identity. Her first novel, *Hullabaloo in the Guava Orchard,* was also widely applauded. Kiran Desai, who is the youngest woman to ever win the Booker Prize, is the daughter of the award-winning Indian novelist Anita Desai, who has thrice been a Booker Prize nominee.

For further recommendations of just some of the many brilliant Indian novels available, see Travel Literature (p22) and Top Picks (p23).

Cinema

Today, India's film industry is the biggest in the world – larger than Hollywood – and Mumbai, the Hindi-language film capital, is affectionately dubbed 'Bollywood'. Bollywood has a worldwide audience of around 3.7 billion – and growing – as compared to Hollywood's estimated 2.6 billion. India's other major film-producing centres include Chennai, Hyderabad and Bengaluru, with a number of other southern centres also producing films in their own regional vernaculars. Bollywood movies in particular have a massive NRI (Non-Resident Indian) following, which has largely been responsible for the recent success of Indian cinema on the international arena. On average, 900 feature films are produced annually in India, each costing anywhere between Rs 2,000,000 and upwards of Rs 500 million, although only a small percentage yield healthy profits.

Broadly speaking, there are two categories of Indian films. Most prominent is the mainstream movie – three hours and still running, these blockbusters are often tear-jerkers and are packed with dramatic twists interspersed with copious song-and-dance performances. There aren't explicit sex scenes, nor is there any kissing (although nowadays smooching is creeping into some films occasionally) in Indian films made for the local market; however, lack of nudity is often compensated for by heroines writhing to music in clinging, wet saris.

The second Indian film genre is art house, which adopts Indian 'reality' as its base. The images are a faithful reproduction of what one sees in the subcontinent and the idiom in which it is presented is usually a Western one. Generally speaking they are, or at least supposed to be, socially and politically relevant. Usually made on infinitely smaller budgets than their commercial cousins, these films are the ones that win kudos at international film festivals. One recent example is India-born Canadian filmmaker Deepa

Legends of Goa, by Mario Cabral E Sa, is an illustrated compilation of Goan folktales that offers an insight into the state's colourful traditions and history.

Encyclopedia of Indian Cinema, by Ashish Rajadhyaksha and Paul Willemen, comprehensively chronicles India's cinema history, spanning from 1896 to the 21st century.

Mehta's widely acclaimed trilogy, *Earth*, *Fire* and *Water*. In 2007, *Water* received a Best Foreign Language Film Oscar nomination.

Mumbai is undeniably the epicentre of the Hindi film industry, but along with Pune (Maharashtra) it also turns out popular Marathi-language films. The classic formula for any mainstream blockbuster is the masala (mixed) movie, which combines family-values moralising, a startling degree of violence and whimsical romantic sequences, all interwoven with plenty of song-and-dance sequences. While some may dismiss this film genre as nothing more than mindless escapism, many masala movies actually do tackle serious social issues, such as caste conflict, religious upheaval, corruption and the economic divide. Admittedly, sometimes it's quite a challenge to decipher the message among the abrupt jumps in plot, the often exaggerated acting and the many song-and-dance routines, but talented filmmakers have a long tradition of mixing current issues with good old-fashioned entertainment, and deserve credit for doing so.

For the latest on the film industry, check out Movie South India (www.india film.com), Bollywood World (www.bollywood world.com) and Tamil Cinema World (www .tamilcinemaworld.com).

As well as the obvious Bollywood blockbusters, most states in South India have their own regional film industry. Tamil-language films from Tamil Nadu and Telugu films from Andhra Pradesh are the most numerous, but there are strong Malayalam films from Kerala and Kannada films from Karnataka. For more information about Bollywood and the possibility of working as a film extra, see Bollywood, p116; for the lowdown on some of Bollywood's biggest stars, check out Star Struck, p128; and for details about Tamil films, see Into the 'Woods, p378.

You can also tour the movie-making complex Ramoji Film City (p281) at Hyderabad.

Music

South India's form of classical music, called Carnatic, traces its origins to Vedic times, some 3000 years ago. There are two basic elements in Indian music, the *tala* and the raga. The *tala* is the rhythm and is characterised by the number of beats; the raga provides the melody. In Carnatic music both are used for composition and improvisation.

While it has many elements in common with its northern counterpart, Hindustani, Carnatic music differs in several important respects: Hindustani has been more heavily influenced by Persian musical conventions (a result of Mughal rule); Carnatic music, as it developed in South India, cleaves more closely to theory. The most striking difference, at least for those unfamiliar with India's classical forms, is Carnatic's greater use of voice.

Appreciating Carnatic Music, by Chitravina Ravi Kiran, is aimed at helping those more familiar with Western music get to grips with this South Indian art form. It's a compact little book with masses of useful information, including a question-and-answer section.

One of the best-known Indian instruments is the sitar (a large stringed instrument) with which the soloist plays the raga. Other stringed instruments include the *sarod* (which is plucked) and the *sarangi* (which is played with a bow).

Also popular is the tabla (twin drums), which provides the *tala*. The drone, which runs on two basic notes, is provided by the oboelike *shehnai* or the stringed *tamboura*. The hand-pumped keyboard harmonium is used as a secondary melody instrument for vocal music.

A completely different genre altogether, *filmi* music entails musical scores from Bollywood movies. These days, a lot of *filmi* music consists of rather cheesy pop-techno tunes, not the lyrically poetic and mellow melodies of the old days. Modern (slower paced) love serenades also feature among the predominantly hyperactive dance songs, offering some respite from the high-energy tunes. With Bollywood cranking out hundreds of movies a year, it's hardly surprising that *filmi* hits tend to come and go in the wink of an eye. To ascertain the latest *filmi* favourites as well as in-vogue Indian pop singers, simply ask at any music store.

BHANGRA MANIA

Originating in the north Indian state of Punjab, bhangra is a wildly rhythmic and innovative form of subcontinental music and dance that has been embraced right around India, including the south. It first came to fruition as part of Punjab's harvest festival celebrations (dating to around the 14th century) then later appeared at weddings and other joyous events.

In terms of dance movements, there are different variations but most entail the arms being held high in the air coupled with the energetic shaking of the shoulders and intermittent kicking of the legs. More traditional forms involve brightly costumed participants dancing in a circle. The most prominent musical instrument used in bhangra is the *dhol* (a traditional two-sided drum), while accompanying lyrics tend to revolve around the themes of love, marriage and assorted social issues.

In the 1980s and '90s, inventive fusion versions of traditional bhangra (which include elements of hip-hop, disco, techno, rap, house and reggae) made big waves on both the domestic and international music/dance arenas, especially in the UK.

Radio and TV have played a paramount role in broadcasting different music styles throughout the country – from soothing bhajans to buzzing bhangra (see above)– to even the remotest corners of South India.

Architecture

From looming temple gateways adorned with a rainbow of delicately carved deities, to whitewashed cube-like village houses, South India has a rich architectural heritage. Traditional buildings, such as temples, often have a superb sense of placement within the local environment, whether perched on a boulder-strewn hill or standing by a large artificial reservoir.

The influence of British architecture is most obvious in cities such as Chennai, Bengaluru and Mumbai, which have many grand neoclassical structures. British bungalows with corrugated iron roofs and wide verandas are a feature of many hill stations, including Udhagamandalam (Ooty; p436). More memorable are the attempts to meld European and Indian architecture, such as in the great 19th-century public buildings of Mumbai and the positively breathtaking Maharaja's Palace in Mysore (for more details see p233).

RELIGIOUS ARCHITECTURE

For Hindus the square is the perfect shape, and complex rules govern the location, design and building of each temple, based on numerology, astrology, astronomy and religious law. Essentially, a temple is a map of the universe. At the centre is an unadorned space, the *garbhagriha* (inner shrine), which is symbolic of the 'womb-cave' from which the universe emerged. This provides a residence for the deity to whom the temple is dedicated.

Above the shrine rises a superstructure known as a *vimana* in South India and a *sikhara* in North India. The *sikhara* is curvilinear and topped with a grooved disk, on which sits a pot-shaped finial, while the *vimana* is stepped, and the grooved disk is replaced with a solid dome. Some temples have a *mandapa* (temple forechamber) connected to the sanctum by vestibules. These *mandapas* may also contain *vimanas* or *sikharas*.

A *gopuram* is the soaring pyramidal gateway tower of a Dravidian temple. The towering *gopurams* of various South Indian temple complexes take ornamentation and monumentalism to new levels. A stunning example is Madurai's Sri Meenakshi Temple (p420).

Stupas, which characterise Buddhist places of worship, evolved from burial mounds. They served as repositories for relics of the Buddha and, later, other

The History of Architecture in India: From the Dawn of Civilisation to the End of the Raj, by Christopher Tadgell, is an illustrated overview of the subject and includes most of the important sites in South India.

venerated souls. A relatively recent innovation is the addition of a *chaitya* (hall) leading up to the stupa itself.

The subcontinent's Muslim invaders contributed their own architectural conventions – arched cloisters and domes among them. Travellers will come across various forms of exquisite temple architecture, India's most striking and revered form of construction – the nation's most spectacular Mughal monument is the milky-white Taj Mahal in Agra. One of the most striking differences between Hinduism and Islam is religious imagery – while Islamic art eschews any hint of idolatry or portrayal of God, it has developed a rich heritage of calligraphic and decorative designs.

Discover more about India's diverse temple architecture (in addition to other temple-related information) at Temple Net (www.templenet.com).

When it comes to mosque architectural styles, the basic elements are largely the same worldwide. A large space or hall is dedicated to communal prayer, while in the hall is a mihrab (niche), which marks the direction of Mecca. Outside the hall there's usually some sort of courtyard with places for devotees to wash their feet and hands before prayers. Minarets are placed at the cardinal points, and it's from here that the faithful are called to prayer. Most large towns and cities will have at least one mosque; some fine examples of Islamic architecture in South India include Hyderabad's Mecca Masjid (p280) and Golconda Fort (p280), and Bijapur's Golgumbaz (p268).

Churches in India reflect the fashions and trends of typically European ecclesiastical architecture, with many also displaying Hindu decorative flourishes. The Portuguese, among others, made impressive attempts to replicate the great churches and cathedrals of their day. Today, Goa has some particularly impressive churches and cathedrals, especially Old Goa – see p187.

FORTS & PALACES

A typical South Indian fort is situated on a hill or rocky outcrop, ringed by moated battlements. It usually has a town nestled at its base, which has developed after the fortifications were built. Gingee (Senji; p395), in Tamil Nadu, is a particularly good example. Vellore Fort (p392), in Tamil Nadu, is one of India's best-known moated forts, while Bidar (see p271) and Bijapur (p269) are home to great metropolitan forts.

Daulatabad (p146), in central Maharashtra, is another magnificent fortress, with 5km of walls surrounding a hilltop fortress. The fortress is reached by passageways filled with ingenious defences, including spike-studded doors and false tunnels, which in times of war led either to a pit of boiling oil or to a crocodile-filled moat!

Few old palaces remain in South India, as conquerors often targeted these for destruction. The remains of the royal complex at Vijayanagar, near Hampi (p257), indicate that local engineers weren't averse to using the sound structural techniques and fashions (such as domes and arches) of their Muslim adversaries, the Bahmanis. Travancore's palace of the maharajas (p319), at Padmanabhapuram, which dates from the 16th century, has private apartments for the king, a zenana (women's quarters), rooms dedicated to public audiences, an armoury, a dance hall and temples. Meanwhile, the Indo-Saracenic Maharaja's Palace (p233), in Mysore, is the best-known and most opulent in the south, its interior a kaleidoscope of stained glass, mirrors and mosaic floors.

Window on Goa, by Maurice Hall, is an authoritative labour of love featuring descriptions of Goa's churches, forts, villages and more.

Sculpture

Sculpture and religious architecture are closely related in South India, and it's difficult to consider them separately. Sculpture is invariably religious in nature and isn't generally an art form through which individuals express their own creativity.

THE RISE & RISE OF CONTEMPORARY INDIAN ART

In the 21st century, paintings by contemporary Indian artists have been selling at record numbers (and prices) around the world. One especially innovative and successful online art auction house, the Mumbai-based **Saffronart** (www.saffronart.com), has reportedly surpassed heavyweights like Sotheby's and Christie's in terms of its online Indian art sales.

Online auctions promote feisty global bidding wars, largely accounting for the high success rate of Saffronart, which also previews its paintings in Mumbai and New York prior to its major cyber auctions. Many bidders are wealthy NRIs (Non-Resident Indians) who not only appreciate Indian art, but have also recognised its investment potential. However there is also mounting demand from non-Indian collectors, with spiralling sales in Europe, the USA, UK, Southeast Asia and the Middle East.

International auction houses are descending upon India, to either set up offices or secure gallery alliances, in order to grab a piece of the action of what they have identified as a major growth market. Although the bulk of demand, on both the domestic and international fronts, is for senior Indian artists' works, such as those of Francis Newton Souza, Tyeb Mehta, Syed Haider Raza, Akbar Padamsee, Ram Kumar and Maqbool Fida Husain, there's a steadily growing interest in emerging Indian artists.

The 7th-century relief Arjuna's Penance (p385), at Mamallapuram (Mahabalipuram), is one of the most sublime examples of early sculpture. Its fresh, lively touch is also reflected in later 9th-century Chola shrine sculptures. The legacy and tradition of sculptors from the Pallava dynasty live on in Mamallapuram, where hundreds of modern-day sculptors work with stone to produce freestanding sculptures of all shapes and sizes (see the Sculpture Museum, p385). Some mix the old with the spanking new – such as a sculpture of Ganesh chatting on a mobile phone!

Unlike in the north of India, a tradition of South Indian sculpture was able to develop without serious interruption from Muslim invasions. But curiously, despite a high level of technical skill, the 17th-century work appears to lack the life and quality of earlier examples. However, South India remains famous for its bronze sculptures, particularly those of the 9th and 10th centuries, created during the highly artistic Chola dynasty (p37). Artisans employed the lost-wax technique to make their pieces, which were usually of Hindu deities, such as Vishnu and – in the south especially – Shiva in his adored form as Lord of the Dance, Nataraja. This technique, still in use in South India, involves carving a model out of wax then painting on a claylike mixture to form a mould. The wax is melted out, leaving a hollow mould into which molten bronze (or silver, copper, lead etc) is poured. Some of the most exuberant sculptural detail comes from the Hoysala period (see the boxed text, p248), and can be seen at the temples of Belur (p248) and Halebid (p248) in Karnataka.

Architecture and Art of Southern India, by George Michell, provides details on the Vijayanagar empire and its successors, encompassing a period of some 400 years.

Dance

Dance is an ancient and revered Indian art form that is traditionally linked to mythology and classical literature. Historically, accomplished artists were a matter of prolific pride among royal houses; the quality of their respective dance troupes was at one stage the cause of intense competition between the maharajas of Mysore and Travancore. Between the 2nd and 8th centuries, trade between South India and Southeast Asia brought a cultural legacy that endures in the dance forms of Bali (Indonesia), Thailand, Cambodia and Myanmar (Burma). Today dance – classical, popular and folk – thrives on city stages, on the cinema screen and in towns and villages throughout South India.

South India has many kinds of folk dance: these include the Puraviattams of Karnataka and Tamil Nadu, where dancers are dressed in horse costumes; the Koklikatai dance of Tamil Nadu, in which dancers move about on stilts that have bells attached; and the Kolyacha fishers' dance from the Konkan Coast. Goa's stylised Mando song and dance is a waltzlike blend of Indian rhythms and Portuguese melody accompanied by Konkani words.

Various forms of trance-dancing and dances of exorcism occur throughout the south, and almost all tribal peoples, including the Todas of Tamil Nadu and the Banjaras of Andhra Pradesh, retain their own unique dance traditions.

The major classical dance forms of South India:

- Bharata Natyam (also spelt *bharatanatyam*) is Tamil Nadu's unique performing art and is believed to be India's oldest continuing classical dance. It was originally known as Dasi Attam, a temple art performed by young women called *devadasis*. After the 16th century, however, it fell into disrepute, largely because it became synonymous with prostitution. It was revived in the mid-19th century by four brothers from Thanjavur (Tanjore), credited with restoring the art's purity by returning to its ancient roots.

- Kathakali, one of South India's most renowned forms of classical dance-drama, is a Keralan form of play, usually based on Hindu epics; also see the boxed text, p349.

- Kuchipudi is a 17th-century dance-drama that originated in the Andhra Pradesh village from which it takes its name. Like Kathakali, its present-day form harks back to the 17th century, when it became the prerogative of Brahmin boys from this village. It often centres on the story of Satyambhama, wife of Lord Krishna.

- Mohiniyattam, from Kerala, is a semiclassical dance form that is based on the story of Mohini, the mythical seductress. Known for its gentle and poetic movements, it contains elements of Bharata Natyam and Kathakali.

- Theyyam, seen in Kannur (Kerala; see the boxed text, p359), is an ancient dance form practised by tribal people and villagers in the north Malabar region. The headdresses, costumes, body painting and trance-like performances are truly extraordinary. The Parasinikadavu Temple (near Kannur) stages theyyam performances; see p359 for details on where to catch a performance.

- Yakshagana is unique to the Tulu-speaking region of Karnataka's south coast. The focus in Yakshagana is less on the dance or movement aspect of performance, since (unlike Kathakali) the actors have vocal roles to play, both singing and speaking. As in Kathakali, the costumes and make-up are not only visually striking but are symbolic of a particular character's personality.

Handicrafts

Over the centuries India's many ethnic groups have spawned a vivid artistic heritage that is both inventive and spiritually significant. Many subcontinental crafts fulfil a practical need as much as an aesthetic one.

There's a plethora of handicrafts produced in South India, with standouts including ceramics, jewellery, leatherwork, metalwork, stone carving, papier-mâché, woodwork and a spectacular array of textiles. To get some shopping ideas, see p478.

POTTERY

The potter's art is steeped in mythology. Although there are numerous stories that explain how potters came to be, they all share the notion that a talent

Indian Classical Dance, by Leela Venkataraman and Avinash Pasricha, is a lavishly illustrated book with good descriptions about the various Indian dance forms, including Bharata Natyam and Kathakali.

Delve into India's vibrant performing-arts scene – especially Indian classical dance – at Art India (www.artindia.net).

THE SPIDERY ART OF MEHNDI

Mehndi is the traditional art of painting a woman's hands (and sometimes feet) with intricate henna designs for auspicious ceremonies, such as marriage. If quality henna is used, the design, which is orange-brown, can last up to one month. The henna usually fades faster the more you wash it and apply lotion.

In touristy areas, *mehndi*-wallahs are adept at doing henna tattoo 'bands' on the arms, legs and even the navel area. If you're thinking about getting *mehndi* applied, allow at least a couple of hours for the design process and required drying time (during drying you can't use henna-applied hands).

It's always wise to request the artist to do a 'test' spot on your arm before proceeding, as nowadays some dyes contain chemicals that can cause allergies or even permanent scarring. If good henna is used, you should not feel any pain during or after the procedure.

---

for working with clay is a gift from the god Brahma. This gives potters a very special status; on occasion they act directly as intermediaries between the spiritual and the temporal worlds.

The name for the potter caste, Kumbhar, is taken from *kumbha* (water pot), which is itself an essential component in a version of the story that explains how potters found their calling. The water pot is still an indispensable item in South India. The narrow-necked, round-based design means that women can carry the water-filled pots on their heads with less risk of spillage. The shape is also symbolic of the womb and thus fertility.

Apart from water pots, potters create a variety of household items, including all manner of storage and cooking pots, dishes and *jhanvan* (thick, flat pieces of fired clay with one rough side used for cleaning the feet). The ephemeral nature of clay-made items means the potter never wants for work. Potters all over Tamil Nadu are kept especially busy at their wheels thanks to such traditions as the Pongal harvest festival (see the boxed text, p366). On the day before the festival starts, clay household vessels are smashed and replaced with new ones.

Potters are also called upon to create votive offerings. These include the guardian horse figures (which can be huge creations) that stand sentry outside villages in Tamil Nadu, images of deities such as Ganesh, and other animal effigies. Clay replicas of parts of the human body are sometimes commissioned by those seeking miraculous cures and are then placed before a shrine. Clay toys and beads are also among a potter's repertoire.

Glazing pottery is rare in South Indian states; one exception is Tamil Nadu, where a blue or green glaze is sometimes applied.

The Arts and Crafts of Tamil Nadu, by Nanitha Krishna, with photography by VK Rajamani, is a beautifully crafted book that has detailed information on a range of crafts, including textiles, bronzes, terracotta, woodcraft, stone-carving, basketry and painting.

TEXTILES

Textiles have always played an important role in South Indian society and trade, and are still the region's biggest handicraft industry. India is famous for *khadi* (homespun cloth) – Mahatma Gandhi's promotion of *khadi* and the symbol of the spinning wheel played a paramount part in the nation's struggle for independence. Although chemical dye is widely used nowadays, natural dyes made from plants, roots, bark and herbs are still in use.

The sari typifies Indian style, and breathtakingly exquisite saris brocaded with pure gold thread are still produced in the tiny village of Paithan – you can view this work at the Paithani Weaving Centre (p146) in Maharashtra. Much thought is put into selecting the base fabric, style of embroidery, colour and thread for handmade saris. All sequined, beaded and salma (continuous spring thread) saris are hand-worked and the fabric is usually rayon, cotton, satin or silk.

Sprinkled with sumptuous colour illustrations, *Traditional Indian Textiles*, by John Gillow and Nicholas Barnard, explores India's stunning regional textiles and includes sections on tie-dye, weaving, beadwork, brocades and even camel girths.

KOLAMS

Kolams, the striking and breathtakingly intricate rice-flour designs (also called *rangoli*) that adorn thresholds in South India, are both auspicious and symbolic. *Kolams* are traditionally drawn at sunrise and are sometimes made of rice-flour paste, which may be eaten by little creatures – symbolising a reverence for even the smallest living things. Deities are deemed to be attracted to a beautiful *kolam*, which may also signal to wandering sadhus that they will be offered food at a particular house. Some people believe that *kolams* protect against the evil eye.

Embroidered shawls have assumed a significant role in the culture of the Toda people from the Nilgiri Hills (see the boxed text, p439) in Tamil Nadu. Embroidered exclusively by women in distinctive red-and-black designs, these beautiful shawls are made of thick white cotton material.

Food & Drink

Through its cuisine, you'll discover that South India is a heavenly banquet expressed in a symphony of colours, aromas, flavours and textures. Traditional South Indian food is markedly different to that of the north; however, both are comprised of regionally diverse dishes, all with their own preparation techniques and ingredients.

Although South Indian meals may at times appear quite simple – mounds of rice and side dishes of *sambar* (soupy lentils), spiced vegetables, plain curd and a splodge of pickles, all served on a banana-leaf plate, within this deceptive simplicity hides a sensual and complex array of taste sensations and time-honoured recipes. Add to this the distinct regional variations – from the colonial-influenced fare of Goa to the traditional seafood specialities of Kerala – along with a bounty of exotic fruits and vegetables – and there's more than enough to get the tastebuds tingling.

Those craving North Indian food won't have to look far to find succulent tandoori creations, *mattar paneer* (peas and unfermented cheese in gravy), butter chicken and piping hot naan, as they're available at numerous South Indian restaurants and hotels. Meanwhile, travellers pining for familiar fast food will find American-style burger and pizza joints scattered throughout the south, with the most variety found in the larger cities such as Mumbai (Bombay), Bengaluru (Bangalore) and Chennai (Madras). Tourist haunts, such as Goa, get special kudos when it comes to satiating foreign palates, with eateries offering everything from banana pancakes and honey-drizzled porridge for breakfast, to spinach ravioli and chicken stroganoff for dinner.

Technically speaking, there's no such thing as an Indian 'curry' – the word, an anglicised derivative of the Tamil word *kari* (black pepper), was used by the British as a term for any dish, including spices.

STAPLES & SPECIALITIES
Rice
Without a doubt, rice is the staple grain in South India. It's served with virtually every meal, and is used to make anything and everything from *idlis* (spongy rice cakes) and dosas (large savoury crepes) to exquisite *mithai* (Indian sweets).

After China, India is the world's second-largest producer and consumer of rice, and the majority of it is grown in the south. Long-grain white rice is the most common and is served boiled with any 'wet' dish, usually a thali in the south. In can be cooked up in a *pulao* (or pilaf; spiced rice dish) or in a spicy biryani, or simply flavoured with a dash of turmeric or saffron.

On average, Indians eat almost 2kg of rice per person per week.

Spices
Spices are integral to any South Indian dish and the subcontinent boasts some of the finest. Indeed Christopher Columbus was searching for the famed black pepper of Kerala's Malabar Coast when he stumbled upon America.

Turmeric is the essence of most Indian curries, but coriander seeds are the most widely used spice, and lend flavour and body to just about every savoury dish. Most Indian 'wet' dishes – commonly known as curries in the West – begin with the crackle of cumin seeds in hot oil. Tamarind is sometimes known as the 'Indian date' and is a particularly popular souring agent in the south. The green cardamom of Kerala's Western Ghats is regarded as the world's best, and you'll find it in savoury dishes, desserts and warming chai (tea). Saffron, the dried stigmas of crocus flowers grown in Kashmir, is so light it takes more than 1500 hand-plucked flowers to yield just 1g. Cinnamon, curry leaves, nutmeg and garlic are also widely used in cooking.

Because of the prices it can fetch, saffron is frequently adulterated, usually with safflower – dubbed (no doubt by disgruntled tourists) as 'bastard saffron'.

A masala is a blend of dry-roasted ground spices (the word loosely means 'mixed'), the most popular being garam masala (hot mix), a combination of up to 15 spices used to season dishes.

Red chillies are another common ingredient. Often dried or pickled (in rural areas you may see chillies laid out to dry on the roadside), they are used as much for flavour as for heat.

India has more than 500 varieties of mangoes, and supplies almost 60% of the world with what is regarded as the king of fruit.

Fruit, Vegetables & Pulses

A visit to any Indian market will reveal a vast and vibrant assortment of fresh fruit and vegetables, overflowing from large baskets or stacked in neat pyramids. The south is especially well known for its abundance of tropical fruits such as pineapples, papaya and mangoes. Naturally in a region with so many vegetarians, *sabzi* (vegetables) make up a predominant part of the diet, and they're served in a variety of inventive ways. Potatoes, cauliflower, eggplant, spinach and carrots are some of the most commonly used vegies, but you'll rarely see them simply boiled up and plopped on your plate. They can be fried, roasted, curried, baked, mashed and stuffed into dosas or wrapped in batter to make deep-fried *pakoras* (fritters). Something a little more unusual is the bumpy-skinned *karela* (bitter gourd) which, like *bhindi* (okra), is commonly prepared dry with spices.

Pulses – lentils, beans and peas – are another major South Indian staple as they form the basis for dhal, the lentil-based dish served with every thali meal.

Dhal

The Anger of Aubergines: Stories of Women and Food, by Bubul Sharma, is an amusing and unique culinary analysis of social relationships, interspersed with lip-smacking recipes.

Dhal, along with rice, is a mainstay of the South Indian diet. Dhal refers to a wide range of pulse dishes, commonly made from lentils, but also from certain beans as well as chickpeas. The pulses are boiled or simmered, then mixed with spices tempered in hot oil or ghee (clarified butter) and perhaps vegetables. The most common forms of dhal in South India are *sambar* and *tuvar* (yellow lentils).

Breads

Although traditional-style breads are more commonly associated with North India, you'll certainly encounter them at many restaurants in the south. Roti, the generic term for Indian-style bread, is a name used interchangeably with chapati to describe the most common variety: the irresistible unleavened round bread made with whole-wheat flour and cooked on a *tawa* (hotplate). Naan is thicker and cooked in a *tandoor* (clay oven), while *paratha* is unleavened flaky bread often found in street stalls.

Dosas & Snacks

A much-loved classic of the south, the dosa is a crepe-like mixture of fermented rice flour and dhal cooked on a griddle. It's traditionally served

---

PAAN

Meals are often rounded off with *paan*, a fragrant mixture of betel nut (also called areca nut), lime paste, spices and condiments wrapped in an edible, silky *paan* leaf. Peddled by *paan*-wallahs, who are usually strategically positioned outside busy restaurants, *paan* is eaten as a digestive and mouth-freshener. The betel nut is mildly narcotic and some aficionados eat *paan* the same way heavy smokers consume cigarettes – over the years these people's teeth can become rotted red and black.

There are two basic types of *paan*: mitha (sweet) and saadha (with tobacco). A parcel of *mitha paan* is a splendid way to finish a satisfying meal. Pop the whole parcel in your mouth and chew slowly, letting the juices secrete around your gob.

with a bowl of hot, orange *sambar* and another bowl of mild coconut *chatni* (chutney). The ubiquitous masala dosa is stuffed with spiced potatoes, onions and curry leaves. Don't miss it!

Breakfast in South India often consists of *idlis*, *vadas* (deep-fried savoury doughnuts, made of lentils) or *uttappams* (thick savoury rice-flour pancakes with finely chopped onions, green chillies, coriander and coconut). These can also be eaten at any time of the day as tiffin, an all-purpose Raj-era term for between-meal snacks.

Meat & Fish

Although South Indian Hindus are largely vegetarian, fish is a staple food in coastal regions. South India is the undisputed 'fish basket' of the nation; in seaside areas of Goa and Kerala you can watch fishermen hauling in the day's catch, which may include tuna, mackerel, kingfish, pomfret, lobster and prawns. In Goa and Kerala, significant Christian populations mean you can find pork and even beef dishes. Chicken is widely available through the region in nonvegetarian restaurants, while goat is particularly popular in Andhra Pradesh.

Dairy

Milk and milk products make a staggering contribution to Indian cuisine: *dahi* (curd/yoghurt) is served with most meals and is handy for countering chilli-hot food; *paneer* is a godsend for the vegetarian majority; the popular *lassi* (yoghurt-based drink) is just one in a host of nourishing sweet and savoury beverages; ghee is the traditional and pure cooking medium, and the best sweets are made with milk. About 60% of milk consumed in India is buffalo milk, a richer, high-protein version, which many prefer to cow's milk.

Sweets

India has a colourful jumble of *mithai*, often sticky and squishy, most of them sinfully sweet. The main categories are *barfi* (a fudgelike milk-based sweet), *halwa* (made with vegetables, cereals, lentils, nuts or fruit), *ladoos* (gram flour and semolina sweetmeats, usually ball-shaped) and those made from *chhana* (unpressed *paneer*) such as *rasgulla* (sweet cream-cheese balls flavoured with rose-water). There are also simpler – but equally scrumptious – offerings such as *jalebis* (orange-coloured whorls of deep-fried batter dunked in syrup) and *gulab jamuns* (deep-fried balls of dough soaked in rose-flavoured syrup).

Payasam (called *kheer* in the north) is one of India's favourite desserts. It's a rice pudding with a light, delicate flavour, and might include cardamom, saffron, pistachios, flaked almonds, cashews or dried fruit. *Kulfi* is a firm-textured ice cream that's especially popular in Mumbai. It's made with reduced milk and flavoured with any number of nuts, fruits and berries. In the hill areas of Maharashtra you'll find *chikki*, a rock-hard, ultrasweet concoction of peanuts and jaggery coffee.

REGIONAL SPECIALITIES

If you think it's all thalis and dosas in South India, think again. One of the pleasures of travelling in this region is the remarkable diversity of cuisine. Most southern states have a particular speciality worth seeking out.

Maharashtra

Maharashtra's capital, Mumbai, offers South India's most diverse dining scene – a veritable melting pot of North and South Indian cuisines. Here you

Making that perfect dosa back home is just a click away on www.top-indian-recipes.com/indian-dosa-recipes.htm.

The legendary Madhur Jaffrey has written best-selling cook books including *A Taste of India*; her fascinating memoirs, *Climbing the Mango Trees*, include 32 family recipes.

Sweet-tooths will adore *The Book of Indian Sweets* by Satarupa Banerjee, which contains a delicious collection of regional recipes, including irresistible Goan *bebinca* (coconut-flavoured layered pudding).

can feast on a classic Gujarati thali, a tandoori platter, fresh seafood from the Konkan Coast, and a host of global creations, from Italian-style wood-fired pizzas to Tex-Mex offerings. A well-known Mumbai dish is Bombay Duck – actually a tiny fish called *bombil,* sun-dried and marinated in spices. Another speciality is *bhelpuri,* a crispy snack of thin rounds of dough mixed with puffed rice, fried vermicelli or lentils, chopped onions, lemon juice, peanuts, herbs and spices, and *chatni,* best eaten at the stalls along Chowpatty Beach. Mumbai's Parsi (Zoroastrian) community adds another dimension to local cuisine with dishes such as *dhansak,* which is chicken or mutton with a mild sauce of vegetables, coriander and dhal. This dish can be found in a number of city restaurants.

The *Chef's Special* series has wonderful (lightweight) cookbooks showcasing various regional cuisines. Titles include *Goan Kitchen, Kerala Kitchen* and *South Indian Kitchen.*

Maharashtrians also enjoy simple, straightforward veg fare, such as rice with *tuvar* dhal, while Marathi nonvegetarian food leans towards fish, fried or curried with the Marathi spice blend *kala* masala. Also worth trying is Kolhapuri mutton, originating from Kolhapur, and served in a fiery gravy of garam masala, copra (dried coconut flesh) and red chillies.

Goa

Goa is famous for its fresh seafood – kingfish, snapper, pomfret, tuna, lobster and tiger prawns hauled in from the Arabian Sea – and the staple dish here is simply known as 'fish curry rice' – a dish of fish served in a spicy sauce over rice.

The Portuguese influence is also strong in Goan cooking. This is the place to sample pork dishes, such as *sorpotel* (pork and liver curry), pork vindaloo (pickled pork curry) and *chourisso* (a delicious Goan sausage). Other Goan specialities include chicken *cafrial* (pieces of chicken coated in a green masala paste) and *ambot tik* (a slightly sour but fiery curry dish), while the Portuguese influence in fish preparations can be seen in *caldeen* and *xacuti* (fish or chicken simmered in coconut milk and spices). *Balchão* is fish or prawns cooked in a dark red and tangy tomato sauce.

Karnataka is the largest producer of commercial coffee in India; as a whole, though, India contributes only 3% of the global output of coffee.

Goans also excel in desserts, the best known being *bebinca,* a mouth-watering coconut-flavoured layered pudding.

Karnataka

Although you can get almost any cuisine you'd care to think of in Bengaluru, traditional Karnatakan cuisine is largely vegetarian, with simple rice, dhal

---

TREMENDOUS THALIS

You'll soon discover in South India that the thali is the lunchtime meal of choice. Cheap, filling, nutritious and delicious, this is Indian food at its simple best. Whereas in North India the thali is usually served on a steel plate with indentations for the various side dishes (thali gets its name from the plate), in the south a typical thali is served on a flat steel plate covered with a fresh banana leaf. When the plate is put in front of you, pour some water on the leaf and spread it around with your right hand. Soon enough a waiter with a large pot of rice will come along and heap mounds of it onto your plate, followed by servings of dhal, *sambar* (soupy lentils), *rasam* (dhal-based broth flavoured with tamarind), chutneys, pickles and *dahi* (curd/yoghurt).

Using the fingers of your right hand, start by mixing the various side dishes with the rice, kneading and scraping it into mouth-sized balls, then scoop it into your mouth using your thumb to push the food in. It's considered bad form to stick your hand right into your mouth or to lick your fingers. If it's getting a bit messy, there should be a finger bowl of water on the table. Watching other diners will help get your thali technique just right. Waiters will continue to fill your plate until you wave your hand over one or all of the offerings to indicate you've had enough.

Thalis are usually served in restaurants between 11am and 3pm.

and *rasam* (dhal-based broth flavoured with tamarind) making up the core diet, along with various masala rice dishes, vegetables, salads and dosas. The Mysore dosa is a treat, spicy and crisp, and stuffed with vegetables and chillies. The major exception to the veg diet is on the Konkan Coast of the state, where Mangalorean seafood is a speciality. Promfret and ladyfish are some of the popular catches, often cooked in a spicy coconut sauce.

Copra (dried coconut flesh) is pressed and made into coconut oil, a very popular cooking medium in Kerala.

Kerala

Spice-rich Kerala has had many visitors to its shores over the centuries including Portuguese, British and Arab traders. The combination of those influences and a coastline reaping some of India's finest seafood makes Keralan cuisine some of the subcontinent's most memorable. Keralan specialities feature fish cooked in coconut oil or simmered in coconut milk and spices, lending it a Southeast Asian quality. Other ingredients in sweet fish curries include cashew nuts and mangoes, while Malabar curries (fish or prawns) are made with coconut milk, tomatoes, ginger and spices cooked in a clay pot.

Kerala's Syrian Orthodox community also eats chicken, mutton and even beef – a popular dish is beef fry (beef slivers cooked with spices and onions). Other dishes include the combination of chicken coconut stew and *appam* (rice pancake), or *meen*, a fish curry. Keralan Muslims from the north Malabar region also make a mean biryani.

101 Kerala Delicacies, by G Padma Vijay, is a detailed recipe book of vegetarian and nonvegetarian dishes from this tropical coast-hugging state.

Tamil Nadu

Like Karnataka, Tamil Nadu epitomises South Indian cuisine, with veg meals based on rice, dhal and *sambar*, interspersed with *idlis* and masala dosas. Vegetarian cuisine rules, and in many small towns this may indeed be all you'll find to eat. Chettinad cuisine is Tamil Nadu's main contribution to cooking with meat, consisting of chicken or mutton dishes in spicy gravy. You can find Chettinad restaurants in Chennai and most large towns.

Puducherry (Pondicherry) offers an unusual French-Indian fusion – numerous restaurants here whip up, with aplomb, bouillabaisse (fish and vegetable soup), baguettes, *coq au vin* (chicken in wine sauce), crème caramel and other similar dishes.

Chettinad, the spicy meat-based cuisine of Tamil Nadu, hails from the Chettiars, a wealthy merchant community.

Andhra Pradesh

Andhra cuisine is made of lentil, vegetable and meat or fish dishes, usually flavoured with tamarind and frequently spiced up with red chillies. Popular dishes include *chapa pulusu*, a flaming red fish curry, and chicken curry in coconut sauce. The state is nationally known for its fiery cuisine and unique blend of Hindu and Muslim cultures. Don't miss a biryani in Hyderabad, an aromatic baked rice dish combined with vegetables, meat (often chicken), spices and nuts. Spicy kebabs wrapped in roti and *achhar gosht* (picklelike meat dish) are Hyderabadi favourites, while pickles and *chatnis* (chutneys made of spices, dhal and chillies) are integral to Andhra cooking. Hyderabad is also the home of the *kulcha*, a soft, leavened Indian-style bread.

DRINKS
Nonalcoholic Drinks

South India grows both tea and coffee but unlike North India, where it has only recently become all the rage to guzzle cappuccinos and lattes, coffee has long been favoured down south. In the larger cities, you'll find some hip coffee chains, such as Barista and Café Coffee Day, offering an excellent range of hot brews as well as tasty cakes and snacks. Meanwhile, on today's tea front, you can enjoy a wide assortment, from peppermint to rosehip and good old-fashioned Indian chai – the ultrasweet milky concoction that still reigns supreme.

In cities and towns particularly you'll come across sugar-cane juice and fruit-juice vendors. Be a little cautious if you decide to try fruit juice; it may have been mixed with ordinary (dodgy) water and many blenders look like they haven't been cleaned for weeks. However, if a stall looks clean and is busy, you should be fine. Coconut water is also popular in the south and you'll see vendors just about everywhere standing by mounds of green coconuts, machete at the ready. Finally, there's lassi, a refreshing and delicious iced curd (yoghurt) drink that comes in sweet and savoury varieties, or mixed with fruit.

For information about drinking water safely, see p512.

Alcoholic Drinks

An estimated three quarters of India's drinking population quaffs 'country liquor' such as the notorious arak (liquor distilled from coconut milk, potatoes or rice) of the south. This is the poor-man's drink and millions are addicted to the stuff. Each year, hundreds of people are blinded or even killed by the methyl alcohol in illegal arak.

In Kerala, Goa and parts of Tamil Nadu, toddy (palm 'beer') is a milky white local brew made from the sap of the coconut palm. It's collected in pots attached to the tree by toddy-tappers and drunk either straight from the pot or distilled. In Goa toddy is called *feni* and is made either from coconut or – the more popular and potent version – from the fruit of the cashew tree. The fermented liquid is double-distilled to produce a knockout concoction that can be as much as 35% proof. Although usually drunk straight by locals, *feni* virgins should consider mixing it with a soft drink. Decorative *feni* bottles can be found in Goan shops and they make a nice gift or souvenir.

About a quarter of India's drinks market comprises Indian Made Foreign Liquors (IMFLs), made with a base of rectified spirit. Recent years have seen a rise in the consumption of imported spirits, with more and more city bars and restaurants flaunting both domestic and foreign labels.

Beer is widely consumed around South India with the more upmarket bars and restaurants stocking an impressive selection of both Indian and foreign brands (Budweiser, Heineken, Corona and the like). Most of the domestic brands are straightforward Pilsners around the 5% alcohol mark; travellers champion Kingfisher.

India's wine-drinking culture is steadily growing despite the domestic wine-producing industry still being at its infancy stages – it does have a long way to go before it is globally competitive. Nevertheless, the favourable South Indian climate and soil have spawned some fine wineries, such as Chateau Indage (Maharasthra), Grover Vineyards (Karnataka) and Sula Vineyards (Maharasthra; also see Wine Country, p142). Offerings include Chardonnay, Sauvignon Blanc, Shiraz and Zinfandel. Other reliable wine-makers to look out for include Sankalp Winery and Renaissance Winery.

India has the world's biggest whisky market with an annual growth rate of around 10%.

TIP FOR BEER DRINKERS

Indian beer often contains the preservative glycerol, which can cause headaches. To avoid a thumping head, open the bottle and quickly tip it upside down, with the top immersed, into a full glass of water. An oily film (the glycerol) descends into the water – when this stops, remove the bottle and enjoy a glycerol-free beer.

CELEBRATIONS

Although most Hindu festivals have a religious core, many are also great occasions for spirited feasting. Sweets are considered the most luxurious of foods and almost every special occasion is celebrated with a mind-boggling range. *Karanjis,* crescent-shaped flour parcels stuffed with sweet *khoya* (milk solids) and nuts, are synonymous with Holi, the most rambunctious Hindu festival, and it wouldn't be the same without sticky *malpuas* (wheat pancakes dipped in syrup), *barfis* and *pedas* (multicoloured pieces of *khoya* and sugar). Pongal (Tamil for 'overflowing') is the major harvest festival of the south and is most closely associated with the dish of the same name, made with the season's first rice, along with jaggery, nuts, raisins and spices. Diwali, the festival of lights, is the most widely celebrated national festival, and some regions have specific Diwali sweets; if you're in Mumbai, dive into delicious *anarsa* (rice-flour cookies).

For details on when to catch these festivals, see p471.

WHERE TO EAT & DRINK

Restaurants in South India fall into five main categories: veg, nonvegetarian (often signposted as 'nonveg'), hotel restaurants, tourist restaurants, and restaurants specialising in regional or ethnic cuisine. The latter are really only found in major cities or tourist areas, such as Mumbai, Pune, Bengaluru, Chennai, Hyderabad and Goa, where you can find versions of Italian, Chinese, Thai, Mediterranean and even Mexican cuisine. Apart from street-food vendors, the most basic place to grab a bite is at a *dhaba* (basic roadside eatery), found throughout the country.

Veg restaurants (often called 'meals' restaurants) are simple places serving *idlis,* dosas and *vada* for breakfast, and thalis for lunch and dinner. Nonveg restaurants have both a vegetarian menu and North Indian meat dishes, usually with chicken, mutton and fish, as well as Chinese offerings.

In coastal resorts, such as those at Goa and Kerala, it's hard to beat the beach shacks for a fresh seafood meal – from fried mussels, prawns and calamari to steamed fish, crab or lobster – washed down with a cold beer as you watch the sun set over the Arabian Sea. The bamboo and palm thatch shacks are usually set up in late October and stay open until late March, when they are dismantled and put away in anticipation of the summer and monsoon.

You'll find terrific watering holes in most major cities such as Mumbai and Bengaluru, which are usually at their liveliest on weekends. The more up-market bars serve an enticing selection of domestic and imported beverages as well as draught beer. Be warned that many bars turn into music-thumping nightclubs anytime after 8pm, although there are quiet lounge-bars to be found in some cities. In smaller towns the bar scene can be seedy, male-dominated affairs – not the kind of place thirsty female travellers should venture into alone. For details about a city's bars, see the Drinking sections of regional chapters.

Stringent licensing laws discourage drinking in some restaurants, but places that depend on the tourist rupee may covertly serve you beer in teapots and disguised glasses – however, don't assume anything, at the risk of causing offence. Very few vegetarian restaurants serve alcohol.

Street Food

Street food is part of everyday life in India, and the sights, smells and sounds of street cooking are a constant banquet for the senses. Whatever the time of day, street vendors are busily frying, boiling, roasting, simmering, mixing or baking some type of food to lure peckish passers-by. The food is usually safe

Street Foods of India, by Vimla and Deb Kumar Mukerji, gives recipes of some of the subcontinent's favourite eats, including southern stars such as masala dosa and *appam* (rice pancakes).

STREET FOOD DOS & DON'TS

Exercise caution when eating street food but as long as you use your common sense you should be fine. Remember, fortune favours the brave.

- Give yourself a few days to adjust to the local cuisine, especially if you're not used to spicy food.

- You know the rule about following a crowd – if the locals are avoiding a particular vendor, you should, too. Also take notice of the profile of the customers – any place frequented by women and families will probably be your safest bet.

- Check how and where the vendor is cleaning the utensils, and how and where the food is covered. If the vendor is cooking in oil, have a peek to check it's clean. If the pots or surfaces are dirty, there are food scraps about or too many buzzing flies, don't be shy to make a hasty retreat.

- Don't be put off when you order some deep-fried snack and the cook throws it back into the wok. It's common practise to partly cook the snacks first and then finish them off once they've been ordered. In fact, frying them hot again will kill any germs.

- Unless a place is reputable (and busy), it's best to avoid eating meat from the street.

- Juice stalls are usually safe if the place looks clean, is busy, and the juice is freshly squeezed in front of you (not stored in a jug).

- Don't be tempted by glistening presliced melon and other fruit, which keeps its luscious veneer with the regular dousing of (often unfiltered) water. Instead, buy fruit and peel it yourself.

to eat, as long as it's cooked fresh in front of you. Any food that has been sitting around in the sun attracting flies is bad news.

Devilishly delicious snacks worth sniffing out on your South Indian wanderings include the Mumbai speciality *bhelpuri*; *pao bhaja*, another Mumbai speciality of spiced vegetables with bread; samosas (pyramid-shaped pastries filled with spiced vegetables and, less often, meat); *vada*; *puri* (puffed-up Indian-style bread); biryani, a Hyderabadi rice-based speciality; and *bhajia* (vegetable fritters). *Idlis* and dosas are also served at some street stalls, with the thin dosa crepe cooked on a griddle right in front of you. For something simpler there are omelettes or egg sandwiches, or cobs of corn roasting on braziers.

Locals gather to eat street food at all times of the day – usually as a between-meal snack rather than a replacement for a meal.

Healthy South Indian Cooking, by Alamelu Vairavan and Patricia Marquardt, emphasises Chettinad cuisines, with almost 200 simple but tasty vegetarian recipes.

Platform Food

One of the thrills of travelling by rail is the culinary circus that greets you at every station. Roving vendors accost arriving trains, yelling and scampering up and down the carriages; fruit, *namkin* (savoury nibbles), omelettes and nuts are offered for sale through the grills on the windows; and platform cooks try to lure you from the train with the sizzle of fresh samosas. Frequent train travellers know which station is famous for which food item – for instance, Lonavla train station in Maharashtra is known for *chikki*.

Vegetarian Cuisine from South India, by Chandra Padmanabhan, is an easy-to-read and beauti-fully illustrated book of recipes. The suggested menus at the back are perfect for anyone planning a vegetarian banquet.

VEGETARIANS & VEGANS

Vegetarians will be in heaven in South India. Tamil Nadu and Karnataka are predominately vegetarian, but every town will have several veg restaurants. Indian restaurants are either pure veg (no eggs or meat), veg (no meat), or nonveg (meat and veg dishes). Devout Hindus (and Jains) avoid foods such as garlic and onions, which are thought to heat the blood and arouse sexual desire. You may come across vegetarian restaurants that make it a point to advertise the absence of onion and garlic in their dishes for this reason.

There's little understanding of veganism (the term 'pure vegetarian' means without eggs), and animal products such as milk, butter, ghee and curd are included in most Indian dishes. If you are vegan your first problem is likely to be getting the cook to completely understand your requirements. For further information, check out www.vegansworldnetwork.org (click on the Directory link, then on India) and www.vegan.com.

HABITS & CUSTOMS

South Indians generally have an early breakfast, then a thali for lunch and/or several tiffin during the day. Dinner, usually large serves of rice, vegetables, curd and spicy side dishes, is eaten quite late. It's not unusual for dinner to start at 9pm or 10pm and any drinking (of alcohol) is almost always done before the meal.

Food is usually eaten with the fingers in South India, or more precisely the fingers of the right hand. The left hand is reserved for toilet duties, so is considered unclean, but it's still customary to wash your hands before every meal. Rice and side dishes are mixed together with the fingers and scooped into the mouth in small handfuls using the thumb to push it in. (Also see Tremendous Thalis for more tips, p78.) Avoid the temptation to lick your fingers – a finger bowl filled with warm water is usually placed on the table to wash your fingers at the end of the meal and serviettes should be on hand to dry them. In most restaurants, foreigners will at least be offered a fork (and perhaps a spoon). In North Indian restaurants it's customary to scoop the food up with traditional Indian breads, such as chapati and naan.

COOKING COURSES

You might find yourself so inspired by Indian food that you want to take home a little Indian kitchen know-how. For those interested in cooking classes, the following recommendations are worth a try:

Cook & Eat (p344) Classes are run in a family kitchen in Kochi (Cochin), Kerala.
India on the Menu (p184) A five-day Indian cookery course held near Panaji (Panjim), Goa.
Kuk@ease (p166) Offers one-day cookery courses in Pune, Maharashtra.

For a comprehensive travellers' guide to India's cuisine, grab Lonely Planet's *World Food India*.

USEFUL WORDS

English	Tamil	Kannada	Konkani	Malayalam	Marathi	Telugu
butter	vennai	benne	mosko	vella	lonee	wenna
coffee	kaappi	kaafi	kaafi	kaappi	kaafi	kaafee
egg	muttai	motte	taanthee	mulla	aanda	gullu
fruit	pazham	hannu	phala	palam	phal	pallu
ice	ais	ays	jell	ays	barfu	ays/ manchugalla
meat	maamisam	maamsa	maas	irachi	maas	maamsama
milk	paal	haalu	dudh	paala	dudh	paalu
rice	arisi	akki	tandul	ari	bhat/tandul (cooked/raw)	biyyam
sugar	sakkarai	sakkare	sakhar	panchasaara	sakhar	chakkera/ pañcadaara
tea	teneer	tee	chay	caaya	chaha	lee/teneeru
vegetables	kaaykarikal	tarakaari	bhaji/verdur	pachakkali	bhajee	kooragaayalu
water	neer	neeru	udhok	vellam	paani	neellu

EAT YOUR WORDS
Food & Drink Glossary

achar	pickle
aloo	potato; also *alu*
aloo tikka	mashed potato patty
appam	rice pancake
arak	liquor distilled from coconut milk, potatoes or rice
barfi	fudgelike sweet made from milk
betel	nut of the betel tree; chewed as a stimulant and digestive in *paan;* also called areca nut
bhajia	vegetable fritter
bhang lassi	blend of lassi and bhang (a derivative of marijuana)
bhelpuri	thin fried rounds of dough with rice, lentil, lemon juice, onion, herbs and chutney
bhindi	okra
biryani	fragrant spiced rice with meat or vegetables
chaat	snack, usually seasoned with chaat masala
chai	tea
chapati	round unleavened Indian-style bread; also known as roti
chatni	chutney
chawal	rice
dahi	curd/yoghurt
dhal	curried lentil dish
dhansak	Parsi dish; meat, usually chicken, with curried lentils and rice
dosa	large savoury crepe
feni	Goan liquor distilled from coconut milk or cashews
ghee	clarified butter
gobi	cauliflower
gram	legumes
gulab jamun	deep-fried balls of dough soaked in rose-flavoured syrup
halwa	soft sweetmeat made with vegetables, cereals, lentils, nuts and fruit
idli	spongy, round, fermented rice cake
jaggery	hard, brown, sugarlike sweetener made from palm sap
jalebi	orange-coloured whorls of deep-fried batter dunked in sugar syrup
karela	bitter gourd
kheer	rice pudding; called *payasam* in the south
korma	curry-like braised dish
kulcha	soft, leavened Indian-style bread
kulfi	flavoured (often with pistachio) firm-textured ice cream
ladoo	sweetmeat ball made with gram flour and semolina; also *ladu*
lassi	yoghurt-and-iced-water drink
masala dosa	large savoury crepe (dosa) stuffed with spiced potatoes
mattar paneer	peas and unfermented cheese in gravy
mithai	Indian sweets
molee	Keralan dish; fish pieces poached in coconut milk and spices
momo	Tibetan steamed or fried dumpling stuffed with vegetables or meat
naan	tandoor-cooked flat bread
namkin	savoury nibbles
pakora	bite-sized piece of vegetable dipped in chickpea-flour batter and deep-fried
paneer	soft, unfermented cheese made from milk curd
pani	water
pappadam	thin, crispy lentil or chickpea-flour circle-shaped wafer; also *papad*
paratha	Indian-style flaky bread (thicker than chapati) made with ghee and cooked on a hotplate; often stuffed with grated vegetables, *paneer* etc
payasam	rice pudding (called *kheer* in the north)
pilaf	see pulao

pulao	rice cooked in stock and flavoured with spices; also *pulau* or *pilaf*
puri	flat savoury dough that puffs up when deep-fried; also *poori*
rasam	dhal-based broth flavoured with tamarind
rasgulla	sweet little balls of cream cheese flavoured with rose-water
sabzi	vegetables
sambar	South Indian soupy lentil dish with cubed vegetables
samosa	deep-fried pastry triangles filled with spiced vegetables/meat
tandoor	clay oven
tawa	flat hotplate/iron griddle
thali	all-you-can-eat meal; in the south a typical thali is served on a flat stainless steel plate (sometimes silver) covered with a fresh banana leaf
tiffin	snack; also refers to meal container often made of stainless steel
tikka	spiced, often marinated, chunks of chicken, *paneer* etc
toddy	alcoholic drink, tapped from palm trees
vada	deep-fried savoury doughnut, made of lentils
vindaloo	Goan dish; fiery curry in a marinade of vinegar and garlic

Environment

THE LAND

With its magnificent mix of landscapes, from emerald green rice paddies and shady coconut groves to postcard-perfect beaches and mountains ranges, South India surely must have been painted before it was created.

The most prominent geographical feature of the region is the range of mountains known as the ghats (literally 'steps'), running down the spine of South India, while most of Maharashtra and Andhra Pradesh sit on the dry Deccan plateau. The Vindhya Range, which stretches nearly the entire width of peninsular India (roughly contiguous with the Tropic of Cancer), is the symbolic division between the north and the south. South of the Vindhya Range lies the Deccan plateau (Deccan is derived from the Sanskrit word *dakshina*, meaning south), a triangular-shaped mass of ancient rock that slopes gently towards the Bay of Bengal. On its western and eastern borders, the Deccan plateau is flanked by the Western and Eastern Ghats. Pockets of the ghats are now protected in forest reserves and national parks.

The Western Ghats (known in Goa and Maharashtra as the Sahyadris) start to rise just north of Mumbai (Bombay) and run parallel to the coast, gaining height as they go south until they reach the tip of the peninsula. The headwaters of southern rivers, such as the Godavari and Cauvery, rise in the peaks of the Western Ghats and drain into the Bay of Bengal.

The Eastern Ghats, a less dramatic chain of low, interrupted ranges, sweep northeast in the direction of Chennai (Madras) before turning northward, roughly parallel to the coast bordering the Bay of Bengal, until they merge with the highlands of central Orissa.

At 2695m, Anamudi in Kerala is South India's highest peak. The Western Ghats have an average elevation of 915m, and are covered with tropical and temperate evergreen forest and mixed deciduous forest. The western coastal strip between Mumbai and Goa, known as the Konkan Coast, is studded with river estuaries and sandy beaches. Further south, the Malabar Coast forms a sedimentary plain into which are etched the sublime waterways and lagoons that characterise Kerala. The eastern coastline (known as the Coromandel Coast where it tracks through Tamil Nadu) is wider, drier and flatter.

Offshore from India are a series of island groups, politically part of India but geographically linked to the landmasses of Southeast Asia and islands of the Indian Ocean. The Andaman and Nicobar Islands sit far out in the Bay of Bengal (they comprise 572 islands and form the peaks of a vast submerged mountain range extending almost 1000km between Myanmar and Sumatra), while the coral atolls of Lakshadweep (300km west of Kerala) are a northerly extension of the Maldives islands, with a land-area of just 32 sq km.

WILDLIFE

South India is home to a diverse range of wildlife that can be seen in the region's many national parks and wildlife sanctuaries. To find out where and when to get close to nature, see the boxed text, p92.

India is one of around a dozen 'megadiversity' countries, which together make up an estimated 70% of the world's biodiversity. South India has three recognised biogeographic zones: the forested, wet and elevated Western Ghats, which run parallel to the west coast from Mumbai to Kerala; the flat, dry Deccan plateau; and the islands, including the Andaman and Nicobar Islands and Lakshadweep.

The Ministry of Environment & Forest (www.envfor.nic.in) is the official Government of India website.

India's national animal is the tiger, its national bird is the peacock and its national flower is the lotus. The national emblem of India is a column topped by thee Asiatic lions.

Animals

Most people know that India is the natural home of the tiger and Indian elephant, but the forests, jungles, coastline, waters and plains actually provide a habitat for a staggering multitude of species.

The tropical forests of the Western Ghats are home to one of the rarest bats on earth – the small fruit-eating *Latidens salimalii* – as well as flying lizards (technically gliders), sloth bears, leopards, hornbills, parrots and hundreds of other bird species (birding enthusiasts should see below for more details).

The Lakshadweep Islands in the Indian Ocean and the Andaman and Nicobar Islands in the Bay of Bengal preserve classic coral atoll ecosystems. Bottlenose dolphins, coral reefs, sea turtles and tropical fish flourish beneath the water, while seabirds, reptiles, amphibians and butterflies thrive on land.

To read up-to-date wildlife issues, click on Indian Jungles (www .indianjungles.com).

ENDANGERED SPECIES

In 1972 the Wildlife Protection Act was introduced to stem the abuse of wildlife, followed by a string of similar pieces of legislation with bold ambitions but few teeth with which to enforce them. A rare success story has been Project Tiger, launched in 1973 to protect India's big mammals. The main threats to wildlife continue to be habitat loss due to human encroachment and poaching by criminals and even corrupt national park officials. The bandit Veerappan (see p46 for more information) is believed to have killed 200 elephants and sold US$22 million of illegally harvested sandalwood during his 30-year crime spree.

India is the world's only country with native lions and tigers, and the forests and mountains also hide dwindling populations of leopards, panthers and other jungle cats. All these species are facing extinction from habitat loss and poaching for the lucrative trade in skins and body parts for Chinese medicine. Spurious health benefits are linked to almost every part of the tiger, from the teeth to the penis, and a whole tiger carcass can fetch upwards of US$10,000. Government estimates suggest that India is losing approximately 1% of its tigers every year to poachers.

The Wildlife Protection Society of India (www.wpsi-india.org) is a prominent wildlife conservation organisation campaigning for animal welfare through education, lobbying and legal action against poachers.

Elephants are poached for ivory – we implore you not to support this trade by buying ivory souvenirs, which are still illegally sold in some parts of India (also see the boxed text, The Majestic Indian Elephant, p88). Rhinos are also threatened by the medicine trade – rhino horn is highly valued as an aphrodisiac and as a material for making handles for daggers in the Persian Gulf. Various species of deer are threatened by those hunting them for food and trophies, while bears and Indian elephants have also diminished in recent decades. Other threatened species include lion-tailed macaques, glossy black Nilgiri langurs and the slender loris, an adept insect-catcher with huge eyes for nocturnal hunting. Sadly, there is still illegal trade in South India for live lorises – their eyes are believed by some to be a powerful medicine for human-eye diseases, as well as a vital ingredient for love potions. South India's hilly regions are the last remaining stronghold of the endangered Nilgiri tahr (cloud goat).

In the Andaman Islands, the once-common dugong (*Dugong dugon;* a large herbivorous aquatic mammal with flipper-like forelimbs) has almost disappeared. It was hunted by mainland settlers for its meat and oil, and has also suffered from a loss of natural habitat (seagrass beds).

A Pictorial Guide to the Birds of the Indian Subcontinent, by Salim Ali and S Dillon Ripley, is a comprehensive field reference to birds found in South India.

BIRDS

Birdlife is where South India really comes into its own, and there are several wetlands and sanctuaries supporting a large percentage of the country's water birds. Many species, including herons, cranes, storks and even flamingos, can be spotted at various sanctuaries – see p97.

In village ponds, you can often see a surprising array of birds, from the common sandpiper to the Indian pond heron, or paddy bird, surveying its domain. Waterways are particularly rich in birdlife; graceful white egrets and colourful kingfishers (including the striking stork-billed kingfisher, with its massive red bill) are common, as are smaller species, such as plovers, water hens and coots. Red-wattled and yellow-wattled lapwings can be readily recognised by the coloured, fleshy growths on their faces.

The waters around the Andaman and Nicobar Islands contain more than 1200 species of tropical fish; on land, more than half of the mammals identified are unique to the islands.

Birds of prey, such as harriers and buzzards, soar over open spaces searching for unwary birds and small mammals. Around rubbish dumps and carcasses, the black or pariah kite is a frequent visitor. Birds inhabiting forested areas include woodpeckers, barbets and malkohas (a colourful group of large, forest-dwelling cuckoos). Fruit-eaters include a number of pigeons (including the Nilgiri wood-pigeon and pompadour green-pigeon), doves, colourful parrots (including Malabar and plum-headed parakeets), minivets and various cuckoo-shrikes and mynahs.

Hornbills are forest-dwelling birds, with massive curved bills, similar to toucans. The largest is the great hornbill, sporting a large bill and a horny growth on its head (called a casque); the Malabar grey hornbill is endemic to the Malabar region.

For details about where and when to see certain bird species, birders should peruse the boxed text, Major National Parks & Wildlife Sanctuaries (p92).

FISH

The still-pristine coral around the archipelagos of Lakshadweep, Andaman and Nicobar supports a diverse marine ecosystem that hosts a myriad of tropical fish, including butterfly fish, parrotfish, the very ugly porcupine fish

---

THE MAJESTIC INDIAN ELEPHANT

Revered in Hindu mythology and admired for its strength and stamina, the elephant traditionally appears in various guises in South India's history and culture.

Today, however, Indian elephants are honoured as well as exploited: tamed elephants are used in religious ceremonies or in logging (though they have largely been replaced by heavy machinery), while farmers fear the destructive capabilities of their wild brethren. Indian elephants weigh up to five tonnes and live in family groups, usually led by the oldest females. At puberty, males leave to pursue solitary lives. Elephants live in forest or grassland habitats and have voracious appetites, eating for up to 18 hours per day and wolfing down some 200kg of food, mostly grass, leaves and shrubs. (In the Andamans, the small population of elephants have been known to swim up to 3km between islands.) While in search of food, elephants have been known to leave the forest and demolish farmers' entire crops, bringing themselves into unwanted human contact. Indeed, humans are the elephant's sole enemy. Along with loss of habitat from urban development and logging, elephants face an ongoing threat from poachers. The tusk of the male elephant is valued for its ivory, and illegal poaching has had serious effects on the gender balance. A recent report indicates that while there are around 20,000 elephants in India, there are only about 1200 male 'tuskers' of breeding age.

The cultural significance of the elephant can be seen at temples and during festivals, where they may be colourfully decorated and lead processions. In Hindu creation myths, the elephant is the upholder of the universe, the foundation of life, while the elephant-headed deity Ganesh is the god of good fortune and remover of obstacles (see p59). Many temples have their own elephant, which takes part in rituals or waits patiently at the entrance with its mahout (keeper), accepting offers or coins with its trunk.

Safaris through forest reserves give you the opportunity to spot elephants in the wild, and some national parks offer elephant treks through the jungle (see p98).

and the light-blue surgeonfish. Along the Goan and Malabar coasts, mackerel and sardines are prevalent, although overfishing from mechanised trawlers is an increasing problem. Other marine life off the coast of South India includes moray eels, crabs and sea cucumbers. Migratory visitors include the sperm whale *(Physeter catodon)*.

INVERTEBRATES

South India has some truly spectacular butterflies and moths, including the Malabar banded swallowtail *(Papilio liomedon)* and the peacock hairstreak *(Thelca pavi)*.

In the Andaman and Nicobar Islands, you may come across the coconut or robber crab *(Birgus latro)*, a 5kg tree-climbing monster that combs the beaches for coconuts.

Leeches are common in the forests, especially during and immediately after the monsoon.

MAMMALS

The nocturnal sloth bear *(Melursus ursinus)* has short legs and shaggy black or brown hair, with a splash of white on its chest. It roams in the forested areas of the national parks, and in the Nilgiris.

The gaur *(Bos gaurus)*, a wild ox (sometimes referred to as the Indian bison), can be seen in major national parks in Karnataka, Goa and Kerala. Up to 2m high, it's born with light-coloured hair, which darkens as it ages. With its immense bulk and white legs, the gaur is easily recognised. It prefers the wet *sholas* (virgin forests) and bamboo thickets of the Western Ghats.

The common dolphin *(Delphinus delphis)* is found off both coastlines of the Indian peninsula, and dugongs, although elusive, can sometimes be spotted off the Malabar Coast and the Andaman Islands.

Antelopes, Gazelles & Deer

You'll see plenty of these grazers in South India's national parks, but keep your eyes peeled for the chowsingha *(Tetracerus quadricornis)*, the only animal in the world with four horns. Also unusual is the nilgai *(Boselaphus tragocamelus)*, which is the largest Asiatic antelope.

The blackbuck *(Antilope cervicapra)* has distinctive spiral horns and an attractive dark coat, making it a prime target for poachers. The dominant males develop dark, almost black, coats (usually dark brown in South India), while the 20 or so females and subordinate males in each herd are fawn in colour.

The slender chinkara *(Gazella gazella;* Indian gazelle*)*, with its light-brown coat and white underbelly, favours the drier foothills and plains. It can be seen in small herds in national parks and sanctuaries in Karnataka and Andhra Pradesh.

The little mouse deer *(Tragulus meminna)* only grows 30cm tall. Delicate and shy, its speckled olive-brown/grey coat provides excellent camouflage in the forest. The common sambar *(Cervus unicolor)*, the largest of the Indian deer, sheds its impressive horns at the end of April; new ones start growing a month later. Meanwhile, the attractive chital *(Axis axis;* spotted deer*)* can be seen in most of South India's national parks, particularly those with wet evergreen forests. The barking deer *(Muntiacus muntjak)* is a small deer that bears tushes (elongated canines) as well as small antlers, and its bark is said to sound much like that of a dog. It's a difficult animal to spot in its habitat, the thick forests of Tamil Nadu, Karnataka and Andhra Pradesh.

At last count, India had 569 threatened species, comprising 247 species of plants, 89 species of mammals, 82 species of birds, 26 species of reptiles, 68 species of amphibians, 35 species of fish and 22 species of invertebrates.

Cheetal Walk: Living in the Wilderness, by ERC Davidar, describes the author's life among the elephants of the Nilgiri Hills and explores how they can be saved from extinction.

Tigers & Leopards

The tiger (*Panthera tigris*) is the prize of wildlife watchers in India but, being a shy, solitary animal, it's a rare sight. India has the world's largest tiger population but most of the famous tiger reserves are in North India. Tigers prefer to live under the cover of tall grass or forest and can command vast areas of territory.

The leopard (*P. pardus*) does not stick exclusively to heavy forest cover, but it is possibly even harder to find than the tiger. Leopards are golden brown with black rosettes, although in the Western Ghats they may be almost entirely black. To find the best places for tiger- and leopard-spotting in the region, see the boxed text, Major National Parks & Wildlife Sanctuaries, p92.

In the early 20th century there were believed to be at least 40,000 wild tigers in India. Current estimates suggest there are fewer than 3500.

Dog Family

The wild dog, or dhole (*Cuon alpinus*), is a tawny predator that hunts during the day in packs that have been known to bring down animals as large as a buffalo.

The Indian wolf (*Canis lupus linnaeus*) has suffered from habitat destruction and hunting, and is now rare in South India. Its coat is fawn with black stipples, and it's generally a much leaner looking animal than its European or North American cousins. For a chance to see the Indian wolf, head to its preferred habitat of dry, open forest and scrubland of the Deccan plateau.

The Indian fox (*Vulpes bengalensis*) has a black-tipped tail and a greyish coloured coat, and because of its appetite for rodents, it can coexist much more comfortably with farming communities than other carnivores.

Primates

You can't miss these cheeky creatures, whether it's passing through signposted 'monkey zones' as you traverse the Western Ghats, or fending off overfriendly macaques at temples.

The little pale-faced bonnet macaque (*Macaca radiata*) is so-named for the 'bonnet' of dark hair that covers its head. These macaques live in highly structured troops where claims on hierarchy are commonly and noisily contested. They are opportunistic feeders – barely a grub, berry or leaf escapes their alert eyes and nimble fingers – and they love to congregate at tourist spots where excited families throw fruit their way. The crab-eating macaque (*M. fascicularis*), found in the Nicobar Islands, looks rather like a rhesus or a bonnet macaque, but has a longer, thicker tail. In contrast, the lion-tailed macaque (*M. silenus*) has a thick mane of greyish hair that grows from its temples and cheeks.

Less shy is the common langur (*Presbytis entellus*) or Hanuman monkey, recognisable by its long limbs and black face. India's most hunted primate is the Nilgiri langur (*P. johni*), which inhabits the dense forests of the Western Ghats, including the *sholas* of the Nilgiri and Annamalai ranges. This vegetarian monkey is pursued by poachers for the supposed medicinal qualities of its flesh and viscera.

The peculiar-looking slender loris (*Loris tardigradus*) has a soft, woolly, brown/grey coat and huge, bushbaby eyes. Nocturnal, this endangered species (see p87) comes down from the trees only to feed on insects, leaves, berries and lizards.

REPTILES & AMPHIBIANS

Of the 32 species of turtles and tortoises in India, you may see the hawksbill, leatherback, loggerhead or endangered olive ridley species in the waters of

South India. Turtles are protected, but it's possible to see them nesting in some areas, notably at Morjim (p204) in Goa. If you're lucky, you may see the Indian star tortoise *(Geochelone elegans)* waddling along the forest floor in Andhra Pradesh.

Three species of crocodiles are found in India, two of them in South India – the mugger, or marsh, crocodile *(Crocodylus palustris)* and the saltwater crocodile *(C. porosus)*. The latter lives in the Andaman and Nicobar Islands, while the mugger is extensively distributed in rivers and freshwater lakes in South India thanks to government breeding programmes. If you don't see them in the wild, you certainly will at the Crocodile Bank (p382), a breeding farm 40km south of Chennai. India has 238 species of snakes including the tiny Perrotet's shield-tail snake *(Plectrurus perroteti)*, found in the Western Ghats, and the fearsome 3m-long king cobra *(Ophiophagus hannah)*.

Plants

India's total forest cover is estimated to be around 20% of the total geographic coverage, despite an optimistic target of 33% set by the Forest Survey of India. The country boasts 49,219 plant species, of which around 5200 are endemic.

Forest types in South India include tropical, wet and semi-evergreen forests of the Andaman and Nicobar Islands and Western Ghats; tropical, moist deciduous forests in the Andamans, southern Karnataka and Kerala; tropical thorn forests, found in much of the drier Deccan plateau; and montane and wet temperate forests in the higher parts of Tamil Nadu and Kerala.

Characteristic of the Nilgiri and Annamalai Hills in the Western Ghats are the patches of moist evergreen forest restricted to the valleys and steep, protected slopes. Known as *sholas*, these islands of dark green are surrounded by expansive grasslands covering the more exposed slopes. They provide essential shelter and food for animals, but their limited size and patchy distribution make *sholas* vulnerable to natural and human disturbances.

Indian rosewood *(Dalbergia latifolia)*, Malabar kino *(Pterocarpus marsupium)* and teak have been virtually cleared from some parts of the Western Ghats, and sandalwood *(Santalum album)* is diminishing across India due to illegal logging for the incense and wood-carving industries. A bigger threat to forestry is firewood harvesting, often carried out by landless peasants who squat on gazetted government land.

Widely found in the south are banyan figs with their dangling aerial roots; bamboo in the Western Ghats; coconut palms on the islands and along the coastal peninsula; Indian coral trees along the coasts, and mangroves in tiny pockets. India is home to around 2000 species of orchid, about 10% of those found worldwide. The Nilgiri Hills is one of the finest places to spot orchids, such as the Christmas Orchid *(Calanthe triplicata)*.

NATIONAL PARKS & WILDLIFE SANCTUARIES

India has 93 national parks and 486 wildlife sanctuaries, which constitute about 4.7% of the country. There are also 14 biosphere reserves, overlapping many of the national parks and sanctuaries, providing safe migration channels for wildlife and allowing scientists to monitor biodiversity. In South India, most of the parks were established to protect wildlife from loss of habitat, so entry is often restricted to tours.

We strongly recommend visiting at least one national park/sanctuary on your travels – the experience of coming face to face with a wild beast will stay with you for a lifetime. Wildlife reserves tend to be off the beaten track and infrastructure can be limited – book transport and accommodation in advance, and check opening times, permit-requirements and entry

---

The Foundation for Revitalisation of Local Health Traditions has a search engine for medicinal plants at www.medicinalplants.in. Travellers with an especially keen interest should get CP Khare's *Encyclopedia Of Indian Medicinal Plants*.

The Kurinji shrub, which only produces bright purple-blue coloured blossoms every 12 years, is unique to the hills of South India's Western Ghats. Unfortunately the next blossom is due in 2016!

Read about wildlife, conservation and the environment in Sanctuary Asia (www.sanctuaryasia.com), a slick publication raising awareness about India's precious natural heritage.

fees before you visit. Many parks close to conduct a census of wildlife in the off season, while monsoon rains can make wildlife-viewing tracks inaccessible.

Almost all parks offer jeep/van tours, but you can also search for wildlife on guided treks, boat trips and elephant safaris. For the various safari possibilities, see p97.

MAJOR NATIONAL PARKS & WILDLIFE SANCTUARIES

Park/sanctuary	Page	Location	Features	Best time to visit
Bondla Wildlife Sanctuary	p215	eastern Goa	botanical garden, fenced deer park & zoo; gaurs & sambars	Nov-Mar
Calimere (Kodikkarai) Wildlife & Bird Sanctuary	p407	near Thanjavur, Tamil Nadu	coastal wetland; blackbucks, dolphins, crocodiles, deer teals, shovellers, curlews, gulls, terns, plovers, sandpipers, shanks, herons, koels, mynahs & barbet	Nov-Jan
Dubare Forest Reserve	p245	Near Madikeri, Karnataka	Interactive camp for retired working elephants	Sep-May
Indira Gandhi (Annamalai) Wildlife Sanctuary	p431	near Pollachi, Tamil Nadu	forested mountains; elephants, gaurs, tigers, panthers, boars, bears, deer, porcupines, civet cats & hornbills	Year-round except in periods of drought
Mahatma Gandhi Marine National Park	p455	Andaman & Nicobar Islands	mangrove, rainforest & coral	Nov-Apr
Molem & Bhagwan Mahavir Wildlife Sanctuary	p216	eastern Goa	tree-top-viewing tower; gaurs, sambars, leopards, spotted deer & snakes	Nov-Mar
Navagaon National Park	p154	east of Nagpur, Maharashtra	hilly forest & bamboo groves around manmade lake; leopards, sloth bears, deer & migratory birds	Oct-Jun
Nilgiri Biosphere Reserve				
Mudumalai National Park	p442	Mudumalai	forest; elephants, tigers, deer, gaurs,	Mar-May
Bandipur National Park	p241	Bandipur	sambars, muntjacs, chevrotains,	(some areas
Nagarhole National Park	p242	Nagarhole	chitals & bonnet macaques	year-round)
Wayanad Wildlife Sanctuary	p357	Tamil Nadu, Karnataka & Kerala		
Periyar Wildlife Sanctuary	p334	Kumily, Kerala	highland deciduous forest & grasslands; langurs, elephants, gaurs, otters, wild dogs, tortoises, kingfishers & fishing owls	Nov-Apr
Ranganathittu Bird Sanctuary	p240	near Mysore, Karnataka	river & island; storks, ibis, egrets, spoonbills & cormorants	Jun-Nov
Sanjay Gandhi National Park	p136	near Mumbai, Maharashtra	scenic area; water birds, butterflies & leopards	Aug-Apr
Tadoba-Andhari Tiger Reserve	p154	south of Nagpur, Maharashtra	deciduous forest, grasslands & wetlands; tigers, chitals, nilgais & gaurs	Feb-May
Vedantangal Bird Sanctuary	p388	near Chengalpattu, Tamil Nadu	lake & island; cormorants, egrets, herons, stork, ibis, spoonbills, grebes & pelicans	Nov-Jan

ENVIRONMENTAL ISSUES

With over one billion people, expanding industrialisation and urbanisation and chemical-intensive farming, India's environment is under threat. An estimated 65% of the country's land is degraded in some way, and the government has fallen short on most of its targets for environmental protection.

Despite dozens of new environmental laws enforced in recent decades, corruption continues to exacerbate environmental degradation – worst exemplified by the flagrant flouting of environmental rules by companies involved in hydroelectricity, uranium and oil exploration and mining. Typically, the people most affected are rural farmers and Adivasis (for more information, see p56), who have limited political representation and few resources to fight the commercial ambitions of big business. Rather than decreeing from on high, some of the most successful environmental schemes have returned power to local communities through the creation of seed banks, micro-loan schemes and water-users cooperatives. Organic and biodynamic farming – based on natural compost and timing farming to natural and lunar cycles – is also gaining ground (for further details, see www.biodynamics.in).

Between 11% and 27% of India's agricultural output is lost due to soil degradation through over-farming, rising soil salinity, loss of tree-cover and poor irrigation. Pollution from industry, human habitation and farming is further affecting the health and quality of life for South India's rural poor. The human cost is heartrending – crushing levels of debt and poverty drive thousands of Indian farmers to suicide every year. Lurking behind all these problems is a basic Malthusian truth: there are simply too many people for India to support at its current level of development.

While the Indian government could undoubtedly do more, some share of blame must also fall on Western farm subsidies that artificially reduce the cost of imported produce, undermining prices for Indian farmers. Western agribusiness may also like to take a cynical bow for promoting the use of nonpropagating GM seed stocks.

As anywhere, tourists tread a fine line between providing an incentive for change and making the problem worse. Many of the environmental problems in Goa (see the boxed text, p216) are a direct result of years of irresponsible development for tourism. Always consider your environmental impact while travelling in South India, including while diving (see p99).

Deforestation

Since Independence, some 5.3 million hectares of Indian forests have been cleared for logging and farming or damaged by urban expansion, mining, industrialisation and river dams. About 8% of South India is forested today. Demand for fuel and building materials, natural fires and traditional slash-and-burn farming, destruction of forests for mining or farmland, and illegal smuggling of teak, rosewood and sandalwood have all contributed to this drastic deforestation.

One of the most dramatic examples of deforestation is in the Andaman and Nicobar Islands where forest cover has been slashed from 90% to a mere 20%. Although protected forest reserves have been established on most islands here, illegal and sanctioned logging continues.

India's first Five Year Plan in 1951 recognised the importance of forests for soil conservation, and various policies have been introduced to increase forest cover. However, almost all have been flouted by corrupt officials, criminals and by ordinary people clearing forests for firewood and allowing grazing in forest areas.

The World Wide Fund for Nature (WWF; www .wwfindia.org) promotes environmental protection and wildlife conservation in India; see the website for offices around the country.

The Goa Foundation (www.goacom.com/goa foundation) is the premier environmental monitoring group in Goa.

The popular guru Jaggi Vasudev has launched an ambitious project to plant 114 million new saplings in Tamil Nadu by 2016, increasing forest cover in the region by 10%.

Marine Environment

The marine life along the 3000km-long coastline of South India and around the outlying archipelagos is under constant threat from pollution, sewage and harmful fishing methods. Ports, dams and tourism all contribute to the degradation of South India's marine environment.

India's seas have been overfished to such an extent that stocks are noticeably dwindling. Trawlers and factory fishing ships have largely replaced traditional log boats, and in some areas – eg the coast of Kerala – fishing communities are struggling to find other sources of income. Over the past decade, the international demand for prawns saw a plethora of prawn farms set up in South India, resulting in vast environmental damage to the coastline and birdlife as well as to farmland. There are now laws in place to curtail the effects of prawn farming, although these are not always adhered to.

Fish Curry & Rice, published by the Goa Foundation, is an incisive study of the Goan environment and the threats facing it.

MANGROVES

About 2.5 million hectares of mangroves have been destroyed in India since 1900. Mangroves are home to migratory birds and marine life, and are the first defence against soil erosion. They also help protect the coast from natural disasters, such as tidal waves and cyclones. Destruction of South India's mangroves has been caused by cattle grazing, logging, water pollution, prawn farming and tidal changes caused by the erosion of surrounding land. On the coast of Tamil Nadu and in the Andaman and Nicobar Islands, there have been efforts to reintroduce mangroves around fishing villages as a protective barrier following the damage caused by the devastating 2004 tsunami.

CORAL REEFS

Three major coral reefs are located around the islands of Lakshadweep, Andaman and Nicobar, and the Gulf of Mannar (near Sri Lanka). Coral is a crucial part of the fragile marine ecology, but is under constant threat from overfishing and bottom-of-the-sea trawling. Other factors contributing to the onslaught against the reefs are shipping, pollution, sewage, poaching, and excessive silt caused by deforestation and urban development on the land.

Mining

Throughout South India, a considerable number of mining rights have been granted with little regard for the environment, and with no requirement to undertake rehabilitation. In 2007 the Goa Forest Department purported that more than 10,000 hectares of forestland was threatened by mining. Nearly half the iron ore exported from India comes from Goa. When open-pit mines have been fully exploited they are often simply abandoned, scarring the hinterland. In Goa and other states of South India, heavy rains flush residues from open-cut mines into the rivers and sea. Some residues seep into the local water table, contaminating the drinking water.

Some licences for the mining of gold, silver, platinum and diamonds in Karnataka, and for gold and mica in the Nilgiris, have also been issued without sufficiently considering the adverse effects on the environment.

Climate Change

Changing climate patterns – linked to global carbon-emissions – have been creating dangerous extremes of weather in India. While India is a major polluter, in carbon emissions per capita it stands far behind America, Australia and Europe in the global league of polluting nations.

Elevated monsoon rainfalls have caused widespread flooding and destruction, including the devastating Maharashtra floods in 2005. Conversely, other areas are experiencing reduced rainfall, causing drought and riots over access to water supplies. Offshore, several islands in the Lakshadweep group have been inundated by rising sea levels.

Water

Arguably the biggest threat to public health in South India is inadequate access to clean drinking water and proper sanitation. With India's population set to double by 2050, agricultural, industrial and domestic water usage are all expected to spiral, despite government policies designed to control water use. Indeed water resources have long been a hot political issue; for instance, Karnataka and Tamil Nadu have been engaged in a heated dispute over the Cauvery River (since Karnataka controls the headwaters) for over a century. In 1990 a dedicated body, the Cauvery River Water Tribunal, was established to resolve the long-running dispute and in 2007 it ruled that Tamil Nadu would be sanctioned a greater amount than it currently receives. The Karnatakan government, who wasn't allocated the amount of water it requested, is appealing the decision.

Across India, ground water is being removed at an uncontrolled rate, causing an alarming drop in water-table levels and supplies of drinking water. Simultaneously, contamination from industry is rendering ground water unsafe to drink across the country. The soft-drink manufacturer Coca-Cola faced accusations that it was selling drinks containing unsafe levels of pesticides, as well as allegations over water shortages near its plants and farmland being polluted with industrial chemicals. Although cleared of claims about the safety of its drinks, Coca-Cola has yet to be held to account on any of the other allegations.

Pollution

While North India is most heavily affected by pollution, the south is by no means without its share of problems. It's hard to find a river or lake that has not been polluted with sewage, rubbish and/or chemical waste. Factories spew chemicals into the sea, rivers and air with little regulative control by understaffed, and often corrupt, local authorities. Tanneries and textile factories are often the worst polluters. Some rivers, such as the Noyyal and the Bhavani, tributaries of the Cauvery, are now virtually unusable for drinking water and irrigation.

Many of the problems experienced today are a direct result of the Green Revolution of the 1960s when a quantum leap in agricultural output was achieved using chemical fertilisers and pesticides. Pesticides used for cash crops, such as cotton and tobacco, upset the ecology – only about 1% of pesticides (which are often those banned elsewhere in the world) actually reach the pests; the rest seeps into the environment.

AIR POLLUTION

Air pollution from industry and vehicle emissions is an ongoing concern in South India, with Mumbai being among the world's most polluted cities, and Chennai, Hyderabad and Bengaluru not that far behind.

Indian diesel reportedly contains around 50 to 200 times more sulphur than European diesel and the ageing engines of Indian vehicles would fail most emissions tests in Europe or America. However, there have been some positive developments – Mumbai, has, for instance, switched over much of its public transport to Compressed Natural Gas (CNG). Several Indian cities have banned polluting industry (largely comprised of various manufacturing factories) completely from urban areas, although often with limited compensation for affected workers.

Air pollution in many Indian cities has been measured at more than double the maximum safe level recommended by the World Health Organization. In Mumbai, vehicular emissions account for around 50% of total pollution.

Noise pollution in major
cities has been measured
at over 90 decibels –
more than one-and-a
half times the recognised
'safe' limit. Bring earplugs!

Despite laws aimed at reducing toxic emissions, industry is still a major polluter. The massive growth of budget air travel is pumping even more greenhouse gases into the atmosphere – concepts such as carbon-balancing hold little sway in a nation embracing the freedom of the skies for the first time.

Another contributing factor is the rapidly rising number of vehicles in modern India – in 1951 there were 306,000 registered vehicles; in 1991 that figure had jumped to a staggering 21 million and today that figure has more than quadrupled and is expected to further swell as the cashed-up middle class surges into the car market.

Plastic Waste

Almost everywhere in South India plastic bags and bottles clog drains, litter city streets and beaches, and even stunt grass growth in the parks. Animals choke on the waste and the plastic also clogs water courses, heightening the risk of malaria and water-borne diseases. Campaigners estimate that about 75% of plastics used are discarded within a week and only 15% are recycled.

Fed up with ineffectual government policies to address the plastic problem, an increasing number of local initiatives are being pursued. For instance, in Kodaikanal shopping bags are now made from paper instead of plastic, while Goa has imposed a number of 'plast-free' zones, including on most of its beaches, and Karnataka's state legislature is considering a total ban on plastic shopping bags.

Tourists can assist by not buying anything in plastic bags or bottles, and encouraging hotels and shops to use environmentally-friendly alternatives. Shopkeepers almost invariably put your purchases in plastic bags, and without turning it into a crusade, it does help to request they use paper bags or nothing at all. Other ways to help include buying tea in terracotta cups at train stations and purifying your own drinking water (see the boxed text, p512).

Activities

Whether it's working up a sweat on a heart-racing forest trek, or splashing in the warm waters of the Arabian Sea, South India has a truly scintillating smorgasbord of things to do. And after all those blood-pumping activities, you can stretch that aching body and nourish your weary soul by enrolling in a mind-cleansing yoga course – just one of a number of spiritual activities on offer.

It would take an entire book to cover all the possibilities out there, but this chapter should keep you content for at least one lifetime.

Choosing an Operator

Regardless of what you decide to pursue, you are advised to exercise caution when choosing a tour operator. We receive reports of substandard operators taking poorly equipped tourists into potentially dangerous situations. Remember that travel agents are only the go-betweens and the final decisions about safety and equipment rest on the people actually operating the trip. Check out all tour operators and activity providers carefully and ensure you know what is included (it is always wise to get all the details in writing) before paying.

Where possible, stick to companies that provide activities themselves and have their own guides. If you go through an agency, choose operators who are accredited by the Travel Agents Association of India (www.travelagentsofindia.com), the Indian Association of Tour Operators (www.iato.in) or the Adventure Tour Operators Association of India (www.indianadventure.com). Note that dodgy operators often change their names to sound like the trusted companies – consult official tourist offices for lists of government-approved operators and seek first-hand recommendations from fellow travellers.

Always check safety equipment before you set off – if anything is below par, let the operator know. If they refuse to make the necessary changes, opt for another company. For any activity, make sure that you have adequate insurance – many travel insurance policies have exclusions for risky activities, including commonplace holiday pursuits, such as diving and trekking (see p474).

OUTDOOR ACTIVITIES

South India has an alluring array of outdoor activities, from diving and trekking to bird-watching and paragliding.

MEETING THE WILDLIFE

The subcontinent has some of the most beautiful flora and fauna on the planet – here are several ways to get up close and personal with nature in this region.

Bird-Watching

Some of the world's major bird-breeding and feeding grounds are found in India.

Some prime bird-watching sites:

Andaman & Nicobar Islands Spot rare drongos and golden orioles on Havelock Island (p456).

Karnataka Gawk at storks, egrets, ibis and spoonbills at Karanji Lake Nature Park (p236).

India Outdoors (www.indiaoutdoors.com) provides information on an incredible range of outdoor activities, from cycling and kayaking to paragliding and horse riding.

The website www .birding.in is a one-stop-shop for bird-watchers in India, with listings of bird-watching sites and all the species you are likely to see.

Kerala See Indian bird species from May to July and migratory birds from October to February at Kumarakom Bird Sanctuary (p333) and Thattekkad Bird Sanctuary (p340). Some other sanctuaries include Ranganathittu Bird Sanctuary (p240), Bandipur National Park (p241) and Nagarhole National Park (p242).

Tamil Nadu Plenty to point binoculars at in Mudumalai National Park (p442), Calimere (Kodikkarai) Wildlife & Bird Sanctuary (p407) and Vedantangal Bird Sanctuary (p388). Come here from December to January for multitudinous waterfowl.

Elephant Safaris

Elephant rides are a tremendous way of getting close to wildlife. Many national parks have their own working elephants, which can be hired for safaris into areas that are inaccessible to jeeps and walkers.

To ascertain the best times to visit major national parks, see the boxed text, p92.

Goa Elephant rides through spice plantations near Ponda (p215).

Karnataka Elephant safaris to India's largest elephant reserve at Bandipur National Park (p241) near Mysore. Interact with retired working elephants at Dubare Forest Reserve (p245) near Madikeri.

Kerala Elephant rides at Periyar Wildlife Sanctuary (p334) and Neyyar Dam Sanctuary (p314) near Trivandrum.

Horse Riding

Most of South India's hill stations offer horse rides, from gentle ambles through town to more serious trails through the forest.

Good places to saddle up:

Maharashtra Horses can be hired at Matheran (p159).

Tamil Nadu Take some rides at Kodaikanal (p429) and Udhagamandalam (Ooty; p438).

Jeep Safaris

In addition to elephant rides, jeep safaris visit national parks, tribal villages and remote temples. You can usually arrange a customised itinerary, either with travel agents or directly with jeep drivers.

Here are some popular options:

Karnataka Jungle Lodges & Resorts (p219) offers safaris to Nagarhole National Park, Bandipur National Park and other reserves.

Kerala You can take wildlife-spotting jeep tours through the Wayanad Wildlife Sanctuary (p357).

Tamil Nadu One of several ways to spot wildlife in Mudumalai National Park (p442).

ADVENTURE ACTIVITIES

Apart from trekking, lovers of the great outdoors can scuba dive, paraglide, raft, kayak and more. Remember to take out adequate insurance cover before you travel.

Boat Tours

Take your pick from languid river rides, scenic lake cruises or motorboat tours of offshore islands.

Several recommended tours:

Andaman & Nicobar Islands Boat and ferry trips to outlying islands from Port Blair (p454) and Mayabunder (p459).

Goa Dolphin-spotting boat trips from Panaji (Panjim; p185), Fort Aguada and Candolim (p191), Calangute (p195), Arambol (Harmal; p205), Colva (p210), and Palolem (p214).

Kerala Days of dreamy drifting on the backwaters around Alappuzha (Alleppey; p328), canoe-tours from Kollam (Quilon; p324) and bamboo-raft tours in Periyar Wildlife Sanctuary (p334).

Mumbai (Bombay) Boat cruises around Mumbai harbour (p119) and Elephanta Island (p136) from Mumbai.

Cultural Tours

Tours to tribal areas are permitted in some regions and provide a captivating window into the traditional way of life among India's Adivasis (see p56 for more details). Responsible operators should employ tribal guides and minimise their impact on communities.

Reputable tribal tours:

Andhra Pradesh Tribal tours to Adivasi communities around Visakhapatnam (p300).

Kerala Tours to Mannakudy tribal areas of Periyar Wildlife Sanctuary (p334).

Cycling & Motorcycling

There are some brilliant organised bicycle or motorcycle tours, or you can rent a bike or motorcycle and design your own itinerary. Recommended motorcycle tours are covered on p500 and towns offering motorcycle hire are mentioned throughout the regional chapters; Goa is particularly geared to tourists.

Top spots for pedal cycling:

Andhra Pradesh Rent bikes at Warangal (p298).

Goa Try the mountain-bike tours around Palolem (p214), and there is bike rental in Panaji (Panjim; p187) and Colva (p210).

Karnataka There is bike hire in Hampi (p263) and Bidar (p272).

Kerala There is bike rental in Munnar (p339) and free use of bikes at budget guesthouses in and around Alappuzha (Alleppey; p326).

Maharashtra Bikes are for rent in Aurangabad (p146), Murud (p156), Lonavla (p162) and Mahabaleshwar (p172).

Tamil Nadu You can rent mountain bikes in Kodaikanal (p430) and push-bikes in Puducherry (Pondicherry; p402).

Diving, Snorkelling & Water Sports

The Andaman Islands are India's leading destination for scuba diving, with world-class dive sites on well-preserved coral reefs, particularly around Havelock Island. Visibility is clearest from December to March/April. The Lakshadweep Islands offer coral atoll diving from mid-October to mid-May. Dive certification courses and recreational dives are also possible in Goa.

> To learn more about South India's Adivasis, read *The Todas of South India – A New Look,* by Anthony Walker, and *Archaeology and History: Early Settlements in the Andaman Islands,* by Zarine Cooper.

RESPONSIBLE DIVING

To help preserve the ecology and beauty of reefs, observe the following guidelines when diving:

- Never use anchors on the reef, and take care not to ground boats on coral.

- Avoid touching or disturbing living marine organisms – they can be damaged by even the gentlest contact. If you must hold on to the reef, only touch exposed rock or dead coral.

- Be conscious of your fins. Even without contact, the surge from fin strokes near the reef can damage delicate organisms. Take care not to kick up clouds of sand, which can smother organisms.

- Practise and maintain proper buoyancy control. Major damage can be done by divers descending too fast and colliding with the reef.

- Don't collect or buy corals or shells.

- Ensure that you carry back your rubbish and any litter you may find; plastics in particular are a serious threat to marine life.

- Don't feed fish.

- Choose a dive company with appropriate environmental policies and practices.

Some recommended sites:

Andaman & Nicobar Islands Growing numbers of surfers are discovering the breaks off the island of Little Andaman (p448), with the best waves between mid-March and mid-May. You'll find India's finest dives around Havelock Island (p448).

Goa Numerous beach resorts offering diving courses, windsurfing and other watersports in Goa (p176).

Kerala World-class dives on the little-visited Lakshadweep Islands (p362).

Dive India (www.dive india.com/sites.html), the Andaman Islands' premier dive company, has a comprehensive list of dive sites on its website.

Hang-gliding & Paragliding

Goa and Maharashtra are the flying capitals of South India. Safety standards have been variable in the past – consult the tourist office for a safety update before leaping into the blue beyond.

A few offerings:

Goa Paragliding flights at Arambol (p205) and Anjuna (p199).

Maharashtra Courses and tandem paragliding flights are found at Lonavla (p161).

Kayaking & River Rafting

South India doesn't have the wild river-rafting opportunities found up north, but there are still some admirable options. The rafting seasons are from around October to January in Goa and Karnataka, and June to September in Maharashtra. The level of rapids varies from modest Grade II to raging Grade IV and most operators offer multiday rafting safaris, as well as short thrill rides.

Some worthy options:

Goa Arrange rafting tours on the Kali River in Calangute with Day Tripper (p195).

Karnataka Kayaking and rafting trips with Getoff ur ass (p225), based in Bengaluru (Bangalore). White-water trips up to Grade IV are possible in Dubare Forest Reserve (p245).

Kerala Canoe trips on the backwaters of Kerala at Greenpalm Homes (p331) near Alappuzha (Alleppey).

Mumbai Rafting in Maharashtra through Mumbai-based Outbound Adventure (p117).

Rock-Climbing

For warm-weather climbers, there are some fabulous sandstone and granite climbing areas in Karnataka at Badami, Ramanagram, Savandurga and Hampi, India's premier bouldering region (see the boxed text, Climbing in Karnataka, p262).

Climbing is on a mixture of bolts and traditional protection. Organised climbs can be arranged, but serious climbers should bring gear from home – pack plenty of nuts, hexacentrics and cams, plus spare rolls of climbing tape for jamming cracks in sharp granite.

Trekking

North India is prime trekking territory; however, South India still has some worthy offerings. Most people opt for organised treks (sometimes mandatory) with local trekking agencies.

If you do make your own arrangements, tell someone where you're going and when you intend returning, and never trek alone.

Popular trekking options:

Andaman & Nicobar Islands There are bird-watching jungle treks on Havelock Island (p456).

Karnataka Treks around Karnataka with Bengaluru-based Getoff ur ass (p225) and agents and guesthouses in Madikeri (p243).

Kerala There are guided wildlife-spotting treks in Periyar Wildlife Sanctuary (p334) and Wayanad Wildlife Sanctuary (p357) and hill treks at Munnar (p337 and p339).

Tamil Nadu Guided treks in the buffer zone around Mudumalai National Park (p442), and hill and jungle treks around Indira Gandhi (Annamalai) Wildlife Sanctuary (p431), Udhagamandalam (Ooty; p438) and Kodaikanal (p428).

HOLISTIC & SPIRITUAL ACTIVITIES

Travellers with an interest in spirituality and alternative therapies will find a host of excellent courses and treatments that are designed to heal the body and mind.

AYURVEDA

Ayurveda is the ancient science of Indian herbal medicine and holistic healing. It uses herbal treatments, massage and a gamut of other therapies. There are clinics, resorts and colleges where you can learn Ayurvedic techniques and receive treatments.

Here are some options:

Goa Therapies and residential courses in Ayurveda, reflexology, aromatherapy, acupressure and yoga at the Ayurvedic Natural Health Centre (p195) near Calangute.

Karnataka Take some naturopathy classes and Ayurvedic therapies in Bengaluru (p225) and Mysore (p236).

Kerala There are various classes and Ayurvedic therapies in Varkala (p320).

Tamil Nadu Courses in Ayurvedic massage are available at Puducherry (p399).

Healthy Living with Ayurveda, by Anuradha Singh, provides an understanding of one's *prakriti* (constitution) and tailoring a diet and exercise regime accordingly.

Spa Treatments

If you simply wish to enjoy the healing effects without the study, there are spas throughout South India, from Ayurvedic hospitals to luxurious health centres at five-star resorts. Be cautious of one-on-one massages by private operators, particularly in tourist towns. Seek recommendations and no matter where you go, if you ever feel uneasy, leave.

Some recommendations:

Goa Numerous beach resorts offering massages and other spa services at Calangute and Baga (p194), Anjuna (p199), Colva and Benaulim (p210), Arambol (p204) and other locations.

Karnataka There are herbal rubs and scrubs in Bengaluru (p225), Mysore (p236) and Gokarna (p255).

Kerala Massages and herbal treatments are available at Varkala (p320) and Kochi (Cochin; p344) and therapeutic breaks at Janakanthi Panchakarma Centre (p324) and Thapovan Heritage Home (p319).

Maharashtra Massages, saunas and spa treatments are available at the Osho Meditation Resort (p165).

Mumbai The pampering of pamperings at Mumbai's finest spa – inside the ITC Hotel Grand Maratha Sheraton & Towers (p124).

Tamil Nadu Posh hotel spas are found in Thanjavur (Tanjore; p410) and Kodaikanal (p429) and massage sessions are available in Mamallapuram (Mahabalipuram; p386) and Puducherry (p399).

YOGA

Many places in South India offer classes and courses in various types of yoga, often with a meditation component. The most common yoga forms are: hatha (following the *shatkarma* system of postures and meditation), *ashtanga* (following the 'eight limbs' system of postures and meditation), *pranayama* (controlled yogic breathing), and Iyengar (a variation of *ashtanga* yoga using physical aids for advanced postures).

To delve into yoga, Ayurveda and other holistic therapies, try clicking on www .indianmedicine.nic.in.

Yoga Courses

There are oodles of yoga courses on offer with some outfits being more reputable than others (especially in tourist towns). Visit several to find one that suits your needs. Many ashrams (spiritual communities or retreats) also have yoga courses (see p102), although some centres require a minimum time-commitment.

ASHRAMS & GURUS

Many people visit India specifically to spend time at an ashram – literally a 'place of striving' – for spiritual sustenance and personal learning. There are literally hundreds of gurus (the word means 'dispeller of darkness' or 'heavy with wisdom') offering their knowledge to millions of keen followers from around the globe.

The atmosphere surrounding an ashram can have a profound and deeply moving effect on visitors; however, you are urged to exercise common sense and discernment, as regrettably not all ashrams (or gurus) are as sincere in their motives as others. Talk to locals and fellow travellers to see which ashram or guru might best suit you. Most ashrams don't require notice of your arrival but it's best to double-check in advance. Gurus may move around without much notice – another good reason to do some homework ahead of your visit.

It's important to realise that ashram life isn't for everyone. Most ashrams have strict codes of conduct, which may include a dress code, daily regimen of yoga and/or meditation, and charitable work at social projects run by the ashram. The diet is almost always vegetarian and you may also be asked to abstain from eggs, tobacco, alcohol, garlic, onions, and 'black drinks', ie anything containing caffeine, including tea and cola. A donation to cover the cost of your accommodation, food and the running expenses of the ashram is in order.

There are many yoga opportunities across the South India region; for those that impose no fees, donations are always appreciated.

The following represent a selection:

Goa A massive range of yoga courses at hotels, spiritual centres and retreats is available in Anjuna (p199), Arambol (p205), Calangute (p195) and Palolem (p214).

Karnataka There are world-renowned courses in *ashtanga*, hatha and Iyengar yoga and meditation in Mysore (p236), plus yoga classes in Bengaluru (Bangalore; p225) and Gokarna (SwaSwara; p256).

Kerala Hatha yoga courses at Sivananda Yoga Vedanta Dhanwantari Ashram (p315) near Thiruvananthapuram (Trivandrum) and yoga classes in Varkala (p320).

Maharashtra There's yogic healing at the Kaivalyadhama Yoga Hospital (p161) in Lonavla and advanced Iyengar yoga courses (for experienced practitioners only) at Ramamani Iyengar Memorial Yoga Institute (p166) in Pune.

Mumbai There are classes in various styles of yoga available in Mumbai (p118).

Tamil Nadu Various hatha yoga classes in Chennai (Madras; p374). Assorted yoga classes and courses available in Mamallapuram (Mahabalipuram; p386) and Puducherry (p399).

> Yoga is one of the oldest therapies in human history, dating back 4000 years. Yoga as we know it today was kick-started around 200 BC by the Hindu scholar Patanjali.

Ashrams

South India has dozens of ashrams – places of communal living established around the philosophies of a guru (spiritual guide). Codes of conduct vary, so make sure you're willing to abide by them before committing. For more information, see the boxed text, above.

Several key offerings:

Andhra Pradesh Puttaparthi (Puttaparthi; p304) is the ashram of controversial but phenomenally popular guru Sri Sathya Sai Baba.

Kerala Matha Amrithanandamayi Mission (Alappuzha; p328) is famed for its female guru Amma – 'The Hugging Mother'.

Maharashtra Brahmavidya Mandir Ashram (Sevagram; p156) was established by Gandhi's disciple Vinoba Bhave. The Osho Meditation Resort (Pune; p165) was founded and led by the teachings of Osho. The Sevagram Ashram (Sevagram; p155) was established by Mahatma Gandhi. The Sivananda Yoga Vedanta Dhanwantari Ashram (Thiruvananthapuram; p315) is a well-regarded yoga centre, renowned for its hatha yoga courses. Sivagiri Mutt (Varkala; p321) is devoted to Sree Narayana Guru.

Tamil Nadu Sri Aurobindo Ashram (Puducherry; p399) was founded by the famous Sri Aurobindo, and has branches around India. The Isha Yoga Center (Coimbatore; p434) is a rural yoga centre offering residential courses and retreats. The Sri Ramana Ashram (Tiruvannamalai; p394) was founded by Sri Ramana Maharishi.

MEDITATION

A number of centres offer courses in *vipassana*, or mindfulness meditation, and Buddhist philosophy; be aware that some courses require students to abide by a vow of silence and may also have other protocols (inquire in advance).

Some popular choices:

Andhra Pradesh There are *vipassana* meditation courses in Hyderabad (p282) and Vijayawada (p301).

Maharashtra Courses lasting 10 to 45 days at the world's largest *vipassana* meditation centre are at Igatpuri (p142).

Tamil Nadu Various *vipassana* courses are available in Chennai (p374).

Famous practitioners of *vipassana* meditation include the Dalai Lama, Richard Gere and novelist Graham Greene. See www.dhamma.org for listings of *vipassana* study centres in and beyond India.

Mumbai (Bombay)

Measure out: one part Hollywood; six parts traffic; a bunch of rich power-moguls; stir in half a dozen colonial relics (use big ones); pour in six heaped cups of poverty; add a smattering of swish bars and restaurants (don't skimp on quality here for best results); equal parts of mayhem and order; as many ancient bazaars as you have lying around; a handful of Hinduism; a dash of Islam; fold in your mixture with equal parts India; throw it all in a blender on high (adding generous helpings of pollution to taste) and presto: Mumbai.

An inebriating mix of all the above and more, this mass of humanity is a frantic melange of India's extremes. It is the country's financial powerhouse and its vogue centre of fashion, film and after-dark frolics. Glistening skyscrapers and malls mushroom amid slums and grinding poverty, and Mumbai slowly marches towards a brave new (air-conditioned) world. But not everyone made the guest list: more than half of the population lives in slums, and religious-based social unrest tugs at the skirt of Mumbai's financial excess.

Only once the initial shell shock of Mumbai's chaos subsides, can one start to appreciate the city's allure: a wealth of Art Deco and grand colonial relics; cacophonic temples; warrens of bazaars; and the odd spiritual bastion of tranquillity. In Mumbai you can dine at some of the finest restaurants in the country, and work off the appetite gyrating at ultrachic bars alongside Bollywood starlets and wannabes. With a pinch of gumption, a dash of adventure, an open wallet and a running start, there's no excuse not to dive into the Mumbai madness head-first.

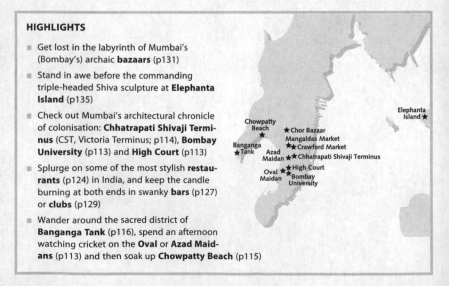

HIGHLIGHTS

- Get lost in the labyrinth of Mumbai's (Bombay's) archaic **bazaars** (p131)
- Stand in awe before the commanding triple-headed Shiva sculpture at **Elephanta Island** (p135)
- Check out Mumbai's architectural chronicle of colonisation: **Chhatrapati Shivaji Terminus** (CST, Victoria Terminus; p114), **Bombay University** (p113) and **High Court** (p113)
- Splurge on some of the most stylish **restaurants** (p124) in India, and keep the candle burning at both ends in swanky **bars** (p127) or **clubs** (p129)
- Wander around the sacred district of **Banganga Tank** (p116), spend an afternoon watching cricket on the **Oval** or **Azad Maidans** (p113) and then soak up **Chowpatty Beach** (p115)

HISTORY

Koli fisherfolk have inhabited the seven islands that form Mumbai as far back as the 2nd century BC. Amazingly, ruminants of this culture remain huddled along the city shoreline today. A succession of Hindu dynasties held sway over the islands from the 6th century AD until the Muslim Sultans of Gujarat annexed the area in the 14th century, eventually ceding it to Portugal in 1534. The only memorable contribution the Portuguese made to the area was christening it Bom Bahai, before throwing the islands in with the dowry of Catherine of Braganza when she married England's Charles II in 1661. The British government took possession of the islands in 1665, but leased them three years later to the East India Company for the paltry annual rent of UK£10.

Then called Bombay, the area flourished as a trading port. So much so that within 20 years the presidency of the East India Company was transferred to Bombay from Surat. Bombay's fort was completed in the 1720s, and a century later ambitious land reclamation projects joined the islands into today's single landmass. Although Bombay grew steadily during the 18th century, it remained isolated from its hinterland until the British defeated the Marathas (the central Indian people who controlled much of India at various times) and annexed substantial portions of western India in 1818.

The fort walls were dismantled in 1864 and massive building works transformed the city in grand colonial style. When Bombay took over as the principal supplier of cotton to Britain during the American Civil War, the population soared and trade boomed as money flooded into the city.

A major player in the independence movement, Bombay hosted the first Indian National Congress in 1885, and the Quit India campaign was launched here in 1942 by frequent visitor Mahatma Gandhi. The city became capital of the Bombay presidency after Independence, but in 1960 Maharashtra

and Gujarat were divided along linguistic lines – and Bombay became the capital of Maharashtra.

The rise of the pro-Maratha regionalist movement, spearheaded by the Shiv Sena (Hindu Party; literally 'Shivaji's Army'), shattered the city's multicultural mould by actively discriminating against Muslims and non-Maharashtrans. The Shiv Sena won power in the city's municipal elections in 1985. Communalist tensions increased and the city's cosmopolitan self-image took a battering when nearly 800 people died in riots that followed the destruction of the Babri Masjid in Ayodhya in December 1992. They were followed by a dozen bombings on 12 March 1993, which killed more than 300 people and damaged the

FAST FACTS

- Population: 16.4 million
- Area: 440 sq km
- Telephone code: ☎ 022
- When to go: October to February

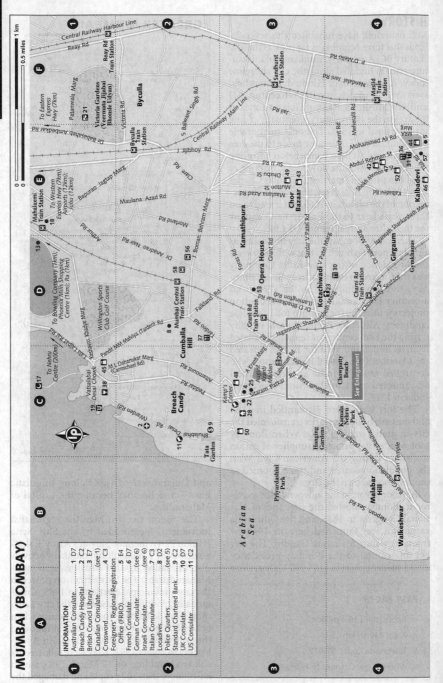

INFORMATION
Australian Consulate.....................1 D7
Breach Candy Hospital..................2 C2
British Council Library....................3 E7
Canadian Consulate....................(see 1)
Crossword....................................4 C3
Foreigners' Regional Registration
  Office (FRRO)............................5 E4
French Consulate...........................6 D7
German Consulate......................(see 6)
Israeli Consulate.........................(see 6)
Italian Consulate...........................7 C3
Locadives.....................................8 D2
Police Quarters..........................(see 5)
Standard Chartered Bank...............9 C2
UK Consulate...............................10 D7
US Consulate...............................11 C2

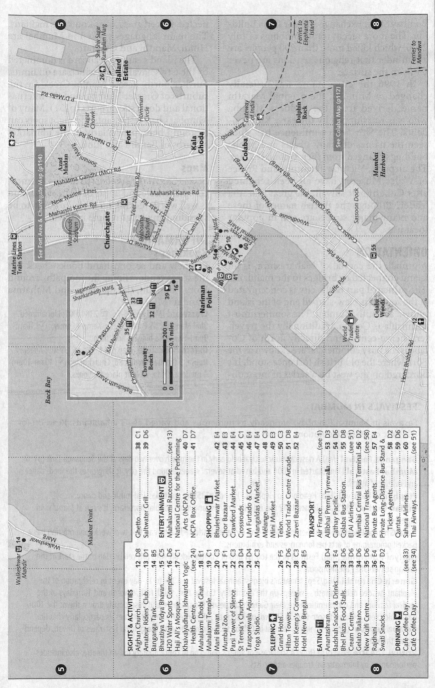

SIGHTS & ACTIVITIES
Afghan Church.................................12 D8
Amateur Riders' Club.......................13 D1
Banganga Tank.................................14 B5
Bharatiya Vidya Bhavan...................15 C5
H2O Water Sports Complex...............16 D6
Haji Ali's Mosque.............................17 C1
Khaivalyadham Ishwardas Yogic
    Health Centre..........................(see 24)
Mahalaxmi Dhobi Ghat.....................18 E1
Mahalaxmi Temple...........................19 C1
Mani Bhavan....................................20 C3
Mumbai Zoo.....................................21 F1
Parsi Tower of Silence.......................22 C3
St Teresa's Church............................23 D4
Taraporewala Aquarium....................24 D4
Yoga Studio......................................25 C3

SLEEPING
Grand Hotel......................................26 F5
Hilton Towers...................................27 D6
Hotel Kemp's Corner.........................28 C3
Hotel New Bengal.............................29 E5

Ghetto...38 C1
Saltwater Grill..................................39 D6

ENTERTAINMENT
Mahalaxmi Racecourse.................(see 13)
National Centre for the Performing
    Arts (NCPA).................................40 D7
NCPA Box Office...............................41 D7

SHOPPING
Bhuleshwar Market...........................42 E4
Chor Bazaar.....................................43 E3
Crawford Market..............................44 E4
Crossroads.......................................45 C1
LM Furtado & Co..............................46 E4
Mangaldas Market............................47 E4
Mélange...48 C3
Mini Market.....................................49 E3
Telon...50 C3
World Trade Centre Arcade...............51 D8
Zaveri Bazaar...................................52 E4

TRANSPORT
Air France....................................(see 1)
Allbhai Premji Tyrewala....................53 D3
Cathay Pacific...................................54 D6
Colaba Bus Station............................55 D8
El Al Airlines.................................(see 58)
Mumbai Central Bus Terminal...........56 D2
National Travels.............................(see 58)
Rajdhani..57 E4
Private Bus Agents............................58 D2
Private Long-Distance Bus Stand &
    Ticket Agents...............................59 D6
Qantas...60 D7
Sahara Airlines.............................(see 51)
Thai Airways.................................(see 51)

EATING
Anantashram....................................30 D4
Badshah Snacks & Drinks..................31 E4
Bhel Plaza Food Stalls.......................32 D6
Cream Centre...................................33 D6
Gelato Italiano..................................34 D6
New Kulfi Centre..............................35 D6
Rajdhani..36 E4
Swati Snacks....................................37 D2

DRINKING
Café Coffee Day............................(see 33)
Café Coffee Day............................(see 34)

Ferries to
Elephanta
Island

Ferries to
Mandwa

Dolphin
Rock

See Colaba Map (p112)

*Mumbai
Harbour*

Colaba
Woods

World
Trade
Centre

Cuffe Pde

Sassoon Dock

Back Bay

Malabar Point

Walkeshwar
Mandir

Walkeshwar
Marg

Chowpatty
Beach

Jagannath
Shankarsheth Marg

200 m
0.1 miles

Marine Lines
Train Station

See Fort Area & Churchgate Map (p114)

Fort

Churchgate

Waterfield
Stadium

New Marine Lines

Maharshi Karve Rd

Maharshi Karve Rd

Mahatma Gandhi (MG) Rd

Azad
Maidan

P D'Mello Rd

Nagar
Chowk

Horniman
Circle

**Kala
Ghoda**

Gateway
of India

Colaba

**Nariman
Point**

**Ballard
Estate**

Shri Shiv Sagar
Ramgulam Marg

Bombay Stock Exchange and Air India Building. The more recent train bombings of July 2006, which killed more than 200 people, are a reminder that religious tensions are never far from the surface.

In 1996 the city's name was officially changed to Mumbai, the original Marathi name derived from the goddess Mumba who was worshipped by the early Koli residents. The Shiv Sena's influence has since seen the names of many streets and public buildings changed from their colonial names. The airports, Victoria Terminus and Prince of Wales Museum have all been renamed after Chhatrapati Shivaji, the great Maratha leader, although the British names of these and many major streets are still in popular local use.

ORIENTATION

Mumbai, the capital of Maharashtra, is an island connected by bridges to the mainland. The principal part of the city is concentrated at the southern, claw-shaped end of the island known as South Mumbai. The southernmost peninsula is Colaba, traditionally the travellers' nerve-centre, and directly north of Colaba is the busy commercial area known as the Fort, where the old British fort once stood. It's bordered on the west by a series of interconnected, fenced, grass areas known as maidans. The main languages spoken in Mumbai are Hindi, Marathi and Gujarati.

The island's eastern seaboard is dominated by the city's naval docks, which are off limits. Further north, across Mahim Creek are the suburbs of Greater Mumbai and the international and domestic airports (p131). Many of Mumbai's best restaurants and night spots can be found here, particularly in the upmarket suburbs of Bandra and Juhu.

Maps

Eicher City Map Mumbai (Rs 250) is the most comprehensive and up-to-date street atlas and is well worth picking up if you're going to be spending any lengthy time in town.

INFORMATION
Bookshops

For new and second-hand books check out the street vendors lining the footpaths around Flora Fountain, the maidans, and Mahatma Gandhi (MG) Rd.

Crossword (Map pp106-7; ☎ 23842001; Mohammed Bhai Mansion, NS Patkar Marg, Kemp's Corner; ☽ 10am-9pm) Mumbai's biggest bookshop.

Oxford Bookstore (Map p114; ☎ 56339309; Apeejay House, 3 Dinsha Wachha Rd, Churchgate; ☽ 10am-10pm) A modern, clean, well-lit place for books.

FESTIVALS IN MUMBAI

Festivals in Mumbai (Bombay) are nearly as numerous and varied as its inhabitants. Read on for the best of these celebrations:

Banganga Festival (Jan) A classical music festival held early in the month over two days at the Banganga Tank (p116).
Mumbai Festival (Jan) Started in 2004 and based at several stages around the city, it showcases the food, dance and culture of Mumbai.
Elephanta Festival (Feb) Head out to Elephanta Island (p135) for more classical music and dance.
Indian Derby (Feb) Staged since 1942 this is India's richest and most popular horserace. It's run at Mahalaxmi Racecourse (p130).
Kala Ghoda Festival (Feb) Getting bigger and more sophisticated each year, this two-week-long offering has a packed programme of arts performances and exhibitions.
Nariyal Poornima (Aug) Festivals in the tourist hub of Colaba kick off with this celebration of the start of the fishing season after the monsoon.
Ganesh Chaturthi (Aug/Sep) Mumbai's biggest annual festival – a 10- to 11-day event in celebration of the elephant-headed deity Ganesh – sweeps up the entire city. On the first, third, fifth, seventh and 10th days of the festival families and communities take their Ganesh statues to the seashore and auspiciously drown them: the 10th day, which sees millions descending on Chowpatty Beach to submerge the largest statues, is particularly chaotic.
Colaba Festival (Oct) A small arts festival in Colaba that can merge with the general festivities of Diwali, depending on the year.
Prithvi Theatre Festival (Nov) A showcase of what's going on in contemporary Indian theatre; also includes performances by international troupes and artists.

READING MUMBAI

Containing all the beauty and ugliness of the human condition it's little wonder that Mumbai has inspired a host of the best writers on the subcontinent as well as international scribes such as VS Naipaul and Pico Iyer. Leading the field are Booker Prize–winner Salman Rushdie (*Midnight's Children, The Moor's Last Sigh* and *The Ground Beneath Her Feet*) and Rohinton Mistry (*A Fine Balance* and *Family Matters*), who have both set many of their novels in the city.

Making a credible grab to be the ultimate chronicle of the modern city is Suketu Mehta's *Maximum City: Bombay Lost and Found*. This incisively researched and elegantly written epic – equal parts memoir, travelogue and journalism – covers Mumbai's riots, gang warfare, Bollywood, bar girls and everything in between. Another doorstopper is Gregory David Robert's factional saga *Shantaram*, about the Australian prison escapee's life on the run in Mumbai's slums and jails. Also well worth dipping into is the anthology *Bombay, Meri Jaan,* edited by Jerry Pinto and Naresh Fernandes, a heady mix of politics, pop culture, literature and history.

Search Word (Map p112; ☎ 22852521; Metro House, Colaba Causeway, Colaba; ⌚ 10:30am-8:30pm) Small and tidy bookshop, also selling magazines.

Strand Book Stall (Map p114; ☎ 22661994, www .strandbookstall.com; Cowasji Patel Rd; ⌚ 10am-8pm Mon-Sat) This old-school bookshop has walls overflowing with new English-language books, particularly nonfiction and titles by Indian authors.

Internet Access

There are many internet cafés across the city. Most charge Rs 30 to 40 per hour and almost all offer phone, fax, photocopying and printing services.

Cyber Online (Map p114; Jiji House, 1st fl, 17 Sukhadwala Rd, Fort; per hr Rs 30; ⌚ 10.30am-11pm Mon-Sat) Fast, new, flat-screen computers.

Sify iWay per 1½hrs Rs 50; Churchgate (Map p114; Prem Ct, J Tata Rd; ⌚ 9am-11pm); Colaba (Map p112; Colaba Causeway; ⌚ 24hrs) The entrance to the Colaba branch is on JA Allana Marg.

Waghela Communications Centre (Map p112; 23-B Nawroji F Rd; per hr Rs 30; ⌚ 8:30am-11:30pm)

Libraries & Cultural Centres

Library books, newspapers, internet access and cultural information and events are available at the following:

Alliance Française (Map p114; ☎ 22035993; 40 New Marine Lines; 3-month/annual membership Rs 200/800; ⌚ 9.30am-5.30pm Mon-Fri, 9.30am-1pm Sat)

American Information Resource Centre (AIRC; Map p114; ☎ 22624590; http://mumbai.usconculate.gov/airc; 4 New Marine Lines, Churchgate; visit Rs 20, annual membership Rs 400; ⌚ library noon-6pm Mon-Fri)

British Council Library (Map pp106-7; ☎ 22790101; www.britishcouncilonline.org; 1st fl, Mittal Tower A Wing, Barrister Rajni Patel Marg, Nariman Point; minimum monthly membership Rs 250; ⌚ 10am-6pm Tue-Sat)

Max Mueller Bhavan (Goethe Institut; Map p114; ☎ 22027542; K Dubash Marg, Fort; ⌚ library 11am-6pm Mon-Fri) For German books.

Media

English-language publications:

City Info Free monthly listings booklet available in many hotels and guesthouses.

Indian Express Has a Mumbai edition.

Mid-Day The main local English-language paper.

Time Out Mumbai Published every two weeks (Rs 30), this is the best round-up of what's going on in the city.

Times of India Has a Mumbai edition.

Medical Services

Bombay Hospital (Map p114; ☎ 22067676; www .bombayhospotal.com; 12 New Marine Lines) Close to Fort and Colaba.

Breach Candy Hospital (Map pp106-7; ☎ 23672888; www.breachcandyhospital.org; 60 Bhulabhai Desai Rd, Breach Candy) Best in Mumbai, if not India.

Royal Chemists (Map p114; ☎ 22004041-3; 89A Maharshi Karve Rd, Churchgate; ⌚ 8:30am-8:30pm) A very reputable pharmacy.

Sahakari Bhandar Chemist (Map p112; ☎ 23648435; Colaba Causeway, Colaba; ⌚ 8am-10pm Mon-Sat, 10am-8pm Sun) Well-stocked and convenient pharmacy.

Money

ATMS

The number of 24-hour ATMs linked to international networks in Mumbai has exploded in recent years and you're rarely far from one.

CURRENCY EXCHANGE

There's no shortage of foreign-exchange offices in Colaba that will change cash and travellers cheques. There are 24-hour exchange bureaus at both airports.

Erudite Forex (Map p112; ☎ 22882706; Colaba Causeway, Colaba; ⏲ 7am-7pm Mon-Sat)
Standard Chartered Bank (⏲ 9.30am-6pm Mon-Sat Breach Candy (Map pp106-7; Bhulabhai Desai Rd); Fort (Map p114; MG Rd)
Thomas Cook (Map p114; ☎ 22078556-8; 324 Dr Dadabhai Naoroji Rd, Fort; ⏲ 9.30am-6pm Mon-Sat)

Photography

Standard Supply Co (Map p114; ☎ 22612468; Image House, W Hirachand Marg, Fort; ⏲ 10am-7pm Mon-Sat) Modern digital processing, print and slide film, video cartridges, memory cards and camera accessories are available here.

Post

The **main post office** (Map p114; ☎ 22621671; ⏲ 9am-8pm Mon-Sat, 10am-5pm Sun) is an imposing building behind Chhatrapatri Shiraji Terminus (CST, Victoria Terminus). **Poste restante** (⏲ 9am-6pm Mon-Sat) is at Counter 1. Letters sent there should be addressed c/o Poste Restante, Mumbai GPO, Mumbai 400 001. You'll need to bring your passport to collect mail. There's an **EMS Speedpost parcel counter** (⏲ 11am-1pm & 1.30-4pm Mon-Sat) to the left of the stamp counters. Regular parcels can be sent from the parcel office behind the main post office building. Directly opposite the post office is a group of parcel-wallahs who will stitch up your parcel for around Rs 40. The **Colaba post office** (☎ 22023549; Henry Rd, Colaba) is convenient.

To send air-freight parcels domestically or internationally (a 10kg box to the UK or USA costs about Rs 6360), try the following:
Blue Dart (Map p114; ☎ 22822495; www.bluedart.com; 25/B J Tata Rd; ⏲ 10am-8.30pm Mon-Sat)
DHL Worldwide Express (⏲ 8am-8pm Mon-Sat Churchgate (Map p114; ☎ 22837187; www.dhl.co.in; Sea Green South Hotel, 145A Marine Dr, Churchgate). Colaba (☎ 22044131; 1B Rahim Mansions, Colaba Causeway)

Telephone

Private phone and fax centres (labelled 'STD/ISD' or 'PCO') in Colaba and the Fort are convenient for STD and international calls (around Rs 12 per minute to the UK, USA or Australia). The cheapest international calls can be made through internet cafés using Net2 Phone. Calls cost from Rs 5 per minute to the USA.

Tourist Information

Government of India tourist office (Map p114; ☎ 22074333; www.incredibleindia.com; 123 Maharshi Karve Rd; ⏲ 8.30am-6pm Mon-Fri, 8.30am-2pm Sat)

MUMBAI IN...

One Day
Start at the granddaddy of Mumbai's colonial giants, **Chhatrapati Shivaji Terminus** (CST, the old Victoria Terminus; p114). Stroll up to **Crawford Market** (p131) and into the maze of other, smaller bazaars here. Exhausted, rest and grab a bite at **Rajdhani** (p125), finishing off with a juice shake from **Badshah Snacks & Drinks** (p125).

Next, taxi it over to Malabar Hill's **Banganga Tank** (p116). Soak in the serenity, and cab it back to **Chowpatty Beach** (p115) for an ice cream at **Cream Centre** (p126). Be sure to pop into the wonderful **Mani Bhavan** (p116) museum dedicated to Gandhi while here.

Spend the late afternoon at the **Oval Maidan** (p113) for a spot of impromptu cricket. Don't forget to glance over at the grand edifices of the **High Court** (p113) and the **University of Mumbai** (p113). Next up is jumpin' Colaba and the **Gateway of India** (opposite), the **Taj Mahal Palace & Tower** (p112) and the colourful **Colaba Market** (opposite). You must be starving by now, so grab some tasty, street-side barbecue at **Bade Miya** (p124) or spoil yourself rotten at **Indigo** (p124). Finally, swap tall tales with fellow travellers over a beer at **Leopold Café & Bar** (p127).

Three Days
Make the trip out to **Elephanta Island** (p135), and spend the afternoon visiting the museums and galleries of **Kala Ghoda** (p113). In the evening, get up to Bandra district for a Goan feast at **Goa Portuguesa** (p126), followed by some seriously hip bar action at **Zenzi** (p128).

Another day could be spent visiting the **Dhobi Ghat** (p117) and the nearby **Mahalaxmi Temple** and **Haji Ali's Mosque** (p117). Spend the afternoon lazing at the **Mumbai Zoo** (p117) or pop into the inner-city enclave of **Kotachiwadi** (p115).

This busy but efficient office opposite Churchgate train station cheerfully provides tourist information for the entire country. Guides can be organised here, and it's the place to find out about the paying guest accommodation scheme (rooms cost around Rs 700 to 1500).
Government of India tourist office booths domestic airport (Map p123; ☎ 26156920; ☼ 7am-11pm); international airport (Map p123; ☎ 26829248; Arrival Hall 2A; ☼ 24hr)
Maharashtra Tourism Development Corporation booth (MTDC; Map p112; ☎ 22841877; Apollo Bunder; ☼ 10am-5pm) Near the Gateway of India. Purchase tickets here for the MTDC bus and boat tours of the city (p120).
MTDC reservation office (Map p114; ☎ 22027762; Madame Cama Rd, Nariman Point; ☼ 9.45am-5.30pm Mon-Sat) The head office of the MTDC gives some information on travel in Maharashtra and can book MTDC hotels throughout the state.

Travel Agencies
Agencies in Colaba tend to charge higher prices for flights, so it's best to go to the Fort area.
Akbar Travels (Map p114; ☼ 10am-7pm Mon-Sat) Reputable flight-booking agent with an army of computer-armed assistants.Opposite CST.
Magnum International Travel & Tours (Map p112; ☎ 22838628; 10 Henry Rd, Colaba) Handy for Colaba.
Thomas Cook (Map p114; ☎ 22048556; 324 Dr Dadabhai Naoroji Rd, Fort; ☼ 9.30am-6pm Mon-Sat) Efficient and reliable.

Visa Extensions
Foreigners' Regional Registration Office (FRRO; Map pp106-7; ☎ 22620111 ext 266; Annexe Bldg No 2, CID, 3rd fl, Sayed Badruddin Rd) Does not officially issue extensions on six-month tourist visas – even in emergencies they will direct you to Delhi (p486). However, some travellers have managed to procure an emergency extension here after a lot of waiting and persuasion.

SIGHTS
Most of the major tourist attractions are based in South Mumbai, though North Mumbai is an alternative accommodation base and home to several trendy bars and restaurants, particularly in the Juhu Beach and Bandra districts.

Colaba
For mapped locations of all the following sights, see Map p112.

The unofficial headquarters of Mumbai's tourist scene, Colaba sprawls down the city's southernmost peninsula. It's a bustling district packed with street stalls, markets, bars and budget to midrange lodgings. **Colaba**

MUMBAI BY NUMBERS

- Number of black taxis: about 40,000
- Population density: 29,000 people per square kilometre
- Average daily income: Rs 134 (US$2.90, or three times national average)
- Daily traffic passing through Chhattapati Shiraji Terminus (CST Victoria Terminus): 2.5 million people
- Percentage of people living in slums: 55%
- Number of Bollywood movies made since 1931: 67,000
- Proportion of Mumbai built on reclaimed land: 60%

Causeway (Shahid Bhagat Singh Marg) dissects the promontory and is the traffic-filled artery connecting Colaba's jumble of side streets and gently crumbling mansions.

Sassoon Dock, south of the main tourist action, is a scene of intense and pungent activity at dawn (around 5am) when colourfully clad Koli fisherwomen sort the catch unloaded from fishing boats at the quay. The fish drying in the sun are *bombil*, the fish used in the dish Bombay duck. Photography at the dock is forbidden without permission from the **Mumbai Port Trust** (☎ 56565656; www.mumbaiporttrust.com). While you're here, it's worth popping into the 1847 Church of St John the Evangelist, known as the **Afghan Church** (Map pp106–7, dedicated to British forces killed in the bloody 1838–43 First Afghan War.

During the more reasonable hours of the day, nearby **Colaba Market** (Lala Nigam St) has plenty of activity and colour and is lined with jewellery shops and fruit-and-veg stalls.

GATEWAY OF INDIA
This bold basalt arch of colonial triumph faces out to Mumbai Harbour at the tip of Apollo Bunder. Derived from the Islamic styles of 16th-century Gujarat, it was built to commemorate the 1911 royal visit of King George V. It was completed in 1924: ironically, the gateway's British architects used it just 24 years later to parade off their last British regiment, as India marched towards Independence.

These days, the gateway is a favourite gathering spot for locals and a top spot for

MUMBAI (BOMBAY)

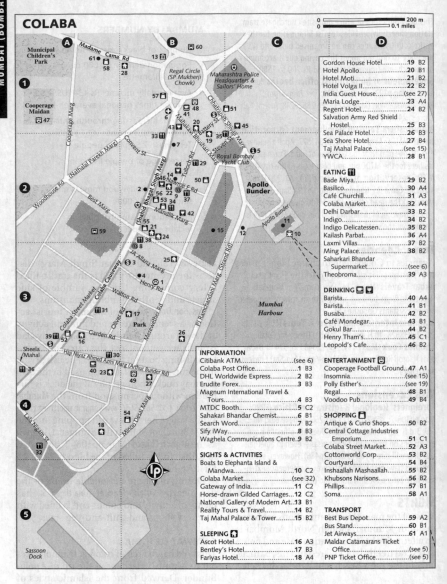

COLABA

0 ——————— 200 m
0 ——————— 0.1 miles

INFORMATION	
Citibank ATM	(see 6)
Colaba Post Office	1 B3
DHL Worldwide Express	2 B2
Erudite Forex	3 B3
Magnum International Travel & Tours	4 B3
MTDC Booth	5 C2
Sahakari Bhandar Chemist	6 B1
Search Word	7 B2
Sify iWay	8 B3
Waghela Communications Centre	9 B2

SIGHTS & ACTIVITIES	
Boats to Elephanta Island & Mandwa	10 C2
Colaba Market	(see 32)
Gateway of India	11 C2
Horse-drawn Gilded Carriages	12 C2
National Gallery of Modern Art	13 B1
Reality Tours & Travel	14 B2
Taj Mahal Palace & Tower	15 B2

SLEEPING	
Ascot Hotel	16 A3
Bentley's Hotel	17 B3
Fariyas Hotel	18 A4
Gordon House Hotel	19 B2
Hotel Apollo	20 B1
Hotel Moti	21 B2
Hotel Volga II	22 B2
India Guest House	(see 27)
Maria Lodge	23 A4
Regent Hotel	24 B2
Salvation Army Red Shield Hostel	25 B3
Sea Palace Hotel	26 B3
Sea Shore Hotel	27 B4
Taj Mahal Palace	(see 15)
YWCA	28 B1

EATING	
Bade Miya	29 B2
Basilico	30 A4
Café Churchill	31 A3
Colaba Market	32 A4
Delhi Darbar	33 B2
Indigo	34 B2
Indigo Delicatessen	35 B2
Kailash Parbat	36 A4
Laxmi Villas	37 B2
Ming Palace	38 B2
Saharkari Bhandar Supermarket	(see 6)
Theobroma	39 A3

DRINKING	
Barista	40 A4
Barista	41 B1
Busaba	42 B2
Café Mondegar	43 B1
Gokul Bar	44 B2
Henry Tham's	45 C1
Leopold's Cafe	46 B2

ENTERTAINMENT	
Cooperage Football Ground	47 A1
Insomnia	(see 15)
Polly Esther's	(see 19)
Regal	48 B1
Voodoo Pub	49 B4

SHOPPING	
Antique & Curio Shops	50 B2
Central Cottage Industries Emporium	51 C1
Colaba Street Market	52 A3
Cottonworld Corp	53 B2
Courtyard	54 B4
Inshaallah Mashaallah	55 B2
Khubsons Narisons	56 B2
Phillips	57 B1
Soma	58 A1

TRANSPORT	
Best Bus Depot	59 A2
Bus Stand	60 B1
Jet Airways	61 A1
Maldar Catamarans Ticket Office	(see 5)
PNP Ticket Office	(see 5)

people-watching. Giant-balloon sellers, photographers, beggars and touts rub shoulders with Indian and foreign tourists, creating all the hubbub of a bazaar. Boats depart from the gateway's wharfs for Elephanta Island and Mandwa.

You can ride in a Victoria – one of the **horse-drawn gilded carriages** that ply their trade along Apollo Bunder. Get them to go around the Oval Maidan at night so you can admire the illuminated buildings – it should cost Rs 300 if you bargain. Hard.

TAJ MAHAL PALACE & TOWER
This sumptuous hotel (see p124) is a fairy-tale blend of Islamic and Renaissance styles

jostling for prime position among Mumbai's famous landmarks. Facing the harbour, it was built in 1903 by the Parsi industrialist JN Tata, supposedly after he was refused entry to one of the European hotels on account of being 'a native'. The Palace side has a magnificent grand stairway that's well worth a quick peek, even if you can't afford to stay or enjoy a drink or meal at one of its several restaurants and bars.

Kala Ghoda

Kala Ghoda, the area wedged between Colaba and the Fort, contains most of Mumbai's main galleries and museums alongside a wealth of colonial buildings. The best way to see these buildings is on a guided (p119) or self-guided (p118) walking tour.

CHHATRAPATI SHIVAJI MAHARAJ VASTU SANGRAHALAYA (PRINCE OF WALES MUSEUM)

Mumbai's biggest and best **museum** (Map p114; ☎ 22844519; K Dubash Marg; Indian/foreigner Rs 10/300, camera/video Rs 30/200; ❂ 10.15am-6pm Tue-Sun), this domed behemoth is an intriguing hodgepodge of Islamic, Hindu and British architecture displaying a mix of dusty exhibits from all over India. Opened in 1923 to commemorate King George V's first visit to India (back in 1905, while he was Prince of Wales), its flamboyant Indo-Saracenic style was designed by George Wittet – who also did the Gateway of India.

The vast collection inside includes impressive Hindu and Buddhist sculpture, terracotta figurines from the Indus Valley, miniature paintings, porcelain and some particularly vicious weaponry. There's also a natural-history section with suitably stuffed animals. Take advantage of the free, multilanguage audioguides as not everything is labelled.

Foreign students with a valid International Student Identity Card (ISIC) can get in for a bargain Rs 6.

GALLERIES

The **National Gallery of Modern Art** (Map p112; ☎ 22881969-70; MG Rd; Indian/foreigner Rs 10/150; ❂ 11am-6pm Tue-Sun) has a bright, spacious and modern exhibition space showcasing changing exhibitions by Indian and international artists. Nearby, **Jehangir Art Gallery** (Map p114; ☎ 22048212; 161B MG Rd; admission free; ❂ 11am-7pm) is one of Mumbai's principal commercial galleries, hosting interesting weekly shows by

Indian artists; most works are for sale. Rows of hopeful local artists often display their work on the pavement outside.

KENESETH ELIYAHOO SYNAGOGUE

Built in 1884, this impossibly sky-blue **synagogue** (Map p114; ☎ 2283 1502; Dr VB Gandhi Marg) still functions and is tenderly maintained by the city's dwindling Jewish community. One of two built in the city by the Sassoon family (the other is in Byculla), the interior is wonderfully adorned with colourful pillars, chandeliers and stained-glass windows – best viewed in the afternoons when rainbows of light shaft through.

Fort Area

For mapped locations of the following sights see Map p114.

Lined up in a row and vying for your attention with aristocratic pomp, many of Mumbai's majestic Victorian buildings pose on the edge of **Oval Maidan**. This land, and the **Cross** and **Azad Maidans** immediately to the north, was on the seafront in those days, and this series of grandiose structures faced west directly onto the Arabian Sea. The reclaimed land along the western edge of the maidans is now lined with a remarkable collection of Art Deco apartment blocks. Spend some time in the Oval Maidan admiring these structures and enjoying the casual cricket matches.

HIGH COURT

A hive of daily activity, packed with judges, barristers and other cogs in the Indian justice system, the **High Court** (Eldon Rd) is an elegant 1848 neogothic building. The design was inspired by a German castle and was obviously intended to dispel any doubts about the authority of the justice dispensed inside, though local stone carvers presumably saw things differently: they carved a one-eyed monkey fiddling with the scales of justice on one pillar. It's permitted (and highly recommended) to walk around inside and check out the pandemonium and pageantry of public cases in progress.

UNIVERSITY OF MUMBAI

Looking like a 15th-century French-Gothic masterpiece plopped incongruously among Mumbai's palm trees, this university on Bhaurao Patil Marg, still commonly known as Bombay University, was designed by Gilbert Scott of London's St Pancras Station fame.

It's possible to take a peek inside both the exquisite **University Library** and **Convocation Hall** but the 80m-high **Rajabai Clock Tower**, decorated with detailed carvings, is off limits.

ST THOMAS' CATHEDRAL

Recently restored to its former glory, this charming cathedral on Veer Nariman Rd is the oldest English building standing in Mumbai (construction began in 1672, though it remained unfinished until 1718). The cathedral is an interracial marriage of Byzantine and colonial architecture and it's airy, white-washed interior is full of exhibitionist colonial memorials. A look at some of the gravestones reveals many colonists died very young of malaria.

CHHATRAPATI SHIVAJI TERMINUS (VICTORIA TERMINUS)

Imposing, exuberant and overflowing with people, this is the city's most extravagant Gothic building, the beating heart of its railway network, and an aphorism for colonial India. Historian Christopher London uttered 'the Victoria Terminus is to the British Raj, what the Taj Mahal is to the Mughal empire.' It's a meringue of Victorian, Hindu and Islamic styles whipped into an imposing, Dalíesque structure of buttresses, domes, turrets, spires and stained-glass windows. Be sure to get close to the jungle-themed façade, particularly around the reservation office: it's adorned with peacocks, gargoyles, cheeky monkeys and lions.

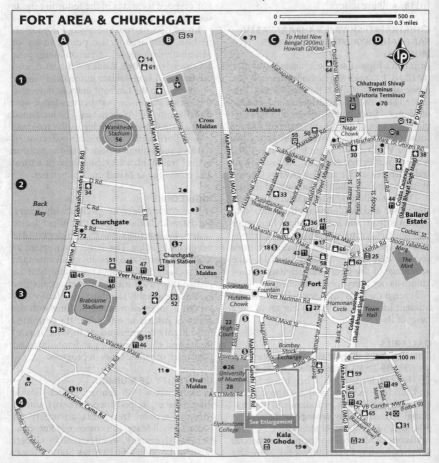

FORT AREA & CHURCHGATE

Designed by Frederick Stevens, it was completed in 1887, 34 years after the first train in India left this site. Today it's the busiest train station in Asia. Officially renamed Chhatrapati Shivaji Terminus (CST) in 1998, it's still better known locally as VT. It was added to the Unesco World Heritage list in 2004.

MONETARY MUSEUM

While you're in the area, it's worth popping into this tiny and thoughtfully-presented **museum** (☎ 22614043; www.museum.rbi.in; Amar Bldg, Sir P Metha Marg; admission Rs 10; ☽ 11am-5pm), run by the Reserve Bank of India. It's an engrossing historical tour of India through coinage: from early concepts of cash, to the first coins of 600 BC, through Indo-European influences, right up to today's Gandhi-covered notes. Also on display is the world's smallest coin, probably found in the crack of an ancient couch.

Marine Drive & Chowpatty Beach

For mapped locations of the following sights see Map pp106–7.

Built on land reclaimed from Back Bay in 1920, **Marine Drive** (Netaji Subhashchandra Bose Rd) arcs along the shore of the Arabian Sea from Nariman Point past Chowpatty Beach (where it's called Chowpatty Seaface) to the foot of Malabar Hill. Lined with flaking Art Deco apartments, this is one Mumbai's most popular promenades and sunset-watching spots. It's twinkling night-time lights earned it the nickname 'the Queen's Necklace'.

Chowpatty Beach remains a favourite evening spot for courting couples, families, political rallies and anyone out to enjoy what passes for fresh air. Eating an evening time *bhelpuri* (crisp fried thin rounds of dough mixed with puffed rice, lentils, lemon juice, onions, herbs and chutney) at the throng of stalls found here is an essential part of the Mumbai experience. Forget about visiting during the day for a dip: the water is toxic.

Kotachiwadi

For mapped locations of the following sights see Mappp106–7.

This *wadi* (hamlet) is a bastion clinging onto Mumbai life as it was before cement trucks and high-rises. A Christian enclave of 30-odd elegant, two-storey wooden mansions, it's 500m northeast of Chowpatty, lying amid Mumbai's predominantly Hindu and Muslim neighbourhoods. These winding laneways allow a wonderful glimpse into a quiet life free of rickshaws and taxis. To find it, aim for **St Teresa's Church** on the corner of Jagannath Shankarsheth Marg and RR Roy Marg (Charni Rd) then duck into the warren of streets directly opposite. Guided walks of the area are occasionally organised by Bombay Heritage Walks (p119).

INFORMATION		
Akbar Travels	1	D2
Alliance Française	2	B2
American Information Resource Centre	3	B2
Blue Dart	4	B3
Bombay Hospital	5	B1
Cyber Online	6	C2
DHL Worldwide Express	(see 37)	
Government of India Tourist Office	7	B3
Main Post Office	8	D2
Max Mueller Bhavan	9	D4
MTDC Reservation Office	10	A4
Oxford Bookstore	11	B4
Parcel Office (Main Post Office)	12	D1
Parcel-wallahs	13	D2
Royal Chemists	14	B1
Sify iWay	15	B3
Standard Chartered Bank	16	C3
Standard Supply Co	(see 30)	
Strand Book Stall	17	C3
Thomas Cook	18	C3

SIGHTS & ACTIVITIES		
Bombay Natural History Society	19	C4
Chhatrapati Shivaji Maharaj Vastu Sangrahalaya (Prince of Wales Museum)	20	C4
Chhatrapati Shivaji Terminus (Victoria Terminus)	21	D1
High Court	22	C3
Jehangir Art Gallery	23	D4
Keneseth Eliyahoo Synagogue	24	D4
Monetary Museum	25	D3
Rajabai Clock Tower	26	C4

St Thomas' Cathedral	27	C3
University of Mumbai	28	C4

SLEEPING 🏠		
Astoria Hotel	29	B3
Hotel City Palace	30	D2
Hotel Lawrence	31	D4
Hotel Oasis	32	D2
Hotel Outram	33	C2
Intercontinental	34	A2
Marine Plaza	35	A3
Residency Hotel	36	C2
Sea Green Hotel	37	A3
Sea Green South Hotel	(see 37)	
Welcome Hotel	38	D2
West End Hotel	39	B1

EATING 🍴		
210°C	(see 46)	
Gaylord	40	A3
Ideal Corner	41	C2
Khyber	42	D4
Mahesh Lunch Home	43	C3
Mocambo Café & Bar	(see 43)	
National Hindu Hotel	44	D2
Pizzeria	45	A3
Relish	(see 46)	
Samrat	46	B3
Suryodaya	47	B3
Tea Centre	48	B3
Trishna	49	D4

DRINKING 🍷		
Barista	50	C1

Cha Bar	(see 11)	
Dome	(see 34)	
Mocha Bar	51	A3
Samovar Café	(see 23)	

ENTERTAINMENT 🎭		
Eros	52	B3
Metro	53	B1
Not Just Jazz By The Bay	(see 45)	
Red Light	54	D4
Sterling	55	C2
Wankhede Stadium	56	B2

SHOPPING 🛍		
Bombay Paperie	57	C4
Bombay Store	58	C3
Fabindia	59	D4
Fashion Street Market	60	C2
Kala Niketan	61	B1
Kashmir Government Arts Emporium	62	D3
Khadi & Village Industries Emporium	63	C2
Planet M	64	D1
Rhythm House	65	D4
Uttar Pradesh Handicrafts Emporium	66	D3

TRANSPORT		
Air India	67	A4
British Airways	68	B3
Bus Stand	69	D1
Central Railways Reservation Centre	70	D1
Indian Airlines	(see 67)	
Private Buses to Goa & Bus Agents	71	C1
Virgin Atlantic	72	A2
Western Railways Reservation Centre	(see 7)	

Malabar Hill

For mapped locations of the following sights see Map pp106–7.

Mumbai's most exclusive neighbourhood of sky-scratchers and private palaces, **Malabar Hill** is at the northern promontory of Back Bay and signifies the top rung for the city's social and economic climbers.

Surprisingly, one of Mumbai's most sacred and tranquil oases lies concealed among apartment blocks at its southern tip. **Banganga Tank** is a precinct of serene temples, bathing pilgrims, meandering, traffic-free streets and picturesque old *dharamsalas* (pilgrims rest houses). The wooden pole in the centre of the tank is the centre of the earth – according to legend Lord Ram created the tank by piercing the earth with his arrow. The classical music **Banganga Festival** is held here in January.

The lush and well-tended **Hanging Gardens** (Pherozeshah Mehta Gardens) on top of the hill are a pleasant but often crowded place for a stroll. For some of the best views of the Chowpatty Beach and the graceful arc of Marine Dr, be sure to visit the smaller **Kamala Nehru Park**, opposite. It's popular with coy courting couples and there's a two storey 'boot house' and colourful animal decorations that the kiddies might like.

Kemp's Corner & Mahalaxmi

For mapped locations of the following sights see Map pp106–7.

MANI BHAVAN

As poignant as it is tiny, this **museum** (☎ 2380 5864; 19 Laburnum Rd; admission free; 🕙 10am-6pm) is housed in the building in which Mahatma

---

BOLLYWOOD

History

Mumbai is the glittering epicentre of India's gargantuan Hindi-language film industry. From silent beginnings with a cast of all-male actors (some in drag) in the 1913 epic *Raja Haishchandra*, to the first talkie in 1931 *Lama Ara*, today the industry churns out more than 900 films a year – more than any other city in the world (yes, Hollywood included). Not surprising considering they have one-sixth of the world's population as a captive audience, as well as a sizable NonResident Indian (NRI) following.

Regional film industries exist in other parts of India, but Bollywood continues to entrance the nation with its winning, escapist formula of masala entertainment – where all-singing, all-dancing good-guys battle evil protagonists (moustache optional) in a never-ending quest for true love. These days, Hollywood-inspired thrillers and over-the-top action extravaganzas vie for moviegoer attentions alongside the more family-orientated saccharine formulas.

Bollywood stars have been known to attain near godlike status in the minds of Indian moviegoers. Their faces plaster advertisement boards the length of the country, and Bollywood star-spotting is a favourite pastime in Mumbai's posher establishments (see boxed text, p128).

Extra, Extra!

Studios often look for extras for background scenes and sometimes need Westerners to add that extra whiff of international flair to a film. Getting a part, though, is a matter of luck. When extras are required the studios usually send scouts down to Colaba, often around the Gateway of India, to conscript travellers for the following day's shooting. You receive between Rs 500 and 1000 for a day's work, but it's clearly not something you do for the money. It can be a long, hot day standing around on the set, without promised food and water; others have described the behind-the-scenes peek as a fascinating experience. Before agreeing to be an extra, always ask for identification from the person who has approached you.

Tours

Though overpriced, **Bollywood Tourism** (☎ 26609909; www.bollywoodtourism.com; child/adult US$75/100) is the only agency so far that offers Bollywood tours. Tours visit the BollywooDrome (a special set showcasing dance sequences and stunts) and take a peek behind the scenes at the shooting of a live Bollywood film – there's always one on somewhere. Lunch is included.

Gandhi stayed during his visits to Bombay from 1917 to 1934. Dedicated to this amazingly insightful leader, the museum showcases the simple room where Gandhi formulated his philosophy of satyagraha (truth, nonviolence and self sacrifice) and launched the 1932 Civil Disobedience campaign that led to the end of British rule. There are rooms showcasing a photographic record of his life, along with dioramas and original documents such as letters he wrote to Adolf Hitler and Franklin D Roosevelt. Nearby August Kranti Maidan is where the campaign to persuade the British to 'Quit India' was launched in 1942.

MAHALAXMI DHOBI GHAT
If you've had washing done in Mumbai, chances are your clothes have already paid a visit to this 136-year-old dhobi ghat (place where clothes are washed). The whole hamlet is Mumbai's oldest and biggest human-powered washing machine: every day hundreds of people beat the dirt out of thousands of kilograms of soiled Mumbai clothes in 1026 open-air troughs. The best view, and photo opportunity, is from the bridge across the railway tracks near Mahalaxmi train station (Map pp106–7).

MAHALAXMI TEMPLE
It's only fitting that in money-mad Mumbai one of the busiest and most colourful temples is dedicated to Mahalaxmi, the goddess of wealth. Perched on a headland, it's the focus for Mumbai's **Navratri** (Festival of Nine Nights) celebrations in September/October. After paying your respects to the goddess, climb down the steps towards the shore and snack on tasty *gota bhaji* (fried lentil balls) at the cliffside Laxmi Bhajiya House.

HAJI ALI'S MOSQUE
Floating like a sacred mirage off the coast, this mosque is one of Mumbai's most striking shrines. Built in the 19th century, it contains the tomb of the Muslim saint Haji – legend has it that Haji Ali died while on a pilgrimage to Mecca and his casket miraculously floated back to this spot. A long concrete causeway reaches into the Arabian Sea, providing access to the mosque. Thousands of pilgrims cross it to make their visit, many donating to the beggars who line the way; but at high tide, water covers the causeway and the mosque becomes an island.

MUMBAI ZOO
Mumbai's **zoo** (Map pp106-7; ☎ 23725799; Victoria Gardens; adult/child Rs 5/2; ☺ 9am-6pm Thu-Tue) is remarkably well-maintained. Set in the sprawling and lush grounds of Victoria Gardens, it's worth visiting not least for its green hillocks, shady grassy bits and soundtrack of birds chirping in place of cars honking. The animals are a little few and far between, with the few local species in large cages including crocs, elephants, rhinos and a few bored lions. There's a small playground, and it's generally a popular place for families and couples to meander.

North Mumbai
NEHRU CENTRE & NEHRU PLANETARIUM
The most striking thing about this **cultural complex** (Dr Annie Besant Rd, Worli), which includes a decent **planetarium** (☎ 24920510; adult/child Rs 40/20; ☺ English show 3pm Tue-Sun) and the serpentine-but-interesting history exhibition **Discovery of India** (admission free; ☺ 11am-5pm) is the bold modern architecture of the buildings. The tower looks like a giant cylindrical pineapple, the planetarium a UFO. There's a theatre here too (see p129).

ACTIVITIES
Horse Riding
The **Amateur Riders' Club** (Map pp106-7; ☎ 5600 5204-5; Mahalaxmi Racecourse) has horse rides for Rs 500 per 30 minutes; escorts cost Rs 250 extra.

Swimming
Despite the heat don't be tempted by the lure of Back Bay, or even the open sea at Chowpatty; the water is filthy. If you want to swim and aren't staying at a luxury hotel, Fariyas Hotel (p122) in Colaba has a tiny terrace pool (Rs 500 for nonguests).

Water Sports
H2O Water Sports Complex (Map pp106-7; ☎ 236 77546; info@h2osports.biz; Marine Dr, Mafatlal Beach; ☺ 10am-10pm Oct-Apr) on the southeast side of Chowpatty Beach rents out jet skis (Rs 950 per 10 minutes) and speed boats (per person per hour Rs 175, minimum four people) or kayaks (per hour Rs 300). It also holds sailing and windsurfing classes and rents fresh-water (river) kayaks.

Outbound Adventure (☎ 26315019, www.outbound adventure.com) runs one-day rafting trips on the Ullas River near Karjat, 88km southeast of Mumbai, from the end of June to early September (Rs 1000 per person). After a good rain rapids can get up to Grade III+, though usually the rafting is much calmer.

WALKING TOUR

Mumbai's distinctive mix of colonial and Art Deco architecture is one of its defining features. This walk takes you past many of the city's key buildings and is a great way to spend anything from a few hours to a whole day. Pick up the guidebook *Fort Walks* at most major bookshops if you wish to explore further.

Starting from the **Gateway of India** (1; p111) walk up Shavaji Marg past the members-only colonial relic **Royal Bombay Yacht Club (2)** on one side and the Art Deco residential-commercial complex **Dhunraj Mahal (3)** on the other towards **Regal Circle (4**; SP Mukherji Chowk). Dodge the traffic to reach the car park in the middle of the circle for the best view of the surrounding buildings, including the old **Sailors Home (5)**, which dates from 1876 and is now the Maharashtra Police Headquarters, the Art Deco cinema **Regal (6**; p129) and the old **Majestic Hotel (7)**, now the Sahakari Bhandar cooperative store.

Continue up MG Rd, past the beautifully restored façade of the **Institute of Science (8)**. Opposite is the **Chhatrapati Shivaji Maharaj Vastu Sangrahalaya (9**; Prince of Wales Museum; p113); step into the front gardens to admire this grand building. Back across the road is the 'Romanesque Transitional' **Elphinstone College (10)** and the inviting **David Sassoon Library (11)**, a good place to escape the heat of the day lazing on planters' chairs on the upper balcony.

Cross back over to Forbes St to visit the **Keneseth Eliyahoo Synagogue (12**; p113) before returning to MG Rd and continuing north along the left-hand side so you can admire the vertical Art Deco stylings of the **New India Assurance Company Building (13)**. In a traffic island ahead lies the pretty **Flora Fountain (14)**, named after the Roman goddess of abundance, and erected in 1869 in honour of Sir Bartle Frere, the Bombay governor responsible for dismantling the fort.

Turn east down Veer Nariman Rd walking towards **St Thomas' Cathedral (15**; p114). Ahead lies the stately **Horniman Circle (16)**, an arcaded ring of buildings laid out in the 1860s around a circular and beautifully kept botanical garden. The circle is overlooked from the east by the neoclassical **Town Hall (17)**, which contains the regally decorated members-only Asiatic Society of Bombay Library and Mumbai's State Central Library.

Start	Gateway of India
Finish	Churchgate train station
Distance	2.5km
Duration	3 hours minimum

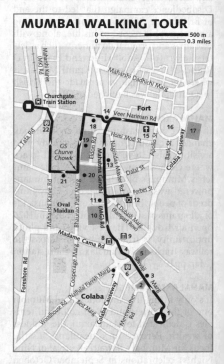

MUMBAI WALKING TOUR

Retrace your steps back to Flora Fountain and continue west past the Venetian Gothic-style **State Public Works Department (18)**. Turn south onto Bhaurao Patil Marg to see the august **High Court (19**; p113) and the equally venerable and ornately decorated **University of Mumbai (20**; p113). The façades of both buildings are best observed from within the **Oval Maidan (21)**. Turn around to compare the colonial edifices with the row of Art Deco beauties lining Maharshi Karve (MK) Rd, culminating in the wedding cake tower of the **Eros Cinema (22)**. End your walk at Churchgate station.

COURSES
Yoga

For serious students, yoga courses are held at the **Kaivalyadhama Ishwardas Yogic Health Centre**

(Map pp106-7; ☎ 22818417; www.kdham.com; 43 Marine Dr, Chowpatty; ☼ 6.30-10am & 3.30-7pm Mon-Sat). Fees are a minimum Rs 300 (students Rs 220), plus Rs 400 extra for a monthly membership, and you are expected to attend a one-hour class, six days a week for at least three months.

The **Yoga Institute** (Map p123; ☎ 26122185; www .yogainstitute.org; Prabhat Colony, Shri Yogendra Marg, Santa Cruz) offers classes, some free, others from Rs 300/200 during your first/second month. The **Yoga Studio** (Map pp106-7; ☎ 24538852; 1st fl Delstar Bldg, 9-9A Patkar Marg, Kemp's Corner), recently opened by director Neetu Watamull, also has drop-in classes (Rs 150) in varying yoga styles with knowledgeable instructors. Monthly rates are Rs 1200.

Language

Professor Shukla is based at **Bharatiya Vidya Bhavan** (Map pp106-7; ☎ 23871860, 24968466; Dr K M Munshi Chowk, Sitaram Patkar Rd, Chowpatty), behind Wilson College, and offers private Hindi, Marathi and Sanskrit classes (Rs 500 per hour). Contact this worldly octogenarian directly to arrange a syllabus and class schedule to suit your needs.

MUMBAI FOR CHILDREN

Here are a few sure-fire recommendations on how to entertain the little darlings while in Mumbai.

For little tykes with energy to burn, visit **Esselworld** (Map p105; ☎ 28452222; Gorai Island, Borivali; admission adult/child Rs 325/260; ☼ 11am-7pm) amusement park and **Water Kingdom** (☎ 28452310; admission Rs 340/270) next door. Both are well-maintained and clean, offer lots of rides, slides and have plenty of shade. It's a Rs 20 ferry ride from Marve Jetty near Malad.

Knock off a few pins at the **Bowling Company** (☎ 24914000; www.thebowlingcompany.com; High Street Phoenix, S B Marg, Lower Parel West; games Rs 59-199; ☼ 11am-11pm daily) or take a trip in one of the **horse-drawn gilded carriages** (p112) that ply their trade along Apollo Bunder.

For a little more education with their recreation, several museums have kid-friendly exhibits, including **Prince of Wales Museum** (p113) with lots of stuffed animals, and **Mani Bhavan** (p116) with fascinating dioramas of Gandhi's life.

The **Mumbai Zoo** (p117) may be a little low on animals, but has lots of tidy and lush grounds as well as several kids' play areas. The **Taraporewala Aquarium** (Map pp106-7; ☎ 22082061; Chowpatty Beach; adult/child Rs 15/10; ☼ 10am-7pm Tue-Sun) is a little sadder, with mostly unsigned, murky tanks. Kids still seem to dig it anyway.

TOURS

The best city tours are offered by **Bombay Heritage Walks** (☎ 23690992, 26835856; www.bombayherit agewalks.com), which is run by two enthusiastic female architects. There's often a monthly public Sunday walk (adult/student Rs 100/50) lasting no more than a couple of hours; otherwise private guided tours are Rs 2500 for up to five people.

Transway International (☎ 26146854; transintl@vsnl .com; ☼ 8am-8pm) runs a Bombay by night tour (US$25) which includes the major sites, an

---

THE PARSI CONNECTION

Mumbai has a strong – but diminishing – Parsi community. The Parsis (descendants of Persian Zoroastrians who first migrated to India after persecution by the Muslims in the 7th century) settled in Bombay in the 17th and 18th centuries. They proved astute businesspeople, enjoyed a privileged relationship with the British colonial powers, and became a very powerful community in their own right while managing to remain aloof from politics.

With the departure of the British, the influence of the Parsis waned in Mumbai, although they continued to own land and established trusts and estates, or colonies, built around their temples, where many of the city's 60,000-plus Parsis still live.

Perhaps the most famous aspect of the Zoroastrian religion is its funerary methods. Parsis hold fire, earth and water sacred and do not cremate or bury their dead. Instead, the corpses are laid out within towers – known as Towers of Silence – to be picked clean by vultures. In Mumbai the Parsi Tower of Silence is on Malabar Hill (although it's strictly off limits to sightseers). But traditions are being eroded by a shortage of vultures around the city, due mainly to urban growth and pollution which has driven the birds away. This has meant that the Parsis have sometimes had to resort to artificially speeding up the natural decomposition of their dead with solar-powered heaters or chemical methods.

arts performance and a drop-off at the night club of your choice.

MTDC (p110) runs uninspiring **bus tours** of the city (Rs 150; Tuesday to Sunday) and one-hour open-deck bus tours of illuminated heritage buildings (Rs 90, weekdays/weekends 7pm/8:30pm). All depart from and can be booked near Apollo Bunder. More enjoyable are the 45-minute boat tours of the bay by night (Rs 60 to 75, between 5:30pm and 9pm) that also run from here. H20 (see p117) also arranges 45-minute day (Rs 180 per person, minimum six people) and night (Rs 280, between 7pm and 10pm) cruises.

The Government of India tourist office (p110) can arrange **multilingual guides** (per half-/full day Rs 350/500). Guides using a foreign language other than English are an extra Rs 180.

Cruises on Mumbai Harbour are a good way to escape the city and offer the chance to see the Gateway of India as it was intended. Short ferry rides (one hour) cost Rs 30 and depart from the Gateway of India.

If you want to do a cruise in luxury, hire the **Taj Yacht** (up to 12 people per hour Rs 12,000); contact the Taj Mahal Palace & Tower (p124) for details.

SLEEPING

You may need to recalibrate your budget upon arrival; Mumbai has the most expensive accommodation in India. Anything under Rs 1000 a double is considered budget here, while midrange options go up to Rs 7000. During the hectic Christmas and Diwali season you may be hard pressed to find a room.

Colaba is compact, has the liveliest foreigner scene and many of the budget and midrange options. The fort area is more spread-out and convenient to sights and the main train stations (CST and Churchgate). Most of the top-end places are dotted around the international and domestic airports, with a smattering of up-market hotels in the Juhu Beach area, convenient for visits to the trendy Bandra district.

To stay with a local family in the city, contact the Government of India tourist office (p110) for a list of homes participating in Mumbai's paying guest scheme. There's a **hotel reservation desk** (☎ 26164790; ☿ 24hr) in the arrivals hall of the domestic and international airports which can book hotels and arrange transfers.

Budget

Apart from Colaba and Fort there are some budget hotels in Vile Parle, a middle-class suburb adjoining the domestic airport, but they are fairly grotty and you'd be better off camping out at the airport for the night if needs be.

COLABA

For mapped locations of the following venues see Map p112.

Salvation Army Red Shield Hostel (☎ 22841824; 30 Mereweather Rd; dm with breakfast Rs 150, d/tr with full board Rs 600/897) This rock-bottom-priced hostel is a Mumbai institution popular with budget travellers counting every rupee. The large, ascetic dorms are reasonably clean, though bed bugs make the odd cameo appearance. It can fill up fast – come just after the 9am kick-out to ensure a spot as there are no reservations. Lockers are available for Rs 15 a day.

Sea Shore Hotel (☎ 22874237; 4th fl, Kamal Mansion, 1 Arthur Bunder Rd; s/d with shared bathroom Rs 375/400, s/d Rs 450/500) At the top of a building housing several budget guesthouses, the neat, intimate and friendly atmosphere makes up for shoe-box-sized rooms. It's worth paying that bit extra for a windowed room with harbour views. On the floor below, India Guest House (☎ 22833769; doubles with shared bathroom Rs 350 to 400) is an OK backup option, but a little low on charm.

Maria Lodge (☎ 22854081, 5/2 Grand Bldg, Arthur Bunder Rd; d without/with AC Rs 400/600; ✖) A sprightly contender in the Colaba budget accommodation race, Maria's rooms may be Lilliputian, but each comes with it's own tiny bathroom and is kept ridiculously clean. The staff gets the thumbs up from travellers for big smiles and helpful advice.

Hotel Volga II (☎ 22885341; 1st fl, Rustam Manzil, Nawroji F Rd; s/d with shared bathroom Rs 500/600, d Rs 700, d AC & TV Rs 1000; ✖) Someone went on a white-tile rampage in this small, ramshackle establishment. It's clean enough and will do the job if other cheapies are full.

YWCA (☎ 22025053; www.ywcaic.info; 18 Madame Cama Rd; dm/s Rs 652/750, s/d with AC Rs 871/1655; ✖) This well-run place has spacious four-bed dorm rooms, which are a good deal considering rates include buffet breakfast and dinner. Other rooms are small but tidy, and they accept both men and women.

ourpick Bentley's Hotel (☎ 22841474; www .bentleyshotel.com; 17 Oliver Rd; d incl breakfast & tax Rs 865-1600; ✖) Bentley's wins the accolade for 'most charming budget option' yet another year running. Spread out over several buildings on Oliver St and nearby Henry Rd, all rooms are spotless and come with TV and optional AC (Rs 220 extra). Look at a few rooms as they come in dozens of sizes and flavours: the most expensive have colonial furniture and sweeping balconies overlooking a garden (rooms 31 and 21), while the cheaper options on Henry Rd are a bit noisier. Reservations recommended.

FORT AREA
For mapped locations of the following venues see Map p114.

Hotel New Bengal (☎ 23401951; Sitaram Bldg, Dr Dadabhai Naoroji Rd; s/d with shared bathroom from Rs 285/425, s/d with bathroom from Rs 650/700; ☒) This Bengali-run hotel occupies a rambling, maze-like building perennially buzzing with Indian businessmen. Rooms, slightly aged but tidy, are an excellent deal. Look at a few, as some have lots of natural light while others flirt with pokiness. It's right in the CST/Crawford Market area.

Hotel Lawrence (☎ 22843618; 3rd fl, ITTS House, 33 Sai Baba Marg; s/d/tr with shared bathroom incl breakfast & tax Rs 400/500/700) Once you get past the ominous-looking, red *paan* (mixture of betel but and leaves for chewing)–stained stairwell (à la B-grade slasher flick), be ready to be pleasantly

surprised by basic, clean rooms and affable management. The foyer has fun, original '70s styling and the location can't be beat.

Hotel Outram (☎ 22094937; Marzaban Rd; small s/d with shared bathroom Rs 468/572, d with AC & bathroom Rs 1195; ☒) This plain but superfriendly place is in a quiet spot between CST and the maidans. Rooms with private bathroom are fairly clean but low on natural light.

Welcome Hotel (☎ 66314488; welcome_hotel@vsnl .com; 257 Colaba Causeway; s/d with shared bathroom from Rs 650/900, s/d from Rs 1000/1400; ☒) With a boggling array of single/double/bathroom/AC combinations, this fastidiously cared-for, marble-coated budget hotel boasts a foyer that adds some much-needed class to the budget category. The top floor rooms are very bright and have awesome views of CST.

Hotel City Palace (☎ 22615515; www.hotelcity palace.net; 121 City Tce, W Hirachand Marg; economy s/d from Rs 675/875, larger s/d from Rs 750/950; ☒) The rather cramped rooms are spotlessly clean and quiet, surprising given its location opposite rowdy CST. A do-able option if you're only in Mumbai for a night or two.

Hotel Oasis (☎ 22697887; www.hoteloasisindia.com; 276 Colaba Causeway; r Rs 780, with AC Rs 1065; ☒) This modern and fun-coloured skinny little hotel is a stone's throw from CST and has spick-and-span rooms, all with TV. Beware that

---

DHARAVI SLUM

An astonishing 55% of Mumbai's population live in shantytowns and slums, and the largest slum in Mumbai, and in all of Asia, is Dharavi.

Established in 1933 atop reclaimed marshland, it incorporates 1.7 sq km sandwiched between Mumbai's two major railway lines and is home to more than one million people. While it may look a bit shambled from the outside, the maze of dusty alleys and sewer-lined streets of this city-within-a-city are actually a collection of abutting settlements. In each part of the slum inhabitants from different parts of India, and with different trades, have set up homes and tiny factories. Potters from Saurasthra live in one area, Muslim tanners in another, embroidery workers from Uttar Pradesh work alongside metal-smiths, while other workers recycle plastics as women dry pappadams in the searing sun. Some of these thriving industries even export their wares: the annual turnover of business from Dharavi is thought to top US$650 million.

Up close, life in the slums seems strikingly normal. Residents pay rent, most houses have kitchens and electricity, and building materials range from flimsy corrugated-iron shacks to permanent, multistorey concrete structures.

Insightful tours of Dharavi are run by **Reality Tours & Travel** (Map p112; ☎ 9820822253; www .realitytoursandtravel.com; Unique Business Centre; 1st fl, Nawroji F Rd, Colaba), allowing you to gain a glimpse into this microcosm of Mumbai life. Tours cost Rs 300/600 by train/car and last 2½ hours to 4½ hours, photography is strictly forbidden and a significant part of the profits go to a Dharavi-based NGO.

Visits to such economically depressed areas can be a sensitive issue, and as a visitor you will need to make up your own mind whether to go at all. If you decide to use a tour company, do your research beforehand and make sure they adhere to ethically sound principles.

the singles are so small you can touch all four walls lying in bed.

Midrange
COLABA

For mapped locations of the following venues see Map p112.

Hotel Moti (☎ 22025714; hotelmotiinternational@yahoo .co.in; 10 Best Marg; s/d from Rs 1500/2000; 🟦) Occupying the ground floor of a gracefully crumbling colonial building, the rooms are a tad plain and shadowy, but absolutely huge and have some nice surprises – such as the ornate stucco ceilings. This place gets positive reports for friendliness.

Hotel Apollo (☎ 22873312; h.apollo@gmail.com; cnr Battery St & Mahakavi Bhushan Marg; s Rs 1850, d Rs 2300-2900; 🟦) Fresh from a trendy modern facelift, the rooms are simple and modestly sized but kept in mint condition and have 'party' showers big enough for two. Some doubles come with a bathtub.

Regent Hotel (☎ 22871853-4; www.regentho telcolaba.com; 8 Best Marg; s/d incl breakfast & tax Rs 2600/2750; 🟦 🖳) This stylish, Arabian-flavoured hotel has marble surfaces a-plenty and an attractive 1st-floor café serving Middle Eastern–style tea. Rooms are comfortable with enclosed balconies.

Sea Palace Hotel (☎ 22841828; www.seapalacehotel .com; 26 PJ Ramchandani Marg; s/d from Rs 1700/3000; 🟦) This freshly renovated property has lots of modern rooms that are heavy on glitz but light on personality. The pricier rooms with sea-views are worth splurging on, and there's an enjoyable patio seating area downstairs looking out onto the sea.

Ascot Hotel (☎ 66385566; www.ascothotel.com; 38 Garden Rd; d incl breakfast & tax Rs 3500-3900; 🟦 🖳) The Ascot soothes you upon entry with contemporary blue-and-yellow tones and a fresh, uncluttered design. The rooms continue the tasteful scheme and are spacious, comfortable and boast decadent bathrooms with bathtubs.

Gordon House Hotel (☎ 22871122; www.ghhotel .com; 5 Battery St; incl breakfasts/d Rs 5500/6000, ste Rs 10,000; 🟦 🖳) This white, mausoleum-like boutique hotel has elegant rooms decorated in Mediterranean, Scandinavian or country styles. Just this side of kitsch, it's fun and has gizmos such as CD players and flat-screen TVs in all rooms. Rooms above its Poly Esther's nightclub (see p129) are noisy but available at a discount if you ask.

Fariyas Hotel (☎ 22042911; www.fariyas.com; 25 Off Arthur Bunder Rd; s/d from Rs 6000/7000; 🟦 🖳 🟦) Straddling the high-end category, this efficient and friendly hotel has dated furnishings, but the rooms are otherwise good. There's a small swimming pool on the 1st-floor terrace, a gym, a restaurant, nail-bar, wi-fi and the Tavern & Beyond pub.

FORT AREA

Residency Hotel (Map p114; ☎ 22625525; residencyhotel@ vsnl.com; 26 Rustom Sidhwa Marg; s/d from Rs 1600/ 1700; 🟦 🖳) This is one of the few comfortable options in the heart of the Fort. It has a marble-clad lobby with friendly staff and speckless rooms decorated with Indian-themed paintings and bright curtains.

Grand Hotel (Map pp106-7; ☎ 22618211; www .grandhotelbombay.com; 17 Shri Shiv Sagar Ramgulam Marg, Ballard Estate; s/d from Rs 2000/2300; 🟦 🖳) The quiet but central location is the big draw, and while it fails to live up to its name, it's not too bad with tidy, dowdily furnished rooms.

West End Hotel (Map p114; ☎ 22039121; www .westendhotelmumbai.com; 45 New Marine Lines; s/d Rs 2800/3200; 🟦 🖳) You'd half expect Austin Powers to be swinging in this Hotel's grey-velour-lined bar, Chez Nous. The hotel has a funky but unintentionally retro feel, and the old-fashioned rooms are plain but roomy, with soft beds. There's wi-fi downstairs.

CHURCHGATE, MARINE DRIVE & KEMP'S CORNER

Hotel Kemp's Corner (Map pp106-7; ☎ 23634646; 131 August Kranti Marg; s/d from Rs 1200/1700; 🟦) With a great spot close to the multitude of fashion stores at Kemp's corner, you might forgive the curt staff and occasional carpet bald-spot of this old-fashioned place. It's worth forking out a bit more for the deluxe double rooms.

Astoria Hotel (Map p114; ☎ 22852626; astoria@hath way.com; Churchgate Reclamation, J Tata Rd, Churchgate; s/d from Rs 2500/3000; 🟦 🖳) This conveniently located, smartly refurbished hotel has immaculate rooms that almost live up to the promise of the sleek, modern lobby. Some of the abodes have room enough to swing two cats and there's a restaurant with wi-fi.

Sea Green Hotel (Map p114; ☎ 22822294; www.sea greenhotel.com; 145 Marine Dr; s/d Rs 2000/2450; 🟦) and **Sea Green South Hotel** (Map p114; ☎ 22821613; www .seagreensouth.com; 145A Marine Dr; s/d Rs 2000/2450; 🟦) are identical Art Deco–styled hotels offering spacious but spartan AC rooms, originally built in the 1940s to house British soldiers. Ask for one of the sea-view rooms as they're the same price. A 20% tax is added to room rates.

JUHU BEACH, BANDRA & AIRPORT AREA

There are half a dozen midrange hotels clustered on Nehru Rd Extension near the domestic airport, though rooms are overpriced and only useful for early or late flights. Juhu's beach area is more convenient for clubbing/culinary excursions to the suburb of Bandra. For mapped locations of the following venues see Map p123.

Iskcon (☎ 26206860; guesthouse.mumbai@pamho.net; 111 Hare Krishna Lane, Juhu; s/d incl tax Rs 1320/1584; with AC incl tax Rs 1452/1971; 🔀) This unique, flamingo-pink building, with undulating exterior walls, is part of a lively Hare Krishna complex. The high-rise is very efficiently managed and rooms are a fairly big and spick-and-span, with large balconies, but no TV or fridge. A good vegetarian buffet restaurant, Govinda's, is on site.

Hotel Columbus (☎ 26182029; hotel_columbus@ rediffmail.com; 344 Nanda Patkar Rd, Vile Parle; s Rs 1650-2000, d Rs 2000-3000; 🔀) This is one of the few midrange hotels in the airport area we'd happily send our grandmother to. Be sure to avoid the slightly skanky budget rooms and opt for the gussied-up deluxe options with simple, bright furniture and fun colour highlights.

Hotel Metro Palace (☎ 26427311; www.unique hotelsindia.com; Ramdas Nayak Rd, Bandra; s/d from Rs 2200/2600; 🔀) One of the only options in the modish Bandra area that doesn't quote it's prices in US dollars, the rooms are very comfortable, have balconies and lovingly conserved flourishes of '80s décor. There is a small army of a superefficient staff on call.

Hotel Airport International (☎ 26182222; www.ho telairport.net; Nehru Rd, Vile Parle; s/d from Rs 2700/3700; 🔀) The pick of the bunch among cheaper airport hotels, it's so close to the domestic airport you can see the runway from most rooms. The decent rooms are clean but decorated in dowdy colours.

Hotel Suba Galaxy (☎ 26831188; www.hotelsub agalaxy.com; NS Phadke Rd, Andheri; s/d Rs 2500/3600; 🔀) This brand new, efficient and business-focused tower is 4km from the airport and offers ultramodern rooms, all nicely finished in dark wood and glass. It's got all the mod cons, with flat-screen TVs and broadband in each room. Oh, and lots of fluffy pillows.

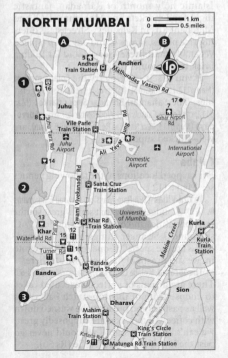

NORTH MUMBAI

SIGHTS & ACTIVITIES	
Yoga Institute	1 A2

SLEEPING 🛏	
Hotel Airport International	2 B2
Hotel Columbus	3 A2
Hotel Metro Palace	4 A3
Hotel Suba Galaxy	5 A1
Iskcon	6 A1
ITC Hotel Grand Maratha Sheraton & Towers	7 B1
JW Marriott	8 A1

EATING 🍴	
Culture Curry	(see 9)
Goa Portuguesa	9 A3
Peshawri	(see 7)
Pot Pourri	10 A3
Seijo and the Soul Dish	11 A3
Sheesha	12 A2

DRINKING 🍸	
Olive Bar & Kitchen	13 A2
Vie Lounge	14 A2
Zenzi	15 A2

ENTERTAINMENT 🎭	
Prithvi Theatre	16 A1

TRANSPORT	
Delta Airlines	17 B1

Top End

COLABA

our pick **Taj Mahal Palace & Tower** (Map p112; ☎ 66653366; www.tajhotels.com; Apollo Bunder, Colaba; tower rooms s/d from US$325/350, palace rooms from US$475/500; ✗ ▯ ☎) A Mumbai landmark since 1903, this distinguished hotel is a world of sweeping arches, staircases and domes, all very far away from the flurry of Colaba life. Every conceivable facility is found within, including superb restaurants, miles of luxury shops, a large outdoor pool, spa, gymnasium, the nightclub Insomnia (p129), even a resident fortune-teller. The plush, heritage-themed rooms in the palace complex are the ones to go for if you want real decadence, although the rooms in the newer tower have better views.

MARINE DRIVE

Marine Plaza (Map p114; ☎ 22851212; hotelmarineplaza@vsnl.com; 29 Marine Dr, Nariman Point; d from US$250; ✗ ▯ ☎) An appealing and showy boutique five-star hotel with Art Deco flourishes and stylish rooms. The rooftop swimming pool has a glass bottom that looks down on the foyer five floors below! The hotel also has a gym, wi-fi, two restaurants and the popular Boston-style Geoffrey's Bar.

Intercontinental (Map p114; ☎ 39879999; www.intercontinental.com; 135 Marine Dr, Churchgate; d incl breakfast from US$315; ✗ ▯ ☎) You'll want to pay a little extra for the splendid sea views at this sophisticated boutique-style hotel. With equally stylish rooms, the cherry on the cake is the smart bar Dome (p127), which elegantly crowns the rooftop.

Hilton Towers (Map pp106–7; ☎ 66324343; www.hilton.com; Marine Dr, Nariman Point; s/d from US$259/279; ✗ ▯ ☎) The Hilton Towers (once the Oberoi Towers) wins out over its neighbour, the Oberoi, both on price and the spiffy design of its restaurants, bars and pool area. Although managed separately, both hotels still share facilities so you can wander happily between the two.

BANDRA, JUHU BEACH & AIRPORT AREA

ITC Hotel Grand Maratha Sheraton & Towers (Map p123; ☎ 28303030; www.itcwelcomgroup.in; Sahar Airport Rd, Andheri; s/d incl breakfast & tax from US$250/275; ✗ ▯ ☎) Easily the hotel in this area with the most luxurious Indian character, from the Jaipur-style lattice windows around the atrium to the silk pillows on the beds and the embalmed palms in the lobby. It's right outside the international airport and has an excellent spa and the celebrated restaurant Peshawri (p127).

JW Marriott (Map p123; ☎ 66933000; mail@jwmarriott mumbai.com; Juhu Tara Rd, Juhu; d incl tax from US$269; ✗ ▯ ☎) Smack in the middle of Juhu Beach is this monument to luxury hotels, sporting no fewer than three pools, one of them filled with heavily filtered sea water. There's a bright foyer encasing a lily pond and the rooms leave little to be desired.

EATING

Munching in Mumbai is a treat. Food options in the metropolis are as diverse as the squillion inhabitants – go on a cultural history tour by sampling Parsi *dhansak* (meat with curried lentils and rice), Gujarati or Keralan thalis ('all-you-can-eat' meals) and everything from Muslim kebabs to Goan vindaloo to Mangalorean seafood. If you find Bombay duck on a menu, remember it's actually *bombil* fish dried in the sun and deep-fried.

Don't miss Mumbai's famous *bhelpuri*; readily available at Chowpatty Beach or at the excellent Swati Snacks (p126). During the Islamic holy month of Ramadan, fantastic night food markets line Mohammed Ali and Merchant Rds in Kalbadevi. Street stalls offering rice plates, samosas and *pav bhaji* (spiced vegetables and bread) for around Rs 15 do a brisk trade around the city.

If you're self-catering try the **Colaba market** (Map p112; Lala Nigam St) for fresh fruit and vegetables. The **Saharkari Bhandar Supermarket** (Map p112; cnr Colaba Causeway & Wodehouse Rd) and **Suryodaya** (Map p114; Veer Nariman Rd; ✦ 7.30am-8.30pm), are well-stocked supermarkets.

Colaba

For mapped locations of the following venues see Map p112.

Laxmi Villas (19A Ram Mansion, Nawroji F Rd; mains Rs 12-70) A budget eatery that serves great southern specialities in comfortable, modern, AC surrounds? Stranger things have happened. Dosas are the speciality, one reader even wrote in 'we still dream of the meals we ate there.'

Theobroma (Colaba Causeway, Colaba; cakes Rs 40-60) There are dozens of perfectly executed cakes to choose from at this top-notch bakery, as well as pastries and breads to be washed down with coffee. All the cakes are supposedly great, we can't know for sure – we could never go past the lavish chocolate truffle (Rs 50).

ourpick Bade Miya (Tulloch Rd; meals Rs 40-60; dinner) As Mumbai as traffic jams, this street-stall-on-steroids buzzes nightly with punters from all walks of Mumbai life lining up for spicy, fresh grilled treats. Grab a chicken tikka roll to go, or snap up one of makeshift street-side tables to sample the *boti kebab* (lamb kebab) or *paneer masala* (cheese and tomato curry).

Kailash Parbat (5 Sheela Mahal, 1st Pasta Lane; mains Rs 50-80) Nothing fancy, but a Mumbai legend nonetheless thanks to its inexpensive Sindhi-influenced vegetarian snacks, mouth-watering sweets and extra-spicy masala chai.

Café Churchill (103B Colaba Causeway; sandwiches Rs 50-90) This tiny, packed place with booth seating does Western comfort food better than most, all served in fiercely-arctic AC. Grab a sandwich or a pasta and finish up with one of its 'happy endings.' Um, dessert that is.

Indigo Delicatessen (Pheroze Bldg, Shivaji Marg; mains Rs 235-350) This new place near Indigo has breakfast anytime (Rs 115 to 185), more casual meals and a selection of imported cheeses (at imported prices), breads and desserts.

Basilico (☎ 67039999; Sentinel House, Arthur Bunder Rd; mains Rs 265-320) A modish, Euro-style bistro, deli and bakery, this place whips up creative fresh pastas, salads and risottos almost as good as mamma used to make. There's lots of veggie options too, such as the yummy conchiglie pasta, with roast zucchini, peppers and garlic (Rs 255).

ourpick Indigo (☎ 66368980; 4 Mandlik Marg; mains Rs 485-685; lunch & dinner) The finest eating option in Colaba, and possibly Mumbai, Indigo offers inventive European cuisine, a long wine list and a sleek ambience including a roof deck lit with fairy lights. The appetizer of lobster brusque with Cajun shrimp crackling appetizer (Rs 345) is a long-time favourite.

Bookings are essential, but if the restaurant is full you can always hang out with the in crowd at the bar.

Also recommended:

Delhi Darbar (Holland House, Colaba Causeway; mains Rs 80-180; lunch & dinner) Excellent Mughlai and tandoori restaurant.

Ming Palace (Colaba Causeway; mains Rs 150-305; lunch & dinner) Quality Chinese, Korean and Japanese food with gargantuan portions.

Kala Ghoda & Fort Area

Rajdhani (Map pp106-7; 361 Sheikh Memon St, Kalbadevthali; thali Rs 25) This smart place, opposite Mangaldaas Market, is a great spot to refuel on a tasty thali while shopping in the Crawford Market area.

National Hindu Hotel (Map p114; 1st flr, cnr Colaba Causeway & Mint Rd; thali Rs 25; lunch & dinner) Keralan run, this concealed, no-frills and grittily authentic working-man's eatery serves nothing but finger-licking (there are no utensils), all-you-can-eat thalis. Expect a fast-moving line out the door and rows of benches inside. Just find a spare seat, say hello to your neighbour, and wait for wandering staff to fill your banana leaf to the brim.

Mocambo Café & Bar (Map p114; 23A Sir P Mehta Rd, Fort; mains Rs 50-170) A modern, convivial and convenient spot for breakfast, sandwiches, a main meal or a cold beer. It has a huge Indian and Western menu, but the breakfast egg-and-brain fry (with fries! Rs 75) may only be for culinary adrenalin junkies.

Mahesh Lunch Home (Map p114; 8B Cowasji Patel St, Fort; mains Rs 70-180; lunch & dinner) A modern version of a hole-in-the-wall come good, this is the place to try Mangalorean seafood at budget prices. It's renowned for its ladyfish, pomfret, lobster and crabs, and its *rawas tikka* (marinated white salmon) and tandoori pomfret are outstanding.

DHABA-WALLAS

A small miracle of logistics, Mumbai's 5000 *dhaba* (snack bars)–wallahs (also called tiffin-wallahs) work tirelessly to deliver hot lunches to hungry office workers throughout the city.

Lunch boxes are picked up each day from restaurants, homes, doting mothers and wives and carried in their hundreds on heads, bicycles and trains. Taken to a centralised sorting station, a sophisticated system of numbers and colours (many wallahs are illiterate) is then used to determine where every lunch must end up. More than 200,000 meals are delivered in Mumbai in this way – always on time, come (monsoon) rain or (searing) shine.

This same intricate supply-chain system has been used for centuries, and wallahs are known to take immense pride in their work. Considering that on average only about one mistake is made every six-million deliveries, they have certainly earned our pat on the back.

Trishna (Map p114; ☎ 22614991; Sai Baba Marg, Kala Ghoda; mains Rs 300-500; ☽ lunch & dinner) We have it on good authority that this might just be the best seafood in town. Specialising in Mangalorean preparations, the crab with butter, pepper and garlic and various shrimp dishes, all brought to your table for inspection, are excellent.

Khyber (Map p114; ☽ 22673227; 145 MG Rd, Fort; mains Rs 330-600; ☽ lunch & dinner) Khyber serves up Punjabi and other North Indian dishes in moody, burnt-orange, Afghan-inspired interiors to a who's who of Mumbai's elite. The food is some of the best the city has to offer, with the meat-centric menu wandering from kebabs, to biryanis, to it's *pièce de résistance*, *raan* (a whole leg of slow-cooked lamb).

Also recommended:

Badshah Snacks & Drinks (Map pp106-7; snacks Rs 15-70) Serving snacks and fruit juices (Rs 29 to 85) to hungry bargain-hunters for more than 100 years; opposite Crawford Market.

Ideal Corner (Map p114; Gunbow St, Fort; mains Rs 30-65; ☽ breakfast & lunch Mon-Fri) A classic Parsi café serving a different menu daily.

Churchgate

For mapped locations of the following venues see Map p114.

Tea Centre (78 Veer Nariman Rd; mains Rs 60-130, set lunch Rs 200) A great place to try out some of India's premium teas, as well as sample some excellent light meals and snacks, this is a serene, colonial-meets-contemporary place with severe AC.

Samrat (Prem Ct, J Tata Rd; mains Rs 80-200; ☽ lunch & dinner) A busy traditional Indian vegetarian restaurant; one of three premises at the same location run by the same company. Relish (mains Rs 65 to 130) is the funkier cousin (open lunch and dinner) with dishes ranging from Lebanese platters to Mexican, while 210° C is an outdoor café and bakery (pastries from Rs 10; open noon to 11pm).

Pizzeria (Soona Mahal, 143 Marine Dr; pizzas Rs 110-350; ☽ lunch & dinner) Serves up passable pizza-pies with ocean views the main draw.

Gaylord (☎ 22821259; Veer Nariman Rd; meals Rs 125-550; ☽ lunch & dinner) Great North Indian dishes served with over-the-top, Raj-era styles dining replete with tuxedo-wearing waiters hanging on your every gesture. It also serves domestic and imported wines (Rs 125 to 550 per glass).

Chowpatty Beach & Around

For mapped locations of the following venues see Map pp106-7.

The evening stalls at Bhel Plaza on Chowpatty Beach are the most atmospheric spots to snack on *bhelpuri* (Rs 10) or *panipuri* (small crisp puffs of dough filled with spicy tamarind water and sprouted gram; Rs 20).

Swati Snacks (248 Karai Estate, Tardeo Rd, Tardeo; mains Rs 35-70; ☽ lunch & dinner) This bustling old-timer has been revamped as a modern cafeteria for discerning grown-ups (all stainless steel and smooth wood). Try out the delicious *bhelpuri*, *panki chatni* (savoury pancake steamed in a banana leaf) and homemade ice cream in delectable flavour combinations such as rose-coconut-pineapple (Rs 40). Don't leave Mumbai without snacking here.

Anantashram (46 Kotachiwadi, Girgaum; ☽ lunch & dinner Mon-Sat) This no-frills restaurant is as renowned for its spartan décor and surliness of its staff as for its supremely delicious cooking and thali meals. Look for it down a small maze of laneways.

Cream Centre (☎ 23679222; 25B Chowpatty Seaface; mains Rs 85-139; ☽ lunch & dinner) With a slick, modern-art-adorned interior, it's only fitting that the fusion menu is equally original. Enjoy pure veg dishes and such hybrids as Indian Mexican cuisine, and of course there's an excellent ice-cream parlour.

Speaking of ice cream, try out these two places to cool off after a Chowpatty stroll:

Gelato Italiano (Chowpatty Seaface; scoop Rs 29-49; ☽ lunch & dinner) Flavours such as custard apple sorbetto or limoncello, yum.

New Kulfi Centre (cnr Chowpatty Seaface & Sardar V Patel Rd; kulfi per 100gm Rs 17-35; ☽ lunch & dinner) Serves kulfi, a pistachio-flavoured sweet similar to ice cream.

North Mumbai

North Mumbai's centres of gravity as far as trendy dining and drinking are concerned lie in Bandra West and Juhu. For mapped locations of the following venues see Map p123.

Culture Curry (Kataria Rd; dishes Rs 70-200; ☽ lunch & dinner) Next door to Goa Potuguesa (below) and run by the same folk, this restaurant offers curries from around India. Guitar-strumming musicians and singers wander between the two connected spaces.

Goa Portuguesa (www.goaportuguesa.com; Kataria Rd, Mahim; dishes Rs 90-200; ☽ lunch & dinner) As good as making a trip to Goa is a visit to this fun restaurant, which specialises in the fiery dishes of the former Portuguese colony.

Pot Pourri (Carlton Ct, cnr of Turner & Pali Rds, Bandra West; mains Rs 100-260; ☿ lunch & dinner) In a great corner from which to peruse Bandra streetlife, decent Western-style cuisine is dished up here – everything from Highland Scotch broth to its famed chicken stroganoff (Rs 190). The reasonable prices scoff at much spendier Bandra establishments.

Sheesha (7th flr, Shoppers Stop, Linking Rd; dishes around Rs 120-230; ☿ lunch & dinner) This funky, roof-top place pays token homage to the Middle East, and is strewn with curvy concrete lounges and cushions ideal for elegant slumming. The food is good but almost secondary to the ambience, with Indian fare mixed alongside Arabic dishes such as kebabs (Rs 120 to 240).

Seijo & the Soul Dish (☎ 26405555; 206 Patkar Marg, Bandra; mains Rs 235-885; ☿ dinner) Serving some of the best pan-Asian fusion dishes around, it's worth coming to this über-hip joint just for the *Bladerunner*-meets-Sushi-bar design concept alone. The surreal, freestanding, egg-shaped loos inside the main dining room will leave you with lots to talk about over sushi, noodles or a Thai curry.

Peshawri (☎ 28303030; ITC Hotel Grand Maratha Sheraton & Towers, Sahar Airport Rd; mains Rs 400-1000; ☿ dinner) Make this Indian North-West Frontier restaurant, conveniently located just outside the international airport, your first or last stop in Mumbai. You will not regret forking out for the sublime leg of spring lamb and amazing dhal Bukhara (a thick black dhal cooked for more than a day!).

DRINKING

Mumbai's lax attitude to alcohol offers up loads of places to get nicely inebriated – from hole-in-the-wall beer bars to brash, multilevel superclubs. Expect to pay around Rs 80 to 130 for a bottle of Kingfisher in a bar or restaurant, a lot more in a club or fashionable watering-hole.

Cafés

Mocha Bar (Map p114; 82 Veer Nariman Rd, Churchgate; ☿ 9am-12:30am) This atmospheric, Arabian-styled café is often filled to the brim with bohemians and students deep in esoteric conversation, or maybe just the latest Bollywood gossip. Cosy, low-cushioned seating, hookah pipes, exotic coffee varieties and world music add up to longer stays than you expected.

Samovar Café (Map p114; Jehangir Art Gallery, 161B MG Rd, Kala Ghoda; ☿ 11am-7pm Mon-Sat) This intimate place inside the art gallery overlooks the gardens of the Prince of Wales Museum and is a great spot to chill out over a beer, mango lassi (Rs 50) or light meal.

The Rs 5 chai-wallahs are still out there, but fancy 'espresso-bars' are where Mumbaikers head for their caffeine jolt these days. Barista and Café Coffee Day vie for dominance across the city in a race to out-Starbucks each other. **Barista** (Colaba Map p112; Colaba Causeway; Colaba Map p112; Arthur Bunder Rd; near CST Map p114; Marzaban Rd) seems to be winning, with slightly more stylish pristine orange- and cream-coloured surroundings, but **Café Coffee Day** (Map pp106-7; Chowpatty Seaface) is not far behind.

The spiffy **Cha Bar** (Map p114; ☿ 66354477; Apeejay House, 3 Dinsha Wachha Marg, Churchgate; ☿ 10am-10pm) at Oxford Bookstore also serves an inspiring range of teas and tasty snacks.

Bars
COLABA & AROUND
For mapped locations of the following venues see Map p112.

Leopold's Café (cnr Colaba Causeway & Nawroji F Rd; ☿ 7.30am-12:30am) Drawn like moths to a Kingfisher flame, most tourists end up at this Mumbai travellers' institution at one time or another. Around since 1871, Leopold's has wobbly ceiling fans, open-plan seating and a rambunctious atmosphere conducive to swapping tales with random strangers. Although there's a huge menu, it's the lazy evening beers that are the real draw.

Busaba (☎ 22043779; 4 Mandlik Marg; ☿ noon-3pm & 7pm-12.30am; ☒) Red walls, framed postcards and old photos give this loungey restaurant-bar a bohemian feel. It's next to Indigo so gets the same trendy crowd, but serves cheaper, more potent cocktails.

Café Mondegar (Metro House, 5A Colaba Causeway; ☿ 8:30am-11:30pm) Mondegar's nightly traveller-based crowd is as 'colourful' as the wall caricatures by a famous Goan artist, but that could be our beer-goggles talking. Expect to shout your draught beer orders over the popular, nonstop CD jukebox.

Henry Tham's (☎ 22023186; Apollo Bunder; ☿ 7pm-1:30am) This superswanky bar-cum-restaurant features towering ceilings, gratuitous use of space and strategically placed minimalist décor. It's the currently darling of the Mumbai jet set and therefore *the* place to see and be seen. To

MUMBAI (BOMBAY)

STAR STRUCK

Mumbai (Bombay) is home of the glitz and glamour of Bollywood (see p116); be sure to study up on some of the industry's A-list players:

- Saif Ali Khan: Dashing son of the Nawab (Prince) of Pataudi, this debonair actor is India's latest homegrown heart-throb.
- Amitabh Bachchan: Now in his 60s, the face of this white-bearded action-film legend graces half the movie-posters and billboards in the country.
- Raj Kapoor: Actor, producer, director and all-round, old-school megastar.
- Salman Khan: An infamous Bolly-bad-boy who plays the quintessential romantic hero onscreen.
- Rani Mukerji: A starlet with classic looks and a real passion for her roles.
- Aishwarya Rai: A former Miss World who has since become one of Bollywood's brightest stars.
- Shah Rukh Khan: Classically trained in theatre, he's a versatile actor with chiselled good looks.

And if you hang out long enough at any of these swanky establishments, you too can rub shoulders with India's celluloid jet-set:

- Henry Tham's (p127)
- Dome (below)
- Vie Lounge (below)
- Zenzi (below)
- Insomnia (opposite)

---

find it, look for the monolithic door – thankfully opened by a doorman.

Gokul Bar (Tulloch Rd; ☽ 11am-1.30am) This classic, workin' man's Indian drinking den can get pretty lively and the beer is cheap (starting at Rs 60). There's an AC section upstairs where the real boozers hang out.

MARINE DRIVE, BREACH CANDY & LOWER PAREL

Ghetto (Map pp106-7; ☎ 23538418; 30B Bhulabhai Desai Marg, Mahalaxmi; ☽ 7pm-1.30am) Mumbai's best and only real dive bar, this smoke-filled, graffiti-covered rocker's hang-out blares rock nightly to a dedicated set of regulars. International movies are screened (for free) every Monday night.

Saltwater Grill (Map pp106-7; Chowpatty Seaface, Chowpatty; ☽ 7:30pm-1:30am) As close as you can get to Mumbai's ocean without swimming in it, this beach bar sits cocooned by it's own palm-frond jungle. Right next to H20, it's a prime contender for the title of 'ultimate sundowner cocktail venue.'

Dome (Map p114; ☎ 39879999, ext 8872; Hotel Intercontinental, 135 Marine Dr, Churchgate; ☽ 6pm-1:30am) What may be the swishest hotel bar in town, this white-on-white rooftop drinking lounge has awesome views of Mumbai's curving seafront. Cocktails beckon the hip young things of Mumbai nightly – get out your Bollywood star-spotting logbook.

BANDRA & JUHU

Vie Lounge (Map p123; ☎ 26603003; Juhu Tara Rd, Juhu; ☽ 7pm-1.30am) Right on Juhu Beach is this glamorous party spot (opposite Little Italy restaurant). Call before dragging yourself all the way out here to check there isn't a private Bollywood bash on.

Zenzi (Map p123; ☎ 56430670; 183 Waterfield Rd, Bandra West; ☽ 11:30am-1.30am) This superstylin' hang-out pad is a favourite among starlet wannabes and well-heeled expats. Comfy lounges are frequently visited by efficient and chatty service and the burnt orange décor is warmly bathed in soft lighting. It's at its best when the canopy is open to the stars after the monsoon season.

Olive Bar & Kitchen (Map p123; ☎ 26058228; Pali Hill Tourist Hotel, 14 Union Park, Khar; ☽ 7.30pm-12.30am) Hip and snooty, this Mediterranean-style restaurant and bar has light and delicious food, soothing DJ sounds and pure Ibiza décor. Thursday is packed: it's the new Saturday, though Saturday hasn't heard the news.

ENTERTAINMENT

The daily English-language tabloid *Mid-Day* incorporates the *List*, a guide to Mumbai entertainment. Newspapers have information on mainstream events and film screenings as does *Time Out Mumbai* (p109). You should also check out www.gigpad.com for live music listings in Mumbai.

Nightclubs

The big nights in clubs are Wednesday, Friday and Saturday when there's usually a cover charge. Dress codes apply so don't rock up in shorts and sandals.

Insomnia (Map p112; ☎ 66666653; Taj Mahal Palace & Tower, Apollo Bunder, Colaba; ☺ 8pm-3am) For Bollywood star-spotting, ultrachic Insomnia remains the place to be seen dropping some serious dough. It doesn't get going till after midnight and the minimum drinks spend is a hefty Rs 600 (Rs 1600 on Friday and Saturday).

Ra (☎ 66614343; Phoenix Mills, 462 Senapati Bapat Marg, Lower Parel; minimum bar tab Rs 1500; ☺ 9pm-1.30am Wed-Sat) If you were wondering where the city's beautiful people come to shake their moneymakers, wonder no more. Ra's glass roof opens wide to the stars, and your wallet will open even wider to pay for it's top-notch cocktails. It's in the Phoenix Mills shopping complex, 1km north of Mahalaxmi Racecourse.

Polly Esther's (Map p112; ☎ 22871122; Gordon House Hotel, 5 Battery St, Colaba; cover per couple Rs 600-1000; ☺ 8.30am-1am Tue-Sat) Wallowing in a cheesy timewarp of retro pop, rock and disco, the Gordon House Hotel's mirror-plated, groovy nightclub still manages to pull a crowd. It comes complete with a *Saturday Night Fever* illuminated dance floor and waiters in Afro wigs.

Red Light (Map p114; ☎ 56346249; 145 MG Rd, Fort; cover Rs 300; ☺ 7pm-midnight) This very trendy bar is a huge hit with Mumbai's student scene, particularly on Wednesday when its thumping hip-hop sessions are on. The fun-house-mirror trip to the loos is not for the faint hearted.

Voodoo Pub (Map p112; ☎ 22841959; 2/5 Kamal Mansion, Arthur Bunder Rd, Colaba; cover Rs 200; ☺ 8pm-1.30am) Famous for hosting Mumbai's only regular gay night (Saturday), this dark and sweaty bar has little going for it on other nights of the week.

Cinema

Going to see a movie in India's film capital is practically mandatory; with well over 100 cinemas around the city there's no excuse not to. Try the following:

Eros (Map p114; ☎ 22822335; MK Rd, Churchgate; tickets Rs 40-100) For Bollywood blockbusters.

Metro (Map p114; ☎ 22030303; MG Rd, New Marine Lines, Fort; tickets Rs 40-100) Also for Bollywood blockbusters.

Regal (Map p112; ☎ 22021017; Colaba Causeway, Colaba; tickets Rs 70-150) Art Deco cinema showing brash Bollywood hits and the occasional Hollywood tripe.

Sterling (Map p114; ☎ 22075187; Marzaban Rd, Fort; tickets Rs 60-87) First-run English-language movies.

Music, Dance & Theatre

Not Just Jazz By the Bay (Map p114; ☎ 22851876; 143 Marine Dr; admission singles/couple Rs 200/300; ☺ 6pm-2am) This is the best, and frankly the only, jazz club in South Mumbai. True to its name, there are also live pop, blues and rock performers most nights, though Sunday- or Monday-night karaoke might be best avoided.

National Centre for the Performing Arts (NCPA; Map pp106-7; ☎ 22833737; www.tata.com/ncpa; cnr Marine Dr & Sri V Saha Rd, Nariman Point; tickets Rs 40-280) This is the hub of Mumbai's music, theatre and dance scene. In any given week, it might host Marathi theatre, dance troupes from Bihar, ensembles from Europe and Indian classical music. The Tata Theatre here occasionally has English-language plays. Many performances are free. The box office (☎ 22824567; open 9am to 1.30pm and 4.30pm to 6.30pm) is at the end of NCPA Marg.

Nehru Centre (☎ 24964676-80; www.nehrucentre mumbai.com; Dr Annie Besant Rd, Worli) Stages occasional dance, music and English-language theatre performances.

Prithvi Theatre (Map p123; ☎ 26149546; www.prith vitheatre.org; Juhu Church Rd, Vile Parle) At Juhu Beach, this is a good place to see both English-language and Hindi theatre. It hosts an annual international theatre festival.

Sport

CRICKET

The cricket season runs from October to April. Test matches and One Day Internationals are played a handful of times a year at **Wankhede Stadium** (Map p114; ☎ 22811795; mcacrick@vsnl.com; D Rd, Churchgate). To buy tickets apply in writing well in advance. One-day match tickets start at Rs 150, for a test match you'll have to pay for the full five days – around Rs 700 for general admission, up to Rs 10,000 for the members stand (replete with lunch and afternoon tea). State match tickets (Rs 25) are available at the gate.

HORSE RACING
Mumbai's horse-racing season runs from November to the end of April.
Mahalaxmi Racecourse (Map pp106-7; ☎ 23071401) Races are held on Sunday and Thursday afternoons (Saturday and Sunday towards the end of the season). Big races, such as the Indian Derby in February, are major social occasions. Entry to the public enclosure costs Rs 30.

FOOTBALL
The **Cooperage Football Ground** (Map p112; ☎ 220 24020; MK Rd, Colaba; tickets Rs 50) is home to the Mumbai Football Association and hosts national- and state-league soccer matches between November and February. Tickets are available at the gate.

SHOPPING
Mumbai is India's great marketplace, with some of the best shopping in the country. Colaba Street Market lines Colaba Causeway with hawkers' stalls and shops selling garments, perfumes and knick-knacks. Electronic gear, pirated CDs and DVDs, leather goods and mass-produced gizmos are for sale at stalls on Dr Dadabhai Naoroji Rd between CST and Flora Fountain, and along MG Rd from Flora Fountain to Kala Ghoda.

Antiques & Curios
Small antique and curio shops line Merewether Rd behind the Taj Mahal Palace & Tower (see Map p112). Prices aren't cheap, but the quality is definitely a step up from government emporiums.

If you prefer Raj-era bric-a-brac, head to Chor Bazaar (Map pp106-7; opposite); the main area of activity is Mutton St where you'll find a row of shops specialising in antiques (many ingenious reproductions, so beware) and miscellaneous junk.
Mini Market (Map pp106-7; ☎ 23472427; 33/31 Mutton St; ☼ 11am-8pm Sat-Thu) Sells original vintage Bollywood posters and other movie ephemera as well as many trinkets.
Phillips (Map p112; ☎ 22020564; www.phillipsantiques .com; Woodhouse Rd, Colaba; ☼ 10am-1.30pm & 2.30-7pm Mon-Sat) Opposite the Regal cinema, this long-running antique shop is known for its quality prints, silver, brassware and glass lamps – all late Victorian.

Fashion
Snap up a bargain backpacking wardrobe at Fashion Street Market, the cheap stalls lining MG Rd between Cross and Azad maidans (Map p114). Hone your bargaining skills.

Designer clobber can be bought at boutiques near Kemp's Corner. Pieces by Indian designers sell for half the price of off-the-shelf gear back home.
Courtyard (Map p112; SP Centre, 41/44 Minoo Desai Marg; ☼ 11am-7.30pm) This collection of boutiques is Mumbai's fashion nexus, with appealing, keenly priced couture clothes, shoes and interior goods by top local designers such as Narendra Kumar and the Gaultier-goes-to-Bollywood look of Manish Arora.
Fabindia (Map p114; Jeroo Bldg, 137 MG Rd, Kala Ghoda; ☼ 10am-7.45pm Tue-Sun) All the vibrant colours of the country are represented in the top-quality, keenly priced cotton and silk fashions, materials and homewares of this modern Indian shop.
Kala Niketan (Map p114; ☎ 22005001; www.kalaniket angroup.com; 95 MK Rd; ☼ 12:30pm-11:30pm) The pick of the bunch of Sari shops lining this part of Queens Rd, the helpful staff will help you sort through the sari-madness. Prices range from Rs 500 all the way to Rs 80,000.

Also recommended are the following:
Khadi & Village Industries Emporium (Map p114; ☎ 33073280/8; 286 Dr Dadabhai Naoroji Rd, Fort) A 1940s time-warp with ready-made traditional Indian clothing, material, shoes and handicrafts.
Mélange (Map pp106-7; ☎ 23534492; www.melange world.com; 33 Altamount Rd, Kemp's Corner), Wall-to-wall, exposed-brick chic selling high fashion garments from 70 Indian designers.
Telon (Map pp106-7; 149 Warren Rd, Kemp's Corner) Fine gents tailor whipping up suits to order (starting at Rs 10,000).

For the massive, modern, sterile AC shopping centre experience, get lost in **Crossroads** (Map pp106-7; 28 Pandit MM Malviya Rd, Breach Candy; ☼ 10am-8pm), Mumbai's biggest (to date).

Handicrafts & Gifts
You can pick up handicrafts from various state-government emporiums in the World Trade Centre Arcade (Map pp106–7) near Cuffe Pde. All the following places have fixed prices and accept credit cards.
Bombay Store (Map p114; ☼ 22885048; Western India House, Sir P Mehta Rd, Fort; ☼ 10.30am-7.30pm Mon-Sat, 10.30am-6.30pm Sun) The place to browse if you're

looking for souvenirs from around India. Although the prices are considerably higher than at the markets or Central Cottage Industries Emporium (below), the range and quality is impressive. It sells rugs, textiles, home furnishings, silverware, glassware, *pietra dura* (marble inlay work) and bric-a-brac.

Bombay Paperie (Map p114; ☎ 66358171; www .bombaypaperie.com; 59 Bombay Samachar Marg, Fort; ✆ 10.30am-6pm Mon-Sat) Sells handmade, cotton-based paper manufactured in the village of Kagzipura near Aurangaba, crafted into charming cards, sculptures and lampshades.

Soma (Map p112; ☎ 22826050; 1st fl, 16 Madama Cama Rd; ✆ 10am-8pm) Soma has home-furnishings and clothing made from hand-block-printed materials at surprisingly reasonable prices, especially considering one bedspread can be hand-stamped up to 14,000 times!

Other stores worth popping into include the following:

Khubsons Narisons (Map p112; ☎ 22020614; 49 Colaba Causeway; ✆ 10:30am-8pm) Selling famous Tantra T-shirts sporting funky original sketches, designs and witty slogans.

Inshaallah Mashaallah (Map p112; ☎ 22049495; Best Marg, Colaba; ✆ 11am-9pm) An Aladdin's cave of olfactory chaos, with local perfumed oils and potions sold in antediluvian bottles.

Cottonworld Corp (Map p112; ☎ 22850069; Mandlik Marg; ✆ 10:30am-8pm Mon-Sat, noon-8pm Sun) Small chain selling quality cotton goods in Indian and Western designs.

Chimanlals (☎ 22077717; 210 Dr DN Rd, Fort) An Aladdin's cave of cards, envelopes and writing materials made from traditional Indian paper. Enter from Wallace St.

Government emporiums worth checking out include the following:

Central Cottage Industries Emporium (Map p112; ☎ 22027537; Shivaji Marg, Colaba; ✆ 10am-7pm)

Kashmir Government Arts Emporium (Map p114; ☎ 22663822; Sir P Mehta Rd, Fort; ✆ 10am-7pm Mon-Sat)

Uttar Pradesh Handicrafts Emporium (Map p114; ☎ 22662702; Sir P Mehta Rd, Fort; ✆ 10.30am-7.30pm Mon-Sat)

Markets

You can buy just about anything in the dense bazaars north of the Fort (see Map pp106–7). The main areas are Crawford Market (fruit and veg), Mangaldas Market (silk and cloth), Zaveri Bazaar (jewellery), Bhuleshwar Market (fruit and veg) and Chor Bazaar (antiques and

---

> **THIEVES BAZAAR**
>
> Nobody is sure exactly how Mumbai's Chor Bazaar (literally 'thieves market') earned its moniker. One popular explanation has it that Queen Victoria, upon arrival to Mumbai in her steam ship, discovered that her violin/purse/jewellery went missing while being unloaded off the ship. Having scoured the city, the missing item was supposedly found hanging in Chor Bazaar's Mutton St, and hence the name.

---

furniture), where Dhabu St is worth a peek for leather goods, and Mutton St specialises in antiques, reproductions and junk.

Colourful Crawford Market (officially called Mahatma Phule Market) is the last outpost of British Bombay before the tumult of the central bazaars begins. Bas-reliefs by Rudyard Kipling's father, Lockwood Kipling, adorn the Norman-Gothic exterior. The meat market is strictly for the brave; it's one of the few places you can expect to be accosted and asked to buy a bloody goat's head.

Music

LM Furtado & Co (Map pp106–7; ☎ 22013163; 540-544 Kalbadevi Rd, Kalbadevi; ✆ 10am-8pm Mon-Sat) The best place in Mumbai for musical instruments – sitars, tablas, accordions and local and imported guitars. It also has a branch around the corner on Lokmanya Tilak Rd.

Poor-quality pirated CDs and DVDs are available on the street for around Rs 200. If you want quality discs, drop by at either **Planet M** (Map p114; ☎ 66353872; Dr Dadabhai Naoroji Rd, Fort; ✆ 11am-9pm Mon-Sat, noon-8pm Sun) or **Rhythm House** (Map p114; ✆ 22842835; 40 K Dubash Marg, Fort; ✆ 10am-8.30pm Mon-Sat, 11am-8.30pm Sun).

GETTING THERE & AWAY
Air
AIRPORTS

Mumbai is the main international gateway to South India and has the busiest network of domestic flights. The **international airport** (☎ 26829000; www.mumbaiairport.com), officially renamed Chhatrapati Shivaji but still known as Sahar, is 4km away from the domestic airport, also called Chhatrapati Shivaji but known as Santa Cruz. A free shuttle bus runs between the airports, which are 30km and 26km north of Nariman Point in downtown Mumbai.

The international airport has two arrivals halls which have foreign-exchange counters offering reasonable rates, a **Government of India tourist office booth** (☎ 2615660, ext 4700; Arrival Hall 2A), a **hotel reservation desk** (☎ 66048772) and a prepaid taxi booth – all open 24 hours.

The **domestic airport** (☎ 26156600) has two terminals with foreign-exchange bureaus, ticketing counters and a restaurant-bar. The Government of India tourist office booth is in terminal B. Note that flights on domestic sectors of Air India routes depart from the international airport.

INTERNATIONAL AIRLINES

Travel agencies are often a better bet than airline offices for booking international flights, and will reconfirm your flight for a small fee.

Air France (Map pp106–7; ☎ 22024818; Maker Chamber VI, Nariman Point)

Air India (Map p114; ☎ 22796666; Air India Bldg, cnr Marine Dr & Madame Cama Rd, Nariman Point)

British Airways (Map p114; ☎ 22820888; 202-B, Vulcan Insurance Bldg, Veer Nariman Rd, Churchgate)

Cathay Pacific (Map pp106–7; ☎ 22029561; 3rd fl, Bajaj Bhavan, Nariman Point)

Delta Airlines (Map p123; ☎ 28267000; Leela Galleria, Andheri-Kurla Rd, Andheri)

El Al Airlines (Map pp106–7; ☎ 22154701; 57 Shopping Arcade, World Trade Centre, Cuffe Parade)

Qantas (Map pp106–7; ☎ 22020343; 42 Sakhar Bhavan, Nariman Point)

Thai Airways (Map pp106–7; ☎ 22823084; 15 Shopping Centre, World Trade Centre, Cuffe Parade)

Virgin Atlantic (Map p114; ☎ 2281289; Marine Dr, Churchgate)

DOMESTIC AIRLINES

Domestic carriers servicing Mumbai include the following:

Air Deccan (☎ 26611601; domestic airport)

Go Air (☎ 9223222111; domestic airport)

Indian Airlines (Map p114; ☎ 22023031, 24hr reservations 1401; Air India Bldg, cnr Marine Dr & Madame Cama Rd, Nariman Point)

Jet Airways (Map p112; ☎ 22855788; Amarchand Mansion, Madame Cama Rd)

Kingfisher (☎ 56469999; domestic airport)

Sahara Airlines (Map pp106–7; ☎ 56374101-4; 7 Tulsiani Chambers, Free Press Journal Marg, Nariman Point)

Spice Jet (☎ 9871803333; www.spicejet.com; domestic airport)

There are flights to more than 30 Indian cities from Mumbai. See right for details of

MAJOR DOMESTIC FLIGHTS FROM MUMBAI

Destination	Fare (US$)	Duration (hr)	Flights per day
Bengaluru	187	1½	18
Chennai	207	1¾	19
Delhi	237	2	34
Goa	127	1	16
Hyderabad	162	1¼	14
Jaipur	202	1¾	14
Kochi	232	1¼	20
Kolkata	287	2¼	21

major flights. The boxed table above shows rough prices for tickets booked in person a few days in advance – expect discounts if booking earlier or online. Kingfisher and Air Deccan offer flights to most of these destinations at the much cheaper Indian fares (up to 70% less).

Bus

Numerous private operators and state governments run long-distance buses to and from Mumbai. Private operators provide faster service, more comfort and simpler booking procedures.

Private long-distance buses depart from Dr Anadrao Nair Rd near Mumbai Central train station (Map pp106–7). Fares for non-AC deluxe buses include:

Destination	Fare (Rs)	Duration (hr)
Ahmedabad	300	13
Aurangabad	250	10
Bengaluru	550	24
Mahabaleshwar	300	7
Panaji	300	14-18
Pune	150	7
Udaipur	450	16

There are also sleeper buses to Goa for Rs 350 to 450. Fares to popular destinations (such as Goa) are up to 75% higher during holiday periods such as Diwali and Christmas. To check on departure times and current prices, try **National Travels** (Map pp106–7; ☎ 23015652; Dr Anadrao Nair Rd; ◷ 6am-10pm).

More convenient for Goa and southern destinations are the private buses that depart twice a day from in front of Azad Maidan, just south of the Metro cinema. Purchase tickets directly from agents located near the bus departure point.

Long-distance state-run buses depart from **Mumbai Central bus terminal** (Map pp106-7; ☎ 23074272) by Mumbai Central train station. Buses service major towns in Maharashtra and neighbouring states. They're marginally cheaper and more frequent than the private services, but they're also decrepit and crowded. Destinations include Pune (Rs 160, four hours), Aurangabad (Rs 200, eight to nine hours) and Mahabaleshwar (Rs 180, seven hours).

Train

Three train systems operate out of Mumbai, but the two most relevant for overseas visitors are Central Railways and Western Railways. See the boxed table (below) for information on key long-distance services.

Central Railways (☎ 134),handling services to the east, south, plus a few trains to the north, operate from CST. The **reservation centre** (Map p114; ☎ 22625959; ☼ 8am-8pm Mon-Sat, 8am-2pm Sun) is around the side of CST where the taxis gather. **Foreign tourist-quota tickets** (Counter 52, ☼ 8am-8pm) can be bought up to 60 days before travel, but must be paid in foreign currency or with rupees backed by an encashment certificate or ATM receipt. Indrail passes (p505) can also be bought at Counter 52. You can buy nonquota tickets with a Visa or MasterCard at the much faster credit-card counters (10 and 11) for a Rs 30 fee.

A few Central Railways trains depart from Dadar (D), a few stations north of CST. Others leave from Churchgate/Lokmanya Tilak (T), 16km north of CST. One these is the *Chennai Express,* the fastest train to Chennai (Madras). Book tickets for all these trains at CST.

MAJOR TRAINS FROM MUMBAI				
Destination	**Train No & name**	**Fare (Rs)**	**Duration (hr)**	**Departure**
Agra	2137 *Punjab Mail*	417/1118/1583	21½	7.10pm CST
Ahmedabad	2901 *Gujarat Mail*	235/604/844	9	9.50pm MC
Aurangabad	7057 *Devagiri Exp*	178/471/666	7½	9.05pm CST
	7617 *Tapovan Exp*	109/369*	7½	6.10am CST
Bengaluru	6529 *Udyan Exp*	377/1031/1472	24½	7.55am CST
Bhopal	2137 *Punjab Mail*	330/872/1229	14	7.10pm CST
Chennai	6011 *Chennai Exp*	389/1065/1521	26½	2:00pm CST
Delhi	2951 *Rajdhani Exp*	1495/2040**	17	4.15pm MC
	9023 *Janata Exp*	405***	30	7.25am MC
	2137 *Punjab Mail*	449/1208/1713	25¼	7.10pm CST
Goa	0111 *Konkan Kanya Exp*	284/769/1093	12	11:00pm CST
	0103 *Mandavi Exp*	284/769/1093	11½	6:55am CST
	2051 *Shatabdi Exp*	197/675*	8	5.30am D
Hyderabad	2701 *Hussainsagar Exp*	317/837/1178	15	9.50pm CST
Indore	2961 *Avantika Exp*	325/861/1212	15	7.05pm MC
Jaipur	2955 *Jaipur Exp*	389/1039/1469	18	6.50pm MC
Kochi	6345 *Netravati Exp*	441/1211/1732	27	11.40pm T
Kolkata	2859 *Gitanjali Exp*	517/1399/1989	30	6:00am CST
	2809 *Howrah Mail*	517/1399/1989	32	8.35pm CST
Pune	2123 *Deccan Queen*	82/270*	3½	5.10pm CST
	1007 *Deccan Exp*	72/240*	4½	7:10am CST
Varanasi	1093 *Mahanagari Exp*	429/1178/1683	29	12:10am CST
	5017 *Gorakhpur Exp*	421/1155/1651	31	6.35am T
Trivandrum	6345 *Netravati Exp*	473/1301/1862	31	11.40pm T

Abbreviations for train stations: CST – Chhatrapati Shivaji Terminus; MC – Mumbai Central; T – Lokmanya Tilak; D – Dadar
   Note: Fares are for sleeper/3AC/2AC sleeper on overnight trips except for: *2nd class/AC seat, **3AC/2AC and ***sleeper.

Western Railways (☎ 131) has services to the north (including Rajasthan and Delhi) from Mumbai Central (MC) train station (often still called Bombay Central). Make these bookings at the crowded **reservation centre** (Map p114; ☎ 22620079; ◷ 8am-8pm Mon-Sun) opposite Churchgate train station. The **foreign tourist-quota counter** (Counter 28) is upstairs next to the Government of India tourist office, same rules apply as at CST station. The credit-card counter is No 20. There's a reservation centre adjacent to Mumbai Central train station for nonquota tickets.

GETTING AROUND
To/From the Airports
INTERNATIONAL
Taxis operate 24 hours a day from the airport. The trip is much faster by night, though a night surcharge is added.

The prepaid-taxi booth at the international airport has set daytime fares to Colaba, the Fort and Marine Dr (Rs 350; Rs 440 for AC), as well as to Juhu (Rs 190), Chowpatty (Rs 320) and to Mumbai Central train station (Rs 270). There's a 25% surcharge between midnight and 5am and a charge of Rs 5 to 10 per bag. The journey to Colaba takes about 45 minutes at night and 1½ to two hours during the day. You could try to negotiate a lower fare with a private taxi, but it's hardly worth the hassle. A tip of 5% to 10% is appreciated. Don't catch an autorickshaw from the airport to the city: they're prohibited from entering downtown Mumbai and can take you only as far as Mahim Creek.

The cheap alternative is to catch an autorickshaw (around Rs 30) to Andheri train station and catch a suburban train (Rs 9, 45 minutes) to Churchgate or CST. You can only do this if you arrive during the day; don't attempt it during rush hours (particularly the manic 7am to 10am morning rush), or if you're weighed down with luggage. At the very least, buy a 1st-class ticket (Rs 76).

Minibuses outside the arrival hall offer free shuttle services to the domestic airport and Juhu hotels.

A taxi from the city centre (eg CST station) to the international airport costs around Rs 300 with a bit of bargaining, plus extra for baggage; taxi drivers in Colaba ask for a fixed Rs 350. It's 30% more between midnight and 5am.

DOMESTIC
Taxis and autorickshaws queue up outside both domestic terminals. There's no prepaid-

taxi counter, but the taxi queue outside is controlled by the police – make sure your driver uses the meter and conversion card. A taxi takes one to 1½ hours to reach the city centre and costs around Rs 300.

If you don't have too much luggage, bus 195 stops on nearby Nehru Rd and passes through Colaba Causeway (Rs 16). Coming from the city, it stops on the highway opposite the airport.

A better alternative is to catch an autorickshaw between the airport and Vile Parle train station (Rs 15), and catch a suburban train between Vile Parle and Churchgate (Rs 9, 45 minutes). Don't attempt this during rush hour.

Boat
Both **PNP** (☎ 22885220) and **Maldar Catamarans** (☎ 22829695) run regular ferries to Mandwa (Rs 100 one-way), useful for access to Murud-Janjira and other parts of the Konkan Coast (p157), avoiding the long bus trip out of Mumbai. Their ticket offices are at Apollo Bunder (near the Gateway of India; Map p112).

Bus
Mumbai's single- and double-decker buses are good for travelling short distances. Fares around South Mumbai cost around Rs 3 for a section, pay the conductor once you're aboard. The service is run by **BEST** (☎ 28227006; www.best undertaking.com), which has its main depot in Colaba (the website has a useful search facility for bus routes across the city). Just jumping on a double-decker bus (such as No 103) is an inexpensive way to have a look around South Mumbai.

Following are some useful bus routes; all of these buses depart from the bus stand at the southern end of Colaba Causeway and pass Flora Fountain:

Destination	Bus No
Breach Candy	132, 133
Chowpatty	103, 106, 107, 123
Churchgate	70, 106, 123, 132
Haji Ali	83, 124, 132, 133
Hanging Gardens	103, 106
Mani Bhavan	123
Mohammed Ali Rd	1, 3, 21
Mumbai Central train station	124, 125
CST & Crawford Market	1, 3, 21, 103, 124

Car

Cars are generally hired for an eight-hour day and with a maximum of 80km travel allowed; additional charges rack up if you exceed these limits.

Agents at the Apollo Bunder ticket booths near the Gateway of India can arrange a non-AC Maruti with driver for a half-day of sightseeing for Rs 600 (going as far as Mahalaxmi and Malabar Hill). Regular taxi drivers often accept a similar price.

Motorcycle

Allibhai Premji Tyrewalla (Map pp106-7; ☎ 23099313; www.premjis.com; 205/207 Dr D Bhadkamkar Rd, Opera House; ⏰ 10am-7pm Mon-Sat) is the place to purchase a new or used motorcycle with a guaranteed buy-back option. For two- to three-week 'rental' periods you'll still have to pay the full cost of the bike upfront. The company prefers to deal with longer-term schemes of two months or more, which work out cheaper anyway. A used 350cc or 500cc Enfield costs Rs 35,000 to 60,000, with a buy-back price of around 60% after three months. A smaller bike (100cc to 180cc) starts at Rs 25,000. It can also arrange shipment of bikes overseas (Rs 18,000 to the UK).

Taxi & Autorickshaw

Every second car on Mumbai's streets seems to be a black-and-yellow Premier taxi (India's version of a 1950s Fiat). They are the most convenient way to get around the city and in South Mumbai drivers almost always use the meter without prompting. Autorickshaws are confined to the suburbs north of Mahim Creek.

Drivers don't always know the names of Mumbai's streets – the best way to find something is by using nearby landmarks. The taxi meters are out of date, so the fare is calculated using a conversion chart, which all drivers must carry. The rate during the day is around 13 times the meter reading, with a minimum fare of Rs 13 for the first 1.6km (flag fall) and Rs 7 per kilometre after this. Costs are around 25% more expensive between midnight and 6am.

Cool Cabs (☎ 28227006) operates correctly metered, blue AC taxis. They're about a third more expensive than regular cabs and can be booked by telephone.

If you're north of Mahim Creek and not heading into the city, it's best to catch autorickshaws. They're metered but also use a conversion chart: the fare is roughly 10 times the meter reading.

Train

Mumbai has an efficient but overcrowded suburban train network.

There are three main lines, making it easy to navigate. The most useful service operates from Churchgate heading north to stations such as Charni Rd (for Chowpatty Beach), Mumbai Central, Mahalaxmi (for the dhobi ghat; p117), Vile Parle (for the domestic airport), Andheri (for the international airport) and Borivali (for Sanjay Gandhi National Park). Other suburban lines operate from CST to Byculla (for Victoria Gardens), Dadar, and as far as Neral (for Matheran). Trains run from 4am till 1am. From Churchgate, 2nd-/1st-class fares are Rs 5/41 to Mumbai Central, Rs 9/76 to Vile Parle or Andheri and Rs 11/102 to Borivali.

Avoid rush hours when trains are jam-packed, even in 1st class – watch your valuables. Women should take advantage of the ladies-only carriages.

GREATER MUMBAI

ELEPHANTA ISLAND

In the middle of Mumbai Harbour, 9km northeast of the Gateway of India, the rock-cut temples on **Elephanta Island** (Map p105; Indian/foreigner Rs 10/250; ⏰ caves 9am-5.30pm Tue-Sun) are a spectacle worth crossing the waters for. Home to a labyrinth of cave-temples carved into the basalt rock of the island, the artwork represents some of the most impressive temple carving in all India. The main Shiva-dedicated temple is an intriguing latticework of courtyards, halls, pillars and shrines, with the magnum opus a 6m tall statue of Sadhashiva – depicting a three-faced Shiva as the destroyer, creator and preserver of the universe. The enormous central bust of Shiva, its eyes closed in eternal contemplation, may be the most serene sight you witness in India.

The temples are thought to have been created between AD 450 and 750, when the island was known as Gharapuri (Place of Caves). The Portuguese renamed it Elephanta because of a large stone elephant near the shore, which collapsed in 1814 and was moved by the British to Mumbai's Victoria Gardens.

The English-language guide service (free with deluxe boat tickets) is worthwhile, tours depart every hour on the half-hour from the ticket booth. If you prefer to explore independently, pick up Pramod Chandra's *A Guide to the Elephanta Caves* from the stalls lining the stairway. There's also a small **museum** on site, which has some informative pictorial panels on the origin of the caves.

Getting There & Away

Launches head to Elephanta Island from the Gateway of India every half-hour from around 9am to 3pm Tuesday to Sunday. Economy boats cost Rs 100 return while more spacious 'deluxe' launches are Rs 120; buy tickets at the booths lining Apollo Bunder. The voyage takes just over an hour.

The ferries dock at the end of a concrete pier, from where you can walk (around three minutes) or take the miniature train (Rs 8) to the stairway leading up to the caves. It's lined with handicraft stalls and patrolled by pesky monkeys. Maharajas-in-training can be carried there by palanquins (one-way/return Rs 150/250).

SANJAY GANDHI NATIONAL PARK

It's hard to believe that within 90 minutes of the teeming metropolis you can be surrounded by the jungle of this 104-sq-km **protected area** (Map p105; ☎ 28866449; adult/child Rs 10/5; ☽ 7.30am-7pm Tue-Sun). Here, bright flora, birds, butterflies and elusive wild leopards replace traffic and crowds, all surrounded by forested hills on the city's northern edge. Urban development and shantytowns are starting to muscle in on the edges of this wild region, but for now much of it remains a refuge of green and calm.

One of the main attractions is the **lion & tiger safari** (Rs 30; ☽ every 20min 9am-12.40pm & 2-5.20pm Tue-Sun), departing from the tiger orientation centre (about 1km in from the main entrance). Expect a whirlwind 20-minute jaunt by bus through the two separate areas of the park housing the tigers and lions.

Inside the main northern entrance is an **information centre** with a small exhibition on the park's wildlife. The best time to see birds is October to April and butterflies August to November.

Another big draw are the 109 **Kanheri Caves** (Indian/foreigner Rs 5/100; ☽ 9.30am-5.30pm Tue-Sun) lining the side of a rocky ravine 5km from the northern park entrance. They were used by Buddhist monks between the 2nd and 9th centuries as *viharas* (monasteries) and *chaityas* (temples), but don't compare to the caves at Ajanta (p150), Ellora (p147) or even Lonavla (p160).

For information on the park, contact Mumbai's main conservation organisation, the **Bombay Natural History Society** (Map p114; ☎ 22821811; www.bnhs.org; Colaba Causeway) in Kala Ghoda.

Getting There & Away

Take the train from Churchgate to Borivali train station (Rs 11, one hour). From there take an autorickshaw (Rs 15) or catch any bus to the park entrance. It's a further 10-minute walk from the entrance to the safari park.

Maharashtra

Sprawling Maharashtra, India's second most populous state, stretches from the gorgeous greens of the little-known Konkan Coast right into the parched innards of India's beating heart. Within this massive framework are all the sights, sounds, tastes, and experiences of India.

In the north there's Nasik, a city of crashing colours, timeless ritual and Hindu legend. In the south you can come face to face with modern India at its very best in Pune, a city as famous for its sex guru as its bars and restaurants. Further south still, the old maharaja's palaces, wrestling pits and overwhelming temples of Kolhapur make for one of the best introductions to India anyone could want. Out in the far east of the state towards Nagpur, the adventurous can set out in search of tigers hidden in a clump of national parks. On the coast a rash of little-trodden beaches and collapsing forts give Goa's tropical dreams a run for their money and in the hills of the Western Ghats, morning mists lift to reveal stupendous views and colonial-flavoured hill stations. But it's the centre, with its treasure house of architectural and artistic wonders (topped by the World Heritage–listed cave temples of Ellora and Ajanta), that really steals the show. Whatever way you look at it, Maharashtra is one of the most vibrant and rewarding corners of India, yet despite this, most travellers make only a brief artistic pause at Ellora and Ajanta before scurrying away to other corners of India, leaving much of this diverse state to the explorers.

HIGHLIGHTS

- Feel dwarfed by the monumental Kailasa Temple, the shining jewel of the cave temples at **Ellora** (p147)
- Follow in the footsteps of pilgrims heading to **Nasik** (p139), and its colourful riverside ghats
- Ponder the reasons for hiding a gallery of Buddhist art in the jungle at **Ajanta** (p150)
- Hunt out serene beaches, elephant temples and tumbling fortresses on the **Konkan Coast** (p156)
- Gallop on a horse to Echo Point in **Matheran** (p158) and then chug back home on a toy train
- Search for snakes and 'zennis' (Zen tennis) courts in **Pune** (p163).

★Ajanta
★Nasik ★Ellora
★ Matheran
★ Pune
★ Konkan Coast

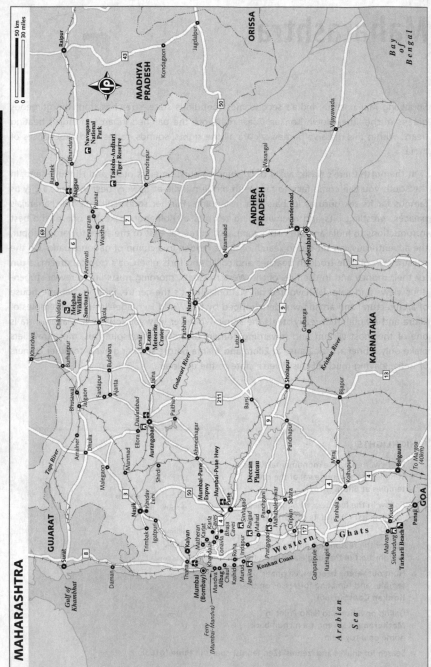

MAHARASHTRA

History

With a relatively small army, Maratha leader Shivaji (1627–80) established a base at Pune and later Raigad, from where he controlled the Deccan and conquered more than 300 forts during his reign. Shivaji, still highly respected, is credited for instilling a strong, independent spirit among the region's people.

From the early 18th century the Maratha empire came under the control of the Peshwas, who retained power until 1819 when, after much tussling, the British barged them aside.

After Independence, western Maharashtra and Gujarat were joined to form Bombay state. Today's state has Mumbai (Bombay) as its capital and was formed in 1960 when the Marathi- and Gujarati-speaking areas were once again separated. The state is currently controlled by a Congress-NCP coalition.

Climate

The monsoon hits most of Maharashtra hard from May through to September. The rest of the year you can expect the coastal and interior regions to be hot; for some respite head to the hill stations of the Western Ghats.

Information

The head office of Maharashtra Tourism Development Corporation (MTDC; Map p114; ☎ 22026713; Madame Cama Rd, Nariman Point; ⊙ 9.45am-5.30pm Mon-Sat) is in Mumbai. Most major towns throughout the state have offices, too, but they're generally only useful for booking MTDC accommodation and tours.

ACCOMMODATION

In Maharashtra rooms costing Rs 1199 or less are charged a 4% tax, while those that are Rs 1200 and up are hit with a 10% tax. Some hotels also levy an extra expenditure tax (up to 10%). Rates in this chapter do not include tax unless otherwise indicated. High-season rates are quoted but prices might rise higher still during holidays such as Diwali.

Getting There & Away

Maharashtra's main transport hub is Mumbai (p131), although Pune, Nasik and Nagpur are also players.

Getting Around

Because the state is so large you might want to consider taking a few internal flights (eg Mumbai to Nagpur) to speed up your explo-

---

FAST FACTS

- Population: 96.8 million
- Area: 307,690 sq km
- Capital: Mumbai (Bombay)
- Main language: Marathi
- When to go: October to March (coast); September to mid-June (hills)

---

rations. Otherwise there are plenty of trains and private long-distance buses, with rickety state transport buses connecting up the more remote places.

NORTHERN MAHARASHTRA

NASIK

☎ 0253 / pop 1.2 million / elev 565m

Standing on the Godavari, one of India's holiest rivers, Nasik (also known as Nashik) is the kind of town where you can't walk more than a couple of steps without tripping over yet another exotic temple or colourful bathing ghat. It's an absorbing and exciting place and has many associations with the Hindu epic Ramayana. Lord Rama and his wife Sita were exiled here and it's where Lakshmana hacked off the *nasika* (nose) of Ravana's sister, thus giving the city its name.

Nasik also serves as a base for pilgrims visiting Trimbak (p142) and Shirdi (79km southeast), birthplace of the original Sai Baba. Every 12 years Nasik plays host to the Kumbh Mela, the largest religious gathering on earth. The next one is due in 2019, but a smaller gathering, Ardha Mela (Half Mela), is held every six years. See also p472.

Orientation

Mahatma Gandhi Rd, better known as MG Rd, a couple of blocks north of the Old Central bus stand, is Nasik's commercial hub. The temple-strewn Godavari River flows through town just east of here.

Information

Cyber Café (8 Twin Centre, Vakil Wadi Rd; per hr Rs 20; ⊙ 10am-10pm Mon-Sat, 10am-3pm Sun) Near Hotel Panchavati.

HDFC Bank (MG Rd) Has a 24-hour ATM.

MAHARASHTRA

MAHARASHTRA

MTDC tourist office (☎ 2570059; Paryatan Bhavan, Old Agra Rd; ⏰ 10.30am-5.30pm Mon-Sat) About 700m south of the Old Central bus stand. Has a pretty useless city map (Rs 5).

State Bank of India (☎ 2502436; Old Agra Rd; ⏰ 10.30am-4pm Mon-Fri, 10.30am-1.30pm Sat) Across from the Old Central bus stand. Changes cash and travellers cheques and has an ATM.

Sights
RAMKUND
This **bathing tank** is the centre of the Nasik world and sees hundreds of colourful pilgrims arriving daily to bathe, pray and, because the waters of the Ramkund provide moksha (liberation of the soul), even to die. For a tourist it all promises one of the most intense experiences in Maharashtra. The scene is further enhanced by the colourful **market** just down river.

TEMPLES
A short walk uphill east of the Ramkund, the **Kala Rama** (Black Rama), is the city's holiest temple. Dating to 1794 and containing unusual black-stone representations of Rama, Sita and Lakshmana, the temple stands on the site

where Lakshmana sliced off Ravana's sisters nose. Nearby is the **Gumpha Panchivati**, where Sita hid from the evil Ravana.

The ramshackle **Sundar Narayan Temple**, at the western end of Victoria Bridge, contains three black Vishnu deities, and the modern **Muktidham Temple**, about 7km southeast of the city and near the train station, has the 18 chapters of the Bhagavad Gita lining its interior walls.

All of the temples listed here are open from 6am to 9pm.

Tours
An all-day tour of Nasik, conducted in Marathi and including Trimbak and Pandav Leni, departs daily at 7.30am from the Old Central bus stand (Rs 94) and returns at 5.30pm.

Sleeping & Eating
Hotel Abhishek (☎ 2514201; hotabhi_nsk@sancharnet.in; Panchavati Karanja; s/d from Rs 215/290) A couple of minutes' walk uphill from the Godavari River, this is the best budget base from which to be totally overwhelmed by sacred India at its best (and nosiest). Rooms are good value with hot showers and TV.

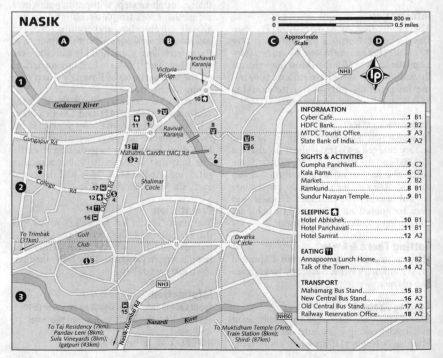

NASIK

0   800 m
0   0.5 miles

Approximate Scale

INFORMATION	
Cyber Café	1 B1
HDFC Bank	2 B2
MTDC Tourist Office	3 A3
State Bank of India	4 A2

SIGHTS & ACTIVITIES	
Gumpha Panchivati	5 C2
Kala Rama	6 C2
Market	7 B2
Ramkund	8 B1
Sundur Narayan Temple	9 B1

SLEEPING	
Hotel Abhishek	10 B1
Hotel Panchavati	11 B1
Hotel Samrat	12 A2

EATING	
Annapoorna Lunch Home	13 B2
Talk of the Town	14 A2

TRANSPORT	
Mahamarg Bus Stand	15 B3
New Central Bus Stand	16 A2
Old Central Bus Stand	17 A2
Railway Reservation Office	18 A2

MAHARASHTRA

FESTIVALS IN MAHARASHTRA

Sarai Gandarvar (Feb; Pune, p163) Classical Indian music and dance performances that last all night.

Matharaj Naag Panchami (Aug; Pune, p163 & Kolhapur, p173) A slithery snake-worshipping festival.

Ganesh Chaturthi (Aug & Sep; Pune, p163) Ganesh Chaturthi is celebrated with fervour across Maharashtra, but one of the best places to be is Pune, 163km southeast of Mumbai, where special arts and cultural events accompany the general mayhem for the elephant-headed deity.

Dussehra Festival (Sep/Oct; Nagpur, p154) Thousands of Buddhists celebrate the anniversary of Dr Ambedkar's conversion to Buddhism.

Kalidas Festival (Nov; Nagpur, p154) A music and dance festival dedicated to the Sanskrit poet Mahakavi Kalidas.

Ellora Dance & Music Festival (Dec/Jan; Aurangabad, p143) Classical music and dance festival held at the Soneri Mahal.

Hotel Samrat (☎ 2577211; fax 2306100; Old Agra Rd; s/d from Rs 450/625, with AC from Rs 775/925; ❄) Its position close to the bus stands means you don't have far to stumble with your bags, and the rooms, which come with balconies and cable TV, are clean and comfortable enough to make for a pleasant stay. Its spick-and-span restaurant is open 24 hours and makes delectable Gujarati thalis (Rs 70).

Hotel Panchavati (430 Chandak Wadi) You can save yourself some time and effort by heading straight for this excellent complex – the four hotels cover every pocket from budget to top-end. Kicking off at the cheaper end of the market is the Panchavati Guesthouse (☎ 2578771; dorms/singles/doubles Rs 250/400/500), which has clean, cramped rooms and very few foreign guests. Brilliant-value midrange rooms with piping-hot showers and spot-on service are on offer at the Panchavati Yatri (☎ 2578782; singles/doubles from Rs 710/910, with AC Rs 920/1040). The Hotel Panchavati (☎ 2575771; singles/doubles from Rs 950/1190, with AC from Rs 1140/1340) is a pricier option for midrange travellers but the rooms are classier. Last of all is the sumptuous Panchavati Millionaire (☎ 2312318; singles/doubles from Rs 1350/1650).

Taj Residency (☎ 2536604499; www.tajhotels.com; MIDC, Ambad; d from US$95; ❄ ▢ ▨) Nasik's most luxurious hotel is on the Nasik–Mumbai Rd, close to Pandav Leni and well away from all the noise and excitement of the town centre. It's a lovely and calm modern business-class hotel, which also has a regarded restaurant.

Annapoorna Lunch Home (MG Rd; snacks & meals Rs 10-80) There might not be any surprises on the menu but it would be hard to find fault with the cheap eats dished out by the friendly waiters here. The list of dosas on offer is almost as long as the dosa itself!

Talk of the Town (Old Agra Rd; dishes Rs 60-150) Set inside a glass-plated building next to the New Central bus stand, Talk of the Town has a long menu of Indian and Chinese favourites, smartly suited waiters and a tranquil atmosphere.

Getting There & Around

BUS

Nasik is a major player on the road-transport scene, with frequent state buses operating at nearly all hours from three different stands.

The **Old Central bus stand** (CBS; ☎ 2309310) is useful mainly for those going to Trimbak (Rs 17, 45 minutes). A block south the **New Central bus station** (☎ 2309308) has services to Aurangabad (semideluxe Rs 153, five hours) and Pune (ordinary/semideluxe Rs 110/170, 4½ hours). The **Mahamarg bus stand** (☎ 2309309), has services hourly to Mumbai (semideluxe Rs 140, 4½ hours) and twice-hourly to Shirdi (Rs 60, 2½ hours).

Many private bus agents are based near the CBS and most buses depart from Old Agra Rd. Destinations include Pune (with/without AC Rs 220/150, 4½ hours), Mumbai (with/without AC Rs 320/150, 4½ hours), Aurangabad (without AC Rs 130, 11.30pm only) and Ahmedabad (with/without AC Rs 500/280, 12 hours). Note that most of the Mumbai-bound buses terminate at Dadar.

TRAIN

The Nasik Rd train station is 8km southeast of the town centre, but a useful **railway reservation office** (☎ 134; ✆ 8am-8pm Mon-Sat, 8am-2pm Sun) is on the 1st floor of the Commissioner's Office, Canada Corner, 500m west of the CBS. The 7am *Panchavati Express* is the fastest train to Mumbai (2nd class/chair Rs 56/211, four hours) and the 9.50am *Tapovan Express* is the only convenient direct train to Aurangabad

(2nd class/chair Rs 56/211, 3½ hours). Local buses leave frequently from Shalimar Circle, a few minutes' walk northeast of the CBS, to the train station (Rs 6). An autorickshaw costs about Rs 70.

AROUND NASIK
Pandav Leni

The 24 Early Buddhist caves of **Pandav Leni** (Indian/foreigner Rs 5/US$2; ☺ 8am-6pm), about 8km south of Nasik along the Mumbai road, date from the 1st century BC to the 2nd century AD. Caves 19 and 23 have some interesting carvings; the rest are virtually empty and of limited interest to the lay-person.

Below the caves is the **Dadasaheb Phalke Memorial** (admission Rs 10; ☺ 10am-9pm), dedicated to the pioneering Indian movie producer of the same name.

Local buses (Rs 7) run past the caves from Shalimar Circle, near the CBS, in Nasik, but the easiest way there is by autorickshaw; a return journey including waiting time costs around Rs 200.

Trimbak

Trimbakeshwar Temple, stands in the centre of Trimbak, 33km west of Nasik, and is one of India's most sacred temples, containing a *jyoti linga*, one of the 12 most important shrines of Shiva. It's open to Hindus only, but it's possible to see into the courtyard. Even with this restriction Trimbak is a fascinating town, whose narrow streets and explosive markets fit every idea of exotic India. Nearby, the waters of the Godavari River tumble into the **Gangadwar bathing tank**, where pilgrims gather to wash away their sins. Non-Hindus are welcome. The real highlight of a visit to Trimbak is to make the four-hour-return hike up the sheer **Brahmagiri Hill** behind the town to the

WINE COUNTRY

India makes chai, not wine – but wait, what's this? A vineyard near Nasik? As it turns out, the fertile soils and cooler climate of Nasik (at around 600m above sea level) aren't that different from Bordeaux at all, making this town the Grand Crux of India's fledgling wine-growing industry. One winery welcoming visitors is **Sula Vineyards** (☎ 0253-2231663; www.sulawines.com; Govardhan, Gangapur-Savargaon Rd; ☺ 12.30-8.30pm), 8km southwest of Nasik. This pioneer of the Indian wine industry has produced decently drinkable drops since 1998. A tasting room has recently been added; call in advance if you're planning on visiting to try out a drop or two.

source of the Godavari. Pilgrims from across the nation clamber up to the flower encrusted summit where the Godavari dribbles forth from a spring and into a couple of temples soaked in incense. On the route up to the top you will pass a number of other temples, shrines and even some caves in which sadhus have made a home. Don't attempt the ascent if rain looks imminent, as the trail can quickly become a dangerous raging torrent.

If you want to stay the night, the **MTDC Resort** (☎ 02594-233143; d Rs 300, tr ste Rs 800) is a modern building housing spacious suites with creature comforts such as cable TV.

Regular buses run from the New Central bus station in Nasik to Trimbak (Rs 17, 45 minutes).

Igatpuri

About 44km south of Nasik on the rail line to Mumbai, the village of Igatpuri is home to

---

THE GOD WHO CAME TO STAY

His calm, smiling face is seen on posters throughout India and many regard him as a living god, but who exactly was Sai Baba? Well his real name, date of birth and knowledge of his childhood are unknown, but at around the age of 16 he appeared in the small town of Shirdi, not far from Nasik, where he spent the rest of his life sleeping alternately in an old Mosque or a Hindu temple and praying in them both equally. His message of tolerance between the faiths and the many miracles attributed to him meant that by the time he died in 1918, he had established a large following. Today, his temple complex in Shirdi draws an average of 40,000 pilgrims a day. However, like Elvis, he is possibly not even dead – in Andhra Pradesh another famous holy man who also commands huge respect, Sathya Sai Baba, claims to be the reincarnation of the original Sai Baba (see p305).

the world's largest *vipassana* (a type of meditation) centre, **Vipassana International Academy** (☎ 02553-244076; www.vri.dhamma.org).

Ten-day residential courses in this strict form of Theravada Buddhist meditation are held throughout the year. *Vipassana* was first taught by Gautama Buddha in the 6th century BC, but was reintroduced to India by teacher SN Goenka in the 1960s.

AURANGABAD

☎ 0240 / pop 872,667 / elev 513m

They say that every dog has its day and for dog-eared Aurangabad that day came when the last Mughal emperor, Aurangzeb, made the city his capital from 1653 to 1707. Though its claim to fame was only brief, the city retains a number of worthwhile historical relics, including a tempting Taj wannabe and some grandly carved caves, but the real reason for traipsing all the way out here is because the city makes an excellent base from which to explore the World Heritage site of Ellora.

Silk fabrics are Aurangabad's traditional trade but the city is now a major industrial centre with beer and bikes being the big earners.

Orientation

The train station, cheap hotels and restaurants are clumped together in the south of the town. The **Maharashtra State Road Transport Corporation bus stand** (MSRTC; Station Rd West) is 1.5km to the north. Northeast of the bus stand is the buzzing Old Town with its narrow streets and distinct Muslim quarter.

Information
BOOKSHOPS
Sharayu (☎ 2335220; 119-A Kailash Market, Station Rd East; ☺ 10.30am-9.30pm) Aurangabad's best selection of English-language books.

INTERNET ACCESS
Café Internet (Shop 12, Station Rd East; per hr Rs 30; ☺ 9.30am-11pm)
Cyber-dhaba (Station Rd West; per hr Rs 20; ☺ 8am-11pm) Also changes money.
Global Access (Konark Estate, Osmanpura; per hr Rs 20; ☺ 9.30am-11pm) Doubles as a travel agent and money exchange centre.

MONEY
ICICI has ATMs on Nirala Bazaar and Station Rd East.

Bank of Baroda (☎ 2337129; Pattan Darwaza Rd; ☺ 10.30am-3pm Mon-Fri, to 12.45pm Sat) Near the Paithan Gate, gives cash advances on Visa and MasterCard.
Trade Wings (☎ 2322677; Station Rd West; ☺ 9am-7pm Mon-Sat, to 1pm Sun) Charges a Rs 50 fee.

POST
Post office (☎ 2331121; Juna Bazaar; ☺ 10am-6pm Mon-Sat)

TOURIST INFORMATION
Government of India tourist office (☎ 2331217; Krishna Vilas, Station Rd West; ☺ 8.30am-6pm Mon-Fri, to 1.30pm Sat) A friendly and helpful tourist office with a decent range of brochures.
MTDC office (☎ 2331513; Station Rd East; ☺ 10am-6pm Mon-Sat)

TRAVEL AGENCIES
Ashoka Tours & Travels (☎ 2390618; Hotel Panchavati, Station Rd West) City and regional tours, car hire and hotel pick-ups.
Classic Tours (☎ 2335598; aurangabad@classicservices .in; MTDC Holiday Resort, Station Rd East) Trusty place to book transport, tours and even accommodation.

Sights
BIBI-QA-MAQBARA
Built in 1679 as a mausoleum for Aurangzeb's wife, Rabia-ud-Daurani, the **Bibi-qa-Maqbara** (☎ 2400620; Indian/foreigner Rs 5/US$2; ☺ dawn-10pm) is known as the 'Poor mans Taj'. This is a slightly ironic comparison considering it was Aurangzeb's father who built the original shortly before being overthrown and imprisoned by his son on account of his extravagance! The comparison is also a little unfair because, despite the obvious weathering, it's still a damn sight more impressive than the average gravestone.

AURANGABAD CAVES
With goats more numerous than tourists, the **Aurangabad caves** (☎ 2400620; Indian/foreigner Rs 5/US$2; ☺ dawn-dusk) might not be a patch on Ellora or Ajanta, but they are very quiet and peaceful. Carved out of the hillside in the 6th or 7th century AD, the 10 caves – consisting of two groups 1km apart (retain your ticket for entry into both sets) – are all Buddhist. Cave 7 with its sculptures of scantily clad lovers in suggestive positions is everyone's favourite. A rickshaw from the Bibi-qa-Maqbara shouldn't cost more than Rs 100 including waiting time.

PANCHAKKI

Panchakki (Water Wheel) takes its name from the mill which in its day was considered a marvel of engineering. Driven by water carried through earthen pipes from the river 6km away, it once ground grain for pilgrims. You can still see the humble machine at work.

Baba Shah Muzaffar, a Sufi saint and spiritual guide to Aurangzeb, is buried here. His **memorial garden** (admission Rs 5; ☼ 6am-8pm) has a series of fish-filled tanks, near a large shade-giving banyan tree.

SHIVAJI MUSEUM

This dull **museum** (☎ 2334087; Dr Ambedkar Rd; admission Rs 5; ☼ 10.30am-1.30pm & 3-6pm Wed-Mon), dedicated to the life of the Maratha hero Shivaji, includes a 500-year-old chain-mail suit and a copy of the Quran handwritten by Aurangzeb.

Tours

Classic Tours (☎ 2335598; www.aurangabadtours.com) run daily tours to the **Ajanta** (Rs 270; ☼ 8am-5.30pm) and **Ellora** (Rs 170; ☼ 9.30am-5.30pm) caves, which include a guide but no admission fees. The Ellora tour also includes all the other major Aurangabad sites, which is a lot to swallow in a day. Tours start and end at the MTDC Holiday Resort (right).

Sleeping

BUDGET

YHA Hostel (☎ 2334892; Station Rd West; dm/d Rs 60/160) The woman who runs this decrepit old hostel is a real gem, but you really do have to be counting your pennies to stay here. Breakfast is available for Rs 17 and a thali dinner costs Rs 25.

Tourist's Home (☎ 2337212; Station Rd West; s/d Rs 150/200) As basic as basic gets and with a truly memorable aroma (think long-dead roadkill), but at least it's cheap and the staff are cool.

Hotel Panchavati (☎ 2328755; www.hotelpanchavati .com; Station Rd West; s/d Rs 300/400, with AC Rs 550/650; ✖) We've received mixed reports about this establishment over the years but it seems that its bad patch has passed and it now offers immaculate rooms that have actually had a bit of love shown to them. The managers are efficient and friendly and it sits easily at the top of the value-for-money class.

Hotel Shree Maya (☎ 2333093; shrimaya_agd@san charnet.in; Bharuka Complex; d with/without AC Rs 495/345; ✖) Presentable and welcoming budget ac-

commodation close to the train station. The plain rooms have TVs and hot showers in the morning, but the real plus is the outdoor terrace where breakfast and other meals are served. It's a good spot to tap into the travellers' grapevine.

MIDRANGE

MTDC Holiday Resort (☎ 2331513; Station Rd East; d low/high season Rs 650/750, with AC Rs 800/900; ✖) Set in its own shady grounds, this slightly disorganised (in the nicest possible way) hotel is one of the better MTDC operations, offering spruce, spacious rooms. Some rooms suffer a bit from road noise. A restaurant, bar and travel agency are on site.

Classic Hotel (☎ 5624314; www.aurangabadhotel .com; Railway Station Rd; s/d from Rs 1000/1200; ✖ ▢) This sparkling new hotel next to the Goldie Cinema has very clean rooms, but is let down by pushy staff.

Hotel Amarpreet (☎ 6621133; www.amarpreethotel .com; Jalna Rd; s/d from Rs 1410/2100; ✖) A chintzy, glitzy lobby leads to slightly less impressive rooms, but it's much cleaner and more professional than any other hotel in its class.

TOP END

President Park (☎ 2486201; www.presidenthotels .com; R-7/2, Chikalthana, Airport Rd; s/d from Rs 2300/2800; ✖ ▢ ▨) On the road to the airport, this classy hotel needs a bit of a polish but the setting around the half-moon pool makes this a good top-end option. Nonguests can use the pool for Rs 175 per hour.

Taj Residency (☎ 2381106; www.tajhotels.com; Ajanta Rd; s/d from US$75/85; ✖ ▢ ▨) Set in 2 hectares of pleasantly landscaped gardens, the Taj is an oasis of well-appointed rooms on the northern fringes of Aurangabad. Most rooms have romantic Mughal-style swings on the balconies.

Eating

Swad Veg Restaurant (Kanchan Chamber, Station Rd East; mains Rs 20-55) As well as a pile of cheap-eat Indian staples there are pizzas (Rs 30 to 40) and lots of ice creams and shakes – all of which is gobbled up under the benevolent gaze of swami Yogiraj Hansthirth. It's quite hard to find – look for an orange circular sign (in Marathi) pointing the way down to the entrance just below the Saraswat Bank.

Ashoka's Fast Food (Nirala Bazaar; mains Rs 20-60) Offering both indoor seating and an outdoor

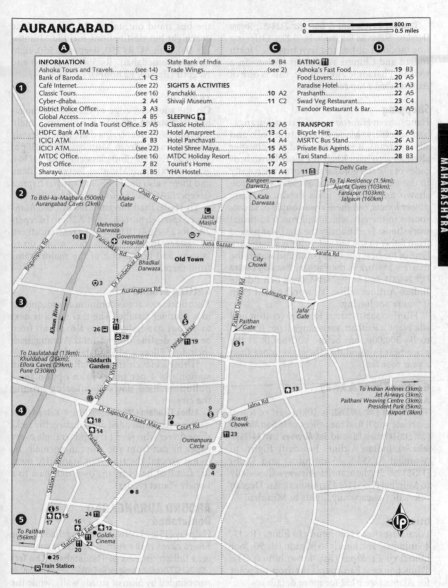

AURANGABAD

0 ——————— 800 m
0 ——————— 0.5 miles

INFORMATION		
Ashoka Tours and Travels............(see 14)		
Bank of Baroda.............................**1** C3		
Café Internet................................(see 22)		
Classic Tours...............................(see 16)		
Cyber-dhaba...............................**2** A4		
District Police Office....................**3** A3		
Global Access..............................**4** B5		
Government of India Tourist Office.**5** A5		
HDFC Bank ATM...........................(see 22)		
ICICI ATM....................................**6** B3		
ICICI ATM....................................(see 22)		
MTDC Office................................(see 16)		
Post Office..................................**7** B2		
Sharayu.......................................**8** B5		

| State Bank of India.......................**9** B4 |
| Trade Wings................................(see 2) |

| SIGHTS & ACTIVITIES |
| Panchakki...................................**10** A2 |
| Shivaji Museum...........................**11** C2 |

| SLEEPING |
| Classic Hotel...............................**12** A5 |
| Hotel Amarpreet..........................**13** C4 |
| Hotel Panchavati.........................**14** A5 |
| Hotel Shree Maya........................**15** A5 |
| MTDC Holiday Resort...................**16** A5 |
| Tourist's Home............................**17** A5 |
| YHA Hostel.................................**18** A4 |

| EATING |
| Ashoka's Fast Food......................**19** B3 |
| Food Lovers.................................**20** A5 |
| Paradise Hotel.............................**21** A3 |
| Prashanth...................................**22** A5 |
| Swad Veg Restaurant...................**23** C4 |
| Tandoor Restaurant & Bar............**24** A5 |

| TRANSPORT |
| Bicycle Hire.................................**25** A5 |
| MSRTC Bus Stand........................**26** A3 |
| Private Bus Agents.......................**27** B4 |
| Taxi Stand..................................**28** B3 |

To Bibi-ka-Maqbara (500m);
Aurangabad Caves (2km)

Makai Gate

Ghati Rd

Rangeen Darwaza

Kala Darwaza

11 — Delhi Gate

To Taj Residency (1.5km);
Ajanta Caves (103km);
Fardapur (103km);
Jalgaon (160km)

Mehmood Darwaza

Government Hospital

Jama Masjid

Panchakki Rd

10

Dr Ambedkar Rd

Bhadkal Darwaza

Old Town

7

Juna Bazaar

City Chowk

Sarata Rd

3

Aurangpura Rd

Gulmandi Rd

Jafar Gate

Paithan Darwaza Rd

26

21

28

6

Nirala Bazaar

19

Paithan Gate

1

Khan River

Siddarth Garden

To Daulatabad (13km);
Khuldabad (26km);
Ellora Caves (29km);
Pune (230km)

Station Rd West

2

13

To Indian Airlines (3km);
Jet Airways (3km);
Paithani Weaving Centre (3km);
President Park (5km);
Airport (8km)

Dr Rajendra Prasad Marg

18

14

Court Rd

Jalna Rd

9

Kranti Chowk

27

23

Osmanpura Circle

Padampura Rd

4

Station Rd West

8

5

17

15

24

12

16

Station Rd East

Goldie Cinema

20

22

25

Train Station

To Paithan (56km)

MAHARASHTRA

---

terrace that is all the rage at night, Ashoka's Punjabi staples, piles of sweet Indian cakes and Western-style burgers make the trek out here well worthwhile.

Prashanth (Siddharth Arcade, Station Rd East; mains Rs 25-90) Prashanth wins trophies from travellers for its delightful vegetarian-only dishes, epic fruit juices and enjoyable patio setting.

Paradise Hotel (Station Rd West; mains Rs 40-60; ⏲ 11am-3pm) Directly opposite the MSRTC bus stand the Paradise Hotel is a reliable lunchtime bet with quick curries and endless thalis.

Food Lovers (Station Rd East; mains Rs 50-200) This restaurant is full of aquariums stuffed with catfish. Oh and the Punjabi and Chinese food isn't bad either.

Tandoor Restaurant & Bar (☎ 2328481; Shyam Chambers, Station Rd East; mains Rs 60-200) Offering fine tandoori dishes and flavoursome North Indian and Chinese vegetarian options in a weirdly Pharaonic atmosphere, this is one of Aurangabad's top restaurants.

Shopping

Hand-woven Himroo material is an Aurangabad speciality. Made from cotton, silk and silver threads, it was developed as a cheaper alternative to Kam Khab, the more lavish brocades of silk and gold thread woven for royalty in the 14th century. Most of today's Himroo shawls and saris are mass-produced using power looms, but there are a couple of showrooms in the city which still run traditional workshops. Traditionally the craft was passed from father to son but today this is a dying art. One of the best places to come and watch the masters at work is the **Paithani Weaving Centre** (☎ 2482811, Jalna Rd; ⏱ 11am-8.30pm), behind the Indian Airlines office. It's worth a visit even if you're not buying.

Himroo saris start at Rs 1000 (cotton and silk blend). Paithani saris range from Rs 5000 to Rs 300,000, but before you baulk at the price bear in mind that they take more than a year to make!

Getting There & Away

AIR

The **airport** (☎ 2483392) is 10km east of town. En route you'll find the offices of **Indian Airlines** (☎ 2485241; Jalna Rd) and **Jet Airways** (☎ 2441392; Jalna Rd). Indian Airlines has daily flights to Mumbai (US$54, 45 minutes) and Delhi (US$129, 3½ hours). Jet Airways flies daily to Mumbai (US$116, 45 minutes). Air Deccan offers dirt-cheap daily flights to Mumbai.

BUS

Local buses head half-hourly to Ellora (Rs 17, 45 minutes) and hourly to Jalgaon (Rs 90, four hours) via Fardapur (Rs 74, two hours). The T-junction near Fardapur is the drop-off point for Ajanta (see p152 for more details).

Buses leave regularly from the **MSRTC bus stand** (☎ 2242165; Station Rd West) to Pune (Rs 140, five hours) and Nasik (Rs 110, five hours). For longer-distance journeys, private luxury buses are more comfortable and better value. The private bus agents congregate around the corner where Dr Rajendra Prasad Marg becomes Court Rd, and a few sit closer to the bus stand on Station Rd West. Deluxe overnight bus destinations include Mumbai (Rs 180, with AC Rs 250, sleeper Rs 550, eight hours), Ahmedabad (Rs 350, 15 hours) and Nagpur (Rs 320, 12 hours).

TRAIN

On the southern edge of town is Aurangabad **train station** (☎ 131). It's not on a main line, but two direct trains daily (often heavily booked) run to/from Mumbai. The 2.30pm *Tapovan Express* (2nd class/chair Rs 94/344, eight hours), from Mumbai, leaves at 6.10am, and there's also the 11.25pm *Devagiri Express* (sleeper/2AC Rs 158/641, nine hours).

To Hyderabad (Secunderabad), the *Manmad Express* departs daily at 7.20pm (sleeper/2AC Rs 236/954, 10 hours). To reach northern or eastern India by train, take a bus up to Jalgaon and board one of the major trains from there.

Getting Around

Autorickshaws are as common as mosquitoes in a summer swamp. The taxi stand is next to the bus stand; share jeeps also depart from here for destinations around Aurangabad, including Ellora and Daulatabad.

Hiring a bicycle from a stall near the train station (Rs 4 per hour) is an option for a pollution-filled day's sightseeing around the city.

Ashok T Kadam (☎ 9890340816; a_t_kadam@yahoo .co.in) is a recommended and trustworthy rickshaw driver who won't try and wrangle every rupee he can from you. He can normally be found around the train/bus stand. He owes the fact that he owns his own rickshaw to a Lonely Planet reader!

AROUND AURANGABAD
Daulatabad

Halfway (13km) between Aurangabad and the Ellora caves is the ruined but truly magnificent hilltop fortress of Daulatabad. The **fort** (☎ 2615777; Indian/foreigner Rs 5/US$2; ⏱ 6am-6pm) is surrounded by 5km of sturdy walls, while the central bastion tops a 200m-high hill – originally known as Devagiri, the Hill of the Gods. It's a peaceful spot, with numerous monkeys and squirrels playing on the battlements and pompous peacocks strutting their stuff on the lawns.

In the 14th century it was renamed Daulatabad, the City of Fortune, by sultan Mohammed Tughlaq, who came up with the crazy scheme of not only building himself a new capital here, but marching the entire population of Delhi 1100km south to populate it. Those who didn't die on the way sloped back to Delhi a couple of years later when Daulatabad proved untenable as a capital.

The climb to the summit takes at least 45 minutes and the rewards are the superb views over the surrounding countryside. On the way up you'll pass through an ingenious series of defences, including multiple doorways with spike-studded doors to prevent elephant charges. A tower of victory, known as the **Chand Minar** (Tower of the Moon), built in 1435, soars 60m above the ground, but unfortunately it's not possible to climb it.

Higher up is the **Chini Mahal**, where Abul Hasan Tana Shah, king of Golconda, died after being imprisoned for 12 years from 1687. It was once coated in blue-and-white tiles but now only a few fractured fragments remain. You will also find a 6m **cannon**, cast from five different metals and engraved with Aurangzeb's name.

Part of the ascent to the top goes through a pitch-black spiralling tunnel – down which the fort's defenders hurled burning coals, arrows or even boiling water at invaders. (Allegedly the fort was once successfully conquered, despite all these elaborate precautions, by simply bribing the guard at the gate.) There's normally a guide waiting near the tunnel to light the way with a flame for a small tip, but on the way down you'll be left to your devices. Note that the crumbling staircases and sheer drops can make life difficult for the elderly, children and vertigo sufferers.

If you take an organised tour from Aurangabad to Daulatabad and Ellora, you won't have time to climb to the summit.

Khuldabad

The scruffy walled town of Khuldabad, the Heavenly Abode, is a cheerful little Muslim pilgrimage town just 3km from Ellora. A number of historical figures are buried here, including Aurangzeb, the last great Mughal emperor. Despite being the Sultan of Brunei of his era, Aurangzeb left instructions that he should be buried in a simple tomb constructed only with the money he had made from sewing together Muslim skullcaps – and an unfussy affair of bare earth in a courtyard of the **Alamgir Dargah** (7am-8pm) is exactly what he

got. The contrast with that of his wife's fantastical mausoleum, the Bibi-qa-Maqbara, in Aurangabad couldn't be greater. Heads must be covered when visiting the tomb and women are not allowed into the inner sanctum.

Generally a calm place, Khuldabad is swamped with millions of pilgrims every April when a robe said to have been worn by the Prophet Mohammed, and kept within the dargah (shrine), is shown to the public. The shrine across the road from the Alamgir Dargah contains hairs of the Prophet's beard and lumps of silver from a tree of solid silver, which miraculously grew at this site after a saint's death.

ELLORA
 02437

The World Heritage–listed **Ellora cave temples** (244440; Kailasa Temple; Indian/foreigner Rs 10/US$5; dawn-dusk Wed-Mon), about 30km from Aurangabad, are the pinnacle of Deccan rock-cut architecture.

Over five centuries, generations of monks (Buddhist, Hindu and Jain) carved monasteries, chapels and temples from a 2km-long escarpment and decorated them with a profusion of remarkably detailed sculptures. Because of the escarpment's gentle slope, in contrast with the sheer drop at Ajanta (p150), many of the caves have elaborate courtyards in front of the main shrines. The masterpiece is the breathtaking Kailasa Temple (Cave 16). Dedicated to Shiva, it is the world's largest monolithic sculpture, hewn from the rock by 7000 labourers over a 150-year period.

Altogether Ellora has 34 caves: 12 Buddhist (AD 600–800), 17 Hindu (AD 600–900) and five Jain (AD 800–1000). The site represents the renaissance of Hinduism under the Chalukya and Rashtrakuta dynasties, the subsequent decline of Indian Buddhism and a brief resurgence of Jainism under official patronage. The sculptures show the increasing influence of Tantric elements in India's three great religions and their coexistence at one site indicates a lengthy period of religious tolerance.

Official guides can be hired at the ticket office in front of the Kailasa Temple for Rs 280 for up to four hours. Most relay an extensive knowledge of the cave architecture. Touts offer a selection of pictorial guidebooks. If you only have time to visit either Ellora or Ajanta then make it Ellora.

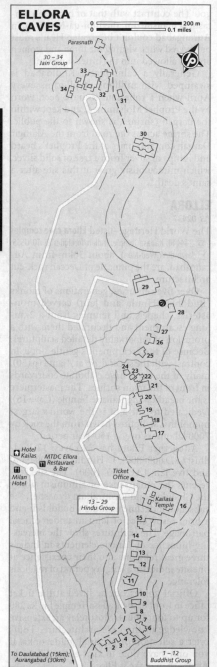

ELLORA CAVES

Parasnath

30 – 34
Jain Group

33

34

32

31

30

29

7

28

27

26

25

24 23
22
21
20
19
18
17

Hotel
Kailas

MTDC Ellora
Restaurant
& Bar

Milan
Hotel

Ticket
Office

Kailasa
Temple 16

13 – 29
Hindu Group

15

14

13

12

11

10

9

8

7

6

1 2 3 4 5

To Daulatabad (15km);
Aurangabad (30km)

1 – 12
Buddhist Group

Sights

KAILASA TEMPLE

Neither a simple cave, nor a plain religious monument, this **rock-cut temple**, built by King Krishna I of the Rashtrakuta dynasty in AD 760, was built to represent Mt Kailasa (Kailash), Shiva's home in the Himalaya. Three huge trenches were cut into the cliff face and then the shape was 'released' with tools – an undertaking that entailed removing 200,000 tonnes of rock! Kailasa covers twice the area of the Parthenon in Athens and is 1½ times as high.

Size aside, the Kailasa Temple is remarkable for its prodigious sculptural decoration. Around the temple are dramatic carved panels, depicting scenes from the Ramayana, the Mahabharata and the adventures of Krishna. The most superb depicts the demon king Ravana flaunting his strength by shaking Mt Kailasa. Unimpressed, Shiva crushes Ravana's pride by simply flexing a toe. This is still a functioning temple and many people come to pray in the main shrine.

Don't forget to explore the dank, bat-filled corners of the complex with their numerous forgotten carvings. Afterwards take a hike up the path to the south of the complex and walk right around the top perimeter of the 'cave', from where you can appreciate its grand scale.

BUDDHIST CAVES

The southernmost 12 caves are Buddhist *viharas* (resting places), except Cave 10, which is a *chaitya* (assembly hall). While the earliest caves are simple, Caves 11 and 12 are more ambitious, probably in an attempt to compete with the more impressive Hindu temples.

Cave 1, the simplest *vihara*, may have been a granary. **Cave 2** is notable for its ornate pillars and its imposing seated Buddha figure facing the setting sun. **Cave 3** and **Cave 4** are unfinished and not as well preserved.

Cave 5 is the largest *vihara* in this group, at 18m wide and 36m long; the rows of stone benches hint that it may have once been an assembly hall.

Cave 6 is an ornate *vihara* with wonderful images of Tara, consort of the Bodhisattva Avalokiteshvara, and of the Buddhist goddess of learning, Mahamayuri, looking remarkably similar to Saraswati, her Hindu equivalent. **Cave 7** is an unadorned hall, but from here you can pass through a doorway to **Cave 8**, the first cave in which the sanctum is detached from the rear wall. **Cave 9** is notable for its wonderfully carved façade.

Cave 10, the Viswakarma (Carpenter's) Cave, is the only *chaitya* in the Buddhist group and one of the finest in India. It takes its name from the ribs carved into the roof, in imitation of wooden beams; the balcony and upper gallery offer a closer view of the ceiling and a frieze depicting amorous couples. A decorative window gently illuminates an enormous figure of the teaching Buddha.

Cave 11, the Do Thal (Two Storey) Cave, is entered through its third, basement level, not discovered until 1876. Like Cave 12 it probably owes its size to competition with the more impressive Hindu caves of the same period.

Cave 12, the huge Tin Thal (Three Storey) Cave, is entered through a courtyard. The (locked) shrine on the top floor contains a large Buddha figure flanked by his seven previous incarnations. The walls are carved with relief pictures, like those in the Hindu caves.

HINDU CAVES

Where calm and contemplation infuse the Buddhist caves, drama and excitement characterise the Hindu group (Caves 13 to 29). In terms of scale, creative vision and skill of execution, these caves are in a league of their own.

All these temples were cut from the top down so that it was never necessary to use scaffolding – the builders began with the roof and moved down to the floor.

Cave 13 is a simple cave, most likely a granary. **Cave 14**, the Ravana-ki-Khai, is a Buddhist *vihara* converted to a temple dedicated to Shiva sometime in the 7th century.

Cave 15, the Das Avatara (Ten Incarnations of Vishnu) Cave, is one of the finest at Ellora. The two-storey temple contains a mesmerising Shiva Nataraja, and Shiva emerging from a lingam (phallic image) while Vishnu and Brahma pay homage.

Caves 17 to **20** and numbers **22** to **28** are simple monasteries.

Cave 21, known as the Ramesvara, features interesting interpretations of the familiar Shaivite scenes depicted in the earlier temples. The figure of goddess Ganga, standing on her *makara* (crocodile), is particularly notable.

The large **Cave 29**, the Dumar Lena, is thought to be a transitional model between the simpler hollowed-out caves and the fully developed temples exemplified by the Kailasa. It has views over the nearby waterfall.

JAIN CAVES

The five Jain caves may lack the artistic vigour and ambitious size of the best Hindu temples, but they are exceptionally detailed. The caves are 1km north of the last Hindu temple (Cave 29) at the end of the bitumen road.

Cave 30, the Chota Kailasa (Little Kailasa), is a poor imitation of the great Kailasa Temple and stands by itself some distance from the other Jain temples.

In contrast, **Cave 32**, the Indra Sabha (Assembly Hall of Indra), is the finest of the Jain temples. Its ground-floor plan is similar to that of the Kailasa, but the upstairs area is as ornate and richly decorated as the downstairs is plain. There are images of the Jain *tirthankars* (great teachers) Parasnath and Gomateshvara, the latter surrounded by wildlife. Inside the shrine is a seated figure of Mahavira, the last *tirthankar* and founder of the Jain religion.

Cave 31 is really an extension of Cave 32. **Cave 33**, the Jagannath Sabha, is similar in plan to 32 and has some well-preserved sculptures. The final temple, the small **Cave 34**, also has interesting sculptures. On the hilltop over the Jain temples, a 5m-high image of Parasnath looks down on Ellora.

Sleeping & Eating

Hotel Kailas (☎ 244446; www.hotelkailas.com; d from Rs 300, cottages from Rs 900) A mixed bag of rooms that range from cheap budget cells that get very hot to clean, stone cottages with warm showers and inviting views over the caves. There's a good restaurant and a lush lawn where you can sit and have a drink.

Locals say the best food emerges from the kitchens of the **Milan Hotel** (dishes Rs 20-50), across the road. Also reliable is the spotless **MTDC Ellora Restaurant & Bar** (dishes Rs 30-150), which will also provide lunch boxes for you so you can have a picnic beside the caves.

Getting There & Away

Buses travel regularly between Aurangabad and Ellora (Rs 17); the last bus returns from Ellora at around 7pm. Share jeeps leave when they're full and drop off outside the bus stand in Aurangabad (Rs 12). A full-day rickshaw tour to Ellora with stops en route costs around Rs 350 and a taxi will be somewhere between Rs 500 and 600.

AJANTA

☎ 02438

A World Heritage site, the **Buddhist caves of Ajanta** (☎ 244226; Indian/foreigner Rs 10/US$5; ⏲ 9am-5.30pm Tue-Sun) – 105km northeast of Aurangabad, and about 60km south of Jalgaon – are the Louvre of central India. The caves date from around 200 BC to AD 650 and, as Ellora developed and Buddhism gradually waned, the glorious Ajanta caves were abandoned and forgotten until 1819, when a British hunting party stumbled upon them. Their isolation contributed to the fine state of preservation in which some of their paintings remain to this day.

Information

Flash photography is banned in the caves; a video-camera permit costs Rs 25. Many of the caves are too dark to see much without a torch, so bring your own if you really want to glimpse any detail. Avoid visiting on weekends or holidays when everybody and their second cousin turns up.

A cloakroom near the main ticket office is a safe place to leave gear (Rs 4 per bag for four hours), so you could even arrive in the morning from Jalgaon, check out the caves and continue to Aurangabad in the evening. There's a short, steep climb to the first cave from the entrance; if you're not up to the hike, a chair carried by four bearers (Rs 400) can be hired at the foot of these steps.

Government of India tourist office guides can be hired at Cave 1 for up to four people for an approximately two-hour tour (Rs 350). They have extensive knowledge and bring the frescoes to life with their stories.

Sights & Activities

THE CAVES

The 30 caves are cut into the steep face of a horseshoe-shaped rock gorge on the Waghore River. Apart from Caves 29 and 30, they are sequentially numbered from one end of the gorge to the other. They do not follow a chronological order; the oldest are mainly in the middle and the newer ones are close to each end. At busy times viewers are allotted 15 minutes within each cave.

Five of the caves are *chaityas* while the other 25 are *viharas*. Caves 8, 9, 10, 12, 13 and part

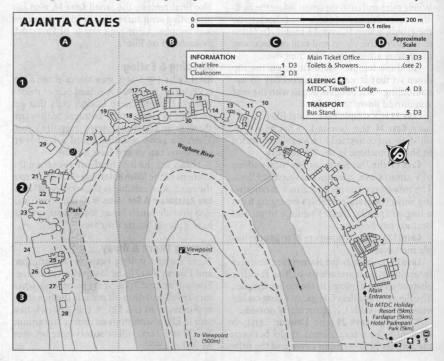

AJANTA CAVES

0	200 m
0	0.1 miles

Approximate Scale

INFORMATION
Chair Hire.................................1 D3
Cloakroom...............................2 D3
Main Ticket Office....................3 D3
Toilets & Showers................(see 2)

SLEEPING 🛏
MTDC Travellers' Lodge............4 D3

TRANSPORT
Bus Stand................................5 D3

Waghore River

Park

🅵 Viewpoint

Main Entrance
To MTDC Holiday Resort (5km);
Fardapur (5km);
Hotel Padmpani Park (5km)

To Viewpoint (500m)

of 15 are older early Buddhist caves, while the others are Mahayana (dated from around the 5th century AD). In the simpler, more austere early Buddhist school, the Buddha was never represented directly – his presence was always alluded to by a symbol such as the footprint or wheel of law.

Of special note are the Ajanta 'frescoes', which are technically not frescoes at all. A fresco is a painting done on a wet surface that absorbs the colour; the Ajanta paintings are more correctly tempera, since the artists used animal glue and vegetable gum mixed with the paint pigments to bind them to the dry surface.

Caves 3, 5, 8, 22 and 28 to 30 are closed and/or inaccessible; Cave 14 is sometimes closed.

Cave 1, a Mahayana *vihara*, was one of the latest to be excavated and is the most beautifully decorated. A veranda at the front leads to a large congregation hall, with elaborate sculptures and narrative murals. Perspective in the paintings, details of dress and daily life, and many of the facial expressions are all wonderfully executed. The colours in the paintings were created from local minerals, with the exception of the vibrant blue made from Central Asian lapis lazuli. Look up to the ceiling to see the carving of four deer sharing a common head.

Cave 2 is also a late Mahayana *vihara* with deliriously ornamented columns and capitals, and some fine paintings. The ceiling is decorated with geometric and floral patterns. Mural scenes include a number of jatakas surrounding the Buddha's birth, including his mother's dream of a six-tusked elephant, which heralded the Buddha's conception.

Cave 4 is the largest *vihara* at Ajanta and is supported by 28 pillars. Although never completed, the cave has some impressive sculptures, including scenes of people fleeing from the 'eight great dangers' to the protection of the Buddha's disciple Avalokiteshvara.

Cave 6 is the only two-storey *vihara* at Ajanta, but parts of the lower storey have collapsed. Inside is a seated Buddha figure and an intricately carved door to the shrine. Upstairs the hall is surrounded by cells with fine paintings on the doorways.

Cave 7 has an atypical design, with porches before the veranda, leading directly to the four cells and the elaborately sculptured shrine.

Cave 9 is one of the earliest *chaityas* at Ajanta. Although it dates from the early Buddhist period, the two figures flanking the entrance door were probably later Mahayana additions. Columns run down both sides of the cave and around the 3m-high dagoba at the far end. The vaulted roof has traces of wooden ribs.

Cave 10 is thought to be the oldest cave (200 BC) and was the one first spotted by the British soldiers who rediscovered Ajanta. Similar in design to Cave 9, it is the largest *chaitya*. The façade has collapsed and the paintings inside have been damaged, in some cases by graffiti dating from soon after the rediscovery.

Cave 16, a *vihara*, contains some of Ajanta's finest paintings and is thought to have

---

WHEN WAS AJANTA'S GOLDEN AGE?

Theories on major archaeological sites continuously undergo review and there's no exception with the Ajanta caves.

American professor Dr Walter M Spink (who has studied the caves for more than 40 years) suggests that the splendour of the later Mahayana group may have been accomplished in less than 20 years – rather than over centuries as previously thought.

Scholars agree that the caves had two periods of patronage: an early group was crafted around the 1st and 2nd centuries BC and a second wave of work began centuries later. Spink pinpoints the Vakataka emperor Harisena as a reigning sponsor in the incredible renaissance of activity. Soon after his rise to the throne in AD 460 the caves began to realise their present forms, until Harisena's unexpected death in AD 477. The site was probably deserted in the AD 480s.

The silver lining to the tragedy is, according to Spink, that the sudden downfall of the eminent Vakataka empire at the pinnacle of the caves' energetic crafting is solely responsible for their phenomenally preserved state today.

If you're interested, Spink's book *Ajanta: A Brief History and Guide* (1994) can be bought from touts near the site.

been the original entrance to the entire complex. The best known of these paintings is the 'dying princess' – Sundari, wife of the Buddha's half-brother Nanda, who is said to have fainted at the news that her husband was renouncing the material life (and her) in order to become a monk. Carved figures appear to support the ceiling in imitation of wooden architectural details, and there's a statue of the Buddha seated on a lion throne teaching the Noble Eightfold Path.

Cave 17, with carved dwarfs supporting the pillars, has Ajanta's best-preserved and most varied paintings. Famous images include a princess applying make-up, a horny prince using the old trick of plying his lover with wine and the Buddha returning home from his enlightenment to beg from his wife and astonished son. A detailed panel tells of Prince Simhala's expedition to Sri Lanka. With his 500 companions he is shipwrecked on an island where ogresses appear as enchanting women, only to seize and devour their victims. Simhala escapes on a flying horse and returns to conquer the island.

Cave 19, a magnificent *chaitya*, has a remarkably detailed façade; its dominant feature is an impressive horseshoe-shaped window. Two fine standing Buddha figures flank the entrance. Inside is a three-tiered dagoba with a figure of the Buddha on the front. Outside the cave to the west sits a striking image of the Naga king with seven cobra hoods around his head. His wife, hooded by a single cobra, sits at his side.

Cave 24, if it had been finished, would be the largest *vihara* at Ajanta. You can see how the caves were constructed – long galleries were cut into the rock and then the rock between them was broken through.

Cave 26, a largely ruined *chaitya*, contains some fine sculptures. On the left wall is a huge figure of the 'reclining Buddha', lying back in preparation for nirvana. Other scenes include a lengthy depiction of the Buddha's temptation by Mara.

Cave 27 is virtually a *vihara* connected to the Cave 26 *chaitya*.

VIEWPOINTS

Two lookouts offer picture-perfect views of the whole horseshoe-shaped gorge. The first is a short walk beyond the river, crossed via one of the concrete bridges below Caves 8 and 27. A further 20-minute uphill walk leads to the lookout from where the British party first saw the caves. It's also possible to take a taxi up to the latter viewpoint from Fardapur.

Sleeping & Eating

Accommodation options close to the caves are limited and you're better off using Jalgaon as a base. However, during the lifetime of this book a luxury holiday complex, just beside the T-junction, is due for completion. In the meantime, if you wish to stay within spitting distance of the caves choose from one of the following.

Hotel Padmpani Park (☎ 244280; padmpanipark@ yahoo.co.in; Aurangabad-Jalgaon Rd; d with/without AC Rs 350/450). Small and clean rooms come with a hospitable welcome.

MTDC Holiday Resort (☎ 244230; Aurangabad-Jalgaon Rd; d with/without AC from Rs 700/600; 🌊) At Fardapur, 1km from the T-junction, there are rumours that the prices of rooms here are going to drop to just Rs 650/450, which makes these adequate and spacious rooms a good deal, but the staff are a bit sleepy.

The MTDC Travellers' Lodge, just beside the ticket office, was closed for much-needed renovations at the time of research. It's expected to reopen sometime during 2007.

As far as filling your stomach goes there is a string of cheap (but not very appetising) restaurants in the 'shopping plaza' – our advice is to pack a picnic and enjoy it in the shady park below Caves 22 to 27.

Getting There & Away

Buses from Aurangabad (p146) or Jalgaon (opposite) will drop you off at the T-junction (where the Aurangabad–Jalgaon Rd meets the road to the caves), 4km from the caves. From here, after paying an 'amenities' fee (Rs 5), race through the 'shopping plaza' to the departure point for the green-coloured Euro I buses (Rs 6, with AC Rs 10), which zoom down to the caves. Buses return on a regular basis (half-hourly, last bus at 6.15pm) to the T-junction.

During the day all MSRTC buses passing through Fardapur stop at the T-junction. After the caves close you can board buses to either Aurangabad or Jalgaon outside the MTDC Holiday Resort in Fardapur, 1km down the main road towards Jalgaon. Taxis are available in Fardapur; Rs 500 should get you to Jalgaon.

JALGAON

☎ 0257 / elev 208m

Built on the passing rail trade, you might be forgiven for thinking of Jalgaon as nothing more than a dreary transit town – which, in fact, it is. However, it's not all bad news because the town keeps a couple of alluring aces stuffed up its sleeve. Firstly, despite a population of some half a million, Jalgaon feels like a small country town full of happy people. Secondly, and much more practically, Jalgaon makes a great base for the Ajanta Caves, 60km to the south.

Information

You can find a couple of banks, ATMs and internet cafés along Nerhu Rd, which is the road running along the top of Station Rd.

Sleeping & Eating

Most of the hotels in Jalgaon have 24-hour checkout.

our pick Hotel Plaza (☎ 2227354; hotelplaza_jal@yahoo .com; Station Rd; dm/s/d from Rs 150/200/250; ❷ ▯) Hotel owners throughout Maharashtra take note. With just a little love, care and a few licks of paint you too could create an establishment like Hotel Plaza. The snow-white rooms are simple and efficient and come in a pick-and-mix range of styles and sizes. The effusive owner is a mine of useful information.

Anjali Guest House (☎ 2225079; Khandesh Mill Complex, Station Rd; s/d from Rs 250/300) Just past the autorickshaw stand. The tiny beds in this guesthouse certainly aren't designed for fat or tall people, but for anyone else it will just about pass for a night. Much better than the rooms is the downstairs vegetarian restaurant which has Kashmiri pilau and *malai kofta* (veggie balls) to die for.

Hotel Kewal (☎ 2223949; shreekewal@ip.eth.net; Station Rd; d with/without AC from Rs 775/525; ❷) Another in India's legion of drab hotels. Despite this, after the Hotel Plaza, this is the best bet in town and the eccentric mix of Pharaonic Egyptian, Hindu Indian and European Romantic wall decorations are certainly memorable.

Hotel Arya (Navi Peth; mains Rs 20-60) Opposite Kelkar Marke, near the clock tower. Serving colourful Indian food that won't set your taste buds aflame. It's so popular you may have to queue for a table.

Silver Palace (mains Rs 45-150) Next door to the Hotel Plaza this restaurant's claims of luxury might be overstating things a tad –

you wouldn't come for here for tea with the Queen, but the food is good, so if she can't make it then it'll do just fine.

Getting There & Away

Several express trains between Mumbai and Delhi or Kolkata (Calcutta) stop briefly at Jalgaon **train station** (☎ 131). Expresses to Mumbai (sleeper/2AC Rs 170/691, eight hours) are readily available. The *Sewagram Express*, leaving from Jalgaon at 10.10pm, goes to Nagpur (sleeper/2AC Rs 170/691, eight hours).

The first run from the **bus stand** (☎ 2229774) to Fardapur (Rs 38, 1½ hours) is at 6am; buses depart every half hour thereafter. The same bus continues to Aurangabad (Rs 77, four hours).

Jalgaon's train station and bus stand are about 2km apart (Rs 12 by autorickshaw). Luxury bus offices on Railway Station Rd offer services to Aurangabad (Rs 120, 3½ hours), Mumbai (Rs 250, nine hours), Pune (Rs 250, nine hours) and Nagpur (normal/sleeper Rs 300/350, 10 hours).

LONAR METEORITE CRATER

Around 50,000 years ago a meteorite slammed into the earth leaving behind this massive crater, which measures some 2km across and 170m deep. It's the only hypervelocity natural impact crater in basaltic rock in the world – impressive stuff, hey! Assuming this means nothing to you then take faith in the fact that, with a shallow green lake in its base, it's as tranquil and relaxing a spot as you could hope to find. The lake itself is highly alkaline and, apparently, taking a dip in its waters is excellent for the skin. Scientists suspect that the meteorite is still embedded about 600m below the southeastern rim of the crater.

In addition to being an all-natural beauty treatment, the crater's edge is home to several **Hindu temples** as well as wildlife, including langur monkeys, peacocks, gazelles and an array of birds. The **Government Rest House**, which is the starting point for the trail down to the bottom, is about 15 minutes' walk from the bus stand.

MTDC Tourist Complex (☎ 07260-221602; dm/d Rs 100/ 450), has a prime location just across the road from the crater, but don't expect much electricity. There's also a basic restaurant here.

Getting There & Away

There are a couple of buses a day between Lonar and Aurangabad (Rs 110, five hours).

Lonar can also be reached by bus from Fardapur with a change at Buldhana.

It's possible to visit Lonar on a day trip from Aurangabad or Jalgaon if you hire a car and driver. A full day there and back from either town will cost at least Rs 1800.

NAGPUR

☎ 0712 / pop 2.1 million / elev 305m

Nagpur, the geographic centre and orange-growing capital of India, is a clean and affluent city which makes a good jumping-off point for a series of trips into the far eastern corner of Maharashtra. In addition to its proximity to Ramtek (opposite) and the ashrams around Sevagram (opposite), Nagpur is a convenient stop for those heading to the isolated **Navagaon National Park**, 135km east, and **Tadoba-Andhari Tiger Reserve**, 150km south of Nagpur. The former has bears, wild dogs and elusive leopards, while the latter hosts gaurs, chitals, nilgais and seldom-spotted tigers.

The countryside around Nagpur might be interesting but the city itself has such a dearth of attractions that locals list a shiny shopping mall and a less shiny prison in the towns' roll call of sites. What is worth prodding about in is the colourful central market – the star buys are the near-fluorescent clay pots. The one time Nagpur is worth visiting for its own sake is during the **Dussehra Festival** (September or October); see the boxed text, below.

Information

Computrek (18 Central Ave; per hr Rs 20) Internet access on the main drag.

Cyber Zoo (54 Central Ave; per hr Rs 15; ☺ 10am-10pm Mon-Sun) Another central internet café.

MTDC office (☎ 2533325; Sanskrutik Bachat Bhavan, Sitabuldi; ☺ 10am-5.45pm Mon-Sat) In the compound opposite Hotel Hardeo.

State Bank of India (☎ 2531099; Kingsway) A two-minute walk west of the train station. Deals with foreign exchange.

Sleeping & Eating

The majority of the budget and midrange hotels are clustered along noisy Central Ave, a 10-minute walk east of the train station. An autorickshaw to Central Ave from the bus stand costs around Rs 20. The accommodation here is more focused on Indian businessmen than tourists.

Hotel Blue Diamond (☎ 2727461; fax 2727460; www .hotelbluediamondnagpur.com; 113 Central Ave; s/d with shared bathroom from Rs 150/200, with private bathroom Rs 250/350, with AC Rs 550/650; ☒) The mirrored ceiling in the reception is straight out of a bad '70s nightclub and the rooms are pretty much the type you'd expect to find above a seedy '70s nightclub. However, it has the cheapest beds in town.

Hotel Blue Moon (☎ 2726061; ktcbaja_ngp@sancha rnet.in; Central Ave; s/d with TV from Rs 350/500) One of the closest hotels to the train station with large, plain and clean rooms that don't win any awards for imagination.

Hotel Skylark (☎ 2724654; fax 2726193; 119 Central Ave; s/d Rs 450/575, with AC Rs 775/850; ☒) This is the best budget hotel, but it's nothing to rave about. Rooms are drab, dreary and none too clean. The receptionist is very helpful and the restaurant, which has regular live music, has a diverse range of Indian and Chinese food (meals Rs 50 to 120).

Hotel Hardeo (☎ 2529116; hardeo_ngp@sancharnet .in; s/d Rs 1700/2200; ☒ 🖳) Around 1km east of

---

UNTOUCHABLE CHAMPION

One of the most highly respected humanitarians in Maharashtra's history was Dr Bhimrao Ramji Ambedkar, a low-caste Hindu who became Law Minister and Scheduled Castes leader. He was born into a Dalit household in the district of Ratnagiri in 1891. After studying in the West, he returned to India to encounter discrimination with even his workmates refusing to hand him anything for fear of ritual pollution. Thus began a lifelong campaign for Dalit rights, in which he unrelentingly sought equality for the depressed classes.

Despite his victories for the people, Dr Ambedkar lost faith that Hindu prejudice against Dalits would ever be eradicated and, on 14 October 1956, he converted to Buddhism in Nagpur, an act that was repeated by an estimated three million low-caste Hindus. Along with vows embracing tenets of the Buddha, he stated, 'I shall believe in the equality of man'.

Every year thousands come to Nagpur during the Hindu Dussehra Festival to commemorate his life. For more information on Dr Ambedkar, Buddhism and the fight for Dalit parity, see www.ambedkar.org.

the train station. You only have to look at the drooping moustache and tail coats of the doorman to know that this business-class hotel is the best of the bunch. Even so the large, clean rooms are past their sell-by date. There's a good restaurant.

Krishnum (Central Ave) This is one of the better eating choices on the main road and once you sample its thalis (Rs 30 to 60), great *upma* (spicy South Indian semolina pancake), fruit juices and other South Indian snacks you'll understand why.

Shivraj (Central Ave; mains Rs 25-80) Directly opposite the Krishnum, the Shivraj has similar South Indian tastes and a mean dosa.

The dozens of *dhabas* (snack bars), food stalls and fruit stands opposite the train station rouse in the evening. Summer is the best time to sample the famed oranges.

Getting There & Away

AIR
Indian Airlines (☎ 2533962) has flights to Hyderabad (US$75, one hour, twice weekly), Mumbai (US$93, 1¼ hours, twice daily), Delhi (US$108, 1½ hours, daily) and Kolkata (US$93, 1½ hours, three weekly). **Jet Airways** (☎ 5617888) has flights to Mumbai (US$126, twice daily). Air Deccan has cheap daily flights to Mumbai and Hyderabad. Kingfisher hooks Nagpur up with Ahmedabad, Bengaluru, Chennai (Madras), Hyderabad and Pune, and IndiGo zooms to Mumbai and Kolkata. Taxis/autorickshaws from the airport to the city centre cost Rs 300/150.

BUS
The main **MSRTC bus stand** (☎ 2726221) is 2km south of the train station and hotel area. Buses head regularly for Wardha (Rs 40, two hours) and Ramtek (Rs 24, 1½ hours). Two buses roar off daily to Jalgaon (semideluxe/deluxe Rs 300/350, 10 hours), and a semideluxe bus to Hyderabad (Rs 350, 12 hours) leaves at 6pm.

TRAIN
Nagpur Junction **train station** (☎ 131), on the Mumbai–Howrah line, is an impressive edifice in the centre of town. The overnight *Vidarbha Express* originates in Nagpur and departs for Mumbai CST (sleeper/2AC Rs 288/1165, 14 hours) at 6.10pm. The same train departs Mumbai at 7.40pm for Nagpur. Heading north to Kolkata the *Mum-*

bai Howrah Mail departs from Nagpur at 11.05am and arrives at Howrah at 5.50am (sleeper/2AC Rs 345/1398, 1138km). Five Mumbai-bound expresses stop at Jalgaon (for Ajanta caves; sleeper/2AC Rs 170/691, seven hours). There are also connections between Nagar and Bengaluru, Delhi and Hyderabad.

AROUND NAGPUR
Ramtek
About 40km northeast of Nagpur, the interesting 600-year-old **temples** (🕙 6am-9pm) of Ramtek squat happily atop the Hill of Rama and are positively bubbling with playful monkeys. It's said in the epic Ramayana that Rama spent time here with Sita and Lakshmi. Autorickshaws will cart you the 5km from the bus stand to the main temple complex for Rs 25 and you can walk back down to the town via the 700 steps at the back of the complex.

On the road to the temples you'll pass the delightful **Ambala Tank**, which is lined with small temples most of which appear to be slowly dissolving back into the lake waters or disappearing into the undergrowth. An hour or so spent poking your nose into nooks and crannies here can make you feel like a real explorer. Boat rides around the lake are available for Rs 20 per person.

The **Kalidas Memorial** (admission Rs 5; 🕙 8am-8.30pm), on the top of the hill beside the main temple complex, is dedicated to the famous classical Sanskrit dramatist Kalidas (also spelled Kalidasa). There is a number of other temples in the area, including a Jain temple at the base of the hill and a **mosque** on the opposite hill.

On the hilltop and not far from the temples, **Rajkamal Resort** (☎ 07114-255620; d with/without AC Rs 900/700; ❄) has large but overpriced rooms that come with TVs. The hotel has a basic restaurant-bar.

Buses run half-hourly between Ramtek and the MSRTC bus stand in Nagpur (Rs 24, 1½ hours). The last bus back to Nagpur is at 8.30pm.

SEVAGRAM
☎ 07152
Sevagram, the Village of Service, is where Mahatma Gandhi set up base in the long run to Independence and established the **Sevagram Ashram** (☎ 284753; 🕙 6.30am-6.30pm).

The peaceful ashram, encompassing 40 hectares of farmland, as well as residences and research centres, is a long way from anywhere and, with very little to see, it's only to be recommended to die-hard Gandhi fans. The highlights of a visit are the original huts that Gandhi lived in, one of which contains the great man's toilet (Western style!), as well as some of his personal effects, including his famous walking stick.

Across the road from the ashram, the **Gandhi Picture Exhibition** (admission free; 10am-6pm Wed-Mon), traces his life through old photographs. For such an important figure, it's unfortunate the exhibition is so dull and poorly presented.

Very basic lodging is available in **Yatri Nivas** (d Rs 80), across the road from the entry gate – book in advance through the ashram. Vegetarian meals are served in the ashram's dining hall.

Getting There & Away

The ashram can be reached from Wardha or Sevagram train stations, both of which are on the Central Railway. There are around five express trains from Nagpur to Sevagram (Rs 16 on the slow country trains or Rs 42 on the faster, one-hour expresses). Express MSRTC buses run more frequently between Nagpur and Wardha (Rs 40, two hours).

Local buses go regularly to the ashram from Wardha (Rs 5, 20 minutes), or an autorickshaw will cost Rs 60 for the 8km trip.

AROUND SEVAGRAM

Just 3km from Sevagram on the road to Nagpur at Paunar is the **Brahmavidya Mandir Ashram** (07152-288388; 6am-10am, 11am-noon & 2-6pm), the ashram of Gandhi's disciple Vinoba Bhave. This persistent soul walked through India asking rich landlords to hand over land for redistribution to the poor – he managed to persuade them to fork out a total of 1.6 million hectares.

With just 33 members, the ashram is run almost entirely by women. Dedicated to *swarajya* (rural self-sufficiency), it's operated on a social system of consensus with no central management. Basic accommodation and board (about Rs 75) in two rooms sharing a bathroom is available; call ahead. The bus from Nagpur runs past the ashram; otherwise it's Rs 50 in an autorickshaw to Paunar from Wardha or Sevagram. There's little for the casual visitor to see.

SOUTHERN MAHARASHTRA

KONKAN COAST

Maharashtra's Konkan Coast – the narrow strip between the Western Ghats and Arabian Sea – will suit those travellers really wishing to deviate from the beaten track. It's a remote, little-explored fringe of superlative beaches, disco-green paddy fields, heaped-up hills and collapsing clifftop forts. It's not the easiest region to travel through; accommodation is scarce, the food monotonous, transport painfully slow and the locals completely unaccustomed to foreigners. However, the Konkan Railway provides access to some of the bigger towns while local buses help connect up the dots. If you want to gain the most from this area then rent a car and driver in Mumbai and drift slowly down the coast to Goa. You may have to spend some nights sleeping in villagers' houses – be generous with how much you give. The rewards for your efforts are beaches of which the Maldives would be jealous!

Murud

02144 / pop 12,551

About 165km south of Mumbai, the sleepy fishing town of Murud is the most obvious first port of call. With a striking beach (though suffering from a little pollution carried down from Mumbai) and the commanding island fortress of **Janjira**, 5km south of the village, you'll be happy you came.

Standing a little way offshore, the fortress was built in 1140 by Siddi Jahor and became the 16th-century capital of the Siddis of Janjira, descendants of sailor-traders from the Horn of Africa. Although constructed on an island, its 12m-high walls seem to emerge straight from the sea. This made the fort utterly impregnable, even to the mighty Marathas – Shivaji tried to conquer it by sea and his son, Sambhaji, attempted to tunnel to it. Today the fort has finally been conquered by none other than Mother Nature: its walls are slowly turning to rubble and its interior back into forest.

The only way to reach Janjira is by local boat (Rs 12 return, 10 minutes) from Rajpuri Port, about 5km south of Murud. Boats depart from 7am to 6pm daily, but require a minimum of 20 passengers. On weekends and holidays you won't have to wait long.

To get to Rajpuri from Murud, either take an autorickshaw (Rs 45) or hire a bicycle (Rs 4 per hour) from the small shop opposite the midroad shrine on Darbar Rd, Murud's main beach road.

Back in Murud you can waste away the days on the beach, peer through the gates of the off-limits **Ahmedganj Palace**, estate of the Siddi Nawab of Murud, or scramble around the decaying mosque and tombs on the south side of town. If you want a quieter spot to swim, there's a near-pristine beach a couple of kilometres to the north.

SLEEPING & EATING

Several accommodation options are strung out along Murud's beach road.

Mirage Holiday Homes (☎ 276744; opposite Kumar Talkies, Darbar Rd; d with/without AC Rs 1500/600; ✷) A small and friendly hotel with a pretty garden and clean, simple rooms – so simple that not all the bathrooms have a roof!

Golden Swan Beach Resort (☎ 274078; www.goldenswan.com; Darbar Rd; d with/without AC from Rs 1800/1000, cottages Rs 4000; ✷) The first place you come to as the bus enters town and also the plushest. The rooms are clean and brightly decorated.

If you want to be right on the sand, the beach to the north of Murud has a number of places to stay either in people's homes or in simple guesthouses.

Both the above serve food, but the Golden Swan Beach Resort offers the best selection. Otherwise, in the town centre, try **Patel Inn** (☎ 274153; mains Rs 40-60), serving fresh fish dishes that make you drool.

GETTING THERE & AWAY

In Mumbai regular ferries (Rs 60, one hour) or hydrofoils (Rs 110, 45 minutes) from the Gateway of India cruise to Mandva. If you take the hydrofoil the ticket includes a free shuttle bus to Alibag (30 minutes), otherwise an autorickshaw will be about Rs 120. Rickety local buses from Alibag head down the coast to Murud (Rs 27, two hours). Alternatively, buses from Mumbai Central bus stand take almost six hours to Murud (Rs 130).

The nearest railhead on the Konkan Railway is about two hours away in Roha.

Ganpatipule

☎ 02357

Ganpatipule, on the coast 375km south of Mumbai, has several kilometres of almost

perfect beaches and clean waters that leave those of Goa for dead. For much of the year life plods along very slowly but woe betide anyone coming here for a bit of peace and quiet during the Indian holidays (Diwali is especially busy). These tourists haven't come for the hedonism of sun and sand though, but rather for the town's seaside **temple** (☎ 235223; ✷ 5am-9pm) with its Swayambhu Ganpati, or 'naturally formed' monolithic Ganesh (painted a lurid orange), allegedly discovered 1600 years ago.

Foreign tourists do not frequent Ganpatipule often and you are likely to be an object of considerable curiosity. For a quieter patch of sand, head towards the beach in front of the MTDC Tent Resort.

There are several places to stay in and around the town but a kilometre or so from the beach is the unforgettable **Hotel Shiv Sagar Palace** (☎ 25147163; shivsagarpalace@yahoo.com; d with/without AC from Rs 1000/1500; ✷). This massive pink structure, full of colonnades, domes and arches looks like a tacky Las Vegas hotel on LSD. The sweeping driveway is big enough to park a 747 on and, once inside the hallowed halls, you'll discover a kitsch world of orange plastic palm trees, towering chandeliers, gold tables and mirrors. It's worth staying for the novelty factor alone. The stunning sea views, good vegetarian restaurant and a professional attitude bring an unexpected class to the place.

The **MTDC Resort** (☎ 235248; fax 235328; d with/without AC from Rs 1400/1200; ✷) is nicely ensconced among the palms and has the prime beachside spot. Its **Tent Resort** (☎ 235248; 2-/4-bed tents Rs 300/500), might be a cheaper option but the tents have no security and can get very hot. The resort offers a variety of water sports, has a **Bank of Maharashtra** (☎ 235304), which can change travellers cheques but not currency, and the **Tarang Restaurant** (mains Rs 40-90), serving local specialities such as Malvani fish curry. MTDC can also organise tours (Rs 1200 day tour, Rs 500 evening tour) of the region that include a boat cruise and village visits.

GETTING THERE & AWAY

One MSRTC bus heads daily to Ganpatipule (semideluxe Rs 250, 10 hours) from Mumbai, leaving the state road transport terminal near Mumbai Central bus stand at 7.30pm. The bus rumbles back to Mumbai from Ganpatipule at 6.00am. Frequent ordinary buses head down to Ratnagiri (Rs 30, one hour).

Ratnagiri

☎ 02352 / pop 70,335

Around 50km south of Ganpatipule, Ratnagiri is the largest town on the south coast and the main transport hub (it's on the Konkan Railway), but for a tourist that's about all that can be said for it. It's a hot, sticky workaday town with little to see and do aside from visiting the former home of freedom fighter Lokmanya Tilak, which is now a small **museum** (Tilak Alley; admission free; 🕑 9am-7pm), and the remnants of the **Thibaw Palace** (Thibaw Palace Rd), where the last Burmese king, Thibaw, was interned under the British from 1886 until his death in 1916. A more exciting option is to take an evening stroll along **Bhatya Beach**, but you certainly wouldn't want to swim or sunbathe here.

There is no shortage of ATMs or internet cafés along the main road into town.

Just west of the bus stands, **Hotel Landmark** (☎ 220120; fax 220124; Thibaw Palace Rd; s/d Rs 495/695, d with AC Rs 995; 🔀) has clean rooms and a restaurant serving good Indian food.

Ratnagiri **train station** (☎ 131) is 10km east of town; all express trains stop here, including the 10.33am *Jan Shatabdi* south to Margao (2nd class/chair Rs 122/390, 3½ hours, Thursday to Tuesday) and north to Mumbai (Rs 137/455, five hours, Friday to Wednesday). The **old bus stand** (☎ 222340), in the town centre, has state buses to Kolhapur (Rs 97, four hours) and Ganpatipule (Rs 30, one hour). The **new bus stand** (☎ 227882), 1km further west, has two buses daily to both Malvan (Rs 110, five hours) and Panaji (Panjim) in Goa (Rs 200, seven hours).

Tarkarli & Malvan

☎ 02365

Two hundred kilometres south of Ratnagiri and within striking distance of Goa, Tarkarli has the compulsory white sand and sparkling blue waters that every tropical beach should have. In fact it's actually considerably nicer and a good deal cleaner than many of the Goan beaches. The only thing it's really lacking is a tourist industry kitted out for foreigners. There are a few places to stay on the bumpy 7km road in from Malvan, the nearest town, the **MTDC Holiday Resort** (☎ 252390; d from Rs 1200) being only the most obvious. Here you will find an array of simple but sturdy (and a little overpriced) chalets and an excellent restaurant. Get up early and you may see turtles on the beach or a school of dolphins playing

in the waters. Also inquire at the resort about backwater tours on its houseboat.

The monstrous **Sindhudurg Fort**, dating from 1664, is easily visible floating on its offshore island and it can be reached by frequent ferry (Rs 27) from Malvan. It's said that the great Chhatrapati Shivaji helped build this almost impregnable island citadel; his hand- and footprints can be found in one of the turrets above the entrance. A village and several temples lie within the 3km of fort walls.

The closest train station is Kudal, 38km west of the coast. Reasonably frequent buses (Rs 35, one hour) run between here and Malvan **bus stand** (☎ 252034). Otherwise an autorickshaw from Kudal to Malvan or Tarkali is Rs 300. Malvan has several buses daily to Panaji, Goa (Rs 85, five hours) and a couple of services to Ratnagiri (Rs 100, six hours). An autorickshaw between Malvan and Tarkarli costs Rs 60.

MATHERAN

☎ 02148 / pop 5139 / elev 803m

Matheran (Jungle Topped), resting atop the Sahyadris Mountains amid a shady forest crisscrossed with walking tracks and breathtaking lookouts, is easily the most gorgeous of Maharashtra's hill stations.

Hugh Malet, collector for the Thane district, 'discovered' Matheran in 1850 while climbing the path known as Shivaji's Ladder; thereafter it quickly became a popular hill station. The place owes its tranquillity to a ban on motor vehicles and bicycles, making it an ideal place to rest the ears and lungs. It's a very friendly town, well geared up for Indian tourists, but less sure of foreigners.

From around mid-June to early October the monsoon-mudded village practically hibernates. Otherwise weekends generally see Matheran clogged with day-trippers, while during the true high season – the peak holiday periods of May to June, Diwali and Christmas – it's packed to the gills and hotel prices get ludicrous.

Getting to Matheran always used to be half the fun; from Neral Junction a narrow-gauge toy train (mini train) chugged along a scenic 21km route to the heart of the village, but the devastating monsoon of 2005, which left hundreds across the state dead and Mumbai crippled, also put a temporary end to such shenanigans thanks to track damage. At the time of research repair work was ongoing and

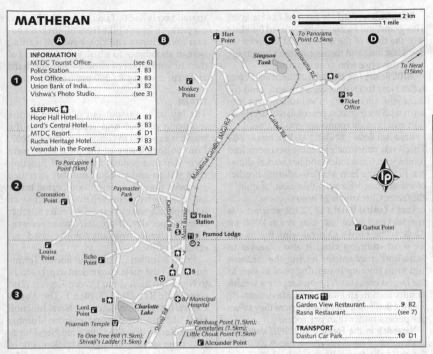

MATHERAN

INFORMATION
MTDC Tourist Office..................(see 6)
Police Station..................**1** B3
Post Office..................**2** B3
Union Bank of India..................**3** B2
Vishwa's Photo Studio..................(see 3)

SLEEPING 🏠
Hope Hall Hotel..................**4** B3
Lord's Central Hotel..................**5** B3
MTDC Resort..................**6** D1
Rucha Heritage Hotel..................**7** B3
Verandah in the Forest..................**8** A3

EATING 🍴
Garden View Restaurant..................**9** B2
Rasna Restaurant..................(see 7)

TRANSPORT
Dasturi Car Park..................**10** D1

MAHARASHTRA

it's hoped that the train will once again be chugging through 'One Kiss Tunnel' by the time this book hits the shelves.

Information
Entry to Matheran costs Rs 25 (Rs 15 for children), which you pay on arrival at the train station or the car park.

Vishwa's Photo Studio (☎ 230354), on Mahatma Gandhi (MG) Rd, sells useful miniguides (Rs 25) and is actually a far better source of information than the so-called **tourist office** (☎ 230540) inside the MTDC Resort next to the car park. The **Union Bank of India** (☎ 230282; MG Rd; 🕙 10am-2pm Mon-Fri, to noon Sat) changes travellers cheques only.

Sights and Activities
You can walk along shady forest paths to most of Matheran's viewpoints in a matter of hours and it's a place suited to stress-free ambling. If you've got the early morning energy then **Panorama Point** is the most dramatic place to glimpse the sunrise, while **Porcupine Point** (also known as Sunset Point) is the most popular (read: packed) as the sun drops. **Louisa Point**

and **Little Chouk Point** also have stunning views and if you're visiting **Echo Point**, be sure to give it a yell. Stop at **Charlotte Lake** on the way back from Echo Point, but don't go for a swim – this is the town's main water supply. You can reach the valley below **One Tree Hill** down the path known as **Shivaji's Ladder**, allegedly trod upon by the Maratha leader himself.

Horses can be hired from people along MG Rd – you will certainly be approached – for rides to lookout points; they cost about Rs 200 per hour.

Sleeping & Eating
A few budget places sit near the train station, but most of the midrange and upscale 'resort' accommodation is between 10 and 20 minutes' walk away (1½ hours from the Dasturi car park). Checkout times vary wildly in Matheran – they can be as early as 7am. Rates quoted here are standard high-season prices, but if it's a very busy weekend then most hotels will do their best to push prices even higher. Regardless, all the accommodation is highly overpriced and standards are some of the lowest in Maharashtra.

Rucha Heritage Hotel (☎ 230072; MG Rd; d from Rs 500) This grand and formal white-pillared building is in the thick of the action. First impressions don't last long and the rooms don't match up, but at this price who's complaining?

MTDC Resort (☎ 230540; fax 230566; d with TV from Rs 650) Next to Dasturi car park and good for those who are too lazy to walk all the way into town with their gear. A peaceful, wooded location and the tidy rooms are good value.

Hope Hall Hotel (☎ 230253; MG Rd; d from Rs 1500) This lovely ramshackle building has overpriced rooms with squat toilets and hot bucket showers. Junior, the Iron Maiden–adoring brother of the woman who runs this joint, is quite a character. Checkout is 24 hours.

Lord's Central Hotel (☎ 230228; www.matheran.com; MG Rd; s/d Rs 800/1600, valley view Rs 1700/3400; 🖳 🖳) The Lord's Central wins the award for most stunning view. It also deserves to win another award for having the cleanest and most inviting swimming pool as well as the largest chess set. The owners are a wealth of information and the rooms are decent. Be warned that when they quote prices they mean per person rather than per room.

Verandah in the Forest (☎ 230296; www.neemranahotels.com; d weekdays/weekends from Rs 2000/2500) Set amid the forest close to Charlotte Lake, the 19th-century aura and period furniture of creaky Barr house will send Raj-lovers' hearts racing. The hotel is completely without modern distractions and the electricity can be a bit hit and miss. It's let down by lousy service and a reception that certainly wouldn't amuse Queen Vic. The set meals (Indian lunch, continental breakfast and dinner) are very good.

Garden View Restaurant (☎ 230550; MG Rd; mains Rs 60-100) Locals insist that the tastiest meals in Matheran come with a garden view. Thalis are the star attraction.

Attached to Rucha Heritage Hotel, **Rasna Restaurant** (☎ 230072; MG Rd; mains Rs 70-110) is good value and includes a few Matheran surprises such as milk shakes and burgers.

Matheran is famed for its locally produced honey and for *chikki*, a rock-hard workout for the jaws made of *gur* (unrefined sugar made from cane juice) and nuts. Find it at the numerous 'chikki marts' and shops on MG Rd.

Getting There & Away
TAXI
From Neral to Matheran taxis cost around Rs 250 and take 20 to 30 minutes. A seat in a shared taxi is Rs 50. Taxis stop at the Dasturi car park, an hour's hike from Matheran's bazaar area. Horses and rickshaws are waiting here in abundance to whisk you in a cloud of dust to your hotel of choice – bargain hard and expect to pay Rs 200 per horse or cart.

TRAIN
The toy train was put out of action by the monsoon of 2005 and repair work to the tracks is expected to continue until late 2007. Prior to the closure of the train there were three departures daily from Neral Junction train station and an equal number of return journeys. During the monsoon period trains were far less frequent. When the repair work is completed, you can expect a similar number of trains per day. If possible, make reservations in advance from any computerised reservation office.

From Mumbai Chhatrapati Shivaji Terminus (CST) the most convenient express train to Neral Junction is the *Deccan Express* (2nd class/chair Rs 34/142, 7.10am). The *Koyna Express* (9am) doesn't arrive at Neral Junction until 10.31am. Most expresses from Mumbai stop at Karjat, down the line from Neral Junction, from where you can backtrack on one of the frequent local trains. Alternatively, take a suburban Karjat-bound train from Mumbai CST and get off at Neral (2nd/1st class Rs 20/120, 2½ hours).

From Pune the 7am *Sahyadri Express* (sleeper/2 AC Rs 101/280, two hours) is the only express stopping at Neral Junction, arriving at 10.09am. Alternatively, take an express that stops at Karjat and get a local train from there.

Getting Around
Matheran is one of the few places left in India where you'll find hand-pulled rickshaws (though even these are more barrow cart than rickshaw); they charge Rs 200 to haul you up from the Dasturi car park to the town. Apart from the rickshaws the only other transport options are your own feet, or a horse. For some reason nobody appears to have thought of attaching a cart to a horse.

LONAVLA
☎ 02114 / pop 55,650 / elev 625m
Lonavla, 106km southeast of Mumbai, caters to weekenders and conference groups coming from the big city and is promoted by the local

tourist board as a 'hill resort'. This is a bit of a misnomer – there are certainly no soaring peaks in the background or precipitous drops to peer fearfully over, but the surrounding countryside is relatively pretty, if a little overdeveloped, and the air cooler and less humid than Mumbai. Lonavla is a long way off being an attractive town – its main drag consists almost exclusively of garishly lit shops flogging chikki, the rock-hard nut brittle sweet that is made in the area. But Lonavla does have one very worthwhile calling card – the nearby Karla and Bhaja Cave Temples, which after those of Ellora and Ajanta, are the best in Maharashtra.

Hotels, restaurants and the main road to the caves are a short walk north of the train station (exit from platform 1). Most of Lonavla

town, which includes a busy market, is south of the station.

Change money in Mumbai or Pune as none of the banks here deal in foreign exchange. Internet access is available at **Balaji Cyber Café** (1st fl, Khandelwal Bldg, New Bazaar; per hr Rs 20; 12.30-10.30pm), immediately south of the train station.

Activities

Set in neatly kept grounds about 2km from Lonavla just off the Mumbai–Pune Hwy on the way to the Karla and Bhaja Caves, the **Kaivalyadhama Yoga Hospital** (☎ 273039; www.kdham .com; s/d Indian Rs 400/600, foreigner from US$15/24;) is favoured by those seeking yogic healing. It was founded in 1924 by Swami Kuvalayanandji

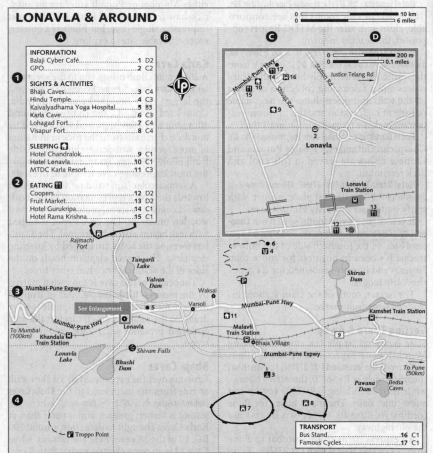

and combines yoga courses with naturopathic therapies. Room rates cover full board and yoga sessions as well as programmes and lectures. The minimum course is seven days. Book in advance.

Mumbai-based **Nirvana Adventures** (☎ 022-26493110; www.nirvanaadventures.com) offers paragliding courses (three-day learner course from €250) or short tandem flights at Kamshet, 25km from Lonavla.

Sleeping & Eating
Lonavla's hotels suffer from inflated prices and low standards. Most places are packed out during weekends and holidays (except through the monsoon). All hotels listed here have a 10am checkout time.

Hotel Lonavla (☎ 272914; Mumbai-Pune Hwy; d Rs 795; ☒) Small fan-only rooms that are comfortable, clean and, after the MTDC Resort (opposite), the best bet in town.

Hotel Chandralok (☎ 272294; fax 272921; Shivaji Rd; d with/without AC from Rs 1200/900; ☒) Set back from the traffic, this is a friendly hotel with dreary rooms and a fascinating collection of stains on the walls and sheets. Rates are negotiable outside of high season and the in-house restaurant makes a remarkable Gujarati thali.

Hotel Gurukripa (Mumbai-Pune Hwy; mains Rs 40-80) Cheap, cheerful and ever reliable Punjabi and Chinese dishes are served in this cool and dark restaurant.

Hotel Rama Krishna (☎ 273600; Mumbai-Pune Hwy; dishes Rs 45-120) The sleekest place in town with spiffy waiters serving tasty Punjabi fare.

If you've got a sweet tooth, search out **Coopers** (☎ 272564; Jaychand Chowk; ☽ 11am-1pm & 3-5pm, closed Wed), on the southern side of the railway tracks. It's been in business for more than 50 years and is justly renowned for its gooey chocolate fudges.

The bazaar, south of the train station, includes a large fruit market.

Getting There & Away
State buses set to ply the smooth-moving Mumbai–Pune Expressway depart continuously from the **bus stand** (☎ 273842) to Mumbai (ordinary/deluxe Rs 56/70, three/two hours), while their AC siblings (Rs 100) rev up just a few times daily. The many buses for Pune (ordinary/deluxe Rs 44/60, two hours) use the old highway.

All express trains from Mumbai to Pune stop at Lonavla **train station** (☎ 273725). Travelling from Mumbai trains take three hours and cost Rs 35/122 in 2nd class/chair. To Pune there are express trains (2nd class/chair Rs 27/122, one hour, 64km) and hourly shuttle trains (Rs 14, two hours).

Bicycles can be hired from **Famous Cycles** (Mumbai-Pune Hwy; per hr Rs 5).

KARLA & BHAJA CAVES
Dating from around the 2nd century BC, these rock-cut caves are among the oldest and finest examples of early Buddhist rock temple art in India. They may not be on the same scale as Ellora or Ajanta, but the lack of visitors, pretty countryside and zero commercialisation make them worthy of a visit.

It's possible to visit the caves in a day from either Mumbai or Pune if you hire an autorickshaw from Lonavla. Karla has the most impressive single cave, but Bhaja is a quieter, more enjoyable site to explore.

Karla Cave
A 20-minute climb brings you to the spectacular **Karla Cave** (Indian/foreigner Rs 5/US\$2; ☽ 9am-5pm), the largest early Buddhist *chaitya* in India. Completed in 80 BC, the *chaitya* is around 40m long and 15m high, and was carved by monks and artisans from the rock in imitation of more familiar wooden architecture. Aside from Ellora's Kailasa Temple this is probably the most impressive cave temple in the state.

A semicircular 'sun window' filters light in towards the cave's representation of the Buddha – a dagoba, or stupa, protected by a carved wooden umbrella. The cave's roof is ribbed with teak beams said to be original. The 37 pillars forming the aisles are topped by kneeling elephants. The carved elephant heads on the sides of the vestibule once had ivory tusks.

The beauty of this cave is somewhat marred by the modern **Hindu temple** built in front of the cave mouth. However the temple is a big draw for the pilgrims you'll meet in the area and their presence adds some colour to the scene.

Bhaja Caves
Crossing over the expressway, it's a 3km walk or ride from the main road to the **Bhaja Caves** (Indian/foreigner Rs 5/US\$2; ☽ 8am-6pm), where the setting is lusher, greener and quieter than at Karla Cave. Thought to date from around 200 BC, 10 of the 18 caves here are *viharas*, while Cave 12 is an open *chaitya*, earlier than Karla,

containing a simple dagoba. Beyond this is a strange huddle of 14 stupas, five inside and nine outside a cave. If you avoid weekends and holidays then there's a good chance you'll be the only visitor here, which helps to lend an air of Indiana Jones–style discovery to your wanderings. From Bhaja Caves you'll see the ruins of the **Lohagad** and **Visapur Forts**, which local kids will happily lead you to for a tip.

Sleeping & Eating

MTDC Karla Resort (☎ 02114-282230; fax 282370; d cottages with/without AC from Rs 1000/600, executive cottage Rs 2500; ✖ ☐) The tidy and spacious rooms on offer here are much better than anything Lonavla can throw at you. Set under the trees, the complex is very peaceful – there's even a little lake where you can go boating. Frequently passing buses and rickshaws can take you either to the caves or back to Lonavla. The resort has a restaurant, and is just off the Mumbai–Pune Hwy.

Getting There & Away

If you don't mind some walking, you can get around the sites within a day by public transport. Frequent local buses run between Lonavla and Karla Cave (Rs 9, 12km); the first leaves Lonavla at 6am. From Karla, walk to Bhaja Caves (minium two hours, 10km), then follow your feet back to Malavli train station (one hour, 3km) to catch a local train to Lonavla. You can trim some walking time by taking an autorickshaw from Karla to Bhaja village (around Rs 70). The last bus from Karla to Lonavla leaves at 7pm.

Autorickshaws are plentiful, but they drive a hard bargain. The price should include waiting time at the sites (about three hours all up), and a return trip from Lonavla to the Karla and Bhaja Caves will cost Rs 400.

PUNE

☎ 020 / pop 3.8 million / elev 457m

A place where old and new India interweave without a second thought, Pune (pronounced Poona) is a thriving centre of academia and business as well as a historic centre and home to the Osho Meditation Resort.

The great Maratha leader Shivaji would be astonished to see how his city has changed in 500 years. He was raised here after the city was granted to his grandfather in 1599. The town fell to the British in 1817 and became their alternative capital during the monsoon.

Many maharajas had palaces here, too, taking advantage of its cooler climate.

Despite the pollution and clogged traffic that typically go with Indian cities, Pune is an interesting place to hang out for a day or two and a great place to glimpse the much touted, but sometimes hard to find, 'New India'.

Orientation

The city sits at the confluence of the Mutha and Mula Rivers. Mahatma Gandhi (MG) Rd, about 1km south of Pune train station, is the main street and is lined with banks, restaurants and shops. Southwest of here, the streets narrow and take on the atmosphere of a traditional bazaar town. Northeast of the train station, Koregaon Park, home of the Osho ashram and ground zero for the Pune backpacker scene, is where the more upmarket restaurants and bars are to be found.

Information
BOOKSHOPS

Crossword (1st fl, Sohrab Hall, RBM Rd; ✇ 10.30am-9pm) On Raibahadur Motilal (RBM) Rd, this offers a diverse collection of books and magazines, as well as a small café.
Manneys Booksellers (7 Moledina Rd; ✇ 9.30am-1.30pm & 4-8pm Mon-Sat)

INTERNET ACCESS
Computology Systems (326 Ashok Vijay Complex, Bootie St; per hr Rs 10; ✇ 9.30am-9.30pm Mon-Sat, 11am-8pm Sun)
Cyber-Net (1B Gera Sterling, North Main Rd, Koregaon Park; per hr Rs 30; ✇ 8am-11.30pm)
Dishnet Hub Internet Centre (Sadhu Vaswani Rd; per hr Rs 30)

MAP
The *Destination Finder* map of Pune (Rs 60) is the best map around. You can find it at most bookshops or at the newspaper stand on platform 1 of the train station.

MONEY
Citibank has 24-hour ATMs at its main branch on East St and at the branches on Bund Garden Rd and North Main Rd. ICICI Bank has an ATM at the Pune train station and another on Koregaon Rd. Southwest of Koregaon Park there is a HSBC ATM, near the Air India office on Mangaldas Rd. On MG Rd you'll find a UTI Bank ATM.
Thomas Cook (☎ 26346171; 2418 G Thimmaya Rd; ✇ 9.30am-6pm Mon-Sat)

MAHARASHTRA

PUNE

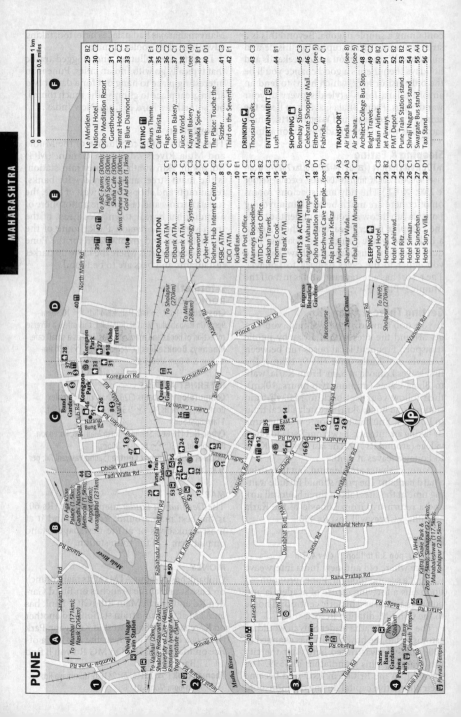

INFORMATION

Citibank ATM.................1	C1
Citibank ATM.................2	C3
Citibank ATM.................3	C3
Computology Systems.......4	C3
Crossword.....................5	C2
Cyber-Net.....................6	C1
Dishnet Hub Internet Centre.....7	C3
HSBC ATM....................8	C1
ICICI ATM.....................9	C1
Main Post Office.............10	E1
Manneys Booksellers........11	C3
MTDC Tourist Office........12	C3
Rokshan Travels..............13	C3
Thomas Cook.................14	C3
UTI Bank ATM................15	C3
...............................16	C3

SIGHTS & ACTIVITIES

Jangali Maharaj Temple.......17	A2
Osho Meditation Resort.......18	D1
Pataleshvara Cave Temple...(see 17)	
Raja Dinkar Kelkar	
Museum.........................19	A3
Shaniwar Wada................20	A3
Tribal Cultural Museum.......21	C2

SLEEPING 🛏

Grand Hotel...................22	C3
Homeland......................23	B2
Hotel Ashirwad...............24	C2
Hotel Ritz......................25	C2
Hotel Simman.................26	C1
Hotel Sunderban.............27	D1
Hotel Surya Villa.............28	D1
.................................29	B2
.................................30	C2

Le Méridien...................29	B2
National Hotel................30	C2
Osho Meditation Resort	
Guesthouse...................31	C1
Samrat Hotel..................32	C2
Taj Blue Diamond...........33	C1

EATING 🍴

Arthurs Theme................34	E1
Café Barista...................35	C3
Flags............................36	C2
German Bakery...............37	C1
Juice World....................38	C3
Kayani Bakery................39	E1
Malaka Spice.................40	D1
Prems..........................41	C3
The Place: Touche the Seventh	
Sizzler..........................42	E1
Third on the Seventh........42	E1

DRINKING 🍷

Thousand Oaks..............43	C3

ENTERTAINMENT 🎭

Lush............................44	B1

SHOPPING 🛍

Bombay Store................45	C3
Celebrate Shopping Mall....46	C3
Either Or.......................(see 5)	
Fabindia.......................47	C1

TRANSPORT

Air India.......................(see 8)	
Air Sahara.....................(see 5)	
Architect College Bus Stop.....48	A4
Bright Travels.................49	C2
Indian Airlines................50	B2
Jet Airways....................51	C1
PMT Depot....................52	B2
Pune Train Station stand....53	B2
Shivaji Nagar Bus stand.....54	A1
Swargate Bus stand.........55	A4
Taxi Stand.....................56	C2

To ABC Farms (300m);
High Spirits (300m);
Shisha Café (300m)

Swiss Cheese Garden (300m);
Gold Ad Labs (1.3km)

POST
Main post office (☎ 26125516; Sadhu Vaswani; ⏱ 10am-6pm Mon-Sat)

TOURIST INFORMATION
MTDC tourist office (☎ 26126867/24373277; I Block, Central Bldg; ⏱ 10am-5.30pm Mon-Sat) Buried in a government complex south of the train station and not of great help. There is also a small MTDC desk at the train station (open 9am to 7pm Monday to Saturday, and to 3pm Sunday).

TRAVEL AGENCIES
Rokshan Travels (☎ 26136304; rokshantravels@ hotmail.com; 1st fl, 19 Kumar Pavilion, East St; ⏱ 10am-6pm) Small, friendly and professional outfit. Staff can arrange bus and train journeys and domestic and international flights, as well as taxis.

Sights & Activities
OSHO MEDITATION RESORT
The Bhagwan Rajneesh's **ashram** (☎ 2066019999; www.osho.com; 17 Koregaon Park) is located in a desirable northern suburb of Pune. Since the Bhagwan's death in 1990, the meditation resort has continued to draw in manifold *sanyasins* (seekers), many of them Westerners. Facilities include a swimming pool, sauna, 'zennis' (Zen tennis) and basketball courts, a massage and beauty parlour, a bookshop and a boutique guesthouse (p167). The main centre for meditation and the nightly white-robed spiritual dance is the Osho Auditorium (a 'cough-free and sneeze-free zone'!). The Osho Samadhi, where the guru's ashes are kept, is also open for silent or music-accompanied meditation.

The commune is big business. Its 'Multiversity' runs a plethora of courses in meditation as well as New Age techniques. If you wish to take part in any of the courses, or even just to visit for the day to meditate you'll have to pay Rs 1280. This covers registration, a mandatory on-the-spot HIV test (sterile needles are used), introductory sessions and your first day's meditation pass. You'll also need two robes (one maroon and one white, from Rs 300 per robe). Meditation is Rs 450/150 (foreigner/Indian) per day and you can come and go as you please. If you want to contribute further, there's the resort's 'Work-as-Meditation' programme.

The curious can watch a video presentation at the visitor centre and take a 10-minute silent tour of the facilities (Rs 10; no children)

at 9am and 2pm daily. Even if you decide not to enter the resort, it's worth checking out the placid 5-hectare gardens, **Osho Teerth** (admission free; ⏱ 6-9am & 3-6pm), behind the commune; the gardens are accessible all day for those with a meditation pass.

RAJA DINKAR KELKAR MUSEUM
This quirky **museum** (☎ 24461556; www.rajakelkar museum.com; 1377-78 Natu Baug, Bajirao Rd; adult/child Rs 200/50; ⏱ 9.30am-6pm) is one of Pune's true delights. The exhibits are the personal collection of Sri Dinkar Gangadhar, who died in 1990. Among the 17,000 or so artworks and curios he collected are a suit of armour made of fish scales and crocodile skin, hundreds of hookah pipes and a superb collection of betel-nut cutters.

KATRAJ SNAKE PARK & ZOO
There is a good representation of Indian wildlife on show at the **Katraj Snake Park & Zoo** (☎ 24367712; Pune-Satara Hwy; adult/child Rs 3/2; ⏱ 10.30am-6pm Jul-Mar, to 7pm Apr-Jun, closed Wed). Located on the southern outskirts of the city, the large, natural-looking enclosures of the zoo are built with the requirements and breeding needs of the inmates in mind. It provides a home to tigers, leopards, bears and monkeys, but it's the reptiles that are the real passion here. The zoo curator is renowned as one of India's most respected herpetologists.

SHANIWAR WADA
The ruins of this fortresslike **palace** (Shivaji Rd; admission US$2; ⏱ 8am-6.30pm) stand in the old part of the city. Built in 1732, the palace of the Peshwa rulers burnt down in 1828, but the massive walls remain, as do the sturdy palace doors with their angry spikes. In the evenings there is an hour-long **sound & light show** (Rs 25; ⏱ 8.15pm Thu-Tue).

PATALESHVARA CAVE TEMPLE
Set across the river is the curious rock-cut **Pataleshvara Cave Temple** (☎ 25535941; Jangali Maharaj Rd; ⏱ 6am-9.30pm), a small, unfinished 8th-century temple similar in style to the grander Elephanta Island near Mumbai. It's an active temple, with people coming here for worship or simply to relax in the gardens. In front of the excavation is a circular Nandi *mandapa* (pillared pavilion). Adjacent is the **Jangali Maharaj Temple** (⏱ 6am-10pm), dedicated to a Hindu ascetic who died here in 1818.

THE ARMANI OF ASHRAMS

Bhagwan Shree Rajneesh (1931–90), or Osho as he preferred to be called, was one of India's most flamboyant 'export gurus' and undoubtedly the most controversial. He followed no particular religion or philosophy and outraged many Indians (and others) with his advocacy of sex as a path to enlightenment, earning him the epithet 'sex guru'. In 1981 Rajneesh took his curious blend of Californian pop psychology and Indian mysticism to the USA, where he set up an agricultural commune and ashram in Oregon. There, his ashram's notoriety as well as its fleet of Rolls Royces (bought to prove that material processions had no meaning!) grew like weeds. Eventually, with rumours and local paranoia about the ashram's activities running amok, the Bhagwan was charged with immigration fraud, fined US$400,000 and deported. An epic journey began during which he and his followers, in their search for a new base, were deported from or denied entry to 21 countries. By 1987 he was back at the Pune ashram, where thousands of foreigners soon flocked for his nightly discourses and meditation courses.

They still come in droves. The unveiling of the capacious Osho Auditorium in 2002 also marked the alteration of the centre's name from 'Osho Commune International' to 'Osho Meditation Resort'. Prices for the 'resort' privileges are continually on the rise, facilities become ever more luxurious and, just in case you were wondering, despite Osho's comments on how nobody should be poor, none of the money generated by the resort goes into helping the poor or disadvantaged of the local community. That, resort authorities claim, is up to someone else.

TRIBAL CULTURAL MUSEUM

About 1.5km east of the Pune train station, this excellent **museum** (☎ 2636207; 28 Queens Garden, Richardson Rd; Indian/foreigner Rs 5/10; ☷ 10.30am-5.30pm) opens up a whole new side of India that most visitors are completely unaware of. The ornate papier-mâché festival masks are like something from the Rio carnival.

GANDHI NATIONAL MEMORIAL

Set in 6.5 hectares of gardens across the Mula River in Yerwada is the grand **Aga Khan Palace** and **Gandhi National Memorial** (☎ 26680250; Ahmednagar Rd; Indian/foreigner Rs 5/100; ☷ 9am-5.45pm). After the Mahatma delivered his momentous Quit India resolution in 1942, the British interned him and other leaders of India's Independence movement here for nearly two years. Both Kasturba Gandhi, the Mahatma's wife, and Mahadoebhai Desai, his secretary for 35 years, died while imprisoned here. Their ashes are kept in memorial samadhis (shrines) in the gardens.

Photos and paintings exhibit moments in Gandhi's extraordinary career, but it's all very poorly presented.

GARDENS

At the **Empress Botanical Gardens** (admission Rs 5; ☷ 6.30am-7pm) cosy couples on park benches enjoy the spots of shade under the trees. In the evening, dozens of food stalls and kiddie carnival rides are set up outside **Peshwa Park** (admission Rs 2; ☷ 9.30am-5.30pm).

RAMAMANI IYENGAR MEMORIAL YOGA INSTITUTE

To attended classes at this famous **institute** (☎ 25656134; www.bksiyengar.com; 1107 B/1 Hare Krishna Mandir Rd, Model Colony), around 7km northwest of the train station, you need to have been practising yoga for at least eight years.

Courses

Kuk@ease (☎ 30938999/09371207599; antimaa@rediffmail .com; C-8, Sapphire Apts, Lane 6, Koregaon Park) offers one-day cookery courses (single person/per person in group of four Rs 1600/600), with equipment and ingredients supplied.

Tours

Good bus tours of Pune leave the **Pune Municipal Transport depot** (PMT; Sasson Rd; ☷ bookings 8am-noon & 3-6pm), near the train station, at 9am daily, returning around 6pm (Rs 128). They quickly cover all of Pune's major sights.

Sleeping

There's no shortage of accommodation all over Pune but the main hubs are around the train station and Koregaon Park, which, with its proximity to the Osho Meditation Resort, has become the main backpackers' hang-out. Many families rent rooms out to passing travellers and, with prices starting at Rs 150 for a room with a shared bathroom and Rs 250 for private bathrooms, this is the cheapest way to grab a good night's sleep. Quality varies widely, so check out a few before deciding. For longer-term stays you can negotiate a room in one of these places from Rs 3000 to 10,000 per month. Rickshaw drivers will know where to look.

BUDGET

Grand Hotel (☎ 26360728; MG Rd; s with shared bathroom/d with private bathroom Rs 250/575) Excluding its private rooms in family homes, the Grand has the cheapest beds in Pune, but it's not a place you would chose for a luxurious break. On the positive side the patio bar is a good place for a beer.

National Hotel (☎ 26125054; 14 Sasson Rd; d/tr Rs 450/550, cottages from Rs 500) Located opposite the train station is this charmingly run-down colonial mansion with verandas and high ceilings set in a pleasing garden. While the rooms are basic, they are clean, and the cottages have little porches.

Homeland (☎ 26127659; homeland@satyam.net.in; 18 Wilson Garden; s/d Rs 450/550, with AC Rs 750/850; ✄) Dirty and run down but if everything else is full it will pass for a night.

Hotel Surya Villa (☎ 26124501; www.hotelsuryavilla .com; 294/1 Koregaon Park; s/d Rs 1000/1200, d with AC Rs 1300; ✄) With light and airy rooms this could have been one of the better Koregaon Park hotels, but sadly you'll be having threesomes (or even twelvesomes) with the numerous cockroaches that have infested the bedrooms. The downstairs café seems to be cockroach-free and is good value.

MIDRANGE

All hotels listed have a noon checkout and accept credit cards.

Hotel Sunderban (☎ 26124949; www.tghotels.com; 19 Koregaon Park; d with shared bathroom from Rs 800, with private bathroom with/without AC from Rs 1300/1000; ✄) Next to the Osho Resort this was a popular, but increasingly neglected, heritage property that at the time of research was about to close for renovations. When it reopens (no date scheduled) it's likely to remain just as popular. The prices listed are pre-renovations.

Samrat Hotel (☎ 26137964; thesamrathotel@vsnl.net; 17 Wilson Garden; s/d Rs 1190/1400, with AC Rs 1600/1800; ✄) Every Indian town has one hotel that shines above all the others and in Pune that honour falls to the Samrat Hotel. This sparkling modern hotel is in a class of its own and represents superb value for money. It's often full so book in advance.

Hotel Ritz (☎ 26122995; fax 26136644; 6 Sadhu Vaswani Path; d with/without AC Rs 2550/1950; ✄) A ramshackle old building with unharnessed potential. It's friendly and certainly one of Pune's better bets. All rooms have TVs and the cheaper ones are at the back next to the garden restaurant, which serves good Gujarati thalis.

Hotel Ashirwad (☎ 26128585; hotelash@vsnl.com; 16 Cannaught Rd; s/d from Rs 2200/2500; ✄) The smug management don't exactly warm you to this place but the rooms are very clean and it sits nicely near the top of the midrange class. The Akshaya restaurant is a worthy choice that serves Punjabi, Mughlai and Chinese vegetarian fare.

Hotel Srimaan (☎ 26133535; srimaan@vsnl.com; 361/5A Bund Gdn Rd; s/d Rs 2300/2800; ✄) Clean and functional but lacking any real spark. It's popular with passing Indian businessmen and is good value.

ourpick Osho Meditation Resort guesthouse (☎ 2066019999; www.osho.com; Koregaon Park; s/d Rs 2400/2900; ✄) If your visit to Pune is to attend the Osho Meditation Resort (p165), then its stylish guesthouse, with minimalist rooms, offers the unique opportunity to breathe in deep lungfuls of specially cleaned air! Book in advance and note that you have to be attending courses at the resort to stay.

TOP END

Taj Blue Diamond (☎ 6025555; bdresv.pune@tajhotels .com; 11 Koregaon Rd; d from US$180; ✄ ▢ ✄) An elegant, top-class business hotel with all the trimmings from courteous staff in saris to pleasantly decorated rooms and a stylish selection of restaurants.

Le Meridien (☎ 26050505; www.lemeridien-pune .com; RBM Rd; d from US$235; ✄ ▢ ✄) Styled on a Mughal palace and full of marble pillars and high ceilings, this is the most sumptuous hotel in Pune. Rooms are compact and comfortable. Other assets include three restaurants, two bars, a nightclub, gym and a small rooftop pool (open to nonguests for Rs 450 per day).

Eating

The opportunity to eat, drink and make merry is one of the highlights of Pune. The biggest concentration of well-priced, high-quality eateries are be found around the Lanes in Koregaon Park. Unless otherwise mentioned the following are open noon to 3pm and 7pm to 11pm daily.

RESTAURANTS

Vaishali (☎ 25672676; FC Rd; mains Rs 70) A long established Pune institution on account of its delicious South Indian dishes.

Shabree Restaurant (Hotel Parichay, 1199/1A FC Rd; mains Rs 70-120) Some of the best, cheap Maharashtran thalis you could hope to find.

Flags (☎ 26141617; G2 Metropole, Bund Garden Rd; mains Rs 75-200) With possibly Pune's longest menu, running the global gamut from Mongolian cauliflower to *yakisoba* (fried Japanese noodles), the highly popular Flags has something to please practically everyone, all wrapped up in a comfy contemporary interior.

Prems (North Main Rd, Koregaon Park; mains Rs 80-150) In a quiet, leafy courtyard tucked away from the main road, Prems is a relaxing and very popular place for a decent mixture of Indian and Continental food. It's as popular with Indians as Westerners.

The Place: Touche the Sizzler (☎ 26134632; 7 Moledina Rd; mains Rs 120-200) As the name suggests, this long-running place specialises in sizzlers, but it also offers Indian, tandoori, seafood and Continental dishes.

Third on the Seventh (☎ 26140715; Lane 7, North Main Rd; mains Rs 120-250) In something of a reversal of trends, this classy joint is run by a British-Indian couple who have returned to Pune from the UK bringing with them a bulging recipe book of 'British-style' curries and Continental food.

our pick **Malaka Spice** (☎ 26136293; Lane 6, North Main Rd; mains Rs 110-300, 11am-11pm) A supertrendy little restaurant with excellent Southeast Asian food and a menu that is part artwork, part travel diary. It's very popular with the young and beautiful of Pune.

Arthur's Theme (☎ 26132710; Lane 6, North Main Rd, mains Rs 120-300) This is a stylish place offering decent French cuisine in a slightly formal atmosphere.

The ABC Farms is a complex of midrange restaurants in Koregaon Park, where healthy, organic food is the order of the day. One of the best restaurants is the **Swiss Cheese Garden** (☎ 26817413; mains Rs 100-400), which, alongside delicious pastas, offers good old-fashioned cheese fondues. Almost next door is the equally enjoyable **Shisha Café** (☎ 26818885; mains Rs 100-180; 10.30am-1.30pm), which is a combination of a jazz bar and an Iranian restaurant, complete with bubbling hookah pipes (Rs 125).

CAFÉS

Juice World (2436/B East St Camp; 8am-1am) As well as producing delicious fresh fruit juices and shakes, this casual café with outdoor seating serves inexpensive snacks such as pizza and *pav bhaji* (spiced vegetables and bread) for around Rs 40.

German Bakery (North Main Rd, Koregaon Park; dishes Rs 50-150, cakes Rs 25-50; 6am-11.30pm) A compulsory halt on the Koregaon Park backpacker scene, but also appreciated by locals. This long-running café, with light and healthy snacks and great cakes makes a brilliant lunch stop. Fruit and vegetables are sterilised and water used for beverages is purified.

Café Barista (Sterling Centre, 12 MG Rd; meals Rs 40-80) A branch of the Western-style coffee chain, which dishes up plain sandwiches and cakes with good coffee.

The family-run Kayani Bakery on East St is famous for its homemade Shrewsbury biscuits, but the sweet attractions run to all manner of cakes.

Drinking & Entertainment

With its massive student population, Pune puts a great deal of effort into nocturnal activities and has a large array of ever-changing bars and clubs. Ask around Koregaon Park for the latest. The bar scene in Pune can be a little cliquey and it really helps if you know some locals.

High Spirits (Koregaon Park) Brand new bar that's caught the attention of the student population. Has a nice open terrace. It's next to the ABC Farms.

Lush (Boat Club Rd) It's cool. It's super trendy. It's *the* place to be seen. It's Lush, Pune's sleekest new lounge bar.

Thousand Oaks (☎ 26343194; thousandoaks@vsnl.com; 2417 East St; admission Fri & Sat Rs 200) This cosy pub-style bar is an old favourite but its DJs can't decide what kind of music they are into.

Gold Ad Labs (☎ 26050101; Queen's Garden Rd; adult Rs 130) New state-of-the-art cinema complex surrounded by modern shopping malls, bright lights and about as much Eastern exotica as McDonalds on a Saturday night – which happens to be almost next door.

Shopping

Pune has some good shopping options.

Bombay Store (322 MG Rd; 10.30am-8.30pm Mon-Sat, 11am-8pm Sun) This place is the best spot for general souvenirs.

Celebrate Shopping Mall (Bund Garden Rd, Koregaon Park) This glass-fronted mall is full of Western high-street labels.

Pune is a good spot to buy modern Indian clothing; try **Either Or** (24/25 Sohrab Hall, 21 Sasson Rd; ☻ 10.30am-8pm, closed Thu) or **Fabindia** (Sakar 10, Sasson Rd; ☻ 10am-7.45pm).

Getting There & Away

AIR

Airline offices in Pune:

Air India (☎ 26128190; Hermes Kunj, 4 Mangaldas Rd)

Air Sahara (☎ 26059003; 131 Sohrab Hall, 21 Sasson Rd)

Indian Airlines (☎ 26052147; 39 Dr B Ambedkar Rd)

Jet Airways (☎ 26123268; 243 Century Arcade, Narangi Bung Rd)

Indian Airlines flies daily to Delhi (US$153, two hours), and to Bengaluru (US$102, 2½ hours), Goa (US$60 45 minutes) and Mumbai (US$102, 30 minutes). Jet Airways flies twice daily to Mumbai (US$81, 30 minutes), Bengaluru (US$146, 1½ hours), Delhi (US$186, two hours), and daily to Chennai (US$169, 2¼ hours) and Kolkata US$336, 2½ hours). Air Sahara flies twice daily to Delhi (US$115, two hours). Of the budget airlines Spice Jet flies to Delhi and Bengaluru, while Kingfisher flies to Ahmedabad, Bengaluru, Coimbatore, Chennai, Delhi, Hyderabad, Jammu and Nagpur. Air Deccan links Pune up with Ahmedabad, Bengaluru, Delhi and Hyderabad, and IndiGo flies to Bengaluru and Delhi.

BUS

Pune has three bus stands: **Pune train station stand** (☎ 26126218), for Mumbai and destinations to the south and west, including Goa, Belgaum, Kolhapur, Mahabaleshwar and Lonavla; **Shivaji Nagar bus stand** (☎ 25536970), for points north and northeast, including Ahmednagar, Aurangabad, Ahmedabad and Nasik; and **Swargate bus stand** (☎ 24441591), for Sinhagad, Bengaluru and Mangalore. Deluxe buses shuttle from the train station bus stand to Dadar (Mumbai) every 30 minutes (semi-deluxe/deluxe Rs 117/240, four hours).

Plenty of private deluxe buses head to most centres, including Panaji in Goa (ordinary/sleeper Rs 300/400, 12 hours – though high season prices sometimes rise to Rs 600!), Nasik (semideluxe/deluxe Rs 200/250, five hours) and Aurangabad (Rs 160, six hours). Make sure you know where the bus will drop you off (going to Mumbai, for instance, some private buses get no further than Borivali). Try **Bright Travels** (☎ 26114222; Connaught Rd); its buses depart from the service station near the roundabout.

For Mumbai the train is the safest option.

TAXI

Long-distance shared taxis (four passengers) link up Pune with Dadar in Mumbai round the clock. They leave from the **taxi stand** (☎ 26121090) in front of Pune train station (per seat Rs 260, AC Rs 320, three hours). Share-taxi services to Nasik and Aurangabad have been discontinued.

TRAIN

Pune is an important rail hub with connections to many parts of the state. The swarming computerised **booking hall** (☎ 131) is in the building to the left of the station as you face the entrance – take a deep breath before crossing the threshold.

The *Deccan Queen, Sinhagad Express* and *Pragati Express* are fast commuter trains to Mumbai, taking three to four hours.

MAJOR TRAINS FROM PUNE

Destination	Train No & name	Fare (Rs)	Duration (hr)	Departure
Bengaluru	6529 *Udyan Exp*	325/1327	21½	11.45am
Chennai	6011 *Chennai Exp*	337/1366	22½	6.05pm
Delhi	1077 *Jhelum Exp*	417/1691	21¾	9.40pm
Hyderabad	7031 *Hyderabad Exp*	230/933	13¼	4.40pm
Mumbai CST	2124 *Deccan Queen*	57/215	3¼	7.15am

Express fares are 2nd class/chair for day trains, sleeper/2AC sleeper for overnight trains; *Deccan Queen* fares are 2nd class/chair. To calculate 1st class and other fares see p503.

Getting Around

The airport is 8km northeast of the city. An autorickshaw there costs about Rs 50, a taxi is Rs 150.

City buses gather at the PMT depot across from Pune train station, but journeys are slower than a wet Sunday. Useful buses include bus 4 to Swargate, bus 5 to Shivaji Nagar bus terminal, and bus 159 to Koregaon Park.

Autorickshaws can be found everywhere. A ride from the Pune train station to Koregaon Park costs about Rs 30 in the daytime and Rs 50 at night.

AROUND PUNE

Sinhagad

Scene of a victory by Shivaji's forces over those of Bijapur in 1670, Sinhagad (Lion Fort), 24km southwest of Pune, is a fun day out. The ruined fort stands on top of a steep hill cluttered with telecommunications towers and tourist stalls; the real attractions are the sweeping views and the chance for a healthy workout on the hike up from the bus stop in Sinhagad village.

If you don't want to walk, jeeps (Rs 25) are usually around to cart you to within a short stroll of the summit. The Pune city bus 50 runs frequently to Sinhagad village from 7am until evening, leaving from either Swargate or the Architect College bus stop opposite Nehru Stadium (Rs 17, 45 minutes). At the time of research the fort was closed and the access road out of action thanks to damage inflicted by heavy monsoon rains.

MAHABALESHWAR

☎ 02168 / pop 12,736 / elev 1372m

High up in the Western Ghats, the hill station of Mahabaleshwar was founded in 1828 by Sir John 'Boy' Malcolm, after which it quickly became the summer capital of the Bombay presidency during the days of the Raj. Today few traces of those times remain, save for a couple of dilapidated buildings. In fact Rudyard Kipling would positively turn in his grave if he could see how down-at-heel the old girl had become and good gosh, you can't even get a properly brewed cup of tea. While the tea and summer balls are long gone what hasn't changed one jot are the delightful views and equally delightful temperatures and it's for these two reasons that Mahabaleshwar attracts hordes of holidaymakers who fill the main street with loud exuberance. If you are after just a hint of peace and quiet then avoid the peak periods during the summer school holidays (April to June), Christmas and Diwali.

The hill station virtually shuts up shop during the monsoon (from late June to mid-September), when an unbelievable 6m of rain falls. Buildings are clad with *kulum* grass to stave off damage from the torrential downpours. After things calm down, the reward is abundantly green landscapes.

Orientation

Most of the action is in the main bazaar (Main Rd, also called Dr Sabane Rd) – a 200m strip of holiday tack. The bus stand is at the western end. A Rs 15 'tourist tax' is payable on arrival.

Information

Mahabaleshwar has no internet facilities.

Bank of Maharashtra (☎ 260290; Main Rd) Changes cash and travellers cheques.

Krsna Travels (☎ 261035; Subhash Chowk, Main Rd, ☽ 9am-8pm) Reliable onward travel information, a variety of local tours and all manner of bus tickets.

MTDC tourist office (☎ 260318; Bombay Point Rd) At the MTDC Resort south of town, has crude maps but helpful staff.

State Bank of India (Masjid St) Has a 24-hour ATM.

Sights & Activities

The hills are alive with the sound of music, though it's usually being blasted out of car windows as people race by in an effort to tick off all the towns viewpoints as quickly as possible. If you can ignore this then fine views can be savoured from **Wilson's Point** (also known as Sunrise Point), which is within easy walking distance of town, as well as **Elphinstone**, **Babington**, **Kate's** and **Lodwick Points**. The latter is dedicated to Peter Lodwick, the first European to set foot in Mahabaleshwar in 1824.

The sunset views at **Bombay Point** are stunning; but you won't be the only one who thinks so. Much quieter, thanks no doubt to being 9km from town, is **Arthur's Seat**, which, should Arthur have ever fallen out of it, would have resulted in him tumbling down a sheer drop of 600m – at least the view would have been good. Attractive waterfalls around Mahabaleshwar include **Chinaman's**, **Dhobi's** and **Lingmala Falls**. On the edge of Venna Lake, a **boathouse** (Temple Rd; ☽ 8am-8pm) rents out rowboats (Rs 160 per hour) and pedal boats (Rs 200 per hour).

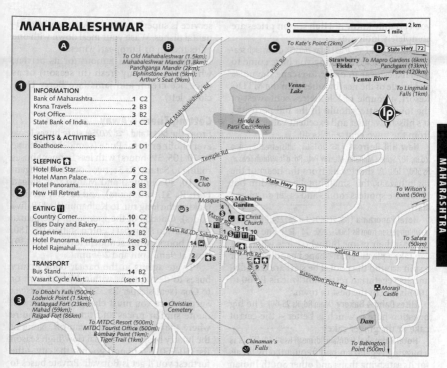

MAHABALESHWAR

INFORMATION	
Bank of Maharashtra	1 C2
Krsna Travels	2 B3
Post Office	3 B2
State Bank of India	4 C2

SIGHTS & ACTIVITIES	
Boathouse	5 D1

SLEEPING	
Hotel Blue Star	6 C2
Hotel Mann Palace	7 C3
Hotel Panorama	8 B3
New Hill Retreat	9 C3

EATING	
Country Corner	10 C2
Elises Dairy and Bakery	11 C2
Grapevine	12 B2
Hotel Panorama Restaurant	(see 8)
Hotel Rajmahal	13 C2

TRANSPORT	
Bus Stand	14 B2
Vasant Cycle Mart	(see 11)

By far the most enjoyable way of seeing a couple of the viewpoints is to follow the forest tracks that run between them. This means you probably won't rub shoulders with anyone but the odd troupe of monkeys. One highly recommended two-hour walk is to stroll down to Bombay Point and then follow the very inappropriately named **Tiger Trail** back into town (maps are available from the MTDC tourist office).

The village of Old Mahabaleshwar has two ancient temples. The **Panchganga Mandir** (🕑 7am-9pm), said to contain the springs of five rivers, including the sacred Krishna River, and the **Mahabaleshwar Mandir** (🕑 6am-9pm), which has a naturally formed lingam.

Tours

The MSRTC conducts sightseeing tours (high season only) for the very rushed. The Mahabaleshwar round (Rs 45, 4½ hours) takes in nine viewpoints plus Old Mahabaleshwar; it leaves the bus stand at 2.30pm. Alternatively, taxi drivers will fall over themselves to get you on their three-hour tour for Rs 300. This amounts to a ride out to Arthur's Seat

and back with a stop at Old Mahabaleshwar along the way. Tours are also available to the lookout points south of town (Rs 280, 2½ hours), Panchgani (Rs 300, three hours) and Pratapgad Fort (Rs 450, three hours).

Sleeping & Eating

Hotel prices are all about supply and demand in Mahabaleshwar – rates soar during peak holiday times; at other times the budget and midrange hotels can be good value. Most of the budget places are around the main bazaar near the bus stand, but dozens of resort-style lodges (most offering full board) are scattered around the village. During the monsoon the vast majority of places shut up shop. Note that many of the midrange and top-end establishments refuse single travellers – men in particular.

Hotel Mann Palace (☎ 261778; Murray Perth Rd; d from Rs 500) One of the towns' better budget options, with great-value, refreshingly well-cared-for rooms.

Hotel Blue Star (☎ 260678; 114 Main Rd; d low/high season Rs 250/1000) During the low season the cheapest beds in town can be found here, but you certainly know it! High season prices are completely ludicrous.

MTDC Resort (☎ 260318; fax 260300; d low/high season from Rs 450/650) Assuming you have come to Mahabaleshwar in order to escape the noise and bustle of the nearby cities then the MTDC Resort, a couple of kilometres southwest of the town centre, should fit the bill perfectly. It's blissfully quiet and excellent value. A taxi from the town centre is Rs 40.

New Hill Retreat (☎ 261361; hillsretreat@yahoo .co.in; 187 School Mohalla, Murray Peth Rd; d low/high season Rs 500/1100) A short walk from the heart of the main bazaar, this small hotel boasts dim but otherwise spotless rooms and eager-to-please staff.

Hotel Panorama (☎ 260404; fax 261234; 28 MG Rd; r low/high season from Rs 1500/2800; ⛶ ⛶) The rooms are past their prime but who cares when you can take a plastic swan-shaped paddle boat for a spin around the pool. The staff are friendly, and its vegetarian restaurant (meals Rs 60 to 100) is one of the best in town.

Elises Dairy & Bakery (Main Rd; Rs 25-60) The big question here is which is better – the carrot cake or the ginger cake?

Hotel Rajmahal (80 Main Rd; meals Rs 30-60) This is a buzzing vegetarian pad frequented by locals for its satisfying thalis and other South Indian and Punjabi eats.

Country Corner (Imperial Stores; Main Rd; snacks & dishes Rs 40-120) So what if they're greasy and un-healthy – the burgers, pizzas and other snacks here are undeniably tasty.

Grapevine (Masjid Rd; dishes Rs 60-160) It's almost worth coming to Mahabaleshwar just to eat at this Mediterranean-flavoured restaurant. The

---

BERRY DELICIOUS

Mahabaleshwar is ripe with some of India's finest strawberries, as well as raspberries, mulberries and gooseberries.

Fruits are harvested from late November to June, with the best crops coming around February. You can visit the farms and buy direct, or get them from the many vendors in Mahabaleshwar's bazaar. The industry also dips into fruit drinks, sweets, fudge and jam. Free factory tours and the chance to tuck into some samples are offered at **Mapro Gardens** (☎ 02168-240112; ⏲ 10am-1pm & 2pm-6.30pm Wed-Mon), between Mahabaleshwar and Panchgani.

---

service is superb as are the Asian and Continental dishes. Wash your meal down with one of its Indian or European wines.

Mahabaleshwar is famous for its berries, which you can buy fresh (in season) or as juice, ice cream and jams (see Berry Delicious, left).

Getting There & Away

From the **bus stand** (☎ 260254) state buses leave every hour or so for Pune (semideluxe/deluxe Rs 70/105, 3½ hours) with less frequent buses rolling to Satara (Rs 31, two hours), Panchgani (Rs 10, 30 minutes) and Mahad (for Raigad Fort; Rs 31, two hours), and several services making the long run to Kolhapur (Rs 110, five hours). Outside of the monsoon, one deluxe bus heads to Mumbai Central Station (Rs 180, seven hours), while semideluxe buses (Rs 139) leave at 9am, 1pm and 2.45pm.

Private agents in the bazaar book luxury buses to destinations within Maharashtra or to Goa (seat/sleeper Rs 550/750, 12 hours via Surur where you must change bus). They all quote similar prices and times, but inquire where they intend to drop you off. None of the luxury buses to Mumbai (low/high season Rs 350/550, 6½ hours) go into the city – the furthest you'll get is Borivali. Private buses to Pune (Rs 190) will bid you adieu at Swargate.

Getting Around

There are heaps of taxis and Maruti vans near the bus stand to take you to the main viewpoints or to Panchgani. For trips around town, the minimum charge is Rs 30 (for up to 2km).

The light traffic makes cycling a sensible option, though take care along the narrow lanes with their blind corners if you ride to the viewpoints. Bikes can be hired from **Vasant Cycle Mart** (Main Rd; ⏲ 8am-9pm) for Rs 10 per hour or Rs 50 for the day.

AROUND MAHABALESHWAR
Pratapgad Fort

Built in 1656, the impressive **Pratapgad Fort** (admission free; ⏲ 7am-7pm) dominates a high ridge 24km west of Mahabaleshwar and was the setting for one of the most enduring legends involving the Maratha leader. In 1659 Shivaji agreed to meet the Bijapuri general, Afzal Khan, below the fort walls in an attempt to end a stalemate. However, the two men arrived armed and Shivaji disembowelled his enemy with a set of iron *waghnakh* (tiger's claws). Khan's tomb marks the site of this painful encounter.

The fort is reached by a 500-step climb, which affords brilliant views. Guides are available from outside the fort for a negotiable fee. To get here from Mahabaleshwar, you can take the 9.30am state bus (Rs 50 return, one hour). It waits at the site for an hour before returning. A taxi to Pratapgad and back costs Rs 450.

Raigad Fort

Over 80km northwest of Mahabaleshwar, all alone on a hilltop, **Raigad Fort** (Indian/foreigner Rs 5/ US$5; ⊙ 8am-5.30pm) has stunning views. This was Shivaji's capital, where he was crowned in 1648 and where he died and was cremated in 1680.

You can hike to the top – it's a 2½-hour steep haul up 1475 steps. Or if that sounds like too much hard work then you can glide up the hill via a **ropeway** (☎ 02145-274831; ⊙ 8.30am-6.30pm). The return ticket (Rs 130) includes a guide, entry into a small museum and the opportunity to view a short film about the site's past.

Raigad is best reached from Mahad (Rs 13, 45 minutes) or you can take a taxi tour direct from Mahabaleshwar (Rs 1100).

KOLHAPUR

☎ 0231 / pop 485,183 / elev 550m

Kolhapur was once the capital of an important Maratha state, but today it's just a forgotten backwood receiving no more than a handful of foreign visitors each month. This is a shame because, with its proximity to Goa, a friendly population and an intriguing temple complex, Kolhapur is one of the best introductions to the splendours of India that you could hope to find.

In August the **Matharaj Naag Panchami**, a snake-worshipping festival, is held here and in Pune.

Orientation

The old town around the Mahalaxmi Temple is around 3km southwest of the bus and train stations, while the 'new' palace is a similar distance to the north. Rankala Lake, a popular spot for evening strolls and the location of the Hotel Shalini Palace, is 5km southwest of the stations.

Information

Internet Zone (Kedar Complex, Station Rd; per hr Rs 20; ⊙ 8am-midnight) Internet access.

MTDC tourist office (☎ 2652935; Assembly Rd; ⊙ 10am-5.45pm Mon-Sat) On the way to the maharaja's palace, opposite the Collector's Office.

State Bank of India (☎ 2660735; Udyamnagar) A short autorickshaw ride southwest of the train station near Hutatma Park. Deals in foreign exchange.

UTI Bank (Station Rd) Has a 24-hour ATM just west of Hotel International.

Sights

SHREE CHHATRAPATI SHAHU MUSEUM

If you think your house is full of old junk then just wait till you get a load of this place. The maharaja's 'new' palace, completed in 1881, houses an extraordinary **museum** (☎ 2538060; admission Rs 24; ⊙ 9.15am-12.30pm & 2.15-6pm), with one of the most bizarre collections of memorabilia in the country. The building, worthy of a visit in its own right, was designed by 'Mad' Charles Mant, the British architect who fashioned the Indo-Saracenic style of colonial architecture, and is a cross between a Victorian train station and the Addams Family mansion.

The maharaja was a bit of an animal lover and he was particularly fond of fluffy wild animals after they'd been shot, stuffed and hung on his wall – the building is a giant horror-house zoo with the stuffed pangolin (a scaly nocturnal anteater) being probably the oddest animal anyone has ever gone hunting for.

Other Mant-designed buildings in Kolhapur include the attractive old **Town Hall**, which now houses a dull museum.

OLD TOWN

Don't fail to devote a few hours to Kolhapur's atmospheric old town. Dominating this compact area is the lively and colourful **Mahalaxmi Temple** (⊙ 5am-10.30pm) dedicated to Amba Bai, or the Mother Goddess. The temple's origins date back to AD 10, but much of what you see is from the 18th Century. It's one of the most important Amba Bai temples in India and therefore attracts an unceasing tide of humanity who flood across the temple and its courtyard. Non-Hindus are welcome and it's a fantastic place for a spot of people-watching.

In the grounds of the nearby Old Palace the **Bhavani Mandap** (Shivaji Rd; ⊙ 6am-8pm) is dedicated to the goddess Bhavani. It also contains a few more of the maharaja's hunting souvenirs.

Kolhapur is famed for the calibre of its wrestlers and at the **Motibag Thalim**, a courtyard beside the entrance to the Bhavani Mandap,

MAHARASHTRA

you can watch young athletes train in a muddy pit. Tourists aren't exactly encouraged and single women travellers may find the sensation of being surrounded by dozens of testosterone filled, sweaty, seminaked men a little uncomfortable. Either way it's certainly a slice of grimy India at its best.

Professional matches are held between June and December in the **Kasbagh Maidan**, a red-earth arena in a natural sunken stadium a short walk south of Motibag Thalim. Events are announced in local papers. Finally, if you're a shopoholic, then the old town streets are rammed with gold jewellery shops where the hard sale of some Indian tourist cities is unheard of.

CHANDRAKANT MANDARE MUSEUM
Dedicated to actor and artist Chandrakant Mandare (1913–2001), this well-maintained **gallery** (☎ 2525256; Rajarampuri, 7th Lane; admission Rs 3; ◷ 10.30am-1pm & 1.30-5.30pm Tue-Sun), houses stills of his movies as well as his fine paintings and sketches.

Sleeping & Eating
Most of the better hotels and restaurants can be found along Station Rd, which appropriately enough is the busy main street running west of the train station.

Hotel Tourist (☎ 2650421; tourist@epages.webindia .com; Station Rd; s/d/tr Rs 375/475/550, s/d with AC from Rs 600/650; ❄) Exceptionally friendly hotel offering the neatest budget beds in town. The only drawback is a little road noise so ask for a room facing away from all the commotion.

Hotel Radha Swami (☎ 6682485; Station Rd; s/d Rs 450/550, with AC Rs 650/750) A useful standby if the next-door Hotel Tourist is full. The rooms are clean but squat toilets and communication difficulties mean that it cannot quite compete with its neighbour.

Hotel International (☎ 2536641; fax 2536644; 517 A1 Shivaji Park; s/d from Rs 600/700, with AC Rs 800/950; ❄) You'd be hard pushed to find any hotel in Maharashtra with bathrooms as immaculately polished as those of the Hotel International. It's a shame the cleanliness levels haven't extended to the bedrooms, but even so this one's a good bet. Meals are Rs 60 to 100.

Hotel Pearl (☎ 6684451; hotelpearl@hotmail.com; 517 A2 Shivaji Park; s/d Rs 1050/1200, with AC Rs 1350/1500 ❄ ▢) The manageress of this classy business hotel should be commended for creating such a beacon of calm. The rooms are large

and well-equipped and the staff have a very professional attitude.

Hotel Shalini Palace (☎ 2630401; fax 2630407; Rankala Lake; d from Rs 1800; ❄) Without doubt one of the saddest hotels in India. This wonderful old British-influenced pile could, with a bit of TLC, be turned into one of the country's finest hotels. Instead it's a shell of its former self. The dirty rooms, should you really want to stay, are ridiculously overpriced. Still it has a certain romance to it – if you really want to stay in a maharaja's palace...

Surabhi (Hotel Sayhadri Bldg; snacks & mains Rs 20- 45) This eatery is one of those clustered around the bus stand, and almost moves it's so busy. The crowds come for its thalis, Kolhapuri snacks such as *misal* (a spicy snack not unlike *bhelpuri*) and lassi.

Other than Surabhi, the hotel restaurants are the best places to eat, with the Hotel Pearl having the tastiest Chinese, Indian and Continental dishes at around Rs 140 for a main.

Getting There & Around
Rickshaws are abundant in Kolhapur and most drivers will give you the correct price or even use their meters (though these are outdated and so they'll use a conversion chart to arrive at the real price) without any great fanfare.

From the **bus stand** (☎ 2650620), services head regularly to Pune (semideluxe Rs 200, 5½ hours), Mahabaleshwar (Rs 110, five hours) and Ratnagiri (Rs 97, four hours), as well as to Belgaum (Rs 60, 2½ hours) and Bijapur (Rs 100, four hours). For popular longer hauls, your body will be happier on a deluxe private bus. Most of the private bus agents are on the western side of the square at Mahalaxmi Chambers, just across from the bus stand. Overnight services with AC head to Mumbai (seat/sleeper Rs 300/550, nine hours) and non-AC overnights go to Panaji (Rs 160, 5½ hours).

The **train station** (☎ 2654389) is 10 minutes' walk west of the bus stand towards the centre of town. Three daily expresses, including the 2.26am *Sahyadri Express*, zoom to Mumbai (sleeper/2AC Rs 146/592, 10 hours) via Pune (Rs 101/338, 41½ hours). A variety of express trains embark daily except Wednesday for the long voyage to Bengaluru (sleeper/2AC Rs 298/1208, 21 hours). You can also fly cheaply between Kolhapur and Mumbai on a daily basis with Air Deccan.

Goa

Those who haven't visted Goa tend to imagine it as some kind of Indian Costa Brava but with more cosmic karma and, thanks to this image, many people vow never to set foot there. However, Goa, like everywhere in India, is never quite what you expect. In places the infamous hash-fuelled days of Goa's golden hippy years are still alive and kicking and in others the all-inclusive package holiday is king. But these are two very narrow sides of the Goan experience and anyone who spends much time here will discover that Goa contains more variety and vitality than almost anywhere else in India. Head into Panaji (Panjim), one of India's smallest and most likeable state capitals, and instead of self-contained tourist resorts and trinket-selling dreadlocks you'll discover a Portuguese pantry of flaking architectural delicacies spiced up with Indian exuberance. Inland, you can stand in greener-than-green fields picking vanilla pods or bathing with elephants.

The main draws of Goa are, of course, the beaches, which are every bit as cliché beautiful as they're supposed to be, but just as much of an attraction is Goa's intriguing fusion of colonial Portugal and modern India. There is almost nowhere else in India where the influence of the former colonial overlords remains as strong as it does in Goa and it's not at all unusual to find crucifixes hanging on walls next to posters of Shiva and groups of elderly Goan men conversing in Portuguese. Goa may not be as cool as it once was but it's certainly just as magical.

HIGHLIGHTS

- Explore the old Portuguese quarter of **Panaji** (Panjim; p181) and savour its rich Mediterranean flavour

- Gaze in awe at the magnificent cathedrals of **Old Goa** (p187), the fallen city that once rivalled Lisbon

- Make footprints on idyllic **beaches** (p204) in the far north of Goa

- Get nostalgic in the crumbling ballrooms of colonial mansions in **Chandor** (p208)

- Barter for souvenirs at the legendary Wednesday flea market and then watch the sunset at **Anjuna** (p199)

- Hire a moped or motorbike and discover the back lanes of the luminous green countryside (p180)

★ Northern Beaches
★ Anjuna
Panaji ★ ★ Old Goa
(Panjim)
★ Chandor

History

In the 3rd century BC Goa formed part of the Mauryan empire. Later it was ruled by the Satavahanas of Kolhapur and eventually passed to the Chalukyas of Badami from AD 580 to 750.

Goa fell to the Muslims for the first time in 1312, but they weren't fans of the beach and eventually left in 1370 under the forceful persuasion of Harihara I of the Vijayanagar mpire. During the next 100 years Goa's harbours were important landing places for ships carrying Arabian horses for the Vijayanagar cavalry.

Blessed as it is by natural harbours and wide rivers, Goa was the ideal base for the seafaring Portuguese, who arrived in 1510 aiming to control the spice route from the East. Jesuit missionaries led by St Francis Xavier arrived in 1542. For a while, Portuguese control was limited to a small area around Old Goa, but by the middle of the 16th century it had expanded to include the provinces of Bardez and Salcete.

The Marathas (the central Indian people who controlled much of India at various points in time) almost vanquished the Portuguese in the late 18th century, and there was a brief occupation by the British during the Napoleonic Wars in Europe. However, it was not until 1961, when the Indian army marched into Goa, that Portuguese occupation finally came to its end on the subcontinent.

Today Goa has one of India's highest per-capita incomes, with farming, fishing, tourism and iron-ore mining forming the basis of its economy.

Climate

The monsoon hits Goa between June and the end of September; many places close up shop during this time. From late October to February the climate is near perfect after which the humidity starts rising.

Information

The **Goa Tourism Development Corporation** (GTDC; www.goa-tourism.com), commonly known as Goa Tourism, has branches in Panaji (p181), Margao (p207) and at Dabolim Airport (Goa's airport, 29km south of Panaji). You can also pick up information on the state from the Government of India tourist office in Panaji (p181).

FAST FACTS

- Population: 1.34 million
- Area: 3701 sq km
- Capital: Panaji (Panjim)
- Main languages: Konkani, Marathi, English and Hindi
- Telephone code: ☎ 0832
- When to go: October to March

ACCOMMODATION

Accommodation prices in Goa are based on high, middle (shoulder) and low seasons. The high season is December to late January, the middle periods are October to late November and February to June, and the low season is July to September (the monsoon). Unless otherwise stated, prices quoted in this chapter are high-season rates. There's a fourth season, when some hotel prices rise again, sometimes to ludicrous heights, over the peak Christmas period from around 22 December to 3 January.

Most places have noon checkout but some are 9am or 10am.

Activities

Water sports such as **parasailing**, **jet-skiing** and **windsurfing** are available on the beaches at Candolim (p191), Calangute and Baga (p195), and Colva (p210). You can try **paragliding** at Arambol (p205) and Anjuna (p199). Although the waters off Goa aren't crystal clear, there are three **scuba-diving** outfits offering boat dives and PADI (Professional Association of Diving Instructors) courses: the very professional Barracuda Diving is based at the Goa Marriott Resort in Miramar (p185); Goa Diving is in Bogmalo (p209); and Goa Dive Center is in Baga (p195).

Boat trips to spot dolphins, go fishing or cruise the backwaters are also available from most beaches, including Arambol (p205) and Palolem (p214) – the boat owners will probably find you. An interesting day trip is to visit one of the **spice plantations** near Ponda (p215), where you get a tour and lunch for around Rs 300. You can go by yourself but most tour operators offer this trip. One of the best tour operators is **Day Tripper** (☎ 2276726; www.daytrip pergoa.com), based in Calangute; it also offers rafting in Karnataka.

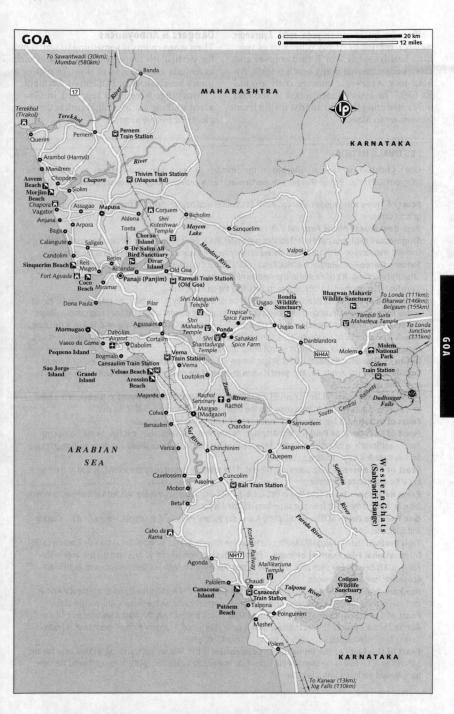

GOA

0 — 20 km
0 — 12 miles

MAHARASHTRA

KARNATAKA

To Sawantwadi (30km);
Mumbai (580km)

Banda

17

Terekhol
(Tirakol)

Terekhol

Querim

Pernem

River

Pernem
Train Station

Arambol (Harmal)

Mandrem

River

Asvem
Beach

Chopdem

Chapora

Thivim Train Station
(Mapusa Rd)

Morjim
Beach

Siolim

Chapora

Assagao

Mapusa

Corjuem

Bicholim

Vagator

Aldona

Shri
Koteshwar
Temple

Anjuna

Arpora

Torda

Mayem
Lake

Sanquelim

Baga

Saligao

Chorao
Island

Valpoi

Calangute

Betim

Dr Salim Ali
Bird Sanctuary

Candolim

Reis
Magos

Ribandar

Divar
Island

Old Goa

Bondla
Wildlife
Sanctuary

Bhagwan Mahavir
Wildlife Sanctuary

To Londa (111km);
Dharwar (146km);
Belgaum (155km)

Sinquerim Beach

Fort Aguada

Coco
Beach

Miramar

Panaji (Panjim)

Karmali Train Station
(Old Goa)

Shri Manguesh
Temple

Usgao

Tambdi Surla
Mahadeva Temple

Dona Paula

Pilar

Shri
Mahalsa
Temple

Tropical
Spice Farm

Ponda

Usgao Tisk

To Londa
Junction
(111km)

Agassaim

Shri
Shantadurga
Temple

Sahakari
Spice Farm

Danblandora

Molem
National
Park

Mormugao

Dabolim
Airport

Cortalim

NH4A

Molem

Vasco da Gama

Dabolim

Verna
Train Station

Colem
Train Station

Pequeno Island

Bogmalo

Cansaulim Train Station

Verna

Sao Jorge
Island

Grande
Island

Velsao Beach

Loutolim

South Central Railway

Dudhsagar
Falls

Arossim
Beach

Majorda

Rachol
Seminary

Zuari River

Rachol

Colva

Margao
(Madgaon)

Chandor

Sanvordem

Benaulim

Sal River

**ARABIAN
SEA**

Varca

Chinchinim

Sanguem

Quepem

Cavelossim

Assolna

Cuncolim

Mobor

Betul

Bali Train Station

Pareda River

Sanguem
River

Konkan Railway

**W e s t e r n G h a t s
(Sahyadri Range)**

Cabo da
Rama

NH17

Shri
Mallikarjuna
Temple

Agonda

Palolem

Chaudi

Talpona River

Cotigao
Wildlife
Sanctuary

Canacona
Island

Canacona
Train Station

Talpona

Patnem Beach

Poinguinim

Masher

Polem

KARNATAKA

To Karwar (13km);
Jog Falls (110km)

GOA

If you're interested in **yoga**, **reiki**, **Ayurvedic massage**, **reflexology** or any other sort of spiritual health regime, you'll find courses and classes advertised at many beach resorts. An hour-long Ayurvedic massage costs around Rs 650. The courses mentioned in the text only run during the peak tourist season from November to March.

Dangers & Annoyances

Theft from rooms is something to watch out for, particularly on party nights at places such as Anjuna and Vagator, or if you're renting a flimsy beach shack at Palolem or Arambol.

Muggings have been reported in Goa – avoid walking alone at night unless there are plenty of people around.

FESTIVALS IN GOA

Goa's Christian heritage is reflected in the number of feast days and festivals that follow the religious calendar. Panaji (Panjim), in particular, has a bumper crop of nonreligious festivals.

Feast of Three Kings (6 Jan; Chandor, p208) At churches local boys re-enact the story of the three kings bearing gifts for Christ.

Pop, Beat & Jazz Music Festival (Feb; Panaji, p181)

Shigmotsav (Shigmo) of Holi (Feb/Mar; statewide) This is Goa's version of the Hindu spring festival Holi. Coloured water and powders are thrown around at everyone and anyone and parades are held in the main towns.

Sabado Gordo (Fat Saturday; Feb/Mar; Panaji, p181) Part of the statewide Carnival, this festival is held on the Saturday before Lent. It's celebrated by a procession of floats and raucous street partying.

Carnival (Mar; statewide) A three-day party heralding the arrival of spring.

Procession of All Saints (Mar/Apr; Old Goa, p187) On the fifth Monday in Lent, this is the only procession of its sort outside Rome. Thirty statues of saints are brought out from storage and paraded around Old Goa's neighbouring villages.

Feast of Our Lady of Miracles (Apr; Mapusa, p190) A Hindu and Christian feast day held 16 days after Easter.

Beach Bonanza (May; Calangute, p194, Colva p210, & Miramar, p184) Several food and entertainment festivals, known as 'Beach Bonanzas', are held at various beach towns.

Igitun Chalne (May; Bicholim) Held at Sirigao Temple in Bicholim province, this fire-walking festival is one of Goa's most distinctive events. The high point is when devotees of the goddess Lairaya walk across burning coals to prove their devotion.

Feast of St Anthony (13 Jun; statewide) It is said that if the monsoon has not arrived by the time of this feast day, a statue of the saint should be lowered into the family well to hasten the arrival of the rain.

Feast of St John (24 Jun; statewide) A thanksgiving for the arrival of the monsoon.

Feast of St Peter & St Paul (29 Jun; statewide) Another monsoon celebration, this time by the fishing community, particularly in the region of Bardez, between Panaji and Mapusa. Dance, drama and music performances are held on makeshift stages floating on the river.

Feast of St Lawrence (Aug; statewide) The end of the monsoon is marked by this festival, as well as the reopening of the Mandovi to river traffic.

Fama de Menino Jesus (2nd Mon in Oct; Colva, p210) Colva's biggest feast day, this festival is when the Menino Jesus (a statue of the infant Jesus said to perform miracles) is paraded.

Goa Heritage Festival (Nov; Panaji, p181) A two-day cultural event held at Campal, featuring music, dancing and traditional food.

Tiatr Festival (Nov; Panaji, p181) Another drama-arts programme held as a competition at the Kala Academy (p186).

International Film Festival of India (IFFI; www.iffi.nic.in; normally for 10 days from the last week of Nov; Panaji, p181) Based in Goa since 2004, this is the largest film festival in India and features numerous exciting arthouse films from across the world.

Konkani Drama Festival (Nov/Dec; Panaji, p181) A programme of Konkani music, dance and theatre held at the Kala Academy (p186) – it's a competition, with prizes awarded to the best performing group at the end.

Feast of St Francis Xavier (3 Dec; Old Goa, p187) Old Goa's biggest bash, this feast is preceded by a 10-day Novena. There are lots of festivities and huge crowds during this period, especially for the Exposition of St Francis Xavier's body, which is held once every 10 years (see boxed text, p189).

Feast of Our Lady of the Immaculate Conception (8 Dec; Margao, p206, & Panaji, p181) A large fair and a church service is held at the Church of Our Lady of the Immaculate Conception (p183) in Panaji. Around the same time, Margao celebrates with a large fair.

Some foreign women find Goa anything but a relaxing beach holiday and reports of harassment are disappointingly common. For many foreign women, beach dress code is dramatically different to that normally preferred by Indian women. This has led to problems with some groups of young Indian men coming to Goa for no other reason than to stare at scantily clad women. It's an unpleasant situation and one that both groups hold a certain amount of responsibility for. Many foreigners do seem to forget that they are no longer at home and that dress standards here are different, and the harassers seem unaware that their behaviour would be considered by foreigners to be unacceptable. The best solution is to aim for the quieter beaches and just give in to the fact that things that might be normal elsewhere, such as topless sunbathing, are taboo in some places and by doing it you are only likely to cause problems for yourself. Though the harassment rarely steps beyond staring or a few comments there have been instances of physical attack.

Note that the monsoonal seas are very dangerous.

DRUGS

Acid, ecstasy, cocaine and hash – the drugs of choice for many party-goers – are illegal (though still very much available) and any attempt to purchase or carry them is fraught with danger. Fort Aguada prison houses some foreigners serving lengthy sentences for drug offences.

Possession of even a small amount of *charas* (hashish) can mean 10 years in prison. Cases of corrupt policemen approaching hapless tourists and threatening to 'plant' drugs on them, or simply demanding a relatively large baksheesh (bribe) on the spot are becoming less common than in the past, but the possibility of such occurrences does remain.

Getting There & Away

AIR

Goa's airport, Dabolim, is 29km south of Panaji, on the coast near Vasco da Gama. Most of India's domestic airlines operate services here, and several direct charter companies fly into Goa from the UK and Europe. Be aware that it's illegal to fly into India on a scheduled flight and out on a charter flight. If you book an international flight from Goa, it will involve a domestic flight to Mumbai (Bombay), or another international airport, and a connection there; there are numerous flights between Goa and Mumbai. Domestic flights are listed in Domestic Scheduled Flights from Goa (below). Between them the budget carriers of Air Deccan, Spice Jet, Kingfisher and IndiGo link Goa up with virtually every decent-sized town in India for prices that are normally much more competitive than their scheduled brothers.

BUS

Long-distance interstate buses operate to/from Panaji, Margao, Mapusa and Calangute, and you can pick up some buses from Chaudi near Palolem. See those sections for more information.

TRAIN

The **Konkan Railway** (www.konkanrailway.com) connects Goa with Mumbai and Mangalore. The main station in Goa is Madgaon in Margao,

DOMESTIC SCHEDULED FLIGHTS FROM GOA				
Destination	Airline code	Price (US$)	Duration (hr)	Frequency
Bengaluru	IC	75	1½	daily
	9W	105	1	daily
Chennai	IC	99	1	daily
Kochi	IC	90	1	daily
Delhi	IC	165	4	daily
	S2	100	2½	2 daily
Mumbai	IC	65	1	3 daily
	S2	45	1	daily
	9W	100	1	3 daily
IC – Indian Airlines; S2 – Sahara Airlines; 9W – Jet Airways				

GOA

WHERE'S THE PARTY?

Goa has long been renowned among Western visitors as a party place where all-night, open-air raves dominated the scene in places such as Anjuna and Vagator. A central government ban on loud music in open spaces between 10pm and 6am was aimed partly at curbing Goa's intrusive party scene, but with a tourist industry to nurture (and a bit of bribery) the authorities have tended to turn a blind eye to parties during the peak Christmas–New Year period. Rave parties are organised at open-air locations such as Disco Valley at Vagator and Bamboo Forest in Anjuna, and occasionally at Arambol, but they are not advertised so you'll have to ask around to find out what's on and be prepared to ride around aimlessly on a motorcycle looking for the right place. More permanent nightclubs have also become established in the Candolim-Calangute-Baga area over the years.

---

but expresses and passenger trains stop at most other stations along the line.

There are two daily expresses between Margao's Madgaon train station and Mumbai's Chhatrapati Shivaji Terminus (CST; the old Victoria Terminus), two between Madgaon and Lokmanya Tilak and one between Madgaon and Dadar (both in northern Mumbai). From Mumbai CST the overnight *Konkan Kanya Express* departs at 11pm (sleeper/3AC Rs 273/771, 12 hours) and the *Mandavi Express* departs at 6.55am. The fastest train (in theory) is the *Shatabdi Express,* which departs from Dadar at 5.35am daily except Wednesday (2nd class/AC seat Rs 197/675, six hours). From Margao to Mumbai, the *Konkan Kanya Express* leaves at 6pm, the *Mandavi Express* at 9.50am and the *Shatabdi Express* at 11.40am.

There are 12 direct trains between Margao and Mangalore (sleeper/3AC Rs 207/533, 4½ hours), most stopping at Mangalore's Kankanadi station.

The South Central Railway operates from Vasco da Gama via Margao and Londa, and runs to Pune, Delhi and Bengaluru (Bangalore). The *Nizamuddin–Goa Express* goes to Delhi (sleeper/3AC Rs 531/1438, 41 hours).

The Delhi–Goa (Margao) *Rajdhani Express* (3AC/2AC/1st class Rs 1985/2915/5430, 25½ hours) leaves Delhi Nizamuddin station Sunday and Tuesday. It also goes from Delhi to Goa every Wednesday and Friday, leaving Margao at 11.30am.

Bookings can be made at Madgaon (p208) and Vasco da Gama stations, or at the train reservation office at Panaji's Kadamba bus stand (p186). Other useful stations on the Konkan route are Pernem for Arambol, Thivim for Mapusa and the northern beaches, Karmali (Old Goa) for Panaji and Canacona for Palolem.

Getting Around

BOAT

Passenger/vehicle ferries cross the state's many rivers. Foot passengers ride for free, and motorcycles cost Rs 4.

BUS

The state-run Kadamba bus company is the main operator of public buses, although there are also private companies running more comfortable buses to Mumbai, Hampi, Bengaluru and several other interstate destinations. Local buses are cheap, services are frequent and they run to just about everywhere, eventually. Express buses run between Panaji and Mapusa, and Panaji and Margao (see p186 for more details).

CAR

Self-drive car hire is not worth the trouble, especially since it's more expensive than a chauffeur-driven car.

MOTORCYCLE

Goa is one of the few places in India where hiring a motorcycle or scooter is both cheap and easy, and the relatively short distances make travel a breeze, although India is no place to learn to ride a motorcycle, or even a scooter. Every other traveller you meet seems to have been involved in a bike accident of some description. Bikes available include old Enfields, more modern Yamaha 100s and the gearless Kinetic Honda scooters. Hire prices vary according to season, length of hire and quality of the bike. In the peak Christmas season, you're looking at paying up to Rs 300 per day for a scooter, Rs 400 for the small bikes and Rs 500 for an Enfield. Outside this time, when there's a glut of idle bikes, especially at the northern beach resorts, you should only pay Rs 150 per day for a scooter, Rs 250 for the small bikes and Rs 350 for an Enfield if you hire for a week or more. In most cases you don't need to provide a deposit, but you'll probably be asked for your passport details (don't hand over the passport itself) and the name of your hotel. Guesthouses, hotels and places where taxi drivers congregate are good places to hire a bike, but you'll get plenty of offers on the street at beach resorts.

TAXI
If the thought of riding a motorbike in Goa turns your knuckles white then taxis are available everywhere and a full day's sightseeing, depending on the distance, is likely to be around Rs 1000.

Motorcycles are a licensed form of taxi in Goa. They are cheap, easy to find, backpacks are no problem and they can be identified by a yellow front mudguard.

NORTH GOA

PANAJI (PANJIM)
pop 98,915

Panaji (also known as Panjim) is a town of shades; the pastel shades of the buildings, romantic shades of the Mediterranean, excitable shades of Latin America and noisy shades of India. It's a town utterly unique to the subcontinent, yet for most travellers it tends to be a quick after thought to a Goan beach holiday. This is a grave mistake because the narrow winding streets of its old Portuguese quarter, and its fine location at the mouth of the broad Mandovi River, make Panaji one of the indisputable highlights of Goa. To get the most out of Panaji spend a couple of days here and make it a base for explorations of nearby Old Goa (p187) and central Goa (p215).

Information
BOOKSHOPS
Hotel Mandovi (☎ 2426270; Dayanand Bandodkar Marg; ⏱ 9am-9pm) Small, well-stocked bookshop in hotel lobby.

Pauline Book & Media Centre (☎ 2231158; Rani Pramila Arcade; ⏱ 10am-7pm Mon-Wed, Fri & Sat, 9am-1pm Thu) Specialising in self-help, spiritual and religious titles. Down a laneway off 18th June Rd.

Singbal's Book House (☎ 2425747; Church Sq; ⏱ 9.30am-1pm & 3.30-7.30pm Mon-Sat)

INTERNET ACCESS
There are plenty of internet cafés. Try the following:

Log In (1st fl, Durga Chambers, 18th June Rd; per hr Rs 30; ⏱ 9am-11pm)

Shruti Communications (31st January Rd; per hr Rs 35; ⏱ 9am-11pm Mon-Sat)

MEDICAL SERVICES
Goa Medical College Hospital (☎ 2458700; Bambolin) Situated 9km south of Panaji on National Hwy 17.

MONEY
Centurion (MG Rd) Has a 24-hour ATM accepting international cards (MasterCard, Cirrus, Maestro, Visa). There's another branch on Dr Atmaram Borkar Rd.

HDFC (18th June Rd) There's another branch nearby.

Thomas Cook (☎ 2221312; Dayanand Bandodkar Marg; ⏱ 9.30am-6pm Mon-Sat year-round, 10am-5pm Sun Oct-Mar) Changes travellers cheques commission-free and gives cash advances on Visa and MasterCard.

UTI Bank (ground fl, Cardozo Bldg) Located next to Paulo Travels, it has an ATM near the bus stand.

POST
Main post office (MG Rd; ⏱ 9.30am-5.30pm Mon-Fri, 9am-5pm Sat) Has a Speedpost parcel service and reliable poste restante (open 9.30am to 4pm).

TELEPHONE
There are also plenty of private Private Call Offices (PCO) and STD/ISD offices.

Central telegraph office (Dr Atmaram Borkar Rd; ⏱ 7am-8.30pm)

TOURIST INFORMATION
Goa Tourism Development Corporation office (GTDC; ☎ 2427972; www.goa-tourism.com; Dr Alvaro Costa Rd; ⏱ 9.30am-5.45pm Mon-Fri) Commonly known as Goa Tourism, GTDC is just south of the Old Pato Bridge. There's not a lot of information to be gleaned here, but you can pick up maps of Goa and Panaji and book local tours.

Government of India tourist office (☎ 2223412; in diatourismgoa@sancharnet.in; Communidade Bldg, Church Sq; ⏱ 9.30am-6pm Mon-Fri, 10am-1pm Sat) This office is far more helpful. Staff here are bright and enthusiastic, and qualified guides can be arranged (from Rs 350/500 per half-/full day depending on the size of the group).

Sights & Activities
Panaji is a city to savour on leisurely strolls, especially true in the atmospheric Sao Tomé, Fontainhas and Altino areas (see p184). The warren of narrow streets, lined with a clutch of churches, sparkling blue-and-white tiles,

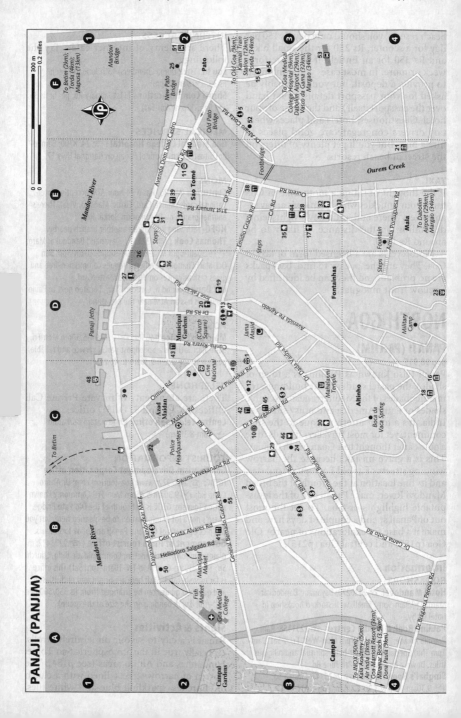

PANAJI (PANJIM)

INFORMATION
Central Telegraph Office...................1 D3
Centurion Bank...................................2 C3
Centurion Bank ATM.........................3 B3
Cozy Nook Travel...............................4 C2
Goa Tourism Development Corporation
 (GTDC) Office..................................5 F3
Government of India Tourist Office....6 D2
HDFC Bank...7 B3
HDFC Bank...8 B3
Hotel Mandovi...................................9 C1
Log In...10 D3
Main Post Office..............................11 E2
Pauline Book & Media Centre..........12 C3
Shruti Communications.................(see 39)
Singbal's Book House.......................13 D2
Thomas Cook....................................14 B2
UTI Bank...15 F3

SIGHTS & ACTIVITIES
Bishop's Palace.................................16 C4
Chapel of St Sebastian......................17 E3
Chief Minister's Residence................18 C4
Church of Our Lady of the Immaculate
 Conception......................................19 D2
Crucifix...20 D2
Gitanjali Gallery............................(see 34)
Goa State Museum...........................21 F4
Institute Menezes Braganza.............22 C2
Matuti Temple..................................23 D4
Panaji Central Library....................(see 22)
Public Observatory...........................24 C3
River Cruises..................................(see 25)
Santa Monica Jetty..........................25 F2
Secretariat Building..........................26 D2
Statue of Abbé Faria.........................27 D1

SLEEPING
Afonso Guest House.........................28 C4
Hotel Fidalgo....................................29 C3
Mayfair Hotel...................................30 C3
Panaji Residency..............................31 E2
Panjim Inn..32 B3
Panjim Peoples.................................33 B3
Panjim Pousada................................34 B3
Park Lane Lodge...............................35 B3
República Hotel................................36 D2
Vaz Residence..................................37 E2

EATING
A Ferradura......................................38 E3
Hotel Venite.....................................39 F2
Lourenzos...40 E2
New Café Hema................................41 B2
Sher-E-Punjab..................................42 C3
Sher-E-Punjab..................................43 D2
Viva Panjim......................................44 B3
Zen Restaurant.................................45 C3

DRINKING
Aces Pub...46 C3
Gadhino Bar......................................47 D2
Hotel Venite..................................(see 39)

ENTERTAINMENT
Casino Goa..48 C1

TRANSPORT
Daud M Aga Cycle Store...................49 C2
Indian Airlines..................................50 B2
Interstate Private Bus Stand.............51 F2
Jet Airways.......................................52 F3
Kadamba Bus Stand..........................53 F3
Paulo Travels.................................(see 54)
Private Bus Agents............................54 F3
Sahara Airlines.................................55 B2
Train Reservation Office................(see 53)

shuttered windows and tiny overhanging balconies, is a pleasure to get lost in. Or wander beside the Mandovi River, where a promenade was laid in 2004 for the 35th International Film Festival India. The annual festival is now a permanent fixture on the Goan calendar.

CHURCH OF OUR LADY OF THE IMMACULATE CONCEPTION

The centre piece of the city is the main **church**, originally consecrated in 1541, which stands above the square in the town centre. Panaji was the first port of call for voyages from Lisbon and newly arrived sailors would visit this strikingly whitewashed church to give thanks for a safe crossing before continuing to Old Goa. Mass is held here daily in English, Konkani and Portuguese.

GOA STATE MUSEUM

An eclectic collection of items awaits visitors to this large **museum** (☎ 2458006; www.goamuseum .nic.in; EDC Complex, Pato; admission free; ☼ 9.30am-5.30pm Mon-Fri), in a rather forlorn area southwest of the Kadamba bus stand. As well as Christian art, Hindu and Jain sculpture and bronzes, and paintings from all over India, exhibits include an elaborately carved table used in the Goa Inquisition, and, just to prove that wasting money on the lottery isn't a recent phenomenon, an antique pair of rotary lottery machines. There is also a small wildlife conservation gallery.

SECRETARIAT BUILDING

Dating from the 16th century, this handsome **colonial building** was originally the palace of the Muslim ruler Adil Shah before becoming the viceroy's official residence in 1759. Now it's government offices. Immediately to the west, the bizarre **statue** of a man apparently about to strangle a woman is of Abbé Faria, a famous Goan hypnotist, and his assistant.

INSTITUTE MENEZES BRAGANZA

On the west side of the Azad Maidan, the institute houses **Panaji Central Library** (Malaca Rd; ☼ 9.30am-1.15pm & 2-5.45pm Mon-Fri) and is worth popping into to see the pretty blue-and-white *azulejos* (glazed ceramic-tile compositions) in the entrance hall.

PUBLIC OBSERVATORY

Reach for the stars at the **observatory** (Swami Vivekanand Rd; ☼ 7-9pm Nov-May) on the rooftop of Junta House.

MIRAMAR

The closest beach to Panaji is at **Miramar**, 3km southwest of the city along Dayanand Bandodkar Marg. It's far from the cream of Goa's beaches but is pleasant enough for a sunset stroll and makes a good short bike ride out the city. On the way you'll pass the Goa Marriot Resort (opposite), where you'll find **Barracuda Diving** (☎ 6656294; www.barracudadiving.com), one of the state's most professional diving operations.

Walking Tour

From the **Church of Our Lady of the Immaculate Conception** (**1**; p183) walk east up the hill along Emidio Gracia Rd (Corte de Oiterio). At the four-way junction, where you'll see fruit-seller barrows, turn right into 31st January Rd. Continue down to the heritage hotel **Panjim Inn** (**2**; opposite).

> **Start & Finish:** Church of Our Lady of the Immaculate Conception
> **Distance:** 6km
> **Duration:** 1½ hours

WALKING TOUR

Take the right fork of the road and continue south past the small **fountain** (**3**; not working) from which Fontainhas gets its name. Keep walking in the same direction until you see the steps off to the right leading uphill to the ornate, salmon-pink **Maruti Temple (4)**, dedicated to the monkey god Hanuman. The temple's veranda provides fine views towards the Mandovi River. Nip behind the temple and follow the road up into the Altinho district.

When you reach a junction with a red 'stop and proceed' sign, turn right and continue around to the **Bishop's Palace (5)**, residence of the Archbishop of Goa. This grand white mansion, with a silver painted Jesus statue outside, lords it over the much-humbler **Chief Minister's Residence (6)** across the road. After gazing through the fence of these two buildings retrace your steps back past the Maruti Temple and back towards the fountain. Turn left at the crossroads just before this and head towards the steps, just before these turn right and head up hill past lots of big old houses. After around 300m you'll see a set of steps on your right descending downhill and marked by a crucifix. Heading down these you'll pass by many colourful houses until you reach the **Chapel of St Sebastian (7)**. Built in the 1880s, its most striking feature is a crucifix that originally stood in the Palace of the Inquisition in Old Goa.

Walk back to 31st January Rd and return to where the road meets up with the fruit stalls. Then, at the junction with Emido Garcia Rd, continue straight over and into the brightly painted streets of Sao Tomé, pausing for a drink at the **Hotel Venite** (**8**; p186). Afterwards continue on to the river, turn left and walk down to the **Secretariat Building (9)**, left again at Jose Falcao Rd and, keeping an eye peeled for the strange flower- and star-coated **crucifix (10)** built into a wall on the right, back to where you started at Church Sq.

Courses

India on the Menu (www.indiaonthemenu.com) is a recommended five-day Indian cookery course offered by London-based **On the Go Tours** (www.onthegotours.com). The programme is based in Betim, just across the river from Panaji, and covers North and South Indian cuisines, Goan cuisine and a market tour. On the final day you can choose to be taught how to cook your favourite Indian dishes by the course tutor. Each of the cooking sessions lasts half a day (including lunch).

Cruises & Tours

GTDC operates entertaining hour-long **cruises** (Rs 100; ☽ dusk cruise 6pm, sundown cruise 7.15pm) along the Mandovi River aboard the *Santa Monica*. They include a live band performing Goan folk songs and dances. On full-moon nights there is a two-hour cruise at 8.30pm (Rs 150). Cruises depart from the Santa Monica jetty next to the huge Mandovi Bridge and tickets can be purchased here. **Royal Cruises** (☎ 2435599), has virtually identical trips from Santa Monica jetty starting around 6.15pm (Rs 100), as well as open-sea 'dolphin cruises' (from mid-October to the end of April only; Rs 300) from 10am to 1pm. Its boats are bigger and rowdier (for the boozy Indian party crowd) than the *Santa Monica*.

GTDC also runs a **Goa By Night bus tour** (Rs 140; ☽ 6.30pm), which leaves from the same spot and includes a river cruise. It also offers a whole bevy of day-long bus tours.

Sleeping

BUDGET

Park Lane Lodge (☎ 2227154; pklaldg@sancharnet.in; d without/with AC Rs 475/650; ☒) Stepping through the doors of this rambling 1930s Portuguese house is like going to visit your grandparents, thanks to all the fuss the owners pour over you. There are six small, simply furnished rooms full of character; checkout is 8am and prices more than double at Christmas.

Vaz Residence (☎ 2432909; d Rs 500) This decent-value budget hotel off 31st January Rd doesn't extend the warmest of welcomes, but it's in a quiet, friendly neighbourhood and has six basic, clean rooms with midget-sized balconies.

Republica Hotel (☎ 2224630; Jose Falcao Rd; d Rs 600) The Republica is an interesting old place with good views from the balcony over to the river and the Secretariat building. But with squat toilets and a general air of neglect it's the least appealing of the budget choices. For some reason it charges Rs 1000 in high season if you book over the phone.

our pick Afonso Guest House (☎ 2222359; d Rs 750) Surrounded by pot plants and set in a beautifully restored yellow Portuguese town house that almost whiffs of Lisbon, this superb family-run budget hotel has immaculately clean, well-cared-for rooms that are a bargain.

MIDRANGE

Mayfair Hotel (☎ 2223317; mayfair@sancharnet.com; Dr Dada Vaidya Rd; s/d from Rs 840/1040; ☒) Bright red-and-yellow-striped walls lead into tidy rooms that are ideal for those who enjoy the hustle of the city centre.

Panaji Residency (☎ 2227103; MG Rd; d without/with AC from Rs 870/990; ☒) This GTDC-run establishment has as much charm and character as a bowl of porridge, but it's a useful standby if all the goodies are taken. Popular with Indian businessmen.

Panjim Inn (☎ 2226523; www.panjiminn.com; 31st January Rd; s/d from Rs 1440/1620; ☒) A delightful hotel, the Panjim Inn is a beautiful 200-year-old pastel pink mansion with period furniture and a large 1st-floor veranda with overhanging vines. All rooms have romantic four-poster beds. The attached restaurant is slow and not such good value. Note that there's a modern, new extension, so call ahead to request one of the genuinely old rooms!

Panjim Pousada (☎ 2226523; www.panjiminn.com; 31st January Rd; s/d from Rs 1440/1620; ☒) Across from Panjim Inn and under the same management, this is a discreet hotel hidden away inside a lovely old Hindu house. The Gitanjali art gallery around the bright central courtyard and the rooms are full of antique wooden furniture.

Hotel Fidalgo (☎ 2226291; www.hotelfidalgo-goa.com; 18 June Rd; s/d from Rs 2000/2500; ☒ ▯ ▣) Sterile but reliable business-class hotel with huge bedroom windows overlooking the city centre and a whole bevy of 24-hour restaurants. Has an inviting pool.

TOP END

our pick Panjim Peoples (☎ 2226523; www.panjiminn.com; 31st January Rd; d high season from Rs 5200; ☒) This is another venture by the Panjim Inn people, and is far and away the most atmospheric hotel in Panaji. The bed heads alone should be in an art gallery and nothing else about the massive, beautifully furnished rooms is likely to disappoint either.

Goa Marriott Resort (☎ 2463333; www.marriott.com; Miramar; d from US$250; ☒ ▯ ▣) Panaji's luxury choice – a relaxed hotel with spacious, soothingly decorated rooms – is at Miramar, 3km from the town centre. The service is perfect, the food in the various restaurants divine, but at the end of the day it lacks the character and sense of place of some of the other Panaji hotels.

Eating

Panaji knows how to relax over a good meal and you'll find plenty of memorable places in which to enjoy Goa's famous food.

New Café Hema (General Bernado Guedes Rd; mains Rs 20-30; ⏰ 6am-7.30pm Mon-Sat, to 12.30pm Sun) This is a cheap, clean place near the municipal market serving a very good fish curry and rice (Rs 20) and cheap veg snacks for under Rs 10. Entrance is at the rear and up some stairs.

Lourenzos (MG Rd; mains Rs 30-100) Brand new, homely bar and restaurant near old Pato Bridge that's popular with local drivers. The owner is a highly eccentric Maradona looka-like who'll probably do his best to get you drinking. South American atmosphere with old Goan favourites.

Viva Panjim (☎ 2422405; 178 31st January Rd; mains Rs 50-160; ⏰ 8-10.30am, 11.30am-3pm & 7-11pm Mon-Sat) A compulsory pit stop on the foreigners' Panaji circuit and for good reason – the cheap Goan and Portuguese staples are tasty and the ambience is that of small town in Portugal. There are a couple of outdoor tables and the chicken *xacuti* (spicy Goan curry made using coconut milk) is delicious.

Sher-E-Punjab (☎ 2227975; 1st fl, Hotel Aroma, Cunha-Rivara Rd; mains Rs 60-150) Simple and quick but reassuringly good, and once bitten no-one is too shy to return. There's also a branch on 18th June Rd.

Hotel Venite (☎ 2425537; 31st January Rd; mains Rs 65-110; ⏰ 8.30am-11pm) With colourful graffiti covered walls and half-a-dozen tiny balconies hanging over the street this Latin-flavoured restaurant is the perfect spot to pause for one of its delicious milk shakes and a light snack.

Zen Restaurant (☎ 2420737; 1st fl, Padmavati Towers, 18th June Rd; mains Rs 100-200) The welcoming statement that the Chinese will eat anything with four legs but a table and anything with two wings but a plane does make you ponder what 'delicacy' might emerge from the kitchens next, but rest assured that this stylish new joint avoids anything dodgy and just sticks to praise-winning Chinese and Thai staples.

our pick **A Ferradura** (Horseshoe; ☎ 2431788; Ourem Rd; mains Rs 150-300) As the only true Portuguese restaurant in Panaji a good meal here can whisk you away to the banks of the Douro River. The main courses aren't for the hungry, but it's a good place for an intimate meal, and serves Portuguese wines and beers.

Drinking

Panaji has a fair smattering of darkened bars full of hard-core feni (liquor distilled from coconut milk or cashews) drinkers, and a few pubs frequented by young Goans rather than foreign tourists. Apart from **Hotel Venite** (31st January Rd), try **Aces Pub** (Swami Vivekanand Rd). It's a tiny, two-tier place that's like a little cocktail bar. **Gadhino Bar** (Dr Dada Vaidya Rd) is a spit-and-sawdust local bar consisting of two tables and a row of drinks bottles.

Entertainment

Kala Academy (☎ 2420451; www.kalaacademy.org; Dayanand Bandodkar Marg) On the west side of the city at Campal is Goa's premier cultural centre, which features a programme of dance, theatre, music and art exhibitions throughout the year. Many shows are in Konkani, but there are occasional English-language productions.

INOX (☎ 2420999; tickets Rs 50-120) This multiplex cinema, which shows English-language and Indian films, is near the Kala Academy.

Casino Goa (☎ 2234044; ⏰ dusk cruise 5.30-8pm Rs 500, dinner cruise from 7.30pm-6am Rs 1500) Aboard a small luxury ship, the MV *Caravela*, moored at the Panaji jetty, opposite Hotel Mandovi, is India's only live gaming casino – it's a fun night out, particularly if the Russian belly dancers are putting on a show. There's a smart dress code and a no-children policy.

Getting There & Away

AIR

Big boy airlines with offices in Panaji include the following:

Air India (☎ 2225172) Near Bal Bhavan, Campal.

Indian Airlines (☎ 2237826; ground fl, Dempo Bldg, Dayanand Bandodkar Marg)

Jet Airways (☎ 2438792; Shop 7-9, Sesa Ghor, Patto Plaza, Dr Alvaro Costa Rd) Near GTDC office.

Sahara Airlines (☎ 2237346; General Bernado Guedes Rd)

A prepaid taxi from the airport to Panaji is Rs 500.

BUS

State-run bus services operate out of Panaji's **Kadamba bus stand** (☎ 2438034). Fares vary depend on the type of bus and include the following:

Destination	Fare (Rs)	Duration (hr)
Bengaluru	400	14
Hospet	177	9
Mangalore	190	10
Mumbai	900 (deluxe)	12-15
Mysore	345	17
Pune	400	12

There are also services to Londa (Rs 70, three hours), where you can get a daily direct train connection to Mysore and Bengaluru, as well as services to Hubli (Rs 103, six hours) and Belgaum (Rs 85, five hours).

Many private operators have offices outside the entrance to the bus stand, with luxury and AC buses to Mumbai, Bengaluru, Hampi and other destinations. Most private interstate buses arrive and depart from a separate bus stand next to the Mandovi Bridge. **Paulo Travels** (☎ 2438531; www.paulotravels .com; ☷ 8am-9.30pm), just north of the bus stand, has nightly AC sleeper coaches to Mumbai (Rs 650, 14 to 18 hours) and Bengaluru (Rs 650, 14 hours), though these prices fluctuate – they rise from mid-December. Ordinary, non-AC buses cost Rs 350 to Mumbai and Rs 350 to Hampi. Luxury buses can also be booked through agents in Margao, Mapusa and the beach resorts, but they still depart from Panaji.

For journeys within Goa, popular routes from Panaji depart from the Kadamba bus stand and include the following:

Calangute Frequent services throughout the day and evening (Rs 7, 45 minutes).

Mapusa Frequent buses run to Mapusa (Rs 7) or there's a separate ticket booth at the Kadamba bus stand for express services (Rs 10, 25 minutes).

Margao Direct express buses run frequently to Margao (Rs 16, one hour). Change at Margao for the beaches of the south.

Old Goa Direct buses to Old Goa leave constantly (Rs 7, 25 minutes).

TRAIN
The train is a better bet than the bus for getting to/from Mumbai and Mangalore, but it can be difficult getting a seat into Goa around Christmas. The nearest train station to Panaji is Karmali, 12km to the east near Old Goa. There's a very busy **reservation office** (☷ 8am-8pm Mon-Sat) upstairs at Panaji's Kadamba bus stand.

Getting Around
Getting taxi and autorickshaw drivers to use their meters is impossible. Agree on the fare before heading off. Short trips around Panaji cost Rs 50; to Old Goa they cost roughly Rs 150.

It's easy enough to hire a motorcycle or scooter in Panaji, though if you intend to spend most of your time at the beach resorts it's more convenient and usually cheaper to hire one there. There are no hire shops as such – ask at your guesthouse or head to the cluster of bikes opposite the main post office on MG Rd. Bicycles can be hired from **Daud M Aga Cycle Store** (☎ 2222670; per day Rs 40; ☷ 8am-8pm Mon-Sat, to noon Sun), opposite Cine Nacional.

OLD GOA
Gazing at Old Goa today it's hard to believe that this fallen city was once able to stand up to Lisbon and demand, 'Who's the man?'. But back in the 1500s and with a population exceeding that of Lisbon and London, that's exactly what Old Goa was able to do. However the good times didn't last long and both the Inquisition and a major epidemic did their best to decimate this decadent and immoral dollop of Portugal. Finally, in 1843, the capital was shifted to the far more prim and proper Panaji.

All that's now left of Golden Goa are half-a-dozen imposing churches and cathedrals (among the largest in Asia) and an awful lot of atmosphere.

Old Goa can get crowded on weekends and in the 10 days leading up to the **Feast of St Francis Xavier** on 3 December. The Archaeological Survey of India publishes the useful guide *Old Goa* (Rs 10), available from the archaeological museum (p188).

Sights
SE CATHEDRAL
Construction of the **Sé de Santa Catarina**, the largest church in Old Goa, began in 1562 and though the building was completed by 1619, the altars were not finished until 1652.

The building's style is Portuguese-Gothic with a Tuscan exterior and Corinthian interior. The remaining tower houses a famous bell, often called the Golden Bell because of its rich sound. The main altar is dedicated to St Catherine of Alexandria, and paintings on either side of it depict scenes from her life and martyrdom.

CONVENT & CHURCH OF ST FRANCIS OF ASSISI
One of the most interesting buildings in Old Goa, the **church** interior contains gilded and carved woodwork, a stunning *reredos* (ornamented screen behind the altar), old murals depicting scenes from the life of St Francis and a floor made of carved gravestones –

complete with family coats of arms dating back to the early 16th century. The church was built by eight Franciscan friars who arrived here in 1517 and constructed a small chapel, which was later pulled down and the present building was constructed on the same spot in 1661.

A convent behind this church is now the **archaeological museum** (admission Rs 5; 🕑 10am-5pm Sat-Thu). It houses portraits of the Portuguese viceroys, sculpture fragments from Hindu temple sites, and stone Vetal images from the animist cult that flourished in this part of India centuries ago.

BASILICA OF BOM JESUS

This basilica is famous throughout the Roman Catholic world. It contains the tomb and mortal remains of St Francis Xavier who, in 1541, was given the task of spreading Christianity among the subjects of the Portuguese colonies in the East.

A former pupil of St Ignatius Loyola, the founder of the Jesuit order, St Francis Xavier embarked on missionary voyages that became legendary and, considering the state

of transport at the time, were nothing short of miraculous.

Apart from the richly gilded altars, the interior of the church is remarkable for its simplicity. Construction began in 1594 and was completed in 1605. The focus of the church is the three-tiered marble tomb of St Francis – his remains are housed in a silver casket, which at one time was covered in jewels.

The **Professed House**, next door to the basilica, is a two-storey laterite building covered with lime plaster. Construction was completed in 1585, despite much opposition to the Jesuits from the local Portuguese. There is a modern **art gallery** attached to the basilica; even if the art isn't to your taste it's worth popping your head in to look through a small window down onto the tomb of St Francis Xavier.

CHURCH OF ST CAJETAN

Modelled on the original design of St Peter's in Rome, this **church** was built by Italian friars of the Order of Theatines, who were sent by Pope Urban III to preach Christianity in the kingdom of Golconda (near Hyderabad).

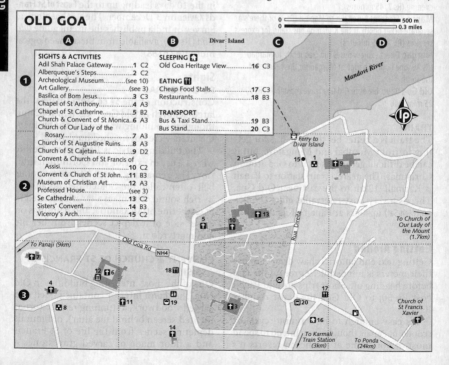

OLD GOA

0 —————— 500 m
0 —————— 0.3 miles

SIGHTS & ACTIVITIES
Adil Shah Palace Gateway...........1 C2
Alberqueque's Steps...................2 C2
Archeological Museum..........(see 10)
Art Gallery.............................(see 3)
Basilica of Bom Jesus.................3 C3
Chapel of St Anthony.................4 A3
Chapel of St Catherine................5 B2
Church & Convent of St Monica...6 A3
Church of Our Lady of the
Rosary.................................7 A3
Church of St Augustine Ruins.......8 A3
Church of St Cajetan.................9 D2
Convent & Church of St Francis of
Assisi................................10 C2
Convent & Church of St John.......11 B3
Museum of Christian Art............12 A3
Professed House.....................(see 3)
Se Cathedral.........................13 C2
Sisters' Convent.....................14 B3
Viceroy's Arch.......................15 C2

SLEEPING 🏠
Old Goa Heritage View.............16 C3

EATING 🍴
Cheap Food Stalls....................17 C3
Restaurants...........................18 B3

TRANSPORT
Bus & Taxi Stand.....................19 B3
Bus Stand.............................20 C3

Divar Island

Mandovi River

Ferry to Divar Island

Rua Direita

Old Goa Rd

NH4

To Paraji (9km)

To Church of Our Lady of the Mount (1.7km)

Church of St Francis Xavier

To Karmali Train Station (3km)

To Ponda (24km)

THE INCORRUPT BODY OF ST FRANCIS XAVIER

Goa's patron saint, Francis Xavier, spent 10 years as a tireless missionary in Asia but it was his death on 3 December 1552 that gave rise to his greatest influence on the region.

He died on the island of Sancian, off the coast of China. A servant is said to have emptied four sacks of quicklime into his coffin to consume his flesh in case the order came to return the remains to Goa. Two months later the body was still in perfect condition – refusing to rot despite the quicklime. The following year it was returned to Goa, where the people were declaring the preservation a miracle.

The church was slower to acknowledge it, requiring a medical examination to establish that the body had not been embalmed. This was performed in 1556 by the viceroy's physician, who declared that all internal organs were still intact and that no preservative agents had been used. He noticed a small wound in the chest and asked two Jesuits to put their fingers into it. He noted, 'When they withdrew them, they were covered with blood which I smelt and found to be absolutely untainted'.

It was not until 1622 that canonisation took place, but by then holy-relic hunters had started work on the 'incorrupt body'. In 1614 the right arm was removed and divided between Jesuits in Japan and Rome, and by 1636 parts of one shoulder blade and all the internal organs had been scattered through Southeast Asia. By the end of the 17th century the body was in an advanced state of desiccation, and the miracle appeared to be over. The Jesuits decided to enclose the corpse in a glass coffin out of view, and it was not until the mid-19th century that the current cycle of 10-yearly expositions began, the next one being in 2014.

The friars were not permitted to work in Golconda, so settled at Old Goa in 1640. The construction of the church began in 1655.

CHURCH OF ST AUGUSTINE (RUINS)

The **church** was constructed in 1602 by Augustinian friars and abandoned in 1835 due to the repressive policies of the Portuguese government, which resulted in the eviction of many religious orders from Goa. It quickly fell into neglect and all that really remains is the enormous 46m tower that served as a belfry and formed part of the façade.

CHURCH & CONVENT OF ST MONICA

This huge, three-storey **laterite building** was completed in 1627, only to burn down nine years later. Reconstruction started the following year, and it's from this time that the buildings date. Once known as the Royal Monastery, due to the royal patronage that it enjoyed, the building is now used by the Mater Dei Institute as a nunnery. It was inaugurated in 1964.

Within the convent, the excellent **Museum of Christian Art** (adult/child Rs 10/free; ⏲ 9.30am-5pm) contains statuary, paintings and sculptures transferred here from the Rachol Seminary. Many of the works of Goan Christian art during the Portuguese era were produced by local Hindu artists.

OTHER HISTORIC SITES

Other monuments of interest are the **Viceroy's Arch**, **Adil Shah's Palace Gateway**, **Chapel of St Anthony**, **Chapel of St Catherine**, **Alburqueque's Steps**, the **Convent & Church of St John**, **Sister's Convent** and the **Church of Our Lady of the Rosary**. For a wonderful view of the city head to the hilltop **Church of Our Lady of the Mount**, 2km east of Se Cathedral.

Sleeping & Eating

Most people visit Old Goa as a day trip and there is little reason to stay out here, but should you want to the GTDC **Old Goa Heritage View** (☎ 2285013; d with/without AC Rs 450/650; 🔀), has simple rooms and zero enthusiasm.

Outside the basilica there are two restaurants, geared primarily to local tourists, where you can order full meals and cold drinks, including beer. They're raised up from the road and are a good spot to relax and take in the scene. You can also get cheap snacks (less than Rs 120) from the food stalls that line the road just north of the Old Goa Heritage View.

Getting There & Away

Frequent buses to Old Goa depart from the Kadamba bus stand at Panaji (Rs 7, 25 minutes) and stop on the east side of the main roundabout.

TORDA

Just 5km north of Panaji, off the main road to Mapusa, is the village of Torda, where you'll find, on a traffic island, the **Houses of Goa Museum** (☎ 2410711; www.archgoa.org; admission Rs 25; ⌚ 10am-7.30pm Tue-Sun). This extraordinary ship-like building houses a small but illuminating collection of materials explaining the unique design and intricacies of Goa's traditional architecture. Inquire also about guided walks through the mangroves surrounding the village. The easiest way here is by autorickshaw from Panaji (around Rs 70).

MAPUSA

pop 40,100

The colourful market town of Mapusa (pronounced 'Mapsa') is the main population centre in the northern *talukas* (districts) of Goa. There's not much to see in Mapusa, aside from a raucous **Friday market** (⌚ 8am-6.30pm) that attracts hordes of vendors and shoppers from all over Goa. Unlike the Anjuna market it's a local event where people shop for cheap clothing and produce, but you can also find a few souvenirs and textiles here. If your idea of India has yet to extend beyond the beach bubbles then this is a great place to see an authentic slice of small-town India.

Information

Several ATMs can be found around the municipal gardens.

Cyber Zone (per hr Rs 40; ⌚ 9.30am-2pm & 2.30-6.30pm Mon-Sat) Internet access, just around the corner from the Hotel Satyaheera.

Other India Bookstore (☎ 2263306; www.goacom.com/oib; Mapusa Clinic Rd; ⌚ 9am-5pm Mon-Fri, to 1pm Sat) Stocks mainly books published in India, including books on Goa or by Goan authors.

Sleeping & Eating

Accommodation at the nearby beaches of Anjuna, Vagator and Calangute is far preferable to what's on offer in Mapusa.

Hotel Vilena (☎ 2263115; Feira Baixa Rd; d with shared/private bathroom Rs 300/450) Noisy, matchbox-sized rooms that just about suffice for a night. Friendly.

Hotel Satyaheera (☎ 2262849; satya_goa@sancharnet.in; d without/with AC from Rs 490/700; ❄) Near the Maruti Temple on the northern roundabout, this is Mapusa's best choice with all the rooms painted a different colour – ask for one of the garish purple rooms just for the novelty value.

Vrundavan (dishes Rs 15-50) Near the Municipal Gardens, this is a simple place offering good, cheap veg thalis for Rs 40.

Bertsy Bar & Restaurant (Market Rd) Basic chicken and beef curries for Rs 30 to 50.

Ruchira Restaurant (mains Rs 30-100) On the rooftop of Hotel Satyaheera, this is one of Mapusa's best restaurants, serving Indian and Continental dishes.

Shopping

Sawant Chapple Shop (⌚ 7am-8pm) For three generations the same family have been churning out handmade leather sandals. Expect to pay between Rs 300 and 600 for a decent pair. It's behind Laxmi Narayan Temple.

Getting There & Away

If you're coming by bus from Mumbai, Mapusa is the jumping-off point for the northern beaches. Private operators such as **India Travel** (☎ 2262635) congregate around the municipal gardens and the taxi and autorickshaw stand. They have buses to Mumbai (normal/sleeper Rs 450/800, 14 hours) and Bengaluru (Rs 500, 15 hours). From the Kadamba bus stand there are state-run buses to Pune (Rs 230, 15 hours) and Belgaum (Rs 47, five hours).

There are frequent local express buses to Panaji (Rs 7, 25 minutes), and buses every 30 minutes to Calangute and Anjuna (both Rs 6). Other buses go to Chapora, Candolim and Arambol (Rs 12). A motorcycle taxi to Anjuna or Calangute costs Rs 80, an autorickshaw Rs 120.

Thivim, about 12km northeast of town, is the nearest train station on the Konkan Railway. Local buses meet trains (Rs 5); an autorickshaw costs around Rs 80.

FORT AGUADA & CANDOLIM

pop 8600

The beaches of Candolim and Sinquerim (below Fort Aguada) are popular with charter and upmarket tourists. The pace is a little less frenetic than at Calangute and Baga up the coast. Independent travellers are rare here, most of the hotels being favoured by package-tour operations. The beach at Fort Aguada is notable for its rocky and attractive headland, while Candolim has the rusting hulk of a grounded tanker, the *River Princess* – it's not a very pretty princess. Some of the best-value beach accommodation in Goa lines the quiet back lanes of both villages.

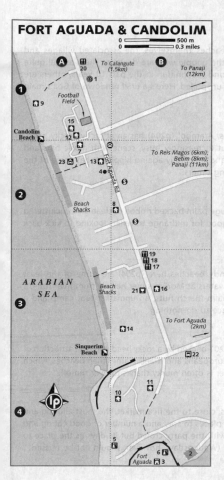

INFORMATION
Online World.................................1 A1

SIGHTS & ACTIVITIES
Aguada Jail..................................2 B4
Fort Aguada.................................3 B4
John's Boat Tours (Elephant Shop)........4 A2
New Lighthouse............................5 B4
Old Lighouse...............................6 B4

SLEEPING
Aguada Hermitage....................(see 10)
Ave Maria..................................7 A2
Casa Sea-Shell.............................8 B2
D'Mello's...................................9 A1
Fort Aguada Beach Resort................10 B4
Marbella Guest House.....................11 B4
Moonlight Bar & Restaurant..............12 A1
Sea Shell Inn..............................13 A2
Taj Holiday Village........................14 B3
Tropicano Beach Resort...................15 A1
Villa Ludovici Tourist Home..............16 B3

EATING
Bomra's Restaurant.......................17 B3
Flambé....................................18 B3
Stone House...............................19 B3
Viva Goa..................................20 A1

DRINKING
Riio..21 B3

TRANSPORT
Sinquerim Bus Stop.......................22 B3
Taxi Stand.................................23 A2

sory, extended stays) are in on drug charges. Needless to say, it's not really much of tourist destination.

There are various boat cruises on offer. The best value are **John's Boat Tours** (☎ 2497450), further up behind Candolim Beach. The half-day dolphin trip (Rs 795, with a no-dolphin, no-pay guarantee) includes lunch and beers on the boat; the popular full-day 'Crocodile Dundee' river trip (Rs 995) includes lunch at a spice plantation and free drinks. It also offers an overnight backwater trip on a Kerala-style houseboat (Rs 4000 full board), and a variety of nonwatery trips.

The Taj Holiday Village (p194) organises paragliding and rents jet-skis and windsurfing equipment.

Sleeping
BUDGET
Some of Goa's best-value places to put up for the night can be found in Fort Aguada and Candolim.

Ave Maria (☎ 2489074; d incl tax Rs 600; 🛒) A hop and a skip from the beach but you need to be skinny to squeeze into the shower. Friendly.

Sights & Activities
Guarding the mouth of the Mandovi River, **Fort Aguada** was constructed by the Portuguese in 1612. It's worth visiting the moated ruins on the hilltop for the views, which are particularly good from the **old lighthouse**. Nearby is the **new lighthouse** (adult/child Rs 5/3; 🕓 4-5.30pm). It's a pleasant 2km ride along a hilly, sealed road to the fort, or you can walk via a steep, uphill path past Marbella Guest House. Beneath the fort, facing the Mandovi, is the **Aguada Jail**. Most of the inmates here (including some tourists on compul-

The post office and banks are located on Fort Aguada Rd, and internet access is available at **Online World** (per hr Rs 30; 🕓 9am-11pm).

GOA

THE BEACH FILES

Goa's biggest attraction is its beaches. The beaches themselves, the associated villages and resorts that have grown up around them, and the people who are drawn to them are all quite different in character. Some have changed beyond recognition in the past 10 years, others are just being discovered and a few pockets remain unspoiled. Here's a brief rundown of Goa's main beaches from north to south.

Arambol (Harmal)

The most northerly of Goa's developed beaches, Arambol (p204) has an attractive rocky headland, a long strip of sand and a chilled-out, but increasingly busy, scene with music bars and some good restaurants; it attracts backpackers and gracefully ageing hippies. It has some of the cheapest accommodation in Goa and lots of long timers.

Mandrem

The next beach south, Mandrem (p204) is one huge palm backed ribbon of clean and uncluttered sand; it's one of Goa's undiscovered gems. It's good for midrange travellers looking to kick back and do absolutely nothing.

Morjim & Asvem

Stretching down to the Chapora River, the sandy beaches here (p204) are some of the least disturbed and most beautiful in the state. The waters at Morjim suffer heavily from river run-off pollution year-round. There are bamboo and palm-thatch huts, an upmarket tent camp and a few beach shacks but essentially it's a quiet place to do nothing.

Vagator

There are three small cove beaches at Vagator (p201 backed by a rocky headland. The attraction of Vagator is the huge party scene, dominated by Europeans and Israelis, rather than beaches, which cannot be described as Goa's prettiest. The water is often murky thanks to river run-off.

Anjuna

Of all the big tourist beaches Anjuna (p199) has, close to the flea market, the most alluring and relaxed stretch of sand. There are also plenty of places to stay and a number of good eating and drinking options. Anjuna retains its popularity with the party crowd but its days as the place to 'see and be seen' are virtually over. Market day (Wednesday), however, should not be missed.

Calangute & Baga

The long sweep of very crowded beach here (p194) is overloaded with beach shacks and sun beds, backed by midrange concrete-block hotels. This is package-tourism central, though many travellers still prefer the upbeat atmosphere here to that further north. The beach can be dirty and women in bikinis won't get a second's peace.

Tropicano Beach Resort (☎ 2489732; 835B Camotim Vaddo; d Rs 600) Six small freshly painted rooms that are as clean as Goa gets, a garden full of drooping trees and a friendly family welcome make the Tropicano Beach Resort a hard place to top.

Villa Ludovici Tourist Home (☎ 2479684; Fort Aguada Rd; d incl breakfast Rs 650) Nowhere else in Candolim can match the fading glory of this charming old colonial house. There are only four rooms, some of which come with creak-

ing four-posters, so book in advance. In the evenings you can sit yourself in a comfortable chair on the shady verandah and sup on a beer.

D'Mello's (☎ 2489650; dmellos_seaview_home@hot mail.com; d small/large Rs 700/1200) The large ocean-facing rooms are some of the best you will find anywhere and feature enormous sliding wooden shutters instead of glass windows. The result is lots of breezes and sunlight filtering into the room and the sensation that

Candolim & Sinquerim

A continuation of Calangute, Candolim(p190) is a mix of upmarket resorts, package hotels, beach shacks and some good restaurants, culminating in the sprawling Taj complex at Sinquerim. Though still busy this beach is likely to come closer to your Goa ideals.

Miramar

Miramar (p184), Panaji's the town beach of Panaji (Panjim), is no place for swimming but it's a popular spot from which to watch the sunset.

Bogmalo

A small and sheltered beach hemmed in by coconut cliffs that sits just 4km south of Dabolim Airport, Bogmalo (p209) has a feeling of exclusivity and can be used as a base for diving. It's close to the sprawling industrial centre of Vasco da Gama and accessed easily from the airport. Very few people come here.

Majorda & Velsao

Blighted by a petrochemical plant in the distance, these beaches north of Colva have a few upmarket resort hotels but little tourist activity.

Colva & Benaulim

The exposed and endless sandy beach here (p210) is similar to Calangute but it's much quieter and still has a noticeable fishing industry. There's a mix of Indian and foreign package tourists and backpackers, but no party scene. Benaulim village is quieter still and a good place to stay long-term. Neither beach is very clean.

Varca & Cavelossim

Five-star luxury resorts here (p213) front relatively empty, undeveloped beaches that meet all the tropical clichés.

Agonda

North of Palolem, the large beach at Agonda (p213) is the most inviting in south Goa. It attracts travellers who are over the scene at Palolem.

Palolem & Patnem

Palolem (p213) used to be the quietest and most idyllic beach in the state but nowadays it's been well and truly discovered. Even so its palm trees continue to attract bus loads of backpackers attempting to escape the stresses of Indian travel. Patnem, a short distance south, is much cleaner, quieter and has some decent surf.

you're floating out on the ocean in a boat. The cheaper rooms are also good.

MIDRANGE

Sea Shell Inn (☎ 2489131; seashellgoa@hotmail.com; Fort Aguada Rd; d incl breakfast Rs 850) On the main road, this whitewashed grand colonial house has eight rooms situated in a newer annexe round the back. Good value. Skimpy breakfast.

Casa Sea-Shell (☎ 2479879; seashellgoa@hotmail .com; Fort Aguada Rd; d Rs 950; ☒) The larger and

more modern sister of the Sea Shell lacks the character of that establishment but does have the plus of a pool.

Moonlight Bar & Restaurant (☎ 2489249; santa natheresa@yahoo.com; d from Rs 1000) Tasteful blue-and-white building with large rooms full of wicker furniture and bathrooms so big you'll need a GPS to navigate around them. Should the tropical sun be making you feel a bit wintry, try the attached restaurant that serves up Sunday roasts.

our pick **Marbella Guest House** (☎ 2479551; marbella_goa@yahoo.com; d incl tax from Rs 1500; ☒) This stunningly renovated Portuguese villa, stuffed full of period furniture and with peaceful, shady gardens, might be the most romantic guesthouse in Goa and alone is reason enough to come to Fort Aguada. Each room is full of lots of little touches that hotels many times its price cannot match. Book ahead.

TOP END

The **Taj Group** (☎ 6645858; www.tajhotels.com) operates a complex of three luxury hotels beside Sinquerim Beach:

Taj Holiday Village (d from US$180; ☒ ☐ ☒) Terracotta roofed cottages, a small putting green and a wonderful pool, but little character.

Aguada Hermitage (s/d from US$295; ☒ ☐ ☒) Originally built to house Commonwealth heads of state this is the most alluring of the three hotels.

Fort Aguada Beach Resort (s & d from US$325; ☒ ☐ ☒) Built into the outer walls of the fort and with epic sea views.

Eating

Viva Goa (Fort Aguada Rd; mains Rs 40-110; ☺ 11am-midnight) This cheap, locals-only spot serves seafood so fresh it might just swim away.

Bomra's Restaurant (☎ 2106236; Fort Aguada Rd; mains Rs 80-170) For a change from the soggy pastas and identikit curries that many places slop onto your plate try this small new Burmese restaurant.

Stone House (☎ 2479909; Fort Aguada Rd; mains Rs 90-170) A mellow soundtrack makes you want to linger in the comfy wicker chairs while choosing from an extensive all cast menu.

Flambé (☎ 26114271; Fort Aguada Rd; mains Rs 100-150; ☺ 8am-midnight) A melange of French and Indian cuisine and a great range of kebabs make for a real change from the everyday menus of many other establishments. It's also one of the few places that's open for service all day.

Down on the beach are dozens of beach shacks serving the obligatory Western breakfasts, seafood and cold drinks.

Drinking

Riio (☎ 5649504; Fort Aguada Rd; ☺ 10.30am-4am) Formerly known as 10 Downing Street, the Riio has jazzed itself up and is now Candolim's hippest bar.

Getting There & Away

Buses run from Panaji (Rs 7, 45 minutes), Mapusa (Rs 6) or Betim to Sinquerim via the Calangute–Candolim road. There are frequent buses travelling between Sinquerim and Calangute (Rs 3). A prepaid taxi from Daoblim Airport to Candolim costs Rs 550.

CALANGUTE & BAGA

pop 15,800

Calangute and Baga were the first beaches to attract hippies travelling overland in the '60s, then the first to secure the rampant package-and charter-tourist market in the '90s. Today they are India's 'kiss me quick' hat capital and the most popular beach resorts in the country with holidaying Indians. For many people it's just a busy, noisy and tacky Indian Costa del Sol and the thought of spending a single night here is enough to make them shudder. For others, the very fact that it is so alien to anything else in India is an attraction in itself, there's certainly no denying that the town has a certain character to it and, if you're searching for a glimpse of how the much-hyped 'New India' holidays, then here she is in all her glory.

Calangute is more of a bucket-and-spade family holiday destination while Baga, up near the mouth of the river, is popular with those wanting to drink, dance and get rowdy. For something a bit more chilled out take a room at the southern end of Calangute, towards Candolim, or among the last remaining patches of greenery on the north side of the Baga River.

Orientation & Information

Most services cluster around the main market and bus stand, from where a road leads down to the beach.

There are many currency-exchange offices scattered around the town that will change cash or travellers cheques, and most give cash advances on Visa and MasterCard. There are 24-hour ATMs accepting foreign cards at the ICICI and UTI banks in the market, and Centurion Bank, about 100m south on the main road.

There are plenty of internet cafés and many hotels offer internet access for guests. The standard charge is Rs 30 an hour. In the market area try Edson's Cyber Café; in Baga try the internet café at Angelina Beach Resort (p197).

Book Palace (☎ 2281129; ☺ 9am-7pm) Next to the football ground on the road to the beach, Book Palace has a good selection of reading material in all languages sold by a man who loves his products.

Literati Bookshop & Café (☎ 2277740; www.literati -goa.com) Tucked away down a dusty lane leading to the beach at the far southern end of Calangute is this refreshingly different bookshop. Piles of good reads are stacked onto shelves throughout the owners' home, and there are bean bags to relax on and coffee to wake up with.

MGM International Travels (☎ 2276249; ☯ 9.30am-6.30pm Mon-Sat) This is a reputable travel agency.

Sights & Activities

Water sports, including parasailing (Rs 700 to 1500), jet-skiing (Rs 900 per 15 minutes), and boat trips are offered about halfway along the beach between Calangute and Baga by **Altantis Water Sports** (☎ 9890047272) and **H2O Tripper** (☎ 2277907).

The **Ayurvedic Natural Health Centre** (☎ 2409275; www.healthandayurveda.com; Chogm Rd, Saligao), 5km inland, offers a range of residential packages (one week single/double US$492/874) that include accommodation and courses, in reflexology, aromatherapy, acupressure and yoga. There's also a range of herbal medicines on offer and a free consultation by a Keralan doctor.

Diving trips and courses are offered by the German-run **Goa Dive Center** (☎ 9822157094; goadivecenter@rediffmail.com; Tito's Rd, Baga; 4-day PADI beginners course Rs 14,500; ☯ 10am-1pm & 4-9pm).

There are two Saturday-night markets in the Baga area that are alternatives to the Anjuna Market; for details p199.

If you're after something a little more laidback, the **Kerkar Art Complex** (☎ 2276017; www .subodhkerkar.com; ☯ 10am-11pm) showcases the colourful paintings and sculptures of local artist Dr Subodh Kerkar; here you'll also find a restaurant (p198), hotel (p197) and an open-air auditorium where classical Indian music concerts are held.

If you're staying awhile and want to rekindle the hippy days by not just playing a guitar around the fire but actually building one yourself (the guitar that is, not the fire), then you can learn how to do it with a tailormade course from **Jungle Guitars** (☎ 9823565117; www .jungleguitars.com; Rs 38,000) based on the north side of the Baga River.

It's not really a sight or activity in the standard sense but stopping by **Star Magic Shop** (☎ 09810483939; Tito's Rd; ☯ 9am-11pm) makes for an entertaining half-hour for the child in all of

us. The magician owner will dazzle you with an array of magic that extends way beyond the average pub card trick – just don't accept the use of one of his lighters! Pay enough and he'll show you the tricks of the trade.

Tours

Day Tripper (☎ 2276726; www.daytrippergoa.com; ☯ 9am-6pm end Oct-end Apr), with its head office in south Calangute, is one of Goa's best tour agencies. It runs a wide variety of trips around Goa, including to Dudhsagar Falls (p216), and also interstate to Hampi and the Kali River (for rafting and bird-watching trips) in Karnataka.

GTDC tours (see p185) can be booked at the **Calangute Residency** (☎ 2276024) beside the beach.

Sleeping

It's a solid line of hotels for about 3km along the main Calangute–Baga road and along lanes between the road and the beach, but few places actually have sea views.

CALANGUTE
Budget

South Calangute is generally quieter and more rustic than further north. In central Calangute there are several good places down Golden Beach Rd, a laneway that runs parallel to the beach.

Johnny's Hotel (☎ 2277458; johnnys_hotel@yahoo .com; d small/large Rs 400/600) Well-established backpackers hotel close to the beach. There's a variety of big, neat rooms, along with rooftop yoga (Rs 250 per hour) and massage (Rs 500 per hour) sessions.

Gabriel's Guest House (☎ 2279486; d from Rs 500; ☒) Halfway down a laneway at the southern end of the beach, Gabriel's is a pleasant family home with crazy mosaic floors and simple, spotless rooms (one with AC) with balconies. There is a simple restaurant.

Angela Guest House (Golden Beach Rd; Rs r 550) It's hard to know which has more character – the Portuguese villa itself or the frail old gentleman who runs it. The four basic rooms are about the cheapest in town. A friendly attached restaurant offers no-fuss meals.

Garden Court Resort (☎ 2276054; r without/with AC Rs 600/1200; ☒) In the thick of things at the roundabout at the start of the Calangute–Baga road is this lovely colonial building full of Catholic religious mementos. The rooms are

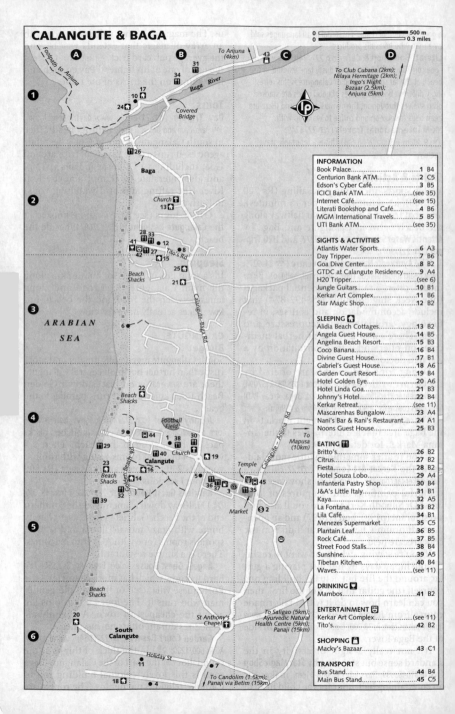

CALANGUTE & BAGA

0   500 m
0   0.3 miles

To Anjuna
(4km)

To Club Cubana (2km);
Nilaya Hermitage (2km);
Ingo's Night
Bazaar (2.5km);
Anjuna (5km)

Baga River

Covered
Bridge

Baga

Church

Beach
Shacks

Tito's Rd

Calangute-Baga Rd

**ARABIAN
SEA**

To
Mapusa
(10km)

Anjuna Rd

Beach
Shacks

Football
Field

Calangute

Church

Temple

To
Market

Golden Beach Rd

Beach
Shacks

Beach
Shacks

**South
Calangute**

Holiday St

St Anthony's
Chapel

To Saligao (5km);
Ayurvedic Natural
Health Centre (5km);
Panaji (15km)

To Candolim (1.5km);
Panaji via Betim (15km)

INFORMATION
Book Palace	1 B4
Centurion Bank ATM	2 C5
Edson's Cyber Café	3 B5
ICICI Bank ATM	(see 35)
Internet Café	(see 15)
Literati Bookshop and Café	4 B6
MGM International Travels	5 B5
UTI Bank ATM	(see 35)

SIGHTS & ACTIVITIES
Atlantis Water Sports	6 A3
Day Tripper	7 B6
Goa Dive Center	8 B2
GTDC at Calangute Residency	9 A4
H20 Tripper	(see 6)
Jungle Guitars	10 B1
Kerkar Art Complex	11 B6
Star Magic Shop	12 B2

SLEEPING
Alidia Beach Cottages	13 B2
Angela Guest House	14 B5
Angelina Beach Resort	15 B3
Coco Banana	16 B4
Divine Guest House	17 B1
Gabriel's Guest House	18 A6
Garden Court Resort	19 B4
Hotel Golden Eye	20 A6
Hotel Linda Goa	21 B3
Johnny's Hotel	22 B4
Kerkar Retreat	(see 11)
Mascarenhas Bungalow	23 A4
Nani's Bar & Rani's Restaurant	24 A1
Noons Guest House	25 B3

EATING
Britto's	26 B2
Citrus	27 B2
Fiesta	28 B2
Hotel Souza Lobo	29 A4
Infanteria Pastry Shop	30 B4
J&A's Little Italy	31 B1
Kaya	32 A5
La Fontana	33 B2
Lila Café	34 B1
Menezes Supermarket	35 C5
Plantain Leaf	36 B5
Rock Café	37 B5
Street Food Stalls	38 B4
Sunshine	39 A5
Tibetan Kitchen	40 B4
Waves	(see 11)

DRINKING
Mambos	41 B2

ENTERTAINMENT
Kerkar Art Complex	(see 11)
Tito's	42 B2

SHOPPING
Macky's Bazaar	43 C1

TRANSPORT
Bus Stand	44 B4
Main Bus Stand	45 C5

large and clean and the old couple in charge are very welcoming.

Coco Banana (☎ 2279068; www.cocobananagoa.com; d Rs 1200) Walter and Marina, the Goan-Swiss couple who run this tight ship, will regale you with their life history and stories of how Goa used to be. They'll love having you to stay, but only so long as you obey the (only partially joking) signs not to have sex in the bathrooms! It's often full so book ahead, and the price rises over the Christmas period.

Midrange & Top End

Mascarenhas Bungalow (☎ 2276375, 9822989825; d Rs 800-1500) Superbly situated just a minute's walk from the beach, this earthy Portuguese house (built in 1901) is run by an easygoing mother-and-son team, Venita and Neil. Set amid whispering coconut trees, there are three unpretentious 'cottages', two of which are like apartments (each with small kitchens) – the upstairs one has a glorious sea-view terrace. Weekly/monthly rates are possible. Jerry and Gina, the pet pooches, love a good back scratch.

Hotel Golden Eye (☎ 2277308; www.hotelgoldeneye .com; d without/with AC Rs 1000/1500; ⛅) If you can overlook the slightly cold and forlorn atmosphere, this place offers great-value apartment-style rooms just a few sandy footsteps from a quieter patch of beach.

Kerkar Retreat (☎ 2276017; www.subodhkerkar.com; d without/with AC Rs 2000/2500; ⛅) If you liked the art then why not live with it for a while? This hotel, located inside the Kerkar Art Complex, could be really memorable but sadly it's a little bit overpriced.

BAGA
Budget

Angelina Beach Resort (☎ 2279145; angelinabeachres ort@rediffmail.com; d without/with AC Rs 550/700; ⛅ 🖳) A large, family-run place with neatly tiled bathrooms and rooms so clean you could eat your dinner off the floor. Well cared for and very welcoming.

Noons Guest House (☎ 2282787; Calungate-Baga Rd; d Rs 600) Set back from the noisy main drag this superb-value guesthouse ran by Maurice is only open in the high season. The nine large rooms come with balconies overlooking the garden. The main house is a century-old Portuguese villa with a guardian soldier statue above the entrance. Guests' rooms are in the modern annexe round the back.

Nani's Bar & Rani's Restaurant (☎ 2276313; r Rs 800-1000) Situated on the tranquil north side of the Baga River, but just a short step from the sandy beach and within sight of all the action Nani's might well have the prime spot in Baga. As if this weren't enough the colonial house is a real gem, with simple and sufficient rooms.

Divine Guest House (☎ 2279546; www.indivinehome .com; d Rs 800, ste Rs 1200) In a beautiful, quiet riverside location this bright red-and-white building with statues of cockerels and herons all over the roof offers clean rooms that are often full. The suites are really good value.

Midrange & Top End

Alidia Beach Cottages (☎ 2279014; alidia@rediffmail .com; d from Rs 800, ste Rs 2500; ⛅) Set back behind the whitewashed church, this old-fashioned house has a lost-in-the-jungle feel to it thanks to thousands of enveloping tropical flowers. It's especially good value in the low season.

Hotel Linda Goa (☎ 2276066; www.hotellindagoa.com; d without/with AC Rs 2100/2600; ⛅ 🖳) A completely nondescript hotel frequented by package tours. It's overpriced but the pool (nonresidents Rs 50) is good.

Nilaya Hermitage (☎ 2276793; www.nilayahermi tage.com; d incl breakfast & dinner from US$375; ⛅ 🖳 🖳) The last word in Goan luxury and, with only 10 rooms, the best chance you'll ever have of sleeping in the same bed as former guest Kate Moss (or, if you prefer, Richard Gere). This is one of those ever-so-exclusive places that most of us are far too ugly, wrinkled and, yes OK, poor to ever be allowed anywhere near. Rates include Dabolim Airport transfers. Please note – Kate or Richard may not actually be in the bed with you at the time.

Eating

Calangute and Baga boast some of the best dining in Goa. There are literally hundreds of small restaurants bringing the tastes of the world to the streets of Goa. For the cheapest eats check out the string of food stalls selling juices, omelettes and curries that appear each evening beside the football field in Calangute.

In the thick of Calangute is the Menezes supermarket, which is a good bet for self-caterers.

CALANGUTE

Infanteria Pastry Shop (Rs 50-100; ⏱ 7.30am-midnight) Next to the Sao João Batista church is this scrummy bakery with homemade cakes just like your mum makes. Also has light snacks and seafood meals. It's normally packed out for breakfast.

Plantain Leaf (mains Rs 50-100) Catering more to the domestic tourism market this is the best Indian vegetarian restaurant around, but it feels a bit like eating in a school canteen.

Kaya (Golden Beach Rd; mains Rs 50-180) The tie-dyed '60s keep rocking in this tiny hippy-flavoured Japanese restaurant. Includes such delights as fried chicken and *okonomiyaki* (a kind of spicy pancake), all of which are cooked up by chefs who are the real deal.

Rock Café (☎ 2282015; Almita 3; mains Rs 80-150) One of the hot spots of the moment that's very popular with expats on account of its speedy service and endless range of goodies from home. It seems to be something of a magnet to all manner of weird and wonderful characters.

Sunshine (mains Rs 80-200) A cute sand-floored, family-run beachside restaurant with chequer tablecloths and tasty seafood.

Hotel Souza Lobo (☎ 2276463; most mains Rs 80-200) The sunset views, cocktails (Rs 120 to 180) and seafood, including mussels (Rs 90) and oysters (Rs 120), are impossible to beat.

Tibetan Kitchen (☎ 2275744; mains Rs 120) If you've never tried *momos* (Tibetan dumplings) or Tibetan tea (it's an acquired taste) then now's your chance to sample the food of the mountain kingdom without altitude sickness. Tucked off the main beach road.

Waves (☎ 2276017; mains Rs 120-280) Surrounded by the art of the Kerkar Art Complex, this relaxed restaurant-bar has high-quality Goan and Western dishes at slightly inflated prices.

BAGA

Britto's (mains Rs 50-150; ⏰ 8am-midnight) Long-running and stylish restaurant that explodes out onto the beach. There's good Goan and Continental foods, appealing cakes and desserts, and live music Monday and Thursday nights.

Lila Café (☎ 2279843; mains Rs 50-180; ⏰ 8.30am-6.30pm) Run by longtime German residents of Goa, the Lila Café offers superb breakfasts (Rs 20 to 100) that some might be tempted to call the best in the state. This relaxed café ain't a bad spot for lunch either.

La Fontana (☎ 275027; Tito's Rd; 3-course menu Rs 250; ⏰ 7-11pm) This place has chatty waiters and tasty food with a Euro twist. There are some less common additions to the menu such as

stuffed potato skins. The cheesy music selection is truly dire.

Citrus (Tito's Rd; mains Rs 150-250; ⏰ 6-11pm) Near Tito's, this trendy vegetarian restaurant is one of the best in Baga and features an exciting menu of innovative fusion food. Book a table in advance.

J&A's Little Italy (☎ 2282364; mains Rs 180-285) Sick of botched pastas and pathetic pizzas? J&A's will set your world to right with its authentic Italian cuisine which includes all those little extras, such as decent olive oil and real Parmesan, that get overlooked by more run-of-the-mill establishments.

Fiesta (☎ 2279894; Tito's Rd; mains Rs 200-295; ⏰ 7pm-midnight Wed-Mon) There's a magical Balearic feel to the alfresco Fiesta, opposite the club Tito's, with its soft lighting, view to the beach and silvery silk-wrapped menus. The food is excellent, but at the end of the day you're here for the glamour as much as the taste.

Drinking & Entertainment

If you thought Calungute and Baga by day weren't what you came to India for, then just wait until the sun goes down. While Calungute, with its early-to-bed attitude, is pretty sedate after dark, Baga is something else altogether – money talks here and Baga is loud, brash, pretentious and undeniably fascinating.

Tito's (☎ 2275028; www.titosgoa.com; Tito's Rd; club cover charge men/man with a woman Rs 500/300, women free; ⏰ 6pm-3am) Possibly the most famous club in India, but since it has reached middle age it has lost a lot of its coolness and, though the hard-drinking Kingfisher lads from Mumbai aren't as welcome now, it's still got a testosterone atmosphere: single women will be harassed mercilessly.

Club Cubana (☎ 2279799; www.clubcubana.net; women/men Rs free/499; ⏰ 9pm-4am Fri-Sun; 🍸) Aiming for a more cosmopolitan crowd than Tito's this stylish out-of-town club likes hip-hop and R&B and has an open-air pool.

Mambos (☎ 2279895; before/after 10pm free/Rs 200) Under the same management as Tito's and right beside the beach, this is the hottest ticket of the moment with the beautiful of Bollywood. A busy night in season is the polar opposite of many people's idea of India.

Getting There & Away

There are frequent buses to Panaji (Rs 7, 45 minutes) and Mapusa (Rs 6) from the bus stand near the beach. Some services also stop at the bus stop near the temple. A taxi from Calangute or Baga to Panaji costs Rs 150 to 200 and takes about 30 minutes. A prepaid taxi from Dabolim Airport to Calangute will set you back Rs 550.

ANJUNA

Famous throughout Goa for its Wednesday flea market (see the boxed text, below), Anjuna's name still pulls in backpackers, European ravers, long-term hippies and, increasingly, midrange tourists taking advantage of comfy new hotels. Of all the more developed beaches in Goa Anjuna's is the best.

Orientation & Information

There are three distinct areas: the main crossroads and bus stand, where paths lead down to the beach; the back part of the village, where you'll find the post office and convenience stores; and the flea market area a couple of kilometres to the south.

Internet access is available at a number of places, including the Manali Guest House (right) and Villa Anjuna (p200), both Rs 40 per hour.

The **Bank of Baroda** (☉ 9.30am-2.30pm) gives cash advances on Visa and MasterCard. There are no ATMs; the closest are in Baga.

Travel agencies where you can make onward travel bookings, get flights confirmed and change foreign currency include **MGM Travels** (☎ 2274317; Anjuna-Mapusa Rd; ☉ 9.30am-6pm

Mon-Sat) and **Kwick Travels** (☎ 2273477; Manali Guest House; ☉ 9am-9pm).

Activities

The long-established **Purple Valley Yoga Centre** (www.yogagoa.com; Hotel Bougainvillea) offers a variety of drop-in classes in Asthanga, hatha and pranayama yoga, as well as meditation, from November to April. It also runs longer residential courses at its retreat in Assagao, 3km east towards Margao.

Paragliding takes place off the headland at the southern end of the beach, but usually only on market day.

Sleeping

Many restaurants and family homes have a few rooms out the back, so ask around and look for 'To Let' signs – there are plenty along the back lanes leading to the flea market. If you arrive before about 15 December you should easily be able to find a place for long-term rent.

BUDGET

Manali Guest House (☎ 2274421; manalionline@siffy .com; s/d Rs 150/200; ☐) A classic backpackers hotel with simple, good-value rooms (often full), a bookshop and a travel agency. The disadvantage is the distance form the beach.

Coutino's Nest (☎ 2274386; shaldon_555@yahoo .co.in; d Rs 300; ☒) Jungle green with a garden to match, this place features six clean rooms and a pleasant rooftop restaurant hidden well away from the bustle.

THE GOA MARKET EXPERIENCE

The ever-expanding Wednesday **flea market** at Anjuna is not just a place to browse for souvenirs – it's an essential part of the Goa experience! The famous market is a wonderful blend of Tibetan and Kashmiri traders, colourful Gujarati and Lamani tribal women, blissed-out hippies and travellers from all over the world. Whatever you need, from a used paperback novel to a tattoo you'll find it here – along with an endless jumble of stalls selling jewellery, carvings, T-shirts, sarongs, chillums and spices. Bargain hard to get a reasonable deal as the traders are wise to unsavvy tourists and start high with their prices.

There's lots of good Indian and Western food, as well as a couple of bars, and when it all gets too much you can wander down to the beach. The best time to visit is early morning (it starts about 8am) or late afternoon (from about 4pm); the latter is good if you plan to stay on for the sunset and party at the Shore Bar (p201).

Anjuna's market can be a bit overwhelming and very hot. For something more relaxing try one of the Saturday-night markets near Baga, where the emphasis is as much on entertainment and food stalls as it is on the usual collection of handicraft, jewellery and clothing stalls. **Ingo's Night Bazaar**, on Arpora Hill, halfway between Baga and Anjuna, is well organised and has a good mix of Indian and Western stalls. **Macky's Bazaar**, on the Baga River, is a smaller Goan-run affair. Both run from around 6pm to midnight.

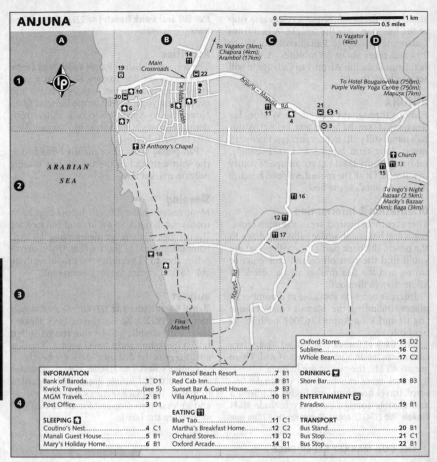

ANJUNA

INFORMATION	
Bank of Baroda................................1 D1	
Kwick Travels..............................(see 5)	
MGM Travels..................................2 B1	
Post Office......................................3 D1	

SLEEPING	
Coutino's Nest.................................4 C1	
Manali Guest House.........................5 B1	
Mary's Holiday Home.......................6 B1	
Palmasol Beach Resort......................7 B1	
Red Cab Inn....................................8 B1	
Sunset Bar & Guest House................9 B3	
Villa Anjuna..................................10 B1	

EATING	
Blue Tao.......................................11 C1	
Martha's Breakfast Home................12 C2	
Orchard Stores...............................13 D2	
Oxford Arcade...............................14 B1	
Oxford Stores................................15 D2	
Sublime..16 C2	
Whole Bean...................................17 C2	

DRINKING	
Shore Bar......................................18 B3	

ENTERTAINMENT	
Paradiso..19 B1	

TRANSPORT	
Bus Stand......................................20 B1	
Bus Stop..21 C1	
Bus Stop..22 B1	

Red Cab Inn (☎ 2274427; redcabinn@rediffmail.com; De Mello Vaddo; d Rs 400-700) It's a bit gloomy, but the split level mezzanine rooms offer top value for your rupees if travelling in a family group. Meanwhile couples wishing to start a family might find the romantic domed room studded with a galaxy of blue lights helpful!

Sunset Bar & Guesthouse (☎ 2273917; d Rs 500) The rooms here are nothing special, but the location certainly is. Well away from the noise of town and sitting right on the most relaxing of Goa's major tourist beaches, this is the perfect place for beach bums.

Mary's Holiday Home (☎ 5613118; junjim@sify .com; d Rs 600) Standing proudly on the cliffs above the sea this is an excellent and therefore frequently full backpackers hotel with help-ful management who know everyone and everything.

Palmasol Beach Resort (☎ 273258; d Rs 600) Some of the tidiest budget rooms in town with friendly owners and plenty of opportunities to kick back in a hammock.

MIDRANGE & TOP END
Villa Anjuna (☎ 2273443; www.anjunavilla.com; d Rs 650-1000;) In a prime location on the main road to the beach is this friendly hotel which has comfortable rooms arranged around a pool (open to nonguests for Rs 200). One of the better-value midrange hotels, it's often full.

Hotel Bougainvillea (☎ 273270; granpas@hotmail .com; d/ste incl breakfast & tax from Rs 1400/1800;

☒ ▣ ☒) Also known as Granpa's Inn, this could be described as a 'budget heritage hotel' and it certainly offers value for money. An old-fashioned hotel with comfortable rooms, billiard tables in the bar and hidden tables for apéritifs in the garden. Home of the Purple Valley Yoga Centre (p199).

Eating

Anjuna has some great places to eat that range from the cheap and cheerful beach shacks at the southern end (near the flea-market site) to a handful of seafood restaurants overlooking the beach, and, best of all, some refreshingly unusual places back in the village.

Whole Bean (☎ 273952; Rs 50-100) Simple, tasty health-food café that focuses on tofu-based meals.

Martha's Breakfast Home (breakfast Rs 50-120) This is a great place to start the day, with delicious pancakes, omelettes, fresh bread and various juices, served in a pleasant, shady garden or on the veranda. There are also rooms to rent.

Blue Tao (mains Rs 60-160) Organic delights emerge from the spick-and-span kitchen of a restaurant that's highly regarded by locals.

Sublime (☎ 982248405; mains Rs 150) One of the most appropriately named restaurants in Anjuna; the food in this newly opened garden restaurant is prepared by a New York–trained chef, Chris, and includes such rare finds as blue-cheese burgers.

The retail needs of the expat community are served by Oxford Stores and Orchard Stores, opposite each other back in the village, and the Oxford Arcade, closer to the beach. Here you can get everything from a loaf of bread to Vegemite and imported cheese.

Drinking & Entertainment

Shore Bar (⊙ 7.30am-midnight) Not as popular as it once was, but market day brings in the crowds and spectacular sunsets still work their magic.

Paradiso (men/women from Rs 200/free); ⊙ 10pm-4am Wed, Fri & Sat) The stunning sea views go unnoticed in this lurid temple to trance, which in season attracts all the top DJs, including old-timer Goa Gil.

Getting There & Away

There are buses every half-hour or so from Mapusa to Anjuna (Rs 6). They park at the end of the road to the beach and continue on to Vagator and Chapora. Some go up to Arambol. The two other bus stops inland from the beach are pick-up and drop-off points. Plenty of motorcycle taxis gather at the main crossroads and you can also hire scooters and motorcycles easily from here.

VAGATOR & CHAPORA

A series of rusty cliffs and headlands bursting out of thickets of greenery help to give Vagator and charming Chapora one of the prettiest settings on the north Goan coast. It's this back drop, rather than the beaches (which are largely forgettable) that have made these two little villages the centre for the wild, outdoor parties that made Goa (in)famous. Large contingents of long-stay backpackers and party people religiously set up camp here for months on end every season.

Information

There are PCO/STD/ISD places in the main street of Chapora. **Soniya Travels** (☎ 2273344; Chapora; ⊙ 9am-11pm) is a good agency for transport bookings, foreign exchange and internet access (Rs 50 per hour).

In Vagator, the **Rainbow Bookshop** (⊙ 9am-2am), opposite Primrose Café, stocks a good range of second-hand and new books and has internet access. Web access is available at several places; check out Jaws, Mira Cybercafé and Bethany Inn, all open from around 9am to midnight daily and charging Rs 50 per hour.

Sights

On the rocky headland separating Vagator from Chapora sits a ruined Portuguese **fort** dating from 1617. Its worth climbing up here

---

EL SHADDAI

Lounging around on Goa's beaches, it's easy to forget that the state shares most of India's social problems. The charitable trust **El Shaddai** (☎ 226650; www.elshaddaigoa.com; 2nd fl, St Anthony Apartments, Mapusa Clinic Rd, Mapusa) has established five homes – three in Assagao, between Vagator and Mapusa, and two in Saligao – where local children live and receive schooling. It also runs a night shelter in Panaji (Panjim).

You can visit the homes and the children daily between 4pm and 6pm. Donations of spare clothing or cash are welcome.

VAGATOR & CHAPORA

0 — 500 m
0 — 0.3 miles

A   **B**

INFORMATION
Bethany Inn..................................(see 5)
Jaws...**1** B5
Mira Cybercafé...........................(see 15)
Rainbow Bookshop.......................**2** B6
Soniya Travels............................**3** B5

SLEEPING 🏠
Bean Me Up Soya Station...............**4** B6
Bethany Inn................................**5** B6
Helinda Restaurant.......................**6** B5
Jackie's Daynite..........................**7** B6
Jolly Jolly Lester..........................**8** A5
Jolly Jolly Roma..........................**9** A6
Julie Jolly.................................**10** B6
Leoney Resort............................**11** A6
Shertor Villa.............................**12** B5

EATING 🍴
Bean Me Up Soya Station..............(see 4)
Le Bluebird..............................**13** A6
Mango Tree Bar and Café..............**14** B5
Marakesh.................................**15** A6
Marikettys...............................**16** B5
Sai Ganesh Fruit Juice Centre.........**17** B5
Sunrise Restaurant......................**18** B5

DRINKING 🍸
Paulo's Antique Bar.....................**19** B5
Tin Tin Bar & Restaurant...............**20** A5

ENTERTAINMENT 🎭
Hill Top Motels..........................**21** B6
Nine Bar.................................**22** A6
Primrose Café...........................**23** B6

TRANSPORT
Main Bus Stand..........................**24** B6

Chapora River

Harbour

Chapora
Fort

To Siolim (6km);
Arambol (13km)

5 Vagator
Beach

ARABIAN Disco
SEA Valley

19 16
18 17
6
3
Temple
12 Chapora

8 14
20
@
Vagator
9

To Mapusa
(10km)

**Little
Vagator
Beach**

22 13 11
Church
24

15 23

7

2

To Petrol
Station
(300m)
4

6

**Ozran
Beach** Spaghetti
Beach

21

To
Anjuna
(2km)

(access is easiest from the Vagator side) for the coastal views.

Sleeping

If you're planning to stay long term it's possible to find a basic room (with shared bathroom) in a private house for around Rs 50 per night; ask around at the budget hotels for recommendations.

VAGATOR

Jolly Jolly Lester (☎ 2273620; www.hoteljollygoa.com; s/d Rs 300/400, d with AC Rs 800; 🕸) Jolly nice rooms are on offer at this tongue-twisting family-run backpacker hotel. The superclean rooms come in a weird array of shapes and sizes, but demand is always heavy. The same family run the equally good and similarly priced Jolly Jolly Roma (☎ 2273001), along the path leading to Little Vagator, and the Julie Jolly (☎ 2273386), near the Primrose Café.

Jackie's Daynite (☎ 2274320; melfordsouza@hotmail .com; Ozran Beach Rd; r Rs 350, cottages Rs 650) Day and night this backpackers hotel offers consistently tidy rooms set around a small garden, promising a quiet retreat from the chaos of the beach.

Bean Me Up Soya Station (☎ 2273479; d with shared/ private bathroom Rs 450/650) Upmarket hippies will find the groovy rooms at this exceptionally well-run hotel perfectly blissful, man. It's certainly the best midrange hotel in Vagator and its acclaimed restaurant (opposite), won't disappoint either.

Bethany Inn (☎ 2273731; www.bethanyinn.com; d from Rs 600, ste with AC Rs 2000; 🕸 💻) The basic rooms aren't earth-shatteringly exciting but the swish AC rooms, in a separate daffodil-yellow building set back from the road, are pretty good. They'll happily negotiate the price on slow days. There's also a travel agency on site.

Leoney Resort (☎ 2273634; fax 2274914; Ozran Beach Rd; d/cottages Rs 1700/2500; 🕸 💻) This resort complex has less personality than a dead dab, but if dead dabs are your thing then the rooms here actually offer some of Vagator's best bang for your buck. The pool (Rs 200 nonresidents) is in tip-top shape. They don't accept charter groups or hippies – though god knows how they class who's a hippy and who isn't.

CHAPORA

Lovely Chapora is generally more popular with long-staying hardcore hippies and tranceheads than Vagator and only has a couple of official hotels, both of which are highly basic.

Helinda Restaurant (☎ 2274345; s/d from Rs 250/350) Clean and relaxed, Helinda has the best rooms in Chapora and is often full.

Shertor Villa (☎ 9822158154; d from Rs 350) Down a quiet side street, the 20 plain rooms here are presided over by a friendly guy who can normally be found over the road at the Noble Nest restaurant.

Eating

VAGATOR

The area's best eating places are situated in Vagator.

Mango Tree Bar & Café (mains Rs 70-120) The food at this flavour-of-the-month restaurant covers all corners of the culinary world and the breakfasts are quickly gaining legendary status. Has regular film screenings but be warned – some of these are near enough pornographic!

Bean Me Up Soya Station (☎ 2273479; main Rs 120-150) On the road towards the Anjuna petrol station, everyone's green and beautifully in touch with nature at this bizarrely named, but very good, vegetarian restaurant. Hosts frequent events that range from gigs to magic shows.

Marrakesh (mains Rs 120-160) Tajines, couscous and other Saharan splendours in Goa's only Moroccan restaurant.

Le Bluebird (☎ 2273695; mains Rs 150-300) Gallic culinary know-how under the palms of Goa make this one of Vagator's finest dining experiences. All the French favourites are here, even bottles of heart-warming Bordeaux.

CHAPORA

There are several small restaurants along the main street of Chapora, including **Sunrise Restaurant** (mains Rs 40-80), which does a decent breakfast and lunch and **Marikettys** (Rs 100; ☻ 6pm-2am), where a Greek expat makes kebabs that you certainly don't need to be

stumbling drunk out of a club to enjoy. A local institution is the **Sai Ganesh Fruit Juice Centre** (Rs 15-30), which could well have Goa's best juices and lassis.

Drinking & Entertainment

Vagator is the centre of Goa's dying party scene. If you're coming here expecting the massive full-moon pilgrimages that brought thousands of the faithful to Vagator's Disco Valley back in the '90s heyday then you're going to be disappointed. Since those times things have become increasingly staid, partially due to a general slump in the dance-music market but, more importantly, it's thanks to a government crackdown on the drugs scene and a ban on amplified music after 10pm. However, hardcore, mainly Israeli, fans are still partying here at more organised venues such as the legendary, open-air, Nine Bar, overlooking Little Vagator Beach, where trance and house music plays to a packed floor until 10pm. Depending on restrictions, the party then moves up to Primrose Café, towards the back of Vagator village, where music continues till 2am or 3am under a canopy of psychedelically painted trees.

Hill Top Motels is another venue with a huge garden of rainbow coloured palms that occasionally hosts outdoor parties past the 10pm music restrictions.

If incessant techno beats aren't your thing then you might get lucky at the **Tin Tin Bar & Restaurant** (☻ 9am-midnight) in Vagator, which has occasional live music and if not, then at least there's a pool table. **Paulo's Antique Bar** (☻ 8.30am-midnight) in Chapora is a tiny, brightly painted local bar with a cracking atmosphere and cold beers.

Getting There & Away

Fairly frequent buses run to both Chapora and Vagator from Mapusa (Rs 12) throughout the

GOA

INTERNATIONAL ANIMAL RESCUE

The **International Animal Rescue** (IAR; ☎ 2268328; iargoa@satyam.net.in; Madungo Vaddo, Assagoa), based near Vagator, does a sterling job tending to the army of stray cats, dogs, cows and other animals in Goa. They are involved in a state-wide sterilisation and rabies immunisation programme and also treat sick and injured animals of all descriptions. If you find a sick or injured animal or befriend a stray cat, dog or any other furry, feathered or scaly friend then take it to them so it can be properly cared for. They are in constant need of financial and physical assistance (dog walkers etc), but even just going on one of the guided tours (11am and 3.30pm) of their centre helps spread the message.

day. Many of these go via Anjuna. The bus stand is near the road junction in Chapora village. Most people hire a motorcycle to get around; inquire at hotels and restaurants.

CHAPORA TO ARAMBOL

The Chapora River, spanned by the Siolim Bridge, is a magical ribbon dividing the mainly devastated beaches of charter and techno Goa from the gorgeous greens and tropical blues of a more undisturbed Goa of old to the north.

Public buses in this region of Goa are few and far between; to fully explore it you'd be advised to rent your own transport, preferably a scooter or motorbike.

Morjim & Asvem

Crossing the bridge to Chopdem, you can head east to **Morjim Beach**, an exposed strip of empty sand with a handful of low-key beach shacks at the southern end and several places to stay at the northern end. Rare olive ridley turtles nest at the southern end of Morjim Beach from September to February, so this is a protected area, which, in theory at least, means no development and no rubbish. Morjim is one of the very few beaches where sitting on the sand doesn't attract hordes of hawkers, dogs and onlookers, but the water does suffer from a bit of river run-off pollution and cannot ever be described as crystal clear.

A short walk down the beach from Montego Bay (see below) is the **Goan Café** (☎ 2244394; anthonylobo2015@yahoo.co.uk; huts/tree houses Rs 600/1000). The three brothers who run this beachside property might well be the friendliest and most helpful hotel owners in Goa! The rooms are basic, but for sheer romance the tree houses are impossible to beat. There's also a great restaurant and they can sort out taxi and bike hire.

Montego Bay (☎ 2244222; www.montegobaygoa .com; tent/hut/cottage with AC Rs 1650/1650/3000; ✷) is for the camper who hates camping: the luxurious 'tents' found here come complete with bathrooms and are nothing like those you used at Scout camp. The huts and cottages are equally good. The restaurant, where you can relax in sunken lounge pits or a hammock, is overpriced.

For a change of scenery, the food at **Britto's** (☎ 2244245), also at the northern end of the beach, is worthy of praise.

our pick **Siolim House** (☎ 2272138; www.siolim house.com; standard/superior d incl breakfast, dinner & tax

Rs 6000/7000; ✷ ▣) is tucked away in the leafy lanes between Chapora and Morjim, and it's a truly special place to stay. Its seven large rooms are all individually designed to an exacting standard and contain more antiques than the British Museum. The service is of a calibre appropriate to such a grand old building and the pool and gardens perfectly maintained. Yes, it's expensive, but it sits near the top of the best hotels in Goa.

Mandrem

The very fact that Mandrem has been ignored for so long is probably the reason why, the moment you step out onto its sands, a tingle will roll down your spine and you'll finally feel as if you've arrived in the Goa of tourist brochure clichés. For the moment there is little to mar the green backdrop and anyone brave enough to step out of the travellers circuit is going to be handsomely rewarded with the finest beach in Goa. Of the few groups of beach shacks, the **Riva Resorts** (☎ 2247088; www.rivaresorts.com; huts/ cottages Rs 1000/1600), formerly known as Dunes, is the largest and most comfortable. It's popular with Indian tourists in the know.

On the bank of the Mandrem River, and with much more character, is the **River Cat Villa** (☎ 2247928; villarivercat@hotmail.com; d from Rs 2400), which is rammed full of sculptures and paintings and feels like an artists retreat. The rooms are beautifully maintained and many have large balconies overlooking the trees. It's one of the most interesting guesthouses north of Calangute and there's a good restaurant serving Continental dishes, too.

ARAMBOL (HARMAL)

Shoved aside by the consumer age, the hippy '60s needed somewhere to hide; San Francisco wouldn't do, Carnaby Street couldn't cope and the Marrakesh Express was suddenly cancelled in a cost-saving exercise. Eventually reaching Arambol's sickle of sand and rash of beautiful, rocky bays the '60s knew it had finally found its never-never land. Ever since then travellers, attracted by the hippy atmosphere, have been drifting up to this blissed-out corner of Goa, setting up camp and, in some cases, never leaving again. In turn, a mushrooming (probably magic) industry of low-key accommodation and facilities has sprung up to cater to these visitors, and in the high season the beach and the road leading down to it gets pretty crowded. For the moment the flower-power guys and girls hold the upper hand, but with all the beaches to the south full up, Arambol is starting to turn developers' hands sweaty with excitement and it can't be long until the sweet '60s are forced off in search of the next Kathmandu.

Information

Arambol village has dozens of travel agencies (handling foreign exchange), including Divya Travels, Pedro Travels and Tara Travels. Internet access is available from several places, such as the reliable Cyberzone, and motorbike hire and other services are also widely available. Most of this is concentrated on the road leading to the northern end of the beach. A word of warning: theft is a big problem in the high season; most of the cheaper beach shacks have minimal security and leaving bags unguarded on the beach is just asking for trouble.

Activities

From November to March it's possible to take **boat trips** to go fishing and dolphin spotting – operators will find you as you hang out on the beach. So-called extreme sports have taken

off in a big way in Arambol with plenty of people offering paragliding and kite-surfing lessons.

Courses

About 2km south of Arambol is the **Himalayan Iyengar Yoga Centre** (www.hiyogacentre.com; 5-day course Rs 1800), which runs hatha yoga courses on the beach between November and March. This is the winter centre of the Dharamsala school.

Arambol Music Academy (☎ 9326131795) offers lessons in classical Indian singing and tabla playing.

Sleeping

Priya Guest House (☎ 2292661; d with shared/private bathroom Rs 200/250) Basic and a fair hike from the action, but it's gained a devoted fan club of repeat visitors. The attached restaurant is something of a social centre.

Residensea (☎ 2292413; pkresidensea_37@hotmail .com; huts Rs 350) Large bamboo huts with shared bathrooms arranged around a simple restaurant with a perfect beachfront location.

La Muella (☎ 9822486314; d Rs 600) New Israeli-run hotel and restaurant venture with six

GOA

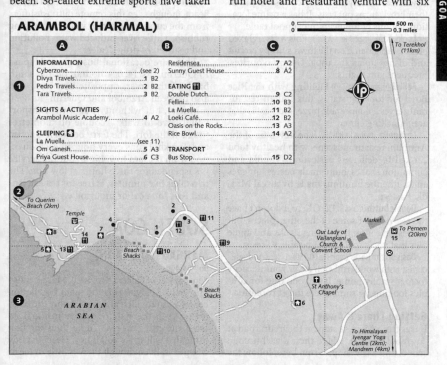

ARAMBOL (HARMAL)

0 _____ 500 m
0 _____ 0.3 miles

To Terekhol (11km)

INFORMATION
Cyberzone..............................(see 2)
Divya Travels...............................**1** B2
Pedro Travels..............................**2** B2
Tara Travels................................**3** B2

SIGHTS & ACTIVITIES
Arambol Music Academy...............**4** A2

SLEEPING
La Muella...............................(see 11)
Om Ganesh..................................**5** A3
Priya Guest House........................**6** C3

Residensea...................................**7** A2
Sunny Guest House.......................**8** A2

EATING
Double Dutch................................**9** C2
Fellini..**10** B3
La Muella....................................**11** B2
Loeki Café...................................**12** B2
Oasis on the Rocks.......................**13** A3
Rice Bowl....................................**14** A2

TRANSPORT
Bus Stop.....................................**15** D2

To Querim Beach (2km)

Temple

Market

To Pernem (20km)

Our Lady of Vailangkani Church & Convent School

Beach Shacks

St Anthony's Chapel

Beach Shacks

ARABIAN SEA

To Himalayan Iyengar Yoga Centre (2km); Mandrem (4km)

dingy rooms that are nevertheless the flavour of the month, no doubt thanks to the yoga classes held up on the roof. Rates are open to negation out of season.

The prime accommodation is the jumble of cliffside **huts** (d small/large Rs 450/600) on the next bay to the north of the main beach. Many remain very basic, but an increasing number now have private bathrooms and running water, and all have breathtaking sea views. Outside high season you can normally negotiate cheaper rates, especially for long stays. Two of the better places are the **Om Ganesh** (☎ 2297675) and **Sunny Guest House** (☎ 2297602) with the Sunny having the edge.

Eating

There's a string of shacks lining the main beach, serving seafood and beer and offering similar menus and prices. Otherwise most places to eat (and drink) are on the busy lane leading down to the beach. All are open from breakfast until around 11pm.

Rice Bowl (mains Rs 30-100) It could equally be called Noodle Bowl or in fact any other kind of bowl, because anything they choose to put in their bowls turns out tasty. It has a prime location, legions of followers and a pool table.

Loeki Café (mains Rs 40-120) This very relaxed place is a big name on the town's hippy circuit and dishes up all the usual Goan favourites. Frequent jam nights.

Fellini (mains Rs 60-150) Fighting with the Rice Bowl for top-dog status, this Italian restaurant serves a memorable pizza and pastas that aren't lacking either.

La Muella (mains Rs 80-150) The new star of the Arambol restaurant scene, with healthy food cooked to delicious perfection. Vanilla and cinnamon shakes, homemade pastas, quiches and authentic hummus made by a real Middle Eastern.

Double Dutch (mains Rs 130) OK, so it doesn't have the sea views of some of the other places, but it does have mouth-watering steaks and apple pies that you simply won't be able to resist.

Oasis on the Rocks (mains Rs 60-250) A seafood specialist with wonderful views over your dinner's former watery home. It's a good one for couples looking for somewhere to get romantic.

Getting There & Away

Buses from Mapusa stop on the main road at Arambol (Rs 12), where there's a church, a school and a few shops. From here, follow the road about 1.5km through the village to get to the main road down to the beach.

TEREKHOL (TIRACOL) FORT

How many times in your life have you woken up in a fairy-tale castle overlooking the Arabian Sea? Well at Terekhol, the northernmost outpost of Goa, you finally have that chance.

ourpick Fort Tiracol Heritage Hotel (☎ 02366-227631; nilaya@sancharnet.in; d/suite incl breakfast & dinner Rs 5500/7500) has seven stylish rooms that come with antique shields on the bedroom walls, studded doors to prevent elephant charges, a whitewashed chapel with a coat of colourful flowers and views that make you want to propose to whoever your with (so don't take your sister). Superb Goan dinners and Continental breakfasts are included in the price. Book ahead. Between 11am and 5pm nonguests can stop by for lunch or a drink.

A trip to the fort makes a good outing on a motorcycle. The winding 11.5km road from Arambol passes through villages and rice paddies and rises up to provide good views over the countryside and Terekhol River. You can also stop for a swim on near-deserted **Querim Beach**, though even this remote outpost suffers from the curse of uncaring visitors dropping rubbish, a little river-induced water pollution and a surfeit of drug dealers.

There are occasional buses from Mapusa to Querim (Rs 14, 1¾ hours), on the south bank of the river, opposite Terekhol, and also between Arambol and Querim (Rs 8, 30 minutes), but without your own transport you'll have to walk a couple of kilometres to reach the fort. The ferry between Querim and Terekhol runs every hour in each direction from 6.15am to 9.45pm, but the service is suspended for three hours at low tide. The trip takes five minutes, is free for pedestrians and Rs 4 for a car or motorbike.

SOUTH GOA

MARGAO (MADGAON)

pop 94,400

The capital of Salcete province, Margao (also known as Madgaon) is the main population centre of south Goa and is probably the busiest town in the state. If you've just arrived from the cities of 'real' India then the first thing that will strike you is how clean and tidy Margao is. Even though there is little to see or

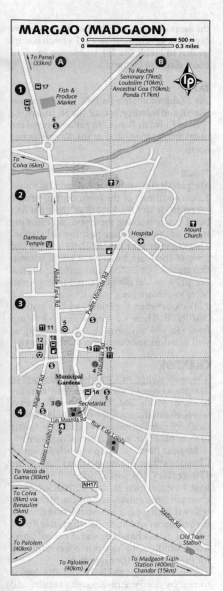

MARGAO (MADGAON)

INFORMATION
Bank of Baroda	1 A4
Centurion Bank ATM	2 A4
Cyberlink	3 A4
Goa Tourism Development Corporation (GTDC) Tourist Office	(see 9)
HDFC Bank ATM	(see 3)
Hindnet	4 A4
Main Post Office	5 A3
UTI Bank ATM	6 A1

SIGHTS & ACTIVITIES
Church of the Holy Spirit	7 A2
Covered Market	8 B4

SLEEPING
Margao Residency	9 A4

EATING
Banjara	10 A3
Café Coffee Day	11 A3
Raissa'a Herbs & Spices	12 A3
Tato	13 A3

TRANSPORT
Advance Reservation Office	14 A4
Bus Stand	15 A1
Buses to Colva, Benaulim & Palolem	16 A4
Kadamba Bus Stand	17 A1
Old Bus Stand	18 A3

turion Bank has an ATM just off Luis Miranda Rd; and UTI Bank has an ATM near the roundabout just south of the main bus stand.

Cyberlink (Caro Centre, Abade Faria Rd; per hr Rs 25; 8.30am-7pm Mon-Sat) Internet access.

GTDC tourist office (☎ 2715204; Margao Residency; 9.30am-1.15pm & 2-5.45pm Mon-Fri) At the south end of the Municipal Gardens and not very helpful.

Hindnet (Valaulikar Rd; per hr Rs 20; 8.30am-11pm) Internet access, just east of the municipal gardens.

Main post office (9am-1.30pm & 2-4pm) On the north side of the municipal gardens.

Sights

Long-term visitors will want to visit Margao for its markets – the **covered market** in the town's centre is one of the largest and most raucous in Goa, and there's a fish and produce market in a vast complex near the Kadamba bus stand. The richly decorated **Church of the Holy Spirit** is worth a look and can be positively exciting when a big service is taking place.

Sleeping

With the beaches of Colva and Benaulim less than 10km away there's no pressing reason to stay in Margao.

Margao Residency (☎ 2715528; Luis Miranda Rd; s/d Rs 550/650, d with AC Rs 780;) This GTDC hotel is

do here it's worth stopping by to see how Goa lives beyond the beaches.

Information

Visa or MasterCard cash advances are available at the Bank of Baroda. HDFC Bank has a 24-hour ATM accepting international cards on the ground floor of the Caro Centre; Cen-

GOA

centrally positioned and has large clean rooms with little balconies.

Eating

Tato (Apna Bazaar Complex, Valualikar Rd; dosas from Rs 14, mains Rs 70; ☽ Mon-Sat) This is a favourite lunch spot with workers from the nearby businesses and it also attracts many passing backpackers.

Banjara (☎ 3222000; D'Souza Chambers, Valualikar Rd; mains Rs 50-110) This dark and cool place with polar AC is Margao's best North Indian restaurant.

Café Coffee Day (Vasaith Arcade; Rs 50-150; ☽ 9am-midnight;) This snack bar–coffee shop chain is ideal for homesick Westerners, with lots of healthy (and some decidedly less healthy) goodies that are a struggle to find out in the sticks. Popular with local students.

Raissa'a Herbs & Spices (☎ 2731699; Priyadarshini Apartments, Rafael Pereira Rd; mains Rs 80-150) One of Margao's most highly regarded restaurants with an excellent selection of Chinese and Indian staples as well as some less common items such as delicious Afghani kebabs.

Getting There & Around

BUS

All local buses operate from the busy Kadamba bus stand 2km north of the town centre, but many also stop at the old bus stand opposite the municipal gardens. Catch buses to Colva, Benaulim and Palolem from Kadamba or from the bus stop on the east side of the municipal gardens.

There are hourly buses from both bus stops to Colva from around 7am to 7pm (Rs 7, 20 minutes). Some go via Benaulim. Buses to Panaji run from the Kadamba bus stand every 15 minutes (ordinary/express Rs 20/25, one hour). There are around eight buses a day direct to Palolem (Rs 30, one hour) and many others heading from either bus stand south to Karwar (Rs 65), stopping in nearby Chaudi. There are also local buses to Vasco de Gama (for the airport), Ponda, Chandor and Rachol.

Services to Mumbai (semideluxe/deluxe Rs 500/700, 14 hours), Bengaluru (Rs 450, 14 hours) and Pune (Rs 400, 10 hours) can be booked at the advance reservation office in the Secretariat Building. Long-distance government buses leave form the Kadamba bus stand. For most interstate trips it's best to use a long-distance private bus. There are private booking offices clustered near the Margao Residency on Luis Miranda Rd and costs are the same or marginally higher than the more expensive government buses. To reach Hampi go first to Hubli (Rs 75), where you can find buses direct to Hampi.

TAXI

Taxis (approximately Rs 100), autorickshaws (Rs 80) and motorcycle taxis (Rs 50, backpacks fine) to Colva or Benaulim gather around the municipal gardens and at the Kadamba bus stand.

TRAIN

Margao's train station, Madgaon, is about 1.5km southeast of the town centre; vehicle access is via the road south of the train line but if you're walking there you can cross the tracks at the footbridge past the old station. There's a **reservation hall** (☎ 2721841) on the 2nd floor of the main building, a **tourist information counter** (☎ 2702298) and retiring rooms. See p179 for details of trains running from Margao to Mumbai.

Taxis between the train and bus stations cost Rs 70. There's a prepaid taxi booth out front (Rs 150 to Colva, Rs 500 to Panaji), as well as autorickshaws and motorcycle taxis.

CHANDOR

The lush village of Chandor, 15km east of Margao, is one of the best respites from the beach in south Goa. Here, more than anywhere else in the state, the opulent lifestyle of Goa's former Portuguese overlords is visible in a couple of decaying colonial mansions.

Braganza House takes up one whole side of Chandor village square and dates back to the 17th century. It's now divided into east and west wings, which stretch outwards from a common front entrance. Ongoing restoration is slowly taking place but, wandering through the ballrooms with their Italian marble floors, Belgian glass chandeliers and carved rosewood furniture, it's hard not to feel a little sad for the lost world they represent.

The **east wing** (☎ 2784227; ☽ 10am-5pm) is owned by the Pereira-Braganza family, and includes a small family chapel containing a carefully hidden fingernail of St Francis Xavier. This side of the house shows its age much more than the other side and the old caretaker who shows you around seems almost on the point of tears when he passes through the ballroom with its sagging ceiling and damaged chandeliers. The old family photos, cheap souvenirs from friends abroad and tacky knick-knacks all add to an overall sense of melancholy.

The **west wing** (☎ 2784201; ◷ 10am-5pm) belonging to the Menezes-Braganza family has clearly had more money invested in its restoration and is crammed with beautiful furniture and a whole museum's worth of Chinese porcelain. The two large rooms behind the entrance halls contain the largest private library in Goa. The elderly and formidable Mrs Menezes-Braganza lives here alone and, once she's waved her maids aside, will act as your guide. She doesn't take nonsense gladly, but is an entertaining host who represents the last of the old Goan-Portuguese families. In general there appears to be a lack of concern about these old houses and, without urgently needed funds for their restoration, you can only wonder what will become of them once the current custodians are gone.

Both homes are open daily, but you may want to call ahead to ensure the owners will be around. There is no official entry fee, but the owners rely on contributions for maintenance and restoration – Rs 100 to 200 per house is reasonable.

A kilometre east past the church is the **Fernandes House** (☎ 2784245; ◷ 10am-5pm Mon-Sat). It's smaller and less grand than the Braganza House, but older and with an interesting history. The original Indian house here dates back more than 500 years, while the Portuguese section was tacked on by the Fernandes family in 1821. The secret basement hideaway, full of gun holes and with an escape tunnel to the river, was used by the family to flee attackers.

South of Chandor, in the village of Quepem, the immaculately renovated **Palacio do Deao** (☎ 2664029; www.palaciododeao.com; ◷ 10am-6pm Mon-Sat) has recently opened to visitors. The beautiful gardens are as much an attraction as the 200-year-old mansion. Evening meals are available with advance notice (mains Rs 250).

The best way to reach Chandor is by taxi from Margao (around Rs 150 round trip) or by motorcycle.

LOUTOLIM

Further relics of a bygone age can be found in the unhurried village of Loutolim, 10km northeast of Margao. There are a number of impressive Portuguese mansions here but the only one officially open to the public is the 250-year-old **Casa Arajao Alvarez** (admission Rs 100; ◷ 9am-6.30pm), though it lacks much of the atmosphere of the houses of Chandor. It's also possible to visit the wonderful **Figueiredo House** (☎ 2777028) if you call ahead. This house, and its sister owners, were memorably featured in William Dalrymple's brilliant book, *The Age of Kali*, where, over tea and mango juice, Mrs Donna Georgina Figueiredo gets all uppity about the 'botheration' that was the Indian 'invasion' of Goa in 1961. It's fascinating reading and a visit to this house makes for an interesting hour or so. It's also possible to stay in one of the dark rooms (doubles from Rs 2500). Anywhere else such a room would be overpriced but here the experience is worth every rupee. Traditional Goan meals are also available if you book in advance.

Also in the village, and set up purely for tourists, **Ancestral Goa** (☎ 2777034; admission Rs 20; ◷ 9am-6.30pm) is a re-creation of Goan village life under the Portuguese a century ago.

Loutolim is best visited by motorcycle or taxi (around Rs 120 round trip) from Margao.

BOGMALO & AROSSIM

Hidden between the airport and a sprawl of industry the forgotten village of Bogmalo, 4km from the airport, has a pleasant, sandy cove dominated by the ugly five-star Bogmalo Beach Resort. Aside from the beach, which is popular with Indian tourists looking for a quiet break, there isn't a great deal to do here. **Goa Diving** (☎ 2555117; www.goadiving.com) is a reputable dive school that offers PADI courses. Guided dives start at Rs 1430, courses at Rs 15,000.

Regular buses run between Bogmalo and Vasco da Gama (Rs 5), from where you can pick up buses to Margao and Panaji.

Accommodation in Bogmalo is more expensive than elsewhere in Goa.

Friendly, family-run **William's Inn** (☎ 2538004; d from Rs 900) has bright yellow rooms that are perfectly clean and represent great value for money. Auntie is certain to fuss over you.

Saritas Guest House (☎ 2538965; www.saritasguest house.com; Rs 900) has a great seaside location but it comes second best to Williams Inn.

Coconut Creek (☎ 2538090; joets@sancharnet.in; cottages incl breakfast from Rs 9500; ✕ 🖳 🖳) is a stylish resort set back from the beach in the coconut groves with modern, minimalist rooms and lots of bamboo furniture. The swimming pool is hard to resist and there's a good restaurant serving Italian and Goan cuisine. Prices drop considerably out of season.

Around the headland, beyond the eyesore petrochemical plant, is Arossim village and beach. Here you'll find the stylish **Park Hyatt Goa Resort & Spa** (☎ 2721234; www.goa.park.hyatt.com; d from US$200; ❄ ▣ ▨). The overriding feature of this sterile top-end resort is the maze of interconnecting pools. Prices vary by the day depending on availability but US$200 should be seen as a ball-park high-season figure.

The best places to eat are John Seagull, where great views come with equally great seafood or, back in the village, Claudis Corner, which is recommended by all the locals.

COLVA & BENAULIM
pop 10,200

It wasn't that long ago that Colva was nothing more than a peaceful little fishing village that attracted a handful of hippies bored of the sex, drugs and rock-and-roll lifestyle of Calangute. However, where hippies go, charter flights follow and in just the blinking of a stoned hippie's eye package tourism had changed paradise forever. Fortunately, the scale of development here is nowhere near that of Calangute – you can still see the fish being brought ashore in the morning.

Colva is popular with Indian families and a middle-aged European crowd, while Benaulim, 2km south, is still a very peaceful village with most of the accommodation in family guesthouses. It's a good place to rent long-term if you're after a relaxing Goan experience, but in both places the beaches are far from immaculate.

Bikes can be hired near the bus stand in Colva and on the beach in Benaulim. With fewer people than the northern beaches and quiet back lanes, occasional robberies do occur in Benaulim. Avoid walking from the beach alone at night.

Information

There are branches of the Bank of Baroda both in Colva (next to the church, on Colva Beach Rd) and Benaulim, near the intersection of Colva and Vasvaddo Beach Rds. You'll find several travel agencies in both Colva and Benaulim that will change cash and travellers cheques and give cash advances on Visa and MasterCard. There's a Centurion Bank ATM accepting foreign cards on the main road in Colva, near Club Margarita.

Amin Crystal Point by the main junction in Benaulim rents out bikes and scooters.
GK Tourist Centre (☎ 2771221; per hr Rs 40; ❨ 9am-10pm) In Benaulim. Internet access and money exchange.
Hello Mae Communication (Colva Beach Rd; per hr Rs 40; ❨ 8am-10pm) Internet access.
Ida Online (Colva Beach Rd; ❨ 10am-1am) Internet access. Above Baskin Robbins.
Meeting Point Travel (☎ 2788626; Colva Beach Rd; ❨ 9am-10pm) Changes cash and travellers cheques.

Activities

Water sports and dolphin tours have arrived at Colva, with **parasailing** and **jet-skiing** available in the high season for around Rs 500 per person and **dolphin tours** for around Rs 300. Just daring to pause on the beach for a second should guarantee touts approaching you with offers of tours. Be warned – we have received some serious complaints, involving intimidation, about some of the touts selling dolphin tours on the seafront.

Sleeping

It's easy to rent houses long-term in Colva, particularly if you arrive early in the season (before December), and Benaulim is probably the best place in Goa for a long-term stay – just ask around in the restaurants and shops. Most houses are a 20-minute walk from the beach.

COLVA
Budget

Joema Tourist Home (☎ 2888782; d Rs 350) One of the few guesthouses with any character, this quiet, flower-scented family home on a dusty side street has four clean, basic but superb-value rooms. The candle-lit garden café is very enjoyable. There are several similar places nearby.

Hotel Lucky Star (☎ 2788071; d Rs 400) A tightly run ship with brightly painted cottages and clean beachfront rooms make this an excellent choice. The attached restaurant (p212) is as good as the rooms.

Midrange

William's Beach Retreat (☎ 2788153; www.goa getaway.com; Colva Beach Rd; d without/with AC Rs from 1800/2500; ❄ ▨) The AC rooms look like something from a '70s porn film and, perhaps because of this, it's a popular hotel with charter groups. The pool, massage centre, restaurant and even the rooms aren't actually

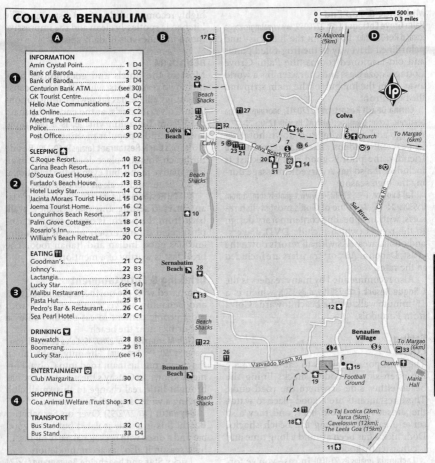

COLVA & BENAULIM

INFORMATION
Amin Crystal Point......................1 D4
Bank of Baroda............................2 D2
Bank of Baroda............................3 D4
Centurion Bank ATM..............(see 30)
GK Tourist Centre........................4 D4
Hello Mae Communications........5 C2
Ida Online....................................6 C2
Meeting Point Travel...................7 C2
Police..8 D2
Post Office...................................9 D2

SLEEPING
C.Roque Resort..........................10 B2
Carina Beach Resort..................11 D4
D'Souza Guest House.................12 D3
Furtado's Beach House...............13 B3
Hotel Lucky Star........................14 C2
Jacinta Moraes Tourist House....15 D4
Joema Tourist Home..................16 C2
Longuinhos Beach Resort..........17 B1
Palm Grove Cottages.................18 C4
Rosario's Inn..............................19 C4
William's Beach Retreat.............20 C2

EATING
Goodman's.................................21 C2
Johncy's.....................................22 B3
Lactangia...................................23 C2
Lucky Star..............................(see 14)
Malibu Restaurant.....................24 C4
Pasta Hut...................................25 B1
Pedro's Bar & Restaurant..........26 C4
Sea Pearl Hotel..........................27 C1

DRINKING
Baywatch...................................28 B3
Boomerang................................29 B1
Lucky Star..............................(see 14)

ENTERTAINMENT
Club Margarita..........................30 C2

SHOPPING
Goa Animal Welfare Trust Shop..31 C2

TRANSPORT
Bus Stand..................................32 C1
Bus Stand..................................33 D4

---

bad but it might not be quite how your travel agent described it.

Longuinhos Beach Resort (☎ 2788068; www .longuinhos.net; s/d with AC Rs 2000/2400; ✕ ⌨) At the north end of the beach, this upmarket place has tidy rooms, spot-on service and a pool.

BENAULIM

Less than 2km south of Colva, Benaulim is much more peaceful and rustic, with numerous guesthouses and small hotels spread over a wide area.

Budget

Jacinta Moraes Tourist House (☎ 2770187; d Rs 150-250) With chickens squawking about the house and garden and a bubbly woman in charge

you're guaranteed a memorable stay. The clean rooms are a bargain at twice the price.

Rosario's Inn (☎ 2770636; d from Rs 250) Rosario's, next to the football ground, is a huge, good-value backpackers inn just a couple of minutes' stroll from the beach. It lacks the character of some of the Benaulim guesthouses.

D'Souza Guest House (☎ 2770583; d Rs 400) As you'd guess from the name this traditional blue house is run by a real Goan-Portuguese family and comes with bundles of homely atmosphere, a lovely garden and three spacious, clean rooms. Book ahead.

Furtado's Beach House (☎ 2770396; d without/with AC from Rs 1000/1500; ✕) Prime beachfront location, spacious rooms set around a courtyard and not much idea about customer service.

Midrange & Top End

Palm Grove Cottages (☎ 2770059; www.palmgrovegoa
.com; d Rs 600-1200; ✳) From the hibiscus- and
palm-lined driveway to the frog-filled ponds
and old-fashioned rooms, the Palm Grove
Cottages ooze class and character. It's a world
away from the hubbub of the main strip and
the beachfront.

Carina Beach Resort (☎ 2770413; bookings@carina
beachresort.com; d without/with AC Rs 950/1250; ✳ ✳)
A large and somewhat run-down hotel set
in peaceful gardens. The management are
friendly, the pool is good and breakfast is
included. It also has Ayurvedic massage during the high season.

Taj Exotica (☎ 2771234; www.tajhotels.com; d from
US$300; ✳ ▢ ✳) One of Goa's most stylish re-
sorts, with an appealing contemporary design
to the rooms (which include DVD players)
and public areas. As with all resorts down the
coast, Dabolim Airport transfers are included
in the rates.

Also recommended by many readers is the
C Roque Resort (☎ 738199; d Rs 350), which is a
15-minute walk up the beach towards Colva
from Furtado's.

Eating

COLVA

The most popular places to eat in Colva are
the open-sided wooden shacks lining the
beach either side of where the road ends.
These restaurants are a good place to watch
the sunset with a cold beer, and they also
serve breakfast. Among the beach shacks,
Dominick's has been around a long time and
is consistently good.

Lactangia (mains Rs 50-100) In case you've forgotten where you are this place has cheap and
cheerful wholesome Indian food.

Lucky Star (mains Rs 50-200) An army of waiters
tend to your every whim as you sedately flick
through a menu of Goan specialities.

Pasta Hut (mains Rs 60-120) In front of the Hotel
Colmar, and a good spot to sit with a happy-
hour cocktail and watch the sun go down. The
Italian dishes keep all the punters happy.

Goodman's (mains Rs 65-150) Fish and chips and
north English accents are the order of the day
at this home-away-from-home restaurant for
the Brits. The big screen TV is the best place
in town to catch up with the footy. It has a
good atmosphere.

Sea Pearl Hotel (☎ 2780176; mains Rs 80-200)
Sit among a jungle of potted plants in this

highly recommended seafood restaurant. The
kitchen is spotlessly clean and the impressive
menu includes lots of daily specials.

BENAULIM

Most of the hotels and guesthouses have
their own restaurants, which is lucky because
Benaulim village has far fewer eating options
than Colva. Johncy's, at the end of the main
road from Benaulim village, is a perennial
favourite and a popular meeting place.

Pedro's Bar & Restaurant (mains Rs 60-120) Beside
the beach, this airy place doesn't believe in an
imaginative menu, but even so the traditional
Goan dishes and steak sizzlers are tasty.

Malibu Restaurant (mains Rs 90-150) With a pleasant alfresco setting, this place, a short walk
back from the beach, is one of the more sophisticated dining experiences in Benaulim
and has good Indian and Italian food. The
breakfast is worthy of a mention, too.

Drinking & Entertainment

Compared with the northern beaches, Colva
and Benaulim are very quiet at night, with
most people content to eat out and enjoy a
few drinks near the beach.

Club Margarita (☎ 2789745; Colva Beach Rd; cover
charge Rs 250; ⏱ 7pm-3am) The only nightclub in
the area is on the main road into Colva. Formerly known as Gatsby's the name change has
brought little real change to this small club
playing a wide range of dance music.

Baywatch (☎ 2772795) Over on Sernabatim
Beach, this is a little isolated but has a good
bar and a disco with occasional party nights. In
high season it also has accommodation.

Lucky Star and beachside **Boomerang** (⏱ 24
hr) are among the more popular bars.

Shopping

Goa Animal Welfare Trust Shop (☎ 2759849; www
.gawt.org; ⏱ 9.30am-12.30pm & 5-8pm Mon-Sat) On the
main junction in Benaulim village this shop,
one of the only charity shops in Goa, is run
by the deserving Goa Animal Welfare Trust,
who does a sterling job dishing out some love
to all the stray animals in south Goa.

Getting There & Away

Buses run from Colva to Margao roughly
every 15 minutes (Rs 10, 20 minutes) from
7.30am to about 7pm, departing from the
parking area at the end of the beach road.
Buses from Margao to Benaulim are also fre-

quent (Rs 6, 15 minutes); some continue south to Varca and Cavelossim. Buses stop at the crossroads known as Maria Hall.

BENAULIM TO PALOLEM

Immediately south of Benaulim are the up-market beach resorts of **Varca** and **Cavelossim**. Boasting an uninterrupted, 10km strip of pristine sand, this is where you'll find a cluster of five-star resorts, all luxurious, self-contained bubbles with pools, extensive private grounds and practically every whim catered for. One of the best is the **Leela Goa** (☎ 2871234; www.ghmhotels.com; d from US$200; ✶ ▢ ▣) at Mobor, 3km south of Cavelossim. Some of the rooms go up to a not very cheap US$3600 per night, but then again if it was good enough for Bill Clinton, it's good enough for you.

On the unlikely chance that you're not a former US President then don't fret – it's still possible to access the beaches, and the coastal road makes a more interesting and enjoyable route towards Palolem than the faster National Hwy. To cross the Sal River estuary, take the ferry from Cavelossim to Assolna – turn left at the sign saying 'Village Panchayat Cavelossim' before you get to Mobor, then continue on for 2km to the river. From there you can ride on to the fishing village of **Betul**.

The road from Betul to Agonda winds over hills and is a little rough in places. You can detour to the old Portuguese fort of **Cabo da Rama**, which has a small church within the fort walls, stupendous views and several old buildings rapidly becoming one with the trees.

Back on the main road there's a turn-off to **Agonda**, a small village with an empty beach that might well be the gem of south Goa. This clean and uncluttered beach actually lives up to expectations and is an idyllic retreat for travellers wanting to escape the tourist resorts. Heading south along the beach road you'll find **Dersy Beach Resort** (☎ 2647503; huts Rs 200, d Rs 300-800), which has spotless doubles, control-freak management and a highly popular restaurant.

Dunhill Resort (☎ 2647328; d Rs 400) has 12 tatty rooms with private bathrooms in which you almost have to stand in the toilet to use the shower. There's also a shady bar and restaurant.

Sunset Bar (☎ 2647381; r Rs 600), at the southern end of the beach, has a spectacular setting on a pile of granite boulders that would be the envy of any five-star resort. The rooms though

are far from five-star and the atmosphere is a little strange.

At the even quieter north end of the beach, **Forget Me Not** (☎ 2647611; cottages Rs 500, r with private bathroom Rs 1500) has a mixture of cheap bamboo huts and a whitewashed mud-brick house.

Another recommended spot is **Madhu Hotel** (☎ 9423813442; r Rs 800), close to the church. It has 10 seasonal huts with bathrooms.

PALOLEM & AROUND

Palolem is the most southerly of Goa's developed beaches and was once the state's most idyllic. Nowadays its beauty is very much dependent on your point of view. For those who believe a beach cannot be paradise without a decent selection of cheap restaurants and hotels, a dose of nightlife and plenty of like-minded people then Palolem is still top of the pops. For those who prefer their paradise to be a little less claustrophobic then Palolem will make you feel queasy. Whatever your opinion one indisputable fact is that Palolem is far from undiscovered – the sheer number of ramshackle camps protruding out of what was once almost pristine jungle has turned Palolem into a kind of tropical Glastonbury – with all the associated good and bad points. In September 2006 the government destroyed all unlicensed businesses and buildings and, for a short time afterwards, Palolem was very much down in the dumps. However it hasn't taken long for the village to get back on its feet and Palolem is once again back in the driving seat and sitting pretty at number one. The following listings feature hotels and restaurants that were fully licensed and unaffected by the bulldozers, but be warned that the situation may change and it is advisable to check ahead.

If Palolem is all too much for you then further north, and reachable by boat, is pretty **Butterfly Beach**, while around the southern headland is a small, rocky cove called **Colomb Bay**, with a couple of basic places to stay, and beyond that is another fine stretch of sand, **Patnem Beach**, with a handful of beach huts and something approaching surf.

Information

Motorcycle hire and foreign exchange is available through several travel agencies, including **Rainbow Travel** (☎ 2643912; ☼ 9am-11pm). **Bliss Travels** (☎ 2643456; ☼ 9am-midnight), near the main entrance to the beach, is a good travel agent with internet access at Rs 40 per hour.

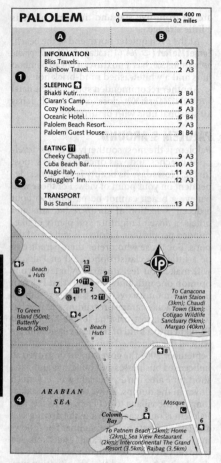

PALOLEM

0 —————— 400 m
0 —————— 0.2 miles

INFORMATION
Bliss Travels...1 A3
Rainbow Travel.....................................2 A3

SLEEPING
Bhakti Kutir...3 B4
Ciaran's Camp.......................................4 A3
Cozy Nook..5 A3
Oceanic Hotel.......................................6 B4
Palolem Beach Resort.........................7 A3
Palolem Guest House..........................8 B4

EATING
Cheeky Chapati....................................9 A3
Cuba Beach Bar.................................10 A3
Magic Italy..11 A3
Smugglers' Inn...................................12 A3

TRANSPORT
Bus Stand...13 A3

Beach Huts

To Green Island (50m); Butterfly Beach (2km)

To Canacona Train Staion (3km); Chaudi Town (3km); Cotigao Wildlife Sanctuary (9km); Margao (40km)

Beach Huts

ARABIAN SEA

Mosque

Colomb Bay

To Patnem Beach (2km); Home (2km); Sea View Restaurant (2km); Intercontinental The Grand Resort (3.5km); Rajbag (3.5km)

Sights & Activities

About 9km southeast of Palolem, and a good day trip, is the rewarding **Cotigao Wildlife Sanctuary** (☎ 2229701; admission/camera/video camera Rs 5/25/100; ☉ 7am-5.30pm). If you go there expecting to see some of its larger inhabitants (including gaurs, sambars, leopards and spotted deer) then you're going to leave empty handed. Instead keep your eyes peeled for the smaller creatures – frogs, snakes, insects, and birds are all easy to see. Early morning is the best time to visit. **Cottages** (d Rs 250/500) are available at the park entrance.

Boat tours to see dolphins or to visit tiny Butterfly Beach are easy to arrange through most travel agents and hotels – a one-hour trip costs around Rs 150 per person. Three-hour **mountain bike tours** (Rs 300) out to Patnem and Rajbag run on demand; ask at Ciaran's Camp (below).

Sleeping

Prior to the bulldozing, the edge of the beach at Palolem was thick with palm-thatch or bamboo huts grouped together in about 30 little 'villages'. Prices for the most basic huts cost from Rs 100 a double (Rs 150 in peak season), rising to Rs 150 or even Rs 300 for the swankier ones. Whether all of these will return is anyone's guess – most likely they will but in reduced numbers and with higher prices. The following are all places that remain standing.

Cozy Nook (☎ 2643550; huts & tree houses Rs 500-1500) Superbly located blue-and-white huts at the northern end of the beach near the river mouth. Prices vary widely depending on room type, of which there are many kinds. We have received a few reports of indifferent service.

Palolem Beach Resort (☎ 2643054; yogishwer@ sancharnet.com; tents Rs 350, d Rs 700) Just a little drunken stumble from the bars and restaurants, this complex is a good one if you want to be in the thick of it all. The large rooms are better than most and the pleasant gardens offer plenty of quiet, shady patches.

Palolem Guest House (☎ 2644880; palolemguest house@hotmail.com; d from Rs 600) If flimsy beach huts aren't for you then this place, five minutes' walk from the beach, offers tidy, tiled rooms with luxuries such as solid brick walls and glass windows! The owners are friendly and there's a good in-house restaurant.

Home (☎ 2643916; home.patnem@yahoo.com; d Rs 1000) This European-run hotel has sparkling white rooms with nice little terraces, and a perfect location on mellow Patnem beach. The atmosphere is very laid-back and friendly.

our pick Bhakti Kutir (☎ 2643472; www.bhaktikutir .com; huts Rs 2000, stone house Rs 2500; ☒) Ensconced in a coconut grove between Palolem and Patnem Beaches and surrounded by a thousand luminous birds, butterflies and flowers, the well-equipped jungle huts here offer something truly different. Refreshingly, almost all waste products are recycled and there are frequent dance, massage and yoga courses. The predominantly vegetarian restaurant is excellent.

Ciaran's Camp (☎ 2643477; johnciaran@hotmail.com; huts Rs 2500) By far the best of the beachside options, with a handful of luxurious, clean and airy huts set in nicely landscaped grounds.

Oceanic Hotel (☎ 2643059; www.hotel-oceanic.com; d standard/deluxe Rs 2000/3500; 🌊) On the road to Patnem Beach, this British-run hotel is in a class above most other places. The rooms, which are full of little luxurious extras, are so sparkling you'll need to put sunglasses on and the pool, oh boy, the pool...

Intercontinental The Grand Resort (☎ 2644777; goaresv@thegrandhotels.net; d incl breakfast from Rs 20,000; 🌊 🖥 🌊) A little further down the coast at Rajbag is Goa's largest resort. This highly desirable hotel is something of a Goan prince's palace – and it even comes with its very own golf course. Nonguests can use the pool for Rs 500 per day.

Eating & Drinking

Apart from the shacks on its beach, Palolem has plenty to offer in the way of restaurants and bars.

Cheeky Chapati (mains Rs 100-200) Has good seafood and a few less-common species such as blue cheese and broccoli quiche. One of the towns better music collections.

Seaview Restaurant (mains Rs 100-200) Located on Patnem Beach, this Canadian-run place receives warm reports and its king prawns are considered worthy of royalty.

Magic Italy (mains Rs 120-160; 🕔 5pm-midnight) Run by an Italian couple, this is one of the best places for authentic wood-fired pizzas and pasta in Goa. There's free filtered water, wine by the glass and candle-lit tables.

Smugglers' Inn (mains Rs 120-200) With full English breakfasts, sausage and mash, and beef and ale pies that could be straight from Yorkshire, this is an unashamedly British place and after weeks of sloppy curries elsewhere in India, few people can resist. The bar area is comfy and there's a nook where you can watch all the latest DVDs and big football matches.

Cuba Beach Bar (mains Rs 100-300) It's not on the beach, nor is it in Cuba, but it's certainly the moment's drinking hole of choice. The food isn't bad either.

Getting There & Away

There are hourly buses to Margao (Rs 25, one hour) from the bus stand on the main road down to the beach. There are also regular buses to Chaudi (Rs 5), the nearest town, from where you can get frequent buses to Margao or south to Karwar and Mangalore. The closest train station is Canacona.

CENTRAL GOA

PONDA & AROUND

The busy inland town of Ponda, 29km southeast of Panaji, is home to a number of unique Hindu temples and several spice plantations that make for an interesting day out.

The Hindu temples were rebuilt from originals destroyed by the Portuguese and their lamp towers are a distinctive Goan feature. The Shiva temple of **Shri Manguesh** at Priol-Ponda Taluka, 5km northwest of Ponda, is one of the best. This tiny 18th-century hilltop temple, with its white tower, is a local landmark. Close by is **Shri Mahalsa**, a Vishnu temple.

Among the other temples, the most architecturally interesting is the **Shri Shantadurga Temple**, 1km southwest of the town centre. Dedicated to Shantadurga, the goddess of peace, this temple sports an unusual, almost pagoda-like structure with a roof made from long slabs of stone.

One of the best spice plantations to visit is the **Tropical Spice Farm** (☎ 2340329; admission Rs 300; 🕤 9am-5pm) You'll be taken on an informative and entertaining 45-minute tour of the spice plantation, learning, among other things, how to pollinate vanilla and how to burn your taste buds out with the world's hottest chillies! An excellent buffet lunch is included in the price and elephant rides are available. The farm is about 6km northeast of Ponda and a taxi/rickshaw will cost Rs 250/170 with waiting time. The **Sahakari Spice Farm**, (☎ 2312394; www.sahakarifarms.com; 🕗 8am-6pm) is closer to Ponda and offers an almost identical tour.

There are regular buses to Ponda from Panaji (Rs 15, 45 minutes), but to visit the temples and a spice plantation you're better off with your own transport.

BONDLA WILDLIFE SANCTUARY

In the foothills of the Western Ghats, 52km from Panaji, lies **Bondla** (admission Rs 5, motorcycle/car Rs 10/50, camera/video Rs 25/100; 🕤 9am-5pm Fri-Wed), the smallest of the Goan wildlife sanctuaries (8 sq km) and the easiest to reach.

For the benefit of tourists expecting to see some animals, there's a botanical garden and a zoo. Large wild fauna includes gaurs and sambars, but you'll have more luck spotting the little, but no less impressive creatures.

GOA

GREEN GOA

Increased tourism, overuse of water, and mining are all posing a threat to the environment in Goa – you can do your bit by conserving water when showering and frequenting the few restaurants that have installed water filters. Mining and water overuse aside, for many tourists the biggest and most obvious environmental problem concerns litter and the general lack of care that Goa's most prized possession – its beaches – receive. Come in the low season or even in the early and late high season and at a few beaches you will find an astonishing level of rubbish strewn across the sands. It seems very strange that a state so dependent on its beaches hasn't taken any real efforts to keep their most precious assets in tip-top condition. True, during the high season the major beaches are given a daily sweep, but this is only for a few weeks of the year. As a visitor, you can and should do your part to help keep the beaches clean (you might even help to change attitudes) by visibly picking up the rubbish (preferably in sight of the culprit) and taking it away with you to dispose of properly. It also doesn't hurt to complain to your hotel about the rubbish levels and suggest that if the local government won't do anything then the tourist industry itself needs to come together and take action to clean the beaches. After all, it would only need a tiny increase in accommodation and restaurant bills to generate enough money to pay for a small army of dedicated year-round beach cleaners.

The **Goa Foundation** (☎ 2263306; www.goacom.com/goafoundation) in Mapusa is the state's main environmental pressure group and has been responsible for a number of conservation projects since its inauguration in 1986. It also produces numerous conservation publications, such as the excellent *Fish Curry & Rice,* which is available from the Other India Bookstore (p190) in Mapusa, other Goan bookshops and on the website.

There's **chalet accommodation** (☎ 2229701; dm/s/d Rs 75/250/350) at the park entrance.

Getting to Bondla is easiest if you have your own transport. By public transport there are buses from Ponda to Usgao village (Rs 5), from where you'll need to take a taxi (Rs 150) the remaining 5km to the park entrance.

MOLEM & BHAGWAN MAHAVIR WILDLIFE SANCTUARY

The forlorn village of Molem is the gateway to the much more rewarding Bhagwan Mahavir Wildlife Sanctuary. The largest of Goa's protected wildlife areas covers 240 sq km, incorporating the 107-sq-km Molem National Park; there's an observation platform a few kilometres into the park from where you may catch a glimpse of animals such as jungle cats, deer and Malayan giant squirrels. Accommodation is available at Molem in the

GTDC **Dhudhsagar Resort** (☎ 2612238; dm Rs 100, d without/with AC Rs 450/600; ⊠).

The sanctuary is east of Panaji (54km from Margao), with its main entrance on NH4A. To reach it by public transport, take any bus to Ponda, then change to a bus to Belgaum or Londa, getting off in Molem.

DUDHSAGAR FALLS

On the eastern border with Karnataka, Dudhsagar Falls (603m) are Goa's most impressive waterfalls – and the second highest in India. However, reaching them is expensive and time-consuming, and they are really only at their best during the monsoon – when they're inaccessible – and immediately after. To get here take an infrequent local train or taxi to Colem station, then a jeep for Rs 1800 (up to five people). The simpler option is to go on a full-day tour from Panaji (p181) or Calangute (p195).

Karnataka

If you're looking for variety in your Indian travel experience, Karnataka fits the bill nicely. The state's capital and international entry point is the IT powerhouse of Bengaluru (Bangalore), a modern, energetic city best savoured for its restaurants and shops. Ancient architectural gems are abundant, including the World Heritage–listed monuments of Hampi and Pattadakal. Practically untouched beaches and devout temple towns dot Karnataka's quiet tropical coast, while in the cool highlands of Kodagu (Coog) you can trek between lush coffee and spice plantations along paths trampled by migrating elephants.

Bedecked in dazzling finery, elephants are also the stars of the show in Mysore's justly famous Dussarah celebrations. The royal city is the jewel in Karnataka's crown, home to a spectacular palace and an atmospheric fresh produce and spice market, as well an internationally renowned centre for yoga. Nearby are superbly crafted Hoysala temples dating from the 12th century and enormous Jain sculptures of Gomateshvara, not to mention the wildlife havens of Bandipur and Nagarhole National Parks, both part of the Nilgiri Biosphere Reserve and home to elusive tigers.

The best time for touring is October to March, when the monsoon ceases lashing the coast and baking temperatures ease in far-northern interior towns such as Bijapur, with its beautiful South Indian Islamic architecture. And although the only thing that Karnataka lacks is snow-covered mountains, you'd still be wise to pack some warm clothes to beat off the winter chill in Bengaluru.

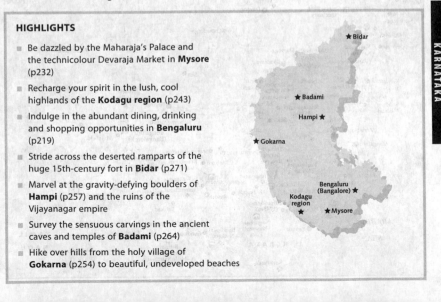

HIGHLIGHTS

- Be dazzled by the Maharaja's Palace and the technicolour Devaraja Market in **Mysore** (p232)
- Recharge your spirit in the lush, cool highlands of the **Kodagu region** (p243)
- Indulge in the abundant dining, drinking and shopping opportunities in **Bengaluru** (p219)
- Stride across the deserted ramparts of the huge 15th-century fort in **Bidar** (p271)
- Marvel at the gravity-defying boulders of **Hampi** (p257) and the ruins of the Vijayanagar empire
- Survey the sensuous carvings in the ancient caves and temples of **Badami** (p264)
- Hike over hills from the holy village of **Gokarna** (p254) to beautiful, undeveloped beaches

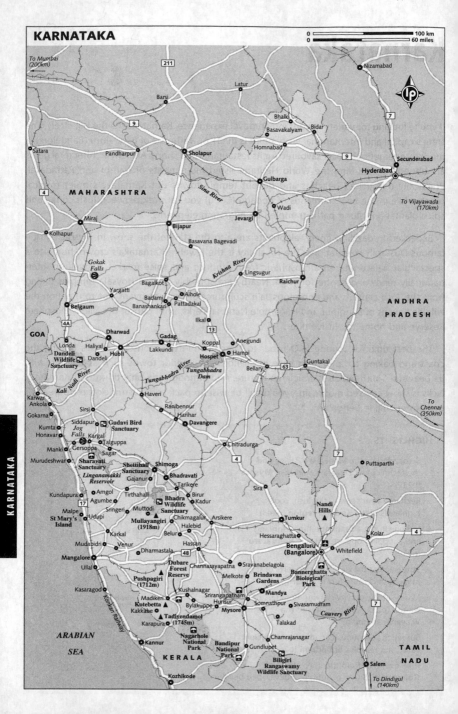

KARNATAKA

0 — 100 km
0 — 60 miles

KARNATAKA

To Mumbai
(200km)

To Vijayawada
(170km)

To Chennai
(350km)

To Dindigul
(140km)

Nizamabad

Barsi

Latur

Bhalki

Basavakalyam
Bidar

Homnabad

Sholapur

Gulbarga

Secunderabad

Hyderabad

Satara

Pandharpur

MAHARASHTRA

Sina River

Wadi

Jevargi

Miraj

Bijapur

Kolhapur

Basavana Bagevadi

Gokak
Falls

Krishna River

Lingsugur

Raichur

Bagalkot

Yargatti

Badami
Aihole

Banashankari
Pattadakal

ANDHRA
PRADESH

Belgaum

Ilkal

GOA

Dharwad

Gadag

Koppal
Anegundi

Londa
Haliyal

Hubli
Lakkundi

Hospet
Hampi

4A

Guntakal

Dandeli
Wildlife
Sanctuary

Dandeli

Bellary

Kali Nadi River

Tungabhadra River

Tungabhadra
Dam

Karwar
Ankola

Haveri

Gokarna

Ranibennur
Harihar

Kumta

Sirsi

Davangere

Honavar

Siddapur

Gudavi Bird
Sanctuary

Jog
Falls

Kargal

Manki

Talguppa

Chitradurga

Puttaparthi

Murudeshwar

Gersoppa

Sagar

Shimoga

Sharavati
Sanctuary

Shettihalli
Sanctuary

Linganamakki
Reservoir

Gajanur

Bhadravati

Sira

Kundapura

Amgol

Tirthahalli

Tarikere

Agumbe

Birur

Nandi
Hills

Malpe

Sringeri

Muttodi

Bhadra
Wildlife
Sanctuary

Kadur

St Mary's
Island

Udupi

Mullayangiri
(1918m)

Chikmagalur

Arsikere

Tumkur

Kolar

Karkal

Beluru

Halebid

Hessaraghatta

Mudabidri

Venur

Dharmastala

Hassan

Bengaluru
(Bangalore)

Whitefield

Mangalore

48

Channarayapatna

Sravanabelagola

Ullal

Dubare
Forest
Reserve

Melkote

Brindavan
Gardens

Bannerghatta
Biological
Park

Pushpagiri
(1712m)

Kushalnagar

Srirangapatnam

Mandya

Kasaragod

Madikeri

Kotebetta

Bylakuppe

Hunsur

Somnathpur

Sivasamudram

Kakkabe

Mysore

Talakad

Karapura

Tadiyendamol
(1745m)

Cauvery River

Kannur

Chamrajanagar

ARABIAN
SEA

Nagarhole
National
Park

Bandipur
National
Park

Gundlupet

TAMIL
NADU

Konkan Railway

Biligiri
Rangaswamy
Wildlife
Sanctuary

Salem

KERALA

Kozhikode

History

Religions, cultures and kingdoms galore have sashayed through Karnataka, from India's first great emperor, Chandragupta Maurya, who in the 3rd century BC retreated to Sravanabelagola after embracing Jainism, to Tipu Sultan who stood up against the encroaching British empire.

In the 6th century the Chalukyas built some of the earliest Hindu temples near Badami. Dynasties such as the Cholas and Gangas played important roles in the region's history, but it was the Hoysalas (11th to 14th centuries), who have left a lasting mark with their architecturally stunning temples at Somnathpur, Halebid and Belur.

In 1327, Mohammed Tughlaq's Muslim army sacked the Hoysala capital at Halebid, but in 1346 the Hindu empire of Vijayanagar annexed it. This dynasty, with its capital at Hampi, peaked in the early 1550s, then fell in 1565 to the Deccan sultanates. Bijapur then became the prime city of the region.

With Vijayanagar's demise, the Hindu Wodeyars (former rulers of Mysore state) quickly grew in stature. With their capital at Srirangapatnam, they extended their rule over a large part of southern India. Their power remained largely unchallenged until 1761 when Hyder Ali (one of their generals) deposed them. The French helped Hyder Ali and his son, Tipu Sultan, to consolidate their rule in return for support in fighting the British. However, in 1799, the British defeated Tipu Sultan, annexed part of his kingdom and put the Wodeyars back on Mysore's throne. This was the real kick off for British territorial expansion in southern India.

The Wodeyars ruled Mysore until Independence. They were enlightened rulers, and the maharaja became the first governor of the post-Independence state. The state boundaries were redrawn along linguistic lines in 1956 and thus the extended Kannada-speaking state of Mysore was born. This was renamed Karnataka in 1972, with Bangalore (now Bengaluru) as the capital. About 66% of the state's population speak Kannada as the main language; other significant languages are Urdu (10%) and Telugu (7.4%).

Information

The website of Karnataka Tourism (www.karnatakatourism.org) is generally more useful than the government tourist information centres around the state.

FAST FACTS

- Population: 52.7 million
- Area: 191,791 sq km
- Capital: Bengaluru (Bangalore)
- Main languages: Kannada, Urdu and Telugu
- When to go: October to March

If you're planning a visit to one of the state's several wildlife parks and reserves, it's worth contacting **Jungle Lodges & Resorts Ltd** (Map p223; ☎ 080-25597021; www.junglelodges.com; 2nd fl, Shrungar Shopping Complex, MG Rd, Bengaluru; ☑ 10am-5.30pm), who organise safari and accommodation packages for Nagarhole and Bandipur National Parks, and several other reserves.

ACCOMMODATION

In Karnataka luxury tax is 4% on rooms costing Rs 151 to 400, 8% on those between Rs 401 and 1000, and 12% on anything over Rs 1000. Some midrange and top-end hotels may add a further service charge. Rates quoted in this chapter do not include taxes unless otherwise indicated.

SOUTHERN KARNATAKA

BENGALURU (BANGALORE)

☎ 080 / pop 5.7 million / elev 920m

Rebranded Bengaluru in November 2006, the city more commonly known as Bangalore is not an obvious charmer. The crazy traffic, associated pollution and creaking infrastructure of this IT boom town will fast drive you demented. However, even though locals rarely sing Bengaluru's praises as a tourist destination, it's not a dead loss. There are a handful of interesting sights, the climate is benevolent, the city's reputation for green spaces is well deserved, and the youthful energy and imagination (not to mention disposable income) of the ITocracy fuels a progressive dining, drinking and shopping scene – one of the best in India, in fact.

History

Legend has it that Bengaluru (meaning 'Town of Boiled Beans') got its name after an old woman served cooked pulses to a lost and hungry Hoysala king. In 1537 the feudal lord

FESTIVALS IN KARNATAKA

Udupi Paryaya (17 Jan; Udupi, p253) Held in even-numbered years, much procession and ritual marks the handover of swamis at the town's Krishna Temple.

Classical Dance Festival (Jan; Pattadakal, p267) Has some of India's best classical dance, without the crowds of Vasantahabba.

Tibetan New Year (Jan/Feb; Bylekuppe, p245) Lamas in the Tibetan refugee settlements, near Kushalnagar, take shifts leading the nonstop *pujas* (prayers) that span the week of Tibetan New Year celebrations, which also include special dances and a fire ceremony.

Vasantahabba (Feb; Nrityagram dance village, p232) The dance village of Nrityagram hosts this free festival featuring traditional and contemporary Indian dance and music.

Shivaratri Festival (Feb/Mar; Gokarna, p254) Two gargantuan chariots barrel down Gokarna's main street on 'Shiva power' as bananas are tossed at them for luck.

Muharram (Feb/Mar; Hospet, p263)This Shi'ia Muslim festival features fire walkers to the accompaniment of mass hoopla.

Vairamudi Festival (Mar/Apr; Melkote, p241) Lord Vishnu is adorned with jewels at Cheluvanarayana Temple, including a diamond-studded crown belonging to Mysore's former maharajas.

Karaga (Apr; Bengaluru, p219) Nine-day festival honouring the goddess Draupadi held at Dharmaraya Swamy Temple in Bengaluru (Bangalore). The highlight is a colourful procession led by a cross-dressed priest and accompanied by half-naked swordsmen.

Ganesh Chaturthi (Aug/Sep; Gokarna, p254) Families quietly march their Ganeshes to the sea at sunset.

Dussehra (Sep/Oct; Mysore, p235) One of India's great Dussehra festivals.

Kadalekayi Parishe (Nov; Bengaluru, p219) Groundnut farmers come from all over the region to the Bull Temple, seeking blessings for their harvests.

Vijaya Utsav (Nov; Hampi, p257) Traditional music and dance re-creates Vijayanagar's glory among Hampi's temples and boulders.

Manjunatheshwara (Nov; Dharmastala, p253) The Jain pilgrimage town has a lively festival season beginning with Diwali and including this three-day event.

Huthri (Nov/Dec; Madikeri, p244) The Kodavas celebrate the start of the season's rice harvests with ceremony, music, traditional dances and much feasting for a week, beginning on a full-moon night.

Laksha Deepotsava (Nov/Dec; Dharmastala, p253) Lakhs of lanterns light up this pilgrimage town in a fitting climax to its festival season.

Kempegowda built a mud fort here, but it remained something of a backwater until 1759, when the city was gifted to Hyder Ali by the Mysore maharaja.

In 1809 the British Cantonment was established, and in 1831 the British moved their regional administrative base from Srirangapatnam to Bengaluru, renaming the city Bangalore in the process. Winston Churchill enjoyed life as a junior officer here, famously leaving a debt (still on the books) of Rs 13 at the Bangalore Club.

Bengaluru's reputation as a science and technology centre was established early in the 20th century; in 1905 it became the first city in India to have electric street lights. Since the 1940s it has been home to Hindustan Aeronautics Ltd (HAL), India's first aircraft manufacturing company. Today the city is best known as a hub for software and electronics development, and business process outsourcing.

Bengaluru's prosperity is changing the city in more ways than just its name. A new international airport is under construction and a new city centre is rising in a clutch of skyscrapers on the old United Breweries site at the Cubbon Park end of Vittal Mallya Rd (Grant Rd).

Orientation

Bengaluru is vast, but the two central areas of particular interest to travellers are Gandhi Nagar (the old part of town) and Mahatma Gandhi (MG) Rd (the heart of British-era Bangalore).

The Central bus stand and the City train station are on the edge of Gandhi Nagar. The crowded streets in this lively, gritty area – known locally as Majestic – teem with shops, cinemas and budget hotels. The Krishnarajendra (City) Market is here and a few remaining historical relics are to the south, including Lalbagh Botanical Gardens.

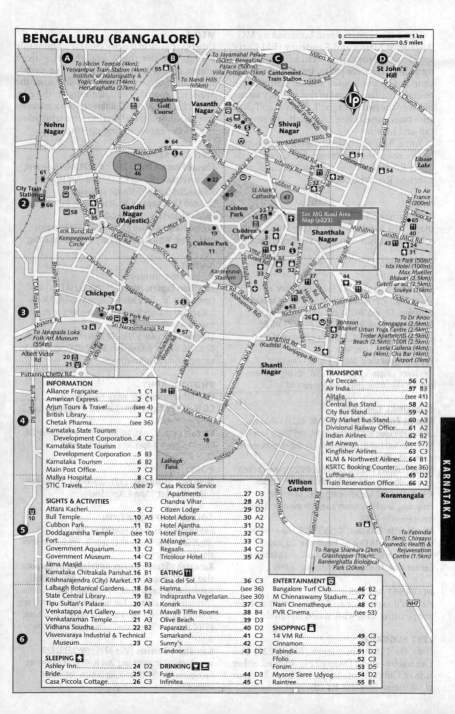

BENGALURU (BANGALORE)

INFORMATION
Alliance Française	1 C1
American Express	2 C1
Arjun Tours & Travel	(see 4)
British Library	3 C2
Chetak Pharma	(see 36)
Karnataka State Tourism Development Corporation	4 C2
Karnataka State Tourism Development Corporation	5 B3
Karnataka Tourism	6 C2
Main Post Office	7 C2
Mallya Hospital	8 C3
STIC Travels	(see 2)

SIGHTS & ACTIVITIES
Attara Kacheri	9 C2
Bull Temple	10 A5
Cubbon Park	11 B2
Doddaganesha Temple	(see 10)
Fort	12 A3
Government Aquarium	13 C2
Government Museum	14 C2
Jama Masjid	15 B3
Karnataka Chitrakala Parishat	16 B1
Krishnarajendra (City) Market	17 A3
Lalbagh Botanical Gardens	18 B4
State Central Library	19 B2
Tipu Sultan's Palace	20 A3
Venkatappa Art Gallery	(see 14)
Venkataraman Temple	21 A3
Vidhana Soudha	22 B2
Visvesvaraya Industrial & Technical Museum	23 C2

SLEEPING
Ashley Inn	24 D2
Bride	25 C3
Casa Piccola Cottage	26 C3
Casa Piccola Service Apartments	27 D3
Chandra Vihar	28 A3
Citizen Lodge	29 D2
Hotel Adora	30 A2
Hotel Ajanta	31 D2
Hotel Empire	32 C2
Mélange	33 C2
Regaalis	34 C2
Tricolour Hotel	35 A2

EATING
Casa del Sol	36 C3
Harima	(see 36)
Indraprastha Vegetarian	(see 30)
Konark	37 C3
Mavalli Tiffin Rooms	38 B4
Olive Beach	39 D3
Paparazzi	40 D2
Samarkand	41 C2
Sunny's	42 C2
Tandoor	43 D2

DRINKING
Fuga	44 D3
Infinitea	45 C1

ENTERTAINMENT
Bangalore Turf Club	46 B2
M Chinnaswamy Stadium	47 C2
Nani Cinematheque	48 C1
PVR Cinema	(see 53)

SHOPPING
14 VM Rd	49 C3
Cinnamon	50 C2
Fabindia	51 D2
Ffolio	52 C3
Forum	53 D5
Mysore Saree Udyog	54 D2
Raintree	55 B1

TRANSPORT
Air Deccan	56 C1
Air India	57 B3
Alitalia	(see 41)
Central Bus Stand	58 A2
City Bus Stand	59 A2
City Market Bus Stand	60 A3
Divisional Railway Office	61 A2
Indian Airlines	62 B2
Jet Airways	(see 57)
Kingfisher Airlines	63 C3
KLM & Northwest Airlines	64 B1
KSRTC Booking Counter	(see 36)
Lufthansa	65 D2
Train Reservation Office	66 A2

KARNATAKA

Some 4km east, the area bounded by MG, Brigade, St Mark's and Residency (FM Cariappa) Rds is Bengaluru's retail and entertainment hub. Here are parks, tree-lined streets, churches, grand houses and the army compounds that are integral to this military town. Between the two areas you'll find the golf club and racecourse, close to which are several top-end hotels.

Some Bengaluru streets are known better by the roads they intersect; 3rd Cross, Residency Rd, for example, refers to the third cross street on Residency Rd.

MAPS

The tourist offices (right) give out decent city maps. The excellent *Eicher City Atlas* is also sold at Bengaluru's many bookshops (below).

Information

BOOKSHOPS

Crossword (Map p223; ACR Tower, Residency Rd; 10.30am-9pm Mon-Sat) Great selection of books, magazines, CDs and DVDs in modern surroundings.

Gangarams Book Bureau (Map p223; 72 MG Rd; 10am-8pm Mon-Sat) A mighty collection of books, plus stationery and postcards.

Premier Bookshop (Map p223; 46/1 Church St; 10am-1.30pm & 3-8pm Mon-Sat) It's tiny but somehow has everything; enter from Museum Rd.

CULTURAL CENTRES

Alliance Française (Map p221; ☎ 41231340; www.allfranceblr.com; 108 Thimmaiah Rd; 10am-1pm & 3-6pm Mon-Sat) French cultural hub offering courses, events, a café and a library.

British Library (Map p221; ☎ 22489220; www.britishcouncilonline.org; 23 Kasturba Rd Cross; 10.30am-6.30pm Mon-Sat) English newspapers, books and magazines, and free internet access for members (annual membership Rs 1000).

Max Mueller Bhavan (☎ 25205305; www.goethe.de/Bangalore; 716 CMH Rd, Indiranagar 1st Stage; 9am-5pm Mon-Fri) Has a good café and a library of German titles. Also runs exhibitions and courses.

INTERNET ACCESS

As you'd expect for an IT city, internet cafés are plentiful as is wi-fi access in hotels.

LEFT LUGGAGE

Both the City train station (Map p221) and Central bus stand (Map p221), located either side of Gubbi Thotadappa Rd, have 24-hour cloakrooms (per day Rs 10).

MEDIA

City Info (www.explocity.com) is a bimonthly listings booklet that's available free from tourist offices and many hotels. The weekly national magazines *India Today* and the *Week* run monthly supplements on the city. Also check out the **Chillibreeze** (www.chillibreeze.com) ebook and travel section for useful information for expats setting up in the city.

MEDICAL SERVICES

Chetak Pharma (Map p221; ☎ 22212449; Basement, Devatha Plaza, Residency Rd; 9am-9pm Mon-Sat, 9.30am-2pm Sun) Well-stocked pharmacy.

Dr Anoo Chengappa (☎ 9886006991; 602 12th Main, HAL 2nd Stage) Makes house calls.

Mallya Hospital (Map p221; ☎ 22277979; mallyahospital.net; Vittal Mallya Rd) With a 24-hour pharmacy.

MONEY

ATMs are common.

American Express (Map p221; ☎ 22254337; 180 Cunningham Rd; 9.30am-6.30pm Mon-Fri, 9.30am-1.30pm Sat) Changes travellers cheques with no commission.

Thomas Cook (Map p223; ☎ 25581357; The Pavilion, 62-63 MG Rd; 9.30am-6pm Mon-Sat) Charges a Rs 50 commission on travellers cheques.

PHOTOGRAPHY

Digital services are easy to come by.

GG Welling (Map p223; 113 MG Rd; 9.30am-1pm & 3-7.30pm Mon-Sat)

GK Vale (Map p223; 89 MG Rd; 9am-8pm Mon-Sat, 10am-1.30pm & 4-8pm Sun) Locals' favourite.

POST

Main post office (Map p221; Cubbon Rd; 8.30am-5.30pm Mon-Sat, 10am-4.30pm Sun).

TOURIST INFORMATION

Government of India tourist office (Map p223; ☎ 25585417; KFC Bldg, 48 Church St; 9.30am-6pm Mon-Fri, 9am-1pm Sat)

Karnataka State Tourism Development Corporation (KSTDC; Map p221; Badami House (☎ 22275883; Badami House, Kasturba Rd; 6.30am-10pm); Karnataka Tourism House (Karnataka Tourism House, 8 Papanna Lane, St Mark's Rd; 6.30am-10pm) For city and local tours; KSTDC also has offices at the City train station and the airport.

Karnataka Tourism (Map p221; ☎ 22352828; www.karnatakatourism.org; 2nd fl, 49 Khanija Bhavan, Racecourse Rd; 10am-5.30pm Mon-Sat, closed alternate Sat)

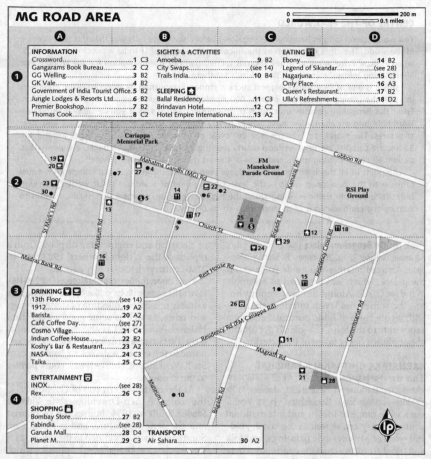

MG ROAD AREA

0 ——————————— 200 m
0 ——————————— 0.1 miles

INFORMATION		
Crossword	1	C3
Gangarams Book Bureau	2	C2
GG Welling	3	B2
GK Vale	4	B2
Government of India Tourist Office	5	B2
Jungle Lodges & Resorts Ltd	6	B2
Premier Bookshop	7	B2
Thomas Cook	8	C3

SIGHTS & ACTIVITIES		
Amoeba	9	B2
City Swaps	(see 14)	
Trails India	10	B4

SLEEPING		
Ballal Residency	11	C3
Brindavan Hotel	12	C2
Hotel Empire International	13	A2

EATING		
Ebony	14	B2
Legend of Sikandar	(see 28)	
Nagarjuna	15	C3
Only Place	16	A3
Queen's Restaurant	17	B2
Ulla's Refreshments	18	D2

DRINKING		
13th Floor	(see 14)	
1912	19	A2
Barista	20	A2
Café Coffee Day	(see 27)	
Cosmo Village	21	C4
Indian Coffee House	22	B2
Koshy's Bar & Restaurant	23	A2
NASA	24	C3
Taika	25	C2

ENTERTAINMENT		
INOX	(see 28)	
Rex	26	C3

SHOPPING		
Bombay Store	27	B2
Fabindia	(see 28)	
Garuda Mall	28	D4
Planet M	29	C3

TRANSPORT		
Air Sahara	30	A2

TRAVEL AGENCIES

Arjun Tours & Travel (Map p221; ☎ 22217054; www.arjuntours.com; 1st fl, Karnataka Tourism House, 8 Papanna Lane, St Mark's Rd; ✆ 9.30am-7.30pm Mon-Fri, 9.30am-5pm Sat) Reliable place to book cars for longer journeys, and to buy transport tickets.

STIC Travels (Map p221; ☎ 2202408; www.stictravel .com; Imperial Court, 33/1 Cunningham Rd; ✆ 9.30am-1pm & 2-6pm Mon-Sat) Agents for STA Travel.

Sights

LALBAGH BOTANICAL GARDENS

Named for its profusion of red roses (Lalbagh means 'Red Garden'), **Lalbagh** (Map p221; ☎ 26579231; admission Rs 5; ✆ dawn-dusk) rivals England's Kew Gardens. Laid out in 1760 by Hyder Ali, this 96-hectare park is a great place

to reconnect with nature; take one of Bangalore Walk's (p225) tours of the garden to discover more about the centuries-old trees and collections of plants from around the world. The main entrance is at the southern end of Kengal Hanumanthiah (KH) Rd; near here is the three-billion-year-old rock on which Kempegowda built one of Bengaluru's original watchtowers.

A beautiful glasshouse, modelled on the original Crystal Palace in London, is the venue for flower shows in the week preceding Republic Day (26 January) and the week before Independence Day (15 August).

BENGALURU PALACE

For an insight into the homelife of the Wodeyars (the current raja still lives here), take a

CENTRE OF THE FLAT WORLD

You won't spend long in Bengaluru (Bangalore) before someone tells you that this is the centre of the world. The city's reputation as the silicon-coated heart of IT India was cemented in 2005, when Pulitzer Prize–winning writer Thomas L Friedman got the inspiration for *The World Is Flat* after visiting Infosys' campus on Bengaluru's southern edge.

Infosys is one of Bengaluru's biggest success stories. Established by seven software engineers in 1981, the company today has over 66,000 employees and revenues of over US$2100 million. Enter the Bengaluru campus (not open to the public) and it's as if you've slipped through a wormhole into an alternative India, where neatly trimmed lawns sprout shiny glass and steel structures. The workforce (average age 26) cycle or use electric golf carts to get around the 32-hectare campus, passing five food courts (serving 14 types of cuisine), banks, a supermarket, basketball court, putting green and state-of-the-art gyms. There's even a hotel!

The point of all this is to prove that Infosys (and by extension India) can compete on equal terms with the developed world – the level playing field of Friedman's 'flat world'. And with bumper-to-bumper traffic crawling along the highway outside, nowhere in Bengaluru seems to sum up the contradictions of modern India so succinctly.

peek inside **Bengaluru Palace** (☎ 23315789; Palace Rd; Indian/foreigner Rs 100/200, camera Rs 500; ☽ 10am-6pm). An aged retainer will guide you around the palace, which was designed to resemble Windsor Castle. Alongside many family photos, the sometimes lavish interiors are hung with a collection of nude portraits, adding a saucy note to the tour. The guards get touchy about photos being taken of the exterior.

KARNATAKA CHITRAKALA PARISHAT

This **visual-arts gallery** (Map p221; ☎ 22261816; www .chitrakalaparishath.com; Kumarakrupa Rd; admission Rs 10; ☽ 10am-6pm Mon-Sat) is Bengaluru's best. You'll see a wide range of Indian and international contemporary art, as well as the lavish gold-leaf work of Mysore-style paintings, and folk and tribal art from across the continent. There are also galleries devoted to Russian master Nicholas Roerich, whose vividly colourful paintings of the Himalayas are outstanding, and his son Svetoslav, who settled in India.

CUBBON PARK

Named after the former British commissioner Sir Mark Cubbon, the 120-hectare **Cubbon Park** (Map p221) is where the city breathes. Inside and on its fringes you'll find the red-painted Gothic-style **State Central Library**, two municipal museums, an art gallery and a bleak **Government Aquarium** (☎ 22867440; adult/child Rs 5/2; ☽ 10am-5.30pm Tue-Sun).

The mechanically minded will find plenty of interest at the quirky **Visvesvaraya Industrial & Technical Museum** (☎ 22864009; Kasturba Rd; admission Rs 15; ☽ 10am-6pm), which includes all manner of electrical and engineering displays, from a replica of the Wright brothers' 1903 flyer to 21st-century virtual-reality games.

Next door, the **Government Museum** (☎ 22864483; Kasturba Rd; admission Rs 4; ☽ 10am-5pm Tue-Sun) houses a drably presented collection of stone carvings and relics, as well as some good pieces from Halebid. Your ticket is also valid for the attached **Venkatappa Art Gallery** (☽ 10am-5pm Tue-Sun), home to the surreal watercolour landscapes of Sri K Venkatappa (1887–1962), court painter to the Wodeyars.

At the northwestern end of Cubbon Park, the colossal neo-Dravidian-style **Vidhana Soudha**, built in 1954, houses the secretariat and the state legislature, and is floodlit on Sunday evenings. It's closed to the public, as is the neoclassical **Attara Kacheri**, opposite, which houses the High Court.

KRISHNARAJENDRA (CITY) MARKET & TIPU'S PALACE

For a pungent taste of traditional urban India, dive into this bustling wholesale fresh-produce **market** (Map p221; ☽ 6am-7pm) and the dense grid of commercial streets that surround it. This is the main Muslim area of the city and you'll also find several mosques here, including the impressively massive lilac-painted **Jama Masjid** (Map p221; Silver Jubilee Park Rd; admission free).

Head south along Krishna Rajandra (KR) Rd, under the elevated highway, and you'll pass the remains of the **fort** (Map p221) originally built by Kempegowda and rebuilt in stone in the 18th century by Hyder Ali. It's not open to the public. On the next block south is Tipu

Sultan's elegant and modest **palace** (Map p221; Albert Victor Rd; Indian/foreigner Rs 5/US$2; ☼ 8am-6pm), notable for its teak pillars and frescoes – although it's not in as good condition as Tipu's beautiful palace in Srirangapatnam (p240).

Next to the palace is the ornate **Venkataraman Temple** (Map p221; KR Rd; ☼ 8.30am-6pm, closed alternate Sat).

BULL TEMPLE & DODDA GANESHA TEMPLE

Built by Kempegowda in the Dravidian style of the 16th century, the **Bull Temple** (Map p221; Bull Temple Rd, Basavangudi; ☼ 6am-1pm & 4-9pm) contains a huge granite monolith of Nandi and is one of Bengaluru's liveliest and most atmospheric. Nearby is the **Dodda Ganesha Temple** (Map p221; Bull Temple Rd, Basavangudi; ☼ 6am-1pm & 4-9pm), with an equally enormous Ganesh idol. Take bus 31, 31E, 35 or 49 to get there.

ISKCON TEMPLE

Built by the wealthy International Society of Krishna Consciousness (Iskcon), better known as the Hare Krishnas, this shiny **temple** (Hare Krishna Hill, Chord Rd; ☼ 7am-1pm & 4-8.30pm), 8km northwest of the town centre, is lavishly decorated in a mix of ultracontemporary and traditional styles. The Sri Radha Krishna Mandir blends souvenir selling with a stunning shrine to Krishna and Radha.

Activities & Courses

AYURVEDA & YOGA

Chiraayu Ayurvedic Health & Rejuvenation Centre (☎ 25500855; 6th block, 17th D Main, Koramangala; ☼ 8.30am-6pm) provides longer-term therapies, as well as a day spa for walk-in relaxation. An hour-long massage costs Rs 700.

People come from around the world for the yoga and naturopathy programmes at the **Institute of Naturopathy & Yogic Sciences** (INYS; ☎ 23717777; Tumkur Rd, Jindal Nagar; per person per day from Rs 600). It's 20km northwest of Bengaluru.

Set on a 30-acre organic farm, **Soukya** (☎ 7945001; www.soukya.com; Soukya Rd, Samethanahalli, Whitefield; ☼ 6am-8.30pm) is an internationally renowned place offering a variety of holistic health programmes, including Ayurvedic treatments and yoga. Packages for two days and one night start at Rs 8900/13,800 for a single/double.

Ayurvedic therapists from Kerala staff **Spa** (☎ 5217239; www.theleela.com; Airport Rd ☼ 6.30am-9pm), a sleek centre with a wide variety of rejuvenation and detox treatments. Prices kick off at Rs 1600 for an hour's massage.

Stylish **Urban Yoga Centre** (☎ 32005720; www .urbanyoga.in; 100ft Rd, Indiranagar; ☼ 6.30am-9pm) has a smart yoga studio offering a range of classes, and sells yoga clothes, accessories and books.

OUTDOOR ADVENTURE

Getoff ur ass (☎ 51161600; www.getoffurass.com; 472, Sri Krishna Temple St; Indiranagar 1st Stage; ☼ 10am-8pm Mon-Sat) sells and rents out all you need for an outdoor-adventure expedition. It also runs a variety of reasonably priced hiking, rafting and kayaking trips in Karnataka and elsewhere in India.

Tours

Bangalore Walks (☎ 9845523660; www.bangalore walks.com) Not to be missed! Sign up for one of the highly informative history or nature walks (Rs 495 including breakfast) and learn to love Bengaluru in a way that many locals have forgotten. Walks run from 7am to 11am every Saturday and Sunday.

City Swaps (Map p223; ☎ 65715056; www.cityswaps .in; 902 Barton Centre, 84 MG Rd; ☼ 10am-8pm Wed-Mon) Guides give a running commentary on open-top double-decker buses, which follow a 14km route around central Bengaluru. A two-hour tour is Rs 200; a day-long hop-on, hop-off ticket is Rs 300.

Karnataka State Tourism Development Corporation (KSTDC; Map p221; Badami House (☎ 22275883; Badami House, Kasturba Rd; ☼ 6.30am-10pm); Karnataka Tourism House (Karnataka Tourism House, 8 Papanna Lane, St Mark's Rd; ☼ 6.30am-10pm) Runs a couple of city tours, all of which begin at Badami House. The basic city tour runs twice daily at 7.30am and 2pm (ordinary/deluxe bus Rs 140/160), and a 16-hour tour to Srirangapatnam, Mysore and Brindavan Gardens departs daily at 7.15am (ordinary/deluxe bus Rs 435/560). KSTDC also has offices at the City train station and the airport.

Sleeping

As a major business destination, Bengaluru's accommodation is generally pricey and in short supply. The cheapest options (anything under Rs 500 a night) are near the bus stand and fill up quickly. Serviced apartments are frequently a better deal than many midrange (Rs 500 to 15,500) and top-end hotels. Wherever you stay, book as far ahead as possible.

BUDGET

Stacks of hotels line Subedar Chatram (SC) Rd, east of the bus stands and City train station. This neighbourhood is loud and seedy – women may not like it – but convenient if you're in transit. If you're in Bengaluru longer than one night, consider staying closer to MG Rd. All hotels listed here have hot water, at least in the mornings.

Chandra Vihar (Map p221; ☎ 22224146; Avenue Rd; s/d from Rs 255/400; ✷) Convenient for the bazaar, which buzzes outside. Rooms are clean and spacious with TV and telephone; some have market views and balconies.

Hotel Adora (Map p221; ☎ 22872280; 47 SC Rd; s/d from Rs 280/380) One of the best of the SC Rd budget options. Downstairs is a good veg restaurant, Indraprastha Vegetarian.

Brindavan Hotel (Map p223; ☎ 25584000; 108 MG Rd; s/d from Rs 390/570; ✷) Book well in advance for this popular cheapie offering large decent rooms with balconies, and an astro-palmist to fulfil other needs. Rates include taxes.

Hotel Ajantha (Map p221; ☎ 25584321; fax 25584780; 22A MG Rd; s/d from Rs 400/600; ✷ 🖳) Old Indian tourism posters decorate the halls of this simple hotel, with a range of well-taken-care-of rooms in a semiquiet compound off MG Rd (ask for a room away from the parking lot).

Citizen Lodge (Map p221; ☎ 25591793; fax 25596811; 3/4 Lady Curzon Rd; r from Rs 450; ✷) The best rooms here are those facing on to the pretty garden at the back of the compound; they include rooms with AC and all the trimmings.

MIDRANGE

Hotel Empire (Map p221; ☎ 25592821; www.hotel empireinternational.com; 78 Central St; s/d from Rs 695/920; ✷ 🖳) Not too big a step up from the budget category, this appealing place offers bright rooms, friendly staff and constant hot water. Note the street – and the crowds who flock to the famous restaurant downstairs – can be noisy, as they are at the hotel's ritzier sister property, Hotel Empire International (Map p223; ☎ 25593743; 36 Church St), which is closer to MG Rd; prices at the Hotel Empire International start at Rs 1250/1650 for a single/double (including breakfast), and the hotel has internet access and AC.

Casa Piccola Serviced Apartments (Map p221; ☎ 22270754; www.casacottage.in; Wellington Park Apartments, Wellington St; r from Rs 1350; ✷) The Oberoi family, who also run the Casa Piccola Cottage, offer a range of equally pleasant one-, two- and three-bedroom apartments in this building and opposite the cottage on nearby Clapham Rd.

Ashley Inn (Map p221; ☎ 25352020; www.aranha homes.com; 11 Ashley Park Rd; r from Rs 1400; ✷) This sweet guesthouse is seconds away from MG

Rd, and has eight pleasantly furnished rooms and a homy atmosphere. There's free wi-fi access. The management company also offers a range of serviced apartments.

Tricolour Hotel (Map p221; ☎ 41279090; www .newindiahotels.com; 15 Tank Bund Rd; s/d incl breakfast Rs 2000/2500; ✷ 🖳) Part of a shopping mall and convenient for both bus and train stations, this new hotel brings a surprising touch of contemporary class to the area. Rates include breakfast.

our pick Casa Piccola Cottage & Service Apartments (Map p221; ☎ 22270754; www.casacottage.in; 2 Clapham Rd; r from Rs 2000; ✷) This beautifully renovated 1915 cottage is a tranquil sanctuary from the madness of the city. Some of the studio rooms have kitchenettes for self-catering. Wi-fi access is available, and rates include breakfast served under a gazebo in the garden.

Ballal Residency (Map p223; ☎ 25597277; www .ballalgrouphotels.com; 74/4 3rd Cross, Residency Rd; s/d Rs 2000/2600; ✷) Set back from the chaos, the Ballal offers big, sparkling clean rooms with all the mod cons, including wi-fi. Downstairs is a popular pure-veg restaurant and sweet shop.

Mélange (Map p221; ☎ 22129700; www.melangeban galore.com; 21 Vittal Mallya Rd; apt from Rs 2500; ✷ 🖳) Occupying part of an apartment block just off Bengaluru's chicest shopping street, you can choose between economy apartments or upgraded ones with guaranteed electricity supply and lots of mod cons.

Villa Pottipati (☎ 23360777; www.neemranahotels .com; 142 8th Cross, 4th Main, Malleswaram; r from Rs 3000; ✷ 🖳 🖳) An inconvenient location away from the centre is the only downside of this small colonial charmer. Raj era–style rooms come with antique furnishings, the gardens include a dunk-sized pool and service is very friendly.

Tristar Apartments (☎ 51185900; www.tristarapt .com; 1216 100ft Rd, HAL 2nd Stage, Indiranagar; apt studio/ deluxe incl breakfast Rs 3750/4500; ✷ 🖳) Handy for the business parks on this side of town, and the restaurants and bars of 100ft Rd, these appealing apartments are dressed in IKEA-style furnishings and have a Jacuzzi on the roof.

Bride (Map p221; ☎ 41144408; www.bridesuites.com; 5 Bride St, Langford Town; r incl breakfast from US$99; ✷ 🖳) Designed by a US architect and tastefully furnished, these suites are spacious and come with big lounges and kitchens that are shared between the rooms on each floor. There's a roof garden with a small gym.

Jayamahal Palace (☎ 23331321; www.jayamahal palace.com; 1 Jayamahal Rd; s/d from US$100/112; ✗ ☐) Originally built by Bangalore's British Resident, this cute palace is set in placid, green gardens. The cheapest rooms are in a new block; they're small but quite good. Some of the suites dazzle but the bathrooms can leave something to be desired.

Regaalis (Map p221; ☎ 411133111; www.regaalis.net; 40/2 Lavelle Rd; r from US$115; ✗ ☐) Slick business hotels like this are sprouting like mushrooms in central Bengaluru. The Regaalis scores with a great location and pleasant decorative touches in the rooms (including massage chairs).

TOP END

Bengaluru has its Tajs (three of them!), its Oberoi and a host of other luxe hotels with matching price tags.

Ista Hotel (☎ 25558888; www.istahotels.com; 1/1 Swami Vivekananda Rd, Ulsoor; s/d from US$350/370; ✗ ☐ ✗) Meaning 'Bliss', Ista delivers accommodation happiness in a cool, minimalist style. Smallish rooms offer sweeping vistas across Ulsoor lake and the city, and the bar and restaurant opening on to the rooftop pool are heavenly.

Park (Map p221; ☎ 25594666; www.theparkhotels.com; 14/7 MG Rd; r from US$350; ✗ ☐ ✗) This Terence Conran–styled hotel is as swish as the vibrantly colourful raw silk curtains coddling the lobby. Rooms are a little cramped but very fashionable. The hotel's i-bar and *magnifico* Italian restaurant i-t.alia are among the places to be seen in Bengaluru.

Eating

Bengaluru's delicious dining scene keeps pace with the whims and rising standards of its hungry, moneyed masses. Unless mentioned otherwise all restaurants are open from noon to 3pm, and 7pm to 11pm. If there's a telephone number, it's advisable to book.

MG ROAD AREA

All the following venues appear on Map p223.

Ulla's Refreshments (1st fl, Public Utility Bldg, MG Rd; mains Rs 40-70; �},9am-10pm) Rise above the MG Rd crowds on Ulla's convivial terrace, where you can dig into simple, tasty North and South Indian fare. Thalis (traditional South Indian and Gujerati 'all-you-can-eat' meal) kick off at Rs 65.

Queen's Restaurant (Church St; mains Rs 50-120) The rustic, tribal décor gives this cosy restaurant the atmosphere of an upmarket mud hut. The delicious Indian food draws in the customers.

Nagarjuna (44/1 Residency Rd; mains Rs 60-125) Not a place to linger, this fast-moving, constantly packed-out joint dishes up spicy-as-hell Andhra specialities on banana leaves.

Only Place (☎ 30618989; 13 Museum Rd; mains Rs 70-200) The burgers, steaks and yummy apple pie couldn't be tastier at this delightful semialfresco restaurant with a relaxed vibe.

Ebony (13th fl, Barton Centre, 84 MG Rd; mains Rs 90-275) Worth visiting for its terrace tables overlooking the city and its savoury mains of the Thai, French and Parsi varieties.

Legend of Sikandar (☎ 51252333; 4th fl, Garuda Mall, Magrath Rd; mains Rs 100-300) Serves Lucknowi, Hyderabadi and North Indian cuisine to general applause.

ELSEWHERE

Mavalli Tiffin Rooms (MTR; Map p221; Lalbagh Rd; dishes Rs 16-80; �},6.30-11am, 12.30-2.45pm, 3.30-7.30pm & 8-9pm) MTR dishes up legendary *masala dosas* (curried vegetables inside a crisp pancake) for breakfast and tiffin (snacks). Be prepared to stand in line, especially for the thalis – a feast of 12 dishes for lunch and dinner.

Konark (Map p221; 50 Residency Rd; mains Rs 30-70) This place serves tasty Indian food in colourful, comfy surroundings. The lunchtime South Indian thali (Rs 75) is a gut buster; for something less filling, opt for the snack dishes, or eggless cakes and pastries.

Paparazzi (Map p221; ☎ 25584242; 10th fl, Royal Orchid Central Hotel, 47/1 Dickenson Rd; mains Rs 200-300) Spicy chicken kebabs (served on a flaming skewer) and decent caesar salads are served with sweeping city views at this supertrendy place. The Rs 200 set lunch is a good option.

Harima (Map p221; ☎ 41325757; 4th fl, Devatha Plaza, 131 Residency Rd; mains Rs 200-300) Practically a homeaway-from-home for Bengaluru's expat Japanese, Harima is pretty much on the mark for its atmosphere and Japanese food, including sushi, noodles, tempura and more obscure dishes, such as *natto* (fermented bean sprouts).

Sunny's (Map p221; ☎ 22243642; 34 Vittal Mallya Rd; mains Rs 200-500) Beloved by the expat and well-to-do Indian set, Sunny's is like a little piece of California transplanted to downtown Bengaluru. The salads, pizzas and pastas are impressive, and the desserts downright sinful.

KARNATAKA

Casa del Sol (Map p221; ☎ 51510101; 3rd fl, Devatha Plaza, 131 Residency Rd; mains Rs 250; ☼ 11am-11pm) This is a relaxed Mediterranean-style bistro with a semialfresco area. Wednesday is disco night, Thursday has free salsa classes and Sunday has a good brunch (Rs 524) with lots of activities for kids.

Olive Beach (Map p221; ☎ 41128400; 16 Wood St, Ashoknagar; mains Rs 425-600) This spot duplicates the groovy Mediterranean style and deliciously authentic food of its Delhi and Mumbai (Bombay) sisters. Book ahead for the great Sunday brunch (Rs 1500) with free-flowing booze.

ourpick Grasshopper (☎ 26593999; 45 Kalena Agrahara, Bannerghatta Rd; 5-/7-course meals Rs 700/1000) You won't regret schlepping 15km south of the city centre to enjoy a delicious, relaxed meal at this restaurant-cum-fashion-boutique in a leafy residential setting. Husband and wife team Sonali and Himanshu design clothes, and fantastic fusion menus of five or seven set courses. Bookings are essential, with weekends being the busiest.

Also recommended:

Samarkand (Map p221; ☎ 41113364; Gem Plaza, Infantry Rd; mains Rs 100-250) For Peshawari cuisine and theatrical décor.

Tandoor (Map p221; ☎ 25584620; Centenary Bldg, 28 MG Rd; mains Rs 100-300) Consistently good tandoori, biryani (steamed rice with meat or vegetables) and kebab dishes.

Drinking

BARS & LOUNGES

For all its reputation as a 'pub city', Bengaluru is also an early-to-bed city with strict last orders at 11.30pm (unless mentioned opening time is 7.30pm). This said, the city does a nice line in plush lounge-type spaces for cocktails and nibbles. Typically the trendiest spots will have a cover charge on Friday or Saturday of around Rs 500 for a couple or a single guy and Rs 300 for women; the cover charge is often refundable against drinks or food.

Beach (1211 100ft Rd, HAL 2nd Stage, Indiranagar) Feel the sand between your toes – literally – at this fun beach-bums' bar in the happening Indiranagar area. Women drink for free on Wednesday.

Cosmo Village (Map p223; 29 Magrath Rd) Setting the Bengaluru lounge-bar standard, this place goes through more make-overs than Paris Hilton, yet still manages to remain popular with both locals and expats.

Fuga (Map p221; 1 Castle St, Ashoknagar) This eye-poppingly slick bar-club-lounge wouldn't look out of place in New York or London. DJ Sasha works the decks and absinthe is the mixer of choice in the cocktail lounge.

Koshy's Bar & Restaurant (Map p223; 39 St Mark's Rd; ☼ 9am-11.30pm) Locals love the British-school-dinner-style meals (mains Rs 50 to 250) dished up at this Bengaluru institution. Skip that and indulge in an unrushed beer in its buzzy, non-AC dining room.

NASA (Map p223; 1A Church St; ☼ 11am-11pm) The antithesis of hip, this old favourite is decked out like a spaceship. It's a trip, especially when those laser shows spark up.

1912 (Map p223; 40 St Mark's Rd) An older crowd hang out at this elegant option with a small courtyard. It's a good spot for a quiet drink, until the DJ – or sometimes a live band – gets things moving later on.

Taika (Map p223; 206-209 The Pavilion, 62-63 MG Rd; ☼ 12.30-3pm & 7.30-11.30pm) This so-called spa lounge offers Ayurvedic food, although it wasn't available when we visited. Really it's just a cool place to twizzle your cocktail stick in a slick rooftop setting. There's a disco at the back.

13th Floor (Map p223; 13th fl, Barton Centre, 84 MG Rd) Come early to grab a spot on the balcony, with all of Bengaluru glittering at your feet. The atmosphere is that of a relaxed cocktail party.

CAFÉS & TEAHOUSES

Bengaluru is liberally sprinkled with good chain cafés, such as **Café Coffee Day** (Map p223; MG Rd; ☼ 8am-11.30pm) and **Barista** (Map p223; 40 St Mark's Rd; ☼ 8am-11.30pm). For something a bit different try one of the following.

Indian Coffee House (Map p223; 78 MG Rd; ☼ 8.30am-8.30pm) Waiters in turbans and fabulous buckled belts dish out South India's best java at this charming old-timer with yellowing formica table tops.

Infinitea (Map p221; www.infini-tea.com; 2 Shah Sultan Complex, Cunningham Rd; ☼ 10.45am-11pm) Infinitea is an amiable modern teahouse that offers a great range of infusions from across the subcontinent. It's also an ideal spot for lunch and snacks.

Cha Bar (Oxford Bookstore, Leela Galleria, Airport Rd; ☼ 10am-10pm) Offering more than 20 different types of tea, Cha Bar allows you to hunker down with a book or magazine from the attached bookshop.

Entertainment

BOWLING
Amoeba (Map p223; ☎ 25594631; 22 Church St; ☉ 11am-11pm) A date with the lanes at this state-of-the-art bowling alley costs Rs 80 to 125 per person, depending on the time of day.

CINEMA
English-language films are popular; tickets are around Rs 60, rising to Rs 220 at the multiplexes.

INOX (Map p223; ☎ 41128888; www.inox.com; 5th fl; Garuda Mall, Magrath Rd)

Nani Cinematheque (Map p221; ☎ 22356262; www.collectivechaos.org/nani.html; 5th fl, Sona Tower, 71 Millers Rd) Classic Indian and European films are screened Friday, Saturday and Sunday.

PVR Cinema (Map p221; ☎ 22067511; www.pvrcinemas.com; Forum, 21 Hosur Rd) Megacinema with 11 theatres.

Rex (Map p223; ☎ 25587350; 12/13 Brigade Rd) Has regional films, too.

SPORT
Bengaluru's winter horse-racing season runs from November to February, and its summer season is from May to July. Races are generally held on Friday and Saturday afternoons. Contact the **Bangalore Turf Club** (Map p221; ☎ 22262391; www.bangaloreraces.com; Racecourse Rd) for details.

For a taste of India's sporting passion up close, attend one of the regular cricket matches at **M Chinnaswamy Stadium** (Map p221; ☎ 22869970; MG Rd). A range of tickets (Rs 50 to 500) is sold on the day, though there are inevitably queues. A good seat in a not-too-crowded area costs about Rs 250. The **Karnataka Cricket Association** (☎ 22869631) has the spin.

THEATRE
Ranga Shankara (☎ 26592777; www.rangashankara .org; 36/2 8th Cross, JP Nagar) All kinds of interesting theatre (in a variety of languages) and dance are held at this cultural centre.

Shopping
Bengaluru's shopping options are abundant, ranging from teeming bazaars (see p224) to glitzy malls. Some good shopping areas include Commercial St (Map p221), Vittal Malya Rd (Map p221) and MG Rd (Map p223) between St Mark's and Brigade Rds.

Cinnamon (Map p221; 11 Walton Rd; ☉ 10.30am-8.15pm) Just off Lavelle Rd, Cinnamon is a chic boutique for clothes, homewares and gifts – perfect for stylish souvenirs.

Fabindia (☎ 25532070; 54 17th Main; ☉ 10am-8pm) This flagship shop contains Fabindia's full range of stylish clothes and homewares in traditional cotton prints and silks. There's a also a small café. From Hosur Rd, make a left at the mosque about 1km past the Forum; Fabindia is on the right. There are also branches on Commerical St (Map p221) and in the Garuda mall (Map p223; McGrath Rd).

100ft (☎ 25277752; 777/1, 100ft Rd, HAL 2nd Stage, Indiranagar; ☉ 11am-11pm) An appealing boutique for colourful clothes, interior design and handicrafts; it also has a restaurant and bar.

Raintree (Map p221; 4 Sankey Rd; ☉ 10am-7pm Mon-Sat, 11am-6pm Sun) This early-20th-century villa has been turned into a stylish gift shop, fashion shop and café; it includes a branch of fab clothes shop Anokhi, which is also found at the Leela Galleria (23 Airport Rd, Kodihalli).

14 VM Rd (Map p221; 14 Vittal Mallya Rd) This classy boutique complex showcases top Indian designers, including Abraham & Thakore, Manish Arora and Neeru Kumar.

Ffolio (Map p221; 5 Vittal Mallya Rd) Head to this shop for high Indian fashion. Ffolio also has a branch at Leela Galleria (23 Airport Rd, Kodihalli).

Bombay Store (Map p223; 99 MG Rd; ☉ 10.30am-8.30pm) This is a smooth one-stop option for gifts ranging from ecobeauty products to linens.

Planet M (Map p223; 9 Brigade Rd; ☉ 10.30am-9pm) Try this shop for all kinds of recorded music and movies.

Mysore Saree Udyog (Map p221; 1st fl, 294 Kamaraj Rd; ☉ 10.30am-8.30pm Mon-Sat) Located near Commercial St, Mysore Saree Udyog is great for top-quality silks and saris.

Bengaluru's malls include **Garuda** (Map p223; McGrath Rd), **Forum** (Map p221; Hosur Rd, Koramangala) and **Leela Galleria** (23 Airport Rd, Kodihalli).

Getting There & Away

AIR
Airline offices are generally open from 9am to 5.30pm Monday to Saturday, with a break for lunch. Domestic carriers serving Bengaluru include the following:

Air Deccan (Map p221; ☎ 39008888, call centre 9845777008; 35 Cunningham Rd)

Air Sahara (Map p223; ☎ 22102777; 39 St Mark's Rd)

Indian Airlines (Map p221; ☎ 25226233; Housing Board Bldg, Kempegowda Rd)

Jet Airways (Map p221; ☎ 25550856, call centre 25221929; Unity Bldg, Jayachamaraja Wodeyar Rd)

KARNATAKA

DAILY FLIGHTS FROM BENGALURU

Destination	One-way price (US$)	Duration (hr)
Ahmedabad	153	3½
Chennai (Madras)	51	¾
Delhi	183	2½
Goa	75	1½
Hyderabad	81	1
Kochi	60	1
Kolkata (Calcutta)	192	2½
Mangalore	102	¾
Mumbai (Bombay)	99	1½
Pune	102	1½
Trivandrum	60	1

Kingfisher Airlines (Map p221; ☎ 41979797; UB Anchorage, Richmond Rd)
Spice Jet (☎ 1800 180 333, 0987-180333; www
.spicejet.com)

There are daily flights to the places listed on above.

Some of Bengaluru's international airline offices:
Air France (☎ 25589397; Sunrise Chambers, 22 Ulsoor Rd)
Air India (Map p221; ☎ 22277747; Unity Bldg, Jayacha-maraja Wodeyar Rd)
Alitalia (Map p221; ☎ 25591936; 66 Infantry Rd)
British Airways (☎ 1800 180 1213, 1800 102 1213) All booking enquiries can be made on these toll-free numbers.
KLM & Northwest Airlines (Map p221; ☎ 22268703; Taj West End, Racecourse Rd)
Lufthansa (Map p221; ☎ 25588791; 44/2 Dickenson Rd)

BUS
Bengaluru's huge, well-organised **Central bus stand** (Map p221; Gubbi Thotadappa Rd) is directly in front of the City train station. **Karnataka State Road Transport Corporation** (KSRTC; ☎ 22870099) buses run throughout Karnataka and to neighbouring states; the Rajahamsa is its comfortable deluxe model. Other interstate bus operators: **Andhra Pradesh State Road Transport Corporation** (APSRTC; ☎ 22873915) **Kadamba Transport Corporation** (☎ 22351958) Goa. **State Express Transport Corporation** (SETC; ☎ 22876974) Tamil Nadu.

Computerised advance booking is available for most buses at the station; **KSRTC** (Map p221; Devantha Plaza, Residency Rd) also has convenient booking counters around town, including one at Devantha Plaza. It's wise to book long-distance journeys in advance.

Numerous private bus companies offer comfier and only slightly more expensive services. Private bus operators (Map p221) line the street facing the Central bus stand, or you can book through an agency (see p223).

Major KSRTC bus services from Bengaluru are listed on below.

TRAIN
Bengaluru's **City train station** (Map p221; Gubbi Thota-dappa Rd) is the main train hub and the place to make reservations. **Cantonment train station** (Map p221; Station Rd) is a sensible spot to disembark if you're arriving and headed for the MG Rd area, while **Yesvantpur train station** (Rahman Khan Rd), 8km northwest of downtown, is the starting point for Goa trains.

MAJOR BUS SERVICES FROM BENGALURU

Destination	Fare (Rs)	Duration (hr)	Frequency
Chennai	222 (R)/455 (V)	6-8	15 daily
Ernakulum	460 (R)/610 (V)	14	16 daily
Hampi	275 (R)	9	1 daily
Hyderabad	360 (R)/625 (V)	10-12	25-plus daily
Jog Falls	300 (D)	8-9	1 daily
Mumbai	961 (V)	18	2 daily
Mysore	125 (R)/155 (V)	2½-3½	25-plus daily
Ooty	225 (R)	8	6 daily
Panaji	458 (R)/656 (V)	11-15	3 daily
Puttaparthi	175 (V)	4	3 daily

D – semideluxe/regular, R – Rajahamsa, V – Volvo AC

MAJOR TRAINS FROM BENGALURU

Destination	Train No & Name	Fare (Rs)	Duration (hr)	Departures
Chennai	2608 *Lalbagh Exp*	118/392	5½	6.30am
	2640 *Brindavan Exp*	118/392	6	2.30pm
	2008 *Shatabdi*	580/1105	5	4.15pm Wed-Mon
Delhi	2627 *Karnataka Exp*	559/1517/2160	42	6.40pm
	2429 *Rajdhani*	2105/2840	35	8pm Mon, Wed, Thu & Sun
Hospet	6592 *Hampi Exp*	203/765/881	9½	10.15pm
Hubli	2079 *Jan Shatabdi*	147/485	7	6am Wed-Mon
Kolkata	2509 *Guwahati Exp*	605/1646/2247	37	11.30pm Wed, Thu & Fri
Mumbai	6530 *Udyan Exp*	377/1031/1472	24	8pm
Mysore	6222 *Mysore Exp*	70/228	3	5.10am
	2614 *Tipu Exp*	70/228	2½	2.15pm
	6216 *Chamundi Exp*	61/198	3	6.15pm
	2007 *Shatabdi*	305/590	2	11am Wed-Mon
Trivandrum	6526 *Kanniyakumari Exp*	330/901/1283	17	9.45pm

Rajdhani fares are 3AC/2AC; *Shatabdi* fares are chair/executive; *Jan Shatabdi* fares are 2nd/chair; and express (Exp) fares are 2nd/chair for day trains and sleeper/3AC/2AC for night trains.

Rail reservations in Bengaluru are computerised. If your train is fully booked, it's usually possible to get into the emergency quota; first, buy a wait-listed ticket, then fill out a form at the **Divisional Railway Office** (Map p221; Gubbi Thotadappa Rd) building immediately north of the City train station. You find out about 10 hours before departure whether you've got a seat (a good chance); if not, the ticket is refunded. The **train reservation office** (☎ 139; ☻ 8am-8pm Mon-Sat, 8am-2pm Sun), on the left as you face the station, has separate counters for credit-card purchases (Rs 30 fee), women and foreigners. Luggage can be left at the 24-hour cloakroom on Platform 1 at the City train station (from Rs 10 per bag per day).

See above for information on major train services.

Getting Around
TO/FROM THE AIRPORT
The airport is about 9km east of the MG Rd area. Prepaid taxis can take you from the airport to the city (Rs 190), but in the other direction you'll probably have to haggle for a price. An autorickshaw will set you back about Rs 60. Bus 333 goes from the City bus stand to the airport (Rs 15, 45 minutes).

A new international **airport** (www.bialairport .com) is scheduled to open in April 2008.

AUTORICKSHAW
The city's autorickshaw drivers are legally required to use their meters. After 10pm, 50% is added onto the metered rate, but you'll usually have to negotiate a fare. Flag fall is Rs 10 and then Rs 5 for each extra kilometre. There's a prepaid autorickshaw stand outside the City train station, as well as a couple along MG Rd and outside the Garuda Mall. From the City train station to MG Rd costs Rs 30.

BUS
Bengaluru has a thorough but often crowded local bus network. Pickpockets abound and locals warn that solo women should think twice about taking buses after dark. Most local buses (light blue) run from the City bus stand (Map p221), next to the Central bus stand; a few operate from the City Market bus stand (Map p221) to the south.

To get from the City train station to the MG Rd area, catch any bus from Platform 17 or 18 at the City bus stand. For the City market, take bus 31, 31E, 35 or 49 from Platform 8.

CAR
Plenty of places around Bengaluru offer car rental with driver or (if you're fearless) self-drive. Standard rates for a Hindustan Motors Ambassador car are Rs 5.5 per kilometre for a

minimum of 250km, plus an allowance of Rs 125 for the driver (a total of Rs 1375 per day). For an eight-hour rental of a Tata Indicar with a driver you're looking at around Rs 850.

We recommend:

Cabs Den (☎ 22483879)
Jyothi Car Rentals (☎ 9845007535, 9845212079)
Mr Gopalan (☎ 9845089554)

AROUND BENGALURU
Bannerghatta Biological Park

The attached zoo is a little grim, but it's well worth making the 25km trek south of Bengaluru to this **nature reserve** (☎ 080-27828425; ⊙ 9am-5.30pm Wed-Mon) to take its hour-long **grand safari** (weekday/weekend Rs 85/110; ⊙ 11am to 4pm) in a minibus through an 11,330-hectare enclosure. Here the Karnataka Forest Department is rehabilitating 34 tigers (including two white ones) and 11 lions rescued from circuses.

It's an easy half-day trip from Bengaluru, but if you want to stay over, **Jungle Lodges & Resorts Ltd** (Map p223; ☎ 080-25597021; www.junglelodges .com; 2nd fl, Shrungar Shopping Complex, MG Rd, Bengaluru; ⊙ 10am-5.30pm) has some log huts here. On the way out or back you could also visit the excellent restaurant and boutique Grasshopper (p228). Bus 366A from City Market runs here (Rs 20, one hour).

Wonder La

Wonder La is a brand-new **water park** (www .wonderla.com; adult/child/senior/disabled Mon-Fri Rs 430/330/280/320, Sat, Sun & hols 540/400/350/400; ⊙ 11am-7pm Mon-Fri, 11am-8pm Sat, Sun & hols) located just under 30km from Bengaluru along the Bengaluru–Mysore highway. The massive park offers dozens of water and 'dry' rides.

Hessaraghatta

Located 30km northwest of Bengaluru, Hessaraghatta is home to **Nrityagram** (☎ 080-28466313; www.nrityagram.org; ⊙ 10am-5.30pm Tue-Sat, 10am-3pm Sun), the living legacy of celebrated dancer Protima Gauri Bedi, who died in a Himalayan avalanche in 1998. Protima established this dance academy in 1989 to revive and popularise Indian classical dance.

Designed in the form of a village by Goa-based architect Gerard da Cunha, the attractive complex offers the long-term study of classical dance within a holistic curriculum. Local children are taught for free on Sunday. Self-guided tours cost Rs 20 or you can call ahead to book a tour, lecture-cum-

demonstration and vegetarian meal (Rs 850, minimum 10 people). A month-long beginners' workshop is held in July for US$1000. Earmark the first Saturday in February for the free dance festival **Vasantahabba** (p220).

Opposite the dance village, **Taj Kuteeram** (☎ 080-22252846; www.tajhotels.com; r from Rs 4300; 😕) combines comfort with rustic charm. It offers Ayurveda and yoga sessions.

Learn how to drive a bullock cart and how to milk a cow at **Our Native Village** (☎ 9880999924; www.ournativevillage.com; Survey 72, Kodihalli, Madurai Hobli; s/d incl full board Rs 3750/4500; 🏊), an ecofriendly organic farm and resort. The resort generates its own power, harvests rainwater, and processes and reuses all its waste.

From Bengaluru's City Market, buses 253, 253D, 253E run to Hessaraghatta (Rs 20, one hour), with bus 266 continuing on to Nrityagram.

Nandi Hills

Rising to 1455m the **Nandi Hills** (admission Rs 5; ⊙ 6am-10pm), 60km north of Bengaluru, were once the summer retreat of Tipu Sultan. It's a good place for hiking with stellar views and two notable **Chola temples**. Avoid weekends if you like your nature quiet. A recommended retreat out here is **Silver Oak Farm** (☎ 9342510445; www.silveroakfarm.com; Sultanpet Village; s/d incl full board from Rs 2250/3250), which has a beautiful hillside position. Buses head to Nandi Hills (Rs 40, two hours) from Bengaluru's Central bus stand.

Janapada Loka Folk Arts Museum

HL Nage Gowda spent decades researching the folk arts and native cultures of the region. The fruits of his labours are on display at this engaging **museum** (☎ 08113-72701143; admission Rs 10; ⊙ 9am-1.30pm & 2.30-5.30pm Wed-Mon), 53km southwest of Bengaluru, which is worth a brief pause if you're driving towards Mysore. Displayed items include 500-year-old shadow puppets, festival costumes and instruments. There's an attached restaurant. Mysore-bound buses (one hour) will get you here; ask to be dropped 3km after Ramanagaram.

MYSORE

☎ 0821 / pop 950,000 / elev 707m

It's not difficult to divine Mysore's charismatic appeal. The historic seat of the Wodeyar maharajas is easy to get around, has a good climate and works hard to promote its regal heritage. Famous for its traditional painting and its silk, sandalwood and incense production, Mysore is now promoting itself as an international centre for Ashtanga yoga. Whether you choose to stretch your body in a traditional yoga pose or take more gentle exercise strolling through the city's magnificent palace and colourful market, Mysore is one Indian city that rewards a slower pace.

History

Mysore was named after the mythical Mahisuru, where the goddess Chamundi slew the demon Mahishasura. The Mysore dynasty was founded in 1399, but up until the mid-16th century its rulers, the Wodeyars, were in the service of the Vijayanagar emperor. With the fall of the empire in 1565, the Mysore rulers were among the first to declare their independence.

Apart from a brief period in the late 18th century when Hyder Ali and Tipu Sultan usurped the throne, the Wodeyars continued to rule until Independence in 1947. In 1956 when the new state was formed, the former maharaja was elected governor.

Orientation

The train station is northwest of the city centre, about 1km from the main shopping street, Sayyaji Rao Rd. The Central bus stand is on Bengaluru–Mysore (BM) Rd, on the northeastern edge of the city centre. The Maharaja's Palace occupies the entire southeastern sector of the city centre. Chamundi Hill is an ever-visible landmark to the south.

Information

ATMs and internet cafés are sprinkled around town.

BOOKSHOPS

Ashok Book Centre (396 Dhanvanthri Rd; ☣ 9.30am-9pm Mon-Sat, 10am-2.30pm Sun)
Geetha Book House (KR Circle; ☣ 10am-1pm & 5-8pm Mon-Sat) On Krishnajara (KR) Circle.
Sauharda Bookstore (1683 Hanumantha Rao St; ☣ 9.30am-1.30pm & 4.30-8.30pm Mon-Sat)

LEFT LUGGAGE

The City bus stand has a cloakroom open from 6am to 11pm; it costs Rs 10 per bag per 12 hours.

MEDICAL SERVICES

Basappa Memorial Hospital (☎ 2512401; 22B Vinoba Rd, Jayalakshmipuram)

MONEY

State Bank of Mysore Nehru Circle (☎ 2538956; cnr Irwin & Ashoka Rds; ☣ 10.30am-2.30pm & 3-4pm Mon-Fri, 10.30am-12.30pm Sat); Sayyaji Rao Rd (☎ 2445691; 10.30am-2.30pm Mon-Fri, 10.30am-12.30pm Sat) Changes cash and Amex travellers cheques.

PHOTOGRAPHY

Rekha Colour Lab (142 Dhanvanthri Rd; ☣ 9am-9.30pm) For digital needs.

POST

Main post office (cnr Irwin & Ashoka Rds; ☣ 10am-6pm Mon-Sat, 10.30am-1pm Sun)

TOURIST INFORMATION

Karnataka Tourism (☎ 2422096; Old Exhibition Bldg, Irwin Rd; ☣ 10am-5.30pm Mon-Sat) Unusually helpful.
KSTDC Transport Office (☎ 2423652; 2 Jhansi Lakshmi Bai Rd; ☣ 6.30am-8.30pm) KSTDC has counters at the train station and Central bus stand, as well as this transport office next to KSTDC Hotel Mayura Hoysala.

Sights
MAHARAJA'S PALACE

The fantastic profile of this walled Indo-Saracenic **palace** (Mysore Palace; ☎ 2434425; www .mysorepalace.org; admission Rs 20, camera Rs 5; ☣ 10am-5.30pm), the seat of the maharajas of Mysore, graces the city's skyline. An earlier palace burnt down in 1897 and the present one, designed by English architect Henry Irwin, was completed in 1912 at a cost of Rs 4.5 million.

The palace's interior – a kaleidoscope of stained glass, mirrors and gaudy colours – is undoubtedly over the top, but it includes awe-inspiring carved wooden doors and mosaic floors, as well as a series of historically interesting paintings depicting life in Mysore during the Edwardian Raj. Hindu temples within the palace grounds include the **Sri Shweta Varahaswamy Temple**; its *gopuram* (gateway tower) influenced the style of the later Sri Chamundeswari Temple on Chamundi Hill. There's also the Royal House of Mysore shop selling exclusive designs of saris and dupattas (scarves worn by Punjabi women).

The entry fee is paid at the southern gate of the grounds; keep your ticket to enter the palace building itself. Cameras must be deposited at the entrance gate – you can only take photos of the outside of the buildings. Some books on historical sites are sold near the exit of the main rooms, though the state archaeology office, in the southwest part of the

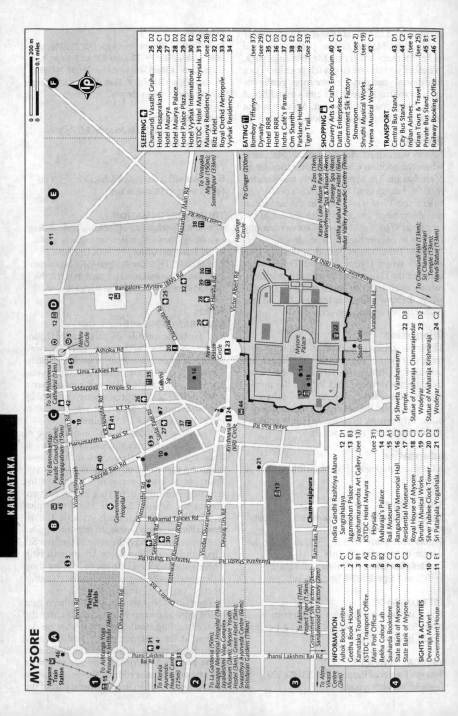

MYSORE

SLEEPING

Chamundi Vasathi Gruha..............	25 D2
Hotel Dasaprakash........................	26 C1
Hotel Maurya..............................	27 C2
Hotel Maurya Palace....................	28 D2
Hotel Palace Plaza.......................	29 D2
Hotel Vyshak International............	30 B2
KSTDC Hotel Mayura Hoysala.......	31 A2
Maurya Residency........................	(see 28)
Ritz Hotel...................................	32 D2
Royal Orchid Metropole...............	33 A2
Vyshak Residency........................	34 B2

EATING

Bombay Tiffanys..........................	(see 37)
Dynasty......................................	(see 29)
Hotel RRR...................................	35 D2
Hotel RRR...................................	36 D2
Indra Café's Paras........................	37 C2
Om Shanthi.................................	38 E2
Parklane Hotel.............................	39 D2
Tiger Trail...................................	(see 33)

SHOPPING

Cauvery Arts & Crafts Emporium..40	C1
Datta Enterprises.........................	41 C1
Government Silk Factory	
Showroom................................	(see 2)
Shruthi Musical Works..................	(see 19)
Veena Musical Works....................	42 C1

TRANSPORT

Central Bus Stand.........................	43 D1
City Bus Stand..............................	44 C2
Indian Airlines.............................	(see 4)
Kiran Tours & Travel.....................	(see 25)
Private Bus Stand.........................	45 B1
Railway Booking Office..................	46 A1

INFORMATION

Ashok Book Centre.........................	1 C1
Geetha Book House........................	2 C2
Karnataka Tourism..........................	3 B1
KSTDC Transport Office...................	4 A2
Main Post Office............................	5 D1
Rekha Colour Lab..........................	6 B2
Sauharda Bookstore.......................	7 C2
State Bank of India........................	8 C1
State Bank of Mysore.....................	9 C2

SIGHTS & ACTIVITIES

Devaraja Market............................	10 C2
Government House.........................	11 E1
Indira Gandhi Rashtriya Manav	
Sangrahalaya.............................	12 D1
Jaganmohan Palace.......................	13 B3
Jayachamarajendra Art Gallery.....	(see 13)
KSTDC Hotel Mayura	
Hoysala....................................	14 C3
Maharaja's Palace..........................	15 A1
Rail Museum.................................	16 C2
Rangacharlu Memorial Hall............	17 C2
Residential Museum.......................	18 C3
Royal House of Mysore..................	19 C1
Shruthi Musical Works...................	20 D2
Silver Jubilee Clock Tower..............	21 C3
Sri Patanjala Yogashala.................	22 D3
Sri Shweta Varahaswamy	
Temple.....................................	22 D3
Statue of Maharaja Chamarajendra	
Wodeyar..................................	23 D2
Statue of Maharaja Krishnaraja	
Wodeyar..................................	24 C2

grounds, has a more complete collection.

Incorporating some of the palace's living quarters and personal effects belonging to the maharaja's family, the **Residential Museum** (admission Rs 20; ⏲ 10.30am-6.30pm) is rather dull next to the lustre of the state rooms.

Ninety-six thousand light bulbs illuminate the building during the 10 days of Dussehra (above) and every Sunday from 7pm to 8pm.

DEVARAJA MARKET
Built during Tipu Sultan's time, the spellbinding **Devaraja Market** (Sayyaji Rao Rd; ⏲ 6am-8.30pm) is one of India's most colourful and lively bazaars. Stalls selling all manner of fruits, vegetables, flower garlands and spices, and conical piles of *kumkum* (coloured powder used for bindi dots on heads of married women as well as other religious rituals) make ideal photographic subjects. Be prepared to bargain when shopping.

CHAMUNDI HILL
Overlooking Mysore from the 1062m-high summit of Chamundi Hill, the **Sri Chamundeswari Temple** (☎ 2590027; ⏲ 7am-2pm & 3.30-9pm), dominated by a towering seven-storey, 40m-high *gopuram*, makes a fine half-day excursion. Pilgrims are supposed to climb the 1000-plus steps to the top; those not needing a karmic boost will find descending easier. A road goes to the top; bus 201 departs from the City bus stand in Mysore for the summit every 40 minutes (Rs 6, 30 minutes). A taxi will cost about Rs 200.

A path that starts near the stalls behind the statue will lead you down the hill, a 45-minute descent taking in 1000 steps and re-energis-ing views. One-third of the way down is a 5m-high **Nandi** (Shiva's bull vehicle) that was carved out of solid rock in 1659. It's one of the largest in India and is visited by hordes of pilgrims. The garlanded statue has a flaky black coating of coconut-husk charcoal mixed with ghee.

You may have rubbery legs by the time you reach the bottom of the hill and it's still about 2km back to Mysore's centre. Fortunately, there are usually autorickshaws nearby, which charge Rs 40 or so for the trip back to town.

JAYACHAMARAJENDRA ART GALLERY
The **Jaganmohan Palace**, just west of the Maharaja's Palace, houses the **Jayachamarajendra Art Gallery** (☎ 2423693; Jaganmohan Palace Rd; adult/child Rs 15/8; ⏲ 8.30am-5pm), which has a collection of kitsch objects and memorabilia from the Wodeyars, including weird and wonderful musical machines, rare instruments, Japanese art, and paintings by Raja Ravi Varma. Built in 1861, the palace served as a royal auditorium.

INDIRA GANDHI RASHTRIYA MANAV SANGRAHALAYA
The Bophal-based **Indira Gandhi Rashtriya Manav Sangrahalaya** (National Museum of Mankind; ☎ 2448231; www.museumofmankindindia.org; Wellington House, Irwin Rd; admission free; ⏲ 10am-5.30pm Tue-Sun) is dedicated to preserving and promoting traditional Indian arts and culture. The Mysore branch functions primarily as a cultural centre and exhibition space showcasing arts from rural India. Monthly demonstrations and lectures are open to the public, as are workshops, which are usually two-week courses in a traditional

KARNATAKA

art form. The museum has excellent rotating exhibitions and a good souvenir shop.

JAYALAKSHMI VILAS COMPLEX MUSEUM

Inside the Mysore University Campus, 3km west of the city centre, this **museum** (☎ 2419348; admission free; ☺ 10am-5.30pm Mon-Sat, closed alternate Sat) housed in a grand mansion specialises in folklore. Displays include a wooden puppet of the 10-headed demon Ravana, leather shadow puppets, rural costumes, a 300-year-old temple cart and a stuffed tiger bearing a portrait of a past maharaja framed with elephant tusks!

RAIL MUSEUM

To see how Indian royals travelled in days past, pop into this **museum** (☎ 9844060012; KRS Rd; adult/child Rs 10/5; ☺ 9.30am-6.30pm Tue-Sun) behind the train station, where you can inspect the Mysore maharani's saloon, a wood-panelled beauty dating from 1899. There are also five steam engines, each with its own story.

OTHER SIGHTS

Mysore is an architectural vaudeville of fine buildings and monuments. Dating from 1805, **Government House** (Irwin Rd), formerly the British Residency, is a Tuscan Doric building set in 20 hectares of **gardens** (admission free; ☺ 5am-9pm).

In front of the north gate of the Maharaja's Palace is the 1920 **statue of Maharaja Chamarajendar Wodeyar** (New Statue Circle), facing the 1927 **Silver Jubilee Clock Tower** (Ashoka Rd). Nearby is the imposing **Rangacharlu Memorial Hall**, built in 1884. The next circle west is the 1950s Krishnaraja Circle, better known as KR Circle, graced by a **statue of Maharaja Krishnaraja Wodeyar**.

Towering **St Philomena's Cathedral** (☎ 2563148; St Philomena St; ☺ 5am-6pm, English mass 7am), built between 1933 and 1941 in neo-Gothic style, is one of the largest in India and has beautiful stained-glass windows.

Mysore's **zoo** (☎ 2440752; Indiranagar; adult/child Rs 25/5, camera Rs 10; ☺ 8.30am-5.30pm Wed-Mon), set in pretty gardens on the eastern edge of the city, dates from 1892. A range of primates, tigers, elephants, bears, birds and rhinos live here.

Activities & Courses

BIRD-WATCHING

Karanji Lake Nature Park (Indiranagar; admission Rs 10, camera/video Rs 10/25; ☺ 8.30am-5.30pm), next to the zoo, is home to a large number of bird species, including great and little cormorants, purple and grey herons, various egrets, black ibises, rose-ringed parakeets, green bee-eaters and painted storks, as well as several kinds of butterfly. The aviary here is sad but fascinating; its enormous great pied hornbill is a sight to see.

AYURVEDA

Emerge Spa (☎ 2522500; www.emergespa.co.in; Windflower Spa & Resort, Maharanapratap Rd, Nazarbad), Mysore's slickest spa operation, offers an hour's Ayurvedic massage starting at Rs 690, as well as a range of Balinese massage, hydrotherapy and beauty treatments.

Classy **Indus Valley Ayurvedic Centre** (☎ 2473437; www.ayurindus.com; Lalithadripura) is set on 16 hectares of gardens, 7km east of Mysore at the foot of Chamundi Hill. Its academic approach to the science of Ayurveda is based strictly on the Vedas (Hindu sacred books), and it offers training programmes for those interested in learning the technique. A whole body massage and steam is Rs 860. Vikram-style yoga classes are held at 7am and 4pm (Rs 210). The best deals are the overnight-stay packages (single/double from Rs 5040/7980).

More of a clinic than a spa, **Kerala Ayurvedic Health Centre** (☎ 5269111; www.keralaayurhealth.com; 10/1 Jhansi Lakshmi Bhai Cross Rd) offers four-hour sessions for around US$20. Training courses and yoga classes are also given.

The outpatient operation of Swaasthya Ayurveda Village (p240), **Swaasthya Ayurveda Centre** (☎ 5557557; www.swaasthya.com; Vijayanagar) offers similar keenly priced, expertly performed treatments. It's 5km west of Mysore's centre, just past the Green Hotel and behind Bharatiya Vidya Bhavan.

YOGA

The following places have put Mysore on the international yoga map. Most courses require at least a month's commitment, and you'll need to book far in advance for Ashtanga Yoga Research Institute and the Atma Vikasa Centre; call or write to the centres for details.

Ashtanga Yoga Research Institute (AYRI; ☎ 2516756; www.ayri.org; 3rd Stage, 235 8th Cross, Gokulam) Ninety-two-year-old K Pattabhi Jois is famous in Ashtanga circles the world over. He taught Madonna her yoga moves.

Atma Vikasa Centre (☎ 2341978; www.atmavikasa .com; Bharathi Mahila Samaja, Kuvempunagar Double Rd) 'Backbending expert' Yogacharya Venkatesh offers courses in yoga, Sanskrit and meditation.

Sri Patanjala Yogashala (Yoga Research Institute; Sri Bramatantra Swatantra Parakala Mutt, Jaganmohan Palace Circle; ☼ 6-8am & 5-7pm) The well-respected Ashtanga practitioner BNS Iyengar (not to be confused with BKS Iyengar, famed exponent of Iyengar yoga) teaches here.

MUSIC

The folks at **Shruthi Musical Works** (☎ 2529551; 1189 3rd Cross, Irwin Rd; ☼ 10.30am-9pm Mon-Sat, 10.30am-2pm Sun) get good reviews for their tabla instruction (Rs 200 per hour).

Tours

The KSTDC's comprehensive Mysore city tour (Rs 125) takes in city sights plus Chamundi Hill, Srirangapatnam and Brindavan Gardens. It starts daily at 8.30am, ends at 8.30pm and is likely to leave you breathless.

Other KSTDC tours include one to Belur, Halebid and Sravanabelagola (Rs 325) every Tuesday, Wednesday, Friday and Sunday at 7.30am, ending at 9pm; and Udhagamandalam (Ooty) every Monday, Thursday and Saturday (Rs 350) leaving at 7am and returning at 9pm. Both these tours run daily in the high season.

All tours leave from the **KSTDC Hotel Mayura Hoysala** (2 Jhansi Lakshmi Bai Rd). Bookings can be made at the KSTDC Transport Office (p233) or at travel agencies around town.

Sleeping

Rooms fill up during Dussehra, so book ahead if you're arriving during the festival. Also check with the tourist office about the local homestay programme, which offers rooms from around Rs 400 per person.

BUDGET

The following have hot water (at least in the morning) and 24-hour checkout.

Mysore Youth Hostel (☎ 2544704; www.yhmysore .com; Gangothri Layout; dm from Rs 40; ▯) All the usual rules and regs, including a 10.30pm curfew, are in place at this well-run, friendly hostel set in quiet, green grounds about 4km from the city centre.

Hotel Dasaprakash (☎ 2442444; www.mysoredas aprakashgroup.com; Gandhi Sq; s/d from Rs 215/420; ▨) This long-time favourite has efficient service, and old wooden furniture in some rooms. Within the complex there's an inexpensive veg restaurant, an ice-cream parlour, a travel agency and an astro-palmist.

Chamundi Vasathi Gruha (☎ 5266162; Chandragupta Rd; s/d Rs 250/550; ▯) This family-run place has a smattering of colonial charm, pumpkin-coloured walls and internet access.

Hotel Maurya (☎ 2426677; Hanumantha Rao St; s/d from Rs 400/600) In the process of upgrading all its well-kept rooms, this justly popular place has obliging staff and a great location among Mysore's winding alleys.

Ritz Hotel (☎ 2422668; hotelritz@rediffmail.com; BM Rd; d/q Rs 450/700) The Ritz's glory days are long gone but its four old-fashioned rooms have charm. The shaded restaurant-bar is a good place for a quiet drink or snack.

MIDRANGE

KSTDC Hotel Mayura Hoysala (☎ 2425349; www.nic .in/kstdc; 2 Jhansi Lakshmi Bai Rd; s/d incl breakfast from Rs 500/650; ▨) This government hotel with clean, good sized rooms is convenient for the train station, but it's also on a busy street, so don't bargain on a quiet night's sleep.

Hotel Maurya Palace (☎ 2435912; www.sangroupof hotels.com; 2716 Sri Harsha Rd; r from Rs 575; ▨) Along with its sister property next door, Maurya Residency (☎ 2523375; room with AC from Rs 745), this is the best of the Sri Harsha Rd hotel gang. The staff are helpful, the tidy rooms well presented and its nonveg restaurant Jewel Rock is beloved by carnivores.

Hotel Palace Plaza (☎ 2430034; www.hotelpalace plaza.com; Sri Harsha Rd; s/d from Rs 600/750; ▨ ▯) Not the most palatial of places, but the rooms here are modern, tastefully decorated and comfortable.

Hotel Vyshak International (☎ 2421777; vyshakint ernational@yahoo.com; 19 Seebaiah Rd; d from Rs 800; ▨) Clean, efficiently run and welcoming – what more could you want? The management also runs the Vyshak Residency (double from Rs 800) across the road.

Ginger (☎ 6633333; www.gingerhotels.com; Nazarbad Mohalla; s/d Rs 999/1199; ▨ ▯) This ultramodern business hotel is painted in warm orange tones. The sleek rooms are good value and come with lots of features, including wi-fi and LCD TVs.

our pick **Green Hotel** (☎ 2512536; www.greenhotel india.com; 2270 Vinoba Rd, Jayalakshmipuram; s/d garden from Rs 1250/1650, palace from Rs 2250/2500) Partly housed in a century-old palace once used as a country retreat for Wodeyar princesses, the award-winning Green Hotel, 5km west of town, is a gem. Not only is it run on ecological principles, it also donates all profits to charity.

KARNATAKA

The palace's elegant atmosphere, complete with beautiful gardens, is impressively intact, and the guest rooms are imaginatively themed. The modern garden wing has fresh (but themeless) rooms.

TOP END

Lalitha Mahal Palace Hotel (☎ 2470470; www.lalitha mahalpalace.com; s/d/ste from US$60/70/230; ☒ ☐ ☎) Only consider staying at this former palace, 5km east of the city centre, if you're prepared to splash out on the suites, which offer a taste of Raj-era life, with canopied beds, period furniture and lots of froufrou. The elevator is similarly precious, with carpeting and a tapestry-upholstered ottoman. As a government-run operation, the hotel's service can be lax.

Windflower Spa & Resort (☎ 2522500; www .thewindflower.com; Maharanapratap Rd, Nazarbad; s/d incl breakfast from Rs 3200/3600; ☒ ☐ ☎) Bali comes to Mysore at this stylish, relaxing resort next to the racecourse. Rooms are huge and come with outdoor showers and private plunge pools. Rates include taxes.

Royal Orchid Metropole (☎ 5255566; www.baljee hotels.com; 5 Jhansi Lakshmi Bai Rd; s/d from Rs 4000/4600; ☒ ☐ ☎) This recently renovated hotel was originally built by the Wodeyars and has bona fide old-world charm. The heritage rooms are particularly nice.

Eating

Mysore is well served by Indian restaurants, but for Western food you're best sticking with the major hotels. Unless otherwise mentioned, restaurants are open from noon to 3pm and 7pm to 11pm.

Bombay Tiffanys (Sayyaji Rao Rd; sweets Rs 2-40; ☯ 7.30am-10pm) For traditional Indian sweets, Bombay Tiffanys has a solid reputation. Try the local delicacy *Mysore pak* (a sweet made from chickpea flour, sugar and ghee).

Vinayaka Mylari (769 Nazarbad Main Rd; snacks Rs 6-22; ☯ 7.30-11.30am & 4-8pm) Locals line up for the dosas (paper-thin, lentil-flour pancakes) and soft Mysore-style *idlis* (rice dumplings) served with delicious coconut chutney at this decades-old operation. A *masala dosa* and coffee make a great breakfast or lunch.

Indra Café's Paras (1740 Sayyaji Rao Rd; mains Rs 30-60; ☯ 7.30am-10pm) Take your pick from South (Rs 30) or North (Rs 60) Indian-style thalis at this popular joint opposite the market, with *chaat* (snack) central (Rs 8 to 20) downstairs.

Parklane Hotel (☎ 2430400; www.parklanemysore .com; 2720 Sri Harsha Rd; mains Rs 35-100) At the time of research the hotel was being upgraded, with plans to add a rooftop pool, but the popular restaurant-bar was still in full swing; by now the famous hanging gardens courtyard should be fully restored, with a new upper terrace for families. Enjoy Chinese, continental and Indian dinners by candlelight at night, and occasional live music.

Hotel RRR (Gandhi Sq; mains Rs 40-70) The speciality at this reliable and usually packed place is spicy Andhra-style veg thalis (Rs 36) served on banana leaves. Some meaty options are available, too. There's a second branch on Sri Harsha Rd.

Om Shanthi (Hotel Siddharta, Guest House Rd; mains Rs 40-80) Om Shanthi is a byword for excellent veg food in Mysore. Its special South Indian thali (Rs 75) is really quite special. Pay first at the counter before sitting down.

Dynasty (Hotel Palace Plaza, Sri Harsha Rd; mains Rs 40-85) There's a touch of class to this ground-floor restaurant, with its check tablecloths, intimate booths and low lighting. The same menu of reliable Indian and continental standards is also served on the rooftop, with views of the palace and Chamundi Hill.

La Gardenia (☎ 2426426; Regaalis Mysore, 3-14 Vinoba Rd; mains Rs 120-150) This place serves tasty and well-presented food in a sophisticated environment, with a good assortment of dishes if you're tired of the Indian options.

our pick Tiger Trail (☎ 5255566; Royal Orchid Metropole; 5 Jhansi Lakshmi Bai Rd; mains Rs 80-200) This delightful restaurant specialising in tandoori dishes serves delicious food in a courtyard that twinkles with torches and fairy lights at night. There's often live classical Indian music performances, and it's a nice spot for high tea, too.

Lalitha Mahal Palace Hotel (☎ 2470470; mains Rs 200-350) Feel like you're dining at Versailles in the Wedgwood-coloured restaurant at the hotel of the same name (left).

Shopping

Mysore is famous for its carved sandalwood, inlay work, silk saris and wooden toys. It is also one of India's major incense-manufacturing centres, peppered with scores of little family-owned *agarbathi* (incense) factories.

Souvenir and handicraft shops are dotted around Jaganmohan Palace and Dhanvanthri Rd, while silk shops line Devaraj Urs Rd.

Cauvery Arts & Crafts Emporium (Sayyaji Rao Rd; 10am-7.30pm) Not the cheapest place, but the selection is extensive and there's no pressure to buy.

Government Silk Factory (☎ 2481803; Mananthody Rd, Ashokapuram; 10am-noon & 2-4pm Mon-Sat) You can see weavers at work here, and buy silks at an on-site shop; there's also a factory showroom on KR Circle, open from 10.30am to 7.30pm.

Sandalwood Oil Factory (☎ 2483345; Ashokapuram; 9am-1pm & 2-5pm Mon-Sat) Buy authentic incense sticks and oil (from Rs 650 for 5ml) at this factory, located about 2km southeast of the Maharaja's Palace, off Mananthody Rd.

Datta Enterprises (355 KR Hospital Rd; 10am-9pm) Get custom-made Ganesh stickers here, starting at Rs 25 each.

Fabindia (☎ 4259009; 451JLB Rd, Chamrajpuram; 10am-8pm) There's a branch of the ever reliable clothing and homewares shop on the way to the silk and sandalwood factories.

Shruthi Musical Works (☎ 2529551; 1189 3rd Cross, Irwin Rd; 10.30am-9pm Mon-Sat, 10.30am-2pm Sun) and **Veena Musical Works** (Kalamma Temple Bldg, Irwin Rd; 10am-8.30pm Mon-Sat, 10am-1.30pm Sun) both sell a variety of traditional musical instruments; you can view the workshop of the latter across the road from the shop.

Getting There & Away
AIR
There are no flights to Mysore (although an airport is in the offing). **Indian Airlines** (☎ 2421846; Jhansi Lakshmi Bai Rd; 10am-1.30pm & 2.15-5pm) has an office next to KSTDC Hotel Mayura Hoysala.

BUS
The **Central bus stand** (☎ 2520853; Bangalore–Mysore Rd) handles all KSRTC long-distance buses. The **City bus stand** (☎ 2425819; Sayaji Rao Rd) is for city, Srirangapatnam and Chamundi Hill buses.

KSRTC bus services from Mysore include those listed on below.

For Belur, Halebid or Sravanabelagola, the usual gateway is Hassan. There's one bus to Sravanabelagola; otherwise you can transfer at Channarayapatna. For Hampi, the best transfer point is Hospet.

The **Private bus stand** (Sayyaji Rao Rd) has services to Hubli, Bijapur, Mangalore, Udhagamandalam (Ooty) and Ernakulum. Book tickets with **Kiran Tours & Travel** (☎ 5559404; 21/2 Chandragupta Rd).

TRAIN
At the **railway booking office** (☎ 131; 8am-8pm Mon-Sat, 8am-2pm Sun), located within the train station, you can reserve a seat on one of six daily expresses to Bengaluru (2nd/chair Rs 70/228, three hours), or on the high-speed *Shatabdi* (chair/executive Rs 275/550, two hours), departing at 2.20pm daily except Tuesday. The *Shatabdi* continues to Chennai (chair/executive Rs 690/1315, seven hours). Several passenger trains also go daily to Bengaluru (Rs 28, 3½ hours), stopping at Srirangapatnam (Rs 9, 20 minutes).

Two passenger and three express trains go daily to Arsikere and Hassan. One express sets off to Mumbai on Thursday at 6.50am (sleeper/3AC/2AC Rs 369/1009/1583).

BUSES FROM MYSORE			
Destination	**Fare (Rs)**	**Duration (hr)**	**Frequency**
Bandipur	35 (O)	2	hourly
Bengaluru	70 (O)/102 (R)/150 (V)	3	every 15min
Channarayapatna	50 (O)	2	hourly
Chennai	384 (V)	6	2 daily
Ernakulum	440 (R)	10	5 daily
Gokarna	240 (O)	12	1 daily
Hassan	60 (O)	3	every 45min
Hospet	200 (O)	8	4 daily
Mangalore	130 (O)/220 (R)	7	hourly
Nagarhole	55 (O)	3	4 daily
Ooty	75 (O)/120 (D)	5	hourly
Sravanabelagola	50 (O)	2½	1 daily

O – Ordinary, D – semideluxe, R – Rajahamsa, V – Volvo

KARNATAKA

Getting Around

Agencies at hotels and around town rent cars from Rs 5 per kilometre for an Ambassador, with a minimum of 250km per day, plus Rs 125 for the driver.

Flag fall on autorickshaws is Rs 12, and Rs 5 per kilometre is charged thereafter. Taxis are meterless, so fares must be negotiated.

AROUND MYSORE
Srirangapatnam
☎ 08236

From this fort, built on a long island in the Cauvery River only 16km from Mysore, Hyder Ali and his son Tipu Sultan ruled much of southern India during the 18th century. In ruins since the British came through like a whirlwind in 1799, the ramparts, battlements and some of the gates of the fort still stand.

Close to the bus station is a handsome twin tower mosque built by Tipu Sultan, and within the fort walls you can also find the dungeon where Tipu held British officers captive, and the handsome **Sri Ranganathaswamy Temple** (☼ 7.30am-1pm & 4-8pm).

Srirangapatnam's star attraction is Tipu's summer palace, the **Daria Daulat Bagh** (☎ 252023; Indian/foreigner Rs 5/US$2; ☼ 9am-5pm), which lies 1km east of the fort. Set in ornamental gardens, the palace is notable for its beautiful interior decoration. Not one inch has been left unadorned, with fascinating floor-to-ceiling murals depicting courtly life and Tipu's campaigns against the British. The man himself can be glimpsed in a portrait by John Zoffony, which was painted in 1780 when Tipu was 30.

About 2km further east the remains of Hyder Ali, his wife and Tipu are housed in the impressive onion-domed **Gumbaz** (☎ 252007; ☼ 8am-8pm). Again it's the tiger-striped interior of this mausoleum that dazzles most.

Head 500m east of Gumbaz for the river banks. A short coracle ride runs for Rs 25 per person. Resist dangling your hand in the water; a crocodile could have it for lunch.

Three kilometres upstream from Srirangapatnam, the **Ranganathittu Bird Sanctuary** (☎ 0821-2481159; Indian/foreigner Rs 10/60, camera/video Rs 20/100; ☼ 8.30am-6pm) is on one of three islands in the Cauvery River. The storks, ibises, egrets, spoonbills and cormorants here are best seen in the early morning or late afternoon on a short **boat ride** (per person Rs 25). There's also a maze made from herbal plants and a restaurant on site.

SLEEPING & EATING
Royal Retreat New Amblee Holiday Resort (☎ 0821-3292475; www.ambleeresort.com; r from Rs 1200; ▨ ▣) A menagerie of rabbits and ducks, and the owner's Rolls-Royce greets you at the Amblee, which offers relatively good accommodation, a pleasant riverside setting and a reasonably priced restaurant.

Swaasthya Ayurveda Village (☎ 217476; www .swaasthya.com; 69 Bommuru Agrahara; r incl full board Rs 960) Set amid lush riverside greenery, this is an idyllic place to stay whether or not you choose to avail yourself of the various reasonably priced Ayurvedic treatments on offer. Rooms are clean and simple, and rates include delicious vegetarian meals, yoga and spoken Sanskrit classes. It's located off Bengaluru–Mysore Rd.

GETTING THERE & AWAY
Take the frequent buses 313 or 316 (Rs 10, one hour) from Mysore's City bus stand. Passenger trains travelling from Mysore to Bengaluru (Rs 9, 20 minutes) also stop here. The stand for private buses heading to Brindavan Gardens (Rs 12, 30 minutes) is just across from Srirangapatnam's main bus stand.

GETTING AROUND
The sights are a little spread out, but walking isn't out of the question. For a quicker look round, tongas (two-wheeled horse carriages) cost about Rs 100 for three hours, and an autorickshaw is about Rs 150 (also for three hours).

Brindavan Gardens
If you think these ornamental **gardens** (☎ 08236-290019; adult/child Rs 10/5, camera Rs 25; ☼ 10am-10pm) laid out below the River Cauvery dam look like the set from a Bollywood movie, then you're on the money – they've been the backdrop to many a shimmying musical number. Locals flock here, particularly on weekends and holidays, and at 7pm, when the illuminated fountains are switched on (to the accompaniment of film tunes).

Within the gardens are two hotels: the no-frills **Hotel Mayura Cauvery** (☎ 08236-257252; s/d Rs 200/350) and the swanky **Royal Orchid Brindavan Garden** (☎ 080-25584242; www.baljeehotels.com), still under construction at the time of research. Its bar promises to be the best spot from which to view the gardens.

The gardens are 19km northwest of Mysore. One of the KSTDC tours stops here, and buses 301, 304, 305, 306 and 365 depart from Mysore's City bus stand hourly (Rs 7, 45 minutes).

Melkote

Life in the devout Hindu town of Melkote, about 50km north of Mysore, revolves around the 12th-century **Cheluvanarayana Temple** (☎ 08236-298739; Raja St; ⏱ 8am-1pm & 5-8pm), with its rose-coloured *gopuram* and ornately carved pillars. Get a work-out on the hike up to the hilltop **Yoganarasimha Temple** (admission free), which offers fine views of the surrounding hills and valleys. The town comes alive for the **Vairamudi Festival** in March or April (p220).

Three KSRTC buses a day shuttle between Mysore and Melkote (Rs 40, 1½ hours).

Somnathpur

The astonishingly beautiful **Keshava Temple** (☎ 08227-270059; Indian/foreigner Rs 5/US$2; ⏱ 9am-5.30pm) stands at the edge of the tranquil village of Somnathpur, approximately 33km east of Mysore. Built in 1268, this star-shaped temple is a masterpiece of Hoysala architecture (see p248), covered with superb stone sculptures depicting various scenes from the Ramayana, Mahabharata and Bhagavad Gita, and the life and times of the Hoysala kings. Unlike the larger Hoysala temples at Belur and Halebid, it's also remarkably complete.

On a tree in the temple grounds there's a red postbox where you can drop your stamped mail to get it postmarked with a temple image.

Somnathpur is 7km south of Bannur and 10km north of Tirumakudal Narsipur. Take one of the half-hourly buses from Mysore to either village (Rs 12, 30 minutes) and change there.

Sivasamudram

About 60km southeast of Mysore, near the twin waterfalls of Barachukki and Gaganachukki, is the relaxing **Georgia Sunshine Village** (☎ 9845754661; www.georgiasunshine.com; Malavalli; d incl full board from Rs 1372; ✖ 🏊). Accommodation is in bungalows (the open-air bathrooms have small gardens) and the home-made food is delicious. The dog-loving hosts can arrange treks to the waterfalls (best viewed in June and July), which are around 5km away.

Frequent buses run from Mysore (Rs 22, one hour) and Bengaluru (Rs 50, three hours) to Malavalli, 14km away. Call ahead and they'll arrange an autorickshaw to bring you the rest of the way for Rs 100.

BANDIPUR NATIONAL PARK

About 80km south of Mysore on the Ooty road, the **Bandipur National Park** (Indian/foreigner Rs 50/150) covers 880 sq km and is part of the Nilgiri Biosphere Reserve, which includes the sanctuaries of Nagarhole, Mudumalai in Tamil Nadu and Wayanad in Kerala. It was once the Mysore maharajas' private wildlife reserve and is home to over 5000 Asiatic elephants – a fifth of the world's population.

Bandipur is also noted for herds of gaurs (Indian bison), chitals (spotted deer), sambars, panthers, sloth bears and langurs. More than 80 tigers reportedly roam here, but they're rarely seen. The vegetation is a hodgepodge of deciduous and evergreen forest and scrubland. The best time to see wildlife is March to April, but November to February has the most temperate climate.

Brief **elephant rides** (per person Rs 50) are available for a minimum of four people. Private cars – with the exception of resort vehicles – are not allowed to tour the park so you're stuck with the Forest Department's diesel-minibus **safari** (per person Rs 25; ⏱ 6am, 7am, 8am, 4pm & 5pm), which lasts one hour. The wildlife seen will be limited, as a bus lumbering through the forest doesn't exactly entice creatures out into the open. On Sundays tourists can outnumber the chitals.

Sleeping & Eating

Forest Department Bungalows (r Rs 500) It's all pretty basic, and at night the grounds are shared with sleeping chitals. Meals are available with advance notice. Reservations should be made at least two weeks in advance with Project Tiger (☎ 0821-2480901; fdptrm@sancharnet.in; Aranya Bhavan, Ashokapuram) in Mysore.

Bandipur Safari Lodge (Mysore-Ooty Rd; s/d incl full board US$65/100) The 12 animal-themed rooms at this government-run operation, 3km outside the park, are comfy. Rates include a jeep safari, an elephant ride and all park fees. Book with Jungle Lodges & Resorts Ltd (Map p223; ☎ 080-25597021; www.junglelodges .com; 2nd floor, Shrungar Shopping Complex, MG Rd, Bengaluru; open 10am to 5.30pm).

Tusker Trails (☎ 080-23618024; www.nivalink .com/tuskertrails/index.html; s/d incl full board US$90/150; 🏊) Rates at this small, simple resort on the eastern edge of the park near Mangala village include two daily safaris.

Getting There & Away

Buses between Mysore (2½ hours) and Udhagamandalam (Ooty; three hours) will drop you at Bandipur National Park or Bandipur Safari Lodge.

NAGARHOLE NATIONAL PARK

West of the Kabini River is the 643-sq-km wildlife sanctuary of **Nagarhole National Park** (Rajiv Gandhi National Park; Indian/foreigner Rs 50/150, camera Rs 50), pronounced *nag*-ar-hole-eh. The lush forests here are home to around 60 tigers, as well as leopards, elephants, gaurs, muntjacs (barking deer), wild dogs, bonnet macaques and common langurs; animal sightings are more common here than in Bandipur.

The park's main entrance is 93km southwest of Mysore. However, the best accommodation and the most beautiful views are at the Kabini Lake side of the reserve, near the village of Karapura, around 80km south of Mysore. **Orange County** (www.orangecounty.in) are building a resort on the far bank of the lake here. If heading to the park by taxi, make sure that your driver knows exactly which side of the park you're staying, as it's quite a distance between the two locations.

If you're not staying at a lodge, the only way to see the park is on the bus **tour** (per person Rs 25; ☿ 6-8am & 4-5pm); the best time to view wildlife is the hot months (April to May), but the winter air (November to February) is kinder. Bookings can be made in advance with the Forest Department in Mysore, or you can just turn up.

Sleeping & Eating

As there's less accommodation at the park's main entrance (and subsequently less noise to scare away the wildlife), this is the place to be if you want to up your chances of spotting a tiger. However, the places to stay here are not nearly as nice as those on Kabini Lake. Unless otherwise mentioned, rates quoted cover accommodation, three meals, and early morning and late afternoon safari tours into the park, either by jeep or boat.

PARK GATE

Forest Department rooms (☎ 0821-2480901; fdptrm@sancharnet.in; r Indian/foreigner Rs 750/1500) These rooms are within the park, close to the main gate. They're overpriced for what you get and you'd be advised to bring mosquito coils. Meals and tours are extra. Book at least two weeks in advance with Project Tiger (☎ 0821-2480901; fdptrm@sancharnet.in; Aranya Bhavan, Ashokapuram) in Mysore.

Jungle Inn (☎ 08222-246022; www.jungleinnnagarhole.com; Km 19 Hunsur–Nagarhole Rd; s/d 1st night US$110/170, additional nights US$60/100) This place is by no means luxurious, but there's a welcoming atmosphere, evening campfires and simple, clean rooms. Many of the organic vegetables and fruit used in the meals are grown on site. The resort is 35km from park reception on the Hunsur road.

Kings Sanctuary (☎ 08222-246444; www.vivekhotels; Km 19 Hunsur–Nagarhole Rd; s/d Indian Rs 7000/8500, foreigner US$190/280; 🔀 🛋) This large resort is only a few years old but it's already looking worn. It's the only upmarket option at this end of the park. The rates for Indians include only one safari, while foreigners get two.

KABINI LAKE

Kabini Lake View (☎ 9880175605; kabinilakeview@yahoo.co.in; Sogahalli, Antrasanthe; Indian/foreigner Rs 2000/US$85) This place offers eight rooms in simple concrete cabins using solar power for lights and water heating. There's little shade on the site, 63km south of Mysore, but it has splendid view of the backwaters and the package includes boat trips to an island for bird-watching.

Kabini River Lodge (☎ 08228-264402; Indian tents/r/cottages Rs 2750/3000/3500, foreigner s/d US$120/240) On the grounds of the former maharaja's hunting lodge beside Kabini Lake is this efficient, government-run resort. For accommodation there's a choice of large canvas tents sheltering beneath corrugated roofs, regular rooms and cottages. Book through Jungle Lodges & Resorts Ltd (Map p223; ☎ 080-25597021; www.junglelodges.com; 2nd floor, Shrungar Shopping Complex, MG Rd, Bengaluru; open 10am to 5.30pm).

Cicada Kabini (☎ 080-41152200, 9945602305; www.cicadaresorts.com; s/d Rs 5000/7000; 🔀 🛋 🛋) This well-thought-out luxury ecoresort brings a dash of contemporary chic to the lakeside. The rates are for accommodation and meals only; safaris (R750) and the use of kayaks and pedal boats (R250) are extra.

Water Woods (☎ 08228-264421; www.waterwoods.net; s/d US$225/325; 🔀) Next to Kabini River Lodge, Water Woods offers just five rooms set in a large and pleasantly furnished lakeside house with tranquil gardens, a multigym and a six-hole golf course. A canoe is available for guests' use.

Getting There & Away

Direct buses depart from Mysore twice daily and can drop you at Jungle Inn. For transport to the lodges around Kabiri Lake, enquire when making a booking.

KODAGU (COORG) REGION

The mountainous Kodagu (or Coorg) region is home to the Kodava people and refugee Tibetans. The geography and cool climate make it a fantastic area for trekking, bird-watching and generally refreshing the soul. Winding roads ramble over forested hills and past spice and coffee plantations, which burst into fragrant white blossoms in March and April.

The best season for trekking is October to March. You should hire a guide who will arrange food, transport and accommodation; see right for recommendations. Most treks last two to three days, but longer treks are possible; the most popular treks are to the peaks of Tadiyendamol (1745m) and Pushpagiri (1712m), and to smaller Kotebetta.

Kodagu was a state in its own right until 1956, when it merged with Karnataka. Local politicians, tired of seeing little financial assistance from Bengaluru for infrastructure and social services, are pushing for statehood to be restored, or at least for more local autonomy.

The region's capital and transport hub is Madikeri, but for the authentic Kodagu experience it's best to base yourself on one the many estates that take in guests. Owners can arrange plantation tours and guides for hiking routes. Avoid weekends, when places get booked up by Bengaluru's IT and call-centre crowd.

Madikeri (Mercara)

☎ 08272 / pop 32,286 / elev 1525m
Also known as Mercara, this bustling market town is spread out along a series of ridges. The main reason for coming here is to organise treks and sort out the practicalities of travel.

ORIENTATION & INFORMATION

In the chaotic centre around the KSRTC and private-bus stands, you'll find most of the hotels and restaurants as well as several ATMs.

If you need to change money, cash travellers cheques or get a credit-card advance, try **Canara Bank** (☎ 229302; Main Rd, Gandhi Chowk; ☼ 10.30am-2.30pm Mon-Fri). Internet cafés are plentiful.

SIGHTS

Madikeri's **fort**, now the municipal headquarters, was built in 1812 by Raja Lingarajendra II. Cows graze around the old church here, home to a quirky **museum** (admission free; ☼ 10am-5.30pm Tue-Sun) displaying dusty, poorly labelled statues and the like.

East of the fort is the Indo-Saracenic-style **Omkareshwara Temple** (☼ 6.30am-noon & 5-8pm), built by the raja in 1820, which is surrounded by a small lake. Reach it via the steps descending past the police station.

The panoramic view from **Raja's Seat** (admission free; MG Rd; ☼ 5.30am-7.30pm) is breathtaking. Behind are gardens, a toy train line for kids and a tiny Kodava-style **temple**.

On the way to **Abbi Falls**, a pleasant 7km hike from the town centre, visit the quietly beautiful **Raja's Tombs**, better known as Gaddige. An autorickshaw costs about Rs 150 return.

ACTIVITIES

A trekking guide is essential for navigating the labyrinth of forest tracks. Most of the estates in Kodagu also offer trekking programmes.

Raja Shekar at **Friends Tours & Travels** (☎ 225672; v_trak@rediffmail.com; College Rd; ☼ 10am-2pm & 4.30-8pm Mon-Sat, 6-7.30pm Sun) works in conjunction with Rao Ganesh at **Sri Ganesh Automobile** (☎ 229102; Hill Rd), just up from the private bus stand. It arranges one- to 10-day treks for Rs 500 per person per day (Rs 700 if you're solo), including guide, accommodation and food. Short walks take only a day or two to prepare. For long treks, trips on obscure routes or big groups, it's best to give a week's notice.

Coorg Trails (☎ 594061; coorgtrails@yahoo.co.in; Main Rd; ☼ 9am-8.30pm) can also arrange day treks for R300 per person and a 22km trek to Kotebetta, including an overnight stay in a village, for Rs 600 per person. The office is near the town hall.

Anoop Chinnappa at the **Dawn** (☎ 223388; outdoorindia@sancharnet.in; Powerhouse Rd) offers guided day walks up on the ridges for Rs 500 per person, and can also arrange longer camping trips to a wildlife sanctuary that has an elephant migratory path running through it.

One-hour sessions at the tiny **Shri Akhila Ravi Ayurshala Ayurvedic clinic** (☎ 594288; Powerhouse Rd; ☼ 9am-6pm), a short walk from the fort, cost Rs 175; a normal course runs seven days.

SLEEPING

Many hotels reduce their rates in the off season (January to March and June to September); all of those listed below have hot water, at least in the morning, and 24-hour checkout.

Dawn (☎ 223388; outdoorindia@sancharnet.in; Powerhouse Rd; dm Rs 125) This is the home of enthusiastic ecowarrior Anoop Chinnappa, who can also organise treks. It's 1km from the bus stand, and although the rooms are basic, they have personality.

Hotel Cauvery (☎ 225492; School Rd; s/d/tr Rs 200/450/550) This ageing hotel, tucked behind Hotel Capitol opposite the private bus stand, is scheduled for a make-over. It has some character, and the amiable owner Ganesh Aiyanna can arrange treks up to Tadiyendamol and elsewhere.

Hilltown Hotel (☎ 223801; www.madikeri.com/hilltown; Hill Town Rd; s/d from Rs 250/600) Down the lane running past Hotel Chitra, the Hilltown is a generally spruce place with fish tanks on the stairs and a pretty garden opposite. Singles are small and some rooms have damp walls. It also has a restaurant (mains Rs 30 to 60).

Hotel Mayura Valley View (☎ 228387; r from Rs 999) The overpriced rooms here fail to match up to the stunning valley view from the windows. Staff are pretty laid back, and the restaurant-bar (meals Rs 30 to 85; open 6.30am to 10.30pm) with a terrace is certainly the best place in town for a drink. It's near Raja's Seat.

Hotel Coorg International (☎ 228071; www.coorginternational.com; Convent Rd; s/d incl half-board from Rs 2400/2900; 🖵 🏊) Madikeri's classiest option isn't such a bad deal considering rates include breakfast and dinner, snacks through the day, and facilities such as cable TV, a small pool, a gym and an Ayurvedic massage room.

EATING

East End Hotel (GT Circle; mains Rs 35-80; ☉ 7am-10.30pm) Some veg dishes are available among the mutton offerings, but the special *masala dosas* (Rs 15) are the real reason to come; they're only available from 7.30am to 10.30am and 4pm to 10.30pm.

Udupi Hotel Vegland (Chickpet, Main Rd; meals Rs 15-20; ☉ 7am-9pm) This standard pure-veg joint near the fort is a friendly local place with cheap, reliable thalis.

Popular Guru Prasad (Main Rd; meals Rs 20; ☉ 6.30am-10pm) The aptly named Popular Guru Prasad serves perfectly steamed *idlis* (Rs 3.50 each) and other veggie options.

Hotel Capitol (School Rd; meals Rs 15-40; ☉ 6am-9.30pm) Head to the nonveg-room-cum-drinking-den at the rear for bacon-and-eggs breakfasts and the local speciality, *pandhi* (pork curry; Rs 35), made from porkers raised on the owner's estate.

THE KODAVAS

The native people of Kodagu are known as Kodavas. Numbering no more than 100,000, they are believed to be descendants of migrating Persians and Kurds or Greeks left behind from Alexander the Great's armies, although no-one's exactly sure. The word 'Kodava' apparently comes from the local words for 'Blessed by Mother Cauvery'.

Kodavas are divided into about 1000 clans. Each clan has its own *aine mane* (clan house), at which the entire clan gathers once a year to pay respects to their ancestors. Although nominally Hindu, Kodavas refuse to recognise any head of religion and are mainly nonvegetarian (their signature dish is pork curry served with rice dumplings). They also worship unique deities, including the Cauvery River. Wedding ceremonies (which rarely involve dowries) include complex dances, mock fighting with sticks, and such symbolic exploits as chopping off a banana leaf with a sword.

The best time to see Kodavas celebrating their unique culture is during their various festivals. Apart from the lively November/December **Huthri** festival (p220), there's Keilpodhu, the end of rice-planting season (held in the first week of September), when men show off their marksmanship by shooting coconuts strung up in tall trees. The **Tula Sankramana** festival, when the goddess Cauvery appears in the form of a gush of water at the river's source, is celebrated in mid-October with a dip in the Cauvery at the Talacauvery Temple.

At these festivals and other special occasions, Kodavas will don their distinctive traditional costumes; the men wear sashes, daggers, black gowns, colourful turbans and plenty of jewellery, while the women are wrapped in bright scarves and saris that are draped with even more complexity than normal.

KARNATAKA

GETTING THERE & AWAY

Five deluxe buses a day depart from the KSRTC **bus stand** (☎ 229134) for Bengaluru (Rs 135, seven hours), stopping in Mysore (Rs 70, 3½ hours) on the way. Deluxe buses also go to Mangalore (Rs 110, four hours, three daily), and frequent ordinary buses head to Hassan (Rs 60, three hours) and Shimoga (Rs 140, eight hours).

Around Madikeri

Many estates in Kodagu offer homestay-style accommodation, ranging in quality from basic to quite luxurious. The following are our pick of places within easy reach of Madikeri; for more options, see p246. Unless otherwise mentioned, rates include meals and trekking guides. Advance bookings should be made.

About 8km southeast of Madikeri is **Capitol Village Resort** (☎ 08272-225492; fax 229455; Chettali-Siddapur Rd; r from Rs 1250), a pleasant lodge nestled among coffee, cardamom and pepper plantations. Superclean rooms have balconies with great views. Meals (breakfast Rs 100, buffet lunch or dinner Rs 150) are extra, as are trekking guides.

our pick **Rainforest Retreat** (☎ /fax 08272-265636; www.rainforestours.com; s/d from Rs 1500/2500; ☼ Oct-end of May) is hard to beat for nature immersion. These ecochic cottages are located on an organic plantation surrounded by forest, and the friendly owners Sujata (a botanist) and Anurag (a molecular biologist) are a fount of knowledge about the region. The trekking is excellent, or you can just lie in a hammock and watch the birds. All proceeds go to the couple's NGO, which promotes environmental awareness and sustainable agriculture. It's 10km west of Madikeri near Gallibedu; call to arrange transport.

Alath-Cad Estate Bungalow (☎ 08274-252190, 9449617665; www.alathcadcoorg.com; Ammathi; r incl breakfast from Rs 1650) is set on a 26-hectare coffee plantation about 28km southeast of Madikeri, 1.5km from the town of Ammathi. Its rooms have solar-heated water and the owners are very friendly. Lunch and dinner are Rs 150 each.

A German-owned organic tea plantation, **Golden Mist** (☎ 08272-265629; www.goldenmist.4t.com; s/d Rs 2000/3000) has rooms for up to four people. It's a lovely place, similar in atmosphere to Rainforest Retreat.

On the way to Gallibedu, **Club Mahindra** (☎ 08272-221790; www.clubmahindra.com; Galibeedu Rd;

d from Rs 2500; ☒ ☒) is an upmarket time-share resort. It's a good place if you're travelling with kids, since it offers plenty of activities, two pools and self-catering suites. Rates are room only.

Luxury tents (far nicer than many hotel rooms!) are the latest addition to **Orange County Resort** (☎ 08274-258481; www.orangecounty.in; Siddapur; d cottages/tents Rs 8500/10,500; ☒ ☒), a fine resort on a 120-hectare plantation, 32km south of Madikeri. Some of the villas have private swimming pools. Rates include taxes; guided treks, boating and Ayurvedic massages are available for extra cost. Make bookings through **Trails India** (☎ 080-25325302; www.trailsindia.com; 2nd floor, St Patrick's Business Complex, Museum Rd) in Bengaluru.

Dubare Forest Reserve

Head to Kushalnagar, Kodagu's second-largest town, and you'll pass the Dubare Forest Reserve. Here, on the banks of the Cauvery River, a camp has been established for 12 elephants retired from working in the jungles. Cross the river (Rs 20) and you can watch the elephants being washed and fed daily at 9.30am. To take part in the full programme (Indian/foreigner Rs 100/250), including an elephant ride, you need to be there by 8.30am.

Bookings can be made through **Jungle Lodges & Resorts Ltd** (Map p223; ☎ 080-25597021; www.junglelodges.com; 2nd fl, Shrungar Shopping Complex, MG Rd, Bengaluru; ☼ 10am-5.30pm), which also runs the reserve's rustic but good **Dubare Elephant Camp** (☎ 9449599755; Indian/foreigner incl full board Rs 1900/US$75). Rates include the elephant-interaction programme.

White-water rafting (per person from Rs 600) is also organised from here for groups of six people or more. The rapids go up to grade 4 and are at their most powerful in August.

Opposite the reserve, next to where the boat leaves, **Dubare Inn** (☎ 08276-267855; Nanjarayapatna; cottages Rs 1400) offers simple, clean brick cottages with river views and an inexpensive **café** (☼ 6am-9pm).

Bylakuppe

☎ 08223

In the exodus from Tibet that followed the 1959 Chinese invasion, thousands of Tibetan refugees settled around Bylakuppe, 5km southeast of Kushalnagar, where the Karnataka government gifted them 1200 hectares of land. The area has since sprouted several villages centred around monasteries where maroon-and-yellow-robed monks are a common sight and Tibetan arts and crafts are practised. The atmosphere in the villages is heart-warmingly welcoming.

Contact Namdroling Monastery (below) or the **Sera Jey Choeling Centre** (☎ 258723; www.serajey monastery.org) if you're interested in visiting the settlements for more than a few days, as you will first need to apply for a Protected Area Permit (PAP) from the Ministry of Home Affairs in Delhi.

The area's highlight is the **Namdroling Monastery** (☎ 254036; www.palyul.org), home to the jaw-droppingly spectacular **Golden Temple** (Padmasambhava Buddhist Vihara; ☯ 7am-8pm), presided over by an 18m-high gold-plated Buddha. The temple is in particularly good form when school is in session and it rings out with the gongs, drums and chanting of hundreds of young novices. You're welcome to sit and meditate on it all; look for the small blue guest cushions lying around. The **Zangdogpalri Temple** (☯ 7am-8pm), a similarly ornate affair, is next door.

Opposite the Golden Temple is a shopping centre; on its top floor you'll find the simple **Paljor Dhargey Ling Guest House** (☎ 258686; p_dhargeyling@yahoo.com; r Rs 250). Add Rs 100 if you'd prefer a room with a TV.

Shanti Family Restaurant (Paljor Dhargey Ling Shopping Centre; mains Rs 30-50; ☯ 7am-9.30pm) is a lively place for fresh juices, milk shakes, a good range of Indian meals and Tibetan dishes, such as *momos* (dumpings) and *thukpa* (noodle soup).

Autorickshaws (shared/alone Rs 10/30) ply the route to Sera from Kushalanagar. Buses run frequently to Kushalnagar from Madikeri (Rs 18, 1½ hour) and Hassan (Rs 50, four hours); most buses on the Mysore–Madikeri route stop at Kushalnagar.

Kakkabe
☎ 08272

The region around the village of Kakkabe is an ideal base if you're planning an assault on Kodagu's highest peak, Tadiyendamol. The small and picturesque **Nalakunad Palace** (admission free; ☯ 9am-5pm), 3km from Kakkabe, is the recently restored hunting lodge of a Kodagu king and dates from 1794. Within walking distance of here you'll find several excellent places to stay.

our pick Honey Valley Estate (☎ 238339; huts & r with shared bathroom from Rs 200, d with private bathroom

from Rs 700) is a wonderful place 1250m above sea level where you can wake to the forest's dawn chorus. The owners' friendliness, environmental mindfulness and scrumptious food (with organic veggies from the farm) fully deserve enthusiastic applause. The estate is only accessible by jeep or by a one-hour uphill walk. Bookings are essential.

Old cannonballs border the garden at **Palace Estate** (☎ 238446, 9880447702; www.palaceestate.co.in; s with shared bathroom Rs 250, d with private bathroom Rs 1200), a beautiful homestay run by a hospitable Kodagu family. The rooms, view and home-cooked meals (breakfast Rs 75, lunch or dinner Rs 110) are all excellent. It's just above the Nalakunad Palace.

Also neighbouring Nalakunad Palace is **King's Cottage** (☎ 238464; d Rs 700), a picturesque place offering seven simply furnished rooms and, again, beautiful views. Breakfast is Rs 50, home-cooked Kodava lunch or dinner Rs 100.

The name of tiny **Misty Woods** (☎ 238561; www .coorgmisty.com; cottages incl full board from Rs 4000), immediately uphill from Nalakunand Palace, aptly sums up the landscape surrounding it. The *vastu sasthra*–style cottages made from hollow bricks are roomy enough to sleep three.

Regular buses run to Kakkabe from Madikeri (Rs 20, 1½ hours) and from Virarajendrapet (also called Virajpet, Rs 14, one hour).

HASSAN
☎ 08172 / pop 117,386

With a reasonable range of hotels, a railhead and other conveniences, Hassan is a handy base for exploring Belur (38km), Halebid (33km) and Sravanabelagola (48km). When we passed through, the town centre was looking like Beirut on a bad day; hopefully the road widening project will have been completed by the time you arrive.

Orientation & Information
The train station is 2km east of the town centre on busy Bengaluru–Mangalore (BM) Rd. The Central bus stand is on the corner of AVK College and Bus Stand Rds. The **tourist office** (☎ 268862; AVK College Rd; ☯ 10am-5.30pm Mon-Fri & alternate Sat), 100m east of the bus stand, is one of Karnataka's more helpful. There are plenty of ATMs and internet cafés; try **Cyber Park** (☎ Harsha Mahal Rd; per hr Rs 30). Banks, however, don't offer foreign exchange. The **Southern Star** (☎ 251816; BM Rd) will change dollars at a bad rate.

Sleeping

Vaishnavi Lodging (☎ 263885; Harsha Mahal Rd; s/d Rs 170/235) Steps away from the bus stand, it's cheap, tidy and the sheets are clean. Ask for a room at the back to keep street noise to a minimum.

Hotel Sri Krishna (☎ 263240; fax 233904; BM Rd; s/d from Rs 325/600; 🖭) Not far from the train station, this place has agreeable rooms and a quality pure-veg eatery (mains Rs 30 to 60).

Hotel Suvarna Regency (☎ 266774; www.hotelsu varnaregency.com; BM Rd; s/d from Rs 350/605; 🖭) This city-centre hotel, just south of Gandhi Sq, offers standard nonflash rooms. Its small swimming pool was out of commission when we dropped by. There's a internet café in the same building.

Southern Star (☎ 251816; www.ushalexushotel sandresorts.com; BM Rd; s/d from Rs 1000/1200; 🖵 🖭) Reasonably good rooms and pleasant service make up for the street noise at this smartish hotel across from Hotel Sri Krishna. Its Karwar Restaurant (mains Rs 40 to 100; open 6am to 11pm) is as posh as it gets for Hassan.

Hoysala Village Resort (☎ 256764; www.trailsindia .com; Belur Rd; d incl breakfast from Rs 2960; 🖭 🖳) This rustic and relaxing place is set in pretty gardens (with a tree house), 6km from Hassan on the road to Belur. Rooms are very spacious and comfortable.

Hotel Hassan Ashhok (☎ 268731) Back in the centre of town, Hotel Hassan Ashhok was undergoing major renovations at the time of research; it looks like it might be quite stylish when finished.

Eating

Hotel Sanman (Municipal Office Rd; meals Rs 12-15; 🕑 6am-10pm) Pay upfront and take your pick from *masala dosas* or a rice plate at this busy joint located about a block south of the bus station.

Hotel GRR (Bus Stand Rd; meals Rs 15-35; 🕑 11am-11pm) Top-of-the-line Andhra-style thalis (Rs 15) on banana leaves are on offer at this friendly place opposite the bus station.

Suvarna Gate (Hotel Suvarna Regency, BM Rd; mains Rs 40-100; 🕑 noon-3.30pm & 6.30-11.30pm) You'll wait a while for your food but it's worth it. The chicken tandoori masala is delicious and the terrace dining room overlooking neatly trimmed hedges has some ambience. Head to the back of the Hotel Suvarna Regency to find it.

Getting There & Away

BUS

Buses leave from the Central bus stand, situated on the corner of AVK College and Bus Stand Rds. If you're planning to visit Belur and Halebid on the same day from Hassan, go to Halebid first as there are more buses from Belur to Hassan and they run until much later.

Buses to Halebid (Rs 15, one hour, every half hour) start running at 6am, with the last bus back leaving Halebid at 7.30pm. Frequent buses go between Hassan and Belur (Rs 20, one hour); the first leaves Hassan at 6am, and the last bus from Belur is at 10pm.

To get to Sravanabelagola, you must take one of the many buses to Channarayapatna (Rs 20, 45 minutes) and change there.

There are frequent services to Mysore (Rs 65, three hours) Bengaluru (ordinary/deluxe Rs 95/160, four hours), and Mangalore (ordinary/deluxe Rs 95/165, four hours).

TAXI

Taxi drivers hang out on AVK College Rd, north of the bus stand. A tour of Belur and Halebid will cost you about Rs 700 for the day. A return taxi to Sravanabelagola will cost the same. Firmly set the price before departure.

TRAIN

The well-organised **train station** (☎ 268222) is about 2km east of town (Rs 10 by autorickshaw); it has a cloakroom (Rs 10) and retiring rooms (Rs 100). Three passenger trains head to Mysore daily (2nd class Rs 22, three hours); the one at 2.20pm is a fast passenger train (two hours). For Bengaluru, take one of the four daily trains to Arsikere (Rs 11, one hour) and change there. Services to Mangalore (2nd class Rs 38, five hours) are expected to be running now.

BELUR & HALEBID

☎ 08177 / elev 968m

The Hoysala temples at Halebid (also known as Halebeed, Halebidu and Halebeedu) and Belur, along with the temple at Somnathpur (p241), are the apex of one of the most artistically exuberant periods of Hindu cultural development. Their sculptural decoration rivals that of Khajuraho (in Madhya Pradesh) and Konark (in Orissa).

If you're staying overnight (although it's not really necessary), Belur is a better bet than Halebid.

KARNATAKA

Belur and Halebid are only 16km apart. Buses shuttle between the two towns every 30 minutes or so from 6.30am to 7pm (Rs 11, 30 minutes). See p247 for details of buses to/from Hassan. Belur also has direct buses to Bengaluru (Rs 120, five hours). To get to Hampi, catch a bus from Belur to Kadur (Rs 14, one hour), then take a bus to Shimoga. Buses leave Shimoga frequently for Hospet, the access town for Hampi.

Belur

The **Channekeshava Temple** (Temple Rd; admission free; ☼ dawn-dusk) is the only one at the three major Hoysala sites still in daily use – try to be there for the *puja* ceremonies at 9am, 3pm and 7.30pm. Begun in 1116 to commemorate the Hoysalas' victory over the Cholas at Ta-lakad, work on the temple continued for over a century. Although its exterior lower friezes are not as extensively sculpted as those of the other Hoysala temples, the work higher up is unsurpassed in detail and artistry. Particularly intriguing are the angled bracket figures de-picting women in ritual dancing poses. Note that the front of the temple is reserved for images of dancers and characters from the Ka-masutra; the back is strictly for gods. Plentiful decorative work also lines the internal sup-porting pillars (no two of which are identical) and lintels. Allegedly every major Hindu deity is represented here.

The temple grounds are worth a wander, with their smaller, ageing temples and 14th-century seven-storey *gopuram*, which has some sensual sculptures explicitly portraying the après-temple activities of dancing girls.

Guides can be hired for Rs 125; they help to bring some of the sculptural detail to life.

The other, lesser, Hoysala temples at Belur are the **Chennigaraya** and the **Viranarayana** temples.

Vishnu Regency (☎ 223011; www.hoysalatourism .com; Kempegowda Rd; d/tr from Rs 400/500; ☐) is clearly the best of Belur's none-too-salubrious hotels. Its simple rooms are clean and fresh smelling, there's a resident astrologer on hand and it has a pleasant **restaurant** (mains Rs 20-65; ☼ 11.30am-10.30pm) serving North Indian and Chinese food. From the bus stand, walk up Temple Rd and turn left at the statue of Kempegowda.

Near Kempegowda's statue is **Shankar Hotel** (Temple Rd; meals Rs 20; ☼ 7am-9.30pm), a busy place serving fine South Indian thalis, *masala dosas*, Indian sweets, snacks and drinks.

Halebid

Construction began on Halebid's **Hoysaleswara Temple** (☼ dawn-dusk) around 1121. Despite more than 80 years of labour it was never completed, but it's still the most outstanding example of Hoysala architecture. The entire outside and some of the interior is covered with a riot of Hindu deities, sages, stylised animals and friezes depicting the life of the Hoysala rulers.

The temple is set in large well-tended gar-dens, adjacent to which is a small **museum** (admission Rs 2; ☼ 10am-5pm Sat-Thu) housing a col-lection of sculptures.

Halebid also has a smaller temple known as **Kedareswara** and a little-visited enclosure con-taining three **Jain** temples, which also have fine carvings. These are peacefully tout free.

HOYSALA ARCHITECTURE

The Hoysalas, who ruled this part of the Deccan between the 11th and 13th centuries, originated in the hill tribes of the Western Ghats and for a long time were feudatories of the Chalukyas. They didn't become fully independent until about 1190, though they first rose to prominence under their leader Tinayaditya (1047–78), who took advantage of the waning power of the Gangas and Rashtrakutas. Under Bittiga (1110–52), later named Vishnuvardhana, they began to take off on a course of their own; it was during his reign that the distinctive temples at Belur and Halebid were built.

Typically, these temples are squat, star-shaped structures set on a platform. They are more human in scale than the soaring temples found elsewhere in India, but what they lack in size they make up for in sheer intricacy.

It's quickly apparent from a study of these sculptures that the arts of music and dance were highly regarded during the Hoysala period. It also seems that these were times of a relatively high degree of sexual freedom and prominent female participation in public affairs.

The Hoysalas converted to Jainism in the 10th century, but took up Hinduism in the 11th century. This is why images of Shaivite, Vaishnavite and Jain sects coexist in their temples.

The saving grace of the otherwise shoddy **KSTDC Mayura Shantala** (☎ 273224; d/q with shared bathroom Rs 250/350) is its reasonably quiet garden compound, which is about the nicest place to grab refreshments in town. Four plain rooms offer shelter if you're really stuck.

SRAVANABELAGOLA

☎ 08176

Atop the bald rock of Vindhyagiri Hill, the 17.5m-high statue of the Jain deity Gomateshvara (Bahubali), said to be the world's tallest monolithic statue, is visible long before you reach the pilgrimage town of Sravanabelagola. Viewing the statue close up is the main reason for heading to this sedate town, whose name means 'the Monk of the White Pond'. The statue's simplicity and serenity is in complete contrast to the complexity and energy of the sculptural work at the Belur and Halebid temples.

In the 3rd century BC, Chandragupta Maurya came here with his guru, Bhagwan Bhadrabahu Swami, after renouncing his kingdom. Bhadrabahu's disciples spread his teachings all over the region, firmly planting Jainism in southern soils. The religion found powerful patrons in the Gangas, who ruled southern Karnataka between the 4th and 10th centuries, the zenith of Jainism's influence.

Information

The helpful **tourist office** (☎ 257254; ⏰ 10am-5.30pm) is in a new complex at the foot of Vindhyagiri Hill. There are plans for the complex to include an audiovisual interpretation display, a café and a gift store. Though there are no entry fees to the sites in Sravanabelagola, donations are encouraged.

Sights

GOMATESHVARA STATUE

The naked statue of **Gomateshvara** (Bahubali; ⏰ 6am-6.15pm), reached via 614 rock-cut steps up Vindhyagiri Hill, was commissioned by a military commander in the service of the Ganga king Rachamalla and carved out of granite by the sculptor Aristenemi in AD 981.

Bahubali's father was the great Emperor Vrishabhadeva, who became the first Jain *tirthankar* (revered Jain teacher), Adinath. Bahubali and his brother Bharatha competed fiercely for the right to succeed their father but, on the point of victory, Bahubali realised the futility of the struggle and renounced his kingdom. He withdrew from the material world, entered the forest and meditated in complete stillness until he attained enlightenment. The statue has vines curling around his legs and an ant hill at his feet, signs of his utter detachment. The gallery around his statue has many smaller images of Jain *tirthankars*.

You must leave your shoes at the foot of the hill; if the rocks are hot it's OK to wear socks. Those who prefer not to tackle the steps can hire a *dholi* (man-carried portable chair) with bearers for Rs 150; the *dholi* can be hired from 7am to 12.30pm and 3pm to 5.30pm.

Every 12 years, millions flock here to attend the Mahamastakabhisheka ceremony, which involves the statue being dowsed in all manner of fluids, pastes, powders, precious metals and stones. The next ceremony will be around January 2018.

TEMPLES

In addition to the Bahubali statue, there are several interesting Jain temples in the town and on Chandragiri Hill, the smaller of the two hills between which Sravanabelagola is nestled.

The **Chandragupta Basti** (Chandragupta Community; ⏰ 6am-6pm), on Chandragiri Hill, is believed to have been built by Emperor Ashoka. The Hoysala-style **Bhandari Basti** (Bhandari Community; ⏰ 6am-6pm), in the southeast corner of town, is Sravanabelagola's largest temple. Nearby, **Chandranatha Basti** (Chandranatha Community; ⏰ 6am-6pm) has well-preserved paintings resembling a 650-year-old comic strip of Jain stories.

Sleeping & Eating

The local Jain organisation **SDJMI** (☎ 257258) handles bookings for its 15 guesthouses; the office is behind the Vidyananda Nilaya Dharamsala, past the post office and before the bus stand on the way into town. Most foreigners find themselves bunked at the simple and well-maintained **Yathri Nivas** (d/tr Rs 135/160).

Hotel Raghu (☎ 257238; d from Rs 200; ❄), Sravanabelagola's only privately owned hotel, offers a range of dingy rooms, some with TV and AC; it's just at the foot of Vindhyagiri Hill. It also has a busy vegetarian **restaurant** (mains Rs 20-40; ⏰ 6am-9pm).

Getting There & Away

No buses go direct from Sravanabelagola to Hassan or Belur – you must go to Channarayapatna (Rs 8, 20 minutes) and catch an onward connection there. Three direct buses a day run to both Bengaluru (Rs 74, 3½ hours) and Mysore (Rs 45, 2½ hours). Nearly all long-distance buses leave before 3pm; if you miss these, catch a local bus to Channarayapatna, 10km north-west, which is on the main Bengaluru–Mangalore road and has lots of connections.

KARNATAKA COAST

MANGALORE

☎ 0824 / pop 398,745

Situated at the point where the Netravati and Gurupur Rivers flow into the Arabian Sea, Managlore has been a pit stop on international trade routes since the 6th century AD. It was the major port of Hyder Ali's kingdom, and today the region's coffee and cashew crops are still shipped out from the modern port, which is 10km north of the city.

Not an especially picturesque place, Mangalore is the largest city on Karnataka's coast, and therefore is a useful place to stop for amenities. It's not without its tourist charms, however, chief of which is quiet Ullal Beach, 12km south of the city.

Orientation

Mangalore is hilly, with winding, disorienting streets. Luckily most hotels and restaurants, the bus stand and the train station are in or around the frenzied city centre, and are easy to find. Less handily, the KSRTC long-distance bus stand is 3km to the north.

Information

ATMs and internet cafés are everywhere, and several banks in town also have foreign-exchange facilities.

Athree Book Centre (Balmatta Rd; ☉ 8.30am-1pm & 2.30-8pm Mon-Sat)

Higginbothams (Lighthouse Hill Rd; ☉ 9.30am-1.30pm & 3.30-7.30pm Mon-Sat) Bookshop.

KSTDC tourist office (☎ 2442926; Lighthouse Hill Rd; ☉ 10am-5pm Mon-Sat) Mostly useless.

Trade Wings (☎ 2427225; Lighthouse Hill Rd; ☉ 9.30am-5.30pm Mon-Sat) Travel agency that's the best place to change travellers cheques.

Sights

Catholicism's roots in Mangalore date back to the arrival of the Portuguese in the 1520s, and today the city is liberally dotted with churches. One of the most impressive is the Sistine Chapel–like **St Aloysius College Chapel**

(Lighthouse Hill; ☉ 8.30am-6pm Mon-Sat, 10am-noon & 2-6pm Sun), with its walls and ceilings painted with brilliant frescoes. Nearby are the restful gardens of **Tagore Park**.

Sultan's Battery (Sultan Battery Rd; admission free; ☉ 6am-6pm), the only remnant of Tipu Sultan's fort, is 4km from the centre on the headland of the old port; bus 16 will get you there. Take bus 19 to **Shreemanthi Bai Memorial Government Museum** (☎ 2211106; admission Rs 2; ☉ 9am-5pm Tue-Sun), which has a motley collection that's worth a browse; check out the leather shadow puppets.

The attractive Keralan-style **Kadri Manjunatha Temple** (Kadri; ☉ 6am-1pm & 4-8pm) houses a 1000-year-old bronze statue of Lokeshwara. *Puja* (prayers) at the temple is at 8am, noon and 8pm; take bus 3, 4 or 6.

Serene **Ullal Beach** is best enjoyed at Summer Sands Beach Resort (opposite), which costs Rs 25 to enter (redeemable against food or drink at its restaurant) and Rs 60 to use the pool. An autorickshaw is Rs 150 one way, or the frequent bus 44A (Rs 7) from the City bus stand will drop you right outside the gate. Buses 44C or 44D also go to Ullal.

Sleeping

The humidity means few hotels are free from damp.

BUDGET

Hotel Surya (☎ 2425736; Balmatta Rd; s/d/tr from Rs 175/225/275; ✷ ▨) Set back from the road near Lalith Restaurant, Hotel Surya has simple rooms with tiled floors and walls that could do with a lick of paint. The staff are friendly.

Hotel Manorama (☎ 2440306; KS Rao Rd; s/d from Rs 250/360; ✷) This cheapie is a clear cut above other budget options. The superclean rooms have a sparse 1940s feel to them; the bathrooms have squat toilets.

Hotel Srinivas (☎ 2440061; www.hotelsrinivas.com; GHS Rd; s/d from Rs 400/525; ✷) Central and reasonably clean, but really nothing to write home about.

MIDRANGE & TOP END

Hotel Poonja International (☎ 2440171; www.hotel poonjainternational.com; KS Rao Rd; s/d from Rs 600/800; ✷) Offers a good location, professional staff and reasonably comfortable no-frills rooms at decent prices.

Nalapad Residency (☎ 2424757; www.nalapad.com; Lighthouse Hill Rd; s/d from Rs 650/750; ✷) Ask for a room with a sea view at the hilltop Nalapad.

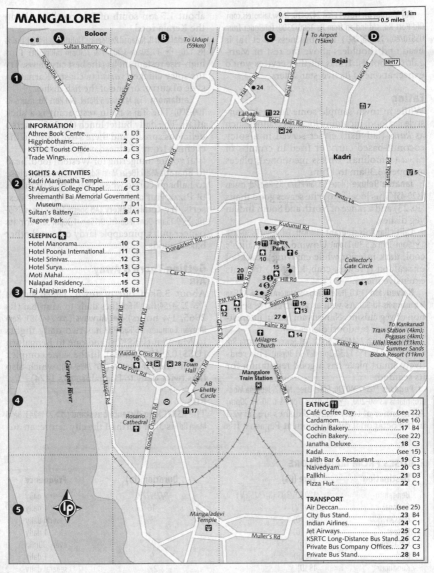

MANGALORE

INFORMATION
Athree Book Centre	**1** D3
Higginbothams	**2** C3
KSTDC Tourist Office	**3** C3
Trade Wings	**4** C3

SIGHTS & ACTIVITIES
Kadri Manjunatha Temple	**5** D2
St Aloysius College Chapel	**6** C3
Shreemanthi Bai Memorial Government Museum	**7** D1
Sultan's Battery	**8** A1
Tagore Park	**9** C3

SLEEPING
Hotel Manorama	**10** C3
Hotel Poonja International	**11** C3
Hotel Srinivas	**12** C3
Hotel Surya	**13** C3
Moti Mahal	**14** C3
Nalapad Residency	**15** C3
Taj Manjarun Hotel	**16** B4

EATING
Café Coffee Day	(see 22)
Cardamom	(see 16)
Cochin Bakery	**17** B4
Cochin Bakery	(see 22)
Janatha Deluxe	**18** C3
Kadal	(see 15)
Lalith Bar & Restaurant	**19** C3
Naivedyam	**20** C3
Pallkhi	**21** D3
Pizza Hut	**22** C1

TRANSPORT
Air Deccan	(see 25)
City Bus Stand	**23** B4
Indian Airlines	**24** C1
Jet Airways	**25** C2
KSRTC Long-Distance Bus Stand	**26** C2
Private Bus Company Offices	**27** C3
Private Bus Stand	**28** B4

KARNATAKA

Nice touches such as terracotta-tile ceilings in the lobby are, sadly, not replicated in the plain rooms.

Moti Mahal (☎ 2441411; www.motimahalmangalore .com; Falnir Rd; s/d incl breakfast from Rs 950/1250; ❄ ☒) The selling point of this average hotel is its big outdoor pool and gym. There are also three restaurants.

Summer Sands Beach Resort (☎ 2467690; www .summer-sands.com; d from Rs 970; ❄ ☒) Set amid leafy grounds beside Ullal Beach, Summer Sands' rustic bungalows are the ideal place for a quiet retreat. The Summer Place Restaurant (mains Rs 40 to 90) has plenty of fresh fish, as well as the sound of the ocean nearby.

Taj Manjarun Hotel (☎ 2420420; www.tajhotels.com; Old Port Rd; s/d Indian from Rs 1800/2300, foreigner from US$70/80; ❄ 🖳 🖭) This business-level Taj is head and shoulders above the rest of Mangalore's hotels. It has all the services you'd expect at one of its five-star sisters.

Eating

While in town sample some Mangalorean-style seafood, including local specialities such as *kane* (ladyfish) either served in a spicy coconut-based curry or fried in crumbs of *rawa* (semolina). Unless mentioned, places are open 6.30am to 11pm.

Janatha Deluxe (Hotel Shaan Plaza, KS Rao Rd; mains Rs 20-45) This local favourite serves good thalis (Rs 23) and a range of North and South Indian veg dishes.

Lalith Bar & Restaurant (Balmatta Rd; mains Rs 30-100; ☷ 9am-3pm & 5.30-11pm) Unwind in the Lalith's cool, dark interior while enjoying a cocktail or seafood (prawns, crab, kingfish) from its extensive menu.

Naivedyam (1st fl, Hotel Mangalore International, KS Rao Rd; mains Rs 40-80) As well as an extensive selection of veg cuisine, Naivedyam has an interesting range of tandoori dishes.

Pallkhi (☎ 2444929; 3rd fl, Tej Towers, Balmatta Rd; mains Rs 85-125; ☷ 12.30-3pm & 7-11.30pm) This relatively smart place has a good reputation for its seafood.

Pegasus (☎ 2240120; Sutej Baug, NH17, Jeppina Mogaru; mains Rs 80-200; ☷ 11.30am-3pm & 6.30-11.30pm) All manner of tasty seafood dishes are served in the octagonal dining room at Pegasus. It's about 1.5 km south of Pumpwell Circle on the Kerala road.

Kadal (7th fl, Nalapad Residency, Lighthouse Hill Rd; mains Rs 120; ☷ 11.30am-3.30pm & 7.30pm-midnight) This high-rise restaurant has the best city views. Try the spicy chicken *varval* (a coastal Karnataka style of curry) or one of the fish dishes.

Cardamom (Taj Manjarun Hotel, Old Port Rd; mains Rs 100-300) The Taj's main restaurant is a slick affair. The daily buffet lunch (Rs 295) offers a delicious spread, and there's live music in the evening from Wednesday to Saturday.

If you're hungering for Western food, head to **Bharath Mall** (Bejai Main Rd; ☷ 10am-10pm) close to Lalbagh Circle where you'll find branches of Pizza Hut and Café Coffee Day. For desserts, try **Cochin Bakery** (AB Shetty Circle; cakes Rs 5-10; ☷ 9.15am-9pm Mon-Fri, 9.15am-1.30pm Sat) for its paneer puffs, pineapple lardy cake and other baked goods.

Getting There & Away

AIR

About 3.5km out of town, **Indian Airlines** (☎ 2254254; Hathill Rd) flies daily to Mumbai (Rs 2965, 1¼ hours). **Jet Airways** (☎ 2441181; Ram Bhavan Complex, KS Rao Rd) has two daily flights to Mumbai (US$175) and one to Bengaluru (US$102, 45 minutes). In the same complex you'll find **Air Deccan** (☎ 2496948), which also flies twice daily to Bengaluru (Rs 1474).

BUS

The **KSRTC long-distance bus stand** (☎ 2211243; Bejai Main Rd) is 3km north of the city centre; an au-

BUSES FROM MANGALORE

Destination	Fare (Rs)	Duration (hr)	Frequency
Bengaluru	180 (D)/303 (R)/375 (V)	9/7½/7½	several daily
Chennai	750 (V)	16	1 daily
Hassan	102 (D)	4½	several daily
Hospet	201 (D)	11	1 daily
Kasaragod	25 (D)	1½	every 30min
Kochi	340 (R)	9	1 daily
Kundupur	48 (D)	2½	several daily
Madikeri	72	4½	several daily
Mumbai	810 (V)	17	1 daily
Mysore	132 (D)/222 (R)/275 (V)	8	several daily
Panaji	170 (D)/302 (R)	9	3 daily
Udupi	29 (D)	1½	several daily

D – semideluxe/regular, R – Rajahamsa, V – Volvo AC

torickshaw there costs about Rs 20. It's quite orderly, with bus services to the destinations listed on opposite.

Private buses heading to destinations including Udupi, Sringeri, Mudabidri and Jog Falls run from opposite the City bus stand. Tickets can be purchased at offices near Falnir Rd.

Be warned that the roads to Managlore from the Deccan plateau (and parts of the coastal highway) are pot-hole hell during the monsoon and usually for several months after.

TRAIN
The main **train station** (☎ 2423137) is south of the city centre. The 12.10pm *Matsyagandha Express* stops at Margao (sleeper/2AC Rs 217/843, five hours) in Goa, and continues to Mumbai (sleeper/2AC Rs 393/1631, 16 hours). The 5.50pm *Malabar Express* heads to Thiruvananthapuram (Trivandrum; sleeper/2AC Rs 261/1096, 15½ hours). Express trains to Chennai (sleeper/2AC Rs 338/1384, 17 hours) depart at 1.15pm and 9.15pm.

Several Konkan Railway trains (to Mumbai, Margao, Ernakulam or Trivandrum) use **Kankanadi train station** (☎ 2437824), 5km east of the city.

Getting Around
The airport is about 22km north of the city. Take bus 47B or 47C from the City bus stand or catch a taxi (Rs 300). Indian Airlines has a free airport shuttle for its passengers.

The City bus stand is opposite the State Bank of India, close to the Taj Manjarun Hotel. Flag fall for autorickshaws is Rs 11, and they cost Rs 11 per kilometre thereafter. For late-night travel, add on 50%. An autorickshaw to Kankanadi station costs around Rs 40, or take bus 9 or 11B.

DHARMASTALA
Inland from Mangalore are a string of Jain temple towns, including Venur, Mudabidri and Karkal. The most interesting is Dharmastala, 75km east of Mangalore on the banks of the Nethravathi River. In a remarkable show of organisation, the town hosts an average 10,000 pilgrims a day, and 10 times as many on major holidays and during the town's festival season (see p220).

Three elephants are on hand to bless pilgrims outside the nondenominational **Manjunatha Temple** (⏲ 6.30am-2pm & 6.30-8.30pm); men entering the temple should do so bare chested

and, preferably, wearing long trousers. Simple free meals are available in the temple's **kitchen** (⏲ 11.30am-2.15pm & 7.30-10pm), which is attached to a hall that can seat up to 3000. It gets through around 2500kg of rice a day!

Elsewhere in this lively town there's a 12m-high **statue of Bahubali**; the **Manjusha Museum** (Rs 2; ⏲ 10am-1pm & 4.30-9pm) housing a collection of Indian stone and metal sculptures, jewellery and local craft products; and, best of all, the **Car Museum** (admission Rs 3; ⏲ 8.30am-1pm & 2-7pm), home to 48 vintage autos, including a 1903 Renault, a monster of a Cadillac from 1954 and a 1983 Datsun!

Should you wish to stay in Dharmastala, contact the helpful **temple office** (☎ 08256-277121; www.shridharmasthala.org), which can arrange accommodation for Rs 50 per person in one of its pilgrim lodges.

There are frequent buses to Dharmastala from Mangalore (Rs 30, two hours).

UDUPI (UDIPI)
☎ 0820
Vaishnavite pilgrims come to Udupi to visit its **Krishna Temple** (☎ 2520598; Car St; ⏲ 5.30am-8.30pm), dating from the 13th century. Surrounded by eight *maths* (monasteries), the atmospheric temple is a hive of activity, with musicians playing at the entrance, elephants on hand for *puja*, and pilgrims constantly coming and going. *Darshan* (viewing of a deity) is available to non-Hindus; men must enter the main shrine bare chested.

Near the temple, above the Corp Bank ATM, the **tourist office** (☎ 2529718; Krishna Bldg, Car St; ⏲ 10am-1.30pm & 2.30-5.30pm Mon-Sat) is a useful source of advice on Udupi and the surrounding area.

Udupi is famed for its vegetarian food – it's particularly well known for creating the *masala dosa*. A good place to sample the local fair is **Woodlands** (Dr UR Rao Complex; ⏲ 8am-9.30pm), a short walk south of the temple. It serves dosas before 11.30pm and after 3.30pm. In between you can get a pretty good thali (Rs 30 to 43).

Udupi is 58km north of Mangalore along the coast; regular buses run here from Mangalore (Rs 29, 1½ hours).

MALPE
☎ 0820
The fishing harbour of Malpe is set on the coast, 4km from Udupi. From Malpe it's possible to take a boat (Rs 70 per person) out to

tiny **St Mary's Island**, where Vasco da Gama is said to have landed in 1498. At weekends the island is busy with groups of locals inspecting the curious hexagonal basalt rock formations that jut out of the sand; during the week you might just have it to yourself.

Paradise Isle Beach Resort (☎ 2537300; www .theparadiseisle.com; s/d Rs 3000/3500; ✗ ☐ ☎) is right on Malpe Beach, about 2km north of the harbour, with a clear view of St Mary's Island. It lacks atmosphere but the rooms are comfortable and clean. Students from the nearby university at Manipal converge here on Saturdays to drink and dance at the hotel's disco. The neighbouring food court is the only spot to grab a meal.

An autorickshaw from Udupi to Malpe is Rs 50.

AMGOL

Head inland for 6km from Kundapura on National Highway 17 to the sleepy village of Basrur on the banks of the Varahi River. A punted boat will then transport you the 200m across to the slender private island of **Amgol** (r per person incl full board Rs 1500), which is no more than 750m long and is home to just five rustic rooms. To stay at this tranquil spot book through **Soans Holidays** (☎ 08254-231683; www.soans.com). On the way to the village is one of the racing areas for Kambla (see Buffalo Surfing, opposite).

MURUDESHWAR
☎ 08385

There are pleasant beaches at this sacred site where the pretty little Shiva temple is overshadowed by a 40m-high idol of the deity (the tallest in the world) and a stupendous 83m-tall *gopuram*. If you think the Shiva statue looks lopsided, it's because one of his four arms blew off in a storm.

Accommodation is no problem, with the **RNS Residency** (☎ 260060, 268901; www.naveenhotels .com; r from Rs 900; ✗ ☎) and the **Naveen Beach Resort** (☎ 260415, 260428; www.naveenhotels.com; r from Rs 1400; ✗) offering decent rooms with sea views. Perched over the waves, the Naveen Beach Restaurant does excellent Punjabi or South Indian thalis (Rs 25 to 45), as well as ice-cream sundaes.

Murudeshwar is just off the coastal highway, 163km north of Mangalore and 70km south of Gokarana. Trains on the **Konkan Railway** (www.konkanrailway.com), which connects Goa with Mumbai and Mangalore, stop here.

JOG FALLS
☎ 08186

Jog Falls might be the highest waterfalls in India, but unless you visit during the monsoon they're not that exciting; the Linganamakki Dam further up the Sharavati River limits the water flow. The longest of the four falls is the Raja, which drops 293m.

The viewing area close to the bus stand is scrappy. The best thing you can do if you come here is to hike to the foot of the falls, accessible by a 1200-plus step path – it will take around one hour to get down and two to get up. Watch out for leeches in the wet season.

The friendly **tourist office** (☎ 244732; ☉ 10am-5pm Mon-Sat) is above the food stalls close to the bus stand.

Jog Falls has two inspection bungalows, usually reserved for VIPs. The **British Bungalow** (☎ 08389-230134; r Rs 100) sits atop the falls about 3km from the bus stand. The **PW Guesthouse** (☎ 08183-226213; per person Rs 250), across from the KSTDC hotel, is pretty fancy.

The **KSTDC Hotel Mayura Gerusoppa** (☎ 244732; s/d Rs 300/400), about 150m from the car park, has enormous, musty rooms.

Stalls near the bus stand serve omelettes, thalis, noodles and rice dishes, plus hot and cold drinks. KSTDC's mediocre **restaurant** (meals Rs 20-40) is just next door.

Jog Falls has buses roughly every hour to Shimoga (Rs 45, three hours) and to Sagar (Rs 13, one hour), two a day to Siddapur (Rs 10, one hour) and three daily to Karwar via Kumta (Rs 38, three hours), where you can change for Gokarna (Rs 12, 45 minutes). There are two painfully slow daily buses to/from Mangalore (Rs 112, eight hours); you may be better off going via Shimoga.

GOKARNA
☎ 08386

Sun worshippers and Hindu pilgrims rub shoulders in the low-key village of Gokarna (Cow's Ear), 50km south of Karwar. The quaint village is a holy place, which you should bear in mind if sunbaking is your objective. Modesty is your best policy; keep shoulders and knees covered, and take your parties to the out-of-town beaches.

Information

There are lots of places to access the internet, including many of the guesthouses.

BUFFALO SURFING

Kambla, the Canarese sport of buffalo racing, first became popular in the early part of the 20th century, when farmers would race their buffaloes home after a day in the fields. Today the best of the races have hit the big time, with thousands of spectators attending. The valuable racing buffaloes are pampered and prepared like thoroughbreds – a good animal can cost more than Rs 300,000.

The events are held in the Dakshina Kannada region between November and March, usually on a weekend. Parallel tracks (120m long) are laid out in a paddy field, and the fastest pairs of buffaloes can cover the distance through water and mud in around 14 seconds. There are two versions: in one, the man runs alongside the buffalo; in the other, he rides on a board fixed to a ploughshare, literally surfing his way down the track behind the beasts. And if you don't think these lumbering beasts can really move, look out!

Shree Radhakrishna Bookstore (Car St; ⊗ 10am-6pm) Good selection of new and second-hand books.
Pai STD Shop (Main St; ⊗ 9am-9pm) Changes cash and travellers cheques and gives advances on Visa.
Sub post office (1st fl, cnr Car & Main Sts)

Sights & Activities

TEMPLES

Foreigners are not allowed inside Gokarna's temples, but you'll certainly bear witness to religious rituals around town. At the western end of Car St is the **Mahabaleshwara Temple**, home to a revered lingam (phallic image of Shiva). Nearby is the **Ganapati Temple**, which honours the role Ganesh played in rescuing the lingam. At the other end of the street is the **Venkataraman Temple**, and 100m south of this is **Koorti Teertha**, the large temple tank (reservoir), where locals, pilgrims and immaculately dressed Brahmins perform their ablutions next to dhobi-wallahs (people who wash clothes) on the ghats (steps or landings).

BEACHES

Gokarna's 'town beach' suffers from litter: the best sands are reached via a footpath that begins on the southern side of the Ganapati Temple and heads southward (if you reach the bathing tank – or find yourself clawing up rocks – you're on the wrong path).

Twenty minutes on the path will bring you to the top of a barren headland with expansive sea views. On the southern side is **Kudle** (*koodlee*), the first in a series of four lovely beaches. Basic snacks, drinks and accommodation are available here.

At the southern end of Kudle Beach, a track climbs over the next headland, and a further 20-minute walk brings you to **Om Beach**, with a handful of chai (tea) shops and shacks. A sealed road provides vehicle access to Om, but it's generally deserted except on holidays and weekends, when day-trippers come by the carload. To the south, the more isolated **Half-Moon Beach** and **Paradise Beach** are a 30-minute and one-hour walk, respectively.

Depending on demand, boats run from Gokarna Beach (look for the fishermen) to Kudle (Rs 100) and Om (Rs 200). An autorickshaw from town costs Rs 200 to Om Beach.

Don't walk between the beaches and Gokarna after dark, and don't walk alone at any time – it's easy to slip on the paths or get lost, and muggings have occurred. For a small fee, most lodges in Gokarana will safely stow valuables and baggage while you chill out in the beach huts.

AYURVEDA

Apart from Ayurveda centres at SwaSwara (p256) and Om Beach Resort (p257), a good range of Ayurvedic treatments are available at the **Kerala Ayurveda Hospital Institute of Medical Technology** (☎ 9945702596; www.keralaayurvedagokarn .com; Kamat Complex, Main St; ⊗ 8am-8pm). Prices kick off with a general massage for Rs 400.

Sleeping

With a few exceptions the choice here is between a rudimentary shack on the beach or a basic but more comfortable room in town.

BEACHES

Both Kudle and Om Beaches have several budget options in the form of huts and rooms – shop around. Huts and basic restaurants open up on Half-Moon and Paradise Beaches from late November to March. Most places provide at least a bedroll, but you will want to bring your own sleeping sheet or sleeping

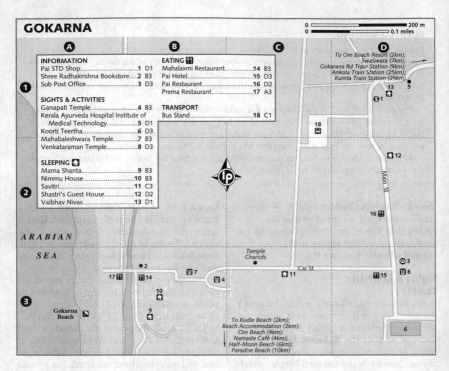

GOKARNA

INFORMATION
Pai STD Shop...........................1 D1
Shree Radhakrishna Bookstore...2 B3
Sub Post Office.......................3 D3

SIGHTS & ACTIVITIES
Ganapati Temple.....................4 B3
Kerala Ayurveda Hospital Institute of
    Medical Technology...........5 D1
Koorti Teertha.......................6 D3
Mahabaleshwara Temple.........7 B3
Venkataraman Temple.............8 D3

SLEEPING
Mama Shanta.........................9 B3
Nimmu House........................10 B3
Savitri...................................11 C3
Shastri's Guest House............12 D2
Vaibhav Nivas.......................13 D1

EATING
Mahalaxmi Restaurant............14 B3
Pai Hotel...............................15 D3
Pai Restaurant.......................16 D2
Prema Restaurant..................17 A3

TRANSPORT
Bus Stand.............................18 C1

To Om Beach Resort (2km);
SwaSwara (7km);
Gokarana Rd Train Station (9km);
Ankola Train Station (25km);
Kumta Train Station (25km)

ARABIAN
SEA

Temple
Chariots

Car St

Gokarna
Beach

To Kudle Beach (2km);
Beach Accommodation (2km);
Om Beach (4km);
Namaste Café (4km);
Half-Moon Beach (6km);
Paradise Beach (10km)

bag. Padlocks are provided and huts are secure. Communal washing and toilet facilities are simple.

Spanish Place (☎ 257311; Kudle Beach; huts with shared bathroom Rs 70, d Rs 250; ☒) This chilled spot in the middle stretch of Kudle Beach has palm-thatch huts, and two lovely garden rooms with private shower but common 'toilet' (ie the bushes).

Namaste (☎ 257141; Om Beach; s with shared bathroom Rs 100, deluxe hut with private bathroom Rs 400; ☒) In and out of season, Namaste is the place to hang. Its spacious restaurant-bar does good food and is the premier Om chill-out spot. In season it also offers basic huts (Rs 50) at Paradise Beach and cottages at Namaste Farm (from Rs 300) on Kudle Beach.

SwaSwara (☎ 0484-2668221; www.swaswara.com; Om Beach; r incl breakfast from US$300; ☒ ☒ ☒) Using the red laterite stone, this beautifully designed and unobtrusive resort provides a luxurious base for a holiday based around yoga and Ayurvedic treatments. Rates include taxes and yoga sessions. Guests are encouraged to pop into the kitchens to learn from the cooks and exchange culinary tips.

GOKARNA

Most guesthouses in town offer discounts in the low season.

Vaibhav Nivas (☎ 256714; off Main St; r with shared bathroom Rs 80, s/d/tr with private bathroom from Rs 75/100/200; ☒) The cell-like rooms at this place tucked away from the main drag come with mosquito nets and hot water in the morning. There's also a rooftop restaurant.

Mama Shanta (☎ 256213; r with shared/private bathroom Rs 100/200; ☺ Oct-May) Just past Nimmu House, you'll find this homestay run by a kindly old soul who rents out very basic rooms a hop away from the beach.

Shastri's Guest House (☎ 256220; dr _murti@rediffmail.com; Main St; r Rs 125-150) The singles are claustrophobic, but the doubles out the back are big and sunny; some have balconies and palm-tree views. New rooms were being added at the time of research.

Nimmu House (☎ 256730; nimmuhouse@yahoo.com; s/d from Rs 150/300; ☒) The best of the budget brigade, Nimmu House has recently renovated a block to provide pleasant tiled-floor rooms with balconies. The management are very friendly.

Savitri (☎ 256720; Car St; d from Rs 200) In the middle of town, this new place offers spotless, simply furnished rooms.

Om Beach Resort (☎ 257052; www.ombeachresort .com; Bangle Gudde; d incl full board US$40; ❉ ▣) This small resort is, confusingly, not at Om Beach but on the headland, about 2km out of Gokarna off the Om Beach road. Accommodation is in nicely decorated rooms in brick cottages with views out to the coast. Rates include taxes. There's a professional Ayurvedic centre on site with various treatment packages available.

Eating

The chai shops on all of the beaches rustle up basic snacks and meals.

Prema Restaurant (meals Rs 20-60; ✆ 8am-9pm) Closest place to the town beach, Prema whips up a decent *masala dosa* (Rs 15) and thali (Rs 30), along with traveller treats, such as coffee milk shakes, and yogurt with muesli and honey.

Mahalaxmi Restaurant (meals Rs 30-70) This popular traveller hang-out promises 'all types of world famous dishes' (ie banana pancakes and cornflakes) in myriad ways. It also has a handful of simple rooms to rent (Rs 150).

Namaste Café (meals Rs 30-80; ✆ 7am-11pm) Om Beach's social centre serves OK Western stand-bys – pizzas and burgers – and some Israeli specials.

A couple of decent vegetarian places in Gokarana:

Pai Hotel (Car St; mains Rs 15-30; ✆ 6am-9.30pm)

Pai Restaurant (Main St; mains Rs 20-40; ✆ 6.30am-9.30pm)

Getting There & Away

BUS

From Gokarna's **bus stand** (☎ 279487), one bus daily heads to Margao (Rs 65, four hours); alternatively you can go to Karwar (Rs 29, 1½ hours, three daily), which has connections to Goa. Direct buses run to Hubli (Rs 86, four hours, five daily), and a daily 6.45am bus goes direct to Mangalore (Rs 129, six hours), continuing on to Mysore (Rs 328, 14 hours). If you miss this, get an hourly local bus to Kumta, 25km south, then one of the frequent Mangalore buses from there. Daily buses set off to Hospet (Rs 165, nine hours) for Hampi at 7am and 2.30pm. There's an ordinary bus to Bengaluru (Rs 257, 12 hours) at 5pm and a deluxe one (Rs 432) at 7pm.

TRAIN

The Konkan Railway is the best way to reach Goa and Mangalore, among other destinations, though only slow passenger trains stop at **Gokarna Rd train station** (☎ 279487), 9km from town. A noon train heads to Margao (Rs 23, two hours); another leaves at 4.25pm (Rs 54, 1½ hours). For Mangalore (Rs 44, five hours), trains depart at 5pm and 3am. Trains head to Kochi (Cochin; sleeper Rs 281, 15 hours) on Saturday and Sunday; you must buy a sleeper ticket and upgrade, if you like, upon boarding. Many of the hotels and small travel agencies in Gokarna can book tickets.

Autorickshaws charge Rs 100 to take you out to the station, but buses go hourly (Rs 7) and also meet arriving passenger trains.

Several express trains stop at Ankola and Kumta stations, both about 25km from Gokarna and accessible by local bus.

CENTRAL KARNATAKA

HAMPI
☎ 08394

The fascinating ruins of the 15th-century city of Vijayanagar, near the village of Hampi, are set in an extraordinary landscape of giant granite boulders, lush paddies and banana plantations. The clock seems to have stopped at this World Heritage site, and you can spend a surprisingly large amount of time gazing at the weirdly balanced rocks, wondering how millions of years of erosion could achieve such formations.

Given its magical atmosphere, Hampi is a major pit stop on the traveller circuit, with November to March (the cooler months) being the peak season. The ruins cover a wide area, but it's possible to see the main sites in a day or two. However, this goes against Hampi's relaxed grain, so plan on lingering for a while.

History

In the Hindu legends of Ramayana, this area was Kishkinda, the realm of the monkey gods. In 1336 the Telugu princes Harihara and Bukka founded the city of Vijayanagar, which over the next couple of centuries grew into one of the largest Hindu empires in Indian history (see the Muslim Invasion & the Vijayanagar Empire, p39).

By the 16th century, the greater metropolitan region of Vijayanagar, surrounded

KARNATAKA

by seven lines of fortification, covered 650 sq km and had a population of about 500,000. Vijayanagar's busy bazaars were centres of international commerce, brimming with precious stones and merchants from faraway lands. This all came to a sudden end in 1565 when the city was ransacked by a confederacy of Deccan sultanates; it subsequently went into terminal decline.

Today's battles are being waged between those who want to protect what's left of Hampi's ruins and the people who now live there. Although it was declared a World Heritage site in 1986, only 58 of the 550 monuments in the area hold heritage-protection status. The businesses occupying Hampi Bazaar have been given their marching orders and a new complex for the area's modern-day needs is under slow construction away from the monuments. **Global Heritage Fund** (www.globalheritagefund.org/where/hampi.html) have more details about Hampi's endangered monuments.

Orientation

Hampi Bazaar and the village of Kamalapuram to the south are the two main points of entry to the ruins. The KSTDC Hotel and the archaeological museum are in Kamalapuram. The main travellers' scene is Hampi Bazaar, a village crammed with budget lodges, shops and restaurants, all dominated by the Virupaksha Temple. The ruins themselves are divided into two main areas: the Sacred Centre, around Hampi Bazaar; and the Royal Centre, to the south around Kamalapuram. To the northeast across the Tungabhadra River is the village of Anegundi. Signposting in some parts of the site is inadequate, but you can't really get lost.

Information

Aspiration Stores (Map p260; 10am-1pm & 4-8pm) For books on the area. Recommended is *Hampi* by John M Fritz and George Michell – a good architectural study.
Canara Bank (Map p260; 241243; 11am-2pm Mon-Tue & Thu-Sat) Changes travellers cheques and gives cash advances on credit cards. The numerous authorised moneychangers around offer slightly worse rates.
Hampi Heritage Gallery (Map p260; 10am-2pm & 3-6pm) Sells books and offers half-day walking or cycling tours for Rs 200.
Sree Rama Cyber Café (Map p260; per hr Rs 50; 7am-11pm) Hampi is brimming with internet cafés – this is a good one. It also burns CDs of digital snaps for Rs 60.

Tourist Office (Map p260; 241339; 10am-5.30pm Sat-Thu) Can arrange guides for Rs 300/500 for a half/full day.

Dangers & Annoyances

Hampi is a safe place, generally free of any aggression. That said, don't wander around the ruins after dark or alone, as muggings and violent attacks are not unknown.

Keep your wits about you with the autorickshaw drivers; some will overcharge outrageously for short trips around the village (you shouldn't have to pay more than Rs 10 for a ride from bus station to any of the lodges) and take commission from some of the lodge owners they recommend.

Sights & Activities

VIRUPAKSHA TEMPLE

The focal point of Hampi Bazaar is the **Virupaksha Temple** (Map p260; 2441241; admission Rs 2; dawn-dusk), one of the city's oldest structures. The main *gopuram*, almost 50m high, was built in 1442, with a smaller one added in 1510. The main shrine is dedicated to Virupaksha, a form of Shiva.

If Lakshmi (the temple elephant) and her attendant are around, you can get a smooch (blessing) from her for a Rs 1 coin. The adorable Lakshmi gets her morning bath at 7.30am, just down the way by the river ghats.

To the south, overlooking Virupaksha Temple, **Hemakuta Hill** (Map p260) has a scattering of early ruins, including Jain temples and a monolithic sculpture of Narasimha (Vishnu in his man-lion incarnation). It's worth the short walk up for the view over the bazaar.

At the east end of Hampi Bazaar is a monolithic **Nandi statue** (Map p260) and shrine. This is the main location for **Vijaya Utsav**, the Hampi arts festival held in November (see p220).

VITTALA TEMPLE

From the eastern end of Hampi Bazaar, a track, best covered on foot, leads left to the **Vittala Temple** (Map p259; Indian/foreigner Rs 10/US$5; 8.30am-5.30pm), about 2km away. The undisputed highlight of the Hampi ruins, the 16th-century temple is in a good state of preservation, though purists may gasp at the cement-block columns erected to keep the main structure from collapsing.

Work likely started on the temple during the reign of Krishnadevaraya (1509–29) and, despite the fact that it was never finished or

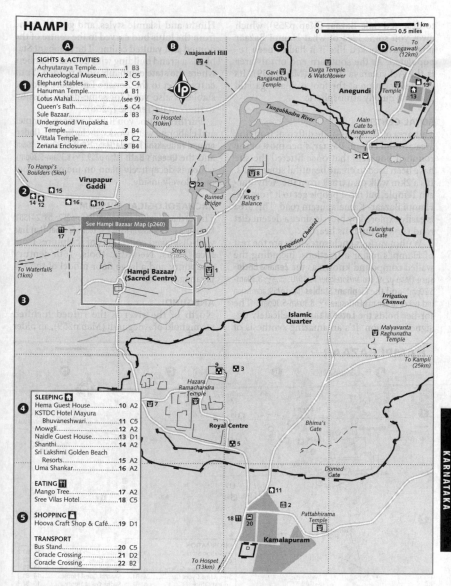

HAMPI

SIGHTS & ACTIVITIES
Achyutaraya Temple	**1** B3
Archaeological Museum	**2** C5
Elephant Stables	**3** C4
Hanuman Temple	**4** B1
Lotus Mahal	(see 9)
Queen's Bath	**5** C4
Sule Bazaar	**6** B3
Underground Virupaksha Temple	**7** B4
Vittala Temple	**8** C2
Zenana Enclosure	**9** B4

SLEEPING
Hema Guest House	**10** A2
KSTDC Hotel Mayura Bhuvaneshwari	**11** C5
Mowgli	**12** A2
Naidle Guest House	**13** D1
Shanthi	**14** A2
Sri Lakshmi Golden Beach Resorts	**15** A2
Uma Shankar	**16** A2

EATING
Mango Tree	**17** A2
Sree Vilas Hotel	**18** C5

SHOPPING
Hoova Craft Shop & Café	**19** D1

TRANSPORT
Bus Stand	**20** C5
Coracle Crossing	**21** D2
Coracle Crossing	**22** B2

KARNATAKA

consecrated, the temple's incredible sculptural work is the pinnacle of Vijayanagar art. The outer 'musical' pillars reverberate when tapped, although this is discouraged to avoid further damage. There's an ornate stone chariot in the temple courtyard containing an image of Garuda. Its wheels were once capable of turning.

Keep your temple entry ticket for same-day admission into the Zenana Enclosure and Elephant Stables in the Royal Centre (see p260).

SULE BAZAAR & ACHYUTARAYA TEMPLE
Halfway along the path from Hampi Bazaar to the Vittala Temple, a track to the right leads

to deserted Sule Bazaar (Map p259), which gives you some idea of what Hampi Bazaar might have looked like if it hadn't been re-populated. At the southern end of this area is the Achyutaraya Temple (Map p259). Its isolated location at the foot of Matanga Hill makes it quietly atmospheric.

ROYAL CENTRE

This area of Hampi is quite different from the area around Hampi Bazaar, since most of the rounded boulders that once littered the site have been used to create beautiful stone walls. It's a 2km walk on a track from the Achyutar-aya Temple, but most people get to it from the Hampi Bazaar–Kamalapuram road. This area is easily explored by bicycle since a decent dirt road runs through its heart.

Within various enclosures here are the rest of Hampi's major attractions, including the walled compound known as the **Zenana Enclosure** (Map p259; Indian/foreigner Rs 10/US$5; 8.30am-5.30pm), and the **Elephant Stables** (Map p259; admission incl ticket to Zenana Enclosure; 8.30am-5.30pm). The former holds the **Lotus Mahal**, a delicately de-signed pavilion. It's an amazing synthesis of Hindu and Islamic styles, and gets its name from the lotus bud carved in the centre of the domed and vaulted ceiling. The Elephant Sta-bles is a grand building with domed chambers where the state elephants once resided. Your entry ticket to the Zenana Enclosure and the stables is also valid for same-day admission to the Vittala Temple (p258).

Further south, you'll find various temples and elaborate waterworks, including the **Underground Virupaksha Temple** (Map p259; 8.30am-5.30pm) and the **Queen's Bath** (Map p259; 8.30am-5.30pm), which is deceptively plain on the outside but quite lovely inside.

ARCHAEOLOGICAL MUSEUM

The **archaeological museum** (Map p259; ☎ 241561; Kamalapuram; admission Rs 5; 10am-5pm Sat-Thu) has well-displayed collections of sculptures from local ruins, Neolithic tools, 16th-century weaponry and a large floor model of the Vi-jayanagar ruins.

ANEGUNDI

North of the river is the ruined fortified stronghold of Anegundi (Map p259), an older

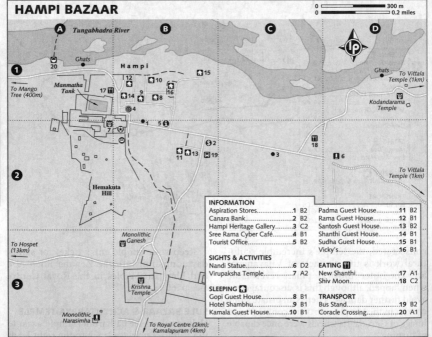

HAMPI BAZAAR

0 .... 300 m
0 .... 0.2 miles

INFORMATION	
Aspiration Stores.................1 B2	
Canara Bank........................2 B2	
Hampi Heritage Gallery........3 C2	
Sree Rama Cyber Café.........4 B1	
Tourist Office.....................5 B2	

Padma Guest House..........11 B2	
Rama Guest House............12 B1	
Santosh Guest House.........13 B2	
Shanthi Guest House.........14 B1	
Sudha Guest House...........15 B1	
Vicky's.............................16 B1	

SIGHTS & ACTIVITIES
Nandi Statue......................6 D2
Virupaksha Temple..............7 A2

EATING 🍴
New Shanthi......................17 A1
Shiv Moon.........................18 C2

SLEEPING 🛏
Gopi Guest House................8 B1
Hotel Shambhu....................9 B1
Kamala Guest House...........10 B1

TRANSPORT
Bus Stand.........................19 B2
Coracle Crossing.................20 A1

To Royal Centre (2km);
Kamalapuram (4km)

THE KISHKINDA TRUST

The **Kishkinda Trust** (TKT; ☎ 08533-267777; wwwthekishkindatrust.org) runs programmes and builds business opportunities in Anegundi that benefit both the local community and help preserve the village's heritage and culture. The first project in 1997 created a cottage industry of crafts using locally produced cloth, banana fibres and river grasses. It now employs over 500 women and the attractive crafts are sold across India; you can view the range at the **Hoova Craft Shop & Café** (9.30am-5pm Mon-Sat, 10am-2.30pm Sun) in the village centre. Internet access and bicycle rental are also available here.

With international support, one of the village's traditional houses has been rehabilitated and turned into an interpretation centre. TKT's latest project is a series of homestays and guesthouses around the village; rates start at Rs 250 per person. The **Naidle Guesthouse** (d Rs 500) sleeps up to seven people. Meals (from Rs 30 to 150) are extra.

---

structure than those at Hampi; within it you'll find a charming village. Free of the rampant commercialism that blights Hampi Bazaar, this is a wonderful place to stay thanks to a heritage-conservation project (see the Kishkinda Trust, above).

Much of the old defensive wall is intact and there are numerous small temples worth a visit, including the whitewashed **Hanuman Temple** (Map p259; dawn-dusk), perched on top of the prominent Anjanadri Hill. Fittingly, lots of cheeky monkeys roam about, so don't walk up wearing bananas.

It takes less than an hour to walk to Anegundi from Hampi Bazaar. At the time of research a new bridge across the Tungabhadra River was nearing completion; until then coracle rides cost Rs 10. Alternatively there's a road to Anegundi from Hospet.

ROCK-CLIMBING

Some of the best low-altitude climbing in India can be had near Hampi. For more information, see p262.

Sleeping

There's little to choose between many of the quaint but basic rooms in Hampi Bazaar and Virupapur Gaddi. If you need AC and cable TV, stay in Hospet (p263), or if you're looking for something quieter then consider staying in Anegundi (see the Kishkinda Trust, above). The prices listed can shoot up by 50% or more during the manic fortnight around New Year's Day, and drop just as dramatically in the low season (from April to September).

HAMPI BAZAAR

All of the following places are shown on Map p260.

Shanthi Guest House (☎ 241568; s/d with shared bathroom Rs 100/150) An oldie but a goodie, Shanthi offers a peaceful courtyard, bicycle rental (Rs 40), a morning bakery delivery and a small shop that operates on an honour system.

Gopi Guest House (☎ 241695; kirangopi2002@ yahoo.com; d Rs 200-400;) The Gopi empire keeps on expanding – apart from the rooftop garden and restaurant, it has recently renovated a block across the road, which contains four pleasant en suite rooms. Management plans to offer free yoga lessons up on the roof.

Vicky's (☎ 241694; vikkyhampi@yahoo.co.in; r Rs 250;) One of the village's larger operations, with 10 brightly painted rooms, a swing chair on the front porch, internet access and the requisite rooftop café.

Hotel Shambhu (☎ 241383; angadiparamesh1@hotmail .com; r Rs 300) Rooms painted in lavender, and a hallway with plants and an opalescent chandelier add a distinctive note to this pleasing place.

Padma Guest House (☎ 241331; s/d Rs 300/400) A range of good rooms are offered by the astute Padma, including some with lovely views of Virupaksha Temple.

Other good options:

Sudha Guest House (☎ 652752; d from Rs 250) Has a good family vibe, and some doubles fit three people.

Kamala Guest House (☎ 592662; ganeshashanker@yahoo.com; r Rs 300) New place with four well-presented rooms.

Rama Guest House (☎ 241962; d Rs 300) Has kept up good standards and added a few more rooms since we last checked.

Santosh Guest House (☎ 241460; hampisachin@yahoo.com; r Rs 350-500) Spotlessly clean; TV available in the most expensive room.

VIRUPAPUR GADDI

Many travellers prefer the tranquil atmosphere of Virupapur Gaddi, immediately across the river from Hampi Bazaar. A small boat (Rs 10) shuttles frequently across the river from 7am, although out of high season the last one leaves at 6pm. When the river is running high during the monsoon, boats may not be able to cross.

Shanthi (Map p259; ☎ 325352; r with shared bathroom Rs 100, bungalows with private bathroom from Rs 250) Shanthi's bungalows have ricefield, river and sunset views, and front porches with couch swings. The restaurant does good thalis (Rs 45) and pizzas (Rs 70 to 85).

Mowgli (Map p259; ☎ 9448217588; mowgli96@hotmail .com; r with shared bathroom Rs 100, bungalows with private bathroom from Rs 250; 🖳) With prime views across the rice fields, shady gardens sheltering hammocks, and thatched-roof bungalows, this is a top-class chill-out spot.

Hema Guest House (Map p259; ☎ 9449103008; dm/ bungalows Rs 100/300) Justifiably one of Virupapur Gaddi's more popular spots, the Hema offers a friendly welcome, simple accommodation and a relaxing restaurant in a beautiful wooden belvedere.

Uma Shankar (Map p259; ☎ 08533-287067; vijaygharti@ hotmail.com; r from Rs 200) Swing seats under a shady porch front the neat rooms at this laid-back place set amid pretty gardens.

Sri Lakshmi Golden Beach Resorts (Map p259; ☎ 08533-287008; d Rs 150-1500; 🌡 🖳) With a traditional resort feel, this place has a wide range of rooms, some in circular cottages with circular beds. At the time of research the large pool was out of commission; once it's up and running nonguests can use it for Rs 50 per hour.

Hampi's Boulders (☎ 08539-265939, 9448034202; Narayanpet; s/d incl full board from Rs 4000/6000; 🌡 🖳) To really get away from it all, head for this very discreet, small-scale wilderness resort, 5km west of Virupapur Gaddi. Inventively designed cottages blend almost seamlessly into the landscape, and the food is excellent.

KAMALAPURAM

KSTDC Hotel Mayura Bhuvaneshwari (Map p259; ☎ 08394-241574; d/tr from Rs 400/500; 🌡) This soulless, government-run place is really only worth it if you can't live without AC (and these rooms kick off at Rs 900). One slender point in its favour is its bar – the only legal one close to Hampi.

Eating

With one exception, Hampi is not renowned for its restaurants. Due to Hampi's religious significance, meat is scarce (if you want a chicken dish, for example, you generally have to order it a day in advance) and alcohol is banned – though travellers have been known to (discreetly) bend the rules. Places are open from 7am to 10pm.

our pick Mango Tree (Map p259; mains Rs 25-70) No visit to Hampi is complete until you've spent a lazy few hours at the Mango Tree. The walk out here through a banana plantation is delicious, the thalis (Rs 45) are a treat, and it does dosas for breakfast and dinner. Hop on the swing that hangs from the eponymous mango tree or lie back on the terraced seating with a book for the afternoon.

Shiv Moon (Map p260; mains Rs 35-90) This friendly place with pleasant views across the river is

---

CLIMBING IN KARNATAKA

Magnificent bluffs and rounded boulders poke up all over Karnataka, offering some of India's best rock-climbing. However, bolting is limited, so you'll need to bring a decent bouldering mat and plenty of gear from home – see p100.

Hampi is the undisputed bouldering capital of India. The entire landscape is made of granite crags and boulders, some bearing the marks of ancient stonemasons. Also interesting is nearby **Badami** (p264), a perfect horseshoe of red sandstone cliffs containing rock-carved temples and some magnificent bolted and traditional routes looking out over an ancient medieval city.

About 40km from Bengaluru, accessible by bus on the Mysore road, is **Ramnagar**, a cluster of towering granite boulders with some of the most popular routes in Karnataka. Other top spots include the granite massif at **Savandurga**, 50km west of Bengaluru near Magadi, and the boulder field at **Turalli**, 12km south of Bengaluru towards Kanakapura, both accessible by bus or taxi from Bengaluru.

Routes and grades are only just being assigned, so this is old-fashioned adventure climbing. **Dreamroutes** (www.dreamroutes.org/etc/allclimbs.html) has more tips on climbing in Karnataka.

away from the hubbub of Hampi Bazaar. It gets good reviews for its ambience and the quality of its food, which includes thalis (Rs 35) and quiche (Rs 90).

Waterfalls (Map p259; mains Rs 50) Around a 2km walk west of Hampi Bazaar, this simple, appealing operation is tucked away beside shady banana plantations on the path towards some interesting rock pools and small waterfalls.

New Shanthi (Map p260; mains Rs 20-45) A hippy vibe hangs over this popular option with an impressive selection of juices, lassis (yogurt and ice-water drinks) and shakes, as well as a good bakery.

Several of Hampi's lodges sport rooftop restaurants; good ones include those at Gopi Guest House (p261), Vicky's (p261) and Rama Guest House (p261). Kamalapuram has a few simple eateries, such as **Sree Vilas Hotel** (Map p259; meals Rs 20; ☺ 5am-8.30pm), opposite the bus stand.

Getting There & Away

While some buses from Goa and Bengaluru will drop you at the bus stand in Hampi Bazaar, you have to go to Hospet to catch most buses out. The first bus from Hospet (Rs 10, 30 minutes, half-hourly) is at 6.30am; the last one back leaves Hampi Bazaar at 8.30pm. An autorickshaw costs Rs 80. See right for transport information for Hospet.

KSRTC has a daily Rajahamsa bus service between Hampi Bazaar and Bengaluru (Rs 280, nine hours) leaving at 8pm. The overnight sleeper bus to/from Goa (Rs 500), which runs November to March, is a popular option – but don't expect a deep sleep. Numerous travel agents in Hampi Bazaar are eager to book onward bus, train and plane tickets, or arrange a car and driver.

Getting Around

Once you've seen the Vittala and Achyutaraya Temples, and Sule Bazaar, exploring the rest of the ruins by bicycle is the thing to do. There are key monuments haphazardly signposted along the road from Hampi Bazaar to Kamalapuram. Bicycles cost Rs 30 to 40 per day in Hampi Bazaar; mopeds can be hired for around Rs 200, plus petrol. You can take your bicycle or motorbike (extra Rs 10) across the river on the boat.

Walking is the only way to see all the nooks and crannies, but expect to cover at least 7km just to see the major ruins. Autorickshaws and taxis are available for sightseeing, and

will drop you as close to each of the major ruins as they can. A five-hour autorickshaw tour costs Rs 300.

Organised tours depart from Hospet; see below for details.

HOSPET

☎ 08394 / pop 163,284

This busy regional centre is the transport hub for Hampi. There's no reason to linger unless you desire an air-conditioned hotel room and cable TV.

Information

Internet joints are common, with connections costing Rs 40 per hour. The bus-stand cloakroom holds bags for Rs 10 per day.

KSTDC tourist office (☎ 228537; Shanbhag Circle; ☺ 7.30am-8.30pm) Offers a Hampi tour (Rs 140), which runs daily October to March and on demand the rest of the year; it departs from the tourist office at 9.30am and returns at 5.30pm. The quality of guides varies enormously. Call ahead as tours won't run with fewer than 10 people.

State Bank of India (☎ 228576; Station Rd; ☺ 10.30am-4pm Mon-Sat) Changes currency; also has a 24-hour ATM that accepts Visa and MasterCard.

Sleeping & Eating

Hotel Malligi (☎ 228101; www.malligihotels.com; Jabunatha Rd; r from Rs 300-3000; ☒ ☒ ☒) This is only worth it if you opt for the more expensive AC rooms, some of which are decorated in a vaguely contemporary style. Amenities including a couple of decent restaurants, a pool (Rs 35 for nonguests and guests in the cheapest rooms; closed Monday), a gym and Ayurvedic masseurs.

Hotel Priyadarshini (☎ 228838; www.priyainnhampi .com; Station Rd; s/d from Rs 900/950; ☒ ☒) Handily located between the bus and train stations, all the fresh, tidy rooms here have balconies and come with TV. Its outdoor nonveg restaurant-bar Manasa (mains Rs 60 to 110) has a good menu, and is shaded by trees with a lovely view of the fields.

Udupi Sri Krishna Bhavan (meals Rs 15-45; ☺ 6am-11pm) Opposite the bus stand, this clean, nononsense spot dishes out North and South Indian fare, including thalis for Rs 23.

Getting There & Away

BUS

The chaotic **bus stand** (☎ 228802) has services to Hampi from Bay 10 every half-hour (Rs 7 to 10, 30 minutes). Several express buses run to

Bengaluru (ordinary/deluxe Rs 175/300, nine hours) in morning and evening batches, and three overnight buses head to Panaji (Panjim; Rs 180, 11 hours) via Margao. Two buses a day go to Badami (Rs 150, six hours), or you can catch one of the many buses to Gadag (Rs 52, 2½ hours) and transfer. There are frequent buses to Hubli (Rs 82, 4½ hours) and Bijapur (Rs 130, six hours), three overnight services to Hyderabad (deluxe Rs 300, 10 hours) and one direct bus, at 9am, to Gokarna (Rs 200, 10 hours). For Mangalore or Hassan, take one of the many morning buses to Shimoga (Rs 160, five hours) and change there.

TRAIN

Hospet's **train station** (☎ 228360) is a 20-minute walk or Rs 10 autorickshaw ride from the centre of town. The daily *Hampi Express* heads to Hubli at 7.45am (2nd class Rs 46, 3½ hours) and Bengaluru at 8pm (sleeper/2AC Rs 212/881, 10 hours), or you can go to Guntakal (Rs 42, 2½ hours) and catch a Bengaluru-bound express there. Every Tuesday, Friday and Saturday, an 8.45am express heads to Vasco da Gama (sleeper/2AC Rs 169/690, 9½ hours).

To get to Badami, catch a Hubli train to Gadag and change there.

HUBLI

☎ 0836 / pop 786,018

The busy, prosperous city of Hubli is a hub for rail routes from Mumbai to Bengaluru, Goa and northern Karnataka. Several hotels and restaurants sit close to the train station; others surround the old bus stand, a 15-minute walk from the train station. Long-distance buses usually stop here before heading to the new bus stand 2km away, where there are few amenities.

Information

Ing Vysya Bank, next to Sagar Palace, has an ATM, and there's an iWay internet café across the road from the Hotel Ajanta.

Sleeping & Eating

Hotel Ajanta (☎ 2362216; Jayachamaraj Nagar; s/d from Rs 120/175) This large and well-run place near the train station has a good range of basic, functional rooms. The vibe is pre-Independence and its ground-floor restaurant (mains around Rs 50) is packed at lunch.

Hotel Samrat Ashok (☎ 2362380; Lamington Rd; s/d from Rs 350/400; 🔀) Above a bookshop on Lam-

ington Rd, this is handy for both the train station and old bus stand. Not to be confused with the Hotel Ashok on the corner.

Sagar Palace (Jayachamaraj Nagar; mains Rs 30-70; ⏰ 11am-3.30pm & 7-11.30pm) A classy pure-veg restaurant and bar serving up good food, including rum-spiked ice-cream sundaes.

Getting There & Away

BUS

Long-distance buses depart from the **new bus stand** (☎ 2221085). There are numerous services to Bengaluru (deluxe Rs 220, 10 hours), Hospet (Rs 85, four hours) and Mangalore (Rs 200, 10 hours). Buses also head to Mumbai (Rs 350, 14 hours, 10 daily), Mysore (ordinary/deluxe Rs 240/480, 12 hours, eight daily), Bijapur (Rs 92, six hours, six daily), Gokarna (Rs 200, five hours, four daily) and Panaji (Rs 103, six hours, six daily), as well as Vasco da Gama and Margao.

Private deluxe buses to Bengaluru (Rs 326) run from opposite the **old bus stand** (Lamington Rd), 2km away.

TRAIN

From the train station, which has a **reservation office** (☎ 2354333; ⏰ 8am-8pm), three expresses head to Hospet (Rs 47, 3½ hours). Around five expresses run daily to Bengaluru (sleeper/2AC Rs 216/777, eight hours), but there's only one direct train to Mumbai (sleeper/2AC Rs 289/1223, 17 hours). Trains run on Tuesday, Friday, Saturday and Sunday to Vasco de Gama (via Margao; sleeper/2AC Rs 143/542, seven hours).

NORTHERN KARNATAKA

BADAMI

☎ 08357 / pop 25,851

Looking at the scuffy village today, it's difficult to believe that Badami was once the capital of the Chalukya empire, which covered much of the central Deccan between the 4th and 8th centuries AD. However, climb up into the red sandstone ridge and explore the magnificent rock-cut cave temples surrounding the village, and you'll find ample evidence of Badami's former status.

Nearby Aihole hosted the earliest Chalukya capital; later the site was moved to Badami, with a secondary capital in Pattadakal. The result of this relocation is that the whole area around Badami is liberally scattered with ancient temples. Badami is the best base for taking in all these sites; a day or two should cover it.

History

Badami was the Chalukyan capital from about AD 540 to 757. At its height the empire was enormous, stretching from Kanchipuram in Tamil Nadu to the Narmada River in Gujarat. The surrounding hills are dotted with temples, fortifications, carvings and inscriptions dating not just from the Chalukyan period, but also from other times when the site was occupied as a fortress. After Badami fell to the Rashtrakutas, it was occupied successively by the Chalukyas of Kalyan (a separate branch of the Western Chalukyas), the Kalachuryas, the Yadavas of Devagiri, the Vijayanagar empire, the Adil Shahi kings of Bijapur and the Marathas.

The sculptural legacy left by the Chalukya artisans includes some of the earliest and finest examples of Dravidian temples and rock-cut caves, as well as the earliest free-standing temple in India. Aihole was a sort of trial ground for new temple architecture, which was further developed at Pattadakal, now a World Heritage site. The forms and sculptural work at these sites inspired the later South Indian Hindu empires that rose and fell before the arrival of the Muslims.

Orientation & Information

Station Rd, Badami's busy main street, has several hotels and restaurants; the more tranquil Badami village is between this road and the hilltop caves. The **tourist office** (☎ 220414; Ramdurg Rd; ☼ 10am-5.30pm), in the KSTDC Hotel Mayura Chalukya, is next to useless.

Mookambika Deluxe hotel changes currency for guests, but at a lousy rate; bring enough cash with you.

Internet (Ramdurg Rd; per hr Rs 60; ☼ 7am-10pm) is available in a house at the back of the KSTDC Hotel Mayura Chalukya compound. You can also try **Hotel Rajsangam** (Station Rd; per hr Rs 100) in the town centre.

Sights

CAVES

Badami's highlight is its beautiful **cave temples** (Indian/foreigner Rs 5/US$2; ☼ dawn-dusk). Nonpushy guides ask Rs 200 for a tour of the caves, or Rs 300 for the whole site.

Cave One

This cave, just above the entrance to the complex, is dedicated to Shiva. It's the oldest of the four caves, probably carved in the latter half of the 6th century. On the cliff wall to the right of the porch is a captivating image of Nataraja striking 81 dance poses (one for every combination of his 18 arms). He holds, among other things, a snake, a musical instrument and a *trishula* (trident).

On the right of the porch area is a huge figure of Ardhanarishvara. The right half of the figure shows features of Shiva, such as matted hair and a third eye, while the left half of the image has aspects of Parvati. On the opposite wall is a large image of Harihara; the right half represents Shiva and the left half Vishnu.

Cave Two

Dedicated to Vishnu, this cave is simpler in design. As with Caves One and Three, the front edge of the platform is decorated with images of pot-bellied dwarfs in various poses. Four pillars support the veranda, and the top of each pillar is carved with a bracket in the shape of a *yali* (mythical lion creature). On the left wall of the porch is the bull-headed figure of Varaha, an incarnation of Vishnu and the emblem of the Chalukya empire. To his left is Naga, a snake with a human face. On the right wall is a large sculpture of Trivikrama, another incarnation of Vishnu, booting out a demon while he holds various weapons in his eight hands. The ceiling panels contain images of Vishnu riding Garuda, *gandharva* (demigod) couples, swastikas and 16 fish arranged in a wheel (yet another incarnation of Vishnu).

Between the second and third caves are two sets of steps to the right. The first leads to a **natural cave**. The eastern wall of this cave contains a small image of Padmapani (an incarnation of the Buddha). The second set of steps – sadly, barred by a gate – leads to the hilltop **South Fort**.

Cave Three

This cave, carved in AD 578 under the orders of Mangalesha, the brother of King Kirtivarma, contains some sculptural highlights.

On the left-hand wall is a large carving of Vishnu, to whom the cave is dedicated, sitting on the coils of the snake. Nearby is an image of Varaha with four hands. The pillars have carved brackets in the shape of *yalis* and the sides of the pillars are also carved. The ceiling panels contain images, including Indra riding an elephant, Shiva on a bull and Brahma on a swan.

Cave Four

Dedicated to Jainism, Cave Four is the smallest of the set and was carved between the 7th and 8th centuries. The pillars, with their roaring *yalis*, are of a similar design to the other caves. The right wall of the cave has an image of Suparshvanatha (the seventh Jain *tirthankar*) surrounded by 24 Jain *tirthankars*. The sanctum contains an image of Adinath, the first Jain *tirthankar*.

OTHER SIGHTS

The caves overlook the 5th-century **Agastyatirtha Tank** and the waterside **Bhutanatha temples** (admission free). On the other side of the tank is an **archaeological museum** (☎ 220157; admission Rs 2; ☉ 10am-5pm Sat-Thu), which houses superb examples of local sculpture, including a remarkably explicit Lajja-Gauri image of a fertility cult that flourished in the area. The stairway just behind the museum climbs through a dramatic sandstone chasm and fortified gateways

to reach the various temples and ruins of the **north fort** (admission free). The fort has expansive views and overlooks the rooftops of Badami.

It's worth exploring Badami's **laneways**, where you'll find old houses with brightly painted carved wooden doorways, the occasional Chalukyan ruin and, of course, flocks of curious children.

Activities

Badami offers some great low-altitude climbing. For more information, see p262.

Sleeping

Many of Badami's hotels offer discounts in the low season.

Mookambika Deluxe (☎ 220067; fax 220106; Station Rd; s/d from Rs 150/300; ☒) The helpful staff at Badami's de facto tourist office can arrange taxis and guides. There's a range of rooms, including pricier ones with AC, but all suffer from street noise.

Hotel New Satkar (☎ 220417; Station Rd; s/d from Rs 275/450; ☒) Rooms at this friendly budget place are painted in beiges and creams; the best are on the 1st floor.

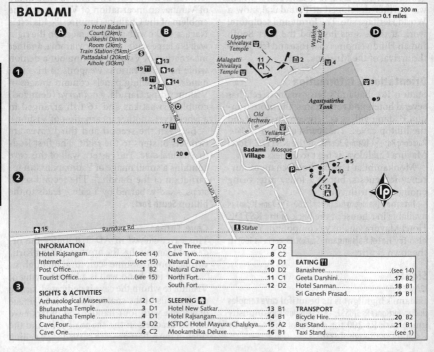

INFORMATION

Hotel Rajsangam	(see 14)
Internet	(see 15)
Post Office	1 B2
Tourist Office	(see 15)

SIGHTS & ACTIVITIES

Archaeological Museum	2 C1
Bhutanatha Temple	3 D1
Bhutanatha Temple	4 D1
Cave Four	5 D2
Cave One	6 C2
Cave Three	7 D2
Cave Two	8 C2
Natural Cave	9 D1
Natural Cave	10 D2
North Fort	11 C1
South Fort	12 D2

SLEEPING

Hotel New Satkar	13 B1
Hotel Rajsangam	14 B1
KSTDC Hotel Mayura Chalukya	15 A2
Mookambika Deluxe	16 B1

EATING

Banashree	(see 14)
Geeta Darshini	17 B2
Hotel Sanman	18 B1
Sri Ganesh Prasad	19 B1

TRANSPORT

Bicycle Hire	20 B2
Bus Stand	21 B1
Taxi Stand	(see 1)

KSTDC Hotel Mayura Chalukya (☎ 220046; Ramdurg Rd; d/tr Rs 400/550; 🖳) The rooms are large and reasonably pleasant at this government-run place in a quiet compound away from the perpetual bustle of the town centre.

Hotel Rajsangam (☎ 221991; www.hotelrajsangam .com; Station Rd; d from Rs 800; 🍴 🖳 🍸) This midrange place with good rooms (the best are the deluxe ones at the back where it's a bit quieter) is a useful addition to Badami's hotel scene. There's also a plunge pool on the roof for a cooling dip with a brilliant view.

Hotel Badami Court (☎ 220230; rafiqmht@blr.vsnl.net.in; Station Rd; s/d incl breakfast from Rs 1975/2500; 🍴 🍸) As good as it gets for Badami, this pleasant place sits in pastoral countryside 2km from the noisy town centre. Rooms are more functional than plush. Nonguests can use the pool for Rs 100.

Eating

Geeta Darshini (Station Rd; snacks Rs 6-10; ☉ 6.30am-9pm) The *idlis* and *masala dosas* come out thick and fast at this popular town-centre joint, and they're all washed down with tiny cups of chai. Perfect for a snack or quick meal.

Sri Ganesh Prasad (Station Rd; meals Rs 15; ☉ 5.30am-10.30pm) Beneath the Hotel Anand Deluxe, this is a cheap and cheery standby for excellent South Indian thalis (Rs 17) and *masala dosas* (Rs 10).

Hotel Sanman (Station Rd; mains Rs 30-50; ☉ 10am-11.30pm) If you need a cold beer with your meal, this is the place to get it. Tables behind curtained booths make it an intimate affair.

Banashree (Station Rd; mains Rs 40-60; ☉ 7am-10.30pm) In front of the Hotel Rajsangam, this bright and welcoming pure-veg restaurant offers everything from a variety of dosas to quasi-Chinese dishes. A better bet than the hotel's nonveg restaurant at the rear, which is more of a smoky bar.

Pulikeshi Dining Room (mains Rs 55-125; ☉ 24hr) People rave about the good range of continental and Indian dishes at this silver-service restaurant in Hotel Badami Court.

Getting There & Away

Buses shuffle off from Badami to Bijapur (Rs 69, 3½ hours, seven daily), Hubli (Rs 54, three hours, seven daily) and Bengaluru (ordinary/deluxe Rs 260/387, 12 hours, five daily). Three buses go direct to Hospet (Rs 84, six hours), or you can catch any of the buses to Gadag (Rs 30, two hours) and go from there. Note that this route is particularly hard on the bum.

Trains only run to Gadag (Rs 15, two hours, three daily), where you can get a connecting train to Hospet or Hubli. They're all 2nd-class passenger trains – but they're still more comfortable than the buses.

Getting Around

Badami's **train station** (☎ 220040) is 5km from town. Tongas (Rs 30), taxis (Rs 55), autorickshaws (Rs 30), and shared vans or large autorickshaws (Rs 4) ply the route. You can hire bicycles in Badami for Rs 5 per hour.

Exploring the surrounding area by local bus is easy, since they're moderately frequent and usually run on time. You can visit both Aihole and Pattadakal in a day from Badami if you get moving early; it's best to start with the morning bus to Aihole (Rs 15, one hour). Frequent buses then run between Aihole and Pattadakal (Rs 8, 30 minutes), and from Pattadakal to Badami (Rs 8, one hour). The last bus from Pattadakal to Badami is at 8pm. Take food and water with you.

Taxis cost at least Rs 650 for a day trip to Pattadakal, Aihole and Mahakuta. Badami's hotels can arrange taxis; alternatively, go to the taxi stand in front of the post office.

AROUND BADAMI
Pattadakal

This riverside village 20km from Badami was the second capital of the Badami Chalukyas; most of its **temples** (☎ 08357-243118; Indian/foreigner Rs 10/US$5; ☉ 6am-6pm) were built during the 7th and 8th centuries AD, but the earliest remains date from the 3rd and 4th centuries AD and the latest structure, a Jain temple, dates from the Rashtrakuta period (9th century). The group of temples is a World Heritage site.

Pattadakal, like Aihole, was a significant site in the development of South Indian temple architecture. In particular, two main types of temple towers were tried out here: curvilinear towers top the Kadasiddeshwra, Jambulinga and Galaganatha temples; and square roofs and receding tiers are used in the Mallikarjuna, Sangameshwara and Virupaksha temples.

The main **Virupaksha Temple** is a huge structure. The massive columns are covered with intricate carvings depicting episodes from the Ramayana and Mahabharata; they show battle scenes, lovers and decorative motifs. Around the roof of the inner hall are sculptures of elephants' and lions' heads. To the east, and facing the temple, is a pavilion containing a massive Nandi. The **Mallikarjuna Temple**, next to the Virupaksha Temple, is almost identical in design but slightly more worn. About 500m south of the main enclosure is the Jain **Papanatha Temple**, with its entrance flanked by elephant sculptures.

See p267 for transport details to/from Badami and Aihole.

Aihole

The Chalukyan regional capital between the 4th and 6th centuries, Aihole (*ay*-ho-leh) teems with at least 100 temples, although many are in ruins and engulfed by the modern village. Here you can see Hindu architecture in its embryonic stage, from the earliest simple shrines, such as those in the Kontigudi Group and the most ancient Lad Khan Temple, to the later and more complex buildings, such as the Meguti Temple.

The most impressive building in Aihole is the **Durga Temple** (☎ 08351-284533; Indian/foreigner Rs 5/US$2; ☼ 8am-6pm), which dates from the 7th century. It's notable for its semicircular apse, which is copied from Buddhist architecture, and for the remains of the curvilinear *sikhara* (Hindu temple spire). Intricate carvings adorn the colonnaded passageway around the sanctuary. The small **museum** (admission Rs 2; ☼ 10am-5pm Sat-Thu) behind the Durga Temple contains further examples of the Chalukyan sculptors' work.

To the south of the Durga Temple are several other collections of buildings, including some of the earliest structures in Aihole – the Gandar, Ladkhan, Kontigudi and Hucchapaya groups, which are of the pavilion type, with slightly sloping roofs. About 600m to the southeast, up a series of steps on a low hilltop, is the Jain **Meguti Temple**. Watch out for snakes!

The unappealing **KSTDC Tourist Home** (☎ 08351-284541; Amingad Rd; d/tr Rs 200/300), 1km from the village centre, is the only accommodation in town. You're better off staying in Badami.

See p267 for transport information.

BIJAPUR

☎ 08352 / pop 245,946 / elev 593m

Ruins and still-intact gems of 15th- to 17th-century Islamic architecture embellish old, dusty Bijapur like so many tatters of faded sultans' finery. It's a fascinating place to explore, blessed by a wealth of mosques, mausoleums, palaces and fortifications, whose austere grace is in complete contrast to the sculptural extravagance of the Chalukyan and Hoysala temples further south.

Bijapur was the capital of the Adil Shahi kings from 1489 to 1686, and was one of the splinter states formed when the Bahmani Muslim kingdom broke up in 1482. The town has a strong Islamic character but is also a centre for the Lingayat brand of Shaivism, which emphasises a single personalised god. The **Lingayat Siddeshwara Festival** runs for eight days in January/February.

Orientation

The two main attractions, the Golgumbaz and the Ibrahim Rouza, are at opposite ends of the town. Between them runs Station Rd (also known as Mahatma Gandhi Rd, or MG Rd), along which you'll find most of the major hotels and restaurants. The bus stand is a five-minute walk from Station Rd; the train station is 2km east of the centre.

Information

Canara Bank (☎ 250163; Azad Rd; ☼ 10.30am-4pm Mon-Fri, 10.30am-1pm Sat) Changes travellers cheques; bring a photocopy of your passport and prepare to wait forever.

Cyber Park (MG Rd; per hr Rs 30; ☼ 9am-10.30pm) Internet access.

Tourist office (☎ 250359; Station Rd; ☼ 10am-5.30pm Mon-Sat) Not much on offer. It's behind KSTDC Hotel Mayura Adil Shahi Annexe.

Sights

GOLGUMBAZ

Set in tranquil gardens, the ill-proportioned but magnificent **Golgumbaz** (☎ 240737; Indian/foreigner Rs 5/US$2; ☼ 6am-5.40pm) is Bijapur's largest monument – both in size and reputation. Dating from 1659, the building is the mausoleum of Mohammed Adil Shah (1626–56), his two wives, his mistress (Rambha), one of his daughters and a grandson. Their caskets stand on a raised platform in the centre of the immense hall, though their actual graves are in the crypt, accessible by a flight of steps under the western doorway.

Octagonal seven-storey towers stand at each of corner of the hall, which is capped by an enormous dome, 38m in diameter; it's said to be the largest dome in the world after St Peter's Basilica in Rome. Climb the steep, narrow stairs up one of the towers to reach

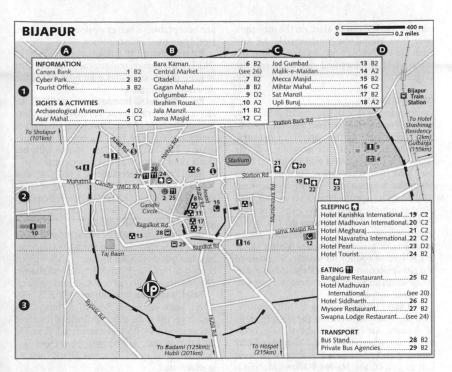

BIJAPUR

INFORMATION
Canara Bank..............................**1** B2
Cyber Park...............................**2** B2
Tourist Office...........................**3** B2

SIGHTS & ACTIVITIES
Archaeological Museum........**4** D2
Asar Mahal..............................**5** C2

Bara Kaman.............................**6** B2
Central Market.....................(see 26)
Citadel...................................**7** B2
Gagan Mahal.........................**8** B2
Golgumbaz.............................**9** D2
Ibrahim Rouza.......................**10** A2
Jala Manzil.............................**11** B2
Jama Masjid...........................**12** C2

Jod Gumbad...........................**13** B2
Malik-e-Maidan.....................**14** A2
Mecca Masjid.........................**15** B2
Mihtar Mahal.........................**16** C2
Sat Manzil.............................**17** B2
Upli Buruj.............................**18** A2

SLEEPING 🏠
Hotel Kanishka International....**19** C2
Hotel Madhuvan International.**20** C2
Hotel Megharaj......................**21** C2
Hotel Navaratna International.**22** C2
Hotel Pearl.............................**23** D2
Hotel Tourist..........................**24** B2

EATING 🍴
Bangalore Restaurant.............**25** B2
Hotel Madhuvan
International......................(see 20)
Hotel Siddharth.....................**26** B2
Mysore Restaurant.................**27** B2
Swapna Lodge Restaurant.....(see 24)

TRANSPORT
Bus Stand..............................**28** B2
Private Bus Agencies..............**29** B2

the 'whispering gallery'; the acoustics are such that if you whisper into the wall a person on the opposite side of the gallery can hear you clearly, and any sound made is said to be repeated 10 times over. Unfortunately people like to test this out with their shouting, so come in the early morning before any school groups arrive.

The gardens house a missable **archaeological museum** (admission Rs 2; ⏰ 10am-5pm Sat-Thu).

IBRAHIM ROUZA

The beautiful **Ibrahim Rouza** (Indian/foreigner Rs 5/ US$2, video Rs 25; ⏰ 6am-6pm) is considered to be one of the most finely proportioned Islamic monuments in India. It was built at the height of Bijapur's prosperity by Ibrahim Adil Shah II (r 1580–1626) for his queen, Taj Sultana. As it happens, he died before her, so he was laid to rest here as well. Unlike the Golgumbaz, which is impressive for its immensity, the emphasis here is on elegance and detail. Its 24m-high minarets are said to have inspired those of the Taj Mahal. It's also one of the few monuments in Bijapur with substantial stone filigree and other decorative sculptural work.

Interred here with Ibrahim Adil Shah and his queen are his daughter, his two sons, and his mother, Haji Badi Sahiba.

CITADEL

Surrounded by fortified walls and a wide moat, the citadel once contained the palaces, pleasure gardens and durbar (royal court) of the Adil Shahi kings. Now mainly in ruins, the most impressive of the remaining fragments is the **Gagan Mahal**, built by Ali Adil Shah I around 1561 as a dual-purpose royal residency and durbar hall.

The ruins of Mohammed Adil Shah's seven-storey palace, the **Sat Manzil**, are nearby. Across the road stands the delicate **Jala Manzil**, once a water pavilion surrounded by secluded courts and gardens. On the other side of Station Rd are the graceful arches of **Bara Kaman**, the ruined mausoleum of Ali Roza.

JAMA MASJID

The finely proportioned **Jama Masjid** (Jama Masjid Rd; ⏰ 9am-5.30pm) has graceful arches, a fine dome and a vast inner courtyard with room for 2250 worshippers. Spaces for the worship-

KARNATAKA

pers are marked out in black on the mosque's floor. Jama Masjid was constructed by Ali Adil Shah I (r 1557–80), who was also responsible for erecting the fortified city walls and the Gagan Mahal.

OTHER SIGHTS

On the eastern side of the citadel is the tiny, walled **Mecca Masjid** (admission free), thought to have been built in the early 17th century. Some speculate that this mosque, with its high surrounding walls and cloistered feel, may have been for women. Further east, the **Asar Mahal** (admission free), built by Mohammed Adil Shah in about 1646 to serve as a Hall of Justice, once housed two hairs from the Prophet's beard. The rooms on the upper storey are decorated with frescoes and a square tank graces the front. A sign states that it's out of bounds for women. The stained but richly decorated **Mihtar Mahal** (admission free) to the south serves as an ornamental gateway to a small mosque.

Upli Buruj (admission free) is a 16th-century, 24m-high watchtower near the western walls of the city. An external flight of stairs leads to the top, where there are a couple of hefty cannons and good views. A short walk west brings you to the **Malik-e-Maidan** (Monarch of the Plains), a huge cannon over 4m long, almost 1.5m in diameter and estimated to weigh 55 tonnes. Cast in 1549, it was brought to Bijapur as a war trophy thanks to the effort of 10 elephants, 400 oxen and hundreds of men. Legend has it that the gunners would jump into the moat after lighting the fuse rather than be deafened. The mouth of the cannon is shaped like a lion (representing Islam), and its razor-sharp jaws are closing on a cartoonish bug-eyed elephant (Hinduism) that's trying to flee.

In the southwest of the city, off Bagalkot Rd, stand the twin **Jod Gumbad** tombs with handsome bulbous domes; an Adil Shahi general and his spiritual adviser, Abdul Razzaq Qadiri, are buried here. The surrounding gardens are a popular picnic spot.

Bijapur's **central market**, just north of MG Rd, is also worth exploring; it's packed with spice merchants, flower sellers, tailors and other traders.

Sleeping

Hotel Tourist (☎ 250655; MG Rd; s/d from Rs 80/150, deluxe Rs 150/250) The very ordinary doubles here

are acceptable; a better option is the clean, freshly painted deluxe rooms.

Hotel Megharaj (☎ 254458; Station Rd; r from Rs 150; ✗) The Megharaj continues to make an effort to keep things nice, and it's a little out of the downtown jumble.

Hotel Navaratna International (☎ 222771; fax 222772; Station Rd; r from Rs 400; ✗) Colourful paintings in the style of Kandinsky and Chagal are a pleasant surprise in the lobby of the Navaratna. The sparkling clean rooms with big shiny floor tiles are also very welcome.

Hotel Kanishka International (☎ 223788; www .kanishka_bijapur.com; Station Rd; d from Rs 450; ✗) The spacious rooms here have big comfy beds and marble floors, and there's a small gym for guests' use. Rates include tax.

Hotel Pearl (☎ 256002; fax 243606; Station Rd; d from Rs 500; ✗) Across the road from the Golgumbaz, this business hotel has some class with its central atrium and brightly painted rooms. Ask for one at the rear to avoid street noise.

Hotel Madhuvan International (☎ 255571; fax 256201; Station Rd; r from Rs 950; ✗) Although it's clearly on the slide, this is still one of the nicer places in town – it's just overpriced. A major plus that it's set well enough away from Station Rd to be quiet. The restaurant (below) is excellent.

Hotel Shashinag Residency (☎ 260344; www .hotelshashinag.com; Solapur-Chitradurga Bypass Rd; s/d incl breakfast from US$30/45; ✗ ▢ ▣) The rooms are large but the housekeeping standards need improvement at what is supposed to be Bijapur's most upmarket choice. Bonuses are a small pool (Rs 30 per hour for nonguests), a playground and a gym. Rates include taxes.

Eating

Unless otherwise mentioned, all places are open from around 6pm to 10pm.

Bangalore Restaurant (MG Rd; meals Rs 18) This modest little pink-painted place does good South Indian veg thalis.

Mysore Restaurant (New Market; meals Rs 20) Locals swear by this place for good-value South Indian veg dishes.

Hotel Madhuvan International (mains Rs 25-50) Delicious food is served either in the garden or inside in AC relief. Try the yummy *masala dosa* or the never-ending North Indian thalis dished out by waiters in red turbans.

Hotel Siddharth (New Market; mains Rs 35-80; ✆ 8am-11pm) On top of the market, the Siddharth offers curtained booths and rooftop seating.

It has a huge selection of vegetarian and meaty dishes, plus booze.

Swapna Lodge Restaurant (MG Rd; mains Rs 30-100; ☽9am-11pm) On the 2nd floor of the building next to Hotel Tourist, Swapna Lodge has good grub, cold beer and a 1970s lounge feel. Its open-air terrace is perfect for evening dining.

Getting There & Away
BUS
From the **bus stand** (☎ 251344), buses run direct to Badami (Rs 60, 4½ hours, seven daily) and Bidar (Rs 150, seven hours, four daily). Buses head every half-hour to Gulbarga (Rs 70, four hours), Hubli (Rs 80, six hours) and Sholapur (Rs 61, two hours). Eight evening buses go to Bengaluru (deluxe Rs 292, 12 hours) via Hospet, and a few buses a day go to Hyderabad (deluxe Rs 312, 10 hours) and Pune (Rs 172, eight hours).

The plentiful private bus agencies near the bus stand run services to Bengaluru (Rs 350) and Mumbai (Rs 380), as well as to Hubli (Rs 140), Mangalore (Rs 370) and other destinations.

TRAIN
From **Bijapur train station** (☎ 244888), there are four daily trains to Sholapur (Rs 21, 2½ hours), which has connections to Mumbai, Hyderabad and Bengaluru. An express to Bengaluru (sleeper/3AC Rs 310/550, 12 hours, three weekly) also passes through, as do 'fast passenger' trains to Mumbai (chair/sleeper Rs 70/151, 12 hours, three weekly) and Hyderabad (sleeper Rs 123, 15½ hours, daily).

Getting Around
Autorickshaws are oddly expensive in Bijapur; Rs 30 (plus haggling) should get you between the train station and the town centre. Between the Golgumbaz and Ibrahim Rouza they cost about Rs 30. Tonga drivers are eager for business but charge around the same. Autorickshaw drivers ask for Rs 200 for four hours around town.

BIDAR
☎ 08482 / pop 172,298 / elev 664m
Tucked away in Karnataka's far northeastern corner, Bidar is an afterthought on most travellers' itineraries. This is a great shame since the old walled town has some amazing ruins and monuments dating from its time as the capital of the Bahmani kingdom

(1428–87), and later the capital of the Barid Shahi dynasty.

Orientation & Information
The modern town centre is strung along Udgir Rd, along which you'll also find the bus station. Fast internet access is available at **Arien Computers** (per hr Rs 20; ☽9.30am-10.30pm) around the corner from the Krishna Regency.

Sights
BIDAR FORT
You can wander peacefully for hours around the magnificent 15th-century **Bidar Fort** (admission free; ☽dawn-dusk), sprawled across rolling hills, 2km east of Udgir Rd. Surrounded by a triple moat hewn out of solid red rock and 5.5km of defensive wall (the second longest in India), the fort has a fairy-tale entrance on a roadway that twists in an elaborate chicane through three gateways.

Inside the fort are many evocative ruins, including the **Rangin Mahal** (Painted Palace) which sports elaborate tilework, woodwork and panels with mother-of-pearl inlay, and the **Solah Kambah Mosque** (Sixteen-Pillared Mosque). There's also a small **museum** (admission free; ☽9am-6pm) in the former royal bath. If you're looking for a guide, call the **archaeological office** (☎ 230418) and ask for Abdul Mumaf.

BAHMANI TOMBS
The huge domed **tombs** (admission free) of the Bahmani kings, in Ashtur, 2km east of Bidar, have a desolate, moody beauty that strikes a strange harmony with the sunny hills around them. These impressive mausoleums were built to house the remains of the sultans – their graves are still regularly draped with fresh satin and flowers – and are arranged in a long line along the edge of the road. The painted interior of Ahmad Shah I's tomb is the most impressive.

OTHER SIGHTS
Dominating the heart of the old town are the remains of **Khwaja Mahmud Gawan Madrasa** (admission free), a college built in 1492. The remnants of coloured tiles on the front gate and one of the minarets gives an idea of how grand the building once was.

Bidri artists (see p272) still tap away at their craft in the back streets on and around Chowbara Rd, near Basveshwar Circle.

KARNATAKA

BIDRI: THE ART OF BIDAR

Around the 14th century, the Persian craftsmen of Bidar came up with an art form known as *bidriware* by moulding metals together to create imaginative blends of blackened zinc, copper, lead and tin. Embossed and overlaid or inlaid with pure silver, *bidriware* designs are heavily influenced by the typically Islamic decorative motifs and features of the time. Finely crafted pieces, such as hookahs, goblets, and jewellery boxes, are exquisitely embellished with interwoven creepers and flowing floral patterns, occasionally framed by strict geometric lines.

Sleeping & Eating

Don't expect much in the way of pampering – the best you can hope for is a clean room with AC and a hot-water shower. Places listed below are all within a few minutes' walk of the bus stand.

Hotel Mayura (☎ 228142; Udgir Rd; r from Rs 150) Across from the bus station and set back from the road is this standard-issue government-run hotel with rooms that have clearly seen better days. The best thing about it is the non-veg restaurant-bar (mains Rs 30 to 80) with a beer garden where you can guzzle in the privacy of a privet-hedge booth.

Krishna Regency (☎ 221991; fax 228388; Udgir Rd; s/d/tr from Rs 275/325/550; ✖) This friendly, efficiently

run hotel with a glass elevator running up the outside of the building is the best option in Bidar. There's a good range of rooms, but some lack natural light and there's no food available.

Sapna International (☎ 220991; fax 240095; Udgir Rd; s/d from Rs 300/350; ✖) On a par with the Krisha in terms of rooms – it's just not as friendly. In its favour are its two restaurants: the pure-veg Kamat and the Atithi, which offers meat dishes and booze. Mains cost Rs 23 to 50.

Jyothi Udupi (Udgir Rd; meals Rs 20-45; ❂ 6am-11pm) This place opposite the bus stand has 21 kinds of dosa, filling South Indian thalis (Rs 20) and an ice-cream sundae named beauty ripples.

Getting There & Away

From the **bus stand** (☎ 228508), frequent services run to Gulbarga (Rs 50, three hours), which has good express-train connections to Mumbai and Bengaluru, as well as to Hyderabad (Rs 69, 3½ hours), Bijapur (Rs 131, eight hours) and Bengaluru (deluxe/AC Rs 380/707, 12 hours).

The train station, around 1km southwest of the bus stand, has daily services to Hyderabad (chair Rs 27, 4½ hours) and Bengaluru (sleeper/2AC Rs 295/801, 17 hours).

Getting Around

Rent a bike at **Diamond Cycle Taxi** (Basveshwar Circle; per day Rs 12; ❂ 7am-10pm) or arrange a tour in an autorickshaw for around Rs 250.

Andhra Pradesh

Aside from tens of millions of pilgrims, not many people make the trip to Andhra Pradesh. But Andhra's a place with subtle charms, quiet traditions and a long history of spiritual scholarship and religious harmony. The state is 95% Hindu, but you wouldn't know it in the capital's Old City, where Islamic monuments and the call of the muezzin are more ubiquitous than the garlanded, twinkling tableaux of Ganesh. The city's rich Islamic history announces itself in Hyderabad's huge, lavish mosques, its opulent palaces and the stately Qutb Shahi tombs – but also, more softly, in a tiny spiral staircase in the Charminar and in the sounds of Urdu floating through the air.

Meanwhile, in the city's north, a 17.5m-high statue of the Buddha announces another Andhran history: the region was an international centre of Buddhist thought for several hundred years from the 3rd century BC. Andhras were practising the dharma from the time of the Buddha (rumour has it that he even once visited). Today ruins of stupas and monasteries defy impermanence around the state, especially at Amaravathi and Nagarjunakonda.

Travelling here is like a treasure hunt: the jewels have to be earned. The stunning Eastern Ghats near Visakhapatnam only emerge after hours on a broad-gauge line. A family workshop filled with exquisite traditional paintings appears after a meander through Sri Kalahasti. And the most famous wait of all, through a long, holy maze filled with pilgrims at Tirumala, is rewarded with a glimpse of Lord Venkateshwara, who, if you're lucky, will grant you a wish.

HIGHLIGHTS

- Buy an old drum and more bangles than you need while soaking up centuries-old ambience at Hyderabad's colourful **Laad Bazaar** (p278)

- Receive loving kindness from Buddha statues in **Hyderabad** (p281), **Nagarjunakonda** (p295) and **Amaravathi** (p301)

- Enjoy the beauty of the spectacular Eastern Ghats as your train chugs through the mountains to the **Araku Valley** (p300)

- Find devotion you didn't know you had for Lord Venkateshwara and mingle with the pilgrims at **Tirumala** (p302) as they shed their hair for their deity

- Picnic atop the ruins of the 16th-century **Golconda Fort** (p280) and then wander in and out of the **royal tombs of the Qutb Shahi kings** (p280) in Hyderbad

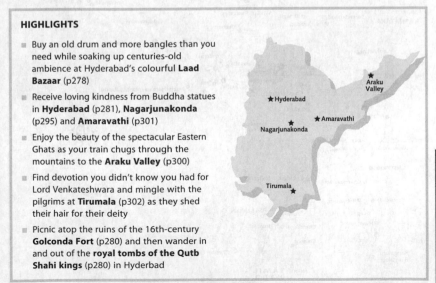

★ Araku Valley

★ Hyderabad

★ Amaravathi

★ Nagarjunakonda

★ Tirumala

History

From the 2nd century BC, the Satavahana empire, also known as the Andhras, reigned throughout the Deccan plateau. It evolved from the Andhra people, whose presence in southern India may date back to 1000 BC. The Buddha's teaching took root here early on, and in the 3rd century BC the Andhras fully embraced it, building huge edifices in its honour. In the coming centuries, the Andhras would develop a flourishing civilisation that extended from the west to the east coasts of South India.

From the 7th to the 10th century the Chalukyas ruled the area, establishing their Dravidian style of architecture, especially along the coast. The Chalukya and Chola dynasties merged in the 11th century to be overthrown by the Kakatiyas, who introduced pillared temples into South Indian religious architecture. The Vijayanagars then rose to become one of the most powerful empires in India.

FAST FACTS

- Population: 75.7 million
- Area: 276,754 sq km
- Capital: Hyderabad
- Main languages: Telugu, Urdu, Hindi
- When to go: October to February

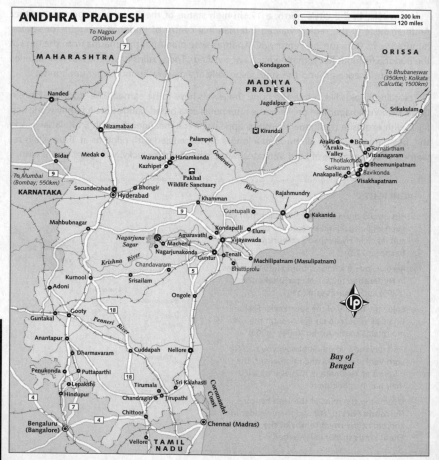

By the 16th century the Islamic Qutb Shahi dynasty held the city of Hyderabad, but in 1687 was supplanted by Aurangzeb's Mughal empire. In the 18th century the post-Mughal rulers in Hyderabad, known as nizams, retained relative control as the British and French vied for trade, though their power gradually weakened. The region became part of independent India in 1947, and in 1956 the state of Andhra Pradesh, an amalgamation of Telugu-speaking areas, plus the predominantly Urdu-speaking capital, was created.

Information

ACCOMMODATION

Most hotels charge a 5% 'luxury' tax, which is not included in the prices quoted in this chapter. All hotels in this chapter have 24-hour checkout unless otherwise stated.

HYDERABAD & SECUNDERABAD

☎ 040 / pop 5.5 million / elev 600m

Hyderabad and Secunderabad, City of Pearls, was once the seat of the powerful Qutb Shahi and Asaf Jahi dynasties. Today Hyderabad's west side is, with Bengaluru (Bangalore), the seat of India's mighty software dynasty; 'Cyberabad' generates jobs, wealth and posh lounges like she was born to do it. Opulence, it would seem, is in this city's genes.

Across town from all this sheen is Cyberabad's gorgeous and aged grandmother, the old Muslim quarter, with centuries-old Islamic monuments and even older charms. In fact, the whole city is laced with architectural gems (just like the garments of Asaf Jahi princesses threaded with gold): ornate tombs, mosques, palaces and homes from the past are tucked away, faded and enchant-

---

FESTIVALS IN ANDHRA PRADESH

Sankranti (Jan; statewide) This important Telugu festival marks the end of harvest season. Kite-flying competitions are held, women decorate their doorsteps with colourful *kolams* (or *rangolis* – rice-flour designs), and men decorate cattle with bells and fresh horn paint.

Industrial Exhibition (Jan/Feb; Hyderabad, above) A huge exhibition with traders from around India displaying their wares, accompanied by a colourful, bustling fair.

Deccan Festival (Feb; Hyderabad, above) Pays tribute to Deccan culture. Urdu *mushairas* (poetry readings) are held, along with Qawwali (Sufi devotional music) and other local music and dance performances.

Shivaratri (Feb/Mar; statewide) During a blue moon, this festival celebrates Shiva with all-night chanting, prayers and fasting. Hordes of pilgrims descend on the auspicious Shiva temples at Sri Kalahasti, Amaravathi and Lepakshi.

Muharram (Feb/Mar; Hyderabad, above) Muharram commemorates the martyrdom of Mohammed's grandson for 14 days in Hyderabad. Shiites wear black in mourning, and throngs gather at Mecca Masjid.

Ugadi (Mar; statewide) Telugu new year is celebrated with *pujas* (offerings or prayers), mango-leaf *toranas* (architraves) over doorways, and sweets and special foods.

Mahankali Jatra (Jun/Jul; statewide) A festival honouring Kali, with colourful processions in which devotees convey *bonalu* (pots of food offerings) to the deity. Secunderabad's Mahankali Temple goes wild.

Mrigasira (Jun/Jul; Hyderabad, above) Also known as Mrugam, this event marks the start of the monsoon with a feast of local fish and a fascinating medical treatment administered to thousands of asthma sufferers. The treatment, more than 150 years old, involves swallowing live fish that have consumed a herbal remedy. It's believed that the remedy was revealed by a sage to the ancestors of the physicians who now dispense it.

Batakamma (Sep/Oct; Hyderabad, above & Warangal, p297) Women and girls in the north of the state participate in this celebration of womanhood. There's dancing and feasting, and the goddess Batakamma is worshipped in the form of elaborate flower arrangements that women make and set adrift on rivers.

Brahmotsavam (Sep/Oct; Tirumala, p302) Initiated by Brahma himself, the nine-day festival sees the Venkateshwara temple adorned in decorations. Special *pujas* and colourful chariot processions are a feature of the festivities, and it's considered an auspicious time for *darshan* (deity viewing).

Pandit Motiram-Maniram Sangeet Samaroh (Nov; Hyderabad, above) This four-day music festival, named for two renowned classical musicians, celebrates Hindustani music.

Lumbini Festival (2nd Fri in Dec; Hyderabad, above & Nagarjunakonda, p295) The three-day Lumbini Festival honours Andhra's Buddhist heritage.

Visakha Utsav (Dec/Jan; Visakhapatnam, p298) A celebration of all things Visakhapatnam, with classical and folk dance and music performances; some events are staged on the beach.

ing, in corners all over town. Keep your eyes open.

Once an important centre of Islamic culture, Hyderabad is southern India's counterpart to the Mughal splendour of Delhi, Agra and Fatehpur Sikri, and a sizeable percentage of Hyderabad's population is Muslim. The city gracefully combines Hindu and Islamic traditions – while a strategically placed 17.5m-high Buddha looks on.

You're likely to be taken aback by the chilled-out kindness of Hyderabadis, and many find the city delightful: lots to see and do with almost no hassle.

History

Hyderabad owes its existence to a water shortage at Golconda in the late 16th century. The reigning Qutb Shahis were forced to relocate, and so Mohammed Quli and the royal family abandoned Golconda Fort for the banks of the Musi River. The new city of Hyderabad was established, with the brand-new Charminar as its centrepiece.

In 1687 the city was overrun by the Mughal emperor Aurangzeb, and subsequent rulers of Hyderabad were viceroys installed by the Mughal administration in Delhi.

In 1724 the Hyderabad viceroy, Asaf Jah, took advantage of waning Mughal power and declared Hyderabad an independent state with himself as leader. The dynasty of the nizams of Hyderabad began, and the traditions of Islam flourished. Hyderabad became a focus for the arts, culture and learning, and the centre of Islamic India. Its abundance of rare gems and minerals – the world-famous Kohinoor diamond is from here – furnished the nizams with enormous wealth. (Get a copy of William Dalrymple's *White Mughals* for a fascinating portrait of the city at this time.)

When Independence came in 1947, the then nizam of Hyderabad, Osman Ali Khan, considered amalgamation with Pakistan – and then opted for sovereignty. Tensions between Muslims and Hindus increased, however, and military intervention saw Hyderabad join the Indian union in 1948.

Orientation

Hyderabad has four distinct areas. The Old Town by the Musi River has bustling bazaars and important landmarks, including the Charminar.

North of the river is Mahatma Gandhi (Imlibun) bus station, Hyderabad (Nampally) station and the main post office. Abid Rd runs through the Abids district, a good budget-accommodation area.

Further north, beyond the Hussain Sagar, lies Secunderabad, with its Jubilee bus station and huge train station, an important stop for many regional trains.

Jubilee Hills and Banjara Hills, west of Hussain Sagar, are where the well heeled – and their restaurants, shops and lounges – reside, and further west is Cyberabad's capital, Hitec (Hyderabad Information Technology Engineering Consulting) City.

Information

BOOKSHOPS

On Sunday, second-hand books are sold on Abid Rd; a few gems nestle among the computer books.

AA Husain & Co (Map p279; ☎ 23203724; Abid Rd; ☺ 10.30am-8.30pm Mon-Sat) Tonnes of Indian and foreign authors.

MR Book Centre (Map p279; ☎ 23205684; Abid Rd; ☺ 10am-9pm Mon-Sat, 11am-10pm Sun) New and secondhand novels; magazines from back home.

Walden (Map p277; ☎ 23413434; Greenlands Rd, Begumpet; ☺ 9am-9pm) Hyderabad's megastore.

CULTURAL CENTRES & LIBRARIES

Alliance Française (Map p277; ☎ 27700734; www .afindia.org; St No 16, West Marredpally, Secunderabad; ☺ 9am-1pm & 2-6pm Mon-Fri, 9am-1pm Sat)

British Library (Map p279; ☎ 23483333; www.british councilonline.org; Secretariat Rd; ☺ 11am-7pm Tue-Sun) Membership costs Rs 1000.

State Library (Map p277; ☎ 24600107; Maulvi Allaudin Rd; ☺ 8am-8pm Fri-Wed) Beautiful old building with more than three million books.

INTERNET ACCESS

Railtel Cyber Express (Map p279; ☎ 64512724; Nampally Station; per hr Rs 23; ☺ 6am-10pm)

Reliance Web World (Map p279; ☎ 30609991; MPM Mall, Abids Circle; per 3 hr Rs 100; ☺ 9.30am-10pm)

LEFT LUGGAGE

All three train stations, as well as Mahatma Gandhi bus station, have left-luggage facilities, charging Rs 10 per bag per day.

MEDIA

Good 'what's on' guides include *Channel 6*, *GO Hyderabad* and *Primetime Prism*. The

HYDERABAD & SECUNDERABAD

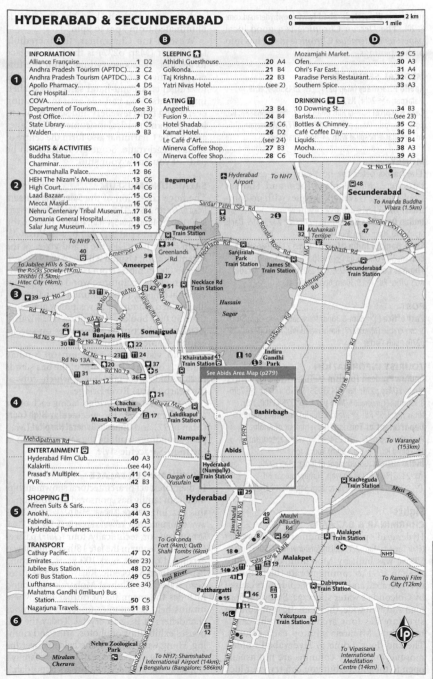

INFORMATION
Alliance Française...........................1 D2
Andhra Pradesh Tourism (APTDC)....2 C2
Andhra Pradesh Tourism (APTDC)....3 C4
Apollo Pharmacy............................4 D5
Care Hospital.................................5 B4
COVA..6 C6
Department of Tourism.............(see 3)
Post Office....................................7 D2
State Library..................................8 C5
Walden...9 B3

SIGHTS & ACTIVITIES
Buddha Statue.............................10 C4
Charminar....................................11 C6
Chowmahalla Palace.....................12 B6
HEH The Nizam's Museum.............13 C6
High Court...................................14 C6
Laad Bazaar.................................15 C6
Mecca Masjid...............................16 C6
Nehru Centenary Tribal Museum....17 B4
Osmania General Hospital..............18 C6
Salar Jung Museum.......................19 C5

SLEEPING 🏠
Athidhi Guesthouse......................20 A4
Golkonda.....................................21 B4
Taj Krishna..................................22 B3
Yatri Nivas Hotel.....................(see 2)

EATING 🍽
Angeethi......................................23 B4
Fusion 9......................................24 B4
Hotel Shadab...............................25 C6
Kamat Hotel................................26 D2
Le Café d'Art.........................(see 24)
Minerva Coffee Shop....................27 B3
Minerva Coffee Shop....................28 C6

Mozamjahi Market.......................29 C5
Ofen...30 A3
Ohri's Far East.............................31 A4
Paradise Persis Restaurant.............32 C2
Southern Spice.............................33 A3

DRINKING 🍷 🍸
10 Downing St.............................34 B3
Barista...................................(see 23)
Bottles & Chimney.......................35 C2
Café Coffee Day...........................36 B4
Liquids..37 B4
Mocha..38 A3
Touch...39 A3

ENTERTAINMENT 🎭
Hyderabad Film Club....................40 A3
Kalakriti.................................(see 44)
Prasad's Multiplex........................41 C4
PVR..42 B3

SHOPPING 🛍
Afreen Suits & Saris......................43 C6
Anokhi..44 A3
Fabindia......................................45 A3
Hyderabad Perfumers...................46 C6

TRANSPORT
Cathay Pacific..............................47 D2
Emirates.................................(see 23)
Jubilee Bus Station.......................48 D2
Koti Bus Station...........................49 C5
Lufthansa...............................(see 34)
Mahatma Gandhi (Imlibun) Bus
   Station....................................50 C5
Nagarjuna Travels........................51 B3

juiciest is **Wow! Hyderabad** (www.wowhyderabad.com; Rs 20). The *Deccan Chronicle* is a good local paper; its *Hyderabad Chronicle* insert has info on happenings.

MEDICAL SERVICES
Apollo Pharmacy (Map p277; ☎ 23433609; NH9, Malakpet; ⏱ 24hr) Rs 200 to deliver.
Care Hospital Banjara Hills (Map p277; ☎ 66668888; Rd No 1); Nampally (Map p279; ☎ 66517777; Mukarramjahi Rd) Reputable hospital with 24-hour pharmacy.

MONEY
The banks offer the best currency-exchange rates here. State Bank of India and Thomas Cook change travellers cheques with no commission. ATMs are everywhere.
Indian Overseas Bank (Map p279; ☎ 24756655; Bank St; ⏱ 10.30am-3pm Mon-Fri)
State Bank of India (Map p279; ☎ 23231986; HACA Bhavan, AG's Office Rd; ⏱ 10.30am-4pm Mon-Fri)
Thomas Cook (Map p279; ☎ 23296521; Nasir Arcade, AG's Office Rd; ⏱ 9.30am-6pm Mon-Sat)

POST
Post office (⏱ 8am-8.30pm Mon-Sat, 10am-6pm Sun) Secunderabad (Map p277; Rashtrapati Rd); Abids (Map p279; Abids Circle)

TOURIST INFORMATION
Andhra Pradesh Tourism (APTDC; www.aptdc.in) Hyderabad (Map p277; ☎ 23453036; Tankbund Rd; ⏱ 7am-8.30pm); Secunderabad (Map p277; ☎ 27893100; Yatri Nivas Hotel, SP Rd; ⏱ 7am-8.30pm) Organises tours.
Department of Tourism (Government of Andhra Pradesh; Map p277; ☎ 23454550; www.aptourism.in; Tankbund Rd; ⏱ 6am-9pm) Tours, too.
Indiatourism (Government of India; Map p279; ☎ 23261360; Netaji Bhavan, Himayatnagar Rd; ⏱ 9.30am-6pm Mon-Fri, to 2pm Sat) Most helpful.

Sights
CHARMINAR & BAZAARS
Hyderabad's principal landmark, the **Charminar** (Four Towers; Map p277; Indian/foreigner Rs 5/100; ⏱ 9am-5.30pm) was built by Mohammed Quli Qutb Shah in 1591 to commemorate the founding of Hyderabad and the end of epidemics caused by Golconda's water shortage. Standing 56m high and 30m wide, the dramatic four-column structure has four arches facing the cardinal points. Minarets sit atop each column. The 2nd floor, home to Hyderabad's oldest mosque, and upper columns are not usually open to the public, but you can try your luck

with the man with the key. The structure is illuminated from 7pm to 9pm.

West of the Charminar, the incredible **Laad Bazaar** (Map p277) is the perfect place to get lost. It has everything from the finest perfumes, fabrics and jewels to musical instruments, second-hand saris and kitchen implements. You can see artisans creating everything from jewellery and scented oils to large pots and musical instruments. The lanes around the Charminar also form the centre of India's pearl trade. Some great deals can be had – if you know your stuff.

SALAR JUNG MUSEUM
The huge collection of the **Salar Jung Museum** (Map p277; ☎ 24523211; Salar Jung Marg; Indian/foreigner Rs 10/150; ⏱ 10am-5pm Sat-Thu), dating back to the 1st century, was put together by Mir Yusaf Ali Khan (Salar Jung III), the grand vizier of the seventh nizam, Osman Ali Khan (r 1910–49). The 35,000 exhibits from every corner of the world include sculptures, wood carvings, devotional objects, Persian miniature paintings, illuminated manuscripts, weaponry and more than 50,000 books. The impressive nizams' jewellery collection is sometimes on special exhibit. Cameras are not allowed.

Avoid visiting the museum on Sunday when it's bedlam. From any of the bus stands in the Abids area, take bus 7, which stops at the nearby Musi River bridge.

Not far west of the bridge, facing each other across the river, are the spectacular **High Court** (Map p277) and **Osmania General Hospital** (Map p277) buildings, built by the seventh nizam in the Indo-Saracenic style.

CHOWMAHALLA PALACE
In their latest act of architectural showmanship, the nizam family has sponsored a restoration of this dazzling **palace** (Khilwat; Map p277; ☎ 24522032; www.chowmahalla.com; Indian/foreigner Rs 25/150; ⏱ 11am-5pm Sat-Thu) – or, technically, four *(char)* palaces *(mahalla)*. Begun in the late 18th century, it was expanded over the next 100 years, absorbing Persian, Indo-Sarocenic, Rajasthani and European styles. The Khilwat Mubarak compound includes the magnificent durbar hall, where nizams held ceremonies under 19 enormous chandeliers of Belgian crystal. Today the hall houses exhibitions of photos, arms and clothing. Hung with curtains, the balcony over the main hall once served as seating for the family's women, who attended all durbars in purdah.

ANDHRA PRADESH

ABIDS AREA

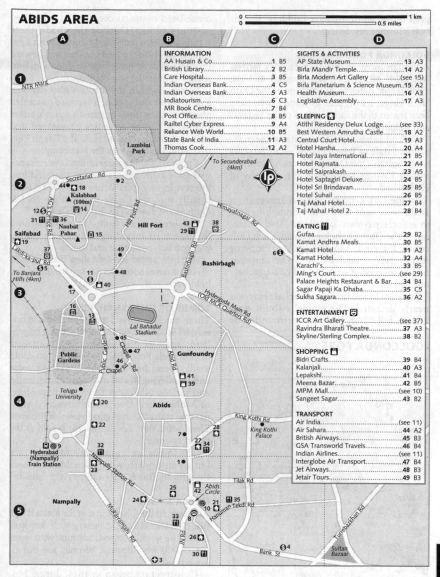

0   1 km
0   0.5 miles

INFORMATION
AA Husain & Co...............................1 B5
British Library.................................2 B2
Care Hospital.................................3 B5
Indian Overseas Bank.....................4 C5
Indian Overseas Bank.....................5 A3
Indiatourism..................................6 C3
MR Book Centre.............................7 B4
Post Office.....................................8 B5
Railtel Cyber Express......................9 A4
Reliance Web World.......................10 B5
State Bank of India........................11 A3
Thomas Cook................................12 A2

SIGHTS & ACTIVITIES
AP State Museum...........................13 A3
Birla Mandir Temple.......................14 A2
Birla Modern Art Gallery ....(see 15)
Birla Planetarium & Science Museum.15 A2
Health Museum..............................16 A3
Legislative Assembly......................17 A3

SLEEPING
Atithi Residency Delux Lodge.........(see 33)
Best Western Amrutha Castle..........18 A2
Central Court Hotel........................19 A3
Hotel Harsha.................................20 A4
Hotel Jaya International..................21 B5
Hotel Rajmata...............................22 A4
Hotel Saiprakash............................23 A5
Hotel Saptagiri Deluxe...................24 B5
Hotel Sri Brindavan........................25 B5
Hotel Suhail..................................26 B5
Taj Mahal Hotel.............................27 B4
Taj Mahal Hotel 2..........................28 B4

EATING
Gufaa...29 B5
Kamat Andhra Meals......................30 B5
Kamat Hotel..................................31 A2
Kamat Hotel..................................32 A4
Karachi's.......................................33 B5
Ming's Court............................(see 29)
Palace Heights Restaurant & Bar.....34 B4
Sagar Papaji Ka Dhaba...................35 C5
Sukha Sagara................................36 A2

ENTERTAINMENT
ICCR Art Gallery.........................(see 37)
Ravindra Bharati Theatre................37 A3
Skyline/Sterling Complex................38 B2

SHOPPING
Bidri Crafts...................................39 B4
Kalanjali.......................................40 A3
Lepakshi.......................................41 B5
Meena Bazar.................................42 B5
MPM Mall................................(see 10)
Sangeet Sagar...............................43 B2

TRANSPORT
Air India.....................................(see 11)
Air Sahara....................................44 A2
British Airways..............................45 B3
GSA Transworld Travels..................46 B4
Indian Airlines...........................(see 11)
Interglobe Air Transport.................47 B4
Jet Airways...................................48 B3
Jetair Tours...................................49 B3

HEH THE NIZAM'S MUSEUM

The 16th-century Purani Haveli was home of the sixth nizam, Fath Jang Mahbub Ali Khan (r 1869–1911), rumoured to have never worn the same thing twice. His 72m-long, two-storey wardrobe of Burmese teak is on display at this **museum** (Purani Haveli; Map p277; adult/student Rs 65/15; 10am-5pm Sat-Thu). Also on exhibit,

in the palace's former servants' quarters, are personal effects of the seventh nizam and gifts from the Silver Jubilee celebration of his reign. The pieces are unbelievably lavish and include some exquisite artwork. The museum's guides do an excellent job putting it all in context.

The rest of Purani Haveli is now a school, but you can wander around the grounds and peek in the administrative building, the nizam's former residence.

GOLCONDA FORT

Although most of this 16th-century **fortress** (Map p280; ☎ 23513984; Indian/foreigner Rs 5/100; ❤ 10am-6pm) dates from the time of the Qutb Shah kings, its origins, as a mud fort, have been traced to the earlier reigns of the Yadavas and Kakatiyas.

Golconda had been the capital of the independent state of Telangana for nearly 80 years when Sultan Quli Qutb Shah abandoned the fort in 1590 and moved to the new city of Hyderabad.

In the 17th century, Mughal armies from Delhi were sent to the Golconda kingdom to enforce payment of tribute. Abul Hasan, last of the Qutb Shahi kings, held out at Golconda for eight months against Emperor Aurangzeb's massive army. The emperor finally succeeded with the aid of a treacherous insider.

It's easy to see how the Mughal army was nearly defeated. The citadel is built on a granite hill 120m high and surrounded by

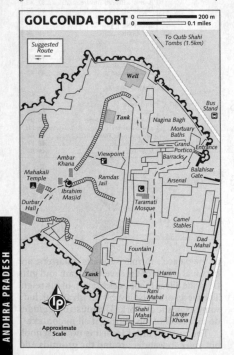

GOLCONDA FORT

0 ———— 200 m
0 ———— 0.1 miles

Suggested Route

To Qutb Shahi Tombs (1.5km)

Well

Tank

Nagina Bagh

Bus Stand

Mortuary Baths

Grand Portico

Entrance

Viewpoint

Ambar Khana

Barracks

Balahisar Gate

Mahakali Temple

Ramdas Jail

Arsenal

Ibrahim Masjid

Durbar Hall

Taramati Mosque

Camel Stables

Dad Mahal

Fountain

Tank

Harem

Rani Mahal

Shahi Mahal

Langer Khana

Approximate Scale

crenellated ramparts constructed from large masonry blocks. Outside the citadel there stands another crenellated rampart, with a perimeter of 11km, and yet another wall beyond this. The massive gates were studded with iron spikes to obstruct war elephants.

Survival within the fort was also attributable to water and sound. A series of concealed glazed earthen pipes ensured a reliable water supply, while the acoustics guaranteed that even the smallest sound from the Grand Portico would echo across the fort complex.

Knowledgeable guides around the entrance will ask Rs 250 for a 1½-hour tour and lose interest in any offer below Rs 150. You can usually find the *Guide to Golconda Fort & Qutb Shahi Tombs* (Rs 20) on sale here.

An autorickshaw from Abids costs around Rs 200 return, including waiting time. Mornings are best for peace and quiet.

A trippy **sound-and-light show** (admission Rs 50; ❤ English version 6.30pm Nov-Feb, 7pm Mar-Oct) is also held here.

TOMBS OF QUTB SHAHI KINGS

These graceful domed **tombs** (admission Rs 10, camera/video Rs 20/100; ❤ 9.30am-6pm) sit serenely in landscaped gardens about 1.5km northwest of Golconda Fort's Balahisar Gate. You could easily spend half a day here taking photos and wandering in and out of the mausoleums and various other structures. The upper level of Mohammed Quli's tomb, reached via a narrow staircase, has good views of the area. *The Qutb Shahi Tombs* (Rs 20) is sold at the ticket counter.

The tombs are an easy walk from the fort, but an autorickshaw ride shouldn't be more than Rs 20. Bus 80S also stops right outside.

MECCA MASJID

Adjacent to the Charminar is the **Mecca Masjid** (Map p277; Shah Ali Banda Rd, Patthargatti; ❤ 9am-5pm), one of the world's largest mosques, with space for 10,000 worshippers. Women are not allowed inside.

Construction began in 1614, during Mohammed Quli Qutb Shah's reign, but the mosque wasn't finished until 1687, by which time the Mughal emperor Aurangzeb had annexed the Golconda kingdom. Several bricks embedded above the gate are made with soil from Mecca – hence the name. The colonnades and door arches, with their inscriptions from the Quran, are made from single slabs

ANDHRA PRADESH

of granite that were quarried 11km away and dragged here by a team of 1400 bullocks.

To the left of the mosque, an enclosure contains the tombs of Nizam Ali Khan and his successors. Guides here offer tours for around Rs 50.

BUDDHA STATUE & HUSSAIN SAGAR

Hyderabad boasts one of the world's largest freestanding stone **Buddha statues** (Map p277), completed in 1990 after five years of work. However, when the 17.5m-high, 350-tonne monolith was being ferried to its place in the **Hussain Sagar** (Map p277), the barge sank. The statue languished underwater until being raised – undamaged – in 1992. It's now on a plinth in the middle of the lake.

Frequent **boats** (☎ 23455315; Rs 30; ◷ 9am-9pm) make the 30-minute return trip to the statue from **Lumbini Park** (Map p279; admission Rs 5; ◷ 9am-9pm), a pleasant place to enjoy Hyderabad's spectacular sunsets and the popular musical fountain. The Tankbund Rd promenade, which skirts the eastern shore of Hussain Sagar, has great views of the Buddha statue.

AP STATE & HEALTH MUSEUMS

The recently renovated **AP State Museum** (Map p279; ☎ 23232267; Public Gardens Rd, Nampally; admission Rs 10, camera/video Rs 20/100; ◷ 10.30am-4.30pm Sat-Thu) hosts a collection of important archaeological finds from the area, as well as a Buddhist sculpture gallery, with some relics of the Buddha and an exhibit on the Andhra's fascinating Buddhist history. The ever-expanding museum also has a Jain sculpture gallery, an exhibition of paintings by Pakistani painter AR Chughtai and an Egyptian mummy. The museum, like the gorgeous **Legislative Assembly building** down the road (both built by the seventh nizam), is floodlit at night.

Well worth a visit is the nearby **Health Museum** (admission free; ◷ 10.30am-5pm Sat-Thu), where you'll see a bizarre collection of medical and public-health paraphernalia.

NEHRU CENTENARY TRIBAL MUSEUM

Andhra Pradesh's 33 tribal groups, based mostly in the northeastern part of the state, comprise several million people. This **museum** (Map p277; ☎ 23391486, ext 306; Mahavir Marg, Masab Tank; admission free; ◷ 10.30am-5pm Mon-Sat), run by the government's Tribal Welfare Department, exhibits photographs, dioramas

of village life, musical instruments and some exquisite Naikpod masks. It's basic, but you'll get a glimpse into the cultures of these fringe peoples. The library here has books on Indian anthropology, traditional medicine and sociology. The museum is across from Chacha Nehru Park.

BIRLA MANDIR TEMPLE & PLANETARIUM

The **Birla Mandir Temple** (Map p279; ◷ 7am-noon & 2-9pm), constructed of white Rajasthani marble in 1976, graces Kalabahad (Black Mountain), one of two rocky hills overlooking the southern end of Hussain Sagar. Dedicated to Lord Venkateshwara, the temple is a popular Hindu pilgrimage centre and affords excellent views over the city, especially at sunset. The religious library here is worth a visit (open 4pm to 8pm).

The **Birla Planetarium & Science Museum** (Map p279; ☎ 23235081; museum/planetarium Rs 17/20; ◷ museum 10.30am-8pm, till 3pm Fri, planetarium shows 11.30am, 4pm, 6pm), as well as the **Birla Modern Art Gallery** (Map p279; admission Rs 10; ◷ 10.30am-6pm), are on the hill adjacent to the temple.

RAMOJI FILM CITY

Movie fans can't miss the four-hour tour of **Ramoji Film City** (☎ 23235678; www.ramojifilmcity.com; admission Rs 250; ◷ 9.30am-5.30pm), an 800-hectare movie-making complex for Telugu, Tamil and Hindi films. This place has everything – dance routines, gaudy fountains, flimsy film sets – and the whole thing wraps up with a Wild West song-and-dance number. The 'Royal Package' (Rs 750) includes AC transport and lunch at a five-star hotel. Buses 205 and 206 from Koti Women's College, 100m northeast of Koti station, take an hour to get here.

Activities

The Theravada **Ananda Buddha Vihara** (Map p277; ☎ 27733161; www.buddhavihara.in; Mahendra Hills; ◷ 5.30am-12.30pm & 4-8.30pm) will eventually include a museum of Buddhist art and a library. At the time of writing, only the temple – on a hill with incredible views – was complete. Meditation sessions are held at 6am and 6pm, but monks and nuns are available anytime to give instruction or just chat about the tradition. Call to inquire about special programmes.

The centre is near the Amrita ashram; take East Maredpally Main Rd through Trimurthy Colony. An autorickshaw from Abids will cost around Rs 75.

ANDHRA PRADESH

Courses

The **Vipassana International Meditation Centre** (Dhamma Khetta; ☎ 24240290; www.dhamma.org; Nagarjuna Sagar Rd, Kusumnagar) has intensive 10-day meditation courses at its peaceful grounds 20km outside the city. Apply by email or at the Hyderabad **office** (☎ 24732569). A shuttle runs to/from Hyderabad on the first and last day of courses.

Tours

APTDC (see p278) conducts tours of the city (full day, Rs 230), Ramoji Film City (Rs 415), Nagarjuna Sagar (weekends only, Rs 360) and Tirupathi (two days, Rs 1600 AC). The evening city tour (Rs 155) takes in Hitec City, the botanic gardens and Golconda Fort's sound-and-light show, though you may spend much of it in traffic. All tours start from the Secunderabad office.

The Department of Tourism (p278) has daytime (Rs 125) and night-time (Rs 175) city tours by AC bus.

Save the Rocks Society (☎ 23552923; www.saverocks .org; 1236 Rd No 60, Jubilee Hills) organises monthly walks through the Andhran landscape and its surreal-looking boulders.

Sleeping

Rooms tend to fill up, so call ahead.

BUDGET

The best cheap hotels are in the Abids area between Abids Circle and Hyderabad train station. Many of the cheaper places seem to be filled with curious gents.

Hotel Suhail (Map p279; ☎ 24610299; Troop Bazaar; s/d/tr from Rs 200/375/395) Tucked away on an alley behind the main post office and the Grand Hotel, the Suhail is an excellent deal. Rooms are large and quiet and have balconies and constant hot water. Troop Bazaar is unlit at night, though; some readers find it sketchy.

Hotel Sri Brindavan (Map p279; ☎ 23203970; fax 23200204; Nampally Station Rd; s/d from Rs 350/450; 🔀) The curved balcony and fresh lemon-yellow paint give this well-ordered place a slight Art Deco feel. Few staff speak English, but rooms are tidy and compact, and AC rooms in the back are surprisingly peaceful. The parking lot even has trees.

Atithi Residency Delux Lodge (Map p279; ☎ 66848491; Mahaprabhu House, JN Rd; s/d from Rs 350/525; 🔀) The Atithi gets an A for effort. Rooms have soothing peach walls, door mouldings and 24-hour

hot water. There's also a travel 'desk', which is really just reception, but staff can help with train booking and car rental. Request a room at the back to avoid street noise.

Hotel Saptagiri Deluxe (Map p279; ☎ 24610333; Nampally Station Rd; r from Rs 450; 🔀) Women guests were spotted here – always a good sign. Set back from Nampally Station Rd, it's quiet, clean, bright and almost tasteful – a step up from the joints you usually find at this price. Rooms come with clean towels!

Hotel Jaya International (Map p279; ☎ 24752929; hoteljaya@sancharnet.in; Hanuman Tekdi Rd; s/d from Rs 495/595; 🔀) There's a reason that the Jaya always seems to be full of student groups: it's the best deal in town. Capacious, sunny rooms have arched balconies with good views, stained-glass lamps and scrubbed bathrooms. It's centrally located, too. But there definitely won't be a room for you if you don't book ahead.

APTDC's paying-guest programme (☎ 23450444) can help find you rooms in private homes for Rs 250 to Rs 600.

If you arrive late at Secunderabad train station, try the clean but noisy **retiring rooms** (dm from Rs 50, s/d from Rs 250/450; 🔀).

MIDRANGE

Taj Mahal Hotel (Map p279; ☎ 40048484; fax 55827373; King Kothi Rd; s/d from Rs 550/750; 🔀) Taj number two is just east of – and second fiddle to – the original (see below). Big, spotless rooms always seem to have a fresh coat of paint. Reception is at the back of the parking lot, past the reception for Taj No 3.

Hotel Rajmata (Map p279; ☎ 66665555; fax 23204133; Public Gardens Rd; s/d Rs 590/690) The Rajmata is very professionally run – the folks at reception are great – and has a helpful travel desk. Rooms here vary; the better ones are big and bright, and since the place is set back from busy Public Gardens Rd, they're not too noisy. It's popular with families.

Taj Mahal Hotel (Map p279; ☎ 24758250; sundar taj@satyam.net.in; cnr Abid & King Kothi Rds; s/d with AC from Rs 800/1150; 🔀) This rambling heritage building has a magnificent exterior, plants peppered about, and some exceedingly charming rooms. Each is different so ask to see a few: the better ones have boudoirs, crystal-knobbed armoires and wood-beam ceilings. All are peaceful. Service is good, too.

Athidhi Guesthouse (Map p277; ☎ 9246544051; www .athidhiguesthouse.com; Rd No 13A, Happy Valley Rd, Banjara

Hills; s/d with AC incl breakfast Rs 1000/1500; ⚅) If you're more interested in the conveniences of home than being close to the action, take a room in one of Athidhi's three-bedroom serviced apartments, set on a tranquil lane in chichi Banjara Hills. Nearby food shops provide all you need to cook in the kitchen.

Also recommended:

Yatri Nivas Hotel (Map p277; ☎ 23461847; www .amogh-india.com; SP Rd, Secunderabad; s/d with AC incl breakfast Rs 1000/1200; ⚅) Indian families mill about the YN compound, which has two restaurants, a bar and trees strung with lights.

Hotel Saiprakash (Map p279; ☎ 24611726; www .hotelsaiprakash.com; Nampally Station Rd; s/d with AC from Rs 1200/1400; ⚅)

Hotel Harsha (Map p279; ☎ 23201188; www .hotelharsha.net; Public Gardens Rd; s/d with AC from US$30/40; ⚅)

TOP END

All the following have central AC, and rates include breakfast.

Golkonda (Map p277; ☎ 66110101; www.thegolkon dahyd.com; Masab Tank; r from US$185; ⚅ ▣) Recently completely overhauled, the Golkonda is growing into its new and improved self: staff are still learning. But rooms are elegant and contemporary, with sumptuous upholstery on chairs and clever touches like a curved glass wall separating the bathroom. Maybe Hyderabad's most chic.

Taj Krishna (Map p277; ☎ 66664242; www.tajhotels .com; Rd No 1, Banjara Hills; s/d from US$350/375; ⚅ ▣ ▣) The sort of opulence you expect for the price: a lobby resembling a *mahal* (palace), marble-inlaid hallway floors, and rooms with elegant furniture and piles of taffeta pillows.

Other recommendations:

Central Court Hotel (Map p279; ☎ 23232323; www .thecentralcourt.com; Lakdi-ka-pul; s/d from Rs 2595/3495; ⚅ ▣) Ever-so-slightly overpriced, but central, spotless and very efficiently run.

Best Western Amrutha Castle (Map p279; ☎ 66633888; www.amruthacastle.com; Saifabad; s/d from US$85/98; ⚅ ▣ ▣) Chains suck, but it looks like a castle!

Eating

Andhra Pradesh's cuisine has two major influences. The Mughals brought tasty biryanis, *haleem* (pounded, spiced wheat with mutton – see the boxed text, p284) and kebabs. The Andhra style is vegetarian and famous for its spiciness. We use the term 'meals' instead of 'thali' in this chapter; the word 'thali' is not used in this part of India, but they mean the same thing.

CITY CENTRE

Mozamjahi Market (Map p277; cnr Mukarramjahi & Jawaharlal Nehru Rds; ☯ 6am-6pm) A great place to buy fruit and veggies (or ice cream), while enjoying the alluring architecture.

Karachi's (Map p279; Mahaprabhu House, JN Rd; snacks Rs 20-40; ☯ 11am-11pm) A tacky, fun fast-food joint with good *chaat* (snacks), veggie burgers, pizza and the enigmatic 'Chinese dosa'.

Kamat Hotel (Map p277; SD Rd, Secunderabad; mains Rs 45-75; ☯ 7.30am-10pm) Each Kamat (other branches are on AG's Office Rd and Nampally Station Rd – see Map p279) is slightly different, but they're all cheap and good. Meals (traditional South Indian all-you-can-eat meals; Rs 25 to Rs 37) are reliably delish.

Kamat Andhra Meals (Map p279; Troop Bazaar; meals Rs 45; ☯ lunch & dinner) Excellent authentic Andhra meals on banana leaves. Its sister restaurants in the same compound – Kamat Jowar Bhakri (Maharashtran), Kamat Restaurant (North and South Indian) and Kamat Coffee Shop – are likewise friendly family joints full of happy diners. No relation to Kamat Hotel.

Sagar Papaji Ka Dhaba (Map p279; Hanuman Tekdi Rd; mains Rs 35-90; ☯ lunch & dinner) Always busy, Papaji's has profoundly delicious veg and nonveg biryanis, curries and tikkas. You can watch the guys making naan and throwing it in the tandoor while you wait for a table.

our pick Hotel Shadab (Map p277; High Court Rd, Patthargatti; mains Rs 40-130; ☯ 5am-11pm) One meal at Shadab and you'll be forever under its spell. The hopping restaurant is *the* place to get biryani and, during Ramadan, *haleem* (see p284). It has even mastered veg biryani (!) and hundreds of other veg and nonveg delights (if you try the chocolate chicken or pineapple mutton, let us know how it goes). Packed with Old Town families and good vibes.

Minerva Coffee Shop (Map p277; Salar Jung Marg; mains Rs 55-85; ☯ 7.30am-11pm) The North Indian meal (Rs 85) in this old-school coffee shop is a delight – five delicious curries, topped off with fruit salad and ice cream. All with a river view. There's a Minerva in Somajiguda, too.

Gufaa (Map p279; ☎ 23298811; Ohri's Cuisine Court, Bashirbagh Rd; mains Rs 130-200; ☯ lunch & dinner) The eccentric Gufaa has faux-rock walls with African masks, leopard-print upholstery, twinkling stars on the ceiling and red roses on the tables.

And it serves Peshawari food. But somehow it works, and even 'dhal with roti' (black dhal stewed with fresh cream and tomatoes, and roti made with chillies) is extraordinary here.

Palace Heights Restaurant & Bar (Map p279; ☎ 24754483; 8th fl, Triveni Complex; mains Rs 130-225; ☏ 11am-11pm) This pearl in the dirty shell of an old city-centre building has a palatial interior and incredible views. The service is excellent, the wine list endless and the nonveg menu – Andhran, Goan, Chinese, Italian, Filipino – extensive.

Also recommended:

Sukha Sagara (Map p279; AG's Office Rd; mains Rs 40-80; ☏ 7am-10pm)

Paradise Persis Restaurant (Map p277; ☎ 55313723; cnr SD & MG Rds, Secunderabad; mains Rs 60-195; ☏ 11am-midnight) Ask any Hyderabadi about biryani, and they'll mention Paradise.

Ming's Court (Map p279; ☎ 23298811; Ohri's Cuisine Court, Bashirbagh Rd; mains Rs 120-250; ☏ lunch & dinner)

BANJARA HILLS
Restaurants

Angeethi (Map p277; ☎ 66255550; 7th fl, Reliance Classic Bldg, Rd No 1; mains Rs 100-285; ☏ lunch & dinner) The setting, designed to resemble an old Punjabi *dhaba* (snack bar), is over the top. But Angeethi does truly outstanding North Indian and Punjabi dishes, such as corn *methi malai* (sweet-corn stew with fenugreek leaves; Rs 105). The lunchtime buffet (Rs 140; Monday to Saturday) is a good deal.

Fusion 9 (Map p279; ☎ 65577722; Rd No 1; mains Rs 235-550; ☏ lunch & dinner) Soft lighting and cosy décor set off pan-fried Norwegian salmon (Rs 550) or Australian pork chops (Rs 800). There's also (less expensive) Mexican, Thai and pizzas, and lots of imported liquor. The Grill Room upstairs serves grilled goods (dinner only) in a tasteful lounge atmosphere.

Other recommendations:

Southern Spice (Map p277; ☎ 23353802; Rd No 2; mains Rs 75-160; ☏ lunch & dinner) Spicy southern goodness.

Ohri's Far East (Map p277; ☎ 23302200; Rd No 12; mains Rs 120-250; ☏ lunch & dinner) Pan-Asian.

Cafés

Ofen (Map p277; ☎ 23372205; Rd No 10; desserts Rs 12-95; ☏ 8am-10.30pm) Cheesecake, chocolate cinnamon roulade and chocolate gugel hopf bread.

Le Café d'Art (Map p277; ☎ 66506661; Rd No 1; light meals Rs 115-185; ☏ 9am-11pm) Most of the beautiful young people here come to smoke hookahs (Rs 250) while lounging in antique

---

BEATING THE BHATTIS

If you're travelling around Andhra Pradesh during Ramadan (known locally as Ramazan), look out for the clay ovens called *bhattis*. You'll probably hear them before you see them. Men gather around, taking turns to vigorously pound *haleem* (a mixture of meat and wheat) inside purpose-built structures. Come nightfall, the serious business of eating begins. The taste is worth the wait.

---

fauteuils and wooden furniture. We recommend it for the art exhibitions, among the best in town.

Drinking
CAFÉS

Barista (Map p277; Ground floor, Reliance Classic Bldg, Rd No 1, Banjara Hills; coffees Rs 20-50; ☏ 8am-10pm)

Café Coffee Day (Map p277; Rd No 1, Banjara Hills; coffees Rs 20-50; ☏ 9am-10pm)

Mocha (Map p277; ☎ 23350133; Rd No 7, Banjara Hills; coffees Rs 20-180; ☏ 9am-11pm) Full of 20-somethings smoking hookahs, but the décor, the garden and the coffee are fabulous.

BARS & LOUNGES

Hyderabad's nightlife has gained momentum in recent years, but drinking establishments are limited by a midnight-curfew law. The following are all open from noon to midnight (but don't get going till 9pm). All serve food and charge covers (Rs 500 to 1000) on certain nights – for couples, that is: guys will need a gal to enter. Beer starts at Rs 140, cocktails at Rs 250.

Liquids (Map p277; ☎ 66259907; Bhaskar Plaza, Rd No 1, Banjara Hills) Regularly featured in the papers' Society pages, Liquids is reigning queen of Hyderabad nightlife.

Touch (Map p277; ☎ 23542422; Trendset Towers, Rd No 2, Banjara Hills) Sporting a sort of feminine *Star Wars* look, with futuristic white furniture and chiffon screens, Touch is all about image. It's a stylish, comfy place to watch the beautiful people.

Begumpet bars/clubs on weekends:

10 Downing Street (Map p277; ☎ 55629323; My Home Tycoon Bldg) Looking British.

Bottles & Chimney (Map p277; ☎ 27766464; SP Rd)

(Continued on page 293)

MICK ELMORE

Locals enjoying popular Chowpatty Beach (p115),
Mumbai (Bombay)

Fuelling the local passion for cricket at
Oval Maidan (p113), Mumbai

PETER PTSCHELINZEW

MICK ELMORE

Impressive rock-cut cave sculptures of Elephanta Island (p135),
Mumbai

The art of selling, well, yes, a gramophone, Chor Bazaar (p131), Mumbai

KAREN TRIST

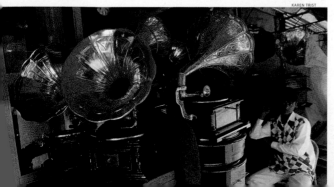

NEIL SETCHFIELD

Seeking out souvenirs at the legendary
flea market (p199) in Anjuna, Goa

PAUL GREENWAY

Striking, whitewashed Church of
Our Lady the Immaculate Conception (p183), Panaji (Panjim), Goa

Strolling the quaint, narrow and winding streets of Fontainhas (p184), Panaji, Goa

PAUL BEI

Clamour for peace at the palm-fringed beach strip that is Palolem (p213), Goa

Gasp at the monumental, powerful rush of Dudhsagar Falls (p216), Goa

Make the pilgrimage to the Basilica of Bom Jesus (p188), Old Goa, Goa

GREG ELMS

Scan the kaleidoscopic tableau of powders at the Devaraja Market (p235), Mysore, Karnataka

PETER PTSCHELINZEW

Examine the exquisite stone chariot at Vittala Temple (p258), Hampi, Karnataka

Marvel at the Indo-Saracenic architecture of the Maharaja's Palace (p233), Mysore, Karnataka

CRAIG PERSH

Experience peace and loving kindness under the golden gaze of the statue of Buddha (p281), Hyderabad, Andhra Pradesh

There's no lovelier spot for a picnic than at the ruins of Golconda Fort (p280), Hyderabad, Andhra Pradesh

Wander through the grounds of the graceful, domed Tombs of Qutb Shahi Kings (p280), Hyderabad, Andhra Pradesh

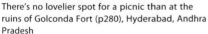

You need never run out of hair oil or cosmetics, Laad Bazaar (p278), Hyderabad, Andhra Pradesh

PAUL HARDING

Relaxing on a *kettuvallam* (rice barge) houseboat (p328) and exploring the 900km network of Keralan backwaters

Getting up close and personal with the rare Nilgiri tahr, Eraviku-lam National Park (p339), Kerala

HIRA PU

PETER PTSCHELINZEW

Cruising along the lush, watery backbone of Kerala's canal highways (p328)

MARK DAFFEY

Sharing the sands with the tropical shadows of
Kovalam (p315), Kerala

GREG ELMS

Spice-rich Malabar curry dishes
(p79) are a Keralan speciality

Patchworks of tea plantations dot the high ranges of Munnar (p337), Kerala

LINDSAY BROWN

CRAIG PERSHOUSE

The huge Nandi (Shiva's bull vehicle) heralds the intricately chiselled stone chariot of Arjuna Ratha (p385), Mamallapuram (Mahabalipuram), Tamil Nadu

Artistic, grand film posters adorning the streetscapes of Chennai (Madras; p364), Tamil Nadu

PAUL BEINSSEN

MICHAEL TAYLOR

Chugging through the stunning Nilgiri Hills on a miniature steam train (p441), Tamil Nadu

(Continued from page 284)

Entertainment

ARTS

Ravindra Bharati Theatre (Map p279; ☎ 23233672; www
.artistap.com; Public Gardens Rd) Regular music, dance
and dramaperformances. Check local papers.

Hyderabad has a burgeoning contemporary-art scene, centred mostly in the Hills:
ICCR Art Gallery (Map p279; ☎ 23236398; Ravindra
Bharati Theatre, Public Gardens Rd; ☒ 11am-8pm)
Kalakriti (Map p277; ☎ 55564466; Rd No 10, Banjara
Hills; ☒ 11am-7pm)
Shishtri (☎ 23540023; Rd No 15, Jubilee Hills;
☒ 11am-7pm)

CINEMA

Hyderabad Film Club (Map p277; ☎ 9391020243; Ameerpet Rd) Shows foreign films, sometimes in conjunction with the Alliance Française.

Cinemas showing English-language movies:
Prasad's Multiplex (Map p277; ☎ 23448989; NTR
Marg) A monstrous IMAX theatre.
PVR (Map p277; ☎ 66467876; Hyderabad Central,
Panjagutta Rd)
Skyline/Sterling Complex (Map p279; ☎ 23222633;
Bashirbagh)

Shopping

The bazaars near the Charminar (see p278)
are the most exciting places to shop: you'll
find exquisite pearls, silks, gold and fabrics
alongside billions of bangles.

Hyderabad Perfumers (Map p277; ☎ 24577294;
Patthargatti; ☒ 10am-8.30pm Mon-Sat) The family-run Hyderabad Perfumers, which has been
in business for four generations, can whip
something up for you on the spot.

Meena Bazar (Map p279; ☎ 24753566; Tilak Rd;
☒ 11am-9.30pm Mon-Sat) Gorgeous saris, *salwar*
(trouser) suits and fabrics at fixed prices.
Even if you're not in the market, come here
to sightsee.

Kalanjali (Map p279; ☎ 23423440; Public Gardens Rd;
☒ 10am-8pm Mon-Sat) With a huge range of arts,
crafts, fabrics and clothing, Kalanjali is a good
place to prepare for the bazaar: the prices are
higher, but you'll get a feel for what things are
worth in a relaxed environment.

Afreen Suits & Saris (Map p277; ☎ 55711802; Patthargatti; ☒ 10.30am-10.30pm) A wide range of silks
and fabrics are sold here for fixed prices; credit
cards accepted.

Sangeet Sagar (Map p279; ☎ 23225346; Bashirbagh Rd;
☒ 11am-9pm Mon-Sat) Great little music shop.

Other places for crafts and clothes:
Fabindia (Map p277; ☎ 23354526; Rd No 9, Banjara
Hills; ☒ 10am-7.30pm Tue-Sun) Clothes in stunning
fabrics at good prices.
Anokhi (Map p277; ☎ 23350271; Rd No 10, Banjara
Hills; ☒ 10.30am-8pm Mon-Sat) Stylish clothes in handblock prints.
Bidri Crafts (Map p279; ☎ 23232657; Gunfoundry;
☒ 10am-9pm Mon-Sat)
Lepakshi (Map p279; ☎ 23235028; Gunfoundry;
☒ 10am-8pm Mon-Sat) Andhra crafts.

Getting There & Away

To handle overcrowding at Hyderabad airport,
a massive new international airport is scheduled to open in mid-2008 at Shamshabad,
about 20km southwest of the city.

AIR

Domestic Airlines

Indian Airlines has the highest domestic fares,
with Jet, Air Sahara and Kingfisher following
close behind. Air Deccan, along with online
budget airlines GoAir, Indigo, Paramount and
spiceJet, has the lowest.

DAILY DOMESTIC FLIGHTS FROM HYDERABAD			
Destination	IA Fare (US$)	Duration (hr)	Other Airlines
Bengaluru	103	1	JA/AS/DN/K
Chennai	103	1	JA/DN/SP
Delhi	175	2	JA/AS/DN/G/SP
Kolkota	175	2	JA/AS/DN
Mumbai	106	1	JA/AS/DN/G/SP
Tirupathi	85	1	DN
Visakhapatnam	100	1	AS/DN

Note: Fares are one way. Airline codes: IA=Indian Airlines, JA=Jet Airways, AS=Air Sahara, DN=Air
Deccan, G=Go Air, K=Kingfisher, SP=spiceJet.

ANDHRA PRADESH

Domestic airlines in Hyderabad:

Air Deccan (☎ 9845777008, airport 27902794)

Air Sahara (Map p279; ☎ 66782020; Secretariat Rd)

Indian Airlines (Map p279; ☎ 1800 1801407; HACA Bhavan, AG's Office Rd)

Jet Airways (Map p279; ☎ 39824444; Adarsh Nagar, Hill Fort Rd)

International Airlines

Air India (Map p279; ☎ call centre 1800 227722, airport 23389711; HACA Bhavan, AG's Office Rd)

British Airways (Map p279; ☎ 23211270, 23296437; Chapel Rd)

Cathay Pacific (Map p277; ☎ 27702234; 44 SD Rd, Secunderabad)

Emirates (Map p277; ☎ 66234444; Rd No 1, Banjara Hills)

GSA Transworld Travels (Map p279; ☎ 23210947; Chapel Rd) For Qantas.

Interglobe Air Transport (Map p279; ☎ 23233590; Chapel Rd) For Air New Zealand, Delta, Indigo, South African, United Airlines and Virgin Atlantic.

Jetair Tours (Map p279; ☎ 23298773; 1st fl, Summit House, Hill Fort Rd) For American, Austrian, Bangladesh Airlines, Gulf Air and Royal Jordanian.

KLM (Map p277; ☎ airport 27905015)

Lufthansa (Map p277; ☎ 23481000; Begumpet) Next to the Lifestyle Building.

Nagarjuna Travels (Map p277; ☎ 23372429; Raj Bhavan Rd, Somajiguda) For Sri Lankan Airlines.

BUS

Hyderabad's long-distance bus stations are mind-bogglingly efficient. **Mahatma Gandhi bus station** (Map p277; ☎ 24614406), better known as Imlibun, has an **advance booking office** (⏱ 8am-9pm). For Nagarjunakonda, take one of the frequent morning buses to Vinukonda or

Macherla and get off en route. For trips to Karnataka, better go with **KSRTC** (☎ 24656430).

Secunderabad's **Jubilee bus station** (Map p277; ☎ 27802203) is less convenient, but does operate Volvo AC buses to Bengaluru (Rs 620, 10 hours, three daily), Chennai (Rs 670, 12 hours, one daily) and Visakhapatnam (Rs 675, 13 hours, one daily).

Private bus companies with super-deluxe services are on Nampally High Rd, near the train station entrance.

TRAIN

Secunderabad (Map p277), Hyderabad (Map p277) – also known as Nampally – and Kacheguda (Map p277) are the three major train stations. Most through trains stop at Secunderabad and Kacheguda, which is more convenient for Abids. See the boxed text, opposite, for key routes. Bookings can be made at Hyderabad and Secunderabad stations from 8am to 8pm Monday to Saturday (to 2pm Sunday). Both stations have a tourist counter. For general inquiries, phone ☎ 131; for reservation status, ☎ 135.

Getting Around

TO/FROM THE AIRPORT

Hyderabad Airport (Map p277) is in Begumpet, 8km north of Abids. Take an autorickshaw from Abids (Rs 60) or a taxi (Rs 150). A prepaid autorickshaw from the airport costs Rs 95.

AUTORICKSHAW

Except in the Old Town, drivers generally use their meters. Flag fall is Rs 10 for the first kilometre, then Rs 5 for each additional

BUSES FROM IMLIBUN			
Destination	Fare (Rs)	Duration (hr)	Departures (daily)
Bengaluru	358(H)/405(A)/620(V)	12/10/10	14
Bidar	69(E)	4	4
Bijapur	212(E)/295(A)	10	7
Chennai	372(H)/670(V)	12	3
Hospet	195(H)/280(A)	12	2
Mumbai	424(E)/720(V)	16/12	6
Mysore	755(V)	13	2
Tirupathi	248(E)/321(H)	12	7
Vijayawada	157(H)/272(V)	6/5	every 15min
Warangal	70(E)	3	half-hourly

E – express, H – hi-tech, A – AC sleeper, V – Volvo AC

ANDHRA PRADESH

MAJOR TRAINS FROM HYDERABAD & SECUNDERABAD

Destination	Train No & Name	Fare (Rs)	Duration (hr)	Departures
Bengaluru	2430 *Rajdhani*	1065/1460	12	6.50pm S (Tue, Wed, Sat & Sun)
	2785 *Secunderabad-Bangalore Exp*	288/756/1061	11	7.05pm K
Chennai	2754 *Hyderabad-Chennai Exp*	301/792/1113	13	4.55pm H
	2760 *Charminar Exp*	317/837/1178	14	6.30pm H
Delhi	2723 *Andhra Pradesh Exp*	469/1264/1794	26	6.25am H
	2429 *Rajdhani*	1725/2335	26	7.25am S (Mon, Tue, Thu & Fri)
Kolkata	2704 *Falaknuma Exp*	449/1208/1713	26	4pm S
	8646 *East Coast Exp*	437/1200/1716	30	10am H
Mumbai	7032 *Hussain Sagar Exp*	306/807/1134	15	2.45pm H
	7032 *Hyderabad-Mumbai Exp*	286/777/1104	15	8.40pm H
Tirupathi	2734 *Narayanadri Exp*	288/756/1061	12	6.05pm S
	2797 *Venkatadri Exp*	281/735/1030	12	8.05pm K
Visakhapatnam	2728 *Godavari Exp*	299/785/1103	11	5.15pm H

S – Secunderabad, H – Hyderabad, K – Kacheguda. Rajdhani fares are 3AC/2AC; express (Exp) fares are sleeper/3AC/2AC.

kilometre. Between 10pm and 5am a 50% surcharge applies.

BUS
Lots of local buses originate at **Koti bus station** (Map p277; Maharani Jhansi Rd; ☾ 24hr), so if you come here you might get a seat. The 'travel as you like' ticket (Rs 30), available from bus conductors, permits unlimited travel anywhere within the city on the day of purchase.

Useful local bus routes:

Bus No	Route
20D	Jubilee station–Nampally
1P	Secunderabad station–Jubilee station
2/2V, 8A/8U,	Charminar–Secunderabad station
1K, 1B, 3SS, 40	Secunderabad station–Koti
20P, 20V, 49, 49P	Secunderabad station–Nampally
65G/66G	Charminar–Golconda
87	Charminar–Nampally
119OR, 142M	Nampally–Golconda
142K	Koti–Golconda

CAR
There are places around Nampally station where you can rent a car and driver; **City Cabs** (☎ 27760000; Begumpet) is reliable for local taxis. For local and longer trips, try **Banjara Travels** (☎ 23394368; Rd No 12, Banjara Hills).

TRAIN
The MMTS trains are a convenient way to get around, particularly between the three main train stations. There are two main lines. Hyderabad (Nampally) to Lingampalli (northwest of Banjara Hills) has 11 stops, including Lakdikapul, Khairatabad, Necklace Rd, Begumpet and Hitec City. The Falaknuma (south of Old Town) to Begumpet line passes by Yakutupura, Dabirpura, Malakpet, Kacheguda and Secunderabad, among others. Trains will be labelled with their start and end point: so, HL is Hyderabad–Lingampalli, FS is Falaknuma–Secunderabad and so on. Trains are new and efficient, but they only run about every 45 minutes. Tickets are Rs 5 to 10.

NAGARJUNAKONDA
☎ 08680

The ancient remains at this site, 150km southeast of Hyderabad, were discovered in 1926 by archaeologist AR Saraswathi. In 1953, when it became known that a massive hydroelectric project would soon create the **Nagarjuna Sagar** reservoir, which would flood the area, a major six-year excavation was undertaken to unearth the area's many Buddhist ruins: stupas, *viharas*, *chaityas* (temples) and *mandapas* (pillared pavilions), as well as some outstanding examples of white-marble depictions of the Buddha's life. The finds were reassembled

ANDHRA PRADESH

STATE OF GOOD KARMA

In its typically understated way, Andhra Pradesh doesn't make a big deal of its vast archeological – and karmic – wealth. But in fact, the ruins of Andhra Pradesh's rich Buddhist history sprinkle the state like so many forgotten pearls of the Buddha's wisdom. Only a few of Andhra's 150 stupas, *viharas* (monastery complexes), caves and other sites have been excavated, turning up rare relics of the Buddha (usually pearl-like pieces of bone, found with offerings like golden flowers). They speak of a time when Andhra Pradesh – or Andhradesa – was a hotbed of Buddhist activity, when monks came from around the world to learn from some of the tradition's most renowned teachers, and when Indian monks set off for Sri Lanka and Southeast Asia via the Krishna and Godavari Rivers and the Bay of Bengal to spread the teaching of the Buddha.

Andhradesa's Buddhist culture, in which sangha (community of monks and nuns), laity and statespeople all took part, lasted around 1500 years from the 6th century BC. There's no historical evidence for it, but some even say that the Master himself visited the area.

Andhradesa's first practitioners were likely the disciples of Bavari, an ascetic who lived on the banks of the Godavari River and sent his followers north to bring back the Buddha's teaching. But the dharma really took off in the 3rd century BC under Ashoka (see p35), who dispatched monks out across his empire to teach and construct stupas enshrined with relics of the Buddha. (Being near these was thought to help people progress on the path to enlightenment.)

Succeeding Ashoka, the Satavahanas and then Ikshvakus were also supportive. At their capital at Amaravathi, the Satavahanas adorned Ashoka's modest stupa with elegant decoration. They built monasteries across the Krishna Valley and exported the dharma through their sophisticated maritime network.

It was also during the Satavahana reign that Nagarjuna lived. Considered by many to be the progenitor of Mahayana Buddhism, the eminent monk was equal parts logician, philosopher and meditator, and he wrote several groundbreaking works (with evocative titles like *Seventy Verses on Emptiness*) that shaped contemporary Buddhist thought. Other important monk-philosophers would emerge from the area in the centuries to follow, making Andhradesa a sort of Buddhist motherland of the South.

Those interested in Buddhist history will find these excavated sites ripe for exploring, but most are out of the way, infrastructure is nil and you may have trouble finding them. If you're game, head to the area around Vijayawada for Chandavaram, Guntupalli or Bhattiprolu, and near Visakhapatnam for Thotlakonda, Sankaram, Ramatirtham and Bavikonda.

---

on Nagarjunakonda, an island in the middle of the dam.

Prehistoric remnants suggest human activity began here around 200,000 years ago. From the 3rd century BC until the 4th century AD, the Krishna River valley was home to powerful empires that supported the sangha (community of monks and nuns), including the Ikshvakus, whose capital was Nagarjunakonda. It's estimated that this area alone had 30 monasteries.

Nagarjunakonda is named after Nagarjuna, a 2nd-century-AD monk and philosopher. He founded the Madhyamika school, which developed into Mahayana Buddhism (see above).

Sights

NAGARJUNAKONDA MUSEUM

This thoughtfully laid-out **museum** (Indian/foreigner Rs 2/US$2; ☉ 9.30am-3.45pm Sat-Thu) has Stone Age picks, hoes and spears on exhibit, but more impressive are its Buddha statues and the carved stone slabs that once adorned stupas. Most of them are from the 3rd century AD and depict scenes from the Buddha's life, interspersed with *mithuna* (paired male and female) figures languorously looking on.

Launches (Rs 45, one hour) depart for the island from Vijayapuri, on the banks of Nagarjuna Sagar, at 8.30am and 1.30pm, and stay for 30 minutes. To do the place justice, take the morning launch out and the afternoon one back. Extra express launches (Rs 60) may run on weekends and holidays. Bring food and water.

Sleeping & Eating

Nagarjunakonda is popular, and accommodation can be tight during weekends and holidays.

Project House (Punnami; ☎ 276540; r from Rs 300; ☒) This place is 5km from the jetty, opposite the main bus stand in Hill Colony. Rooms are basic but clean enough, and the veg restaurant is OK.

Nagarjuna Resort (☎ 08642-242471; r from Rs 450; ☒) The most convenient place to stay, right across the road from the boat launch, has spacious rooms with geysers. Those in front have good views, and there's a multicuisine restaurant.

Vijay Vihar Complex (☎ 277362; fax 276633; r with AC from Rs 1060; ☒) Two kilometres up the hill from Project House is this fancy place overlooking the lake. Rooms have balconies with excellent views. The restaurant has a range of veg and nonveg dishes.

Getting There & Away

The easiest way to visit Nagarjunakonda is with **APTDC** (☎ 040-2789310). Tours (Rs 360) depart from Hyderabad on weekends at 7.30am from Yatri Nivas Hotel (see p283), returning at 9.30pm.

You can also make your own way there from Hyderabad or Vijayawada. From Hyderabad, take a bus to Macherla or Vinukonda, which will stop at Nagarjuna Sagar. The nearest train station is 22km away at Macherla, where buses leave regularly for Nagarjuna Sagar.

WARANGAL

☎ 0870 / pop 528,570

Warangal was the capital of the Kakatiya kingdom, which covered the greater part of present-day Andhra Pradesh from the late 12th to early 14th centuries until it was conquered by the Tughlaqs of Delhi. The Hindu Kakatiyas were great builders and patrons of Telugu literature and arts, and it was during their reign that the Chalukyan style of temple architecture reached its pinnacle.

If you're interested in Hindu temple development, then it's worth the trip to Warangal, which is also a friendly town, and Palampet (see p298). It's possible – but not leisurely – to visit both places on a long day trip from Hyderabad, 157km away.

Most buses and trains will stop en route at Bhongir, about 60km from Hyderabad. It's well worth jumping down for a couple of hours to climb the fantastical-looking 12th-century Chalukyan **hill fort** (Rs 3) from which the town gets its name. Looking like a gargantuan stone egg, the hill is mostly ringed by stairs.

Orientation & Information

Warangal, Hanamkonda and Kazhipet are sister towns. The Warangal train station and bus stand are opposite each other, and the post office and police station are on Station Rd. Main Rd connects Warangal and Hanamkonda.

There are some **internet cafés** (MG Rd; per hr Rs 20) near Hotel Ratna. The **State Bank of Hyderabad** (Station Rd) has an ATM. The **Department of Tourism** (☎ 2459201; Hanamkonda-Kazhipet Rd, opposite REC; ◷ 10.30am-5pm Sun-Fri & holidays) is helpful and can advise on trips in Warangal and beyond.

Sights

FORT

Warangal's **fort** (Indian/foreigner Rs 5/US$2; ◷ dawn-dusk) was a massive construction with three distinct circular strongholds surrounded by a moat. Four paths with decorative gateways, set according to the cardinal points, led to the Swayambhava, a huge Shiva temple. The gateways are still obvious, but most of the fort is in ruins.

The fort is easily reached from Warangal by bus, bike or autorickshaw (Rs 75 return, including waiting time).

HANAMKONDA

Built in 1163, the **1000-Pillared Temple** (◷ 6am-6pm) on the slopes of Hanamkonda Hill, 400m from the Hanamkonda crossroads, is a fine example of Chalukyan architecture in a peaceful, leafy setting. Dedicated to three deities – Shiva, Vishnu and Surya – it has been carefully restored with intricately carved pillars and a central, very impressive Nandi of black basalt.

Down the hill and 3km to the right is the small **Siddheshwara Temple**. The **Bhadrakali Temple**, featuring a stone statue of Kali, seated with a weapon in each of her eight hands, is high on a hill between Hanamkonda and Warangal.

Sleeping

Warangal has a range of good budget hotels.

Vijaya Lodge (☎ 2501222; fax 2446864; Station Rd; s/d from Rs 130/200) About 100m from the train station, the Vijaya is a great deal, with tidy, compact rooms, layers of fresh, pastel paint on the walls and an almost domestic touch.

Hotel Ratna (☎ 2500645; fax 2500096; MG Rd; s/d from Rs 299/400; ☒) The Ratna has shiny floors and professional staff – including friendly, English-speaking houseboys – and it accepts credit cards. Its veg restaurant, Kavya, gets good reviews (mains Rs 40 to 85).

Hotel Surya (☎ 2441834; fax 2441836; Station Rd; s/d incl breakfast from Rs 390/450; ▓) Near the stations, this modern and well-run hotel has smart rooms, which are only just beginning to fade, constant hot water and a good restaurant downstairs.

Eating

Warangal has several meals places (we use the term 'meals' instead of thali in this chapter), some of which have seen better days. The hotel restaurants are good bets.

Sri Raghavendra Bhavan (Station Rd; meals Rs 22; ◷ 5.30am-10.30pm) A little neighbourhood joint with the best meals in Warangal. It's close to Hotel Surya.

Kanishka (☎ 2578491; Main Rd, Hanamkonda; mains Rs 30-80; ◷ 6.30am-10.30pm) The Hotel Ashoka, a Hanamkonda institution, has a busy compound with this excellent veg restaurant, a non-veg restaurant, a bar-restaurant and a pub.

Surabhi (Station Rd; mains Rs 40-75; ◷ 11am-3pm & 7-11pm) Surprisingly good food in somewhat elegant surroundings at the Hotel Surya. The menu includes such wonders as the 'Surabhi special dosa', stuffed with carrots, *paneer* (unfermented cheese), onions and ghee (Rs 30).

Getting There & Away

Bus services run to Vijayawada (Rs 190, seven hours, seven daily) from Warangal. Frequent buses to Hyderabad (Rs 74, 3½ hours) depart from Hanamkonda bus station, an Rs 6 bus ride away.

Warangal is a major rail junction. Trains go regularly to Hyderabad (2nd/chair Rs 71/232, three hours), Vijayawada (sleeper/3AC/2AC Rs 125/321/448, four hours) and Chennai (sleeper/3AC/2AC Rs 281/735/1030, 10 hours). Many trains go to Delhi daily.

Getting Around

Bus 28 goes to the fort and regular buses go to all the other sites. You can rent bicycles at **Ramesh Kumar Cycle Taxi** (Station Rd; per hr Rs 4; ◷ 8am-10pm). A shared autorickshaw ride costs Rs 6.

AROUND WARANGAL
Palampet

About 65km northeast of Warangal, the stunning **Ramappa Temple** (◷ 6am-6.30pm), built in 1234, is an attractive example of Kakatiya architecture, although it was clearly influenced by Chalukya and Hoysala styles. Its pillars

are ornately carved and its eaves shelter fine statues of female forms.

Just 1km south, the Kakatiyas constructed **Ramappa Cheruvu** to serve as temple tank. The artificial lake now assumes a natural presence in the landscape.

The easiest way to get here is by private car, but frequent buses also run from Hanamkonda to Mulugu (Rs 25). From Mulugu, you can take a bus (Rs 4, every half-hour) or shared jeep (Rs 5) to the village of Palampet. The temple is about 500m from here.

VISAKHAPATNAM

☎ 0891 / pop 1.3 million

Visakhapatnam – also called Vizag (*vie*-zag) – is Andhra Pradesh's second-largest city, though it feels more like an ageing beach-resort town. It's famous for shipbuilding and steel manufacturing, and now it's also an up-and-comer in the call-centre, software and film industries. But we love it for its kitschy coasts. The run-down boardwalk along Ramakrishna Beach has lots of spunk, and the beach at nearby Rushikonda is one of Andhra's best. Vizag is also a base for visits to the Araku Valley (see p300).

Orientation

Vizag's train station sits in a hive of shops and hotels on the western edge of town, near the port. Dwarakanagar, Vizag's commercial centre, is 1.5km northeast of the train station, and the bus stand, known as RTC Complex, is 2km due east. Waltair and its Ramakrishna Beach are about 2km southeast of RTC.

Information

ATMs are all around. RTC Complex has several internet cafés, some open 24 hours.

APTDC RTC Complex (☎ 2788820; ◷ 6am-10pm); train station (☎ 2788821; ◷ 5am-11pm) Information and tours.

iWay (☎ 3293692; 1st Lane, Dwarakanagar; per hr Rs 25; ◷ 8.30am-11pm) Secure web browsing. Next to Pollocks School.

Pages Book Shop (☎ 6450555; Old Jail Rd, Daba Gardens; ◷ 9.30am-9.30pm)

Thomas Cook (☎ 2588112; Eswar Plaza, Dwarakanagar; ◷ 9am-6.30pm Mon-Sat) Next to ICICI Bank.

Train station cloak room (per day Rs 10, locker per day Rs 15; ◷ 24hr)

Sights & Activities

The long beaches of **Waltair** overlook the Bay of Bengal, with its mammoth ships and brightly painted fishing boats. Its coastal **Beach**

Rd, lined with parks and weird sculptures, is great for long walks.

The best beaches for swimming are at **Rushikonda**, 8km north. On the way, **Kailasagiri Hill** has gardens, playgrounds, and a gargantuan Shiva and Parvati. The views from the hill and the **Kailasagiri Passenger Ropeway** (☎ 6510334; admission Rs 44; ☯ 11am-1pm & 2-8pm) are awesome. Movies or cricket matches are sometimes shown across Beach Rd, at the festive **Tenetti Beach**.

At Simhachalam Hill, 10km northwest of town, is a fine 11th-century **Vishnu Temple** (☯ 6-10am & 4-6pm) in Orissan style. You can give *puja* to the deity, who's covered with sandalwood paste. Bus 6 A/H goes here.

Tours
APTDC operates full-day tours of the city (Rs 245) and of Araku Valley (see p300).

Sleeping
VISAKHAPATNAM
Budget and midrange hotels huddle around the train station, which has **retiring rooms** (r from Rs 200; ☒). Waltair has a much better vibe, but few budget hotels. Prices may rise for Dussehra/Diwali holidays, when Bengalis swarm to Vizag.

Sree Kanya Lodge (☎ 2564881; Bowdara Rd; s/d from Rs 175/350; ☒) Near the train station but out of the bustle, Sree Kanya is mostly characterless but clean and bright, with sheets folded in little squares on the beds, friendly staff, balconies in most rooms and a good restaurant.

Jaabily (☎ 2706468; www.jaabilybeachinn.com; Beach Rd; r from Rs 595; ☒) The Jaabily has an eclectic, overpriced assortment of so-so rooms, an old beach-cabana feel and a colourful but gritty spot near the beach. Checkout is noon.

Taj Residency (☎ 2567756; www.tajhotels.com; Beach Rd; s/d from US$100/110; ☒ ▢ ▢) The usual Taj classiness, with great views. Slightly frayed at the edges, but where else can you stay at a Taj for this price? Checkout is noon.

Other recommendations:
Hotel Morya (☎ 2731112; hotelmorya@yahoo.co.in; Bowdara Rd; r from Rs 350; ☒)
Hotel Daspalla (☎ 2564825; www.daspallagroup.com; Suryabagh; s/d incl breakfast from Rs 1200/1400; ☒ ▢) Looking like the inside of an Ambassador car, it's Vizag's classic. Has a bar named Dimple.

RUSHIKONDA
Sai Priya Resort (☎ 2790333; www.saipriya.com; cottages/r from Rs 550/900; ☒ ▢) Modern rooms and cool cottages of bamboo and cane in a tranquil setting on the shore. Checkout is a rude 8am, though, and the service charge is a whopping 10%. Nonguests can use the pool for Rs 50.

Punnami Beach Resort (☎ 2788826; r with AC from Rs 1350; ☒) Set on a cliff top over the beach, the Punnami has spacious rooms with crappy bathrooms and fabulous bay views.

Eating & Drinking
At night, guys barbecue fish (Rs 80) along Ramakrishna Beach, and the beachfront restaurants at Rushikonda, next to Punnami, are hopping.

New Andhra Hotel (Sree Kanya Lodge, Bowdara Rd; mains Rs 25-75; ☯ lunch & dinner) An unassuming little place with *really* good, *really* hot Andhra dishes. Meals and biryani are top-notch.

Masala (☎ 2750750; Signature Towers, 1st fl, Asilmetta; mains Rs 60-110; ☯ lunch & dinner) Near Sampath Vinayaka Temple, Masala does out-of-this-world Andhra, tandoori and Chinese. Try the *chepa pulusu* (Andhra-style fish; Rs 85).

Café Coffee Day (coffees Rs 20-50) Up the road from Masala.

Getting There & Away
AIR
Vizag's **airport** (☎ 2572020) is 13km west of town. An autorickshaw there should cost Rs 120. Bus 38 will take you there for Rs 6.

Air Deccan (☎ 2543352, 9849677008; Prantosini Apartments No 7, CBM Compound; ☯ 9am-8pm) Daily flights: Hyderabad, Chennai, Tirupathi and Bengaluru.

Air Sahara (☎ 6672333; Kalyani Estates, near Big Bazaar, Dwarkanagar) Daily flights: Hyderabad and Mumbai; frequent flights to Bengaluru, Delhi and Kolkata.

Indian Airlines (☎ 2746501, 1800 1801407; LIC Bldg) Daily flights: Chennai, Hyderabad, Mumbai (via Hyderabad) and Delhi.

BOAT
Boats depart every now and then for Port Blair in the Andaman Islands (see p450). If you want to try your luck, bookings for the 56-hour journey can be made at the **Shipping Office** (☎ 2565584, 2562661; Av Bhanoji Row; ☯ 8am-5pm) in the port complex.

BUS
You'll probably take the train to/from Vizag, but its **bus stand** (☎ 2746400) is well organised, with frequent services to Vijayawada (deluxe/Volvo Rs 225/404, nine hours) and Hyderabad (ordinary/Volvo Rs 382/676, 14/12 hours).

TRAIN

Visakhapatnam Junction station is on the Kolkata–Chennai line. The overnight *Coromandel Express* (sleeper/3AC/2AC Rs 338/896/1263, 13½ hours) is the fastest of the five daily trains running to Kolkata. Heading south, it goes to Vijayawada (sleeper/3AC/2AC Rs 189/476/659, 5½ hours) and Chennai (sleeper/3AC/2AC Rs 315/831/1170, 13 hours). Many other trains head to Vijayawada daily; seven others go to Chennai.

AROUND VISAKHAPATNAM

Andhra's best train ride is through the magnificent Eastern Ghats to the **Araku Valley**, 120km north of Vizag. The area is home to isolated tribal communities, and the tiny **Museum of Habitat** (admission Rs 5; ☼ 9am-12.30pm & 1.30-5.30pm) has fascinating exhibits of indigenous life. APTDC runs a tour from Vizag (see p298; Rs 430), which takes in a performance of Dhimsa, a tribal dance, and the million-year-old limestone **Borra Caves** (Rs 25; ☼ 10am-5pm), 30km from Araku.

The **Punnami Hill Resort** (☎ 958936-249204; cottages from Rs 300; ☒), near the museum, has cottages with good views. But it's more fun to stay at the forest retreat of **Jungle Bells** (Tyda; cottages from Rs 650; ☒), 45km from Araku. It hurts to say the name, true. But its wooden cottages – including the 'igloo hut' – are tucked away in woods. Book at APTDC (see p298).

The Kirandol passenger train (Rs 24, five hours) leaves Vizag at 7.45am and Araku at 3pm. It's a slow, spectacular ride on a broadgauge line; sit on the right-hand side coming out of Vizag for the best views. For Jungle Bells, get off at Tyda station, 500m from the resort.

VIJAYAWADA

☎ 0866 / pop 1 million

Vijayawada, at the head of the delta of the mighty Krishna River, is considered by many to be the heart of Andhra culture and language. It's also an important Hindu site, both for its Durga temple and the Krishna Pushkaram, held every 12 years, when Lord Pushkara is believed to reside in the River Krishna. Nearby Amaravathi, meanwhile, was a centre of Buddhist learning and practise for many centuries.

Vijayawada's a big, bustling city and an important port, but it's also surrounded by hills, intersected by canals, ringed by fields of rice and palm, and imbued with a charm that takes time to emerge.

Orientation

The Krishna River cuts across the southern end of the city. The bus station is just north of the river, and the train station is in the centre of town, near the Governorpet neighbourhood, which has lots of hotels.

Information

Apollo Pharmacy (☎ 2432333; Vijaya Talkies Junction, Karl Marx Rd; ☼ 6am-11pm)

APTDC (☎ 2571393; MG Rd; ☼ 7am-8pm) Across from PWD Grounds. Not particularly helpful.

Care Hospital (☎ 2470100; Siddhartha Nagar)

Cloakrooms (per day Rs 10; ☼ 24hr) At the train and bus stations.

Department of Tourism (☎ 2577577; Train Station; ☼ 10am-5pm)

State Bank of Hyderabad (☎ 2574832; 1st fl, Vijaya Commercial Complex, Governorpet; ☼ 10.30am-3pm Mon-Fri) Changes currency and travellers cheques. Near Vijayawada.net.

Vijayawada.net (☎ 2574242; Rajagopalachari St, Governorpet; per hr Rs 20; ☼ 9.30am-9.30pm Mon-Sat, 10am-6.30pm Sun) Off Prakasam Rd, towards Apsara Theatre.

Sights

CAVE TEMPLES

Four kilometres southwest of Vijayawada, the stunning 7th-century **Undavalli cave temples** (Indian/foreigner Rs 5/US$2; ☼ 9am-6pm) cut a fine silhouette against the palm trees and rice paddies. Shrines are dedicated to the Trimurti – Brahma, Vishnu and Shiva – and one cave on the third level houses a huge, beautiful statue of reclining Vishnu while seated deities and animals stand guard out the front. Bus 301 goes here.

The east side of Vijayawada is also peppered with defunct cave temples, like the very damaged but nonetheless interesting 6th- to 7th-century **Mogalarajapuram Caves**.

VICTORIA JUBILEE MUSEUM

The best part of this **museum** (☎ 2574299; MG Rd; admission Rs 3; ☼ 10.30am-5pm Sat-Thu) is the building itself, built in 1877 to honour Queen Victoria's coronation jubilee. Later, in 1921, it hosted the Congress meeting where a new tricolour flag was introduced. Mahatma Gandhi added a wheel to the design and made it the Indian National Congress's official flag.

The interesting architecture outshines the museum's small collection of art and arms. But the garden, where temple sculpture from around the state lines shady paths, is lovely.

KANAKA DURGA TEMPLE
This **temple** (Indrakila Hill; ☼ 5am-9pm) is dedicated to Kanaka Durga, the goddess and protector of the city. Legend has it that she eradicated powerful demons from the area. She now receives continual gratitude from her followers, who credit her with Vijayawada's prosperity. Avoid mornings and bring lots of change for blessings.

GHATS
Vijayawada's Krishna River has 10 ghats running along its shores. The Krishnaveni ghat, just across from the bus stand, is a fascinating place to sit and watch the world – and its laundry, swimming kids and prayers – go by.

Courses
MEDITATION
Dhamma Vijaya (Vipassana Meditation Centre; ☎ 08812-225522; www.dhamma.org; Eluru-Chintalapudi Rd, Pedavegi Mandalam) offers intensive 10-day *vipassana* meditation courses free of charge. Frequent trains run from Vijayawada to Eluru (2nd/chair Rs 52/197, one hour). The centre is 15km from Eluru; call for details.

Sleeping & Eating
The train station's clean and spacious **retiring rooms** (dm/s/d from Rs 50/120/250; ▩) are a great option. The bus station has **dorms** (☎ 3297809; from Rs 100) for gents.

Sree Lakshmi Vilas Modern Cafe (☎ 2572525; Besant Rd, Governorpet; s with shared bathroom Rs 90, s/d with private bathroom from Rs 150/300) With black-and-white check floors and thick wooden banisters, this place has a heavy 1940s vibe. Housekeeping, however, is not its strong suit. The veg restaurant (meals Rs 24) is excellent, with fresh juices (Rs 10) and mismatched wooden chairs.

Hotel Santhi (☎ 2577351; Apsara Theatre Junction, Governorpet; s/d from Rs 350/450; ▩) Well-organised Santhi feels like a midrange place despite its prices, with its pastel-pink and mint-green rooms, two-tone cabinets and newish bathrooms.

Hotel Grand Residency (☎ 6668505; grandvja@sify.com; Prakasam Rd; s/d with AC from Rs 825/925; ▩) Light, airy rooms that aren't huge but very smart, with some style, eg lacquered furniture. Reserve in advance if you can. The restaurant, Tulips (mains Rs 30 to 95; open for dinner), has good veg and nonveg, and the hotel also has a bar.

Cross Roads (Prakasam Rd; mains Rs 50-95; ☼ lunch & dinner) There's sometimes a wait at this popular family place specialising in quality kebabs, biryani and North Indian dishes. Save room for ice cream.

Other recommendations:
Hotel Sree Vasudev (☎ 2571345; Mudda Subbaiah St, Governorpet; s/d from Rs 90/130) Just behind Sree Lakshmi. Slightly less character, slightly cleaner toilets.
Jayalakshmi Cool Magic (Prakasam Rd, Governorpet; mains Rs 25-45; ☼ 9.30am-10.30pm) Outdoor patio seating and chicken *masala dosas*.

Getting There & Away
The bus stand has a helpful **inquiry desk** (☎ 2522200). Frequent services run to Hyderabad (deluxe/Volvo Rs 170/280, six hours), Amaravathi (Rs 22, 1½ hours), Warangal (deluxe Rs 120, six hours) and Visakhapatnam (deluxe/Volvo Rs 230/400, 10 hours).

Vijayawada is on the main Chennai–Kolkata and Chennai–Delhi railway lines. The daily *Coromandel Express* runs to Chennai (sleeper/3AC/2AC Rs 214/544/758, seven hours) and, the other way, to Kolkata (sleeper/3AC/2AC Rs 401/1073/1518, 20 hours). Speedy *Rajdhani* (Thursday and Saturday) and *Jan Shatabdi* (daily except Tuesday) trains also ply the Chennai–Vijayawada route.

Plenty of trains run to Hyderabad (2nd/chair Rs 115/386, 6½ hours) and Tirupathi (sleeper/3AC/2AC Rs 181/480/708, seven hours).

The **computerised advance booking office** (inquiry ☎ 133, 2577775; reservations ☎ 136, 2578955) is in the station basement.

AROUND VIJAYAWADA
Amaravathi
Amaravathi, 60km west of Vijayawada, was once the Andhran capital and a significant Buddhist centre. India's biggest **stupa** (Indian/foreigner Rs 5/100; ☼ 8am-6pm), measuring 27m high, was constructed here in the 3rd century BC, when Emperor Ashoka sent the monk Bhikku Mahadeva south to spread the Buddha's teaching. All that remains are a mound and some stones, but the nearby **museum** (admission Rs 2; ☼ 10am-5pm Sat-Thu) has a small replica of the stupa, with its intricately carved pillars, marble-surfaced dome and carvings of the life of the Buddha. It also has the relics once enshrined in the stupa and a reconstruction of part of the surrounding gateway. It's worth the trip, but most of Amaravathi's best sculptures are in London's British Museum and Chennai's Government Museum (p371).

About 1km down the road is the **Dhyana Buddha**, a 20m-high seated Buddha built on the site where the Dalai Lama spoke at the 2006 Kalachakra.

Buses run from Vijayawada to Amaravathi every hour or so (Rs 22, 1½ hours), and APTDC organises tours on Sundays for Rs 200, subject to demand.

Kondapalli

Situated strategically on the old Machilipatnam–Golconda trade route, **Kondapalli fort** (admission Rs 5; ☼ 10.30am-5pm) was built in 1360 by the Reddy kings, and was held by the Gajapathis, the Qutb Shahis, the Mughals and the nizams before becoming a British military camp in 1767. Today it's a quiet, lovely ruin. On weekdays, you'll likely have the place to yourself and you can easily spend a few hours hiking around. Kondapalli village, 1km downhill, is famous for its wooden dolls. The fort is 21km from Vijayawada; an autorickshaw costs Rs 300 return.

TIRUMALA & TIRUPATHI

☎ 0877 / pop 302,000

The holy hill of Tirumala is one of the most visited pilgrimage centres in India – and indeed the world: it's said that Venkateshwara Temple eclipses Jerusalem, Rome and Mecca for sheer numbers of pilgrims.

There are never fewer than 5000 pilgrims here at any one time – the daily average is 40,000 and the total often reaches 100,000 – and *darshan* (deity viewing) runs around the clock. Temple staff alone number 12,000, and the efficient **Tirumala Tirupathi Devasthanams** (TTD; www.tirumala.org) administers the crowds. It also runs *choultries* (guesthouses) for pilgrims in Tirumala and Tirupathi, the service town at the bottom of the hill. The private hotels and lodges are in Tirupathi, so a fleet of buses constantly ferries pilgrims the 18km up and down the hill.

Tirumala is an engrossing place, but receives few non-Hindu visitors. The crowds can be overwhelming, but Tirumala somehow has a sense of serenity and ease about it and is worth a visit, even if you're not a pilgrim.

Information

You'll find most of your worldly needs in Tirupathi, conveniently clustered around the bus station and, about 500m away, the train station. G Car St becomes Tilak Rd further from the train station.

Apollo Pharmacy (☎ 2252314; G Car St; ☼ 24hr) Beware imposters.
APTDC (☎ 2289120; Sridevi Complex, Tilak Rd; ☼ 7am-9pm)
Cloakrooms (per day Rs 8; ☼ 24hr) At the train and bus stations.
Cybermate (☎ 3093968; Tilak Rd; per hr Rs 15; ☼ 8.30am-9.30pm)
Net Hill (TP Area; per hr Rs 15; ☼ 9am-9.30pm) Next to the bus stand.
Police station (☎ 2289006; Railway Station Rd)

Sights

VENKATESHWARA TEMPLE

Devotees flock to Tirumala to see Venkateshwara, an avatar of Vishnu. Among the many powers attributed to him is the granting of any wish made before the idol at Tirumala. Many pilgrims also donate their hair to the deity – in gratitude for a wish fulfilled, or to renounce ego – so hundreds of barbers attend to devotees. Tirumala and Tirupathi are filled with tonsured men, women and children.

Legends about the hill itself and the surrounding area appear in the Puranas, and the temple's history may date back 2000 years. The main **temple** is an atmospheric place, though you'll be pressed between hundreds of devotees when you see it. The inner sanctum itself is dark and magical; it smells of incense, resonates with chanting and may make you religious. There, Venkateshwara sits gloriously on his throne, inspiring bliss and love among his visitors. You'll have a moment to make a wish and then you'll be out again.

'Ordinary *darshan*' requires a wait of several hours in the claustrophobic metal cages ringing the temple. 'Special *darshan*' tickets (Rs 50) can be purchased a day in advance in Tirupathi. These come with a *darshan* time and get you through the queue faster.

Foreigners are advised to have VIP 'cellar' *darshan*, which involves minimal waiting. Bring your passport, a photocopy and Rs 100 to the Joint Executive Officer's (JEO) office at Tirumala, about 2km from the Tirupathi bus drop-off. The free red buses go here.

Tours

If you're pressed for time, APTDC runs two-day tours (Rs 1550) to Tirumala from Hyderabad. KSTD (see p222) and TNTDC (see p370) offer the same tours from Bengaluru and Chennai, respectively. APTDC also has a full-day tour

(Rs 300) of the many important temples in the Tirupathi area.

Sleeping & Eating

Most non-Hindu visitors stay in Tirupathi, which has a range of good accommodation.

TIRUMALA

Vast **dormitories** (beds free) and **guesthouses** (Rs 100-2500) surround the temple, but these are intended for pilgrims. If you want to stay, check in at the Central Reception Office, near the Tirumala bus stand, or reserve online at www.ttdsevaonline.com (reservations not accepted for festivals).

Huge **dining halls** (meals free) in Tirumala serve thousands of meals daily to pilgrims. There are also veg restaurants serving meals for Rs 10.

TIRUPATHI

Hotels are clustered around the bus stand (TP Area) and train station, which has nice **retiring rooms** (dm/r from Rs 45/150; 🍴).

Hotel Mamata Lodge (☎ 2225873; fax 2225797; 1st fl, 170 TP Area; s/d/tr/q Rs 150/250/300/300) A friendly, spic-and-span cheapie. Some of the sheets are stained, but they're tucked in tight and lovingly patched with white squares. Avoid the downstairs lodge of the same name.

Hotel Woodside (☎ 2284464; 15 G Car St; s/d incl breakfast from Rs 300/350; 🍴) The cheerful Woodside has royal-blue walls and plaid curtains (unlike the dreary Woodside Annexe down the road). The restaurant downstairs has great, spicy meals (Rs 23) and lots of windows.

Hotel Annapurna (☎ 2250666; 349 G Car St; d/tr/q from Rs 450/600/800; 🍴) Rooms at the reigning best value in town are pink and clean and new. Since the hotel's on a corner (across from the train station), rooms are bright but noisy. AC rooms are at the back and therefore quieter.

Hotel Sindhuri Park (☎ 2256430; www.hotelsindhuri.com; 119 TP Area; s/d from Rs 890/990; 🍴 💻) Rooms at the professional Sindhuri Park are well appointed and have central AC; some have views of the Pushkarna Tank out the front.

Hotel Universal Deluxe (49 G Car St; mains Rs 20-50; 🕐 5.30am-11.30pm) A bustling standby.

Hotel Vikram (☎ 2225433; TP Area; mains Rs 20-65; 🕐 5am-11pm) Excellent meals (Rs 22) and juices and full of happy families.

Punjabi Dhaba (☎ 5560827; G Car St; mains Rs 30-75; 🕐 7am-11pm) North Indian standbys and the delicious Special Punjabi Thali (Rs 60).

Other places to stay:

Hotel Mayura (☎ 2225925; mayura@nettlinx.com; 209 TP Area; r from Rs 750; 🍴)

Bhimas Deluxe (☎ 2225521; www.bhimas.com; 34-38 G Car St; r from Rs 850; 🍴) Has light-wood furniture, soft lighting and fancy towel racks, but could use a lick of paint.

Getting There & Away

It's possible to visit Tirupathi on a (very) long day trip from Chennai. If travelling by bus or train, you can buy 'link tickets', which include transport from Tirupathi to Tirumala.

AIR

Indian Airlines (☎ 2283992; Tirumala Bypass Rd; 🕐 10am-5.30pm), 2km outside of town, has daily flights to Hyderabad (US$85, one hour). **Air Deccan** (☎ 2285471) plies the same route daily for less. The easiest way to book either of these is with **Mitson Travels** (☎ 2225981; 192 Railway Station Rd; 🕐 9am-7.30pm Mon-Sat, to 12.30pm Sun), across from the train station's 'parcel office'.

BUS

Tirupathi's mega **bus station** (☎ 2289900) has frequent buses to Chennai (Rs 55, four hours) and Hyderabad (deluxe/Volvo Rs 330/560, 12/10 hours). Tonnes of APSRTC and KSTDC buses go to Bengaluru (deluxe/Volvo Rs 178/275, six/five hours), and three buses head to Puttaparthi daily (Rs 132, eight hours).

Private buses depart from the TP Area, opposite the bus stand.

TRAIN

Tirupathi station is well served by express trains. The **reservation office** (☎ 2225850; 🕐 8am-8pm Mon-Sat, 8am-2pm Sun) is across the street.

Getting Around

BUS

Tirumala Link buses run out of two bus stands in Tirupathi: next to the main bus stand and outside the train station. The scenic 18km trip to Tirumala takes one hour (Rs 44 return); if you don't mind heights, sit on the left side for views. A prepaid taxi is Rs 250.

WALKING

TTD has constructed probably the best footpath in India for pilgrims to walk up to Tirumala. It's about 15km and takes four to six hours. Leave your luggage at the toll gate at Alipiri near the Hanuman statue. It will be transported free to the reception centre. It's

ANDHRA PRADESH

TRAINS FROM TIRUPATHI

Destination	Fare (Rs)	Duration (hr)	Daily Departures
Bengaluru	166/437/617(A)	7	2
Chennai	63/209(B)	3	3
Madurai	248/661/948(A)	12	4
Mumbai	357/975/1391(A)	24	1
Secunderabad	263/712/1061(A)	12	6
Vijayawada	201/510/708(A)	7	6

A – sleeper/3AC/2AC; B – 2nd/chair

best to walk in the cool of the evening, but there are shady rest points along the way, and a few canteens.

AROUND TIRIMULA & TIRUPATHI
Alamelumangapuram

A visit to Tirumala isn't technically complete until you've paid respect to Venkateshwara's consort, Padmavathi Devi, at her less crowded **temple** in Tiruchanur, 5km from Tirumala. Legend has it that Padmavathi once appeared on a lotus in the tank here. Prepaid taxis from Tirupathi train station, 30km away, cost Rs 350.

Chandragiri Fort

Only a couple of buildings remain from this 15th-century **fort** (☎ 2276246; Indian/foreigner Rs 5/100; ⏱ 8am-6pm), 14km west of Tirupathi. Both the Rani Mahal and the Raja Mahal, which houses a small **museum** (⏱ 10am-5pm Sat-Thu), were constructed under Vijayanagar rule and resemble structures in Hampi's Royal Centre. There's a nightly **sound-and-light show** (admission Rs 30; ⏱ 8pm Mar-Oct, 7.30pm Nov-Feb), narrated by Bollywood stars. Buses for Chandragiri (Rs 6) leave from outside Tirupathi train station every 15 minutes. A prepaid taxi is Rs 250 return.

Sri Kalahasti

Around 36km east of Tirupathi, Sri Kalahasti is known for its **Sri Kalahasteeswara Temple**, which derives its name from the legend of three animals that worshipped Shiva: a snake, spider and elephant.

Sri Kalahasti is also, along with Machilipatnam near Vijayawada, a centre for the ancient art of *kalamkari*. These paintings are made with natural ingredients: the cotton is primed with *myrabalam* (resin) and cow's milk; fig-

ures are drawn with a pointed bamboo stick dipped in fermented jaggery and water; and the dyes are made from cow dung, ground seeds, plants and flowers. You can see the artists at work in the Agraharam neighbourhood, 2.5km from the bus stand.

Buses leave Tirupathi for Sri Kalahasti every 10 minutes (Rs 20, 45 minutes); a prepaid taxi is Rs 475 return.

PUTTAPARTHI
☎ 08555

Prasanthi Nilayam (Abode of Highest Peace), in the southwestern corner of Andhra Pradesh at Puttaparthi, is the main ashram of Sri Sathya Sai Baba, who has a huge following in India and around the globe. He set up this ashram 40 years ago, and spends most of the year here.

Sleeping & Eating

Most people stay at the **ashram** (☎ 287164; www .sathyasai.org), a small village with all amenities. Accommodation and food are cheap but very basic. Advance bookings aren't taken.

Sri Pratibha Guest House (☎ 289599; Gopuram St, 1st Cross; r from Rs 300) On an alley behind the canteen, Sri Pratibha is away from the chaos of Main Rd. Rooms are big, bright and airy.

Sri Sai Sadan (☎ 287507; Hanuman Temple Main Rd; r from Rs 600; ⚡) Spacious rooms have balconies with good views, but the roof-garden restaurant is the kicker.

Sri Annapoorna Hotel (meals Rs 18; ⏱ 6am-10pm) Down the alley next to the bus station, Sri Annapoorna has great chai, tiffin and spicy meals.

World Peace Café (German Bakery; Main Rd; mains Rs 40-95; ⏱ 7.30am-10.30pm) This breezy rooftop place has herbal teas, healthy foods and good filter coffee. Customers meditate at their ta-

---

THE GOD OF BIG THINGS

Many times a year, the population of Puttaparthi swells to more than 50,000. The drawcard, of course, is Sai Baba. Puttaparthi is his birthplace and where he established his main ashram, Prasanthi Nilayam.

It's difficult to overestimate the pulling power of this man who, aged 14, declared himself to be the reincarnation of Sai Baba, a saintly figure who died in 1918 (p142).

In November 2000 an estimated one million people gathered at the ashram to celebrate Sai Baba's 75th year. The massive gig resembled an Olympics opening ceremony. Sai Baba's elaborately adorned elephant, Sai Gita, led a procession of bands, dancing troupes and flag bearers from 165 countries. Many devotees regard Sai Baba as a true avatar.

Everything about Sai Baba is big: the Afro hairdo; the big name-devotees, including film stars, politicians and cricket superstar Sachin Tendulkar; and the money (millions of dollars) pumped into the nearby hospital, schools and university. And there's the big controversy. Allegations of sexual misconduct have led some devotees to lose faith. Others, however, regard such controversy as simply another terrestrial test for their avatar.

---

bles amidst saffron lassis and spirulina milkshakes.

Bamboo Nest (Chitravathi Rd, 1st fl; mains Rs 45-60; ⏰ 9.30am-2pm & 4.30-9pm) This Tibetan place has a memorable veg wonton soup (Rs 35) and good *momos* (dumplings).

Other recommendations:

Sai Towers (☎ 287270; www.saitowers.com; Main Rd; s/d from Rs 485/1220) A swanky joint.

Sai Krishna Italian Restaurant (Samadhi Rd, ⏰ 7am-1.30pm & 5-8.30pm; mains Rs 40-95)

Getting There & Around

Puttaparthi is most easily reached from Bengaluru; eight KSRTC buses (deluxe/Volvo Rs 150/205, four hours) and six trains (sleeper/ 3AC/2AC Rs 145/351/478, three hours) head here daily. A *Rajdhani* train (3AC/2AC Rs 405/545, 2½ hours) runs four days a week. Booking for KSRTC buses is next to the bus station.

Uncomfortable APSRTC buses run to/from Tirupathi (Rs 132, eight hours, three daily) and Chennai (Rs 273, 12 hours, two daily), but for other destinations, the train's the way to go.

The bus station has a **train reservation booth** (⏰ 8am-11.30pm & 3-5.30pm Mon-Sat, 8am-2pm Sun). For Hyderabad, an overnight train goes daily to Kacheguda (sleeper/3AC/2AC Rs 230/618/875, 10 hours), and a *Rajdhani* express goes to Secunderabad four days a week (3AC/2AC Rs 910/1230, 8½ hours). Overnight train 8564 runs to Visakhapatnam (sleeper/ 3AC/2AC Rs 33/120/1283, 20 hours), stopping at Vijayawada. The daily *Udyan Express* (6530) heads to Mumbai (sleeper/3AC/2AC Rs 330/901/1283, 21 hours).

Indian Airlines flies erratically from Mumbai (US$121).

An autorickshaw to/from the train station is Rs 40.

LEPAKSHI

About 65km from Puttaparthi is Lepakshi, site of the **Veerbhadra Temple**. The town gets its name from the Ramayana: when demon Ravana kidnapped Rama's wife, Sita, the bird Jatayu fought him but fell, injured, at the site of the temple. Rama called to him to get up: 'Lepakshi' derives from the Sanskrit for 'Get up, bird'.

Look out for the 9m-long monolithic Nandi bull – India's largest – at the town's entrance. From here, you can see the temple's Naga-lingam, a lingam crowned with a spectacular seven-headed cobra. The temple is known for its unfinished Kalyana Mandapam (Marriage Hall), which depicts the wedding of Parvati and Shiva, and its Natyamandapa (Dance Hall), with its carvings of dancing gods. The temple's most stunning feature, though, are the Natyamandapa's ceiling paintings.

Ramana, an excellent guide, brings the temple to life (Rs 100 is an appreciated offering). Bring plenty of small change for the inner sanctum.

To get here, take a Puttaparthi–Bengaluru bus and alight at Kodakonda Checkpost. From there, take a Gorantla–Hindupur bus (Rs 6) or an autorickshaw (Rs 250 return) to Lepakshi. The local Puttaparthi–Gorantla bus also stops at Lepakshi. A private car from Puttaparthi is Rs 900.

KERALA

Kerala

Kerala is where India slips down into second gear, stops to smell the roses and always talks to strangers. A strip of land between the Arabian Sea and the Western Ghats, its perfect climate flirts unabashedly with the fertile soil, and everything glows. An easy-going and successful socialist state, Kerala has a liberal hospitality that stands out as its most laudable achievement.

The backwaters that meander through Kerala are the emerald jewel in South India's crown. Here, spindly networks of rivers, canals and lagoons nourish a seemingly infinite number of rice paddies and coconut groves, while sleek houseboats cruise the water highways from one bucolic village to another. Along the coast, slices of perfect, sandy beach beckon the sun-worshipping crowd, and far inland the mountainous Ghats are covered in vast plantations of spices and tea. Exotic wildlife also thrives in the hills, for those who need more than just the smell of cardamom growing to get their juices flowing.

This flourishing land isn't good at keeping its secret: adventurers and traders have been in on it for years. The serene Fort Cochin pays homage to its colonial past, each building whispering a tale of Chinese visitors, Portuguese traders, Jewish settlers, Syrian Christians and Muslim merchants. Yet even with its colonial distractions, Kerala manages to cling to its vibrant traditions: Kathakali – a blend of religious play and dance; *kalarippayat* – a gravity-defying martial art; and *theyyam* – a trance-induced ritual. Mixed with some of the most tastebud-tingling cuisine in India and you can imagine how hard it will be to leave before you even get here.

HIGHLIGHTS

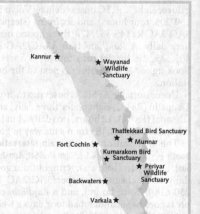

- Cruise the hydro-highways of Kerala's **back-waters** (p328) on a houseboat; an entry in our top 10 things-to-do-before-you-die list
- Kick back on shimmering beaches by day and feast on cliff-side seafood by night at **Varkala** (p319)
- Soak in the culture and serenity of captivating **Fort Cochin** (p343), a trading-post city echoing hundreds of years of colonial history
- Go elephant spotting at **Wayanad** (p357) or **Periyar Wildlife Sanctuary** (p334), then grab your logbook for some bird-watching at **Kumarakom Bird Sanctuary** (p333) or **Thattekkad Bird Sanctuary** (p340)
- See an ancient ritual of spirit possession called *theyyam* around **Kannur** (Cannanore, p359)
- Take in a kaleidoscope of green at tea plantations around **Munnar** (p337)
- Get oiled, rubbed and treated with the aromatic herbs used in **Ayurvedic massage** (p321)

Kannur ★
★ Wayanad Wildlife Sanctuary

Thattekkad Bird Sanctuary ★
Fort Cochin ★   ★ Munnar
Kumarakom Bird Sanctuary ★
★ Periyar Wildlife Sanctuary
Backwaters ★
Varkala ★

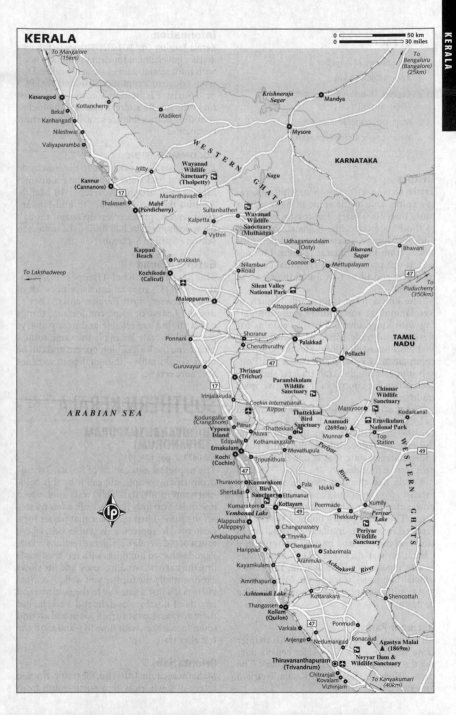

KERALA

0   50 km
0   30 miles

To Mangalore (15km)

To Bengaluru (Bangalore) (25km)

Kasaragod
Bekal
Kottancherry
Kanhangad
Nileshwar
Valiyaparamba

Madikeri

Krishnaraja Sagar

Mandya

Mysore

KARNATAKA

Iritty

Kannur (Cannanore)

17

Thalasseri
Mahé (Pondicherry)

Mananthavadi

Wayanad Wildlife Sanctuary (Tholpetty)

Nagu

WESTERN GHATS

Sultanbatheri

Kalpetta

Vythiri

Wayanad Wildlife Sanctuary (Muthanga)

Udhagamandalam (Ooty)

Bhavani Sagar

Bhavani

Kappad Beach

Purakkatri

Nilambur Road

Coonoor

Mettupalayam

47

To Lakshadweep

Kozhikode (Calicut)

Silent Valley National Park

To Puducherry (350km)

Malappuram

Attappadi

Coimbatore

Shoranur

Cheruthuruthy

Palakkad

TAMIL NADU

Ponnani

Guruvayur

Thrissur (Trichur)

Pollachi

17

Irinjalakuda

Parambikulam Wildlife Sanctuary

Chinnar Wildlife Sanctuary

ARABIAN SEA

Cochin International Airport

47

Marayoor

Kodaikanal

Kodungallur (Cranganore)

Vypeen Island

Parur

Thattekkad

Thattekkad Bird Sanctuary

Anamudi (2695m) ▲

Eravikulam National Park

Aluva

Edapally

Kothamangalam

Munnar

Top Station

Ernakulam

Muvattupula

Periyar River

Kochi (Cochin)

Tripunithura

47

WESTERN GHATS

49

Thuravoor

Kumarakom Bird Sanctuary

Pala

Idukki

Shertallai

Ettumanur

Kumarakom

Kottayam

Kumily

Vembanad Lake

49

Peermade

Periyar Lake

Alappuzha (Alleppey)

Changanassery

Thekkady

Ambalappuzha

Tiruvilla

Periyar Wildlife Sanctuary

Harippad

Chengannur

Sabarimala

Achankovil River

Kayamkulam

Aranmula

Amrithapuri

Ashtamudi Lake

Kottarakara

Shencottah

Thangasseri

Kollam (Quilon)

Ponmudi

47

Varkala

Anjengo

Nedumangad

Bonacaud

Agastya Malai ▲ (1869m)

Neyyar Dam & Wildlife Sanctuary

Thiruvananthapuram (Trivandrum)

Chitranjali
Kovalam
Vizhinjam

To Kanyakumari (40km)

KERALA

History

Traders have been drawn to the whiff of Kerala's spices and to the shine of its ivory for more than 3000 years. The coast was known to the Phoenicians, the Romans, the Arabs and the Chinese, and was a transit point for spices from the Moluccas (eastern Indonesia). It was probably via Kerala that Chinese products and ideas first found their way to the West.

The kingdom of Cheras ruled much of Kerala until the early Middle Ages, competing with kingdoms and small fiefdoms for territory and trade. Vasco da Gama's arrival in 1498 opened the floodgates to European colonialism as Portuguese, Dutch and English interests fought Arab traders, and then each other, for control of the lucrative spice trade.

The present-day state of Kerala was created in 1956 from the former states of Travancore, Cochin and Malabar. A tradition of valuing the arts and education resulted in a post-Independence state that is one of the most progressive in India.

Kerala had the first freely elected communist government in the world, coming to power in 1957 and holding power regularly since. The participatory political system has resulted in a more equitable distribution of land and income, and impressive health and education statistics (see p311). Many Malayalis (speakers of Malayalam, the state's official language) work in the Middle East, and remittances play a significant part in the economy.

National Parks

All national parks mentioned in this chapter close for one week for a tiger census during the months of January or February. The dates differ, so check with Kerala Tourism for exact dates.

Information

Kerala Tourism (☎ 0471-2321132; www.keralatourism .org) is a government tourism promotion body with information offices – usually called District Tourism Promotion Council (DTPC) or Tourist Facilitation Centres – in most major towns. Be aware of places with official-sounding names that are actually private tour companies.

ACCOMMODATION

Parts of Kerala – particularly the beachside towns and backwater hubs – have a distinct high season around November to March. Around the mid-December to mid-January peak season, prices creep up again, though great deals are to be had during the monsoon season (April to September).

Getting Around

The Kerala State Road Transport Corporation (KSRTC) runs an extensive network of buses between most Keralan cities. They're not the fastest or most comfortable things on earth, but are reliable and nearly always punctual. Private buses ply the same routes, plus some the KSRTC don't cover, and can be more comfortable – though departure times are more erratic.

SOUTHERN KERALA

THIRUVANANTHAPURAM (TRIVANDRUM)

☎ 0471 / pop 889,191

The unpretentious capital of Kerala, Trivandrum (many people still call it by this colonial name, understandably) rests upon seven low hills. You only have to walk a few metres off the fume-filled racetrack that passes for a main road to appreciate its gentler side, where much of old Kerala's ambience remains intact. Pagoda-shaped buildings with red-tiled roofs line the narrow, winding lanes, and life slows exponentially the further you walk. For most visitors it's just a gateway to the golden-sand resorts of nearby Kovalam and Varkala, but there are some great attractions in and around town for visitors with time to wander off the traveller trail.

Orientation

Mahatma Gandhi (MG) Rd, the traffic-clogged artery of town, runs 4km north–south from

---

FESTIVALS IN KERALA

Across the state on any night (but especially during festival season from November to mid-May) there are literally hundreds of vivid temple festivals being held, featuring an array of performing arts and rituals, music and the odd elephant procession. Some highlights:

Ernakulathappan Utsavam (Jan/Feb; Shiva Temple, Ernakulam, Kochi (Cochin), p345) Hugely significant for residents of Kochi, the climax of this eight-day festival brings a procession of 15 splendidly decorated elephants, ecstatic music and fireworks.

Bharni Utsavam (Feb/Mar; Chettikulangara Bhaghavathy Temple, Chettikulangara village, near Kayamkulam, p326) This one-day festival is dedicated to the popular Keralan goddess Bhagavathy. It's famous for its *kootiattam* (traditional Sanskrit drama) ritual and the spectacular procession to the temple of larger-than-life effigies.

Thirunakkara Utsavam (Mar; Thirunakkara Shiva Temple, Kottayam, p331) There's all-night Kathakali dancing on the third and fourth nights of this 10-day festival; on the last two nights there are processions of caparisoned elephants.

Pooram Festival (Apr; Asraman Shree Krishna Swami Temple, Kollam (Quilon), p324) There are full-night Kathakali performances during this 10-day festival; on the last day there's a procession of 40 ornamented elephants in Asraman Maidan.

Thrissur Pooram (Apr/May; Vadakkumnatha Temple, Thrissur (Trichur), p354) The elephant procession to end all elephant processions. Thrissur is Kerala's festival hot spot; see the Thrissur section for more details.

Nehru Trophy Snake Boat Race (2nd Sat in Aug; Punnamadakalyal, Alappuzha (Alleppey), p330) The most popular of Kerala's boat races.

Aranmula Boat Race (Aug/Sep; near Shree Parthasarathy Temple, Aranmula, p334) This water regatta recreates a ritualistic journey in honour of Krishna. It's a spectacularly exciting event, with crowds cheering as rowers shout along with the songs of the boatmen.

Onam (Aug/Sep; statewide) Kerala's biggest cultural celebration is the 10-day Onam, when the entire state celebrates the golden age of mythical King Mahabali. This is primarily a family affair, with an emphasis on feasting and decorating the home in anticipation of the king's visit.

Ashtamudi Craft & Art Festival (Dec/Jan; Asraman Maidan, Kollam (Quilon), p324) This festival, held every second year, features folk art from all over India, with workshops, demonstrations and exhibitions.

---

the museums and zoo to the Sri Padmanab-haswamy Temple area.

Information

BOOKSHOPS & LIBRARIES

Alliance Française (☎ 2320666; aftinfo@afindia.org; Forest Office Lane, Vazhuthacaud; ☺ 9am-1pm & 2-6pm Mon-Sat) Library and cultural events.

British Library (☎ 2330716; www.britishcouncilonline .org; YMCA Rd; ☺ 11am-7pm Mon-Sat) Open only to members (Rs 900 per year), but visitors can usually browse.

DC Books (☎ 2453379; www.dcbooks.com; Statue Rd; ☺ 9.30am-7.30pm Mon-Sat) Kerala's excellent bookshop chain, with a respectable selection of fiction in English and nonfiction books on India.

Modern Book Centre (☎ 2331826; Gandhari Amman Kovil Rd; ☺ 9.30am-1.30pm & 2.30-8.30pm Mon-Sat)

INTERNET ACCESS

Almikkice (MG Rd; per hr Rs 20; ☺ 7.30am-11.30pm) he best and friendliest of several internet places in this small mall.

Yahoo Internet City (Manjalikulam Rd; per hr Rs 20; ☺ 9am-9.30pm) Fast connections in cartoon-coloured cubicles.

MEDICAL SERVICES

General hospital (☎ 2307874; Statue Rd) About 1km west of MG Rd.

MONEY

There are ATMs that accept foreign cards all along MG Rd. Travellers cheques can be processed at the Canara Bank.

PHOTOGRAPHY

Paramount Digital Colour Lab (☎ 2331643; MG Rd; ☺ 8.30am-9pm) Prints and produces CDs from digital; sells memory cards and digital accessories.

POST & TELEPHONE

There are several STD/ISD kiosks around town.

Main post office (☎ 2473071; MG Rd)

TOURIST INFORMATION

Tourist Facilitation Centre (☎ 2321132; Museum Rd; ☺ 10am-5pm) Supplies maps and brochures.

Tourist Reception Centre (☎ 2330031; Central Station Rd; ☺ 9am-5pm Tue-Sun) Arranges KTDC tours (see p312) and car rental.

KERALA

THIRUVANANTHAPURAM (TRIVANDRUM)

0 ————— 500 m
0 ————— 0.3 miles

INFORMATION
Alliance Française	1	C3
Almikkice	2	A4
Andhra Bank ATM	(see 29)	
British Library	3	B4
Canara Bank & ATM	4	A5
Canara Bank & ATM	(see 44)	
DC Books	5	A4
Federal Bank ATM	6	A4
General Hospital	7	A4
HDFC ATM	8	C2
ICICI ATM	9	A5
Main Post Office	10	A4
Modern Book Centre	11	A5
Paramount Digital Colour Lab	12	A5
Tourist Facilitation Centre	13	B3
Tourist Reception Centre	(see 29)	
Yahoo Internet City	(see 34)	

SIGHTS & ACTIVITIES
Ayurveda College	14	A5
CVN Kalari Sangham	15	A6
Napier Museum	16	B3
Natural History Museum	17	C3
Puthe Maliga Palace Museum	18	A6
Reptile House	19	B3
Sri Chitra Art Gallery	20	B2
Sri Padmanabhaswamy Temple	21	A6
Ticket Counter (for Zoo and Museums)	22	B2
Zoological Gardens	23	B2

SLEEPING
Greenland Lodge	24	B5
Homeland	25	A5
Hotel Geeth	26	A4
Hotel Highland Park	27	B5
Hotel Regency	28	B5
KTDC Hotel Chaithram	29	B5
KTDC Hotel Mascot	30	B3
Kukie's Holiday Inn	31	A5
Manjalikulam Tourist Home	(see 34)	
Muthoot Plaza	32	B4
Omkar Lodge	33	A5
Pravin Tourist Home	34	A5
Wild Palms Home Stay	35	A4
YWCA International Guesthouse	36	A4

To Sivananda Yoga Vedanta
Dhanwantari Ashram (30km);
Neyyar Dam (31km);
Ponmudi (58km)

To Wild Palms
On Sea (20km);
Varkala (51km);
Kochi (222km)

EATING
Ananda Bhavan	37	A4
Azad Restaurant	38	A5
Indian Coffee House	(see 13)	
Kalavara Family Restaurant	39	A4
Kerala House Family Restaurant	40	A4
Maveli Café	41	B5
Prime Square	42	B5
Regency	43	A4
Spencer's Daily	44	A4
Tiffany's Restaurant	(see 32)	

ENTERTAINMENT
Sree Kumar Cinema	(see 29)	

SHOPPING
Connemara Market	45	B3
Sankers Coffee & Tea	46	A5
SMSM Institute	47	B4

TRANSPORT
Air India	48	C2
Airtravel Enterprises	49	B3
East Fort Bus Stand (Buses & Taxis to Kovalam)	50	A6
Indian Airlines	(see 30)	
Jet Airways	51	D2
KSRTC Bus Stand	52	B5
Municipal Bus Stand	53	A6

To Academy of Magical
Sciences (4km);
Poojapura (4km)

To Airport (6km);
Veli Tourist Park (8km)

To Margi Kathakali
School (200m)

To Padmanabhapuram
Palace (85km);
Kanyakumari (88km)

To Kovalam (15km)

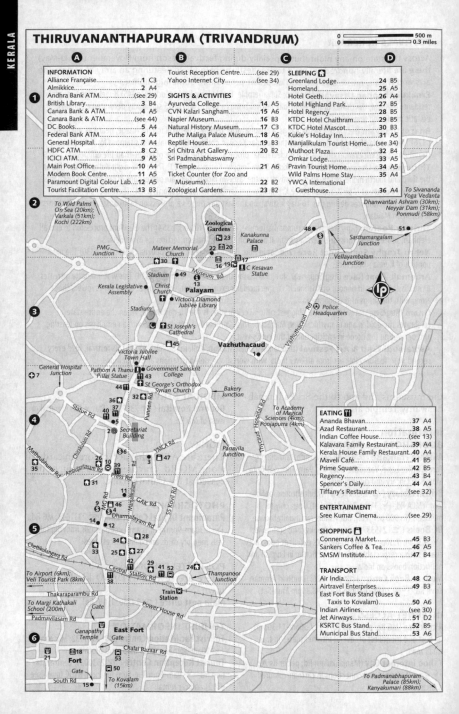

Sights & Activities
ZOOLOGICAL GARDENS & MUSEUMS
This well-cultivated collection of museums, a gallery and an excellent zoo are a peaceful haven from the flurry of the city.

The modern **zoological gardens** (admission Rs 6, camera Rs 20; ⊙ 9am-5.15pm Tue-Sun) are among the most impressive in the subcontinent. There are shaded paths meandering through miles of woodland and lakes, where animals happily carouse in massive, open enclosures that mimic their natural habitats. There's also a separate **reptile house** (entrance with zoo ticket), where dozens of the slithery things do their thing and cobras frequently flare their hoods – just don't ask what the cute guinea pigs are for.

A single Rs 6 entry ticket, purchased at the **ticket counter** (⊙ 10am-4pm), covers the following **gallery and museums** (⊙ 10am-5pm Tue & Thu-Sun, 1-5pm Wed) in the park. Housed in an absorbing Keralan-style wooden building from 1880, the **Napier Museum** has an eclectic display of bronzes, Buddhist sculptures, temple carts and ivory carvings. The painted carnivalesque interior is stunning and worth a look in its own right. The dusty **Natural History Museum** has hundreds of stuffed animals and birds, a fine skeleton collection and the odd empty display case. The **Sri Chitra Art Gallery** has paintings of the Rajput, Mughal and Tanjore schools, and works by Ravi Varma.

SRI PADMANABHASWAMY TEMPLE
This 260-year-old **temple** (⊙ 4am-7.30pm) is Thiruvananthapuram's spiritual heart and the city's erstwhile guardian. Spilling over 2400 sq metres, its main entrance is the 30m tall, seven-tier eastern *gopuram* (gateway tower). In the inner sanctum, the deity Padmanabha reclines on the sacred serpent and is made from over 10,000 *salagramam* (sacred stones) that were purportedly, and no doubt slowly, transported from Nepal by elephant.

The temple is officially open to Hindus only, but the path around to the right of the gate offers good views of the *gopuram*.

PUTHE MALIGA PALACE MUSEUM
The **Puthe Maliga Palace Museum** (admission Rs 20; ⊙ 8.30am-1pm & 3-5.30pm Tue-Sun) is housed in the 200-year-old palace of the Travancore maharajas. Based on typical Keralan architecture, it has carved wooden ceilings, marble sculptures and even imported Belgian glass – it took 5000 workers four years to complete. Inside you'll find Kathakali images, an armoury, portraits of Maharajas, ornate thrones and other artefacts.

The annual **classical music festival** is held here in January/February.

VELI TOURIST PARK
At the junction of Veli Lake and the Arabian sea, 8km west of the city, this unique **park** (☎ 2500785; admission Rs 5; ⊙ 8am-7.30pm) showcases strikingly oversized sculptures by local artist Kanai Kunhiraman. It's well designed, and the ponds, mammoth concrete conches and quasi-erotic curves of the artwork make for an interesting backdrop for a picnic or a stroll.

LEADER OF THE PACK

In 1957, Kerala was first in the world to freely elect a communist government. While communism's hammer and sickle hasn't had much luck in running other parts of the world, Kerala's unique blend of democratic-socialist principles has a pretty impressive track record.

Kerala has been labelled 'the most socially advanced state in India' by Nobel prize–winning economist Amartya Sen. Land reform and a focus on infrastructure, health and education have played a large part in Kerala's success. The literacy rate (91%) is the highest of any developing nation in the world, though a strong history of education goes back centuries to the days of magnanimous Rajas and active missionaries. The infant mortality rate in Kerala is one-fifth of the national average, while life expectancy stands at 73 years, 10 years higher than the rest of the country.

The picture is not all rosy, however. A lack of any industrial development or foreign investment means that many educated youth have their ambitions curtailed. This might explain why Kerala also has the highest suicide rates and liquor consumption statistics in the country. A big hope for the future is the recent boom in tourism, with Kerala emerging as one of India's most popular new tourist hot spots. So, thanks for coming, and congratulations on being a part of the solution.

KERALA

AYURVEDA

The students at **Ayurveda College** (☎ 2460190; MG Rd; ☻ 8am-1pm) perform massage and general *panchakarma* (cleansing and purification) treatments (after consultation with a doctor) free of charge. Expect to wait in line, and expect Indian hospital, rather than Western resort-style, ambience.

Courses

Margi Kathakali School (☎ 2478806; Fort), behind Fort School, conducts courses in Kathakali (see the boxed text, p349) and *kootiattam* for genuine students – absolute beginners as well as advanced. Fees average Rs 200 per 1½-hour class. Visitors can peek at the uncostumed practise sessions held 10am to noon Monday to Friday.

CVN Kalari Sangham (☎ 2474182; South Rd; ☻ 10am-1pm & 5-6.30pm) offers three-month courses (Rs 1000 per month) in *kalarippayat* (see boxed text, p349) for serious students with some experience in martial arts. Contact **Sathyan** (☎ 2474182) for details. Daily **training sessions** (☻ 7-8.30am Mon-Sat) are open for public viewing.

Tours

KTDC offers tours, leaving from the **KTDC Hotel Chaithram** (Central Station Rd). The **Kanyakumari Day Tour** (per person Rs 250; ☻ 7.30am-9pm Tue-Sun) visits Padmanabhapuram Palace (p319), Kanyakumari (p423) and the nearby Suchindram Temple. The **Thiruvananthapuram City Day Tour** (half-/full-day tours Rs 80/130) visits Trivandrum's major sights plus Kovalam beach (half-day 8.30am to 1pm, 2 to 7pm; full day 8.30am to 7pm). Avoid Mondays when some places are closed.

Sleeping

BUDGET

The best hunting ground is along the quieter Manjalikulam Rd – streetside rooms in MG Rd hotels are *very* noisy.

Omkar Lodge (☎ 2451803; MG Rd; s/d Rs 130/230) While Omkar offers little more than cramped, bare rooms, it does throw in a free ration of mosquito cream every night! Rooms are clean enough, though the street noise isn't exactly a sweet lullaby.

Kukie's Holiday Inn (☎ 2478530; Lukes Lane; s/d Rs 150/325) This gem of a cheapie lies enveloped in golden, verdant silence at the end of a small lane. The rooms are very simple but thoughtfully maintained and offer frilly bits,

like wicker chairs and bright paintwork. Some of the best bang-for-buck around.

Pravin Tourist Home (☎ 2330443; Manjalikulam Rd; s/d Rs 170/253) Pravin's rooms are an outstanding example of our favourite Indian budget-hotel label: BBC (Basic But Clean).

Greenland Lodge (☎ 2328114; Thampanoor Jn; s/d Rs 184/276) Greenland greets you with lots of serenity-inducing pastel colours. Spick-and-span rooms are excellent value, have lots of space and come with hybrid squat/Western toilets. Best of all, it's efficiently run by smiling staff. You get free mosquito coils nightly.

YWCA International Guesthouse (☎ 2477308; 4th fl, MG Rd; s/d/tr Rs 250/350/450, d with AC Rs 600; ☒) While the rooms are a bit tattered around the edges, they're well kept and offer space in spades. Those facing away from the street are much quieter. They have a 10pm curfew, as well as the slowest elevators in all of India.

MIDRANGE

Homeland (☎ 2338415; Manjalikulam Rd; s/d Rs 350/490, with AC Rs 675/800; ☒) Homeland has spotless, austere rooms in a brand-spanking new hotel. It is characterless midrange quality for near budget prices.

Hotel Regency (☎ 2330377; www.hotelregency.com; Manjalikulam Cross Rd; s/d Rs 375/600, with AC Rs 800/950; ☒) With small, cosy rooms, a leafy entryway, lots of hush and plenty of smiles, this is an excellent choice for a good night's rest.

Manjalikulam Tourist Home (☎ 2330776; Manjalikulam Rd; s/d Rs 400/600, with AC Rs 700/750; ☒) The rooms here are massive and tidy but spartan, except for a few odd grandmotherly touches like pink floral curtains.

Hotel Highland Park (☎ 2338800; Manjalikulam Rd; s/d Rs 450/600, with AC Rs 750/850; ☒) This is relatively new and in very good nick, though the single rooms are really cramped. Don't mistake this for its older sister-hotel, Hotel Highland, across the road.

Wild Palms Home Stay (☎ 2471175; wildpalm@md3 .vsnl.net.in; Mathrubhumi Rd; s Rs 895-1495, d Rs 1095-1895; ☒) The only pad in this price range that offers any real character – where else would you have a *Venus de Milo* statue greet you in the front garden? This lavish but comfortable family home has spacious rooms, handsome furniture and a friendly vibe (breakfast included).

Hotel Geeth (☎ 2471987; www.geethinternational.in; Ambujarilasam Rd; s/d from Rs 900/1500; ☒) Nothing too flash going on here, but the agreeable rooms all come with AC and lounge chairs, cable TV and eager staff for good measure. The top-floor restaurant comes recommended.

Wild Palms On Sea (☎ 2756781; Puthenthope; s/d from Rs 1295/1595) A resort-style place about 20km from town on a secluded beach (Rs 350 by taxi), run by the same owners as Wild Palms Home Stay.

TOP END

KTDC Hotel Mascot (☎ 2318990; hotelmascot@vsnl.net; Mascot Sq; s/d from Rs 2400/2900; ✂ ▯ ▧) Lots of stylish period touches, massive hallways and an imposing reception area lend this place the sort of charisma missing from modern-mausoleum hotels. There's a monster pool and an Ayurvedic spa, and it's convenient for visits to the zoo, museums and galleries.

Muthoot Plaza (☎ 2337733; www.sarovarhotels.com; Punnen Rd; s/d from Rs 3300/3800, ste from Rs 6500; ✂ ▯) In an unabashedly modern, cool-aqua glass tower, even the cheaper rooms are plush and top value. It's studiously focused on business travellers, with free breakfast and damned efficient service.

Eating

For some unusual refreshments with your meal, look out for *karikku* (coconut water) and *sambharam* (buttermilk with ginger and chilli).

Ananda Bhavan (MG Rd; dishes Rs 15-20; ☽ lunch & dinner) This veg restaurant hones its skills on South Indian and tandoori dishes. It's a classic Keralan sit-down-and-dig-in-with-your-hands type situation.

Maveli Café (Central Station Rd; dishes Rs 15-45) Part of the Indian Coffee House chain, Maveli serves its standard tucker in a unique, narrow, four-storey spiralling tower lined by bench tables. Equal parts funhouse and Indian diner, it's a must-see. There's a traditional branch of Indian Coffee House (Museum Rd; ☽ 8.30am-6pm) opposite the zoo.

Kerala House Family Restaurant (Statue Rd; mains Rs 25-55) Don't expect much in the way of décor (think formica), but do expect one mean fish-curry masala (Rs 50). The fish *pollichathu* (baked in banana leaf), with ginger, vegetables and spices, is also top-notch.

Kalavara Family Restaurant (Press Rd; dishes Rs 30-105; ☽ lunch & dinner; ✂) A favourite of Trivandrum's middle class, this place does commendable lunchtime biryanis (Rs 41 to 75) and a range of Keralan fish dishes; the fish *molee* (fish pieces in coconut sauce, Rs 59) is excellent and there's atmospheric rooftop dining.

There are plenty of good places to eat near the bus and train stations:

Azad Restaurant (MG Rd; nonveg mains Rs 17-40) Popular place with a juice bar attached.

Prime Square (Central Station Rd; mains from Rs 25) Keralan specialities and a great-value fish curry (Rs 28).

There's a choice of good hotel buffets at places like **Tiffany's Restaurant** (Muthoot Plaza; lunch Rs 350, dinner Rs 450) and **Regency** (MG Rd; buffet Rs 275) at the South Park Hotel. **Spencer's Daily** (MG Rd; ☽ 9am-9pm) is a well-stocked supermarket with lots of Western food, and even tampons!

Entertainment

Academy of Magical Sciences (☎ 2358910; www.magicmuthukad.com; Poojapurra) Ever wanted to learn how on earth they do that Indian rope trick? This is your chance. This academy works to preserve traditional Indian magic, give recognition to street magicians and train students in the art of illusion. It holds regular shows and has a shop selling magic kits. Fun.

For a quick Bolly- or Hollywood fix, try **Sree Kumar Cinema** (☎ 2331222; Central Station Rd; admission Rs 30-35; ☽ 11am-11pm).

Shopping

Wander around Connemara Market to see vendors selling vegetables, fish, live goats, fabric, clothes, spices and more bananas than you've ever seen in one place.

Sankers Coffee & Tea (☎ 2330469; MG Rd; ☽ 9am-9pm Mon-Sat) You'll smell the fresh coffee well before you reach this dainty little shop. It sells Nilgiri Export OP Leaf Tea (Rs 240 per kilogram) and a variety of coffee and nuts.

SMSM Institute (☎ 2330298; YMCA Rd; ☽ 9am-8pm Mon-Sat) Contrary to intuition, this place is not dedicated to the study of text messaging, but is a Kerala Government–run handicraft emporium with an Aladdin's den of reasonably priced goodies. A giant dancing-Shiva statue will greet you at the entrance.

Getting There & Away

AIR

Both **Indian Airlines** (☎ 2314781; Museum Rd; ☽ 10am-1pm & 1.45-5.35pm Mon-Sat) and **Jet Airways** (☎ 2728864; Sasthamangalam Junction; ☽ 9am-5.30pm Mon-Sat) have offices in Trivandrum.

Jet Airways and Indian Airlines fly daily to Mumbai (Bombay, US$262). **Air India** (☎ 2500585; International Airport; ☽ 9am-5.30pm Mon-Sat) flies to Kochi (US$115), while Indian Airlines flies to Bengaluru (Bangalore, US$162), Chennai (Madras, US$157) and Delhi (US$442).

There are regular flights from Trivandrum to Colombo and Male; see p493.

All airline bookings can be made at the efficient **Airtravel Enterprises** (☎ 2334202; fax 2331704; New Corporation Bldg, MG Rd; 🕑 9.30am-6pm Mon-Sat, 9.30am-5pm Sun).

BUS

For buses operating from the **KSRTC bus stand** (☎ 2323886), opposite the train station, see the table, below.

There's also a daily 8.45am bus to Thekkady (Rs 141, eight hours) for Periyar Wildlife Sanctuary.

For Tamil Nadu, State Express Transport Corporation (SETC) buses leave from the eastern end of the KSRTC bus stand for Chennai (Rs 306, 17 hours, eight daily) and Madurai (Rs 135, seven hours, nine daily). There's one daily bus at 3.45pm for Udhagamandalam (known as Ooty; Rs 258, 14 hours) and one at 2pm for Puducherry (Pondicherry, Rs 265, 16 hours).

Buses leave for Kovalam Beach (Rs 8, every 15 minutes) between 5.40am and 10pm from the southern end of the East Fort bus stand on MG Rd.

TRAIN

Trains are often heavily booked, so it's worth visiting the **reservation office** (🕑 8am-8pm Mon-Sat, to 2pm Sun).

A bunch of trains run up the coast via Kollam and Ernakulam to Thrissur. Beyond Thrissur, many others branch off east via Palakkad (Palghat) to Tamil Nadu. You can travel to Coimbatore (sleeper/3AC/2AC Rs 194/514/728, 11 hours) for connections to Ooty.

BUSES FROM TRIVANDRUM (KSRTC BUS STAND)

Destination	Fare (Rs)	Duration (hr)	Frequency
Alleppey	90	3½	every 15min
Kanyakumari	40	2	6 daily
Kochi	124	5	every 15min
Kollam	42	1½	every 15min
Neyyar Dam	20	1½	every 40min
Thrissur	168	7½	every 30min
Varkala	32	1¼	hourly

Trains that travel up the coast as far as Mangalore in Karnataka include the daily *Parasuram Express* (2nd class/AC chair Rs 154/547, 16 hours, 6.35am) and *Malabar Express* (sleeper/3AC/2AC Rs 261/705/1000, 6.30pm).

There are frequent trains to Varkala (2nd class/AC chair Rs 24/142, around 45 minutes), Kollam (Rs 31/167, 1¼ hours) and Ernakulam (2nd class/3AC/2AC Rs 60/335/470, 4½ hours), with three passing through Alleppey (2nd class/AC chair Rs 47/180, three hours). There are daily services to Calicut (sleeper/3AC/2AC Rs 190/505/716, 11 hours) and Kanyakumari (Rs 131/213/291, two hours).

Getting Around

The **airport** (☎ 2501537) is 6km from the city and 15km from Kovalam; take local bus 14 from the East Fort bus stand (Rs 5). Prepaid taxi vouchers from the airport cost Rs 206 to the city and Rs 313 to Kovalam.

Autorickshaws patrol the streets and are the easiest transport around the city. Standard rates (assuming you can convince drivers to use the meter) are Rs 10 flagfall, then Rs 5 per kilometre, but all rules go out the window at night – 50% over the meter is fair. Agree on a fare beforehand. A cheap way to get around is to hop on and off any of the crowded buses plying the length of MG Rd (Rs 3).

AROUND TRIVANDRUM
Neyyar Dam Sanctuary

This **sanctuary** (☎ 2272182; Indian/foreigner Rs 10/100; 🕑 9am-4pm Tue-Sun), 32km north of Trivandrum, is set around an idyllic lake created by the 1964 Neyyar dam. The verdant forest lining the shoreline is home to gaurs, sambar deer, sloth, elephants, lion-tailed macaques and the occasional tiger.

The sanctuary office organises 40-minute **lion safaris** (Rs 250 per car, plus Rs 10 each for guide), though you're more likely to see monkeys than big cats. For improved spotting opportunities it's better to sneak around on a three-hour guided **trek** (Indian/foreigner Rs 400/800 per group of up to 10 people). There's a **Crocodile Protection Centre** (Indian/foreigner Rs 5/10) nearby and you can go for a dip in the lake's pristine waters (Rs 50). The **elephant rehabilitation centre** (Kappukadu; 🕑 9am-5pm), 7km up the road, offers 30-minute rides for Rs 100.

You can get here by frequent bus from Trivandrum (Rs 16, 1½ hours). A taxi costs

Rs 650 return (with two hours waiting time) and a very bumpy rickshaw costs half that.

Sivananda Yoga Vedanta Dhanwantari Ashram

Just before Neyyar Dam, this **ashram** (☎ /fax 0471-2273093; www.sivananda.org/ndam), established in 1978, is renowned for its hatha yoga courses. Courses run for a minimum of two weeks and cost Rs 650 per day for accommodation in a double room (Rs 450 in dormitories). Low season (April to October) rates are Rs 100 less. There's an exacting schedule (6am to 10pm) of yoga practice, meditation and chanting; and students rave about the food (included in the rates). Prior bookings are required. Month-long yoga-teacher training and Ayurvedic massage courses are also available – it's often best to go when one of these is running.

KOVALAM

☎ 0471

The frenzied beachfront development, bloated prices and indefatigable souvenir-sellers of Kovalam are almost worth putting up with for its lovely slice of sand and perfectly swaying palms. Permanently tattooed on European charter-group itineraries, these days there is little room left for the budgeteers that pioneered India's tourism industry. Nevertheless, Kovalam clings to some remnants of charm, particularly once you step off the main-beach drag into the rice paddies and palm groves that stretch far inland. It can be a good place to kick back for a few days, particularly during quieter times.

Orientation

Kovalam consists of two coves (Lighthouse Beach and Hawah Beach) separated from less-populated beaches north and south by rocky headlands. The town proper is at Kovalam Junction, about 1.5km from the beaches.

Information

Just about every shop and hotel wants to change your money, but ask around for the best rate. There are Federal Bank and ICICI ATMs at Kovalam Junction. There are also plenty of small, uniformly slow internet places charging Rs 30 to 50 per hour and lots of STD/ISD facilities around.

Bookshop (☻ 7am-11pm) A good range of books to rent/buy/exchange, underneath the German Bakery.

Post office (☻ 10am-1pm Mon-Sat)

Top Shop Cyber Cafe (per hr Rs 30; ☻ 9.30am-midnight) Off the beach up a steep hill, this is the only serious internet joint.

Tourist facilitation centre (☎ 2480085; ☻ 10am-5pm) Very helpful, inside the entrance to the Kovalam Beach Resort.

United Books (NUP Beach Rd; ☻ 9am-9pm) A kooky collection of books on Kerala, Indian spirituality and English-language trash lit.

Upasana Hospital (☎ 2480632; ☻ 9.30am-10pm Mon-Sat, 9.30m-12pm Sun) Has two English-speaking doctors who can take care of minor injuries.

Dangers & Annoyances

Women are likely to grow tired of the parade of male Indian daytrippers who stroll along the beach in the hope of glimpsing female flesh – it's more annoying than dangerous, however. Theft does occur, both from hotels and the beach. Lock the doors and windows and watch your possessions at the beach.

There are strong rips at both ends of Lighthouse Beach that carry away several swimmers every year. Swim only between the flags in the area patrolled by lifeguards.

Kovalam has frequent blackouts and the footpaths further back behind Lighthouse Beach are unlit, so carry a torch (flashlight) after dark.

Sleeping

Kovalam is bumper to bumper with hotels, though budget places cost more than usual and are fewer in number every year. Beachfront properties are the most expensive and have great sea views, but many of these cater to package groups. There are lots of better-value, smaller places tucked away in the labyrinth of paths behind the beach among palm groves and rice paddies.

Prices quoted are for the November to March high season; outside of these times expect huge discounts. During the Christmas and New Year rush savvy owners double their prices. Rooms offered are usually doubles, though single travellers often bargain a small discount.

BUDGET

Pink Flower (☎ 2383908; d Rs 250) It's worth seeking this place out, at least for the look of surprise on friendly Mr Sadanandan's face that you managed to find his little guesthouse. Tucked well away in the palms behind several hotels, this lovingly kept place has several humble, spotless rooms that may just be the cheapest digs in Kovalam.

Hotel Holiday Home (☎ 2486382; d Rs 300-800) This great place has spacious, if a bit dark, bungalow-style rooms facing each other over a small garden. There's a tangible chill-out vibe, helped along by its tranquil setting in a maze of paths behind the main beach. It's popular with long-term travellers.

Hotel Surya (☎ 2481012; kovsurya@yahoo.co.in; d downstairs/upstairs Rs 350/500, with AC Rs 1200; 🖫) This run-of-the-mill place has small, dark, downstairs rooms and bigger upstairs ones with TV, fridge and a communal balcony.

Dwaraka Lodge (☎ 2480411; d Rs 400) This concrete building is a little grimy, but inside you get clean sheets, a loo and a room with ocean views. What more do you want at this price?

Moon Valley Cottage (☎ 9847049643; sknairkovalam@yahoo.com; d from Rs 400, upstairs apt per week Rs 5000) There's nothing but swaying palms all the way back here, and this place makes the most of it with a thatched-roof, top-floor hangout where you can practically reach out and fondle the coconuts. The rooms are typically basic and clean.

Green Valley Cottages (☎ 2480636; indira_ravi@hotmail.com; s/d Rs 500/600) Also way back in the paddy fields, this serene spot is the place to revel in serious hush time. The rooms are ruthlessly austere, perfect for monks-in-training looking to escape pesky distractions like room furnishings.

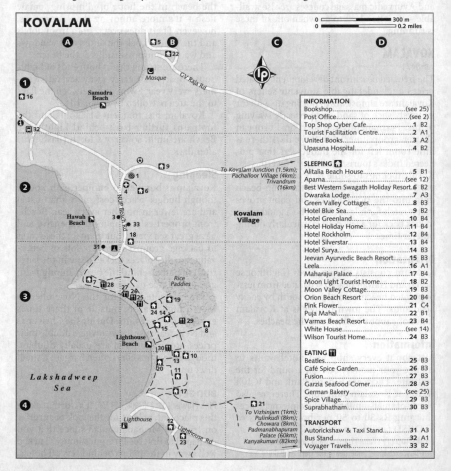

KOVALAM

0 _____ 300 m
0 _____ 0.2 miles

INFORMATION
Bookshop.....................................(see 25)
Post Office...................................(see 2)
Top Shop Cyber Cafe.........................1 B2
Tourist Facilitation Centre..................2 A1
United Books..................................3 A2
Upasana Hospital.............................4 B2

SLEEPING
Alitalia Beach House.........................5 B1
Aparna.......................................(see 12)
Best Western Swagath Holiday Resort.6 B2
Dwaraka Lodge................................7 A3
Green Valley Cottages........................8 B3
Hotel Blue Sea...............................9 B2
Hotel Greenland.............................10 B4
Hotel Holiday Home..........................11 B4
Hotel Rockholm..............................12 B4
Hotel Silverstar............................13 B4
Hotel Surya.................................14 B3
Jeevan Ayurvedic Beach Resort......15 B3
Leela.......................................16 A1
Maharaju Palace.............................17 B4
Moon Light Tourist Home.................18 B3
Moon Valley Cottage........................19 B3
Orion Beach Resort.........................20 B4
Pink Flower.................................21 C4
Puja Mahal.................................22 B1
Varmas Beach Resort........................23 B4
White House................................(see 14)
Wilson Tourist Home........................24 B3

EATING
Beatles.....................................25 B3
Café Spice Garden..........................26 B3
Fusion......................................27 B3
Garzia Seafood Corner......................28 A3
German Bakery..............................(see 25)
Spice Village...............................29 B3
Suprabhatham...............................30 B3

TRANSPORT
Autorickshaw & Taxi Stand.............31 A3
Bus Stand...................................32 A1
Voyager Travels.............................33 B2

Mosque
CV Raja Rd
Samudra Beach
Hawah Beach
Lakshadweep Sea
Rice Paddies
Kovalam Village
Lighthouse Beach
Lighthouse
To Kovalam Junction (1.5km); Pachalloor Village (4km); Trivandrum (16km)
To Vizhinjam (1km); Pulinkudi (8km); Chowara (8km); Padmanabhapuram Palace (60km); Kanyakumari (82km)
Lighthouse Rd

LUNGI OR DHOTI?

No, it's not a dress, or a kilt, or a frock the men in Kerala are all wearing, it's called a lungi. Made from cotton and patterned in different designs, men sporting lungis are a common sight in southern India, as well as in Bangladesh and Myanmar.

The lungi is traditionally a colourful piece of fabric, often sewn together to form a tube, and knotted around the waist. It comes in many colours and is worn mostly as casual dress. If the lungi is white, it's called *mundu*, which is worn at formal occasions like weddings. Men will fold their lungi or *mundu* in half while working or during hot weather (ie most of the time), though this is never done in formal situations. Interestingly, Muslim men wear their lungi tucked to the left, while Hindus and Christians wear theirs to the right.

Now before you think you're an expert on the subject, don't get this confused with the dhoti (called a *vesthi* in Kerala), which is a white, open rectangular piece of cloth wrapped around the waist and worn throughout India on official occasions. It is generally acceptable for foreigners to wear a lungi/*mundu*/*vesthi*/dhoti. Try it out – there's nothing like having a cool breeze running between your legs on a scorching Kerala day.

Wilson Tourist Home (☎ 9847363831; d Rs 500-900, with AC Rs 1300 incl breakfast; ✷ ☖) Wilson has large courtyard rooms set around a garden, with swing chairs on the balconies and Keralan darkwood touches. The cheaper rooms aren't much to write home about.

White House (☎ 3091963; whitehousekovalam@walla .com; d Rs 600) Next door to Hotel Surya, this is a clone offering 'same-same but different'.

MIDRANGE

Hotel Silverstar (☎ 2482983; www.silverstar-kovalam .com; d incl breakfast Rs 600-800) Fresh from a round of renovations, the spick-and-span rooms here have enough space to swing at least two cats. The hotel's set back in the heart of the village, which means it's quiet, but the large balconies don't have much of a view. Mosquito nets are provided and there's a roof terrace.

Hotel Greenland (☎ 2486442; hotelgreenlandin@yahoo .com; s/d Rs 600/800) The humungous refurbished rooms in this multilevel complex sport natural light and small kitchenettes for self-catering. It's a very friendly place that cooks up yummy food on request.

Maharaju Palace (☎ 2485320; www.maharajupal ace.in; d Rs 1100) More of a quiet retreat than a palace, this boutiquey place has far more character than anything else in its class. The few medium-sized rooms are decorated with artsy touches and have a large shared balcony sporting comfortable lounging chairs. There's a charming, secluded little garden out the front.

Aparna (☎ 2480950; s/d Rs 1250/1500) Immediately behind Hotel Rockholm, this is similar and has slightly better-kept rooms, but with less character.

Hotel Rockholm (☎ 2480306; www.rockholm .com; Lighthouse Rd; s/d Rs 1350/1500, with AC Rs 1850/2000; ✷ ☖) Overlooking crashing waves and near a secluded beach, this place clings to leftover '80s chic. AC rooms are slightly bigger and have romantic window seats.

Varmas Beach Resort (☎ 2480478; www.calanguete beach.com; Lighthouse Rd; d Rs 1500, with AC Rs 2500; ✷) This is the best-looking place in Kovalam, with a Kerala-style façade, rooms with wooden furniture and rattan sitting areas on the balconies. Throw in some exceptional views and access to an isolated beach and shazam – we have a winner!

Jeevan Ayurvedic Beach Resort (☎ 2480662; www .jeevanresort.com; d Rs 2100-3500; ✷ ☖) This resort has a great burnt-orange/blue colour scheme, decent-sized rooms with bathtubs and an alluring pool that practically plays footsies with the ocean.

Also recommended:

Orion Beach Resort (☎ 2480999; www.orion beachresort.com; d downstairs/upstairs Rs 700/1500) Your rupees pay for the balconies with awesome seaviews, but there's not much left over for anything more than rudimentary rooms.

Moon Light Tourist Home (☎ 2480375; moonlight@satyam.net.in; d Rs 1500, with AC Rs 1750; ✷ ☖) Friendly place with a dash of character and a few great balcony rooms. Nonguests can use the pool for Rs 150.

Hotel Blue Sea (☎ 2480555; www.hotelbluesea.net; r Rs 1000-2500, with AC Rs 3500; ✷ ☖) Something different: great rooms inside circular, three-storey towers with polished floors and round verandas.

KERALA

TOP END

Best Western Swagath Holiday Resort (☎ 2481148; www.swagathresorts.com; r Rs 1400-3600, with AC Rs 1800-4000, ste Rs 6000; ❄ ☒ ▯) Set in a cultivated, fairytale-perfect garden overlooking coconut palms. The rooms are big and well furnished, but with a whiff of the chain hotel about them. The place is kid-friendly, with a small playground and kiddie pool, and there is one ridiculously charming garden villa (Rs 2000), complete with white picket fence.

Leela (previously Kovalam Beach Resort; ☎ 2480101; www.theleela.com; s/d from US$295/320, ste from Rs 9000; ❄ ☒) This hotel is glamorously located around extensive grounds on the headland north of Hawah Beach. There are three (three!) swimming pools, an Ayurvedic centre, gym and all the luxury you'd expect for the price. Rooms aren't huge, but are sumptuously decorated with colourful textiles and Keralan artwork.

Eating

Open-air restaurants line the beach area displaying the catch of the day nightly – just pick a fish, settle on a price (per serve around Rs 150, tiger prawns over Rs 400) and decide how you want it prepared. Menus and prices are indistinguishable, so it's more about which ambience takes your fancy. Restaurant are open from around 7.30am to midnight.

Suprabhatham (meals Rs 45-75) This vegetarian place dishes up excellent, dirt-cheap and truly authentic Keralan cooking. It's secluded and intimate, out in the palm groves with an option to dine under the stars to a nightly orchestra of crickets.

Garzia Seafood Corner (mains Rs 50-200) Long-term visitors rate this lime-green place as a reasonable seafood option.

Spice Village (dishes Rs 50-220) A romantic lily-pond oasis, this place calls itself 'traditional Keralan', though the requisite pasta and Chinese dishes make their cameo appearances. Nevertheless, it does some excellent Keralan seafood, like its fish *pollichathu* (marinated fish wrapped in a banana leaf and grilled, Rs 130).

Beatles (mains Rs 60-180) Offering the usual Kovalam food suspects, what sets Beatles apart is the funky gnarled wood décor, with vines dripping from every corner. The jungle continues upstairs with awesome sea views to boot.

Café Spice Garden (mains Rs 60-300) Modishly decked out in brightly coloured cushions, there's a wide-ranging menu that includes a dangerously long list of cocktails. The seafood gets particularly good reports.

German Bakery (mains Rs 80-160) The most popular breakfast hang-out, this rooftop bakery has a winning range of breakfasts, strong coffee, fresh pastries, quiches and a varied selection of main courses, including stir-fried tofu (Rs 100) and seafood pizza (Rs 140). We love its version of the French breakfast: croissant, café au lait and a cigarette (Rs 60).

Fusion (mains Rs 90-200) This funky pad has an inventive menu where East meets West – and they even seem to get along pretty well. Its fusion dishes have Indian and continental choices colliding to form yummy new taste combinations.

Entertainment

During the high season, a shortened version of Kathakali is performed most nights somewhere – inquire about locations and times from the Tourist Facilitation Centre (p315). The intricate make-up process starts at around 5pm, the performance around 6.30pm. On weekends cultural programmes involving music and dance are sometimes performed on the beach – look out for signs.

Western videos are shown twice a night in some restaurants. Dedicated bars are thin on the ground, but beer is available in most of the restaurants (around Rs 80) and some serve cocktails (Rs 80 to 100) to an endless soundtrack of reggae, trance and classic rock.

Getting There & Away

BUS

There are local buses between Kovalam and Trivandrum every 20 minutes between 5.30am and 9.30pm (Rs 8, 30 minutes); catch them from the entrance to Leela resort. Buses to Ernakulum leave at 6am, 6.30am and 2.30pm (Rs 125, 5½ hours), stopping at Kallambalam (for Varkala, Rs 38, 1½ hours), Kollam (Rs 47, 2½ hours) and Alleppey (Rs 92, four hours).

TAXI & AUTORICKSHAW

A taxi between Trivandrum and Kovalam Beach is Rs 250. Autorickshaws should be around Rs 100, depending on the season. Prepaid taxis from Trivandrum airport to Lighthouse Beach cost Rs 313.

A great way to get around to remote beaches is on your own wheels. **Voyager Travels** (☎ 2485217) rents out scooters/Enfields for around Rs 450/550 per day – though its opening hours can be unpredictable.

AROUND KOVALAM
Samudra Beach
Samudra Beach, about 4km north of Kovalam by road, has a couple of resorts jostling for space with local fishing villages. Although more peaceful, the steep and rough beach is not as good for swimming.

Alitalia Beach House (☎ 2480042; s/d Rs 600/1000) The unique, octagonal rooms here have neat furniture, poster beds with mosquito nets, rooftop seating and windows on six sides – perfect for that fresh ocean breeze.

Puja Mahal (☎ 2481245; www.hotelpujamahal.com; s/d Rs 2000/2500; 🔀 🖳) This new hotel has made some rather curious interior-design decisions – concrete, jungle scenes anyone? The rooms are perfectly comfortable, but the star attraction remains the refreshing pool.

Pulinkudi & Chowara
Around 8km south of Kovalam are some luxury alternatives to Kovalam's crowded beaches.

Dr Franklin's Panchakarma Institute (☎ 2480870; www.dr-franklin.com; Chowara; s €15-50, d €20-65; 🖳) For those serious about Ayurvedic treatment, this is a reputable and less expensive alternative to some flashier resorts. Daily treatment costs €35, with a full meal plan an additional €16. Accommodation is clean and comfortable but not resort style (though sea-view rooms are available). Options include packages for spine problems and slimming, as well as general rejuvenation and stress relief.

Thapovan Heritage Home (☎ 2480453; www.thapovan.com; s/d Rs 3000/3850) This is the way to live the simple life (no pool, AC, TV) in the complete luxury of gorgeous Keralan teak cottages filled with handcrafted furniture. It's set among perfectly manicured grounds that roll down a hillside and overlook acres of swaying palm groves. Ayurvedic treatments available range from one-hour massages to 28-day treatment marathons. It's a few kilometres from the nearest beach.

Bethsaida Hermitage (☎ 2267554; www.bethsaida-c.org; Pulinkudi; r €55-80) A resort with a difference: this is a charitable organisation that helps support a nearby orphanage. As a bonus, it's also a luxurious beachside escape, with rolling, sculpted gardens, seductively slung hammocks, palms galore and shade in spades.

It offers a variety of cottages, from rainbow-painted, half-ovals scattered down a hillside, to spacious, cool Kerala-style huts.

Surya Samudra Beach Garden (☎ 2480413; www.surya samudra.com; Pulinkudi; r incl breakfast €120-350; 🔀 🖳) This luscious, small resort has six types of cottages, many of which are constructed from transplanted traditional Keralan houses, with spectacular carved ceilings and open-air bathrooms. There are private beaches, an infinity pool and Ayurvedic treatments – all on 21 acres of wonderfully cultivated grounds.

PADMANABHAPURAM PALACE
With several large lumberyards worth of carved ceilings and polished-teak beams, this **palace** (admission Rs 10, camera/video Rs 25/1200; 🕑 9am-5pm Tue-Sun) is considered the best example of traditional Keralan architecture today. Parts of it date back to 1550, though as the egos of successive rulers left their mark, it expanded into the magnificent conglomeration of 14 palaces it is today.

The largest wooden palace complex in Asia, it was once the seat of the rulers of Travancore, a princely state taking in parts of Tamil Nadu as well as Kerala. Fetchingly constructed of teak and granite, the exquisite interiors include rosewood ceilings carved in floral patterns, Chinese-influenced screens, and floors finished to a high-black polish. Getting one of the English-speaking guides that hang around inside the gate is worthwhile (around Rs 50 to 100).

Padmanabhapuram is around 60km southeast of Kovalam. Catch a local bus from Kovalam (or Trivandrum) to Kanyakumari and get off at Thuckalay, from where it's a short autorickshaw ride or 15-minute walk. Alternatively, take one of the tours organised by the KTDC (see p312), or hire a taxi (about Rs 1000 return).

VARKALA
☎ 0470 / pop 42,273
The sensational cliffs of Varkala might just be its saving grace, holding back the kind of development that has left nearby Kovalam gasping for air. With a strand of golden beach nuzzling the cliff edge, and more Bob Marley music that you can poke a dreadlocked backpacker at, the vibe here remains faithfully laid-back. Varkala's beaches are protected by soaring bluffs, while all the on-land action is perched precariously, but beautifully, along

the crumbling precipice above. Sure, the number of new hotels is creeping up each year, but it's still a great place to while away the days, even weeks, with tonnes of sleeping options and some excellent dining spots (with dramatic, cliffside sunsets on the house).

Orientation & Information

The main beach is accessed from either Beach Rd, or by several steep stairways cut into the north cliff. The town and the train station are about 2km from the beach. There's a State Bank of India ATM in Varkala town and there are plenty of slow internet places along the clifftop (around Rs 40 per hour) – save your emails often as power cuts are not uncommon.

Bureau de Change (☎ 2606623; Temple Junction; ☼ 9am-7pm) Cashes travellers cheques, does credit-card cash advances, and is helpful for bus and train times.

Police aid post (☼ Nov-Feb) At the helipad.

Post office (☼ 10am-2pm Mon-Sat) North of Temple Junction.

Dangers & Annoyances

The beaches at Varkala have very strong currents; even experienced swimmers have been swept away. This is one of the most dangerous beaches in Kerala, so be careful and swim between the flags or ask the lifeguards for the best place to swim.

Indian male gawkers are starting to discover the bikini-clad attractions at Varkala. However, with police patrolling beaches to keep male starers a-walkin' and the hawkers at bay, there had been no serious incidents when we were there. It still pays to dress sensitively, especially if you're going into Varkala town.

It seems like every man and his dog has an Ayurvedic-related product to sell, from treatments, to massage, to Ayurvedic tea and even Ayurvedic toilets. Most people aren't qualified practitioners – it's best to ask for recommendations before you go get herbalised (see opposite). Women should always be treated by a female practitioner.

Sights & Activities

Varkala is a temple town, and **Janardhana Temple** is the main event – its technicolour Hindu spectacle sits hovering above Beach Rd. It's closed to non-Hindus, but you may be invited into the temple grounds where there is a huge

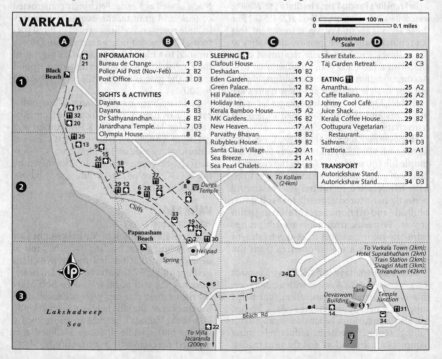

VARKALA

0 —————— 100 m
0 —————— 0.1 miles
Approximate Scale

INFORMATION	
Bureau de Change	1 D3
Police Aid Post (Nov-Feb)	2 B2
Post Office	3 D3

SIGHTS & ACTIVITIES	
Dayana	4 C3
Dayana	5 B3
Dr Sathyanandhan	6 B2
Janardhana Temple	7 D3
Olympia House	8 B2

SLEEPING	
Clafouti House	9 A2
Deshadan	10 B2
Eden Garden	11 C3
Green Palace	12 B2
Hill Palace	13 A2
Holiday Inn	14 D3
Kerala Bamboo House	15 A2
MK Gardens	16 B2
New Heaven	17 A1
Parvathy Bhavan	18 B2
Rubybleu House	19 B2
Santa Claus Village	20 A1
Sea Breeze	21 A1
Sea Pearl Chalets	22 B3

Silver Estate	23 B2
Taj Garden Retreat	24 C3

EATING	
Amantha	25 A2
Caffe Italiano	26 A2
Johnny Cool Café	27 B2
Juice Shack	28 B2
Kerala Coffee House	29 B2
Oottupura Vegetarian Restaurant	30 B2
Sathram	31 D3
Trattoria	32 A1

TRANSPORT	
Autorickshaw Stand	33 B2
Autorickshaw Stand	34 D3

To Kollam (24km)

Black Beach

Durga Temple

Cliffs

Papanasham Beach

Spring

Helipad

Lakshadweep Sea

Beach Rd

To Villa Jacaranda (200m)

Devaswom Building

Tank

Temple Junction

To Varkala Town (2km); Hotel Suprabhatham (2km); Train Station (2km); Sivagiri Mutt (3km); Trivandrum (42km)

banyan tree and shrines to Ayyappan, Hanuman and other Hindu deities.

Sivagiri Mutt (☎ 2602807; www.sivagiri.org) is the headquarters of the Sree Narayana Dharma Sanghom Trust, the ashram devoted to Sree Narayana Guru (1855–1928), Kerala's most prominent guru. This is a popular pilgrimage site and the swami is happy to talk to visitors. If you're serious about studying meditation and philosophy here, it's possible to stay (rooms Rs 200 to 250).

Practically everyone offers Ayurveda, yoga or massage (see also Dangers & Annoyances, opposite). A recommended place for Ayurvedic beauty treatments is **Dayana** (☎ 2609464; manicure & pedicure Rs 250, facials Rs 400-1000; ☼ 9am-7pm), which has a shack on the beach and a shop on Beach Rd (women only). Mr Omanakuttan at **Olympia House** (☎ 3291783) is a qualified massage instructor, in both Ayurveda and other schools, and has an excellent reputation. His wife sees female clients. **Eden Garden** (☎ 2603910; www.eden-garden.net), a popular Ayurvedic resort, offers single treatments and packages; see p322 for accommodation details. Readers also have good things to say about **Dr Sathyanandhan** (☎ 2602950; smAyurveda@hotmail.com), near Seaview. Single massage treatments cost between Rs 500 and Rs 900, depending on the type.

For tabla (traditional drum) lessons contact **Mr Venu** (☎ 9895473304), who has been playing and teaching for 15 years and will come to your residence for banging instructions (Rs 250 to 300 per hour).

Boogie boards can be rented from places along the beach for Rs 100, but be wary of very strong currents (see Dangers & Annoyances, opposite).

Sleeping

Most places to stay are along the north cliff; some open only for the tourist onslaught in November. The quieter places are either inland or at the far northern end of the cliff; although the number of guesthouses is inexorably increasing here, too. Prices given are average high-season (November to March) rates, which fluctuate wildly with the ebb and flow of demand – expect astronomical prices around the Christmas holidays and bargains in the off season.

The commission racket is alive and well – make sure that your rickshaw takes you to the place you've asked for.

BUDGET

Rubybleu House (☎ 9995040495; www.rubybleuhouse.com; dm Rs 75, s/d Rs 200/300) This gem of a guesthouse has basic, colourful rooms in a rambling house deep among the palm groves. There's a small jungle/garden with rare plants from around the world and the friendly hippy vibe is administered by the very informative Leon and his partner Katalin (who's a qualified reiki instructor). They have an awesome 6000-CD music collection and an eclectic Buddhist/rock-and-roll library. Long-termers love this place.

AYURVEDA

With its roots in Sanskrit, the word Ayurveda is derived from *ayu* (life) and *veda* (knowledge); it is the knowledge or science of life. Principles of Ayurvedic medicine were first documented in the Vedas some 2000 years ago, but it may even have been practised centuries earlier.

Ayurveda sees the world as having an intrinsic order and balance. It argues that we possess three *doshas* (humours): *vata* (wind or air); *pitta* (fire); and *kapha* (water/earth). Known together as the *tridoshas*, deficiency or excess in any of them can result in disease – an excess of *vata* may result in dizziness and debility; an increase in *pitta* may lead to fever, inflammation and infection. *Kapha* is essential for hydration.

Ayurvedic treatment aims to restore the balance, and hence good health, principally through two methods: *panchakarma* (internal purification) and massage. The herbs used for both grow in abundance in Kerala's moist climate, and every village has its own Ayurvedic pharmacy.

Having an occasional Ayurvedic massage, something offered at tourist resorts all over Kerala, is relaxing, but you have to go in for the long haul to reap any real benefits – usually 15 days or longer. Expect a thorough examination followed by an appropriate Ayurvedic diet, exercises and a range of treatments, as well as regular massages.

If you want to learn more, pick up a copy of *Ayurveda: Life, Health & Longevity* by Dr Robert E Svoboda, or check out www.ayur.com.

Silver Estate (☎ 9387755309; mohdrafi20@rediffmail.com; s/d Rs 250/300) Silver Estate gets rave reviews for the friendliness of its staff. It has typically basic rooms with hammocks out the front, and is back far enough from the beach to be blissfully quiet. There's a child-care centre run from here during the high season.

MK Gardens (☎ 2603298; mkgarden_2005@yahoo.com; r Rs 250-300) In a massive house well off Varkala's 'Vegas strip,' the rooms are plain but enormous, with palm-top views that come together to spell 'good budget value'.

New Heaven (☎ 2156338; newheavenbeachresort@yahoo.com; r Rs 500-700) Just back from the northern cliffs, New Heaven has easy access to Black Beach and great top-floor views. Rooms are tidy and have big, blue bathrooms.

Kerala Bamboo House (☎ 9895270993; www.keralabamboohouse.com; huts Rs 700-800) For a slightly upmarket bamboo-hut experience, this wonderful place has dozens of pretty, Balinese-style huts with handsome interiors of antique wood and painted bamboo. Cooking classes are run nightly (Rs 500), there are culture shows and yoga classes in the Keralan-styled pavilion.

Also recommended:

Parvathy Bhavan (☎ 2602596; d Rs 300-400) An elementary homestay with bare, tiled rooms popular with the ultra-budget brigade.

Holiday Inn (r Rs 300-400) Clean, plain rooms near the tank with – wait for it – holy water straight from the tap!

MIDRANGE

Eden Garden (☎ 2603910; www.eden-garden.net; d Rs 800-1200) Delightfully situated overlooking silent paddy fields, this place has a few small, orderly and well-decorated double rooms set around a lush lilypond. There are dining gazebos on stilts over the pools and an Ayurvedic resort (see above). You'll need to lather yourself in mosquito repellent by night.

Santa Claus Village (☎ 9249121464; www.santaclausvillageresort.com; s Rs 900-1700, d Rs 1400-1900, s/d with AC Rs 2000/2200; 🅿 🕮) Even though the cheesy name is only funny once a year, this place is surprisingly well designed, with traditional Keralan-themed buildings, nice bits of furniture and lots of teak-wood flair. The two deluxe rooms come with huge bay windows facing out to sea.

Green Palace (☎ 2610055; greenpalace@eth.net; s/d from Rs 1000/1200, with AC Rs 2400/3000; 🅿) The Palace's rooms, while big and orderly, are nondescript and don't really follow through on the façade's promises of luxury. There's a trim lawn leading down to the cliff edge, illuminated at night by a brash runway of coloured fairylights.

Sea Pearl Chalets (☎ 2605875; seapearlvarkala@hotmail.com; d Rs 1250) Precariously dangling off the southern cliffs of Varkala, these small but charismatic concrete wigwams boast unbeatable views. They're definitely worth checking out before they tumble into the ocean.

Sea Breeze (☎ 2603257; www.seabreezevarkala.com; r Rs 1500, with AC Rs 2500; 🕮) The large and orderly rooms in this hefty building all offer great sea views and share a large veranda – perfect for nightly sunset adulation. The friendly owners have their restaurant under a beachside coconut grove.

Also recommended:

Clafouti House (☎ 2601414; www.clafouti.com; d Rs 700-900) Intimate, homey atmosphere, with bright double rooms straight out of the '80s.

Hill Palace (☎ 2610142; www.hillpalace.com; d Rs 800) Chintzy but always clean and freshly painted, with balconies facing the ocean.

Deshadan (☎ 3204242; www.deshadan.com; r incl breakfast Rs 3000; 🕮 🕮) In a notable, burnt-red complex with rooms decorated in themes from regions of India.

TOP END

Villa Jacaranda (☎ 2610296; www.villa-jacaranda.biz; d Rs 3300-4400) The ultimate in understated luxury, this romantic retreat has several huge, bright, beautiful rooms with balconies, individually decorated with a chic blend of modern and period touches. Front rooms have sea views; the roof-terrace room is really impressive.

Taj Garden Retreat (☎ 2603000; www.tajhotels.com; r US$120-145; 🕮 🖳 🍽) Luxury, '80s-style: this opulent but slightly dated resort has big rooms, an Ayurvedic centre, bar and health club. The Sunday lunch buffet (12.30pm to 3pm; Rs 400) is deservedly popular – particularly since you get to use the pool. Cocktails all round, then!

Eating

Restaurants in Varkala are open from around 7.30am to midnight and offer pretty much the same mix of Indian, Asian and Western fare. It's best to join in the nightly Varkala cliff-side saunter till you find a place that suits your mood.

Oottupura Vegetarian Restaurant (mains from Rs 30) Bucking the trend and serving only veggie options, this great budget restaurant has a respectable range of dishes, including breakfast *puttu* (wheat and coconut flour with milk, bananas and honey, Rs 35).

Juice Shack (juices Rs 50, snacks Rs 30-100; ☻7am-7.30pm) A funky little health-juice bar that doubles as Varkala's own intranet, where long-termers come to gossip and share the latest news the old way.

Kerala Coffee House (breakfast/mains around Rs 50/100) With oodles of atmosphere and top service, this perennially popular hang-out has tableclothed dining under the swaying palms (221 days since the last coconut-related injury at time of writing). It serves cocktails (around Rs 70) and has particularly tasty pizzas (Rs 70 to 90), all served to a dancy, reggae soundtrack.

Johnny Cool Café (meals Rs 60-150) Run by dreadlocked hipster Manu, this place serves superb Western and Indian food – but be warned, it may take a while to come out. Quite a while if Manu has to run down to the market to grab ingredients. It's always worth the wait, however; there's no set menu so just turn up and ask what's going.

Trattoria (meals Rs 70-150) This friendly and efficient Tibetan-managed place does some of the most consistently well-prepared Western food in town (lasagne in particular, Rs 80 to 105). Meals from the other directions of the compass ain't bad either.

Also recommended:

Sathram (Temple Junction; meals Rs 20-30) Eat with the autorickshaw drivers at this no-frills Keralan diner.

Caffe Italiano (meals Rs 40-200) Leafy, vine-side dining.

Amantha (thalis Rs 30, meals Rs 50-100) A tiny, barely standing family-run hut.

Culinary adventurers should ask around town about certain Varkalan households that prepare outstanding home-cooked meals on request.

Drinking

Although most of the places along the cliff aren't licensed, most will serve beer (around Rs 70), sometimes in a discreet teapot and with a watchful eye for patrolling police.

Entertainment

Kathakali performances are organised during December and January; look out for signs advertising location and times.

Getting There & Away

There are frequent trains to Trivandrum (2nd class/AC chair Rs 24/142, 45 minutes) and Kollam (Rs 20/142, 35 minutes), and three a day to Alleppey (Rs 38/155, two hours). It's easy to get to Kollam in time for the morning backwater boat to Alleppey (see the boxed text, p328). From Temple Junction, four daily buses go to/from Trivandrum (Rs 36, 1½ hours) and one express bus goes to Kollam at 11.15am (Rs 34, one hour). Many slower buses also head to Kollam, or alternatively you can catch a bus or autorickshaw to the highway junction 7km away for more frequent express buses rumbling north.

Getting Around

An autorickshaw between the train station and the beach is Rs 30 to 40, a taxi about Rs 60. Beware that many drivers will try to shoehorn you into the hotel that pays them the highest commission – it's often best to be dropped off at the Helipad and walk to your chosen hotel. Many places along the cliff-top rent Enfields/scooters for Rs 350/250 per day.

KOLLAM (QUILON)

☎ 0474 / pop 379,975

Kollam is a tranquil trading town and the secret southern approach to Kerala's backwaters. One of the oldest ports in the Arabian Sea, it was once a major commerce hub that saw Roman, Arab, Chinese and later Portuguese, Dutch and British traders jostle ships into port, eager to get their hands on spices and the region's valuable cashew crops. The town's shady streets and antediluvian market are worth a wander, and the calm waterways of the surrounding Ashtamudi Lake are still fringed with coconut palms, cashew plantations and traditional villages.

Information

There are a couple of ATMs around town.

Cyber Zone (☎ 2766566; per hr Rs 15; ☻ 9.30am-9.30pm) The fastest of the numerous internet cafés at the Bishop Jerome Nagar Complex.

DTPC information centre (☎ 2745625; contact@dtpckollam.com; ☻ 8.30am-7pm) Very helpful; near the KSRTC bus stand.

Post office (☎ 2746607)

UAE Exchange (☎ 2751240; Tourist Bungalow Rd; ☻ 9.30am-5.30pm Mon-Sat, to 1pm Sun)

Sights

The lively **Shrine of Our Lady of Velankanni** is dedicated to a patron saint from neighbouring Tamil Nadu. There aren't many places in the

KERALA

world you can see sari-clad Christian iconography worshipped with such Hindu exuberance. On the next street south, the **Mukkada Bazaar** has been a commercial hub of activity for hundreds of years. Here, spice merchants sit atop bags of bright powders, porters ferry goods deftly on their heads and shop fronts are draped in mysterious herbs (many used for Ayurvedic treatments).

At **Kollam Beach** you can stroll past picturesque Keralan fishing hamlets, where fishermen mend nets and dozens of fishing boats colour the shoreline. There's a rowdy **fish market** here, where customers and fisherfolk alike pontificate on the value of the catch of the day – get there early in the morning. The beach is 2km south of town, a Rs 20 rickshaw ride away.

The **Police Museum** (admission Rs 3; 9am-6pm) has a random collection of old uniforms, dusty muskets, and a macabre room displaying photographs of violent-crime victims. It's not for everyone, but the 100-year-old banyan tree sprouting from a well out the back is impressive, and 100% gore-free.

The **Pooram festival** (April) is held in Kollam annually, while the **Ashtamudi Craft and**

Art festival (December/January) every two years.

Activities

Janakanthi Pancharkarma Centre (2763014; Vaidyasala Nagar, Asraman North; s/d Rs 400/500, with AC Rs 500/750) is a lakeside Ayurvedic resort, 5km from Kollam, popular for its seven- to 21-day treatment packages (seven-day packages start from around Rs 15,000). You can also just visit for a rejuvenation massage and herbal steam bath (Rs 500). A return boat trip from the jetty in Kollam should cost around Rs 300.

Tours

Canoe-boat tours (per person Rs 300; 9am & 2pm) through the canals of Munroe Island and across Ashtamudi Lake are organised by the DTPC. On these excellent excursions (with knowledgeable guides) you can observe daily life in this isolated village area, and see *kettuvallam* (rice barge) construction, toddy (palm beer) tapping, coir-making (coconut fibre), prawn and fish farming, and do some bird-watching and perhaps a quick spice-garden tour.

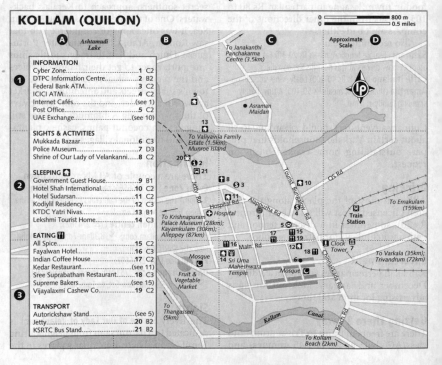

KOLLAM (QUILON)

INFORMATION	
Cyber Zone	1 C2
DTPC Information Centre	2 B2
Federal Bank ATM	3 C2
ICICI ATM	4 C2
Internet Cafés	(see 1)
Post Office	5 C2
UAE Exchange	(see 10)

SIGHTS & ACTIVITIES	
Mukkada Bazaar	6 C3
Police Museum	7 D3
Shrine of Our Lady of Velankanni	8 C2

SLEEPING	
Government Guest House	9 B1
Hotel Shah International	10 C2
Hotel Sudarsan	11 C2
Kodiylil Residency	12 C3
KTDC Yatri Nivas	13 B1
Lekshmi Tourist Home	14 C3

EATING	
All Spice	15 C2
Fayalwan Hotel	16 C3
Indian Coffee House	17 C2
Kedar Restaurant	(see 11)
Sree Suprabatham Restaurant	18 C3
Supreme Bakers	(see 15)
Vijayalaxmi Cashew Co	19 C2

TRANSPORT	
Autorickshaw Stand	(see 5)
Jetty	20 B2
KSRTC Bus Stand	21 B2

Sleeping

BUDGET

The DTPC office keeps a list of **homestays** (d Rs 200-500) in and around Kollam.

Lekshmi Tourist Home (☎ 2741067; Main Rd; s/d Rs 130/200) This primitive pilgrims' lodge may have stained walls and musty rooms, but at least the sheets are clean and there's plenty of light.

Government Guest House (☎ 2743620; d without/ with AC Rs 220/240; ✷) Wafting in the remnants of faded grandeur, this Raj relic (3km north of the centre on Ashtamudi Lake) has immense, crumbling rooms with high ceilings and wooden floors. They're a bargain but isolated.

Kodiylil Residency (☎ 9847913832; Main Rd; s/d Rs 300/400, s/d with AC Rs 500/800; ✷) This new hotel brings a desperately needed touch of class to the budget category. Bright red walls are lit by mood lighting, rooms come in shades of lime, and have stylishly modern furniture and TVs. Shame about the complete lack of windows.

MIDRANGE

KTDC Yatri Nivas (☎ 2745538; s Rs 275-330, d Rs 330-500) Though the rooms are run-down and slightly dysfunctional, they're sanitary and all have balconies overlooking the backwaters. A fun taxi-boat ride across the lake is Rs 35.

Hotel Sudarsan (☎ 2744322; Alappuzha Rd; www .hotelsudarsan.com; s Rs 450, s/d with AC from Rs 750/850; ✷) Welcoming but overpriced, all the non-AC rooms in the front wing are spacious but very noisy. The executive rooms at the back (s/d Rs 1400/1650) are smaller and quieter.

Hotel Shah International (☎ 2742362; Tourist Bungalow Rd; r Rs 400-450, d with AC Rs 800-1300; ✷) With a once funky, but now dated, mirrored-ceiling approach to design, this is a slightly shabby and institutional hotel. The big, bright executive rooms (Rs 1300) with AC and bathtub are OK value.

Valiyavila Family Estate (☎ 9847132449; www .kollamlakeviewresort.com; Panamukkom; s/d Rs 1300/1500, deluxe with AC Rs 2300/2500; ✷) The pick of Kovalam's sleeping bunch, this estate crowns a breezy peninsula surrounded by leisurely backwaters on three sides. The enormous rooms have Jacuzzis and lots of windows to enjoy the views, the morning breeze and the extraordinary sight of pert bosoms (belonging to their misshapen sculpture – the 'Goddess of Light'). Call ahead for a boat pick-up or catch one of the nine daily public ferries from Kovalam (Rs 3).

Eating

Fayalwan Hotel (Main Rd; meals Rs 10-40) This is a real Indian working-man's diner, packed to the rafters come lunchtime. There are concrete booths and long benches for sitting and tucking in – try its mutton biryani (Rs 40).

Sree Suprabatham Restaurant (Chinnakkada Rd; meals Rs 20-30) This veg restaurant is popular with local families and there's a remarkable spread of breakfast dishes, especially dosas (from Rs 15).

All Spice (Musaliar Bldgs; mains Rs 30-110; ✷ lunch & dinner) Desperate for a Western fast-food fix? Burgers (Rs 29 to 55), pizza (Rs 50 to 90), hot dogs (Rs 35) and excellent tandoori items can be followed up with ice-cream desserts – all served in a disconcertingly shiny cafeteria-style atmosphere.

Kedar Restaurant (Alappuzha Rd; mains Rs 35-130) The restaurant at Hotel Sudarsan does good Indian food; the tangy fish curry (Rs 60) is the pick of the bunch.

Also recommended:

Supreme Bakers (Musaliar Bldgs; ✷ 9am-8pm) Selection of Indian and Western cakes and sweets.

Indian Coffee House (Main Rd) Reliable for a decent breakfast and strong coffee.

Vijayalaxmi Cashew Co (Main Rd; ✷ 9.30am-8pm) A major exporter of Kollam's famous cashews; quality nuts are around Rs 250 per 500g.

Getting There & Away

BOAT

See the boxed text, p328, for information on cruises to Alleppey. There are public ferry services across Ashtamudi Lake to Guhanandapuram (one hour) and Perumon (two hours), leaving from the jetty. Fares are around Rs 10 return.

BUS

Kollam is situated on the well-serviced Trivandrum–Kollam–Alleppey–Ernakulam bus route, with superfast/superexpress (sic) buses going every 10 or 20 minutes to Trivandrum (Rs 42, 1½ hours), Alleppey (Rs 52, two hours) and Kochi (Rs 84, 3½ hours). Buses depart from the KSRTC Bus Stand.

TRAIN

There are frequent trains to Ernakulam (2nd class/AC chair Rs 46/177, 3½ hours, 12 daily) and Trivandrum (Rs 31/167, 1¼ hours, nine daily), as well as four daily trains to Alleppey (Rs 33/142, 1½ hours).

Getting Around

Most autorickshaw trips should cost around Rs 20, but drivers will ask for more at night. There's a prepaid stand near Supreme Bakers.

AROUND KOLLAM
Krishnapuram Palace Museum

Two kilometres south of Kayamkulam (between Kollam and Alleppey), this restored palace (☎ 2441133; admission Rs 3; ⏰ 10am-1pm & 2-5pm Tue-Sun) is a grand example of Keralan architecture. Now a museum, the two-storey palace houses paintings, antique furniture and sculptures. Its renowned 3m-high mural depicts the Gajendra Moksha, or the liberation of Gajendra, the chief of the elephants, as told in the Mahabharata. The **Bharni Utsavam Festival** is held at the nearby Chettikulangara Bhaghavathy Temple in February/March.

Buses (Rs 22) leave Kollam every few minutes for Kayamkulam. Get off at the bus stand near the temple gate, 2km before Kayamkulam.

ALAPPUZHA (ALLEPPEY)

☎ 0477 / pop 282,727

A slice of Venice in the heart of Kerala, Alleppey is a mix of shady streets set around a grid of canals spilling into the vast watery highways of the region. The most popular place to organise a foray into the backwaters, this is the base for most of the houseboat-action in Kerala (and even more houseboat agents), and home to the famous Nehru Trophy Snake Boat Race. It's worth stopping in Alleppey to soak in some tropical village life before making a beeline for the backwaters.

Orientation

The bus stand and boat jetty are close to each other; the hotels are spread far and wide. The train station is 4km southwest of the town centre. The beach is about 2km west of the city centre; it's a nice, shaded walk, but there's no shelter at the beach itself and swimming is dangerous.

Information

There are several ATMs around town.

Danys Bookshop (☎ 2237828; Hotel Royale Park; ⏰ 10am-1pm & 5.30-9pm) Has a small but good-quality selection of books about India, and some English fiction.

DTPC Tourist Reception Centre (☎ 2253308; www .alappuzhatourism.com; ⏰ 8.30am-6pm) Fairly helpful office.

Mailbox (☎ 2339994; Boat Jetty Rd; per hr Rs 40; ⏰ 8.30am-11.30pm) Internet access.

National Cyber Park (☎ 2238688; YMCA Compound; per hr Rs 30; ⏰ 10am-10pm Mon-Sat) Internet access.

Tourist Police (☎ 2251161; ⏰ 24hr)

UAE Exchange (☎ 1800 4259585; cnr Cullan & Mullackal Rds; ⏰ 9.30am-6pm Mon-Sat, to 1pm Sun) Changes cash and travellers cheques.

Tours

Any of the dozens of travel agencies in town can arrange canoe-boat tours of the backwaters; see also the boxed text, p328.

The DTPC organises motor-boat rental, with several different itineraries possible in the high season (November to March). Boats cost Rs 25 per hour for up to 10 people.

Sleeping

Look out for guesthouse and heritage home accommodation in Alleppey; it's better value and a much nicer choice than the profoundly uninspiring hotels.

There are several relaxed options to stay on the backwaters a few kilometres north of Alleppey; all arrange pick-ups and drop offs from town.

BUDGET

St George Lodgings (☎ 2251620; CCNB Rd; s/d Rs 106/190, with shared bathroom Rs 75/135) It's amazing what a fresh lick of yellow paint can do to a place – this once-grimy cheapie is now eminently sleepable. There are loads of different rooms, but all are very basic. The communal bathrooms have quite a waft.

Vrindavanam Heritage Home (☎ 2263321; Zacharia Bazaar; r Rs 250-550) Definitely the best budget deal around. The better rooms are in a beautifully preserved, 180-year-old home set around a small, luxuriant courtyard garden. The cheaper rooms are in a separate building and are inlaid with bamboo and thatch, have pretty, frilly touches and bright, hand-painted art. It's walking distance to the beach.

Palmy Residency (☎ 2235938; www.geocities.com /palmyresorts; r Rs 300-500) Run by the same superfriendly folk at Palmy Resort, this new little place is very central and has four lovely, quiet rooms of varying size – all with mosquito netting and flyscreens and free bicycles. It's just north of the footbridge.

Gowri Residence (☎ 2236371; www.gowriresidence .com; d from Rs 400, with AC Rs 900; 🖳) A friendly heritage home with a selection of spacious and

ALAPPUZHA (ALLEPPEY)

INFORMATION
Canara Bank	1 B2
Danys Bookshop	(see 18)
DTPC Tourist Reception Centre	2 B2
Federal Bank ATM	(see 18)
Mailbox	3 A2
National Cyber Park	4 A1
State Bank ATM	5 A2
Tourist Police	(see 2)
UAE Exchange	6 B3
UTI Bank ATM	7 B3

SLEEPING
Hotel Raiban	8 A5
Palmy Residency	9 B1
St George Lodgings	10 B4
Springs Inn	11 B1

EATING
Hot Kitchen	12 B3
Hotel Aryas	13 A5
Indian Coffee House	14 A5
Indian Coffee House	15 B2
Kream Korner	16 A3
Kream Korner	17 B4
Royal Park Hotel	18 A2
Sree Durga Bhavan Udipi Hotel	19 A3

TRANSPORT
Bus Stand	20 B2
Jetty	21 B2

Springs Inn (☎ 9847750000; Punnamada Rd; r Rs 500) Three nifty little rooms in a comely Keralan-style house.

MIDRANGE & TOP END

Johnson's (☎ 2245825; www.johnsonskerala.com; d Rs 650) In a garishly painted mansion filled with funky furniture, this place has big and bright rooms with lots of greenery and enormous balconies. The owners have unusual expansion plans that involve bathtubs on the balconies, as well as cheaper rooms (Rs 250 to 400) out the back. It's not signposted.

Sona (☎ 2235211; www.sonahome.com; Shornur Canal Rd; d Rs 700) Run by a gracious family, this heritage home has cool, spacious rooms with lots of character, high rosewood ceilings, four-poster beds with nets and secluded verandas overlooking a well-kept garden. It's 1km north of town.

Palmy Lake Resort (☎ 2235938; www.geocities.com /palmyresorts; Punnamada Rd East; cottages Rs 750) With four handsome cottages, two in bamboo and two in concrete, there's loads of charm and peace draped over this small homestay, 3.5km north of Alleppey. It's set among palm groves near the backwaters and the wonderful owners provide meals on request.

Palm Grove Lake Resort (☎ 2235004; palmgrove _lr@yahoo.com; Punnamada; cottages d Rs 1200-1500) On

comfortable rooms with mosquito nets. The owners will pick you up and drop you off in town any time, there are free bicycles, and good food is served in gazebos in the garden or on your veranda.

Also recommended:

Hotel Raiban (☎ 2251930; s/d Rs 200/300, d with AC Rs 800;) Basic, clean rooms in an institutional setting.

KERALA

THE BACKWATERS

The undisputed main attraction of a trip to Kerala is travelling through the 900km network of waterways that fringe the coast and trickle far inland. Long before the advent of roads these waterways were the slippery highways of Kerala, and many villagers today still use paddle-power as transport. Trips through the backwaters cross shallow, palm-fringed lakes studded with cantilevered Chinese fishing nets, and travel along narrow, shady canals where coir (co-conut fibre), copra (dried coconut meat) and cashews are loaded onto boats. Along the way are small villages with mosques, churches, temples and schools, villagers going about their daily chores and tiny settlements where people live on narrow spits of reclaimed land only a few metres wide.

Kerala Tourism (www.keralatourism.org) produces a *Backwater Map*.

Tourist Cruises

The popular cruise between Kollam and Alleppey (adult/student Rs 300/250) departs at 10.30am and arrives at 6.30pm, operating daily from August to March and every second day at other times. Many hotels in Kollam and Alleppey take bookings for one or other of these services; some offer cheaper rates but you'll end up paying the difference on board.

Generally, there are two stops: a 1pm lunch stop (be aware that you'll pay extra for every element over the standard meal!) and a brief afternoon chai stop. The crew has an ice box full of fruit, soft drinks and beer to sell. Bring sunscreen and a hat.

It's a scenic and leisurely way to get between the two towns, but as a backwater experience the cruise is limited by the fact that the boat travels along the major highways of the canal sys-tem and you won't see much of the close-up village life that makes the backwaters so magical. Some travellers have reported becoming bored with the eight-hour trip.

Another option is to take the trip halfway (Rs 150) and get off at the **Matha Amrithanan-damayi Mission** (☎ 0476-2896399; www.amritapuri.org; Amrithapuri), the ashram of Matha Amrith-anandamayi. One of India's very few female gurus, Amrithanandamayi is known as Amma (Mother) and is called 'The Hugging Mother' because of the *darshan* (blessing) she practises, often hugging thousands of people in marathon all-night sessions. The ashram runs official tours at 5pm each day, or you may be able to get someone to show you around when you arrive off the boat. It's a huge complex, with around 2000 people living here permanently – monks and nuns, students, Indian families and Westerners. There's food available, Ayurvedic treatments, yoga and meditation, as well as souvenirs from the cult of Amma, everything from books to postcards of her toes. Amma travels around for much of the year, so you might be out of luck if you're after a cuddle.

Visitors should dress conservatively and there is a strict code of behaviour. You can stay at the ashram for Rs 150 per day (including simple vegetarian meals) and pick up an onward or return cruise a day or two later. Alternatively, you can take a (free) ferry to the other side of the canal anytime. From here a rickshaw will take you the 10km to Karunagappally (around Rs 100) and you can take one of the frequent buses from there to Alleppey (Rs 30, 1½ hours).

The DTPC offices in Alleppey (p326) and Kollam (p323) run some sightseeing tours on tourist boats during the high season.

Houseboats

Renting a houseboat designed like a *kettuvallam* (rice barge) could be one of your most expensive experiences in India, but it's worth every darned rupee. Drifting through quiet canals lined with coconut palms, eating deliciously authentic Keralan food, meeting local villagers and sleeping on the water under a galaxy of stars – it's a world away from the clamour of India.

Houseboats cater for groups (with up to eight bunks) or couples (one or two double bed-rooms). Food (and an onboard chef to cook it) is generally included in the quoted cost. The houseboats can be chartered through the DTPC in Kollam or Alleppey, or through a multitude of private operators.

This is the biggest business in Kerala and some operators are unscrupulous. The boats come in a range of qualities, from veritable rust buckets to floating palaces – try to lay eyes on the boat you'll be travelling in before agreeing on a price. Make sure that everything (eg food) has been included in your price.

Travel-agency reps will be pushing their boats as soon as you set foot in Kerala and most of the bad experiences we hear about are from people who booked their trip outside the backwater hub towns. Your choice is greater in Alleppey (350 boats and counting!), but it's also the more popular base and you're quite likely to get caught in something approaching backwater-gridlock there in the high season.

It's possible to travel by houseboat between Alleppey and Kollam, or between Alleppey and Kochi, over 24 hours but only on larger boats that operate an inboard motor. These larger boats not only cost more but aren't as environmentally friendly. Those that are propelled by punting with two long bamboo poles obviously don't allow you to cover as much distance (no more than 15km in 24 hours, usually a round trip from Alleppey), but can be a wonderfully relaxing way to travel.

Prices are hugely variable. Expect a boat for two people for 24 hours to cost anything from Rs 3500. Shop around outside the high season to negotiate a bargain; in the peak season you'll definitely pay more.

Village Tours & Canoe Boats

Village tours usually involve small groups of five to six people, a knowledgeable guide and an open canoe or covered *kettuvallam*. The tours (from Kochi, Kollam or Alleppey) are from 2½ to six hours in duration and cost around Rs 300 to 600 per person. They include visits to villages to watch coir-making, boat building, toddy (palm beer) tapping and fish farming, and on the longer trips a traditional Keralan lunch is provided. The Munroe Island trip from Kollam (see p324) is an excellent tour of this type; the tourist desk in Ernakulam also organises recommended tours (see p344).

In Alleppey, rented canoe boats offer a nonguided laze through the canals on a small, covered canoe for up to four people (Rs 600 for four hours) – the ultimate way to spend a relaxing afternoon.

Public Ferries

If you want the local backwater transport experience, or a shorter trip, there are State Water Transport boats between Alleppey and Kottayam (Rs 12, 2½ hours, five boats daily from 7.30am to 5.30pm). The trip crosses Vembanad Lake and has a more varied landscape than the Alleppey cruise.

Environmental Issues

Environmental problems, such as pollution, land reclamation, and industrial and agricultural development, seriously threaten the backwaters and the communities that live on their banks. It's estimated that the backwaters are only at one-third of their mid-19th-century levels. Many migratory birds no longer visit the backwaters. Another very obvious problem is the unhindered spread of water hyacinth (African moss or Nile cabbage), which clogs many stretches of the canals.

Pollution from houseboat motors is becoming a real problem as their numbers swell every season. The Keralan authorities have introduced an ecofriendly accreditation system for houseboat operators. Among the categories an operator must fulfil before being issued with the 'Green Palm Certificate' are the installation of solar panels and sanitary tanks for the disposal of waste, as well as trying to minimise the use of outboard motors. Although the system is still new, ask operators whether they have the requisite certification. There's been talk of running boats on cleaner natural gas, though we've yet to see this being implemented. Seriously consider choosing a punting, rather than motorised, boat.

Punnamada Lake, close to the starting point of the Nehru Cup race, this is an upmarket option, with stylish cottages in natural materials with secluded verandas, outdoor showers and perfect patio views of the lake.

Raheem Residency (☎ 2239767; www.raheem residency.com; Beach Rd; s/d from €117/130; 🏊 🕮) The top-end option of choice, this is a romantic, architecturally acclaimed refurbishment of an 1860s mansion. All rooms have bathtubs, dashing antique furniture and appropriate period fixtures. The common areas are airy and comfortable, and there's a thoughtfully stocked library.

Also recommended:

Cherukara Nest (☎ 2251509; lakes_lagoon@satyam .net.in; d Rs 550, with AC Rs 1200; 🏊) Gracious, century-old family home, with roomy doubles and lots of character. Breakfast included.

Anamika (☎ 242044; www.anamikahome.com; VCSB (Boat Jetty) Rd; d incl breakfast Rs 1500-2000) Elegant Syrian Christian home with four massive, breezy rooms, agreeable furniture and lamp lighting.

Eating

Hot Kitchen (Mullackal Rd; thali Rs 22-28) This place comes highly recommended for veg meals and South Indian breakfasts – it gets packed at lunchtime.

Vembanad Restaurant (AS Rd; mains Rs 30-150) At the Alleppey Prince Hotel, it's well worth making the trip out here. One of the better eating options around, you can dine pool side to live music (nightly from 6.30pm).

Kream Korner (Mullackal Rd; dishes Rs 40-80) This place has two locations with a relaxed atmosphere and is popular with Indian and foreign families. There's a multicuisine menu with tandoori choices, and the cold coffee with ice-cream (Rs 22) beats a frappuchino any day

Royal Park Hotel (YMCA Rd; meals Rs 45-210; 🏊) Excellent food is served up in this swish hotel's restaurant, and it has the same menu in the upstairs licensed bar, so you can have a Kingfisher with your tasty butter chicken masala (Rs 70).

Chakara Restaurant (☎ 2230767; Beach Rd; 3 courses €12; 🕚 lunch & dinner) The restaurant at Raheem Residency is the most expensive, and best, place in town. The menu is creative and combines elements of traditional Keralan and European cuisine. Grover's Estate wine is available at Rs 990 per bottle.

Also try:

Indian Coffee House (Mullackal Rd & YMCA Rd; snacks Rs 4-12)

Hotel Aryas (Collectorate Rd; meals Rs 12-20) Has a cheap veg restaurant.

Sree Durga Bhavan Udipi Hotel (Cullan Rd; thali Rs 24) Veg food and more thalis.

Getting There & Away
BOAT
Ferries run to Kottayam from the jetty on VCSB (Boat Jetty) Rd; see p329.

BUS
There are frequent services that operate along the Trivandrum–Kollam–Alleppey–Ernakulam route, with buses to Trivandrum (Rs 90, 3½ hours, every 20 minutes) also stopping at Kollam and Kochi (Rs 36, 1½ hours). Buses to Kottayam (Rs 28, 1¼ hours, every 30 minutes) are considerably faster than the ferry.

TRAIN
There are frequent trains to Ernakulam (2nd class/AC chair Rs 28/142, 1½ hours) and Trivandrum (Rs 47/180, three hours).

NEHRU TROPHY SNAKE BOAT RACE

This famous regatta on Vembanad Lake in Alleppey takes place on the second Saturday of August each year, with scores of giant, low-slung *chundan vallam* (snake boats) competing. Each boat is over 30m long with a raised, snaking prow, and is crewed by up to 100 rowers singing in unison and shaded by gleaming silk umbrellas. Watched avidly by thousands of cheering spectators, the annual event celebrates the seafaring and martial traditions of ancient Kerala with floats and performing arts.

Tickets entitle you to seats on bamboo terraces, which are erected for the races. Prices range from Rs 75 to 500 for the best seats in the Tourist Pavilion, which offers views of the finishing point and separates you from gatherings of rowdy men. Take food, drink and an umbrella.

Other less famous but no less spectacular boat races are held around the backwaters between June and September. Ask at any KTDC office for details.

AROUND ALLEPPEY

Kerala's backwaters snake in all directions from Alleppey, and while touring on a houseboat is a great experience, taking time to slow down and stay in a village can be even more rewarding.

A mere 10km from Alleppey, and run by the erudite and ever-helpful Thomas, **Greenpalm Homes** (☎ 2724497, 9495557675; greenpalms@sifi .com; Chennamkary; s/d/tr with full board Rs 1000/1500/1750) is a series of bucolic homestays that seems like a universe away. Set in a typical and ridiculously picturesque backwater village, you sleep in basic rooms in villagers' homes among the rice paddies. Your hosts double as guides to the village and its traditions, and will prepare three Keralan meals a day. It's wonderfully quiet, there are no roads in sight and you can rent bicycles (Rs 20/100 per hour/day), take canoe trips (Rs 150) or ask about cooking classes.

To get here, call ahead and catch one of the hourly ferries from Alleppey to Chennamkary (Rs 5, 1¼ hours). Please remember this is a traditional village; dress appropriately.

KOTTAYAM

☎ 0481 / pop 172,867

Sandwiched between the Western Ghats and the backwaters, Kottayam is more renowned for being Kerala's centre of the spice and rubber trade than for its aesthetic appeal. It's a good place to make a connection between these two regions, or to pop into the pretty backwater village of Kumarakom.

Kottayam is a bookish town: the first Malayalam-language printing press was established here in 1820 and it was the first district in India to achieve 100% literacy. Today it's home to the newspaper *Malayala Manorama* (with the second-largest circulation in India) and is the headquarters of DC Books, Kerala's excellent bookshop chain. A place of churches and seminaries, Kottayam was a refuge for the Orthodox church when the Portuguese began forcing Keralan Christians to switch to Catholicism in the 16th century (see the boxed text right).

The **Thirunakkara Utsavam Festival** is held in March at the Thirunakkara Shiva Temple.

Orientation & Information

The KSRTC bus stand is 1km south of the centre, the boat jetty a further 2km (at Kodimatha), while the train station is 1km north

---

> ### SYRIAN CHRISTIANS IN SOUTH INDIA
>
> Tradition has it that Christianity was first brought to India in the first century, when St Thomas (one of the original apostles) found his way to the subcontinent and evangelised a family of Brahmins. With strong early ties to the Middle East, Christians in Kerala aligned themselves with the Syrian Patriarch from around the 4th century onwards.
>
> The 16th century brought the Portuguese to Kerala, along with missionaries eager to convert locals to their Roman brand of Catholicism. Then the arrival of the Anglican British in the 18th century led to further challenges to India's unique Christianity. Today, small communities of Syrian Christians still survive in Kerala, professing a faith that dates all the way back to one adventurous apostle.

---

of Kottayam. There are a couple of ATMs in Kottayam.

DC Books Heritage Bookshop (☎ 2300501; Good Shepherd St; ☽ 9.30am-7.30pm Mon-Sat) Excellent collection of literature, philosophy and travel titles.

DTPC office (☎ 2560479; ☽ 10am-5pm Mon-Sat) At the boat jetty.

Sify iWay (☎ 2563418; KK Rd; per hr Rs 25; ☽ 8.30am-8.30pm Mon-Sat) Fast internet connections.

UAE Exchange (☎ 2303865; 1st fl, MC Rd; ☽ 9.30am-6pm Mon-Sat, ☽ 9.30am-12.30pm Sun) For changing cash or travellers cheques.

Sleeping

Accommodation for all budgets is pretty dire. Try checking for **homestays** (☎ 2560479; around Rs 500-1000) at the DTPC office, but most of these will be outside town.

Ambassador Hotel (☎ 2563293; KK Rd; s/d from Rs 200/250, d with AC Rs 600; ✷) Definitely the pick of the budget litter, the rooms are spartan but speckless, spacious and quiet. There's a bakery, an adequate restaurant and a huge painting of the *Last Supper* to greet you in the lobby.

Hotel Venad (☎ 2568012; MC Rd; s/d Rs 250/300) Venad's rooms are central, a little weathered and depressingly dark. It's do-able for a night's rest, though street-facing rooms will have to contend with the racket of the street.

Hotel Aida (☎ 2568391; MC Rd; s/d Rs 350/700, with AC Rs 500/850; ✷) Looking like a very lost ski-chalet

KERALA

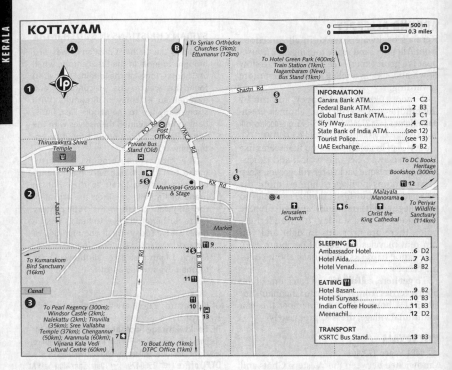

KOTTAYAM

To Syrian Orthodox Churches (3km); Ettumanur (12km)

Shastri Rd

To Hotel Green Park (400m); Train Station (1km); Nagambaram (New) Bus Stand (1km)

PO Rd
Post Office
Thirunakkara Shiva Temple
Private Bus Stand (Old)
YMCA Rd

Temple Rd

Azad La

Municipal Ground & Stage

KK Rd

To DC Books Heritage Bookshop (300m)

Malayala Manorama

Jerusalem Church

Christ the King Cathedral

To Periyar Wildlife Sanctuary (114km)

Market

To Kumarakom Bird Sanctuary (16km)

Canal

MC Rd

B Rd

To Pearl Regency (300m); Windsor Castle (2km); Nalekattu (2km); Tiruvilla (35km); Sree Vallabha Temple (50km); Chengannur (50km); Arannmula (60km); Vijnana Kala Vedi Cultural Centre (60km)

To Boat Jetty (1km); DTPC Office (1km)

INFORMATION	
Canara Bank ATM	1 C2
Federal Bank ATM	2 B3
Global Trust Bank ATM	3 C1
Sify iWay	4 C2
State Bank of India ATM	(see 12)
Tourist Police	(see 13)
UAE Exchange	5 B2

SLEEPING 🏠	
Ambassador Hotel	6 D2
Hotel Aida	7 A3
Hotel Venad	8 B2

EATING 🍴	
Hotel Basant	9 B2
Hotel Suryaas	10 B3
Indian Coffee House	11 B3
Meenachil	12 D2

TRANSPORT	
KSRTC Bus Stand	13 B3

0   500 m
0   0.3 miles

from the outside, the rooms inside are comfortable, but on the dark and dowdy side.

Pearl Regency (☎ 2561123; www.pearlregencyktm.com; MC Rd; s/d from Rs 1200/1400; 🅇 🖳) A slick new business-focused contender, this place has roomy, but boring, abodes. It's all run very efficiently, and there's an internet centre, coffee shop and restaurant on site. It's good value.

Windsor Castle (☎ 2363637; www.thewindsorcastle.net; MC Rd; s/d Rs 2500/3000, cottages Rs 5000; 🅇 🖳) This grandiose carbuncle of a building has the best rooms in Kottayam – minimally furnished, spacious and with bathtub – but they're still overpriced. Luxurious cottages are strewn around lake-side grounds, with Chinese fishing nets for the snaphappy.

Eating

Hotel Suryaas (TB Rd; dishes Rs 10-30; 🅇) Packed at mealtimes, this popular eatery serves North and South Indian food as well as the ubiquitous thali (Rs 35).

Hotel Green Park (Nagampadon; meals Rs 30-90; 🅇) The restaurant at this hotel serves up great Indian victuals, both veg and nonveg, in either its fan room or in AC comfort.

Meenachil (2nd fl, KK Rd; Rs 40-80; 🕑 lunch & dinner) With a friendly family atmosphere, this tidy, modern place does good biryanis, veg and nonveg dishes, and tandoori, to the sound of cheesy muzak.

Nalekattu (MC Rd; dishes Rs 60-125; 🕑 lunch & dinner) The traditional Keralan restaurant at the Windsor Castle is in an open-walled pavilion and serves delicious Keralan specialities, such as chemeen (mango curry, Rs 125) and tharavu (duck in rich coconut gravy, Rs 110).

Also try:

Indian Coffee House (TB Rd) We just can't get enough of this South Indian institution.

Hotel Basant (TB Rd; meals Rs 22) Popular lunchtime place with set meals.

Getting There & Away
BOAT
Ferries run to Alleppey; see p329.

BUS
The KSRTC bus stand has buses to Trivandrum (Rs 86, four hours, every 20 minutes) and Kochi (Rs 44, two hours, every 30 minutes). There are also buses to Kumily for Peri-

yar Wildlife Sanctuary (Rs 66, four hours, every 30 minutes) and Munnar (Rs 92, 5½ hours, five daily). Private buses, which are a little faster and more comfortable, depart from the Nagambaram (New) Bus Stand for Kochi (Rs 37, 1½ hours, every 15 minutes) and Kumily (Rs 63, every hour).

TRAIN
Kottayam is well served by express trains running between Trivandrum (2nd class/3AC/ 2AC Rs 50/251/399, three hours, 10 daily) and Ernakulam (Rs 28/188/266, 1½ hours, 12 daily).

Getting Around
An autorickshaw from the jetty to the KSRTC bus stand is around Rs 30, and from the bus stand to the train station about Rs 20. Most trips around town cost Rs 15.

AROUND KOTTAYAM
Kumarakom
Kumarakom, 16km west of Kottayam and on the shore of Vembanad Lake, is an unhurried backwater town with a smattering of resplendent, top-end sleeping options. You can arrange houseboats through Kumarakom's less-crowded canals, but expect to pay considerably more than in Alleppey.

Arundhati Roy, author of the 1997 Booker Prize–winning *The God of Small Things*, was raised in the nearby Aymanam village.

SIGHTS
Kumarakom Bird Sanctuary (☎ 2525864; Indian/foreigner Rs 5/45; ⏲ 6am-5.30pm) is on the 5-hectare site of a former rubber plantation and is the haunt of a variety of domestic and migratory birds. October to February is the time for travelling birds, such as the garganey teal, osprey, marsh harrier and steppey eagle, while May to July is the breeding season for local species, such as the Indian shag, pond herons, egrets and darters. Early morning is the best viewing time.

Buses between Kottayam's KSRTC stand and Kumarakom (Rs 8, 30 minutes, every 15 minutes) stop at the entrance to the sanctuary.

SLEEPING
Mooleppura Guest House (☎ 2525980; r without/with AC Rs 600/1100; ⊠) If you are on a budget, this has small, bucolic rooms in a friendly family home 500m south of the sanctuary entrance.

Tharavadu Heritage Home (☎ 2525230; www .tharavaduheritage.com; r without/with AC Rs 1200/1800; ⊠) Tharavadu means 'large family house', an apt description. Rooms are in the perfectly restored, 1870s teak family mansion, or in individual, creekside cottages. All are well crafted, some with glistening teak-wood beams, and others with big bay windows and relaxing patios. It's 4km before the bird sanctuary

Taj Garden Retreat (☎ 2524377; retreat.kumara kom@tajhotels.com; s/d US$150/160, cottage r US$245, villa US$385; ⊠ ⓢ) The height of secluded luxury, this excellent resort has rooms in a lovingly restored colonial house, cottages on a private lagoon in extensive grounds and luxury villas on the lake. It's right next door to the bird sanctuary, so wannabe ornithologists don't have to leave their porch.

Coconut Lagoon (☎ 2524491; reservations 0484-2668221; coconutlagoon@cghearth.com; cottages US$190-375; ⊠ ⓢ) This sprawling resort has beautiful *tharawad* (ancestral home) cottages. There's a list of activities as long as your arm, including cooking classes, traditional music lessons and village walks. It's reachable by boat from the private jetty just north of the sanctuary entrance. This place might seem familiar to those who have read Arundhati Roy's *The God of Small Things*.

Ettumanur
The **Shiva Temple** at Ettumanur, 12km north of Kottayam, has inscriptions dating from 1542, but parts of the building may be even older than this. The temple is noted for its exceptional woodcarvings and murals similar to those at Kochi's Mattancherry Palace. The annual **festival**, involving exposition of the idol (Shiva in his fierce form) and elephant processions, is held in February/March.

Sree Vallabha Temple
Devotees make offerings at this temple, 2km from Tiruvilla, in the form of traditional, regular all-night **Kathakali** performances that are open to all. Tiruvilla, 35km south of Kottayam, is on the rail route between Ernakulam and Trivandrum.

Vijnana Kala Vedi Cultural Centre
This French-run **centre** (☎ 0468-2214483; www .vijnanakalavedi.org; Tarayil Mukku) at Aranmula, 10km from Chengannur, offers highly recommended courses in Indian arts with expert teachers. You can choose to study from

a range of 15 subjects, including Ayurveda, Kathakali or Kathakali make-up, *mohiniattam* and *bharatanatyam* (classical dances), Carnatic or percussive music, mural painting, Keralan cooking, languages (Malayalam, Sanskrit and Hindi) and *kalarippayat*. Classes are generally individual and are held for a minimum of three hours per day, Monday to Friday.

Fees, which include lessons, accommodation in the village and all meals, are US$230/650 per week/month – less for longer stays. You can volunteer to teach English to children in the village schools, which will entitle you to a discount on your fees. Short stays of one to three nights are also possible (US$32 per night), though you will need to book well ahead.

The **Aranmula Boat Race** is held here in August/September.

THE WESTERN GHATS

PERIYAR WILDLIFE SANCTUARY
☎ 04869

Periyar (☎ 224571; www.periyartigerreserve.org; Indian/foreigner Rs 25/300; ⏰ 6am-6pm), South India's most popular wildlife sanctuary, encompasses 777 sq km, with a 26-sq-km artificial lake created by the British in 1895. It's home to bison, sambar, wild boar, langur, over 1000 elephants and at least 46 tigers. This is an established tourist spot, and can sometimes feel like Disneyland-in-the-Ghats, but the mountain scenery on the road up, the lake cruise and a jungle walk make for an enjoyable visit. Bring warm and waterproof clothing.

Orientation
Kumily, 4km from the sanctuary, is a small strip of hotels, spice shops and Kashmiri emporiums. Thekkady is the centre inside the park with the KTDC hotels and boat jetty. When people refer to the sanctuary, they tend to use Kumily, Thekkady and Periyar interchangeably.

Information
DC Books (☎ 222548; ⏰ 8.30am-9.30pm) Has a small but decent-quality selection of fiction and books about India.
DTPC office (☎ 222620; ⏰ 10am-5pm Mon-Sat) Behind bus stand.
IR Communications (per hr Rs 40; ⏰ 7am-10pm)

Spider-Net Cafe (☎ 223727; per hr Rs 40; ⏰ 9.30am-9.30pm)
State Bank of Travancore (⏰ 10am-3.30pm Mon-Fri, to 12.30pm Sat) Changes travellers cheques and currency; the ATM accepts foreign cards.
Wildlife Information Centre (☎ 222028; ⏰ 6am-6pm) Above the boat jetty in Thekkady.
Wildlife Interpretation Centre (⏰ 7.30am-7.30pm) This excellent centre at Spice Village (see p336) has a resident naturalist showing slides between 7.30pm and 9.30pm and answering questions about the park. Guests and diners at its restaurant can attend free of charge.

Sights & Activities
VISITING THE PARK
Two-hour **KTDC boat trips** (lower/upper deck Rs 45/100; ⏰ 7am, 9.30am, 11.30am, 2pm & 4pm) around the lake are the usual way of touring the sanctuary. The boat trip itself is enjoyable enough, though any wildlife you see will be from afar. The smaller, more decrepit **Forest Department boats** (per person Rs 15; ⏰ 9.30am, 11.30am, 2pm & 4pm) offer a chance to get a bit closer to the animals, and are driven by sanctuary workers who may offer some commentary. Entry to the park doesn't guarantee a place on the boat; get to the **ticket office** (⏰ 6.30am-5.30pm) one hour before a scheduled trip to buy tickets (no advance reservations). The first and last departures offer the best wildlife-spotting prospects, and October to March are generally the best times to see animals.

Guided three-hour **jungle walks** (per person Rs 100; ⏰ 7am, 10.30am & 2pm) cover 4km or 5km and are a better way to experience the park close up, accompanied by a trained tribal guide. Note that leeches are common after rain.

A number of more adventurous explorations of the sanctuary can be arranged by the **Ecotourism Centre** (☎ 224571; ⏰ 8am-6pm). These include two-/three-day 'tiger trail' **treks** (per person Rs 3000/5000), full-day **hikes** (per person Rs 1000), three-hour **night treks** (per person Rs 500) and full-day **bamboo rafting** (per person Rs 1000) on the lake. See the website www.periyartiger reserve.org for more information on what is available.

A small outfit called **Tribal Heritage Tour** (per person Rs 100 ⏰ 8am-4pm) does engaging 1½-hour tours through Mannakudy tribal village inside the sanctuary (you will need your park day-ticket). The walk includes a visit to the small village **museum**, which has some old tools and paintings done by villagers.

Agencies around town arrange all-day 4WD **Jungle Safaris** (per person Rs 1500; ☻ 5am-6pm), which cover over 40km of trails in jungle bordering the park. Tours include meals as well as a paddleboat trip. You can arrange **elephant rides** (per 30 min Rs 250) at **Indian Spices** (☎ 222868; Thekkady Rd).

SPICE GARDENS & PLANTATIONS

Spice tours (costing around Rs 400/600 by autorickshaw/taxi and lasting two to three hours) can be arranged anywhere and are really insightful if you get a knowledgeable guide. Spice gardens are small domestic gardens, whereas plantations are bigger commercial affairs where you may also see harvesting and processing. If you want to see a tea factory in operation (worth it for the smell alone), do it here – tea-factory visits are not permitted in Munnar.

If you'd rather do it independently, you can visit a few excellent spice gardens several kilometres from Kumily: **Abraham's Spice Garden** (☎ 222919; ☻ 6.30am-7.30pm) has been going for 54 years and does one-hour tours of their 1-hectare garden for Rs 50. At **Spice Paradise** (☎ 222868; ☻ 7am-7pm) there is a 4-hectare garden interplanted with Ayurvedic herbs among the usual spices. Two-hour tours are Rs 100.

AYURVEDA

One highly recommended place for the Ayurvedic experience is **Santhigiri Ayurveda** (☎ 223979; Vandanmedu Junction), offering both massage (from Rs 500) and long-term treatments.

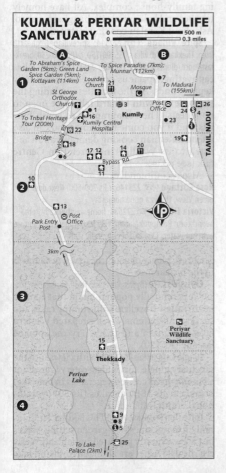

KUMILY & PERIYAR WILDLIFE SANCTUARY

INFORMATION	
DC Books	**1** A1
DTPC Office	**2** B1
IR Communications	(see 18)
Spider-Net Café	**3** B1
State Bank of Travancore ATM	**4** B1
Wildlife Information Centre	**5** B4
Wildlife Interpretation Centre	(see 18)

SIGHTS & ACTIVITIES	
Ecotourism Centre	**6** A2
Indian Spices	(see 22)
Santhigiri Ayurveda	**7** B1
Ticket Office	**8** B4

SLEEPING ⌂	
Aranya Nivas	**9** B4
Coffee Inn	**10** A2
El Paradiso	**11** A2
Green View Homestay	**12** A2
Leelapankai	**13** A2
Mickey Homestay	**14** B2
Periyar House	**15** A3
Prime Castle	**16** A1
Rose Cottage	**17** A2
Spice Village	**18** A2
Victoria House	**19** B2

EATING ⊞	
Chrissie's Café	**20** B2
Coffee Inn	(see 10)
Hotel Lakeshore	**21** A1
Jungle Café	(see 10)

ENTERTAINMENT ⊟	
Mudra	**22** A1

TRANSPORT	
Bicycle Hire Shacks	**23** B1
Bus Stand	**24** B1
Jetty	**25** B4
Tamil Nadu Bus Station	**26** B1

Sleeping & Eating
INSIDE THE SANCTUARY

The Ecotourism Centre can arrange accommodation in a **forest cottage** (d with meals Rs 2000).

The KTDC has three hotels in the park. It's a good idea to make reservations (at any KTDC office), particularly for weekends. Note that there's effectively a curfew at these places – guests are not permitted to wander the sanctuary after 6pm.

Periyar House (☎ 222026; periyar@sancharnet.in; s/d with breakfast & dinner from Rs 800/1250) This faux-brick, school camp–like complex has plain, slightly musty and definitely overpriced rooms.

Aranya Nivas (☎ 222023; aranyanivas@sancharnet .in; s/d from Rs 3100/3950; 🏊) Bright, clean abodes in an imposing, pseudo-stone building with token period touches. There are no real views, but the pool is in a lush forest setting.

Lake Palace (☎ 222023; aranyanivas@sancharnet.in; s/d ste with all meals Rs 6750/7850) The only place where you can stay in the midst of the sanctuary and view elephants over breakfast, this is an appealingly restored former game lodge with a Raj-era ambience. Transport is only by boat across the lake. Make reservations through Aranya Nivas.

KUMILY

There's a growing homestay scene in Kumily offering better bang-for-your-rupee than the town's uninspiring hotels.

Green View Homestay (☎ 211015; www.sureshgreen view.com; Bypass Rd; s Rs 150, d incl breakfast Rs 300-600) With loads of greenery, there are great large and airy doubles here, all with balconies and small sitting areas – though the singles are tiny. The garden out the back has hammocks to laze in and the hosts are very friendly.

our pick Coffee Inn (☎ 222763; coffeeinn@sancharnet .in; Thekkady Rd; huts/cottages Rs 200/250, r Rs 400-500) This is a charming, friendly place with a range of simple accommodation, from cute bamboo huts and tree houses to comfortable cottages and nicely finished rooms. Best of all, it abuts the sanctuary and it has its own secluded animal-spotting hut. Their restaurant is also top-notch.

Mickey Homestay (☎ 223196; www.mickeyhomestay .com; Bypass Rd; r Rs 250-600) In a fetching and lush family house, the five rooms here come in all shapes, sizes and configurations. All have homey touches and massive balconies with rattan furniture and hanging bamboo seats.

Ask about long-distance trekking and mountain-biking adventures (including a jungle walk all the way to Alleppey!).

Leelapankai (☎ 9349197934; Thekkady Rd; r Rs 700) Leelapankai's dainty, individual thatched-roof cottages sit up on a hill overlooking the sanctuary. They're plain on the inside, but the views of the park from the porches and restaurant are first rate.

Prime Castle (☎ 223469; Thekkady Rd; d Rs 850-1200) In a gaudy pink complex, the rooms inside are well maintained, spacious and many have chichi bathrooms. The budget annexe (Rs 100 per person) has small, dark, cheap rooms.

El Paradiso (☎ 222350; www.goelparadiso.com; Bypass Rd; r Rs 950) El Paradiso has fastidiously neat, massive rooms in a large and welcoming family-house complex. All have homely touches and balconies with hanging bamboo. Ask about Keralan cooking instruction.

Spice Village (☎ 222314; spicevillage@cghearth .com; Thekkady Rd; villa s US$190-250, d US$200-250, breakfast/lunch/dinner Rs 300/500/500; 🏊) This place has captivating, spacious cottages in beautifully kept grounds. All the facilities (including the Raj-style bar with billiard table) are open to nonguests. The restaurant does lavish buffets, and if you come for dinner you can also attend a Keralan cooking demonstration and listen to its Wildlife Interpretation Centre talk (see p334).

Also recommended:

Rose Cottage (☎ 223146; r Rs 200-500) Next door to Green View, this is a good homestay.

Victoria House (☎ 222684; homestaythekkady@emai lworld.com; Rosappukandam; r Rs 300) Huge plain rooms with hot water, TVs, and very friendly staff.

There are plenty of good cheap veg restaurants in the bazaar area.

Chrissie's Café (Bypass Rd; snacks Rs 30-60, meals Rs 100-120) A perennially popular haunt that continues to satisfy travellers with yummy cakes and snacks, and extremely well-prepared Western faves like pizza and pasta. Try the spinach lasagne (Rs 120).

Jungle Café (meals Rs 40-80) With views into the sanctuary jungle, this budget eatery is great for a *masala dosa* (curried vegetables in pancake) breakfast (Rs 18), pancakes (Rs 30) or traditional South Indian fare.

Coffee Inn (meals Rs 60-120) This laid-back restaurant, in a peaceful spice-garden setting, serves just a few expertly prepared Indian and Western meals. Dishes are all made fresh and take a while – but the patient are well rewarded. Cheeky monkeys from the neighbouring sanctuary often make guest appearances.

You can also try **Hotel Lakeshore** (dishes Rs 20-60), a local favourite for veg and nonveg dishes.

Entertainment

Mudra (☎ 9447157636; admission Rs 125; ☯ shows 4.30pm & 7pm) Kathakali shows twice a day; make-up starts 30 minutes before the show begins.

Getting There & Away

Buses originating or terminating at Periyar start and finish at Aranya Nivas, but they also stop at the Kumily bus station, at the eastern edge of town.

Eight buses daily operate between Kochi and Kumily (Rs 98, six hours). Buses leave every 30 minutes for Kottayam (Rs 66, four hours), and there are two direct buses daily to Trivandrum at 8.45am and 5pm (Rs 148, eight hours). Four morning buses and one afternoon bus go to Munnar (Rs 68, 4½ hours).

Tamil Nadu buses leave every 30 minutes to Madurai (Rs 40, four hours) from the Tamil Nadu bus stand just over the border.

Getting Around

Kumily is about 4km from Periyar Lake; you can catch the bus (almost as rare as the tigers), take an autorickshaw (Rs 40) or set off on foot; it's a pleasant, shady walk into the park. **Bicycle rental** (per hr Rs 4; ☯ 6.30am-8pm) is available from a couple of shacks near the bus stand.

MUNNAR

☎ 04865 / elev 1524m

With a *Sound-of-Music*-in-India backdrop of rolling mountain scenery, craggy peaks, manicured tea estates and crisp mountain air, Munnar really hits the spot after the sticky heat of the lowlands. Once known as the High Range of Travancore, today Munnar is the commercial centre of some of the world's highest tea-growing estates. But don't be fooled by the noisy and grubby namesake town of the region; the real attractions lie in the surrounding hills.

Information

There are ATMs near the bridge, south of the bazaar.

DTPC Tourist Information Office (☎ 231516; ☯ 8.30am-7pm) Marginally helpful.

State Bank of Travancore (☎ 230274; ☯ 10am-3.30pm Mon-Sat, to noon Sun) Changes travellers cheques.

Tourist Information Service (☎ 231136; ☯ 9am-6pm) Run by local legend Joseph Iype, a walking Swiss-army knife of Munnar information, this office has maps, local history, travel tips and much more.

Triveni Communications (☎ 230966; per hr Rs 40; ☯ 8am-10pm) New computers put this place a nose ahead of some sad competition.

Sights & Activities

The main reason to be in Munnar is to explore the verdant hillocks that surround it (see below for tour options). Travel agencies and autorickshaw drivers, as well as most passers-by, want to organise a day of sightseeing for you; shop around. The DTPC can organise half-day, full-day and two- to four-day **treks** around Munnar.

You can do your own 12km day-trek around the patchwork of plantations surrounding Munnar to visit the **Pothamedu Viewpoint** and the roaring **Atthukad Waterfalls**. Head south on the road towards Ernakulum, cross the bridge just after the government checkpoint, take a right and continue up the road. Take a path leading to the viewpoint just after Copper Castle Resort. Continue on to the waterfalls, from where you can take a shortcut back to the Ernakulum–Munnar Rd and either walk, or catch one of the frequent buses, back to Munnar. A rickshaw to the waterfalls or to the viewpoint and back costs Rs 150.

Tata Tea Museum (☎ 230561; adult/child Rs 50/25; ☯ 10am-4pm Mon-Sat) is, unfortunately, about as close as you'll get to a working tea factory around Munnar. It's a slightly sanitised and deserted version of the real thing, but it still shows the basic process. A collection of old bits and pieces from the colonial era, including photographs and a 1905 tea-roller, are also kept here.

Tours

The DTPC runs a couple of fairly rushed full-day tours to points around Munnar:

Chinnar Wildlife Tour (per person Rs 300; ☯ 9am-7pm) Goes to Chinnar Wildlife Sanctuary (p339).

Sandal Valley Tour (per person Rs 300; ☯ 9am-6pm) Visits several viewpoints, waterfalls, plantations, a sandalwood forest and villages.

Tea Valley tour (per person Rs 250; ☯ 10am-6pm) Visit Echo Point, Top Station and Rajamalai (for Eravikulam National Park), among other places.

KERALA

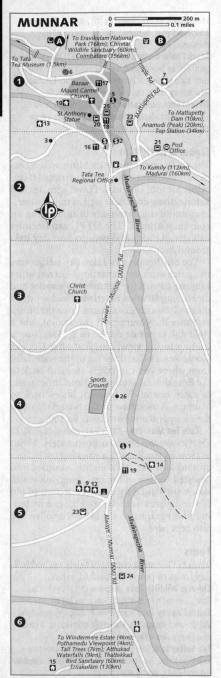

MUNNAR

INFORMATION

DTPC Tourist Information Office	1	B4
Federal Bank ATM	2	B2
Forest Information Centre	3	A2
State Bank of Travancore ATM	4	A2
Tourist Information Service	5	B1
Triveni Communications	6	A1

SLEEPING

Edassery Eastend	7	B1
Green View	8	A5
JJ Cottage	9	A5
Kaippallil Homestay	10	A1
Royal Retreat	11	B6
SMM Cottage	12	A5
Westend Cottages	13	A1
Westwood Riverside Resort	14	B5
Zina Cottages	15	A6

EATING

Hotel Saravan Bhavan	16	A2
Rapsy Restaurant	17	A1
Silver Spoon	18	A1
SN Restaurant	19	B5

TRANSPORT

Buses to Coimbatore	20	A1
Buses to Kumily & Madurai	21	B2
Buses to Top Station	22	B1
Gokulam Bike Hire	23	A5
Jeep & Rickshaw Stand	(see 22)	
KSRTC Bus Station	24	B6
Private Buses to Kumily	25	A1
Raja Cycles	26	B4

Sleeping

There are several cheap-and-nasty hotels right in Munnar town, but these are best avoided. Prices are a bit higher than in comparable Indian towns, though there are several neat homestay and top-end options around.

Kaippallil Homestay (☎ 230203; www.kaippallil.com; r Rs 200-800) Up the hill and away from (most of) the clatter of the bazaar, Kaippallil has several unique rooms in an attractively landscaped house. There are inviting sitting areas and the rooms are eclectically but tastefully decorated, some with balconies and great views. The budget rooms share bathrooms and are a tad dark.

SMM Cottage (☎ 230159; r Rs 350-500) Right next to JJ Cottage and Green View, this brisk homestay will do if the others are full.

JJ Cottage (☎ 230104; d Rs 350-800) The mothering family at this genial homestay will go out of their way to make sure your stay is comfortable. The varied and uncomplicated rooms are very clean, bright and have TV and geyser hot water.

Green View (☎ 230940; www.greenviewmunnar.com; r Rs 500-600) Next door to JJ Cottage, this offers the same thing with less attentive staff.

Zina Cottages (☎ 230349; d incl tax Rs 600-800) Just on the outskirts of town but already immersed in lush tea plantations, these cosy rooms are an excellent deal. Stunning vistas come standard, as does the piles of information provided by gregarious owner Mr Iype from the Tourist Information Service (see p337).

Westwood Riverside Resort (☎ 230884; www.westwoodmunnar.com; AM Rd; r Rs 1800-2600) You might be forgiven for thinking you'd stumbled onto a ski lodge. There's lots of polished wood around and the rooms are refreshingly pleasant for a cookie-cutter standard, midrange hotel.

Edassery Eastend (☎ 230451; www.edasserygroup.com; Mattupetty Rd; cottages Rs 1950-2300) With a Disneyland-perfect miniature garden, these blandly comfortable and spacious rooms are probably a tad overpriced.

You can also try:

Westend Cottages (☎ 230954; d Rs 250-450, with shared bathroom Rs 250) A few darkish but clean doubles in a friendly family home.

Royal Retreat (☎ 230240; www.royalretreat.co.in; r Rs 1200-1500) Comfortable rooms; OK value by Munnar's standards.

There are some excellent top-end accommodation options in plantations in the hills around Munnar, where the mountain serenity is unbeatable.

Tall Trees (☎ 230641; Pothamedu; cottages Rs 4500-5500) Spread around thick forest and far away from the clamour of the world, this back-to-nature retreat has comfy cottages with natural-wood finishes, each with balconies opening to infinite nature views. There's a kids' playground and sprawling grounds dotted with cardamom trees. It's 7km from Munnar.

Windermere Estate (☎ 230512; www.windermeremunnar.com; Pothamedu; r & cottages incl breakfast US$125-195) Windermere is a boutique-meets-country-retreat and manages to be both luxurious and intimate at the same time. There are farmhouse rooms and newer, swankier cottages with spectacular views. Book ahead.

Eating

Early morning food stalls in the bazaar serve breakfast snacks and cheap meals.

Hotel Saravan Bhavan (dishes Rs 15-50) Try this popular place for top-value veg banana-leaf meals (Rs 18).

SN Restaurant (AM Rd; meals Rs 20-80) This seems to always be full of people digging into morning dosas (Rs 15 to 25) and other Indian dishes. The butter chicken is outstanding (Rs 60).

Rapsy Restaurant (Bazaar; dishes around Rs 25-40) This place is packed at lunchtime, with locals lining up for Rapsy's famous *paratha* or biryani (from Rs 25). It also makes a stab at international dishes like Spanish omelette (Rs 25) and Israeli *shakshuka* (scrambled eggs with tomatoes and spices Rs 30).

Silver Spoon (AM Rd; meals Rs 40-100; ☽ lunch & dinner) Beneath the Munnar Inn, this popular family eatery has some tables overlooking the river and a great Keralan fish-curry meal, with 12 all-you-can-eat dishes to savour (Rs 60).

Getting There & Away

Roads around Munnar are in poor condition and can be seriously affected by monsoon rains, so bus times may vary. The main **KSRTC bus station** (AM Rd) is south of the town, but it's best to catch buses from stands in town, where more frequent private buses also depart. See Map p338 for bus departure locations.

There are around 10 buses a day to Ernakulam in Kochi (Rs 84, 4½ hours), and a few daily services to Kottayam (Rs 92, five hours), Kumily (Rs 68, five hours) and Trivandrum (Rs 176, nine hours). There are Tamil Nadu buses to Coimbatore (Rs 80, six hours, two daily) and Madurai (Rs 88, six hours, one daily at 2.30pm).

Getting Around

Raja Cycles (per hr Rs 8; ☽ 8.30am-7.30pm) rents bicycles. **Gokulam Bike Hire** (☎ 9447237165; per day Rs 250; ☽ 7.30am-7pm) has several motorbikes for rent.

Autorickshaws ply the hills around Munnar with bone-shuddering efficiency; they charge from Rs 150 to nearby places and up to Rs 650 for a full day's sightseeing.

AROUND MUNNAR

Eravikulam National Park (Indian/foreigner Rs 15/200; ☽ 7am-6pm Sep-May), 16km from Munnar, is home to the rare, but almost tame, Nilgiri tahr (a type of mountain goat). From Munnar, an autorickshaw/taxi costs Rs 150/300 return; a government bus takes you the final 4km from the checkpoint (Rs 20).

Chinnar Wildlife Sanctuary (☽ 7am-6pm), about 10km past Marayoor and 60km northeast of Munnar, hosts deer, leopards, elephants and the endangered grizzled giant squirrel.

Trekking (Rs 100 for three hours) and **tree house** or **hut stays** (huts Rs 500-1000) within the sanctuary are available, as well as ecotour programs like river-trekking, cultural visits, and waterfall treks (Rs 35 to Rs 100). For details contact the **Forest Information Centre** (☎ 231587; enpmunnar@sify.com; ⊗ 10am-5pm Mon-Sat) in Munnar. There is also accommodation in Marayoor. Buses from Munnar heading to Coimbatore can drop you off at Chinnar (Rs 28, 1½ hours).

Top Station, on Kerala's border with Tamil Nadu, has spectacular views over the Western Ghats. From Munnar, four daily buses (Rs 25, from 7.30am) make the steep 32km climb in around an hour. Taxis (Rs 800) and rickshaws (Rs 400) also make the return trip from Munnar.

Thattekkad Bird Sanctuary (Indian/foreigner Rs 10/100; ⊗ 6am-6pm) is a serene 25-sq-km park, home to over 270 species, including Malabar grey hornbills, parakeets, jungle nightjar, cuckoo, grey drongo, jungle babbler, darters and rarer species, such as the Sri Lankan frogmouth and rose-billed roller. You can rent private guides (Rs 150 to 200) in the sanctuary, and there's a canteen with basic food and drinks just inside the gate. There's a **Treetop Machan** (dm Rs 900) in the sanctuary that you can stay in; contact the **assistant wildlife warden** (☎ 0485-2588302) at Kothamangalam. Otherwise, **Hornbill Inspection Bungalow** (☎ 0484-2310324; www.thehornbillcamp.com; s/d Rs 900/1800) has basic rooms outside the sanctuary, though you might be better off asking around about homestays (around Rs 600 including meals).

Thattekkad is on the Ernakulam–Munnar road. Take a direct bus from Ernakulam to Kothamangalam, from where a Thattekkad bus travels the final 12km (Rs 6, 25 minutes).

PARAMBIKULAM WILDLIFE SANCTUARY

Resting in a deep valley around the Parambikulam, Thunakadavu and Peruvaripallam Dams, **Parambikulam Wildlife Sanctuary** (Indian/foreigner Rs 25/100; ⊗ 7am-6pm) extends for 285 sq km. It's home to elephants, bison, gaur, sloth bears, wild boars, sambar, chital, crocodiles, tigers, panthers and some of the largest teak trees in Asia. There's also an elephant camp at Kozhikamthi and you can go boating on the reservoir. The sanctuary is best avoided during monsoon (June to August) and it sometimes closes in March and April.

For entry to the sanctuary, permission is required from the **divisional forests officer** (☎ 04253-244500) at Thunakadavu. Three-hour jeep tours (Rs 750) are available and short treks can also be organised from here.

There are Forest Rest Houses at Thunakadavu, Thellikkal and Anappady, and a **tree-top hut** (d Rs 1000) at Thunakadavu; book through the divisional forests officer.

The best access to the sanctuary is by bus from Pollachi (40km from Coimbatore and 49km from Palakkad) in Tamil Nadu. There are at least two buses in either direction between Pollachi and Parambikulam via Anamalai daily (Rs 15, 1½ hours).

CENTRAL KERALA

KOCHI (COCHIN)

☎ 0484 / pop 1.36 million

If you listen closely, you can hear the collective sigh breathed by travellers upon setting foot in laid-back Fort Cochin. Kochi has been luring wanderers and traders for over 600 years and remains a living homage to its varied colonial past: giant fishing nets influenced by Chinese merchants, a 16th-century synagogue, ancient mosques, Portuguese houses built half a millennia ago and the crumbling residuum of the British Raj. The result is an unlikely blend of medieval Portugal, Holland and an English country village grafted on to the tropical Malabar Coast. It's a delightful place to spend some time, soak in the history, peruse art galleries and nap in some of the finest heritage accommodation in India.

Mainland Ernakulam is the hectic transport hub and cosmopolitan heart of Kerala, where neon lights and upmarket chainstores rule the roost. The historical towns of Fort Cochin and Mattancherry, however, are wonderfully serene – thick with the smell of the past and with more goats than rickshaws patrolling the streets.

Orientation

Kochi is made up of a gaggle of islands and peninsulas, including mainland Ernakulam; the islands of Willingdon, Bolgatty and Gundu in the harbour; Fort Cochin and Mattancherry on the southern peninsula; and Vypeen and Vallarpadam Islands, north of Fort Cochin. All are linked by ferry, with bridges connecting Ernakulam to Willingdon Island and the

Fort Cochin/Mattancherry peninsula; the new Goshree bridge links Ernakulam with Bolgatty, Vallarpadam and Vypeen Islands. The main train station, the bus stand and KTDC Tourist Reception Centre are in Ernakulam, while Fort Cochin and Mattancherry have all the historical sites and most of the better-value accommodation.

Information
BOOKSHOPS
Current Books (Map p346; ☎ 3231590; ⏲ 9.30am-7.30pm Mon-Sat) A branch of DC Books and of the same quality.

DC Books (Map p346; ☎ 2391295; Banerji Rd, Ernakulam; ⏲ 9.30am-7.30pm Mon-Sat, 3-8pm Sun) A typically great English-language selection.

Idiom Bookshop Fort Cochin (Map p342; ☎ 2217075; Bastion St; ⏲ 9am-9pm Mon-Sat, 10am-6pm Sun); Mattancherry (Map p342; opp boat jetty; ⏲ 10am-6pm) Top range of good-quality new and used books.

INTERNET ACCESS
Café de Net (Map p342; Bastion St, Fort Cochin; per hr Rs 30; ⏲ 9am-10.30pm) Comfortable, fast, drinks served.

Net Park (Map p346; Convent Rd, Ernakulam; per hr Rs 15; ⏲ 9am-9pm)

Open Door Internet Café (Map p346; Carrier Station Rd, Ernakulam; per hr Rs 20; ⏲ 7.30-12.30am)

Sify iWay (Map p342; ☎ 2215438; per hr Rs 30; ⏲ 8.30am-10.30pm) Fast computers and AC comfort, at the back of a Shop-n-Save.

MONEY
There are scores of ATMs along MG Rd in Ernakulam, and a few in Fort Cochin.

Thomas Cook (Map p341; ☎ 2374205; MG Rd; ⏲ 9.30am-5.30pm Mon-Sat)

UAE Exchange (⏲ 9.30am-6pm Mon-Sat, to 1pm Sun); Ernakulam (Map p346; ☎ 2383317; Shanmugh Rd); Fort Cochin (Map p342; ☎ 2812530; KB Jacob Rd)

POST
College post office (Map p346; ☎ 2369302; Convent Rd, Ernakulam; ⏲ 9am-4pm Mon-Fri, to 9pm Sat)

Ernakulam post office branches Hospital Rd (Map p346; ☎ 2355467; ⏲ 9am-8pm Mon-Sat, 10am-5pm Sun); MG Rd (Map p346); Broadway (Map p346)

Main post office (Map p342; Post Office Rd, Fort Cochin; ⏲ 9am-5pm Mon-Fri, to 3pm Sat)

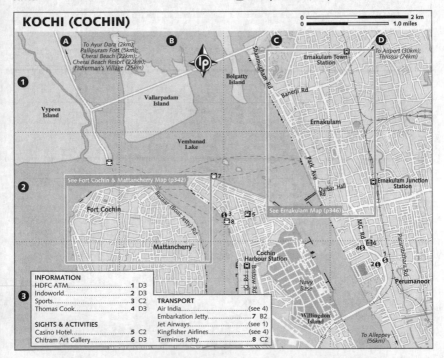

KOCHI (COCHIN)

0   2 km
0   1.0 miles

To Ayur Dara (2km);
Pallipuram Fort (5km);
Cherai Beach (22km);
Cherai Beach Resort (22km);
Fisherman's Village (25km)

Bolgatty Island

Vypeen Island

Vallarpadam Island

Vembanad Lake

Ernakulam Town Station

To Airport (30km);
Thrissur (74km)

Banerji Rd

Ernakulam

Park Ave

Durbar Hall Rd

Ernakulam Junction Station

See Fort Cochin & Mattancherry Map (p342)

Fort Cochin

Mattancherry

See Ernakulam Map (p346)

MG Rd

Parambithara Rd

Cochin Harbour Station

Navy Base

Perumanoor

Willingdon Island

To Alleppey (56km)

INFORMATION	
HDFC ATM	1 D3
Indoworld	2 D3
Sports	3 C2
Thomas Cook	4 D3
SIGHTS & ACTIVITIES	
Casino Hotel	5 C2
Chitram Art Gallery	6 D3

TRANSPORT	
Air India	(see 4)
Embarkation Jetty	7 B2
Jet Airways	(see 1)
Kingfisher Airlines	(see 4)
Terminus Jetty	8 C2

KERALA

FORT COCHIN & MATTANCHERRY

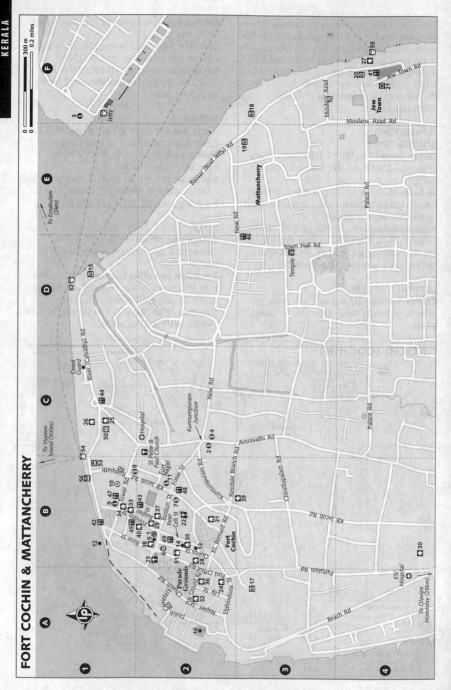

INFORMATION		
Café de Net.......................1	B2
Federal Bank ATM...............2	C2
Government of India Tourist		
Office...........................3	F1
ICICI ATM.........................4	C2
Idiom Bookshop.................5	B2
Indoworld......................(see 29)	
Main Post Office.................6	B2
Sify iWay.......................(see 29)	
South India Bank ATM...........7	B2
State Bank of India ATM..........8	B1
Tourist Desk Information		
Counter.........................9	B2
Tourist Police...................10	B1
UAE Exchange..................11	B2
SIGHTS & ACTIVITIES		
Bishop's House.................(see 17)	
Chinese Fishing Nets............12	B1
Cochin Ayurvedic Centre........13	B2
Cook & Eat.....................14	B2
Draavidia Art & Performance		
Gallery.........................15	D1
Dutch Cemetery................16	A2
Indo-Portuguese Museum........17	A3
Kashi Art Gallery................18	F3

Lila Studio.......................19	E3
Mattancherry Palace............20	F4
Pardesi Synagogue..............21	F4
Santa Cruz Basilica.............22	B2
St Francis Church...............23	B2
SLEEPING		
Ann's Residency...............24	A2
Ballard Bungalow...............25	C1
Brunton Boatyard..............26	C1
Caza Maria.....................27	F4
Delight Home Stay.............28	B2
Elite Hotel......................29	B2
Green Woods Bethlehem........30	B4
Kapithan Inn...................31	B2
Malabar House.................32	A2
Oy's Homestay.................33	B1
Princess Inn....................34	B1
Raintree Lodge.................35	B2
Spencer Home.................36	A2
Spice Holidays Homestay........37	B2
Vasco Homestay................38	B2
Vintage Inn....................39	B3
Walton's Homestay.............40	B2
EATING		
Caza Maria.....................41	F4

Fishmongers...................42	B1
History Restaurant..............(see 26)	
Kashi Art Café..................43	B2
Malabar Junction...............(see 32)	
New Ananda Bhavan............44	C1
Old Courtyard..................45	B1
Ramathula Hotel...............46	D3
Salt 'n' Pepper..................47	B1
Solar Café.....................(see 15)	
Talk of the Town...............48	B2
Teapot.........................49	B2
ENTERTAINMENT		
Kerala Kathakali Centre..........50	C1
SHOPPING		
Cinnamon......................51	B2
Kairali.........................(see 56)	
TRANSPORT		
Customs Jetty..................52	D1
Fort Cochin Bus Stand..........53	B1
Jetty (Ferry to Vypeen Island)...54	B1
Mattancherry Jetty.............55	F4
Tourist Taxi Stand...............56	B1
Vasco Tourist Information		
Centre.........................(see 38)	

TOURIST INFORMATION

There's a tourist information counter at the airport. Many places distribute a brochure that includes a passable map and walking tour entitled 'Historical Places in Fort Cochin'.

Government of India Tourist Office (Map p342; ☎ 2668352; indtourismkochi@sify.com; Willingdon Island; ◷ 9am-5.30pm Mon-Fri, to 1pm Sat) A huge range of brochures and maps of India.

KTDC Tourist Reception Centre (Map p346; ☎ 2353234; Shanmugham Rd, Ernakulam; ◷ 8am-7pm) Organises tours.

Tourist Desk Information Counter Ernakulam (Map p346; ☎ 2371761; touristdesk@satyam.net.in; ◷ 8.30am-6pm); Fort Cochin (Map p342) A private agency at the main ferry jetty in Ernakulam that is very knowledgeable about Kochi and beyond.

Tourist police Ernakulam (Map p346; ☎ 2353234); Fort Cochin (Map p342; ☎ 2215055)

Sights

FORT COCHIN

The tip of Fort Cochin is strung with the unofficial emblem of Kerala's backwaters: cantilevered Chinese fishing nets (Map p342). A legacy of traders from the court of Kubla Khan in around the 1400s, these enormous, spider-like contraptions require at least four men to operate the counterweights – they're mainly used at high tide. Unfortunately, modern fishing techniques are making the nets less and less profitable.

Said to be India's oldest European-built church, **St Francis Church** (Map p342) was constructed in 1503 by Portuguese Franciscan friars. The church's original wooden structure was rebuilt in stone around the mid-16th century. Vasco da Gama, who died in Cochin in 1524, was buried on this spot for 14 years before his remains were taken to Lisbon; you can still visit his tombstone in the church.

The **Indo-Portuguese Museum** (Map p342; ☎ 215400; Indian/foreigner Rs 10/25; ◷ 9am-1pm & 2-6pm Tue-Sun), in the garden of the Bishop's House, preserves the heritage of one of India's earliest Catholic communities, including vestments, statues, silver processional crosses and altarpieces from the Cochin diocese. The basement contains remnants of the Portuguese Fort Immanuel.

The **Dutch Cemetery** (Map p342), consecrated in 1724, contains the worn and dilapidated graves of Dutch traders and soldiers; ask at St Francis Church if you want to have a look around.

The imposing Catholic **Santa Cruz Basilica** (Map p342) was originally built on this site in 1506, though the current building dates to 1902. Inside you'll find artefacts from the different eras in Cochin and a striking, pastel-coloured interior.

MATTANCHERRY PALACE

Built by the Portuguese in 1555, **Mattancherry Palace** (Dutch Palace; Map p342; ☎ 2226085; Bazaar Rd;

admission Rs 2; ⏰ 10am-5pm Sat-Thu) was presented to the raja of Cochin, Veera Kerala Varma (1537–61), as a gesture of goodwill (and probably as a means of securing trading privileges). The Dutch renovated the palace in 1663, hence its alternative name, the Dutch Palace.

The star attractions here are the astonishingly preserved Hindu **murals**, depicting scenes from the Ramayana, Mahabharata and Puranic legends in intricate detail. The central hall on the 1st floor, once a coronation hall, is now a portrait gallery of maharajas from 1864. There's an impressive collection of palanquins (hand-carried carriages), bejewelled outfits and splendidly carved ceilings in every room. The ladies' bedchamber downstairs features a cheerful Krishna using his six hands and two feet to engage in foreplay with eight happy milkmaids.

Photography is prohibited.

PARDESI SYNAGOGUE & JEW TOWN
Originally built in 1568, the **synagogue** (Map p342; admission Rs 2; ⏰ 10am-noon & 3-5pm Sun-Fri, closed Jewish holidays) was destroyed by the Portuguese in 1662 and rebuilt two years later when the Dutch took Kochi. It features an ornate gold pulpit and hand-painted, willow-pattern floor tiles from China. It's magnificently illuminated by chandeliers and coloured-glass lamps. The graceful clock tower was built in 1760. There is an upstairs balcony for women who worshipped separately according to Orthodox rites.

The synagogue is smack bang in the middle of **Jew Town**, a bustling port area and centre of the Kochi spice trade. Scores of small firms huddle together in old, dilapidated buildings and the air is filled with the biting aromas of ginger, cardamom, cumin, turmeric and cloves. These days, the lanes right around the Dutch Palace and the synagogue are filled with antique and tourist curio shops rather than pungent spices. Look out for the Jewish names on some of the buildings.

ART GALLERIES
Kochi is a leader in encouraging contemporary local artists.

Chitram Art Gallery (Map p341; ☎ 2374012; MG Rd, Ernakulam; ⏰ 9.30am-8pm Mon-Sat) Has a few excellent pieces by both well-known and emerging Indian artists.

Draavidia Art & Performance Gallery (Map p342; ☎ 3296812; Bazaar Rd; ⏰ 10am-6pm) Shows off art by Keralan artists in an airy upstairs gallery. It also holds classical music concerts for Rs 100 from November to March at 6pm.

Kashi Art Gallery (Map p342; ☎ 215769; Bazaar Rd, Mattancherry; ⏰ 10am-6pm) Changing exhibitions, local artists, often experimental.

Lila Studio (Map p342; www.anandagaya.com; Bazaar Rd; ⏰ 10am-6pm Mon-Sat) Mostly showing works by co-director, painter and sculptor Gayatri Gamuz.

Activities
SWIMMING
Nonguests can swim in the garden pool of **Casino Hotel** (Map p341; Willington Island; per person Rs 250). For a dip in the ocean, you can make a day trip to the attractive **Cherai beach** on Vypeen Island (see p352).

AYURVEDA
Ayur Dara (☎ 2502362; www.ayurdara.de; Murikkumpadam, Vypeen Island; 1-/7-day treatment incl lunch Rs 1000/7000; ⏰ 9am-5pm) Run by a world-renowned Ayurvedic practitioner, it's 4km from the Vypeen Island ferry (autorickshaw Rs 30). Appointment necessary.

Cochin Ayurvedic Centre (Map p342; ☎ 2217103; fort_hs@yahoo.com; Santa Cruz School Rd, Fort Cochin; massage treatment from Rs 500; ⏰ 9am-7pm) Recommended Ayurvedic massage and treatment.

Kerala Ayurveda Chikitsa Kendram (Map p346; ☎ 2376916; Kannanthodathu Lane, Ernakulam; rejuvenation massage Rs 500, steam bath Rs 200; ⏰ 9.30am-5.30pm) Full range of treatments available.

Courses
Mrs Leelu Roy runs a highly recommended class called **Cook & Eat** (Map p342; ☎ 2215377; simonroy@hotmail.com; Quiros St; class Rs 400; ⏰ 11am & 6pm) in a great big family kitchen. Several homestays also run cooking demonstrations for guests – ask around.

The **Kerala Kathakali Centre** (see p350) has lessons in classical Kathakali dance, music and make-up (from Rs 350 per hour).

Tours
The private Tourist Desk Information Counter runs a full-day backwater tour (Rs 550) on a houseboat through the wider canals and lagoons, and a canoe through the small canals and villages. Lunch and hotel pick-up are provided. See the boxed text, p329, for more information.

The KTDC runs half-day backwater tours (Rs 350) at 8.30am and 2.30pm, and tourist boat tours around Fort Cochin (Rs 100) at the same times. It also has full-day backwater trips (Rs 650) at 8.30am, where you stop to see local weaving factories, spice gardens and most importantly toddy (palm beer) tapping!

Festivals & Events

The eight-day **Ernakulathappan Utsavam festival** culminates in a procession of 15 decorated elephants, ecstatic music and fireworks.

Sleeping

Fort Cochin is a great place to escape the noise and chaos of the mainland – it's tranquil and romantic, with superior accommodation choices. Budget-priced rooms, however, are becoming rarer each season. Ernakulam is buzzing, and more convenient for onward travel, but accommodation is uninspiring. Book well ahead during December and January.

BUDGET

Fort Cochin

Oy's Homestay (Map p342; ☎ 2215798; oyshomestay@ yahoo.com; Burgher St; s Rs 150-400, d Rs 250-500) Oy's has a warren of eclectic and funky rooms. They run the whole gamut from big, bright and cheery to small, dark and dreary.

Princess Inn (Map p342; ☎ 2217073; princessinnfo rtkochi@gmail.com; Princess St; s Rs 250, d Rs 350-550) A shining example of what a fresh lick of paint can do: sprucing up what would otherwise be dull, small rooms with cheery bright colours, comfy communal spaces and spotless bathrooms. Great value.

Spice Holidays Homestay (Map p342; ☎ 2216650; spiceholidays@yahoo.com; Burgher St; s/d from Rs 350/500) The friendly owners here more than make up for the plain rooms, which lack window real estate. The courtyard and welcoming sitting area is a plus.

Vasco Homestay (Map p342; ☎ 2216267; vascoinfor mations@yahoo.co.uk; Rose St; d Rs 400-700) The long-timer has just two subdivided rooms in an elegant Portuguese mansion, thought to be the house where Vasco da Gama died. Its corner room is sensational value: it's enormous, has poster beds with mosquito netting, a few simple decorations and bay windows looking onto St Francis church.

Green Woods Bethlehem (Map p342; ☎ 3247791; greenwoodsbethlehem1@vsnl.net; opp ESI Hospital; r Rs 400-800, with AC Rs 1000; 🔀) This excellent option is in a residential area enclosed in its own, thick jungle of plants and palms, 1½km south of Fort Cochin. There are a few humble, but extremely cosy, rooms, top-floor ones with bird's eye-to-eye views of the treetops. The

family (who look ready to adopt everyone who walks through the door) often cook enough dinner for everyone to join in. Breakfast on their inviting rooftop is included and they often hold cooking classes/demonstrations.

You can also try:

Elite Hotel (Map p342; ☎ 2215733; elitejoy@yahoo .com; Princess St; s Rs 350, d Rs 400-800) An old-school backpacker favourite, the plain rooms are barely OK value these days.

Vintage Inn (Map p342; ☎ 2215064; www.vintage resorts.in; Residale Branch Rd; s Rs 300-500, d Rs 600-800, d with AC Rs 1200; 🔀) Away from the action, with clean, bright and roomy but unexciting digs.

Ernakulam

Piazza Residency (Map p346; ☎ 2376508; Kalathipara-mbil Rd; s Rs 170-250, d Rs 240-370) Rooms here are carpeted and a little tattered, but come in a variety of sizes and have tolerable wooden furniture.

Sapphire Tourist Home (Map p346; ☎ 2381238; Cannon Shed Rd; d Rs 275-325) Close to the main boat jetty, this place has cheerful, bright rooms – not bad value at this price.

Maple Tourist Home (Map p346; ☎ 2355156; Cannon Shed Rd; d Rs 285-450, with AC Rs 680; 🔀) This place has solid-value rooms right near the boat stations. Some are still fresh and sparkling clean from a refurbishment, and all come with TV.

Bijus Tourist Home (Map p346; ☎ 2361661; www.bijus touristhome.com; Market Rd; s/d from Rs 325/420, d with AC Rs 800; 🔀) A friendly, ever-popular choice, handy for the main jetty. Rooms are smart, simple and comfy, and the place is efficiently run

MIDRANGE

Fort Cochin

Walton's Homestay (Map p342; ☎ 2215309; cewalton@redffmail.com; Princess St; r Rs 800-1000) You'll be in good care with the affable Waltons as your hosts. They have big and light rooms, all white with blue trim, a lush garden out the back and a second-hand bookshop downstairs. They also have a big garden cottage with AC (Rs 1500 to 1800).

Ann's Residency (Map p342; ☎ 2218024; www .annsresidency.com; Post Office Rd; r Rs 1000-1850, with AC Rs 1850-2300; 🔀) A friendly homestay that has 11 varied and bright rooms, all with poster beds and mosquito nets. There's an open-air restaurant and some rooms have balcony views looking onto the school classes next door.

Spencer Home (Map p342; ☎ 2215049; spencerhom estyfc@rediffmail.com; Parade Ground Rd; d Rs 1200) This

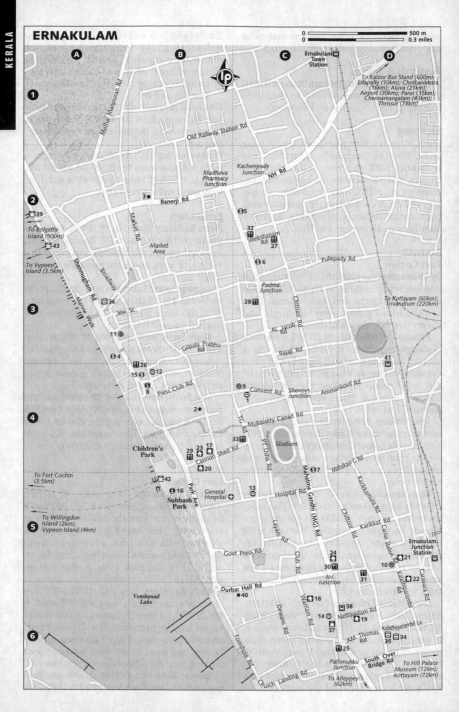

INFORMATION		
College Post Office	1	C4
Current Books	2	B4
DC Books	3	B2
Federal Bank ATM	4	A3
Federal Bank ATM	(see 7)	
HDFC Bank ATM	5	C2
Idbi Bank ATM	6	C3
ING Bank ATM	7	C4
KTDC Tourist Reception Centre	8	B4
Net Park	9	C4
Open Door Internet Café	10	D5
Penta Menaka Building	11	A3
Post Office	12	B4
Post Office	13	C5
Post Office	14	C6
State Bank of India ATM	15	B4
Tourist Desk Information		
Counter	16	B5
Tourist Police	(see 8)	
UAE Exchange	(see 4)	

SIGHTS & ACTIVITIES		
Kerala Ayurveda Chikitsa		
Kendram	(see 34)	

SLEEPING		
Bijus Tourist Home	17	B4
Hotel Aiswarya	18	C6
Hotel Excellency	19	D6
Maple Tourist Home	20	B4
Paulson Park Hotel	21	D5
Piazza Residency	22	D5
Sapphire Tourist Home	23	B4
Yuvarani Residency	24	C5

EATING		
Chinese Garden	25	D6
City Park Restaurant	(see 23)	
Coffee Beanz	26	B4
Frys Village		
Restaurant	27	C2
Indian Coffee House	28	C3

Indian Coffee House	29	B4
Indian Coffee House	30	C5
Pizza Hut	31	D5
Spencer's Daily	32	C2
Spices Food Joint	33	C4

ENTERTAINMENT		
Art Kerala	34	D6
See India Foundation	35	D6
Shenoy Cinema	36	A3

SHOPPING		
Kairali	37	C6

TRANSPORT		
Bus to Fort Cochin	38	D6
High Court Jetty	39	A2
Indian Airlines	40	C6
KSRTC Bus Stand	41	B4
Main Jetty	42	B5
Private Ferry	43	A2

handsomely restored heritage home has snug rooms around a quiet garden courtyard – complete with huge Chinese fishing net. Check out the amazingly intricate gold antique lock on one of the doors.

Delight Home Stay (Map p342; ☎ 2217658; www .delightfulhomestay.com; Post Office Rd; r Rs 1200-1500, with AC Rs 2500; ✷) Delightful it is. There are many uniquely styled rooms, all beautifully remodelled and immediately alluring. There's frilly white woodwork all around, a trim garden and an imposing sitting room covered in wall-to-wall polished teak. Keralan cooking classes are held here.

Raintree Lodge (Map p342; ☎ 3251498; www.fort cochin.com; Peter Celli St; r Rs 1800; ✷) The intimate and comfortable rooms have an agreeable blend of modern and period odds and ends. Try to get an upstairs room with a balcony looking onto the quiet street.

Also recommended:

Kapithan Inn (Map p342; ☎ 2226560; www.kap ithaninn.com; s/d from Rs 600/750, cottages Rs 1800-3000; ✷) Quiet and pleasant, with bright, restful rooms.

Ballard Bungalow (Map p342; ☎ 2215854; www .cochinballard.com; River Rd; d Rs 1200, with AC Rs 2200; ✷ ▢) A gorgeous colonial building with airy, spacious rooms. Price includes breakfast.

Ernakulam

Respectable midrange options in Ernakulam are few and far between.

Hotel Aiswarya (Map p346; ☎ 2364454; Warriam Rd; s/d Rs 400/600, d with AC Rs 900; ✷) Top marks for its central location and a respectable score its for clean, bright rooms. This is a fair midrange choice.

Paulson Park Hotel (Map p346; ☎ 2378240; www .paulsonparkhotel.com; Carrier Station Rd; s/d from Rs 500/800, with AC Rs 900/1200; ✷) Right near the station, this spick-and-span, quiet place boasts a fantasy-inspired indoor garden (was that a unicorn?). The cheaper rooms are minimalist, but the pricier rooms have just enough decoration to make them feel welcoming.

Hotel Excellency (Map p346; ☎ 2378251; www.hotel excellency.com; Nettipadam Rd; s/d from Rs 600/700, with AC Rs 900/1000; ✷ ▢) It feels a little like a hospital but rooms are neat and very tidy. Look at a few rooms; some are bigger than others.

Yuvarani Residency (Map p346; ☎ 2377040; www .yuvaraniresidency.com; MG Rd; s/d from Rs 850/1000, with AC Rs 1250/1600; ✷) Even though all that glitters is not gold here, the rooms are perfectly comfortable and finished with all the stylish dark-wood fixtures your heart might desire. It's set back from MG Rd enough to shield the noise, making it the best midrange choice in town.

Mattancherry & Jew Town

Caza Maria (Map p342; ☎ 2225678; cazamaria@rediffmail .com; Jew Town Rd; r with breakfast Rs 1600 & 1900) Right in the heart of Jew Town, this place has just two magnificently decorated, gigantic rooms overlooking the bazaar. Fit for a maharaja, it definitely has idiosyncratic style.

TOP END
Fort Cochin

Malabar House (Map p342; ☎ 2216666; www.mala barhouse.com; Parade Ground Rd; r €175, ste €250-300, incl breakfast; ✷ ▢) If you have money to burn, let this be your pyre. What may just be the best boutique hotel in India, Malabar flaunts its

KERALA

uber-hip blend of modern colours and period fittings like it's not even trying. The suites are huge and lavishly appointed, although the standard rooms could use more space.

Brunton Boatyard (Map p342; ☎ 2215461; brunton boatyard@cghearth.com; River Rd; r US$275, ste US$385; ☒ ☑) This imposing hotel faithfully reproduces 16th- and 17th-century Dutch and Portuguese architecture in a grand 26-room complex. All of the smallish rooms look out over the harbour, and have bathtub and balconies with a refreshing sea breeze that's better than AC. There are two restaurants and a bar; breakfast is included.

Around Cochin

our pick Olavipe Homestay (☎ 0478-2522255; www .olavipe.com; Olavipe; s/d incl meals Rs 5000/6500) This gorgeous 1890s traditional Syrian-Christian home is on a 16-hectare farm surrounded by backwaters, 28km south of Cochin. A restored mansion of rosewood and glistening teak, it has several large and breezy rooms – all wonderfully finished with original period décor (only the ceiling fans are new). There are lots of shady awnings and sitting areas, a fascinating archive with six generations of family history, and the gracious owners will make you feel like a welcome friend rather than a guest. You can visit nearby backwater villages from here, use their paddle boat, or help out with the working shrimp farm or plant pollination. A taxi to/from Fort Cochin is Rs 600 to 700.

Eating & Drinking

Covert beer consumption is *de rigueur* at most of the Fort Cochin restaurants, and more expensive in the licensed ones (Rs 80 to 165).

FORT COCHIN

In some places you can blow a night's accommodation on a single dish, but with some genuinely interesting food on offer you'll get the urge to splurge.

Teapot (Map p342; Peter Celli St; snacks Rs 30-50, meals Rs 150) This stylish haunt is the perfect venue for high tea, with quality teas, sandwiches and full meals served in chic minimalist, airy rooms. Witty accents include antique teapots, old tea chests for tables and a gnarled, tea tree–based glass table. The death by chocolate (Rs 50) is truly coco homicide, trust us.

Solar Café (Map p342; Bazaar Rd; meals Rs 30-75; ☺ 10am-6pm) This arty and funky café at Draavidia Gallery (p344) serves up breakfast and lunch in a brightly coloured and friendly setting. It has some upstairs veranda seats overlooking the hubbub of the street below.

Talk of the Town (Map p342; cnr KB Jacobs Rd & Bastion St; meals Rs 30-120) Upstairs, casual and breezy, don't miss out on the cheap and expertly prepared Indian dishes whipped up here.

Kashi Art Café (Map p342; Burgher St; breakfast/lunch Rs 70/75; ☺ 8.30am-7pm) Something of an institution, this place has a hip-but-casual vibe, along with hip-but-casual service. The coffee is as strong as it should be, and the daily Western breakfast and lunch specials are excellent. You can fill plastic water bottles for Rs 5 per litre, and a small gallery shows off local artists.

Old Courtyard (Map p342; ☎ 2216302; Princess St; mains from Rs 160) Seafood focused, the small but thoughtful international menu is well executed – Spanish-style beef (Rs 250) and baked mussels (Rs 150) get our vote.

Malabar Junction (Map p342; ☎ 2216666; Parade Ground Rd; mains Rs 300-1000) Set in an open-sided pavilion, this classy restaurant at Malabar House is movie-star cool. There's a seafood-based, European-style menu and Grover's Estate (quaffable, Indian) wine by the bottle (Rs 1200) or glass (Rs 250).

Also recommended:

New Ananda Bhavan (Map p342; River Rd; dishes Rs 11-35) Herbivores: make a beeline for this basic but spotless veggie restaurant.

Salt 'n' Pepper (Map p342; Tower Rd; dishes Rs 35-120; ☺ 24 hr) Superbly average food, but the street-side tables bustle nightly with punters having a special-teapot tipple (Rs 80).

History Restaurant (Map p342; ☎ 2215461; River Rd; mains Rs 350-425) At the Brunton Boatyard, this restaurant has a marvellous historical menu tracing Kochi's Jewish, Syrian, Arabic and Portuguese history.

Behind the Chinese fishing nets are a couple of **fishmongers** (Map p342; seafood per kg Rs 50-300), from whom you can buy fish (or prawns, scampi, lobster), then take your selection to a shack where they will cook it and serve it to you (about Rs 40 per kilogram of fish).

ERNAKULAM

Spices Food Joint (Map p346; Cannon Shed Rd; dishes Rs 7-35; ☺ 5am-12pm) A family-run hole-in-the-wall restaurant captained by the gregarious Sherief. The cheap veg, chicken and meat biryanis (Rs 18 to 35), as well as fish-curry meals (Rs 15), are deservedly popular.

Frys Village Restaurant (Map p346; Veekshanam Rd; dishes Rs 15-70; ☻ lunch & dinner) This cafeteria-like family restaurant is the best place in town for authentic Keralan food, especially seafood, such as fish *pollichathu* and crab roast (both Rs 65).

City Park Restaurant (Cannon Shed Rd; dishes Rs 60-90) City Park has a well-prepared and varied menu (Indian, Chinese, continental). The masala tea is especially tangy (Rs 8).

Chinese Garden (Warriom Rd; dishes Rs 75-150; ☻ lunch & dinner) Good Chinese food served in a plush-red, moodily lit interior.

Other options:

Spencer's Daily (Veekshanam Rd; ☻ 7.30am-10.30pm) Well-stocked supermarket.

Indian Coffee House (Cannon Shed Rd) Also has branches on Jos Junction and MG Rd near Padma Junction.

Coffee Beanz (Shanmugham Rd; breakfasts Rs 20-60; ☻ lunch & dinner; 🕸) For a hip coffee hit.

Pizza Hut (Durbar Hall Rd; medium pizza Rs 90-120; ☻ lunch & dinner) For when the junk-food cravings win. Delivery is available.

MATTANCHERRY & JEW TOWN
Ramathula Hotel (Map p342; Lobo Junction, Mattancherry; biryani Rs 22-38; ☻ lunch & dinner) This place is legendary among locals for its chicken and meat biryanis – get here early or you'll miss out. It's better known by the chef's name, Kayee.

Caza Maria (Map p342; ☎ 2225678; Boat Jetty Rd; mains from Rs 100-200; ☻ lunch & dinner) Run by an expat Frenchman, this is an enchanting space with good music but slightly bland food. There's a small menu of Indian and a few French dishes (*poisson à la Provençale*, Rs 140). Service is great and the ambience delightful.

Entertainment
CINEMAS
Shenoy Cinema (Map p346; Shanmugham Rd, Ernakulam; tickets Rs 40) Screens films in Malayalam, Hindi, Tamil and English.

KATHAKALI
There are several places in Kochi where you can view Kathakali (see the boxed text, below).

TRADITIONAL KERALAN ARTS

Kathakali
The art form of Kathakali crystallised at around the same time as Shakespeare was scribbling his plays, though elements of it stem from 2nd-century temple rituals. The Kathakali performance is the dramatised presentation of a play, usually based on the Hindu epics the Ramayana, the Mahabharata and the Puranas. All the great themes are covered – righteousness and evil, frailty and courage, poverty and prosperity, war and peace.

Drummers and singers accompany the actors, who tell the story through their precise movements, particularly mudras (hand gestures) and facial expressions. Traditionally, performances took place in temple grounds and went from 8pm until dawn; now shorter performances in other open-air locales, as well as indoor halls, are also popular.

Preparation for the performance is lengthy and disciplined. Paint, fantastic costumes, highly decorated headpieces and meditation transform the actors both physically and mentally into the gods, heroes and demons they are about to play.

You'll can see cut-down performances in tourist hot spots all over the state, and there are Kathakali schools in Trivandrum (see p312) and near Thrissur (see p355) that encourage visitors. Many temple festivals across the state feature traditional all-night Kathakali shows; ask at DTPC offices.

Kalarippayat
Kalarippayat is an ancient tradition of martial training and discipline. Still taught throughout Kerala, some believe it is the forerunner of all martial arts. Its roots can be traced back to the 12th century, when skirmishes among the many feudal principalities in the region were common.

Masters of *kalarippayat*, called Gurukkal, teach their craft inside a special arena called a *kalari*. The *kalari* is part gymnasium, part school and part temple. Its construction follows traditional principles: its rectangular design is always aligned east–west and Hindu deities are represented in each corner.

Kalarippayat movements – the foundation of choreography that uses the actors' bodies and gestures as the primary tools of expression – can be traced in Kerala's performing arts, such as Kathakali and *kootiattam* (traditional Sanksrit drama), and in ritual arts such as *theyyam*.

The performances are certainly made for tourists, but they're also a great introduction to this intriguing art form. The standard programme starts with the intricate make-up application, followed by a commentary on the dance and then the performance. All places charge around Rs 125.

See India Foundation (Map p346; ☎ 2376471; Kalathiparambil Lane, Ernakulam; ☽ make-up 6pm, show 6.30-8pm) One of the oldest Kathakali theatres in Kerala, it has small-scale shows with an emphasis on the religious and philosophical roots of Kathakali.

Art Kerala (Map p346; ☎ 2375238; Kannanthodath Lane, Ernakulam; ☽ make-up 6pm, show 7-8.15pm) Started in 1977, this place stages rooftop performances and provides a printout of the night's story.

Kerala Kathakali Centre (Map p342; ☎ 2215827; www.kathakalicentre.com; River Rd, Fort Cochin; ☽ make-up 5pm, show 6.30-8pm) This place stages big, showy performances. It provides useful printed translations of the night's story. Classes in classical dance, music and make-up (from Rs 350 per hour) are also available.

Shopping

Broadway in Ernakulam (p346) is good for local shopping, spice shops, clothing and a bazaar feel. Around Convent and Market Rds there's a huddle of tailors, and on and around Market Rd, between Jew and Press Club Rds, is the textiles centre. On Jew Town Rd in Mattancherry (Map p342), there's a plethora of shops selling antiques and reproductions. Many shops in Fort Cochin operate lucrative commission rackets, with rickshaw drivers getting huge kickbacks (which are added to your price) just for dropping tourists at the door.

Kairali (Map p346; ☎ 2354507; MG Rd, Ernakulam; ☽ 9am-8pm Mon-Sat) This is one of many handicraft shops around here, a government emporium with quality items at fixed prices. There's a much smaller Kairali (Map p342; ☎ 221544; River Rd; ☽ 9am-7pm Mon-Sat) in Fort Cochin.

Cinnamon (Map p342; ☎ 2217124; Post Office Rd, Fort Cochin; ☽ 10am-7pm Mon-Sat) This exquisite shop sells high-quality, individually designed Indian clothes and homewares.

Getting There & Away
AIR
Book flights through the following airlines:
Air India (Map p341; ☎ 2351295; MG Rd; ☽ 9.30am-1pm & 1.45-5.30pm Mon-Sat)

Indian Airlines (Map p346; ☎ 2370235; Durbar Hall Rd; ☽ 9.45am-1pm & 1.45-5pm)
Jet Airways (Map p341; ☎ 2293231; MG Rd; ☽ 9am-7pm Mon-Sat, to 4pm Sun)
Kingfisher Airlines (Map p341; ☎ 2351144; Sreekandath Rd; ☽ 9am-6pm Mon-Sat)

Jet Airways has three daily services to Mumbai (US$239), one daily to Chennai (US$164) and Delhi (US$442), and two daily to Bengaluru (US$126). Indian Airlines flies daily to these cities for the same prices, and also has two flights a week to Goa (US$172) and daily flights to Trivandrum (US$142). Kingfisher flies to most of these destinations for nearly 70% less.

BUS
The **KSRTC bus stand** (Map p346; ☎ 2372033; ☽ reservations 6am-10pm) is in Ernakulam, along the railway, halfway between the train stations, near Ammankovil Rd. Many buses passing through Ernakulam originate in other cities – you may have to join the scrum when the bus pulls in. You can make reservations up to five days in advance for buses originating here. There's a separate window for reservations to Tamil Nadu. See the boxed text, below, for more information on buses from Ernakulam.

In addition, two daily buses (6am and 9pm) run up the coast through Calicut to Kannur (Cannanore), Kasaragod and onto Mangalore (Rs 304).

MAJOR BUSES FROM ERNAKULAM

The following bus services operate from the KSRTC bus stand.

Destination	Fare (Rs)	Duration (hr)	Frequency
Alleppey	33	1½	every 20min
Bengaluru	304	14	6 daily
Calicut	118	5	hourly
Chennai	425	15	2 daily
Coimbatore	127	4½	9 daily
Kanyakumari	166	8	2 daily
Kollam	84	3½	every 20min
Kottayam	38	2	every 20min
Kumily (for Periyar)	73	5	6 daily
Madurai	167	9	2 daily
Thrissur	40	2	every 15min
Trivandrum	127	5	every 20min

There are a number of private bus companies that have super-deluxe, AC, video buses daily to Bengaluru, Chennai, Mangalore and Coimbatore; prices are around 75% higher than the government buses, and there are shops and stands selling tickets all over Ernakulam. The main private bus stand (the Kaloor bus stand) is north of the city.

TRAIN

Ernakulam has two train stations, Ernakulam Town and Ernakulam Junction. Reservations for both stations have to be made at the Ernakulam Junction **reservations office** (🕙 8am-8pm Mon-Sat, 8am-2pm Sun).

There are daily trains to Trivandrum (2nd class/3AC/2AC Rs 60/335/470, 4½ hours, 13 daily), via either Alleppey (Rs 28/188/266, 1½ hours) or Kottayam (Rs 28/188/266, 1½ hours). There are also trains to Thrissur (Rs 30/188/266, two hours, 10 daily), Calicut (Rs 57/281/402, five hours, seven daily) and Kannur (Rs 75/361/518, seven hours, seven daily). For long-distance trains, see the boxed text, below.

Getting Around
TO/FROM THE AIRPORT

Kochi International Airport (☎ 2610113) is at Nedumbassery, 30km northeast of Ernakulam. Taxis to Ernakulam cost around Rs 400, and from Fort Cochin around Rs 550.

BOAT

Ferries are the fastest form of transport between Fort Cochin and the mainland. The stop on the eastern side of Willingdon Island is called Embarkation (Map p342); the west

one, opposite Mattancherry, is Terminus (Map p341); and the main stop at Fort Cochin is Customs (Map p342), with another stop at the Mattancherry Jetty near the synagogue (Map p342). Ferry fares are all around Rs 2.50; buy tickets on board.

Ernakulam

There are services to Fort Cochin every 40 minutes (4.40am to 9.30pm) from the main jetty (Map p346). There are six daily ferries directly to/from the Mattancherry Jetty (5.55am to 6.45pm). The ticket office in Ernakulam opens 10 minutes before each sailing.

Ferries run every 20 minutes to Willingdon and Vypeen Islands (6am to 10pm) – although with the new bridge to Vypeen these are often empty.

Fort Cochin

Ferries run from Customs Jetty to Ernakulam from 6.20am to 9.50pm. Ferries also run between Customs Jetty and Willingdon Island about 18 times a day from 6.40am to 9.30pm (Monday to Saturday).

Car and passenger ferries cross to Vypeen Island from Fort Cochin virtually nonstop from 6am until 10pm.

LOCAL TRANSPORT

There are no real bus services between Fort Cochin and Mattancherry Palace, but it's an enjoyable 30-minute walk through the busy warehouse area along Bazaar Rd. Autorickshaws should cost around Rs 20, but you'll need to haggle. Most autorickshaw trips around Ernakulam shouldn't cost more than Rs 25.

MAJOR TRAINS FROM ERNAKULAM

The following are major long-distance trains departing from Ernakulam Town.

Destination	Train No & Name	Fare (Rs Sleeper/3AC/2AC)	Duration (hr)	Departures
Bengaluru	6525 *Kanyakumari–Bangalore Exp*	261/705/1000	11	6.05pm
Chennai	2624 *Trivandrum–Chennai Mail*	293/771/1082	12	7.10pm
Delhi*	2625 *Kerala Exp*	589/1601//2282	48	3.50pm
Mangalore	6329 *Malabar Exp*	190/505/716	10½	11.50pm
Mumbai	1082 *Kanyakumari–Mumbai Exp*	477/1313/1878	41	12.50pm
Parasuram	6349 *Parasuram Exp*	116/395**	10	11.15am

* Departs from Ernakulam Junction
** Fare in 2nd class/AC chair

To get to Fort Cochin after ferries stop running, catch a bus in Ernakulam on MG Rd (Rs 6), south of Durbar Hall Rd. Taxis charge round-trip fares between the islands, even if you only go one way – Ernakulam Town train station to Fort Cochin should cost around Rs 150.

Vasco Tourist Information Centre (Map p342; ☎ 2216215; vascoinformations@yahoo.co.uk; Bastion St, Fort Cochin) rents bicycles/scooters for Rs 45/200 per day.

AROUND KOCHI
Tripunithura
Hill Palace Museum (☎ 0484-2781113; admission Rs 15; ♥ 9am-12.30pm & 2-4.30pm Tue-Sun) at Tripunithura, 12km southeast of Ernakulam en route to Kottayam, was formerly the residence of the Kochi royal family and is an arresting, 49-building palace complex. It now houses the collections of the royal families, as well as 19th-century oil paintings, old coins, sculptures and paintings, and temple models. From Kochi, catch the bus to Tripunithura from MG Rd or Shanmugham Rd, behind the Tourist Reception Centre; an autorickshaw should cost around Rs 225 return with one-hour waiting time.

Cherai Beach
On Vypeen island, 25km from Fort Cochin, **Cherai Beach** might just be Kochi's best-kept secret. It's an enchanting stretch of undeveloped white sand, with miles of lazy backwaters just 300m back from the seashore. Best of all, it's close enough to visit on a day trip from Kochi.

If you plan on staying for more than a day, there are a handful of stylish but unobtrusive resorts around.

Cherai Beach Resort (☎ 0484-2481818; www .cheraibeachresorts.com; Vypeen Island; r Rs 1000-2500, with AC Rs 3500; 🅿 🖳) This excellent collection of unique cottages lies around a meandering lagoon, with the beach on one side and backwaters on the other. Bungalows are individually designed using natural materials, in conjunction with either curving walls, split-levels or lookouts onto the backwaters – there's even a tree growing inside one room. We love the tiny, individually hammocked islets connected by walkways. There is a restaurant serving daily buffets (breakfast/lunch/dinner Rs 100/300/300) and even lagoon-side wi-fi.

For a budget option, you can try the irregularly open **Fisherman's Village** (r Rs 500-750;

♥ Nov-Mar) a few kilometres further north. It has simple bungalows right near the shore, but the beach here is rocky. At the time of research it was being rehabilitated by a Frenchman.

To get here from Fort Cochin, catch a vehicle ferry to Vypeen Island (per person/scooter Rs 1.50/3) and either hire an autorickshaw from the jetty (around Rs 250) or catch one of the frequent buses (Rs 10, one hour).

Parur & Chennamangalam
Nowhere is the tightly woven religious cloth that is India more apparent than in Parur, 35km north of Kochi. The oldest **synagogue** (Rs 2; ♥ 9am-5pm Tue-Sun) in Kerala has been wonderfully renovated and sits in Chennamangalam, around 8km from Parur. It has notable door and ceiling wood reliefs in dazzling colours and an intricately carved wooden ark. Just outside is the oldest tombstone in India, inscribed with the Hebrew date corresponding to 1269. There's a **Jesuit church** and the ruins of a Jesuit college nearby. The Jesuits first arrived in Chennamangalam in 1577 and soon after the first book in Tamil (the written language then used in this part of Kerala) was printed on this spot. From here you can also walk to the **Hindu temple** on the hill overlooking the Periyar River. On the way you'll pass a 16th-century **mosque**, as well as Muslim and Jewish **burial grounds**.

In Parur town, you'll find the **agraharam** (place of Brahmins) – a small street of closely packed and brightly coloured houses. It was settled by Tamil Brahmins, though it may as well have been garden gnomes judging by the houses' fairytale-like appearance.

Parur is compact and locals can point you in the right direction, though Chennamangalam is best visited with a guide. **Indoworld** (Map p341; ☎ 0484-2367818; www.indoworldtours.com; Heera House, MG Rd, Ernakulam; ♥ 8am-8pm Mon-Sat, to 2.30pm Sun) can organise tours (around Rs 600 plus guide). It also has an **office** (Map p342; Princess St) in Fort Cochin.

For Parur, catch a bus from the KSRTC bus stand in Kochi (Rs 15, one hour, every 10 minutes). From Parur catch a bus (Rs 3) or autorickshaw (Rs 45) to Chennamangalam.

THRISSUR (TRICHUR)
☎ 0487 / pop 330,067
While the rest of Kerala has its fair share of celebrations, Thrissur remains the cultural cherry on the festival cake. With a list of brash festivals as long as a temple elephant's

trunk, the whole region supports multiple institutions that are nursing the dying classical Keralan performing arts back to health. It is a busy, bustling place, home to a community of Nestorian Christians, whose denomination dates back to the 3rd century AD. The popular Sri Krishna Temple (33km northeast of Thrissur; see p355) and performing-arts school Kerala Kalamandalam (see p355) are nearby. Plan to get here during the rambunctious festival season (November to mid-May).

Orientation & Information

There's HDFC, UTI and Federal Bank ATMs in town, accepting all foreign cards.
DTPC office (☎ 2320800; Palace Rd; ☸ 10am-5pm Mon-Sat)

Lava Rock Internet Café (Kuruppam Rd; per hr Rs 20; ☸ 8.30am-10.30pm)
Paragon Web Inc (2nd fl, High Rd; per hr Rs 15; ☸ 8am-10.30pm)
UAE Money Exchange (☎ 2445668; TB Rd; ☸ 9am-6.30pm Mon-Sat, 9.30am-1pm Sun) Next to the Casino Hotel.

Sights & Activities

One of the oldest in the state, **Vadakkunathan Kshetram Temple** crowns the hill at the epicentre of Thrissur. Finished in classic Keralan architecture, only Hindus are allowed inside, though the mound surrounding the temple has sweeping metropolis views and is a popular spot to loiter. There are also a number of inspiring churches, including **Our Lady of**

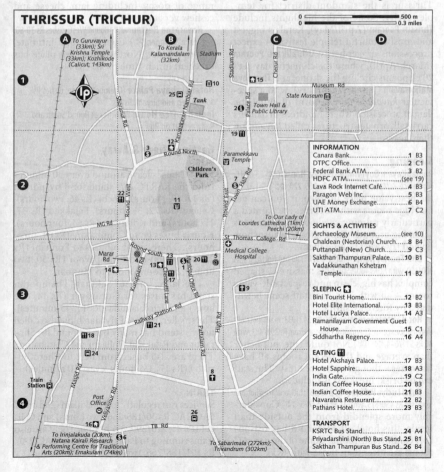

THRISSUR (TRICHUR)

INFORMATION	
Canara Bank	1 B3
DTPC Office	2 C1
Federal Bank ATM	3 B2
HDFC ATM	(see 19)
Lava Rock Internet Café	4 B3
Paragon Web Inc.	5 B3
UAE Money Exchange	6 B4
UTI ATM	7 C2

SIGHTS & ACTIVITIES	
Archaeology Museum	(see 10)
Chaldean (Nestorian) Church	8 B4
Puttanpalli (New) Church	9 C3
Sakthan Thampuran Palace	10 B1
Vadakkunathan Kshetram Temple	11 B2

SLEEPING	
Bini Tourist Home	12 B2
Hotel Elite International	13 B3
Hotel Luciya Palace	14 A3
Ramanilayam Government Guest House	15 C1
Siddhartha Regency	16 A4

EATING	
Hotel Akshaya Palace	17 B3
Hotel Sapphire	18 A3
India Gate	19 C2
Indian Coffee House	20 B3
Indian Coffee House	21 B3
Navaratna Restaurant	22 B2
Pathans Hotel	23 B3

TRANSPORT	
KSRTC Bus Stand	24 A4
Priyadarshini (North) Bus Stand	25 B1
Sakthan Thampuran Bus Stand	26 B4

Lourdes Cathedral, a massive cathedral with an underground shrine; Puttanpalli (New) Church, which has towering, pure-white spires visible from all round town; and the Chaldean (Nestorian) Church, which is unique in its complete lack of pictorial representations of Jesus.

The Archaeology Museum (admission Rs 6; 9am-5pm Tue-Sun) is in the 200-year-old Sakthan Thampuran Palace. Wandering through its arrow-guided maze you get to see some worthy artefacts, including 12th-century Keralan bronze sculptures, earthenware pots big enough to cook children in, decadent remnants of Kochi's royalty, and an extraordinary 1500kg wooden treasury box covered with iron spikes and locks.

In a state where festivals are a way of life, Thrissur is the standout district for temple revelry. Some of the highlights include Thrissur Pooram (April/May), Kerala's biggest and most colourful temple festival – expect processions of elephants; Uthralikavu Pooram (March/April), where the climactic day sees 20 elephants circling the shrine; and Thypooya Maholsavam (January/February), with a spectacular *kavadiyattam* (a form of ritualistic dance) procession where hundreds of dancers carry tall, ornate structures called *kavadis* on their heads.

Sleeping

Ramanilayam Government Guest House (☎ 2332016; cnr Palace & Museum Rds; s/d Rs 165/220; ✗) This is the best-value place in town, if you can get in. Huge rooms with balconies are painted a particularly calming shade of green, and it's set in big grounds. Ring ahead, or just show up and try sweet talking them.

Bini Tourist Home (☎ 2335703; Round North; s/d Rs 300/350, with AC Rs 400/550) This massive U-shaped complex has big, clean and respectable-value rooms – all with TV. The staff seem bewildered by foreign visitors.

Hotel Elite International (☎ 2421033; mail@hotelelit einternational.com; Chembottil Lane; s/d from Rs 391/483, with AC Rs 517/644; ✗ 🖳) Not quite elite, but better than average and the decent rooms all have balconies – though some are noisy. The staff can be brisk. Breakfast is included.

Hotel Luciya Palace (☎ 2424731; luciyapalace@hotmail .com; s/d Rs 450/575, with AC Rs 675/775; ✗) Considerably more splendid from the outside than inside, this hotel off Marar Rd has reasonably comfortable rooms. Some of the non-AC rooms are nicer than those with AC.

Siddhartha Regency (☎ 2424773; cnr TB & Veliyan-nur Rds; s/d Rs 750/900; ✗ 🖳) This is excellent value, with comely rooms decked out in simple but pleasant décor – and there's a pool!

Eating

Pathans Hotel (Round South; dishes from Rs 20) Clean and cafeteria-esque, this atmospheric place is popular with families for lunch and has a sweets counter downstairs.

Hotel Sapphire (Railway Station Rd; dishes Rs 20-60) Another place bustling for lunch-time biryanis (Rs 32 to Rs 49), this one's close to the train and bus stations for a quick meal between trips.

India Gate (Palace Rd; dishes around Rs 25) In the same building as the HDFC Bank, this is a bright, pure-veg place serving an unbeatable range of dosas, including jam, cheese and cashew versions.

Navaratna Restaurant (Round West; dishes Rs 30-80; lunch & dinner; ✗) Cool dark and intimate, this upmarket, North Indian veg place has excellent lunch-time meals (Rs 60).

Also try:

Hotel Akshaya Palace (Chembottil Lane; dishes Rs 15-50) Veg and biryani dishes.

Indian Coffee House Branches at Round South and Railway Station Rd.

Getting There & Away

BUS

KSRTC buses leave around every 30 minutes from the KSRTC bus stand for Trivandrum (Rs 170, 7½ hours), Kochi (Rs 46, two hours), Calicut (Rs 72, 3½ hours), Palakkad (Rs 37, 1½ hours) and Kottayam (Rs 64, four hours). Hourly buses go to Coimbatore (Rs 61, three hours). There are also buses to Ponnani (Rs 25, 1½ hours) and Prumpavoor (Rs 30, two hours), for connections to Munnar.

The large, private Sakthan Thampuran stand has buses for Guruvayur (Rs 14, one hour) and Irinjalakuda (Rs 11, 45 minutes). The smaller, private Priyadarshini (also called north) stand has many buses bound for Shoranur and Palakkad, Pollachi and Coimbatore. There are also buses from here to Cheruthuruthy (Rs 17, 1½ hours, every 10 minutes).

TRAIN

Services run regularly to Ernakulam (2nd class/ 3AC/2AC Rs 30/188/266, two hours) and Calicut (Rs 41/213/295, 3½ hours). There are also trains running to Palakkad (sleeper/3AC/2AC Rs 101/188/266, two hours) via Shoranur.

AROUND THRISSUR

The Hindu-only **Sri Krishna Temple** at Guruvayur, 33km northwest of Thrissur, is perhaps the most famous in Kerala. Said to be created by Guru, preceptor of the gods, and Vayu, god of wind, the temple is believed to date from the 16th century and is renowned for its healing powers. The temple's elephants (over 50 at last count) are kept at an old Zamorin palace, Punnathur Kota. An annual and spectacular **Elephant Race** is held here in February or March.

Kerala Kalamandalam (☎ 04884-262418; www .kalamandalam.com), 32km northeast of Thrissur at Cheruthuruthy, is a champion of Kerala's traditional art renaissance. Using an ancient Gurukula system of learning, students undergo intensive study in Kathakali, *mohiniattam* (classical dance), *kootiattam* (traditional Sanskrit drama), percussion, voice and violin. Structured **visits** (per person incl lunch US$18; ⊗ 9.30am-1pm) are available, including a tour around the theatre and classes. Individually tailored introductory courses are offered one subject at a time (between six and 12 months; around Rs 1500 per month, plus Rs 1500 for accommodation).

Natana Kairali Research & Performing Centre for Traditional Arts (☎ 0480-2825559; natanakairali@gmail .com), 20km south of Thrissur near Irinjalakuda, offers training in traditional arts, including rare forms of puppetry and dance. Short appreciation courses (usually about one month) are available to foreigners. In December each year, the centre holds five days of *mohiniyattam* (dance of the temptress) performances, a form of classical Keralan women's dance.

NORTHERN KERALA

KOZHIKODE (CALICUT)

☎ 0495 / pop 880,168

Always a prosperous trading town, Calicut was once the capital of the formidable Zamorin dynasty. Vasco da Gama first landed near Calicut in 1498, on his way to snatch a share of the subcontinent for king and country (Portugal that is). These days, trade depends mostly on exporting Indian labour to the Middle East. There's not a lot for tourists to see, though it's a good break in the journey and is the jumping-off point for Wayanad Wildlife Sanctuary.

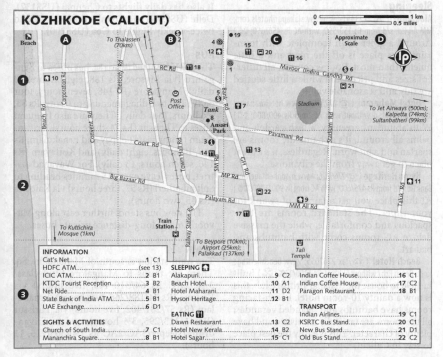

KOZHIKODE (CALICUT)

INFORMATION		
Cat's Net...............................1 C1		
HDFC ATM..............................(see 13)	**SLEEPING**	
ICIC ATM................................2 B1	Alakapuri...............................9 C2	Indian Coffee House.............16 C1
KTDC Tourist Reception............3 B2	Beach Hotel............................10 A1	Indian Coffee House.............17 C2
Net Ride.................................4 B1	Hotel Maharani......................11 D2	Paragon Restaurant..............18 B1
State Bank of India ATM............5 B1	Hyson Heritage......................12 B1	
UAE Exchange.........................6 D1		**TRANSPORT**
	EATING	Indian Airlines......................19 C1
SIGHTS & ACTIVITIES	Dawn Restaurant...................13 C2	KSRTC Bus Stand...................20 C1
Church of South India...............7 C1	Hotel New Kerala..................14 B2	New Bus Stand......................21 D1
Mananchira Square..................8 B1	Hotel Sagar...........................15 C1	Old Bus Stand.......................22 C2

Information

There are HDFC and State Bank of India ATMs in town.

Cat's Net (Mavoor Rd; per hr Rs 20) Open 24 hours – though not always in a row.

KTDC Tourist Reception (☎ 2722391; Malabar Mansion, SM Rd) Rudimentary tourist information.

Net Ride (Bank Rd; per hr Rs 20; ☉ 9am-10pm Mon-Sat)

UAE Exchange (☎ 2723164; Mavoor Rd; ☉ 9.30am-6pm Mon-Sat, to 1.30pm Sun).

Sights

Mananchira Square was the former courtyard of the Zamorins, and preserves the original spring-fed tank. The 650-year-old **Kuttichira Mosque** is in an attractive four-storey wooden building supported by wooden pillars and painted brilliant aqua, blue and white. Burnt down by the Portuguese in 1510, it was rescued and rebuilt to tell the tale. The **Church of South India** was established by Swiss missionaries in 1842 and has unique Euro-Keralan architecture.

Calicut's **beach**, north of the Beach Hotel, is a lovely place to stroll in the late afternoon.

Sleeping

Alakapuri (☎ 2723451-54; www.alakapurihotels.com; MM Ali Rd; s/d from Rs 150/550, with AC Rs 450/650; ✖) Around a green lawn (complete with fountain!) this place is off the road and a little quieter than most. Rooms come in all different sizes and prices, and while a little scuffed are tidy and reasonable value.

Hotel Maharani (☎ 2723101; www.hotelmaharani .com; Taluk Rd; d without/with AC from Rs 400/800; ✖) With abundant greenery, a lush garden and palms all around, it's a shame the rooms are spartan and a bit worn. Regardless, it's a great place to get away from the city noise.

Hyson Heritage (☎ 2766726; www.hysonheritage.com; Bank Rd; s/d from Rs 475/600, with AC from Rs 900/1200; ✖) At this place you get a fair bit of swank for your rupee. The standard rooms are tidy, spacious and comfortable, while the massive deluxe AC rooms come with bathtubs and bad art.

Beach Hotel (☎ /fax 2762055; www.beachheritage .com; Beach Rd; r without/with AC Rs 1200/1400; ✖) Built in 1890 to house the Malabar British Club, this is now a dainty 10-room hotel. Beach-facing rooms have bathtubs and secluded verandas; all the rooms are tastefully furnished and have plenty of character. This is easily the best place to stay in Calicut.

Eating

Hotel Sagar (Mavoor Rd; dishes from Rs 20; ☉ 6am-2am) This is a stylish and breezy veg and nonveg place with biryanis (including fish, Rs 60) and meals at lunchtime.

Paragon Restaurant (Kannur Rd; dishes Rs 28-90) Not as flash as the sign would have you believe, this place comes highly recommended for veg and nonveg dishes and is packed to the rafters come lunchtime to prove it.

Dawn Restaurant (GH Rd; dishes Rs 60-150, buffet Rs 126; ✖) The restaurant at the Hotel Malabar does multicuisine well, serving inventive Indian dishes and Keralan specials to truly awful, loud muzak.

For tasty, cheap meals also try the following:

Indian Coffee House (Mavoor Rd) Great for breakfast; there's also a branch on GH Rd.

Hotel New Kerala (SM Rd; dishes Rs 12-50) Full daily for lunch-time set meals (Rs 30) and biryanis.

Getting There & Away

AIR

Jet Airways (☎ 2740518; 29 Mavoor Rd) flies daily to Mumbai (US$200) – as does **Indian Airlines** (☎ 2766243; Eroth Centre, Bank Rd) for the same price. It also has daily flights to Chennai (US$137), Delhi (US$382) and Coimbatore (US$77), and twice-weekly flights to Goa (US$200).

BUS

The **KSRTC bus stand** (Mavoor Rd) has buses to Bengaluru (via Mysore, Rs 188, eight hours, 10 daily), Mangalore (Rs 148, seven hours, four daily) and to Udhagamandalam (Ooty; Rs 83, 5½ hours, four daily). There are also frequent buses to Thrissur (Rs 74, three hours), Trivandrum (going via Alleppey and Ernakulam; Rs 248, 10 hours, eight daily) and Kottayam (Rs 146, seven hours, 13 daily). For Wayanad district, buses leave every 15 minutes heading to Sultanbatheri (Rs 57, three hours) via Kalpetta (Rs 45, two hours).

The new bus stand, further east along Mavoor Rd, has long-distance private buses.

TRAIN

The train station is south of Mananchira Sq. There are trains to Mangalore (2nd class/3AC/2AC Rs 64/310/445, five hours) via Kannur (Rs 34/188/266, two hours), Ernakulam (Rs 57/281/402, five hours) via Thrissur (Rs 41/213/295, 3½ hours), and to Trivandrum (sleeper/3AC/2AC Rs 190/505/716, 11 hours).

Heading southeast, there are trains to Coimbatore (sleeper/3AC/2AC Rs 101/271/388, five hours), via Palakkad (Rs 101/221/316, three hours). These trains then head north to the centres of Bengaluru, Chennai and Delhi.

Getting Around
Calicut has a glut of autorickshaws. It's about Rs 10 from the station to the KSRTC bus stand or most hotels.

WAYANAD WILDLIFE SANCTUARY
☎ 04936
If Kerala is 'God's Country', this must be his garden of Eden. Part of a remote forest reserve that spills over into national parks in Karnataka and Tamil Nadu, Wayanad lies cocooned in the hills of the Western Ghats. Famed among Keralans for its jaw-dropping beauty, the landscape is a green medley of rice paddies, untouched forests, spice plantations and more rice paddies (the name translates to 'country of paddy fields'). A convenient stopover point between Bengaluru or Mysore and Kochi, the region gets surprisingly few visitors, though it's one of the few places you're almost guaranteed to spot wild elephants. Other wildlife that roam the forests here include sambar and spotted dear, Indian bison, langur monkeys and, drumroll, occasionally tigers.

Orientation & Information
The sanctuary, covering an area of 345 sq km, consists of two separate pockets – **Muthanga** in the east of the district, on the border of Tamil Nadu, and **Tholpetty** in the north, on the border with Karnataka. Three major towns in Wayanad district make good bases for exploring the sanctuary – **Kalpetta** in the south, **Sultanbatheri** (also known as Sultan Battery) in the east and **Mananthavadi** in the northwest.

The extremely helpful **DTPC office** (☎ 04936-202134; www.dtpcwayanad.com; Kalpetta; ☽ 10am-5pm Mon-Sat) can help organise tours, permits and trekking. There's a **UAE Exchange** (☎ 04936-207636; Main Rd; ☽ 9.30am-6pm Mon-Sat, 9.30am-1.30pm Sun) in Kalpetta, and Federal Bank or Canara Bank ATMs can be found in each of the three main towns, as well as internet cafés.

Sights & Activities
VISITING THE SANCTUARY
Entry to both parts of the **sanctuary** (Indian/foreigner Rs 10/100, camera/video Rs 25/150; ☽ 7am-5pm) is only permitted with a park guard (Rs 200); you can organise this through the DTPC office, with your hotel or at the park's entrance offices.

At Tholpetty, early morning 1½-hour **jeep tours** (Rs 500 incl guide) are a great way to spot wildlife; afternoon tours are also available. Pachyderm Palace (see p358) arranges wildlife-spotting treks into the areas surrounding the Tholpetty sanctuary.

At Muthanga, two-hour **jeep tours** (Rs 350 incl guide) and four-hour **guided walks** (Rs 300) are available.

The DTPC and most hotels arrange guided **jeep tours** (up to five people, Rs 1700 to Rs 2000) of the sanctuaries and surrounding sights.

OTHER SIGHTS & ACTIVITIES
There are some top opportunities for **trekking** around the district, including the precipice of **Chembra Peak**, at 2100m the tallest summit; **Vellarimala**, with great views and lots of wildlife-spotting opportunities; **Pakshipathalam**, a formation of large boulders deep in the forest; and a number of **waterfalls**. Permits are necessary and available from forest officers in South or North Wayanad. The accommodating DTPC office in Kalpetta organises permits, trekking guides (Rs 500 per day), camping equipment (Rs 200 per person) and transport – pretty much anything you might need to organise your own trek. It also runs four-hour bamboo rafting trips (Rs 950) from June to December.

Thought to be one of the oldest on the subcontinent, **Thirunelly Temple** (☽ dawn-dusk) is around 10km from Tholpetty. While non-Hindus cannot enter, the ancient and intricate pillars and stone carvings, set against a backdrop of soaring, mist-covered peaks, is an astounding sight no matter what your creed.

The 13th-century **Jain temple** (☽ 8am-noon & 2-6pm), near Sultanbatheri, has splendid stone carvings and is an important monument to the region's strong historical Jain presence. Close by, near Ambalavayal, are the **Edakal Caves** (admission Rs 5; ☽ 9am-5pm), with petroglyphs thought to date back over 3000 years and awe-inspiring views of Wayanad district. In the same area, **Wayanad Heritage Museum** (Ambalavayal; admission Rs 5; ☽ 9am-5pm) exhibits headgear, weapons, pottery, carved stone and other artefacts dating back to the 15th century that shed light on Wayanad's significant Adivasi population (around 17%

of the total population). The labelling is poor, but the friendly guardian is happy to explain what's on display.

The picture-perfect **Pookot Lake** (admission Rs 5; ☺ 9am-6pm) is 3km before Vythiri. Geared up for visitors, it has well-maintained gardens, a cafeteria, playground and paddle/row boats for rent (Rs 30/50 per 20 minutes). It's still peaceful, particularly if you take a half-hour stroll around the lake's perimeter.

Sleeping & Eating

There's a **seramby** (wooden hut; d Rs 900) at Tholpetty near the sanctuary entrance, though you'll have to bring your own food. Contact the **wildlife warden** (☎ 04936-220454; ☺ 10am-5pm Mon-Fri) at Sultanbatheri for details.

PPS Tourist Home (☎ 04936-203431; www.pps touristhome.com; Kalpetta; s/d Rs 150/250, deluxe d Rs 500-550; ☒) This agreeable and friendly place in the middle of Kalpetta has rooms that are clean, good sized and comfy. You can arrange trips to Wayanad (Rs 1700 per carload) here or hikes up Chembra Peak (Rs 600, six hours).

Hotel Regency (☎ 04936-220512; Sultanbatheri; s/d from Rs 350/400, with AC from Rs 750/800; ☒) The best deal in Sultanbatheri, this new place is not particularly inspired, but with large, restful, tidy and quiet rooms it's still a winner. The deluxe rooms differ from the standard ones in price only.

Pachyderm Palace (☎ 0484-2371761; touristdesk@ satyam.net.in; Tholpetty; r per person incl meals Rs 1250-1500) This comfortable house lies huddled outside the gate of Tholpetty Wildlife Sanctuary – handy for early morning treks, tours and ad hoc wildlife viewing. The varied rooms are simple and spotless, but the stilt-bungalows surrounded by forest are the pick of the litter. The Keralan food is outstanding. Make reservations through the Tourist Desk in Ernakulam (see p343).

Stream Valley Cottages (☎ 0436-255860; www .streamvalleycottages.com; Vythiri; d Rs 2500) These huge, modern cottages are set by a small stream among the hills, about 2.5km off the main road before Vythiri. Fully self-contained, with kitchen, separate living area and balcony, there's peace here aplenty. Traditional Keralan meals are available (Rs 250 per day).

Tranquil (☎ 04936-220244; www.tranquilresort.com; Kuppamudi Estate, Kolagapara; s/d €190/240, deluxe s/d €270/340; ☒) This truly charming and luxurious homestay is in the middle of 160 hectares of pepper, coffee, vanilla and cardamom

plantations. The elegant house has sweeping verandas filled with plants and handsome furniture. The owners are excellent hosts and arrange tours of the area (included). They also have the most luxurious treehouse we've ever seen (single/double €240/300). Prices include meals and tax.

You could also try:

Dew Drops (☎ 04935-242; Mysore Rd, Mananthavadi; s from Rs 150/200) The only half-decent place to stay in Mananthavady.

Green Gates Hotel (☎ 04936-202001; www.green gateshotel.com; Kalpetta; s/d Rs 1250/1500, cottages s/d Rs 2750/3000; ☒ ☒) Well-designed cottages with a blend of modern and natural materials.

Getting There & Around

Buses brave the windy roads between Calicut and Sultanbatheri (Rs 57) via Kalpetta (Rs 45) every 30 minutes. Private buses also run between Kannur and Mananthavadi every 45 minutes (Rs 48, 2½ hours). One bus per day passes through Sultanbatheri at 1pm on its way to Udhagamandalam (Ooty; Rs 76, four hours), and buses for Mysore leave every 30 minutes.

Local buses connect Mananthavadi, Kalpetta and Sultanbatheri every 10 to 20 minutes (Rs 12 to Rs 18, 45 minutes to 1¼ hours). You can rent jeeps to get from one town to the next; they cost about Rs 450 to 600 each way – look for them lined up near the bus stands.

There are plenty of autorickshaws for trips around the district, and the DTPC can arrange car rental (from around Rs 1300 per day).

KANNUR (CANNANORE)

☎ 0497 / pop 498,175

Under the Kolathiri rajas, Kannur was a major port bristling with international trade – explorer Marco Polo christened it a 'great emporia of spice trade'. Since then, the usual colonial suspects, including the Portuguese, Dutch and British, have had a go at shaping Kannur. Today it's an agreeable, though unexciting, town known mostly for its weaving industry and cashew trade, with an excellent beach at Costa Malabari and incredible *theyyam* possession performances (see opposite).

Information

The **DTPC** (☎ 2706336; ☺ 10am-6pm Mon-Sat), opposite the KSRTC bus stand, and the **information counter** (☺ 8am-7pm) at the train station can supply maps of Kannur and a few brochures.

There are Federal Bank and State Bank of India ATMs adjacent to the bus stand, and an HDFC ATM about 50m from it, along with a **UAE Exchange** (☎ 2708818; Mahatma Mandir Junction; ☻ 9.30am-5.30pm Mon-Sat, to 1.30pm Sun).

Sights

Kannur is the best place to see the ritual dance **theyyam** (see the boxed text, below); there should be a *theyyam* on somewhere reasonably close by most nights of the year. To find it, ask at Costa Malabari (see right), or try the **Kerala Folklore Academy** (☎ 2778090), near Chirakkal Pond, Valapattanam.

The Portuguese built **St Angelo Fort** (admission free; ☻ 9am-6pm) in 1505 from brilliantly red laterite stone on the promontory northwest of town. It's serene and has excellent views of some palm-fringed beaches.

Established in 1955, the **Kausallaya Weavers' Co-Operative** (☎ 2835279; ☻ 9am-6pm) is the largest in Kannur and occupies a creaky building clicking with the sound of looms. You can stop by for a quick tour – it's 8km south of Kannur. This region is known for the manufacture of beedis, those tiny Indian cigarettes deftly rolled in green leaves. One of the largest, and purportedly best, manufacturers is the **Kerala Dinesh Beedi Co-Operative** (☎ 2835280; ☻ 8-5pm Tue-Sat), with a factory at Thottada, 7km south of Kannur. Either of these cooperatives is a Rs 80 (return) autorickshaw ride from Kannur town.

Kairail (☎ 0460-2243460), located 20km north of Kannur, is starting to offer houseboat trips on the unspoilt northern Kerala backwaters. Day cruises for up to 10 people cost Rs 3500, and 24-hour overnight trips for two are Rs 5000.

Sleeping & Eating

Centaur Tourist Home (☎ 2768270; MA Rd; s/d Rs 175/290, with shared bathroom Rs 120/230) This basic, spacious, clean rooms, across the road from the train station. There are plenty of similar lodges in this area.

Palmgrove Heritage Retreat (☎ 2703182; Mill Rd; s/d from Rs 200/350, with AC Rs 700/800; ☒) In a big heritage house packed with antique furniture and bric-a-brac, there's a variety of quiet, smallish-but-snug rooms set around lots of greenery.

Government Guest House (☎ 2706426; d Rs 220, with AC Rs 575; ☒) Ostensibly only for government officials (but it will let visitors in if there's room), this is great value – huge, bright rooms, all with balcony, in a sprawling complex by the ocean. Phone ahead.

Mascot Beach Resort (☎ 2708445; s/d Rs 700/900, with AC Rs 1000/1200; ☒ ☒) Near the Government Guest House, this also has grand views of the ocean from its comfy AC rooms, though the cheaper options are tucked away and a bit dark.

our pick **Costa Malabari** (☎ 0484-2371761; touristdesk@satyam.net.in; r Rs 1250-1500 per person incl meals) In a small village and five minutes' walk

---

THEYYAM

Kerala's most popular ritualistic art form, *theyyam*, is believed to predate Hinduism and to have developed from folk dances performed in conjunction with harvest celebrations. An intensely local ritual, it's often performed in the *kavus* (sacred groves) that are abundant throughout northern Kerala (there are up to 800 in Kannur district alone).

Theyyam refers to both the form or shape of the deity or hero portrayed, and to the ritual. There are around 450 different *theyyam*s, each with a distinct costume; face paint, bracelets, breastplates, skirts, garlands and especially headdresses are exuberant, intricately crafted and sometimes huge (up to 6m or 7m tall). Today's *theyyam* performances have morphed to incorporate popular Hindu deities and even Muslim characters.

The performer prepares for the ritual with a period of abstinence, fasting and meditation, which extends into the laborious make-up and costume session. During the performance, the performer loses his physical identity and speaks, moves and blesses the devotees as if he were the deity. There is frenzied dancing and wild drumming, and a surreal, otherworldly atmosphere is created, the kind of atmosphere in which a deity indeed might, if it so desired, manifest itself in human form.

The *theyyam* season is October to May, during which time there will be an annual ritual at each *kavu*. *Theyyam*s are also often held to bring good fortune to important events, such as marriages and house warmings. See above for details on how to find one.

from an idyllic and secluded beach, this place has a few bright, spacious rooms in an old hand-loom factory. There's a huge communal space and lots of comfy lounging areas dot the outside, plus it has expanded to include a second house perched dramatically on a sea cliff. The home-cooked Keralan food is plentiful and, frankly, might just be the best in the country. Kurien, your gracious host, is an expert on the astonishing *theyyam* ritual (see boxed text, p359) and can help arrange a visit. It's 8km from Kannur town; a taxi from the train station is around Rs 80. Make reservations at the Tourist Desk in Ernakulam.

Getting There & Away

There are frequent daily buses to Mysore (Rs 136, eight hours) and a few to Mangalore (Rs 76, four hours). Most departures to Calicut (Rs 52, 2½ hours) and Ernakulam (Rs 170, eight hours) leave in the afternoon and evening. There's one bus daily to Udhagamandalam (Ootyl; via Wayanad, Rs 170, nine hours). Frequent private buses to Mananthavadi (for Wayanad, Rs 48, 2½ hours) leave from the private bus stand, located between the KSRTC stand and the train station.

There are several daily trains to Mangalore (2nd class/3AC/2AC Rs 44/221/316, three hours), Calicut (Rs 34/188/266, two hours) and Ernakulam (Rs 75/361/518, seven hours).

BEKAL & AROUND
☎ 0467

Bekal (and nearby Palakunnu and Udma) in Kerala's far north boast unspoilt white-sand beaches. Word on the street is they form the palm-fringed finish line for several large-scale, luxury resorts hoping to transform the area into the next Kovalam. As yet, there are few decent places to stay (and none near a beach) and getting around can be a real pain, making it a DIY destination for off-the-beaten-track adventurers. Because it's a predominantly Muslim area, it's important to keep local sensibilities in mind, especially at the beach.

The laterite-brick **Bekal Fort** (Indian/foreigner Rs 5/100; ⏱ 8am-5pm), built between 1645 and 1660, sits on Bekal's rocky headland and houses a small Hindu temple and plenty of goats.

Kappil Beach, 6km north of Bekal, has fine sand and calm water, but beware of shifting sandbars.

Bekal Boat Stay (☎ 0476-3953311; bekalboats@ rediffmail.com; Kottappuram), 22km south of Bekal, is one of the first enterprises in the region to offer houseboat trips (Rs 6000/8000 per 24 hours for two/four people).

Sleeping & Eating

Sleeping options are mostly scattered between Kanhangad (12km south) and Kasaragod (10km north).

K-Tees Residency (☎ 3950208; www.kteesresidency .com; Bekal; s/d from Rs 200/350) The only place near Bekal passing muster in the hygiene department, it's squished between the railway and the road and has big, clean rooms.

Hotel Bekal International (☎ 2204271; www.hotel bekal.com; Kanhangad; s/d from Rs 200/350, d with AC from Rs 550; 🖭) The most comfortable hotel around, it's 12km south of Bekal. The huge complex has a green fetish, in everything from walls to '70s chairs, and a big choice of spacious, immaculate (green) rooms.

Gitanjali Heritage (☎ 2234159; www.gitanjaliheritage .com; s/d with meals US$50/75) Five kilometres from Bekal, this place is deep in the inland villages, surrounded by paddy fields. It's an intimate homestay in a graceful heritage home, with comfortable, higgledy-piggledy rooms filled with ancestral furniture and polished wood.

Getting There & Around

Frequent local trains stop at Kotikulum, in the village of Palakunnu 3km from Bekal. Kanhangad, 13km south, is the major stop. There are many buses to/from Kasaragod (Rs 10, 20 minutes), the nearest big town, and an autorickshaw at Bekal Junction can take you to/from Palakunnu and Udma (Rs 20 to 30).

LAKSHADWEEP

pop 60,595

A string of 36 palm-covered coral islands 300km off the coast of Kerala, Lakshadweep is as stunning as it is difficult to get to. Only 10 of the islands are inhabited, mostly with Sunni Muslim fishermen, and foreigners are only allowed to stay on a handful of these. With fishing and coir production the main sources of income, local life on the islands remains highly traditional and a caste system divides the islanders between Koya (land owners), Malmi (sailors) and Melachery (farmers).

The real attraction of the islands lies under the water: the 4200 sq km of pristine archipelago lagoons, unspoiled coral reefs and warm waters are a magnet for flipper-toting travellers and divers alike. Lakshadweep can only be visited on a pre-organised package trip – all listed accommodation prices are for the peak October to May season and include permits and meals.

Information

Sports (Society for the Promotion of Recreational Tourism & Sports; Map p341; ☎ 0484-2668387; www.lakshadweeptourism.com; IG Rd, Willingdon Island; ☻ 10am-5pm Mon-Sat) is the main tourism organisation.

PERMITS

Foreigners are limited to staying in pricey resorts; a special permit (one month's notice) is required and is organised by tour operators, hotels or Sports in Kochi. Foreigners and Indians can stay on Bangaram, Agatti and Kadmat, and Indians can stay in resorts on Minicoy and Kavaratti.

Getting There & Away

Indian Airlines has daily 9.15am flights Monday to Saturday from Kochi to Agatti Island (US$200 each way, 1¼ hours). The plane

is a tiny Dornier 228 propeller aircraft and passengers are restricted to 10kg of luggage. Book well in advance. As this book went to press, Kingfisher Airlines had just started up flights between Kochi and Agatti Island with bigger planes and for half the price (around US$200 return). Flights leave Kochi Tuesday, Thursday and Saturday at 12.50pm and return the same day at 2.40pm – though this may all change so its best to check its website (www.flykingfisher.com) for the latest information. A 1½-hour transfer by boat from Agatti to Bangaram costs an extra US$50 return. A boat trip to Agatti from Kochi is US$50 one way (16 to 20 hours).

For Kadmat, there are scheduled boat departures from Kochi between October and May (US$75 return in AC seats, including food, 18 to 20 hours each way) – allow a stay of three to five days plus travelling time. Get in touch with Sports in Kochi for details.

BANGARAM ISLAND

The 50-hectare island is fringed with pure sand, and the sight of the moon slipping beneath the lagoon horizon is very nearly worth

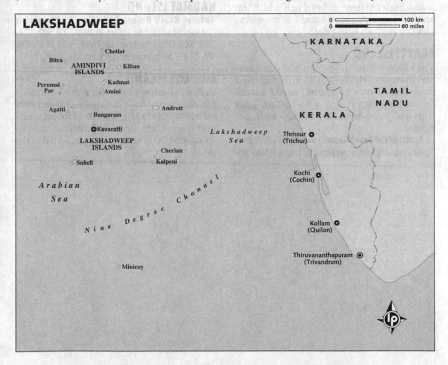

LAKSHADWEEP

KARNATAKA

Chetlat

Bitra

AMINDIVI
ISLANDS   Kiltan

Perumal
Par   Kadmat

Amini

Agatti   Andrott

Bangaram

● Kavaratti

LAKSHADWEEP
ISLANDS   Cherian

Suhell   Kalpeni

*Arabian
Sea*

*Lakshadweep
Sea*

TAMIL
NADU

KERALA

Thrissur ○
(Trichur)

Kochi ○
(Cochin)

Kollam ○
(Quilon)

Thiruvananthapuram ◉
(Trivandrum)

N i n e   D e g r e e   C h a n n e l

Minicoy

0   100 km
0   60 miles

KERALA

DIVING

Lakshadweep is a diver's dream, with excellent visibility and a plethora of marine life living on undisturbed coral reefs. The best time to dive is between mid-October and mid-May when the seas are calm and visibility is 20m to 40m. During the monsoon the weather and strong currents severely limit these opportunities and many dive outfits close up shop.

Lacadives (☎ 022-66627381-82; www.lacadives.com; E-20 Everest Bldg, Taredo Rd, Mumbai) runs dive centres on Bangaram and Kadmat Islands. Costs can vary: a CMAS one-star course costs US$400, while experienced divers pay US$40 per dive (plus equipment rental), with discounts available for multiple dives. Information is available through the hotels or directly through Lacadives in Mumbai; its website also has details about accommodation packages. The diving school on Agatti Island is run by **Goa Diving** (☎ 0832-2555117; www.goadiving.com).

From Kadmat Island, dives range from 9m to 20m in depth and some of the better sites include the North Cave, the Wall, Jack Point, Shark Alley, the Potato Patch, Cross Currents and Sting Ray City. Around Bangaram, good spots include the 32m-deep wreck of the *Princess Royale*, Manta Point, Life, Grand Canyon and the impressive sunken reef at Perumal Par.

Because of weight restrictions on aircraft (10kg), most divers rely on equipment provided on the islands. For a guide to environmentally friendly diving, see the boxed text, p99.

---

the expense. Activities include diving, snorkelling, deep-sea fishing and sailing.

Bangaram Island Resort (www.cghearth.com; s/d with full board Oct-Apr US$280/290, 4-person deluxe cottages with meals US$525) is run by the **CGH Earth group** (☎ 0484-2668221; bangaramisland@cghearth.com), and is administered from its hotel in Kochi. Shop around before you leave home – some operators can secure a better deal.

AGATTI ISLAND

The village on this 2.7-sq-km island has several mosques, which you can visit if dressed modestly. There's no alcohol on the island. Snorkelling, kayaking, glass-bottom boat trips and jaunts to nearby islands can be arranged.

Agatti Island Beach Resort (☎ 0484-2362232; www.agattiislandresorts.com; tw per person for 3 nights US$305-345,

with AC US$430-470; 🔀) sits on two beaches at the southern tip of the island and offers a range of packages. The resort has simple, low-rise beach cottages, designed to be comfortably cool without AC, and a restaurant for 20 people.

KADMAT ISLAND

Kadmat Beach Resort (☎ 0484-2668387; laksports _2004@vsnl.net; s/d for Indians Rs 2000/3000, with AC Rs 2500/4000, s/d for foreigners US$75/125, with AC US$100/175; 🔀) is administered by Sports (see p361).

MINICOY ISLAND

Indians wishing to stay on remote Minicoy can rent newly built cottages at **Swaying Palm** (s/d Rs 2000/3000, with AC Rs 2500/4000; 🔀). Boat transport from Kochi (tourist/1st/deluxe class Rs 3500/6000/7000 return) must be added to the prices.

Tamil Nadu

If thoughts of temples and tigers appeal, then Tamil Nadu – land of the Tamils and heartland of southern India – is the place to be. Long coastlines and forested mountains form stunning backdrops to this, the cradle of Dravidian civilisation. Manifestations of its ancient culture are everywhere, from vast temple compounds with steeply stepped, riotously coloured *gopurams* (gateway towers) to beautifully detailed rock carvings, and classical music and dance that are both complex and compelling. Pilgrims pour into the ancient sites of Kanchipuram, Chidambaram, Kumbakonam, Trichy (Tiruchirappalli), Thanjavur (Tanjore), Madurai, Kanyakumari and Rameswaram – far outnumbering tourists.

While only the very lucky few will see a tiger, the state's national parks and reserves remain important refuges for much of India's wildlife including elephants, several species of rare monkeys and gaurs (a type of bison). The historic hill stations of Ooty (Udhagamandalam, reached by the famous miniature train, and Kodaikanal are perfect bases for exploring and provide cool, calm, green contrast to the bustle of the cities.

The eastern coast fronting the Bay of Bengal has a few resorts and sleepy fishing villages, but Tamil Nadu isn't a beach destination and only Mamallapuram (Mahabalipuram), south of Chennai (Madras), attracts chilled-out tourists. The 2004 tsunami swept along this coast; rehabilitation was comparatively swift near tourist areas, but many local communities are still recovering.

HIGHLIGHTS

- Gorge on fresh seafood and explore some of South India's finest rock carvings in laid-back **Mamallapuram** (Mahabalipuram; p382)
- Ride the toy train, stay in a Raj-era hotel and trek the hills around **Ooty** (Udhagamandalum; p436)
- Experience a small corner of France in India and an early morning yoga session in **Puducherry** (Pondicherry p395)
- Join the pilgrims and devotees filing into Madurai's **Sri Meenakshi Temple** (p420), a riot of Dravidian sculpture and one of South India's finest
- Dust off the binoculars and field guides around **Mudumalai National Park** (p442), where Tamil Nadu's best wildlife viewing is on your doorstep
- See local artisans practising their crafts in traditional workshops at **DakshinaChitra** (p382), a remarkable cultural centre on the coast road south of Chennai (Madras)
- Watch the sun rise and set over two oceans at **Kanyakumari** (p423), on the southernmost tip of the continent

TAMIL NADU

FAST FACTS

- Population: 62.1 million
- Area: 130,058 sq km
- Capital: Chennai (Madras)
- Main language: Tamil
- When to go: November to March

History

It's thought the first Dravidians were part of early Indus civilisations and that they came south to the area about 1500 BC. By 300 BC the region was controlled by three major dynasties – Cholas in the east, Pandyas in the central area and Cheras in the west. This was the classical period of Tamil literature – the Sangam Age – that continued until around AD 300.

The domains of these three dynasties changed many times over the centuries. The Pallava dynasty became influential, particularly in the 7th and 8th centuries, when it constructed many of the monuments at Mamallapuram (p382). Although all of these dynasties were engaged in continual skirmishes, their steady patronage of the arts served to consolidate and expand Dravidian civilisation.

In 1640 the British negotiated the use of Madraspatnam (now Chennai) as a trading post. Subsequent interest by the French, Dutch and Danes led to continual conflict and, finally, almost total domination by the British, when the region became known as the Madras Presidency. Small pocketed areas, including Puducherry (Pondicherry) and Karaikal, remained under French control.

Many Tamils played a significant part in India's struggle for Independence, which was finally won in 1947. In 1956 the Madras Presidency was disbanded and Tamil Nadu was established as an autonomous state.

Information

The state tourism body is **Tamil Nadu Tourism** (www.tamilnadutourism.org) with tourist offices of varying uselessness in most cities and large towns around the state. It also runs a fairly average chain of hotels.

ACCOMMODATION

Accommodation over Rs 200 in Tamil Nadu (but not Puducherry) is subject to a government 'luxury' tax – 5% on rooms between Rs 200 and 500, 10% on rooms between Rs 501 and 1000 and 12.5% on rooms over Rs 1000. There's often an additional 'service tax' at upmarket hotels. Prices throughout this chapter do not include tax, unless stated otherwise. There are few surprises with hotels in Tamil Nadu – the exceptions are Puducherry, which has some lovely heritage hotels, and Ooty and Kodaikanal which have everything from forest lodges to Raj-era mansions.

PERMITS

As well as for the areas listed below, permits are required for trekking in some areas of the Nilgiri Hills around Mudumalai National Park (see p442). Reputable guides should have the required permits for tourist trekking; researchers and academics need to apply separately.

Conservator of Forests (☎ 24321139; 8th fl, Panangal Bldg, Saidapet, Chennai) The Conservator of Forests issues permits for all areas other than the Vedantangal Bird Sanctuary, but will only do so for researchers.

Wildlife Warden's Office (WWO; Map pp368-9; ☎ 24321471; 4th fl, DMS office, 259 Anna Salai, Teynampet, Chennai) Issues permits in advance for accommodation at Vedantangal Bird Sanctuary.

Dangers & Annoyances

Ambling through temples is clearly a highlight of Tamil Nadu. Dealing with temple touts is not. Genuine guides exist and can greatly enhance your experience – a fair rate for a knowledgeable guide is about Rs 60 per hour – but you'll need to search them out. Many self-appointed guides demand big bucks in exchange for very little, often work as a front for nearby craft or tailor shops and, although they're widespread, Kanchipuram, Trichy and Madurai seem to be their breeding grounds. As always, get recommendations from other travellers, question the knowledge of anyone offering guide services and agree on a price before you set out.

CHENNAI (MADRAS)

☎ 044 / pop 6.4 million

Chennai has neither the cosmopolitan, prosperous air of Mumbai (Bombay), the optimistic buzz of Bengaluru (Bangalore) or the historical drama of Delhi. It's muggy, polluted, hot as hell and difficult to get around. Traditional tourist attractions are few. Even the movie stars are, as one Chennaiker put it, 'not that hot'.

But the locals are a little friendlier than average here, the streets a little wider and, in spite of its booming IT, business-outsourcing and auto industries, the pace much slower than in most Indian cities half its size. Chennai is so modest you wouldn't even know it's an economic powerhouse, much less a queen of showbiz: India's fourth-largest city is also its most humble.

Chennai (formerly Madras) prefers to quietly hold onto tradition, thank you very much. Even its tendency to spread out – the city sprawls over 70 sq km with no real centre – seems like an attachment to the small coastal villages from which it descends. And it remains deeply conservative – the lungi (a type of sarong) is very much in fashion, alcohol

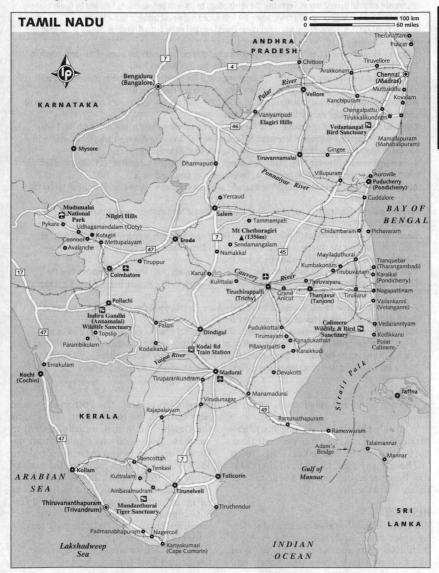

TAMIL NADU

FESTIVALS IN TAMIL NADU

Many of Tamil Nadu's most colourful festivals revolve around temples – there's something going on somewhere in the state all year round.

International Yoga Festival (4-7 Jan; Puducherry (Pondicherry), p395) Puducherry's ashrams and yoga culture are put on show with workshops, classes and music and dance events. Held throughout the city, the event attracts yoga masters from all over India.

Pongal (mid-Jan; statewide) As the rice boils over the new clay pots, this festival symbolises the prosperity and abundance a fruitful harvest brings. For many, the celebrations begin with temple rituals, followed by family gatherings. Later it's the animals, especially cows, which are honoured for their contribution to the harvest.

Music festival (Jan; Thiruvaiyaru, p411) Held near Thanjavur, this music festival is held in honour of the saint and composer Thyagaraja.

Teppam Float Festival (Jan/Feb; Madurai, p418) A popular event held on the full moon of the Tamil month of Thai, when statues of deities are floated on the huge Mariamman Teppakkulam Tank.

Natyanjali Dance Festival (Feb/Mar; Chidambaram, p403) The five-day festival attracts performers from all over the country to the Nataraja Temple to celebrate Nataraja (Shiva) – the Lord of Dance.

Arubathimoovar Festival (Mar/Apr; Chennai, p364) A colourful one-day festival when bronze statues of the 63 saints of Shiva are paraded through the streets of Mylapore.

Chithrai Festival (Apr/May; Madurai, p418) The main event on Madurai's busy festival calendar is this 14-day event that celebrates the marriage of Meenakshi to Sundareshwara (Shiva). The deities are wheeled around the Sri Meenakshi Temple in massive chariots that form part of long, colourful processions.

Summer festivals (May-Jun; Ooty, p436 & Kodaikanal, p427) Tamil Nadu's hill stations both hold similar festivals which feature boat races on the lake, horse racing (in Ooty), flower shows and music.

Bastille Day (14 Jul; Puducherry, p395) Street parades and a bit of French pomp and ceremony are all part of the fun at this celebration.

Avanimoolam (Aug/Sep; Madurai, p418) Marks the coronation of Sundareshwar, when temple chariots are exuberantly hauled around the city.

Karthikai Deepam Festival (Nov/Dec; statewide) Held during full moon, Tamil Nadu's 'festival of lights' is celebrated throughout the state, with earthenware lamps and firecrackers, but the best place to see it is Tiruvannamalai (see the boxed text, p394), where the legend began.

Vaikunta Ekadasi (Paradise Festival; mid-Dec; Trichy (Tiruchirappalli; p411) This 21-day festival brings the Sri Ranganathaswamy Temple to life when the celebrated Vaishnavaite text, Tiruvaimozhi, is recited before an image of Vishnu.

Festival of Carnatic Music & Dance (mid-Dec–mid-Jan; Chennai, p364) One of the largest of its type in the world, this festival is a celebration of Tamil music and dance.

Mamallapuram Dance Festival (Dec-Jan; Mamallapuram, p382) A four-week dance festival showcasing dances from all over India, with many performances on an open-air stage against the imposing backdrop of Arjuna's Penance. Dances include the Bharata Natyam (Tamil Nadu), Kuchipudi (Andhra Pradesh) tribal dance, Kathakali (Kerala drama), puppet shows and classical music. Performances are held only from Friday to Sunday.

is frowned upon and religious devotion is going strong.

With only a handful of tourist sights, Chennai doesn't demand too much of your time. But poke around the markets of George Town or Theagaraya Nagar, take a stroll along Marina Beach at sunset, and get a little taste of village life in the city.

HISTORY

The Chennai area has always attracted seafarers, spice traders and cloth merchants. More than 2000 years ago, its residents engaged with Chinese, Greek, Phoenician, Roman and Babylonian traders. The Portuguese would later arrive in the 16th century, followed by the Dutch. The British, initially content to purchase spices and other goods from the Dutch, decided to end their monopoly in 1599, when the Dutch increased the price of pepper. In 1639, the British East India Company established a settlement in the fishing village of Madraspatnam and completed Fort St George in 1653. George Town was granted municipal charter in 1688 by James II, making it India's oldest municipality.

In the 18th century, the supremacy of the British East India Company was challenged by the French. Robert Clive (Clive of India), a key player in the British campaign, recruited an army of 2000 sepoys (Indian soldiers in British service) and launched a series of military expeditions which developed into the Carnatic Wars. In 1756 the French withdrew to Pondicherry (now Puducherry), leaving the relieved British to develop Fort St George.

In the 19th century, the city became the seat of the Madras presidency, one of the four divisions of British Imperial India. After Independence, it continued to grow into what is now a significant southern gateway.

ORIENTATION

Bordered on the east by the Bay of Bengal, Chennai is a combination of many small districts. George Town, a jumble of narrow streets, bazaars and the court buildings, is in the north, near the harbour. To the southwest are the major thoroughfare of Anna Salai (Mount Rd) and the two main train stations: Egmore, for most destinations in Tamil Nadu, and Central, for interstate trains. The area around Egmore station is a budget-hotel district, as is Triplicane, at the north end of Marina Beach.

INFORMATION
Bookshops

Bookpoint (Map p372; ☎ 28523019; 160 Anna Salai; ⊙ 10am-8pm Mon-Sat, 4-8pm Sun)

Higginbothams (Map p372; ☎ 28513519; 814 Anna Salai; ⊙ 9am-8pm Mon-Sat, 10.30am-7.30pm Sun)

Landmark (⊙ 9am-9pm Mon-Sat, 10.30am-9pm Sun) Anna Salai (Map p372; ☎ 28495995; Spencer Plaza, Phase II); Nungambakkam (Map pp368-9; ☎ 28221000; Apex Plaza, Nungambakkam High Rd)

Cultural Centres

All of the following have libraries and sponsor concerts, films and events.

Alliance Française de Madras (Map pp368-9; ☎ 28279803; www.af-madras.org; 24/40 College Rd, Nungambakkam; ⊙ 9am-6.45pm Mon-Fri, 9am-1pm Sat, library closed Mon morning)

American Information Resource Center (Map pp368-9; ☎ 28112000; americanlibrary.in.library.net; Gemini Circle, Anna Salai; ⊙ 9.30am-5pm Mon-Fri) Bring ID.

British Council Library (Map p372; ☎ 42050600; www.britishcouncilonline.org; 737 Anna Salai; ⊙ 11am-7pm Mon-Sat) Monthly membership is Rs 100.

Goethe-Institut (Max Mueller Bhavan; Map pp368-9; ☎ 28331314; D Khader Nawaz Khan Rd; ⊙ 9am-4pm Mon-Fri, library 11am-6pm Tue-Sat)

Internet Access

The Central Station also has a 24-hour internet café.

Emerald Internet (Map p372; ☎ 52141648; 35 Triplicane High Rd; per hr Rs 15; ⊙ 9am-10.30pm)

Internet Zone (Map p372; ☎ 42145885; 1 Kennet Lane, Egmore; per hr Rs 25; ⊙ 8am-10pm)

iWay (Map pp368-9; ☎ 6551755; 59 Dr Radhakrishnan Salai; per hr Rs 20; ⊙ 24hr)

SGee (Map p372; ☎ 42310391; 20 Vallabha Agraharam St; per hr Rs 20; ⊙ 24hr) 'Happy hour' (per hour Rs 10) is 2pm to 6pm.

Left Luggage

Egmore and Central Stations have left-luggage counters, as do the international and domestic airports (Rs 10 per 24 hours).

Medical Services

Apollo Hospital (Map p372; ☎ 28293333, emergency 1066, pharmacy line 42068474; 21 Greams Lane) Some of its 24-hour pharmacies deliver.

TOP FIVE TEMPLES

Tamil Nadu is nirvana for anyone wanting to explore South Indian temple culture and architecture. Many are important places of pilgrimage for Hindus, where daily *puja* (offering or prayer) rituals and colourful festivals will leave a deep impression on even the most temple-weary traveller. Others stand out for the stunning architecture, soaring *gopurams* (gateway towers) and intricately carved, pillared *mandapas* (pavilions in front of a temple). Almost all have free admission. There are so many that it pays to be selective, but the choice is subjective. Here's our top five.

■ Sri Meenakshi Temple, Madurai (p420)

■ Arunachaleswar Temple, Tiruvannamalai (p394)

■ Brihadishwara Temple, Thanjavur (p409)

■ Rock Fort Temple, Trichy (Tiruchirappalli; p412)

■ Nataraja Temple, Chidambaram (p403)

TAMIL NADU

CHENNAI (MADRAS)

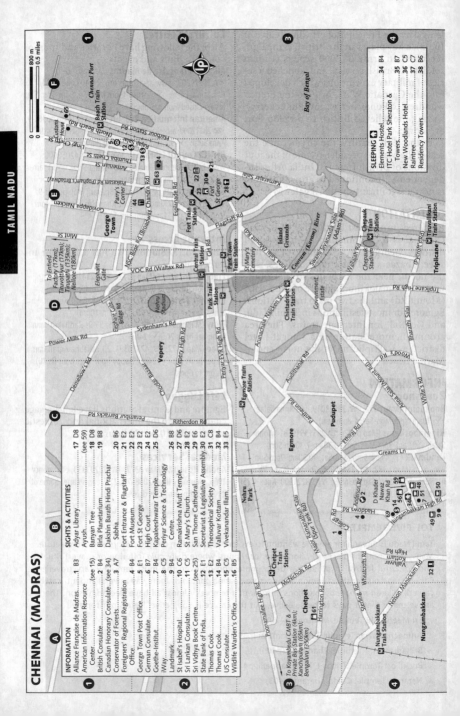

INFORMATION
Alliance Française de Madras.....1 B3
American Information Resource
  Center..............................(see 15)
British Consulate.........................2 B4
Canadian Honorary Consulate...(see 34)
Conservator of Forests..................3 A7
Foreigners' Regional Registration
  Office..................................4 B4
George Town Post Office...............5 E1
German Consulate........................6 B7
Goethe-Institut...........................7 B4
iWay..8 C5
Landmark..................................9 B4
St Isabel's Hospital....................10 C6
Sri Lankan Consulate..................11 C5
Sri Vidhya Book Centre..............(see 25)
State Bank of India.....................12 E1
Thomas Cook...........................13 E2
Thomas Cook...........................14 B4
US Consulate...........................15 C5
Wildlife Warden's Office.............16 B5

SIGHTS & ACTIVITIES
Adyar Library.........................17 D8
Ayush.................................(see 59)
Banyan Tree..........................18 D8
Birla Planetarium.....................19 B8
Dakshan Barath Hindi Prachar
  Sabha...............................20 B6
Fort Entrance & Flagstaff............21 E2
Fort Museum..........................22 E2
Fort St George........................23 E2
High Court............................24 E2
Kapaleeshwarar Temple.............25 D6
Periyar Science & Technology
  Centre...............................26 B8
Ramakrishna Mutt Temple..........27 D6
St Mary's Church......................28 E2
San Thome Cathedral................29 E6
Secretariat & Legislative Assembly..30 E2
Theosophical Society.................31 C8
Valluvar Kottam.......................32 B4
Vivekanandar Illam...................33 E5

SLEEPING
Elements Hostel.......................34 B4
ITC Hotel Park Sheraton &
  Towers..............................35 B7
New Woodlands Hotel................36 C5
Raintree...............................37 C7
Residency Towers....................38 B6

TO FORT ST GEORGE / George Town / Vepery / Egmore / Pudupet / Nungambakkam / Chetpet / Triplicane / Chennai Port / Bay of Bengal

TAMIL NADU

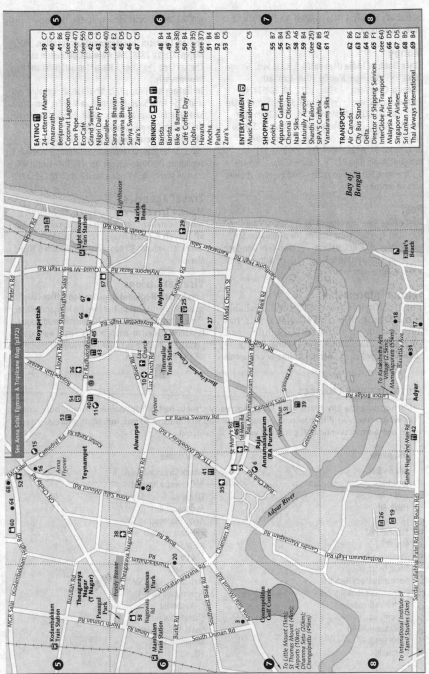

EATING
24-Lettered Mantra....39 C7
Amaravathi....40 C5
Benjarong....41 B6
Coconut Lagoon....(see 47)
Don Pepe....(see 55)
EcoCafé....(see 40)
Grand Sweets....42 C8
Nilgiri Dairy Farm....43 C5
Romalee....(see 40)
Saravana Bhavan....44 E2
Saravana Bhavan....45 D5
Suriya Sweets....46 C7
Zara's....47 C5

DRINKING
Barista....48 B4
Barista....49 B4
Bike & Barrel....(see 38)
Café Coffee Day....50 B4
Dublin....(see 35)
Havana....(see 37)
Mocha....51 B4
Pasha....52 B5
Zara's....53 C5

ENTERTAINMENT
Music Academy....54 C5

SHOPPING
Anokhi....55 B7
Apparao Galleries....56 B4
Chennai Citicentre....57 D5
Nalli Silks....58 A6
Naturally Auroville....59 B4
Shanthi Tailors....(see 25)
SIPA'S Craftlink....60 B5
Varadarams Silks....61 A3

TRANSPORT
Air Canada....62 B6
City Bus Stand....63 E2
Delta....64 B5
Director of Shipping Services....65 F1
InterGlobe Air Transport....(see 64)
Malaysia Airlines....66 D5
Singapore Airlines....67 D5
Sri Lankan Airlines....68 B5
Thai Airways International....69 B4

St Isabel's Hospital (Map pp368-9; ☎ 24991081; 18 Oliver Rd, Mylapore)

Money

State Bank of India (Map pp368-9; Rajaji Salai, George Town; ◷ 10am-4pm Mon-Fri, 10am-1pm Sat)

Thomas Cook Anna Salai (Map p372; ☎ 28492424; Spencer Plaza, Phase I; ◷ 9.30am-6.30pm); Egmore (Map p372; ☎ 28553276; 45 Montieth Rd; ◷ 9.30am-6pm Mon-Sat); George Town (Map pp368-9; ☎ 25342374; 20 Rajaji Salai; ◷ 9.30am-6pm Mon-Sat); Nungambakkam (Map pp368-9; ☎ 28274941; Eldorado Bldg, 112 Nungambakkam High Rd; ◷ 9.30am-6.30pm Mon-Fri, 9.30am-noon Sat) Changes currency and travellers cheques with no commission.

Post

Post office Anna Salai (Map p372; ◷ 8am-8.30pm Mon-Sat, 10am-4pm Sun, poste restante 10am-6pm Mon-Sat); Egmore (Map p372; Kennet Lane; ◷ 10am-6pm Mon-Sat); George Town (Map pp368-9; Rajaji Salai; ◷ 8am-8.30pm Mon-Sat, 10am-4pm Sun)

Tourist Information

The free **CityInfo** (www.explocity.com), available at the tourist office and at some hotels, has information on restaurants, nightlife and what's on. Also check out **Chennai Best** (www .chennaibest.com) and **Chennai Online** (www.chennai online.com). Local newspapers list upcoming events.

Indian Tourism Development Corporation (ITDC; Map p372; ☎ 28281250; www.attindiatourism.com; Cherian Cres; ◷ 10am-5.30pm Mon-Sat) Hotel and tour bookings only.

Indiatourism (Map p372; ☎ 28460285; indtour@vsnl .com; 154 Anna Salai; ◷ 9am-6pm Mon-Fri, 9am-1pm Sat) Great for maps and information. Also has counters at the Tourism Complex and both airports.

Tamil Nadu Tourism Complex (TTDC; Map p372; ☎ 25367850; www.tamilnadutourism.org; 2 Wallajah Rd, Triplicane; ◷ 10am-5.30pm Mon-Fri) State tourist offices from all over India, including Tamil Nadu (☎ 25383333).

Travel Agencies

Madura Travel Service (Map p372; ☎ 28192970; www.maduratravel.com; Kennet Lane, Egmore; ◷ 24hr)

SP Travels & Tours (Map p372; ☎ 28604001; sptravels1@eth.net; 90 Anna Salai; ◷ 9.30am-6.30pm Mon-Sat)

Visa Extensions

Foreigners' Regional Registration Office (Map pp368-9; Shastri Bhavan, Haddows Rd, Nungambakkam; ◷ 9.30am-5.30pm Mon-Fri) Travellers have managed to procure visa extensions here after a lot of waiting and persuasion. If you're lucky, the (very complex) applications take 10 days to process.

STREET NAME CHANGES

It's not only the city that's been renamed. Many streets had official name changes, only some of which stuck. As if that weren't enough, building numbers changed, too. Most addresses have an 'old' and 'new' number, generally written as new/old.

Old name	New name
Adam's Rd	Swami Sivananda Salai
Broadway	NSC Chandra Bose Rd
C-in-C Rd	Ethiraj Rd
Harris Rd	Audithanar Rd
Lloyd's Rd	Avvai Shanmughan Salai
Marshalls Rd	Rukmani Lakshmi Pathy Rd
Mount Rd	Anna Salai
Mowbray's Rd	TTK Rd
North Beach Rd	Rajaji Salai
Nungambakkam High Rd	Mahatma Gandhi Salai
Poonamallee High Rd	Periyar High Rd
Popham's Broadway	Prakasam Rd
Pycroft's Rd	Bharathi Salai
Triplicane High Rd	Quaid-Milleth High Rd
South Beach Rd	Kamarajar Salai
Waltax Rd	VOC Rd

TAMIL NADU

DANGERS & ANNOYANCES

Getting around is likely to be your biggest problem in Chennai. Autorickshaw drivers are tough to bargain with (meters aren't used) and may dispute an agreed-upon fare on arrival. Avoid giving money up front, even if you've hired the auto for the day.

Drivers may offer Rs 50 one-hour 'sightseeing' rides to anywhere in the city, but usually this means you'll be ferried to craft emporiums: don't fall for it.

If you have a serious problem with a driver, mentioning a call to the **traffic police** (☎ 103) can defuse the conflict. See p381 for details on other modes of transport.

SIGHTS
Egmore & Central Chennai
GOVERNMENT MUSEUM

Housed across several British-built buildings known as the Pantheon Complex, this excellent **museum** (Map p372; ☎ 28193238; www.chennaimuseum.org; 486 Pantheon Rd; Indian/foreigner/student Rs 15/250/75, camera/video Rs 200/500; ☉ 9.30am-5pm Sat-Thu) is Chennai's best.

The main building has a fine **archaeological section** representing all the major South Indian periods including Chola, Vijayanagar, Hoysala and Chalukya in sculpture and temple art. Further along is a fascinating **natural history and zoology** section with a motley collection of skeletons (including a blue whale and Indian elephant) and stuffed birds and animals from around the world. Look out for the desiccated cat in a glass case!

In Gallery 3, the **bronze gallery** has a superb and beautifully presented collection of Chola art. Among the impressive pieces is the bronze of Ardhanariswara, the androgynous incarnation of Shiva and Parvati, and the numerous representations of Natesa or Nataraja, the four-armed dancing Shiva stomping on a demon.

The same ticket gets you into the **National Art Gallery**, in Building 5 to the left of the main entrance. It features an excellent collection of 10th- to 18th-century Mughal, Rajasthani and Deccan artworks. On either side of the gallery are the **children's museum** and an interesting **modern art gallery**.

VIVEKANANDAR ILLAM

The **Vivekananda House** (Map pp368-9; ☎ 28446188; Kamarajar Salai, Triplicane; adult/child Rs 2/1; ☉ 10am-noon & 3-7pm Thu-Tue) is fascinating not only for the displays on the famous 'wandering monk', but also for the building in which it's housed. The semicircular seafront structure was formerly known as the Ice House and was once used to store massive ice blocks transported by ship from North America. Swami Vivekananda stayed here in 1897 on his return from the USA and preached his ascetic philosophy to adoring crowds. The museum now houses a collection of photographs and memorabilia from the swami's life, a gallery of religious historical paintings and the 'meditation room' where Vivekananda stayed.

VALLUVAR KOTTAM

This **memorial** (Map pp368-9; Valluvar Kottam High Rd, Kodambakkam; ☉ 9am-7.30pm) honours the Tamil poet Thiruvalluvar and his classic work, the *Thirukural*. Thiruvalluvar, a weaver by trade, lived around the 1st century BC in present-day Chennai, and apparently wrote the poem when asked to record his eminent verbal teachings. The *Thirukural* suggests ways to contemplate life's enigmas and strategies for right understanding and conduct. Today, the poem is a moral code for millions, and Thiruvalluvar is considered a saint. The three-level memorial replicates ancient Tamil architecture and contains inscriptions of the *Thirukural*'s 1330 couplets.

South Chennai
The following sights appear on the Chennai (Madras) map, pp368–9.

Chennai's most active temple, the ancient Shiva **Kapaleeshwarar Temple** (Kutchery Rd, Mylapore; ☉ 4am-noon & 4-8pm) is constructed in the Dravidian style and displays the architectural elements – rainbow-colour *gopuram*, *mandapas* (pavilions in front of a temple) and a huge tank – found in the famous temple cities of Tamil Nadu.

The tranquil, leafy grounds of the **Ramakrishna Mutt Temple** (RK Mutt Rd; ☉ 4.30-11.45am & 3-9pm, puja 8am) are a world away from the chaos outside. Orange-clad monks glide around and there's a reverential feel here. The temple itself is a handsome shrine open to followers of any religion for meditation.

Built in 1504, then rebuilt in neogothic style in 1893, **San Thome Cathedral** (☎ 24985455) is a soaring Roman Catholic church between Kapaleeshwarar Temple and Marina Beach. In the basement is a chapel housing the tomb of St Thomas the Apostle (Doubting Thomas).

TAMIL NADU

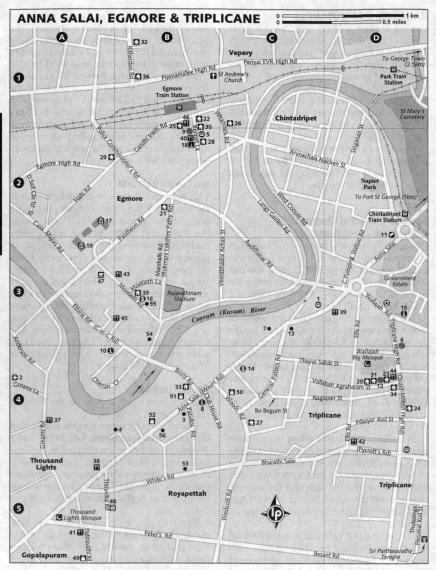

ANNA SALAI, EGMORE & TRIPLICANE

During an early morning or evening stroll along the 13km sandy stretch of **Marina Beach** you'll pass cricket matches, kids flying kites, fortune tellers, fish markets and families enjoying the sea breeze. Don't swim here – strong rips make it dangerous. About 2km further south in Besant Nagar, **Elliot's Beach** is a more affluent place, popular with young couples.

Between the Adyar River and the coast, the 100 hectares of the **Theosophical Society** (Adyar Bridge Rd; ☼ 8-10am & 2-5pm Mon-Fri, 8-10am Sat) provide a peaceful retreat from the city. The grounds contain a church, mosque, Buddhist shrine and Hindu temple, as well as a huge variety of native and introduced trees, including a 400-year-old **banyan tree**. The **Adyar**

INFORMATION			Hotel Comfort	23	D4	Spencer's Daily	(see 51)
Anna Salai Post Office	1	C3	Hotel Himalaya	24	D4	Vasanta Bhavan	46 B1
Apollo Hospital	2	A4	Hotel Impala Continental	25	B1	Vasantha Bhavan	(see 22)
Bookpoint	3	B4	Hotel New Park Plaza	26	C1		
British Council Library	4	B4	Hotel Orchid Inn	27	C4	DRINKING 🍷	
Egmore Post Office	5	B2	Hotel Regent	28	B2	Café Coffee Day	47 A3
Emerald Internet	6	D3	Krishna Park	29	A2		
Higginbothams	7	C3	New Victoria Hotel	30	B1	ENTERTAINMENT 🎭	
Indiatourism	8	B4	Paradise Guest House	31	D4	Sathyam Cinema	48 A5
Internet Zone	9	B2	Salvation Army Red Shield Guest				
ITDC	10	A4	House	32	B1	SHOPPING 🛍	
Landmark	(see 51)		Taj Connemara	33	B4	Amethyst	49 A5
Madura Travel Service	(see 9)		Thaj Regency	34	B4	Fabindia	50 C4
Maldives Honorary Consulate	11	D2	Vestin Park	35	B3	Fabindia	(see 51)
SGee	12	D4	YWCA International Guest			Spencer Plaza	51 B4
SP Travels & Tours	13	C3	House	36	B1	Victoria Technical Institute	52 B4
State Bank of India	14	C4					
Tamil Nadu Tourist Complex	15	D3	EATING 🍴			TRANSPORT	
Thomas Cook	16	B3	Amethyst	(see 49)		Air Deccan	53 B5
Thomas Cook	(see 51)		Gallopin' Gooseberry	37	A4	Air France	(see 55)
			Gyan Vaishnava Punjabi			Air India	54 B3
SIGHTS & ACTIVITIES			Dhaba	38	A5	Air Sahara	(see 53)
Government Museum	17	A2	Hotel Comfort	(see 23)		American Airlines	(see 55)
Mahabodhi Society of Sri Lanka	18	B2	Hotel Saravana Bhavan	39	D4	Cathay Pacific	(see 53)
National Art Gallery	19	A3	Hotel Saravana Bhavan	40	B2	Gulf Air	(see 55)
			Hotel Saravana Bhavan	41	A5	Indian Airlines	(see 54)
SLEEPING 🏨			Jam Bazaar	42	D4	Jet Airways	55 B3
Broadlands Lodge	20	D4	Kitchen K	43	B3	KLM	(see 54)
Hotel Ashoka	21	B2	Maharaja Restaurant	44	D4	Lufthansa	56 B4
Hotel Chandra Park	22	B1	Ponnusamy Hotel	45	B3	Private Bus Stand	(see 40)

Library (🕐 9am-5pm) here has a huge collection of books on religion and philosophy. If you're interested in the Theosophical Society's philosophy, call into the public relations office and chat with the director.

To the west, near Guindy, is the **Periyar Science & Technology Centre** (☎ 24416751; admission Rs 15; 🕐 10am-5.30pm). You can learn your weight on Pluto and other titbits from its kitschy science exhibits. The **Birla Planetarium** (admission Rs 20; 🕐 shows 10.45am, 1.15pm & 3.45pm) is next door.

George Town

The following sights appear on the Chennai (Madras) map, pp368–9.

FORT ST GEORGE

Built around 1653 by the British East India Company, the **fort** (🕐 10am-5pm) has undergone many alterations over the years. Inside the vast perimeter walls is now a precinct housing the **Secretariat & Legislative Assembly**, so there's plenty of daily activity here but not much of historical interest. The 46m-high **flagstaff** at the front is a mast salvaged from a 17th-century shipwreck. The main entrance to the fort is on Kamarajar Salai (near the flagstaff).

The **Fort Museum** (☎ 25670389; Indian/foreigner Rs 2/100, video Rs 25; 🕐 10am-5.30pm Sat-Thu), in the old Exchange Building near the fort entrance,

has military memorabilia from the British and French East India Companies, as well as the Raj and Muslim administrations. There's a scale model of the fort in Gallery 2 and some fine prints of early colonial Madras upstairs.

St Mary's Church, completed in 1680, was the first English church in Madras and India's oldest surviving British church.

HIGH COURT

This red Indo-Saracenic structure (1892) at Parry's Corner is George Town's main landmark. It's said to be the largest judicial building in the world after the Courts of London. You can wander around the court buildings and sit in on sessions.

Other Sights

LITTLE MOUNT & ST THOMAS MOUNT

It's believed that from around AD 58, St Thomas lived in hiding at **Little Mount** (Chinnamalai; Saidapet). The cave still bears what some believe to be Thomas' handprint, left when he escaped through an opening that miraculously appeared. Three kilometres on, **St Thomas Mount** (Parangi Malai) is thought to be the site of Thomas' martyrdom in AD 72. Little Mount and St Thomas Mount are about 1km from the Saidapet and St Thomas Mount Mass Rapid Transport System (MRTS) stations, respectively.

TAMIL NADU

TAMIL NADU

WORKERS IN THE SHADOWS

They leave their slum dwellings early to begin work in the city by 6am. They move swiftly and silently along the city streets, keeping to the shadows and mostly working in pairs. The waste-pickers – mostly women, sometimes children – spend up to 10 hours a day rummaging through domestic and industrial waste and separating it into bags of metal, plastic, paper, cloth and other recyclables. Usually they sell their bundles to middlemen who then sell to recycling companies. For this dangerous and dirty work they earn around Rs 45 a day. With assistance from NGOs, some waste-pickers have formed cooperatives, bypassing the middlemen and boosting their earning potential.

ENFIELD FACTORY

Motorcycle fans will enjoy visiting the famous **Enfield factory** (☎ 42230245; www.royalenfield.com; Tiruvottiyur), 17km north of Chennai, where bikes have been made since 1955. Half-hour tours run on Saturday at 9.30am and cost Rs 500.

ACTIVITIES

Go for a 45-minute *abhyangam* (oil treatment; Rs 500) or an extended Ayurvedic programme at **Ayush** (Map pp368–9; ☎ 65195195; www.leverayush.com; D Khader Nawaz Khan Rd, Nungambakkam; ✆ 7am-7pm).

COURSES
Language
Dakshin Barath Hindi Prachar Sabha (Map pp368–9; ☎ 24341824; Thanikachalam Rd, Theagaraya Nagar) Hindi courses in all levels.
International Institute of Tamil Studies (☎ 22540992; www.ulakaththamizh.org; Central Polytechnic Campus, Adyar) Three-month courses in Tamil. Can recommend teachers for shorter-term study.

Meditation
Dhamma Setu (Vipassana Meditation Centre; ☎ 24780953; info@setu.dhamma.org; www.dhamma.org; Pazhan Thandalam Rd, Thirumudivakkam) Intensive 10-day courses in the SN Goenka tradition of *vipassana* meditation. See p101 for more details.
Mahabodhi Society of Sri Lanka (Map p372; ☎ 28192458; 12 Kennet Lane, Egmore) Dhamma talks, meditation and special *pujas* (offerings or prayers) on full-moon and other days.

Vivekanandar Illam (Map pp368–9; ☎ 28446188; Kamarajar Salai, Triplicane) Free one-hour classes on Wednesday nights.

Yoga
Ayush (Map pp368–9; ☎ 65195195; www.leverayush.com; D Khader Nawaz Khan Rd, Nungambakkam; ✆ 6-11am & 5-8pm) Courses for 21 days (Rs 1200) or one hour (Rs 150).
Vivekanandar Illam (Map pp368–9; ☎ 28446188; Kamarajar Salai, Triplicane) Eight-week sessions are Rs 500. Call ahead to take a single class.

TOURS

TTDC (p370) conducts half-day city tours (Rs 120) and day trips to Mamallapuram (Rs 330), Puducherry (Rs 400) and Tirupathi (Rs 640). Book at ITDC (p370) or TTDC.

SLEEPING

Egmore, on and around Kennet Lane, is good for budget accommodation and all the touts and chaos that go with it. It's also convenient for the train stations. Many prefer the (slightly) less chaotic Triplicane – budget and midrange places huddle around Triplicane High Rd. The top hotels are scattered around the quieter areas south and west of the centre. Places fill up in peak season (December to February), so call ahead.

Budget
EGMORE
Salvation Army Red Shield Guest House (Map p372; ☎ 25321821; 15 Ritherdon Rd; dm/s/d Rs 80/300/350; ✕) This popular cheapie in a quiet spot north of Egmore Station has helpful staff and ageing but clean bathrooms (with bucket hot water for dorm-dwellers). Entrance is on BKN Ave.
Hotel Regent (Map p372; ☎ 28191801; 11 Kennet Lane; s/d Rs 200/315) In the centre of Kennet Lane's chaos, but set back from the road, the Regent is almost tranquil. Very clean rooms surround a shady, freshly swept courtyard.
Hotel Impala Continental (Map p372; ☎ 28191423; 12 Gandhi Irwin Rd; s/d incl tax from Rs 220/372) Impala is one of Egmore's better-value budget places, with clean, spacious double rooms. You'll find it full if you don't book ahead.
Krishna Park (Map p372; ☎ 28190026; 61 Halls Rd; s/d from Rs 325/550; ✕) Near the station but away from its bustle, it has special touches such as stainless-steel buckets and towel racks in the bathroom, smiling staff, and glow-in-the-dark stars on the ceiling of Room 303.

TRIPLICANE

Broadlands Lodge (Map p372; ☎ 28545573; broad landshotel@yahoo.com; 18 Vallabha Agraharam St; s/d with shared bathroom from Rs 200/300, with private bathroom from Rs 300/350) A longtime travellers' hang-out, Broadlands Lodge is falling apart and not very clean, but the old colonial-style place ranks number one for personality. Rooms are set around a leafy central courtyard, and the upper-storey rooms No 43 and 44 are spectacular. The shared bathrooms are dank and hot water is by bucket.

Paradise Guest House (Map p372; ☎ 28594252; paradisegh@hotmail.com; 17 Vallabha Agraharam St; s/d/tr from Rs 250/300/400; ☒) With gleaming tiles, a breezy (but unfinished) rooftop and friendly staff, we thought this was the best value in Triplicane – even though hot water is by the bucket. Some rooms don't have much view so ask to see a few; those on the upper floors are newer.

Hotel Himalaya (Map p372; ☎ 28547522; 54 Triplicane High Rd; s/d/tr Rs 350/400/550; ☒ ▣) This is a great budget/midrange choice with plain but comfortable rooms, a 24-hour internet café and travel desk. Some effort has been made at aesthetics: cheesy landscape photos pepper the walls, and a blue sky is painted on the elevator interior.

Other recommendations:

Thaj Regency (Map p372; ☎ 28529524; 300 Triplicane High Rd; s/d from Rs 200/265; ☒)

Hotel Comfort (Map p372; ☎ 28587661; www .hotelcomfort.com; 22 Vallabha Agraharam; s/d from Rs 400/500; ☒)

Midrange

EGMORE

Hotel Chandra Park (Map p372; ☎ 28191177; www .hotelchandrapark.com; 9 Gandhi Irwin Rd; s/d with AC incl breakfast from Rs 550/750; ☒) The new Chandra Park is priced mysteriously low. The lobby is classy, with lotus flowers floating in a pool and a mosaic of a Bharata Natyam dancer. Standard rooms are small but have clean towels and tight white sheets. Wisely set back from the road.

YWCA International Guest House (Map p372; ☎ 25324234; ywcaigh@indiainfo.com; Poonamallee High Rd; s/d/tr from Rs 650/800/1100; ☒) The YWCAIGH has a monastic feel to it, with off-the-charts cleanliness, a painting of Jesus in the hallway, and no TVs in rooms but, rather, a cosy hallway TV lounge. Geese amble around the leafy compound, which is, unbelievably, just near the train station.

Hotel Ashoka (Map p372; ☎ 28553377; www.ballal grouphotels.com; 47 Pantheon Rd; s/d incl breakfast from Rs 800/900; ☒) If 1950s Miami and a spaceship had a baby, it would be the Hotel Ashoka. Rooms are old-school, with a thousand layers of white paint around the windows and dated room-number plaques, while cottages (single/double Rs 1700/2250) have a lounge ambience: lush red carpeting, fridges and cocoonlike tubs. The compound includes an 'ice cream park' with a counter built around a big tree. Chennai's funkiest.

Other recommendations:

New Victoria Hotel (Map p372; ☎ 28193638; www .newvictoriahotel.com; 3 Kennet Lane; s/d incl breakfast from Rs 975/1250; ☒) Good deluxe rooms.

Hotel New Park Plaza (Map p372; ☎ 30777777; parkplaza@eth.net; 29 Whannels Rd; s/d incl breakfast from Rs 1500/2000; ☒) Has a rooftop bar-restaurant and just underwent a mega-renovation.

Vestin Park (Map p372; ☎ 28527171; www.vestinpark .com; 39 Montieth Rd; s/d incl breakfast from Rs 2000/2500; ☒) Fancy for the price; it's a 'business star' hotel.

TRIPLICANE

Hotel Orchid Inn (Map p372; ☎ 28522555; 19 Woods Rd; s/d from Rs 600/700; ☒) A short walk from Anna Salai, the Orchid has slightly more style than most midrange places. Rooms have interesting details such as ceiling moulding trimmed in lavender or gold, and bathrooms have newish blue tile (and bucket hot water). The 'suite', ambitiously named 'Cloud 9' (singles/doubles Rs 1000/1250), has purple-and-coral walls and tubular furniture.

MYLAPORE & NUNGAMBAKKAM

New Woodlands Hotel (Map pp368–9; ☎ 28113111; www .newwoodlands.com; 72-75 Dr Radhakrishnan Salai; s/d from Rs 550/1050; ☒ ▣) A sprawling complex with 170 rooms and a certain eccentric character, New Woodlands is a Chennai institution. The doubles have seen better days, but singles are a good deal, with balconies overlooking the compound's many trees. Rooms have wi-fi connectivity.

Elements Hostel (Map pp368–9; ☎ 42142552; www .elementshostel.com; 26A Wallace Garden, 3rd St; dm/s/d incl breakfast from Rs 375/1000/1800; ☒ ▣) It's pricey for a hostel, but this is a *boutique* hostel' and you're paying for the amenities: spotless, homy bathrooms with 24-hour hot water, kitchen access, cellphones for rent, an internet centre and a spot in Nungambakkam's chichi shopping area. Plus, it has a swing set. It's a little hard to find; look for the basketball net out front.

Top End

The following hotels have central AC, multicuisine restaurant and bar, and they accept credit cards. Unless stated otherwise, checkout is noon.

Residency Towers (Map pp368-9; ☎ 28156363; www.theresidency.com; Sir Theagaraya Nagar Rd; s/d from Rs 3700/4200; 🔀 🖭 🖭) At this price, it's like Residency Towers doesn't know what a good thing it has going: five-star elegance with a lot more personality – and 24-hour checkout. Every floor is decorated differently, but rooms all have sliding doors in front of windows to block out light and noise, dark wood furniture and thoughtful touches.

Raintree (Map pp368-9; ☎ 42252525; www.raintree hotels.com; 120 St Mary's Rd, Mylapore; s/d from US$160/170; 🔀 🖭 🖭) At the eco-friendly Raintree, floors are made of bamboo (which is an annual), wastewater is treated and used for gardening, and electricity conservation holds pride of place. But then the sleek, minimalist rooms are some of the most stylish and comfortable around, and the rooftop pool (which doubles as insulation) has a gorgeous wooden terrace with views of the sea.

Also recommended:

Taj Connemara (Map p372; ☎ 66000000; www.tajho tels.com; Binny Rd; s & d from US$215-240; 🔀 🖭 🖭) Built in the Raj era, it still retains some regal charm.

ITC Hotel Park Sheraton & Towers (Map pp368-9; ☎ 24994101; www.itcwelcomgroup.com; TTK Rd, Alwarpet; s/d from US$230/255; 🔀 🖭 🖭)

EATING

Chennai has a good range of 'meals' joints, which serve thalis (traditional South Indian 'all-you-can-eat' meals) for lunch and dinner, and tiffin (snacks) such as idlis (rice dumplings) and dosas (lentil-flour pancakes) the rest of the day. It's tempting – and feasible – to eat every meal at one of Chennai's 17 bustling Saravana Bhavans, which you can count on for quality vegetarian food.

The Mylapore area has many good independent restaurants, so head there if you're looking for something more refined.

Restaurants

EGMORE

Vasanta Bhavan (Map p372; 33 Gandhi Irwin Rd; mains Rs 40-60; 🕑 5am-11pm; 🔀) Excellent 'meals' (Rs 30).

The older Vasantha Bhavan down the street at No 10 is not as good but has more charm and also sweets.

Ponnusamy Hotel (Map p372; Wellington Estate, 24 Ethiraj Rd; mains Rs 40-85; 🕑 lunch & dinner) This well-known nonveg place serves curry, biryani (steamed rice with meat or vegetables) and Chettinad specialities. Unusual dishes include pigeon fry and rabbit masala.

Kitchen K (Map p372; 10 Montieth Rd; mains Rs 50-95; 🕑 lunch & dinner) Earth tones, clay pots and wrought-iron chairs make for a soothing ambience at this café serving Hyderabadi and northern dishes. Cake Walk (open 10am to 10pm) next door has tiramisu, apple pie and black forest cake, among other indulgences (Rs 40).

Hotel Saravana Bhavan Egmore (Map p372; 21 Kennet Lane; 🕑 6am-10.30pm); George Town (Map pp368-9; NSC Bose Rd (Broadway Chandra Rd); Mylapore (Map pp368-9; 101 Dr Radhakrishnan Salai; 🕑 6am-11.30pm); 🕑 7am-11pm); Thousand Lights (Map p372; 293 Peter's Rd; 🕑 lunch & dinner); Triplicane (Map p372; Shanthi Theatre Complex, 48 Anna Salai; 🕑 7am-11pm) Dependably delish, 'meals' at the Saravana Bhavans run around Rs 50, though the Mylapore locale has some 'special meals' for Rs 95 and up. The Thousand Lights branch is more upscale, with an Rs 160 buffet and silver cutlery.

TRIPLICANE

Maharaja Restaurant (Map p372; 207 Triplicane High Rd; mains Rs 25-40; 🕑 6am-11pm) Maharaja is a popular veg joint for 'meals' (Rs 22) and early morning tea and idlis.

Hotel Comfort (Map p372; 22 Vallabha Agraharam; mains Rs 30-100; 🕑 dinner) The menu is typical Indian and Chinese, but the rooftop garden is cosy and relaxed, with lots of plants around and great views. You can get a cold beer here, too.

THOUSAND LIGHTS & GOPALAPURAM

Gyan Vaishnava Punjabi Dhaba (Map p372; 260 Anna Salai; mains Rs 40-100; 🕑 lunch & dinner) When asked about his excellent pure-veg Punjabi, Jain and other northern dishes, Mr Vaishnava opened his arms and said, 'I'm giving quality… with love.' And that's the truth.

Gallopin' Gooseberry (Map p372; ☎ 23450872; 1st fl, 11 Greams Rd; dishes Rs 75-125; 🕑 11am-11pm) This American diner–style place does fab Cajun, mushroom and tikka burgers (around Rs 85), as well as pasta and sandwiches. It also delivers. The Fruit Shop next door has exotic juices and shakes (Rs 10 to 70).

Amethyst (Map p372; ☎ 28353581; Padmavathi Rd; light meals Rs 85-200; ☺ 10am-9.30pm) Sitting on the patio amid the gardens of this heritage house (see also p378) will make you feel like someone else entirely. Tea comes with cucumber-and-mint-chutney sandwiches at teatime (Rs 125; 5pm to 7pm).

MYLAPORE

Amaravathi (Map pp368-9; ☎ 28116416; cnr Cathedral & TTK Rds; mains Rs 50-95; ☺ 11am-3.30pm & 7-11pm) Amaravathi serves hot Andhran specialities on banana leaves. Try the biryani or mango prawn masala (an Andhran interpretation of a Keralan classic; Rs 85), but we'd stay away from the mutton-bone soup.

Coconut Lagoon (Map pp368-9; ☎ 42020428; cnr Cathedral & TTK Rds; mains Rs 55-200; ☺ noon-3pm & 7-11.45pm) Excellent Keralan and Goan fare with a focus on seafood delicacies, such as *kari meen polli chathu* (fish masala steamed in banana leaf).

Zara's (Map pp368-9; ☎ 28111462; 74 Cathedral Rd; tapas Rs 65-195; ☺ 1-3pm & 6.30-11pm) An ultra-cool tapas bar with a genuine Spanish flavour, it has everything from squid and olives to tortilla and sangria. Make reservations on weekends. See also right.

Benjarong (Map pp368-9; ☎ 24322640; 537 TTK Rd; mains Rs 130-400; ☺ 12.15-2.45pm & 7.15-11.30pm) From the finely crafted furniture and calming ambience to the attentive service and superbly presented food, this Thai restaurant is an experience. Most mains are around Rs 200, and the three-course special lunch (Rs 158 to 230) will make you feel like royalty.

Other spots:

Romallee (Map pp368-9; cnr Cathedral & TTK Rds; mains Rs 45-100; ☺ 6-11pm) Open-air Hyderabadi barbecue.

EcoCafé (Map pp368-9; Chamiers Rd; mains Rs 100-140; ☺ 8am-10.30pm) So-so food in an atmospheric garden, under arty lamps hanging from an almond tree.

Don Pepe (Map pp368-9; ☎ 28110413; 73 Cathedral Rd; mains Rs 120-180; ☺ noon-3pm & 6-11.30pm) Classy Mexican.

Quick Eats

It's OK to love ghee.

Grand Sweets (Map pp368-9; 24 Gandhi Nagar 2nd Main Rd, Adyar; ☺ 9am-7.30pm) Chennai's favourite sweets.

Suriya Sweets (Map pp368-9; 66 1st Main Rd, RA Puram; ☺ 6.30am-10.30pm) Chennai's second-favourite sweets, with an organic veggie market.

Self-Catering

Nilgiri Dairy Farm (Map pp368-9; ☎ 28110049; 103 Dr Radhakrishnan Salai; ☺ 9.30am-8pm, closed Tue) A great supermarket.

Spencer's Daily (Map p372; ☎ 42140784; Spencer Plaza, Phase I, Anna Salai; ☺ 9.30am-9pm)

24-Lettered Mantra (Map pp368-9; ☎ 24618400; 11 Vishwanathan St, RA Puram; ☺ 9.30am-1pm & 3-8pm Mon-Sat) It's out of the way, but this little shop has all-organic cooking staples and spices.

Jam Bazaar (Map p372; cnr Ellis Rd & Bharathi Salai) The colourful way to get fruit, vegetables and spices.

DRINKING
Cafés

Chennai is very much in the throes of India's cappuccino addiction.

Café Coffee Day (coffee Rs 20-50; ☺ 10am-11pm) Egmore (Map p372; Alsa Mall, Montieth Rd); Nungambakkam (Map pp368-9; Nungambakkam High Rd)

Barista (Map pp368-9; Rosy Towers, Nungambakkam High Rd; D Khader Nawaz Khan Rd; coffee Rs 20-50; ☺ 7.30am-11.30pm)

Mocha (Map pp368-9; D Khader Nawaz Khan Rd; coffee Rs 20-180; ☺ 11am-11pm) The young and beautiful go to Mocha for coffee, hookahs (Rs 150 to 325) and snacks (Rs 50 to 150) in exceedingly arty surrounds. Lovely outdoor garden.

Bars & Nightclubs

Chennai's nightlife scene is on the move but it's no Bengaluru or Mumbai. Bars and clubs are legally supposed to close at midnight (though the clubs occasionally stay open later), and are restricted to hotels. Exceptions are the seedy, government-operated 'wine shops', where men consume cheap local rum.

Some midrange hotels have AC bars with cold beers for Rs 120. Try the rooftop bars at Hotel Comfort (p375) or New Park Plaza (p375) and Tropicana Bar at New Victoria Hotel (p375).

Nightclubs charge a cover of Rs 300 to 500 on weekends (or even weekdays), and gents will require a lady chaperone to enter.

Zara's (Map pp368-9; ☎ 28111462; 74 Cathedral Rd; cocktails Rs 225-325; ☺ 1-3pm & 6.30-11pm) Where the cool people come on weekends for tapas (see left), sangria, house-infused vodka (jalapeno, almond, cinnamon) and inventive mocktails. Dress nice, guys: no shorts or sandals allowed.

Bike & Barrel (Map pp368-9; Residency Towers, Sir Theagaraya Rd; ☺ 11.30am-11.30pm) Better vibe than most bars; walls full of memorabilia, barrels for tables

TAMIL NADU

and a motorcycle hanging from the ceiling. Beer is Rs 140 and pub grub is available.

Dublin (Map pp368-9; ITC Park Sheraton, 132 TTK Rd; 6pm-midnight, closed Tue) An Irish pub-club with three levels of dancing. Cover charged after 10pm.

Other clubs:

Pasha (Map pp368-9; 42144000; The Park, 601 Anna Salai; 8-11.45pm Wed-Sat) Egyptian-themed.

Havana (Map pp368-9; 42252525; Raintree, 120 St Mary's Rd, Mylapore; 7-11.30pm Tue-Sun) Cuban-themed, with cigars and everything.

ENTERTAINMENT
Classical Music & Dance

Music Academy (Map pp368-9; 28115162; cnr TTK Rd & Dr Radhakrishnan Salai) This is Chennai's most popular public venue for Carnatic classical music and Bharata Natyam dance. Check newspapers for events. Expect to pay Rs 250 for a good seat, although many performances are free.

Kalakshetra Arts Village (24521169; kshetra@vsnl .com; Dr Muthulakshmi Rd, Tiruvanmiyu; 10am-6pm) Founded in 1936, Kalakshetra is committed to reviving classical dance and music. See one of the regular performances, or a class (9am to 11am and 2pm to 4.30pm Monday to Friday). Four-month courses are held in music and dance for Rs 600 per month.

Cinema

Chennai has more than 100 cinemas, a reflection of the vibrant film industry here. Most screen Tamil films, but **Sathyam Cinema** (Map p372; 28512425; 8 Thiruvika Rd) often shows English-language films in addition to Tamil and Hindi blockbusters. Tickets cost Rs 55 to 110. Check local papers for show times.

SHOPPING

Chennai's shopping landscape is changing. Traditional stores are extending services to keep up with the spread of the mall epidemic, while new, sophisticated boutiques are responding to both with panache.

Theagaraya Nagar (aka T Nagar; Map pp368-9) has great shopping, especially at Pondy Bazaar and around Panagal Park. Nungambakkam's shady D Khader Nawaz Khan Rd (Map pp368-9) is an exceedingly pleasant lane of shops, cafés and galleries.

Most of the finest Kanchipuram silks turn up in Chennai (and Bengaluru), so consider doing your silk shopping here.

Victoria Technical Institute (Map p372; 2852 3141; 765 Anna Salai; 9.30am-6pm Mon-Fri, 9.30am-1.30pm Sat) Most of the revenue from the quality crafts here goes to the artisans, and some to charity.

SIPA'S Craftlink (Map pp368-9; 28257544; 70 Kodambakkam High Rd, Nungambakkam; 9.30am-8pm Mon-Sat) South India's first fair-trade craft shop.

Amethyst (Map p372; 28351627; Padmavathi Rd, Gopalapuram; 11am-8pm) See what's the latest at this collection of shops in Sundar Mahal, a lovely heritage building. Clothes, jewellery and home décor by India's hottest designers.

Anokhi (Map pp368-9; 24311495; 85/47 Chamiers Rd, RA Puram; 10am-8pm) Hand-block-printed

---

INTO THE 'WOODS

Tamil film fans – and they're known for their fanaticism – will tell you that their movies have always been technically superior to Hindi films. Far from living in Bollywood's shadow, Kollywood – named for Kodambakkam, the neighbourhood preferred by many studios and film people – has its own tradition of filmmaking founded on high-quality production, slightly more realistic plot lines and much more realistic heroes (ie they like them chubby and moustachioed).

Kollywood style, though, is changing. Bollywood's famous 'masala' format – that crowd-pleasing mix of drama, comedy, romance and action – is rubbing off on Tamil films, and vice versa. Bollywood's been remaking Tamil blockbusters, while the big-name celebs in Mumbai (Bombay) are working in Kollywood. (The effect of watching Aishwarya Rai lip-synch to dubbed Tamil can be unsettling.)

For better or worse, it's working. Kollywood doesn't outdo Tollywood (the Telugu film industry) for output, but it comes second to Bollywood for revenue. Some say it even rivals it for distribution, with obsessed Tamil fans queuing up not only in Tamil Nadu's 1800 cinemas, but also in Sri Lanka, Malaysia, South Africa, Europe and the USA. The popularity of Telegu-dubbed Tamil movies over home-grown Tollywood films even led the Andhra Pradesh government to pass a law banning dubbing! Meanwhile, some Hindi film studios, hearing the ch-ching of Kollywood's success, have begun to get in on the action and produce Tamil films themselves – films which, to be sure, will be remade someday in Bollywood.

TRADITIONAL TRADERS

George Town, the area that grew around the fort, retains much of its original flavour. This is the wholesale centre of Chennai (Madras). Many backstreets, bordered by NSC Bose Rd, Krishna Koil St, Mint St and Rajaji Salai, are entirely given over to selling one particular type of merchandise as they have for hundreds of years – paper goods in Anderson St, fireworks in Badrian St and so on. Even if you're not in the market for anything, wander the mazelike streets to see another aspect of Indian life flowing seamlessly from the past into the present.

clothes with which all the women we know are obsessed. Have iced tea afterwards at Eco-Café (p377).

Apparao Galleries (Map pp368-9; ☎ 28332226; 7 Wallace Garden, 3rd St, Nungambakkam; ☙ 11am-7pm Mon-Sat) Rotating exhibitions of contemporary art and photography.

Fabindia (Map p372) Spencer Plaza (☎ 42158015; ☙ 11am-8pm); Woods Rd (☎ 42027015; ☙ 10am-8pm) The Woods Rd shop has home and food sections, along with fabulous clothes.

Naturally Auroville (Map pp368-9; ☎ 28330517; D Khader Nawaz Khan Rd, Nungambakkam; ☙ 10.30am-8pm Mon-Sat) *Objets* (pottery, bedspreads) and

fine foods (organic coffees and cheeses) from Auroville.

Varadarams Silks (Map pp368-9; ☎ 28363867; 88 Harrington Rd, Chetpet; ☙ 10am-7.30pm Mon-Sat) A good selection of low-priced Kanchipuram silk in a relaxed atmosphere.

Nalli Silks (Map pp368-9; ☎ 24344115; 9 Nageswaran Rd, Theagaraya Nagar; ☙ 9.30am-9.30pm) The granddaddy of silk shops.

The area around Kapaleeshwarar Temple has fun shopping; try **Sri Vidhya Book Centre** (Map pp368-9; ☎ 24611345; Sannathi St; ☙ 9am-9pm), for a well-chosen stock of religious and cultural books, and **Shanthi Tailors** (Map pp368-9; ☎ 24643783; Sannathi St; ☙ 9.30am-8.30pm Mon-Sat) if you're a Bharata Natyam dancer – or want to look like one.

The best of the commercial shopping malls include **Spencer Plaza** (Map p372; Anna Salai), and **Chennai Citicentre** (Map pp368-9; Dr Radhakrishnan Salai).

GETTING THERE & AWAY
Air
Anna International Airport (☎ 22560551) in Tirusulam, 16km southwest of the centre, is efficient and not too busy, making Chennai a good entry or exit point. **Kamaraj domestic terminal** (☎ 22560551) is next door in the same building.

DOMESTIC AIRLINES
Air Deccan, along with online budget airlines GoAir, Indigo, Paramount and spiceJet,

DOMESTIC FLIGHTS FROM CHENNAI (MADRAS)

Destination	Airline	Fare (US$)	Duration (hr)	Frequency
Bengaluru	IC	75	45min	2 daily
	9W	72	1	6 daily
Delhi	IC	211	2½	5 daily
	9W	177	2½	11 daily
Goa	IC	121	3	1 weekly
Hyderabad	IC	103	1	3 daily
	9W	97	1	3 daily
Kochi	IC	106	1	8 weekly
Kolkata	IC	184	2	2 daily
	9W	167	2	5 daily
Mumbai	IC	133	2	11 daily
	9W	112	2	12 daily
Port Blair	IC	175	2	1 daily
	9W	147	2	3 daily
Trivandram	IC	103	1½	2 daily
	9W	112	1½	1 daily

Note: Fares are one-way only. Airline codes: IC – Indian Airlines; 9W – Jet Airways.

tend to have the cheapest domestic fares. Indian Airlines tends to have the highest, with Jet, Sahara and Kingfisher following close behind.

Domestic airlines with offices in Chennai:

Air Deccan (Map p372; ☎ 42033209, airport 22560505; www.airdeccan.com; Desabhandu Plaza, White's Rd, Royapettah; ⌚ 8am-8pm)

Air Sahara (Map p372; ☎ 22560909, 42110202; Desabhandu Plaza, White's Rd, Royapettah)

Indian Airlines (Map p372; ☎ 23453366, airport 22561971; www.indian-airlines.com; 19 Marshalls Rd, Egmore)

Jet Airways (Map p372; ☎ domestic 39872222, international 1800225522; www.jetairways.com; 41/43 Montieth Rd, Egmore; ⌚ 9am-8pm Mon-Sat, 9am-7pm Sun) Flies internationally, as well.

INTERNATIONAL AIRLINES

Air Canada (Map pp368-9; ☎ 55713413; 101 HD Raja St, Eldhams Rd, Teynampet)

Air France (Map p372; ☎ 28554916; Thapar House, 43-44 Montieth Rd, Egmore)

Air India (Map p372; ☎ 28578146; Marshalls Rd, Egmore)

American Airlines (Map p372; ☎ 18001807300; Thapar House, 43-44 Montieth Rd, Egmore)

Cathay Pacific Airways (Map p372; ☎ 42140941; Desabhandu Plaza, White's Rd, Royapettah)

Delta (Map pp368-9; ☎ 28226156; Maalavika Centre, 144-145 Kodambakkam High Rd)

Gulf Air (Map p372; ☎ 28554417; Thapar House, 43-44 Montieth Rd, Egmore)

InterGlobe Air Transport (Map pp368-9; ☎ 2822 6149; Maalavika Centre, 144-145 Kodambakkam High Rd) For Air New Zealand, South African, United and Virgin Atlantic.

KLM (Map p372; ☎ 28524427; Marshalls Rd, Egmore)

Lufthansa (Map p372; ☎ 30213500, airport 22569393; 167 Anna Salai) No walk-ins.

Malaysia Airlines (Map pp368-9; ☎ 42191919; 90 Dr Radhakrishnan Salai)

Singapore Airlines (Map pp368-9; ☎ 28473982; Westminster, 108 Dr Radhakrishnan Salai)

Sri Lankan Airlines (Translanka Air Travels; Map pp368-9; ☎ 43921100; 4 Kodambakkam High Rd, Nungambakkam)

Thai Airways International (Map pp368-9; ☎ 42173311; 31 Haddows Rd)

Boat

Passenger ships sail from the George Town harbour to Port Blair in the Andaman Islands (see p449) every 10 days. The **Director of Shipping Services** (Map pp368-9; ☎ 25226873; fax 25220841; Shipping Corporation Bldg, Rajaji Salai; ⌚ 10am-3pm Mon-Fri) sells tickets (Rs 1522 to 5892) for the 60-hour trip. You'll need two photos and three photocopies each of your passport and visa.

Bus

Most Tamil Nadu (SETC) and other government buses operate from the massive **Chennai Mofussil Bus Terminus** (CMBT; ☎ 23455858, 24794705; Jawaharlal Nehru Salai, Koyambedu), better known as Koyambedu CMBT, 7km west of town.

Buses 15 or 15B from Parry's Corner or Central Station, and 27B from Anna Salai or Egmore station, all head there (Rs 4, 40 minutes). An autorickshaw charges around Rs 120 for the same ride.

Frequent SETC, Karnataka (KSRTC) and Andhra Pradesh (APRSTC) buses cover the following destinations, usually in the morning and late afternoon:

Destination	Fare* (Rs)	Duration (hr)
Bengaluru	175	9
Chidambaram	82	7
Hyderabad	372	12
Kodaikanal	208	14
Madurai	180	10
Mamallapuram	40	2
Mysore	209	11
Ooty	221	14
Puducherry	59	4
Thanjavur	135	9
Tirupathi	63	4
Trichy	150	8
* Fares are for ordinary buses.		

Several companies operate Volvo AC buses to the same destinations from the less overwhelming private-bus station next door; try **KPN** (☎ 24797998) or **Rathi Meena** (☎ 24791494). Private operators also depart from opposite Egmore train station. These superdeluxe buses usually leave at night and cost two to three times more than ordinary buses.

Train

Interstate trains and those heading west generally depart from Central Station (Map pp1030–1), while trains heading south depart from Egmore (Map p1034). The **Train Reservation Complex** (☎ general 131, reservations 1361; ⌚ 8am-8pm Mon-Sat, 8am-2pm Sun) is on the west side of Central Station; the Foreign Assistance Tourist Cell is on the 1st floor. Egmore's **booking office** (☎ 28194579) keeps the same hours.

MAJOR TRAINS FROM CHENNAI (MADRAS)

Destination	Train No & name	Fare (Rs)	Duration (hr)	Departure
Bengaluru	2007 *Shatabdi Exp**	510/995	5	6am CC
	2609 *Bangalore Exp*	117/392	5	1.15pm CC
Delhi	2433 *Rajdhani Exp*	2005/2710	28	6.10am CC
	2621 *Tamil Nadu Exp*	497/1400/2016	33	10pm CC
Hyderabad	2759 *Charminar Exp*	317/837/1178	14½	6.10pm CC
	2753 *Hyderabad Exp*	301/792/1113	13	4.45pm CC
Kochi	6041 *Alleppey Exp*	243/741/1052	11½	9.15pm CC
Kolkata	2842 *Coromandel Exp*	449/1234/1764	27½	9am CC
	6004 *Howrah Mail*	449/1234/1764	30½	10pm CC
Madurai	6127 *MS Guruvayur Exp*	215/574/814	8	7.25am CC
	2635 *Vaigai Exp*	142/479	8	12.25pm CE
Mumbai	6012 *Mumbai Exp*	389/1065/1521	26	11.45am CC
Mysore	2007 *Shatabdi Exp***	655/1265	7	6am CC
	6222 *Kaveri Exp*	215/574/814	10½	9.45pm CC
Tirupathi	6053 *Tirupathi Exp*	63/209	3	1.50pm CC
Trichy	2605 *Pallavan Exp*	111/372	5½	3.30pm CE
Trivandrum	2695 *Trivandrum Exp*	342/907/1279	15½	4.15pm CC

CC – Chennai Central, CE – Chennai Egmore
*Daily except Tuesday
**Daily except Wednesday

Shatabdi fares are chair/executive; Rajdhani fares are for 3AC/2AC; Express and Mail fares are 2nd/chair car for day trains, sleeper/3AC/2AC for overnight trains.

The table, above, lists some popular Chennai routes. For Goa there's only one direct train a week: Friday's *Chennai–Vasco Express*.

GETTING AROUND
To/From the Airport
The cheapest way to reach the airport is by MRTS train to Tirusulam station, 500m across the road from the terminals.

An autorickshaw should cost you about Rs 200/300 for a day/night trip.

Both terminals have prepaid taxi kiosks, where tickets are Rs 240 (Egmore) or Rs 260 (to Anna Salai or Triplicane).

Autorickshaw
Fares are relatively high: locals pay Rs 20 for a short trip down the road. From Egmore to George Town, Triplicane or Anna Salai should cost no more than Rs 40, to Nungambakkam, Rs 50. Prices are at least 25% higher after 10pm. There's a prepaid booth outside Central Station.

See p371 for more on details Chennai's autorickshaws.

Bus
Chennai's bus system is worth getting to know. The main city bus stand is at Parry's Corner (Map pp368–9), and fares are between Rs 4 and 10. Some useful routes follow.

Bus No	Route
1	Parry's-Central-Triplicane
5D	Koyambedu CMBT-Guindy-Adyar-Mylapore
9, 10	Parry's-Central-Egmore-T Nagar
11/11A	Parry's-Anna Salai-T Nagar
15B	Parry's-Central-Koyambedu CMBT
18	Parry's-Saidapet
19S	Parry's-Central-Adyar
27B	Egmore-Chetpet-Koyambedu CMBT
31	Parry's-Central-Vivekananda House
32	Central-Triplicane-Vivekananda House
51M	T Nagar-St Thomas Mount

Car & Taxi
For an extended hire, organise a driver through a travel agent or large hotel. You might pay a little more, but the driver should be reliable and you'll have a point of contact should something go wrong. Non-AC rates

TAMIL NADU

are around Rs 450 per half-day (five hours) within the city, and Rs 5 per kilometre, with a daily 250km minimum, beyond city limits. Note that the clock starts ticking when the driver leaves the office.

We like **Shankaran** (☎ 24713874; lmt_shankaran@yahoo.co.in). **Manjoo Cabs** (☎ 23813083; manjoocabs@yahoo.com) is a drivers' cooperative.

Train

Efficient MRTS trains run every 15 minutes from Beach station to Fort, Park (at Central Station), Egmore, Chetpet, Nungambakkam, Kodambakkam, Mambalam, Saidapet, Guindy, St Thomas Mount, Tirusulam (for the airport), and on down to Tambaram. The second line branches off at Park and hits Light House and Tirumailar (at Kapaleeshwarar Temple). Tickets cost between Rs 5 and 10.

NORTHERN TAMIL NADU

CHENNAI TO MAMALLAPURAM

Chennai's urban sprawl continues a fair way south before opening up on the East Coast Rd to Mamallapuram. Along this stretch, known as the Coromandel Coast, are several small beach resorts and wonderful artists' communities, along with less fortunate tsunami-ravaged fishing villages still slowly being rebuilt.

In the village of Injambalkkam, 18km south of Chennai, the **Cholamandal Artists' Village** (☎ 044-24490092; cholamandalartvillage.com; admission free; ☾ 9.30am-6.30pm), set on 4 hectares of land, was created in 1966 as a cooperative where artists and sculptors could live, work and exhibit. Still thriving, the group of traditional thatch-roofed buildings and gardens includes galleries and studios where there are usually artists at work and fine contemporary paintings and sculptures on show and for sale. A new gallery and public exhibition space was being built in 2006, and there are two simple studio-cum-guesthouses available for visiting artists only (Rs 500 per day; book well in advance).

At Muttukadu, 12km south of Cholamandal, is **DakshinaChitra** (☎ 044-27472603; www.dakshinachitra.net; Indian student/adult Rs 25/50, foreign student/adult Rs 70/175; ☾ 10am-6pm, closed Tue), a remarkable cultural centre and arts complex displaying traditional arts and crafts from Tamil Nadu, Kerala, Karnataka and Andhra Pradesh. Established by the Madras Crafts Association, the village incorporates traditional buildings and workshops including silk-weavers' houses, potters' sheds and merchants' homes. Static arts and craft displays are complemented by daily interactive demonstrations of pottery, basket weaving, puppet making and palm-leaf decoration (Rs 5 to 25), and free weekend activities include a puppet show and glass blowing. A truly delightful cool, tiled 12-room **guesthouse** (☎ 98414 22149; r without/with AC Rs 550/800) is in the grounds (though you might want to check you're not coinciding with a school overnight excursion). You can also book rooms through the centre.

To reach these places, take any bus heading south to Mamallapuram (bus 188 or 118, Rs 22, one hour) and ask to be let off; an AC taxi for a full day tour costs about Rs 1200.

Crocodile Bank (☎ 04114-242511; adult/child Rs 20/10, camera/video Rs 10/75; ☾ 8am-5.30pm, closed Mon), 40km south of Chennai, is a well-regarded breeding farm for crocodiles, alligators and turtles. There are hundreds of reptiles here, including the Indian mugger and gavial crocodiles and the saltwater crocs of the Andaman and Nicobar Islands. The leafy grounds support more than 50 bird species; keep an eye open for jewel-like kingfishers bobbing above the croc pools. Late afternoon is feeding time (Rs 20). An attached **snake farm** (adult/child Rs 5/3; ☾ 10am-1pm & 2-5pm) produces antivenin.

About 5km north of Mamallapuram in the village of Salavankuppam, beside the East Coast Rd, the **Tiger Cave** is a rock-cut shrine, possibly dating from the 7th century. It's dedicated to Durga and has a small *mandapa* featuring a crown of carved *yali* (mythical lion creature) heads.

MAMALLAPURAM (MAHABALIPURAM)

☎ 044 / pop 12,049

Mamallapuram is Tamil Nadu's only true travellers' enclave, a mix of sun, seafood and sand with a dash of seediness thrown in. But it's much more than that. Famous for its ancient rock carvings, especially the Shore Temple, it was once the second capital and seaport of the Pallava kings of Kanchipuram. The village is listed as a World Heritage site and remains a renowned centre for stone carving; you'll see and hear the constant tapping of hammer and chisel as artisans chip away at exquisite sculptures.

Less than two hours by bus from Chennai, with a reasonably good beach, an excellent combination of cheap accommodation, fish restaurants, handicraft shops, spectacular stone carvings dotted around the town and Tamil Nadu's most highly regarded dance festival (see the boxed text, p366), it's easy to see why travellers make a beeline here from Chennai and hang around for a while. The local community was affected by the 2004 tsunami but worked hard to get back to sort-of normal as quickly as possible; check out the 'before and after' photos in some of the beachfront restaurants.

Orientation & Information

Mamallapuram village is tiny and laid-back, with most of the action on East Raja, Othavadai and Othavadai Cross Sts; the latter runs parallel to the beach. The surrounding sites of interest can be explored on foot or by bicycle.

BOOKSHOP
JK Bookshop (☎ 9840442853; Othavadai St; ☺ 8.30am-9pm) A small bookshop where you can buy or swap (Rs 50) books in several languages, including English, French and German. Proceeds support village schools established by the owner.

INTERNET ACCESS
You'll find internet access everywhere.
Hotel Lakshmi Internet (Othavadai Cross St; per hr Rs 40; ☺ 9am-10pm) Reliable fast connection.

MEDICAL SERVICES
St Mary's Health Centre (☎ 27442334; ☺ 9am-12.30pm & 4.30-6.30pm) Near the tourist office.

Suradeep Hospital (☎ 27442390; 15 Thirukkulam St; ☺ 24hr) Recommended by travellers.

MONEY
The best places to change cash or travellers cheques are the private exchange offices on East Raja St. Other suggestions:
LKP Forex (East Raja St; ☺ 9.30am-6.30pm Mon-Sat)
Prithvi Exchange (☎ 243265; East Raja St; ☺ 9.30am-7pm Mon-Sat)
State Bank of India ATM (East Raja St; ☺ 24hr)

POLICE
All Women Police Station (GK Mandapam St)
Police Station (Kovalam Rd)

POST
Post office (☺ 8am-4pm Mon-Fri) Down a small lane just east of the tourist office.

TOURIST INFORMATION
Tourist office (☎ 27442232; East Raja St; ☺ 10am-5.45pm Mon-Fri) Staff can provide you with a map, bus timetables and a bit of aimless conversation.

Sights

You can easily spend a full day exploring the temples, *mandapas* and rock carvings around Mamallapuram. Apart from the Shore Temple and Five Rathas, admission is free.

SHORE TEMPLE
Standing alone and majestic facing the Bay of Bengal (but enclosed by a steel fence), this small but romantic **temple** (combined ticket with Five Rathas Indian/foreigner Rs 10/250, video Rs 25; ☺ 6.30am-6pm), weathered by the wind and sea, represents the final phase of Pallava art. Originally constructed around the middle of the 7th

---

THE ROCK CARVINGS OF MAMALLAPURAM

The images carved into the rocks around Mamallapuram (Mahabalipuram) are like no other in Tamil Nadu. Much religious stonework in the state is alive with complex depictions of gods and goddesses, and images of ordinary folk are conspicuous because of their absence. Yet the splendid carvings at Mamallapuram are distinctive for the simplicity of their folk-art origins. The sculptures show scenes of everyday life – women milking buffaloes, pompous city dignitaries, young girls primping and posing on street corners or swinging their hips in artful come-ons.

Most of the temples and rock carvings here were completed during the reigns of Narasimha Varman I (AD 630–68) and Narasimha Varman II (AD 700–28). But this is not an art form consigned to history. Approximately 200 sculptors line the streets and chisel their stone from dawn to dusk. Indeed Mamallapuram's historical reputation for skilled carvers remains sufficiently intact – the town's craftsmen are frequently commissioned to create sculptures for new temples around the world.

MAMALLAPURAM (MAHABALIPURAM)

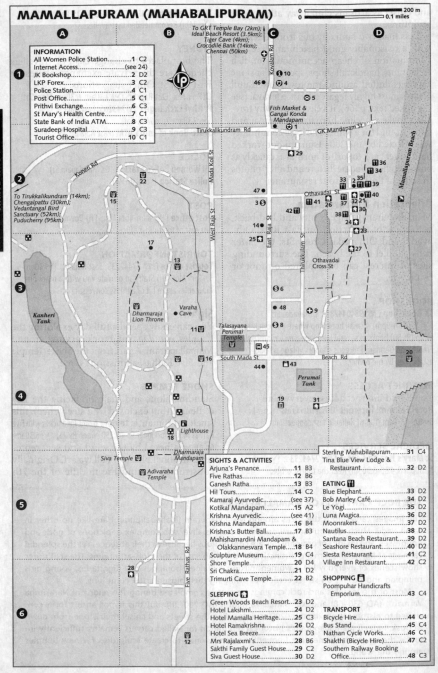

INFORMATION
All Women Police Station........1	C2
Internet Access.........................(see 24)	
JK Bookshop.............................2	D2
LKP Forex.................................3	C2
Police Station..........................4	C1
Post Office...............................5	C1
Prithvi Exchange.....................6	C1
St Mary's Health Centre..........7	C1
State Bank of India ATM..........8	C3
Suradeep Hospital...................9	C3
Tourist Office.........................10	C1

SIGHTS & ACTIVITIES
Arjuna's Penance...................11	B3
Five Rathas...........................12	B6
Ganesh Ratha........................13	B3
Hi! Tours...............................14	C2
Kamaraj Ayurvedic...........(see 37)	
Kotikal Mandapam................15	A2
Krishna Ayurvedic.............(see 41)	
Krishna Mandapam...............16	B4
Krishna's Butter Ball.............17	B3
Mahishamardini Mandapam &	
Olakkannesvara Temple......18	B4
Sculpture Museum.................19	C4
Shore Temple........................20	D4
Sri Chakra.............................21	D2
Trimurti Cave Temple............22	B2

SLEEPING
Green Woods Beach Resort....23	D2
Hotel Lakshmi.......................24	D2
Hotel Mamalla Heritage........25	C3
Hotel Ramakrishna................26	D2
Hotel Sea Breeze...................27	D3
Mrs Rajalaxmi's.....................28	B6
Sakthi Family Guest House....29	C2
Siva Guest House..................30	D2

Sterling Mahabilapuram........31	C4
Tina Blue View Lodge &	
Restaurant.........................32	D2

EATING
Blue Elephant.......................33	D2
Bob Marley Café...................34	D2
Le Yogi.................................35	D2
Luna Magica.........................36	D2
Moonrakers..........................37	D2
Nautilus...............................38	D2
Santana Beach Restaurant.....39	D2
Seashore Restaurant.............40	D2
Siesta Restaurant..................41	C2
Village Inn Restaurant...........42	C2

SHOPPING
Poompuhar Handicrafts	
Emporium..........................43	C4

TRANSPORT
Bicycle Hire..........................44	C4
Bus Stand.............................45	C4
Nathan Cycle Works..............46	C1
Shakthi (Bicycle Hire)...........47	C2
Southern Railway Booking	
Office................................48	C3

To GRT Temple Bay (2km);
Ideal Beach Resort (3.5km);
Tiger Cave (4km);
Crocodile Bank (14km);
Chennai (50km)

To Tirukkalikundram (14km);
Chengalpattu (30km);
Vedantangal Bird
Sanctuary (52km);
Puducherry (95km)

Tirukkalikundram Rd

GK Mandapam St

Mamallapuram Beach

Konen Rd

Mada Koil St

West Raja St

East Raja St

Thirukkulam St

Othavadai St

Othavadai Cross St

Fish Market &
Gangai Konda
Mandapam

South Mada St

Beach Rd

Talasayana
Perumal
Temple

Perumal
Tank

Kanheri
Tank

Dharmaraja
Lion Throne

Varaha
Cave

Dharmaraja
Mandapam

Siva Temple

Adivaraha
Temple

Lighthouse

Five Rathas Rd

Kovalam Rd

TAMIL NADU

century, it was later rebuilt by Narasimha Varman II (also known as Rajasimha). The temple's two main spires contain shrines for Shiva. Facing east and west the original linga (phallic images of Shiva) captured the sunrise and sunset. A third and earlier shrine is dedicated to the reclining Vishnu. A remarkable amount of temple carving remains, especially inside the shrines. The temple is now protected from further erosion by a huge rock wall. Like many of Mamallapuram's sights, it's spectacularly floodlit at night.

FIVE RATHAS

A fine example of Pallava architecture is the **Five Rathas** (Five Rathas Rd; combined ticket with Shore Temple Indian/foreigner Rs 10/250, video Rs 25; ☑ 6.30am-6pm), rock-cut temples resembling chariots. Just 300m from the sea, they were hidden in the sand until excavated by the British 200 years ago.

The Five Rathas derive their names from the champions of the Mahabharata; the Pandavas and their collective wife, Draupadi.

The first *ratha*, **Draupadi Ratha**, on the left after you enter the gate, is dedicated to the goddess Durga. Within, the goddess stands on a lotus, her devotees on their knees in worship. Outside, the huge sculpted lion stands proudly in front of her temple.

Behind the goddess shrine, a huge Nandi (Shiva's bull vehicle) heralds the next chariot, the **Arjuna Ratha**, dedicated to Shiva. Numerous deities, including Indra, the rain god, are depicted on the outer walls.

The next temple chariot, **Bhima Ratha**, honours Vishnu. Within its walls a large sculpture of this deity lies in repose.

The outside walls of **Dharmaraja Ratha**, the tallest of the chariots, portray many deities, including the sun god, Surya, and Indra. The final *ratha*, **Nakula-Sahadeva Ratha**, is dedicated to Indra. The fine sculptured elephant standing next to the temple represents his mount. As you enter the gate, approaching from the north, you see its back first, hence its name **gajaprishthakara** (elephant's backside). This life-sized image is regarded as one of the most perfectly sculptured elephants in India.

ARJUNA'S PENANCE

This **relief carving** (West Raja St) on the face of a huge rock depicts animals, deities and other semidivine creatures as well as fables from the Hindu Panchatantra books. The panel (30m by 12m) is divided by a huge perpendicular fissure that's skilfully encompassed into the sculpture; originally, water, representing the Ganges, flowed down it.

It's one of the most convincing and unpretentious rock carvings in India, with the main relief showing Shiva standing with a wizened Arjuna, balanced on one leg in a state of penance. A guide (around Rs 30) can be useful to help explain the reliefs.

GANESH RATHA & AROUND

This *ratha* is northwest of Arjuna's Penance. Once a Shiva temple, it became a shrine to Ganesh (the elephant-headed god) after the original lingam was removed. Just north of the *ratha* is a huge boulder known as **Krishna's Butter Ball**. Immovable, but apparently balancing precariously, it's a favourite photo opportunity. The nearby **Kotikal Mandapa** is dedicated to Durga.

Nearby, the **Trimurti Cave Temple** honours the Hindu trinity – Brahma, Vishnu and Shiva – with a separate section dedicated to each deity.

MANDAPAMS

Many *mandapas*, featuring fine internal sculptures, are scattered over the main hill. Among them is **Krishna Mandapa**, one of the earliest rock-cut temples and predating the penance relief. Its carvings of a pastoral scene show Krishna lifting up the mythical Govardhana mountain to protect his kinsfolk from the wrath of Indra. Others include **Mahishamardini Mandapa**, just a few metres southwest of the lighthouse. Scenes from the Puranas (Sanskrit stories dating from the 5th century AD) are depicted on the *mandapa* with the sculpture of the goddess Durga considered one of the finest.

Above the *mandapa* are the remains of the 8th-century **Olakkannesvara Temple**, and spectacular views of Mamallapuram. Photography is forbidden here for 'security reasons' – there's a nuclear power station a few kilometres south.

SCULPTURE MUSEUM

This **museum** (East Raja St; adult/child Rs 2/1, camera Rs 10; ☑ 9am-5.30pm) contains more than 3000 local sculptures in stone, wood, metal and even cement. Some fine paintings are also on display and the front courtyard is littered with sculptures.

GETTING BETTER AT DOING GOOD

'Great work was done here after the tsunami. The difficulty is in keeping the development sustainable and long term once it's no longer front-page news.'

Paul Knight, director of NGO Earth Aid Asia in Mamallapuram (Mahabalipuram), is musing on the long-term effects of the disaster. 'It became apparent to us that communities inland were also suffering, but indirectly; for example, in poor tribal villages where families relied on occasional day labour to buy food, both work and money dried up and people miles from the coast were literally starving. From the relationships we built with some of these communities then, we're continuing with health, education and income-generating projects – the things they've told us are their priorities – which will both improve their quality of life and help to bring in some money.' You can learn more about Earth Aid's work – and opportunities for volunteers – by dropping into the office in **Bharathi Street** (☎ 9884252252; www.earthaidindia.org). It may also be possible to support its work by staying at its guesthouse.

The needs of poor villagers are not as visible as those of the children who beg for funds for the many orphanages in Mamallapuram. Sometimes it's hard to define their presence as anything less than child exploitation when they should really be in school or playing. If you want to give to the kids, do your homework. Ask around town to get an idea of how children's homes are regarded locally, and give financial donations to reputable charities that support the children in the long term.

Activities

BEACH

The village is only about 200m from the wide beach, north of the Shore Temple, where local fishers pull in their boats. The beach is cleaner further north, or to the south of the Shore Temple, and you can take long unimpeded walks, although at high tide you need to walk over the rocks in front of the Shore Temple. It's not a great place for swimming – there are dangerous rips – but it's possible to go fishing in one of local outriggers; negotiate a price with the owner. Despite the beach scene, Western swimwear is not the norm here and you (and local people) may feel more comfortable if you cover up.

THERAPIES

There are numerous places offering massage, reiki, yoga and Ayurvedic practices. Sessions cost around Rs 350 for 30 to 45 minutes. **Krishna** (Siesta; Othavadai St) is recommended by both male and female travellers, as is **Kamaraj Ayurvedic** (☎ 27442115; full body Rs 300, face & neck Rs 150), which can be contacted through Moonrakers restaurant (p388).

Sri Chakra (Othavadai St; massage per hr Rs 300; ⏰ 8am-9pm) offers Ayurvedic massage as well as yoga sessions (Rs 150) at 7am.

There are many other operators in town with similar rates and timings. As always, and especially for such an intimate service, ask fellow travellers, question the masseur carefully and if you have any misgivings, don't proceed.

Tours

To tour Mamallapuram on two wheels, **Hi! Tours** (☎ 27443260; www.hi-tours.com; 123 East Raja St) runs bicycle tours (Rs 250, minimum four people) to local villages and sights, including the Tiger Cave and Tirukkalikundram Temple. The tours run from 8am to 2pm and include guide and lunch. Hi! Tours also organises day trips to Kanchipuram (p389) and Vedantangal Bird Sanctuary (p388).

Sleeping

Mamallapuram is full of traveller accommodation. If you don't mind roughing it too much, you can stay in basic home accommodation with families in the backstreets near the Five Rathas and elsewhere around the village. The rooms and facilities are very simple but travellers' reports are positive. The usual cost is around Rs 50 per day or Rs 300 per week.

The main budget and midrange places are on Othavadai and Othavadai Cross Sts, and top-end hotels are north of town on the road to Chennai.

BUDGET

Mrs Rajalaxmi's (☎ 27442460; r Rs 50) One of several cheap family-run places near the Five Rathas, this is friendly and homy but pretty basic.

Rooms have fans and electricity, and there's a communal squat toilet.

Sakthi Family Guest House (☎ 27442577; 6 East Raja St; r Rs 60-150) This rambling old house in the town centre is owned by the affable Mrs Chandra Palani, headmistress of the local primary school. Rooms outside the house are *very* basic and guests are treated like part of the furniture. There's no sign, but you'll find it hidden down a lane behind the town hall building.

Hotel Ramakrishna (☎ 27442331; 8 Othavadai St; s/d/tr Rs 100/150/250) This is a large place on three floors around a central parking area with no garden. Rooms are simple, but clean and good value.

Tina Blue View Lodge & Restaurant (☎ 27442319; 34 Othavadai St; r Rs 150-300) Run by the friendly Xavier, Tina Blue is one of Mamallapuram's originals so it looks a bit old hat, but it's set in a leafy garden with chairs and tables outside the rooms and has a bamboo-and-thatch restaurant on stilts.

Siva Guest House (☎ 27443234; sivaguesthouse@hotmail.com; 2 Othavadai Cross St; d without/with AC Rs 250-800; ☒) Deservedly popular with travellers, Siva gets consistently good reports. Rooms are spotless and each has a small veranda.

Green Woods Beach Resort (☎ 27443243; green woods_resort@yahoo.com; 7 Othavadai Cross St; d without/with AC Rs 300/750; ☒) Although not flash, Green Woods is homely and popular, with a garden and some pleasant rooftop rooms; No 4 has good balcony space.

Hotel Lakshmi (☎ 27442463; d without AC Rs 200-500, with AC Rs 850; ☒ 🖥 🖷) At the end of Othavadai Cross St and with beach access, the former Lakshmi Lodge is a long-standing backpacker place. With a tanklike swimming pool and a popular 1st-floor café hang-out, it's maintaining a standard, but the owners can be a little overbearing.

MIDRANGE & TOP END

Hotel Mamalla Heritage (☎ 27442060; 104 East Raja St; s/d Rs 850/1050; ☒ 🖷) In town, this standard midrange place has spacious, comfortable rooms, all with fridge, the pool's a decent size, and there's a quality veg and rooftop restaurant.

Hotel Sea Breeze (☎ 27443035; seabreezehotel@hotmail.com; Othavadai Cross St; r from Rs 1075; ☒ 🖷) The biggest draw here is the shady garden and pool (nonguests can use it for Rs 150) which give the air of a more upmarket resort.

Rooms are pretty standard but bright and spacious.

Ideal Beach Resort (☎ 27442240; www.idealresort.com; s/d Rs 1400/1700, cottages from Rs 2200; ☒ 🖥 🖷) With a landscaped tropical garden setting and comfortable rooms or cottages, this low-key beachfront resort is popular with package tours. The design is small and secluded enough to have an intimate atmosphere and there's a lovely open-air poolside restaurant. It's about 3.5km north of town.

Sterling Mahabalipuram (☎ 27442287; Shore Temple Rd; d Rs 4950; ☒ 🖷) In a quiet location near the Shore Temple and set in sprawling, shady grounds, this is a pleasant if overpriced place. Facilities include a bar, restaurant, children's play area, big pool and large old-fashioned rooms.

GRT Temple Bay (☎ 27443636; www.grttemplebay.com; r from Rs 5500; ☒ 🖥 🖷) Best of the town's northern resorts, the pool here is beachside, there's a gym, and most of the stylish rooms have sea views and balconies.

Eating & Drinking

One of the pleasures of Mamallapuram is eating out. Palm-thatched beachside restaurants serve up fresh seafood to the gentle sounds of the ocean. Be sure to ask about prices, though, as most seafood varies by weight or availability and king prawns and lobster can turn out to cost more than you expected. Restaurants are neatly clustered around Othavadai St and the beach, and all have extensive breakfast menus, and vegetable, Continental and Chinese dishes. Most places – licensed or not – serve beer but be sensitive to the 11pm local curfew; if you persuade a restaurant to allow you to linger longer over last drinks, it's the owner, not you, who faces a hefty fine. All places listed are open for breakfast, lunch and dinner.

Siesta (Othavadai St; dishes Rs 30-60) On the shaded and breezy rooftop of Sri Murugan Guest House, this tapas restaurant offers – among other things – authentic Spanish omelette, *patatas bravas* (fried potatoes in a spicy sauce), garlic mushrooms and paella.

Village Inn Restaurant (☎ 27442151; Thirukkulam St; mains Rs 45-85, beer Rs 75) Tucked away off the main strip, there's cane furniture, a couple of tables on the veranda and Indian classical music playing in the background, with inexpensive seafood, steaks (order in advance) and, surprisingly, Scotch eggs.

Nautilus (Othavadai Cross St; mains from Rs 50) This bustling French-run eatery is popular for its espresso coffee and European dishes such as ratatouille, salads, stuffed tomatoes or steak and chips, along with the usual seafood and Indian fare.

Le Yogi (☎ 27442571; Othavadai St; mains from Rs 50) Run by a French and Indian couple, this is the place to come for good wholemeal bread, salads, crepes and pasta. Sit up at tables, or loll with a coffee on the comfy floor cushions.

Moonrakers (Othavadai St; mains Rs 60-150) Run by three friendly brothers, Moonrakers' food has long been popular with its big menu of seafood, beef and chicken dishes plus breakfast fare such as pancakes and muffins. It's also a busy late-night hang-out where you can get a beer and meet other travellers. Chinese lamps, wagon wheels and wooden carvings decorate the place. Across the road, the newer and more comfortable Blue Elephant Restaurant – run by another brother! – is also recommended.

If beachside ambience and the strains of Bob Marley are what you're after, Bob Marley Café, Seashore Restaurant, Santana Beach Restaurant and Luna Magica are all recommended for fresh seafood; you'll get a good plate of fish for around Rs 70, with other meals from about Rs 40. All are open from about 7am and make a good setting for breakfast too.

Shopping
Mamallapuram wakes each day to the sound of sculptors' chisels on granite. You can browse hassle-free and buy from the fixed-price **Poompuhar Handicrafts Emporium** (☎ 27442224; South Mada St; ☾ 10am-7pm, closed Wed) or from the craft shops that line the main roads (prices negotiable). Sculptures range from Rs 300 (for a small piece to fit in your baggage) to Rs 400,000 for a massive Ganesh that needs to be lifted with a mobile crane.

Getting There & Away
Mamallapuram's small but busy bus stand is on the corner of East Raja and South Mada Sts. The most direct service to/from Chennai (Rs 22, two hours, 30 daily) is on buses 188 and 118. The express (ECR) buses are fastest. To Chennai airport take bus 108B (Rs 23, two hours, four daily).

To Puducherry (Rs 35, two hours, nine daily) take bus 188A. To Kanchipuram (Rs 20, two hours, 11 daily) via Tirukkalikundram

and Chengalpattu (Chingleput) take buses 212A or 212H.

To get to Madurai catch a bus to Chengalpattu (Rs 9, one hour, 33 daily) and then a train from there.

Taxis are available from the bus station. Long-distance trips require plenty of bargaining. It's about Rs 900 to Chennai or the airport.

You can make train reservations at the **Southern Railway Booking Office** (East Raja St).

Getting Around
The easiest way to get around is on foot, though on a hot day it's quite a hike to see all the monuments. You can hire bicycles from several places, including the bicycle shops near the bus station, **Nathan Cycle Works** (Kovalam Rd; ☾ 8am-6pm) near the post office, or **Shakthi** (137 East Raja St; ☾ 8am-8pm), for around Rs 30 per day. Shakthi also hires mopeds for around Rs 150 a day, as do several other shops and restaurants around town.

AROUND MAMALLAPURAM
About 14km west of Mamallapuram, Tirukkalikundram is a pilgrimage centre with the hilltop **Vedagirishvara Temple** (admission Rs 2; ☾ 8.30am-1pm & 5-7pm) dedicated to Shiva. It's often called the Eagle Temple; according to legend two eagles come here each day at noon from Varanasi, a good 2000km away. They often don't turn up on time.

You climb the 550 smooth steps to the hilltop bare-footed. Once there, the temple contains two beautiful shrines and at intervals there are 360-degree views of the larger Bhaktavatsaleshavra Temple, the temple tanks, rocky hills and rice paddies. It's lovely – if busy – in the late afternoon but the middle of the day, while making for a hot climb, is very peaceful when the temple itself is closed. You can get here by bus or bicycle from Mamallapuram.

VEDANTANGAL BIRD SANCTUARY
Located about 52km from Mamallapuram, this wildlife **sanctuary** (admission Rs 5; ☾ 6am-6pm) is one of the best bird-watching places in South India and is an important breeding ground for waterbirds – cormorants, egrets, herons, ibises, spoonbills, storks, grebes and pelicans – that migrate here from October to March. At the height of the breeding season (December and January) there can be up to

30,000 birds nesting in the mangroves, and the best viewing times are early morning and late afternoon; head for the watchtower and look down on the noisy nests across the water. At other times of the year there are no migrants, but enough resident birds to keep keen birders happy.

Big, basic and comfortable rooms are available at the **Forest Department Resthouse** (d Rs 300), a lovely quiet spot 500m before the sanctuary. You're supposed to book in advance with the **WWO** (Map pp368-9; ☎ 24321471; 4th fl, DMS office, 259 Anna Salai, Teynampet) in Chennai – good luck if you try to do that – but in practice the caretaker will probably find a room for you if one's available. You may or may not be offered food if you arrive unexpectedly; come with snacks just in case, or if you have transport be prepared to drive 10km or so to the nearest evening food stall.

To get there by public transport, first get to Chengalpattu, an hour's bus ride from Mamallapuram (see opposite). From here you can take a bus to Vedantangal via Padalam, where you may have to change buses at the road junction. Most Vedantangal buses go directly to the sanctuary entrance, others to the village bus station, from where the sanctuary is a 1km walk south. Visitors also often make a day trip by AC taxi from Mamallapuram; this should cost around Rs 1000.

KANCHIPURAM
☎ 044 / pop 188,000

Famous throughout India for its silk saris, the temple town of Kanchipuram (Kanchi) is also a treasure-trove of Hindu temples and art from the Pallava, Chola and Pandyan dynasties. Many travellers make a day trip here from Chennai or Mamallapuram, which isn't a bad idea as its attraction for pilgrims and tourists has led to a culture of harassment at some temples and silk shops.

Orientation & Information

The city is on the main Chennai–Bengaluru road, 76km southwest of Chennai.

There's no tourist office, but for information online check out www.hellokanchipuram.com. On Kamaraja St there's a small cluster of cheap internet cafés. None of Kanchipuram's banks will touch travellers cheques, but ATMs

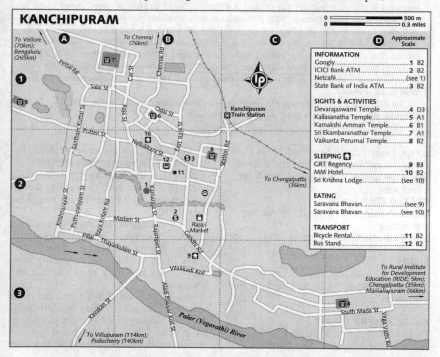

KANCHIPURAM

INFORMATION	
Googly...1 B2	
ICICI Bank ATM...........................2 B2	
Netcafé...................................(see 1)	
State Bank of India ATM.............3 B2	

SIGHTS & ACTIVITIES	
Devarajaswami Temple..................4 D3	
Kailasanatha Temple.....................5 A1	
Kamakshi Amman Temple.............6 B1	
Sri Ekambaranathar Temple..........7 A1	
Vaikunta Perumal Temple.............8 B2	

SLEEPING	
GRT Regency................................9 B3	
MM Hotel....................................10 B2	
Sri Krishna Lodge....................(see 10)	

EATING	
Saravana Bhavan.....................(see 9)	
Saravana Bhavan...................(see 10)	

TRANSPORT	
Bicycle Rental..............................11 B2	
Bus Stand...................................12 B2	

To Vellore (70km); Bengaluru (265km)
To Chennai (76km)
Approximate Scale
0   500 m
0   0.3 miles
Kanchipuram Train Station
To Chengalpattu (36km)
Pettai Rd
Salai St
Car St
Chennai Rd
Raja St
Odai St
East Raja St
Station Rd
Nellukkara St
Santhaik Kuttai St
Putteri St
Krishnavaral St
Putthi palayam St
Raya Kolam Rd
Kamaraji St
Madam St
Rajampet St
Pillai Thayarkulam St
Rajaji Market
Gopuh Rd
Vilakkadi Koil
Kavakan St
Alladi Pillayar Koil St
Palar (Vegavathi) River
To Villupuram (114km); Puducherry (140km)
South Mada St
Vegavathi Rd
To Rural Institute for Development Education (RIDE; 5km); Chengalpattu (35km); Mamallapuram (66km)

TAMIL NADU

TAMIL NADU

CHILD LABOUR & THE SILK INDUSTRY

The sari is synonymous with Indian style, and a brocade bridal sari from Kanchipuram is among the most coveted of garments. The more expensive ones are shot through with gold and silver and can fetch up to Rs 25,000 and weigh around 1.5kg.

About 80% of Kanchipuram's population depend on hand-weaving for a living, and most of the work is done in private homes as part of a larger cooperative. Such a diffuse operation is notoriously difficult to police. Despite national legislation prohibiting child labour, it is estimated that some 4000 school-aged children in Kanchipuram still work full time in the industry, though the situation has improved markedly in the past five years.

Owners of silk looms pay poor families a significant sum of money to buy the children's labour. The opportunity to receive an amount of money that most families could never otherwise dream about is a powerful lure. The payment is in the form of a loan, which families must later repay. When they are unable to pay, silk loom owners offer further loans at high interest rates, thereby perpetuating the cycle of indebtedness and culture of child labour, which is a foundation of this lucrative industry.

One organisation which is challenging the system is the **Rural Institute for Development Education** (RIDE; ☎ 27268393; www.rideindia.org; 46 Periyar Nagar, Little Kanchipuram 631503), a secular NGO. This impressive agency operates in more than 200 villages in the Kanchipuram district by taking children away from the looms (and from other work such as stone masonry) and placing them into one of 11 special RIDE transition schools for six to 12 months, before facilitating their entry into the government education system.

There are many ways that travellers can assist the institute in its work. Volunteers are welcomed in training teachers, counselling, and helping staff write proposals for funding and project development. Qualified teachers can also, with advance notice, assist with teaching in the schools. Volunteers should be prepared to commit for at least one week, preferably longer, and are accommodated in the organisation's guesthouse. A volunteer fee of US$100 per week covers costs.

If you're just passing through, RIDE offers a 24-hour programme that includes accommodation, and visits to some or all of: a local village to see the silk-weaving industry at work and meet its participants; a RIDE school; and silk-weaving factories and silk stores which support child-free labour. The cost is Rs 1300 per person; there are abridged half-day programmes for Rs 850. If you're in town to buy silk, think about contacting RIDE, which can put you in direct touch with a weaver; your transaction is then only between you and them, with no commissions or fees paid to salespeople.

The RIDE office is near Pachapayya James College, about 5km east of Kanchipuram. It's a Rs 50 rickshaw ride, and there are good signs on the roadside.

accept foreign cards. Some hotels (and silk shops) accept foreign cash and credit cards.

Googly (144 Kamaraja St; per hr Rs 25; ☉ 9am-9pm) Internet access.

ICICI Bank ATM (Gandhi Rd)

Netcafé (148 Kamaraja St; per hr Rs 25; ☉ 9am-9pm) Internet access.

State Bank of India ATM (Hospital Rd)

Sights
All the temples are open from 6am to 12.30pm and 4pm to 8.30pm. Most have free admission.

KAILASANATHA TEMPLE
Dedicated to Shiva, Kailasanatha Temple is the oldest temple in Kanchipuram and

for many it is also the most beautiful. Reflecting the freshness of early Dravidian architecture, it was built by the Pallava king Rayasimha in the late 7th century, though its front was added later by his son, King Varman III.

The remaining fragments of 8th-century murals are a visible reminder of how magnificent the original temple must have looked. There are 58 small shrines honouring Shiva and Parvati and their sons, Ganesh and Murugan.

Non-Hindus are allowed into the inner sanctum here, where there is a prismatic lingam – the largest in town and third-largest in Asia. The guide and priest here are generous with information and, set in a quiet residential area, this is the most pleasant temple to visit.

SRI EKAMBARANATHAR TEMPLE
This temple is dedicated to Shiva and is one of the largest in Kanchipuram, covering 12 hectares. Its 59m-high *gopuram* and massive outer stone wall were constructed in 1509 by Krishnadevaraya of the Vijayanagar empire, though construction was originally started by the Pallavas, with later Chola extensions. The temple's name is said to derive from Eka Amra Nathar – Lord of the Mango Tree – and there is an old mango tree, with four branches representing the four Vedas (sacred Hindu texts). Non-Hindus cannot enter the sanctum. If you wish to support the temple, get an official receipt for your donation.

KAMAKSHI AMMAN TEMPLE
This imposing temple is dedicated to the goddess Parvati in her guise as Kamakshi, who accedes to all requests. To the right of the temple's entrance is the marriage hall, which has wonderful ornate pillars, and directly ahead is the main shrine topped with gold; again, non-Hindus cannot enter the sanctum. Each February/March carriages housing statues of deities are hauled through the streets in a colourful procession. The goddess' birthday is in October/November.

DEVARAJASWAMI TEMPLE
Dedicated to Vishnu, this enormous **monument** (admission Rs 2, camera/video Rs 5/100) was built by the Vijayanagars and is among the most impressive of Kanchipuram's temples. It has a beautifully sculptured '1000-pillared' hall (only 96 of the original 1000 remain) as well as a marriage hall commemorating the wedding of Vishnu and Lakshmi. One of the temple's most notable features is a huge chain carved from a single piece of stone which can be seen at each corner of the *mandapa*. The annual temple festival is in May.

Every 40 years the waters of the temple tank are drained, revealing a huge statue of Vishnu. You may like to hang around for the next viewing – in 2019.

VAIKUNTA PERUMAL TEMPLE
Dedicated to Vishnu, this temple was built shortly after the Kailasanatha Temple. The cloisters inside the outer wall consist of lion pillars and are representative of the first phase in the architectural evolution of the grand 1000-pillared halls. The main shrine, on three levels, contains images of Vishnu in standing, sitting and reclining positions.

Sleeping & Eating
Don't get too excited about the accommodation options in Kanchi. The cheap pilgrims' lodges are pretty dire, so unless you are on a tight budget, head for one of the better-value midrange places. Most hotels and lodges are clustered together in the noisy town centre, within a few minutes' walk from the bus station.

Sri Krishna Lodge (☎ 27222831; 60 Nellukkara St; s/d Rs 160/230) One of the few OK cheapies, the cheerful staff makes up for the drab and tatty interior.

MM Hotel (☎ 27227250; www.mmhotels.com; 65 Nellukkara St; d without/with AC Rs 400/700; ✖) A good-value, busy and clean hotel, frequented by Indian businesspeople. Saravana Bhavan veg restaurant is next door, with a welcome AC dining room.

GRT Regency (☎ 27225250; adminkanchi@grtregency.com; 487 Gandhi Rd; s/d Rs 975/1250; ✖) While it's not the best setting on the noisy main road, the rooms here are the probably the cleanest and most comfortable you'll find in Kanchi. Another Saravana Bhavan restaurant is next door at Hotel Jaybala International.

Getting There & Away
The busy bus stand is in the centre of town. See the table, below, for bus services.

Regular suburban trains leave from Beach, Fort or Egmore stations in Chennai direct to Kanchipuram (Rs 18, two hours).

BUSES FROM KANCHIPURAM

Destination	Fare (Rs)	Duration (hr)	Frequency
Bengaluru	100	6	2 daily
Chennai	22.50	2	every 10min
Mamallapuram	20	2	9 daily
Puducherry	30	3	12 daily
Tiruvannamalai	32	3	22 daily
Trichy	90	7	5 daily
Vellore	20	1½	every 15min

Getting Around

Bicycles can be hired (per hour/day Rs 3/40) from stalls around the bus station. An autorickshaw for a half-day tour of the five main temples (around Rs 200) will inevitably involve a stop at a silk shop.

VELLORE

☎ **0416 / pop 388,211**

Vellore, 145km west of Chennai, is a dusty bazaar town whose well-preserved Vijayanagar Fort and temple are the main features on the tourist trail. The city is also famed for its Christian Medical College (CMC) Hospital – a leader in research and health care, recognised as one of the finest hospitals in India. The hospital attracts international medical students as well as patients from all over India, giving this small town a cosmopolitan feel.

Information

There are several internet cafés along Ida Scudder Rd in front of the hospital and Surfzone is next to the State Bank of India.

State Bank of India (102 Ida Scudder Rd) Money can be exchanged here and there's an ATM.

Tourist office (🕒 10am-5.45pm Mon-Fri) Inside the fort complex, to the right of the main gate.

Sights

The solid walls and dry moat of the splendid **Vellore Fort** dominate the west side of town. It was built in the 16th century and passed briefly into the hands of the Marathas in

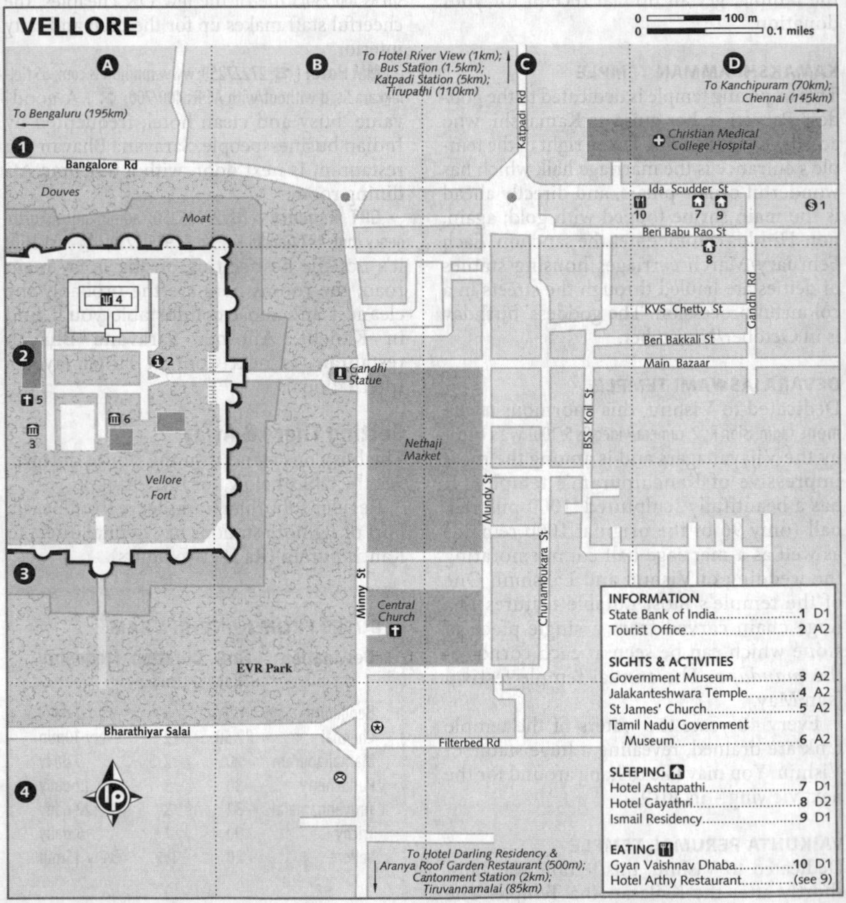
VELLORE
0 100 m
0 0.1 miles
A
B
C
D
To Hotel River View (1km); Bus Station (1.5km); Katpadi Station (5km); Tirupathi (110km)
To Kanchipuram (70km); Chennai (145km)
To Bengaluru (195km)
1
2
3
4
Christian Medical College Hospital
Bangalore Rd
Katpadi Rd
Douves
Moat
Ida Scudder St
Beri Babu Rao St
KVS Chetty St
Beri Bakkali St
Main Bazaar
Gandhi Rd
Gandhi Statue
Nethaji Market
BSS Koil St
Mundy St
Chunambukara St
Minny St
Vellore Fort
Central Church
EVR Park
Bharathiyar Salai
Filterbed Rd
To Hotel Darling Residency & Aranya Roof Garden Restaurant (500m); Cantonment Station (2km); Tiruvannamalai (85km)
INFORMATION
State Bank of India 1 D1
Tourist Office 2 A2
SIGHTS & ACTIVITIES
Government Museum 3 A2
Jalakanteshwara Temple 4 A2
St James' Church 5 A2
Tamil Nadu Government Museum 6 A2
SLEEPING
Hotel Ashtapathi 7 D1
Hotel Gayathri 8 D2
Ismail Residency 9 D1
EATING
Gyan Vaishnav Dhaba 10 D1
Hotel Arthy Restaurant .... (see 9)

1676 and the Mughals in 1708. The British occupied the fort in 1760 following the fall of Srirangapatnam and the death of Tipu Sultan. These days it houses various government offices, parade grounds, a university, a church and an ancient mosque, and a police recruiting school.

At the west side of the fort complex, the small **national government museum** (admission free; ☼ 9am-5pm, closed Fri) contains sculptures dating back to Pallava and Chola times. Next door, pretty **St James' Church** (1846) is only open for Sunday services.

On the east side, the **Tamil Nadu government museum** (Indian/foreigner Rs 5/100; ☼ 9am-5pm, closed Fri) displays hero stones in the forecourt, dating from the 8th century and depicting the stories of war heroes in battle. The dusty exhibits inside have seen much better days, but the small collection of tribal clothes and artefacts is interesting.

Near the fort entrance, the **Jalakanteshwara Temple** (☼ 6am-1pm & 3-8pm), a gem of late Vijayanagar architecture, was built about 1566; check out the small detailed sculptures on the walls of the marriage hall. During the invasions by the Adil Shahis of Bijapur, the Marathas and the Carnatic nawabs (Muslim ruling princes), the temple was occupied by a garrison and temple rituals ceased. Now it's once again a place of worship.

Sleeping & Eating

Vellore's cheapest hotels are concentrated along the roads south of and parallel to the hospital, mostly catering to people in town for treatment; there are many to choose from on Beri Babu Rao St. Decent midrange hotels are scattered further afield.

Hotel Gayathri (☎ 2227714; 22 Beri Babu Rao St; s/d Rs 140/170) This dingy place has impersonal service and squat toilets, but at least the shared balconies let in some light.

Hotel Ashtapathi (☎ 2224602; Ida Scudder St; r without/with AC Rs 325/525; ✱) It's small, clean and good value here, but ask for a room off the noisy roadside. There's a decent veg restaurant attached.

Ismail Residency (☎ 2223216; Ida Scudder St; r Rs 400; ✱) A five-room lodge with tatty but spotless rooms, this is next door to the clean Hotel Arthy restaurant.

Hotel River View (☎ 2225251; New Katpadi Rd; d without/with AC Rs 470/700; ✱) North of the town centre and close to the bus station, this hotel

BUSES FROM VELLORE			
Destination	Fare (Rs)	Duration (hr)	Frequency
Chennai	46-60	3	every 10min
Bengaluru	74/85	5	every 30min
Kanchipuram	20	2	every 15min
Tirupathi	40	2½	every 30min
Tiruvannamalai	24	2	every 5min
Trichy (direct)	99	7	4 daily

benefits from a relatively quiet location and pleasant gardens, but the 'river view' is hardly that. Rooms are spacious, the Shikar garden restaurant serves a barbecue every evening and there's a bar.

Darling Residency (☎ 2213001; 11/8 Officers Line; s/d Rs 750/850; ✱) Recognised as the best hotel in town, the rooms here are clean and comfortable, and there's even a small fitness room with exercise bike. The rooftop Aranya Roof Garden Restaurant (open lunch and dinner) is cool and breezy, serving salads (Rs 25), a variety of pasta, *tandoor* oven and Chinese food for around Rs 60, and good ice cream. It's recommended by visiting medicos and locals alike.

Cheap veg restaurants line Ida Scudder St, or try **Gyan Vaishnav Dhaba** (thalis Rs 25) for good Punjabi food.

Getting There & Away

BUS

The bus stand is about 500m from the Hotel River View, 1.5km to the north of town. For services, see above.

TRAIN

Vellore's main train station is 5km north at Katpadi. Bus 192 (Rs 2) shuttles between the station and town. There are at least six daily express trains to/from Chennai Central (2nd class/sleeper Rs 42/67), which continue to Bengaluru (Rs 65/104).

TIRUVANNAMALAI

☎ 04175 / pop 130,301

The small, unassuming town of Tiruvannamalai, 85km south of Vellore, is something of a hidden gem in a region overwhelmed by significant temples. Flanked by Mt Arunachala, this is an important Shaivite town where Shiva is revered as Arunachaleswar, an aspect of fire. At each full moon the hill swells with thousands of pilgrims who circumnavigate the base of the mountain, but at any time you'll see gatherings of Shaivite priests, sadhus (spiritual men) and devotees gathered around the temple. Tiruvannamalai is also home to the Sri Ramanasramam Ashram.

The main post office is just off the road to Gingee; there are several internet cafés in town and opposite the ashram. Although the State Bank of India won't change travellers cheques, its ATM accepts international cards.

Sights & Activities

ARUNACHALESWAR TEMPLE

Covering some 10 hectares, this vast **temple** (☉ 6am-1pm & 5.30-10pm) is one of the largest, and most captivating, in India. Although it dates from the 11th century, much of the structure is actually from the 17th to 19th centuries. It has four large unpainted *gopurams,* one at each cardinal point, with the eastern one rising to 66m with 13 storeys.

The main (eastern) entrance to the temple is reached by a covered walkway lined with trinket sellers, merchants, half-naked sadhus and orange-clad priests – the atmosphere here in the evenings is noisy and electric. You may be approached to donate rice cakes for the poor that, at Rs 50 for 10, you can then hand to recipients; this may be preferable to handing a few rupees to a beggar. Once inside the temple, there's a 1000-pillared *mandapa* on the right and the large tank on the left, then another gateway leads through a central courtyard containing the main shrine, a Shiva lingam where *puja* is performed daily at 8am, 10am, 6pm, 8pm and 9.30pm. You're likely to wander here comfortably without attracting too much attention.

MT ARUNACHALA

This 800m-high boulder-strewn hill, known locally as Girivalam, looms over the town. On full-moon and festival days thousands of pilgrims circumnavigate the 14km base of the mountain. If you're not quite that devoted, an autorickshaw will take you around – stopping at small temples and shrines along the way – for around Rs 120. An alternative is to pick up a circle map from the ashram office, hire a bicycle (per hour Rs 3) from the road near the entrance, and bike your way around.

For a superb view of the Arunachaleswar Temple, climb part or all the way up the hill (about four hours return). There's a signed path that leads up through village homes near the northwest corner of the temple, passing two caves, **Virupaksha** and **Skandasramam**. Sri Ramana Maharshi lived and meditated in these caves for more than 20 years from 1899 to 1922, after which he and his growing band of spiritual followers established the ashram.

SRI RAMANA ASHRAM

This tranquil **ashram** (☎ 237292; www.ramana-maharshi.org; ☉ office 8am-11am & 2-5pm), 2km southwest of Tiruvannamalai, draws devotees of Sri Ramana Maharshi, a guru who died in 1950 after nearly 50 years in contemplation. It's a very relaxed place, set in green surrounds, where visitors are able to meditate or take part in *puja* at the shrine where the guru achieved *samadhi* (ecstatic state involving conscious exit from the body) and to use the bookshop. Day visits are permitted but *devotees only* may stay at the ashram by applying in writing, preferably at least three months in advance.

THE LINGAM OF FIRE

Legend has it that Shiva appeared as a column of fire on Mt Arunachala in Tiruvannamalai, creating the original symbol of the lingam. Each November/December full moon, the **Karthikai Deepam Festival**, one of India's oldest festivals, celebrates this legend throughout India but the festival is particularly significant at Tiruvannamalai. Here, a huge fire, lit from a 30m wick immersed in 2000L of ghee, blazes from the top of Mt Arunachala for days. In homes, lamps honour Shiva and his fiery lingam. The fire symbolises Shiva's light, which eradicates darkness and evil.

At festival time up to half a million people come to Tiruvannamalai. In honour of Shiva, they scale the mountain or circumnavigate its base (14km). On the upward path, steps quickly give way to jagged and unstable rocks. There's no shade and the sun is relentless. And the journey must be undertaken in bare feet – a mark of respect to the deity. None of this deters the thousands of pilgrims who quietly and joyfully make their way to the top and the abode of their deity.

Sleeping & Eating

There are budget lodges in the busy area around the temple and in the calmer surrounds near the ashram. During festival time (November/December) prices can rise by a staggering 1000%.

Arunachala Ramana Home (☎ 236120; s/d Rs 150/200) Recommended as basic, clean and friendly. It's close to the fabulous Manna Café which will answer any need you may have for non-Indian food, including salads (Rs 25), juices, pastas and cakes. Plenty of chai (tea) stalls and veg cafés are nearby.

Hotel Ganesh (☎ 2226701; 111A Big St; d without/with AC Rs 245/645; ❄) On the busy bazaar road running along the north side of the temple, Ganesh is a little haven of peace and excellent value. Some of the rooms are a bit poky, but they're clean enough and the hotel's inner courtyard balcony is a pleasant place to sit. There's a decent veg restaurant downstairs.

Hotel Arunai Anantha (☎ 237275; hotelarunai anantha@yahoo.co.in; s/d Rs 1100/1250; ❄ ⚕) The big draws at this hotel, about 1km beyond the ashram, are the landscaped gardens and swimming pool. For deluxe rooms add Rs 300; they're worth it for the extra size and comfort.

Getting There & Away

There are buses every half-hour to Chennai (Rs 62, 3½ hours) and Vellore (Rs 23, two hours). There are at least three daily buses to Puducherry (Rs 31, three hours). A taxi to Puducherry (via Gingee) costs around Rs 800.

Only local passenger trains currently use Tiruvannamalai train station – two trains a day pass through between Vellore and Villupuram (where you can change for Puducherry).

GINGEE (SENJI)

☎ 04145

The twin ruined forts of **Rajagiri & Krishnagiri** (King & Queen Fort; Indian/foreigner Rs 5/100; ⏰ 9am-5pm) crown the hilltops as you pass through rural countryside near Gingee (*shin*-gee), 37km east of Tiruvannamalai. Constructed mainly in the 16th century by the Vijayanagars (though some structures date from the 13th century), the fort has been occupied by various armies, including the forces of Adil Shah from Bijapur and the Marathas, who assumed control from 1677. In 1698 the Mughals took over. Then came the French, who remained until the British defeated them at Puducherry.

Nowadays the forts are delightfully free of human activity – except for the odd picnicker or herd of goats you may find you've got the place to yourself. A walk around will take half a day, especially if you cross the road and make the steep ascent to the top of Krishnagiri. Buildings within the main fort (on the south side of the road) include a granary, a Shiva temple, a mosque and – most prominent – the restored audience hall.

It's easy to day trip to Gingee from Puducherry (67km) or Tiruvannamalai (37km). Buses leave every 30 minutes from Tiruvannamalai (Rs 11.50, one hour). Ask to be let off at 'the fort', 2km before Gingee town. An autorickshaw from Gingee to the fort costs about Rs 25 one way.

PUDUCHERRY (PONDICHERRY)

☎ 0413 / pop 220,749

With its seafront promenade, wide boulevards, enduring pockets of French culture and architecture, and a popular ashram, charming Puducherry – whose name officially changed from Pondicherry in October 2006 – is unlike anywhere else in South India. That's hardly surprising – the former French colony was settled in the early 18th century as a colonial enclave and it retains a mildly Gallic air superimposed on a typical Indian background.

The French relinquished their control of the Union Territory of 'Pondy' (as the city is still universally known) some 50 years ago, but reminders of the colonial days remain; the *tricoleur* flutters over the grand French consulate, there's a *hôtel de ville* (town hall), and local police wear red *kepis* (caps) and belts. Don't expect a subcontinental Paris though – this is still India, with all the autorickshaws, choked streets, bazaars and Hindu temples of any city.

A big draw in Puducherry is its alluring restaurants – many serving an approximation of French cuisine – and some superb hotels that make use of the town's French architectural heritage. Without the crippling taxes of Tamil Nadu, beer is relatively cheap and accommodation good value.

Many travellers come here to study yoga or meditation at the Sri Aurobindo Ashram, so there's always a large contingent of foreigners in Puducherry. In any case, this easy-going coastal city is firmly on the travellers' itinerary and you may find yourself staying here longer than you had intended.

TAMIL NADU

TAMIL NADU

Orientation

Puducherry is split from north to south by a partially covered canal. The more 'French' part of town is on the east side (towards the sea) and the more typically Indian part to the west. With its grid design, navigating the town is easy, but there are still some eccentricities with street names. Many have one name at one end and another at the other, while others use the French 'rue' instead of 'street'. See the boxed text, opposite, for more information.

Information

Puducherry keeps European hours and takes a long lunch break; expect most businesses to be closed from about 1pm to 3.30pm.

INFORMATION		
Alliance Française	**1**	C5
Canara Bank	**2**	C3
Coffee.Com	**3**	B4
Fabindia	(see 50)	
Focus Books	**4**	C3
French Bookshop	**5**	C5
French Consulate	**6**	D2
ICICI Bank	**7**	C2
ICICI Bank	**8**	C1
LKP Forex	(see 48)	
Main Post Office	**9**	C3
Maison Colombani	**10**	D5
New Medical Centre	**11**	B4
Puducherry Tourist Office	**12**	D4
Sify i-way	**13**	C4
Sify i-way	**14**	C2
Sify i-way	(see 37)	
UTI Bank ATM	**15**	B1

SIGHTS & ACTIVITIES		
Church of Our Lady of the Immaculate		
Conception	**16**	C3
Gandhi Statue	**17**	D3
Hôtel de Ville (Town Hall)	**18**	D4
Jayalakshmi Fine Arts Academy	**19**	C3
Notre Dame de Agnes	**20**	D4

Prana Ayurvedic Massage	(see 45)	
Puducherry Museum	**21**	D3
Sacred Heart Church	**22**	B5
Sri Aurobindo Ashram	**23**	D2
Sri Aurobindo Information Centre	**24**	C3
Sri Manakula Vinayagar Temple	**25**	C2

SLEEPING 🏠		
Ajantha Beach Guest House	**26**	D5
Ajantha Sea View	(see 26)	
Dumas Guest House	**27**	D5
Ganga Guest House	**28**	A4
Hotel de Pondicherry	**29**	D5
Hotel Surguru	**30**	B1
International Guest House	**31**	C3
Park Guest House	**32**	D5
Patricia Coloniale Heritage Guest		
House	**33**	C5
Surya Swastika Guest House	**34**	C2
Villa Helena	**35**	C4

EATING 🍴		
Au Feu de Bois	**36**	C4
Coffee.Com	(see 3)	
Grinde Sridharan General Merchants	**37**	D5
Hot Breads	(see 46)	
Hotel Aristo	**38**	B2

kasha ki aasha	**39**	C4
La Coromandale	**40**	D4
La Terrasse	**41**	C5
Market	**42**	B2
Nilgiri Supermarket	**43**	C3
Rendezvous	**44**	C4
Satsanga	**45**	C5
Your Daily Bread	**46**	C3

DRINKING 🍷 🍸		
Seagulls Restaurant	**47**	D5
Space Coffee & Arts	**48**	C4

SHOPPING 🛍		
Auroboutique	(see 23)	
Casablanca	**49**	C2
Fabindia	**50**	C5
Kalki	**51**	C2
kasha ki aasha	(see 39)	
La Boutique d'Auroville	**52**	C2
Sri Aurobindo Handmade Paper		
Factory	**53**	C1

TRANSPORT		
Bicycle Hire	**54**	C5
SDP Bike Hire	**55**	C2
Vijay Arya Moped Rental	**56**	C2

TAMIL NADU

BOOKSHOPS

Fabindia (☎ 2226010; 59 Suffren St; ⏰ 9.30am-7.30pm) Opposite the Alliance Française and above the craft shop is a good choice of English-language titles.

Focus Books (☎ 2345513; 204 Mission St; ⏰ 9.30am-1.30pm & 3.30-9pm Mon-Sat) Excellent selection of books, especially contemporary Indian writing, and postcards.

French Bookshop (☎ 2338062; Suffren St; ⏰ 9am-12.30pm & 3.30-7.30pm) This small shop next to the Alliance Française carries many French titles.

CULTURAL CENTRES

Alliance Française (☎ 2338146; afpondy@satyam.net
.in; 58 Suffren St; ⏰ 9am-noon & 3-6pm Mon-Sat) The French cultural centre has a library, computer centre, art gallery, and conducts French-language classes. Films are shown on Sunday at 6pm. The monthly newsletter, *Le Petit Journal*, details forthcoming events. Maison Colombani, its associated exhibition and performance space, is on Dumas St.

INTERNET ACCESS

Coffee.Com (236 Mission St; per hr Rs 20; ⏰ 10am-1am) Hip café with high-speed connections and great coffee.

RENAMED STREETS	
Street name	**Alternative name**
Mission St	Cathedral St
Ambour Salai	HM Kasim St
AH Madam St	Kosakadai St
Beach Rd	Goubert Ave
Lal Bahabhur St	Bussy St
Gingee Salai	NC Bose St

Sify i-way Lal Bahabhur St (per hr Rs 20; ⏰ 8am-midnight); Nehru St (per hr Rs 25; ⏰ 24hr); St Louis St (per hr Rs 25; ⏰ 7.30am-11pm) Part of the i-way chain, these have fast connections and cheap internet phone calls.

MEDICAL SERVICES

New Medical Centre (☎ 343434; 470 Mahatma Gandhi (MG) Rd; ⏰ 24hr)

MONEY

Canara Bank (Gingy St; ⏰ 10am-2pm & 2.30-3.30pm Mon-Fri, 10am-12.30pm Sat) Changes cash and travellers cheques, plus an ATM.

ICICI Bank ATM (Mission St & AH Madam St)

LKP Forex (☎ 2224008; 2A Labourdonnais St; ⏰ 9.30am-7.30pm Mon-Fri, 9.30am-6.30pm Sat) Good place to change a wide range of currencies and travellers cheques, plus money transfers.

UTI Bank ATM (Anna Salai)

POST

Main post office (Rangapillai St; ⏰ 9am-7pm Mon-Sat, 10am-5pm Sun) Post restante is available 10am to 5pm Monday to Saturday.

TOURIST INFORMATION

Puducherry tourist office (☎ 2339497; 40 Goubert Ave; ⏰ 9am-5pm) Enthusiastic staff and a decent free map.

Sights & Activities
FRENCH QUARTER

The best way to view the slightly tattered heritage buildings and broad streets of the French Quarter (bounded roughly by NSC Bose St, SV Patel Rd and Goubert Ave) is to take

Puducherry's **heritage walk**. Start at the north end of Goubert Ave, the seafront promenade, and wander south, past the **French consulate** and the **Gandhi Statue**. Turn right at the **town hall** on Rue Mahe Labourdonnais, past the shady **Bharathi Park**. From there it's a matter of pottering south through **Dumas**, **Romain Rolland** and **Suffren Sts**. Focus Books (p397) sells heritage walking trail brochures (Rs 9).

SRI AUROBINDO ASHRAM

Founded in 1926 by Sri Aurobindo and a Frenchwoman known as 'the Mother', this **ashram** (cnr rue de la Marine & Manakula Vinayagar Koil St) propounds spiritual tenets that represent a synthesis of yoga and modern science. After Aurobindo's death spiritual authority passed to the Mother, who died in 1973 aged 97. These days, the ashram underwrites many cultural, educational and social welfare activities in Puducherry.

A constant flow of visitors files through the **main ashram building** (8am-noon & 2-6pm Mon-Sat), which has the flower-festooned samadhi (tomb venerated as a shrine) of Aurobindo and the Mother in the central courtyard, where devotees gather and meditate. Opposite the main building, in the educational centre, you can sometimes catch a film, play or lecture, and there are occasional evening music performances in the library. For other information, call at the **ashram information centre** (☎ 2233604; bureaucentral@sriaurobindoashram.org; cnr Rangapillai & Ambour Salai; 6am-8pm).

PUDUCHERRY MUSEUM

This **museum** (St Louis St; adult/child Rs 2/1; 9.40am-1pm & 2-5.20pm Tue-Sun), housed in an interesting old colonial building, features a well-presented collection, including sculptures from the Pallava and Chola dynasties, fine bronzes, coins and an archaeological display of artefacts from the days of Roman trade with India. There's a striking collection of French colonial paraphernalia which includes a 19th-century *pousse pousse* (like a rickshaw, except pushed along), a horse-drawn carriage, colonial furniture, an antique grandfather clock and a bed slept in by the peripatetic Dupleix, the colony's most famous governor.

CHURCHES & TEMPLES

Puducherry has several churches built by French missionaries which contribute greatly to the city's Mediterranean flair. The **Church of Our Lady of the Immaculate Conception** (Mission St) was completed in 1791. Its medieval architecture is in the style of many of the Jesuit constructions of that time. The **Sacred Heart Church** (Subbayah Salai) is an impressive sight with its Gothic architecture, stained glass and striking brown and white colours. The mellow pink-and-cream **Notre Dame de Anges** (Dumas St), built in 1858, looks sublime in the late afternoon light. The smooth limestone interior was made using eggshells in the plaster.

Although Puducherry is not often associated with temples, the Hindu faith is celebrated here with as much vigour as anywhere – there are said to be more than 150 temples in the Puducherry area and you'll often stumble across the entrance to an almost-hidden temple while wandering the central streets, particularly west of the canal. One of the most vibrant in the city is **Sri Manakula Vinayagar Temple** (Manakula Vinayagar Koil St; 5.45am-12.30pm & 4-9.30pm), dedicated to Ganesh. Renovations have furnished its sanctum with Rajasthan marble and its *vimana* (a tower over the sanctum) with a gold roof. It's tucked away down a backstreet just south of the Sri Aurobindo Ashram, and also contains more than 40 skilfully painted friezes.

BOTANICAL GARDENS

Established by the French in 1826, the **botanical gardens** (admission free; 10am-5pm) form a green oasis on the southwest side of the city.

BEACHES

The long stretch of city 'beach' is virtually devoid of sand, but the promenade is a fun place to walk at dawn and dusk when it seems that all of Puducherry takes its daily constitutional exercise. There are a few decent beaches to the north and south of town; Quiet, Reppo and Serenity Beaches are all north of the centre within 8km of Puducherry. Chunnambar, 8km south, has Paradise Beach, some resort accommodation, water sports and backwater boat cruises. The tourist office (p397) has details.

Courses
ARTS

Jayalakshmi Fine Arts Academy (☎ 2342036; goodsin@vsnl.net.in; 221 Mission St; 9.30am-1.30pm & 3.30-8.30pm Mon-Sat, 7am-12.30pm Sun) is an established place with classes in *bharatanatyam* (dance), singing, *veena* (stringed instrument), tabla (drums) and a range of other musical instruments. Private tuition fees start at Rs 200 per hour for a minimum of five hours, and there's a one-off registration fee (Rs 350).

YOGA & AYURVEDA

Puducherry's International Yoga Festival is held annually in early January.

International Centre for Yoga Education & Research (ICYER; ☎ 2241561; www.icyer.com; 16A Mettu St, Chinnamudaliarchavady, Kottukuppam) Also known as the Ananda Ashram, established by Swami Gitananda, this renowned centre conducts annual six-month yoga teacher-training courses and 10-day summer courses. Its city office is Yoganjali Natyalayam (25 2nd Cross Iyyana Nagar), near the bus stand.

Prana Ayurvedic Massage (☎ 2331214; 101 Canteen St) Ayurvedic massage (Rs 400 an hour), steam bath (Rs 150) and yoga classes (Rs 150 an hour). Inquire at Satsanga restaurant (p400).

Sri Aurobindo Ashram (☎ 23396483; bureaucentra l@sriaurobindoashram.org; Rangapillai St) Study and/or practise yoga (see also opposite).

Tours

The Puducherry tourist office runs half-day sightseeing tours (Rs 90, 2pm to 6pm) that take you to the water sports complex at Chunnambar, Hanuman Temple, Auroville and Sri Aurobindo Ashram. Full-day tours (Rs 110, 9.30am to 6pm) cover the same area plus the botanical gardens, paper factory, Sacred Heart Church and a couple of Hindu temples; both tours need a minimum of six people to operate.

Sleeping

Puducherry has some of South India's best accommodation in the midrange and top-end bracket – charming old colonial houses and gorgeously decorated guesthouses. At the budget end there's ashram accommodation and basic Indian lodges. The most pleasant part of town is east of the canal, but accommodation is scattered far and wide.

BUDGET

If you've come to Puducherry to sample ashram life, the best budget places are the guesthouses run by Sri Aurobindo Ashram. They're well maintained, well located and you'll be around like-minded souls. However, the accommodation is set up for ashram devotees, and rules include a 10.30pm curfew, and smoking and alcohol ban. For informa-

tion and reservations, contact the **information centre** (☎ 2233604; bureaucentral@sriaurobindoashram .org; cnr Rangapillai & Ambour Salai Sts; ⏰ 6am-8pm).

Surya Swastika Guest House (☎ 2343092; 11 Iswaran Koil St; d without/with bathroom Rs 100/150) You get just what you pay for in this small old-style guesthouse, with its simple rooms.

International Guest House (☎ 2336699; Gingy St; old wing from Rs 100, new from Rs 450; ❄) The most central of the ashram guesthouses, this large, ordered place fronts the canal in the city centre.

Park Guest House (☎ 233644; Goubert Ave; d without/ with AC Rs 400/600; ❄) This is the most sought-after ashram address in town thanks to its wonderful seafront position. All front rooms point to the sea and have their own porch or balcony, and there's a large lawn area for morning yoga or meditation.

MIDRANGE & TOP END

Ganga Guest House (☎ 2222675; 479 Bharathi St; r Rs 500-600) A fabulous colonnaded old house, decked out in deep reds and yellows and awash in Bollywood posters, offers rooms here. Those on the rooftop get a breeze, and some have balconies.

Villa Pondicherry (☎ 2356253; www.pondy.org; 23 Dr Ambedkar Salai; d with shared/private bathroom from Rs 550/650; ❄) This ageing but charming colonial family residence is about 1km south of the train station next to St Francis Xavier Church. The five rooms and central lounge certainly have character and fun décor, but some may find it a little too homely. It's not well signposted – look for the red door and small brass plaque under the veranda.

Dumas Guest House (☎ 2225726; 31 Dumas St; s/d Rs 600/750; ❄) A tall, thin rabbit warren of nooks and crannies, this tidy six-room guesthouse opened in 2006 in a good location.

Ajantha Beach Guest House (☎ 2338898; 1 rue Bazar St Laurent; d with sea view Rs 600-1200; ❄) The location is the main selling point for this place – right on the beachfront promenade. The four sea-view rooms are plain but comfortable and have balconies; the others are drab and windowless.

Hotel Surguru (☎ 2339022; www.hotelsurguru .com; 104 SV Patel Salai; s/d Rs 730/890; ❄) If you're content in a comfortable but characterless business-type hotel, Surguru is the best value in Puducherry. It's large and modern, with bright, spacious rooms and satellite TV. There's a good veg restaurant and credit cards are accepted.

Hotel de Pondichery (☎ 2227409; 38 Dumas St; r from Rs 1350-2450; ⊠) Yet another heritage home, this recently renovated place has 10 lovely colonial-style rooms and outdoor sitting terraces. It's more old-world than luxurious but rooms are private and quiet, set back from the courtyard restaurant.

Villa Helena (☎ 2226789; villahelena@satyam.net.in; 22 Lal Bahabhur St; r Rs 1500-2500; ⊠) This is a superb colonial home with a touch of class at reasonable prices. The five rooms are immaculate and individually designed and the spacious courtyard is elegant and tranquil. If it's full, ask about the owner's other properties.

Ajantha Sea View (☎ 2349032; www.ajanthaseaview hotel.com; 50 Goubert Ave; r from Rs 1750; ⊠) With full beachfront balconies, these rooms have the best view in town. Go for the corner deluxe rooms, full of light with windows on two sides.

Patricia Coloniale Heritage Guest House (☎ 2224 720; colonialeheritage@rediffmail.com; 54 Romain Roland St; r incl breakfast Rs 1800-3000; ⊠) For an intimate, peaceful stay, Patricia's is hard to beat. The delightful colonial home is run by a friendly family and the six rooms all have exotic but original character with stained-glass window panes, traditional Indian furniture and a lovely central garden where breakfast is served in a sunken courtyard. If it's full, ask the owners about their other properties.

Eating

If you've been on the road in Tamil Nadu for a while you'll find Puducherry's restaurant scene a revelation. There are several French-Indian places, some good open-air restaurants, beer is relatively cheap and you can sample both Indian and imported wines. At the other end of the scale, you can eat cheaply at the ashram. Places listed are open for breakfast, lunch and dinner unless otherwise specified.

La Coromandale (30 Goubert Ave; mains Rs 30) As the saying goes, the simple things in life are often the best. Tasty South Indian thalis, rice, noodles, cold drinks and a relaxed atmosphere for meeting and chatting are the attractions of this open-fronted restaurant, situated on the promenade and popular with locals.

Coffee.Com (☎ 2339079; 236 Mission St; ⊙ 10am-1am) This internet café and meeting spot serves up great baguettes (Rs 50 to 70), pasta dishes (Rs 130 to 180), good coffee, pastries and milkshakes.

kasha ki aasha (☎ 2222963; www.kasha-ki-aasha .com; 23 rue Surcouf; ⊙ 8am-7pm, closed Sun) You'll get a great pancake breakfast, good lunches (try the European-style thali) and delicious cakes served on the pretty rooftop of this colonial house-cum-craftshop-cum-café. Loll on comfy chairs under the fans, read magazines, drink organic tea and coffee and chat with the all-women staff.

Hotel Aristo (Nehru St; mains around Rs 80-150; ⊙ lunch & dinner Sat-Thu) The rooftop restaurant at Aristo continues to be a great choice and is usually crowded in the evenings. Dishes include walnut chicken with brown rice (delicious but generally made with cashews!) and grilled prawns. A small Kingfisher (known here as 'secret tea') is Rs 40.

La Terrasse (☎ 2220809; 5 Subbayah Salai; pizzas Rs 80-175; ⊙ Thu-Tue) This simple semi-open-air place near the southern end of the promenade has a wide menu but is deservedly best known for good pizzas and safe salads. No alcohol is served.

Au Feu de Bois (☎ 2341821; 28 Lal Bahabhur St; pizzas Rs 100-140; ⊙ lunch & dinner Tue-Sun) With a wood-fired pizza oven, this no-frills place serves pizzas only in its small rooftop courtyard and rustic dining room.

Satsanga (☎ 2225867; 30-32 Labourdonnais St; mains around Rs 100-150) In the covered backyard of a rambling colonial house, Satsanga serves up tasty French and Italian food and is a good place for a casual salad lunch (Rs 70) or dinner. It's also great for breakfast from 9am (Rs 25 to 50) – freshly baked bread, crepes, fruit and yogurt – or coffee with the morning paper in hand, relaxing in low-slung chairs under the balcony.

Rendezvous (☎ 2330238; 30 Suffren St; mains Rs 100-275; ⊙ lunch & dinner Wed-Mon) The food here is regarded by many locals and expats as the best in town. Served rooftop or in AC comfort, the menu includes such French classics as bouillabaisse, quiches and *coq au vin* (chicken with red wine), along with burgers, pizzas, Indian and Chinese. Wine as well as beer is served.

SELF-CATERING

Nilgiri Supermarket (cnr Mission & Rangapillai Sts; ⊙ 9.30am-9pm) A well-stocked, modern place in which to shop for groceries in air-conditioned comfort. Credit cards are accepted.

Grinde Sridharan General Merchants (☎ 2221232; grspondy@sify.com; 25 St Louis St; ⊙ 9am-1pm & 4-9pm Mon-Sat) An excellent, long-established grocery store with plenty of imported goods and an exchange facility for cash and travellers cheques.

Neighbouring bakeries Your Daily Bread and Hot Breads are on Ambour Salai, selling terrific French bread, croissants and other baked goodies from 7am daily. The main fresh produce market is west of MG Rd, between Nehru and Rangapillai Sts.

Drinking & Entertainment

With low taxes on alcohol, Puducherry has a reputation for cheap booze. The reality is you'll really only find cheap beer (Rs 30) in 'liquor shops' or the darkened bars attached to them. While you can sometimes get a large Kingfisher for Rs 60, the better restaurants charge up to Rs 100. There are a few exceptions and the greatest concentration of local bars can be found along the northern stretch of Anna Salai (West Blvd).

Seagulls Restaurant (19 Dumas St; ⏰ 11.30am-11.30pm) Although this is a restaurant, the waiters generally look bewildered if you order food. But the location, with a balcony overlooking the sea and views north along the promenade, makes it great for a beer (cheap at Rs 60) on a warm evening; an expansive downstairs veranda was being constructed when we visited.

Coffee.Com (☎ 2339079; www.coffeedotcom.net; 236 Mission St; ⏰ 10am-1am) Puducherry's cosmopolitan vibe is typified by this hip little internet hang-out. It's a meeting place where you can go online, read magazines, drink espresso coffee and there's a widescreen TV and a selection of DVDs (Rs 100 per hour).

Space Coffee & Arts (☎ 2356253; 2 Labourdonnais St; ⏰ 6pm-midnight) Space is a funky little semi-open-air café for juice, coffee or beer (Rs 75) and tapas (from Rs 60) in the evening, and it's also a gallery and performing-arts venue with traditional dance often performed on Saturday.

Shopping

Shopping in Puducherry, especially on Nehru St, Mission St and MG Rd, is a strange blend of Indian-bazaar-meets-Western-style opulence, with sari and textile stalls competing for space with modern, neon-lit speciality shops.

Sri Aurobindo Handmade Paper Factory (☎ 2334 763; 50 SV Patel Salai; ⏰ 8.30am-noon & 1.30-5pm Mon-Sat) Fine handmade paper is sold at the shop here, and you can ask at the counter about tours of the factory. There's a wider choice of goods at Auroboutique near the ashram; all sales support its work.

Fabindia (☎ 2226010; www.fabindia.com; 59 Suffren St; ⏰ 9.30am-7.30pm) Opposite Alliance Française, this shop has a stunning variety of quality woven goods and furnishings, traditionally made but with a contemporary feel; clothing, however, seems designed more for whippet-thin models than for most people. In operation since 1960, one of its selling points is its 'fair, equitable and helpful relationship' with the village producers of the goods. Upstairs is the very good French Bookshop (p397).

La Boutique d'Auroville (Nehru St; ⏰ 9.30am-1pm & 3.30-8pm Mon-Sat) It's fun browsing through the crafts here, including jewellery, batiks, *kalamkari* (similar to batik) drawings, carpets and woodcarvings; you can also pick

BUSES FROM PUDUCHERRY (PONDICHERRY)

Destination	Fare (Rs)	Duration (hr)	Frequency	Type
Bengaluru	125	8	6 daily	Deluxe
Chennai	55	3½	83 daily	Exp
Chidambaram	23	1½	50 daily	State
Coimbatore	159	9	6 daily	Deluxe
Kanchipuram	40	3	5 daily	State
Karaikal	43	3½	15 daily	State
Kumbakonam	33	4	6 daily	State
Mamallapuram	33	2	5 daily	State
Nagapattinam	48	4	4 daily	State
Tirupathi	90	6	9 daily	Deluxe
Tiruvannamalai	25	3½	9 daily	State
Trichy	73	5	4 daily	Deluxe

TAMIL NADU

up an Auroville map (Rs 10) if you're planning to visit.

kasha ki aasha (☎ 2222963; www.kasha-ki-aasha .com; 23 rue Surcouf; ☻ 8am-7pm Mon-Sat) Fabulous fabrics and gorgeous garments and crafts that are sourced directly from their makers are sold in this lovely old colonial house. The roof terrace serves great coffee and light meals.

For a modern take on Indian souvenirs and fashions, check out the excellent **Casablanca** (165 Mission St; ☻ 9am-10pm Mon-Sat & 9am-9pm Sun). Opposite, **Kalki** (☎ 2339166; 134 Mission St; ☻ 9.30am-8.30pm Mon-Sat) showcases and sells exquisite-quality clothes and crafts.

Getting There & Away
BUS
The bus stand is 500m west of town. See p401 for details of services.

TAXI
Air-conditioned taxis from Puducherry to Chennai cost around Rs 2700 and to Chennai airport Rs 2500.

TRAIN
There are two direct services a day to Chennai (Rs 58, five hours), and one to Tirupathy. There's a computerised booking service for southern trains at the station.

Getting Around
One of the best ways to get around is by walking. Large three-wheelers shuttle between the bus stand and Gingy St for Rs 5, but they're hopelessly overcrowded. Cycle- and autorickshaws are plentiful – an autorickshaw across town costs about Rs 30.

Since the streets are broad and flat, the most popular transport is pedal power. Bicycle hire shops line many of the streets, especially MG Rd and Mission St. You'll also find hire shops in Subbayah Salai and Goubert Ave. The usual rental is Rs 5 per hour, or Rs 20 per day, but some places ask Rs 70.

Mopeds or motorbikes are useful for getting out to the beaches or to Auroville and can be rented from a number of shops and street stalls. The going rate is Rs 100 a day for a gearless scooter and Rs 125 for a motorbike, with a discount for several days' hire. You need to show some ID (such as a driving licence) and leave Rs 500 deposit. Try **Vijay Arya** (23 Aurobindo St) for moped hire.

AUROVILLE
☎ 0413
Just over the border from Puducherry is the international community of Auroville – a project in 'human unity' that has ballooned to encompass more than 80 rural settlements spread over 20km, and about 1800 residents. Two-thirds of these are foreigners, representing around 38 different nationalities.

Auroville is not a tourist attraction, and casual visitors may find it a bit bewildering and unwelcoming. Each settlement has its own area of work interest and expertise – from traditional medicinal plants to renewable energy to organic farming to women's groups, to name just a few – and most Aurovillians are busy simply getting on with their work and lives in these communities off the main road. But if you're at all interested in the philosophy it's worth the ride out to the visitors centre to find out how it all works, to eat some great food at the café, and maybe stay at a guesthouse in one of the settlements that suits your interests.

At the spiritual and physical centre of Auroville is an astonishing structure called the Matrimandir, looking something like a cross between a giant golden golf ball and a NASA space project. It contains a silent inner chamber lined with white marble and housing a solid crystal (the largest in the world) 70cm in diameter. Rays from the sun are beamed into this crystal from a tracking mirror in the roof. On cloudy days, solar lamps do the job. But you won't actually see this; the Matrimandir is not open to casual visitors. A section of the **gardens** (☻ 10am-1pm & 2-4.30pm daily except Sun afternoon), from which you can see the structure, can be visited; you need to pick up a pass (free) from the information service (below).

Information
There's a photographic exhibition and video room at the **Auroville Information Service** (admission free; ☻ 9am-1pm & 1.30-5.30pm), which also issues garden passes for external views of the Matrimandir (from 9.45am to 12.30pm and 1.45pm to 4pm only). In the same complex, the **visitors centre** (☎ 2622239; www.auroville.org; ☻ 9am-6pm) contains a bookshop, café, and Boutique d'Auroville, which sells Aurovillian handicrafts.

Sleeping & Eating
People with a serious interest in the aims of Auroville can stay with any one of the 40 community groups here. A stay of no shorter than

---

AUROVILLE: THE INTERNATIONAL VISION

Auroville is the brainchild of the Mother, 'an experiment in international living where people could live in peace and progressive harmony above all creeds, politics and nationalities'. Designed by French architect Roger Anger, its opening ceremony on 28 February 1968 was attended by the president of India and representatives of 124 countries, who poured the soil of their lands into an urn to symbolise universal oneness.

The geographical layout of Auroville was seen as a reflection of this striving for unity. At the community's centre stands the Matrimandir, which the Mother called the soul of Auroville. Four zones – cultural, international, industrial and residential – were to radiate out from the Matrimandir to cover an area of 25 sq km, although as yet only 10 sq km has been realised.

In the words of the Mother, the founding vision of Auroville is that 'There should be somewhere upon earth a place that no nation could claim as its sole property, a place where all human beings of goodwill, sincere in their aspiration, could live freely as citizens of the world…'

---

a week is preferred and while work isn't obligatory, it's much appreciated. Accommodation isn't offered in exchange for work; rooms range from Rs 150 to 1000, and guests are also required to contribute Rs 60 per day for the 'maintenance and development' of Auroville.

There are more than 40 guesthouses in Auroville. The best way to find what you're looking for – that is, to match your interests with the community you'll stay in – is to check out the website and, preferably, get suggestions from and make arrangements with the **Auroville Guest Service** (☎ 2622704; avguests@auroville .org.in) before arriving.

Although there are stores and small roadside eateries in Auroville, and communities have communal dining areas, many Aurovillians gather at the Solar Kitchen – powered by solar energy – which dishes out more than 400 meals daily from its buffet. The café at the visitors centre is open to day visitors.

Getting There & Away

The best way to enter Auroville is from the coast road, at the village of Periyar Mudaliarchavadi, near the turn-off to Repos Beach. Ask around as it's not well signposted. A return autorickshaw ride is about Rs 150, but a better option is to hire a moped or bicycle. It's about 12km from Puducherry to the visitors centre.

CENTRAL TAMIL NADU

CHIDAMBARAM

☎ 04144 / pop 67,942

Chidambaram's great temple complex of Nataraja, the dancing Shiva, is a Dravidian architectural highlight and one of the holiest

Shiva sites in South India. Chidambaram can be visited as a day trip from Puducherry, or as a stopover between Puducherry and Kumbakonam or Trichy.

Of the many festivals, the two largest are the **10-day chariot festivals**, which are celebrated in April/May and December/January. In February/March the five-day **Natyanjali Dance Festival** attracts performers from all over the country to celebrate Nataraja – the Lord of Dances.

Orientation & Information

The small town is developed around the Nataraja Temple with streets named after the cardinal points. This is an easy town for walking, with accommodation close to the temple and the bus stand a five-minute walk to the southeast. The train station is about 1km further south.

Cybase (Pillaiyar Koil St; ⊙ 9am-9pm) Fast internet access.

ICICI Bank ATM (Hotel Saradharam & South Car St)

Post office (North Car St; ⊙ 10am-3pm Mon-Sat)

Tourist office (☎ 238739; Railway Feeder Rd; ⊙ 9am-5pm Mon-Fri) You may be able to pick up a brochure but the office is frequently deserted.

UAE Exchange (Pillaiyar Koil St; ⊙ Mon-Sat) The only place in town to exchange money.

Sights

NATARAJA TEMPLE

Chidambaram's star attraction, this **Shiva temple** (⊙ courtyard & shrines 6am-12.30pm & 4-10.30pm) draws a regular stream of pilgrims and visitors. The region was a Chola capital from 907 to 1310 and the Nataraja Temple was erected during the later time of the administration. The high-walled 22-hectare complex has four

TAMIL NADU

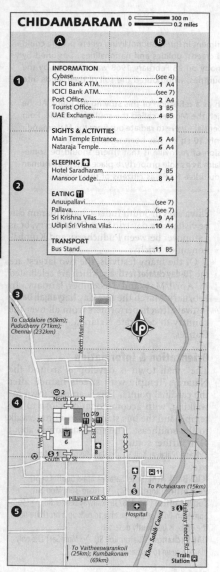

CHIDAMBARAM

0 _____ 300 m
0 _____ 0.2 miles

INFORMATION	
Cybase	(see 4)
ICICI Bank ATM	1 A4
ICICI Bank ATM	(see 7)
Post Office	2 A4
Tourist Office	3 B5
UAE Exchange	4 B5

SIGHTS & ACTIVITIES	
Main Temple Entrance	5 A4
Nataraja Temple	6 A4

SLEEPING 🏠	
Hotel Saradharam	7 B5
Mansoor Lodge	8 A4

EATING 🍴	
Anuupallavi	(see 7)
Pallava	(see 7)
Sri Krishna Vilas	9 A4
Udipi Sri Vishna Vilas	10 A4

TRANSPORT	
Bus Stand	11 B5

To Cuddalore (50km);
Puducherry (71km);
Chennai (232km)

North Main Rd

North Car St

West Car St
East Car St
South Car St

VOC St

To Pichavaram (15km)

Pillaiyar Koil St

Hospital

To Vaitheeswarankoil
(25km); Kumbakonam
(69km)

Khan Sahib Canal

Railway Feeder Rd

Train
Station

towering *gopurams* with finely sculptured icons depicting Hindu myths. The temple is renowned for its prime examples of Chola artistry and has since been patronised by numerous dynasties. The main temple entrance is at the east *gopuram*, off East Car St.

In the northeast of the complex, to the right as you enter, is the 1000-pillared **Raja**

Sabha (King's Hall), open only on festival days, and to the left of that is the **Sivaganga** (Temple Tank) – guides will explain the stories from paintings and sculptures that surround it. In the southeast of the complex is an impressive statue of the elephant-headed god, Ganesh.

Directly opposite the main entrance a large statue of Shiva's escort, Nandi, looks towards the hall leading to the inner sanctum. Although non-Hindus are officially not allowed inside the gold-roofed inner sanctum itself, it's possible to walk down the corridor and observe rituals such as the fire ceremony (usually held before the afternoon and evening closing), where worshippers light goblets of fire and bells clang. Afternoon *puja* at around 5pm is also worth seeing.

Brahmin priests will usually take you in for a fee (anywhere from Rs 30 up to 300, depending on the language skills and knowledge of the guide) and guide you around the temple complex. Since the Brahmins work as a cooperative to fund the temple you may wish to support this magnificent building by way of donation (or hiring a guide), but don't feel bound to do so.

Sleeping & Eating

Chidambaram has many cheap pilgrims' lodges clustered around the temple.

Hotel Saradharam (☎ 221336; www.hotelsaradharam .co.in; 19 VGP St; d without/with AC Rs 500/800; ❄) The busy and friendly Hotel Saradharam is the top hotel in town and is conveniently located across from the bus stand. It's starting to look its age, though.

If you're on a budget and need to stay here overnight, possibly the best of the pilgrims' lodges is **Mansoor Lodge** (☎ 221072; 91 East Car St; s/d Rs 150/200), close to the temple with clean, good-value rooms.

Predictably, the best places to eat are in hotels. **Anuupallavi** (mains Rs 25-70; ☺ lunch & dinner) is an excellent AC multicuisine restaurant; in the same hotel is a veg restaurant, **Pallava** (☺ breakfast, lunch & dinner). Near the temple entrance, **Udipi Sri Vishna Vilas** (thalis Rs 25; ☺ breakfast, lunch & dinner) is a busy, clean place for South Indian veg food and thalis, as is Sri Krishna Vilas across the road.

Getting There & Away

The bus stand is very central – within walking distance to the temple and accommodation.

There are hourly buses to Chennai; bus 157 (Rs 75, seven hours) is the quickest. Puducherry (Rs 21, two hours) and Kumbakonam (Rs 22, 2½ hours) buses run regularly. There are also direct buses to Madurai (Rs 120, eight hours, five daily).

Chidambaram is on a metre gauge rail line rather than a main line but the train is useful for getting to Kumbakonam, where you can change trains for Thanjavur or Trichy. There's one daily express train to Kumbakonam (2nd class/sleeper Rs 31/49, two hours) and several passenger trains. The station is a 20-minute walk southeast of the temple (Rs 30 by autorickshaw).

AROUND CHIDAMBARAM

About 15km east of town, **Pichavaram** is an area of tidal canals and backwaters, fringed by mangroves. You can spend a pleasant hour or two being rowed around the waterways and enjoying the bird life and calm surrounds. Boat hire (per hour Rs 125; maximum five people) is available every day, and is busy with local visitors at the weekend. A basic three-room **guesthouse** (per room Rs 265) is avail-

able beside the boat-hire place, and you can order food there.

KUMBAKONAM
☎ 0435 / pop 160,827

Kumbakonam is a busy, dusty commercial centre, nestled along the Cauvery River some 37km northeast of Thanjavur. Here you can visit the many superb Chola temples scattered around town, or head east to the coastal towns of the Cauvery Delta. It's also an easy day trip from Thanjavur.

There's no tourist office in Kumbakonam, and road names and signs here are more erratic than usual. The best place to exchange travellers cheques is at the **UAE Exchange** (☎ 2423212; 134 Kamarajar Rd) near the train station. You'll find an ICICI Bank ATM almost opposite **Ashok Net Café** (☎ 2433054; 24 Ayikulam Rd; per hr Rs 20; ☺ 9am-10.30pm).

Sights

Dozens of colourfully painted *gopurams* point skyward from Kumbakonam's 18 temples, most dedicated to Shiva or Vishnu, but probably only the most dedicated temple-goer

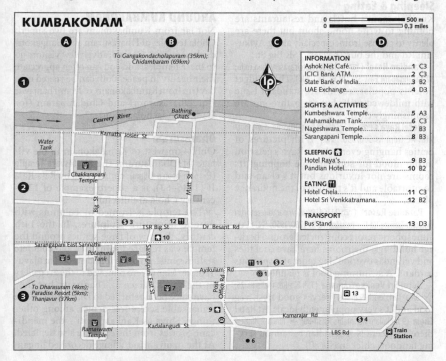

KUMBAKONAM

0 —————— 500 m
0 —————— 0.3 miles

INFORMATION
Ashok Net Café...................................1 C3
ICICI Bank ATM....................................2 C3
State Bank of India.............................3 B2
UAE Exchange.....................................4 D3

SIGHTS & ACTIVITIES
Kumbeshwara Temple.......................5 A3
Mahamakham Tank............................6 C3
Nageshwara Temple..........................7 B3
Sarangapani Temple..........................8 B3

SLEEPING 🏠
Hotel Raya's..9 B3
Pandian Hotel..................................10 B2

EATING 🍽
Hotel Chela......................................11 C3
Hotel Sri Venkkatramana................12 B2

TRANSPORT
Bus Stand...13 D3

would tackle visiting more than a few. All temples are open from 6am to noon and 4pm to 10pm, and admission is free.

The largest Vishnu temple in Kumbakonam, with a 50m-high east gate, is **Sarangapani Temple**, just off Ayikulam Rd. The temple shrine, in the form of a chariot, was the work of the Cholas during the 12th century.

Kumbeshwara Temple, about 200m west and entered via a nine-storey *gopuram*, is the largest Shiva temple. It contains a lingam said to have been made by Shiva himself when he mixed the nectar of immortality with sand.

The 12th-century **Nageshwara Temple**, from the Chola dynasty, is also dedicated to Shiva in the guise of Nagaraja, the serpent king. On three days of the year (in April or May) the sun's rays fall on the lingam. The main shrine here is in the form of a chariot.

The huge **Mahamakham Tank**, 600m southeast of the Nageshwara Temple, is the most sacred in Kumbakonam. It's believed that every 12 years the waters of the Ganges flow into the tank, and at this time a festival is held; the next is due in 2016.

Sleeping & Eating

Kumbakonam's hotels and restaurants are nothing to write home about but there are plenty to choose from, especially along Ayikulam Rd and the busy bazaar, TSR Big St.

Pandian Hotel (☎ 2430397; hotelrayas@yahoo.co.in; 52 Sarangapani East St; s/d Rs 140/200) This budget hotel is popular; rooms are standard issue with mildewed walls but the bathrooms are astonishingly clean.

Hotel Raya's (☎ 2422545; 18 Post Office Rd; d without/ with AC from Rs 500/850; ✷) With pictures of deities hanging everywhere, Raya's gets you in the mood for some temple hopping. Its rooms are not luxurious but it's clean and comfortable and it's the best of the midrange places.

Paradise Resort (☎ 2416469; www.paradiseresortindia.com; Tanjore Rd Darasuram; s/d Rs 1750/1950; ✷) An atmospheric resort constructed around heritage buildings, the rooms here have cool tiles and verandas overlooking quiet and spacious gardens. A swimming pool is planned.

Hotel Sri Venkkatramana (TSR Big Rd; thalis Rs 25; ☺ breakfast, lunch & dinner) serves good fresh veg food and it's very popular with locals. At **Hotel Chela** (9 Ayikulam Rd; mains Rs 30-80; ☺ lunch & dinner) there's a decent North Indian restaurant serving tandoori chicken (Rs 80).

BUSES FROM KUMBAKONAM

Destination	Fare (Rs)	Duration (hr)	Frequency
Chennai (No 303)	118	7	every 30min
Chidambaram	31	2½	every 20min
Coimbatore	110	10	1 daily (7pm)
Madurai	65	5	8 daily
Puducherry	40	4½	every 20min
Thanjavur	14.50	1½	every 10min

Getting There & Away

The bus stand and train station are about 2km east of the town centre. For details of bus services, see above.

For the Cauvery Delta area there are buses running every half-hour to Karaikal (Rs 16, two hours), via Tranquebar and then on to Nagapattinam.

The overnight *Rock Fort Express* is the only major train to/from Chennai (sleeper/3AC Rs 130/365), going via Thanjavur and Trichy. Passenger trains run to Chidambaram (Rs 31, two hours) and Thanjavur.

AROUND KUMBAKONAM

Not far from Kumbakonam are two superb Chola temples at Dharasuram and Gangakondacholapuram. Comparatively few visitors go to these temples, and you can often appreciate their beauty in peace. Both can be visited on a day trip from Kumbakonam, or from Thanjavur (for Dharasuram) and Chidambaram (for Gangakondacholapuram).

Dharasuram

Only 4km west of Kumbakonam in the village of Dharasuram, the **Airatesvara Temple** (☺ 6am-noon & 4-8pm), constructed by Raja Raja II (1146–63), is a superb example of 12th-century Chola architecture.

The temple is fronted by columns with unique miniature sculptures. In the 14th century, the row of large statues around the temple was replaced with brick and concrete statues similar to those found at the Thanjavur Temple. Many were removed to the art gallery in the raja's palace at Thanjavur, but they have since been returned to Dharasuram. The remarkable sculptures depict, among other things, Shiva as Kankalamurti – the mendicant. Stories from the epics are also depicted. At the main shrine, a huge decorated lingam stands, the natural light illuminating it from dawn to dusk.

You can get to Dharasuram by bus (Rs 5) or autorickshaw (Rs 60 return, including waiting time).

Gangakondacholapuram

This **Brihadishwara Temple** (🕙 6am-noon & 4-8pm), 35km north of Kumbakonam, was built by the Chola emperor Rajendra I (1012–44) in the style of the temple at Thanjavur, built by his father. Later additions were made in the 15th century by the Nayaks. The ornate tower is almost 55m high and weighs 80 tonnes. Within the recesses of the temple walls stand many beautiful statues, including those of Ganesh, Nataraja and Harihara.

Buses go from Kumbakonam bus stand to the temple every half-hour (Rs 11, 1½ hours); early morning is the quietest time to visit.

CAUVERY DELTA

The Cauvery River rises in the Western Ghats and flows eastwards before emptying into the Bay of Bengal. Its delta is a fertile farming area and there are a number of coastal towns of interest.

The Nagapattinam district here was the worst affected part of Tamil Nadu when the 2004 tsunami struck, with up to 7000 lives lost and thousands more left homeless. In 2006 damage was still evident all along the coast, and there were the many local and international aid agencies working in the area.

Tranquebar (Tharangambadi)

About 80km south of Chidambaram, Tranquebar was a Danish post, established in 1620. The solid, pink-hued seafront **Danesborg Fort** (Indian/foreigner Rs 5/50; 🕙 10am-1pm & 2-5.45pm, closed Fri), occupied by the British in 1801, houses a small but fascinating **museum** on the region's Danish history. The quiet roadway leading to the fort is entered by an impressive 1792 gateway, and an exuberant Sunday service is held in the nearby 1718 church.

Stay directly opposite the fort in the exquisitely comfortable heritage **Bungalow on the Beach** (☎ 04364-288065; www.neemranahotels.com; r from Rs 4000; 🏊); the pool was still under construction when we visited, but the rooms and views were fabulous. Just next door – and still with sea views – is its budget option **Hotel Tamil Nadu** (☎ 04364-288065; www.neemranahotels.com; r from Rs 600). To get there take a bus from Chidambaram (Rs 28, 2½ hours).

Vailankanni (Velanganni)

☎ 04365 / pop 10,104

Vailankanni is the site of the Roman Catholic **Basilica of Our Lady of Good Health** and its associated sacred sites. Thousands of Christian pilgrims file through the impressive white neogothic structure, which was elevated to the status of basilica in 1962 during the Pope's visit.

An annual nine-day festival culminates on 8 September, the celebration of Mary's birth, and the weeks running up to it see many thousands of pilgrims walking the 300km or so from Chennai and elsewhere; the days before and during the festival see the town packed to bursting. There's a hectically devout but amiable atmosphere, with many interested Hindu visitors. Tragically, many pilgrims were here for Christmas when the 2004 tsunami struck. At least 2000 people were killed and 120 shops leading down to the beach were washed away. The church itself was untouched.

In town there are many lodges, especially in the square by the bus station and around the basilica. **VJ Lodge** (☎ 263861; r without/with AC Rs 250/500; 🏊) is a good, tatty and spotless option, or ask at the Church Rooms Booking Office, also on the square. Just out of town is **Bethesda Inn** (☎ 263336; Nagapattinam Main Rd; r Rs 1300; 🏊), a quieter midrange option, with a garden swimming pool planned. Room rates everywhere double during the festival.

Daily bus services travel between Vailankanni and Chennai, Coimbatore, Bengaluru, Kanyakumari and Thiruvananthapuram (Trivandrum).

Calimere (Kodikkarai) Wildlife & Bird Sanctuary

This 333-sq-km **sanctuary** (per person/vehicle Rs 5/ 15; 🕙 6am-6pm) of scrubby evergreen forest, saltpans and coast is 90km southeast of Thanjavur. Noted for its vast flocks of migratory waterfowl, Calimere's tidal mud flats and saltpans are home to teals, shovelers, curlews, terns, plovers, sandpipers, shanks, herons and more from October to March.

In the drier times of the year there are always bush birds to see, and resident black bucks, sambars and spotted deer on the plains. To get the most from your visit, you'll need at least a bicycle (negotiate with a local) and binoculars. If you have a vehicle, a local guide (not officially compulsory, but in fact

TAMIL NADU

impossible to bypass; pay around Rs 50) will join you at the park entrance for an hour or so to make a 15km round trip through the sanctuary, pointing out wildlife and stopping at an 1890 lighthouse and watchtower on the shore.

There are two lodges run by the forest department. One is in the village at the end of the road, a big and very obvious (unsigned) building on the right. Rooms here are Rs 100 for two people, and you can get food at the basic stalls outside. A better option if you have a vehicle is **Thambusamy Rest House** (r Rs 100), 1km or so off the main road and beside the new lighthouse; you can walk to a watchtower and there's a shady, neglected garden. You'll need to bring food with you.

The easiest way to get to Calimere is by bus (Rs 6, every hour) or taxi from Vedaranniyam, which is 12km away and linked by frequent buses to Nagapattinam or Thanjavur.

THANJAVUR (TANJORE)

☎ 04362 / pop 215,725

Dominated by the superb World Heritage–listed Brihadishwara Temple, and a sprawling Maratha Palace complex, Thanjavur is an easy-going town and a worthy detour off the Chennai–Madurai route.

The town is famous also for its distinctive art style, a combination of raised and painted surfaces. Krishna is the most popular deity depicted, and in the Thanjavur school his skin is white, rather than the traditional blue-black.

THANJAVUR (TANJORE)

INFORMATION	
BBC Net.......................................1 D4	
Main Post Office.......................2 D4	
Raja Netcafé..............................3 C3	
State Bank of India..................4 C2	
Tourist Office............................5 C3	
VKC Forex..................................6 C3	

SIGHTS & ACTIVITIES	
Brihadishwara Temple............7 B3	
Thanjavur Royal Palace &	
Museums................................8 C1	

SLEEPING	
Hotel Gnanam..........................9 C2	
Hotel Oriental Towers...........10 D4	
Hotel Tamil Nadu.................(see 5)	
Hotel Valli...............................11 D4	

Hotel Yagappa.......................12 C4	
Raja Rest House...................(see 5)	

EATING	
Cluster of Vegetarian	
Restaurants..........................13 C2	
Oriental Supermarket........(see 10)	
Sathars....................................14 C3	
Sri Venkata Lodge.................15 C2	

SHOPPING	
Poompuhar.............................16 C3	

TRANSPORT	
Bicycle Hire.............................17 C2	
Bicycle Hire.............................18 C4	
Local Bus Stand......................19 C2	
SETC Bus Stand.......................20 C2	

To Ideal River View Resort (10km); Thiruvaiyaru (13km)

To Kumbakonam (37km); Chidambaram (106km)

Old Town

To ICICI Bank ATM (300km)

South Main Rd

KRA Hospital

Anna Salai (Market Rd)

Abraham Pandither Rd

South Rampart

West Main St

Hospital Rd

Clocktower

Sivaganga Tank

Grand Anicut Canal Rd

Grand Anicut Canal

To Tiruchirappalli (Trichy; 40km); Chennai (351km)

Mosque

Kutchery Rd

Train Station

To Tiruvarur (55km)

To New Bus Station (2.5km); Tiruchirappalli (Trichy; 54km); Madurai (155km)

Vallam Rd (Trichy Rd)

To Nagapattinam (79km)

0   400 m
0   0.2 miles

Thanjavur is set on a fertile delta and the accompanying harvests make the town a great place to be during Pongal (harvest) celebrations in January.

Thanjavur was the ancient capital of the Chola kings, whose origins go back to the beginning of the Christian era. The Cholas' era of empire building was between AD 850 and 1270; at the height of their power, they controlled most of the Indian peninsula. The stylised bronze work for which they were famous is still produced in town.

Information

BBC Net (MKM Rd; per hr Rs 15; 9.30am-9.30pm)
Fast internet access in the basement of the Nallaiyah Shopping Complex.

ICICI Bank ATM (South Main Rd & New Bus Station)

Main post office (9am-7pm Mon-Sat, 10am-4pm Sun) Near the train station.

Raja Netcafé (2378175; 30 Gandhiji Rd; per hr Rs 20; 9am-11pm) Internet access.

Tourist office (230984; 10am-5.45pm Mon-Fri) On the corner of the Hotel Tamil Nadu complex.

VKC Forex (Golden Plaza; Gandhiji Rd; 9.30am-9pm) Changes cash and travellers cheques.

Sights

BRIHADISHWARA TEMPLE & FORT

Built by Raja Raja in 1010, the magnificent **Brihadishwara Temple** (6am-1pm & 3-8pm) is the crowning glory of Chola temple architecture and the highlight of Thanjavur. Known locally as the 'Big Temple', this fascinating monument is one of only a handful in India with World Heritage listing and is worth a couple of visits – preferably early morning and late afternoon, when the setting sun bathes the sandstone tower and walls in a syrupy glow.

Set in spacious, well-tended grounds, the temple has several pillared halls and shrines and 250 linga enshrined along the outer walls. Inscriptions record the names of dancers, musicians and poets – a reminder of the significance of this area to the development of the arts. A huge covered statue of the bull, Nandi – 6m long by 3m high – faces the inner sanctum. Created from a single piece of rock, it weighs 25 tonnes and is one of India's largest Nandi statues.

Unlike most South Indian temples where the *gopurams* are the highest towers, here it is the 13-storey *vimana* above the sanctum at 66m that reaches further into the sky. Its impressive gilded top is the original. The sanctum contains a 4m-high lingam with a circumference of 7m.

To the right of the temple entrance the temple elephant is usually on hand to take a coin donation with its trunk.

THANJAVUR ROYAL PALACE & MUSEUMS

The decaying splendour of huge corridors, spacious halls, observation and arsenal towers and shady courtyards in this labyrinthine and atmospheric complex were constructed partly by the Nayaks of Madurai around 1550 and partly by the Marathas.

At the main entrance of the **palace** (foreign adult/child Rs 50/25, Indian Rs 5/2, incl entry to the Durbar Hall & bell tower; 9am-6pm), follow the signs to the magnificent **Durbar Hall** (Royal Court), one of two such halls where the king held audiences. It's unrestored but in reasonable condition, especially the murals at the eastern end beneath which you can see part of a 6km secret passage running under the palace.

In the former Sadar Mahal Palace is the **Raja Serfoji Memorial Hall** (admission Rs 2) with a small collection of thrones, weapons and photographs. The **Royal Palace Museum** (admission Rs 1, camera/video Rs 30/250) shows off an eclectic collection of regal memorabilia, including wonderful embroidered shoes and hats, most of it dating from the early 19th century when the enlightened and far-sighted Serfoji II ruled. His sixth descendant still lives here; pick up *Raja Serfoji II* (Rs 25), his very readable monograph about his extraordinary ancestor, from any of the ticket desks.

The **art gallery** (admission Rs 15, camera/video Rs 30/250), between the Royal Palace Museum and the bell tower, has a superb collection of detailed Chola bronze statues from the 9th to 18th centuries in the smaller durbar hall. Nearby, the **bell tower** is worth the climb for the views right across Thanjavur and over the palace itself. The spiral stone staircase is dark, narrow and slippery; and watch your head!

The **Saraswati Mahal Library** is between the gallery and the palace museum. Established around 1700, its collection includes more than 30,000 palm-leaf and paper manuscripts in Indian and European languages. The library is closed to the public but you can visit the interesting **museum** (admission free; 10am-1pm & 1.30-5.30pm Tue-Thu), where exhibits range from the Ramayana written on palm leaf, to exquisite miniatures, to explicit prints of Chinese torture methods in 1804.

TAMIL NADU

Sleeping

BUDGET

There's a bunch of nondescript cheap lodges opposite the central bus stand with rooms for around Rs 150 a double.

Raja Rest House (s/d Rs 100/150) Once you get past the dilapidated and mildewed state of this building it's clean enough for the price, and very central, behind Hotel Tamil Nadu. Smiling staff are not included here.

Hotel Valli (☎ 231580; arasu_tnj@rediffmail.com; 2948 MKM Rd; s/d from Rs 185/240, r with AC Rs 600; 🕸) Near the train station, Valli is the best bet for budget travellers. The rooms are clean and the staff friendly and helpful. It's in a reasonably peaceful location beyond the greasy backyard workshops.

Hotel Yagappa (☎ 230421; 1 Vallam Rd; d without AC Rs 195-400, with AC Rs 700; 🕸) Just off Trichy Rd and near the station, Yagappa is a big place with a variety of rooms and a half-decent garden with requisite restaurant. The more expensive doubles are spacious with some unusual furnishings.

Hotel Tamil Nadu (☎ 231325; Gandhiji Rd; d without/with AC from Rs 275/550; 🕸) Although this is a former raja's guesthouse, set in a quiet, leafy courtyard with huge rooms and wide balconies, that's where the royal treatment ends. It's full of character, but some of the rooms look like they haven't been cleaned since the Raj era and the staff give the impression they want to be somewhere else.

MIDRANGE & TOP END

Hotel Gnanam (☎ 278501; www.hotelgnanam.com; Market Rd; s/d Rs 800/900; 🕸 🖳) Clean as a pin and busy with well-to-do locals, this central hotel with two good restaurants is great value.

Hotel Oriental Towers (☎ 230724; www.hotelorientaltowers.com; 2889 Srinivasam Pillai Rd; s/d from Rs 1100/1300; 🕸 🖳 🛦) With a business centre, gym, sauna, spa, massage and 4th-floor swimming pool (Rs 100 for nonguests), this is a business hotel around the corner from the train station. Ask for the rooms with temple view; they're a good size and comfortable. Service is willing and there are a couple of restaurants and a bar.

Ideal River View Resort (☎ 250633; www.idealresort.com; s/d Rs 1600/2200; 🕸 🖳 🛦) Although 10km northwest of the city, this tranquil resort is by far the nicest place to stay near Thanjavur. Set in beautiful gardens beside the Vennar River are immaculate, brightly furnished cottages with roomy balconies. There's a good open-air restaurant beside the river, a great pool, an Ayurvedic centre, and yoga classes on request. In busy season a shuttle runs into Thanjavur at 10am (returning at 4.30pm) and you can call ahead for a free pick-up.

Eating

There's a cluster of simple veg restaurants, open for breakfast, lunch and dinner, near the local bus stand and along Gandhiji Rd.

Sathars (☎ 331041; 167 Gandhiji Rd; mains Rs 35-85) Good service and quality food make this place popular. Downstairs is a veg restaurant with lunchtime thalis, upstairs is an AC section with great-value nonveg food – whole tandoori chicken for Rs 85 or prawn masala Rs 50.

Nearby to Sathars is the veg-only **Sri Venkata Lodge** (Gandhiji Rd; thalis Rs 25). For self-caterers, the excellent **Oriental Supermarket** (🕘 9am-9pm), below Hotel Oriental Towers, stocks a bit of everything.

Shopping

Thanjavur is a good place to shop for handicrafts and arts, especially around the palace area. Numerous shops along East Main Rd and Gandhiji Rd sell everything from quality crafts and ready-made clothes to inexpensive kitsch. For fixed prices and hassle-free shopping, **Poompuhar** (Gandhiji Rd; 🕘 10am-8pm Mon-Sat) is good for leatherwork, carvings, jewellery and other crafts.

To see bronze-casters at work, call craftsman **Mr Kathirvel** (☎ 098432-35202), whose extended family have, for several generations, used the lost-wax method to make bronze artefacts in a backyard kiln; it's a window into the small cottage industries on which Indian craft still thrives. He lives out towards Trichy Rd; call for directions.

Getting There & Away

BUS

The two city bus stands are for local and SETC buses. SETC has a computerised **reservation office** (☎ 230950; 🕘 7.30am-9.30pm). The New Bus Station, 2.5km south of the centre, services local areas and destinations south. Bus 74 shuttles between the three bus stations (Rs 3.50). For details of services, see opposite.

TRAIN

The station is conveniently central at the south end of Gandhiji Rd. Thanjavur is off

BUSES FROM THANJAVUR (TANJORE)

Destination	Fare (Rs)	Duration (hr)	Frequency
Chennai	105-135	8	20 daily
Chidambaram*	50	4	every 30min
Kumbakonam*	15	1	every 30min
Madurai*	50	4	every 15min
Ooty	125	10	8.30pm only
Tirupathi	147	11	8pm only
Trichy*	20	1½	every 5min

* New Bus Station

the main Chennai–Madurai line, so there's only one express train direct to Chennai – the overnight *Rock Fort Express* (sleeper/3AC Rs 181/485, 9½ hours) departing at 8.30pm. For more frequent trains north or south, including to Madurai, take a passenger train to Trichy (Rs 12, 1½ hours, eight daily) and change there. There's one daily express (6.50am) and a couple of passenger trains to Kumbakonam (Rs 10, one hour).

The *Thanjavur-Mysore Express* leaves daily at 7.15pm for Bengaluru (sleeper/3AC Rs 205/493, 11 hours) and Mysore (sleeper/3AC Rs 220/598, 14½ hours).

Getting Around

The main attractions of Thanjavur are close enough to walk between, but it can make for a long tiring day. Autorickshaws will take you on a tour of the temple and palace for around Rs 50 or hire a local taxi (non-AC/AC per half-day Rs 500/700). Both will want to get you into the craft emporiums. Bicycles can be hired from stalls opposite the train station and local bus stand (per hour Rs 3).

An autorickshaw into town from the New Bus Station costs around Rs 150.

AROUND THANJAVUR

About 13km north of Thanjavur, **Thiruvaiyaru** hosts the January **international music festival** in honour of the saint and composer Thyagaraja, whose birthplace is at Tiruvarur, 55km east of Thanjavur. The **Thyagararajaswami Temple** here boasts the largest temple chariot in Tamil Nadu, which is hauled through the streets during the 10-day **car festival** in April/May. Regular buses run from Thanjavur to Thiruvaiyaru for Rs 4.

TIRUCHIRAPPALLI (TRICHY)

☎ 0431 / pop 847,131

Tiruchirappalli, universally known as Trichy, is a sprawling but extremely enjoyable city with two extraordinary temples – one perched high above the town on a rocky mount – and many travellers find Trichy more enjoyable than the clamour of the more renowned Madurai. It's a well-serviced regional transport centre, always busy with locals especially during auspicious marriage seasons when gorgeously clothed families abound in every hotel.

Trichy's long history dates back to before the Christian era when it was a Chola citadel. During the 1st millennium AD, both the Pallavas and Pandyas took power many times before the Cholas regained control in the 10th century. When the Chola empire finally decayed, Trichy came into the realm of the Vijayanagar emperors of Hampi until their defeat in 1565 in the forces of the Deccan sultans. The town and its most famous landmark, the Rock Fort Temple, were built by the Nayaks of Madurai.

Orientation

Trichy's places of interest are scattered over a large area from north to south, but for travellers the city is conveniently split into three distinct areas. The Trichy Junction, or Cantonment, area in the south has most of the hotels and restaurants, the bus and train stations, tourist office and main post office, all conveniently within walking distance of each other. This is where you'll likely arrive and most likely stay. The Rock Fort Temple and main bazaar area is 2.5km north of here; and the other important temples are a further 3km to 5km north again, across the Cauvery River. Fortunately, the whole lot is connected by an excellent bus service.

Information

INTERNET ACCESS

Sify i-way (per hr Rs 30; ⏱ 9am -9pm) Chinnar Bazaar (Map p412); McDonald's Rd (Map p414); Williams Rd (Map p414)

MEDICAL SERVICES

Seahorse Hospital (Map p414; ☎ 2462660; Royal Rd) A large hospital in the Cantonment.

MONEY

Delight Forex (Map p414; ⏱ 9.30am-5.30pm Mon-Sat)
ICICI ATM (Map p414; Junction Rd) In front of the train station.

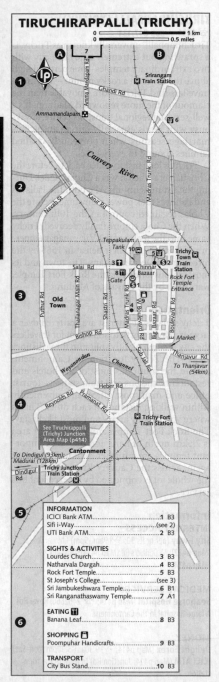

TIRUCHIRAPPALLI (TRICHY)

INFORMATION
ICICI Bank ATM.................................1 B3
Sifi i-Way...................................(see 2)
UTI Bank ATM..................................2 B3

SIGHTS & ACTIVITIES
Lourdes Church...............................3 B3
Natharvala Dargah............................4 B3
Rock Fort Temple.............................5 B3
St Joseph's College........................(see 3)
Sri Jambukeshwara Temple.....................6 B1
Sri Ranganathaswamy Temple...................7 A1

EATING 🍴
Banana Leaf..................................8 B3

SHOPPING 🛍
Poompuhar Handicrafts........................9 B3

TRANSPORT
City Bus Stand..............................10 B3

ICICI Bank ATM (Map p412; West Boulevard Rd)
IDBI Bank ATM (Map p414; Dindigul Rd)
UTI Bank ATM (Map p412; Chinnar Bazaar) Near the Rock Fort Temple entrance.
UTI Bank ATM (Map p414; Junction Rd)

TOURIST INFORMATION
Tourist office (Map p414; ☎ 2460136; 1 Williams Rd; 🕙 10am-5.45pm Mon-Fri) Has brochures for various Tamil Nadu locations.

TRAVEL AGENT
Indian Panorama (☎ 2433372; www.indianpanorama .in) Trichy-based and covering all of India, this professional and reliable agency/tour operator is run by an Australian-Indian couple.

Sights
ROCK FORT TEMPLE
The spectacular **Rock Fort Temple** (Map p412; admission Rs 1.50, camera/video Rs 10/50; 🕙 6am-8pm) is perched 83m high on a massive rocky outcrop. Here, it's not so much the temple itself as the setting and joining the pilgrimage to the top that make it special. This smooth rock was first hewn by the Pallavas who cut small cave temples into the southern face, but it was the Nayaks who later made use of its naturally fortified position. There are two main temples: **Sri Thayumanaswamy Temple**, halfway to the top (check out the bats snoozing in the stairwell roof near here!), and **Vinayaka Temple**, at the summit, which is dedicated to Ganesh. It's a stiff climb up the 437 stone-cut steps, but worth the effort – the view from the top is wonderful, with eagles wheeling beneath you. Non-Hindus are not allowed into either temple, but occasionally – for a small fee – temple priests waive this regulation, particularly at the summit temple.

SRI RANGANATHASWAMY TEMPLE
The superb **Sri Ranganathaswamy temple complex** (Map p412; camera/video Rs 50/150; 🕙 6am-1pm & 3-9pm), about 3km north of the Rock Fort, is dedicated to Vishnu. Although mentioned in the *sangam* poetry of the early academy of Tamil poets, temple inscriptions date its existence from the 10th century. With the Vijayanagar victory the temple was restored to the structure that exists today. Many dynasties have had a hand in its construction, including the Cheras, Pandyas, Cholas, Hoysalas, Vijayanagars and Nayaks – and work continues. The largest *gopuram*, the main entrance, was completed in 1987, and now measures 73m.

At 60 hectares, the complex with its seven concentric walled sections and 21 *gopurams* is possibly the largest in India. The scale of the buildings along the outermost walls retains a sense of the original tradition of poor people and beggars at the first wall, Chettiar traders and financiers at the second, then Brahmins at the third. Inside the fourth wall is a kiosk where you can buy a ticket (Rs 10) and climb the wall for a panoramic view of sorts of the entire complex. Non-Hindus may go to the sixth wall but are not allowed into the gold-topped sanctum. Guides and priests ask high fees to show you around this temple – at least Rs 200 an hour. About half that is reasonable; agree on a fee beforehand.

A **Temple Charlot Festival** where statues of the deities are paraded aboard a fine chariot is held here each January, but the most important festival is the 21-day **Vaikunta Ekadasi** (Paradise Festival) in mid-December, when the celebrated Vaishnavaite text, Tiruvaimozhi, is recited before an image of Vishnu.

Bus 1 from Trichy Junction or Rock Fort stops right outside this temple.

SRI JAMBUKESHWARA TEMPLE

Much smaller and often overlooked, the nearby **Sri Jambukeshwara Temple** (Map p412; camera/ video Rs 20/150; 6am-1pm & 3-9pm) is an oasis of calm and serenity after the clamour of Sri Ranganathaswamy Temple. It was built around the same time, and is dedicated to Shiva and Parvati. Being one of the five temples honouring the elements – in this case, water – the temple is built around a partly immersed Shiva lingam. Non-Hindus may not enter the sanctum, but beyond the second wall is an interesting chamber lined with linga and statues of gods.

If you're taking bus 1, ask for 'Tiruvana-koil'; the temple is about 100m east of the main road.

OTHER SIGHTS

Completed in 1896, the soaring, bone-white **Lourdes Church** (Map p412) is opposite the Teppakkulam Tank. Modelled on the neogothic basilica in Lourdes, France, it was renovated in January 1998 and an annual procession, the **Feast of Our Lady of Lourdes**, is held on 11 February. Its entrance is on Madras Trunk Rd, through the calm green gardens of **St Joseph's College** where an eccentric and dusty **museum** (admission free; 10am-noon & 2-4pm Mon-Sat) contains the natural history collections of the Jesuit priests' summer excursions to the Western Ghats in the 1870s. Bang on the door and the caretaker will let you in.

Natharvala Dargah (Map p412), the tomb of the popular Muslim saint, Nathher, is an impressive building with a 20m-high dome with pinnacles. It's a popular pilgrimage site.

Built in 1812, **St John's Church** (Map p414) in the junction area has louvred side doors that open to turn the church into an airy pavilion.

Sleeping

Most of Trichy's accommodation is in the Junction-Cantonment area around the bus station and a short walk north of the train station.

BUDGET

Hotel Tamil Nadu (Map p414; ☎ 2414346; McDonald's Rd; d without/with AC Rs 300/500;) A decent enough government-run hotel, on a quiet street, with good restaurant attached. It's always busy; book ahead if you can.

Hotel Meega (Map p414; ☎ 2414092; hotelmeega@ rediffmail.com; 3 Rockins Rd; d without/with AC Rs 325/500;) This is a good-value hotel – the rooms are smallish but clean, bright and more midrange than budget standard. There's a popular veg restaurant downstairs.

Ashby Hotel (Map p414; ☎ 2460652; www.ashbyhotel .com; 17A Junction Rd; d without/with AC from Rs 425/850;) Although it looks a bit worse for wear from the outside, Ashby's Raj-era, old-world atmosphere – with non-AC rooms opening out onto a leafy courtyard garden – is full of character. Rooms are spacious (though the AC rooms at the back are very uninteresting), and there's a bar and garden restaurant. Be prepared to contend with somewhat overbearing staff.

Hotel Mathura (Map p414; ☎ 2414737; www.hotel mathura.com; 1 Rockins Rd; s without/with AC Rs 325/595, d Rs 415/685;) Right next door to Hotel Meega, Mathura is another good choice. The rooms are clean and comfortable with thick foam mattresses but be sure to ask for a quiet room towards the back. There's a busy restaurant at the front and credit cards are accepted.

Hotel Annamalai (Map p414; ☎ 2412880; hotelanna malai@yahoo.com; McDonald's Rd; d without/with AC Rs 550/800;) Despite its decidedly insalubrious reception area, the staff is friendly and rooms on this comparatively quiet side street are big, clean and comfortable with decent bathrooms.

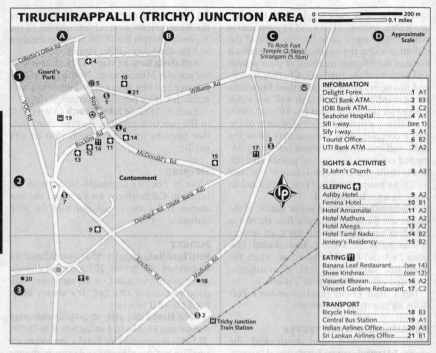

TIRUCHIRAPPALLI (TRICHY) JUNCTION AREA

INFORMATION
Delight Forex	1 A1
ICICI Bank ATM	2 B3
IDBI Bank ATM	3 C2
Seahorse Hospital	4 A1
Sifi i-way	(see 1)
Sify i-way	5 A1
Tourist Office	6 B2
UTI Bank ATM	7 A2

SIGHTS & ACTIVITIES
St John's Church	8 A3

SLEEPING
Ashby Hotel	9 A2
Femina Hotel	10 B1
Hotel Annamalai	11 A2
Hotel Mathura	12 A2
Hotel Meega	13 A2
Hotel Tamil Nadu	14 B2
Jenney's Residency	15 B2

EATING
Banana Leaf Restaurant	(see 14)
Shree Krishnas	(see 12)
Vasanta Bhavan	16 A2
Vincent Gardens Restaurant	17 C2

TRANSPORT
Bicycle Hire	18 B3
Central Bus Station	19 A1
Indian Airlines Office	20 A3
Sri Lankan Airlines Office	21 B1

MIDRANGE & TOP END

Femina Hotel (Map p414; ☎ 2414501; try_fem ina@sancharnet.in; 109 Williams Rd; d without/with AC from Rs 550/1300; 🛒 🖳) Femina is one of those Indian business hotels that manages to be affordable even if you're on a budget – and the staff doesn't look at travellers as if they've just crawled out of a swamp. There's a small shopping arcade, 24-hour coffee shop and a couple of very good restaurants. Nonguests can use the pool and small gym (per hour Rs 75).

Jenneys Residency (Map p414; ☎ 2414414; www .jenneysresidency.com; McDonald's Rd; s/d from US$30/40; 🛒 🖳) Jenneys is enormous, semiluxurious and in a relatively quiet location. The best rooms are on the top floors but all are well appointed; be aware that a 25% luxury tax will be added. Hotel facilities include shops, a health club and a truly bizarre Wild West theme bar.

Eating

Most hotels have their share of good restaurants – such as the multicuisine Madras Restaurant at Jenneys Residency (above) – and most have bars.

Shree Krishnas (Map p414; Rockins Rd; 🕑 breakfast, lunch & dinner) The restaurant in front of Hotel Mathura has a popular veg section serving topnotch thalis (Rs 20) – it's always packed at lunchtime. There's a little veranda and snack bar at the front from where you can watch the bustle of the bus stand across the road.

Vasanta Bhavan (Map p414; Rockins Rd; 🕑 breakfast, lunch & dinner) Next door to Shree Krishnas, good veg North Indian food such as *paneer tikka masala* (spicy curd cheese, Rs 30) with naan (flat bread; Rs 12) is a tasty option.

Banana Leaf (Map p412; ☎ 271101; Madras Trunk Rd; mains Rs 20-75; 🕑 lunch & dinner) One of the few good choices close to the Rock Fort Temple, this is an intimate little place with a big menu of inexpensive Indian and Chinese dishes – tandoori chicken (Rs 70), crab masala (Rs 45) and the intriguing rabbit masala (Rs 70). It's rustic rather than gourmet, but the food and service are fine. Another branch is next to the Hotel Tamil Nadu in the Trichy Junction area.

Vincent Gardens Restaurant (Map p414; Dindigul Rd; mains Rs 30-70; 🕑 lunch & dinner) There's a pleasant outdoor setting, and the limited veg and nonveg menu is done well. Take mosquito repellent in the evening.

Shopping

Trichy's best shopping is in the bazaar area south of the Rock Fort Temple (Map p412). Wandering along Big Bazaar Rd and Chinnar Bazaar in the evening is a fabulous assault on the senses – these areas are constantly packed with people and, from tiny stalls to flashy department stores, lit up like Times Square on New Year's Eve.

Poompuhar Handicrafts (Map p412; West Boulevard Rd; 9am-8pm) For fixed-price crafts, check out this place.

Getting There & Away

Trichy is virtually in the geographical centre of Tamil Nadu and it's well connected by air, bus and train.

AIR

As well as domestic flights, Trichy's airport has flights to Sri Lanka. **Indian Airlines** (Map p414; 2341063; 4A Dindigul Rd) flies four days a week to Chennai (US$120). Air Deccan also flies daily to Chennai.

Sri Lankan Airlines (Map p414; 2462381; 9am-5.30pm Mon-Sat, 9am-1pm Sun), at Femina Hotel, flies daily to Colombo (Rs 3800).

BUS

Most buses head to the central bus station on Rockins Rd. If you're travelling to Kodaikanal, a good option is to take one of the frequent buses to Dindigul (Rs 25, two hours) and change there. For details of services, see the table, right.

TRAIN

Trichy is on the main Chennai–Madurai line so there are lots of rail options in either direction. Of the nine daily expresses to Chennai, the quickest are the *Vaigai Express* (2nd/chair class Rs 85/297, 5½ hours) departing Trichy at 9.10am, and the *Pallavan Express*, which leaves at 6.30am. The best overnight train is the *Rock Fort Express* (sleeper/3AC Rs 136/382, 7½ hours) at 9.40pm.

For Madurai the best train is the *Guruvaya Express* (2nd class/sleeper Rs 47/75, three hours), which leaves at 1pm. The *Mysore Express* goes daily to Bengaluru (sleeper/3AC Rs 160/450, 11½ hours) and Mysore (sleeper/3AC Rs 200/562, 15 hours).

BUSES FROM TRICHY (TIRUCHIRAPPALLI)

Destination	Fare (Rs)	Duration (hr)	Frequency
Bengaluru	150	8	3 daily
Chennai	110-142	7	every 5min
Chidambaram	51	3½	hourly
Coimbatore	73	7	every 30min
Kodaikanal	62	6	3 daily
Madurai	35	3	every 10min
Ooty	100	8	1 daily
Puducherry	70	5	3 daily
Thanjavur	15	1½	every 5min
Tirupathi	144	9	5 daily

Getting Around

TO/FROM THE AIRPORT

The 7km ride into town is Rs 1250 by taxi and Rs 60 by autorickshaw. Otherwise, take bus 7, 59, 58 or 63 to/from the airport (30 minutes).

BICYCLE

Trichy lends itself to cycling as it's flat; it's a reasonably easy ride from Trichy Junction to the Rock Fort Temple, but a long haul to Srirangam and back. There are a couple of places on Madurai Rd (Map p414) near the train station where you can hire bicycles (per hr Rs 5).

BUS

Trichy's local bus service is mercifully efficient and easy to use. Bus 1 (A or B) from the main bus station on Rockins Rd goes every few minutes via the Rock Fort Temple, Sri Jambukeshwara Temple and the main entrance to Sri Ranganathaswamy Temple (Rs 4). To see them all, get off in that order (ask the conductor or driver where the stops are), as it runs in a one-way circuit.

SOUTHERN TAMIL NADU

TRICHY TO RAMESWARAM

Several little-visited historical and cultural gems in this area combine to make a great road trip to Rameswaram, or a day tour from either Trichy or Madurai.

Much of the property of this former princely state (1640–1948) is on display in the wonderful **Pudukkottai Museum** (Indian/foreigner Rs 3/100; 9.30am-5pm), located in a renovated palace

TAMIL NADU

building in Pudukkottai town. It's an eclectic collection, including musical instruments and megalithic burial artefacts, textiles and jewellery, some remarkable paintings and miniatures and much more! There are decent English-language signs, too.

Simple and imposing, the renovated **Tirumayam Fort** (Indian/foreigner Rs 5/100; ☉ 9am-5pm) is worth a climb to the top for 360-degree views of the landscape and the old town walls, and a shady rest with the goats under a banyan tree.

Nothing can adequately prepare visitors for the extraordinary residences of the Chettiars, historically a group of canny businesspeople, bankers and traders from the area of Chettinad. More palaces than houses, these vast constructions of red-tiled roofs, stained glass, carved Burmese teak, sculpted granite and opulent Italian marble – often painted rainbow candy-colours – are stunning. The heritage township of **Kanadukathan**, off a dusty road with no hint of the wonders ahead, is the place to stop and wander. Some houses welcome visitors to potter through the courtyards and public rooms if the family is not in residence or, to experience life in such a place, the 126-room **Chettinadu Mansion** (☎ 04565-273080; www.chettinadmansion.com; r Rs 3300), built between 1902 and 1912, has opened seven fabulous guest rooms. Cheaper accommodation is available 12km away in Karaikkudi; **Hotel Udhayam** (☎ 04565-237440; r without/with AC Rs 195/770; ⊠) is a decent option.

It's an easy day tour from either Trichy (taxi without/with AC Rs 1000/1500) or Madurai (a little more). Otherwise catch one of the many daily buses from Trichy to Karaikkudi (Rs 52, three hours) and get on and off at the sights along the way. Coming from Madurai, get a bus to Karaikkudi and then take a local bus, or hire a taxi. Kanadukathan is about a 500m walk off the main road.

Regular buses run between Karaikkudi, via Ramanathapuram, to Rameswaram.

RAMESWARAM

☎ 04573 / pop 38,035

Rameswaram is one of the most significant pilgrimage centres in South India for both Shaivites and Vaishnavaites. It was here that Rama (an incarnation of Vishnu and hero of the Ramayana) offered thanks to Shiva. At the town's core is the Ramanathaswamy Temple, one of the most important temples in India, and here you'll see a representation of India in miniature, with pilgrims including everyone from urbane sophisticates to colourfully clad Rajasthani tribespeople.

Rameswaram is on an island in the Gulf of Mannar, and is connected to the mainland at Mandapam by one of India's great engineering wonders, the Indira Gandhi bridge, which was opened in 1988. The town was once an important ferry port linking India and Sri Lanka, but the service ceased when things got ugly in Sri Lanka. At the time of writing it shows no signs of resuming, though regular boatloads of Tamil refugees do manage to make the crossing.

Apart from a regular influx of pilgrims, Rameswaram is a sleepy fishing village with a pleasantly laid-back atmosphere and the pungent smell of drying fish hanging in the air – take a stroll down to the harbour in the early morning to see the fishing boats come in and the catch being sorted.

Orientation & Information

Most hotels and restaurants are clustered around the Ramanathaswamy Temple. The bus stand, 2km to the west, is connected by shuttle bus to the town centre.

You can't change money here but the **State Bank of India** (East Car St) has an ATM accepting international cards.

Sights

RAMANATHASWAMY TEMPLE

A fine example of late Dravidian architecture, this **temple** (camera Rs 25; ☉ 4am-1pm & 3-8.30pm) is most renowned for its four magnificent corridors lined with elaborately sculpted pillars. Construction began in the 12th century AD and later additions included a 53m-high *gopuram*. The 22 *theerthams* (tanks) within the complex are believed by devotees to have particular powers and pilgrims are expected to bathe in, and drink from the waters in each *theertham*. The number of *theerthams* is said to correspond with the number of arrows in Rama's quiver, which he used to generate water on the island. Only Hindus may enter the inner sanctum, which is adorned with paintings depicting the origins of Rameswaram.

Even when the temple is closed, it is possible to take a peaceful amble through the extensive corridors.

DHANUSHKODI & ADAM'S BRIDGE

About 18km southeast of town, **Dhanushkodi** is a long, windswept surf beach and sandpit with an end-of-the-world feel. Other than the beach

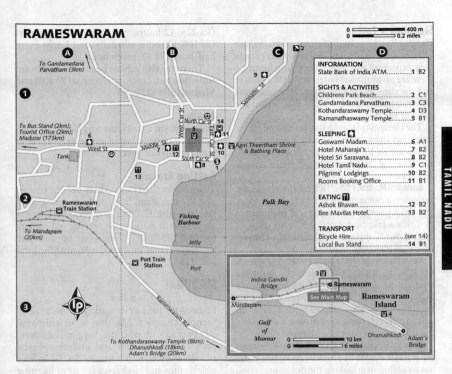

INFORMATION
State Bank of India ATM.............1 B2

SIGHTS & ACTIVITIES
Childrens Park Beach...................2 C1
Gandamadana Parvatham.............3 C3
Kothandaraswamy Temple...........4 D3
Ramanathaswamy Temple............5 B1

SLEEPING
Goswami Madam........................6 A1
Hotel Maharaja's.......................7 B2
Hotel Sri Saravana.....................8 B2
Hotel Tamil Nadu.......................9 C1
Pilgrims' Lodgings....................10 B2
Rooms Booking Office...............11 B1

EATING
Ashok Bhavan..........................12 B2
Bee Mavilas Hotel.....................13 B2

TRANSPORT
Bicycle Hire...........................(see 14)
Local Bus Stand.......................14 B1

TAMIL NADU

and some straggling fishing shanties, there's not much here, but it's a pleasant walk to the end of the peninsula where you can gaze out at **Adam's Bridge**, the chain of reefs, sandbanks and islets that almost connects Sri Lanka with India, 33km away. Legend says that these are the stepping stones created by Rama to follow Ravana, in his bid to rescue Sita in the epic Ramayana. Buses (Rs 5, hourly) from the local bus stand on East Car St stop about 4km before the beach so you have to walk the rest of the way. Otherwise, an autorickshaw (45 minutes one way) costs Rs 250 return, including one hour waiting time.

About 10km before Dhanushkodi, the **Kothandaraswamy Temple** is the only structure to survive the 1964 cyclone that destroyed the village. Legend has it that Rama, overcome with guilt at having killed Ravana, performed a *puja* on this spot and thereafter the temple was built. It is also believed that Vibhishana, brother of Sita's kidnapper Ravana, surrendered to Rama here.

GANDAMADANA PARVATHAM

This **temple**, located 3km northwest of Rameswaram, is a shrine reputedly containing Rama's footprints. The two-storey *mandapa* is on a small hill – the highest point on the island – and has good views out over the coastal landscape. Pilgrims visit here at dawn and dusk.

To visit the temple, it's an easy and interesting bicycle ride through the backstreets of villages and past the humungous TV transmitter.

Activities

At **Childrens Park Beach**, a shady stretch of relatively clean sand with a few swings and fishing boats, touts hang around offering a two-hour **snorkelling trip**. This amounts to a short paddle out in a canoe to a virtually nonexistent reef, but it's fun to go for a swim and you might see some fish. The going rate is about Rs 100 per person for two people.

Festivals & Events

Car Festival (Feb/Mar) During the festival, a huge decorated chariot with idols of the deities installed is hauled through the streets in a pulsating parade.

Thiru Kalyana (Jul/Aug) This festival celebrates the celestial marriage of Shiva and Parvati.

TAMIL NADU

Sleeping & Eating

Hotels, mainly geared towards pilgrims, are often booked out during festivals. Don't come here expecting anything resembling luxury – there are no upmarket hotels and at the budget end the choices are a bit grim. Near the temple, music blasts out from 4.30am and for most of the day.

The cheapest places to stay are the pilgrims' lodgings run by the temple, where basic double rooms are Rs 100 to 200. There's a **rooms booking office** (East Car St) opposite the main temple entrance.

Goswami Madam (☎ 221108; goswamimm@sanchar .net.in; West St; r without/with AC Rs 125/555; ✿) A spare and clean guesthouse funded and maintained by private Hindu donors, this is an oasis of calm about 10 minutes' walk from the temple, where all guests are welcome.

Hotel Maharaja's (☎ 221271; 7 Middle St; d without/ with AC incl tax Rs 294/519; ✿) Near the temple's west entrance, this is one of Rameswaram's better choices and is reasonably priced. Rooms are simple and most open out onto a common balcony though some have private balconies – the upper floors have good temple views.

Hotel Sri Saravana (☎ 223367; South Car St; r without/ with AC from Rs 315/600; ✿) New in 2006, this hotel has a rooftop overlooking the ocean and cool, clean, tiled rooms; good value and one of the few with sea views.

Hotel Tamil Nadu (☎ 221277; Sannathi St; dm Rs 80, d without/with AC from Rs 300/700; ✿) The breezy ocean-front location is the main reason to choose this hotel. The rooms are worn, but most have balconies or sit-outs and the staff is refreshingly cheery. It's extremely popular with pilgrims, so book if you can. The restaurant (mains Rs 10 to 75, open breakfast, lunch and dinner) has all the atmosphere of a school canteen but it's very popular for its thalis (Rs 30) and is one of the few places in town serving a range of nonveg food such as butter chicken (Rs 60), local fish and (sometimes) chips, and noodles. There's also a bar (open 6pm to 10pm).

A number of inexpensive vegetarian restaurants along West Car St, such as Ashok Bhavan, serve thalis (Rs 15). Bee Mavilas Hotel is a basic, local lunch place that serves fish fries, curries and decent biryanis.

Getting There & Away

BUS

Buses run to Madurai every 10 minutes (Rs 49, four hours). There are SETC buses to Chennai (Rs 228, 12 hours, one daily), Kanyakumari (Rs 108, 10 hours, two daily) and Trichy every half-hour (Rs 82, seven hours).

There are also private buses and minibuses from the town centre to Chennai (Rs 400) and Madurai (Rs 125).

TRAIN

Rameswaram's train line was closed in 2006 for an upgrade to broad gauge. It will take at least a couple of years to reopen.

Getting Around

Town buses (Rs 1) travel between the temple and the bus stand from early morning until late at night. Cycling is a good way to get around with many stalls renting old rattlers for Rs 5 per hour – there's one opposite the temple entrance on East Car St, near the local bus stand.

MADURAI

☎ 0452 / pop 1.19 million

Famous for the awe-inspiring Sri Meenakshi Temple complex, Madurai is an animated city packed with pilgrims, beggars, business-people, bullock carts and underemployed rickshaw drivers. It's one of South India's oldest cities and has been a centre of learning and pilgrimage for centuries. A textile centre from way back, the city was also the setting for Mahatma Gandhi's decision, in 1921, to wear nothing but *khadi* (homespun cloth), and tailors' shops are everywhere in town.

Madurai's landmark temple in the heart of the old town is a riotously baroque example of Dravidian architecture with *gopurams* covered from top to bottom in a breathtaking profusion of multicoloured images of gods, goddesses, animals and mythical figures. The temple seethes with activity from dawn to dusk, its many shrines attracting pilgrims and tourists from all over the world; 10,000 visitors may come here on any one day.

Madurai is on virtually every traveller's Tamil Nadu itinerary – it has excellent transport links and some good midrange accommodation – but be prepared for oppressive touts.

History

Tamil and Greek documents record the existence of Madurai from the 4th century BC. It was popular for trade, especially in spices, and was also the home of the *sangam,* the

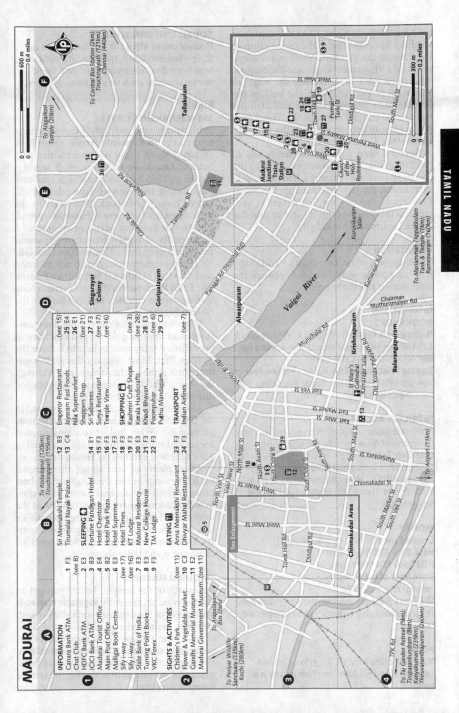

academy of Tamil poets. Over the centuries Madurai has come under the jurisdiction of the Cholas, the Pandyas, Muslim invaders, the Hindu Vijayanagar kings, and the Nayaks, who ruled until 1781. During the reign of Tirumalai Nayak (1623–55), the bulk of the Sri Meenakshi Temple was built, and Madurai became the cultural centre of the Tamil people, playing an important role in the development of the Tamil language.

Madurai then passed into the hands of the British East India Company. In 1840 the company razed the fort, which had previously surrounded the city, and filled in the moat. Four broad streets – the Veli streets – were constructed on top of this fill and to this day define the limits of the old city.

Orientation

The main post office, tourist office and many hotels are conveniently wedged between the train station and the temple.

Information

BOOKSHOPS

Malligai Book Centre (11 West Veli St; 🕙 9am-2pm & 4.30-9pm Mon-Sat) Opposite the train station, with a fair selection of books, maps and cassettes.

Turning Point Books (Town Hall Rd; 🕙 10am-9pm Mon-Sat) A 4th-floor bookshop opposite New College with many English-language titles.

INTERNET ACCESS

There are internet places everywhere in town. Convenient ones include the following:

Chat Club (Town Hall Rd; per hr Rs 20; 🕙 9am-11.30pm) Below Turning Point Books.

Sify i-way (110 & 114 West Perumal Maistry St; per hr Rs 30; 🕙 7am-11pm & 24hr) Adjoining Park Plaza and Supreme hotels.

MONEY

Canara Bank ATM (West Perumal Maistry St)

HDFC Bank ATM (West Veli St)

ICICI Bank ATM (North Chitrai St)

State Bank of India (West Veli St) Has foreign-exchange desks and an ATM.

VKC Forex (Zulaiha Towers, Town Hall Rd; 🕙 9am-7pm) This is an efficient place to change travellers cheques and cash.

POST

Main post office (West Veli St; 🕙 9am-5pm Mon-Sat, parcel office 🕙 9.30am-7pm) Poste restante is at counter 8.

TOURIST INFORMATION

Madurai tourist office (☎ 2334757; 180 West Veli St; 🕙 10am-5pm Mon-Fri, 11am-1pm Sat) Helpful staff when they're there, with brochures and maps. Tourist counters of sorts are also at the train station and airport.

Sights

SRI MEENAKSHI TEMPLE

With its colourful, intricately carved temple towers, the **Sri Meenakshi Temple** (camera Rs 30; 🕙 6am-12.30pm & 4-9pm) is a spectacular pastiche of Dravidian architecture. It was designed in 1560 by Vishwanatha Nayak and built during the reign of Tirumalai Nayak, but its history goes back 2000 years to the time when Madurai was a Pandyan capital. The temple complex occupies an area of 6 hectares. Its 12 highly decorative *gopurams* range in height from 45m to 50m (the tallest is the southern tower) and are adorned with carvings of celestial and animal figures. The **Puthu Mandapam** in the east forms a long and impressive entrance hall that leads to the eastern *gopuram*.

Within the walls of the temple, long corridors lead towards gold-topped sanctums of the deities. It is the custom here to honour the goddess first. Most pilgrims therefore enter the temple at the southeastern corner, through the Ashta Shakti Mandapam, and proceed directly to the Meenakshi shrine.

Also within the temple complex, housed in the 1000-Pillared Hall, is the **Temple Art Museum** (admission Rs 7; 🕙 7am-7pm). It contains painted friezes and stone and brass images, as well as one of the best exhibits on Hindu deities.

Allow plenty of time to see this temple. Early mornings or late evenings are the best times to avoid crowds, and there's often classical dance somewhere in the complex at the weekends. 'Temple guides' charge negotiable fees, rarely below Rs 200, so prepare to negotiate and be aware that they are often a front for emporiums and tailor shops.

MADURAI MARKETS

Just north of the temple, before you get to North Avani St, the daily **vegetable market** is a labyrinth of bustling laneways strewn with aromatic herbs and vegetables. In the thick of it, on the 1st floor of a nondescript cement building, is the gorgeous **flower market**. Vendors dexterously heap mountains of marigolds and jasmine onto scales for the temple flower sellers here.

TIRUMALAI NAYAK PALACE

Located about 1.5km southeast of the Meenakshi Temple, this Indo-Saracenic **palace** (Indian/foreigner Rs 10/50, camera/video Rs 30/100; ☉ 9am-1pm & 2-5pm) was built in 1636 by the ruler whose name it bears. Today, only the imposing entrance gate, main hall and Natakasala (Dance Hall) remain. The rectangular courtyard, 75m by 52m, is known as the Swargavilasa or Celestial Pavilion and it gives clues to the original grandeur of the building, regarded as one of the finest secular buildings in South India.

There's a nightly **sound-and-light show** (Rs 10) which can be fun; the mosquitoes and people carrying on conversations throughout come at no extra cost. The English version is at 6.45pm and it's in Tamil at 8pm. The palace is a 20-minute walk from the temple.

MUSEUMS

Housed in the *tamukkam* (old exhibition pavilion), of the Rani Mangammal is the excellent **Gandhi Memorial Museum** (admission free, camera Rs 50; ☉ 10am-1pm & 2-5.30pm), set in spacious and relaxing grounds. The maze of rooms contains an impressively moving and detailed account of India's struggle for Independence from 1757 to 1947, and the English-language signs pull no punches about British rule. Included in the exhibition is the blood-stained dhoti (long loincloth) that Gandhi was wearing at the time he was assassinated in Delhi; it's here because he first took up wearing the dhoti in Madurai in 1921. The **Gandhian Literary Society Bookstore** (☉ closed Sun) is behind the museum.

The **Madurai Government Museum** (Indian/foreigner Rs 10/100; ☉ 9.30am-5.30pm, closed Fri) is next door in the same grounds. Inside is a dusty collection of archaeological finds, sculpture, bronzes, costumes and paintings. A shady **children's park** (admission Rs 2; ☉ 10am-8pm) with pay-as-you-go rides and slides is alongside the museums' entrance driveway.

MARIAMMAN TEPPAKKULAM TANK

This vast tank, 5km east of the old city, covers an area almost equal to that of Sri Meenakshi Temple and is the site of the popular **Teppam (Float) Festival**, held in January/February, when devotees boat out to the goddess temple in the middle. When it's empty (most of the year) it becomes a cricket ground for local kids. The tank was built by Tirumalai Nayak in 1646 and is connected to the Vaigai River by underground channels.

Tours

The tourist office organises half-day sightseeing tours that include the Tirumalai Nayak Palace and Gandhi Memorial Museum, and finish at the Sri Meenakshi Temple. Tours start at 7am and 3pm and cost Rs 125 per person (minimum six people).

Sleeping

Most of Madurai's accommodation is concentrated in the area between the train station and the Sri Meenakshi Temple. There are loads of places to stay, with plenty of good hotels in the midrange bracket that are reasonably priced and excellent value.

BUDGET

Town Hall Rd, running eastwards from the train station, has a knot of cheap and not-so-cheerful hotels.

KT Lodge (☎ 2345387; 29 Town Hall Rd; s/d Rs 185/250) Upstairs rooms are good value here, big and airy, with TV. It's right in the thick of things, so you'll need your earplugs.

Hotel Times (☎ 2342651; 15-16 Town Hall Rd; s Rs 190, d Rs 300-420; ✄) Hotel Times is a gloomy place, but it's reasonably clean and mercifully quiet if you stay towards the back. Avoid the windowless rooms.

TM Lodge (☎ 2341651; www.maduraitmlodge.com; 50 West Perumal Maistry St; s/d Rs 200/320, d with AC & TV Rs 550; ✄) One of the brighter budget places in the area, this is efficiently run with clean linen and reasonably well-kept rooms. The upper rooms are definitely lighter and airier, some with private sit-outs.

New College House (☎ 2342971; collegehouse_mdu@yahoo.co.in; 2 Town Hall Rd; r without/with AC from Rs 200/670; ✄) This is a huge complex virtually opposite the train station. The 250 rooms are varied – from minuscule to spacious – so check out a few as the cheaper rooms are tired and old, and street noise penetrates.

MIDRANGE & TOP END

Madurai's best-value accommodation is in the midrange hotels along West Perumal Maistry St near the train station, and most offer free pick-ups from the airport or train. Rooms without AC are a bargain and worth making that step up from the budget joints. Most have rooftop restaurants with temple and sunset views.

Hotel Chentoor (☎ 2350490; www.hotelchentoor .com; 106 West Perumal Maistry St; s/d Rs 420/460, with AC from Rs 750/850; ☎) Chentoor is one of the first high-rise hotels you come to when walking north along West Perumal Maistry St. The standard rooms are smallish but very clean and comfortable, several AC rooms have temple views and balconies, and the rooftop restaurant is breezy.

Madurai Residency (☎ 2343140; www.madurairesidency.com; West Marret St; r with AC from Rs 425/490, r with AC from Rs 850; ☎) This is a good-value hotel, with bright, clean rooms – some with temple view – and the highest rooftop restaurant views in town. Breakfast is included with AC rooms.

Hotel Supreme (☎ 2343151; www.supremehotels.com; 110 West Perumal Maistry St; s/d from Rs 460/500, r with AC from Rs 840; ☎) This is another large, well-presented hotel though its growing popularity has brought a noticeable decline in service. However, rooms are comfortable with large windows; many of the AC rooms have balconies and great temple views. Its restaurant is popular and there's a bar decked out like a spaceship!

Hotel Park Plaza (☎ 3011111; www.hotelparkplaza.net; 114 West Perumal Maistry St; s/d Rs 1075/1350; ☎) The Plaza's lobby is slightly more upmarket than its neighbours, and rooms are standard midrange, comfortable and simply furnished. The front rooms have temple views from the 3rd floor up. There's a good rooftop restaurant and the (inappropriately named) Sky High Bar – on the 1st floor.

Fortune Pandiyan Hotel (☎ 2537090; www.fortunepandiyanhotel.com; Alargakoil Rd; s/d Rs 2500/3000; ☎ ☎) New in 2005, one of this smart hotel's big draws is a clean swimming pool in a garden setting. Nonguests can use it for Rs 100, and there's a women-only session between 11am and 1pm daily; there's also exercise equipment in the fitness room.

our pick **Taj Garden Retreat** (☎ 2371601; www.tajhotels.com; 40 TPK Rd; s/d from Rs 3700/4200; ☎ ☎ ☎) In a stunning hilltop location of landscaped grounds and an 1890 colonial building, this is the best hotel in Madurai. Located 5km west of the city in Pasumalai, it's either peaceful or inconvenient, depending on your point of view.

Eating

Along West Perumal Maistry St, the rooftop restaurants of a string of hotels offer breezy night-time dining and temple views; most also have AC restaurants open for breakfast and lunch.

Jayaram Fast Foods (Dindigul Rd; mains Rs 25-75; ☎ lunch & dinner) With a busy bakery downstairs and a spotless AC restaurant upstairs, this makes a pleasant change from thali places. Ice cream and fruit salad is a favourite with families and courting couples, and the menu includes soups, spring rolls, pizzas and burgers.

Surya Restaurant (110 West Perumal Maistry St; mains Rs 30-70; ☎ dinner) The rooftop restaurant of Hotel Supreme offers a superb view over the city, multicuisine veg food including pasta, spectacular lunchtime thalis and cold beer.

Dhivyar Mahal Restaurant (☎ 2342700; 21 Town Hall Rd; mains Rs 30-80; ☎ lunch & dinner) One of the better multicuisine restaurants not attached to a hotel, Dhivyar Mahal is clean and bright. Roast leg of lamb (Rs 80) makes an interesting change, half tandoori chicken is Rs 80 and prawn masala is Rs 75.

Emperor Restaurant (☎ 2350490; 106 West Perumal Maistry St; mains Rs 30-80; ☎ breakfast, lunch & dinner) An all-day rooftop dining area, the restaurant at the Hotel Chentoor appears to be an afterthought, but the food, views and service are all good and nonveg food is served.

Temple View (☎ 3011111; 114 West Perumal Maistry St; mains Rs 55-140; ☎ dinner) The nightly rooftop restaurant at the Hotel Park Plaza serves multicuisine veg and nonveg dishes. Butter chicken masala is Rs 80 and the tandoori chicken (half a chicken Rs 110) is especially succulent.

Taj Garden Retreat (☎ 2371601; www.tajhotels.com; 40 TPK Rd; mains from Rs 150; ☎ breakfast, lunch & dinner) The indoor/outdoor restaurant is perched in the gardens above the city, with stunning sunset views. If you're hankering for spag and salad in relaxed surrounds, this is the place to come.

Among the cheap and cheerful South Indian veg restaurants in the old town is **Anna Meenakshi Restaurant** (West Perumal Maistry St), a busy place good for thalis (Rs 30). **Sree Sabarees** (West Perumal Maistry St) always has a crowd at the outside chai and snacks stand; stop by for a cuppa (Rs 3.50) or eat veg food inside.

Shoppers Shop (Town Hall Rd; ☎ 8am-11pm) and **Nila Supermarket** (Algarkoil Rd; ☎ 7am-11pm) are well-stocked grocery stores including a good selection of Western foods.

Shopping

Madurai teems with cloth stalls and tailors' shops. A great place for getting cottons and printed fabrics is Puthu Mandapam, the pillared former entrance hall at the eastern side of Sri Meenakshi Temple. Here you'll find rows of tailors, all busily treadling away and capable of whipping up a good replica of whatever you're wearing in an hour or two. Quality, designs and prices vary greatly depending on the material and complexity of the design, but you can have a shirt made up for Rs 150.

The fixed-price government shops are conveniently located together in West Veli St, including Poompuhar, Kerala Handicrafts and Khadi Bhavan (*khadi* is the homespun cloth made famous by Gandhi's decision, taken in Madurai, to wear it). Every tout, driver, temple guide and tailor's brother will lead you to the Kashmiri craft shops in North Chitrai St, offering to show you the temple view from the rooftop – the views are good, and so is the inevitable sales pitch.

Getting There & Away
AIR
Indian Airlines (☎ 2341234, airport 2690771; West Veli St; ☺ 10am-5pm Mon-Sat) flies daily to Mumbai and Chennai. Jet Airways also flies daily to Chennai, as does newcomer **Paramount Airways** (☎ 1800 180 1234; www.paramountairways.com). Air Deccan flies daily to Bengaluru. None of these airlines three has an office in town, but airport counters open at flight times.

BUS
Most long-distance buses arrive and depart from the **central bus station** (☎ 2580680; Melur Rd), 6km northeast of the old city. It appears chaotic but is actually a well-organised 24-hour operation. Local buses shuttle into the city every few minutes for Rs 2. Autorickshaw drivers charge Rs 70.

Private bus companies offer superdeluxe coaches with video services to Chennai and Bengaluru (Rs 220 to 300) but the state bus companies have similar services and while travel agencies sell tickets – often at an inflated price – you may end up on a state bus anyway. The table, right, lists prices for government buses; some express services run to Bengaluru, Chennai, Mysore and Puducherry.

The Arapalayam bus stand, northwest of the train station on the river bank, has hourly buses to Kumili (Rs 45, 4½ hours) for the Periyar Wildlife Sanctuary. There are regular stopping services to Coimbatore (Rs 75, six hours) and to Kodaikanal, with an express to Kodaikanal leaving daily at 12.45pm (Rs 40, four hours). Buses to Palani leave every half-hour (Rs 35, five hours).

BUSES FROM MADURAI			
Destination	**Fare (Rs)**	**Duration (hr)**	**Frequency**
Bengaluru	182	12	4 daily
Chennai	144-186	10	every 30min
Chidambaram	85	8	3 daily
Kochi	144	8	2 daily
Kanyakumari	90	6	hourly
Mysore	260	16	1 daily (via Ooty)
Puducherry	105	8	2 daily
Rameswaram	59	4	every 30min
Tirupathi	180	5½	6 daily
Trichy	40	3	every 10min
Trivandrum	215	9	2 daily

TRAIN
Madurai Junction is on the main Chennai–Kanyakumari line. There are at least nine daily trains to Chennai, including the overnight *Pearl City Express* (sleeper/3AC Rs 200/550, 10 hours) at 10.30pm and the *Vaigai Express* (2nd class/chair class Rs 114/397, eight hours) at 6.45am. Chennai trains stop at Trichy (2nd class/sleeper Rs 47/75, three hours). To Kanyakumari there are three daily services (sleeper/3AC Rs 107/300, six hours).

Other services include Madurai to Coimbatore (2nd class/sleeper Rs 62/98, 6½ hours) and Bengaluru (sleeper/3AC Rs 179/502), as well as Trivandrum and Mumbai.

Getting Around
The airport is 12km south of town and taxis cost Rs 200 to the town centre. Autorickshaws ask around Rs 100. Alternatively, bus 10A from the central bus station goes to the airport but don't rely on it being on schedule.

Central Madurai is small enough to get around on foot.

KANYAKUMARI (CAPE COMORIN)
☎ 04652 / pop 19,678

Approached through a surreal landscape of wind farms, Kanyakumari is the 'Land's End' of the Indian subcontinent, where the Bay of Bengal meets the Indian Ocean and the Arabian Sea. Chaitrapurnima (Tamil for the April full-moon day) is the time to experience simultaneous sunset and moonrise over the ocean.

Kanyakumari has great spiritual significance for Hindus, and is dedicated to the goddess Devi Kanya, an incarnation of Parvati. Pilgrims come here to visit the temple and bathe in the sacred waters. Although wildly overdeveloped, the town and fishing beaches still manage a certain relaxed charm and there's enough to keep you occupied for a day or so.

Orientation & Information

The main temple is right on the point of Kanyakumari and leading north from it is a small bazaar lined with restaurants, stalls and souvenir shops.

Internet (Main Rd; per hr Rs 50; ☽ 10am-8pm) Slow and expensive internet access.

Janaki Forex (☽ 9.30am-6pm Mon-Sat) Off South Car St. Change cash and travellers cheques here.

Post office (Main Rd; ☽ 8am-6pm Mon-Fri) About 300m north of the tourist office.

Sea Gate Net (per hr Rs 20; ☽ 9am-9pm) Slow but less expensive internet access here, opposite the Vivekanandapuram entrance gate.

State Bank of India ATM (Main Rd)

Tourist office (☎ 246276; Main Rd; ☽ 8am-6pm Mon-Fri) Get a useful, free *In and Around Kanniyakumari* brochure here.

Sights & Activities

KUMARI AMMAN TEMPLE

According to legend, the *kanya* (virgin) goddess Devi single-handedly conquered demons and secured freedom for the world. At this **temple** (☽ 4.30am-12.30pm & 4-8pm) pilgrims give her thanks for the safety and liberty she at-

KANYAKUMARI (CAPE COMORIN)

0 .... 200 m
0 .... 0.1 miles

INFORMATION	
Internet....................................1	B2
Janaki Forex...........................2	C2
Post Office..............................3	B2
State Bank of India ATM.........4	B2
Tourist Office.........................5	B3

SIGHTS & ACTIVITIES	
Gandhi Memorial....................6	B4
Government Museum..............7	B3
Kumari Amman Temple...........8	C4
Statue of Thiruvalluvar...........9	C4
Vivekananda Exhibition.........10	B3
Vivekananda Memorial..........11	D4

SLEEPING	
Hotel Maadhini.....................12	C2
Hotel Samudra......................13	C3
Hotel Seaview.......................14	C2
Hotel Tamil Nadu..................15	A3
Manickhan Tourist Home.......16	C2
Saravana Lodge....................17	C3
TTDC Youth Hostel...............18	B3
Vivekas Tourist Hotel............19	B1

EATING	
Archana Restaurant.........(see 12)	
Hotel Saravana 1..................20	C3
Hotel Saravana 2..................21	C3
Hotel Seaview................(see 14)	

TRANSPORT	
Autorickshaw Stand..............22	B2
Bus Stand.............................23	A2
SETC Booking Office.............24	B3

To Nagercoil (18km)

Kanyakumari Train Station

Gunganatham Temple

To Vivekanandapuram (1km); Vivekananda Kendra (1km); Sea Gate Net (1km); Thiruvananthapuram (87km); Madurai (235km)

Playing Fields

To Catholic Church (50m)

Tank

Hospital

To Baywatch (1.5km)

Kovalam Rd

Police Station

Main Rd

South Car St

East Car St

Samnathi St

Vinayakar Kovil Temple

Main Bazaar

Ferry Jetty

Beach Rd

Lookout

ARABIAN SEA

Bay of Bengal

Ghats

Mandapam & Bathing Ghats

INDIAN OCEAN

TAMIL NADU

tained for them. Unusually, men must remove their shirts here. Cameras are forbidden.

In May/June there is a **Car Festival** where an idol of the deity is taken in procession.

GANDHI MEMORIAL

This striking **memorial** (admission by donation; ☻ 7am-7pm) resembling an Orissan temple and with elements of Hindu, Islamic and Christian architecture in its design, was used to store some of the Mahatma's ashes. Each year, on Gandhi's birthday (2 October), the sun's rays fall on the memorial stone where his ashes were safely kept. Guides may ask for an excessive donation, but Rs 10 is enough.

VIVEKANANDA EXHIBITION & VIVEKANANDAPURAM

In a quirky, purpose-built terracotta building, this **exhibition** (Main Rd; admission Rs 2; ☻ 8am-noon & 4-8pm) details the life and extensive journey across India made by the Indian philosopher Swami Vivekananda (the 'Wandering Monk'; 1863–1902), who developed a synthesis between the tenets of Hinduism and concepts of social justice. Although the storyboards are labelled in English, there's a lot to digest in one visit; if you're overwhelmed, concentrate on enjoying the photos and Swamiji's letters.

A more interesting pictorial exhibition can usually be found at **Vivekanandapuram** (☎ 247012; admission free; ☻ 9am-1pm & 5-9pm), a spiritual mission and ashram 3km north of town. The exhibition was closed for renovation in late 2006, but – when open – covers not only the life of Vivekananda in prints, sketches and pictures but is a snapshot of Indian philosophy, religion, leaders and thinkers.

VIVEKANANDA MEMORIAL

This **memorial** (admission Rs 10; ☻ 8am-5pm) is on a rocky island about 400m offshore. Swami Vivekananda meditated here in 1892 before setting out to become one of India's most important religious crusaders. The *mandapam*, which was built here in Vivekananda's memory in 1970, reflects architectural styles from all over India. Regardless of the number of pilgrims filing through the memorial, it remains a very peaceful and reverent place. From the island there's a fine view back over the fishing harbour and to distant mountains and wind turbines.

The huge **statue** on the smaller island is not of Vivekananda but of Tamil poet Thiruval-

luvar. India's 'Statue of Liberty' was the work of more than 5000 sculptors. It was erected in 2000 and honours the poet's 133-chapter work *Thirukural* – hence its height of exactly 133ft (40.5m).

Ferries shuttle between the port and the islands between 8am and 4pm; the cost is Rs 20 for the circuit.

GOVERNMENT MUSEUM

The **museum** (Main Rd; Indian/foreigner Rs 5/100; ☻ 9.30am-5.30pm Sat-Thu) houses a standard display of archaeological finds and temple artefacts.

BAYWATCH

Tired of temples? This impressive **amusement park** (☎ 246563; www.baywatch.co.in; adult/child Rs 240/180; ☻ 10am-7pm) is a great way to spend the day, especially if you've got kids in tow. The entry ticket gives unlimited access to a wave pool with water slides (women should swim in at least knee-length shorts and shirt for propriety!) and a host of rides. Its adjacent **wax museum** (adult/child Rs 50/40), the first and – as we write – the only one in India, contains figures of notable nationals.

Sleeping

Some hotels, especially the midrange places around the bazaar, have seasonal rates, so you may find that prices double here during April and May, and late October to January. Many places also charge more for a 'sea view' or 'rock view' and few offer single rates.

BUDGET

TTDC Youth Hostel (☎ 246257; dm Rs 50) This hostel is part of Hotel Tamil Nadu. The dormitories and common bathrooms are pretty dire but you can't beat the price and the location is great.

Vivekananda Kendra (☎ 247177; ngc_vkendra@sancharnet.in; Vivekanandapuram; dm Rs 75, r from Rs 150, with AC from Rs 500; ✵) Though 2km from town, this big ashram guesthouse trumps other budget places in terms of peace, quiet and general cleanliness; the three-bed AC room (Rs 700) with private sitting room is great value. Spacious grounds with peacocks lead down to a sunrise viewpoint of the ocean and statue. A free shuttle bus runs hourly into town.

Vivekas Tourist Hotel (☎ 246192; Main Rd; d from Rs 195) Rooms here are simple but very spacious and reasonably clean; it's just opposite the train station.

Saravana Lodge (☎ 246007; Sannathi St; r Rs 200-300) Just outside the temple entrance all rooms have TV and private bathroom with squat toilet; it's very clean and good value. Go for the breezy upstairs rooms.

MIDRANGE & TOP END

Hotel Tamil Nadu (☎ 246257; Beach Rd; r without/with AC Rs 450/750; 🗙) Despite the usual quirks of a government-run hotel, this is a great location if you want to be a beachfront walk away from the chaos of town; balcony rooms have ocean, though not temple, views.

Hotel Samudra (☎ 246162; Sannathi St; r without/with sea view Rs 470/670, with AC Rs 970; 🗙) Right in the bazaar and near the temple, this hotel is a bit faded but the rooms (especially those overlooking the tank and temple) and service are fine.

Manickhan Tourist Home (☎ 246387; d without/with AC Rs 550/1100; 🗙) Many of the rooms at this friendly hotel have been recently and flamboyantly renovated. Most have balconies and many overlook the ocean.

Hotel Maadhini (☎ 246787; East Car St; r ground fl/sea view Rs 500/700, with AC from Rs 1200; 🗙) Next door to Manickhan Tourist Home, this hotel offers much the same, plus an excellent garden restaurant.

Hotel Seaview (☎ 247841; seaview@sancharnet.in; East Car St; d without/with AC Rs 1400/1950, with sea view Rs 1750/2550; 🗙) The deliciously cool marble lobby signals that this is one of the top places to stay in town. Rooms are neat, clean and well furnished but you pay more for the sea views here than elsewhere.

Eating

There are plenty of fruit stalls and basic veg restaurants in the bazaar area, open for breakfast, lunch and dinner.

Archana Restaurant (East Car St; mains Rs 25-95) At the Hotel Maadhini, this restaurant is one of the more atmospheric places to eat, especially in the evening when the garden section is open. There's a good menu including tandoori chicken, seafood and Chinese, and you can watch chapatis (unleavened Indian bread) being made before your eyes.

Hotel Seaview (East Car St; mains Rs 30-150) This upmarket hotel also has an excellent AC multicuisine restaurant specialising in fresh local seafood.

Hotel Saravana has two clean, busy veg restaurants with thalis (Rs 25) and good chai.

BUSES FROM KANYAKUMARI (CAPE COMORIN)			
Destination	Fare (Rs)	Duration (hr)	Frequency
Bengaluru	333	15	1 daily
Chennai	280	16	6 daily
Kodaikanal	132	10	1 daily
Kovalam	40	3½	1 daily
Madurai	76	6	8 daily
Rameswaram	108	9	2 daily
Trivandrum	31	3	2 daily

Getting There & Away

BUS

The surprisingly sedate bus stand is a 10-minute walk west of the centre along Kovalam Rd and there's a handy **SETC booking office** (⏱ 7am-9pm) on Main Rd. For details of services, see the table, above.

TRAIN

The train station is about 1km north of the bazaar and temple. The daily *Chennai Egmore Express* departs for Chennai at 5.15pm (sleeper/2AC/3AC Rs 189/321/1026, 13 hours) and the 6.35am *Tiruchirappalli–Howrah Express* to Chennai departs on Saturday. The same trains stop at Madurai and Trichy.

To Trivandrum there are two daily express trains (2nd class/3AC Rs 33/183, two hours, 87km).

For the real long-haulers or train buffs, the weekly *Himsagar Express* runs all the way to Jammu Tawi (in Jammu and Kashmir), a distance of 3734km, in 66 hours – the longest single train ride in India.

THE WESTERN GHATS

The Western Ghats stretch out like a mountainous spine for around 1400km from the north of Mumbai, across Maharashtra, Goa, Karnataka and Kerala, before petering out at the southernmost tip of Tamil Nadu. The hills (with an average elevation of 915m) are covered with evergreen and deciduous forest, and are the source of all the major rivers in South India. They also form a diverse biological and ecological haven with 27% of all India's flowering plants, 60% of all medicinal plants and an incredible array of endemic wildlife, along with several tribal groups whose traditional lifestyle is fast being eroded.

For travellers these mountain areas mean opportunities to trek and see wildlife, and to hang out in Tamil Nadu's climatically cool hill stations of Ooty and Kodaikanal.

KODAIKANAL (KODAI)

☎ 04542 / pop 32,931 / elev 2100m

Kodaikanal is a stunningly situated and easy-going hill station on the southern crest of the Palani knolls, some 120km northwest of Madurai. It's surrounded by wooded slopes, waterfalls and precipitous rocky outcrops and the winding route up and down is breathtaking.

TAMIL NADU

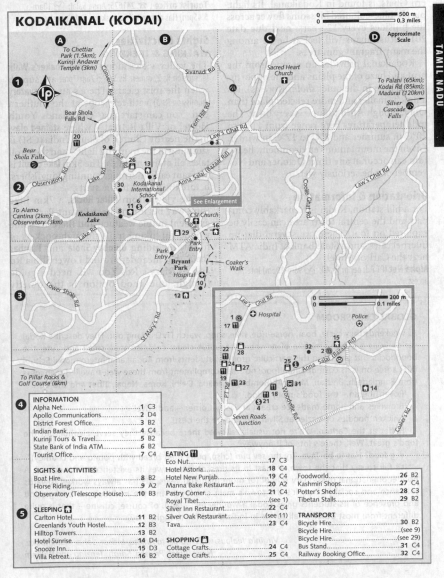

KODAIKANAL (KODAI)

INFORMATION
Alpha Net	1 C3
Apollo Communications	2 D4
District Forest Office	3 B2
Indian Bank	4 C4
Kurinji Tours & Travel	5 B2
State Bank of India ATM	6 B2
Tourist Office	7 C4

SIGHTS & ACTIVITIES
Boat Hire	8 B2
Horse Riding	9 A2
Observatory (Telescope House)	10 B3

SLEEPING
Carlton Hotel	11 B2
Greenlands Youth Hostel	12 B3
Hilltop Towers	13 B2
Hotel Sunrise	14 D4
Snooze Inn	15 D3
Villa Retreat	16 B2

EATING
Eco Nut	17 C3
Hotel Astoria	18 C4
Hotel New Punjab	19 C4
Manna Bake Restaurant	20 A2
Pastry Corner	21 C4
Royal Tibet	(see 1)
Silver Inn Restaurant	22 C4
Silver Oak Restaurant	(see 11)
Tava	23 C4

SHOPPING
Cottage Crafts	24 C4
Cottage Crafts	25 C4
Foodworld	26 B2
Kashmiri Shops	27 C4
Potter's Shed	28 C3
Tibetan Stalls	29 B2

TRANSPORT
Bicycle Hire	30 B2
Bicycle Hire	(see 9)
Bicycle Hire	(see 29)
Bus Stand	31 C4
Railway Booking Office	32 C4

Kodai is the only hill station in India set up by Americans, when missionaries established a school for European children here in 1901. The legacy of this is the renowned Kodaikanal International School, whose cosmopolitan influence is felt throughout the town.

The Kurinji shrub, unique to the Western Ghats, is found in Kodaikanal. Its light, purple-blue-coloured blossoms flower across the hillsides every 12 years; next due date 2018! Australians will feel at home among the many fragrant gum trees.

Kodaikanal provides an escape from the heat and haze of the plains and the opportunity to hike in the quiet *sholas* (forests). It's a much smaller and more relaxed place than Ooty, though April to June is *very* busy. The mild temperatures here range from 11°C to 20°C in summer and 8°C to 17°C in winter. Given the mountainous environment, heavy rain can occur at any time; October and November can be seriously wet.

Orientation & Information

For a hill station, Kodai is remarkably compact and the central town area can easily be explored on foot. There are several dial-up internet cafés, and a State Bank of India ATM near the Carlton Hotel.

Alpha Net (PT Rd; per hr Rs 40; ☑ 9am-10pm) Internet access.

Apollo Communications (Anna Salai; per hr Rs 40; ☑ 9am-8pm) Spacious internet access.

Indian Bank (Anna Salai; ☑ 10am-2pm & 2.30-3.30pm Mon-Fri, 10am-12.30pm Sat) With foreign-exchange desk.

Kurinji Tours & Travel (☎ 240008; kurinjitravels@san charnet.in; Lake Rd; ☑ 9am-6pm) Reliable help with onward travel arrangements.

Tourist office (☎ 241675; Anna Salai; ☑ 10am-5.45pm) Has answers if you ask the right questions.

Sights & Activities
WALKING & TREKKING

The valley views along paved **Coaker's Walk** (admission Rs 2, camera Rs 5; ☑ 7am-7pm) are superb when the mist clears. There's an **observatory** (admission Rs 3) with telescope at the southern end. You can start near Greenlands Youth Hostel or Villa Retreat – where **stained glass** in the nearby Church of South India (CSI) is stunning in the morning light – and the stroll takes all of five minutes. The 5km **lake circuit** is pleasant early morning, counting kingfishers, before the tourist traffic starts.

The views from **Pillar Rocks**, a 7km hike (one-way beginning near Bryant Park), are excellent in fine weather, and there are some wonderful hiking trails through pockets of forest, including **Bombay Shola** and **Pambar Shola**, that meander around Lower Shola Rd and St Mary's Rd. You will need a guide though; one good option is the quietly

---

GLOBAL CLASSROOM

At weekends they cycle, boat, horse-ride, hike, shop, watch DVDs, hang out. They describe Kodai variously as a bubble; middle of nowhere; beautiful; clean; cold; isolated; small and cute; the boondocks. But one thing this particular group of students from Kodaikanal International School (KIS) agree on is its cosmopolitan food; no small compliment from these well-travelled teenagers from Bangladesh, Bhutan, Mumbai (Bombay), Canada, Delhi, Korea, Nepal, Tibet and the USA.

'Royal Tibetan – the food's really good.'

'Brownies and home-made ice cream at Pastry Corner – addictive!'

'Chicken noodles or sizzler at Silver Inn; they're the best!'

'Buffet at the Carlton. We're not usually allowed there because they serve alcohol, but the food's great. Well, there's lots of it anyway.'

'Veg food? Has to be Tava. Try the *sev puri* (crisp, puffy fried bread with potato and chutney).'

It's fair to say that the town, at least in its present form, owes its existence to the school. A nondenominational missionary school for more than 100 years, KIS has always worked towards tolerance and social justice; it's the town's main employer; and the multicultural background and presence of its students gives Kodai a worldly feel – and, of course, cuisine – that is quite different from most other small towns in India. Food for thought, hey?

Virginia Jealous, with thanks to Ankita, Intisar, John, Mallimalika, Nitya, Preet, Prioska, Sarah, Tenzing and William

knowledgeable Vijay Kumar of **Nature Trails Kodai** (☎ 242791, 99942-77373; www.nature-trails.net; per person per hr Rs 50, minimum 2 people), or talk to the helpful folk at Manna Bake Restaurant (p430). Guides (per hour around Rs 70) of varying quality can also be arranged through the tourist office; its booklet *Trekking Routes in Kodaikanal* details walks ranging from 8km to 27km.

PARKS & WATERFALLS

Near the start of Coaker's Walk is **Bryant Park** (admission Rs 5; ☽ 9.30am-5pm), landscaped and stocked by the British officer after whom it is named. **Chettiar Park** (admission free; ☽ 8.30am-5pm), about 1.5km uphill from town on the way to the Kurinji Andavar Temple, is a small and pretty landscaped park. There are numerous waterfalls, at their most impressive after rain of course. **Silver Cascade**, on the road outside Kodai, is often full of interstate tourists bathing and the compact **Bear Shola Falls** is in a pocket of forest about a 20-minute walk from the town centre.

BOATING & HORSE RIDING

The lake at Kodai is beautifully landscaped and it appears to be *de rigueur* for families to get out on a boat. Both the Kodaikanal Boat & Rowing Club, and Tamil Nadu Tourist Development Corporation, rent similar boats for similar prices: Rs 20 to 40 for a two-seater pedal boat to Rs 140 (including boatman) for a Kashmiri *shikara* (covered gondola) for 30 minutes.

At the bicycle hire area by the lake you'll be accosted by guides renting horses. The fixed rate is Rs 130 per hour unaccompanied or Rs 200 with a guide but you can take a short ride for Rs 80. Some of these horses should be retired.

Sleeping

Hotel prices can jump by up to 300% during high season (from 1 April to 30 June). Prices listed here are low-season rates.

Most hotels in Kodai have a 9am or 10am checkout time in high season but for the rest of the year it's usually 24 hours.

BUDGET

Hotel Sunrise (☎ 241358; d Rs 200) This is a down-at-heel but friendly enough place, in a good location. The view from the front (though not from most of the simple rooms) is excellent.

Greenlands Youth Hostel (☎ 240899; dm Rs 100, d Rs 200-800) Near the southern end of Coaker's Walk, this remains the number-one choice for budget travellers, as much for the fine views as the cheap rooms. There's a crowded dormitory and a range of rooms from very basic doubles on the edge of the valley to more spacious rooms with balcony, fireplace and TV. Staff are cheery, the location is peaceful and treks can be arranged here.

Snooze Inn (☎ 240837; Anna Salai; d Rs 300-425) Snooze Inn is well run and good value, with a charming elderly gentleman often at the front desk. Rooms are plain but clean and all have TV; ask for one towards the back, these are quieter, with forest views.

MIDRANGE & TOP END

Villa Retreat (☎ 240940; www.villaretreat.com; Club Rd, Coaker's Walk; r Rs 690-890, cottages Rs 1890) At the northern end of Coaker's Walk, the terrace garden of this lovely old stone-built family hotel offers awesome valley views. The best rooms, somewhat overpriced, are the cottages with panoramic views. Most rooms have fireplaces and TV, and there's a cosy restaurant.

Hilltop Towers (☎ 240413; httowers@sancharnet.in; Club Rd; d/ste from Rs 750/1100) Near the Kodaikanal International School, Hilltop is a neat hotel with bright clean rooms and polished teak floors; those with views are particularly welcoming, as is the helpful staff.

Alamo Cantina (☎ 240566; the.alamo.kodai@gmail .com; r incl breakfast from Rs 1500) Just about ready to open when we visited, this quirky two-room log cabin – a 3km drive from town, but with a 20-minute walking short cut – is all terracotta, wood and bison horns, set in quiet pasture with forest behind.

Carlton Hotel (☎ 240056; www.krahejahospitality .com; Lake Rd; d/cottages Rs 3670/7150) Kodai's most prestigious hotel overlooks the lake, blending colonial style with five-star luxury and a price tag to match. Rooms are bright, spacious and some have private balconies with lake views. Leather chairs huddle around a central stone fireplace in the main lounge which adjoins an excellent bar, billiard room and restaurant. There's also a children's playground, gym, sauna, massage and private boathouse.

Eating

PT Rd is the best place for cheap restaurants and it's here that most travellers and students from the international school congregate.

There's a whole range of different cuisines available, including a strong Tibetan influence. Don't expect an early breakfast in Kodai outside of your hotel; not much gets up and running before 9.30am.

Manna Bake Restaurant (☎ 243766; Bear Shola Falls Rd; dishes Rs 20-50; ☷ breakfast & lunch daily, dinner only Mon-Sat, order by 3pm) This tiny family-run café is a must for its simple home-cooked Western vegetarian food (sandwiches, pizza and soup) and homely atmosphere. The wholemeal bread is legendary and many a cold and hungry traveller has gorged on Ivy's apple crumble and custard (Rs 35). It's a 15-minute walk from town near Bear Shola Falls (fork right off Observatory Rd, then right down a very steep lane *before* the entrance to Hotel Clifton), and tucked down a leafy driveway.

Hotel Astoria (☎ 240524; Anna Salai; mains Rs 20-50, thalis Rs 30-50; ☷ breakfast, lunch & dinner) The veg restaurant here is always packed at lunchtime for its excellent all-you-can-eat thalis.

Tava (PT Rd; mains Rs 30; ☷ lunch & dinner Thu-Tue) A clean, fast and cheap veg option, there's a wide menu here and it's often packed; try the cauliflower-stuffed *gobi paratha* (spicy cauliflower bread) and *sev puri* (crisp, puffy fried bread with potato and chutney).

Royal Tibet (PT Rd; ☷ lunch & dinner) A very popular place, this serves tasty noodle soups and other Himalayan fare; steamed *momo* (dumplings; Rs 40) are good.

Silver Inn Restaurant (☎ 241374; PT Rd; mains Rs 30-100; ☷ breakfast, lunch & dinner) This country-style, family-run restaurant is a great place for brunch (full English breakfast is Rs 150) and the menu ranges from homemade fettuccine and pizzas, huge and delicious sizzler plates (Rs 110) and good salad to Indian and Chinese dishes.

Hotel New Punjab (PT Rd; mains Rs 30-100; ☷ lunch & dinner) For North Indian and tandoori dishes this is the best place in Kodai. Succulent tandoori chicken is Rs 100.

Silver Oak Restaurant (☎ 240056; Lake Rd; buffet lunch & dinner Rs 350; ☷ breakfast, lunch & dinner) The restaurant at the Carlton Hotel puts on lavish buffet meals, though you might feel a bit out of place in hiking gear. After eating you can relax in the atmospheric bar or sit by the roaring fire in the lounge.

SELF-CATERING

Eco Nut (☎ 243296; PT Rd; ☷ 10am-5pm, closed Sun) This interesting shop sells a wide range of locally produced organic health food – wholewheat bread, muffins, cheese, salad greens – and essential oils, herbs and herb remedies.

Pastry Corner (Anna Salai; ☷ 9am-9pm) Pick up great picnic sandwiches and yummy brownies (Rs 5; after 3pm) here, or squeeze onto the benches with a cuppa to watch the world go by.

The local Sunday market, at the northern end of PT Rd, is a colourful riot of fresh produce, and **Foodworld** (Lake Rd; ☷ 9am-7.30pm) supermarket stocks pretty much everything else; there's also a Pastry Corner counter here.

Excellent homemade chocolates and dried fruit are sold all over town.

Shopping

The many handicraft stores stock good craftwork, and several reflect the local low-key but long-term commitment to social justice.

Cottage Crafts Shops (☎ 240160; Anna Salai & PT Rd; ☷ 10am-8pm) Run by the voluntary organisation Coordinating Council for Social Concerns in Kodai (Corsock), these shops sell goods crafted by disadvantaged groups; about 80% of purchase price returns to the craftspeople.

On PT Rd you'll find small Kashmiri shops, as well as the **Potter's Shed** (☷ 9am-8pm Thu-Tue, 9am-5pm Wed) with fine ceramics; proceeds go to help needy children.

By the lakeside entrance to Bryant Park Tibetan stalls sell warm clothing and shawls – good, cheap stuff to keep you warm on chilly nights.

Getting There & Away

The nearest train station is Kodai Road, at the foot of the mountain, where taxis (around Rs 800) and buses (Rs 10) wait. There's a train booking office in town.

Don't expect a bus to be leaving from Kodaikanal in the next five minutes. Tickets for private buses can be booked at travel agents near the bus stand. For details of main bus departures from Kodaikanal see the table, opposite.

Getting Around

The central part of Kodaikanal is compact and very easy to get around on foot. There are no autorickshaws (believe it or not) but plenty of taxis willing to take you to various sightseeing points. Charges are fixed and relatively high – the minimum charge is Rs 60, and sightseeing tours cost from Rs 300 for two hours to Rs 700 for six hours.

BUSES FROM KODAIKANAL (KODAI)			
Destination	**Fare (Rs)**	**Duration (hr)**	**Frequency**
Bengaluru	283	11	1 daily
Bengaluru *	450	11	1 daily
Chennai	203-400	11	2 daily
Coimbatore	50	5	1 daily
Kochi*	400	8	1 daily
Madurai	34	3½	hourly
Madurai*	150	3	2 daily
Ooty	250	8	1 daily
Palani	20	2	8 daily
Trichy	57	5	3 daily
*private buses			

If you fancy a ride around the lake or you're fit enough to tackle the hills, mountain bikes can be hired from several **bicycle stalls** (per hr/day Rs 10/75; ☹ 8am-6pm) around the lake.

AROUND KODAIKANAL

At the foothills of the Western Ghats, about three hours' drive below Kodaikanal off the Palani–Dindigul road, lies the extraordinary **Cardamom House** (☎ 0451-2556765, 09360-691793; www.cardamomhouse.com; r from Rs 2700). Created with love and care by a retired Brit, this low-key, comfortable guesthouse and gardens – at the end of a scenic road beside bird-rich Lake Kamarajar – runs on solar power, uses water wisely, farms organically, trains and employs only locals (who produce terrific meals), and supports several village development initiatives. You'll need to book well in advance, hire a driver to take you there, and prepare for some serious relaxation.

INDIRA GANDHI (ANNAMALAI) WILDLIFE SANCTUARY

One of three wildlife sanctuaries in the Western Ghats along the Tamil Nadu–Kerala border, this cool, misty mountain park covers almost 1000 sq km of mostly teak forest and evergreen jungle. It's home to elephants, gaurs, tigers, panthers, spotted deer, wild boars, bears, porcupines and civet cats, and the Nilgiri tahr – commonly known as the ibex – may also be spotted. The park also has a renowned medicinal plant garden and interpretive centre (check out the astrological medicine chart and beauty hints if you're feeling travel-weary), and is home to the tribal group of Kada people, many of whom

work here. The park's elephant training centre can be visited on the guided vehicle tour.

The **park reception centre** (per person Rs 50, camera/video Rs 10/50; ☹ day visitors 6am-6pm) at Topslip, where trekking guides can be arranged and where there are several lodges, is about 35km southwest of Pollachi. While wildlife is often seen on the drive in, and you can wander around the reception centre surroundings, access to the inner forest is limited to tours (Rs 625 for a 25-seater bus, irrespective of numbers; one hour) or guided treks (Rs 100, maximum four people, four hours). Tours and treks run on demand. A day visit from Pollachi, using public transport, is feasible (see below).

Sleeping & Eating

Forest accommodation is available at and near Topslip. It *must* be booked in advance in Pollachi at the **WWO** (☎ 04259-2225356; Meenkarai Rd; ☹ 9am-5pm Mon-Fri), but hours and service here are erratic at best. Rooms in several simple lodges at Topslip are Rs 300; the somewhat more comfortable New Tree Tops lodge is Rs 1000; and dorm beds are available for Rs 20 at Ambulli Illam, 2km from the reception centre. There's a basic canteen at Topslip.

It's a fairly good bet you'll need to overnight in Pollachi; try **Sakthi Hotels** (☎ 04259-223050; sakthifibreproducts@vsnl.net; Coimbatore Rd; d Rs 200, with AC Rs 495; 🖭).

Getting There & Away

The sanctuary is between Palani and Coimbatore. Regular buses travelling from both places stop at the nearest large town, Pollachi, which is also on the Coimbatore–Dindigul train line.

From Pollachi, buses leave the bus stand for Topslip at 6.15am, 11.15am and 3.15pm, returning at 9.30am, 1pm and 6.30pm. A taxi from Pollachi to the sanctuary costs around Rs 600 one way.

COIMBATORE

☎ 0422 / pop 1.46 million

Although a large business and industrial city, Coimbatore is mainly a transport junction for travellers – a convenient stop if you're heading to the hill stations of Ooty or Kodaikanal. Sometimes known as the Manchester of India for its textile industry, Coimbatore is an easygoing place with plenty of accommodation and eating options.

Information

Email facilities are available throughout the city, especially around the bus stands, and there are 24-hour ATMs dotted around the city.

Blazenet (Nehru St; per hr Rs 20; ☺ 9am-12.30pm) Internet access.

HSBC ATM (Racecourse Rd) Next to Annalakshmi Restaurant.

ICICI ATM (Avanashi Rd) Opposite Nilgiri's Nest.

Main post office (Railway Feeder Rd; ☺ 10am-8pm Mon-Sat, 10am-2pm Sun) A few hundred metres north-west of the train station, reached via a pedestrian underpass from the platforms.

Tourist office (☺ 10am-5.45pm) Small office inside the train station.

VKC Forex (Raheja Centre, Avanashi Rd; ☺ 10am-6pm Mon-Sat) Change cash and travellers cheques.

Sleeping

Low-budget and midrange accommodation is in abundance in the bus stand area and down the bustling and narrow Geetha Hall Rd, directly opposite the train station. More upmarket places are along Avanashi Rd.

New Vijaya Lodge (☎ 2301570; Geetha Hall Rd; s/d Rs 120/190) A basic but clean and friendly little hotel, this has good-value rooms with an internet café downstairs.

Hotel Vaidurya (☎ 4392777; www.hotelvaidurya.com; 73 Geetha Hall Rd; s/d from Rs 275/500, with AC Rs 650/750; ✷) Vaidurya is a smart midrange place, with small but pleasant rooms in the main building; the cheaper rooms in the annexe are less inviting.

Hotel Blue Star (☎ 2230635; 369A Nehru St; s/d from Rs 300/450, r with AC Rs 700; ✷) A sprawling hotel, this has simple, clean rooms; the top floor was recently renovated and is much nicer than downstairs. Management is friendly and it's convenient for the bus stands.

Legend's Inn (☎ 4350000; Geetha Hall Rd; s/d Rs 400/600, with AC Rs 750/850; ✷) New in 2005, this hotel is a gem with comfortable furnishings, bamboo blinds, and sparkling bathrooms (long may they last).

Nilgiri's Nest (☎ 2214309; nilgiris@md3.vsnl.net.in; 739A Avanashi Rd; s/d from Rs 1250/1500; ✷) This intimate, well-run hotel has comfortable rooms, an excellent restaurant and supermarket and food hall attached.

Residency (☎ 2201234; www.theresidency.com; 1076 Avanashi Rd; s/d from Rs 3200/3500; ✷ ▢ ✷) Coimbatore's finest hotel has all the trimmings, along with friendly staff and immaculate rooms. There's a well-equipped health club

COIMBATORE

INFORMATION
Blazenet.................................1 A3
HSBC ATM..........................(see 12)
ICICI ATM............................2 B5
Internet Cafés.....................3 B3
Internet Café.....................(see 9)
Main Post Office................4 A6
VKC Forex..........................5 B5

SLEEPING
Hotel Blue Star..................6 A3
Hotel Vaidurya..................7 B6
Legend's Inn......................8 A6
New Vijaya Lodge.............9 A6
Nilgiri's Nest......................10 B5
Residency..........................11 B5

EATING
Annalakshmi Restaurant...12 B5
Gayathiri Bhavan...............13 A3
Malabar..............................14 A3

TRANSPORT
Central Bus Station............15 B4
Thiruvalluvar Bus Station...16 B3
Town Bus Stand.................17 B3
Ukkadam Bus Station........18 A6

and pool, two excellent restaurants, a coffee shop and a bookshop in the lobby.

Eating

There are numerous places around the train station serving thalis for around Rs 25. Another good place for inexpensive restaurants is along Sastri Rd and Nehru St just north of the central bus station. Avanashi Rd is Coimbatore's trendy area with several high-quality restaurants, and a fast foodhall and supermarket underneath Nilgiri's Nest (opposite).

Gayathiri Bhavan (Nehru St; mains Rs 40-80; ☼ breakfast, lunch & dinner) This popular veg restaurant has an interesting menu, an AC dining hall and an inviting outdoor seating area where you may have to wait for a table. The 'kebab corner' features marinated diced cottage cheese, capsicum, onion and vegetable kebabs, and there's a great range of juices, ice creams and shakes.

Malabar (Sastri Rd; mains Rs 50-100; ☼ lunch & dinner) In the KK Residency Hotel, this restaurant specialises in Keralan and North Indian food. The Malabar chicken roast (Rs 100) is a spicy treat and there are seafood choices such as tandoori pomfret.

Annalakshmi (☎ 2212142; 106 Racecourse Rd; set meals Rs 150; ☼ lunch & dinner Tue-Sun) The top veg restaurant in town, this is run by devotees of Swami Shatanand Saraswati; the price of your meal helps support the Shivanjali educational trust for underprivileged children.

Getting There & Away

AIR

The airport is 10km east of town. **Indian Airlines** (☎ 2399821; 1604 Trichy Rd) flies daily between Coimbatore and Mumbai (US$160), Delhi (US$325) and Kozhikode (Calicut; US$50) and three times a week to Chennai (US$100) and Bengaluru (US$65).

Jet Airways (☎ 2212034) flies daily to Bengaluru (US$75) and Chennai (US$100). Newcomer **Paramount Airways** (☎ 1800 180 1234; www .paramountairways.com) also flies to Chennai. **Air Deccan** (☎ 2599885) offers cheap flights to Bengaluru (Rs 1400). These three airlines have counters at the airport, open to coincide with flight times.

BUS

There are three bus stands in the city centre.

From the **Central Bus Station** (☎ 2431521) services depart to nearby northern destinations such as Ooty (Rs 31, 3½ hours, every 30 minutes) and Mettupalayam (Rs 10.50, one hour, every 10 minutes).

From **Thiruvallur bus station** (☎ 25249690) you can catch state and interstate buses to Bengaluru (Rs 160 to 225, nine hours, 10 daily), Mysore (Rs 60, five hours, every hour) and Chennai (Rs 199 to 275, 11½ hours, seven daily). The town bus stand is for local city buses.

Ukkadam bus station, south of the city, is for buses to nearby southern destinations including Palani (Rs 25, three hours, every 20 minutes), Pollachi (Rs 10, one hour, every five minutes) and Madurai (Rs 70, five hours, every 30 minutes).

TRAIN

Coimbatore Junction is on the main line between Chennai and Ernakulam (Kerala). For Ooty, catch the daily *Nilgiri Express* at 5.15am; it connects with the miniature railway departure from Mettupalayam to Ooty at 7.10am. The whole trip to Ooty takes about seven hours.

Getting Around

For the airport take bus 20 from the town bus stand or bus 90 from the train station (Rs 4).

MAJOR TRAINS FROM COIMBATORE

Destination	Train name	Fare (Rs)	Duration (hr)	Departure
Bengaluru	Kanyakumari-Bangalore Exp	148-416	9	10.35pm daily
Chennai	Kovai Exp	116-404	7½	1.40pm daily
	Cheran Exp	116-404	8½	10pm daily
Kochi	Sabari Exp	93-261	5	8.50am daily
Madurai	Coimbatore-Madurai Exp	60-102	6	10.45pm daily
Ooty	Nilgiri Exp (via Mettupalayam)	22-35	7	5.15am daily
Pollachi		24	1½	5 daily

Many buses ply between the train station and the town bus stand (Rs 1.50).

Autorickshaw drivers charge around Rs 40 between the bus and train stations.

AROUND COIMBATORE

ISHA YOGA CENTER

This **ashram** (☎ 0422-2615345; www.ishafoundation .org; ⏱ 6am-8pm), in Poondi, 30km west of Coimbatore, is also a yoga retreat and place of pilgrimage. The centrepiece is a multi-religious temple housing the Dhyanalingam, said to be unique in that it embodies all seven chakras of spiritual energy. Visitors are welcome to the temple to meditate, or to take part in one- to two-week Isha yoga courses, for which you should register in advance. The ashram was founded by spiritual leader and yogi Sadhguru Jaggi Vasudev and is home to an order of Bhramhacharya monks and devotees.

METTUPALAYAM

This commercial town is the starting point for the miniature train to Ooty. There's little of interest for travellers, but if you want to avoid a predawn start in Coimbatore to make the 7.20am connection here, there is plenty of accommodation available. Try **Nanda Lodge** (☎ 04254-222555; Ooty Main Rd; s/d Rs 195/290), which is basic but clean and right opposite the bus station, through which there's a short cut to the train station. **Hotel EMS Mayura** (☎ 04254-227936; 212 Coimbatore Rd; r without/with AC Rs 450/800; 🍴), a decent enough midrange hotel, is 2km from the station. An autorickshaw to the station will cost about Rs 30.

COONOOR

☎ 0423 / pop 101,000 / elev 1850m

Coonoor is one of the three **Nilgiri hill stations** – Ooty, Kotagiri and Coonoor (see the Nilgiri Hills map, p434) – that lie above the southern plains.

Climbing up out of the busy market area and looking down over the sea of red tile rooftops to the slopes behind, there's a strong sense of what hill stations were originally all about: peace, cool climate and some beautiful scenery. Although smaller than Ooty, Coonoor's centre doesn't come across as being any less busy, especially the area around the

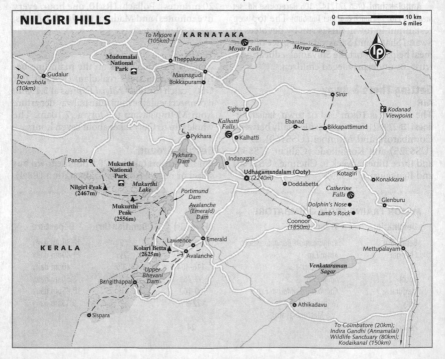

NILGIRI HILLS

train station, bus stand and market, which is a bustling, choking mess with tenacious touts. Thankfully you leave all this behind at your accommodation, most of which is in quieter Upper Coonoor, 1km to 2km above the town centre.

Sights & Activities

In Upper Coonoor the 12-hectare **Sim's Park** (adult/child Rs 5/2, camera/video Rs 25/250; ☻ 8.30am-6pm) is a peaceful oasis of manicured lawns and more than 1000 plant species, including magnolia, tree ferns and camellia. Buses heading to Kotagiri can drop you here.

There are several popular viewpoints around Coonoor. **Dolphin's Nose**, about 10km from town, exposes a vast panorama encompassing Catherine Falls across the valley. Heading out here early is the best bet for avoiding the mist. On the way back, drop into **Guernsey Tea Factory** (☎ 2230205; admission Rs 10; ☻ 8am-6pm) and take a short guided tour of the fragrant processing plant. Afterwards stop at **Lamb's Rock**, named after the British captain who created a short path to this favourite picnic spot in a pretty patch of forest. The easiest way to see these sights – all are on the same road – is on a taxi tour for around Rs 400 and, if you're feeling energetic, walk the 6km or so back into town from Lamb's Rock (it's mostly, but not entirely, downhill).

Sleeping & Eating

Hotel Vivek Coonoor (☎ 2230658; Figure of Eight Rd; dm Rs 100, r from Rs 300-500) Many of the wide range of rooms here have balconies (screened to avoid the 'monkey menace') from which you can hear the tea-pickers plucking the leaves below you. There's also a monster dormitory. It's clean, well run and has a bar and restaurant.

YWCA Wyoming Guesthouse (☎ 2234426; s/d Rs 200/400) This ramshackle guesthouse in Upper Coonoor is a budget favourite. Although ageing and draughty, the 150-year-old colonial house oozes character with wooden terraces and quiet, good views over Coonoor. Take an autorickshaw (around Rs 30) for ease, or catch a town bus to Bedford from where it's a 10-minute walk – you'll need to ask directions.

Taj Garden Retreat (☎ 2230021; www.tajhotels .com; Church Rd; s/d from US$70/85) On the hilltop beside the All Saints Church, this fine hotel has beautiful gardens and enormous comfortable colonial rooms with polished floorboards,

bathtubs and open fireplaces. The 'superior' rooms have a separate sitting room. The hotel also has an excellent multicuisine restaurant and a bar, and for the more health conscious, a gym, Ayurvedic and yoga centre.

Tryst (☎ 2207057; www.trystindia.com; d incl breakfast & dinner Rs 3900) If you're looking for a gregarious accommodation experience that's both quirky and classy, check out the website of this extraordinary guesthouse and book ahead. It's beautifully located in a former tea plantation manager's bungalow.

Your best bet for eating is your hotel restaurant, though there are several eating places around the town centre below the train station.

Getting There & Away

Coonoor is on the miniature train line between Mettupalayam (28km) and Ooty (18km) – see p441. Buses to Ooty (Rs 6.50, one hour) and Kotagiri (Rs 8, one hour) leave roughly every 15 minutes.

KOTAGIRI

☎ 04266 / pop 29,184

Kotagiri is a quiet village 28km east of Ooty. The oldest of the three Nilgiri hill stations, the village itself is dusty and uninspiring but the surrounding landscape of tea estates, tribal Kota settlements and rolling hills is a world away from the overdevelopment of Ooty.

From Kotagiri you can visit **Catherine Falls**, 8km away near the Mettupalayam road (the last 3km is by foot only, and the falls only flow after rain), **Elk Falls** (6km) and **Kodanad Viewpoint** (22km), where there's a view over the Coimbatore Plains and Mysore Plateau. A half-day taxi tour to all three will cost around Rs 600. The scenery on the road down to Mettupalayam is gorgeous, so you may want to detour this way if you're heading down from Ooty.

A couple of very basic lodges are in the small town centre and a splendid 1915 colonial building, **Stone House Retreat** (☎ 273300; www.naharhotels.com; r Rs 2000), offers fabulous views and atmosphere but charges like a wounded bull for all extras.

Getting There & Away

Buses stop at the edge of town, about 1km from the centre. Buses to Ooty depart hourly (Rs 15, two hours), crossing one of Tamil Nadu's highest passes. Buses to Mettupalayam leave every 30 minutes and to Coonoor every 15 minutes.

UDHAGAMANDALAM (OOTY)

☎ 0423 / pop 93,921 / elev 2240m

Ooty is South India's most famous hill station, established by the British in the early 19th century as the summer headquarters of the then-Madras government and memorably nicknamed 'Snooty Ooty'.

Until about 20 years ago it resembled an unlikely combination of southern England and Australia: single-storey stone cottages, bijou-fenced flower gardens, leafy winding lanes and tall eucalyptus stands, all surrounded by the tea plantations that were the town's original *raison d'être*. Times have changed and, if not for the climate and the rolling hills, Ooty's centre resembles any overburdened provincial Indian town.

But Ooty has an undeniable charm and the nearby hills and forest are sensational for trekking. Life here is relaxed and just a few kilometres out of town you are in the peace of the hills with superb views. The journey up to Ooty on the miniature train is romantic and the scenery stunning – try to get a seat on the left-hand side where you get the best views across the mountains.

From April to June (the *very* busy season) Ooty is a welcome relief from the hot plains and in the colder months (October to March) it's crisp, clear and surprisingly cool. You'll need warm clothing – which you can buy very cheaply here – as the overnight temperature occasionally drops to 0°C.

Orientation & Information

Ooty sprawls over a large area among rolling hills and valleys. In between the lake and the racecourse are the train station and the bus station. From either of these it's a 10-minute walk to the bazaar area and a 20-minute walk to Ooty's commercial centre, Charing Cross.

BOOKSHOPS & LIBRARY

Higginbothams Commercial Rd (☎ 2443736; ☼ 9.30am-1pm & 3.30-7.30pm Mon-Sat); Commissioner's Rd (☎ 2442546; ☼ 9am-1pm & 2-5.30pm Mon-Sat) Good selection of contemporary English-language Indian and other fiction, and great postcards.
Nilgiri Library (Bank Rd; temporary membership Rs 350; ☼ 9.30am-1pm & 2.30-6pm, reading room 9.30am-6pm, closed Fri) Quaint little haven in a lovely crumbling 1867 building with a good collection of more than 40,000 books, including rare titles on the Nilgiris and hill tribes.

INTERNET ACCESS

Global Net (Commercial Rd; per hr Rs 25; ☼ 9.30am-9pm)
Internet cafés Church Hill Rd (per hr Rs 30; ☼ 10am-9pm); Commercial Rd (per hr Rs 20; ☼ 10am-10pm)

MONEY

Canara Bank ATM (Commercial Rd)
State Bank of India (Bank Rd; ☼ 10am-4pm Mon-Fri & 10am-2pm Sat) Changes travellers cheques and has an ATM.
State Bank of India ATM (Commercial Rd)
UK Forex (Commercial Rd) Changes travellers cheques and cash.
UTI Bank ATM (Ettines Rd)

NATIONAL PARK INFORMATION

Wildlife Warden Office (WWO; ☎ 2444098; ☼ 10am-5.45pm Mon-Fri) Manages Mudumalai National Park including advance booking for park accommodation (see p442).

POST

Charing Cross post office (Ettines Rd; ☼ 9.30am-5.30pm Mon-Fri)
Main post office (Havelock Rd; ☼ 9am-5pm Mon-Sat) Diagonally opposite St Stephen's Church.

TOURIST INFORMATION

Tourist office (☼ 2443977; ☼ 10am-5.45pm Mon-Fri) Maps, brochures and tour information.

Sights

ST STEPHEN'S CHURCH

Built in 1829, the immaculately maintained **St Stephen's Church** (Church Hill Rd; ☼ 10am-1pm & 3-5pm Mon-Sat, services 8am & 11am Sun) is the oldest in the Nilgiris. Its huge wooden beams came from the palace of Tipu Sultan in Srirangapatnam and were hauled the 120km by a team of elephants. Marble plaques on the walls, and the quiet and overgrown cemetery, commemorate many an Ooty Britisher including John Sullivan, the town's founder.

BOTANICAL GARDENS

Established in 1848, these beautifully maintained **gardens** (adult/child Rs 10/3, camera/video Rs 30/100; ☼ 8am-6.30pm) include some enormous mature trees as well as native shrubs and lush garden beds. There's also a fossilised tree trunk believed to be around 20 million years old.

CENTENARY ROSE PARK

With its terraced lawns and colourful flowerbeds – best between May and July – this

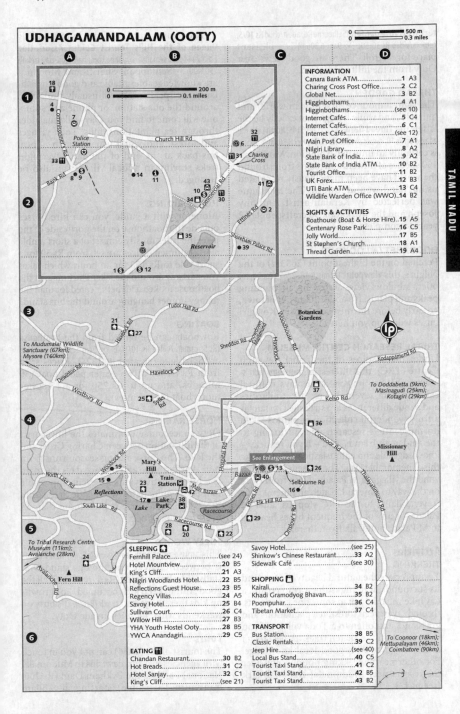

UDHAGAMANDALAM (OOTY)

TAMIL NADU

INFORMATION
Canara Bank ATM	1 A3
Charing Cross Post Office	2 C2
Global Net	3 B2
Higginbothams	4 A1
Higginbothams	(see 10)
Internet Cafés	5 C4
Internet Cafés	6 C1
Internet Cafés	(see 12)
Main Post Office	7 A1
Nilgiri Library	8 A2
State Bank of India	9 A2
State Bank of India ATM	10 B2
Tourist Office	11 B2
UK Forex	12 B3
UTI Bank ATM	13 C4
Wildlife Warden Office (WWO)	14 B2

SIGHTS & ACTIVITIES
Boathouse (Boat & Horse Hire)	15 A5
Centenary Rose Park	16 C5
Jolly World	17 B5
St Stephen's Church	18 A1
Thread Garden	19 A4

SLEEPING
Fernhill Palace	(see 24)
Hotel Mountview	20 B5
King's Cliff	21 A3
Nilgiri Woodlands Hotel	22 B5
Reflections Guest House	23 B5
Regency Villas	24 A5
Savoy Hotel	25 B4
Sullivan Court	26 C4
Willow Hill	27 B3
YHA Youth Hostel Ooty	28 B5
YWCA Anandagiri	29 C5

EATING
Chandan Restaurant	30 B2
Hot Breads	31 C2
Hotel Sanjay	32 C1
King's Cliff	(see 21)
Savoy Hotel	(see 25)
Shinkow's Chinese Restaurant	33 A2
Sidewalk Café	(see 30)

SHOPPING
Kairali	34 B2
Khadi Gramodyog Bhavan	35 B2
Poompuhar	36 C4
Tibetan Market	37 C4

TRANSPORT
Bus Station	38 B5
Classic Rentals	39 C2
Jeep Hire	(see 40)
Local Bus Stand	40 C5
Tourist Taxi Stand	41 C2
Tourist Taxi Stand	42 B5
Tourist Taxi Stand	43 B2

terraced **rose garden** (Selbourne Rd; adult/child Rs 10/5, camera/video Rs 30/50; ☽ 9am-6.30pm) is a pleasant place for a stroll. There are good views over Ooty from the hilltop location.

THREAD GARDEN

The signs announce 'first time in world' and 'miracle', and while it might not exactly be the latter, the **Thread Garden** (☎ 2445145; North Lake Rd; admission Rs 10, camera/video Rs 15/30; ☽ 8.30am-7.30pm) is certainly an unusual exhibition. More than 150 species of flowers and plants from around the world have been meticulously re-created using 'hand-wound' thread. The technique was perfected by Keralan artist Anthony Joseph and the work took 50 craftspeople 12 years to complete.

DODDABETTA LOOKOUT

Perched on the highest point (2633m) of the Nilgiris, this **viewpoint** (admission Rs 2; ☽ 7am-6pm) offers fabulous views across the surrounding peaks and plains. It's about 10km out of town; go early before the mist sets in. Any Kotagiri buses will drop you here.

TRIBAL RESEARCH CENTRE MUSEUM

Under the auspices of the Tribal Research Centre (TRC), this interesting **museum** (admission free; ☽ 10am-5pm Mon-Fri) displays cultural exhibits from several tribes; the similarities and subtle differences are striking. Upstairs is a truly wonderful collection of photos taken on the centre's research trips including to the Andaman Islands, and – if you're lucky – knowledgeable and enthusiastic staff will make this a memorable visit. The museum is just beyond the village of M Palada, 11km from Ooty on the way to Emerald. Catch an Emerald bus (several daily) to the TRC stop just after M Palada, or any of the frequent buses heading to M Palada and walk from there.

Activities
TREKKING

To appreciate the natural beauty of Ooty and its surrounds, walking is the way to go and a day hike will take you to some fine viewpoints, through evergreen forest, tea plantations and grassland, and often to a Toda village. If you want to get off the beaten track it's best to get a reliable guide with good local knowledge. For other nearby trekking options, consider the resorts near Mudumalai National Park (see p442).

The senior guides of the long-standing **Queen of the Hills Tourist Guides Association** (☎ 2444449; seniappan@yahoo.com; half-/full-day trek Rs 250/400) – Seniappan, Sheriff and Mohan – are knowledgeable, affable and good English-language speakers. You'll usually find them around the bus station, or phone and someone will come to find you. Day walks meander through tea plantations, hills, Toda villages and forest, and you'll usually catch a local bus back at the end of the day. Overnight treks staying in a local village can also be arranged.

HORSE RIDING

Alone or with a guide, you can hire horses outside the boathouse on the north side of the lake; the rides mostly consist of a short amble along bitumen. Prices are set, from Rs 50 for a short ride to Rs 150 for an hour, which takes you partway around the lake. The horses at the boathouse looked a lot better cared for than the mangy ponies hanging around the bus stand.

BOATING

Rowboats can be rented from the **boathouse** (Rs 5, camera/video Rs 10/100; ☽ 9am-5.30pm) by the artificial lake (created in 1824). Prices start from Rs 60 for a two-seater pedal boat (30 minutes) and up to Rs 250 for a 15-seater motorboat (20 minutes).

HORSE RACING

Ooty's racecourse dominates the lower part of the hill station between Charing Cross and the lake. The horse-racing season runs from mid-April to June and on race days the town is a hive of activity; it's an event impossible to miss if you're in town. Outside the season, the 2.4km racecourse is little more than an overgrown paddock.

JOLLY WORLD

This **amusement park** (admission Rs 5; ☽ 9am-7.30pm) is between the lake and the bus stand with stalls, sideshows, rides (Rs 5 to 50) and all the good stuff to keep kids occupied. For grown-up kids there's a **go-kart track** (Rs 60). It's busy on weekends when families invade Ooty.

Tours

The tourist office (p436) can put you in touch with agencies that run day trips to Mudumalai National Park via the Pykhara Dam (Rs 200; minimum 15 people) starting at 9.30am

TAMIL NADU

HILL TRIBES OF THE NILGIRI

For centuries, the Nilgiris have been home to hill tribes. While retaining integrity in customs, dress, principal occupation and language, the tribes were economically, socially and culturally interdependent.

The Toda tribe lived on the western plateau in the area now called Ooty. Their social, economic and spiritual system centred on the buffalo. The produce derived from the buffalo (mainly milk and ghee) was integral to their diet and it was used as currency – in exchange for grain, tools, pots and even medical services. Most importantly, the dairy produce provided offerings to the gods as well as fuel for the funeral pyre. It was only at the ritual for human death that the strictly vegetarian Toda killed a buffalo, and they killed not for food but to provide company for the deceased. Other traditional customs that continue today include the division of labour; men care for the buffaloes and women embroider shawls used for ritual, as well as practical purposes. Today, only about 1500 Toda remain.

The Badaga migrated to the Nilgiri Hills in the wake of Muslim invasions in the north, and are thus not officially a tribal people. With knowledge of the world outside the hills, they became effective representatives for the hill tribes. Their agricultural produce, particularly grain, added a further dimension to the hill diet, and they traded this for buffalo products from the Toda.

The Kotas lived in the Kotagiri area and were considered by other tribes to be lower in status. Artisans of leather goods and pots, the Kotas were also musicians. The Kotas still undertake ceremonies in which the gods are beseeched for rains and bountiful harvests.

The Kurumbas inhabited the thick forests of the south. They gathered bamboo, honey and materials for housing, some of which they supplied to other tribes. They also engaged in a little agriculture, and at sowing and harvest times they employed the Badaga to perform rituals entreating the gods for abundant yields. Kurumba witchcraft was respected and sought after by the other tribes.

The Irulus, also from the southern slopes, produced tools and gathered honey and other forest products that they converted into brooms and incense. They are devotees of Vishnu and often performed special rituals for other tribes.

British settlement in the Ooty area from the early 19th century had a significant impact on tribal life. Some tribes adapted quickly, especially the Badaga. Being cultivators, they continued their traditional pursuits in untraditional ways; they cultivated the cash crops (tea and coffee) of the new settlers, but they were no longer able to provide the grains that were essential to the economy of the other tribes. Eventually, tribal systems, especially economic and cultural ones, began to collapse. Displaced tribes have been 'granted' land by the Indian government. But the cultivation of land is anathema to the Toda, who see themselves as caretakers of the soil – for them, to dig into the land is to desecrate it.

Today many tribal people have assimilated to the point of invisibility. Some have fallen into destructive patterns associated with displacement and alienation. Others remain straddled across two cultures, maintaining vestiges of their traditions while embracing customs and beliefs of the dominant culture.

and returning at 7pm, with just a quick spin through the park. Trips to Coonoor and surrounds are also possible.

A better alternative is to hire a taxi for the day and go as you please. The rates are set at Rs 450 for a four-hour trip around Ooty, or Rs 1100 for a full day.

Sleeping

Ooty has some of Tamil Nadu's best and/or most atmospheric accommodation if you're prepared to pay for it. It's a sellers' market in the busy high season (1 April to 15 June) when many hotel prices double and checkout time is often 9am. Prices listed here are for the low season when most places are good value. In town you'll be close to all amenities plus the inevitable noise and pollution, but peace, tranquillity and some wonderful midrange hotels can be found just a few kilometres away. Some guesthouses have open fires, either in bedrooms or in a common lounge, and there's generally a small charge for firewood and cleaning.

If you arrive by train with no accommodation booking, you can leave your bags at the station for a reasonable Rs 10 while you look around.

BUDGET

YHA Youth Hostel Ooty (☎ 2447506; ootyyouth hostel@hotmail.com; 42 South Lake Rd; dm member/nonmember Rs 75/100, d Rs 300/400) Ten minutes' walk from the bus stand, this small hostel is quietly located by the lake but can get busy with local youth groups in high season.

YWCA Anandagiri (☎ 2442218; Ettines Rd; dm Rs 110, r & bungalow incl tax from Rs 345-650) The YWCA has many things going for it, not least the good location overlooking the racecourse, within walking distance of the town centre and bus stand. It's set in spacious grounds with a main building, and a cluster of separate cottages. There are two comfy large, colonial-style lounges, a library and dining room with fireplace, and most rooms are spacious and clean.

Reflections Guest House (☎ 2443834; North Lake Rd; d from Rs 350-600) This family-run place overlooks the lake in a peaceful location between the bus stand and the boathouse. Rooms are simple and clean with hot water in the morning – the ones above the main house have sit-outs and good lake views. Home-cooked meals can be ordered, and there's a lounge with TV and open fire.

Hotel Mountview (☎ 2443307; Racecourse Rd; r Rs 400-500) Perched on a quiet driveway directly above the bus station, these eight simple, big rooms in a once-elegant old bungalow are good value and well located.

MIDRANGE & TOP END

Nilgiri Woodlands Hotel (☎ 2442451; Racecourse Rd; d/cottage incl tax Rs 600/750) This Raj-era hotel is looking decidedly the worse for wear but it's full of mildewy faded character. Manicured gardens, and the gabled roof and red-tiled cottages, are a reminder of old Ooty.

Willow Hill (☎ 2444037; willow@sancharnet.in; 58/1 Havelock Rd; d Rs 800-1500) Sitting high above the town, Willow Hill's large windows provide some great views of Ooty. The rooms, all with wooden floors, are spacious and comfortable in the style of an alpine chalet, with the most expensive rooms offering a private garden. It's not as stylish as some, but it's friendly and affordable and there's a reasonable restaurant.

King's Cliff (☎ 2452888; www.kingscliff-ooty.com; Havelock Rd; d Rs 1275-1975) High above Ooty on Strawberry Hill, this is a delightful hotel built into a colonial mansion with wood panelling, antique furnishings and brilliant views. It's an intimate retreat with only nine rooms, and all have individual character along with fireplaces. Deluxe rooms have a private covered porch, and breakfast is included. There's a very comfortable lounge and popular fine restaurant.

Regency Villas (☎ 2442555; regency@sancharnet.in; Fernhill Post; r/cottages Rs 1800/1600) In a state of splendidly decaying grandeur, the rooms, furnishings and palatial bathrooms at what was the Maharaja of Mysore's former guesthouse have to be seen to be believed. Seeming little-changed over the last 100 years, you're paying for nostalgia and loads of atmosphere rather than modern creature comforts. When we visited in 2006, the Maharaja's summer pad next door, the extraordinary Fernhill Palace, was still undergoing a massive renovation programme in preparation for reopening as a seriously luxurious hotel.

Sullivan Court (☎ 2441416; sullivancourt@vsnl.com; Selbourne Rd; s/d from Rs 2600/2900) Ooty's most modern hotel, Sullivan Court boasts a stunning lobby with glass elevator, plush rooms, a good restaurant, children's play area, and gym – it's excellent value if you're after contemporary comfort rather than old-fashioned style.

Savoy Hotel (☎ 2444142; www.tajhotels.com; 77 Sylks Rd; s/d from US$70/85) The Savoy is one of Ooty's oldest hotels, with parts of it dating back to 1829. Big cottages are arranged around a beautiful garden of flowerbeds, lawns and clipped hedges. Quaint rooms have large bathrooms, polished floors, log fires and bay windows. Modern facilities include a 24-hour bar, excellent multicuisine dining room, an Ayurvedic centre, gym and tennis courts.

Eating

Most of the hotels have their own restaurants, and some of the top-end places are great for lavish meals and atmospheric dining rooms. There are plentiful cheap eats in town.

Hotel Sanjay (☎ 2443160; Charing Cross; mains Rs 35-85; ☙ breakfast, lunch & dinner) This is a basic but bustling place with generous servings of veg and nonveg fare and a bar on the 1st floor.

Sidewalk Café (Commercial Rd; dishes Rs 40-60, pizzas Rs 45-125; ☙ lunch & dinner) A cross between an American diner and an Italian café is something you'd expect to find in Mumbai rather than the mountains, but it's a welcome change of scene. In bright, modern décor, efficient staff wheel out wood-fired veg pizzas, burgers, sandwiches (try the chilli cheese or mushroom toast), salads and awesome desserts and smoothies; there's even a cappuccino machine.

Chandan Restaurant (mains Rs 50-75, thalis Rs 50-70; ☺ lunch & dinner) At Hotel Nahar, Chandan serves up delicious veg dishes in elegant surroundings. Thalis are served at lunchtime or choose from a range of biryanis and Chinese dishes.

Shinkow's Chinese Restaurant (☎ 2442811; 38/83 Commissioner's Rd; mains Rs 50-150; ☺ lunch & dinner) Shinkow's is an Ooty institution and the simple menu of chicken, pork, beef, fish, noodles and rice dishes is usually pretty good.

Both the **Savoy Hotel** (mains from around Rs 140; ☺ lunch & dinner) and **King's Cliff** (mains Rs 80-200; ☺ lunch & dinner) have atmospheric restaurants with log fires and quality multicuisine food. The latter has no alcohol permit, but you can bring your own.

QUICK EATS

There are plenty of basic veg places on Commercial and Main Bazaar Rds and you can get a spicy biryani for Rs 10 at street stalls near the bus stand.

Hot Breads (Charing Cross; ☺ 8am-10pm) This is a popular bakery turning out a huge range of breads, pastries, pies and sweets – go early for the fresh stuff. (Don't be put off by the Chinese shopfront; it's advertising the upstairs restaurant.)

Like Kodai, Ooty is famous for its delicious **home-made chocolates** (per 100g around Rs 50).

Shopping

Ooty can be a fun place to shop, but don't expect anything out of the ordinary. The main places to shop are along Commercial Rd where you'll find Kashmiri shops as well as government outlets for Kairali and Khadi Gramodyog Bhavan. Poompuhar is on Coonoor Rd.

There's no need to lug warm clothes up to Ooty – you can pick up jackets from Rs 100 and hats and gloves from Rs 10 at shops along Commercial Rd (near the bus stand) or at the **Tibetan market** (☺ 9am-8pm) almost opposite the entrance to the Botanical Gardens.

Getting There & Away

Without doubt the most romantic way to arrive in Ooty is aboard the miniature train,

and you'll need to book ahead in the high season. Buses also run regularly up and down the mountain, both from other parts of Tamil Nadu and from Mysore in Karnataka.

BUS

The state bus companies all have **reservation offices** (☺ 9am-5.30pm) at the busy bus station. There are two routes to Karnataka – the main bus route via Gudalur and the shorter, more arduous route via Masinagudi. The latter is tackled only by minibuses and winds through 36 hairpin bends! For details of bus services, see below.

Connect with trains to Chennai or Kochi (Cochin, Kerala) at Coimbatore.

To get to Mudumalai National Park (Rs 23, 2½ hours, 12 daily), take one of the Mysore buses that will drop you at park headquarters at Theppakadu, or one of the small buses that go via the narrow and twisting Sighur Ghat road. Some of these rolling wrecks travel only as far as Masinagudi (Rs 10, 1½ hours), from where there are buses every two hours to Theppakadu.

Local buses leave every 30 minutes for Kotagiri (Rs 10, two hours) and every 10 minutes to Coonoor (Rs 6.50, one hour).

TRAIN

The miniature train – one of the Mountain Railways of India given World Heritage status by Unesco in 2005 – is the best way to get here. There are fine views of forest, waterfalls and tea plantations along the way, especially from the front 1st-class carriage; the steam engine pushes, rather than pulls, the train up the hill, so the front carriage leads the way. Departures and arrivals at Mettupalayam connect with those of the *Nilgiri Express*, which runs between Mettupalayam and Chennai. The miniature train departs Mettupalayam for Ooty

BUSES FROM OOTY (UDHAGAMANDALAM)

Destination	Fare (Rs)	Duration (hr)	Frequency
Bengaluru	155-250	8	7 daily
Chennai	228	15	2 daily (overnight)
Coimbatore	37	3	every 20min
Mettupalayam	17	2	every 20min
Mysore	69-100	4	11 daily

at 7.20am daily (1st/2nd class Rs 117/12; five hours, 46km). If you want a seat in either direction, be at least 45 minutes early or make a reservation (Rs 25) at least 24 hours in advance.

From Ooty the train leaves at 3pm and takes about 3½ hours. There are also two daily passenger trains between Ooty and Coonoor (1½ hours).

Getting Around

Plenty of autorickshaws hang around the bus station – a ride from the train or bus stations to Charing Cross should cost about Rs 25, and a list of autorickshaw fixed prices is on a sign at the steps on Commercial Rd leading to the tourist information office.

Taxis cluster at several stands in town. There are fixed fares to most destinations including to Coonoor (Rs 300), Kotagiri (Rs 400), Gudalur, Mudumalai National Park and Coimbatore (all Rs 600).

You can hire a bicycle at the bazaar if you ask around, but many of the roads are steep so you'll end up pushing it uphill (great on the way down though!). Motorcycles can be hired from **Classic Rentals** (Ettines Rd; 9am-6pm) at RCM Tours & Travels. A Kinetic Honda, TVS scooter or 100cc Yamaha costs Rs 350 for 24 hours, or Rs 50 per hour. A deposit of Rs 500 is usually required.

MUDUMALAI NATIONAL PARK

☎ 0423

In the foothills of the Nilgiris, this 321-sq-km **park** (admission Rs 35), and the surrounding forest outside the park boundaries, are the best places for wildlife viewing in Tamil Nadu. Part of the Nilgiri Biosphere Reserve (3000 sq km), the reserve's vegetation ranges from grasslands to semi-evergreen forests that are home to chitals (spotted deer), gaurs (bisons), tigers, panthers, wild boars and sloth bears. Otters and crocodiles inhabit the Moyar River. The park's wild elephant population numbers about 600.

A good time to visit Mudumalai is between December and June although the park may be closed during the dry season, February to March. Heavy rain is common in October and November.

The admission price includes a Rs 20 minibus tour.

Orientation & Information

The main service area in Mudumalai is Theppakadu, on the main road between Ooty and Mysore. Here you'll find the park's **reception centre** (☎ 526235; 6.30-9am & 3-6pm) and some park-run accommodation.

The closest village is Masinagudi, 7km from Theppakadu.

Tours

It's not possible to hike in the park and tours are limited to the sanctuary's minibuses. Private vehicles are not allowed in the park, except on the main Ooty–Mysore road that runs through it. **Minibus tours** (per person Rs 35 includes Rs 15 park entry fee, 45 mins) run between 7am and 9am, and 3pm and 6pm making a 15km loop through part of the park.

The once-popular elephant safaris stopped some years ago due to the animals' ill-health; if they do restart, this is the best way to see the park, especially in the early morning.

Guides can be hired for **trekking** outside the park boundaries, which also provides some rich wildlife habitat. Talk to the guys who hang around the park entry station, or ask at your resort; all have their own knowledgeable, English-speaking guides. Expect to pay around Rs 150 per person for a couple of hours of guided walking, or around Rs 350 per person for a four-hour combined jeep and walking tour; negotiate prices and group size in low season.

Sleeping & Eating

All budgets are catered for – there are cheap and midrange lodges inside the park at Theppakadu; budget rooms and midrange cottages in Masinagudi; and midrange jungle resorts in Bokkapuram (4km south of Masinagudi). For meals at the resorts, expect to pay from Rs 400 per person, per day.

IN THE PARK

For most accommodation in the park, book in advance, in person, with the WWO in Ooty (p436). In low season, you *may* be able to get accommodation if it's available by asking directly at the park reception centre. The following three park-run places are walking distance from park reception and on the banks of the river.

Minivet Dormitory (r per person Rs 35) A clean place, with two four-bed rooms, each with private bathroom with cold water only.

Theppakadu Log House (d/q Rs 330/560) and **Sylvan Lodge** (d/q Rs 330/560) are the pick of the places in the park. Overlooking the river, they're comfortable, well maintained and good value. There's a kitchen at Sylvan Lodge that prepares meals for booked guests.

The government-run **Tamil Nadu Hotel** (☎ 252 6580; dm/d/q Rs 75/295/495) is in the same cluster of buildings; it provides basic accommodation and basic meals.

MASINAGUDI

There are several lodges on the main road in Masinagudi as well as the odd place for a meal. Unless you arrive after dark, there's little of interest in town; better head for the park or the nearby resorts. If you need to stay, try the following:

Kongu Lodge (☎ 2526131; Main Rd; s/d Rs 250/400), This simple place doubles as a bar and women travelling alone may feel uncomfortable here. A jeep ride from Masinagudi to the park costs around Rs 80, or wait for one of the buses passing through between Ooty and Theppakadu.

Bamboo Banks Farm (☎ 2526211; bambanks@ sancharnet.in; cottages s/d Rs 825/1125) A couple of kilometres out of town towards Bokkapuram, long-established Bamboo Banks Farm offers four big, comfortable private cottages in the lush gardens of a family-run property. The landscape is beautiful but tamed here; you'll need transport to travel the few kilometres to wilderness areas.

BOKKAPURAM

This area south of Masinagudi is home to a gaggle of fine forest resorts, mostly family-run businesses with a warm, homely atmosphere, high standards and breathtaking views. The attraction here is wildlife – trekking in the jungle, jeep safaris, night safaris and bird-watching. Many resorts provide a pick-up service from nearby towns such as Ooty (starting from Rs 500), otherwise hire any jeep in Masinagudi. It's best to book rooms in advance, particularly in the high season. Each resort offers a range of services including visits to Mudumalai National Park, hikes with a guide, fishing and horse riding, all of which cost extra.

Jungle Trails (☎ 2526256; r from Rs 600) There are just a couple of simple rooms at this quiet escape, run for many years by Mark, a quirky and passionate local conservationist. Day visitors (per person Rs 100) are welcome to sit on the comfortable veranda, drink tea and watch the bush (from 6.30am to 8.30am and 4.30pm to 6.30pm). It's just past the bottom of the Sighur Ghat road that winds down from Ooty.

Jungle Hut (☎ 2526240; r from Rs 1200;) A big draw here is the water hole and swimming pool (great for steamy jungle days), and kids' playground. The rooms, though, are looking a bit tired and not such good value compared with others nearby.

Forest Hills Guest House (☎ 2526216; www.forest hillsindia.com; s/d/tr from Rs 850/1100/1400, huts Rs 1250) Forest Hills is a family-run, family-sized guesthouse (10 rooms on 5 hectares) with a few cute bamboo huts, some clean spacious rooms and a fabulous watchtower for wildlife- and bird-watching. Staff are great and the food is terrific, and there's a slight colonial air here with a gazebo-style bar, games rooms and barbecue pit.

Jungle Retreat (☎ 2526470; www.jungleretreat.com; dm Rs 400, bamboo huts & standard r Rs 1500, cottage Rs 2500) This is one of the most stylish resorts in the area, with lovingly built stone cottages decked out with classic furniture, and sturdy bamboo huts, all spread out to give a feeling of seclusion. It's possible to camp, and there's a dormitory for groups. The bar, restaurant and common area is a great place to meet fellow travellers and the owners are knowledgeable and friendly with a large area of private forest at their disposal.

Getting There & Away

Buses from Ooty to Mysore and Bengaluru stop at Theppakadu (Rs 23, 2½ hours, 11 daily). Bus services run every two hours between Theppakadu and Masinagudi.

The longer route that these buses take to or from Ooty is via Gudalur (67km). The direct route to Masinagudi, however, is an interesting 'short cut' (Rs 10, 1½ hours, 36km) which involves taking one of the small government buses that make the trip up (or down) the tortuous Sighur Ghat road. The bends are so tight and the gradient so steep that large buses simply can't use it. Private minibuses heading to Mysore also use this route but if you want to get off at Masinagudi, you'll have to pay the full fare (Rs 125).

Andaman & Nicobar Islands

Andaman & Nicobar Islands

Once known as Kalapani – Black Waters – for their role as a feared penal settlement, the Andaman and Nicobar Islands are now a relaxed tropical island outpost that belongs to India but is geographically closer to Southeast Asia. Superb, near-deserted beaches, incredible corals and marine life, an intriguing colonial past and the remnants of a Stone Age culture lure travellers to these mysterious islands, 1000km off the east coast of India in the Bay of Bengal.

Until the beginnings of colonial rule, the islands were populated mainly by indigenous peoples, but today the majority of the Andamans' population are mainland settlers or their descendants who live in and around Port Blair, the capital, on South Andaman. The territory comprises 572 tropical islands (of which 36 are inhabited), with unique wildlife and lush forests, although the Nicobar Islands are off-limits to tourists.

The islands are close to the epicentre of the undersea earthquake that caused the 2004 Boxing Day tsunami, which, in turn, led to devastating loss of life and homes on the southerly Nicobar Islands and Little Andaman. Apart from flooding on low-lying areas of South Andaman Island and damage to the reefs near Wandoor, the main Andaman island group escaped major damage, though other islands such as Havelock and Interview noticeably tilted with the earth movement. Pre-tsunami, small-scale tourist infrastructure had been slowly developing but the almost total absence of tourists during 2005, coupled with the cost and energy of repairing the damage, demoralised many islanders and there's still much to do to revive these beautiful islands' tourism facilities.

HIGHLIGHTS

- Snorkel the reefs, lounge on the beaches and cruise through mangrove swamps on **Havelock Island** (p456)

- Scuba dive among the coral and big fish of the islands' world-class sites, accessible from **Havelock Island** (p457)

- Explore the ghosts of the colonial past on **Ross Island** (p455) – the former 'Paris of the East'

- Take a road trip through the jungle heart of the Andamans to the quiet coastal beaches and islands around **Mayabunder** and **Diglipur** (p459)

- Relive the horror of Port Blair's origin as a penal colony at the **Cellular Jail** (p451)

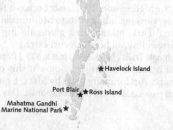

★Diglipur

★Havelock Island

Port Blair ★★Ross Island

Mahatma Gandhi Marine National Park★

History

It's not known when the first inhabitants arrived on the Andaman and Nicobar Islands but their presence was documented in the 2nd century by Greek astronomer Ptolemy, and again in the 7th century by Chinese monk Xuan Zang during his 17-year journey through India.

In the late 17th century, the islands were annexed by the Marathas, whose empire consumed vast areas of India. Two centuries later the British found a use for them as a penal colony, initially to detain 'regular' criminals from mainland India and later to incarcerate political dissidents – the freedom fighters for Indian independence. During WWII, the islands were occupied by the Japanese, who were regarded with ambivalence by the islanders. Some initiated guerrilla activities against them, while others regarded them as liberators from British colonialism.

Following Independence in 1947, the Andaman and Nicobar Islands were incorporated into the Indian Union. Since then,

massive migration from the mainland has inflated the island population from only a few thousand to more than 350,000. During this influx, tribal land rights and environmental protection were disregarded to some extent, but now local lobby groups are becoming more vocal.

Climate

Sea breezes keep temperatures within the 23°C to 31°C range and the humidity at around 80% all year. The southwest monsoons come to the islands between roughly mid-May and early October, and the northeast monsoons between November and December. The best

ANDAMAN & NICOBAR
ISLANDS

EARTHQUAKES & AFTERSHOCKS

The Andaman and Nicobar Island chain is no stranger to earthquakes and tremors. In 1941 an earthquake measuring 7.7 on the Richter scale rocked South and Middle Andaman, destroying many buildings and causing the British administrative centre on Ross Island to be abandoned. A resulting tsunami wave of about 1m reportedly reached the east coast of India, and more than a dozen earthquakes and aftershocks were felt over the next six months on the islands.

It was a far more devastating event at 7.58am on 26 December 2004, when an undersea earthquake measuring 9.0 occurred off the northeastern tip of Sumatra (Indonesia). It was not the tremors that caused the most damage, but the powerful tsunami that swept across the Bay of Bengal and Andaman Sea, devastating parts of Indonesia, Sri Lanka, India, the Maldives, Thailand and the Nicobar Islands. Soon after, a massive aftershock occurred beneath the Andaman and Nicobar Islands, causing more damage and uplifting several islands along the west coast of the Andaman chain (including Interview Island) by as much as 2m. The tsunami's effect on the low-lying Nicobar Islands was severe. When the wave hit the islands, including Great Nicobar, Car Nicobar, Little Andaman, Nancowrie, Katchall and many smaller islands, thousands were caught in its wake. Official figures show 6100 confirmed dead, many more missing and thousands left homeless, evacuated to relief camps in Port Blair. Initial access to some islands proved difficult, so many people were left stranded for days, without food or water, waiting for help. The islands' tribal people suffered few fatalities; responding to signs in the natural world, most had moved to higher ground before the wave hit.

Fortunately the northerly and more densely populated Andaman Island chain was largely spared. Low-lying parts of South Andaman were flooded, leaving many homeless, and water surged into shore areas of Port Blair and islands such as Havelock, but with little lasting damage.

British geologist Dr Mike Searle says some 1300km of the boundary between the Indian plate to the west and the Burma-Andaman-Sumatra plate to the east, was ruptured, while the Indian plate is presently pushing under the Burma-Andaman-Sumatra plate to the east. While such a catastrophe will hopefully never again be seen again, these remote islands are clearly a seismic hotspot.

ANDAMAN ISLANDS

time to visit is between December and early April, when the days are warm, but not oppressive, and the nights pleasant.

Geography & Environment

The islands form the peaks of a vast submerged mountain range that extends for almost 1000km between Myanmar (Burma) and Sumatra in Indonesia. The majority of the land area is taken up by the Andamans at 6408 sq km. The Nicobar Islands begin 50km south of Little Andaman.

The isolation of the Andaman and Nicobar Islands has led to the evolution of many endemic species of both plants and animals. Of 62 identified mammals, 32 are unique to the islands. Among these are the Andaman wild pig, the crab-eating macaque, the masked palm civet and species of tree shrews and bats. Almost 50% of the islands' 250 bird species are endemic, and include eagles, ground-dwelling megapodes, swiftlets (*hawabill*), doves, teals and hornbills. The isolated beaches provide excellent breeding grounds for turtles. While dolphins are frequently sighted, the once abundant dugongs have all but vanished.

Mangroves are an important aspect of the landscape, offering a natural protective barrier to both land and sea. Further inland the tall evergreen and moist deciduous forests contain many important tree species, including the renowned padauk – a hardwood with light and dark colours occurring in the same tree.

Information

Even though they're 1000km east of the mainland, the Andamans still run on Indian time. This means that it can be dark by 5pm and light by 4am. The peak season is December and January, and in September and October domestic holidaymakers can fill literally every bed in Port Blair; book accommodation in advance if you're travelling at these times.

Andaman & Nicobar Tourism (A&N Tourism; Map p452; ☎ 232747; www.tourism.andaman.nic.in; Port Blair; ⏱ 8.30am-1pm & 2-5pm Mon-Fri, 8.30am-noon Sat) is the main tourism body for the islands.

ACCOMMODATION

Accommodation choices and standards are on the way up in the Andamans, despite the slow progress of tourism recovery after the tsunami. Just a few years ago the only places to stay outside Port Blair were tatty government guesthouses and basic forest rest houses.

FESTIVALS IN THE ANDAMAN ISLANDS

The 10-day **Island Tourism Festival** is held in Port Blair, usually in January. Dance groups come from surrounding islands and the mainland, and various cultural performances are held at the Exhibition Complex. One of the festival's more bizarre aspects is the Andaman dog show, but there's also a flower show, a baby show and a fancy-dress competition! For information, check the website of **A&N Tourism** (www.tourism .andaman.nic.in).

These days you can stay in cheap bamboo huts or a handful of romantic upmarket resorts on Havelock and Neil Islands. Although taxes are low, accommodation is expensive by Indian standards – some of the midrange and top-end places in Port Blair are grossly overpriced for the quality – but budget travellers can find a cheap lodge in Port Blair or a simple hut by the beach on Havelock for less than Rs 150.

Prices shoot up in the peak season (15 December to 15 January). Prices given in this chapter are for midseason (1 October to 30 April, excluding peak). May to September is low season.

Camping is currently not permitted on public land or national parks in the islands.

PERMITS

Most senior civil servants come to Port Blair on two-year postings from the mainland. With such a turnover of staff, be aware that rules and regulations regarding tourism and permits are subject to sudden changes.

All foreigners need a permit to visit the Andaman Islands, and it's issued free on arrival. The 30-day permit (which can be extended to 45 days), allows foreigners to stay in Port Blair. Overnight stays are also permitted on South and Middle Andaman (excluding tribal areas), North Andaman (Diglipur), Long Island, North Passage, Little Andaman (excluding tribal areas), Havelock and Neil Islands.

The permit also allows day trips to Jolly Buoy, South Cinque, Red Skin, Ross, Narcondam, Interview and Rutland Islands, as well as The Brothers and The Sisters.

To obtain the permit, air travellers simply present their passport and fill out a form on arrival at Port Blair airport. Permits are usu-

ally issued for as long as you ask, up to the 30-day maximum.

Boat passengers will probably be met by an immigration official on arrival, but if not should seek out the immigration office at Haddo Jetty immediately – you won't be able to travel around without the permit (police will frequently ask to see it, especially when disembarking on another island, and hotels may also need the details). Check current regulations regarding boat travel with:

A&N Tourism office (Map p452; ☎ 232747; http:// tourism.andaman.nic.in; Port Blair; ☒ 8.30am-1pm & 2-5pm Mon-Fri, 8.30am-noon Sat)

Foreigners' Registration Office Chennai (Madras; ☎ 044-28278210); Kolkata (Calcutta; ☎ 033-22473300)

Shipping Corporation of India (SCI; www.shipindia .com) Chennai (☎ 044-25231401; Rajaji Salai); Kolkata (☎ 033-22482354; 1st fl, 13 Strand Rd); Port Blair (Map p452; ☎ 233347; Aberdeen Bazaar)

National Parks & Sanctuaries

Additional permits are required to visit some national parks and sanctuaries. To save a lot of running around, take advantage of the 'single window' system for permits and information at the A&N Tourism office (see opposite) in Port Blair, where there's now also a **Forestry Department Desk** (☒ 8.30-11am & 3-5pm, closed Sun). Here you can find out whether a permit is needed, how to go about getting it, how much it costs and whether it is in fact possible to get one (it's not always).

If you plan to do something complicated, you'll be sent to the **Chief Wildlife Warden** (CWW; Map p452; ☎ 233549; Haddo Rd; ☒ 8.30am-noon & 1-4pm Mon-Fri) where your application should consist of a letter stating your case, the name of the boat and the dates involved; all things being equal, the permit should be issued within the hour.

For most day permits it's not the hassle of getting it but the cost that hurts. For areas such as Mahatma Gandhi Marine National Park, and Ross and Smith Islands near Diglipur, the permits cost Rs 50/500 for Indians/ foreigners. For Saddle Peak National Park, also near Diglipur, the cost is Rs 25/250.

Students with valid ID often only pay minimal entry fees, but must produce a letter from the Chief Wildlife Warden in Port Blair authorising the discount.

The Nicobar Islands are normally off limits to all except Indian nationals engaged in research, government business or trade.

Activities

DIVING

Crystal-clear waters, superb coral, kaleido-scopic marine life and some virtually undis-covered sites make the Andaman Islands a world-class diving destination.

Dive Operators

There are currently two professional dive outfits based on Havelock Island, and the main dive season – depending on the mon-soon – runs from about November to about April. The centres offer fully equipped boat dives, Discover Scuba Diving courses (around US$100), open water (US$350) and advanced courses (US$270), as well as Divemaster train-ing. Prices vary depending on the location, number of participants and duration of the course, but diving in the Andamans is not cheap (compared with Southeast Asia) at around US$45/70 for a single/double boat dive. In national parks there's an additional cost of Rs 1000 per person per day payable directly to the park.

Barefoot Scuba (Map p456; ☎ in Port Blair 237656; www.barefootindia.com) Based at Café del Mar at No 3 Village in Havelock, this dive operation is connected with Barefoot at Havelock resort.

Dive India (Map p456; ☎ 282187; www.diveindia.com) Based at Island Vinnie's Tropical Beach Cabanas, midway between Villages No 3 and 5, this operator offers a variety of dive and accommodation packages.

Another long-term dive operator, **Andaman Dive Club** (Map p456; ☎ 282002; www.andamandiveclub .com), is based at No 1 Village, though he's been off-island for a while. If around, he's also recommended.

Dive Sites

Much of the Andamans' underwater life can be seen between 10m and 20m, and there are sites suitable for all levels of dive experience. The greatest range of options is off Havelock Island where sites include Mac Point, Aquar-ium, Barracuda City, Turtle Bay, Seduction Point, Lighthouse, The Wall, Pilot Reef and Minerva Lodge. Neil Island sites are also vis-ited on day-dives from Havelock. Check out www.diveindia.com for detailed information on these and other dive sites.

SNORKELLING

Much easier and cheaper to arrange than diving, snorkelling can be highly rewarding. Snorkelling gear – though not always good gear – is available for hire, but you may prefer to bring your own or buy some from Port Blair (or the Indian mainland, where it's cheaper and the choice is greater). Havelock Island is one of the best, and certainly easiest, places for snorkelling as many accommoda-tion places organise boat trips out to other-wise inaccessible coral reefs and islands, and you can snorkel offshore on Neil Island.

The closest place to Port Blair for snor-kelling is North Bay. Other relatively easily accessible snorkelling sites include Red Skin and Jolly Buoy, near Wandoor.

SURFING & FISHING

Intrepid surfing travellers have been whisper-ing about **Little Andaman** since it first opened up to foreigners several years ago. Although the island is still quite remote, surfers con-tinue to drift down there for the reliable waves off the east coast. **SEAL** (http://seal-asia.com) offers a couple of live-aboard surfing charters a year, with pick-up and drop-off in Port Blair, be-tween mid-March and mid-May.

The Andamans also have game fishing op-portunities. The occasional charter boat out of Phuket makes **live-aboard trips** (www.andaman island-fishing.com), usually around March.

Getting There & Away

Getting to the Andamans can be an adventure in itself if you take the boat from Chennai or Kolkata. It's a long journey and you'll need to plan ahead as there's usually only one or two sailings a fortnight from each mainland city. Flying from Chennai, Kolkata or Delhi is relatively quick and easy but book ahead to ensure a seat in high season.

AIR

Indian Airlines (Chennai ☎ 044-28555201; Kolkata ☎ 033-22110730; Port Blair Map p452; ☎ 233108; ☑ 9am-1pm & 2-4pm Mon-Sat) flies daily to Port Blair from Chennai (US$230) and Kolkata (US$245). **Jet Airways** (Chennai ☎ 044-28414141; Port Blair ☎ 236922; ☑ 9am-7pm Mon-Sat, 9am-3pm Sun) flies at least once daily from Chennai (US$235). Air Deccan flies daily from Chennai, and Air Sahara flies daily from Delhi; their airport counters open to coincide with flights.

There's been talk for some years about di-rect flights from Phuket (Thailand) to Port Blair, but these seem to have been shelved after the tsunami, and at least until the airport

ISLAND INDIGENES

The Andaman and Nicobar Islands' indigenous peoples constitute just 12% of the population and, in most cases, their numbers are decreasing.

Onge

Two-thirds of Little Andaman's Onge Island was taken over by the Forest Department and 'settled' in 1977. The 100 or so remaining members of the Onge tribe live in a 25-sq-km reserve covering Dugong Creek and South Bay, and were (temporarily) relocated to refugee camps in Port Blair following the tsunami. Anthropological studies suggest that the Onge population has declined due to demoralisation through loss of territory.

Sentinelese

The Sentinelese, unlike the other tribes in these islands, have consistently repelled outside contact. Every few years, contact parties arrive on the beaches of North Sentinel Island, the last redoubt of the Sentinelese, with gifts of coconuts, bananas, pigs and red plastic buckets, only to be showered with arrows, although in recent years encounters have been a little less hostile. About 250 Sentinelese remain.

Andamanese

Now numbering only about 40, it seems impossible that the Andamanese can escape extinction. There were around 7000 Andamanese in the mid-19th century but friendliness to the colonisers was their undoing, and by 1971 all but 19 of the population had been swept away by measles, syphilis and influenza epidemics. They've been resettled on tiny Strait Island.

Jarawa

The 350 remaining Jarawa occupy the 639-sq-km reserve on South and Middle Andaman Islands. In 1953 the chief commissioner requested an armed sea plane bomb Jarawa settlements and their territory has been consistently disrupted by the Andaman Trunk Rd, forest clearance and settler and tourist encroachment. Hardly surprisingly, most Jarawa remain hostile to contact although encounters with outsiders are becoming more common.

Shompen

Only about 250 Shompen remain in the forests on Great Nicobar. Seminomadic hunter-gatherers who live along the riverbanks, they have resisted integration and avoid areas occupied by Indian immigrants.

Nicobarese

The 30,000 Nicobarese are the only indigenous people whose numbers are not decreasing. The majority have converted to Christianity and have been partly assimilated into contemporary Indian society. Living in village units led by a head man, they farm pigs and cultivate coconuts, yams and bananas. The Nicobarese, who probably descended from people of Malaysia and Myanmar, inhabit a number of islands in the Nicobar group, centred on Car Nicobar, the region worst affected by the tsunami.

is upgraded to full international status. Check the tourism department's **website** (http://tourism .andaman.nic.in) for updates.

BOAT

There are usually four to six sailings a month between Port Blair and the Indian mainland –

fortnightly to/from Kolkata (56 hours) and weekly (in high season) to/from Chennai (60 hours) on four vessels operated by **SCI** (Map p452; ☎ 233347; www.shipindia.com; Aberdeen Bazaar, Port Blair). The schedule is erratic, so check with the SCI in advance or see the **A&N Tourism** (www.tourism .andaman.nic.in) website, which usually posts an up-to-date schedule. Also, take the sailing times with a large grain of salt – travellers have reported sitting on the boat at Kolkata harbour for up to 12 hours, or waiting to dock near Port Blair for several hours. So with hold-ups, and variable weather and sea conditions, the trip can take three full days or more. The service from Chennai goes via Cap Nicobar once a month, taking an extra two days, but only residents may disembark. There is usually a service once a month from Visakhapatnam in Andhra Pradesh (see p299 for more details).

If you're buying your return ticket in Port Blair, go to the 1st floor of the A&N Tourism office where they can reserve you a berth under the tourist-quota system; you then take the approval letter to the Directorate of Shipping Services' ticket office at Phoenix Bay Jetty. This process can take some days, so it's simpler to arrange return tickets on the mainland when purchasing your outward ticket.

Ships currently in use are the MV *Nancowry* and MV *Swarajdweep* from Chennai, the MV *Nicobar* and MV *Akbar* from Kolkata, and MV *Harshavardan* from both ports.

Classes vary slightly between the boats, but the cheapest class of accommodation is bunk (Rs 1510), which can be difficult to get. Next up is 2nd or B class (Rs 3870, 16 berths), 1st or A class (Rs 4860, four to six berths) and deluxe cabin (Rs 5880). Food (tiffin for breakfast, and thalis for lunch and dinner) costs around Rs 150 per day. Almost everyone complains; bring something (fruit in particular) to supplement your diet. Some bedding is supplied, but if you're travelling bunk class, bring a sleeping sheet and be prepared for fetid toilets. Many travellers take a hammock to string up on deck.

Getting Around

All roads – and ferries – lead to Port Blair, but getting around the islands can be a slow process, particularly to outlying islands. The main island group – South, Middle and North Andaman – is connected by road, with ferry crossings and bridges. Buses run south from Port Blair to Wandoor, and north to Bharatang, Rangat, Mayabunder and finally to Diglipur, 325km north of the capital. But don't expect to cover any more than 30km an hour, even in a taxi.

Of course, a boat is the only way to reach most islands and both the rigour and romance of ferry travel is alive and well here – you'll often see flying fish and even dolphins from crowded decks. It's relatively quick and easy to get to Havelock and Neil Islands, and there are regular ferries to Rangat, Mayabunder and Diglipur among others. The best source of information about inter-island ferry schedules is in the daily newssheets in Port Blair; the *Andaman Herald* and *Daily Telegrams* list sailing times up to a week in advance.

A subsidised inter-island helicopter service, launched in 2003, remains in service to destinations including Havelock Island (Rs 850; twice weekly) and Diglipur (Rs 2125; once weekly). Bookings must be made at the islands' **Secretariat** (☎ 230093) in Port Blair.

Indian mainland train bookings can also be made in the Secretariat complex, at the **Railway Bookings Centre** (⏰ 8am-12.30pm & 1-2pm) which is very useful for onward travel plans.

PORT BLAIR
pop 100,186

The green, ramshackle capital sprawls around a harbour on the east coast of South Andaman and is the administrative nerve centre of the islands. There's plenty to see in town relating to the islands' colonial past plus a couple of interesting museums, and as this is the only place to change money, reliably access the internet and book (and wait for) onward transport, most travellers will spend at least a couple of days here. If you want to experience the more natural beauty of the Andamans – above and below the water – book a ferry and move on to Havelock or one of the other islands.

Orientation

Most of the hotels, the bus station and inter-island ferries from Phoenix Bay Jetty are around or above the Aberdeen Bazaar area. The airport is about 4km south of town.

Information
EMERGENCY
Aberdeen Police Station (☎ 233077, 32100; MG Rd)
GB Pant Hospital (☎ 232102; GB Pant Rd)

INTERNET ACCESS
Browsenet@Hitech (MA Rd; per hr Rs 30; ⏰ 8.30am-9.30pm, closed Sun)
Net Across (Junglighat Main Rd; per hr Rs 20; ⏰ 9am-10pm) Next door to the India Tourism office.
Samsuva's Internet (MG Rd; per hr Rs 40; ⏰ 9am-8pm) Between post office and YMCA.

MONEY

Port Blair is the only place in the Andamans where you can change cash or travellers cheques, and find an ATM.

ICICI ATM (cnr Foreshore & MA Rds)

Island Travels (☎ 233358; islandtravels@yahoo.com; Aberdeen Bazaar; ⊙ 9am-1pm & 2-6pm Mon-Sat) This is one of several travel agencies with foreign-exchange facilities.

State Bank of India (MA Rd; ⊙ 9am-noon & 1-3pm Mon-Fri, 10am-noon Sat) Travellers cheques and foreign currency can be changed here.

UTI Bank (cnr MG Rd & MA Rd, Aberdeen Bazaar) Near the youth hostel.

POST

Main post office (MG Rd; ⊙ 9am-5pm Mon-Sat)

TOURIST INFORMATION

A&N Tourism office (☎ 232747; www.tourism .andaman.nic.in; Kamaraj Rd; ⊙ 8.30am-1pm & 2-5pm Mon-Fri, 8.30am-noon Sat) This is the main island tourist office and the place to book government accommodation.

India Tourism (☎ 233006; 2nd fl, 189 Junglighat Main Rd; ⊙ 8.30am-12.30pm & 1-5pm Mon-Fri) Formerly the Government of India tourist office, it has little information about mainland India but its staff are eager to help.

Sights & Activities

CELLULAR JAIL NATIONAL MEMORIAL

Built by the British over a period of 18 years from 1890, and preserved as a shrine to India's freedom fighters, the **Cellular Jail National Memorial** (GB Pant Rd; admission Rs 5, camera/video Rs 10/50; ⊙ 9am-12.30pm & 1.30-5pm, closed Mon) is well worth a visit to understand the islands' colonial past and its significance in the memory of the Indian people. Originally seven wings containing 698 cells radiated from a central tower, but only three remain. These remnants, however, give a fair impression of the 'hell on earth' that the prisoners here endured. There's an art gallery, museum, martyrs' memorial, the original gallows, and good views from what was once the central tower.

An informative and atmospheric **sound-and-light show** (adult/child Rs 20/10) depicts the jail's brutal history. It's in Hindi nightly at 6pm and usually in English at 7.15pm but check this, as language and timing vary depending on numbers of local and overseas visitors in town. No refunds for bad weather!

SAMUDRIKA MARINE MUSEUM

Run by the Indian navy, this interesting **museum** (☎ 232012, ext 2214; Haddo Rd; adult/child Rs 10/5,

camera/video Rs 20/40; ⊙ 9am-5.30pm Tue-Sun) is a good place to get a handle on the islands' eco-system. Across several galleries you'll find informative displays on the islands' tribal communities, plants, animals and shells (check out the giant clam shell), as well as rooms dedicated to corals and marine archaeology.

ANTHROPOLOGICAL MUSEUM

With excellent displays of tools, clothing and photographs of the indigenous islanders, this **museum** (☎ 232291; Indian/foreigner Rs 10/50; ⊙ 9am-1pm & 1.30-4.30pm, closed Thu) helps unlock the mysteries of local tribal cultures. There are authentic reconstructions of tribal dwellings with decent – if old fashioned – information in English, and a small selection of Andaman-related books in the gift shop.

MINI-ZOO

Some of the 200 animal species unique to the islands can be seen in rusting cages at the small and rather sad **zoo** (Haddo Rd; adult/child Rs 2/1; ⊙ 8am-5pm, closed Mon). These include the Nicobar pigeon, the Andaman pig (the staple diet of some tribal groups) and the crab-eating macaque. Feeding time is 8.30am to 9am, and there's a short film shown at 10am and 3pm.

FOREST MUSEUM & CHATHAM SAW MILL

Located on Chatham Island (reached by a road bridge), the **saw mill** (admission Rs 2; ⊙ 8am-2.30pm, closed Sun) was set up by the British in 1836 and was one of the largest wood processors in Asia. Inside is the forest museum, which displays locally grown woods, including the padauk, and has displays on the history of timber milling on the island. It may not be to everyone's taste – especially conservationists – but it gives a different perspective on the islands' colonial history and economy.

AQUARIUM & SWIMMING POOL

The **aquarium** (Mahabir Singh Rd; adult/child Rs 5/3; ⊙ 9am-1pm & 2-4.45pm, closed Wed & 2nd Sat of month) displays some of the 350 species found in the Andaman Sea – many pickled in formaldehyde – as well as more interesting live specimens in small tanks, including puffer fish, batfish and tiger fish. Opposite the aquarium, the Olympic-sized public **swimming pool** (admission Rs 25; ⊙ Mon- Sat) is clean enough, and open to men only 6.30am to 8am and 5pm to 6pm, to women only 4pm to 5pm, and to families 6pm to 7pm. It's closed at other times.

ANDAMAN & NICOBAR ISLANDS

ANDAMAN & NICOBAR ISLANDS

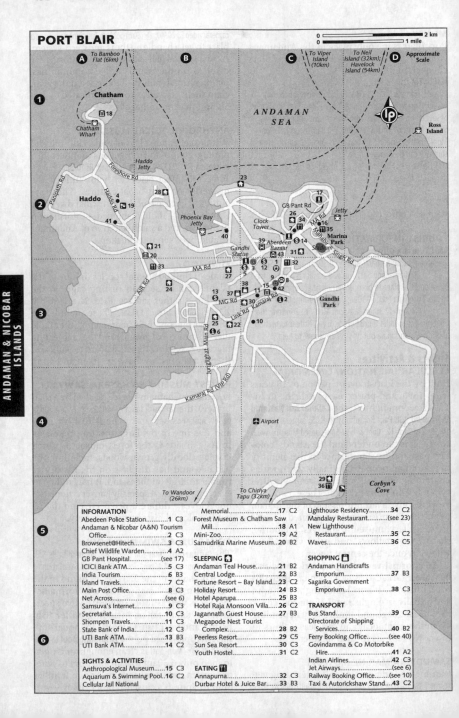

PORT BLAIR

INFORMATION
Abedeen Police Station............1 C3
Andaman & Nicobar (A&N) Tourism
Office.............................2 C3
Browsenet@Hitech............3 C3
Chief Wildlife Warden............4 A2
GB Pant Hospital..............(see 17)
ICICI Bank ATM....................5 C3
India Tourism.......................6 B3
Island Travels.......................7 C2
Main Post Office...................8 C3
Net Across......................(see 6)
Samsuva's Internet...............9 C3
Secretariat........................10 C3
Shompen Travels................11 C3
State Bank of India.............12 C3
UTI Bank ATM...................13 B3
UTI Bank ATM...................14 C2

SIGHTS & ACTIVITIES
Anthropological Museum...15 C3
Aquarium & Swimming Pool..16 C2
Cellular Jail National

Memorial..........................17 C2
Forest Museum & Chatham Saw
Mill..................................18 A1
Mini-Zoo..........................19 A2
Samudrika Marine Museum..20 B2

SLEEPING
Andaman Teal House............21 B2
Central Lodge.....................22 B3
Fortune Resort – Bay Island..23 C2
Holiday Resort....................24 B3
Hotel Aparupa....................25 B3
Hotel Raja Monsoon Villa....26 C2
Jagannath Guest House.......27 B3
Megapode Nest Tourist
Complex.........................28 B2
Peerless Resort..................29 C5
Sun Sea Resort..................30 B3
Youth Hostel.....................31 C2

EATING
Annapurna..........................32 C3
Durbar Hotel & Juice Bar.......33 B3

Lighthouse Residency............34 C2
Mandalay Restaurant..........(see 23)
New Lighthouse
Restaurant........................35 C2
Waves...............................36 C5

SHOPPING
Andaman Handicrafts
Emporium.........................37 B3
Sagarika Government
Emporium.........................38 C3

TRANSPORT
Bus Stand..........................39 C2
Directorate of Shipping
Services..........................40 B2
Ferry Booking Office............(see 40)
Govindamma & Co Motorbike
Hire................................41 A2
Indian Airlines....................42 C3
Jet Airways......................(see 6)
Railway Booking Office........(see 10)
Taxi & Autorickshaw Stand....43 C2

CORBYN'S COVE

Corbyn's Cove, 4km east of the airport and 7km south of the town, is the nearest beach to Port Blair – a small curve of sand backed by palms. It's popular for swimming, sunset-viewing and lazing around, and is packed with picnicking locals on Sunday and holidays.

Tours

Possible day tours include trips to Wandoor Beach and Chiryu Tapu, or to Mt Harriet. There are few scheduled tours, but the following agencies can arrange private tours (which basically mean hiring a car and driver).

Andaman Teal House (☎ 232642; Haddo Rd) An A&N Tourism agency.

Island Travels (☎ 233034; islandtravels@yahoo.com; Aberdeen Bazaar) The most helpful and clued-up of the agencies, used to dealing with international travellers.

Shompen Travels (☎ 233028; Kamaraj Rd) Provides local tours.

Sleeping

Accommodation is quite scattered in Port Blair, but most places are within a few kilometres of each other around MA Rd and Aberdeen Bazaar. Within each price range there's a huge variety in quality, and accommodation in general is higher priced than its equivalent on the mainland. Checkout is usually 8am, to get ready for early-flight arrivals.

BUDGET

Youth Hostel (☎ 232459; dm/d Rs 50/100) Opposite the stadium, this is a rare Indian YHA, although the only discount is for students (Rs 30). It's still the cheapest place around but it's often filled with groups. Management can be unwilling to accommodate foreigners.

Central Lodge (☎ 243791; Link Rd; s/d with shared bathroom Rs 70/120, with private bathroom Rs 80/150) Set back from the road, this is a basic wooden building. Small rooms are a bit grim but it's a popular cheapie – a throwback to simple lodgings on the backpacker trail of old, minus the banana pancakes.

Jagannath Guest House (☎ 232148; 72 MA Rd; dm/s/d Rs 60/200/300) This is a reasonably good budget choice, not least because the management is accustomed to travellers. Rooms are simple but relatively clean and most have a small balcony.

Holiday Resort (☎ 234231; Prem Nagar; s/d Rs 350/500, with AC Rs 600/800; ✷ 💻) Don't be fooled by the name – this isn't a resort or much of a place for a holiday, but it's central, cleanish and straddles budget and midrange mainly because there are AC rooms with TVs.

Hotel Raja Monsoon Villa (☎ 241133; s/d Rs 400/550, with AC Rs 550/900) Centrally located, this tatty, clean and friendly family-run hotel is in a side-street of small shops and tea stalls opposite the town's main mosque.

Many cheap lodges line Aberdeen Bazaar.

MIDRANGE

Andaman Teal House (☎ 234060; Haddo Rd; d without/with AC Rs 400/800; ✷) Run by A&N Tourism (bookings must be made through the tourist office), this is reasonably central and has a range of ageing rooms spilling through gardens and down the hillside. The AC rooms at the top are better, with TV, carpet and furniture – the others are bare and musty.

Hotel Aparupa (☎ 246582; hotelaparupa@yahoo.com; Link Rd; s/d Rs 750/1050, with AC Rs 900/1200; ✷) This smart hotel has 26 smallish but immaculate rooms with tile floors, TV and central AC. There's a good little restaurant with a view of sorts and a bar.

Sun Sea Resort (☎ 238330; MG Rd; s/d from Rs 900/1250; ✷) New in 2006, at these prices (which include breakfast) this is the best value in town. Clean, comfortable and central – with a truly unique exterior, a purple bar and an AC restaurant – it is, however, nowhere near the sea.

Megapode Nest Tourist Complex (☎ 232207; aniidco@vsnl.com; off Haddo Rd; s/d from Rs 1000/1400, cottages Rs 2000; ✷) At Haddo, on the hill above the bay, the Megapode Nest is good value in the upper midrange. Many of the rooms have harbour views and there are large AC doubles and generous yurt-style AC cottages. Prices include breakfast, and it's pleasant to sit in the garden with a cold beer.

TOP END

Major credit cards are accepted at the following hotels and prices include breakfast. They have their charms, but don't expect luxury; they're overpriced for the facilities offered.

Fortune Resort – Bay Island (☎ 234101; bayislandresort@fortuneparkhotels.com; Marine Hill; s/d from Rs 2749/3960; ✷ 💻) Port Blair's top hotel boasts a great location, perched above the ocean with fine sea views from its terraced garden and balcony restaurant. The rooms, while comfortable with polished floors, balconies, neat furnishings, are small and make sure to ask for a sea-facing room. There's a swimming pool and a good restaurant and bar.

Peerless Resort (☎ 229263; pblbeachinn@sancharnet .in; s/d Rs 2250/3650, cottage d Rs 4500; ⚑) The location is the main plus for Peerless Resort – just back from Corbyn's Cove Beach. Otherwise, the rooms are ageing, undersized and in need of serious maintenance and a good clean, although most have a balcony and sea views. The manicured gardens are pleasant, and there's a tennis court, bar and restaurant.

Eating

Port Blair has a range of eating places – from cheap Indian thali places around the bazaar to multi-cuisine hotel restaurants. Good seafood is available at a few places, and those listed are open for breakfast, lunch and dinner unless stated otherwise.

Annapurna (MG Rd; from Rs 20) This spotless veg restaurant, just south of Aberdeen Bazaar, whips up good fresh *paratha* for breakfast and afternoon snacks, as well as main meals; go early or late to avoid local tour groups in peak season.

Durbar Hotel & Juice Bar (near junction Haddo & MA Rd; mains from Rs 20) For cheap clean eats and juices, try this place; the lunchtime side dish of spicy fish fillet (Rs 10) goes well with a thali (Rs 20).

New Lighthouse Restaurant (Marina Park; mains Rs 25-75, seafood Rs 150-350) A decaying structure next to the aquarium, this has a breezy semi-open-air section with a view over the water across sundry piles of rubbish. Fresh seafood – including whole fish, crab and lobster (prices depend on weight and season) – is the main attraction, and you can also get breakfast or a beer here.

Lighthouse Residency (MA Rd, Aberdeen Bazaar; mains Rs 45-110; ☯ lunch & dinner) Modern and trying hard to be chic, this once bright restaurant and cocktail bar had been seriously overtaken by mould when we visited. However there's AC, the beer's cold, and Thai and Chinese dishes make a welcome addition to the Indian favourites.

Waves (Corbyn's Cove; mains Rs 30-95; ☯ lunch & dinner) This breezy open-air beachfront restaurant is a good spot for lunch or an evening meal beneath the palms; indoors it's a bit dismal. Seafood is available (Malai prawns Rs 75, crab and lobster by weight), along with Thai and Indian dishes. You can get a beer at the resort next door.

Mandalay Restaurant (Marine Hill) The open-deck restaurant at Fortune Resort – Bay Island is enjoyable for the views alone, and you can feast in season on the daily buffets (breakfast Rs 200, lunch and dinner Rs 350).

Shopping

Aberdeen Bazaar is lined with stalls selling cheap clothing and household goods. Island crafts such as fine wood carvings, shell jewellery, bamboo and cane furniture, are available from a handful of emporiums and speciality shops. Most of the shells on sale are collected legally – a good emporium can show proof of this – but, as always, be aware of your home countries' restrictions on importing them.

Andaman Handicrafts Emporium (☎ 240141; MG Rd, Middle Point)

Sagarika Government Emporium (MG Rd, Middle Point)

Getting There & Away

See p448 for details on transport to and from the Andaman Islands.

BOAT

Most inter-island ferries depart from Phoenix Bay Jetty. Advance tickets for boats can be purchased from the ticket counters between 9am and 11am the day before travel. On some boats, such as the Neil and Havelock Island ferries, tickets can be purchased on the boat but in high season you risk missing out.

From Chatham Wharf there are hourly passenger ferries to Bamboo Flat (Rs 3, 15 minutes).

BUS

The bus stand in Port Blair has a clear, current timetable hanging from the roof.

Services include four daily buses to Wandoor (Rs 8, 1½ hours). There's a daily bus at 4.30am to Diglipur (Rs 120, 12 hours). A direct bus goes to Mayabunder at 5am and 10.30am (Rs 95, nine hours) and to Rangat at 5.45am and 10.50am (Rs 65, six hours).

If you want to take the scenic 48km road trip to Bamboo Flat and Mount Harriet, there's a bus at 8.15am and 4pm (Rs 15, 1½ hours); returning by ferry will take only 15 minutes.

Getting Around

The central area is easy enough to get around on foot, but if you want to get out to Corbyn's Cove, Haddo or Chatham Island, you'll need some form of transport. A taxi or autorick-shaw from the airport to Aberdeen Bazaar costs around Rs 50. From Aberdeen Bazaar to Phoenix Bay Jetty is about Rs 25 and to Haddo Jetty it's around Rs 35.

A good way to explore the island south of Port Blair is by moped or motorbike. They can be hired through **Govindamma & Co** (☎ 232999; gdmyamaha@yahoo.co.in; off Haddo Rd) for Rs 150 per day for a gearless scooter or Rs 200 per day for a 125cc motorbike. Rs 1000 deposit is required and helmets (of sorts) are supplied. Go to their Yamaha workshop on 2nd DP St, opposite the Hindi Medium School on Haddo Rd but call ahead to check availability.

Bicycles are good for getting around the town and the immediate Port Blair area. They can be hired from stalls in Aberdeen Bazaar for Rs 40 per day.

AROUND PORT BLAIR & SOUTH ANDAMAN
Ross Island
An essential half-day trip from Port Blair, this eerie place was once the administrative headquarters for the British. **Ross Island** (admission Rs 20) is where all the action was in those heady colonial days and newspapers of the day fondly called it the 'Paris of the East'. However, the manicured gardens and grand ballrooms were destroyed by an earthquake in 1941. Six months later, after the Japanese entered WWII, the British transferred their headquarters to Port Blair. The island was again damaged by the tsunami in 2004.

Many of the buildings still stand as evocative ruined shells slowly being consumed by trees. Landscaped paths cross the island and all of the buildings are labelled. There's a small museum with historical displays and photos of Ross Island in its heyday.

Ferries to Ross Island (Rs 16, 20 minutes) depart from the jetty behind the Aquarium in Port Blair at 8.30am, 10.30am, 12.30pm and 2pm Thursday to Tuesday; check current times when you buy your ticket, as times can be affected by tides.

Viper Island
The afternoon boat trip to **Viper Island** (admission Rs 5) is worthwhile to see the sobering remains of the ochre-coloured brick jail and the gallows built by the British in 1867. Viper is named after a 19th-century British trading ship that was wrecked nearby.

A harbour cruise to Viper Island leaves from the jetty behind the Aquarium daily at 3pm (Rs 65, 45 minutes each way) stopping at the island for about 20 minutes. On Wednesday (when no boats are going to Ross Island), there are more frequent ferries.

North Bay
This is the most easily accessible snorkelling bay to Port Blair. A combined boat tour to Ross and Viper Islands and North Bay leaves daily from the jetty behind the Aquarium (per person Rs 250; ☽ 9.30am-5pm), allowing 2½ hours to snorkel and explore the bay.

Mt Harriet
Mt Harriet (365m) is across the inlet, north of Port Blair, and there's a road up to the top with good views and good birding. To reach Mt Harriet, take the Bamboo Flat passenger ferry (Rs 3, 15 minutes), which leaves regularly from Chatham Jetty. From Bamboo Flat the road runs 7km along the coast and up to the summit. Taxis will do the trip for around Rs 250 if you don't want to walk.

Wandoor
Wandoor, a tiny speck of a village 29km southwest of Port Blair, is the jumping-off point for **Mahatma Gandhi Marine National Park** (Indian/foreigner Rs 50/500), which covers 280 sq km and comprises 15 islands. The diverse scenery includes mangrove creeks, tropical rainforest and reefs supporting 50 types of coral. The marine park's snorkelling sites at **Jolly Buoy** and **Red Skin** islands, damaged during the tsunami, have reopened and boats leave somewhat erratically from Wandoor Jetty for visits to both (per person Rs 300); check the current situation at the Forestry Department desk at A&N Tourism in Port Blair. You can pick up your permit there, or at the office next to the Wandoor Jetty. However, if Havelock or Neil Islands are on your Andamans itinerary, you may find it easier and cheaper to wait until you reach them for your underwater experience.

Buses run from Port Blair to Wandoor (Rs 8, 1½ hours). About 2km beyond the Wandoor Jetty are a number of quiet, sandy beaches with some excellent snorkelling.

Chiriya Tapu
Chiriya Tapu, 30km south of Port Blair, is a tiny village with beaches and mangroves.

There's a beach about 2km south of Chiriya Tapu that has some of the best snorkelling in the area. There are seven buses a day to the village from Port Blair (Rs 8, 1½ hours) and it's possible to arrange boats from here to Cinque Island.

Cinque Island

The uninhabited islands of North and South Cinque, connected by a sandbar, are part of the wildlife sanctuary south of Wandoor. The islands are surrounded by coral reefs, and are among the most beautiful in the Andamans. Visiting boats usually anchor off South Cinque and passengers transfer via dinghy to the beach.

Only day visits are allowed but, unless you're on one of the day trips occasionally organised by travel agencies, you need to get permission in advance from the Chief Wildlife Warden (p447). The islands are two hours by boat from Chiriya Tapu or 3½ hours from Wandoor, and are covered by the Mahatma Gandhi Marine National Park permit (Indian/ foreigner Rs 50/500).

HAVELOCK ISLAND

With one of the Andaman's most dazzling beaches and plenty of cheap bamboo-hut accommodation, Havelock is the island of choice for travellers wanting to kick back and enjoy the slow (but not comatose) pace of island life. It's easily accessible from Port Blair, and offers excellent snorkelling and scuba-diving opportunities. Although Havelock is the most developed of the islands, it's still very low-key and simple – a world away from the beach resorts of mainland India or Southeast Asia.

Inhabited by Bengali settlers since the 1950s, Havelock is about 54km northeast of Port Blair and covers 100 sq km. Only the northern third of the island is settled, and each village is referred to by a number. Boats dock at the jetty at No 1 Village; the main bazaar is 2km south at No 3 Village; and most of the accommodation is strung along the east coast between villages No 2 and No 5.

Sights & Activities

Radha Nagar Beach (also called No 7), on the northwestern side of the island about 12km from the jetty, is a gorgeous stretch of squeaky clean white sand – though some seaweed gets thrown up during monsoon – and crystal-clear water backed by native forest. Don't miss a sunset here. In peak season you can take a short **elephant ride** (adult/child Rs 20/10) through the beach's shady forest. Ten minutes' walk along the beach to the northwest is the gorgeous **'lagoon'** stretch of sheltered sand and calm water.

Elephant Beach, where there's good snorkelling, is further north and reached by a 40-minute walk through a muddy elephant logging trail and swamp; it's well-marked (off the cross-island road), but is hard going after rain. The beach itself virtually disappeared after the tsunami and at high tide it's impossible to reach – ask locally.

A highlight of Havelock is **snorkelling** or **fishing**, and the best way to do either is on

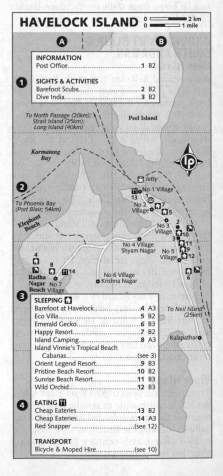

HAVELOCK ISLAND 0 — 2 km / 0 — 1 mile

INFORMATION	
Post Office	1 B2

SIGHTS & ACTIVITIES	
Barefoot Scuba	2 B2
Dive India	3 B2

To North Passage (20km);
Strait Island (25km);
Long Island (40km)

Peel Island

Karmatang Bay

To Phoenix Bay (Port Blair; 54km)

Elephant Beach

Jetty
No 1 Village
13
No 2 Village 7 5
No 3 Village 2 10
No 4 Village 3 11
Shyam Nagar No 5 Village 9 12
4
8
14
Radha Nagar No 7 No 6 Village
Beach Village Krishna Nagar 6

To Neil Island (25km)

Kalapathar

SLEEPING	
Barefoot at Havelock	4 A3
Eco Villa	5 B2
Emerald Gecko	6 B3
Happy Resort	7 B2
Island Camping	8 A3
Island Vinnie's Tropical Beach Cabanas	(see 3)
Orient Legend Resort	9 B3
Pristine Beach Resort	10 B2
Sunrise Beach Resort	11 B3
Wild Orchid	12 B3

EATING	
Cheap Eateries	13 B2
Cheap Eateries	14 A3
Red Snapper	(see 12)

TRANSPORT	
Bicycle & Moped Hire	(see 10)

THE GOOD, THE BAD & THE UGLY

Havelock has become a magnet for budget travellers over the last few years. This is a mixed blessing for islanders, who are delighted by the income they bring, but considerably less delighted by the behaviour of a noticeable minority. Here's the gist of conversations we had repeatedly with locals:

'I don't understand why when we agree a price for something, a room or a tour or motorbike hire, later they shout at me and want me to make a smaller price. Why do they break their word?'

'Some of them are so aggressive. They don't know how to have a conversation or how to ask for something, they only know how to shout. Now I don't have anything to do with those ones, you can tell them a mile off.'

'I think they think we're stupid. They eat almost all the meal and then complain that it wasn't what they ordered and want us to give it free or to make them another one.'

'Well my family can't go to the beach and I can't go out fishing sometimes, when my boat's on-shore and men and women are sunbathing naked on the sand beside it. We don't take our clothes off in front of strangers. They never see us like that, so why do they think it's OK and that we don't mind?'

Fair comments.

---

a boat trip organised by one of the accommodation places. Trips cost from Rs 300 to 1000, depending on the number of people and the distance. Wild Orchid organises full-day trips (per couple from Rs 2000) that take you through a mangrove swamp and to some great snorkelling sites.

Havelock is also the premier spot for **scuba diving** on the Andamans; **Barefoot Scuba** and **Dive India** are the two professional dive outfits here (see p448 for more information).

Some resorts can organise guided **jungle treks** for keen walkers or birders, though be warned that the forest floor turns to slippery and very gluggy mud after rain, and walking is hard work. The inside rainforest is spectacular, giving new meaning to the notion of tall trees, and the **bird-watching** – especially on the forest fringes – is rewarding; look out for the blue-black racket-tailed drongo trailing his fabulous tail feathers and, by way of contrast, the brilliant golden oriole.

About 5km beyond Village No 5 is Kalapathar, where an **elephant training camp** is sometimes open to visitors. Beyond Kalapathar the road peters out into deep forest, and there are some good snorkelling spots accessible by boat along the coast.

Sleeping & Eating

Heading south along the coast from the jetty there's a string of simple huts and a couple of more upmarket places at No 5 Village or west to No 7 Village. The listings that follow are in geographical order beyond the jetty.

Pristine Beach Resort (☎ 282344; alexpristine@ hotmail.com; huts Rs 100-150, cottages with private bathroom Rs 250-400) Run by an affable couple, these cute huts, good restaurant and a licence to serve alcohol make this a cut above most places. The bar stays open late for night owls (but quietly enough to allow other guests to sleep). It's on a nice bit of beach.

Island Vinnie's Tropical Beach Cabanas (☎ 282187; www.islandvinnie.com; cabanas without/with bathroom Rs 450/1200) New in 2006, these comfortably furnished pink canvas tents, raised on individual verandas, wouldn't look out of place in a desert setting, and so far they're surviving the monsoon climate. Packages are offered for divers, and for visitors who are staying more than 10 days.

Wild Orchid (☎ 282472; www.wildorchidandaman .com; d cottages without/with AC Rs 2100/2500; ☒) Set back from a secluded beach, this is a mellow, friendly place with tastefully furnished cottages designed in traditional Andamanese style. Modern bathrooms, four-poster beds and verandas, and roomy public spaces with comfortable seating add to the comfort factor. There's also a masseur on-site in season, and a bar. The restaurant here, Red Snapper (mains Rs 100 to 250), is one of few genuinely good places to eat on the island and certainly scores on ambience. Fresh seafood is usually available (often caught by the owner or guests!) and the menu can include terrific homemade pasta, Thai curries and Continental dishes, as well as Indian favourites. Book your table early in peak season.

Emerald Gecko (☎ 282170; www.emerald-gecko.com; small huts Rs 200-300, large huts Rs 1000-1500) This is a step up in quality from other hut resorts. There are four comfortable double-storey huts with open-roofed bathrooms, lovingly constructed from bamboo rafts that have drifted ashore from Myanmar. There are some budget huts too, and a restaurant with a good creative menu designed by the same folk as Wild Orchid, and a bar. It's low-key and peaceful.

Island Camping (furnished tents Rs 150-500) Island Camping has tented accommodation in an enviable location among the palms at the end of the road to Radha Nagar Beach. All tents have solid floors, raised camp beds and mosquito nets. It's open from November to March; book through A&N Tourism in Port Blair.

Barefoot at Havelock (☎ 282151, in Port Blair 237656; www.barefootindia.com; cottages Rs 3600-5300; 🔀) For the location alone – ensconced in bird-filled forest grounds just back from Radha Nagar Beach – this is the Andamans most luxurious resort, conscious of its use of natural resources. Accommodation is in 18 beautifully designed timber and bamboo-thatched cottages with four-poster beds, stylish bathrooms and verandas, and attention to privacy. Staff and food service still have some way to go to match the quality of accommodation.

Numerous small places have set up under the palm trees, with accommodation in sturdy bamboo huts with lights and fans for around Rs 150 to 300, and all have their own simple, open-sided restaurants. Popular hot spots at the time of research:

Happy Resort (☎ 282061; Village No 2)
Eco Villa (☎ 282072; Village No 2)
Sunrise Beach Resort (Village No 3)
Orient Legend Resort (☎ 282389; Village No 3)

There are cheap eateries serving thalis and fish dishes near the jetty, and on the road leading to No 7 beach.

Getting There & Away

Ferry times are changeable, but there are always direct sailings to and from Havelock from Phoenix Jetty in Port Blair at least once daily, and often twice or more (tourist ferry Rs 150; 2½ hours). Check times in the local newssheet or at the jetty, and you're best to book at least a day in advance at the Port Blair passenger terminal. The ticket office is open between 9am and 11am.

Several ferries a week link Havelock with Neil Island, and also with Rangat in Middle Andaman, where buses continue north to Diglipur.

Getting Around

A local bus connects the jetty and villages on a roughly hourly circuit, but having your own transport is useful on Havelock. You can rent mopeds or motorbikes (per day Rs 150) and bicycles (per day Rs 40 to 50) from the shop outside Pristine Beach Resort, from the stall with the sign in Village No 3, or ask at your hotel.

An autorickshaw from the jetty to No 3 Village is Rs 30, to No 5 is Rs 50 and to No 7 it's Rs 200.

NEIL ISLAND

If you *really* want to slow down, and are looking for peace, isolation and near-deserted beaches without being a castaway, Neil Island, 40km northeast of Port Blair, is a good place to get off the ferry. Much quieter than nearby Havelock Island, Neil is populated by Bengali settlers involved in fishing and agriculture. This is the place to lie on the beach, jungle-walk, snorkel, cycle through paddy fields and farms, and then lie on the beach some more.

Sights & Activities

Neil Island's beaches are numbered 1 to 5, and the road distance between them is 8km. **No 1 Beach** is the prettiest and most accessible, a 40-minute walk 3km west of the jetty and village. Most of the accommodation places are close to No 1 Beach and the island's best **snorkelling** is around the coral reef at the far (western) end of this beach. At low tide it's difficult getting over the coral into the water; conversely, at high tide the beach is underwater so plan your activities around tide times. **No 2 Beach**, on the north side of the island, has a natural bridge rock formation in the water; a cycle ride and short walk will take you to it. A track up the small hill behind Gyan Garden Restaurant leads to a **viewpoint** across the island and out to sea. **No 5 Beach**, reached via the village road to the eastern side of the island, is an enclosed stretch with a bit of swell. It's a pleasant bike ride out here (about 5km from the village); just cycle to the end of the road, and walk 50m or so straight ahead to the beach.

You should be able to hire snorkelling gear around town (per day Rs 100), but don't bank on it. Hire of a fishing boat to go to offshore snorkelling or fishing spots will cost per day between Rs 800 and 900; several people can fit on board, depending on the size of the boat. Bicycles are available for hire at several shops in the village (per day Rs 40).

Contact the charming **Saha** (☎ 282620, 9474212840), Neil Island's unofficial Mr Fixit, for help with accommodation, tours and transport.

Sleeping & Eating

In the village, a few hundred metres from the jetty, there's a market, a few shops, a couple of basic restaurants and the A&N Tourism guesthouse. West of the jetty along No 1 Beach are three small 'resorts' with basic huts and marginally more comfortable cottages; all have great potential and great locations but are in various stages of decay. All provide food.

Cocon Huts (☎ 282528; huts Rs 50, cottages Rs 350-400) The first place you come to, about 500m from the village market, has a good waterfront location but its bar has become a serious local drinking hole, and it can sometimes get pretty uncomfortable for guests.

Tango Beach Resort (☎ 282583; huts Rs 50, cottages Rs 500) Further west, this is a similar set up minus the drinkers, with a couple of concrete cottages as well as huts. It's closer to the better part of No 1 Beach.

Pearl Park Resort (☎ 282510; huts Rs 100, cottages & rooms Rs 400-1000) Pearl Park is set quietly beyond the end of the road, in a beautiful garden of palms and flowering plants a short stroll from the western end of No 1 Beach. As well as thatch huts, there are two dilapidated but once-charming Nicobarese-style cottages on stilts, and a couple of concrete hotel-style rooms.

Hawa Bill Nest (☎ 282630; dm Rs 150, d Rs 800; 🗷) It's not often that a charmless government-run hotel comes out ahead in the comfort and cleanliness stakes, but at the time of research it was true on Neil Island. Five minutes' walk from the village beach, it's convenient if not as atmospheric as the other options; book through A&N Tourism in Port Blair.

Providing somewhat erratic service out of season, but popular when/if they're up and running, **Gyan Garden Restaurant** and **Green Heaven Restaurant** are two informal and relaxed outdoor eateries and hang-outs between the village and No 1 Beach.

There are plans afoot for accommodation and food at No 5 Beach; check with the folk at Wild Orchid on Havelock Island to see what's become of those.

Getting There & Away

A ferry makes a round trip each morning from Phoenix Bay Jetty in Port Blair (Rs 36, two hours). Twice a week the Rangat ferry calls at Neil after Havelock, which is useful if you want to visit both islands.

An autorickshaw will take you to No 1 Beach from the jetty for Rs 50.

MIDDLE & NORTH ANDAMAN

The Andaman Trunk Rd runs north from Port Blair to Bharatang Island and Middle Andaman – both linked by small roll-on roll-off ferries – then onto North Andaman linked by road bridges. It's *very* slow going, but consider at least the northern part of the road – say between the jetties at Rangat and Diglipur – as an alternative to taking the ferry in both directions. Relentlessly thick jungle opening to mangrove-fringed waterways with only occasional cultivated clearings make this a spectacularly lush and green journey, especially with the knowledge that tribal people still live traditional lives in the deep forest. The road runs beside Jarawa reserves on the west coasts of South and Middle Andaman, but as most traditional Jarawa people are busy getting on with their lives in the forest you're unlikely to encounter them unless they're beside the road (see Close Encounters of the Worst Kind, p460). Motorcycles are forbidden beyond the checkpoint, 40km outside of Port Blair.

You can get to Rangat, in Middle Andaman, several times a week from Port Blair or Havelock Island by ferry (Rs 80/25, nine hours) or daily by bus (Rs 70, eight hours). **Hawksbill Nest** (☎ 279022; four-bed dm Rs 600, d without/with AC Rs 450/850; 🗷) is about 15 minutes north of Rangat, and any northbound bus will drop you there; bookings must be made at A&N Tourism in Port Blair. Hawksbill turtles do nest on the beaches of nearby Cuthbert Bay between November and February.

Mayabunder & Around

In Mayabunder there's an unexpected gem in the shape of **Sea'n'Sand** (☎ 273454; thanzin_the _great@yahoo.co.in; r Rs 200-500), a simple lodge, restaurant and bar overlooking the water 1km south of the town centre. Run by Titus and Elizabeth, along with their young family, it's low-key and will appeal to travellers looking for an experience away from the crowds. Titus organises a range of **boat-based day tours** (per tour from Rs 500-2500) that, depending on the season

CLOSE ENCOUNTERS OF THE WORST KIND Virginia Jealous

It's mid-afternoon during a torrential monsoon downpour, and our convoy of public buses, local tour vehicles, goods trucks and police escort crawls slowly along the narrow Andaman Trunk Rd, through the Jarawa tribal reserve.

There is the occasional glimpse of Jarawa people standing beside the road with a police guard – there to protect them from us, I realise, as my bus goes past. People thrust mobile phone cameras out of the windows, fling sweets and bananas, laugh and make monkey noises, and make crude gestures. How the groups of naked and shivering tribal adolescents feel about being on display like this isn't immediately apparent as we go past in a blur, further showering them with water. No-one is reprimanded or arrested or fined. Later I am told that this happens during every transport convoy, every day.

The considerable legal restrictions about contact with tribal people – no gifts, no photography, no 'feeding' – and the considerable police presence in the reserve clearly isn't effective. Many in the islands' government and civil society are lobbying to close the road to the general public and to leave the Jarawa in peace. After this trip I hope they succeed.

and how he feels about you, may include **Forty One Caves** where *hawabills* (swiftlets) make their highly prized edible nests; easy snorkelling off **Avis Island**; or a coast-and-forest-wilderness experience on **Interview Island**.

GETTING THERE & AWAY

Mayabunder, 71km north of Rangat, is linked by daily buses from Port Blair (Rs 95, 10 hours) and by once- or twice-weekly ferries.

Diglipur & Around

Diglipur, three hours by road north of Mayabunder, is the main town of North Andaman and as far north as you can get in the island chain. The town itself and nearby Kalipur are the only places on North Andaman where foreigners can stay. Ferries arrive at the Aerial Bay Jetty from where it's 11km southwest to Diglipur village and the bus stand, basic restaurants, market and a couple of lodges. Ferry tickets can be booked at the Administration Block in town. Kalipur is on the coast 8km southeast of the jetty.

SIGHTS & ACTIVITIES

The twin islands of **Smith** and **Ross**, connected by a narrow sand bar, are accessible by boat and here you can walk through forest, or swim and snorkel in the shallow waters. Since this is designated as a marine sanctuary, you must get a permit (Indian/foreigner Rs 50/500) from the **Forest Office** (6am-2pm, closed Sun) opposite the Aerial Bay Jetty. You can charter a boat to take you for the day from the village near the jetty for around Rs 500.

At 732m, **Saddle Peak** is the highest point in the Andamans. You can trek through subtropical forest to the top and back from Kalipur in about six hours. Again a permit is required from the Forest Office (Indian/foreigner Rs 25/250) and a local guide will make sure you don't get lost – ask at Pristine Beach Resort. **Snorkelling** behind the small island off the beach near Pristine Resort, and just around the coast at Radha Nagar Beach, is good; limited snorkelling gear is available for hire (per day Rs 100).

Leatherback and green turtles nest along the Diglipur coastline between December and March.

SLEEPING & EATING

There are two places to stay opposite each other at Kalipur, 8km southeast of the Aerial Bay Jetty. Buses run along this route (Rs 8); an autorickshaw costs about Rs 100.

Pristine Beach Resort (☎ 201837; huts Rs 200-500) Huddled among the palms between paddy fields and the beach, Pristine is a pretty spot with several simple bamboo huts on stilts, a restaurant and friendly owners. It gets very busy in peak season.

Turtle Resort (☎ 272553; r without/with AC Rs 400/800; ✖) Set on a small hill with rural views from the balconies, this A&N Tourism hotel provides some level of comfort, despite being a little run-down and musty and having a forlorn feel. It's best to book ahead through A&N Tourism in Port Blair, though you'll be able to get a room on-site if one's available.

GETTING THERE & AWAY

Diglipur, about 80km north of Mayabunder, is served by daily buses to/from Port Blair (Rs 120, 12 hours), as well as buses to Mayabunder (Rs 30, 2½ hours) and Rangat (Rs 50, 4½ hours). There are also daily ferries from Port Blair to Diglipur, returning overnight from Diglipur (seat/berth Rs 81/150, 10 hours).

LITTLE ANDAMAN

Little Andaman is still an outpost and one of the more remote inhabited islands in the group at 120km south of Port Blair.

The island is home to members of the Onge tribe, who were relocated to a tribal reserve in 1977 when the government began developing the island for agriculture and logging of forest timber. Settlement and opening up of the island has had a serious impact on the Onge through loss of environment and hunting grounds – only 100 or so remain. The tribal reserve is out of bounds to visitors.

The populated east coast of Little Andaman was badly affected by the tsunami and most of the population temporarily evacuated to Port Blair. Tourism and other development plans have been severely hampered; relief work was still underway at the time of research, and we didn't get the opportunity to visit. The big attractions here were pristine beaches such as **Netaji Nagar Beach**, 11km north of Hut Bay, and **Butler Bay**, a further 3km north, good for surfing and swimming but not for snorkelling; unfortunately this was the area worst hit by the tsunami. Inland, **White Surf** and **Whisper Wave waterfalls** offer a forest experience.

Andaman & Nicobar Islands Forest Plantation Development Corporation (ANIFPDCL; ☎ in Port Blair 232866; pblvanvikas@sancharnet.com) had been actively developing a 1500-hectare **red oil palm plantation** about 11km from Hut Bay, but this was also damaged during the tsunami and its future is uncertain. ANIFPDCL also managed the two guesthouses on the island, but these were not functioning at the time of writing.

Ferries land at the Hut Bay Jetty on the east coast and from there most of the accessible beaches and attractions are to the north. Boats sail from Port Blair about three times a week.

Directory

CONTENTS

Accommodation 462
Business Hours 465
Children 465
Climate Charts 466
Courses 467
Customs 468
Dangers & Annoyances 468
Discounts 470
Embassies & High Commissions in India 470
Festivals & Events 471
Food 473
Gay & Lesbian Travellers 473
Holidays 473
Insurance 474
Internet Access 474
Laundry 474
Legal Matters 475
Maps 475
Money 475
Photography 477
Post 477
Shopping 478
Solo Travellers 483
Telephone 484
Time 485
Toilets 485
Tourist Information 485
Travel Permits 486
Travellers with Disabilities 486
Visas 486
Volunteering 487
Women Travellers 489

ACCOMMODATION

South India has accommodation to suit all budgets, from squalid dives at rock-bottom prices, to flashy five-star offerings. Rates vary regionally and popular tourist centres often see considerable price hikes during the tourist season (for further details, see p464).

Places to stay are arranged in price order – scroll through the listings to find properties that meet your budget and accommodation preferences.

Tariffs in this book are based on high-season rates and don't include taxes unless otherwise indicated. If the rates are seasonal, this will be indicated.

Verify the check-out time when you check in – some hotels have a fixed check-out time while others give you 24 hours (ie your time starts when you check in). Reservations are usually fine by phone without a deposit, but it's wise to call and confirm your booking the day before you arrive. Room quality within a budget or midrange property can distinctly vary, so try to inspect a few rooms first.

Credit cards are accepted at most top-end hotels and some midrange places; budget hotels require cash. Most hotels ask for a deposit at check-in – ask for a receipt and be wary of any request to sign a blank impression of your credit card; if the hotel insists, go to the nearest ATM and pay cash.

Sound pollution can be irksome (especially in urban centres), so pack good-quality earplugs and request a quiet room.

Accommodation Options

As well as conventional hotels, there are some charming family-run guesthouses and unique boutique-style possibilities. Standout options are indicated with the Our Pick icon – **ourpick** – in this book's regional chapters.

BUDGET & MIDRANGE HOTELS

Apart from the more character-filled guesthouses, most budget and midrange hotels are modern concrete blocks. Shared bathrooms are usually only found at the cheapest hotels. Shoestring travellers may like to consider bringing their own sheets (or sleeping-bag liner) and pillowcases, as some budget lodgings can have shabby, stained linen, and more than a few travellers have encountered bed bugs. Away from tourist areas, cheaper hotels may not take foreigners because they don't have the necessary foreigner-registration forms.

BOOK ACCOMMODATION ONLINE

For more accommodation reviews and recommendations by Lonely Planet authors, check out the online booking service, Haystack, at www.lonelyplanet.com.

PRACTICALITIES

- Electricity is 230V to 240V, 50 Hz AC and sockets are the three round-pin variety (two-pin sockets are also found). Blackouts are more common during summer and the monsoon.

- Officially India is metric. Terms you're likely to hear are: lakhs (one lakh = 100,000) and crores (one crore = 10 million).

- Major English-language dailies include the *Hindustan Times, Times of India, Indian Express, Hindu* and *Economic Times*. Regional English-language and local-vernacular publications are found nationwide and include *Mid-Day*, the *Herald* and the *Deccan Herald*.

- Incisive current-affair reports appear in *Frontline, India Today,* the *Week, Sunday* and *Outlook*. For India-related travel articles, get *Outlook Traveller*.

- The national (government) TV broadcaster is Doordarshan. More widely watched are satellite and cable TV; channels include BBC, Discovery, Star Movies and MTV. TV (and radio) programme/frequency details appear in most major English-language dailies.

- Government-controlled All India Radio (AIR) nationally transmits local and international news. There are also private channels broadcasting news and current affairs, music, talkback and more.

It's rare to find hostel-style dormitory beds geared at travellers (as opposed to itinerant truck drivers) in South India, except at some railway retiring rooms (right), youth hostels and tourist bungalows (right).

Some of the best budget accommodation can be found at backpacker-friendly haunts, such as the beach resorts of Goa and Kerala – where you can opt for a cheap bamboo-and-thatch hut – and Hampi and Mamallapuram (Mahabalipuram).

Midrange properties offer more comfort than their budget brothers, but can be a veritable mixed bag: some have lacklustre, boxlike rooms while others ooze with personality. They mostly come with private bathroom and usually satellite TV. Some places offer noisy 'air-coolers' that cool air by blowing it over cold water. These are one step up from a ceiling fan (found in virtually all budget and midrange lodgings) and one step below air-conditioning. Being water-filled, air-coolers are somewhat ineffective in humid conditions.

Note that some budget and midrange places lock their doors at night – let the hotel know in advance if you're arriving or coming back to your room late in the evening.

CAMPING
There are few camping sites around South India, but travellers with their own vehicles can usually find hotels with gardens where they can park and camp for a nominal charge that includes communal bathroom facilities.

GOVERNMENT ACCOMMODATION & TOURIST BUNGALOWS
The Indian government maintains a network of guesthouses for travelling officials and public workers, known variously as Rest Houses, Dak Bungalows, Circuit Houses, PWD (Public Works Department) Bungalows and Forest Rest Houses. These places may accept travellers if no government employees need the rooms, but permission is sometimes required from local officials and you'll have to find the *chowkidar* (caretaker) to open the doors.

'Tourist Bungalows' are run by state governments; their facilities and service vary enormously. Some offer cheap dorm beds as well as decent private rooms. Details are normally available through the state tourism office.

HOMESTAYS
Staying with a local family can be a refreshing change from dealing purely with tourist-oriented people. Homestays (also known as Paying Guest Houses) offer budget and midrange options. Contact the local tourist office for lists of families involved in homestay schemes, or see the entries in the regional chapters.

RAILWAY RETIRING ROOMS
Many large train stations offer accommodation for travellers in possession of an ongoing train ticket or Indrail Pass (see p505). The rooms – which can range from threadbare to surprisingly nice – are handy if you have an early morning train departure, although

GET TO KNOW YOUR BATHROOM

Certain terminology is commonly used in the Sleeping sections throughout this book; mostly 'private bathroom' and 'shared bathroom'. However, several other terms may be used as well. 'Common bath', 'without bath' or 'shared bath' mean communal bathroom facilities. 'Attached bath', 'private bath' or 'with bath' indicates that the room has its very own bathroom. Unless otherwise stated, places to stay listed in this book have private bathrooms.

'Running' or 'constant' water indicates that there is water available around the clock (although it's not always the case in reality). 'Bucket water' means that water is, as the name suggests, available in buckets. Many hotels only have running cold water in bathrooms, but can provide hot water in buckets (sometimes only between certain hours and often for a small charge).

Hotels that advertise 'room with shower' can sometimes be misleading. Even if a bathroom does have a shower, it's a good idea to check that it actually works before accepting the room. Some hotels surreptitiously disconnect showers to save costs, while the showers at other places render a mere trickle of water.

A geyser is a small hot-water tank, often found in budget and (to a lesser extent) midrange hotels. Some geysers need to be switched on an hour or so before use.

Regarding toilets, unless squat toilets are specifically mentioned in this book, bathrooms have sit-down toilets. In South India, squat toilets may be referred to as 'Indian' or 'floor' toilets, while the sit-down variety is known as 'Western' or 'commode'. Budget and midrange hotels may have rooms with both styles, so if you prefer a sit-down toilet, ask for it.

they can be noisy! There is usually a choice of dormitories and/or private rooms (24-hour check-out).

TEMPLES & PILGRIMS' RESTHOUSES

Accommodation is available at some ashrams (spiritual communities), gurdwaras (Sikh temples) and *dharamsalas* (pilgrims' resthouses) for a donation, but these places are intended for genuine pilgrims so do exercise judgment about the appropriateness of staying. Always abide by any protocols.

TOP-END HOTELS

Found in South India's larger cities and tourist traps, top-end hotels range from swanky five-star chains, to less glamorous four-star properties. Most have swimming pools, fancy restaurants and assorted amenities (gyms, beauty salons, business centres etc). Most top-end hotels have rupee rates for Indian guests and separate US dollar rates for foreigners (including Non-Resident Indians, or NRIs). Officially, you are supposed to pay the dollar rates in foreign currency or by credit card, but many places will accept rupees adding up to the dollar rate.

While the luxury chain hotels are all pretty predictable, there are some more unique places worth seeking out, such as the heritage hotels in Puducherry (Pondicherry), resort

hotels in Goa and Kerala, colonial mansions in Udhagamandalam (Ooty) and the sublime Taj Mahal Palace & Tower in Mumbai (Bombay; p124).

Costs

Prices for accommodation vary widely as you travel around the region, so it is hard to pinpoint exact accommodation costs, or provide an average room rate, but most hotels fall somewhere within the following ranges: in budget establishments, single rooms range from Rs 100 to 400, and doubles from Rs 200 to 600; midrange single rooms range from Rs 300 and 1300, and doubles from Rs 450 to

COPYCAT ALERT

Be aware that in tourist hot spots (eg Goa and Kerala) fledgling hotels may 'borrow' the name of a thriving competitor to confuse travellers. To avoid landing at a (usually inferior) copycat hotel, ensure that you know the *exact* name of your preferred hotel, and before paying your rickshaw/taxi driver double-check that you have indeed been taken to the right place, as some cheeky chaps will hastily try to offload you at copycat hotels, where they receive a commission at your expense.

1800; top end single and double rooms start from around Rs 1900 and go up to US$150 or more.

Note that many hotels raise their room rates annually – be prepared for an increase on the rates we've provided. Expect air-conditioned (AC) rooms to generally cost at least several hundred rupees more than non-AC rooms.

SEASONAL VARIATIONS

In popular tourist hangouts (hill stations, beaches, places of pilgrimage etc) most hoteliers crank up their high-season prices. Tourist hubs such as Goa can triple their rates in season – advance bookings are often essential at these times.

The definition of the high and low seasons varies depending on location. For beaches such as Goa and Kerala high season is basically a month before and two months after Christmas; in the hill stations it's usually from April to July when domestic tourists flock to the hills for some cool relief. Some hotels charge higher rates for the Christmas and New Year period, or over major festivals, such as Diwali. (For festival details see p471; the Festivals In…boxes at the start of regional chapters focus on local events.) For any major festival, it's wise to make your accommodation arrangements well in advance. Conversely, in the low season, prices at even normally expensive hotels can be delightfully affordable. It's always worth asking for a better rate if the hotel doesn't seem busy.

Regional chapters have details on seasonal rates for individual areas.

TAXES & SERVICE CHARGES

State governments slap a variety of taxes on hotel accommodation (except at the cheapest hotels) and these are added to the cost of your room. Taxes vary from state to state and are detailed in the regional chapters. Many upmarket hotels also levy an additional 'service charge' (usually around 10%). Rates quoted in this book exclude taxes unless otherwise indicated.

BUSINESS HOURS

Official business hours are from 9.30am to 5.30pm Monday to Friday, but offices may open later and close earlier. Government offices may also open on certain Saturdays. Most offices have an official lunch hour from around 1pm. Shops generally open from around 10am and stay open until 6pm or later; some close on Sunday. Airline offices generally keep to standard business hours Monday to Saturday.

Most banks are open from 10am to 2pm Monday to Friday (until 4pm in some areas), and from 10am to noon (or 1pm) on Saturday. Exact branch hours vary from town to town so check locally. Foreign-exchange offices open longer hours, usually seven days per week.

Main post offices are usually open from 10am to 5pm Monday to Friday, until noon on Saturday. Some larger post offices have a full day on Saturday and a half-day on Sunday – see regional chapters for details.

Restaurant opening hours vary regionally – you can rely on most places to be open from around 8am to 10pm. Exceptions are noted in the Eating listings of the regional chapters.

CHILDREN

Being a family-oriented society, India is a very child-friendly destination. Despite the wonderful acceptance of children, travelling with kids in India can be hard work, requiring constant vigilance – be especially cautious near roads, as traffic can be very heavy and erratic. Any long-distance road travel should include adequate stops, as rough roads can make travel more draining than usual. Always carry sufficient drinking water.

See Lonely Planet's *Travel with Children*, and the travelling with children section of Lonely Planet's **Thorn Tree forum** (thorntree.lonely planet.com) for more advice.

Practicalities
ACCOMMODATION

Many hotels have 'family rooms' and almost all will provide an extra bed for a small additional charge, though cots are rare. Upmarket hotels may offer baby-sitting facilities and/or kid's activity programmes – inquire in advance. Upmarket hotels also have cable TV with English-language children's channels.

FOOD & DRINK

Children are welcome in most restaurants, but usually only upmarket places and fast-food chains have high chairs and children's menus. Nappy-changing facilities are usually restricted to the (often cramped) restaurant toilet. Getting children to eat unfamiliar food can be another challenge, though Western fast food is widely available. Bottled water, cartons of fruit juice and bottles of fizzy pop are easy to find; be cautious of fresh juice sold at street stalls, as unfiltered water may be added.

HEALTH
Pay close attention to hygiene as health risks, such as diarrhoea, can be much more of a threat to children than adults – for details see p511. If your child takes special medication, bring along an adequate stock in case it's not easily found locally. Note that rabid animals (dogs and monkeys in particular) may also pose a risk. Check with a doctor before departure about recommended jabs and drug courses for children.

TRANSPORT
Long-distance road travel should incorporate sufficient food and toilet breaks. Rough roads coupled with chaotic traffic conditions mean that travel sickness can be a problem (bring along appropriate medication if you're concerned). Note that child seats – or indeed any kind of seatbelts – are rare. Trains are usually the most comfortable mode of travel, especially for long trips. Internal air travel can save time and tempers.

Discounts
On Indian trains, under-fours travel free and children aged five to 12 pay half-price. Most airlines charge 10% of the adult fare for infants and 50% for under-12s. Many tourist attractions charge a reduced entry fee for children under 12 (under 15 in some states).

TRAVEL WITH INFANTS
Standard baby products such as nappies (diapers) and milk powder are available in most large cities and tourist centres. If you've got a fussy baby, consider bringing powdered milk or baby food from home. Also bring along high-factor sunscreen, a snug-fitting wide-brimmed hat and a washable changing mat for covering dirty surfaces. Breast-feeding in public is generally not condoned by Indian society.

Sights & Activities
Allow several days for your child to acclimatise to the explosion of sights, smells, tastes and sounds of South India. Start with short outings and make sure to include child-friendly attractions (these are generally more prevalent in the bigger cities). There are, for instance, good museums in Bengaluru (Bangalore; p223), Chennai (Madras; p371) and Mumbai (p119), some with child-friendly interpretive displays. Popular planetariums include the Nehru Centre & Nehru Planetarium (p117) in Mumbai, Chennai's Birla Planetarium (p373) and the Birla Planetarium & Science Museum(p281) in Hyderabad. Theme parks and water parks are also taking off in a big way – check out Wonder La (p232) in Bengaluru and Baywatch (p425) in Kanyakumari (Cape Comorin).

Zoos, such as the ones in Mumbai (p117), Kerala (p311), and Pune's Katraj Snake Park & Zoo (p165) should also win a warm response. Wildlife safaris, particularly those offering elephant rides, are also worth considering (see p98).

Beaches make memorable family outings. Some of the country's finest include those of Goa (see the boxed text, p192), Kerala (p306), Puducherry (p398) and Gokarna (p255).

Hill stations are perfect for serene forest picnics, cooler weather, and family-friendly activities, such as paddle boating and pony rides. Top spots include Udhagamandalam (Ooty; p436) and Kodaikanal (Kodai; p427).

South India's bounty of festivals may also capture your child's imagination, although some kids may get a bit spooked by the crowds. For festival details, see p471 and the Festivals In…boxed texts near the start of regional chapters.

Travelling off-the-beaten track can be a mixed blessing – you generally won't find the facilities and comforts of the cities, but you'll find less traffic, both human and mechanical, and with that, more peace.

For further destination-specific sights and activities that may appeal to your children, peruse the regional chapters.

CLIMATE CHARTS
South India has a largely tropical climate that can be roughly divided into two distinct seasons – the wet (monsoon) and the dry. It's warm year-round – except in the elevated hills – but May to September are the hottest months. For comprehensive details, check out p21.

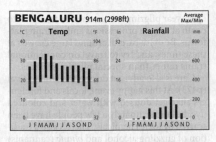

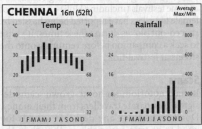

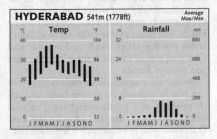

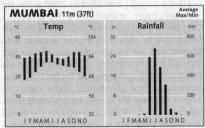

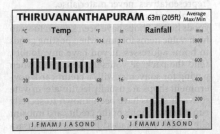

COURSES

You can learn all sorts of new skills in India, ranging from yoga and meditation to Indian cooking and how to speak Tamil. To find out about local courses, inquire at tourist offices, ask fellow travellers or browse local newspapers and noticeboards. For courses in adventure sports check out p98 and for information on cooking courses see p83). Other recommended courses include the following listings.

Languages

Language courses require time to derive lasting benefits – some courses stipulate a minimum time commitment.

Here are some possibilities:

Karnataka Sanskrit courses at the Atma Vikasa Centre (p236) in Mysore.

Kerala Short courses in Malayalam, Hindi and Sanskrit at the Vijnana Kala Vedi Cultural Centre (p333) near Kottayam.

Mumbai Beginners courses in Hindi, Marathi and Sanskrit at Bharatiya Vidya Bhavan (p119) in Mumbai.

Tamil Nadu Various Hindi and Tamil courses in Chennai (p374).

Martial Arts

Courses are available in the traditional Keralan martial art of *kalarippayat* – a form of sword-and-shield fighting incorporating elements of Ayurveda and *marma* (the precursor to Chinese acupressure massage). Major centres include **CVN Kalari Sangham** (p312) in Thiruvananthapuram (Trivandrum) and the **Vijnana Kala Vedi Cultural Centre** (p333) near Kottayam.

Music & Performing Arts

You're going to get the most benefit from these courses if you commit for at least several weeks. Most centres provide instruments.

Some good options:

Goa Courses in classical Indian singing and tabla in Arambol (p205).

Karnataka Classical Indian dance classes at Nrityagram (p232) in Hessaraghatta, and tabla classes at Shruthi Musical Works (p237) in Mysore.

Kerala Courses in Kathakali (traditional Keralan dance opera) and *kootiattam* (traditional Sanskrit drama) in Thiruvananthapuram (Trivandrum; p312), and dance centres near Thrissur (p355) and Kottayam (p333).

Tamil Nadu Courses in classical Tamil dance and music at the Kalakshetra Arts Village (p378) in Chennai. Courses in *bharatanatyam* (classical dance), singing and musical instruments in Puducherry (p398).

DIRECTORY

Yoga & Holistic Courses

India has thousands of yoga centres offering courses of varying duration, as well as courses in Ayurveda, meditation and other therapies. See p101 for details.

CUSTOMS

Visitors are allowed to bring 1L of alcohol and 200 cigarettes or 50 cigars or 250g of tobacco into India duty free. Officials may ask tourists to enter expensive items such as video cameras and laptop computers on a 'Tourist Baggage Re-export' form to ensure they are taken out of India when you depart (this is rarely policed). There are no duty-free allowances when entering India from Nepal.

Technically you're supposed to declare any amount of cash or travellers cheques over US$10,000 on arrival, and more than Rs 10,000 should not be taken out of India. There are additional restrictions on the export of antiques and products made from animals – see the boxed text, p479.

DANGERS & ANNOYANCES

In India, as with anywhere else, a sensible level of caution is your best weapon against crime and scams. Scams change as dodgy characters try to stay ahead of the game, so chat with other travellers as well as tourism officials to stay abreast of the latest hazards.

Also see the India branch of Lonely Planet's **Thorn Tree forum** (thorntree.lonelyplanet.com) – travellers often post warnings about problems they've encountered. Women should also read the advice on p489.

Contaminated Food & Drink

Most bottled water is legit, but always ensure the lid seal is intact and check that the bottom of the bottle hasn't been tampered with. Crush plastic bottles after use to prevent them being misused later, or better still, bring along water-purification tablets or a filtration system to avoid adding to India's plastic-waste mountain (also see p96).

In past years, some private medical clinics have provided patients with more treatment than necessary to procure larger payments from travel insurance companies – get a second opinion if possible.

Festivals

The sheer mass of humanity at India's festivals provides an incredible spectacle, but almost every year pilgrims are crushed or trampled to death at temple processions and on train platforms. Be extra careful around large crowds at these times, and try to travel on conventional trains rather than special pilgrim services.

Care is also advised during the Holi festival (p473). At this happy event, locals and foreigners alike get doused with water and coloured dye, but unfortunately a few people have been scarred by toxic chemicals. There's also a tradition of guzzling alcohol and *bhang* (cannabis) at some festivals (including Holi) – a number of female travellers have reported being hassled by spaced-out blokes during these times. It's wise to seek a companion before venturing onto the streets at festival time.

Scams

India is notorious for home-grown scams designed to separate travellers from their money. Don't be fooled – any deal that sounds too good to be true, invariably is, though in the south thankfully you won't find as much of the gem and carpet scams that are rampant up north. The main places to be wary in South India are big cities, such as Mumbai and Chennai, and at tourist centres, such as Goa and parts of Kerala.

Be highly suspicious of claims that you can purchase goods cheaply in India and sell them easily at a profit elsewhere. Precious stones and carpets are favourites for this con. Operators who practise such schemes are deceptively friendly and after buttering you up with invitations to their home, free meals etc, they begin pouring out sob stories about not being able to obtain an export licence. And therein lies the opportunity for you to 'get rich quick' – by carrying or mailing the goods home and selling them to the trader's overseas 'representatives' at a profit. Many such con artists will provide forged testimonials from other travellers. Without exception, the goods are worth a fraction of what you paid and the 'representatives' never materialise.

It also pays to be cautious when sending goods home. Shops have been known to swap high-value items for junk when posting goods to home addresses. If you have any doubts, send the package yourself. Be careful when paying for souvenirs with a credit card: government shops are usually legitimate; private souvenir shops have been known to secretly run off extra copies of the credit card imprint slip, which will be used for phoney transactions later. Insist that the trader carries out any credit-card transaction on the counter in front of you.

While it's only a minority of traders who are involved in dishonest schemes, many souvenir vendors are involved in the commission racket – see right. For region-specific scams, see the Dangers & Annoyances sections in regional chapters.

TRANSPORT SCAMS

Unscrupulous travel agencies may make extra money by scamming travellers for tours and travel tickets. Make sure you are clear about what is included in the price of any tour (get this in writing) to avoid charges for hidden 'extras' later on.

When buying a bus, train or plane ticket anywhere other than the registered office of the transport company, make certain you are getting the ticket class you paid for. It's not unknown for travellers to book a deluxe bus or air-conditioned train berth and arrive to find a bog-standard ordinary bus, or a less-comfortable sleeper seat.

Swimming

Beaches can have dangerous rips and currents and there are drowning deaths each year. Always check locally before swimming anywhere in the sea and be careful of currents when swimming in any rivers.

Theft & Druggings

Theft is a risk in India, as anywhere else. On buses and trains, keep luggage securely locked (minipadlocks and chains are available at most train stations) and lock your bags to the metal baggage racks or the wire loops found under seats; padlocking your bags to the roof racks on buses is also a sensible policy.

Thieves tend to target popular tourist train routes, such as Mumbai to Goa. Be extra alert just before the train departs; thieves often take advantage of the confusion and crowds. Airports are another place to exercise caution; after a long flight you're unlikely to be at your most alert.

Occasionally tourists (especially those travelling solo) are drugged and robbed during train or bus journeys, although reports of this are relatively rare in South India. A friendly stranger strikes up conversation, offers you a spiked drink (to send you to sleep) then makes off with your valuables. It's wise

to politely decline drinks or food offered by strangers (use your instincts), particularly if you're alone.

Unfortunately some travellers make their money go further by helping themselves to other people's – take extra care in dormitories. For lost credit cards, immediately call the international lost/stolen number; for stolen/lost travellers cheques, contact the closest local branch or the American Express/Thomas Cook offices in Mumbai (p109), Chennai (p370) or Delhi (see p477).

A good travel-insurance policy is essential (see p474) – keep the emergency contact details handy and familiarise yourself with the claims procedure. Keep photocopies of your passport, including the visa page, separately from your passport along with a copy of your airline ticket, or email scans to yourself via the internet.

PERSONAL SECURITY

The safest place for your money and your passport is next to your skin, either in a concealed moneybelt or a secure pouch under your shirt. If you carry your money in a wallet, keep it in your front trouser pocket, never the back pocket.

In dodgy-looking hotels, put your money-belt under your pillow when you sleep and never leave your valuable documents and money in your hotel room when you go out (even under the mattress). Better hotels will have a safe for valuables. For peace of mind, you may also want to use your own padlock in hotels where doors are locked with a padlock (common in cheaper hotels). If you cannot lock your hotel room securely from the inside at night, request another room – if that fails, consider staying somewhere else.

It's wise to peel off at least US$100 and store it away separately from your main stash, just in case. Also separate big notes from small bills so you don't publicly display large wads of cash when tipping or paying for sundry services (eg taxi fares, shoe-polishing).

Touts & Commission Agents

With so many businesses dependent on tourism, competition is fierce in India. Many hotels and shops drum up extra business by paying commission to local fixers who bring tourists through the doors. These places tend to be unpopular for a reason – prices will invariably be raised (by as much as 50%, occasionally even more!) to pay the fixer's commission. To get around this, ask taxi- or rickshaw-drivers to drop you at a landmark rather than your intended destination, so you can walk in unaccompanied and pay the normal price.

Train and bus stations are often swarming with touts – if anyone asks if this is your first trip to India say you've visited several times, as this is usually a ruse to gauge your vulnerability. You'll often hear far-fetched stories about the hotels that refuse to pay commissions being 'full', 'under renovation' or 'closed'. Be on your toes and check things out yourself. Also be very sceptical of phrases such as 'my brother's shop' and 'special deal at my friend's store' – these places usually pay commission.

On the flip side, touts can be beneficial if you arrive in a town without a hotel reservation when some big festival is on, or during the peak season – they'll know which places have beds.

Trekking

Trekking off the beaten track carries risks – we strongly recommend hiring local guides and porters or joining an organised trek before heading off into potentially dangerous terrain – see p100 for more information.

DISCOUNTS

For information on discounts for children and infants, see p466.

Seniors

Indian Airlines and Sahara Airlines offer 50% discounts on domestic air travel for foreign travellers aged 65 or over; Jet Airways offers 25% off. However, promotional fares and tickets on budget airlines are often cheaper than discounted full fares. Ask travel agents about discounts on other air carriers. If you're over 60 you're entitled to a 30% discount on the cost of train travel. Bring your passport as proof of age.

Student & Youth Travel

Student cards are of limited use nowadays as most concessions are based on age. Hostels run by the Indian Youth Hostels Association are part of the Hostelling International (HI) network; an HI card usually entitles you to discount rates. YMCA/YWCA members should also receive some discounts on accommodation.

Foreigners aged 30 or under receive a 25% discount on domestic air tickets. This applies to full-priced tickets, so standard budget-airline fares may be cheaper still. Foreign students studying in India get 50% off train fares.

EMBASSIES & HIGH COMMISSIONS IN INDIA

Most foreign diplomatic missions are based in Delhi, but some have consulates in Mumbai and Chennai. Most missions operate from 9am to 5pm Monday to Friday with a lunch-break between 1pm and 2pm.

If your country's mission is not listed here, that doesn't necessarily mean it's not represented in India – for details consult the phone directory or tourist office.

Australia Delhi (☎ 011-41399900; www.ausgovindia.com; 1/50G Shantipath, Chanakyapuri); Mumbai (Map pp106-7; ☎ 022-66692000; fax 6669 2005; 36 Maker Chambers VI, 220 Nariman Point)

Bangladesh (☎ 011-24121389; www.bhcdelhi.org; EP39 Dr Radakrishnan Marg, Chanakyapuri, Delhi)

Bhutan (☎ 011-26889230; Chandragupta Marg, Chanakyapuri, Delhi)

Canada Delhi (☎ 011-41782000; www.dfait-maeci.gc.ca/new-delhi; 7/8 Shantipath, Chanakyapuri); Mumbai (Map pp106-7; ☎ 67494444; mmbai@international.gc.ca; 6th fl, Fort House, 221 Dr DN Rd)

France Delhi (☎ 011-24196100; www.france-in-india.org; 2/50E Shantipath, Chanakyapuri); Mumbai (Map pp106-7; ☎ 022-66694000; www.consulfrance-bombay.org; 7th fl, Hoechst House, Nariman Point)

Germany Delhi (☎ 011-26871837; www.new-delhi.diplo.de; 6/50G Shantipath, Chanakyapuri); Mumbai (Map pp106-7; ☎ 022-22832422; fax 22025493; 10th fl, Hoechst House, Nariman Point; ☽ 9am-12pm Mon-Fri); Chennai (Map pp368-9; ☎ 44-24301600; www.chennai.diplo.de; 9 Boat Club Rd, RA Puram)

Ireland (☎ 011-24626741; www.irelandinindia.com; 230 Jor Bagh, Delhi)

Israel Delhi (☎ 011-30414500; delhi.mfa.gov.il; 3 Aurangzeb Rd); Mumbai (Map pp106-7; ☎ 022-22822822; info@mumbai.mfa.gov.il)

Italy Delhi (☎ 011-26114355; www.ambnewdelhi.esteri.it; 50E Chandragupta Marg, Chanakyapuri); Mumbai (Map pp106-7; ☎ 022-23804071; www.italianconsulatemumbai.com; 'Kanchanjunga', 1st fl, 72G Deshmukh Marg)

Japan (☎ 011-26876564; www.in.emb-japan.go.jp; 50G Shantipath, Chanakyapuri, Delhi)

Malaysia (☎ 011-26111291; www.kln.gov.my/perwakilan/newdelhi; 50M Satya Marg, Chanakyapuri, Delhi)

Maldives Delhi (☎ 011-41435701; www.maldiveshighcom.co.in; B2 Anand Niketan); Chennai (Map p372; ☎ 44-28535111; Royal Textile Mills, 855 Anna Salai)

Myanmar (☎ 011-24678822; 3/50F Nyaya Marg, Delhi)
Nepal (☎ 011-23327361; Barakhamba Rd, Delhi)
Netherlands (☎ 011-24197600; www.holland-in-india
.org; 6/50F Shantipath, Chanakyapuri, Delhi)
New Zealand (☎ 011-26883170; www.nzembassy
.com; 50N Nyaya Marg, Chanakyapuri, Delhi)
Pakistan (☎ 011-24676004; 2/50G Shantipath,
Chanakyapuri, Delhi)
Singapore (☎ 011-41019801; www.mfa.gov.sg/new
delhi; N88 Panchsheel Park, Delhi)
South Africa (☎ 011-26149411; www.sahc-india.com;
B18 Vasant Marg, Vasant Vihar, Delhi)
Sri Lanka Delhi (☎ 011-23010201; www.slmfa.gov.lk;
27 Kautilya Marg, Chanakyapuri); Chennai (Map pp368-9;
☎ 44-24987896; www.slmfa.gov.lk; 196 TTK Rd, Alwarpet)
Switzerland (☎ 011-26878372; www.eda.admin.ch;
Nyaya Marg, Chanakyapuri, Delhi)
Thailand (☎ 011-26118104; www.thaiemb.org.in; 56N
Nyaya Marg, Chanakyapuri, Delhi)
UK Delhi (☎ 011-24192100; www.ukinindia.com; Shan-
tipath, Chanakyapuri); Mumbai (Map pp106-7; ✆ 022-
66502222; Maker Chambers IV, 2nd fl, 222 Jamnalal Bajaj
Rd, Nariman Point; ✆ 8am-4pm Mon-Thu, 8am-1pm Fri);
Chennai (Map pp368–9; ☎ 44-42192151; 20 Anderson Rd;
✆ 8.30am-4pm)
USA Delhi (☎ 011-24198000; http://newdelhi.usembassy
.gov; Shantipath, Chanakyapuri); Mumbai (Map pp106-7;
☎ 022-23633611; Lincoln House, 78 Bhulabhai Desai Rd);
Chennai (Map pp368–9; ☎ 44-28574242; http://chennai
.usconsulate.gov/; Gemini Circle, 220 Anna Salai)

FESTIVALS & EVENTS

India officially follows the Gregorian calendar;
however most holidays and festivals follow
the Indian or Tibetan lunar calendars, tied to
the cycle of the moon, or the Islamic calendar, which shifts forward 11 days each year
(12 days in a leap year). As a result, the exact
dates of festivals change from year to year.

The India-wide holidays and festivals listed
here are arranged according to the Indian
lunar (and occasionally Gregorian) calendar,
which starts in Chaitra (March or April).
Contact local tourist offices for exact dates
or check the web – festivals.iloveindia.com
and www.festivalsofindia.in have extensive
listings, or visit the regional websites for
the state governments listed on india.gov.in
/knowindia/districts.php.

Many festivals in India occur during
purnima (full moon), which is traditionally
auspicious.

The 'wedding season' generally falls in
the cooler period from around November to
March (wedding dates revolve around auspi-

cious timings set by astrologers). During this
period you're likely to see at least one wedding
procession on the street – a merry mix of singing, dancing and a loud brass band.

The following represent major national
festivals – for details about regional events
see the Festivals In... boxed texts near the
beginning of each regional chapter.

Chaitra (March/April)

Mahavir Jayanti Jain festival commemorating the birth
of Mahavira, the founder of Jainism.
Ramanavami Hindus celebrate the birth of Rama with
processions, music and feasting as well as readings and
enactments of scenes from the Ramayana.
Easter Christian holiday marking the Crucifixion and
Resurrection of Christ.
Eid-Milad-un-Nabi Islamic festival celebrating the birth
of the Prophet Mohammed; it falls on 20 March 2008,
9 March 2009 and 26 February 2010.

Vaisakha (April/May)

Buddha Jayanti Buddhists celebrate the birth, enlightenment and attainment of nirvana by the historical
Buddha; it can fall in May, April or early June.

Jyaistha (May/June)

Only regional festivals currently fall in this period – see the
regional chapters for details.

Asadha (June/July)

Rath Yatra (Car Festival) Effigies of Lord Jagannath
(Vishnu as 'Lord of the World') are hauled through cities on
people-powered chariots.

Sravana (July/August)

Naag Panchami Hindu festival dedicated to Ananta, the
serpent upon whose coils Vishnu rested between universes.
Snakes are venerated as totems against monsoon flooding
and other evils.
Raksha Bandhan (Narial Purnima) On the full moon,
girls fix amulets known as *rakhis* to the wrists of brothers
and/or close male friends to protect them in the coming
year. Brothers reciprocate with gifts. Some people also
worship the Vedic sea god Varuna.

Bhadra (August/September)

Independence Day This public holiday on 15 August
marks the anniversary of India's Independence from Britain
in 1947.
Drukpa Teshi A Buddhist festival celebrating the first
teaching given by Siddhartha Gautama (the founder of
Buddhism).
Ganesh Chaturthi Hindus celebrate the birth of the
elephant-headed god, Ganesh, with verve, particularly

in Mumbai. Clay idols of Ganesh are paraded through the streets before being ceremonially immersed in rivers, water tanks or the sea.

Janmastami The anniversary of Krishna's birth is celebrated with wild abandon, particularly in Mathura (Krishna's birthplace).

Shravan Purnima On this day of fasting, high-caste Hindus replace the sacred thread looped over their left shoulder.

Pateti Parsis celebrate the Zoroastrian New Year at this time, particularly in Mumbai.

Ramadan (Ramazan) Thirty days of dawn-to-dusk fasting marking the ninth month of the Islamic calendar, when the Quran was revealed to the Prophet Mohammed; the fast starts on 13 September 2007, 1 September 2008, 22 August 2009 and 11 August 2010.

Asvina (September/October)

Navratri (Festival of Nine Nights) This Hindu festival leading up to Dussehra celebrates the goddess Durga. Special dances are held and the goddesses Lakshmi and Saraswati also get special praise. Festivities are particularly vibrant in Maharashtra.

Dussehra Dussehra celebrates the victory of the Hindu god Rama over the demon king Ravana, and the triumph of good over evil. Dussehra is especially big in Mysore, where effigies of Ravana and his cohorts are ritually burned.

Durga Puja Also symbolising the triumph of good over evil, Durga Puja commemorates the victory of the goddess Durga over buffalo-headed demon Mahishasura. Celebrations take place on the same dates as Dussehra.

Gandhi Jayanti This public holiday is a solemn celebration of Mohandas (Mahatma) Gandhi's birth anniversary in October at many places associated with his life, including the Gandhi National Memorial (p166) in Pune and the Sevagram Ashram (p155) in Maharashtra.

Eid al-Fitr Muslims celebrate the end of Ramadan with three days of festivities, starting 30 days after the start of the fast.

Kartika (October/November)

Diwali (Deepavaali) On the 15th day of Kartika, Hindus celebrate the 'festival of lights' for five days, giving gifts (usually sweets), lighting fireworks and burning butter and oil lamps to lead Rama home from exile.

Govardhana Puja A Vaishnavite Hindu festival marking the lifting of Govardhan Hill by Krishna, celebrated by Krishna devotees around India.

Aghan (November/December)

Nanak Jayanti The birthday of Guru Nanak, the founder of Sikhism, is celebrated with prayer readings and processions.

Eid al-Adha Muslims commemorate Ibrahim's readiness to obey God even to the point of sacrificing his son; the festival falls on 20 December 2007, 8 December 2008, 27 November 2009 and 16 November 2010.

KUMBH MELA

Held every three years at locations that hopscotch around the plains, the Kumbh Mela is the largest religious congregation on earth. This vast celebration attracts tens of millions of Hindu pilgrims, including mendicant Nagas (naked sadhus) from certain Hindu monastic orders. The Kumbh Mela doesn't belong to any particular caste or creed – devotees from all branches of Hinduism come together to experience the electrifying sensation of mass belief and to take a ceremonial dip in the sacred Ganges, Shipra or Godavari Rivers. Teams of astrologers gather every Kumbh to pinpoint the most auspicious moment for the mass bathing to begin.

The origins of the festival go back to the battle for supremacy between good and evil. In the Hindu creation myths, the gods and demons fought a great battle for a *kumbh* (pitcher) containing the nectar of immortality. Vishnu got hold of the container and spirited it away, but in flight four drops spilt on the earth – at Allahabad (Uttar Pradesh), Haridwar (Uttaranchal), Nasik (Maharashtra) and Ujjain (Madhya Pradesh). Kumbh Mela celebrations are held every three years in one of these four cities, and every 12 years Allahabad plays host to the even larger Maha (Great) Kumbh Mela, with even bigger crowds.

The last Maha Kumbh Mela took place in Allahabad in 2001, attracting around 100 million celebrants – equivalent to a third of the population of America or thirty times the number of people who attend the annual haj to Mecca. Controlling these multitudes takes thousands of officials and vast tent cities are erected to provide accommodation and meals for the devotees. The Kumbh is invariably an international media circus, with news agencies from around the globe competing for the best shot of the naked Naga sadhus leading the charge into the river.

The schedule for Kumbh Melas can be bewildering because of the overlapping cycles, but the next Kumbh Mela in the lifetime of this book is at Haridwar in 2010. You can find dates and general information on the website www.kumbhamela.net.

Pausa (December/January)
Christmas Day Christians celebrate the birth of Christ on 25 December.
Losar Tibetan New Year – celebrated by Tantric Buddhists all over India. Exact dates vary from region to region.

Magha (January/February)
Republic Day This public holiday on 26 January celebrates the founding of the Republic of India in 1950; the most spectacular celebrations are in Delhi, which holds a huge military parade along Rajpath and the Beating of the Retreat ceremony three days later.
Pongal A four-day Tamil festival marking the end of the harvest season. Families in the south prepare pots of *pongal* (a mixture of rice, sugar, dhal and milk), symbolic of prosperity and abundance, then feed them to decorated and adorned cattle.
Vasant Panchami Honouring Saraswati, the goddess of learning, Hindus dress in yellow and place books, musical instruments and other educational objects in front of idols of the goddess to receive her blessing.

Phalguna (February/March)
Holi One of the most exuberant Hindu festivals, when people celebrate the beginning of spring by throwing coloured water and *gulal* (powder) at anyone in range. On the night before Holi, bonfires are built to symbolise the destruction of the evil demon Holika.
Muharram Shiite Muslims commemorate the martyrdom of the Prophet Mohammed's grandson, Imam; the festival starts on 10 January 2008, 29 December 2009 and 18 December 2010.
Shivaratri This day of Hindu fasting recalls the *tandava* (cosmic dance) of Lord Shiva. Temple processions are followed by the chanting of mantras and anointing of linga (phallic symbols).

FOOD
Sampling the local cuisine is undoubtedly one of the highlights of a visit to South India. To get a taste of what's on offer, see p75 and the Eating listings of regional chapters. As well as restaurants, look out for all the wonderful street stalls, snack joints, market vendors, takeaway counters and sweet shops that make eating on the move in India such a pleasure. Places to eat are generally open from early morning (or lunchtime) to late at night – see p465 for more information.

GAY & LESBIAN TRAVELLERS
Technically, homosexual relations for men are illegal in India and the penalties for transgression can theoretically be up to life imprison-

ment. There's no law against lesbian sexual relations.

There are low-key gay scenes in Mumbai and Bengaluru. Physical contact and public displays of affection are generally frowned upon for heterosexual couples as well as gay and lesbian couples. In fact, men holding hands is far more common than heterosexual couples holding hands, though this is generally a sign of friendship rather than sexual orientation.

For more details, see p53.

Publications & Websites
The Mumbai publication, *Bombay Dost*, is a gay and lesbian magazine available from 105A Veena-Beena Shopping Centre, Bandra West, Mumbai, as well as at a limited number of bookshops and newsstands in various Indian cities.

For further information about India's gay scene, there are some excellent websites:
Gay Bombay (www.gaybombay.org)
Humrahi (www.geocities.com/WestHollywood /Heights/7258)
Humsafar (www.humsafar.org)
Indian Dost (www.indiandost.com/gay.php)

Support Groups
Several organisations in Chennai and Bengaluru offer support to the gay and lesbian community:
Good As You (☎ 080-22230959; www.sawnet.org/orgns /good_as_you.html; Bengaluru) Runs a weekly support group for gay, lesbian, bisexual and transgender people.
Sahodaran (☎ 044-8252869; www.sahodaran .faithweb.com; 127, Sterling Rd, Nungambakkam, Chennai) A support group for gay men; holds social group meetings weekly (in English) – contact the office for details.
Sangama (☎ 080-22868680; www.sangamaonline.org; Flat 13, Royal Park Apartments, 34 Park Rd, Tasker Town, Bengaluru 560051) Deals with crisis intervention and provides community outreach services for gay and bisexual men and women, transgenders and *hijras* (transvestites and eunuchs).
Swabhava (☎ 080-22230959; http://swabhava_trust .tripod.com; 54 Nanjappa Rd, Shanthinagar, Bengaluru 560027) This NGO works directly with issues affecting lesbians, gays, bisexuals and transsexuals, through research, documentation, advocacy and training programmes. Volunteers are welcome.

HOLIDAYS
In India there are officially three national public holidays: Republic Day (26 January), Independence Day (15 August) and Gandhi Jayanti (2 October). However, various states may also have their own designated holidays.

There are usually also holidays during major festivals (often only followed by particular religious denominations), which include Diwali, Dussehra and Holi (all Hindu), Nanak Jayanti (Sikh), Eid al-Fitr (Muslim), Mahavir Jayanti (Jain), Buddha Jayanti (Buddhist) and Easter and Christmas (Christian). For more on religious festivals, see p471.

Most businesses (offices, shops etc) and tourist sites close on public holidays, but transport is usually unaffected as many locals travel for religious celebrations. Make any transport and hotel reservations well in advance if you intend visiting during major festivals.

INSURANCE

Every traveller should take out travel insurance. Make sure that your policy covers theft of property and medical treatment, as well as air evacuation. Be aware that some policies place restrictions on potentially dangerous activities such as scuba diving, skiing, motorcycling, trekking, paragliding or climbing. When hiring a motorcycle in India, make sure the rental policy includes at least third-party insurance – see p500.

There are hundreds of different policies so read the small print carefully and make sure your activities are covered. In some areas, trekking agents will only accept customers who have cover for emergency helicopter evacuation. Some policies pay doctors and hospitals directly; others expect you to pay upfront and claim the money back later (keep all documentation for your claim). It's crucial to get a police report in India if you've had anything stolen; insurance companies may refuse to reimburse you without one. For health concerns also see p506.

Worldwide coverage to travellers from over 44 countries is available online at www.lonelyplanet.com/travel_services.

INTERNET ACCESS

Internet cafés are widespread in South India and connections are usually quite fast, except in the more remote areas. Bandwidth load tends to be lowest in the morning and early afternoon. Internet charges vary regionally, but most places charge anywhere between Rs 10 and Rs 60 per hour, usually with a 15-minute minimum.

It's a good idea to write and save your messages in a text application before pasting them into your browser – power cuts are fairly common and all too often your hard-crafted email can vanish into the ether. Be wary of sending sensitive financial information from internet cafés; some internet cafés use keystroke-capturing technology to steal passwords and read emails. Using online banking on any nonsecure system is generally risky.

If travelling with a laptop, most internet café's can supply you with internet access over a LAN Ethernet cable, or you can join an international roaming service with an Indian dial-up number or take out an account with a local ISP. Major ISPs in India include **Sify** (www.sify.com/products), **BSNL** (www.bsnl.co.in) and **VSNL/Tata Indicom** (www.vsnl.in). Make sure your modem is compatible with the telephone and dial-up system in India (an external global modem may be necessary).

Another useful investment is a fuse-protected universal AC adaptor, to protect your circuit board from power surges. Plug adaptors are available throughout India but bring spare plug fuses from home. Wi-fi internet access is offered at many luxury hotels and some coffee shops in big cities, but security is a consideration – avoid sending credit-card details or other personal data over a wireless connection. For more information about travelling with a portable computer, check out www.teleadapt.com.

In this book, hotels offering internet access to guests are marked with the internet icon ▣ . See also p24 for useful India resources on the web.

LAUNDRY

Almost all hotels offer a same- or next-day laundry service, with the majority of these charging per item of clothing. Most (excluding top-end hotels, which invariably have in-house laundries) employ the services of dhobi-wallahs (washerpeople), who will diligently bash your wet clothes against rocks and scrubbing boards, returning them spotlessly clean and ironed, but possibly missing a button or two. If you don't think your clothes will stand up to the treatment, wash them yourself or give them to a drycleaner. Washing powder can be bought cheaply virtually everywhere.

Be aware that it can take longer to dry clothes during the humid monsoon and note that some hotels discourage washing clothes in their rooms.

LEGAL MATTERS

If you're in a sticky legal situation, immediately contact your embassy (see p470). However, be aware that all your embassy may be able to do is monitor your treatment in custody and arrange a lawyer. In the Indian justice system, the burden of proof is often on the accused and long stays in prison before trial are not uncommon.

You should always carry your passport – police are entitled to ask you for identification in all sorts of situations.

Corruption is an issue, so the less you have to do with local police the better (unless getting a written police report for your insurance in the event of theft).

Drugs

India is known for recreational drugs, such as marijuana and hashish. Possession of any illegal drug is treated as a serious criminal offence. If convicted, the *minimum* sentence is 10 years, with no chance of remission or parole.

Cases can take several years to appear before a court, while the accused waits in prison, and there's usually a hefty monetary fine on top of any custodial sentence. The police have been getting particularly tough on foreigners (especially in places like Goa) who use drugs, so you should take this risk very seriously.

Claims of foreigners having drugs planted on them, or being extorted on 'suspicion' of possessing drugs, are not unknown, especially in backpacker centres.

Marijuana grows wild throughout India, but picking and smoking it is still an offence, except in towns where *bhang* (cannabis) is legally sold for religious rituals.

Smoking

Smoking in public places is now illegal in Delhi, Shimla (Himachal Pradesh), Gangtok (Sikkim) and all of Kerala, and a number of cities have also banned spitting and littering. The punishment for breaking these rules is a fine of at least Rs 100. This is variably enforced, but the police do have the power, so heed the street signs. So far, restaurants are exempt from the smoking ban, although some eateries do have dedicated nonsmoking sections.

MAPS

There's a dearth of high-quality maps in India. Better map series include TTK Discover India (covering states and cities), Nest & Wings (www

.nestwings.com) for maps and guidebooks; and **Eicher** (maps.eicherworld.com) for street atlases and city maps. The **Survey of India** (www.surveyofindia .gov.in) also publishes decent city, state and country maps, but some titles are restricted for security reasons. **Nelles** (www.nelles-verlag.de), which produces regional maps, is also recommended. All of these maps are available at good bookshops or you can buy online from the **India Map Store** (www.indiamapstore.com).

Throughout South India, state government tourist offices stock local maps, which are often dated and lacking in essential detail, but good enough for general orientation.

MONEY

The Indian rupee (Rs) is divided into 100 paise (p). Coins come in denominations of five, 10, 20, 25 and 50 paise and Rs 1, 2 and 5; notes come in Rs 10, 20, 50, 100, 500 and 1000. The Indian rupee is linked to a basket of currencies and its value is generally stable – see the Quick Reference on the inside front cover for exchange rates.

ATMs linked to international networks are common in most South Indian towns. However, carry cash or travellers cheques as backup in case the power goes out, the ATM is out of order or you lose or break your plastic.

Remember, you must present your passport whenever changing currency and travellers cheques. Commission for foreign exchange is becoming increasingly rare – if it is charged, the fee is usually nominal. For information about travelling costs, see p21. See p469 for tips on keeping your money safe.

ATMs

Twenty-four hour ATMs are found in most large towns and cities, though the ATM may not be in the same place as the bank branch. The most commonly accepted cards are Visa, MasterCard, Cirrus, Maestro and Plus. Banks in South India that reliably accept foreign cards include Citibank, HDFC, ICICI, UTI, HSBC and the State Bank of India. Away from major towns, always carry cash or travellers cheques as back-up.

Banks impose higher charges on international transactions, but this may be cancelled out by the favourable exchange rates between banks. Reduce charges by making larger transactions less often. Always check in advance whether your card can access banking networks in India and ask for details of charges.

Note that several travellers have reported ATMs snatching back money if you don't remove it within around 30 seconds. Conversely, other machines can take more than 30 seconds to actually release cash, so don't panic if the money doesn't appear instantaneously.

The ATMs listed in this book's regional chapters accept foreign cards (but not necessarily all types of cards). Always keep the emergency lost and stolen numbers for your credit cards in a safe place, separate from your cards, and report any loss or theft immediately.

Cash

Major currencies such as US dollars, UK pounds and euros are easy to change throughout India, although some bank branches insist on travellers cheques only. Private moneychangers usually accept a wider range of currencies, but Pakistani, Nepali and Bangladeshi currencies can be harder to change away from the border. When travelling off the beaten track, always carry a decent stock of rupees.

Whenever changing money, check every note. Banks staple bills together into bricks which puts a lot of wear and tear on the currency. Do not accept any filthy, ripped or disintegrating notes, as these may not be accepted as payment. If you get lumbered, change them to new bills at branches of the Reserve Bank of India in major cities.

Shopkeepers, taxi-wallahs etc seem to rarely have small change, making it wise to maintain a constant stock of smaller currency. Try to stockpile Rs 10, Rs 20 and Rs 50 notes – change bigger bills into these denominations every time you change money.

Before leaving India you can change any leftover rupees back into foreign currency, most easily at the airport. Note that some airport banks will only change a minimum of Rs 1000. You may require encashment certificates (see right) or a credit-card receipt and you may also have to show your passport and airline ticket.

Credit Cards

Credit cards are accepted at a growing number of shops, upmarket restaurants and midrange and top-end hotels, and you can also usually use them to pay for flights and train tickets. However be wary of scams – see p468. MasterCard and Visa are the most widely accepted cards, and cash advances on major credit cards are possible at some banks without

ATMs. For details about whether you can access home accounts in India, inquire at your bank before leaving.

Encashment Certificates

By law, all foreign currency must be changed at official moneychangers or banks. For every transaction, you will receive an encashment certificate, which will allow you to re-exchange rupees into foreign currency when departing India (see left). You'll need to have encashment certificates totalling the amount of rupees you intend changing back to foreign currency. Printed receipts from ATMs may also be accepted as evidence of an international transaction at some banks.

Traditionally, money-exchange receipts have also been required when paying for tourist quota train tickets in rupees, but this requirement has largely been relaxed in recent times.

International Transfers

If you run out of cash, someone at home can wire you money via moneychangers affiliated with **Moneygram** (www.moneygram.com) or **Western Union** (www.westernunion.com). A hefty fee is added to the transaction. To collect cash, bring your passport and the name and reference number of the person who sent the funds.

Moneychangers

Private moneychangers are usually open for longer hours than banks, and they are found almost everywhere (many also double as internet cafés and travel agents). Compare rates with those at the bank, and always check you are given the correct amount.

Tipping, Baksheesh & Bargaining

In midrange and top-end hotels and restaurants, a service fee is usually already added to your bill and tipping is optional. Elsewhere, a tip is appreciated. Hotel bellboys expect around Rs 20 to carry bags, and hotel staff expect similar gratuities for services above and beyond the call of duty. It's not mandatory to tip taxi or rickshaw drivers, but a tip for good service is encouraged (see p497).

Baksheesh can be defined as a 'tip' (aka bribe) and it also refers to giving alms to beggars. Many Indians implore tourists not to hand out sweets, pens or money to children, as it is positive reinforcement to beg. To make a lasting difference, donate to a school or reputable charitable organisation; see p487 for details.

Apart from at fixed-price shops, bargaining is the norm – see The Art of Haggling, p482.

Travellers Cheques
All major brands are accepted in India, but some banks may only accept cheques from American Express (Amex) and Thomas Cook. Pounds sterling and US dollars are the safest currencies, especially in smaller towns. Charges for changing travellers cheques vary from place to place and bank to bank.

Always keep an emergency cash stash in case you lose your travellers cheques, and keep a record of the cheques' serial numbers separate from your cheques, along with the proof-of-purchase slips, encashment vouchers and photocopied passport details.

To replace lost travellers cheques you need the proof-of-purchase slip and the numbers of the missing cheques (some places require a photocopy of the police report and a passport photo). If you don't have the numbers of your missing cheques, Amex (or whichever company has issued them) will contact the place where you bought them.

If you do lose your cheques, contact the Amex or Thomas Cook office in the closest city, or call the head offices in Delhi:
American Express (Amex; ☎ 011-23719506; A-Block, Connaught Place, Delhi; ☺ 9.30am-6.30pm Mon-Fri, to 2.30pm Sat)
Thomas Cook (☎ 011-23342171; Hotel Janpath, Janpath, Delhi; ☺ 9.30am-7.30pm Mon-Fri, to 6pm Sat)

For Thomas Cook office locations in Mumbai see p109, and for Chennai see p370.

PHOTOGRAPHY
For useful tips and techniques on travel photography, read Lonely Planet's *Guide to Travel Photography*, *Travel Photography: Landscapes* and *Travel Photography: People & Portraits*.

Digital
Memory cards for digital cameras are available from photographic shops in most large cities, and increasingly in small places, too. However, the quality of memory cards is variable – some do not carry the advertised amount of data. Expect to pay upwards of Rs 1000/1600 for a 512MB/1GB card. To be safe, regularly back up your memory card to CD – internet cafés offer this service for Rs 50 to 100 per disc.

Some photographic shops make prints from digital photographs for roughly the standard print and processing charge.

Print & Slide
Colour print film-processing facilities are readily available in most South Indian cities. Film is relatively cheap and the quality is usually good, but you'll only find colour slide film/processing in the major cities and tourist traps. On average, print and processing costs around Rs 6 per 4in by 6in colour print plus Rs 15 to 20 for processing. Passport photos are available from many photo shops for around Rs 100 (10 to 12 shots).

Always check the use-by date on local film and slide stock. Make sure you get a sealed packet and that you're not handed a roll that has been sitting in a glass cabinet in the sunshine for the last few weeks. Be wary of buying film from street hawkers – unscrupulous characters have been known to load old/damaged film into new-looking canisters. It's best to only buy film from reputable stores – and preferably film that's been refrigerated.

Restrictions
India is touchy about anyone taking photographs of military installations – restrictions can also include train stations, bridges, airports and sensitive border regions. Photography is officially prohibited from the air, though airlines rarely enforce this. On flights to strategically important destinations, cameras may be banned from the cabin (or you may need to remove the batteries).

Many places of worship – temples, monasteries and mosques – also prohibit photography. Respect these proscriptions and always ask when in doubt as taking photographs of forbidden images can cause serious offence. For etiquette about photographing people, see p51.

POST
Mail and poste restante services are generally good, although the speed of delivery will depend on the efficiency of any given office. Airmail is faster than seamail, although it's best to use courier services (such as DHL) to send and receive items of value – expect to pay around Rs 2700 per kilogram to Europe, Australia or the USA. Private couriers are cheaper but goods may be repacked into large packages to cut costs and things sometimes go missing.

DIRECTORY

Receiving Mail

To receive mail in India, ask senders to address letters to you with your surname in capital letters and underlined, followed by: poste restante, GPO (main post office), and the city or town in question. Many 'lost' letters are simply misfiled under given/first names, so check under both your names and ask senders to provide a return address in case you don't collect your mail. Letters sent via poste restante are generally held for around one month before being returned. To claim mail, you'll need to show your passport. It's best to have any parcels sent to you by registered post.

Sending Mail

Posting an aerogramme/postcard anywhere overseas costs Rs 8.50/8 and airmail letters cost from Rs 15 (1g to 20g). For postcards, stick on the stamps *before* actually writing on them, as post offices can give you as many as four stamps per card. Sending a letter by registered post adds around Rs 15 to the stamp cost.

To eliminate the risk of stamp theft, do request stamps to be franked in front of you before posting.

Posting parcels is quite straightforward; prices vary depending on weight and you have a choice of airmail (delivery in one to three weeks), seamail (two to four months), or Surface Air-Lifted (SAL) – a curious hybrid where parcels travel by air and sea (one month). Parcels must be packed in white linen and the seams sealed with wax. Most local tailors offer this service, or there may be a parcel service at the post office. Carry a permanent marker to write on any information requested by the desk. The post office can provide the necessary customs declaration forms and these must be stitched or pasted to the parcel. If the contents are specified as a gift under the value of Rs 1000, you don't pay duty at the delivery end.

Parcel post has a maximum of 20kg to 30kg depending on the destination; charges vary depending on whether they go by air or sea.

As an indication, a 1kg parcel costs the following (prices in rupees):

Destination	Airmail	SAL	Seamail
Australia	570	535	450
Europe	645	525	500
USA	645	595	480

It is sometimes cheaper to send packages under 2kg in weight as registered letters (packed the same way as parcels). You also have the option of the EMS (express mail service; delivery within three days) for around 30% more than the normal airmail price.

Books or printed matter can go by inexpensive bookpost (maximum 5kg), but the package must be wrapped leaving a gap that reveals the contents for the customs inspection – tailors are experienced in creating this in such a way that nothing falls out. Overseas rates depend on the weight not the country – a 1kg bookpost parcel costs around Rs 260 to any international destination. **India Post** (www.indiapost.gov.in) has an online calculator for other international postal tariffs.

Be cautious with places that offer to mail things to your home address after you have bought them. Government emporiums are usually fine but in most other places it pays to do the posting yourself (see p468 for more information).

SHOPPING

You'll find a treasure trove of things to buy in South India, from exquisite textiles and carpets to stunning jewellery and handicrafts. Specialities from all over the country can be found. Rajasthani crafts, such as sequinned and mirrored embroidery or colourful saris, and Kashmiri shawls, carpets and carvings, can be found everywhere, especially at tourist-oriented markets (such as the Anjuna flea market in Goa, see p199) and city shopping centres. Kashmiris especially are among India's most ubiquitous traders!

Be very cautious when buying items that include delivery to your country of residence. You may be told that the price includes home delivery and all customs and handling charges, but this is not always the case. Also be wary of being led to shops by touts – see p469. Also see the warning on exporting antiques (opposite).

Unless you're at fixed-price shops (such as cooperatives and government emporiums), you'll invariably have to bargain – see the boxed text, p482.

Opening hours for shops vary – exceptions to standard hours are indicated in the shopping listings in regional chapters.

Only a small proportion of the money brought to India by tourism reaches people in rural areas. You can make a greater contribution by shopping at community shops and

PROHIBITED EXPORTS

To protect India's cultural heritage, the export of many antiques is prohibited. Many 'old' objects are fine but the difficulties begin if something is verifiably more than 100 years old. Reputable antique dealers know the laws and can make arrangements for an export clearance certificate for any ancient items that you are permitted to export. If in doubt, contact Delhi's **Archaeological Survey of India** (ASI; ☎ 011-23010822; asi@del3.vsnl.net.in; Janpath; ⊗ 9.30am-1pm & 2-6pm Mon-Fri) next to the National Museum.

The Indian Wildlife Protection Act bans any form of wildlife trade. Don't buy any products that endanger threatened species and habitats – doing so can result in heavy fines and even imprisonment. This includes shawls made from *shahtoosh* wool (wool from a rare Tibetan antelope, known as the chiru), ivory, and anything made from the fur, skin, horns or shell of any endangered species. Realistically, the only way to be sure is to avoid animal products completely. Products made from certain rare plants are also forbidden for export.

Note that your home country may have additional laws forbidding the import of restricted items and wildlife parts. The penalties can be severe, so know the law before you buy.

cooperatives, set up to protect and promote traditional cottage industries and provide education, training and a sustainable livelihood for rural families. Many of these projects focus on refugees, low-caste women, the disabled and other socially disadvantaged groups. Prices are usually fixed and a share of the money goes directly into social projects such as schools, healthcare and training. Shopping at the national network of Khadi & Village Industries emporiums will also contribute to rural communities.

Bronze Figures, Metalwork, Stone-Carving & Terracotta

Bronze figures of various deities are available around South India, especially in and around major temple towns. The bronze makers (called *shilpis*) still employ the centuries' old lost-wax method of casting, a legacy of the Chola period when bronze sculpture reached its apogee in skill and artistry. A wax figure is made, a mould is formed around it and the wax is melted and poured out. The molten metal is poured in and when it's solidified the mould is broken open. Figures of Shiva as Nataraja (lord of the cosmic dance) are among the most popular. Small copper bowls, cigarette boxes and paan containers are still handmade in Hyderabad, while bell metal lamps are a particularly good buy in Thrissur.

Bidriware is a craft named after the town of Bidri (in northern Karnataka) where silver is inlaid into gunmetal (an alloy of zinc, copper, lead and tin). Hookah pipes, lamp bases and jewellery boxes are made in this manner. Bidri employs the technique of sand-casting, where

artisans make a mould from sand, resin and oil (also see the boxed text, p272).

In Mamallapuram (Mahabalipuram; p382) craftsmen have revived the ancient artistry of the Pallava sculptors using local granite and soapstone – souvenirs range from tiny stone elephants to enormous deity statues weighing half a tonne. Tamil Nadu is also known for the bronzeware from Thanjavur (Tanjore; p409) and Tiruchirappalli (Trichy; p411).

At temples across South India you can buy small terracotta or plaster effigies of assorted deities.

Carpets

The majority of carpets you'll see for sale in South India come from Kashmir, Rajasthan or Uttar Pradesh. Kashmiri rugs are either made of pure wool, wool with a small percentage of silk to give them a sheen (known as 'silk touch') or pure silk. The latter are more for decoration. Kashmiri carpets cost anywhere from Rs 200 to 8000 per square foot, with wool being cheaper than silk. The number of knots per square inch (from 200 to 1800) also affects the price.

The price of a carpet will be determined by the number and the size of the hand-tied knots, the range of dyes and colours, the intricacy of the design and the material. Silk carpets cost more and look more luxurious but wool carpets last longer. Expect to pay upwards of US$200 for a good quality 3ft by 5ft (or 3ft by 6ft depending on the region) wool carpet and US$2000 for a similar-sized carpet in silk. Tibetan carpets are slightly cheaper, reflecting the relative simplicity of the designs – many

CARPETS & CHILD LABOUR

Children have been employed as carpet weavers in India for centuries, and many childcare charities from Europe and America are campaigning against the use of child labour by the carpet industry. There are thought to be at least 30,000 child carpet weavers in India, and 10% of these children are believed to have been trafficked from neighbouring countries.

Unfortunately, the issue is not as cut and dried as campaigners would like to suggest. In poor rural areas, education is often not an option, both for economic and social reasons, and the alternative to child labour may not be school but hunger for the whole family. Even with the benefit of education, there are often no skilled jobs around. We encourage travellers to buy from carpet-weaving cooperatives that employ adult weavers *and* provide education for their children, thus breaking the cycle of child labour.

The **Carpet Export Promotion Council of India** (www.india-carpets.com) is campaigning to eliminate child labour from the carpet industry by penalising factories that use children and by founding schools to provide an alternative to carpet making. Ultimately, the only thing that will stop child labour completely is compulsory education for children. However, the economic and social obstacles are significant.

Unfortunately for the buyer, there is no easy way of knowing whether a carpet has been made by children. Shops are unlikely to admit using child labour and most of the international labelling schemes for carpets have been discredited. The carpets produced by Tibetan refugee cooperatives are almost always made by adults but Uttar Pradesh is the undisputed capital of child labour in India. Government emporiums and charitable cooperatives are by far the best places to buy.

refugee cooperatives sell 3ft by 5ft carpets for US$100 or less.

Most places can ship carpets home for a fee – though it may be safest to ship things independently to avoid scams – or you can carry them in the hold (allow 5kg to 10kg of your baggage allowance for a 3ft by 5ft carpet).

Kashmir and Rajasthan produce coarsely woven woollen *numdas* (or *namdas*), which are much cheaper than knotted carpets. Various parts of India produce flat weave *dhurries* (kilim-like cotton rugs). Kashmiris also produce striking *gabbas* made from chainstitched wool or silk. All these types of carpets can also be found for sale in South India.

Jewellery

South India's most significant jewellery-making centres are Hyderabad, Bengaluru, Mysore, Udhagamandalam (Ooty) and Thanjavur (Tanjore). South Indian jewellery is generally distinguished from that made in the north by its use of motifs inspired by nature – lotus buds, flowers, grass stalks and, in Kerala, birds. Throughout South India you can find finely crafted gold and silver rings, anklets, earrings, toe-rings, necklaces and bangles. Pieces can often be crafted to order.

Virtually every town has at least one bangle shop. These sell an extraordinary variety of inexpensive bangles, made from plastic, glass, brass, shell and wood.

If you feel like being creative and making your own necklace, loose beads of agate, turquoise, carnelian and silver can be found for sale. Buddhist meditation beads made of gems or wood make nifty souvenirs; prices cost around Rs 25 for wooden beads to Rs 500 for an amber string.

Pearls are produced by most seaside states. They're a speciality of Hyderabad (see p293) and pearls are crafted into jewellery in many other Indian states. You'll find them at most state emporiums. Prices vary depending on the colour and shape – you pay more for pure white pearls or rare colours like black and red, and perfectly round pearls are more expensive than misshapen or elongated pearls. However, the quirky shapes of Indian pearls are often more alluring than the perfect round balls. A single strand of seeded pearls can cost as little as Rs 200, but better-quality pearls start at Rs 600.

Leatherwork

As the cow is sacred in India, leatherwork here is made from buffalo-hide, camel, goat or some other substitute. Chappals, those wonderful leather sandals found all over India, are a particularly popular traveller's purchase. In Maharashtra, the town of Kolhapur is especially famous for its chappals, and they are also well-made in Pune and Matheran, with prices generally starting at around Rs 150.

Rajasthan (especially Jaipur) is famed for its *jootis* (traditional pointy-toed shoes); those for men often have curled-up toes. These *jootis* can be found throughout South India at bazaars and shopping centres.

In the larger cities, such as Chennai, Bengaluru and Mumbai, you'll find impressive, moderately priced leather handbags, wallets and other leather accessories.

Musical Instruments

Quality musical instruments are available in the larger South Indian cities, but there tends to be more variety in North Indian centres such as Delhi.

Decent tabla sets with a wooden tabla (tuned treble drum) and metal *doogri* (bass tone drum) cost upwards of Rs 3000. Cheaper sets are generally heavier and sound inferior. Sitars range from Rs 4000 to 15,000 – a good-quality starter sitar with inlay work will cost upwards of Rs 7000. The sound of each sitar will vary with the wood used and the shape of the gourd so try a few. Note that some cheaper sitars can warp in colder or hotter climates. On any sitar, make sure the strings ring clearly and check the gourd carefully for damage. Spare string sets, sitar plectrums and a second screw-in 'amplifier' gourd are sensible additions.

Other popular Indian instruments include the *shennai* (Indian flute; from Rs 250), the sarod (like an Indian lute; from Rs 8000) and the harmonium (from Rs 3500).

Paintings

Reproductions of Indian miniature paintings are widely available, but quality varies – the best are almost as good as the real thing, while cheaper ones have less detail and use inferior colours. Beware of paintings purported to be antique – it's highly unlikely and, in addition, paintings more than 100 years old can't be exported from India.

In Kerala and Tamil Nadu, you'll come across miniature paintings on leaf skeletons depicting deities as well as domestic and rural scenes. Meanwhile, in Andhra Pradesh you can buy lovely cloth paintings called *kalamkari,* portraying deities and historic events – see www.kalamkariart.org for more on this interesting art form.

The village of Raghurajpur (Orissa) is an artists' colony that makes *patta chitra* painting, which involves preparing cotton cloth with a mixture of gum and chalk that is then polished to make it tough. Outlines of characters from India's mythologies and deities are drawn with exceedingly fine paintbrushes and then coloured in. Another craft practised in the same village is carving onto dried palm leaf sections with a fine stylus, after which the incisions are dyed with a wash of colour. There's another artists' colony, adopting similar styles, at the Cholamandal Artists' Village (p382) south of Chennai in Tamil Nadu.

Throughout the country (especially in capital cities) look out for shops and galleries selling brilliant contemporary paintings by local artists. Mumbai is the centre of the flourishing Indian contemporary art scene; you can see some of this art at the National Gallery of Modern Art (p113).

Papier-Mâché

Artisans in Srinagar (Kashmir) have been producing lacquered papier-mâché for centuries and papier-mâché ware is now sold right across India. The basic shape is made in a mould from layers of paper (often recycled newsprint), then painted with fine brushes and lacquered for protection. Prices depend upon the complexity and quality of the design and the amount of gold leaf used. Many pieces feature delicate patterns of animals and flowers, or hunting scenes from Mughal miniature paintings. You can find papier-mâché bowls, boxes, letter holders, coasters, trays, lamps and Christmas decorations (stars, crescent moons, balls and bells).

Shawls, Silk & Saris

Indian shawls are famously warm and lightweight and can be bought throughout the subcontinent. Shawls are made from all sorts of wool, from lamb's wool to fibres woven from yak, pashmina goat and angora rabbit hair. Many are embroidered with incredibly intricate designs. However, *shahtoosh* shawls should be avoided because rare Tibetan antelopes (known as chiru) are killed to provide the wool.

The undisputed capital of the Indian shawl is the Kullu Valley in Himachal Pradesh, which has dozens of women's cooperatives producing sublime woollen varieties. Prices range from about Rs 200 for a simple lamb's wool shawl to Rs 6000 for a stylish angora. The most intricately embroidered shawls cost upwards of Rs 10,000. Ladakh and Kashmir are major centres for *pashmina* production, but these shawls are also distributed throughout South India. You'll pay at least Rs 6000 for the authentic 'slides through a wedding ring' article. Be aware that many so-called *pashmina* shawls are actually made from a mixture of yarns.

Aurangabad (p146) is the traditional centre for the production of *himroo* shawls, sheets and saris. Made from a blend of cotton, silk and silver thread, these garments cost from about Rs 500 and are often decorated with motifs from the Ajanta cave paintings. The divine silk and gold-thread saris produced at Paithan near Aurangabad (see the Paithani Weaving Centre, p146) are some of India's finest – prices range from around Rs 6000 to a mind-blowing Rs 300,000.

Saris are a very popular souvenir, and they can be readily adapted to other purposes. Real silk saris are the most expensive, and the silk usually needs to be washed before it becomes soft. The 'silk capital' of India is Kanchipuram (p389) in Tamil Nadu. Note the boxed text on child labour, p390.

Textiles

Textile production is India's major industry and around 40% of production takes place at the village level, where it is known as *khadi* (homespun cloth) – hence the government-backed *khadi* emporiums around the country.

These inexpensive superstores sell all sorts of items made from homespun cloth, including the popular 'Nehru jackets' and kurta (long shirt with either short collar or no collar) pyjamas, and sales benefit rural communities.

You will find a truly amazing variety of weaving and embroidery techniques around the country. In tourist centres, such as Goa, textiles are stitched into shoulder bags, wall hangings, cushion covers, bedspreads, clothes and much more.

Appliqué is an ancient art in India, with most states producing their own version, usually featuring abstract or anthropomorphic patterns. The traditional lampshades and *pandals* (marquees) used in weddings and festivals are produced using the same technique.

Batik can be found throughout South India, especially in the larger cities such as Mumbai. It is often used for saris and *salwar kameez* (dresslike tunic and trouser combination). *Kalamkari* cloth from Andhra Pradesh is an associated but far older craft. It traditionally emerged around South India's temples – the designs reflect elements of temple murals, and are largely used as decorative cloths during devotional ceremonies and festivals.

Big Indian cities, such as Mumbai, Bengaluru and Chennai, are super places to pick up *haute couture* (high fashion) by talented Indian designers, as well as more moderately priced Western fashions.

THE ART OF HAGGLING

Government emporiums, department stores and modern shopping centres usually charge fixed prices. Anywhere else you need to bargain, and bargain hard. Shopkeepers in tourist hubs are accustomed to travellers who have lots of money and little time to spend it, so you can expect to be charged double or triple the 'real' price. Souvenir shops are probably the least likely places of all to charge you the real going rate.

The first 'rule' to haggling is never to show too much interest in the item you want to purchase. Secondly, don't buy the first item that takes your fancy. Wander around and price things, but don't make it too obvious – if you return to the first shop, the vendor will know it's because they are the cheapest and the price, therefore, probably won't budge.

Decide how much you would be happy paying and then express a casual interest in buying. If you have absolutely no idea of what something should really cost, start by slashing the price by half. The vendor will make a show of being shocked at such a low offer, but the game is set and you can now work up and down respectively in small increments until you reach a mutually agreeable price. You'll find that many shopkeepers lower their so-called 'final price' if you head out of the shop saying you'll 'think about it'.

Haggling is a way of life in India, but it should never turn ugly. Keep in mind exactly how much a rupee is worth in your home currency to put things in perspective. If a vendor seems to be charging an unreasonably high price, simply look elsewhere.

Block-printed and woven fabrics are sold by fabric shops all over India, often in vivid colours. Each region has its own speciality. The India-wide chain store **Fab India** (www.fabindia .com) works to preserve traditional patterns and fabrics, transforming then into highly accessible items for home decoration and Indian and Western fashions.

Woodcarving

Mysore is known as South India's main centre of sandalwood carving. While sandalwood was once purely reserved for carving deities, nowadays all manner of things are made, from solid pieces of furniture to keyrings and delicate fans. Sandalwood carvings of Hindu deities are still one of Karnataka's specialities, but you'll pay a fortune for the real thing – a 4in-high Ganesh costs around Rs 3000 in sandalwood, compared to Rs 300 in kadamb wood. However, it will release fragrance for years. Rosewood is used for making furniture, and carving animals is a speciality of Kerala. The religious icons produced from wood inlay in Goa also have a certain chintzy appeal.

Kerala, along with coastal Karnataka, is a centre for marquetry, which uses woods of various hues (including rosewood) and, in Mysore, ivory substitutes. Carved wooden furniture and other household items, either in natural finish or lacquered, are also made in various locations. Woodcarvers' skills are very much in evidence in the major temple towns of Tamil Nadu.

Wooden boxes and chests, once major dowry items, are available in the antique shops of Fort Cochin in Kerala. Although the wooden versions are still made by local artisans, metal cupboards and trunks are replacing them and they are becoming rarer. Dowry boxes are usually made from the wood of the jackfruit tree (sometimes rosewood), and are reinforced with brass hinges and brackets.

Wooden toys are also produced in many regions of South India; brightly painted buses and trucks are a highlight of Thiruvananthapuram (Trivandrum).

Other Buys

Indian spices are legendary around the planet. Most South Indian towns have shops and markets selling locally produced spices at cash-and-carry prices.

Attar (essential oil) shops can be found throughout the country; Mysore is renowned for its sandalwood oil, while Mumbai (p130)

is a major centre for the trade of traditional fragrances, and for the valuable oud (stringed musical instrument similar to a lute), made from a rare mould that grows on the bark of the agarwood tree. In Tamil Nadu, Udhagamandalam (Ooty) and Kodaikanal produce aromatic and medicinal oils from herbs, flowers and eucalyptus.

Indian incense is exported worldwide with Bengaluru and Mysore (p238) being major producers. Incense from Auroville (see p402), an ashram near Puducherry, is also of a high standard. Beware, however, that there are many inferior copies of the quality brands.

One speciality of Goa is *feni* (cashew or coconut liquor), a head-spinning spirit that often comes in decorative bottles. India is also gaining a reputation for the wines produced by vineyards in southern states; Sula, Grover and Chateau Indage are all reputable labels. Excellent Indian tea is also widely sold in South India.

Fine, quality handmade paper – often fashioned into cards, boxes and notebooks is particularly impressive in Puducherry (see the Sri Aurobindo Handmade Paper Factory; p401). Lavishly embellished Indian cards and paper and envelope sets are available in Mumbai's Chimanlals (p131).

You can find a phenomenal range of books in India – see the Bookshops sections of individual regional chapters for recommendations. Also good value are music CDs featuring Indian artists.

SOLO TRAVELLERS

Perhaps the most significant issue facing solo travellers is cost. Single-room rates at guesthouses and hotels are sometimes not much lower than double rates; some midrange and top-end places don't even offer a single tariff. However, it's always worth trying to negotiate a lower rate for single occupancy.

In terms of transport, you'll save money if you find others to share taxis and autorickshaws. This is also advisable if you intend hiring a car with driver.

Although most solo travellers experience no major problems in South India, remember that some less honourable souls (locals and travellers alike) may view lone tourists as an easy target for theft. Don't be paranoid, but, like anywhere else in the world, it's wise to stay on your toes in unfamiliar surroundings. The main traveller hotels and restaurants are

DIRECTORY

good places to swap stories, get up-to-the-minute travel tips and find people to travel with. You might also try advertising for travel companions on Lonely Planet's **Thorn Tree forum** (thorntree.lonelyplanet.com).

For information specific to women, see p489.

TELEPHONE

There are few payphones in India, but private PCO/STD/ISD call booths do the same job, offering inexpensive local, interstate and international calls at much lower prices than calls made from hotel rooms. Many booths are open 24 hours and a digital meter displays how much the call is costing and provides a printed receipt when the call is finished. Faxes can be sent from some call booths or from the local telephone exchange.

Call booths charge the full rate from around 9am to 8pm. After 8pm the cost slides, with the cheapest time to call being between 11pm and 6am. Interstate calls are half-rate on Sunday. Direct international calls from call booths range from Rs 22 to 40 per minute depending on the country you are calling. Hotels charge considerably more at all times. International calls for as little as Rs 5 per minute can be made through internet cafés using Net2phone, Skype and other internet-phone services.

Some booths also offer a 'call-back' service where you ring home, provide the phone number of the booth and wait for people at home to call you back, for a fee of Rs 5 to 10 on top of the cost of the preliminary call.

India has both the **White Pages** (www.indiawhitepages.com) and **Yellow Pages** (www.indiayellowpages.com) online. Note that getting a line can be difficult in remote country and mountain areas – an engaged signal may just mean that the exchange is overloaded, so keep trying.

Mobile Phones

India is becoming increasingly mobile-phone crazy and there is roaming coverage for international GSM phones in most large towns and cities. Mobile-phone numbers in India usually have 10 digits, typically starting with '9'. To avoid expensive roaming costs (often highest for incoming calls), get hooked up to the local mobile-phone network.

Mobiles bought in Western countries are often locked to a particular network; you'll have to get the phone unlocked, or buy a local phone (available from Rs 2300) to use an Indian SIM card.

In most towns you simply buy a prepaid mobile-phone kit (SIM card and phone number, plus a starter allocation of calls) for around Rs 150 from a phone shop or local PCO/STD/ISD booth, internet café or grocery store. Thereafter, you must purchase new credits on that network, sold as scratch-cards in the same shops and call centres. Credit must usually be used within a set time limit and costs vary with the amount of credit on the card. The amount you pay for a credit top-up is not the amount you get on your phone – state taxes and service charges come off first. For some networks, recharge cards are being replaced by direct credit, where you pay the vendor and the credit is deposited straight to your phone – ask which system is in use before you buy.

Calls made within the state/city in which you bought the SIM card are cheap – less than Rs 1 per minute – and you can call internationally for less than Rs 25 per minute. SMS messaging is even cheaper. The more credit you have on your phone, the cheaper the call rate. However, some travellers have reported unreliable signals and problems with international texting (with messages or replies being delayed or failing to get through).

The most popular (and reliable) companies are Airtel, Hutch (Orange in some states), Idea and BSNL. Note that most SIM cards are state specific – they can be used in other states but you pay for calls at roaming rates and you will be charged for incoming calls as well as outgoing calls.

As the mobile-phone industry is evolving, mobile rates, suppliers and coverage are all likely to develop over the life of this book.

Phone Codes

Regular phone numbers have an area code followed by up to eight digits. The government is slowly trying to bring all numbers in India onto the same system, so area codes can change and new digits may be added to numbers with limited warning. It pays to keep abreast of new developments as you travel around the country.

To make a call *to* India from overseas, dial the international access code of the country you're in, then ☎ 91 (international country code for India), then the area code (drop the initial zero when calling from abroad), then the local number. See this book's regional chapters for area codes.

To make an international call *from* India, dial ☎ 00 (international access code from India), then the country code (of the country you are calling), then the area code and the local number.

Also available is the Home Country Direct service, which gives you access to the international operator in your home country. For the price of a local call, you can then make reverse-charge (collect) or phonecard calls. The number is typically constructed ☎ 000 + the country code of your home country + 17.

Some countries and their Home Country Direct numbers:

Country	Telephone Number
Australia	☎ 0006117
Canada	☎ 000167
Germany	☎ 0004917
Italy	☎ 0003917
Japan	☎ 0008117
The Netherlands	☎ 0003117
New Zealand	☎ 0006417
Spain	☎ 0003417
UK	☎ 0004417
USA	☎ 000117

TIME

India is 5½ hours ahead of GMT/UTC, 4½ hours behind Australian Eastern Standard Time (EST) and 10½ hours ahead of American EST. The local standard time is known as IST (Indian Standard Time), although many affectionately dub it 'Indian Stretchable Time'. The floating half hour was added to maximise daylight hours over such a vast country. See the World Time Zones map, p546.

TOILETS

Public toilets are generally confined to the major cities and tourist sites. The cleanest toilets are usually at places such as restaurants and fast-food chains, museums, upmarket shopping complexes and cinemas. There are public urinals and squat toilets in many towns (an entry fee of Rs 1 to 2 applies) but they tend to be quite filthy. Upmarket restaurants almost always have sit-down toilets, but carry your own toilet paper in case there is just a tap and a jug; for more about Indian toilets see the boxed text, Get to Know Your Bathroom (p464).

When it comes to effluent etiquette, it's customary to use your left hand and water, not toilet paper. A strategically placed tap, usually with a plastic jug nearby, is available in most bathrooms. If you prefer to use toilet paper, it is widely sold in cities and towns. However, paper (as well as sanitary napkins and tampons) goes in the bin beside the toilet, not into the narrow and easily blocked drains.

TOURIST INFORMATION
Local Tourist Offices

The first stop for information should be the tourism website of the **Government of India** (www.incredibleindia.org). Here you'll find information in English, French, German, Spanish, Korean and Hindi. For details of regional offices around India, click on Links at the bottom of the homepage. You can also find useful information on the official state government websites – there's a list on india.gov.in/knowindia/districts.php.

In addition to the national (Government of India) tourist office, each state maintains its own tourist office. The state offices vary widely in their efficiency and usefulness. Some are run by enthusiastic souls; others have grumpy or disinterested staff who can be abrupt to the point of rudeness. Apart from dispensing verbal information, most tourist offices have a healthy stock of brochures (no charge) and often a free local map. Many state governments also operate a chain of tourist bungalows (see p463), a number of which house state tourism offices.

For details about specific tourist offices, see the Information sections of this book's regional chapters.

Tourist Offices Abroad

The Government of India operates tourist offices abroad:

Australia (☎ 02-9264 4855; info@indiatourism.com.au; Level 2, Piccadilly, 210 Pitt St, Sydney, NSW 2000)

Canada (☎ 416-962 3787; indiatourism@bellnet.ca; 60 Bloor St, West Ste 1003, Toronto, Ontario, M4W 3B8)

France (☎ 01 45 23 30 45; indtourparis@aol.com; 11-13 Blvd Haussmann, F-75009, Paris)

Germany (☎ 069-2429490; info@india-tourism.com; Basler Strasse 48, D-60329, Frankfurt am-Main 1)

Italy (☎ 02-8053506; info@indiatourismmilan.com; Via Albricci 9, Milan 20122)

Japan (☎ 03-3571 5062; indtour@blue.ocn.ne.jp; Art Masters Ginza Bldg, 6-9 fl, 6-5-12 Ginza, Chūō-ku, Tokyo 104-0061)

DIRECTORY

South Africa (☎ 011-3250880; goito@global.co.za; Craighall 2024, Hyde Lane, Lancaster Gate, Johannesburg 2000)

The Netherlands (☎ 020-6208991; info.nl@india-tourism.com; Rokin 9/15, 1012 KK Amsterdam)

UK (☎ 020-7437 3677; info@indiatouristoffice.org; 7 Cork St, London W1S 3LH)

USA Los Angeles (☎ 213-380 8855; indiatourismla@aol.com; 3550 Wiltshire Blvd, Room 204, Los Angeles, CA 900102485); New York (☎ 212-586 4901; ad@itonyc.com; 1270 Avenue of the Americas, Suite 1808, NY 100201700)

TRAVEL PERMITS

Even with a visa, you're not permitted to travel everywhere in South India. Some national parks and forest reserves require a permit if you intend to go trekking, and a permit (issued free) is required to visit the Andaman Islands (see p447) and another to visit Lakshadweep (p361).

TRAVELLERS WITH DISABILITIES

India's crowded public transport, crush of people in urban areas and variable infrastructure can test even the hardiest able-bodied traveller. If you're physically handicapped or visually impaired, these pose even more of a challenge. However, seeing the way mobility-impaired locals whiz through city traffic on modified bicycles proves that nothing is impossible.

India has limited wheelchair-friendly hotels (mostly top end), restaurants and offices. Staircases are often steep and lifts frequently stop at mezzanines between floors. Footpaths, where they exist, are often riddled with holes, littered with debris and packed with pedestrians, hindering movement. Try to book ground floor hotel rooms, and if you use crutches, bring along spare rubber caps for the tips as they can wear down quickly.

If your mobility is considerably restricted, you could consider travelling with an able-bodied companion. Additionally, hiring a car with a driver will make moving around a whole lot easier (see p497).

The following organisations may offer further advice and there are also some good sites on the web, including www.access-able.com.

Mobility International USA (MIUSA; ☎ 541-3431284; www.miusa.org; 132 E Broadway, Suite 343, Eugene, Oregon 97401, USA)

Royal Association for Disability and Rehabilitation (Radar; ☎ 020-7250 3222; www.radar.org.uk; 12 City Forum, 250 City Rd, London EC1V 8AF, UK)

VISAS

You must get a visa *before* arriving in India and these are easily available at Indian missions worldwide – see your local directories for listings. You won't be issued a visa to enter India unless you hold an onward ticket, which is taken as sufficient evidence that you intend to leave the country.

Six-month multiple-entry tourist visas (valid from the date of issue) are granted to nationals of most countries regardless of whether you intend staying that long or re-entering the country. There are additional restrictions on travellers from Bangladesh and Pakistan, as well as certain Eastern European, African and Central Asian countries. Check any special conditions for your nationality with the Indian embassy in your country.

Visas are priced in the local currency – Brits pay UK£30, Americans pay US$60, Australians pay A$75 (an extra A$15 service fee applies at consulates) and Japanese citizens pay ¥1200.

Extended visas are possible for people of Indian descent (excluding those in Pakistan and Bangladesh) who hold a non-Indian passport and live abroad. Contact your embassy for the latest details.

For visas lasting more than six months, you need to register at the Foreigners' Regional Registration Office (FRRO; see opposite) within 14 days of arriving in India – inquire about these special conditions when you apply for your visa.

Visa Extensions

Fourteen-day extensions are possible under exceptional circumstances from the Foreigners' Regional Registration Office (FRRO; see opposite), found in some of India's major cities (for Mumbai, see p111; for Chennai, see p370); however, many may direct travellers to Delhi for extensions. Don't get your hopes up. The only circumstances where this might conceivably happen, is if you were robbed of your passport just before you planned to leave the country at the end of your visa. A few travellers have reported success in obtaining extensions in Mumbai with a bit of persistence, but don't count on it.

You can only get another six-month tourist visa by leaving the country – many travellers hop over to Sri Lanka, Nepal or on a cheap flight to Bangkok, but be aware that some travellers report difficulties getting another visa in Kathmandu.

If you do find yourself needing to request an extension, you should contact the **Foreigners' Regional Registration Office** (FRRO; ☎ 011-26195530; frrodelhi@hotmail.com; Level 2, East Block 8, Sector 1, Rama Krishna Puram, Delhi; ☙ 9.30am-1.30pm & 2-3pm Mon-Fri), just around the corner from the Hyatt Regency hotel in Delhi. This is also the place to come for a replacement visa if you've had your lost/stolen passport replaced (required before you can leave the country). Regional FRROs are even less likely to grant an extension.

Assuming you meet the stringent criteria, the FRRO is permitted to issue an extension of 14-days, free for nationals of all countries except Japan (Rs 390), Sri Lanka (Rs 135 to 405, depending on the number of entries), Russia (Rs 1860) and Romania (Rs 500). You must bring your confirmed air ticket, one passport photo and a photocopy of your passport (information and visa pages). Note that this system is designed to get you out of the country promptly with the correct official stamps, not to give you two extra weeks of travel.

VOLUNTEERING

Numerous charities and international aid agencies have branches in South India and, although they're generally staffed by locals, there are opportunities for foreigners. You are more use to the charity concerned if you write in advance and, if you're needed, stay for long enough to be of help. A week on a hospital ward may salve your own conscience, but you may actually do little more than get in the way of the people who work there long term – stick to manual tasks such as litter clearing and support roles unless you are able to offer a long-term commitment or are requested to provide specific services.

Flexibility in what you are prepared to do is also vital. Some charities are inundated with foreign volunteers to help babies in an orphanage for instance, but few are willing to work with adults with physical or intellectual disabilities.

If you're a Bollywood fan there may be opportunities for working as an extra (see the boxed text, p116). For details about Chennai's film industry, see the boxed text, Into the 'Woods (p378)

Agencies Overseas

There are hundreds of international volunteering agencies, and it can be bewildering trying to assess which ones have ethical policies.

The organisation Ethical Volunteering (www .ethicalvolunteering.org) has some excellent guidelines for choosing an ethical agency.

There are some tried and tested international projects such as Britain's **Voluntary Service Overseas** (VSO; www.vso.org.uk) that place volunteers in serious professional roles, though the time commitment can be as much as two years. The international organisation **Indicorps** (www.indicorps.org) matches volunteers to projects across India in all sorts of fields, particularly social development. There are special fellowships for people of Indian descent living outside India. Many Indian NGOs also offer volunteer work – for listings try clicking on www.indianngos.com.

To find sending agencies in your area, look at Lonely Planet's *Volunteering, Gap Year* and *Career Break* books, or use the web – searching for 'Volunteering' on your home version of Google should bring up pages of agencies and listings of volunteer opportunities.

Some good starting sites:
Working Abroad (www.workingabroad.com)
World Volunteer Web (www.worldvolunteerweb.org)
Worldwide Volunteering (www.worldwidevolunteer ing.org.uk)

Aid Programmes in India

Following are some of the programmes operating in South India that may have opportunities for volunteers. You should contact them in advance, rather than turning up on their doorstep expecting to be offered a position. Donations of money or clothing from travellers may also be warmly welcomed.

Note that unless otherwise indicated, volunteers are expected to cover their own costs (accommodation, food, transport etc).

ANDHRA PRADESH
Confederation of Voluntary Associations (COVA; ☎ 040-24572984; www.covanetwork.org; 20-4-10, Charminar, Hyderabad) This is an umbrella organisation for around 800 NGOs predominantly based in Andhra Pradesh, working with women, children, civil liberties and sustainable agriculture. Volunteers are matched to programmes that need their skills (long-term volunteers preferred).
Karuna Society for Animals and Nature (☎ 08555-287214; www.karunasociety.org; 2/138/C Karuna Nilayam, Prasanthi Nilayam Post; Anantapur 515134) With an animal hospital and sanctuary, this organisation works to rescue sick and mistreated animals. There are opportunities for volunteer vets.

GOA

Children Walking Tall (☎ 01623-450944; www .childrenwalkingtall.com; 54 Clipstone Dr, Forest Town, Mansfield, Notts, NG19 0JJ, UK) This British-based organisation has opportunities for volunteer child-carers, teachers and medics at its projects for homeless children and orphans near Mapusa. The minimum placement is three months and every volunteer needs a criminal background check.

Goa Foundation (☎ 08322-263305; www.olb.com; c/o Other India Bookstore, Mapusa, Goa 403507) Goa's leading environmental group runs occasional voluntary programmes including litter clean-ups – contact it for current details.

KARNATAKA

Ashoka Trust for Research in Ecology and the Environment (Atree; ☎ 080-23533942; www.atree .org; 659 5th A Main Rd, Hebbal, Bengaluru 560024) This organisation is committed to sustainable development issues related to conservation and biodiversity. It takes volunteers with experience or a keen interest in conservation and environmental issues.

Equations (☎ 080-25457607; www.equitabletourism .org; 415, 2nd C Cross, 4th Main Rd, OMBR Layout, Banaswadi Post, Bengaluru 560043) Works to promote 'holistic tourism' and protect local communities from exploitation through lobbying, local training programmes and research publications.

Family Services (☎ 98440-26222; www.thefamily india.org; 68, 2nd fl, Transpade Towers, Koramangala Industrial Layout, Jyothi Nivas College Rd, Bengaluru 560095) Runs a school for slum kids – it's possible to visit at the weekends to help out. It also runs programmes in Delhi and Mumbai.

It may also be possible to volunteer at the Bengaluru gay and lesbian support groups Sangama and Swabhava (see p473).

MAHARASHTRA

Nimbkar Agricultural Research Institute (☎ 02166-222396; http://nariphaltan.virtualave.net/; Phaltan-Lonand Rd, Tambmal, PO Box 44, Phaltan, Maharashtra) Based near Paltan, this has a focus on sustainable development, animal husbandry and renewable energy. Volunteer internships lasting two to six months are available for agriculture, engineering and science graduates to assist with their research.

Sadhana Village (☎ 020-25380792; www.sadhana -village.org; Priyankit, 1 Lokmanya Colony, Opposite Vanaz Paud Rd, Pune 411038) A residential care centre for intellectually disabled adults, 30km from Pune. Volunteers assist in workshops, cultural activities and community-development programmes for women and children. Meals and accommodation are provided, but the organisation receives no government funding so donations are greatly appreciated.

MUMBAI

Child Rights and You (CRY; ☎ 022-23063647/51; www.cry.org; 189A Anand Estate, Sane Guruji Marg; Mumbai) This independent trust organises fundraising for more than 300 projects India-wide, including a dozen projects in Mumbai helping deprived children. There are long- and short-term opportunities for people of all backgrounds.

Concern India Foundation (☎ 022-22880129; www.concernindia.org; 3rd fl, Ador House, 6K Dubash Marg, Mumbai 400001) This charitable trust supports development-oriented organisations working with vulnerable members of the community. The focus is on establishing sustainable projects run by local people. The foundation can arrange volunteer placements matched to your skills and interests in Mumbai and around India (six months minimum). Volunteers should preferably speak Hindi.

Saathi (☎ 022-23520053; www.saathi.org; Agripada Municipal School, Farooque Umarbhouy Lane, Mumbai, 400011) Works with adolescent street children. It also has a project in Ahmedabad (Gujarat) for children affected by communal violence. Volunteers should be willing to commit at least three months and work full time for the organisation during the project.

Vatsalya Foundation (☎ 022-24962115; Anand Niketan, King George V Memorial, Dr E Moses Rd, Mahalaxmi, Mumbai 400011) Works with Mumbai's street children, focusing on rehabilitation into mainstream society. There are long- and short-term opportunities in teaching and sports activities.

TAMIL NADU

Freedom Foundation (☎ 044-25567228; www .thefreedomfoundation.org; 15 United Colony, Red Hills Rd, Kolathur, Chennai) Provides services to people living with HIV/AIDs, including treatment at its clinic and work skills training. It also campaigns for HIV education and prevention. There are opportunities for counsellors, trainers, teachers and carers.

Missionaries of Charity (☎ 044-25956928; 79 Main Rd, Royapuram, Chennai) There are volunteer opportunities at this charity, which is part of Mother Teresa's Kolkata-based care operation.

Rejuvenate India Movement (RIM; ☎ 044-22235133; www.india-movement.org; A-1, Monisha Sriram Flats, 9 Kulothungan Cross St, Chittlapakkam, Chennai 600064) Based in Chennai, this organisation can arrange three-week to one-year placements for skilled volunteers on development projects run by partner NGOs in 14 villages in Tamil Nadu. There are also opportunities in Karnataka. Spoken Hindi is an asset.

Rural Institute for Development Organisation
(RIDE; ☎ 04112-268393; www.charityfocus.org/India
/host/RIDE; 46 Periyar Nagar, Little Kanchipuram) This NGO
works with around 200 villages in Kanchipuram to remove
children from forced labour and into transition schools.
Volunteers can contribute in teaching, administrative and
support roles. See the boxed text, p390, for more about
child labour.

Unite for Sight
(www.uniteforsight.org/intl_volunteer)
This international eye-care charity has regular month-long
openings for volunteer assistants, teachers, nurses, and
optical health professionals to help at its partner eye-care
clinics in Chennai and around India – see the website for
details.

WOMEN TRAVELLERS

Solo women travellers are likely to receive some
form of unwanted male attention while in India,
whether it's constant staring or the occasional
groping on public transport. Women travellers
have reported far less hassles in the South, but
no matter where you are, the way you dress and
act in public can have a profound impact on
how you're treated. Even on the beach resorts
of Goa and Kerala – where locals have become
accustomed to the sight of scantily clad foreigners – local sensibilities must be respected.
Regrettably, the skimpy clothing and culturally
inappropriate behaviour of a minority of foreign women seems to have had a ripple effect on
the perception of foreign women in general. An
increasing number of female travellers have reported some form of sexual harassment (mainly
lewd comments) despite making an effort to
act and dress conservatively. Most harassment
cases are reported in prominent tourist destinations such as Goa (see p178). While there's no
need to be concerned to the point of paranoia,
you should be aware that your behaviour and
dress code is under scrutiny.

Getting stared at is, unfortunately, something you'll have to get used to. Just be thick-
skinned and don't allow it to get the better
of you. It's best to refrain from returning
stares, as this may be considered a come-on;
dark glasses can help. A good way to block
out stares in restaurants is to take a book or
postcards to write home. Other harassments
encountered include: provocative gestures,
jeering, getting 'accidentally' bumped into
on the street and being followed. Exuberant
special events (such as the Holi festival) can
be notorious for this (see p468).

Based on feedback we've received, women
travelling with a male partner are less likely
to be hassled. However, a foreign woman of
Indian descent travelling with a non-Indian
male may cop disapproving stares from locals.

Ultimately, there are no sure-fire ways of
shielding yourself from sexual harassment,
even for those who do everything 'right'.
You're essentially going to have to use your
own judgement and instincts as there isn't a
blanket rule that applies to every case. If the
warnings in this section make travel in India
seem a little daunting, remember that most
men are certainly not out to bother you, and
the problems mentioned here are just things
to be aware of.

Sanitary pads and tampons (there's a limited
variety of the latter) are available from many
pharmacies in large cities and tourist centres. Carry additional stocks for travel off the
beaten track.

Staying Safe

Women have reported being molested by
masseurs and other therapists, although most
cases have been registered in North India.
Always try to check the reputation of any
teacher or therapist before going to a solo
session. If at any time you feel uneasy, leave.
For gynaecological health issues, seek out a
female doctor.

To keep conversations with unknown men
short, get to the point as quickly and politely
as possible. Getting involved in inane conversations with men can be misinterpreted as a
sign of sexual interest. Questions such as 'do
you have a boyfriend?' or 'you are looking very
beautiful' are indicators that the conversation
may be taking a steamy tangent. Some women
prepare in advance by wearing a pseudo wedding ring, or by announcing early on that
they are married or engaged (regardless of
whether they are or not). For many, this has
proved effective in keeping interactions 'lust-
free'. If, despite your efforts, you still get the
uncomfortable feeling that your space is being
encroached upon, the chances are that it is. A
firm request to keep away is usually enough
to take control of the situation, especially
if it's loud enough to draw attention from
passers-by. Alternatively, the silent treatment
can be a remarkably good way of getting rid
of unwanted male company.

When interacting with men on a day-to-
day basis, it's polite to adhere to the local
practice of not shaking hands. Instead, relay
respect by saying *namaste* – the traditional,

respectful Hindu greeting, often accompanied by a small bow with the hands brought together at the chest or head level.

Female film-goers will probably feel more comfortable (and decrease the chances of potential harassment) by going to the cinema with a companion, as it's uncommon for women to see a movie alone.

Lastly, it's wise to arrive in towns before dark and, of course, always avoid walking alone at night, especially in isolated areas. Unlit back lanes in Goa should be avoided after dark – a rising number of sexual assaults have been reported in recent years.

Taxis & Public Transport

Officials recommend that solo women prearrange an airport pick-up from their hotel if their flight is scheduled to arrive late at night. If that's not possible, catch a prepaid taxi, and make a point of (in front of the driver) writing down the car registration and driver's name and giving it to one of the airport police.

Avoid taking taxis alone late at night (when many roads are deserted) and never agree to having more than one man (the driver) in the car – ignore claims that this is 'just his brother' or 'for more protection'. Women are advised against wearing expensive-looking jewellery as it can make them a target for muggers.

On extended train and bus travel, being a woman has some glowing advantages. When buying tickets, women can queue-jump without consequence and avail of the special ladies-only carriages on many trains. Women have reported less hassle by opting for the more expensive classes on trains, especially for overnight trips. If you're travelling overnight in a three-tier carriage, try to get the uppermost berth, which will give you more privacy (and distance from potential gropers).

On public transport, don't hesitate to return any errant limbs, put some item of luggage in between you and, if all else fails, find a new spot. You're also within your rights to tell him to shove off – loudly enough to

attract public attention and shame the guy into leaving you alone.

What to Wear

Warding off sexual harassment is often a matter of common sense and adjusting your behaviour to match the prevailing social norms in India. What you wear can help enormously. Steer clear of sleeveless tops, shorts, mini-skirts (ankle-length skirts are recommended), skimpy, see-through or tight clothing. Baggy clothing that hides the contours of your body is the way to go.

In some areas, like Goa and Mumbai, there's generally a more liberal attitude towards dress. Swimwear is fine on most of Goa's beaches and party clothes are OK for nightclubs, but away from these areas, take your cues from local women. Many Indian women wear saris, *salwar kameez* (traditional dresslike tunic and trouser combination), or knee-length shorts and a T-shirt whenever swimming in public view. When returning from the beach, use a sarong to avoid stares on the way back to your hotel.

Wearing Indian dress, when done properly, makes a positive impression and, although we've had a few reports of women still being groped, most were pleasantly surprised by the effect it had in curtailing harassment. The *salwar kameez*, widely worn by Indian women, is regarded as respectable attire and wearing it will reflect your veneration for local dress etiquette. It's practical, comfortable, attractive, and comes in a range of designs and prices. A cotton *salwar kameez* is also surprisingly cool in the hot weather. The dupatta (long scarf) that is worn with this outfit is handy if you visit a shrine that requires your head to be covered.

Wearing a *choli* (small tight blouse worn underneath a sari) or a sari petticoat (which some foreign women mistake for a skirt) in public is rather like strutting around half-dressed – not a good idea.

You can read personal experiences proffered by fellow women travellers at www.journeywoman.com.

Transport

CONTENTS

Getting There & Away	**491**
Entering the Country	491
Air	491
Land	494
Sea	494
Getting Around	**495**
Air	495
Bicycle	496
Boat	496
Bus	496
Car	497
Hitching	498
Local Transport	498
Motorcycle	499
Share Jeeps	502
Tours	502
Train	502

GETTING THERE & AWAY

South India is most easily accessed via its major international airports of Mumbai (Bombay) and Chennai (Madras). Some countries also offer charter flights to Goa. For details, see right. The south can also be reached overland from elsewhere in India – for details, see p494.

The following sections contain information on transport to and around South India. Flights and tours can also be booked online at www.lonelyplanet.com.travel_services.

ENTERING THE COUNTRY

Entering India by air or land is relatively straightforward, with standard immigration and customs procedures (see p468).

Passport

To enter India you need a valid passport, visa and an onward/return ticket; there are restrictions on entry for some nationalities (see Visas, p486, for more information). If your passport is lost or stolen, immediately contact your country's representative (see p470). It's wise to keep photocopies of your airline ticket and the identity and visa pages from your passport in case of emergency.

AIR

Airports & Airlines

India is a big county so it makes sense to fly into the nearest airport to the area you want to visit. The main international airports in South India are Mumbai's Chhatrapati Shivaji International Airport (see p131) and Chennai's Anna International Airport (see p379). There are fewer international services to Bengaluru (Bangalore; for international airline offices in Bengaluru see p229), although there are plans to boost these in the coming years – inquire with a travel agent or surf the web for the latest updates.

Direct charter flights from the UK and Europe land at Goa's Dabolim Airport (p179) and, while you can get some cheap deals, you must also return via a charter flight (see p179 for details). There are also some charter flights to Thiruvananthapuram (Trivandrum) in Kerala, but double-check as to whether these are operating at the time of your visit. There are a growing number of departure alternatives to the two main South Indian airports, mostly heading out via the Arab Gulf States or Sri Lanka. Kochi (Cochin) and Kozhikode (Calicut) have connections to the Arab Gulf States, while Thiruvananthapuram (Trivandrum) has flights to Sri Lanka and the Maldives (see p313).

India's national carrier is **Air India** (www.airindia.com) and the state-owned domestic carrier

> **THINGS CHANGE...**
>
> The information in this chapter is particularly vulnerable to change. Check directly with the airline or a travel agent to make sure you understand how a fare (and the ticket you may buy) works, and be aware of the security requirements for international travel. Shop carefully. The details given in this chapter should be regarded as pointers and are not a substitute for your own careful, up-to-date research.

TRANSPORT

CLIMATE CHANGE & TRAVEL

Climate change is a serious threat to the ecosystems that humans rely on, and air travel is one of the fastest-growing contributors to the problem. Lonely Planet regards travel, overall, as a global benefit, but we believe that everyone has a responsibility to limit their personal impact on global warming.

Flying & Climate Change

Every form of motorised travel generates CO_2 (the main cause of human-induced climate change) but planes are far and away the worst offenders, not just because of the fuel they consume, but because they release greenhouse gases high into the atmosphere. Two people taking a return flight between Europe and the US will contribute as much to climate change as an average household's gas and electricity consumption over a whole year.

Carbon Offset Schemes

Climatecare.org and other websites use 'carbon calculators' that allow travellers to offset the level of greenhouse gases they are responsible for with financial contributions to sustainable travel schemes and tree planting projects that offset the effects of global warming – including projects in India.

Lonely Planet, together with Rough Guides and other concerned partners in the travel industry, support the carbon offset scheme run by climatecare.org. Lonely Planet offsets all of its staff and author travel. For more information check out our website: www.lonelyplanet.com.

Indian Airlines (www.indian-airlines.nic.in) also offers flights to 20 countries in Asia and the Middle East. The more reliable private airlines **Jet Airways** (www.jetairways.com) and **Air Sahara** (www.air sahara.net) offer flights to Colombo, Kathmandu and the Maldives. Jet has recently started long-haul flights to London, Bangkok, Kuala Lumpur and Singapore, while Sahara has introduced flights to Singapore. For details about India's domestic airlines, see p495.

Airlines flying to/from India:
Aeroflot (code SU; www.aeroflot.org)
Air Canada (code AC; www.aircanada.com)
Air France (code AF; www.airfrance.com)
Air India (code AI; www.airindia.com)
Air Sahara (www.airsahara.net)
Alitalia (code AZ; www.alitalia.com)
American Airlines (code AA; www.aa.com)
Austrian Airlines (code OS; www.aua.com)
Biman Bangladesh Airlines (code BG; www.bimanair .com)
British Airways (code BA; www.british-airways.com)
Cathay Pacific Airways (code CX; www.cathaypacific.com)
Druk Air (code KB; www.drukair.com.bt)
El Al Israel Airlines (code LY; www.elal.co.il)
Emirates (code EK; www.emirates.com)
Finnair (code AY; www.finnair.com)
Gulf Air (code GF; www.gulfairco.com)
Indian Airlines (www.indian-airlines.nic.in)

Japan Airlines (code JL; www.jal.com)
Jet Airways (www.jetairways.com)
Kenya Airways (code KQ; www.kenya-airways.com)
KLM – Royal Dutch Airlines (code KL; www.klm.com)
Kuwait Airways (code KU; www.kuwait-airways.com)
Lufthansa Airlines (code LH; www.lufthansa.com)
Malaysia Airlines (code MH; www.malaysiaairlines.com)
Pakistan International Airlines (code PK; www.piac .com.pk)
Qantas Airways (code QF; www.qantas.com.au)
Qatar Airways (code QR; www.qatarairways.com)
Royal Nepal Airlines Corporation (code RA; www .royalnepal.com)
Singapore Airlines (code SQ; www.singaporeair.com)
South African Airlines (code SA; www.flysaa.com)
Sri Lankan Airlines (code UL; www.srilankan.aero)
Swiss International Airlines (code LX; www.swiss .com)
Thai Airways International (code TG; www.thaiair.com)

Departing India

Most airlines no longer require reconfirmation of international tickets, although it's still a good idea to call to check that flight times haven't changed. Almost all airlines ask you to check in three hours before international departures – remember to factor in the Indian traffic when planning your trip to the airport.

The majority of Indian airports have free luggage trolleys, but porters will eagerly offer to lug your load for a negotiable fee. For flights originating in India, hold bags must be passed through the X-ray machine in the departures hall, and baggage tags are required for the security check for all cabin bags, including cameras.

Tickets

An onward or return air ticket is a condition of the Indian tourist visa, so few visitors buy international tickets inside India itself. International fares to India fluctuate according to the low, shoulder and high seasons. The cheapest time to visit is generally during the hotter months (around June to late August). The departure tax of Rs 500 (Rs 150 for most South and Southeast Asian countries) and the Rs 200 passenger service fee is included in the price of almost all tickets.

The fares we've given in this section represent average starting fares available at the time of research. Contact a travel agent or surf the web to get up-to-the-minute fares and flight schedules. Advertisements for discount travel agencies appear in the travel pages of major newspapers and listings magazines. Note that fares on airline websites are sometimes just as cheap as going through an agent. Alternatively, try the following international online ticket agencies:

Ebookers (www.ebookers.com)
Expedia (www.expedia.com)
Flight Centre International (www.flightcentre.com)
Flights.com (www.tiss.com)
STA Travel (www.statravel.com)
Travelocity (www.travelocity.com)

AFRICA

There are direct flights to India from South Africa and East Africa. Return fares to Mumbai are US$600 from Nairobi, and US$500 from Cape Town or Johannesburg.

ASIA
Bangladesh

Dhaka is the air hub for Bangladesh. Biman Bangladesh and Indian Airlines offer flights between Dhaka and Kolkata (Calcutta; from US$200 return) or Delhi (from US$500 return).

Japan

Tokyo/Narita is the main hub for flights between Japan and India. Flights to Chennai or Mumbai start at US$540 return.

Maldives

A return or onward ticket is a condition of travel to the Maldives. Excursion fares to Malé from Thiruvananthapuram (Trivandrum) on Indian Airlines start at US$200 return.

Myanmar (Burma)

Return flights between Yangon (Rangoon) and Kolkata cost around US$350. Alternatively, you can connect through Bangkok, Singapore or Kuala Lumpur for around US$500.

Nepal

Royal Nepal Airlines and half-a-dozen Indian carriers offer flights from Kathmandu to several Indian cities. One-way/return fares include Mumbai (from US$230/450) and Bengaluru (from US$230/450). You'll need an onward ticket to enter India on a one-way ticket from Nepal.

Pakistan

Be aware that flights between India and Pakistan are often suspended when relations between the two countries sour. At the time of writing, flights were operating. A return fare from Karachi to Mumbai is US$200.

Singapore, Malaysia, Hong Kong & China

There are extensive air connections between Southeast Asia and Mumbai, Bengaluru and Chennai. Return flights between Singapore, Hong Kong or Kuala Lumpur and India start at US$550. Several airlines have recently started flights from Beijing and Shanghai to Mumbai (from around US$550).

Sri Lanka

Sri Lankan Airlines and several Indian carriers have connections between Colombo and various Indian cities. Return fares include Mumbai (US$390), Bengaluru (US$270) and Thiruvananthapuram (Trivandrum; US$200).

Thailand

Bangkok is the most popular departure point from Southeast Asia to India. Return fares from Bangkok include Mumbai (US$500) and Chennai (US$700).

AUSTRALIA

Qantas has a flight from Sydney to Mumbai via Darwin, or you can fly to Chennai,

TRANSPORT

Mumbai or Bengaluru with a stop in Southeast Asia. Return fares range from A$1200 to A$1700, depending on the season.

CANADA

From eastern and central Canada, most flights go via Europe; from Vancouver and the west coast, flights tend to go via Asia. Return fares from Vancouver or Toronto to Mumbai start at around C$1500.

CONTINENTAL EUROPE

There are connections to Mumbai, Chennai or Bengaluru from most European capitals, either directly or with a stop in the Middle East. For destination-specific details, inquire with travel agents or surf the web.

NEW ZEALAND

Flights between India and New Zealand go via Southeast Asia. Return tickets from Auckland to Mumbai or Chennai start at NZ$1400.

UK & IRELAND

Discount air travel is big business in London. Flights from London or Manchester to Mumbai, Chennai or Bengaluru range from UK£350 to UK£600.

USA

America has plenty of discount travel agents, or 'consolidators', particularly in San Francisco, Los Angeles and New York. Fares to India vary – bank on upwards of US$1100 from the East Coast and US$1300 or more from the West Coast. Consult travel agents and scan the web for the best deal.

LAND

It's possible, of course, to get to South India overland via the long haul through North India. The classic hippie route from Europe to Goa involves travelling via Turkey, Iran and Pakistan. Other overland options are via Bangladesh or Nepal.

If you enter India by bus or train you'll be required to disembark at the border for standard immigration and customs checks. You must have a valid Indian visa in advance as no visas are available at the border. The standard Indian tourist visa allows multiple entries within a six-month period (see p486).

Drivers of cars and motorbikes will need the vehicle's registration papers, liability insurance and an International Driving Permit. You'll also need a *Carnet de passage en douane,* which acts as a temporary waiver of import duty. To find out the latest requirements for the paperwork and other important driving information, contact your local automobile association. For details on travelling through South India by motorcycle, see p499; for road rules, see p501.

The security situation in Nepal has significantly improved since the ceasefire in 2006. Nevertheless, you should still check the latest security status before crossing into Nepal by land – local newspapers and international news websites are good places to start. Political and weather conditions permitting, there are five land border crossings between India and Nepal: Sunauli (Uttar Pradesh) to Bhairawa (central Nepal); Raxaul (Bihar) to Birganj (central Nepal); Panitanki (West Bengal) to Kakarbhitta (eastern Nepal); Jamunaha (Uttar Pradesh) to Nepalganj (western Nepal); and Banbassa (Uttaranchal) to Mahendranagar (western Nepal). The Sunauli to Bhairawa route is the most popular crossing.

Crossing between India and Pakistan by land depends on the state of relations between these South Asian neighbours – transport links between the two countries can be abruptly halted if relations take a dive, so it certainly pays to double-check the current situation. Assuming the crossings are open, there are straightforward routes into Pakistan from Delhi and Amritsar (Punjab) by bus or train. However, clearing the border formalities can take anywhere between two and five hours – compared to one or two hours if you travel independently. At the time of writing, motorcycles were not permitted to cross the border.

For those travelling from India to Bangladesh, the daily bus service between Kolkata and Dhaka is the most convenient option.

Phuentsholing is the main entry and exit point between India and Bhutan but you need a full Bhutanese visa to enter the country, which must be obtained at least 15 days before your trip from a registered travel agent listed under the **Department of Tourism, Bhutan** (www.tourism.gov.bt).

SEA

There are currently no international passenger boat services to or from South India. There are several sea routes to surrounding islands but none leave Indian sovereign territory – for details, see p496. There has been talk of a passenger ferry service between southern India and Colombo in Sri Lanka but this has yet to materialise. Inquire locally to see if there has been any progress.

GETTING AROUND

AIR
South India is well serviced by domestic airlines, with air connections to the major cities as well as dozens of smaller towns. The three big carriers – Indian Airlines, Jet Airways and Air Sahara – charge rupee fares for Indian citizens and higher US-dollar fares for foreigners (often payable in rupees). Most budget airlines charge the same (low) rupee fare to everyone, regardless of nationality. Reconfirmation is normally only required if your ticket was bought outside India, but call a few days ahead to be safe. Airlines may issue a replacement for lost tickets at their discretion, but refunds are rare. For details about airfare discounts see p470.

Check-in for domestic flights is an hour before departure and hold luggage must be X-rayed and stamped before you check in. Every item of cabin baggage needs a baggage label, which must be stamped as part of your security check. In a few cases, you may need to identify your bags on the tarmac before they are loaded on the plane – inquire when checking in.

Some smaller airlines will only take off if there are enough passengers to cover costs. Passengers usually receive a refund for cancellations, but several travellers have reported being booked onto other airlines at inflated prices by airline staff. If your flight is cancelled demand a refund and make the onward booking yourself.

The baggage allowance is 20kg (10kg for smaller aircraft) in economy class, 30kg in business.

Airlines in South India
In recent years, there has been a massive surge in domestic flights right around India. The state-owned carrier **Indian Airlines** (www.indian-airlines.nic.in) still has the largest network, but its record on safety and reliability is unenviable and the private airlines **Jet Airways** (www.jetairways.com) and **Air Sahara** (www.airsahara.net) are catching up fast. Then there are India's new budget airlines, offering discounted rupee fares for flights around the country.

In fact, some analysts say the whole industry is seriously over-inflated. Until the bubble bursts, this is a sensational time to fly around India, but fares change daily and there is no guarantee that all the airlines will still be around after the expected slump occurs. As a rough indication, fares for a one-hour flight range from US$150 on an established carrier to Rs 1000 with a budget airline.

A nifty booklet containing updated domestic air schedules and fares is *Excel's Timetable of Air Services Within India* (Rs 45; published monthly). It's available at city newsstands and bookshops.

New airlines are set to continue springing up, so it's worth talking to local travel agents and perusing the web for the latest routes and carriers.

At the time of writing, the airlines listed here were serving destinations across India – this book's regional chapters and the airline websites have details of routes, fares and booking offices.

Air Deccan (www.airdeccan.net) Budget fares and an expanding list of nationwide destinations.

Air India (www.airindia.com) India's national carrier operates a number of domestic flights, generally leaving from the international terminals of Indian airports (check in advance).

Air Sahara (www.airsahara.net) This private operator offers domestic services throughout India and international flights.

GoAir (www.goair.in) New budget carrier connecting Goa with major hubs across India.

Indian Airlines (www.indian-airlines.nic.in) With its subsidiary Alliance Air, the state domestic carrier has flights across India and international services to 20 neighbouring countries, but a poor record on safety and service.

IndiGo (www.goindigo.in) A new budget carrier set to grow substantially in coming years.

Jagson Airlines (www.jagsonairline.com) Limited services using tiny Dornier planes.

Jet Airways (www.jetairways.com) Rated by many as India's best airline, serving the entire country, plus a handful of international destinations.

Kingfisher Airlines (www.flykingfisher.com) Yep, it's an airline owned by a beer company, connecting an increasing number of cities India-wide.

Spicejet (www.spicejet.com) Discount seats to hubs across India.

Air Passes
Air passes don't represent great value if you're only travelling around South India. On top of that, given the recent deregulation of the

Indian airline industry, they rarely work out cheaper than buying individual discounted tickets.

The three big Indian carriers – Indian Airlines, Jet Airways and Air Sahara – all offer air passes. Indian Airlines 'Discover India' pass costs US$630/895 for 15/21 days, plus US$21 tax for each flight sector. You can travel on any flight, except the flight to the Lakshadweep Islands, but you can't visit the same place twice. There's also the Indian Airlines 'India Wonder' fare, which costs US$300 plus US$21 tax per flight sector for one week's travel. The pass is valid for North India or South India, and you must specify one or the other when you book. Again, Lakshadweep is off-limits.

BICYCLE

South India offers oodles of variety for the cyclist, from pretty coastal routes to roads passing fragrant spice plantations and coconut groves.

Road rules are virtually nonexistent throughout India; cities and national highways are particularly hazardous places to cycle, making it more enjoyable to stick to quieter back roads. Be conservative about the distances you expect to cover – an experienced cyclist can manage 60km to 100km a day on the plains, 40km to 60km on sealed mountain roads, and 40km or less on dirt roads.

There are no restrictions on bringing a bicycle into India, though it may be cheaper to hire or buy a bike after you arrive. Mountain bikes with off-road tyres give the best protection against India's potholed and puncture-inducing roads. Roadside cycle mechanics abound but bring spare tyres and brake cables, lubricating oil and a chain-repair kit, as well as plenty of puncture-repair patches. Bikes can often be carried for free, or for a small luggage fee, on the roofs of public buses – handy for uphill stretches. Contact your airline for information about transporting your bike and customs formalities in your home country.

Read up on bicycle touring before you travel – Rob van de Plas' *Bicycle Touring Manual* (Bicycle Books, 1987) and Stephen Lord's *Adventure Cycle-Touring Handbook* (Trailblazer Publications, 2006) are good places to start. Consult local cycling magazines and cycling clubs for useful information and advice. For India-specific information, contact the **Cycle Federation of India** (☎ /fax 011-23392578; Yamuna Velodrome, IGI Sports Complex, New Delhi; ⊙ 10am-5pm Mon-Fri).

Hire

Big tourist centres and other places where travellers hang around – eg Goa and Hampi (Karnataka) – are the easiest places to find bicycles for hire. Expect to pay between Rs 30 and Rs 100 per day for a roadworthy, Indian-made bike. Hire places may require a security deposit (cash or airline ticket). For good places to rent a bike, see p99.

Purchase

A reliable mountain-bike from reputable brands, such as Hero, Atlas, Hercules or Raleigh, starts at Rs 2000, and extras such as panniers, stands and bells are readily available. Reselling should be quite easy – ask at local cycle or hire shops or put up an advert on travel noticeboards. You should be able to get around 50% back of what you originally paid if it was a new bike and is still in reasonably good condition.

BOAT

Scheduled ferries connect mainland India to Port Blair in the Andaman Islands (see p449); the journey takes around 60 hours from Chennai (see p380). There are also sporadic ferries from Visakhapatnam (Andhra Pradesh) to the Andaman Islands (see p299). From October to May, there are boat services from Kochi (Cochin; Kerala) to the Lakshadweep Islands (around 20 hours; see p361).

There are numerous internal ferry services across rivers, as well as various boat cruises, such as the famous backwater trips through Kerala – see the regional chapters for further details and also have a look at Boat Tours (p98).

BUS

Bus travel in South India is comprehensive, inexpensive and effectively fills the gaps not served by trains (trains are preferable for long-distance journeys). Services are fast and frequent; however, roads can be perilous and buses are often driven with wilful abandon. Avoid night buses unless there is no alternative. All buses make regular snack and toilet stops, providing a break from the rattle and shake but adding hours to journey times.

Vehicles run by the state government bus companies are usually the safest and most reliable options, and seats can be booked up to a month in advance. Private buses can be cheaper, but drivers are notorious speed-demons and conductors cram as many passengers on board as possible to maximise profits. There are some upmarket private bus companies that are much more comfortable and worth the extra money. Earplugs are a boon on all long-distance buses to muffle the often deafening music. On any bus, sit between the axles to minimise the effect of bumps and potholes.

Luggage is either stored in compartments underneath the bus (sometimes for a small fee) or it can be carried free of charge on the roof. Conductors will haul your bags up for a modest tip.

If your bags go on the roof, make sure they are locked and securely tied to the metal baggage rack – some unlucky travellers have lost their luggage thanks to bumpy roads coupled with poor securing. Theft is a minor risk so keep an eye on your bags at snack and toilet stops. Never leave your day pack unattended inside the bus and always keep valuables in your money belt.

Classes

Both state and private companies offer 'ordinary' buses – ageing rattletraps with wonky windows that blast in dust and hot air – or more expensive 'deluxe' buses, which range from less decrepit versions of ordinary buses to flashy Volvo tour buses with AC and reclining two-by-two seating. Travel agents in tourist towns offer more expensive private two-by-two buses, which tend to leave and terminate at conveniently central stops. Be warned that agents have been known to book people onto ordinary buses at superdeluxe prices. Timetables and destinations are usually displayed on signs or billboards at travel agencies and tourist offices.

Costs

The cheapest buses are 'ordinary' government buses but prices vary from state to state – expect to pay Rs 40 to 60 for a three-hour-long daytime journey and Rs 200 to 300 for an all-day or overnight trip. Add around 50% to the ordinary fare for deluxe services, double the fare for AC, and triple or quadruple the fare for a two-by-two service.

Reservations

Deluxe buses can usually be booked in advance – up to a month in advance for government buses – at the bus stand or local travel agents. Reservations are rarely possible on 'ordinary' buses and travellers often get left behind in the mad rush for a seat. To maximise your chances of securing a seat, either send a travelling companion ahead to grab some space, or pass a book or article of clothing through an open window and place it on an empty seat. This 'reservation' method rarely fails. If you board a bus midway through its journey, you will have to stand until a seat becomes free.

At many bus stations there is a separate women's queue, although this isn't always obvious as signs are often in local script and men frequently join the melee. Local women will push to the front of queues – you'll stand a much better chance of getting served if you follow their example.

CAR

Self-drive car rental in South India is possible, but considering that it's such terrific value hiring a car *and* driver, it makes little sense to get behind the wheel on India's hair-raising roads. However you choose to travel, avoid doing so at night when driving conditions are more challenging.

Hiring a Car & Driver

Hiring a car and driver is an excellent way to sightsee, and the cost comes down dramatically if you find other travellers with whom to split the fare. You can also get to off-the-beaten-track places a lot quicker than you could with bus connections. Most towns have taxi stands where you can arrange tours and charter trips. Some taxi companies will only

ROAD DISTANCES (KM)

	Bengaluru (Bangalore)	Chennai (Madras)	Mumbai (Bombay)	Panaji (Panjim)	Thiruvananthapuram (Trivandrum)
Bengaluru (Bangalore)	---				
Chennai (Madras)	337	---			
Mumbai (Bombay)	995	1332	---		
Panaji (Panjim)	576	913	540	---	
Thiruvananthapuram (Trivandrum)	635	716	1526	986	---

TRANSPORT

operate in a designated area, dictated by their government permit.

Try to find a driver who speaks at least some English and is familiar with the region you'll be touring. For multiday trips, the fare should cover the driver's meals and accommodation, but confirm this when you book (and get it in writing). Drivers make their own sleeping and eating arrangements in the evening. Before setting off, it's not a bad idea to inspect the car and meet the driver.

Finally, it's *essential* to set the ground rules from day one. Many travellers have complained of having their holiday completely dictated by their driver. Politely, but firmly, let the driver know from the outset that you're the boss – it can make the difference between a carefree journey and a strained one.

COSTS

The cost of charter trips depends on the distance. Keep in mind that one-way trips almost always cost as much as return trips (to cover the expense of the vehicle going back to the company's base).

Expect to pay Rs 1500 to 2000 for a day trip, which includes petrol and waiting time at sights along the way. For trips beyond a week, try to negotiate a better deal. Some taxi unions set a time limit or a maximum kilometre distance for day trips – if you go over, you'll have to pay extra. To avoid problems later, confirm in advance that the fare covers petrol, sightseeing stops, all your chosen destinations, and meals and accommodation for the driver. Sightseeing trips around a single city are usually cheaper – Rs 550 is a reasonable starting point for an eight-hour city tour (with an 80km limit).

If you cross a state border, there is often an additional fee, and you also have to pay extra for any car-parking or car-entry fees you may incur. Be clear about these additional costs before setting off and get it in writing so there are no misunderstandings later.

You'll generally pay the bulk of the fee at the end of the trip, although the driver may request an advance to cover petrol (ask for a written record of this at the time). If you're happy with the service at the end of the trip, a tip to the driver is in order.

Self-Drive Hire

Self-drive car hire (you'll need a valid International Driving Permit) is possible in South India's larger cities, but given the unnerving driving conditions most travellers opt for a car with driver. International rental companies with representatives in India:

Budget (www.budget.com)
Hertz (www.hertz.com)

HITCHING

Travellers who decide to hitch should understand that they are taking a small but potentially serious risk. Women are strongly advised against hitching alone.

Hitching is not much of an option in South India anyway, as the concept of a 'free ride' – considering the inexpensive public transport options available – is relatively unknown.

LOCAL TRANSPORT

Buses, cycle-rickshaws, autorickshaws, taxis, boats and urban trains provide transport throughout South India. On any form of transport without a fixed fare, agree on the fare *before* you start your journey, and make sure that it covers your luggage and every passenger. If you don't, expect heated altercations when you get to your destination. Even where local transport is metered, drivers may refuse to use the meter, demanding an elevated 'fixed' fare. If this happens, find another vehicle. Parked taxis in tourist areas almost always ask for inflated fares – moving taxis are more likely to use their meters. On some routes, particularly to airports, it may be difficult to get a metered fare.

Costs for public transport vary from town to town (see regional chapters for details). Fares usually increase at night (by up to 100%) and some drivers charge a few rupees extra for luggage. Carry plenty of small bills for taxi and rickshaw fares as drivers rarely have change. It's also a good idea to carry a business card of the hotel in which you are staying, as your pronunciation of roads etc may be incomprehensible to drivers.

Many taxi and autorickshaw drivers are knee-deep in the commission racket – for more information, see p469.

Autorickshaw, Tempo & Vikram

The Indian autorickshaw is basically a three-wheeled motorised contraption with a tin or canvas cover, providing room for two passengers and luggage. You may also hear autorickshaws being referred to as autos, scooters or *túk-túk*. Autorickshaws are cheaper than taxis and they are usually metered, although getting the driver to turn the meter on can prove challenging. If you are going to a fairly obscure destination, it helps to have it written down in the local dialect to show the driver.

On the downside, autos are annoyingly noisy (from the clunky two-stroke engine) and the open spaces let in blasts of dusty and/or polluted air.

Tempos and *vikrams* are basically outsized autorickshaws with room for more passengers, running on fixed routes for a fixed fare. In country areas, you may also see the fearsome-looking 'three-wheeler' – a crude, tractorlike tempo with a front wheel on an articulated arm.

Bus

Urban buses, particularly in the big cities, are fume-belching, human-stuffed mechanical monsters that travel at breakneck speed (except during morning and evening rush hour, when they can be endlessly stuck in traffic). It's usually far more convenient and comfortable to opt for an autorickshaw or taxi.

Boat

Various kinds of local ferries offer transport along rivers in South India and many will also carry bikes and motorcycles for a fee. Kerala is especially renowned for its breathtaking backwater boat cruises (see the boxed text, p328).

Cycle-Rickshaw

Cycle-rickshaws are becoming scarce in South India these days, but you'll still find them in some cities, such as Puducherry (Pondicherry). A cycle-rickshaw is a pedal cycle with two rear wheels, supporting a bench seat for passengers. Most have a canopy that can be raised in wet weather, or lowered to provide extra space for luggage. As with taxis and autorickshaws, fares should be agreed upon before heading off to avoid disagreements once you reach your destination. Given the extremely strenuous nature of this type of work, tips are heartily encouraged.

Taxi

Most South Indian cities and towns have taxis, and these are usually metered. However, getting drivers to use the meter can be a veritable hassle. Drivers may claim that the meter is broken and request a hugely elevated 'fixed'

PREPAID TAXIS

Most Indian airports and many train stations have a prepaid-taxi booth, normally just outside the terminal building. Here, you can book a taxi to town for a fixed price (which will include baggage), and therefore minimise the chances of price hikes and commission scams. However, make sure you hold on to the payment coupon until you actually reach your chosen destination, just in case the driver has any other ideas! Smaller airports and stations may have prepaid autorickshaw booths instead.

---

fare. Threatening to get another taxi will often miraculously fix it. In tourist areas, some taxis flatly refuse to use the meter – if this happens to you, look around for another cab. To avoid shenanigans, avail youself of prepaid taxi services when travelling from the airport or train station (see the boxed text, above).

Getting a metered ride is only half the battle. Meters are almost always outdated, so fares are calculated using a combination of the meter reading and a complicated 'fare adjustment card'. Predictably, this system is open to abuse. If you spend a few days in any town, you'll soon get a feel for the difference between a reasonable fare and an outright rip-off. Many taxi drivers supplement their earnings with commissions – refuse any unplanned diversions to shops, hotels or travel agencies; also see p469.

Other Local Transport

In some towns, tongas (horse-drawn two-wheelers) and victorias (horse-drawn carriages) still operate. Mumbai and Chennai have suburban trains that leave from ordinary train stations. See regional chapters for further details.

MOTORCYCLE

In terms of motorcycles as public transport, Goa is the only place in South India where they are a licensed form of conveyance. They take one person on the back and are a quick, inexpensive way to cover short distances.

Despite the horrendous traffic, India is an amazing country for long-distance motorcycle touring. Motorcycles handle the pitted roads far better than four-wheeled vehicles, and you'll have the added bonus of being able to stop when and where you wish. However, motorcycle touring can be quite an undertaking – there are some excellent motorcycle tours (see right) that will save you the rigmarole of going it alone.

The classic way to motorcycle around India is on an Enfield Bullet, still built to the original 1940s specifications. As well as making a satisfying chugging sound, these bikes are fully manual, making them easy to repair (parts can be found everywhere in India). On the other hand, Enfields are less reliable than many of the newer, Japanese-designed bikes.

Weather is an important factor to consider if you are planning on doing a lot of motorcycle travel – for the best times to visit certain regions, see the Fast Facts boxed texts at the start of regional chapters. At the time of research, it was not possible to cross into Pakistan by motorcycle – check if the law has since changed. It is still possible to cross into Nepal, Bangladesh and Bhutan with the correct paperwork – contact the relevant diplomatic mission for details.

Driving Licence

You are technically required to have a valid International Driving Permit to hire a motorcycle in India; however, many places are happy with the driving licence from your home country. In tourist areas, you may be able to rent a small motorcycle without a driving licence, but you definitely won't be covered by insurance in the event of an accident.

Fuel & Spare Parts

Spare parts for Indian and Japanese machines are widely available in South Indian cities and towns. If you are going to remote regions, carry basic spares (valves, fuel lines, piston rings, etc). Ensure you carry enough extra fuel if you intend travelling to distance areas (always seek local advice about fuel availability before setting off).

For all machines (particularly older ones), make sure you regularly check and tighten all nuts and bolts, as Indian roads and engine vibration tend to work things loose quite quickly. Check the engine and gearbox oil level regularly (at least every 500km) and clean the oil filter every few thousand kilometres. Given the variable road conditions, the chances are you'll make at least a couple of visits to a puncture-wallah – it's advisable

to start your trip with new tyres and carry spanners to remove your own wheels.

Hire

If you are planning an independent trip, motorcycles can be rented throughout South India, with tourist magnets, such as Goa, having the widest options (see also p180).

Japanese- and Indian-made bikes in the 100cc to 150cc range are cheaper than the big 350cc to 500cc Enfields. As a deposit, you'll probably be asked to leave your air ticket, passport (it's best to avoid this option, as you should always carry your passport with you when travelling in India), or a big cash lump sum. A 500cc Enfield costs around Rs 13,000/23,000 for three/eight weeks. See the regional chapters for further information about prices and recommended rental firms.

Insurance

Only hire a bike with third-party insurance – if you hit someone without insurance the consequences can be severe. Reputable companies will include third-party cover in their policies. Those that do not are probably not reputable.

You must also arrange insurance if you buy a motorcycle. The minimum level of cover is third-party insurance – available for Rs 300 to 500 per year. This will cover repair and medical costs for any other vehicles, people or property you might hit, but no cover for your own machine. Comprehensive insurance (recommended) costs Rs 500 to 2000 per year.

Organised Motorcycle Tours

A number of companies offer organised motorcycle tours with a support vehicle, mechanic and a guide. Below are a few reputable companies (see their websites for contact details, itineraries and prices) that have South Indian itineraries:

Blazing Trails (www.jewelholidays.com)
Classic Bike Adventures (www.classic-bike-india.com)
H-C Travel (www.hctravel.com)
Indian Motorcycle Adventures (homepages.ihug
.co.nz/~gumby)
Indian Shepherds (www.asiasafari.com)
Royal Expeditions (www.royalexpeditions.com)
Wheels of India (www.wheelofindia.com)

Purchase

If you are planning a longer tour while in South India, consider purchasing a motorcycle. Secondhand bikes are widely available and the paperwork is a lot easier than buying a new machine. Finding a secondhand machine is a matter of asking around. Check travellers notice boards and approach local motorcycle mechanics and other bikers. Because of the number of bikes and the fact that locals are accustomed to foreigners, Goa is the best place in South India to start your search.

A decent outfit in Mumbai is **Allibhai Premji Tyrewalla** (Map pp106-7; ☎ 022-23099313; www.premjis .com; 205/207 Dr D Bhadkamkar [Lamington] Rd), which sells new and secondhand motorcycles with a buy-back option.

Real enthusiasts should check out the En-field factory in Chennai (p374).

COSTS

A well-looked-after secondhand 350cc En-field will cost Rs 18,000 to 40,000; the 500cc model will cost Rs 35,000 to 65,000. Prices for new Enfield models are listed on www .royalenfield.com. It's advisable to get any secondhand bike serviced before you set off (you'll pay anywhere from Rs 10,000 to 15,000). When reselling your bike, expect to get between half and two-thirds of the price you paid if the bike is still in reasonable con-dition. Shipping an Indian bike overseas is pretty complicated and expensive – ask the shop you bought the bike from to explain the process.

As well as the cost of the bike, you'll have to pay for insurance – see opposite. Helmets are available for Rs 1000 to 1500, and extras, such as panniers, luggage racks, protection bars, rear-view mirrors, lockable fuel caps, petrol filters and extra tools, are easy to come by. One useful extra is a customised fuel tank, which will increase the range you can cover between fuel stops. An Enfield 500cc gives about 25km/L; the 350cc model gives slightly more.

OWNERSHIP PAPERS

There is plenty of paperwork associated with owning a motorcycle. The registration papers are signed by the local registration authority when the bike is first sold and you'll need these papers when you buy a secondhand bike. Foreign nationals cannot change the name on the registration. Instead, you must fill out the forms for a change of ownership and transfer of insurance. If you buy a new bike, the company selling it must register the machine for you, adding to the cost.

For any bike, the registration must be re-newed every 15 years (for around Rs 5000) and you must make absolutely sure that there are no outstanding debts or criminal pro-ceedings associated with the bike. The whole process is extremely complicated and it makes sense to seek advice from the company selling the bike. Allow around two weeks to get the paperwork finished and get on the road.

Road Conditions

Given the challenging road conditions in India, this is not a country for novice rid-ers. Hazards range from cows and chickens meandering across the carriageway to broken-down trucks, pedestrians crossing out of the blue, perpetual potholes and unmarked speed humps. Rural roads sometimes have grain crops strewn across them to be threshed by passing vehicles – a serious sliding hazard for bikers.

Try not to cover too much territory in one day and avoid travelling after dark if at all possible – many vehicles drive without lights and dynamo-powered motorcycle headlamps are useless while negotiating potholes at low revs. On busy national highways expect to average 50km/h without stops; on winding back roads and dirt tracks this can drop to 10km/h.

For long hauls, transporting your bike by train can be a very convenient option. Pur-chase a standard train ticket for the journey, then take your bike to the station parcel office along with your passport, registration papers, International Driving Permit and insurance documents. Packing-wallahs will adeptly wrap your bike in protective sacking for around Rs 100 and you must fill out various forms and pay the shipping fee – around Rs 1600 for a 350cc or smaller bike – plus an insurance fee of 1% of the declared value of the bike. Bring the same paperwork to collect your bike from the goods office at the far end. If the bike is left waiting at the destination for more than 24 hours, you will pay a storage fee of around Rs 30 per day.

Road Rules

Traffic in India is officially required to stick to the left but, in reality, most people drive all over the road. Observe local speed limits (these vary from state to state) and give way to any larger vehicles. Locals tend to use the horn more than the brake, but travellers should heed the advice of the Border Roads Organisation: it is better to be Mr Late than Late Mr!

SHARE JEEPS

In mountain areas, such as those around Aurangabad in Maharashtra, share jeeps supplement the bus service, charging similar fixed fares. Jeeps (nominally designed for five or six passengers, but often carrying up to 10) run from jeep stands and 'passenger stations' at the junctions of major roads.

TOURS

Tours are available all over South India, run by tourist offices, local transport companies and travel agencies. Organised tours can be an inexpensive way to see several places on one trip, although you rarely get much time at each place. If you arrange a tour through the local taxi office (or any reputable car-hire outfit), you'll have more freedom about where you go and how long you stay (also see p497).

Drivers often double as guides, or you can hire a qualified local guide for a fee. However, be wary of (often ill-informed and pushy) touts claiming to be professional guides in tourist towns. Ask the local tourist office about recommended guides and insist on seeing evidence from guides who claim to be accredited.

See this book's regional chapters for information about recommended local tours; for more on treks and tours see (p97).

International Tour Agencies

Many international companies offer tours to all parts of India, from straightforward sightseeing trips to adventure tours and activity holidays. To find tours that specifically match your interests, quiz travel agents and surf the web.

Some marvellous places to start include the following:

Dragoman Overland (www.dragoman.com) One of several overland tour companies offering trips to and around India on customised vehicles.

Essential India (www.essential-india.co.uk) Various tailor-made and special-interest trips and treks in North and South India, with a responsible tourism ethos.

Exodus (www.exodustravels.co.uk) A wide array of specialist trips, including tours with a holistic, wildlife and adventure focus.

India Wildlife Tours (www.india-wildlife-tours.com) All sorts of wildlife tours, plus horse-riding safaris, fishing tours and bird-watching.

Indian Encounters (www.indianencounters.com) Tailor-made and special-interest tours, including wildlife, cookery, arts and horse riding.

Intrepid Travellers (www.intrepidtravel.com) A huge range of tours, from sight-seeing to cycling, river cruising, festivals, wildlife and cooking tours.

Peregrine Adventures (www.peregrine.net.au) Trekking, wildlife and cultural tours in various regions, including South India.

Sacred India Tours (www.sacredindia.com) Offers tours with a spiritual or holistic focus, including yoga, meditation and Ayurvedic trips.

World Expeditions (www.worldexpeditions.com.au) Options include cooking tours, trekking tours, walking tours, cycling tours and volunteering-based trips.

TRAIN

A trip to India just wouldn't be the same without riding the rails. A train trip here is more than merely a journey, it is a cultural experience, a vast melting pot of sights and smells, chai-wallahs (tea vendors), impossibly crowded stations and scenic window gazing. The train network in India is extensive and ticket prices are reasonable. Around 14 million passengers travel by train in India every day, and Indian Railways is the second-largest employer in the world, with a staggering 1.6 million workers.

At first, the process of booking a seat can seem bewildering, but behind the scenes things are remarkably well organised – see Reservations (p504) for tips on buying a ticket. Trains are far preferable to buses for long-distance and overnight trips. Some cities also have suburban train networks, although these can get unbearably crowded during peak hours.

Train services to certain destinations are often increased during major festivals, but almost every year people get crushed to death in stampedes on overcrowded platforms. Something else to be aware of is passenger drugging and theft, although this is fortunately not as rampant in South India as in the north – see p469.

We've listed useful train services throughout this book but there are hundreds of services. It's worth buying a copy of *Trains at a Glance* (Rs 45), available at train-station bookstands, and better bookshops and newsstands. It contains comprehensive timetables covering all the main lines, or you can use the train search engine on the **Indian Railways website** (www.indianrail.gov.in). Another useful

TOP FIVE TRAIN JOURNEYS

If you have a passion for train travel, don't miss these...

- Mountain Railway – the miniature steam train from Mettupalayam to Udhagamandalam (Ooty) climbs up through the stunning Nilgiri Hills (p441)
- Konkan Railway – the trip from Mumbai (Bombay) to Goa passes between the scenic coast and the Western Ghats (see p179)
- Matheran Toy Train – a miniature diesel train running from Neral (north of Mumbai) to the hill station of Matheran (p160)
- *Rajdhani Express* – from Thiruvananthapuram (Trivandrum) in Kerala to Goa, this train takes you up the tropical coast in style (p314)
- Visakhapatnam to the Araku Valley through the Eastern Ghats – a superb ride from the coast through the rugged Eastern Ghats to the tribal communities in Araku Valley (p300)

resource is www.seat61.com/India.htm. Big stations often have English-speaking staff who can help you with selecting the best train. At smaller stations, midlevel officials, such as the deputy station master, usually speak English, and are worth approaching if you're in need of assistance.

Many trains have separate women-only carriages, which should be specifically requested when making a ticket booking.

Classes

Trains and seats come in a variety of classes. Express and mail trains usually have general (2nd class) compartments with unreserved seating – often a real free-for-all – and a series of more comfortable compartments that you can reserve. On day trains, there may be a chair car with padded reclining seats and (usually) AC, or an executive chair car, with superior seats and more space.

For overnight trips, you have several choices. Sleeper berths are arranged in groups of six, with two roomier berths across the aisle, in air-cooled carriages. Air-conditioned carriages have either three-tier AC (3AC) berths, in the same configuration as sleepers, or two-tier AC (2AC) berths in groups of four on either side of the aisle. Some trains also have flashier 1st-class AC (1AC) berths, with a choice of two- or four-berth compartments with locking doors.

Bedding is provided in all AC sleeping compartments and there is usually a meal service, plus regular visits from the coffee and chai-wallah. In sleeper class, bring your own bedding (an Indian shawl is perfect for the job). In all sleeping compartments, the lower

berths convert to seats for daytime use. If you'd rather sleep, book an upper berth. Note that there is usually a locked door between the reserved and unreserved carriages – if you get trapped on the wrong side, you'll have to wait until the next station to change.

There are also special train services connecting major cities. *Shatabdi Express* trains are same-day services with seating only, in AC executive chair and AC chair cars. Both classes are comfortable, but the tinted glass windows cut down the views considerably.

The best views are from the barred but unglazed windows of non-AC sleeper and general carriages.

Rajdhani Express trains are long-distance overnight services between Delhi and state capitals, with a choice of 1AC, 2AC, 3AC and 2nd class. Reserved tickets on both *Shatabdi* and *Rajdhani* trains are more expensive but fares include meals. Prices of all tickets reflect the level of comfort – see below. In all classes, a padlock and a length of chain are very useful for securing your luggage to the baggage racks.

For a brilliant description of the various train classes (including pictures), feast your eyes on www.seat61.com/India.htm.

Costs

Fares are calculated by distance and class of travel – see Express Train Fares in Rupees, p505. *Rajdhani* and *Shatabdi* trains are slightly more expensive, but the price does include meals. Most air-conditioned carriages have a catering service (meals are brought to your seat, but you should carry some tissues to use as serviettes as they're often lacking). In unreserved classes, pack samosas (deep-fried pastry triangles filled with spiced vegetables/meat) or other portable snack foods. You can search for exact fares on www.indianrail.gov.in. Seniors get discounted train tickets – see p470.

Major stations offer 'retiring rooms', which can be handy if you have a valid ticket or Indrail Pass – see p463. Another useful facility is the left-luggage office (cloakroom). Locked bags (only) can be stored for a small daily fee if you have a valid train ticket. For peace of mind, securely chain your bag to the baggage rack and check the opening times to make sure you can get your bag when you need it.

Reservations

No reservations are required for general (2nd class) compartments. You can reserve seats in all chair car, sleeper, and 1AC, 2AC and 3AC carriages up to 60 days in advance at any station with a computerised booking system. Advance bookings are strongly recommended for all overnight journeys.

The reservation procedure is fairly straightforward – obtain a reservation slip from the information window and fill in the starting station, the destination station, the class you wish to travel in and the name and number of the train (this is where *Trains at a Glance* comes into its own). You then join the long queue to the ticket window, where your ticket will be printed.

In larger cities, there are dedicated ticket windows for foreigners and credit-card payments. Elsewhere, you'll have to join a general queue and pay in rupees. A special tourist

quota is set aside for foreign tourists travelling between popular stations. These seats can only be booked at dedicated reservation offices in major cities (details are given in the relevant regional chapters), and you'll need to show your passport and visa as ID. A recent change of rules means that you can pay for tourist quota seats in rupees, British pounds, US dollars or euros, and in cash or Thomas Cook and American Express travellers cheques (change is given in rupees).

Trains are frequently overbooked, but many passengers cancel. You can buy a ticket on the 'wait list' and try your luck; a refund is available if you fail to get a seat – ask the ticket office about your chances. Refunds are available on any ticket, even after departure, with a penalty – the rules are complicated so check when you book.

If you don't want to go through the hassle of buying a ticket yourself, many travel agencies and hotels will purchase your train ticket for a small commission, but beware of ticket scams.

Internet bookings are also possible on the website www.irctc.co.in, and you can choose an e-ticket, or have the tickets sent to you within India by courier. The website www.seat61.com/India.htm has some excellent advice on online bookings; scroll down to the 'How to book – from outside India' heading.

Reserved tickets show your seat/berth number (or wait list number) and the carriage number. When the train pulls in, keep an eye out for your carriage number written on the side of the train (station staff can point you in the right direction if you get confused). A

RIDING THE RAILS IN STYLE

If you're seeking a luxurious way of seeing parts of South India, the following rail journeys should tickle your fancy.

In Maharashtra, the *Deccan Odyssey* offers seven nights of opulence covering the main tourist spots of Maharashtra and Goa. The train leaves Mumbai (Bombay) every Wednesday (October to April), heading south through the resorts and fort towns of the Konkan Coast to Goa, then looping inland to Pune, Aurangabad (for Ellora), Jalgaon (for Ajanta) and Nasik. Fares per person start at US$485/350/285 per day for single/double/triple occupancy (US$395/295/240 in April). You can do the trip one way for a minimum of three days; the seven-day package costs an extra US$100 for guided tours of Mumbai and Goa. Make reservations through Mumbai's **Maharashtra Tourism Development Corporation** (MTDC; Map p114; ☎ 022-22027762; www.maharashtratourism.gov.in/mtdc; Madame Cama Rd, Nariman Point, Mumbai 400020; ⏰ 9.45am-5.30pm Mon-Sat).

The tourist authorities in Karnataka have been planning a similar upmarket train tour for years, but nothing has so far materialised. For progress updates contact **Karnataka Tourism** (www.karnatakatourism.org).

| EXPRESS TRAIN FARES IN RUPEES | | | | | | |
Distance (km)	1AC	2AC	3AC	Chair car (CC)	Sleeper (SL)	Second (II)
100	400	226	158	122	56	35
200	653	269	256	199	91	57
300	888	502	348	271	124	78
400	1107	626	433	337	154	97
500	1325	749	519	404	185	116
1000	2159	1221	845	657	301	188
1500	2734	1546	1070	832	381	238
2000	3309	1871	1295	1007	461	288

list of names and berths is also posted on the side of each reserved carriage – a beacon of light for panicking travellers!

Train Passes

The Indrail Pass permits unlimited rail travel for the period of its validity, but it offers limited savings and you must still make reserva-tions. Passes are available for one to 90 days of travel and you can book through overseas travel agents, or station ticket offices in major Indian cities – click on the 'Information/Inter-national Tourist' link on www.indianrail.gov.in for prices. Children aged between five and 12 pay half fare. There's no refund for either lost or partially used tickets.

TRANSPORT

Health

CONTENTS

Before You Go   **506**
Insurance   506
Vaccinations   506
Internet Resources   507
Further Reading   507
In Transit   **508**
Deep Vein Thrombosis (DVT)   508
Jet Lag & Motion Sickness   508
In South India   **509**
Availability of Healthcare   509
Infectious Diseases   509
Traveller's Diarrhoea   511
Environmental Hazards   512
Women's Health   514

There is huge geographical variation in India, from tropical beaches to the Himalayan mountains. Consequently, environmental issues such as heat, cold, and altitude can cause significant health problems. Hygiene is generally poor in India so food and water-borne illnesses are common. Many insect-borne diseases are present, particularly in tropical areas. Medical care is basic in many areas so it is essential to be well prepared before travelling to India.

Travellers tend to worry about contracting infectious diseases when in the tropics, but these rarely cause serious illness or death in travellers. Pre-existing medical conditions and accidental injury (especially traffic accidents) account for most life-threatening problems. Becoming ill in some way, however, is very common. Fortunately most travellers' illnesses can be prevented with some common-sense behaviour or treated with a well-stocked traveller's medical kit.

The following advice is a general guide only and does not replace the advice of a doctor trained in travel medicine.

BEFORE YOU GO

Pack medications in their original, clearly labelled containers. A signed and dated letter from your physician describing your medical conditions and medications, including generic names, is very useful. If carrying syringes or needles, be sure to have a physician's letter documenting their medical necessity. If you have a heart condition, bring a copy of your ECG taken just prior to travelling.

If you take any regular medication, bring double your ordinary needs in case of loss or theft. You'll be able to buy many medications over the counter in India without a doctor's prescription, but it can be difficult to find some of the newer drugs, particularly the latest antidepressant drugs, blood pressure medications and contraceptive pills.

INSURANCE

Even if you are fit and healthy, don't travel without health insurance – accidents do happen. Declare any existing medical conditions you have – the insurance company will check if your problem is pre-existing and will not cover you if it is undeclared. You may require extra cover for adventure activities such as rock climbing and scuba diving. If your health insurance doesn't cover you for medical expenses abroad, consider getting extra insurance. If you're uninsured, emergency evacuation is expensive; bills of over US$100,000 are not uncommon.

It's a good idea to find out in advance if your insurance plan will make payments directly to providers or if it will reimburse you later for overseas health expenditures. (In many countries doctors expect payment in cash.) Some policies offer lower and higher medical-expense options; the higher ones are chiefly for countries that have extremely high medical costs, such as the USA. You may prefer a policy that pays doctors or hospitals directly rather than you having to pay on the spot and claim from your insurance company later. If you do have to claim later, make sure you keep all relevant documentation. Some policies ask that you telephone back (reverse charges) to a centre in your home country where an immediate assessment of your problem will be made.

VACCINATIONS

Specialised travel-medicine clinics are your best source of information; they stock all available vaccines and will be able to give specific recommendations for you and your trip. The doctors will take into account factors such as past vaccination history, the length of your trip, activities you may be undertaking and underlying medical conditions, such as pregnancy.

Most vaccines don't give immunity until at least two weeks after they're given, so visit a doctor four to eight weeks before departure. Ask your doctor for an International Certificate of Vaccination (otherwise known as the 'yellow booklet'), which will list all the vaccinations you've received.

Recommended Vaccinations

The World Health Organization (WHO) recommends these vaccinations for travellers to India (as well as being up to date with measles, mumps and rubella vaccinations):

Adult diphtheria and tetanus Single booster recommended if none in the previous 10 years. Side effects include sore arm and fever.

Hepatitis A Provides almost 100% protection for up to a year; a booster after 12 months provides at least another 20 years' protection. Mild side effects such as headache and sore arm occur in 5% to 10% of people.

Hepatitis B Now considered routine for most travellers. Given as three shots over six months. A rapid schedule is also available, as is a combined vaccination with Hepatitis A. Side effects are mild and uncommon, usually headache and sore arm. In 95% of people lifetime protection results.

Polio At the time of writing, polio was still present in India. Only one booster is required as an adult for lifetime protection. Inactivated polio vaccine is safe during pregnancy.

Typhoid Recommended for all travellers to India, even if you only visit urban areas. The vaccine offers around 70% protection, lasts for two to three years and comes as a single shot. Tablets are also available; however the injection is usually recommended as it has fewer side effects. Sore arm and fever may occur.

Varicella If you haven't had chickenpox discuss this vaccination with your doctor.

These immunisations are recommended for long-term travellers (more than one month) or those at special risk:

Japanese B Encephalitis Three injections in all. Booster recommended after two years. Sore arm and headache are the most common side effects. Rarely, an allergic reaction comprising hives and swelling can occur up to 10 days after any of the three doses.

Meningitis Single injection. There are two types of vaccination: the quadrivalent vaccine gives two to three years' protection; meningitis group C vaccine gives around 10 years' protection. Recommended for long-term backpackers aged under 25.

HEALTH ADVISORIES

It's usually a good idea to consult your government's travel-health website before departure, if one is available:
Australia (www.dfat.gov.au/travel/)
Canada (www.travelhealth.gc.ca)
New Zealand (www.mfat.govt.nz/travel)
South Africa (www.dfa.gov.za/travelling)
UK (www.doh.gov.uk/traveladvice/)
USA (www.cdc.gov/travel/)

Rabies Three injections in all. A booster after one year will then provide 10 years' protection. Side effects are rare – occasionally headache and sore arm.

Tuberculosis (TB) A complex issue. Adult long-term travellers are usually recommended to have a TB skin test before and after travel, rather than vaccination. Only one vaccine given in a lifetime.

Required Vaccinations

The only vaccine required by international regulations is yellow fever. Proof of vaccination will only be required if you have visited a country in the yellow-fever zone within the six days prior to entering India. If you are travelling to India from Africa or South America you should check to see if you require proof of vaccination.

INTERNET RESOURCES

There is a wealth of travel health advice on the internet – www.lonelyplanet.com is a good place to start. Some other suggestions:
Centers for Disease Control and Prevention (CDC; www.cdc.gov) Good general information.
MD Travel Health (www.mdtravelhealth.com) Provides complete travel health recommendations for every country; updated daily.
World Health Organization (WHO; www.who.int/Ith/) Its superb book *International Travel & Health* is revised annually and available online.

FURTHER READING

Lonely Planet's *Healthy Travel – Asia & India* is a handy pocket size and packed with useful information including pretrip planning, emergency first-aid, immunisation and disease information, and what to do if you get sick on the road. Other recommended references include *Travellers' Health* by Dr Richard Dawood and *Travelling Well* by Dr Deborah Mills – check out the website of **Travelling Well** (www.travellingwell.com.au).

MEDICAL CHECKLIST

Recommended items for a personal medical kit:

- Antifungal cream, eg clotrimazole
- Antibacterial cream, eg muciprocin
- Antibiotic for skin infections, eg amoxicillin/clavulanate or cephalexin
- Antihistamine – there are many options, eg cetrizine for daytime and promethazine for night
- Anti-inflammatory, eg ibuprofen
- Antiseptic, eg Betadine
- Antispasmodic for stomach cramps, eg Buscopam
- Contraceptive method
- Decongestant, eg pseudoephedrine
- DEET-based insect repellent
- Diarrhoea medication – consider an oral rehydration solution (eg Gastrolyte), diarrhoea 'stopper' (eg loperamide) and antinausea medication (eg prochlorperazine); antibiotics for diarrhoea include norfloxacin or ciprofloxacin, for bacterial diarrhoea azithromycin, for giardia or amoebic dysentery tinidazole
- First-aid items such as scissors, elastoplasts, bandages, gauze, thermometer (but not mercury), sterile needles and syringes, safety pins and tweezers
- Indigestion tablets, eg Quick Eze or Mylanta
- Iodine tablets (unless you are pregnant or have a thyroid problem) to purify water
- Laxative, eg Coloxyl
- Migraine medication if you suffer from them
- Paracetamol
- Pyrethrin to impregnate clothing and mosquito nets
- Steroid cream for allergic/itchy rashes, eg 1% to 2% hydrocortisone
- Sunscreen and hat
- Throat lozenges
- Thrush (vaginal yeast infection) treatment, eg clotrimazole pessaries or Diflucan tablet
- Ural or equivalent if prone to urine infections

IN TRANSIT

DEEP VEIN THROMBOSIS (DVT)

Deep vein thrombosis (DVT) occurs when blood clots form in the legs during plane flights, chiefly because of prolonged immobility. The longer the flight, the greater the risk. Though most blood clots are reabsorbed uneventfully, some may break off and travel through the blood vessels to the lungs, where they may cause life-threatening complications.

The chief symptom of DVT is swelling or pain of the foot, ankle, or calf, usually but not always on just one side. When a blood clot travels to the lungs, it may cause chest pain and difficulty in breathing. Travellers with any of these symptoms should immediately seek medical attention.

To prevent the development of DVT on long flights you should walk about the cabin, perform isometric compressions of the leg muscles (ie contract the leg muscles while sitting), drink plenty of fluids, and avoid alcohol and tobacco.

JET LAG & MOTION SICKNESS

Jet lag is common when crossing more than five time zones; it results in insomnia, fatigue, malaise or nausea. To avoid jet lag, try drinking plenty of fluids (nonalcoholic) and eating light meals. Upon arrival, seek exposure to natural sunlight and readjust your schedule (for meals, sleep etc) as soon as possible.

Antihistamines such as dimenhydrinate (Dramamine), promethazine (Phenergan) and meclizine (Antivert, Bonine) are usually the first choice for treating motion sickness. Their main side effect is drowsiness. A herbal alternative is ginger, which works like a charm for some people.

IN SOUTH INDIA

AVAILABILITY OF HEALTHCARE

Medical care is hugely variable in India. Some cities now have clinics catering specifically to travellers and expatriates. These clinics are usually more expensive than local medical facilities, but are worth utilising, as they will offer a superior standard of care. Additionally, they understand the local system, and are aware of the safest local hospitals and best specialists. They can also liaise with insurance companies should you require evacuation. Recommended clinics are listed under Information in the regional chapters in this book. It is difficult to find reliable medical care in rural areas.

Self-treatment may be appropriate if your problem is minor (eg traveller's diarrhoea), you are carrying the relevant medication and you cannot attend a recommended clinic. If you think you may have a serious disease, especially malaria, do not waste time; travel to the nearest quality facility to receive attention. It is always better to be assessed by a doctor than to rely on self-treatment.

Before buying medication over the counter, always check the use-by date and ensure the packet is sealed. Don't accept items that have been poorly stored (eg lying in a glass cabinet exposed to the sun).

INFECTIOUS DISEASES
Avian Flu

'Bird flu' or influenza A (H5N1) is a subtype of the type A influenza virus. This virus typically infects birds and not humans; however, in 1997 the first documented case of bird-to-human transmission was recorded in Hong Kong. Currently very close contact with dead or sick birds is the principal source of infection and bird-to-human transmission does not easily occur.

Symptoms include high fever and typical influenza-like symptoms with rapid deterioration leading to respiratory failure and death in many cases. The early administration of antiviral drugs, such as Tamiflu, is recommended to improve the chances of survival. At this time it is not routinely recommended for travellers to carry Tamiflu with them – immediate medical care should be sought if bird flu is suspected. At the time of writing there have been no recorded cases in travellers or expatriates.

There is currently no vaccine available to prevent bird flu. For up-to-date information check these two websites:

- www.who.int/en/
- www.avianinfluenza.com.au

Coughs, Colds & Chest Infections

Around 25% of travellers to India will develop a respiratory infection. This usually starts as a virus and is exacerbated by environmental conditions such as pollution in the cities, or cold and altitude in the mountains. Commonly a secondary bacterial infection will intervene – marked by fever, chest pain and coughing up discoloured or blood-tinged sputum. If you have the symptoms of an infection, seek medical advice or commence a general antibiotic.

Dengue Fever

This mosquito-borne disease is becomingly increasingly problematic in the tropical world, especially in the cities. As there is no vaccine available it can only be prevented by avoiding mosquito bites. The mosquito that carries dengue bites day and night, so use insect avoidance measures at all times. Symptoms include high fever, severe headache and body ache (dengue was previously known as 'breakbone fever'). Some people develop a rash and experience diarrhoea. There is no specific treatment, just rest and paracetamol – do not take aspirin as it increases the likelihood of haemorrhaging. See a doctor to be diagnosed and monitored.

Hepatitis A

A problem throughout the region, this food- and water-borne virus infects the liver, causing jaundice (yellow skin and eyes), nausea and lethargy. There is no specific treatment for hepatitis A, you just need to allow time for the liver to heal. All travellers to India should be vaccinated against hepatitis A.

Hepatitis B

The only sexually transmitted disease that can be prevented by vaccination, hepatitis B is spread by body fluids. The long-term consequences can include liver cancer and cirrhosis.

Hepatitis E

Transmitted through contaminated food and water, hepatitis E has similar symptoms to hepatitis A, but is far less common. It is a severe problem in pregnant women, and can result in the death of both mother and baby. There is currently no vaccine, and prevention is by following safe eating and drinking guidelines.

HIV

HIV is spread via contaminated body fluids. Avoid unsafe sex, unsterile needles (including in medical facilities) and procedures such as tattoos. The growth rate of HIV in India is one of the highest in the world.

Influenza

Present year-round in the tropics, influenza (flu) symptoms include fever, muscle aches, runny nose, cough and sore throat. It can be severe in people over the age of 65 or in those with medical conditions such as heart disease or diabetes – vaccination is recommended for these individuals. There is no specific treatment, just rest and paracetamol.

Japanese B Encephalitis

This viral disease is transmitted by mosquitoes and is rare in travellers. Like most mosquito-borne diseases, it is becoming a more common problem in affected countries. Most cases occur in rural areas and vaccination is recommended for travellers spending more than one month outside of cities. There is no treatment, and a third of infected people will die, while another third will suffer permanent brain damage.

Malaria

For such a serious and potentially deadly disease, there is an enormous amount of misinformation concerning malaria. You must get expert advice as to whether your trip actually puts you at risk. For most rural areas, the risk of contracting malaria far outweighs the risk of any tablet side effects. Before you travel, seek medical advice on the right medication and dosage for you.

Malaria is caused by a parasite transmitted by the bite of an infected mosquito. The most important symptom of malaria is fever, but general symptoms such as headache, diarrhoea, cough or chills may also occur. Diagnosis can only be made by taking a blood sample.

Two strategies should be combined to prevent malaria – mosquito avoidance, and antimalarial medications. Most people who catch malaria are taking inadequate or no antimalarial medication.

Travellers are advised to prevent mosquito bites by taking these steps:

■ Use a DEET-containing insect repellent on exposed skin. Wash this off at night, as long as you are sleeping under a mosquito net. Natural repellents such as citronella can be effective, but must be applied more frequently than products containing DEET.
■ Sleep under a mosquito net impregnated with pyrethrin.
■ Choose accommodation with screens and fans (if not air-conditioned).
■ Impregnate clothing with pyrethrin in high-risk areas.
■ Wear long sleeves and trousers in light colours.
■ Use mosquito coils.
■ Spray your room with insect repellent before going out for your evening meal.

There are a variety of medications available. The effectiveness of the chloroquine and Paludrine combination is now limited in many parts of south Asia. Common side effects include nausea (40% of people) and mouth ulcers.

The daily tablet doxycycline is a broad-spectrum antibiotic that has the added benefit of helping to prevent a variety of tropical diseases, including leptospirosis, tick-borne disease and typhus. The potential side effects include photosensitivity (a tendency to sunburn), thrush (in women), indigestion, heartburn, nausea and interference with the contraceptive pill. More serious side effects include ulceration of the oesophagus – you can help prevent this by taking your tablet with a meal and a large glass of water, and never lying down within half an hour of taking it. It must be taken for four weeks after leaving the risk area.

Lariam (mefloquine) has received much bad press, some of it justified, some not. This weekly tablet suits many people. Serious side effects are rare, but include depression, anxiety, psychosis and fits. Anyone with a history of depression, anxiety, another psychological disorder or epilepsy should not take Lariam. It is considered safe in the second and third trimesters of pregnancy. Tablets must be taken for four weeks after leaving the risk area.

The new drug Malarone is a combination of atovaquone and proguanil. Side effects are uncommon and mild, most commonly nausea and headache. It is the best tablet for scuba divers and for those on short trips to high-risk areas. It must be taken for one week after leaving the risk area.

Rabies

Around 30,000 people die in India each year from rabies. This uniformly fatal disease is spread by the bite or lick of an infected animal – most commonly a dog or monkey. You should seek medical advice immediately after any animal bite and commence postexposure treatment. Having pretravel vaccination means the postbite treatment is greatly simplified. If an animal bites you, gently wash the wound with soap and water, and apply iodine-based antiseptic. If you are not prevaccinated you will need to receive rabies immunoglobulin as soon as possible, and this is almost impossible to obtain in much of India.

STDs

Sexually transmitted diseases most common in India include herpes, warts, syphilis, gonorrhoea and chlamydia. People carrying these diseases often have no signs of infection. Condoms will prevent gonorrhoea and chlamydia but not warts or herpes. If after a sexual encounter you develop any rash, lumps, discharge or pain when passing urine seek immediate medical attention. If you have been sexually active during your travels, have an STD check on your return home.

Tuberculosis

While TB is rare in travellers, those who have significant contact with the local population (such as medical and aid workers, and long-term travellers) should take precautions. Vaccination is usually only given to children under the age of five, but adults at risk are recommended pre- and posttravel TB testing.

The main symptoms are fever, cough, weight loss, night sweats and tiredness.

Typhoid

This serious bacterial infection is also spread via food and water. It gives a high and slowly progressive fever, headache and may be accompanied by a dry cough and stomach pain. It is diagnosed by blood tests and treated with antibiotics. Vaccination is recommended for all travellers who are spending more than a week in India. Be aware that vaccination is not 100% effective so you must still be careful with what you eat and drink.

TRAVELLER'S DIARRHOEA

This is by far the most common problem affecting travellers – between 30% and 70% of people will suffer from it within two weeks of starting their trip. In over 80% of cases, traveller's diarrhoea is caused by a bacteria (there are numerous potential culprits), and therefore responds promptly to treatment with antibiotics. Treatment with antibiotics will depend on your situation – how sick you are, how quickly you need to get better, where you are etc.

Traveller's diarrhoea is defined as the passage of more than three watery bowel actions within 24 hours, plus at least one other symptom such as fever, cramps, nausea, vomiting or feeling generally unwell.

Treatment consists of staying well hydrated; rehydration solutions like Gastrolyte are the best for this. Antibiotics such as norfloxacin, ciprofloxacin or azithromycin will kill the bacteria quickly.

Loperamide is just a 'stopper' and doesn't get to the cause of the problem. It can be helpful though (eg if you have to go on a long bus ride). Don't take loperamide if you have a fever, or blood in your stools. Seek medical attention quickly if you do not respond to an appropriate antibiotic.

Amoebic Dysentery

Amoebic dysentery is very rare in travellers but is often misdiagnosed by poor-quality labs. Symptoms are similar to bacterial diarrhoea, ie fever, bloody diarrhoea and generally feeling unwell. You should always seek reliable medical care if you have blood in your diarrhoea. Treatment involves two drugs: tinidazole or metronidazole to kill the parasite in your gut and then a second drug to kill the

HEALTH

cysts. If left untreated complications such as liver or gut abscesses can occur.

Giardiasis

Giardia is a parasite that is relatively common in travellers. Symptoms include nausea, bloating, excess gas, fatigue and intermittent diarrhoea. The parasite will eventually go away if left untreated, but as this can take months, the best advice is to seek medical treatment. The treatment of choice is tinidazole, with metronidazole being a second-line option.

ENVIRONMENTAL HAZARDS
Air Pollution

Air pollution, particularly vehicle pollution, is an increasing problem in most of India's major cities. If you have severe respiratory problems, speak with your doctor before travelling to any heavily polluted urban centres. This pollution also causes minor respiratory problems such as sinusitis, dry throat and irritated eyes. If troubled by the pollution leave the city for a few days and get some fresh air.

Diving & Surfing

Divers and surfers should seek specialised advice before they travel to ensure their medical kit contains treatment for coral cuts and tropical ear infections, as well as the standard problems. Divers should ensure their insurance covers them for decompression illness; get specialised dive insurance through an organisation such as **Divers Alert Network** (DAN; www.danasiapacific.org). Have a dive medical before you leave your home country – there are certain medical conditions that are incompatible with diving.

Food

Eating in restaurants is the biggest risk factor for contracting traveller's diarrhoea. Ways to avoid it including eating only freshly cooked food, and avoiding shellfish and food that has been sitting in buffets. Peel all fruit, cook vegetables and soak salads in iodine water for at least 20 minutes. Eat in busy restaurants with a high turnover of customers. See p82 for more on safe eating.

Heat

Many parts of India are hot and humid throughout the year. For most people it takes at least two weeks to adapt to the hot climate.

Swelling of the feet and ankles is common, as are muscle cramps caused by excessive sweating. Prevent these by avoiding dehydration and excessive activity in the heat. Take it easy when you first arrive. Don't eat salt tablets (they aggravate the gut); drinking rehydration solution or eating salty food helps. Treat cramps by stopping activity, resting, rehydrating with double-strength rehydration solution and gently stretching.

Dehydration is the main contributor to heat exhaustion. Symptoms include feeling weak, headache, irritability, nausea or vomiting, sweaty skin, a fast, a normal or slightly elevated body temperature and a weak pulse. Treatment involves getting out of the heat and/or sun, fanning the sufferer and applying cool wet cloths to the skin, laying the sufferer flat with their legs raised and rehydrating with water containing a quarter of a teaspoon of salt per litre. Recovery is usually rapid and it is common to feel weak for some days afterwards.

Heat stroke is a serious medical emergency. Symptoms come on suddenly and include weakness, nausea, a hot dry body with a body temperature of over 41°C, dizziness, confusion, loss of coordination, fits and eventually collapse and loss of consciousness. Seek medical help and commence cooling by getting the person out of the heat, removing their clothes, fanning them and applying cool wet cloths or ice to their body, especially to the groin and armpits.

DRINKING WATER

- Never drink tap water.
- Bottled water is generally safe – check the seal is intact at purchase.
- Avoid ice.
- Avoid fresh juices – they may have been watered down with unfiltered water.
- Boiling water is the most efficient method of purifying it.
- The best chemical purifier is iodine. It should not be used by pregnant women or those with thyroid problems.
- Water filters should also filter out viruses. Ensure your filter has a chemical barrier such as iodine and a small pore size, eg less than four microns.

HEALTH

Prickly heat is a common skin rash in the tropics, caused by sweat being trapped under the skin. The result is an itchy rash of tiny lumps. Treat it by moving out of the heat and into an air-conditioned area for a few hours, and by having cool showers. Creams and ointments clog the skin so they should be avoided. Locally bought prickly heat powder can be helpful.

Tropical fatigue is common in long-term expatriates based in the tropics. It's rarely due to disease and is caused by the climate, inadequate mental rest, excessive alcohol intake and the demands of daily work in a different culture.

High Altitude

If you are going to altitudes above 3000m you should get information on preventing, recognising and treating Acute Mountain Sickness (AMS). The biggest risk factor for developing altitude sickness is going too high too quickly – you should follow a conservative acclimatisation schedule such as can be found in all good trekking guides – and you should never go to a higher altitude when you have any symptoms that could be altitude related. There is no way to predict who will get altitude sickness and it is often the younger, fitter members of a group who succumb.

Symptoms usually develop during the first 24 hours at altitude but may be delayed up to three weeks. Mild symptoms include headache, lethargy, dizziness, difficulty sleeping and loss of appetite. AMS may become more severe without warning and can be fatal. Severe symptoms include breathlessness; a dry, irritative cough (which may progress to the production of pink, frothy sputum); severe headache; lack of coordination and balance; confusion; irrational behaviour; vomiting; drowsiness; and unconsciousness.

Treat mild symptoms by resting at the same altitude until recovery, which usually takes a day or two. Paracetamol or aspirin can be taken for headaches. If symptoms persist or become worse, however, immediate descent is necessary; even 500m can help. Drug treatments should never be used to avoid descent or to enable further ascent.

The drugs acetazolamide and dexamethasone are recommended by some doctors for the prevention of AMS; however, their use is controversial. They can reduce the symptoms, but they may also mask warning signs; severe and fatal AMS has occurred in people taking these drugs.

To prevent acute mountain sickness:

- Ascend slowly – have frequent rest days, spending two to three nights at each rise of 1000m.
- It is always wise to sleep at a lower altitude than the greatest height reached during the day, if possible. Also, once above 3000m, care should be taken not to increase the sleeping altitude by more than 300m per day.
- Drink extra fluids. The mountain air is dry and cold and moisture is lost as you breathe.
- Eat light, high-carbohydrate meals.
- Avoid alcohol and sedatives.

Insect Bites & Stings

Bedbugs don't carry disease but their bites are very itchy. They live in the cracks of furniture and walls and then migrate to the bed at night to feed on you. You can treat the itch with an antihistamine. Lice inhabit various parts of your body but most commonly your head and pubic area. Transmission is via close contact with an infected person. They can be difficult to treat and you may need numerous applications of an antilice shampoo such as pyrethrin. Pubic lice are usually contracted from sexual contact.

Ticks are contracted after walking in rural areas. Ticks are commonly found behind the ears, on the belly and in armpits. If you have had a tick bite and experience symptoms such as a rash at the site of the bite or elsewhere, fever or muscle aches you should see a doctor. Doxycycline prevents tick-borne diseases.

Leeches are found in humid rainforest areas. They do not transmit any disease but their bites are often intensely itchy for weeks afterwards and can easily become infected. Apply an iodine-based antiseptic to any leech bite to help prevent infection.

Bee and wasp stings mainly cause problems for people who are allergic to them. Anyone with a serious bee or wasp allergy should carry an injection of adrenaline (eg an Epipen) for emergency treatment. For others pain is the main problem – apply ice to the sting and take painkillers.

Skin Problems

Fungal rashes are common in humid climates. There are two common fungal rashes that affect travellers. The first occurs in moist areas such as the groin, armpits and between the toes. It starts as a red patch that slowly spreads and is usually itchy. Treatment involves keeping the skin dry, avoiding chafing and using an antifungal cream such as clotrimazole or Lamisil. Tinea versicolor is also common – this fungus causes small, light-coloured patches, most commonly on the back, chest and shoulders. Consult a doctor.

Cuts and scratches become easily infected in humid climates. Take meticulous care of any cuts and scratches to prevent complications such as abscesses. Immediately wash all wounds in clean water and apply antiseptic. If you develop signs of infection (increasing pain and redness) see a doctor. Divers and surfers should be particularly careful with coral cuts, as they become easily infected.

Sunburn

Even on a cloudy day sunburn can occur rapidly. Always use a strong sunscreen (at least factor 30), making sure to reapply after a swim, and always wear a wide-brimmed hat and sunglasses outdoors. Avoid lying in the sun during the hottest part of the day (10am to 2pm). You can get burnt very easily when you are at high altitudes so be vigilant once above 3000m. If you become sunburnt stay out of the sun until you have recovered, apply cool compresses and take painkillers for the discomfort. One-percent hydrocortisone cream applied twice daily is also helpful.

WOMEN'S HEALTH

In most places in India, supplies of sanitary products (pads, rarely tampons) are readily available. Birth control options may be limited, so bring adequate supplies of your own form of contraception. Heat, humidity and antibiotics can all contribute to thrush. Treatment is with antifungal creams and pessaries such as clotrimazole. A practical alternative is a single tablet of fluconazole (Diflucan). Urinary tract infections can be precipitated by dehydration or long bus journeys without toilet stops; bring suitable antibiotics. For gynaecological health issues, seek out a female doctor.

Pregnant women should receive specialised advice before travelling. The ideal time to travel is in the second trimester (between 16 and 28 weeks), when the risk of pregnancy-related problems is at its lowest and pregnant women generally feel at their best. Always carry a list of quality medical facilities available at your destination and ensure you continue your standard antenatal care at these facilities. Avoid rural travel in areas with poor transport and substandard medical facilities. Most of all, ensure that your travel insurance policy covers all pregnancy-related possibilities, including premature labour.

Malaria is a high-risk disease for pregnant women, and WHO recommends that they do not travel to areas with chloroquine-resistant malaria. None of the more effective antimalarial drugs are completely safe in pregnancy.

Traveller's diarrhoea can quickly lead to dehydration and result in inadequate blood flow to the placenta. Many of the drugs used to treat various diarrhoea bugs are not recommended in pregnancy. Azithromycin is considered safe.

Language

CONTENTS

Tamil	515
Kannada	517
Konkani	518
Malayalam	518
Marathi	519
Telugu	520

There is no one 'Indian' language as such. The constitution recognises 18 official languages, including English. The non-English varieties fall roughly into two main groups: Indic (or Indo-Aryan) and Dravidian. There were also over 1600 minor languages and dialects.

The native languages of the regions covered in this book are Tamil, Kannada, Konkani, Malayalam, Marathi, Oriya, and Telugu. They mostly belong to the Dravidian language family, although these have been influenced to varying degrees during their development by Hindi and Sanskrit. As the predominant languages in specific geographic areas they have in effect been used to determine the regional boundaries for the southern states.

Major efforts have been made to promote Hindi as the 'official' language of India, and to gradually phase out English. While Hindi is the predominant language of the north, it bears little relation to the Dravidian languages of the south; subsequently very few people in the south speak Hindi. Resistance to change has been strongest in the state of Tamil Nadu, and as a result, Tamil is still very much the predominant language of South India. English is also widely spoken.

TAMIL

Tamil is the official language in the South Indian state of Tamil Nadu and the Union Territory of Pondicherry.

Tamil is classed as a South Dravidian language, and is one of the major Dravidian languages of South India. The exact origins of the Dravidian family are unknown, but it is believed to have arrived in India's north west around 4000 BC, gradually splitting into four branches with the passage of time. Tamil became isolated to India's south as the Indo-Aryan language varieties such as Hindi became more dominant in the north.

Along with Sanskrit, Tamil is recognised as one of the two classical languages of India. It has a very rich historical tradition dating back more than 2000 years. Since then three forms have been distinguished: Old Tamil (200 BC to AD 700), Middle Tamil (AD 700 to AD 1600) and Modern Tamil (AD 1600 to the present).

Modern Tamil is diglossic in nature, meaning that it has two distinct forms: literary or classical (used mainly in writing and formal speech), and spoken (used in everyday conversation). The spoken form has a wide range of dialects, varying in social, cultural and regional dimensions. Irrespective of the differences, a common variety called Standard Spoken Tamil is widely used in mass media and by all Tamils in their day-to-day life.

Tamil has its own alphabetic script, which isn't used in this language guide. Our transliteration system is intended as a simplified method of representing the sounds of Tamil using the Roman alphabet. As with all such systems it's not exact and should be seen only as an approximate guide to the pronunciation of the language.

PRONUNCIATION
Vowels

a	as the 'u' in 'run'
aa	as in 'rather'
e	as in 'met'
i	as in 'bit'
ee	as in 'meet'
o	as in 'hot'
oo	as in 'boot'
u	as in 'put'

Vowel Combinations

ai	as in 'aisle'
au	as the 'ow' in 'how'

Consonants

g	as in 'go'
k	as in 'kit'
ñ	as the 'ni' in the word 'onion'; as in the Spanish *señor*
s	as in 'sit'
zh	as the 's' in 'pleasure'

Retroflex Consonants

Some consonants in Tamil and the other languages of India are a little more complicated because they represent sounds not found in English. The most common variants are called 'retroflex' consonants, where the tongue is curled upwards and backwards so that the underside of the tip makes contact with the alveolar ridge (the ridge of tissue on the roof of the mouth a little behind the teeth). Retroflex consonants are represented in this guide by a dot below the letter (in Tamil, these are ḷ, ṇ and ṭ). If the lingual gymnastics prove too much you'll find that you can still make yourself understood by ignoring the dot and pronouncing the letter as you would in English.

ACCOMMODATION

hotel	hotal/vituti
guesthouse	viruntinar vituti
youth hostel	ilaiñar vituti
camping ground	tangumitam

Do you have any rooms available?	araikal kitaikkumaa?
for one/two people	oruvar/iruvarukku
for one/two nights	oru/irantu iravukal
How much is it per night/per person?	oru iravukku/oru nabarukku evallavu?
Is breakfast included?	kaalai sirruṇṭiyuṭan serttaa?

CONVERSATION & ESSENTIALS

Hello.	vaṇakkam
Goodbye.	poyiṭṭu varukiren
Yes/No.	aam/illai
Please.	tayavu ceytu
Thank you.	nanri
That's fine, you're welcome.	nallatu varuka
Excuse me.	mannikkavum
Sorry/Pardon.	mannikkavum
Do you speak English?	neenkal aankilam pesuveerkalaa?
How much is it?	atu evvalavu?
What's your name?	unkal peyar enna?
My name is ...	en peyar ...

NUMBERS

0	boojyam
1	onru
2	irantu
3	moonru
4	naanku
5	aintu
6	aaru
7	ezhu
8	ettu
9	onpatu
10	pattu
100	nooru
1000	aayiram
2000	irantaayiram
100,000	latsam (written 1,00,000)
1,000,000	pattu latsam (written 10,00,000)
10,000,000	koti (written 1,00,00,000)

SHOPPING & SERVICES

bank	vangi
chemist/pharmacy	aruntukkataikkaarar/ maruntakam
... embassy	... tootarakam
market	maarkkeṭ
medicine	maruntu
newsagent	niyoos ejensi
post office	tabaal nilayam
public telephone	potu tolaipesi
stationers	elutuporul vanikar
tourist office	surrulaa seyti totarpu aluvalakam
What time does it open/close?	tirakkum/mootum neram enna?
big	periya
small	siriya

TIMES & DAYS

What time is it?	mani ettanai?
day	pakal
night	iravu
week	vaaram
month	maatam
year	varutam
today	inru
tomorrow	naalai

yesterday	*nerru*
morning	*kaalai*
afternoon	*matiyam*

Monday	*tinkal*
Tuesday	*sevvaay*
Wednesday	*putan*
Thursday	*viyaazhan*
Friday	*velli*
Saturday	*sani*
Sunday	*ñaayiru*

TRANSPORT

Where is a/the ...?	*... enke irukkiratu?*
Go straight ahead.	*neraaka sellavum*
Turn left/right.	*valatu/itatu pakkam tirumbavum*
near	*arukil*
far	*tooram*

What time does the	*eppozhutu atutta ...*
next ... leave/arrive?	*sellum/varum?*
boat	*paṭaku*
bus (city)	*peruntu (nakaram/ulloor)*
bus (intercity)	*peruntu (veliyoor)*
tram	*traam*
train	*rayil*

I'd like a ... ticket.	*enakku oru ... ṭikkeṭ veṇum*
one-way	*vazhi*
return	*iru vazhi*
1st class	*mutalaam vakuppu*
2nd class	*irantaam vakuppu*

SIGNS – TAMIL

வழி உள்ளே	Entrance
வழி வெளியே	Exit
திறந்துள்ளது	Open
அடைக்கப்பட்டுள்ளது	Closed
தகவல்	Information
அனுமதி இல்லை	Prohibited
காவல் நிலையம்	Police Station
மலசலகூடம்	Toilets
ஆண்	Men
பெண்	Women

---

left luggage	*tavara vitta saamaan*
timetable	*kaala attavanai*
bus stop	*peruntu nilayam*
train station	*rayil nilayam*

I'd like to hire a ...	*enakku ... vaatakaikku venum*
car	*kaara*
bicycle	*saikkil*

KANNADA

Kannada (also known as Kanarese) is also a Dravidian language and it is the official language of the state of Karnataka in India's south west. After Telugu and Tamil it's the third most common Dravidian language of South India.

The earliest known example of Kannada literature is Kavirajamarga, which dates back to the 9th century AD, and today the modern language is represented by a thriving tradition covering all literary genres.

See the pronunciation guide in the Tamil section of this chapter for an explanation of the retroflex consonants (ḍ, ḷ, ṇ, ṣ and ṭ).

CONVERSATION & ESSENTIALS

Hello.	*namaste* or *namaskaara*
Excuse me.	*kṣamisi*
Please.	*dayaviṭṭu*
Thank you.	*vandanegaḷu*
Yes/No.	*havdu/illa*
How are you?	*hege ideeri?*
Very well, thank you.	*bahaḷa oḷḷeyadu vandanegaḷu*
What's your name?	*nimma hesaru enu?*
My name is ...	*nanna hesaru ...*
Do you speak	*neevu ingliṣ mataaḍteeraa?*
English?	
I don't understand.	*nanage artha aagalla*
Where is the hotel?	*hoṭel ellide?*
How far is ...?	*... eṣṭu doora?*
How do I get to ...?	*naanu allige hogodu hege?*
How much?	*eṣṭu?*
This is expensive.	*idu dubaari*
What is the time?	*gaṇṭe eṣṭu?*

medicine	*auṣadhi*
big	*dodda*
small	*cikka*
today	*ivattu*
day	*hagalu*
night	*raatri*
week	*vaara*
month	*tingalu*
year	*varṣa*

NUMBERS

1	*ondu*
2	*eradu*
3	*mooru*
4	*naalku*
5	*aydu*
6	*aaru*
7	*elu*

8	*entu*
9	*ombhattu*
10	*hattu*
100	*nooru*
1000	*ondu saavira*
2000	*radu saavira*
100,000	*lakṣa* (written 1,00,000)
1,000,000	*hattu lakṣa* (written 10,00,000)
10,000,000	*koti* (written 1,00,00,000)

KONKANI

After a long and hard-fought battle Konkani was finally recognised in 1992 as the official language of the small state of Goa on India's southwest coast. Until then, argument had raged that Konkani was actually no more than a dialect of Marathi, the official language of the much larger neighbouring state of Maharashtra.

Even though Konkani is virtually the only universally understood language of Goa, centuries of colonial rule, significant dialectal variation and as many as five different scripts meant that defining it as an official language would always be problematic. The issue was further complicated by the varying loyalties of Goa's population: the high caste and predominantly Catholic and Hindu Brahmin families who spoke Portuguese, English and Konkani, and the lower caste, mainly Hindu families who tended to speak Marathi as a first language and some Konkani as a second language. Despite these obstacles Konkani went on to be added to the Indian Constitution as the country's 18th national language.

CONVERSATION & ESSENTIALS

Hello.	*paypadta*
Excuse me.	*upkar korxi*
Please.	*upkar kor*
Thank you.	*dev borem korum*
Yes/No.	*oi/naah*
How are you?	*kosso assa?* (m)
	kossem assa? (f)
Very well, thank you.	*bhore jaung*
What's your name?	*tuje naav kide?*
Do you speak English?	*to English hulonk jhana?*
I don't understand.	*mhaka kay samzona na*
Where is a hotel?	*hotel khoy aasa?*
How far is ...?	*anig kitya phoode ...?*
How do I get to ...?	*maka kashe ... meltole?*
How much?	*kitke poishe laqthele?*

This is expensive.	*chod marog*
What's the time?	*vurra kitki jali?*
medicine	*vokot*
big	*hodlo*
small	*dhakto*
today	*aaj*
day	*dees*
night	*racho*
week	*athovda*
month	*mohino*
year	*voros*

NUMBERS

1	*ek*
2	*don*
3	*tin*
4	*char*
5	*panch*
6	*sou*
7	*sat*
8	*att*
9	*nov*
10	*dha*
20	*vis*
30	*tis*
40	*chalis*
50	*ponnas*
60	*saatt*
70	*sottor*
80	*oixim*
90	*novodh*
100	*xembor*
200	*donshe*
1000	*ek hazaar*
2000	*don hazaar*
100,000	*lakh* (written 1,00,000)
10,000,000	*crore* (written 1,00,00,000)

MALAYALAM

Like Tamil, Malayalam belongs to the Dravidian language family. Though there are obvious lexical links between the two languages, with many words sharing common roots, Malayalam includes a far greater number of borrowings from ancient Indian Sanskrit. Its divergence from Tamil began some time after the 10th century AD, with the first official literary record of it dating back to Ramacharitam, a 'pattu' poem written in the late 12th century. The modern form of the Malayalam script developed from the 16th century literary works of Tuñcatt Ezuttacchan.

Malayalam is the official language of the state of Kerala on India's far southwestern coast.

See the pronunciation guide in the Tamil section of this chapter for an explanation of the retroflex consonants (ḍ, ḷ, ṇ, ṛ, ṣ and ṭ).

CONVERSATION & ESSENTIALS

Hello.	namaste
Excuse me.	ksamikkoo
Please.	dayavucheytu
Thank you.	nanni
Yes/No.	aanaate/alla
How are you?	sukhamaaṇo?
Very well, thank you.	sukham tanne
What's your name?	ninnaluṭe pera entaaṇua?
My name is ...	ente peru ...
Do you speak English?	ninnaḷ ingleeṣa samsaarikkumo?
I don't understand.	enikka aṛiyilla
Where is the hotel?	hottal eviṭeyaaṇa?
How far is ...?	... vetra dooramaaṇa?
How do I get to ...?	... aviṭe ennane pokaṇam?
How much?	eṭra?
This is expensive.	vila kootutal aaṇa
What's the time?	mani eṭrayeyi?

medicine	marunnu
big	valiya
small	cheṛiya
today	inna
day	divasam
night	raaṭri
week	aalca
month	maasam
year	varsam

NUMBERS

1	onna
2	raṇḍa
3	moonna
4	naala
5	ancha
6	aaṛa
7	ela
8	eṭṭa
9	ombata
10	patta
100	nooṛa
1000	aayiram
2000	raṇḍaayiram
100,000	lakṣam (written 1,00,000)
1,000,000	patta lakam (written 10,00,000)
10,000,000	koṭi (written 1,00,00,000)

MARATHI

Marathi is the official language of the state of Maharashtra and is one of India's national languages. Like its close linguistic relative, Konkani (the official language of Goa), it belongs to the Indo-Aryan language family. As a result of linguistic influences from neighbouring regions you may notice considerable dialectal variation in Marathi as you move around Maharashtra.

CONVERSATION & ESSENTIALS

Hello/Goodbye.	namaskar
Excuse me.	maaf kara
Please.	krupaya
Yes.	ho
No.	nahi
How are you?	tumhi kase aahat?
Very well, thank you.	mee thik aahe, dhanyawad
What's your name?	aapla nav kai aahe?
Do you speak English?	tumhala english yeta ka?
I don't understand.	mala samjat nahi
Where is a hotel?	hotel kuthe aahe?
How do I get to ...?	... kasa jaycha mhanje sapdel?
How much?	kevdhyala?/kai kimmat?
This is expensive.	khup mahag aahe
What's the time?	kiti vajle?

medicine	aushadh
big	motha/mothi (m/f)
small	lahan
today	aaj
day	divas
night	ratra
week	aathavda
month	mahina
year	varsha

NUMBERS

1	ek
2	don
3	tin
4	char
5	pach
6	saha
7	sat
8	aath
9	nou
10	daha
100	shambhar
200	donshe
1000	ek hazar

2000	don hazar
100,000	ek lakh (written 1,00,000)
10,000,000	daha koti (written 1,00,00,000)

TELUGU

Telugu is a Southeast Dravidian language spoken mainly in the state of Andhra Pradesh on India's east coast; it became the state's official language in the mid-1960s. With around 70 million speakers it is the most predominant of South India's four major Dravidian languages. Its literary history dates back to the 11th century AD when the poet Nannaya produced a translation of parts of the Mahabharata. While Sanskrit has played a major role in Telugu literature over the centuries, there is an increasing tendency for written works to reflect the more colloquial variety of Modern Standard Telugu. See the pronunciation guide in the Tamil section of this chapter for an explanation of the retroflex consonants (ḍ, ḷ, ṇ and ṭ).

CONVERSATION & ESSENTIALS

Hello.	namaste/namaskaaram
Excuse me.	ksamiñchaṇḍi
Please.	dayatsesi
Thank you.	dhanyawaadaalu
Yes.	awunu
No.	kaadu
How are you?	elaa unnaaru?/
	elaa baagunnaaraa?
Very well, thank you.	baagunnaanu dhanyawaadaalu
What's your name?	mee peru emiṭi?/nee peru emiṭi?
My name is ...	naa peru ...

Do you speak English?	meeku anglam waccha?
I don't understand.	naaku artham kaawaṭamledu
Where is the hotel?	hoṭal ekkada undi?
How far is ...?	... enta dooram?
How do I get to ...?	... nenu akkaḍiki weḷḷaṭam elaa?
How much?	enta?
This is expensive.	idi chaalaa ekkuwa
What's the time?	gaṇṭa enta?/taym enta?

medicine	awsadham/mandu
big	pedda
small	tsinna
today	eeroju/eenaaḍu/neḍu
day	pagalu
night	raatri
week	waaram
month	nela/maasam
year	eḍu/samwatsaram

NUMBERS

1	okaṭi
2	reṇḍu
3	mooḍu
4	naalugu
5	aydu/ayidu
6	aaru
7	eḍu
8	enimidi
9	tommidi
10	padi
100	nooru/wanda
1000	weyyi/weyi
2000	reṇḍuwelu
100,000	laksa (written 1,00,000)
1,000,000	padilaksalu (written 10,00,000)
10,000,000	koṭi (written 1,00,00,000)

Glossary

This glossary has a sprinkling of words and terms you are likely to come across during your South Indian wanderings. For food and drink definitions, see p84 and for an understanding of the different vernaculars spoken in South India, have a look at p515.

abbi – waterfall
Adivasi – tribal person
agarbathi – incense
Agni – major deity in the *Vedas*; mediator between men and the gods; also fire
ahimsa – discipline of nonviolence
AIR – All India Radio, the national broadcaster
air-cooler – big, noisy water-filled cooling fan
amrita – immortality
Ananda – *Buddha's* cousin and personal attendant
Ananta – serpent on whose coils Lord *Vishnu* reclined
Annapurna – form of Durga; worshipped for her power to provide food
apsara – heavenly nymph
Aranyani – Hindu goddess of forests
Ardhanariswara – Lord *Shiva's* half-male, half-female (Parvati) form
Arjuna – *Mahabharata* hero and military commander who married Subhadra (*Krishna's* incestuous sister), took up arms and overcame many demons; he had the *Bhagavad Gita* related to him by Krishna, led Krishna's funeral ceremony and finally retired to the Himalaya.
Aryan – Sanskrit for 'noble'; those who migrated from Afghanistan and Central Asia and settled in northern India
Ashoka – ruler in the 3rd century BC; he is responsible for spreading Buddhism throughout South India
ashram – spiritual community or retreat
ASI – Abbreviation for the Archaeological Survey of India; an organisation involved in monument preservation
attar – essential oil; used as a base for perfumes
autorickshaw – noisy, three-wheeled, motorised contraption for transporting passengers, livestock etc for short distances; found throughout the country, they are cheaper than taxis
Avalokiteshvara – in Mahayana Buddhism, the *bodhisattva* of compassion
avatar – incarnation, usually of a deity
Ayurveda – the ancient and complex science of Indian herbal medicine and healing
azad – free (Urdu), as in Azad Jammu and Kashmir

baba – religious master or father; term of respect
bagh – garden
baksheesh – tip, donation (alms) or bribe
banyan – Indian fig tree; spiritual to many Indians
beedi – small, hand-rolled leaf cigarette
Bhagavad Gita – Hindu Song of the Divine One; *Krishna's* lessons to *Arjuna*, the main thrust of which was to emphasise the philosophy of *bhakti;* it is part of the *Mahabharata*
bhajan – devotional song
bhakti – surrendering to the gods; faith
bhang – dried leaves and flowering shoots of the marijuana plant
bhangra – rhythmic Punjabi music/dance; popular throughout India
Bharata – half-brother of *Rama;* ruled while Rama was in exile
bhavan – house, building; also spelt *bhawan*
Bhima – *Mahabharata* hero; he is the brother of Hanuman and renowned for his great strength
bindi – forehead mark (often dot shaped) worn by women
BJP – Bharatiya Janata Party; Hindu nationalist political party
bodhisattva – literally 'one whose essence is perfected wisdom'; in Early Buddhism, bodhisattva refers only to the *Buddha* during the period between his conceiving the intention to strive for Buddhahood and the moment he attained it; in *Mahayana* Buddhism, it is one who renounces nirvana in order to help others attain it
Bollywood – India's answer to Hollywood; the booming film industry of Mumbai (Bombay)
Brahma – Hindu god; worshipped as the creator in the *Trimurti*
Brahmin – member of the priest/scholar *caste,* the highest Hindu caste
Buddha – Awakened One; the originator of Buddhism; also regarded by Hindus as the ninth incarnation of Lord *Vishnu*
bund – embankment or dike

cantonment – administrative and military area of a *Raj*-era town
Carnatic music – classical music of South India
caste – a Hindu's hereditary station (social standing) in life; there are four castes: the *Brahmins,* the *Kshatriyas,* the *Vaishyas* and the *Shudras;* the Brahmins occupy the top spot
chaitya – Sanskrit form of 'cetiya', meaning shrine or object of worship; has come to mean temple, and more specifically, a hall divided into a central nave and two side aisles by a line of columns, with a votive *stupa* at the end

chandra – moon; the moon as a god

chappals – sandals or leather thonglike footwear; flip-flops

charas – resin of the marijuana plant; also referred to as 'hashish'

chillum – pipe of a hookah; commonly used to describe the pipes used for smoking *ganja* (dried flowering tips of the marijuana plant)

chinkara – gazelle

chital – spotted deer

choli – small tight-fitting blouse worn with a sari

chowk – town square, intersection or marketplace

chowkidar – night watchman; caretaker

crore – 10 million

dagoba – see *stupa*

Dalit – preferred term for India's *Untouchable* caste

dargah – shrine or place of burial of a Muslim saint

darshan – offering or audience with someone; auspicious viewing of a deity

Deccan – meaning 'South', this refers to the central South Indian plateau

devadasi – temple dancer

Devi – Lord *Shiva's* wife; goddess

dhaba – basic restaurant or snack bar; especially popular with truck drivers

dharamsala – pilgrims' rest house

dharma – for Hindus, the moral code of behaviour or social duty; for Buddhists, following the law of nature, or path, as taught by the *Buddha*

dhobi – person who washes clothes; commonly referred to as *dhobi*-wallah

dhobi ghat – place where clothes are washed by the *dhobi*

dhol – traditional, large, two-sided Punjabi drum

dholi – people-powered portable 'chairs'; people are carried in them to hilltop temples etc

dhoti – like a *lungi*, but the ankle-length cloth is then pulled up between the legs; worn by men

dhurrie – rug

dowry – money and/or goods given by a bride's parents to their son-in-law's family; it's illegal but still widely exists in many arranged marriages

Draupadi – wife of the five Pandava princes in the *Mahabharata*

Dravidian – general term for the cultures and languages of the deep south of India, including Tamil, Malayalam, Telugu and Kannada

dupatta – long scarf for women often worn with the *salwar kameez*

durbar – royal court; also a government

Durga – the Inaccessible; a form of Lord *Shiva's* wife, *Devi*, a beautiful, fierce woman riding a tiger/lion; a major goddess of the *Shakti* sect

dwarpal – doorkeeper; sculpture beside the doorways to Hindu or Buddhist shrines

Emergency – controversial period in the 1970s when then prime minister, Indira Gandhi, suspended many political rights

Eve-teasing – sexual harassment

filmi – slang term describing anything to do with Bollywood movies

gaddi – throne of a Hindu prince

Ganesh – Hindu god of good fortune and remover of obstacles; popular elephant-headed son of *Shiva* and *Parvati*, he is also known as Ganpati; his vehicle is a ratlike creature

Ganga – Hindu goddess representing the sacred Ganges River; said to flow from Lord *Vishnu's* toe

garbhagriha – the inner, or 'womb' chamber of a Hindu temple

Garuda – man-bird vehicle of Lord *Vishnu*

gaur – Indian bison

geyser – hot-water unit found in many bathrooms

ghat – steps or landing on a river, range of hills, or road up hills

giri – hill

gopuram – soaring pyramidal gateway tower of Dravidian temples

gumbad – dome on an Islamic tomb or mosque

gurdwara – Sikh temple

guru – holy teacher; in Sanskrit literally *goe* (darkness) and *roe* (to dispel)

Guru Granth Sahib – Sikh holy book

haj – Muslim pilgrimage to Mecca

haji – Muslim who has made the *haj*

Hanuman – Hindu monkey god, prominent in the *Ramayana*, and a follower of *Rama*

hartal – strike

haveli – traditional, often ornately decorated, residences

hijra – eunuch, transvestite

hindola – swing

hookah – water pipe used for smoking ganja (dried flowering tips of the marijuana plant) or strong tobacco

imam – Muslim religious (exemplary) leader

IMFL – Indian-made foreign liquor

Indo-Saracenic – style of colonial architecture that integrated Western designs with Islamic, Hindu and Jain influences

Indra – significant and prestigious Vedic god; god of rain, thunder, lightning and war

Jagannath – Lord of the Universe; a form of *Krishna*

jhula – bridge

ji – honorific that can be added to the end of almost anything as a form of respect; thus 'Babaji', 'Gandhiji'

jooti – traditional, often pointy-toed, slip-in shoes

jyoti linga – most important shrines to Lord *Shiva*, of which there are 12

Kailasa – sacred Himalayan mountain; home of Lord *Shiva*

kalamkari – designs painted on cloth using vegetable dyes

Kali – the ominous-looking evil-destroying form of *Devi*; commonly depicted with black skin, dripping with blood, and wearing a necklace of skulls

kameez – woman's shirtlike tunic

Kannada – state language of Karnataka

khadi – homespun cloth; Mahatma Gandhi encouraged people to spin this rather than buy English cloth

Khalistan – former Sikh secessionists' proposed name for an independent Punjab

Khalsa – Sikh brotherhood

Khan – Muslim honorific title

kolam – elaborate chalk, rice-paste or coloured powder design; also known as *rangoli*

Konkani – state language of Goa

Krishna – Lord *Vishnu's* eighth incarnation, often coloured blue; he revealed the *Bhagavad Gita* to *Arjuna*

Kshatriya – Hindu caste of soldiers or administrators; second in the caste hierarchy

kurta – long shirt with either short collar or no collar

lakh – 100,000

Lakshmana – half-brother and aide of *Rama* in the *Ramayana*

Lakshmi – *Vishnu's* consort, Hindu goddess of wealth; she sprang forth from the ocean holding a lotus

lama – Tibetan Buddhist priest or monk

lingam – phallic symbol; auspicious symbol of Lord *Shiva*; plural 'linga'

lungi – worn by men, this loose, coloured garment (similar to a sarong) is pleated at the waist to fit the wearer

maha – prefix meaning 'great'

Mahabharata – Great Hindu Vedic epic poem of the Bharata dynasty; containing approximately 10,000 verses describing the battle between the Pandavas and the Kauravas

mahal – house or palace

maharaja – literally 'great king'; princely ruler

maharani – wife of a princely ruler or a ruler in her own right

mahatma – literally 'great soul'

Mahavir – last *tirthankar*

Mahayana – the 'greater-vehicle' of Buddhism; a later adaptation of the teaching which lays emphasis on the *bodhisattva* ideal, teaching the renunciation of nirvana (ultimate peace and cessation of rebirth) in order to help other beings along the way to enlightenment

mahout – elephant rider or master

maidan – open (often grassed) area; parade ground

Makara – mythical sea creature and *Varuna's* vehicle; crocodile

Malayalam – state language of Kerala

mandapa – pillared pavilion; a temple forechamber

mandir – temple

Mara – Buddhist personification of that which obstructs the cultivation of virtue, often depicted with hundreds of arms; also the god of death

Maratha – central Indian people who controlled much of India at various times and fought the *Mughals* and *Rajputs*

marg – road

masjid – mosque

mehndi – henna; ornate henna designs on women's hands (and often feet), traditionally for certain festivals or ceremonies (eg marriage)

mela – fair or festival

mithuna – pairs of men and women; often seen in temple sculpture

Mohini – Lord *Vishnu* in his female incarnation

moksha – liberation from *samsara*

mudra – ritual hand movements used in Hindu religious dancing; gesture of Buddha figure

Mughal – Muslim dynasty of subcontinental emperors from Babur to Aurangzeb

Naga – mythical serpentlike beings capable of changing into human form

namaste – traditional Hindu greeting (hello or goodbye), often accompanied by a respectful small bow with the hands together at the chest or head level

Nanda – in Hinduism, cowherd who raised *Krishna*; in Buddhism, *Buddha's* half-brother.

Nandi – bull, vehicle of Lord *Shiva*

Narasimha – man-lion incarnation of Lord *Vishnu*

Narayan – incarnation of Lord *Vishnu* the creator

Nataraja – Lord *Shiva* as the cosmic dancer

nilgai – antelope

nizam – hereditary title of the rulers of Hyderabad

NRI – Non-Resident Indian; of economic significance to modern India

paise – the Indian rupee is divided into 100 paise

palanquin – boxlike enclosure carried on poles on four men's shoulders; the occupant sits inside on a seat

Pali – the language; related to Sanskrit, in which the Buddhist scriptures were recorded; scholars still refer to the original Pali texts

Panchatantra – series of traditional Hindu stories about the natural world, human behaviour and survival

Parasurama – *Rama* with the axe; sixth incarnation of Lord *Vishnu*

Parsi – adherent of the Zoroastrian faith

Partition – formal division of British India into two separate countries, India and Pakistan, in 1947

Parvati – a form of *Devi*

PCO – Public Call Office from where you can make local, interstate and international phone calls (cheaper than hotels)

pietra dura – marble inlay work characteristic of the Taj Mahal

Pongal – Tamil harvest festival

pradesh – state

pranayama – study of breath control; meditative practice

prasad – temple-blessed food offering

puja – literally 'respect'; offering or prayers

Puranas – set of 18 encyclopaedic Sanskrit stories, written in verse, relating to the three gods, dating from the 5th century AD

purdah – custom among some conservative Muslims (also adopted by some Hindus, especially the *Rajputs*) of keeping women in seclusion; veiled

Purnima – full moon; considered to be an auspicious time

qawwali – Islamic devotional singing

Radha – favourite mistress of *Krishna* when he lived as a cowherd

raga – any of several conventional patterns of melody and rhythm that form the basis for freely interpreted compositions

railhead – station or town at the end of a railway line; termination point

raj – rule or sovereignty; British Raj (sometimes just Raj) refers to British rule

raja – king; sometimes *rana*

Rajput – Hindu warrior caste, former rulers of north-western India

rakhi – amulet

Rama – seventh incarnation of Lord *Vishnu*

Ramadan – the Islamic holy month of sunrise-to-sunset fasting (no eating, drinking or smoking); also referred to as Ramazan

Ramayana – the story of *Rama* and *Sita* and their conflict with *Ravana* is one of India's best-known epics

rana – king; sometimes *raja*

rangoli – see *kolam*

rani – female ruler or wife of a king

rathas – rock-cut *Dravidian* temples

Ravana – demon king of Lanka who abducted *Sita*; the titanic battle between him and *Rama* is told in the *Ramayana*

rickshaw – small, two- or three-wheeled passenger vehicle

sadhu – ascetic, holy person; one who is trying to achieve enlightenment; often addressed as *swamiji* or *babaji*

sagar – lake, reservoir

sahib – respectful title applied to a gentleman

salai – road

salwar – trousers usually worn with a *kameez*

salwar kameez – traditional dresslike tunic and trouser combination for women

samadhi – in Hinduism, ecstatic state, sometimes defined as 'ecstasy, trance, communion with God'; in Buddhism, concentration; also a place where a holy man has been cremated/buried, usually venerated as a shrine

sambar – deer

samsara – Buddhists, Hindus and Sikhs believe earthly life is cyclical; you are born again and again, the quality of these rebirths being dependent upon your karma in previous lives

Sangam – ancient academy of Tamil literature; means literally 'the meeting of two hearts'

sangha – community of monks and nuns

Saraswati – wife of Lord *Brahma*; goddess of learning; sits on a white swan, holding a *veena*

Sati – wife of Lord *Shiva*; became a *sati* ('honourable woman') by immolating herself; although banned more than a century ago, the act of *sati* is still occasionally performed

satyagraha – nonviolent protest involving a hunger strike, popularised by Mahatma Gandhi; from Sanskrit, literally meaning 'insistence on truth'

Scheduled Castes – official term used for the *Untouchables* or *Dalits*

sepoy – formerly an Indian solider in British service

shahadah – Muslim declaration of faith ('There is no God but Allah; Mohammed is his prophet')

Shaivism – worship of Lord *Shiva*

Shaivite – follower of Lord *Shiva*

Shakti – creative energies perceived as female deities; devotees follow Shaktism

shikara – covered gondola-like boat used on lakes

Shiv Sena – Hindu nationalist party, particularly influential in Maharasthra

Shiva – the Destroyer; also the Creator, in which form he is worshipped as a lingam

Shivaji – great Maratha leader of the 17th century

shola – virgin forest

Shudra – caste of labourers

sikhara – Hindu temple-spire or temple

Sita – the Hindu goddess of agriculture; more commonly associated with the *Ramayana*

sitar – Indian stringed instrument

Sivaganga – water tank in temple dedicated to Lord *Shiva*

Skanda – Hindu god of war, Lord *Shiva's* son

stupa – Buddhist religious monument composed of a solid hemisphere topped by a spire, containing relics of the Buddha; also known as a 'dagoba' or 'pagoda'

Sufi – Muslim mystic

Sufism – Islamic mysticism

Surya – the sun; a major deity in the *Vedas*

swami – title of respect meaning 'lord of the self'; given to initiated Hindu monks

tabla – twin drums

Tamil – language of Tamil Nadu; people of *Dravidian* origin

tandava – Lord *Shiva's* cosmic victory dance

tank – reservoir; pool or large receptacle of holy water found at some temples

tatty – woven grass screen soaked in water and hung outside windows to cool the air

tempo – noisy three-wheeler public transport vehicle; bigger than an autorickshaw

theertham – temple tank

Theravada – orthodox form of Buddhism practiced in Sri Lanka and Southeast Asia that is characterised by its adherence to the *Pali* canon; literally, 'dwelling'

tirthankars – the 24 great Jain teachers

tonga – two-wheeled horse or pony carriage

toy train – narrow-gauge train; minitrain

Trimurti – triple form; the Hindu triad of Lord *Brahma*, Lord *Shiva* and Lord *Vishnu*

Untouchable – lowest caste or 'casteless', for whom the most menial tasks are reserved; the name derives from the belief that higher castes risk defilement if they touch one; now known as *Dalit*

Vaishya – member of the Hindu caste of merchants

Varuna – supreme Vedic god

Vedas – Hindu sacred books; collection of hymns composed in preclassical Sanskrit during the second millennium BC and divided into four books: Rig-Veda, Yajur-Veda, Sama-Veda and Atharva-Veda

veena – stringed instrument

vihara – Buddhist monastery, generally with central court or hall off which open residential cells, usually with a Buddha shrine at one end

Vijayanagar empire – one of South India's greatest empires; lasted from the 14th to 17th centuries AD; the Vijayanagar capital was in Hampi in Karnataka

vikram – *tempo* or a larger version of the standard tempo

vimana – principal part of Hindu temple; a tower over the sanctum

vipassana – the insight meditation technique of *Theravada* Buddhism in which mind and body are closely examined as changing phenomena

Vishnu – part of the *Trimurti*; Lord Vishnu is the Preserver and Restorer who so far has nine avatars: the fish Matsya, the tortoise Kurma, the wild boar Naraha, *Narasimha*, Vamana, *Parasurama*, *Rama*, *Krishna* and *Buddha*

wallah – man; added onto almost anything, eg *dhobi-wallah*, chai-wallah, taxi-wallah

yali – mythical lion creature

zakat – tax in the form of a charitable donation; one of the five 'Pillars of Islam'

zenana – area of a home where women are secluded; women's quarters

Behind the Scenes

THIS BOOK

The 2nd edition of *South India* was coordinated by Richard Plunkett and the 3rd edition was coordinated by Paul Harding. This is the 4th edition of *South India*; its regional chapters have been taken directly from the 12th edition of *India*. The front matter, Directory and Transport chapters were based on text written by Sarina Singh and Joe Bindloss for *India* 12. Dr Trish Batchelor wrote the Health text.

This guidebook was commissioned in Lonely Planet's Melbourne office, and produced by the following:

Commissioning Editors Sam Trafford, Emma Gilmour
Coordinating Editor Gina Tsarouhas
Coordinating Cartographer Amanda Sierp

Coordinating Layout Designer Carol Jackson
Managing Editor Suzannah Shwer
Managing Cartographer Shahara Ahmed
Assisting Editors Susan Paterson, Laura Stansfeld, Fionnuala Twomey, Kate Whitfield
Assisting Designers Margie Jung, Cara Smith, Carlos Solarte
Cover Designer Tamsin Wilson
Colour Designer Evelyn Yee
Project Manager Sarah Sloane
Language Content Coordinator Quentin Frayne

Thanks to Vera Andrades, Melanie Dankel, Sally Darmody, Andrea Dobbin, Ryan Evans, Nicole Hansen, Jim Hsu, Averil Robertson, Vivek Wagle, Udayan Wagle, Tashi Wheeler and Celia Wood.

LONELY PLANET: TRAVEL WIDELY, TREAD LIGHTLY, GIVE SUSTAINABLY

The Lonely Planet Story

The story begins with a classic travel adventure: Tony and Maureen Wheeler's 1972 journey across Europe and Asia to Australia. There was no useful information about the overland trail then, so Tony and Maureen published the first Lonely Planet guidebook to meet a growing need.

From a kitchen table, Lonely Planet has grown to become the largest independent travel publisher in the world, with offices in Melbourne (Australia), Oakland (USA) and London (UK). Today Lonely Planet guidebooks cover the globe. There is an ever-growing list of books and information in a variety of media. Some things haven't changed. The main aim is still to make it possible for adventurous individuals to get out there – to explore and better understand the world.

The Lonely Planet Foundation

The Lonely Planet Foundation proudly supports nimble nonprofit institutions working for change in the world. Each year the foundation donates 5% of Lonely Planet company profits to projects selected by staff and authors. Our partners range from Kabissa, which provides small nonprofits across Africa with access to technology, to the Foundation for Developing Cambodian Orphans, which supports girls at risk of falling victim to sex traffickers.

Our nonprofit partners are linked by a grass-roots approach to the areas of health, education or sustainable tourism. Many projects we support – such as one with BaAka (Pygmy) children in the forested areas of Central African Republic – choose to focus on women and children as one of the most effective ways to support the whole community.

Sometimes foundation assistance is as simple as helping to preserve a local ruin like the Minaret of Jam in Afghanistan; this incredible monument now draws intrepid tourists to the area and its restoration has greatly improved options for local people.

Just as travel is often about learning to see with new eyes, so many of the groups we work with aim to change the way people see themselves and the future for their children and communities.

THANKS
SARINA SINGH
In India, special thanks to my dear friends Mamta and Anup Bamhi for allowing me, yet again, to raid their phenomenal book collection. Many thanks also to everyone who wrote into Lonely Planet with feedback and to those travellers I met on the road, for sharing their stories. At Lonely Planet, warm thanks to Sam Trafford for making this edition a delight to work on and to Emma Gilmour and Gina Tsarouhas for their hard work and invaluable support. And a big thank you to the authors – for burning the midnight oil to make this book what it is.

STUART BUTLER
Big thank you to the many unnamed people who helped out in their own little way and another thanks to the small number of people trying to keep Goa green – keep up the good work. Huge thanks to Anita Jasani and her daughter Anisha for all their help in Pune, Ashok Kadam in Aurangabad, the manager of the Shiv Sagar hotel in Ganpatipule, the guys from the Goan Café in Morjim, anyone who let me get intrusive with my cameras and Sarina, Sam and Tashi at Lonely Planet HQ. Finally, and most importantly, thanks again to Heather for everything she does.

VIRGINIA JEALOUS
In Tamil Nadu, thanks to Shankar for 5000km of safe, companionable and jasmine-scented driving; to Anita and others for demystifying Auroville; and to Leigh and Kodai International School for the working space when the town's power went out for four days. In the Andamans, thanks to Lynda for interrupting her holiday and for providing great information, conversation and wine; to Alex for the motorbike tour of Havelock; and to Titus for managing to get me on the wedding party's bus for the 12-hour journey back to Port Blair (now that was a trip to remember).

AMY KARAFIN
My sincere thanks go to the people of Andhra Pradesh – past and present – for making the place so interesting. I'm also deeply grateful to: Marini and Hari Hariharan; Akash Bhartiya; Baskar and Sheela Subramanian; Mom and Dad; Jayasree Anand; the guy at Tirumala who let me stare at God; Sabrina Katakam and the Modis in Secunderabad; Tom Szollossy; Raghu Raman; the original members of the Barry Karafin International Executive Club; Venerable Kalawane Mahanama Thero (for the metta); the Machado family; Sarina Singh

and Sam Trafford; and SN Goenka and everyone at Dhamma Giri and Dhamma Khetta. *Bhavatu sabba mangalam.*

SIMON RICHMOND
Fellow Lonely Planet colleagues, particularly Sarina, Joe, Amy and Sam, made working on this guide a pleasure. In Bengaluru, Arun at Bangalore Walks was an inspiration on how best to enjoy that, sometimes infuriatingly chaotic, city. Benjamine and the Oberoi family were splendid hosts and thanks also to Shabari for engineering a visit to the Club. Van Vahle was great company in person and by text. My unflappable and ever dependable driver Srinivas Murthi did a splendid job of ferrying me around the state. A huge thank you to Sridamurthi at Mysore's Karnataka Tourism for pulling out all the stops to get me a ringside seat for the Dussehra parade. Finally, to Tonny who was, as ever, patient, supportive and loving.

RAFAEL WLODARSKI
Thanks goes out to the all the helpful folk who smoothed my speedy path through India, particularly the staff at tourist and KTDC offices far and wide. A big bucket of thanks goes out to the people that went beyond the call of duty to help make this book possible: Naresh Fernandez, Piyush, Deborah, Abha Bahl, Chris and Krishna and Pandi the taxi driver in Mumbai, Saithili in Bangalore, Leon in Varkala. Prabhath (Joseph) in Kollam, Anoop and Afsal in Alleppey, Elfie and Shannon in the backwaters, a huge thanks to PJ Varghese, Kurien and Mr Vanu, Santhosh in Cochin, Piyush from Locadives. Thanks also to Sarina Singh and Joe Bindloss for their steady captainship, and to Sam Trafford for sending me to India. Very special thanks are reserved, as always, for Suzanna.

OUR READERS
Many thanks to the travellers who used the last edition and wrote to us with helpful hints, useful advice and interesting anecdotes:

A Ea Akasha, Husain Akbar, Dennis Akkerman, Hazel Armstrong **B** Tania Babic, Elisabeth Banks, Bryan Barragan, Sohaila Bastami, Chris Beech, Mark Beilby, Peter Besier, Arjan de Beus, Mary Bider, Margaret Blake, Mauro Borneo, Sarah Bothwell, Ramon Bramona, Dirk & Silvia Broecher, Eric Brouwer, Roel Brouwer, Jessica Brown, Doris Buchholzer **C** Davide Calamia, Linda Cane, Chris Castagnera, David Cavalla, Colin Chapman, Frederik Claeye, Ranald Coyne **D** Nicky Dawson, Edna Dolan, Stuart Dutson **E** Chris Eaton, Niels Ellegaard **F** Adonis Flokiou, Stanley Freeman **G** Elisabeth Gardner, Paul Garenfeld, Katherine Garrood, Shayne Gary, Navin Ghosh, Anne Giannini **H** Justin Hannemann, Lincoln Harris, Alexander Heitkamp, Tom Hoppel, Brigitte Horrenberger,

SEND US YOUR FEEDBACK

We love to hear from travellers – your comments keep us on our toes and help make our books better. Our well-travelled team reads every word on what you loved or loathed about this book. Although we cannot reply individually to postal submissions, we always guarantee that your feedback goes straight to the appropriate authors, in time for the next edition. Each person who sends us information is thanked in the next edition – and the most useful submissions are rewarded with a free book.

To send us your updates – and find out about Lonely Planet events, newsletters and travelnews–visitouraward-winningwebsite: **www.lonelyplanet.com/contact**.

Note: we may edit, reproduce and incorporate your comments in Lonely Planet products such as guidebooks, websites and digital products, so let us know if you don't want your comments reproduced or your name acknowledged. For a copy of our privacy policy visit www.lonelyplanet.com/privacy.

Anthony Hurley **J** Wanda Jarvis, Fiona Jeffrey, Meredith Josey **K** Anand Kaper, Shannon Katary, Anna Kettley, Marcel Kummer **L** Jeanette Lancaster, Jules Lasson, Ceri Lawley, P Lawrence, James Leask, Rens de Leeuw, Michele Lefranc, Mara Leporati, Reetta Leppanen, Morten Lindgren **M** Eric Maier, Elodie Mantha, John & Diana Martin, Karen Mcgrath, Roy Messenger, Sergio Minder, Sonal Mody, Aymeric Moizard, Leah & Alex Monsey, Zakss Monsey, Gabriel Morris, Thomas Mueller, Sandip Mukherjee **N** Pete Nelson, Eugénie Nottebohm, Tomas Novak **P** Marlis Pantal, Mukesh Patel, Helen Peers, Georgia Pomaki, Christian Portelatine, Martin Potter, Patsy Pouvelle, Ansula Press, Peter Pullicino **R** Anne-Gaelle Rabaud, Sabin Ranabhat, Martina Ravanello, Janet Reigstad, Andy Ridout, Arianna Rinaldo, David Roig **S** Rudie Schonenberg, Kees & Ineke Schouten, Matthias Von Schumacher, Martina Sester, Alice Shiner, Robert Shroyer, E Sivakumar, Lene Smith, Peter Smith, Toni Sonet, Jeffrey Spencer, Alexander Stein, Robert Sterling, Nurani Subramanian **T** Robert Tattersall, Sandra Taylor, Malcolm Thornton, Dudley Tolkien, Fredrik Tukk **U** Bee Ung, Andreas Unterkircher **V** Jens Volmer, Joel Voyer **W** Trudy Watson, Mark Webb, Romy Wessner, Martin Weston, Anna Whalen, Mandy Whitton, Jennifer Widom and Fiona Wilson.

ACKNOWLEDGMENTS

Many thanks to the following for the use of their content:

Globe on title page ©Mountain High Maps 1993 Digital Wisdom, Inc.

Index

1000-Pillared Temple 297

A
accommodation 462-5, *see also
    individual locations*
    children, travel with 465
    internet resources 462
    taxes 465
Achyutaraya Temple 259
activities 97-103, *see also individual
    activities*
    internet resources 97
    outdoor 97-100
    spiritual 101-3
acute mountain sickness 513
Adivasi people 56, 99
Afghan Church 111
Aga Khan Palace 166
Agatti Island 362
Agonda 193, 213
agriculture 93
Ahmedganj Palace 157
aid programmes 487-9
    El Shaddai 201
    Kishkinda Trust 261
AIDS 52
Aihole 268
air pollution 95-6, 512
air travel 491-4, 495-6
    air fares 493-4
    air passes 495-6
    airlines 491-2, 495
    airports 491-2
    to/from Mumbai 131-2
    to/from South India 491-4
    within South India 495-6
Airatesvara Temple 406-7
Ajanta 150-2, **150**
Alamelumangapuram 304
Alappuzha 326-30, **327**
Albuquerque, Alfonso de 40
Alleppey 326-30, **327**
Amaravathi 301-2
Ambedkar, Bhimrao Ramji 154
Amgol 254
amoebic dysentery 511-12

000 Map pages
000 Photograph pages

amphibians 90-1
AMS 513
Andaman Islands 444-61, **446**
Andamanese people 449
Andhra Pradesh 273-305, **274**
    cuisine 79
    festivals 275
Anegundi 260-1
animals 87-91, *see also individual
    animals,* wildlife sanctuaries
    International Animal Rescue 203
    sacred animals 61
Anjuna 192, 199-201, **200**
antelopes 89
antiques 130
Araku Valley 300
Arambol 192, 204-6, **205**
Archaeological Survey of India 479
architecture 69-71
    books 69, 70, 71
    Chalukyan 297
    Dravidian 265, 390, 403-4, 420
    Hoysala 248
    Islamic 268
    Kakatiya 298
    Keralan 319
    modernist 117
    Pallava 385
area codes, *see inside front cover*
Arikkamedu 37
Arjuna Ratha 385, *292*
Arossim 210
arts 66-74, *see also individual arts*
    courses 467
Arunachaleswar Temple 394
Aryan tribes 35
Ashoka 36, 37, 62
ashrams 102-3
    Brahmavidya Mandir Ashram 156
    Isha Yoga Center 434
    itineraries 31
    Osho Meditation Resort 165, 166
    Sevagram 155-6
    Sivananda Yoga Vedanta
        Dhanwantari Ashram 315
    Sri Aurobindo 398
    Sri Ramana Ashram 394
    Vivekanandapuram 425
Asvem 192, 204
ATMs 475-6

Atthukad Waterfalls 337
Aurangabad 143-6, **145**
Auroville 402-3
autorickshaws 498-9
avian flu 509
Avis Island 460
Ayurveda 101, 321
    Baga 195
    Bengaluru 225
    Calangute 195
    Chennai 374
    Goa 178
    Gokarna 255
    Kochi 344
    Kollam 324
    Madikeri 243
    Mamallapuram 386
    Mysore 236
    Periyar Wildlife Sanctuary 335
    Puducherry 399
    Thiruvananthapuram 312
    Varkala 321
Ayyappan 60
Azad Maidan 113

B
backwaters, Keralan 328-9,
    4, *290*
Badaga people 439
Badami 264-7, **266**
Baga 192, 194-9, **196**
Bahmani empire 39
baksheesh 476-7
Bandipur National Park 92, 241
Bangalore 219-32, **221**, **223**
Banganga Tank 116
Bangaram Island 361-2
Bannerghatta Biological Park 232
banyan trees 372
bargaining 476-7, 482
Basilica of Bom Jesus 188, *287*
Basilica of Our Lady of Good Health
    407
bathrooms 464, 485
bazaars, *see* markets
beaches, *see also individual beaches*
    Andaman & Nicobar Islands 453,
        455-9, 460, 461
    Chennai 372
    Cherai Beach 352

Chowara 319
Chowpatty Beach 115, 126, 5, 285
Dhanushkodi 416
Ganpatipule 157
Goa 192-3, 7, 287
Gokarna 255
itineraries 32
Kappil Beach 360
Kollam 324
Konkan Coast 156-8
Kovalam 315, 291
Mangalore 250
Mamallapuram 386
Marina Beach 372
Murudeshwar 254
Pulinkudi 319
Rushikonda 298
Samudra Beach 319
Sinquerim 190, 193
Tarkarli 158
Varkala 319-20
Visakhapatnam 298
bears 87, 154, 340
Bedi, Protima Gauri 232
beer 80
Bekal 360
Belur 247-9
Benaulim 193, 210-13, **211**
Bengaluru 219-32, **221, 223**
accommodation 225-7
activities 225
attractions 223-5
courses 225
drinking 228
entertainment 229
food 227
internet access 222
medical services 222
money 222
shopping 229
tourist information 222
tours 225
travel to/from 229-31
travel within 231-2
berries 172
Betul 213
Bhadrakali Temple 297
Bhagwan Mahavir Wildlife
Sanctuary 216
Bhandari Basti 249
bhangra 69
Bharata Natyam 72
Bhattis 284
Bhatya Beach 158
Bhutanatha Temples 266

Bibi-qa-Maqbara 143
bicycle travel, see cycling
Bidar 271-2
Bijapur 268-71, **269**
bird flu 509
bird-watching 87-8, 97-8
books 87
Calimere (Kodikkarai) Wildlife &
Bird Sanctuary 407-8
Havelock Island 457
internet resources 98
Karanji Lake Nature Park 236
Kumarakom Bird Sanctuary 333
Sanjay Gandhi National Park
92, 136
Thattekkad Bird Sanctuary 340
Vedantangal Bird Sanctuary 92,
388-9
Birla Mandir Temple 281
Birla Planetarium 373
boat travel 494-5, 496, 499
boat trips 98
Alappuzha 326
Arambol 205
backwaters, Keralan 328-9, 4, 290
Candolim 191
canoe boats 328-9, 331
Goa 176
houseboats 328-9
Mumbai 120
Palolem 214
Panaji 185
Periyar Wildlife Sanctuary 334
Bogmalo 193, 209-10
Bokkapuram 443
Bollywood 67, 116, 128, 378, 292
Bombay, see Mumbai
Bondla Wildlife Sanctuary 92, 215-16
books 23, see also literature
architecture 69, 70, 71
birds 87
cinema 67
cricket 56
cultural considerations 37, 52,
56, 67
environmental issues 94
food 76, 77, 78, 81, 82, 83
handicrafts 73
health 101, 507-8
history 35, 36, 38, 39, 40, 41, 44,
46, 64, 67, 99
music 68
photography 477
politics 47
religion 58, 60, 61, 62, 63

sacred Hindu texts 60
spirituality 62
textiles 73
travel 22-4
women in South India 65
border crossings 494
Brahma 59
Brahmagiri Hill 142
Brahmavidya Mandir Ashram 156
Brihadishwara Temple 407
Brindavan Gardens 240-1
British in India 42, 105, 366-7
bronze figures 479
Buddha 63
Buddha Jayanti 471
Buddha statue 281, **289**
Buddhism 62, 296
meditation 103
buffalo racing 57, 255
Bull Temple 225
bus travel
to/from Mumbai 132-3
within Mumbai 134
within South India 496-7, 499
business hours 465
Butler Bay 461
Butterfly Beach 213
buzzards 88
Bylakuppe 245-6

C
Calangute 192, 194-9, **196**
Calicut 355, **357**
Calimere (Kodikkarai) Wildlife & Bird
Sanctuary 92, 407-8
camping 463
canal trips, see boat trips
Candolim 190-4, **191**
Cannanore, see Kannur
Cape Comorin 423-6, **424**
car travel 497-8
costs 498
driving licences 500
hire 497-8
insurance 500
road distances 497
road rules 501-2
Carpet Export Promotion Council of
India 480
carpets 479-80
cash 476
caste system 50, 52
cathedrals, see churches
Cauvery River 34, 407-8
Cavelossim 193, 210-13

INDEX

caves
  Ajanta 150-2, **150**
  Aurangabad 143, **145**
  Badami 265-6
  Bhaja Caves 162-3
  Borra Caves 300
  Edakal Caves 357
  Elephanta Island 135-6, **285**
  Ellora 147-9, **148**, 9
  Kanheri Caves 136
  Karla Cave 162
  Mogalarajapuram Caves 300
  Pandav Leni 142
  Pataleshvara Cave Temple 165
  Rock Fort Temple 412
  Tiger Cave 382
  Undavalli cave temples 300
cell phones 484
Centenary Rose Park 436-8
ceramics 479, see also pottery
chai 80, **12**
Chaldean (Nestorian) Church 354
Chalukya empire 38
Chandor 208-9
Chandragiri 304
Chandrakant Mandare Museum 174
Chandranatha Basti 249
Channekeshava 248
Chapora 201-4
Chapora River 204
charities, see aid programmes
Charminar 278
Cheluvanarayana Temple 241
Chennai 364-82, **368-9**, 292
  accommodation 374
  activities 374
  attractions 371-4
  courses 374
  drinking 377-8
  Egmore 371, 374, 375, 376, **372**
  entertainment 378
  food 376-7
  history 366-7
  internet access 367
  medical services 367-70
  money 370
  shopping 378-81
  tourist information 370
  travel to/from 379-81
  travel within 381-2
  Triplicane 375, 376, **372**

Chennamangalam 352
Chennigaraya 248
Cherai Beach 352
Chettinad cuisine 79, 82
Chhatrapati Shivaji Maharaj Vastu
  Sangrahalaya (Prince of Wales
  Museum) 113
Chhatrapati Shivaji Terminus (Victoria
  Terminus) 114-15
Chidambaram 403-5, **404**
child labour 53, 390, 480
children, travel with 465-6
  Mumbai 119
Childrens Park Beach 417
Chinnar Wildlife Sanctuary 339-40
Chiriya Tapu 455-6
chitals 154, 241, 442
Chola empire 37-9, 406, 407, 411
Cholamandal Artists' Village 382
Chor Bazaar 131, **285**
Chowara 319
Chowmahalla palace 278
Chowpatty Beach 115, 126, **5**, **285**
Christianity 61-2
churches
  Afghan Church 111
  Basilica of Bom Jesus 188, **287**
  Basilica of Our Lady of Good
    Health 407
  Chaldean (Nestorian) Church 354
  Church & Convent of St Monica 189
  Church of Our Lady of the
    Immaculate Conception
    (Panaji) 183, **286**
  Church of Our Lady of the
    Immaculate Conception
    (Puducherry) 398
  Church of St Augustine 189
  Church of St Cajetan 188-9
  Church of South India (Kodaikanal)
    428
  Church of South India (Kozhikode)
    356
  Church of the Holy Spirit 207
  Convent & Church of St Francis of
    Assisi 187-8
  Jesuit church 352
  Lourdes Church 413
  Notre Dame de Anges 398
  Our Lady of Lourdes Cathedral
    353-4
  Puttanpalli (New) Church 354
  Sacred Heart Church 398
  St Aloysius College Chapel 250
  St Francis Church 343

St James' Church 393
St John's Church 413
St Mary's Church 373
St Philomena's Cathedral 236
St Stephen's Church 436
St Thomas' Cathedral 114
San Thome Cathedral 371
Santa Cruz Basilica 343
Sé de Santa Catarina 187
Churchill, Winston 220
cinema
  Bollywood 67, 116, 128,
    378, **292**
  books 67
  festivals 178
  history 43
  internet resources 68
  Mumbai 129
  Ramoji Film City 281
  Tamil films 378
Cinque Island 456
classical dance 72
climate 21, 466-7
  climate change 94-5, 492
climbing, see rock-climbing
clinics, medical 468
clothing 317
  saris 52, 481-2
cloud goats 87, **290**
Cochin, see Kochi
coffee 78, 79
Coimbatore 431-4, **432**
Colomb Bay 213
Colva 193, 210-13, **211**
commission agents 469-70
communism 311
conservation 87
consulates, see high commissions
Convent & Church of St Francis of
  Assisi 187-8
cooking courses 83-5, 166, 184,
  334, 344
Coonoor 434-5
Coorg, see Kodagu (Coorg) region
Copra 79
coral reefs 94
Corbyn's Cove 453
costs 21-2
  accommodation 464-5
  bus travel 497
  car travel 498
  children, travel with 466
  motorcycle travel 501
  train travel 503-4
Cotigao Wildlife Sanctuary 214

courses 467-8
  arts 467
  cooking 83-5, 166, 184, 334, 344
  dance 312, 344, 398-9
  guitar-making 195
  Kathakali 334
  language 119, 334, 374
  martial arts 467
  meditation 103, 282, 301, 374
  music 205, 237, 334, 398-9
  painting 334
  performing arts 71, 467
  Ramamani Iyengar Memorial Yoga
    Institute 166
  yoga 101-2, 118-19, 161-2, 178,
    195, 199, 205, 225, 236-7, 315,
    374, 399
cows 61
crafts, see handicrafts
cranes 87
credit cards 476
cricket 56-7
  Mumbai 129-30
Criminal Tribes 52
crocodiles 91, 314, 340, 382, 442
cruises, see boat trips
cuckoo-shrike 88
cultural considerations 49-74
  books 37, 52, 56, 67
  caste system 50, 52
  child labour 53
  death 50
  food 83
  gay & lesbian people 53-4
  internet resources 49
  poverty 54
  religious etiquette 51
customs regulations 468
cycle-rickshaws 499
cycling 99, 214, 496
  hire 496

D
Dalit people 52
Dalrymple, William 209
dance 69, 71-2, 232
  courses 312, 344, 398-9
  festivals 366
Daulatabad 146-7
Deccan plateau 86
deep vein thrombosis (DVT) 508
deer 89, 214, 241, 242, 431
deforestation 93-4
dengue fever 509
Denotified Tribes 52

Devaraja Market 235, 5, 288
Devarajaswami Temple 391
dhaba-wallahs 125
dhal 76
Dhanushkodi 416
Dharasuram 406-7
Dharavi 121
Dharmastala 253
dholes 90
dhotis 317
diarrhoea, traveller's 511-12
digital photography 477
Diglipur 460
diphtheria 507
disabilities, travellers with 486
diving & snorkelling 99-100
  Andaman Islands 448
  Avis Island 460
  Baga 195
  Bogmalo 209
  Calangute 195
  Childrens Park Beach 417
  Goa 176
  Havelock Island 456-7
  health 512
  Jolly Buoy 455
  Lakshadweep 362
  Miramar 184, 193
  Mt Harriet 455
  Neil Island 458-9
  North Bay 455
  Radha Nagar Beach 456, 460
  Red Skin 455
  responsible travel 99
  Ross Island 460
  Smith Island 460
  Wandoor 455
Diwali (Deepavaali) 472
Dodda Ganesha Temple 225
dolphin spotting 87, 89, 92
  Calangute 195
  Andaman Islands 446, 450
  Arambol 205
  Calimere (Kodikkarai) Wildlife &
    Bird Sanctuary 407
  Candolim 191
  Colva 210
  Goa 176
  Palolem 214
  Panaji 185
  Tarkali 158
dosas 76-7
dowry 50, 65
Dravidian 265, 390, 403-4, 420
drinking water 95, 512

drinks 79-80
  customs 83
driving, see car travel
driving licences 500
druggings 469
drugs 179, 475
Drukpa Teshi 471
Dubare Forest Reserve 92, 245
Dudhsagar Falls 216, 287
dugongs 87
Durga Puja 472
Durga Temple 268
Dussehra 235, 472
Dutch Cemetery 343
Dutch in India 41

E
earthquakes 445
East India Company 41
Eastern Ghats 86
economy 33-4, 37, 46, 47, 48, 49,
    54, 55
Edakal Caves 357
education 33, 311
Eid al-Adha 472
Eid al-Fitr 472
Eid-Milad-un-Nabi 471
El Shaddai 201
electricity 463
Elephant Beach 456
Elephant Race 355
Elephant Stables 260, 5
Elephanta Island 135-6, 285
elephants 88, 242, 245, 314, 334, 340,
    354, 431, 457
  books 89
  safaris 98
Elliot's Beach 372
Ellora 147-9, **148**, 9
embassies 470-1
emergencies, see inside front cover
Emergency, the 46
employment 33, 54, 55
Empress Botanical Gardens 166
encashment certificates 476
environment 86-96
environmental issues 33-4, 93-6
  books 94
  fishing 94
  Goa 216
  internet resources 87
  Keralan backwaters 329
  tsunami 48, 386, 445
Eravikulam National Park 339
Ernakulathappan Utsavam festival 345

INDEX

essential oils 483
etiquette 51
    photography 477
Ettumanur 333
exchange rates, *see inside front cover*
exports, prohibited 479

F
farming 93
ferry travel, *see* boat travel,
    boat trips
festivals 23, 471-3
    Andaman Islands 447
    Andhra Pradesh 275
    Car Festival 417, 425
    cinema 178
    dance 366
    Dussehra 235
    Elephant Race 355
    food 81
    Goa 178
    handicrafts 309
    Karthikai Deepam Festival 366,
        394
    Kerala 309
    Maharashtra 141
    Mumbai 108
    music 366, 411
    Nehru Trophy Snake Boat Race 330
    safe travel 468
    Tamil Nadu 366
    Temple Chariot Festival 413
    Thiru Kalyana 417
    Thrissur Pooram 354
    Thypooya Maholsavam 354
    Uthralikavu Pooram 354
    yoga 366
figs, banyan 91
fish 88-9
fishing 448
flamingos 87
flea market, Anjuna 199, 286
Fontainhas 184, 286
food 75-85, 291
    books 76, 77, 78, 79, 81, 82, 83
    children, travel with 465-6
    cooking courses 83-5, 166, 184,
        334, 344
    cultural considerations 83
    customs 83
    dhaba-wallahs 125

000 Map pages
000 Photograph pages

etiquette 51
    festivals 81
    internet resources 77
    safe travel 82, 468, 512
    vegetarian travellers 81
football 57
Foreigners' Regional Registration
    Office 487
forest reserves, *see* national parks,
    wildlife sanctuaries
Fort Aguada 190-4, **191**
Fort Cochin 343, **342-3**, 8
forts 70-1
    Anegundi 260-1
    Badami 265, 266
    Bengaluru 224
    Bidar 271
    Brihadishwara 409
    Cabo da Rama 213
    Chandragiri 304
    Chapora 201-2
    Danesborg 407
    Daulatabad 146-7
    Fort Aguada 191
    Fort St George 373
    Golconda Fort 280, **280**, 289
    Janjira 156
    Kondapalli 302
    Krishnagiri 395
    Madikeri 243
    Pratapgad Fort 172-3
    Raigad Fort 173
    Rajagiri 395
    St Angelo Fort 359
    Sindhudurg Fort 158
    Sinhagad 170
    Srirangapatnam 240
    Terekhol 206
    Tirumayam 416
    Vellore Fort 392-3
    Warangal 297
foxes 90
FRRO 487

G
galleries, *see also* museums
    art gallery (Thanjavur) 409
    Birla Modern Art Gallery 281
    Chitram Art Gallery 344
    contemporary art 71
    Draavidia Art & Performance
        Gallery 344
    Jayachamarajendra Art Gallery 235
    Jehangir Art Gallery 113
    Kashi Art Gallery 344

National Art Gallery 371
National Gallery of Modern
    Art 113
Sri Chitra Art Gallery 311
Venkatappa Art Gallery 224
Gama, Vasco da 40, 343, 355
Ganapati Temple 255
Gandhi, Indira 46-7
Gandhi Jayanti 472
Gandhi, Mahatma 43-4, 45
    Gandhi Memorial Museum 421
    Gandhi National Memorial 166
Gandhi National Memorial 166
Ganesh 59-60
Ganesh Chaturthi 471-2, 6
Ganesh Ratha 385
Gangadwar bathing tank 142
Gangakondacholapuram 407
Ganpatipule 157
gardens, *see* parks & gardens
Gateway of India 111-13
gaurs 154, 431
gay travellers 473
gazelles 89
geography 86
geology 86
Georgia Sunshine Village 241
ghats 86
    Eastern Ghats 86
    Mahalaxmi Dhobi Ghat 117
    Vijayawada 301
    Western Ghats 86, 426-43
giardiasis 512
Gingee 395
glycerol 80
Goa 175-216, **177**, 7
    activities 176-8
    Ayurveda 178
    cuisine 78
    environmental issues 216
    festivals 178
Gods 58-60
Gokarna 254-7, **256**
Golconda Fort 280, **280**, 289
Golden Temple 246
Gomateshvara statue 249
Govardhana Puja 472
government 33-4, 46-8
government accommodation 463
green turtles 460
Gurus 102

H
Haji Ali's Mosque 117
Halebid 247-9

Half-Moon Beach 255
Hampi 257-63, **259**, **260**, 5
handicrafts 72-4
    Bidar 272
    DakshinaChitra 382
    festivals 309
    Mumbai 130-1
    Mysore 238-9
handmade paper 483
hang-gliding 100
Hanging Gardens 116
Hanuman Temple 261
Harappan people 35
Harmal 192, 204-6, **205**
harriers 88
Hassan 246
Havelock Island 456-8, **456**
health 506-14
    alternative therapies 101-3
    books 101, 507-8
    children, travel with 466
    environmental hazards 512-14
    internet resources 101, 507
    vaccinations 506-7
heat illness 512-13
hepatitis 507, 509-10
herons 87
Hessaraghatta 232
high commissions 470-1
High Court 113
hijras 53
hiking, *see* trekking
Hill Palace Museum 352
hill stations
    Coonoor 434-5
    Kodaikanal 427-31
    Kotagiri 435
    Mahabaleshwar 170-2, **171**
    Matheran 158-60
    Nilgiri Hills 434
    Udhagamandalam 436
Hill Tribes 439
Hinduism 58-61
history 33, 35-48
    Bahmani empire 39
    books 35, 36, 38, 39, 40, 41, 44,
        46, 64, 67, 99
    British in India 42, 105, 366-7
    Chalukya empire 38
    Chola empire 37-9
    Christianity 40-1
    cinema 43
    early civilisations 35
    East India Company 41
    economy 37

Emergency, the 46
Gandhi, Indira 46-7
Gandhi, Mahatma 43-4, 45
independence 43-4
Inquisition 41
internet resources 36
Karnataka 36-7
Kashmir 34, 47
Maratha dynasty 41-2
Mughal empire 41-2
Muslim rulers 39-40
Pallava empire 38
Pandya empire 38
Partition 43-4
Portuguese in India 40, 44, 46
Tamil people 36
trading routes 37
Vijayanagar empire 39-40
hitching 498
HIV 52, 510
Holi 473
holidays, *see* festivals
holistic therapies 101-3
homestays 463
hornbills 88
horse racing 57, 130
    Udhagamandalam 438
horse riding 98
    Kodaikanal 429
    Mumbai 117
    Udhagamandalam 438
Hospet 263-4
hotels 462-3, 464
houseboats 328-9, **290**
Hoysaleswara Temple 248
Hubli 264
Hussain Sagar 281
Hyderabad 275-95, **277**,
    279, 11
    accommodation 282-3
    activities 281
    attractions 278-81
    courses 282
    drinking 284
    entertainment 293
    food 283-4
    history 276
    internet access 276
    medical services 278
    shopping 293
    tourist information 278
    tours 282
    travel to/from 293-4
    travel within 294-5
hygiene 95

I
Igatpuri 142-3
immigration 491, 494
incense 483
independence 43-4
Independence Day 471
Indian National Congress (Congress
    Party) 43
Indira Gandhi (Annamalai) Wildlife
    Sanctuary 92, 431
Indo-Portuguese Museum 343
influenza 509, 510
information technology 34, 48, 55,
    224
Inquisition 41
insurance 474
    car 500
    health 506
    motorcycle 500
    travel 474
International Animal Rescue 203
internet access 474
internet resources 24
    accommodation 462
    activities 97
    air tickets 493
    architecture 70
    bird-watching 98
    cinema 68
    conservation 91
    culture 40, 49
    dance 72
    environmental issues 86, 87, 93
    food 77
    gay & lesbian travellers 473
    health 101, 507
    history 36
    literature 66
    media 58
    plants 91
    politics 48
    religion 58
    safe travel 468
    sports 57
    Tamil people 40
    wildlife 91
    women in South India 64
Interview Island 460
invertebrates 89
Irula people 439
Isha Yoga Center 434
Iskcon temple 225
Islam 61
IT industry 34, 48,
    55, 224

itineraries 25-32
　ashrams 31
　beaches 32
　festivals 32
　Mumbai 110
　pilgrimages 31

J
Jainism 62
Jalgaon 153
Janardhana Temple 320-1
Janata People's Party 46
Janjira 156
Janmastami 472
Japanese B Encephalitis 507, 510
Jarawa people 449, 460
jeep tours 340, 357
jeeps, share 502
Jehangir Art Gallery 113
Jesuit church 352
jet lag 508-9
jewellery 480
Jog Falls 254
Judaism 62-3

K
Kada people 431
Kadmat Island 362
Kailasa Temple 148
Kailasagiri Hill 299
Kailasanatha Temple 390
Kakkabe 246
Kala Rama 140
kalarippayat 57, 349
Kalipur 460
Kamakshi Amman Temple 391
Kamala Nehru Park 116
Kambla 57, 255
Kanadukathan 416
Kanaka Durga Temple 301
Kanchipuram 389-92, **389**
Kanheri Caves 136
Kannur 358-60
Kanyakumari 423-6, **424**
Kapaleeshwarar Temple 371
Kappil Beach 360
Karanji Lake Nature Park 236
Karla Cave 162
karma 59

000 Map pages
000 Photograph pages

Karnataka 217-72, **218**
　cuisine 78-9
　festivals 220
Karthikai Deepam Festival 394
Kashmir 34, 47
Kathakali 72, 312, 333, 349-50, 355
　courses 334, 344
Katraj Snake Park & Zoo 165
kayaking 100
Keneseth Eliyahoo Synagogue 113
Kerala 306-62, **307**
　cuisine 79
Keshava Temple 241
kettuvallams 329
Khuldabad 147
kingfishers 88
Kishkinda Trust 261
kitesurfing 205
Kochi 340-52, **341**
　accommodation 345-8
　activities 344
　courses 344
　drinking 348-9
　entertainment 349-50
　Ernakulam 345, 347, 348-9, 351, **346-7**
　festivals 345
　food 348-9
　Fort Cochin 341, 343, 345-8, 351, **342-3**, 8
　internet access 341
　Jew Town 344, 347, 349
　Mattancherry 347, 349, **342**
　money 341
　shopping 350
　tourist information 343
　tours 344-5
　travel to/from 350-1
　travel within 351-2
Kodagu (Coorg) region 243-6
Kodai 427-31, **427**
Kodaikanal 427-31, **427**
Kodaikanal International School 428
Kodava people 243, 244
Kolams 74
Kolhapur 173-4
Kollam 323-6, **324**
Kollywood 378
Kondapalli 302
Konkan Coast 156-8
Konkan Railway 503, 12
Koorti Teertha 255
Kota people 439
Kotagiri 435
Kottayam 331-3, **332**

Kovalam 315-19, **316**, 291
Kozhikode 355, **357**
Krishna Temple 253
Krishnadevaraya 39, 40
Krishnapuram Palace Museum 326
kuchipudi 72
Kudle Beach 255
Kumarakom 333
Kumarakom Bird Sanctuary 333
Kumari Amman Temple 424-5
Kumbakonam 405-6, **405**
Kumbeshwara Temple 406
Kumbh Mela 472
Kumily 336-7
Kurinji shrub 91
Kurumba people 439
Kuttichira Mosque 356

L
Laad Bazaar 278, 11, 289
lakes
　Karanji Lake Nature Park 236
　Pookot Lake 358
　Vembanad Lake 330
Lakshadweep 360-2, **361**
Lakshmi 59
language 515-20
　courses 119-36, 334, 374, 467
　food 83, 84-5
langurs 87
lapwings 88
laundry services 474
leatherback turtles 460
leatherwork 480-1
leeches 513
legal matters 475
　photography restrictions 477
leopards 87, 90, 154, 214, 242
Lepakshi 305
lesbian travellers 473
Liberation Tigers of Tamil Eelam 47
lions 87, 136, 314
literacy rate 33
literature 22-4, 66-7, 109, see also books
　internet resources 66
　travel 22-4
litter 216
Little Andaman 461
Little Mount 373
Lonar Meteorite Crater 153-4
Lonavla 160-2, **161**
lorises 87
Losar 473
Lourdes Church 413

Loutolim 209
lungi 317, 365

M
macaques 87
Madgaon 206-8, **207**
Madikeri 243-5
Madras, see Chennai
Madurai 418-23, **419**
magazines 58
Mahabaleshwar 170-2, **171**
Mahabalipuram 382-8, **384**
Mahabharata, the 60
Mahalaxmi Dhobi Ghat 117
Mahalaxmi Temple 117, 173
Mahamakham Tank 406
Maharaja's Palace 233, 5, **288**
Maharashtra 137-74, **138**
    cuisine 77-8
    Matheran 159
Mahatma Gandhi Marine National
    Park 92, 455
Mahavir Jayanti 471
Majorda 193
malaria 510-11
malkohas 88
Mallikarjuna Temple 268
Malpe 253-4
Malvan 158
Mamallapuram 382-8, **384**
mammals 89-90
Mandrem 192, 204
Mangalore 250-3, **251**
mangroves 94
Mani Bhavan 116-17
Mapro Gardens 172
maps 475
Mapusa 190
Maratha dynasty 41-2
Margao 206-8, **207**
Mariamman Teppakkulam Tank 421
Marina Beach 372
marine environment 94
markets
    Anjuna 199
    Chor Bazaar 131, 285
    Devaraja Market 235, 5, **288**
    Krishnarajendra (city) market &
        Tipu's Palace 224
    Laad Bazaar 278, 11, **289**
    Mukkada Bazaar 324
marriage 49-50
martial arts 57
    courses 467
Masinagudi 443

Matharaj Naag Panchami 173
Matheran 158-60
Matheran Toy Train 503
Mattancherry 347, **342-3**
Mauryan empire 36
Mayabunder 459-60
measures, see inside front cover
Mecca Masjid 280-1
medical services 509, see also health
meditation 103
    courses 103, 282, 301, 374
    Osho Meditation Resort 165, 166
    vipassana 103
Meguti Temple 268
mehndi 73
Melkote 241
meningitis 507
Mercara 243-5
metalwork 479
metric conversions, see inside front
    cover
Mettupalayam 434
Middle Andaman 459-61
miniature steam train 436, 503, 292
Minicoy Island 362
mining 94
Miramar 184, 193
mobile phones 484
Mohiniyattam 72
Molem 216
Molem & Bhagwan Mahavir Wildlife
    Sanctuary 92
Monetary Museum 115-16
money 21-2, 475-7
    discounts 470
moneychangers 476
monkeys 90, 153, 242
monsoons 21, 466-8
Morjim Beach 192, 204
mosques
    Haji Ali's Mosque 117
    Jama Masjid (Bengaluru) 224
    Jama Masjid (Bijapur) 269-70
    Kuttichira Mosque 356
    Mecca Masjid 270, 280-1
    Solah Kambah 271
motion sickness 508-9
motorcycle travel 99, 499-502
    costs 501
    driving licences 500
    hire 500
    insurance 500
    road distances 497
    road rules 501-2
    tours 500

Mt Arunachala 394
Mt Harriet 455
Mudumalai National Park 92, 442-3
Mughal empire 41-2
Muharram 473
Mukkada Bazaar 324
Muktidham Temple 140
Mumbai 104-36, **105**, **106-7**, 5
    accommodation 120-4
    activities 117-18
    attractions 111-17
    Chowpatty Beach 115, 126,
        5, **285**
    Churchgate 122-3, 126, **114-15**
    Colaba 111-13, 120-2, 124-5,
        127-8, **112**
    courses 118-19
    drinking 127-8
    entertainment 129-30
    food 124-7
    Fort Area 113-15, 121-2, 125-6,
        114-15
    history 105-8
    internet access 109
    itineraries 110
    medical services 109
    money 109
    North Mumbai 117, 126-7
    shopping 130-1
    tourist information 110-11
    tours 119-20
    travel to/from 131-5
    travel within 134-5
    walking tour 118, **118**
Mumbai Zoo 117
Munnar 337-9, **338**, 291
Murud 156-7
Murudeshwar 254
Murugan 59
museums, see also galleries
    Amaravathi 301
    Anthropological Museum 451
    AP State Museum 281
    archaeological museum (Badami)
        266
    archaeological museum (Hampi)
        260
    archaeological museum (Old
        Goa) 188
    archaeology museum 354
    Bengaluru Government Museum
        224
    Birla Planetarium & Science
        Museum 281
    Car Museum 253

INDEX

INDEX

museums *continued*
  Chandrakant Mandare Museum 174
  Chhatrapati Shivaji Maharaj Vastu Sangrahalaya (Prince of Wales Museum) 113
  Forest Museum 451
  Fort Museum 373
  Goa State Museum 183
  Government Museum (Chennai) 371
  Government Museum (Kanyakumari) 425
  Health Museum 281
  Heh the Nizam's Museum 279–80
  Hill Palace Museum 352
  Houses of Goa Museum 190
  Indo-Portuguese Museum 343
  Janapada Loka Folk Arts Museum 232
  Jayalakshmi Vilas Complex Museum 236
  Karnataka Chitrakala Parishat 224
  Krishnapuram Palace Museum 326
  Lila Studio 344
  Madurai Government Museum 421
  Mani Bhavan 116–17
  Manjusha Museum 253
  Monetary Museum 115–16
  Museum of Christian Art 189
  Museum of Habitat 300
  Nagarjunakonda Museum 296
  Napier Museum 311
  national government museum 393
  Natural History Museum 311
  Nehru centenary Tribal museum 281
  Police Museum 324
  Puducherry Museum 398
  Pudukkottai Museum 415–16
  Puthe Maliga Palace Museum 311
  rail museum (Mysore) 236
  Raja Dinkar Kelkar Museum 165
  Royal Palace Museum (Thanjavur) 409
  Salar Jung Museum 278
  Samudrika Marine Museum 451
  Sculpture Museum 385
  Shivaji Museum 144
  Shree Chhatrapati Shahu Museum 173

Shreemanthi Bai Memorial Government Museum 250
Tamil Nadu government museum 393
Tata Tea Museum 337
Temple Art Museum 420
Tribal Cultural Museum 166
Tribal Research Centre museum 438
Victoria jubilee museum 300
Visvesvaraya Industrial & Technical Museum 224
wax museum 425
Wayanad Heritage Museum 357–8
music 68–9
  books 68
  courses 205, 237, 334, 398–9, 467
  festivals 366, 411
musical instruments 481
mynahs 88
Mysore 232–40, **234**, 5
  accommodation 237–8
  activities 236–7
  attractions 233–6
  courses 236–7
  food 238
  history 233
  medical services 233
  money 233
  shopping 238–9
  tourist information 233
  tours 237
  travel to/from 239
  travel within 240

N
Naag Panchami 471
Nagarhole National Park 92, 242–3
Nagarjunakonda 295–7
Nageshwara Temple 406
Nagpur 154–5
Nalakunad Palace 246
Namdroling Monastery 246
Nanak Jayanti 472
Nandi Hills 232
Napier Museum 311
Nasik 139–42, **140**
Nataraja Temple 403–4
National Gallery of Modern Art 113
national parks 91–6, *see also* wildlife sanctuaries
  Bandipur National Park 92, 241
  Bannerghatta Biological Park 232
  Dubare Forest Reserve 92, 245
  Eravikulam National Park 339

Mahatma Gandhi Marine National Park 92, 455
Mudumalai National Park 92, 442–3
Nagarhole National Park 242–3
Navagaon National Park 92, 154
Nilgiri Biosphere Reserve 92, 241
Sanjay Gandhi National Park 92, 136
Natural History Museum 311
Navagaon National Park 92, 154
Navratri (Festival of Nine Nights) 472
Nehru, Jawaharlal 43, 46
Nehru Planetarium 117
Nehru Trophy Snake Boat Race 326, 330
Neil Island 458–9
Nestorian Christian people 353
Netaji Nagar Beach 461
newspapers 58, 463
Neyyar Dam Sanctuary 314–15
Nicobar Islands 444–61
Nicobarese people 449
nilgais 154
Nilgiri Biosphere Reserve 92, 241
Nilgiri Hills 434–43, **434**
  hill tribes 439
Nilgiri tahr 87, 290
noise pollution 96
North Andaman 459–61
North Bay 455
Notre Dame de Anges 398

O
Old Goa 187–9, **188**
Om Beach 255
Onge people 449
Ooty 436–42, **437**
orchids 91
organised tours 502
Osho Meditation Resort 165, 166
Our Lady of Lourdes Cathedral 353–4
Oval Maidan 113, 285

P
paan 76
Padmanabhapuram 319
Paez, Domingo 39–40
painting 71
  courses 334
paintings 481
palaces 70–1
  Aga Khan Palace 166
  Ahmedganj Palace 157
  Bengaluru Palace 223–4

Chowmahalla Palace 278
Daria Daulat Bagh 240
Hill Palace Museum 352
Krishnapuram Palace Museum 326
Maharaja's Palace 233, 5, **288**
Nalakunad Palace 246
Padmanabhapuram Palace 319
Palacio do Dea 209
Rangin 271
Sakthan Thampuran Palace 354
Sat Manzil 269
Shaniwar Wada 165
Taj Mahal Palace 112-13
Thanjavur Royal Palace 409
Thibaw Palace 158
Tipu's Palace 224-5
Tirumalai Nayak Palace 421
Palampet 298
Pallava empire 38
Palolem 213-15, **214**, 287
Panaji 181-7, **182-3**
Panchakki 144
Panchganga Mandir 171
Pandav Leni 142
Pandya empire 38
Panjim 181-7, **182-3**
panthers 87, 241, 340, 431, 442
papier-mâché 481
Paradise Beach 255
paragliding 100
    Anjuna 199
    Goa 176
Parambikulam Wildlife Sanctuary 340
Pardesi Synagogue 344
parks & gardens
    botanical gardens (Puducherry)
        398
    botanical gardens
        (Udhagamandalam) 436
    Brindavan Gardens 240-1
    Bryant Park 429
    Chettiar Park 429
    Cubbon Park 224
    Empress Botanical Gardens 166
    Hanging Gardens 116
    Kamala Nehru Park 116
    Karanji Lake Nature Park 236
    Lalbagh Botanical Gardens 223
    Lumbini Park 281
    Mapro Gardens 172
    Sim's Park 435
    Tagore Park 250
    Thread Garden 438
    Veli Tourist Park 311
parrots 88

Parsi 119
Partition 43-6
Parur 352
passports 491
Pataleshvara Cave Temple 165
Pateti 472
Patnem Beach 193, 213
Pattadakal 267-8
performing arts 71, 467
Periyar Wildlife Sanctuary 92,
    334-7, 6
permits, travel 486
    Andaman Islands 447
    Lakshadweep 361
    Tamil Nadu 364
petroglyphs 357
photography 477
    etiquette 51
Pichavaram 405
pigeons 88
pilgrimages 31
    Brahmagiri Hill 142
    Dharmastala 253
    Isha Yoga Center 434
    Khuldabad 147
    Madurai 418-23
    Mt Arunachala 394
    Rameswaram 416-18
    Rock Fort Temple 412
    Sivagiri Mutt 321
    Sravanabelagola 249
    Tirukkalikundram 388
    Tirumala 302-4
    Tirupathi 302-4
    Tiruvannamalai 393-5
planetariums
    Chennai 373
    Nehru Planetarium 117
planning 20-4, see also itineraries
    discounts 470
plants 91, 426-7, 431
    sacred plants 61
    Sim's Park 435
plastic 96
plovers 88
poaching 46, 88
Police Museum 324
polio 507
politics 33-4, 43-4, 46-8
    books 47
    Gandhi, Indira 46-7
    internet resources 48
pollution 95-6, 512
Ponda 215
Pondicherry 395-402, **396-7**

Pongal 473
Pookot Lake 358
population 33, 54-7
Port Blair 450-5, **452**
Portuguese in India 44
Portuguese occupations 188
postal services 477-8
pottery 72-3
poverty 54, 121
Pratapgad Fort 172-3
primates 90, 153, 242
prohibited exports 479
Project Tiger 87
prostitution 54
Puducherry 395-402, **396-7**
Pulinkudi 319
Pune 163-70, **164**
    accommodation 166-7
    activities 166
    courses 166
    drinking 168
    entertainment 168
    food 167-8
    internet access 163
    money 163
    shopping 168-9
    tourist information 165
    tours 166
    travel to/from 169-70
    travel within 170
Puthe Maliga Palace Museum 311
Puttanpalli (New) Church 354
Puttaparthi 304-5

Q
Querim 206
Quilon 323-6, **324**
Quit India 45

R
rabies 507, 511
Radha Nagar Beach 456, 460
radio 58, 463
rafting 334
    Bengaluru 225
    Calangute 195
    Dubare Forest Reserve 245
    Mumbai 117
    Periyar Wildlife Sanctuary 334
    Wayanad Wildlife Sanctuary 357
Raigad Fort 173
railway accommodation 463-4
Raja Dinkar Kelkar Museum 165
Raksha Bandhan (Narial Purnima)
    471

Ramadan (Ramazan) 472
Ramakrishna Mutt Temple 371
Ramamani Iyengar Memorial Yoga
    Institute 166
Ramanathaswamy Temple 416
Ramanavami 471
Ramappa Temple 298
Ramayana, the 60-9
Rameswaram 416-18, **417**
Ramkund 140
Ramoji Film City 281
Ramtek 155
Ranganathittu Bird Sanctuary 92
Rangat 459
Rath Yatra 471
Ratnagiri 158
rave parties 180
recycling 96
religion 58-64, *see also* spirituality
    books 58, 60, 61, 62, 63
    etiquette 51
    festivals 472
    religious architecture 69-70
    sacred Hindu texts 60
    tribal religions 64
reptiles 90-1
reserves, *see* national parks, wildlife
    sanctuaries
responsible travel 96, 457, 460
    air travel 492
    diving 99
restaurants 81
rhinoceroses 87
rice 75
rice barges 329
rickshaws, *see* autorickshaws,
    cycle-rickshaws
river rafting 100
rock carvings 357
    Shore Temple 383
rock-climbing 100
    acute mountain sickness 513
    Hampi 261
    Karnataka 262
Ross Island 455, 460
Rowlatt Acts 45
Rushikonda 298, 299

S
Sacred Heart Church 398
safaris 98

000 Map pages
000 Photograph pages

safe travel 468-70
    drinking water 95
    internet resources 468
    road conditions 501
    road rules 501-2
    street food 82
    women travellers 489-90
saffron 75
Saffronart 71
Sai Baba 142, 305
St Aloysius College Chapel 250
St Angelo Fort 359
St Francis Church 343
St Francis Xavier 189, 208
St James' Church 393
St John's Church 413
St Mary's Church 373
St Mary's Island 254
St Philomena's Cathedral 236
St Thomas 371, 373
St Thomas' Cathedral 114
St Thomas Mount 373
St Thomas the Apostle 62
Sakthan Thampuran Palace 354
Samudra Beach 319
San Thome Cathedral 371
sandalwood oil 483
sandpipers 88
Sanjay Gandhi National Park 92, 136
Santa Cruz Basilica 343
Sarangapani Temple 406
saris 52, 481-2
scams 464, 468-9
scuba diving, *see* diving &
    snorkelling
sculpture 70-1
Sé de Santa Catarina 187
Secunderabad 275-95, **277**
    accommodation 282-3
    activities 281
    attractions 278-81
    courses 282
    drinking 284
    entertainment 293
    food 283-4
    internet access 276
    medical services 278
    shopping 293
    tourist information 278
    tours 282
    travel to/from 293-4
    travel within 294-5
Senji 395
Sentinelese people 449
Sevagram 155-6

Shaniwar Wada 165
share jeeps 502
shawls 481-2
Shiva 59
Shiva Temple 333
Shivaji, Chhatrapati 42
Shivaji Museum 144
Shivaratri 473
Shompen people 449
shopping 478-83
    Anjuna flea market 199, 286
    antiques 130
    handicrafts 130-1, 238-9, 382
    markets 131, 199
    music 131
    prohibited exports 479
    weaving 146
Shravan Purnima 472
Shree Chhatrapati Shahu Museum 173
Shri Mahalsa 215
Shri Manguesh 215
Shri Shantadurga Temple 215
Shrine of Our Lady of Velankanni
    323-4
Siddheshwara Temple 297
Sikhism 63-4
silk 481-2
silk industry 390
Sindhudurg Fort 158
Sinhagad 170
Sinquerim 190, 193
Sivagiri Mutt 321
Sivananda Yoga Vedanta Dhanwantari
    Ashram 315
Sivasamudram 241
sloth bears 442
sloths 340
Smith Island 460
smoking 475
snakes 61, 91
snorkelling, *see* diving & snorkelling
soccer 57
solo travellers 483-4
spa treatments 101
special events, *see* festivals
spice plantations 215, 335
spices 75-6, 331
spirituality, *see also* religion
    activities 101-3
    books 62
    Buddha 63
    worship 60-1
sports 56-7
Sravanabelagola 249
Sree Vallabha Temple 333

Sri Aurobindo 398
Sri Chamundeswari Temple 235
Sri Chitra Art Gallery 311
Sri Ekambaranathar Temple 391
Sri Jambukeshwara Temple 413
Sri Kalahasti 304
Sri Krishna Temple 355
Sri Kalahasteeswara Temple 304
Sri Meenakshi Temple 420
Sri Padmanabhaswamy Temple 311
Sri Ramana Ashram 394
Sri Shweta Varahaswamy Temple 233
Srirangapatnam 240
STDs 511
stings, insect 513
stone-carving 479
storks 87
street food 81-2
stupas
    Amaravathi 301
    Andhra Pradesh 296
sunburn 514
Sundar Narayan Temple 140
surfing, *see also* kitesurfing,
    windsurfing
    Andaman Islands 448
    buffalo surfing 255
    Butler Bay 461
    health 512
swimming, *see also* beaches
    ghats 301
    safety 21, 469
synagogues
    Chennamangalam 352
    Keneseth Eliyahoo Synagogue 113
    Pardesi Synagogue 344

T
Tadoba-Andhari Tiger Reserve
    92, 154
Tagore, Rabindranath 66
tahrs, Nilgiri 87, **290**
Taj Mahal Palace 112-13
Tamil films 378
Tamil Nadu 363-443, **365, 10**
    cuisine 79
    festivals 366
    temples 367
    Tamil people 36
Tanjore 408-11, **408**
tanks
    Banganga Tank 116
    Gangadwar bathing tank 142
    Mahamakham Tank 406
    Mariamman Teppakkulam Tank 421

Tarkarli 158
Tata Tea Museum 337
taxes 139, 275, 364
taxi travel 499
    women travellers 490
tea plantations 337, *291*
teak trees 340
telephone services 484-5
temples, *see also individual temples*
    Aihole 268
    Airatesvara Temple 406-7
    Alamelumangapuram 304
    Arunachaleswar Temple 394
    Badami 265-6
    Belur 248
    Bengaluru 224-5
    Bijapur 268-70
    Chennai 371
    Elephanta Island 135-6, *285*
    Ellora 147-9, **148,** 9
    Ettumanur 333
    Five Rathas 385
    Gandamadana Parvatham 417
    Ganpatipule 157
    Gokarna 255
    Hampi 258-61
    Halebid 248
    Hyderabad & Secunderabad
        278-81
    itineraries 31, 367
    Kanchipuram 389-91
    Karla Cave 162
    Kumbakonam 405-6, **405**
    Mahabaleshwara Temple 255
    Mahalaxmi Temple 117, 173
    Mamallapuram 383-5
    Melkote 241
    Murudeshwar 254
    Mysore 233-5
    Nandi Hills 232
    Naslk 140
    Nataraja Temple 403-4
    Pattadakal 267-8
    Ponda 215
    Puducherry 398
    Pune 165
    Rameswaram 416-17
    Ramtek 155
    rock carvings 383
    Sravanabelagola 249
    Sri Meenakshi Temple 420
    Tamil Nadu 367, **10**
    Thirunelly Temple 357
    Thyagararajaswami Temple 411
    Tiruchirappalli 412-13

Trimbakeshwar Temple 142
Undavalli cave temples 300
Varkala 320-1
Vedagirishvara Temple 388
Veerbhadra Temple 305
Venkateshwara Temple 302
Vijayawada 300-1
Warangal 297
tempos 498-9
Tenetti 299
tennis 57, 165
Terekhol 206
terracotta 479
terrorism 34, 48
tetanus 507
textiles 73-4, 431, 482-3
thalis 78
Thanjavur 408-11, **408**
Thanjavur Royal Palace 409
Tharangambadi 407
Thattekkad Bird Sanctuary 340
theatre
    Bengaluru 229
    festivals 108, 178
    Hyderabad 293
    Mumbai 129
    Panaji 186
theft 469
theyyam 72, 359
Thibaw Palace 158
Thirunelly Temple 357
Thiruvaiyaru 411
Thiruvalluvar 371
Thiruvananthapuram 308-14, **310**
Thrissur 352-4, **353**
Thypooya Maholsavam 354
Tibet
    Bylakuppe 245-6
    refugees 243, 245-6
ticks 513
tigers 87, 90
    Andhari Tiger Reserve 154
    Bannerghatta Biological Park 232
    Indira Gandhi (Annamalal) Wildlife
        Sanctuary 431
    Mudumalai National Park 442
    Nagahole National Park 242
    Parambikulam Wildlife
        Sanctuary 340
    Perlyar Wildlife Sanctuary 334
    Sanjay Gandhi National Park 136
time 485, **547**
tipping 476-7
Tiracol 206
Tiruchirappalli 411-15, **412, 414**

INDEX

INDEX

Tirukkalikundram 388
Tirumala 302-4
Tirumalai Nayak Palace 421
Tirupathi 302-4
Tiruvannamalai 393-5
Toda people 439
toddy 80
toilets 464, 485
Tollywood 378
tombs & shrines
  Bahmani 271
  Bibi-qa-Maqbara 143
  Jod Gumbad 270
  Natharvala Dargah 413
tombs & shrines *continued*
  Shrine of Our Lady of Velankanni
    323-4
  Tombs of Qutb Shahi Kings 280,
    289
tongas 499
Top Station 340
Torda 190
tortoises 90-1
tourist bungalows 463
tourist information 485-6
tours 502
  boat trips 98
  bus 185
  canoe boats 328-9
  cultural tours 99
  jeep safaris 98
  motorcycle 500
  operators 97
  tea plantations 337
  walking tours 118-19
  wildlife safaris 98, 136, 232, 241
touts 469-70
Towers of Silence 63
toy train, *see* miniature steam
  train
trading routes 37
traditional medicine, *see* Ayurveda
train travel 502-5
  classes 503
  costs 503-4
  itineraries 503
  Konkan Railway 503, 12
  miniature steam train 436, 503,
    292
  platform food 82
  retiring rooms 463-4

train fares 505
train passes 505
travel to/from Mumbai 133-5
travel within Mumbai 135
travel within South India 502-5
Tranquebar 407
travel permits 486
  Andaman Islands 447
  Lakshadweep 361
  Tamil Nadu 364
travel to/from South India 491-5
travellers cheques 477
Treaty of Mangalore 42
trekking 100
  acute mountain sickness 513
  Chinnar Wildlife Sanctuary 339-40
  Kodagu (Coorg) region 243
  Kodaikanal 428-9
  Munnar 337
  Nandi Hills 232
  Periyar Wildlife Sanctuary 334
  safety 470
  tours 119
  Udhagamandalam 438
  Wayanad Wildlife Sanctuary
    357
Tribal Cultural Museum 166
Trichur 352-4, **353**
Trichy 411-15, **412**, **414**
Trimbakeshwar Temple 142
Trimurti Cave 385
Tripunithura 352
Trivandrum 308-14, **310**
tsunami 48, 386, 445
tuberculosis 507, 511
turtles 90-1, 460
TV 58, 463
typhoid 507, 511

U
Udhagamandalam 436-42, **437**
Udupi 253
Ullal Beach 250
Union Territories 44
universities
  High Court 113
  University of Mumbai 113-14
Untouchable people, *see* Dalit
  people
Uthralikavu Pooram 354

V
vaccinations 506-7
Vadakkunathan Kshetram Temple 353
Vagator 192, 201-4

Vaikunta Perumal Temple 391
Vailankanni 407
Varca 193, 213
Varicella 507
Varkala 319-23, **320**
Vasant Panchami 473
Vasudev, Jaggi 93
Vedantangal Bird Sanctuary 92,
  388-9
Veerappan 46
Veerbhadra Temple 305
vegan travellers 82-3
vegetarian travellers 82-3
  books 79
  food 81
Velanganni 407
Veli Tourist Park 311
Vellore 392-3, **392**
Velsao 193
Vembanad Lake 330
Venkateshwara Temple 302
victorias 499
Vijayanagar 257-8
Vijayanagar empire 39-40
Vijayawada 300-1
Vijnana Kala Vedi Cultural Centre
  333-4
vikrams 498-9
Vindhya Range 86
vipassana 103
Viper Island 455
Virupaksha 258, 5
Visakhapatnam 298-300
visas 486-7, *see also* passports
Vishnu 59
Vittala 258-9, **288**
Vivekanandapuram 425
Vizag 298-300
volunteering 386, 487-9

W
walking, *see* trekking
Waltair 298
Wandoor 455
Warangal 297
waste, plastic 96
water
  environmental issues 95
  health 512
water sports 99-100
  Baga 195
  Calangute 195
  Colva 210
  Goa 176
  Mumbai 117-18

000 Map pages
000 Photograph pages

waterfalls
Atthukad Waterfalls 337
Bear Shola Falls 429
Dudhsagar Falls 216, 287
Jog Falls 254
Silver Cascade 429
Wayanad Heritage Museum
357-8
Wayanad Wildlife Sanctuary
92, 357-8
weather 21, 466-7
weaving 146, 359, 382
weights, *see inside front cover*
Wellesley, Richard 43
Western Ghats 86, 426-43
whisky 80
Wildlife Protection Act 87
wildlife safaris 98
Bannerghatta Biological Park
232
Bandipur National Park 241
Sanjay Gandhi National Park
92, 136
wildlife sanctuaries 91-2, *see also*
national parks
Bhagwan Mahavir Wildlife
Sanctuary 216
Bondla Wildlife Sanctuary 92,
215-16
Calimere (Kodikkarai) Wildlife &
Bird Sanctuary 92, 407-8
Chinnar Wildlife Sanctuary
339-40
Cotigao Wildlife Sanctuary 214
Indira Gandhi (Annamalai) Wildlife
Sanctuary 92, 431
Kumarakom Bird Sanctuary
333

Molem & Bhagwan Mahavir
Wildlife Sanctuary 92
Neyyar Dam Sanctuary 314-15
Parambikulam Wildlife
Sanctuary 340
Periyar Wildlife Sanctuary 92,
334-7, **335**, 6
Ranganathittu Bird Sanctuary
92, 240
Tadoba-Andhari Tiger Reserve
92, 154
Thattekkad Bird Sanctuary 340
Vedantangal Bird Sanctuary 92,
388-9
Wayanad Wildlife Sanctuary 357-8
windsurfing
Candolim 191
Goa 176
Mumbai 117
wineries 80, 142
wolves 90
women in South India 64-5
women travellers 489-90
health 514
woodcarving 483
woodpeckers 88
World Heritage sites
Ajanta 29, 150-2, **150**
Brihadishwara Temple 409
Chhatrapati Shivaji Terminus
(Victoria Terminus) 114-15
Elephanta Island 29, 135-6, 285
Ellora 29, 147-9, **148**, 9
Hampi 29
itineraries 29
Mahabalipuram 382-8
Mamallapuram 29, 382-8
Old Goa 29, 187-9

Pattadakal 29, 267-8
Thanjavur 29, 408-11, **408**
Vijayanagar 257-8
World Wide Fund for Nature 93
wrestling 173-4
WWF 93

Y
yakshagana 72
yoga 101-3, *see also* ashrams
festivals 366
Isha Yoga Center 434
Ramamani Iyengar Memorial Yoga
Institute 166
yoga courses 101-2
Anjuna 199
Arambol 205
Bengaluru 225
Calangute & Baga 195
Chennai 374
Goa 178
Lonavla 161-2
Mumbai 118-19
Mysore 236-7
Puducherry 399
Sivananda Yoga Vedanta
Dhanwantari Ashram 315

Z
Zangdogpalri Temple 246
zennis 165
zoos
Katraj Snake Park & Zoo 165
Mumbai Zoo 117
Mysore 236
Port Blair 451
Thiruvananthapuram 311
Zoroastrianism 63

INDEX

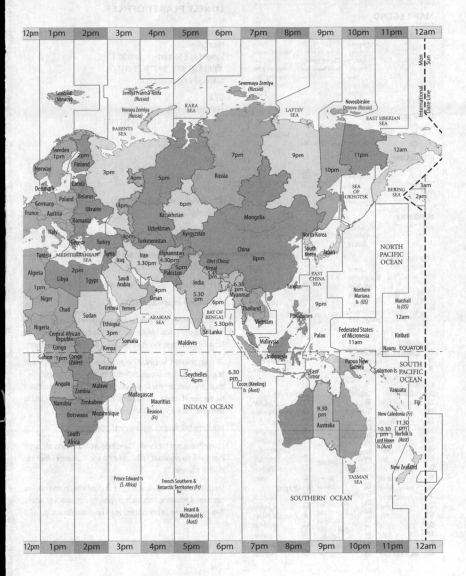

MAP LEGEND

ROUTES

Tollway			Mall/Steps
Freeway			Tunnel
Primary			Pedestrian Overpass
Secondary			Walking Tour
Tertiary			Walking Tour Detour
Lane			Walking Trail
Under Construction			Walking Path
Unsealed Road			Track
One-Way Street			

TRANSPORT

Ferry			Rail
Metro			Rail (Underground)
Bus Route			Tram

HYDROGRAPHY

River, Creek			Canal
Intermittent River			Water
Swamp			Lake (Dry)
Mangrove			Lake (Salt)
Reef			Mudflats

BOUNDARIES

International			Regional, Suburb
State, Provincial			Ancient Wall
Disputed			Cliff

AREA FEATURES

Airport			Land
Area of Interest			Mall
Beach, Desert			Market
Building			Park
Campus			Reservation
Cemetery, Christian			Rocks
Cemetery, Other			Sports
Forest			Urban

POPULATION

● CAPITAL (NATIONAL)	◉	CAPITAL (STATE)
● Large City	●	Medium City
● Small City	○	Town, Village

SYMBOLS

Sights/Activities
- Beach
- Buddhist
- Castle, Fortress
- Christian
- Hindu
- Islamic
- Jain
- Jewish
- Monument
- Museum, Gallery
- Point of Interest
- Pool
- Ruin
- Sikh
- Skiing
- Trail Head
- Zoo, Bird Sanctuary

Eating
- Eating

Drinking
- Drinking
- Café

Entertainment
- Entertainment

Shopping
- Shopping

Sleeping
- Sleeping
- Camping

Transport
- Airport, Airfield
- Border Crossing
- Bus Station
- General Transport
- Parking Area
- Petrol Station
- Taxi Rank

Information
- Bank, ATM
- Embassy/Consulate
- Hospital, Medical
- Information
- Internet Facilities
- Police Station
- Post Office, GPO
- Telephone
- Toilets

Geographic
- Lighthouse
- Lookout
- Mountain, Volcano
- National Park
- Pass, Canyon
- River Flow
- Waterfall

LONELY PLANET OFFICES

Australia
Head Office
Locked Bag 1, Footscray, Victoria 3011
☎ 03 8379 8000, fax 03 8379 8111
talk2us@lonelyplanet.com.au

USA
150 Linden St, Oakland, CA 94607
☎ 510 893 8555, toll free 800 275 8555
fax 510 893 8572
info@lonelyplanet.com

UK
72–82 Rosebery Ave,
Clerkenwell, London EC1R 4RW
☎ 020 7841 9000, fax 020 7841 9001
go@lonelyplanet.co.uk

Published by Lonely Planet Publications Pty Ltd
ABN 36 005 607 983

© Lonely Planet Publications Pty Ltd 2007

© photographers as indicated 2007

Cover photograph: Fishermen combing through nets, Michael S Yamashita/Corbis/APL. Many of the images in this guide are available for licensing from Lonely Planet Images: www.lonelyplanetimages.com.

Printed by SNP Security Printing Pte Ltd, Singapore